www.mhhe.com/belch

Advertising and Promotion

An Integrated Marketing Communications Perspective

The McGraw-Hill/Irwin Series in Marketing

Alreck & Settle
THE SURVEY RESEARCH HANDBOOK, SECOND EDITION

Anderson, Hair & Bush
PROFESSIONAL SALES MANAGEMENT, SECOND EDITION

Arens
CONTEMPORARY ADVERTISING, SIXTH EDITION

Bearden, Ingram & LaForge
MARKETING: PRINCIPLES & PERSPECTIVES, SECOND EDITION

Belch & Belch
ADVERTISING & PROMOTION: AN INTEGRATED MARKETING COMMUNICATIONS APPROACH, FIFTH EDITION

Bernhart & Kinnear
CASES IN MARKETING MANAGEMENT, SEVENTH EDITION

Berkowitz, Kerin, Hartley & Rudelius
MARKETING, SIXTH EDITION

Bowersox and Closs
LOGISTICAL MANAGEMENT, FIRST EDITION

Bowersox and Cooper
STRATEGIC MARKETING CHANNEL MANAGEMENT, FIRST EDITION

Boyd, Walker & Larreche
MARKETING MANAGEMENT: A STRATEGIC APPROACH WITH A GLOBAL ORIENTATION, THIRD EDITION

Cateora & Graham
INTERNATIONAL MARKETING, TENTH EDITION

Churchill, Ford, Walker, Johnston, & Tanner
SALES FORCE MANAGEMENT, SIXTH EDITION

Churchill & Peter
MARKETING, SECOND EDITION

Cole & Mishler
CONSUMER AND BUSINESS CREDIT MANAGEMENT, ELEVENTH EDITION

Cravens
STRATEGIC MARKETING, SIXTH EDITION

Cravens, Lamb & Crittenden
STRATEGIC MARKETING MANAGEMENT CASES, SIXTH EDITION

Crawford & Di Benedetto
NEW PRODUCTS MANAGEMENT, SIXTH EDITION

Dwyer & Tanner
BUSINESS MARKETING, FIRST EDITION

Etzel, Walker & Stanton
MARKETING, TWELFTH EDITION

Futrell
ABC'S OF RELATIONSHIP SELLING, SIXTH EDITION

Futrell
FUNDAMENTALS OF SELLING, SIXTH EDITION

Hair, Bush & Ortinau
MARKETING RESEARCH, FIRST EDITION

Hasty and Rearden
RETAIL MANAGEMENT, FIRST EDITION

Hawkins, Best & Coney
CONSUMER BEHAVIOR, EIGHTH EDITION

Hayes, Jenster & Aaby
BUSINESS TO BUSINESS MARKETING, FIRST EDITION

Johansson
GLOBAL MARKETING, SECOND EDITION

Lambert & Stock
STRATEGIC LOGISTICS MANAGEMENT, THIRD EDITION

Lambert, Stock & Ellram
FUNDAMENTALS OF LOGISTIC MANAGEMENT, FIRST EDITION

Lehmann & Winer
ANALYSIS FOR MARKETING PLANNING, FOURTH EDITION

Lehmann & Winer
PRODUCT MANAGEMENT, SECOND EDITION

Levy & Weitz
RETAILING MANAGEMENT, FOURTH EDITION

Mason & Perreault
THE MARKETING GAME, SECOND EDITION

McDonald
DIRECT MARKETING: AN INTEGRATED APPROACH, FIRST EDITION

Meloan & Graham
INTERNATIONAL AND GLOBAL MARKETING CONCEPTS AND CASES, SECOND EDITION

Monroe
PRICING, SECOND EDITION

Oliver
SATISFACTION: A BEHAVIORAL PERSPECTIVE ON THE CONSUMER, FIRST EDITION

Patton
SALES FORCE: A SALES MANAGEMENT SIMULATION GAME, FIRST EDITION

Pelton, Strutton, Lumpkin
MARKETING CHANNELS: A RELATIONSHIP MANAGEMENT APPROACH, FIRST EDITION

Perreault & McCarthy
BASIC MARKETING: A GLOBAL MANAGERIAL APPROACH, THIRTEENTH EDITION

Perreault & McCarthy
ESSENTIALS OF MARKETING: A GLOBAL MANAGERIAL APPROACH, EIGHTH EDITION

Peter & Donnelly
A PREFACE TO MARKETING MANAGEMENT, EIGHTH EDITION

Peter & Donnelly
MARKETING MANAGEMENT: KNOWLEDGE AND SKILLS, SIXTH EDITION

Peter & Olson
CONSUMER BEHAVIOR AND MARKETING STRATEGY, FIFTH EDITION

Rangan
BUSINESS MARKETING STRATEGY: CASES, CONCEPTS & APPLICATIONS, FIRST EDITION

Rangan, Shapiro & Moriaty
BUSINESS MARKETING STRATEGY: CONCEPTS AND APPLICATIONS, FIRST EDITION

Rossiter & Percy
ADVERTISING COMMUNICATIONS AND PROMOTION MANAGEMENT, SECOND EDITION

Stanton, Spiro & Buskirk
MANAGEMENT OF A SALES FORCE, TENTH EDITION

Sudman & Blair
MARKETING RESEARCH: A PROBLEM SOLVING APPROACH, FIRST EDITION

Ulrich & Eppinger
PRODUCT DESIGN AND DEVELOPMENT, SECOND EDITION

Walker, Boyd and Larreche
MARKETING STRATEGY: PLANNING AND IMPLEMENTATION, THIRD EDITION

Weitz, Castleberry and Tanner
SELLING: BUILDING PARTNERSHIPS, FOURTH EDITION

Zeithaml & Bitner
SERVICES MARKETING, SECOND EDITION

Advertising and Promotion

An Integrated Marketing Communications Perspective

Fifth Edition

George E. Belch & Michael A. Belch
Both of San Diego State University

Boston Burr Ridge, IL Dubuque, IA Madison, WI
New York San Francisco St. Louis
Bangkok Bogotá Caracas Lisbon London Madrid Mexico City
Milan New Delhi Seoul Singapore Sydney Taipei Toronto

McGraw-Hill Higher Education

*A Division of The **McGraw-Hill** Companies*

ADVERTISING AND PROMOTION:
AN INTEGRATED MARKETING COMMUNICATIONS PERSPECTIVE

Published by Irwin/McGraw-Hill, an imprint of the McGraw-Hill Companies, Inc. 1221 Avenue of the Americas, New York, NY, 10020.

This book is printed on acid-free paper.

domestic 1 2 3 4 5 6 7 8 9 0 VNH/VNH 0 9 8 7 6 5 4 3 2 1 0
international 1 2 3 4 5 6 7 8 9 0 VNH/VNH 0 9 8 7 6 5 4 3 2 1 0

ISBN 0-07-231445-1

Vice president/Editor-in-chief: *Michael W. Junior*
Publisher: *David Kendric Brake*
Developmental editor: *Barrett Koger*
Marketing manager: *Kim Kanakes*
Senior project manager: *Susan Trentacosti*
Production supervisor: *Heather D. Burbridge*
Senior supplement coordinator: *Cathy L. Tepper*
Media technology producer: *Burke Broholm*
Cover images: © *PhotoDisc*
Senior designer: *Kiera Cunningham*
Photo research coordinator: *Sharon Miller*
Compositor: *Precision Graphics Services, Inc.*
Typeface: *10.5/12 Times Roman*
Printer: *Von Hoffmann Press, Inc.*

Library of Congress Cataloging-in-Publication Data

Belch, George E. (George Edward)
Advertising and promotion : an integrated marketing communications perspective / George E. Belch & Michael A. Belch. -- 5th ed.
p. cm. -- (The McGraw-Hill/Irwin series in marketing)
Includes bibliographical references and index.
ISBN 0-07-231445-1
1. Advertising. 2. Sales promotion. 3. Communication in marketing. I. Belch, Michael A. II. Title. III. Series.

HF5823.B387 2001
659.1--dc21 00-040688

INTERNATIONAL EDITION ISBN 0-07-118026-5

www.mhhe.com

To Gayle and Melanie

With a special dedication to the kids:

Danny, Derek, Jessica, and Trevor Milos

Preface

The Changing World of Advertising and Promotion

Nearly everyone in the modern world is influenced to some degree by advertising and other forms of promotion. Organizations in both the private and public sectors have learned that the ability to communicate effectively and efficiently with their target audiences is critical to their success. Advertising and other types of promotional messages are used to sell products and services as well as to promote causes, market political candidates, and deal with societal problems such as the AIDS crisis and alcohol and drug abuse. Consumers are finding it increasingly difficult to avoid the efforts of marketers, who are constantly searching for new ways to communicate with them.

Most of the people involved in advertising and promotion will tell you that there is no more dynamic and fascinating a field to either practice or study. However, they will also tell you that the field is undergoing dramatic changes that are changing advertising and promotion forever. The changes are coming from all sides—clients demanding better results from their advertising and promotional dollars; lean but highly creative smaller ad agencies; sales promotion and direct-marketing firms, as well as interactive agencies, who want a larger share of the billions of dollars companies spend each year promoting their products and services; consumers who no longer respond to traditional forms of advertising; and new technologies that may reinvent the very process of advertising. As the new millennium begins, we are experiencing perhaps the most dynamic and revolutionary changes of any era in the history of marketing, as well as advertising and promotion. These changes are being driven by advances in technology and developments that have led to the rapid growth of communications through interactive media, particularly the Internet.

For decades the advertising business was dominated by large, full-service Madison Avenue-type agencies. The advertising strategy for a national brand involved creating one or two commercials that could be run on network television, a few print ads that would run in general interest magazines, and some sales promotion support such as coupons or premium offers. However, in today's world there are a myriad of media outlets—print, radio, cable and satellite TV, and now the Internet—competing for consumers' attention. Marketers are looking beyond the traditional media to find new and better ways to communicate with their customers. They no longer accept on faith the value of conventional advertising placed in traditional media. The large agencies are recognizing that they must change if they hope to survive in the 21st century. Keith Reinhard, chairman and CEO of DDB Worldwide, notes that the large agencies "have finally begun to acknowledge that this isn't a recession we're in, and that we're not going back to the good old days."

In addition to redefining the role and nature of their advertising agencies, marketers are changing the way they communicate with consumers. They know they are operating in an environment where advertising messages are everywhere, consumers channel-surf past most commercials, and brands promoted in traditional ways often fail. New-age advertisers are redefining the notion of what an ad is and where it runs. Stealth messages are being woven into the culture and embedded into movies and TV shows or made into their own form of entertainment.

Marketers are also changing the ways they allocate their promotional dollars. Spending on sales promotion activities targeted at both consumers and the trade has surpassed advertising media expenditures for years and continues to rise. In an article titled "Agencies: Change or Die," Joe Cappo, *Advertising Age* senior vice president, wrote, "What is happening in the advertising industry right now is a massive revolution that is changing the rules of marketing. This revolution is taking place not only in the United States, but in all affluent countries where advertising and media are well developed." In his new book *The End of Marketing as We Know It,* Sergio Zyman, the former head of marketing for Coca-Cola, declares traditional marketing is "not dying, but dead." He argues that advertising in general is overrated as part of the marketing mix and notes that all elements of the marketing mix communicate, such as brand names, packaging, pricing, and the way a product is distributed. The information revolution is exposing consumers to all types of communications and marketers need to better understand this process.

A number of factors are fueling this revolution. The audiences that marketers seek, along with the media and methods for reaching them, have become increasingly fragmented. Advertising and promotional efforts have become more regionalized and targeted to specific audiences. Retailers have become larger and more powerful, forcing marketers to shift money from advertising budgets to sales promotion. Marketers expect their promotional dollars to generate immediate sales and are demanding more accountability from their agencies. The Internet revolution is well under way and the online audience is growing rapidly, not only in the United States and Western Europe, but in many other countries as well. Many companies are coordinating all their communications efforts so they can send cohesive messages to their customers. Some companies are building brands with little or no use of traditional media advertising. Many advertising agencies have acquired, started, or become affiliated with sales promotion, direct-marketing, interactive agencies, and public relations companies to better serve their clients' marketing communications needs. Their clients have become "media-neutral" and are asking that they consider whatever form of marketing communication works best to target market segments and build long-term reputations and short-term sales.

This text will introduce students to this fast-changing field of advertising and promotion. While advertising is its primary focus, it is more than just an introductory advertising text because there is more to most organizations' promotional programs than just advertising. The changes discussed above are leading marketers and their agencies to approach advertising and promotion from an integrated marketing communications (IMC) perspective, which calls for a "big picture" approach to planning marketing and promotion programs and coordinating the various communication functions. To understand the role of advertising and promotion in today's business world, one must recognize how a firm can use all the promotional tools to communicate with its customers.

To the Student: Preparing You for the New World of Advertising and Promotion

Some of you are taking this course to learn more about this fascinating field; many of you hope to work in advertising or some other promotional area. The changes in the industry have profound implications for the way today's student is trained and educated. You will not be working for the same kind of communication agencies that existed 5 or 10 years ago. If you work on the client side of the business, you will find that the way they approach advertising and promotion is changing dramatically.

Today's student is expected to understand all the major marketing communication functions: advertising, direct marketing, interactive media, sales promotion, public relations, and personal selling. You will also be expected to know how to research and evaluate a company's marketing and promotional situation and how to use these various functions in developing effective communication strategies and programs. This book will help prepare you for these challenges.

As professors we were, of course, once students ourselves. In many ways we are perpetual students in that we are constantly striving to learn about and explain how advertising and promotion work. We share many of your interests and concerns and are often excited (and bored) by the same things. Having taught in the advertising and promotion area for a combined 40-plus years, we have developed an understanding of what makes a book in this field interesting to students. In writing this book, we have tried to remember how we felt about the various texts we used throughout the years and to incorporate the good things and minimize those we felt were of little use. We have tried not to overburden you with definitions, although we do call out those that are especially important to your understanding of the material.

We also remember that as students we were not really excited about theory. But to fully understand how integrated marketing communications works, it is necessary to establish some theoretical basis. The more you understand about how things are supposed to work, the easier it will be for you to understand why they do or do not turn out as planned.

Perhaps the question students ask most often is, "How do I use this in the real world?" In response, we provide numerous examples of how the various theories and concepts in the text can be used in practice. A particular strength of this text is the integration of theory with practical application. Nearly every day an example of advertising and promotion in practice is reported in the media. We have used many sources, such as *Advertising Age, AdWeek, BrandWeek, The Wall Street Journal, Business Week, Fortune, Forbes, Marketing Tools, Sales & Marketing Management, Business Marketing, Promo,* and many others, to find practical examples that are integrated throughout the text. We have spoken with hundreds of people about the strategies and rationale behind the ads and other types of promotions we use as examples. Each chapter begins with a vignette that presents an example of an advertising or promotional campaign or other interesting insights. Every chapter also contains several **IMC Perspectives** that present in-depth discussions of particular issues related to the chapter material and show how companies are using integrated marketing communications. **Global Perspectives** are presented throughout the text in recognition of the increasing importance of international marketing and the challenges of advertising and promotion and the role they play in the marketing programs of multinational marketers. **Ethical Perspectives** focus attention on important social issues and show how advertisers must take ethical considerations into account when planning and implementing advertising and promotional programs.

There are also a number of **Career Profiles** which highlight successful individuals working in various areas of the field of advertising and promotion.

Each chapter features beautiful four-color illustrations showing examples from many of the most current and best-integrated marketing communication campaigns being used around the world. We have included more than 350 advertisements and examples of numerous other types of promotion, all of which were carefully chosen to illustrate a particular idea, theory, or practical application. Please take time to read the opening vignettes to each chapter, the IMC, Global, and Ethical Perspectives, and the Career Profiles and study the diverse ads and illustrations. We think they will stimulate your interest and relate to your daily life as a consumer and a target of advertising and promotion.

To the Instructor: A Text That Reflects the Changes in the World of Advertising and Promotion

Our major goal in writing the fifth edition of *Advertising and Promotion* was to continue to provide you with the most comprehensive and current text on the market for teaching advertising and promotion from an IMC perspective. The fifth edition focuses on the many changes that are occurring in areas of marketing communications and how they influence advertising and promotional strategies and tactics. We have done this by continuing with the *integrated marketing communications perspective* we introduced in the second edition. More and more companies are approaching advertising and promotion from an IMC perspective, coordinating the various promotional mix elements with other marketing activities that communicate with a firm's customers. A recent study found that an overwhelming majority of marketing managers believe IMC can enhance the effectiveness and impact of their marketing communications efforts. Many advertising agencies are also developing expertise in direct marketing, sales promotion, event sponsorship, the Internet, and other areas so they can meet all their clients' integrated marketing communication needs—and, of course, survive.

The text is built around an integrated marketing communications planning model and recognizes the importance of coordinating all of the promotional mix elements to develop an effective communications program. Although media advertising is often the most visible part of a firm's promotional program, attention must also be given to direct marketing, sales promotion, public relations, interactive media, and personal selling.

This text integrates theory with planning, management, and strategy. To effectively plan, implement, and evaluate IMC programs, one must understand the overall marketing process, consumer behavior, and communications theory. We draw from the extensive research in advertising, consumer behavior, communications, marketing, sales promotion, and other fields to give students a basis for understanding the marketing communications process, how it influences consumer decision making, and how to develop promotional strategies.

While this is an introductory text, we do treat each topic in some depth. We believe the marketing and advertising student of today needs a text that provides more than just an introduction to terms and topics. The book is positioned primarily for the introductory advertising, marketing communications, or promotions course as taught in the business/marketing curriculum. It can also be used in journalism/communications courses that take an integrated marketing communications perspective. In addition to its thorough coverage of advertising, this text has chapters on sales promotion, direct marketing and marketing on the Internet, personal selling, and publicity/public relations. These chapters stress the integration of advertising with other promotional mix elements and the need to understand their role in the overall marketing program.

Organization of This Text

This book is divided into seven major parts. In Part One we examine the role of advertising and promotion in marketing and introduce the concept of integrated marketing communications. Chapter 1 provides an overview of advertising and promotion and its role in modern marketing. The concept of IMC and the factors that have led to its growth are discussed. Each of the promotional mix elements is defined and an IMC planning model shows the various steps in the promotional planning process. This model provides a framework for developing the integrated marketing communications program and is followed throughout the text. Chapter 2 examines the role of advertising and promotion in the overall marketing program, with attention to the various elements of the marketing mix and how they interact with advertising and promotional strategy. We have also included coverage of market segmentation and positioning in this chapter so students can understand how these concepts fit into the overall marketing programs as well as their role in the development of an advertising and promotional program.

In Part Two we cover the promotional program situation analysis. Chapter 3 describes how firms organize for advertising and promotion and examines the role of ad agencies and other firms that provide marketing and promotional services. We discuss how ad agencies are selected, evaluated, and compensated as well as the changes occurring in the agency business. Attention is also given to other types of marketing communication organizations such as direct marketing, sales promotion, and interactive agencies as well as public relations firms. We also consider whether responsibility for integrating the various communication functions lies with the client or the agency. Chapter 4 covers the stages of the consumer decision-making process and both the internal psychological factors and the external factors that influence consumer behavior. The focus of this chapter is on how advertisers can use an understanding of buyer behavior to develop effective advertising and other forms of promotion.

Part Three analyzes the communications process. Chapter 5 examines various communication theories and models of how consumers respond to advertising messages and other forms of marketing communications. Chapter 6 provides a detailed discussion of source, message, and channel factors.

In Part Four we consider how firms develop goals and objectives for their integrated marketing communications programs and determine how much money to spend trying to achieve them. Chapter 7 stresses the importance of knowing what to expect from advertising and promotion, the differences between advertising and communication objectives, characteristics of good objectives, and problems in setting objectives. We have also integrated the discussion of various methods for determining and allocating the promotional budget into this chapter. These first four sections of the text provide students with a solid background in the areas of marketing, consumer behavior, communications, planning, objective setting, and budgeting. This foundation lays the foundation for the next section where we discuss the development of the integrated marketing communication program.

Part Five examines the various promotional mix elements that form the basis of the integrated marketing communications program. Chapter 8 discusses the planning and development of the creative strategy and advertising campaign and examines the creative process. In Chapter 9 we turn our attention to ways to execute the creative strategy and some criteria for evaluating creative work. Chapters 10 through 13 cover media strategy and planning and the various advertising media. Chapter 10 introduces the key principles of media planning and strategy and examines how a media plan is developed. Chapter 11 discusses the advantages and disadvantages of the broadcast media (TV and radio) as well as issues regarding the purchase of radio and TV time and audience measurement. Chapter 12 considers the same issues for the print media (magazines and newspapers). Chapter 13 examines the role of support media such as outdoor and transit advertising and some of the many new media alternatives.

In Chapters 14 through 17 we continue the IMC emphasis by examining other promotional tools that are used in the integrated marketing communications process. Chapter 14 looks at the rapidly growing areas of direct marketing. This chapter examines database marketing and the way by which companies communicate directly with target customers through various media. Chapter 15 provides a detailed discussion of interactive media and marketing on the Internet and how companies are using the World Wide Web as a medium for communicating with customers. We discuss how this new medium is being used for a variety of marketing activities including advertising, sales promotion and even the selling of products and services. Chapter 16 examines the area of sales promotion including both consumer-oriented promotions and programs targeted to the trade (retailers, wholesalers and other middlemen). Chapter 17 covers the role of publicity and public relations in IMC as well as corporate advertising. Basic issues regarding personal selling and its role in promotional strategy are presented in Chapter 18.

Part Six of the text consists of Chapter 19, where we discuss ways to measure the effectiveness of various elements of the integrated marketing communications program, including methods for pretesting and post-testing advertising messages and campaigns. In Part Seven we turn our attention to special markets, topics, and perspectives that are becoming increasingly important in contemporary marketing. In Chapter 20 we examine the global marketplace and the role of advertising and other promotional mix variables such as sales promotion, public relations, and the Internet in international marketing.

The text concludes with a discussion of the regulatory, social, and economic environments in which advertising and promotion operate. Chapter 21 examines industry self-regulation and regulation of advertising by governmental agencies such as the Federal Trade Commission, as well as rules and regulations governing sales promotion, direct marketing and marketing on the Internet. Because advertising's role in society is constantly changing, our discussion would not be complete without a look at the criticisms frequently levied, so in Chapter 22 we consider the social, ethical, and economic aspects of advertising and promotion.

Chapter Features

The following features in each chapter enhance students' understanding of the material as well as their reading enjoyment.

Chapter Objectives

Objectives are provided at the beginning of each chapter to identify the major areas and points covered in the chapter and guide the learning effort.

Chapter Opening Vignettes

Each chapter begins with a vignette that shows the effective use of integrated marketing communications by a company or ad agency or discusses an interesting issue that is relevant to the chapter. These opening vignettes are designed to draw the students into the chapter by presenting an interesting example, development, or issue that relates to the material covered in the chapter. Some of the companies whose advertising and promotion programs are profiled in the opening vignettes include Mazda, Gap, Hewlett-Packard, Jenny Craig, Fosters, Jack in the Box, AOL, Time Warner, *Fast Company* magazine, and the TBWA/Chiat/Day advertising agency.

IMC Perspectives

These boxed items feature in-depth discussions of interesting issues related to the chapter material and the practical application of integrated marketing communications. Each chapter contains several of these insights into the world of integrated marketing communications. Some of the companies/brands whose IMC programs are discussed in these perspectives are General Motors, Enron, IBM, Nortel Networks, Subaru, Savin, Apple Computer, Chevrolet Trucks, and Intel.

Global Perspectives

These boxed sidebars provide information similar to that in the IMC Perspectives, with a focus on international aspects of advertising and promotion. Some of the companies/brands whose international advertising programs are covered in the Global Perspectives are the Ford Motor Company, Coca-Cola, Pepsi Cola, IBM, Colgate, New Balance, and McDonalds'.

Ethical Perspectives

These boxed items discuss the moral and/or ethical issues regarding practices engaged in by marketers and are also tied to the material presented in the particular chapter. Issues covered in the Ethical Perspectives include the use of the Internet to preempt negative publicity, subliminal advertising, the use of shock ads by companies such as Calvin Klein, Benetton, and others, the controversy over the use of sweepstakes in the direct marketing of magazine subscriptions, invasion of consumer privacy by direct marketers as well as Internet companies, the issue of whether advertisers can influence the editorial content of the media, and the advertising of hard liquor on television.

Career Profiles

Also included are Career Profiles of successful individuals working in the communications industry. Some examples of the individuals featured in the Career Profiles are an agency vice president/management supervisor, an assistant account executive, a creative director for a promotion agency, a media sales person for a major magazine, a director of research for a major media company, a vice president and director of research for a public relations firm, and a vice president/client service director for a Canadian direct and interactive agency.

Key Terms

Important terms are highlighted in boldface throughout the text and listed at the end of each chapter with a page reference. These terms help call students' attention to important ideas, concepts, and definitions and help them review their learning progress.

Chapter Summaries

These synopses serve as a quick review of important topics covered and a very helpful study guide.

Discussion Questions

Questions at the end of each chapter give students an opportunity to test their understanding of the material and to apply it. These questions can also serve as a basis for class discussion or assignments.

Four-Color Visuals

Print ads, photoboards, and other examples appear throughout the book. More than 400 ads, charts, graphs, and other types of illustrations are included in the text.

Changes in the Fifth Edition

We have made a number of changes in the fifth edition to make it as relevant and current as possible, as well as more interesting to students.

- **A Continuing Emphasis on Integrated Marketing Communications** The fifth edition continues to place a strong emphasis on approaching the field of advertising and promotion from an integrated marketing communications perspective. We continue to focus on how the various elements of an organization's promotional mix are combined to develop a total marketing communications program that sends a consistent message to customers. The first chapter now includes an updated discussion of the evolution of IMC and factors that have contributed to the increased attention to IMC on both the client and agency side, including the rapid growth of the Internet. Chapter 3 focuses even more attention on other communication agencies, such as sales promotion and direct-response firms, as well as interactive agencies. More attention is also given to setting objectives for IMC programs (Chapter 7) and measuring their effectiveness (Chapter 19).
- **New Chapter on the Internet and Interactive Media** The fifth edition has added an entire new chapter to provide detailed coverage of interactive media with a focus primarily on how companies are using the Internet as an integrated marketing communications tool. This chapter discusses objectives and strategies for using the Internet and integrating it into marketing communications programs. Advantages and disadvantages of Web advertising are discussed, along with issues such as audience measurement and methods for determining the effectiveness of Internet advertising. Discussion of the Internet as an integrated marketing communications tool is also incorporated throughout the book.
- **New Chapter Opening Vignettes** *All* of the chapter opening vignettes in the fifth edition are new and were chosen for their currency and relevance to students. They demonstrate how various companies and advertising agencies use advertising and other IMC tools. They also provide interesting insights

into some of the current trends and developments that are taking place in the advertising world.

- **New and Updated IMC Perspectives** All of the boxed items focusing on specific examples of how companies and their communications agencies are using integrated marketing communications are new or updated, and provide insight into many of the most current and popular advertising and promotional campaigns being used by marketers. The IMC Perspectives also address interesting issues related to advertising, sales promotion, direct marketing, marketing on the Internet, and personal selling.
- **New and Updated Global and Ethical Perspectives** Nearly all of the boxed items focusing on global and ethical issues of advertising and promotion are new; those retained from the fourth edition have been updated. The Global Perspectives examine the role of advertising and other promotional areas in international markets. The Ethical Perspectives discuss specific issues, developments, and problems that call into question the ethics of marketers and their decisions as they develop and implement their advertising and promotional programs.
- **New Career Profiles** In the fourth edition we added a new feature called Career Profiles that discuss the career path of successful individuals working in various areas of advertising and promotion including clients, advertising agencies, and the media. These profiles provide the students with insight into various types of careers that are available in the area of advertising and promotion on the client and agency side as well as in media. They discuss the educational backgrounds of the individuals profiled, some of the responsibilities and requirements of their positions, and their career paths. This feature has been very popular among students and in the fifth edition we provide eight new profiles. Moreover, these profiles have been written by individuals themselves and provide students with insight into the educational background of the person, how they got started in the field of advertising and promotion, their current responsibilities, and interesting aspects of their jobs as well as experiences.
- **Contemporary Examples** The field of advertising and promotion changes very rapidly, and we continue to keep pace with it. Wherever possible we updated the statistical information presented in tables, charts, and figures throughout the text. We reviewed the most current academic and trade literature to ensure that this text reflects the most current perspectives and theories on advertising, promotion, and the rapidly evolving area of integrated marketing communications. We also updated most of the examples and ads throughout the book. *Advertising and Promotion* continues to be the most contemporary text on the market, offering students as timely a perspective as possible.
- **Same Number of Chapters and More Concise Writing** The fifth edition still has 22 chapters even though we have added a new chapter on the Internet and interactive media. To maintain the same length, the chapter on business-to-business communications was eliminated by integrating this material into other chapters and using business-to-business examples throughout the text. The fifth edition has been carefully edited to continue making the writing style tighter and more concise. In making these changes, we were careful not to reduce relevant content or the many examples that are such a popular feature of this text. However, students will find the writing in the new edition more active, direct, and succinct and thus easier to read.

Support Material

A high-quality package of instructional supplements supports the fifth edition. Nearly all of the supplements have been developed by the authors to ensure their coordination with the text. We offer instructors a support package that facilitates the use of our text and enhances the learning experience of the student.

Instructor's Manual

The instructor's manual is a valuable teaching resource that includes learning objectives, chapter and lecture outlines, answers to all end-of-chapter discussion questions, transparency masters, and further insights and teaching suggestions. Additional discussion questions are also presented for each chapter. These questions can be used for class discussion or as short-answer essay questions for exams.

Manual of Tests

A test bank of more than 1,500 multiple-choice questions has been developed to accompany the text. The questions provide thorough coverage of the chapter material, including opening vignettes and IMC, Global, and Ethical Perspectives, and are categorized by level of learning (definitional, conceptual, or application).

Computerized Test Bank

A computerized version of the test bank is available to adopters of the text.

Instructor CD-ROM

This exciting presentation CD-ROM allows the professor to customize a multimedia lecture with original material from the supplements package. It includes video clips, commercials, ads and art from the text, electronic slides and acetates, the computerized test bank, and the print supplements.

Electronic Slides

A disk containing nearly 300 PowerPoint® slides is available to adopters of the fifth edition for electronic presentations. These slides contain lecture notes, charts, graphs, and other instructional materials.

Home Page

A home page on the Internet can be found at

www.mhhe.business/marketing/

It contains Web Exploration Links (hot links to other Web sites) as well as various other items of interest. For instructors, the home page will offer updates of examples; chapter opener vignettes; IMC, Global, and Ethical Perspectives; additional sources of advertising and promotion information; and downloads of key supplements. Adopters will be able to communicate directly with the authors through the site (contact your McGraw-Hill/Irwin representative for your password).

Four-Color Transparencies

Each adopter may request a set of over 100 four-color acetate transparencies that present print ads, photoboards, sales promotion offers, and other materials that do not appear in the text. A number of important models or charts appearing in the text are also provided as color transparencies. Slip sheets are included with each transparency to give the instructor useful background information about the illustration and how it can be integrated into the lecture.

Video Supplements

A video supplement package has been developed specifically for classroom use with this text. The first set of videos contains nearly 200 television and radio commercials that are examples of creative advertising. It can be used to help the instructor explain a particular concept or principle or give more insight into how a company executes its advertising strategy. Most of the commercials are tied to the chapter openings, IMC and Global Perspectives, or specific examples cited in the text. Insights and/or background information about each commercial are provided in the instructor's manual written specifically for the videos. The second set of videos contains longer segments on the advertising and promotional strategies of various companies and industries. Included on this video are three segments showing campaigns chosen as 1999 Ogilvy Award Winners by the Advertising Research Foundation. Each segment shows how research was used to guide the development of an effective advertising campaign. Other segments include highlights of promotions that won Reggie Awards (given each year to the best sales promotion campaigns), and case studies of the integrated marketing communications programs used by Airwalk, Mazda, and Chicken of the Sea International.

Acknowledgments

While this fifth edition represents a tremendous amount of work on our part, it would not have become a reality without the assistance and support of many other people. Authors tend to think they have the best ideas, approach, examples, and organization for writing a great book. But we quickly learned that there is always room for our ideas to be improved on by others. A number of colleagues provided detailed, thoughtful reviews that were immensely helpful in making this a better book. We are very grateful to the following individuals who worked with us on earlier editions. They include Lauranne Buchanan, *University of Illinois;* Roy Busby, *University of North Texas;* Lindell Chew, *University of Missouri–St. Louis;* Catherine Cole, *University of Iowa;* John Faier, *Miami University;* Raymond Fisk, *Oklahoma State University;* Geoff Gordon, *University of Kentucky;* Donald Grambois, *Indiana University;* Stephen Grove, *Clemson University;* Ron Hill, *University of Portland;* Paul Jackson, *Ferris State College;* Don Kirchner, *California State University–Northridge;* Clark Leavitt, *Ohio State University;* Charles Overstreet, *Oklahoma State University;* Paul Prabhaker, *Depaul University, Chicago;* Scott Roberts, *Old Dominion University;* Harlan Spotts, *Northeastern University;* Mary Ann Stutts, *Southwest Texas State University;* Terrence Witkowski, *California State University–Long Beach;* Robert Young, *Northeastern University*; Terry Bristol, *Oklahoma State University;* Roberta Ellins, *Fashion Institute of Technology;* Robert Erffmeyer, *University of Wisconsin–Eau Claire;* Alan Fletcher, *Louisiana State University;* Jon B. Freiden, *Florida State University;* Patricia Kennedy, *University of Nebraska;* Don Kirchner, *California State University—Northridge;* Susan Kleine, *Arizona State University;* Tina Lowry, *Rider University;* Elizabeth Moore-Shay, *University of Illinois;* Notis Pagiavlas, *University of Texas–Arlington;* William Pride, *Texas A&M University;* Joel Reedy, *University of South Florida;* Denise D. Schoenbachler, *Northern Illinois University;* James Swartz, *California State University–Pomona,* Robert H. Ducoffe, *Baruch College; and* Robert Gulonsen, *Washington University.*

We are particularly grateful to the individuals who provided constructive comments on how to make this edition better: Craig Andrews, *Marquette University;* Subir Bandyopadhyay, *University of Ottawa;* Beverly Brockman, *University of Alabama;* John H. Murphy II, *University of Texas–Austin;* Glen Reicken, *East Tennessee State University;* Michelle Rodriquez, *University of Central Florida;* and Elaine Scott, *Bluefield State College.* We also received many valuable comments from survey respondents.

We would also like to acknowledge the cooperation we received from many people in the business, advertising, and media communities. This book contains several hundred ads, illustrations, charts, and tables that have been provided by advertisers and/or their agencies, various publications, and other advertising and industry organizations. Many individuals took time from their busy schedules to provide us with requested materials and gave us permission to use them. A special thanks to all of you.

A manuscript does not become a book without a great deal of work on the part of a publisher. Various individuals at Irwin/McGraw-Hill have been involved with this project over the past several years. Our sponsoring editor on the fifth edition, Jill Braaten, provided valuable guidance and was instrumental in making sure this was much more than just a token revision. A special thanks goes to Barrett Koger, our developmental editor, for all of her efforts and for being so great to work with. Thanks also to Susan Trentacosti for doing a superb job of managing the production process. We also want to acknowledge the outstanding work of Charlotte Goldman for her help in obtaining permissions for most of the ads that appear throughout the book. Thanks to the other members of the product team, Kiera Cunningham, Sharon Miller, Cathy Tepper, Heather Burbridge, and Burke Broholm, for all their hard work on this edition.

We would like to acknowledge the support we have received from the College of Business at San Diego State University. On a more personal note, a great deal of thanks goes to our families for putting up with us over the past few years while we were revising this book. Gayle, Danny, Derek, Melanie, and Jessica have had to endure the deviation from our usually pleasant personalities and dispositions for a fifth time, while Trevor has now made it through two rounds. Once again we look forward to returning to normal. Finally, we would like to acknowledge each other for making it through this ordeal again. Our mother will be happy to know that we still get along after all this—though it is definitely getting tougher—most of the time.

George E. Belch
Michael A. Belch

Contents in Brief

Contents

Advertising and Promotion

An Integrated Marketing Communications Perspective

Chapter One

An Introduction to Integrated Marketing Communications

Chapter Objectives

- To examine the promotional function and the growing importance of advertising and other promotional elements in the marketing programs of domestic and foreign companies.
- To introduce the concept of integrated marketing communications (IMC) and consider how it has evolved.
- To examine reasons for the increasing importance of the IMC perspective in planning and executing advertising and promotional programs.
- To introduce the various elements of the promotional mix and consider their roles in an IMC program.
- To examine how various marketing and promotional elements must be coordinated to communicate effectively.
- To introduce a model of the IMC planning process and examine the steps in developing a marketing communications program.

Mazda Gets Moving

Mazda has been selling cars and trucks in the highly competitive U.S. market for more than three decades. Its various models have always received high marks from consumers in areas such as styling, performance, reliability, and value. Sporty models such as the rotary engine RX-7, which was Mazda's signature car for many years, and the Miata roadster helped the company sell nearly 400,000 cars and trucks per year in the United States throughout the decade of the 80s and into the early 90s. However, during the mid-90s Mazda embarked on an ill-conceived expansion that included the introduction of six new models in less than a year and a lack of focus in its marketing and advertising plans. From 1994 to 1997 Mazda's U.S. sales dropped nearly 70 percent and reached their lowest level in 15 years. When Richard Beattie took over as president of Mazda North American Operations in early 1997, he said he found an inefficient company with an "image that was bouncing all around." Most of the advertising for the various Mazda models touted the prices and functional features of the cars, with little attention being given to image and positioning. A change in marketing strategy as well as advertising philosophy was clearly needed if Mazda was to regain its strong position in the U.S. market.

To begin its recovery, a new marketing strategy was developed that called for Mazda to refocus its efforts and target a younger generation of drivers who appreciate cars with sporty features and want to make a statement about themselves with their cars. In the fall of 1997 Mazda parted ways with its advertising agency of 27 years and awarded its $250 million business to a new agency, W. B. Doner & Co., now known as Doner. The new agency was given the task of building an image that would capture Mazda's overall personality and set its vehicles apart from other cars. The agency was also asked to develop an advertising theme that could be used for the Mazda brand rather than trying to establish a separate image for each model. Doner developed a simple but powerful slogan for Mazda, "Get In. Be Moved." The slogan is seen as more than just an advertising tagline; it's a brand promise. Mazda's group manager of brand strategy and communication notes, "It's an invitation to the consumer, a motivation and a promise that you come to Mazda, you get in, and we promise that you'll be moved by what our cars have to offer."

One of the first challenges Doner undertook was to develop a campaign to completely reposition Mazda's subcompact Protegé model. The Protegé was positioned as a step up from a compact sedan but retained compact attributes such as fuel efficiency and price. The dual market for the Protegé included entry-level young buyers and older, empty nesters who wanted a smaller second car. However, the new advertising strategy for the Protegé called for positioning it as a cool, fun, hip-to-drive vehicle for young, individualistic females. The ads would target young professional women in their early 20s to mid-30s and promote euro-chic styling, room for friends, value reliability, and cool features such as CD players and air-conditioning.

To launch the repositioning campaign for the Protegé, Doner developed several television commercials that combine computer-generated backgrounds with live action and feature a group of hip 20-somethings carpooling in a Protegé. One of the most popular spots, "Protegé World," shows the group driving a Protegé through a surrealistic cityscape accompanied by a vocal set to music from the Nails' "88 Lines about 44 Women," bemoaning the trials and tribulations of their workday lives. As the car drives off the screen, the voice-over describes how the Protegé "is a change from your high-maintenance relationships."

In addition to using commercials, Mazda also gave the redesigned Protegé a major push on the Internet. Mazda kicked off what it called "the world's largest online automotive launch party" with banner ads on a number of websites and portals such as Yahoo!, Excite, America Online's Autocenter, Carpoint, and MTV. The ads lead visitors to the Protegé section of Mazda's website, which was created by Mazda's interactive agency. Once there they could start the "Protegé Road Trip," where users picked the traits and a photograph of an imaginary travel companion before starting on a cyber journey that included choosing virtual roads to take. Fun facts about the car were offered along the way. While online, travelers could also enter a sweepstakes to win a new Protegé and play trivia games supplied by the game-show site Uproar. Mazda also mailed a CD-ROM with music, movie reviews, and interviews to people who requested more information while visiting the Protegé website.

The new campaign has been very successful in repositioning the Protegé and attracting younger buyers. Sales of the Protegé increased 33 percent in the fourth quarter of 1998 and nearly 20 percent in 1999. The "Get In. Be Moved" tagline is also being used in campaigns for other Mazda models, including the Miata roadster and the 626 and Millenia sedans. Mazda's U.S. sales increased in 1998 and in 1999, and Mazda appears to be on the move once again.

Sources: John O'Dell, "New Agency Breathes New Life into Mazda," *Los Angeles Times,* May 27, 1999, pp. C1, 6; Tanya Gazdik, "Doner Gets Moved," *ADWEEK,* January 25, 1999, pp. 59–61; Jean Halliday, "Redesigned Protegé Take Road Trip," *Advertising Age,* October 12, 1998, pp. 41–42.

The success of Mazda's "Get In. Be Moved" campaign illustrates the importance of having a well-planned and executed marketing communications strategy. However, it also provides an excellent example of how the roles of advertising and other forms of promotion are changing in the modern world of marketing. In the past, marketers such as Mazda relied primarily on advertising through traditional mass media to promote their products. Today many companies are taking a new approach to marketing and promotion: They integrate their advertising efforts with a variety of other communication techniques such as websites on the Internet, direct marketing, sales promotion, publicity, and public relations (PR) and event sponsorships. They are also recognizing that these communication tools are most effective when they are coordinated with other elements of the marketing program.

The various marketing communication tools used by Mazda to promote the Protegé as well as its other cars and trucks show how marketers are using an *integrated marketing communications* approach to reach their customers. Mazda runs advertising in a variety of media including television, radio, magazines, newspapers, and billboards as well as on the Internet. Banner ads on the Internet and in other media encourage consumers to visit the Mazda website (www.mazdausa.com), which provides updated information about the company's various models, prices, financing options, and local dealers and even allows consumers to build their own car (Exhibit 1–1). Publicity for Mazda and for its various models is generated through press releases and PR activities as well as product placements in movies and television shows. Mazda sponsors motor sports such as auto racing and motocross to reach not only its target audience but also other groups and/or individuals who can influence the image of its cars. Promotional efforts for Mazda's cars and trucks are extended to the dealerships, where point-of-purchase displays and materials are provided along with training, contests, and incentives for salespeople. For example, for the Protegé launch Mazda provided dealers with a "launch in a box kit" that contained materials needed to create local advertising and to convert the showroom into a "Protegé World" that was consistent with the national launch advertising.

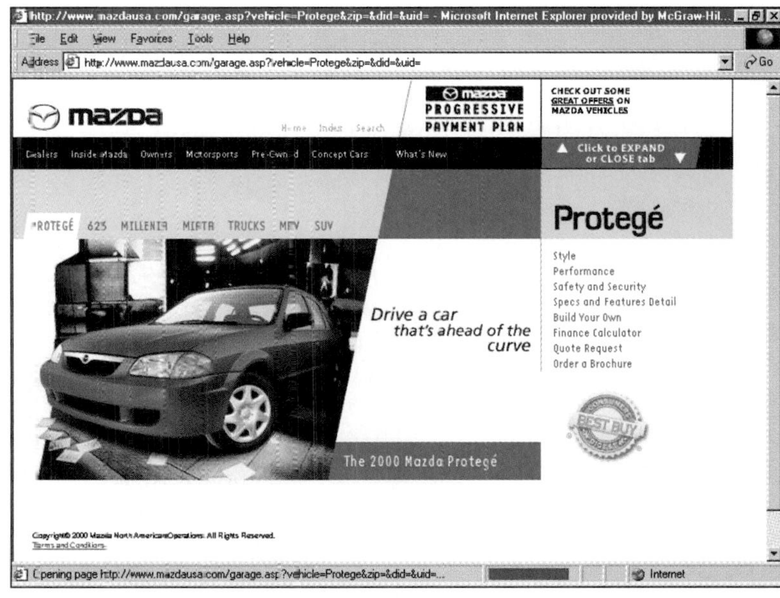

Exhibit 1–1 Mazda provides consumers with information about its various models through its website on the Internet

Mazda and thousands of other companies recognize that the way they must communicate with consumers and promote their products and services is changing rapidly. The fragmentation of mass markets, the explosion of new technologies that are giving consumers greater control over the communication process, the rapid growth of the Internet and electronic commerce, the emergence of global markets, and economic uncertainties are all changing the way companies approach marketing as well as advertising and promotion. Developing marketing communications programs that are responsive to these changes is critical to the success of every organization. However, advertising and other forms of promotion will continue to play an important role in the integrated marketing programs of most companies.

The Growth of Advertising and Promotion

Advertising and promotion are an integral part of our social and economic systems. In our complex society, advertising has evolved into a vital communications system for both consumers and businesses. The ability of advertising and other promotional methods to deliver carefully prepared messages to target audiences has given them a major role in the marketing programs of most organizations. Companies ranging from large multinational corporations to small retailers increasingly rely on advertising and promotion to help them market products and services. In market-based economies, consumers have learned to rely on advertising and other forms of promotion for information they can use in making purchase decisions.

Evidence of the increasing importance of advertising and promotion comes from the growth in expenditures in these areas. In 1980, advertising expenditures in the United States were $53 billion, and $49 billion was spent on sales promotion techniques such as product samples, coupons, contests, sweepstakes, premiums, rebates, and allowances and discounts to retailers. By 2000, an estimated $233 billion was spent on local and national advertising, while sales promotion expenditures increased to more than $250 billion![1] Companies bombarded the U.S. consumer with messages and promotional offers, collectively spending more than $30 a week on every man, woman, and child in the country—nearly 50 percent more per capita than in any other nation.

Promotional expenditures in international markets have grown as well. Advertising expenditures outside the United States increased from $55 billion in 1980 to nearly $230 billion by 2000.[2] Both foreign and domestic companies spend billions more on sales promotion, personal selling, direct marketing, event sponsorships, and public relations, all important parts of a firm's marketing communications program.

The tremendous growth in expenditures for advertising and promotion reflects in part the growth of the U.S. and global economies. For example, Global Perspective 1–1 discusses how expansion-minded marketers are taking advantage of growth opportunities in various regions of the world. The growth in promotional

Career Profile

Mike Morisette

Vice President, Management Supervisor at Doner Advertising

I attended Oakland University (OU) in Rochester, Michigan, and graduated in 1989 with a bachelor's degree in marketing. Prior to attending OU, I spent a year at a tech school and pursued a degree in electrical engineering. My next move involved working toward a degree in culinary arts. It was at that point that I took my first marketing course and knew I had found my career path (since drumming for a rock band never took off!). My impression, as I started college, was that much of what I would learn in required classes would not apply to "real world" experience. However, I have been pleasantly surprised by the amount of course work that has applied to my advertising career.

While in college, I had the opportunity to gain hands-on marketing and advertising experience through involvement in student organizations such as the collegiate chapter of the American Marketing Association (AMA) and the Student Activity Board. The experience was invaluable and helped me land my first advertising job with Young & Rubicam, as well as win an Outstanding Achievement Award from *The Wall Street Journal.*

"Advertising is challenging and rewarding . . . you won't have time to get bored."

As president of the AMA chapter at OU, I met with recruiters from advertising and marketing organizations to coordinate a new program for our members. Luck was on my side—one of the recruiters ran the traffic department at Young & Rubicam and encouraged me to forward my resume when I was close to graduating.

Y&R hired me in an entry-level capacity as a traffic coordinator working on the Lincoln-Mercury account. After a promotion to assistant account executive, I was transferred to the St. Louis field office and later to the Dallas office to work as an account executive. While in Dallas, I joined Doner to work on the Ford Dealer Advertising Association business. The latest move sent me to Southern California to help open a new Doner office and service the new Mazda account.

As a vice president, management supervisor, my responsibilities fall into two broad categories: client-service responsibilities and agency responsibilities. In my current position as a brand asset manager on the Mazda business, I am responsible for the planning, development, and implementation of marketing and advertising programs that nurture and enhance the Mazda brand—specifically the Mazda Protegé, B-Series, and Tribute—which ultimately lead to the achievement of client sales and profit objectives.

In account management, you have the opportunity to shape projects every step of the way. To be effective, you must be able to step into a new pair of shoes every time you enter a different department; you must empathize with the challenge of each discipline and be a source of knowledge and motivation. Also, you must have the stomach for the occasional all-nighter, fueled by cold pizza and microwave popcorn! In the end, there is a strong sense of pride and accomplishment for projects that bear your team's fingerprint.

A major appeal of working in an advertising agency is that it is a *people* business. You deal with diverse groups such as the account planning and research groups, the creative team, the media team, and a host of others. The interaction provides an opportunity for intellectual stimulation and outright fun!

Tight deadlines, unlimited advertising and promotional options, shrinking marketing budgets, and increased client expectations are typical agency challenges. The good news is you work with dynamic marketing partners and people who can meet the challenges and provide creative solutions to marketing and advertising problems. Ad agencies and marketing organizations are constantly seeking individuals with diverse backgrounds and solid experience who can thrive in an entrepreneurial environment sometimes described as "controlled chaos." Advertising is challenging, changing, and rewarding . . . you won't have time to get bored in this business!

Global Perspective 1–1

Marketers Go Global

When companies want to launch a new advertising campaign or introduce a new product or service, they sometimes use a media scheduling technique called "roadblocking," in which they buy airtime on all four major television networks simultaneously. The goal is to get the attention of as many TV viewers across the country as possible. However, on the evening of November 1st, 1999, the Ford Motor Company had a slightly more ambitious goal: seizing the attention of television viewers *all over the world*. In what was billed as an advertising first, Ford bought two minutes of airtime in the 9 P.M. spot on every major commercial TV network around the globe for the debut of a global image campaign tied to the end of the millennium. The two-minute spot is a montage of nearly 60 emotional scenes that jump from Australia to China to Brazil to the United States and involves nine countries in all. Interspersed at various points are the logos of the various brands of automobiles owned by the world's number-two automaker: Ford, Lincoln, Mercury, Volvo, Jaguar, Mazda, and Aston Martin. The goal of the commercial is to show how Ford vehicles relate to people around the world on many different levels in many different cultures and convey the message that it is time to say good-bye to the old millennium and hello to the new one.

Ford's worldwide launch of this image-building ad is an example of how many companies are looking beyond their borders and developing marketing and promotional programs for global markets. These companies are truly global marketers that are selling their products and services to consumers around the world. Diago PLC, the world's biggest spirits company, began the new millennium with a unified global advertising campaign for its Johnnie Walker Red and Black Label Scotch whiskies. PriceWaterhouseCoopers, one of the "Big Five" accounting firms, recently launched a $50 million global campaign that uses the tagline "Join us. Together we can change the world." The ads target potential corporate clients as well as many of the more than 50,000 new workers the firm wants to hire for offices around the world.

Despite recent economic problems, the world's largest markets are developing in Asia, and marketers are using a variety of integrated marketing communications techniques to pursue the opportunities in countries such as China, India, and Thailand. Intel has placed television and billboard ads throughout China to establish brand awareness for its microprocessors, which serve as the brains of personal computers. The company also distributed nearly 1 million bike reflectors—which glow in the dark with the words "Intel Inside Pentium Processor"—throughout China's biggest cities. Citicorp's Citibank unit has captured a high percentage of the credit-card market in many Southeast Asian countries, such as Malaysia and Thailand, by relying primarily on a sales force of 600 part-timers who are paid a fee for each applicant approved.

Global marketers are also recognizing the tremendous marketing opportunities for selling sports in countries around the world. Companies are lining up to take advantage of the integrated marketing opportunities associated with corporate sponsorship of sporting events. Nike paid a record-setting $200 million to sponsor the Brazilian national soccer team through the year 2006. The company also sponsors four teams in China's new professional soccer league, including one owned by the People's Liberation Army. MasterCard, Pepsi, Gillette, and Canon have deals to sponsor Asian soccer broadcasters such as the Fox Sports Network,

which is part of Rupert Murdock's Star TV Asian satellite network, and ESPN is purchasing the broadcast rights for popular Asian sports such as cricket and soccer as well as golf and volleyball.

The Internet revolution is well under way and is no longer limited to upscale, well-educated Americans. Currently, the Internet does not have the same presence in Asia as it does in the United States, Canada, and Europe, and there are still significant barriers to electronic commerce in countries such as China, India, and other developing nations. However, many Chinese companies are beginning to develop websites to reach consumers both at home and abroad, and more are expected to market their products and services online or risk losing sales to foreign companies.

Advances in technology, travel, and communications are turning the world into a global consumer village, and people everywhere want to be part of it. Companies are recognizing that the world is increasingly becoming one global marketplace and that emerging markets in Asia as well as other parts of the world offer tremendous opportunities for growth. They also know that advertising and other promotional tools will play an important role in reaching the new global consumers.

Sources: Ernest Beck, "Johnnie Walker Scotch Tries a New Tack," *The Wall Street Journal,* November 16, 1999, p. B8; Robert L. Simison, "Ford to Debut Ad at Same Time Globally," *The Wall Street Journal,* October 27, 1999, p. B8; Elizabeth MacDonald, "PriceWaterhouse Issues Global Invitation," *The Wall Street Journal,* March 9, 1999, p. B8; Fara Warner and Karen Hsu, "Intel Gets a Free Ride in China by Sticking Its Name on Bicycles," *The Wall Street Journal,* August 7, 1996, p. B5.

expenditures also reflects the fact that marketers around the world recognize the value and importance of advertising and promotion. Promotional strategies play an important role in the marketing programs of companies as they attempt to communicate with and sell their products to their customers. To understand the roles advertising and promotion play in the marketing process, let us first examine the marketing function.

What Is Marketing?

Before reading on, stop for a moment and think about how you would define marketing. Chances are that each reader of this book will come up with a somewhat different answer, since marketing is often viewed in terms of individual activities that constitute the overall marketing process. One popular conception of marketing is that it primarily involves sales. Other perspectives view marketing as consisting of advertising or retailing activities. For some of you, market research, pricing, or product planning may come to mind.

While all these activities are part of marketing, it encompasses more than just these individual elements. The American Marketing Association, which represents marketing professionals in the United States and Canada, defines **marketing** as

> the process of planning and executing the conception, pricing, promotion, and distribution of ideas, goods, and services to create exchanges that satisfy individual and organizational objectives.[3]

Effective marketing requires that managers recognize the interdependence of such activities as sales and promotion and how they can be combined to develop a marketing program.

Marketing Focuses on Exchange

The AMA definition recognizes that **exchange** is a central concept in marketing.[4] For exchange to occur, there must be two or more parties with something of value to one another, a desire and ability to give up that something to the other party, and a way to communicate with each other. Advertising and promotion play an important role in the exchange process by informing consumers of an organization's product or service and convincing them of its ability to satisfy their needs or wants.

Not all marketing transactions involve the exchange of money for a tangible product or service. Nonprofit organizations such as charities, religious groups, the arts, and colleges and universities (probably including the one you are attending) receive millions of dollars in donations every year. Nonprofits often use ads like the one in Exhibit 1–2 to solicit contributions from the public. Donors generally do not receive any material benefits for their contributions; they donate in exchange for intangible social and psychological satisfactions such as feelings of goodwill and altruism.

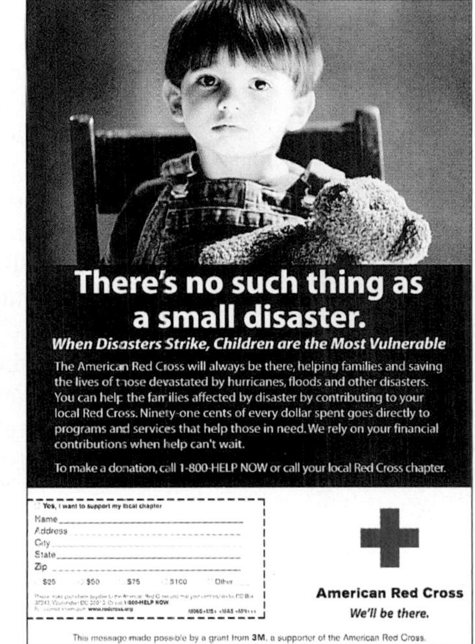

Exhibit 1–2 Nonprofit organizations use advertising to solicit contributions and support

Relationship Marketing

Today, most marketers are seeking more than just a one-time exchange or transaction with customers. The focus of market-driven companies is on developing and sustaining *relationships* with their customers. This has led to a new emphasis on **relationship marketing,** which involves creating, maintaining, and enhancing long-term relationships with individual customers as well as other stakeholders for mutual benefit.[5]

The movement toward relationship marketing is due to several factors. First, companies recognize that customers have become much more demanding. Consumers desire *superior customer value,* which includes quality products and services that are competitively priced, convenient to purchase, delivered on time, and supported by excellent customer service. They also want personalized products and services that are tailored to their specific needs and wants. Advances in information technology, along with flexible manufacturing systems and new marketing processes, have led to **mass customization,** whereby a company can make a product or deliver a service in response to a particular customer's needs in a cost-effective way.[6] New technology is making it possible to configure and personalize a wide array of products and services including computers, automobiles, clothing, golf clubs, cosmetics, mortgages, and vitamins. Consumers can log on to websites such as Mattel Inc.'s barbie.com and design their own Barbie pal doll or Fingerhut's myjewelry.com to design their own rings. Technological developments are also likely to make the mass customization of advertising more practical as well.[7]

Another major reason why marketers are emphasizing relationships is that it is often more cost-effective to retain customers than to acquire new ones. Marketers are giving more attention to the *lifetime value* of a customer because studies have shown that reducing customer defections by just 5 percent can increase future profit by as much as 30 to 90 percent.[8] Exhibit 1–3 shows an ad for Dell Computer, a company that recognizes the importance of developing long-term relationships with its customers.

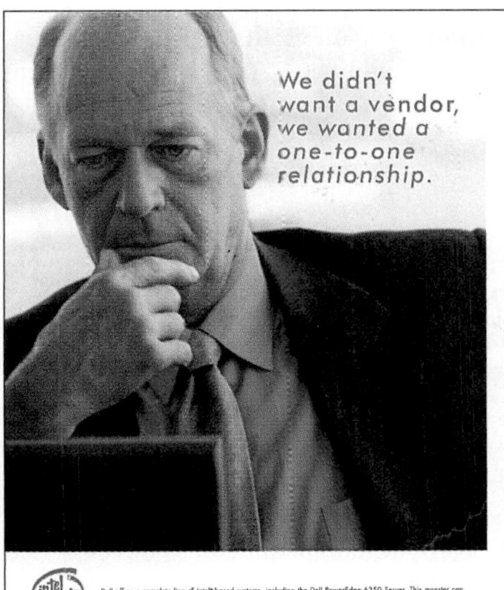

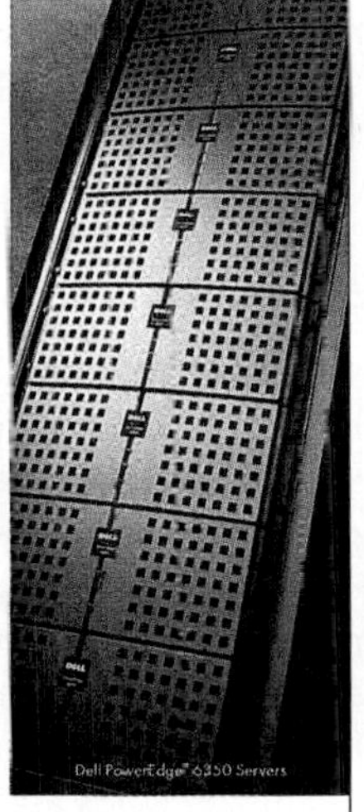

Exhibit 1–3 Dell Computer recognizes the importance of developing relationships with customers

The Marketing Mix

Marketing facilitates the exchange process and the development of relationships by carefully examining the needs and wants of consumers, developing a product or service that satisfies these needs, offering it at a certain price, making it available through a particular place or channel of distribution, and developing a program of promotion or communication to create awareness and interest. These four Ps—product, price, place (distribution), and promotion—are elements of the **marketing mix.** The basic task of marketing is combining these four elements into a marketing program to facilitate the potential for exchange with consumers in the marketplace.

The proper marketing mix does not just happen. Marketers must be knowledgeable about the issues and options involved in each element of the mix. They must also be aware of how these elements can be combined to provide an effective marketing program. The market must be analyzed through consumer research and this information used to develop an overall marketing strategy and mix.

The primary focus of this book is on one element of the marketing mix: the promotional variable. However, the promotional program must be part of a viable marketing strategy and be coordinated with other marketing activities. A firm can spend large sums on advertising or sales promotion, but it stands little chance of success if the product is of poor quality, is priced improperly, or does not have adequate distribution to consumers. Marketers have long recognized the importance of combining the elements of the marketing mix into a cohesive marketing strategy. Many companies also recognize the need to integrate their various marketing communication efforts, such as media advertising, direct marketing, sales promotion, and public relations, to achieve more effective marketing communications.

Integrated Marketing Communications

For many years, the promotional function in most companies was dominated by mass media advertising. Companies relied primarily on their advertising agencies for guidance in nearly all areas of marketing communication. Most marketers did use additional promotional and marketing communication tools, but sales promotion and direct marketing agencies as well as package design firms were generally viewed as auxiliary services and often used on a per-project basis. Public relations agencies were used to manage the organization's publicity, image, and affairs with relevant publics on an ongoing basis but were not viewed as integral participants in the marketing communications process.

Many marketers built strong barriers around the various marketing and promotional functions and planned and managed them as separate practices, with different budgets, different views of the market, and different goals and objectives. These companies failed to recognize that the wide range of marketing and promotional tools must be coordinated to communicate effectively and present a consistent image to target markets.

The Evolution of IMC

During the 1980s, many companies came to see the need for more of a strategic integration of their promotional tools. These firms began moving toward the process of **integrated marketing communications (IMC),** which involves coordinating the various promotional elements and other marketing activities that communicate with a firm's customers.[9] As marketers embraced the concept of integrated marketing communications, they began asking their ad agencies to coordinate the use of a variety of promotional tools rather than relying primarily on media advertising. A number of companies also began to look beyond traditional advertising agencies and use other types of promotional specialists to develop and implement various components of their promotional plans.

Many agencies responded to the call for synergy among the various promotional tools by acquiring PR, sales promotion, and direct marketing companies and touting themselves as IMC agencies that offer one-stop shopping for all of their clients' promotional needs.[10] Some agencies became involved in these nonadvertising areas to gain control over their clients' promotional programs and budgets and struggled to offer any real value beyond creating advertising. However, the advertising industry soon recognized that IMC was more than just a fad. Terms such as *new advertising, orchestration,* and *seamless communication* were used to describe the concept of integration.[11] A task force from the American Association of Advertising Agencies (the "4As") developed one of the first definitions of integrated marketing communications:

> a concept of marketing communications planning that recognizes the added value of a comprehensive plan that evaluates the strategic roles of a variety of communication disciplines—for example, general advertising, direct response, sales promotion, and public relations—and combines these disciplines to provide clarity, consistency, and maximum communications impact.[12]

The 4As' definition focuses on the process of using all forms of promotion to achieve maximum communications impact. However, advocates of the IMC concept, such as Don Schultz of Northwestern University, argue for an even broader perspective that considers *all sources of brand or company contact* that a customer or prospect has with a product or service.[13] Schultz and others note that integrated marketing communications calls for a "big-picture" approach to planning marketing and promotion programs and coordinating the various communication functions. It requires that firms develop a total marketing communications strategy that recognizes how all of a firm's marketing activities, not just promotion, communicate with its customers.

Consumers' perceptions of a company and/or its various brands are a synthesis of the bundle of messages they receive or contacts they have, such as media advertisements, price, package design, direct marketing efforts, publicity, sales promotions, websites, point-of-purchase displays, and even the type of store where a product or service is sold. Integrated marketing communications seeks to have all of a company's marketing and promotional activities project a consistent, unified image to the marketplace. It calls for a centralized messaging function so that everything a company says and does communicates a common theme and positioning.

Many companies have adopted this broader perspective of IMC. They see it as a way to coordinate and manage their marketing communications programs to ensure that they give customers a consistent message about the company and/or its brands. For these companies, the IMC approach represents an improvement over the traditional method of treating the various marketing and communication elements as virtually separate activities. However, as marketers become more sophisticated in their understanding of IMC, they recognize that it offers more than just ideas for coordinating all elements of the marketing and communications programs. The IMC approach helps companies identify the most appropriate and effective methods for communicating and building relationships with their customers as well as other stakeholders such as employees, suppliers, investors, interest groups, and the general public.

Tom Duncan and Sandra Moriarty note that IMC is one of the "new generation" marketing approaches being used by companies to better focus their efforts in acquiring, retaining, and developing relationships with customers and other stakeholders. They have developed a communication-based marketing model that emphasizes the importance of managing *all* corporate or brand communications, as they collectively create, maintain, or weaken the customer and stakeholder relationships that drive brand value.[14] Messages can originate at three levels—corporate, marketing, and marketing communications—since all of a company's corporate activities, marketing mix activities, and marketing communications efforts have communication dimensions and play a role in attracting and keeping customers.

At the corporate level, various aspects of a firm's business practices and philosophies, such as its mission, hiring practices, philanthropies, corporate culture, and ways of responding to inquiries, all have dimensions that communicate with customers and other stakeholders and affect relationships. For example, Nike received a

Exhibit 1–4 Montblanc uses a variety of marketing mix elements including price, product design, brand name, and distribution strategy to create a high-quality, upscale image for its writing instruments

great deal of negative publicity from allegations concerning its use of youth labor and the working conditions in some of its factories in Southeast Asia that weakened its image among many younger consumers.[15] The company has had to engage in major public relations efforts to address these allegations and rebuild its corporate image with these consumers.

At the marketing level, as was mentioned earlier, companies send messages to customers and other stakeholders through all aspects of their marketing mixes, not just promotion. Consumers make inferences about a product on the basis of elements such as its design, appearance, performance, pricing, service support, and where and how it is distributed. For example, a high price may symbolize quality to customers, as may the shape or design of a product, its packaging, its brand name, or the image of the stores in which it is sold. Montblanc uses classical design and a distinctive brand name as well as a high price to position its pens as high-quality, high-status writing instruments. This upscale image is enhanced by the company's strategy of distributing its products only through boutiques, jewelry stores, and other exclusive retail shops. Notice how the marketing mix elements that help shape the brand's distinctive image are mentioned in the Montblanc ad shown in Exhibit 1–4.

At the marketing communications level, Duncan and Moriarty note that all messages should be delivered and received on a platform of executional and strategic consistency in order to create coherent perceptions among customers and other stakeholders. This requires the integration of the various marketing communication messages and the functions of various promotional facilitators such as ad agencies, public relations firms, sales promotion specialists, package design firms, direct response specialists, and interactive agencies. The goal is to communicate with one voice, look, and image across all the marketing communications functions and to identify and position the company and/or the brand in a consistent manner.

Many companies are realizing that communicating effectively with customers and other stakeholders involves more than traditional marketing communication tools. Many marketers, as well as advertising agencies, are embracing the IMC approach and adopting total communication solutions to create and sustain relationships between companies or brands and their customers. Some academics and practitioners have questioned whether the IMC movement is just another management fad.[16] However, the IMC approach is proving to be a permanent change that offers significant value to marketers in the rapidly changing communications environment they are facing in the new millennium.[17] We will now discuss some of the reasons for the growing importance of IMC.

Reasons for the Growing Importance of IMC

The move toward integrated marketing communications is one of the most significant marketing developments that occurred during the 1990s, and the shift toward this approach is continuing as we begin the new century. The IMC approach to marketing communications planning and strategy is being adopted by both large and small companies and has become popular among firms marketing consumer products and services as well as business-to-business marketers. There are a number of reasons why marketers are adopting the IMC approach. A fundamental reason is that they understand the value of strategically integrating the various communication functions rather than having them operate autonomously. By coordinating their marketing communications efforts, companies can avoid duplication, take advantage of synergy among various promotional tools, and develop more efficient and effective marketing communications programs. Advocates of IMC argue that it is one of the easiest ways for a company to maximize the return on its investment in marketing and promotion.[18]

The move to integrated marketing communications also reflects an adaptation by marketers to a changing environment, particularly with respect to consumers, technology, and media. Major changes have occurred among consumers with respect to demographics, lifestyles, media use, and buying and shopping patterns. For example, cable TV and more recently digital satellite systems have vastly expanded the number of channels available to households. Some of these channels offer 24-hour shopping networks; others contain 30- or 60-minute direct response appeals known as *infomercials,* which look more like TV shows than ads. Every day more consumers are surfing the Internet's World Wide Web. Online services such as America Online and Prodigy provide information and entertainment as well as the opportunity to shop for and order a vast array of products and services. Marketers are responding by developing home pages where they can advertise their products and services interactively as well as transact sales. For example, travelers can use American Airlines' AA.com website to plan flights, check for special fares, purchase tickets, and reserve seats, as well as make hotel and car-rental reservations (Exhibit 1–5).

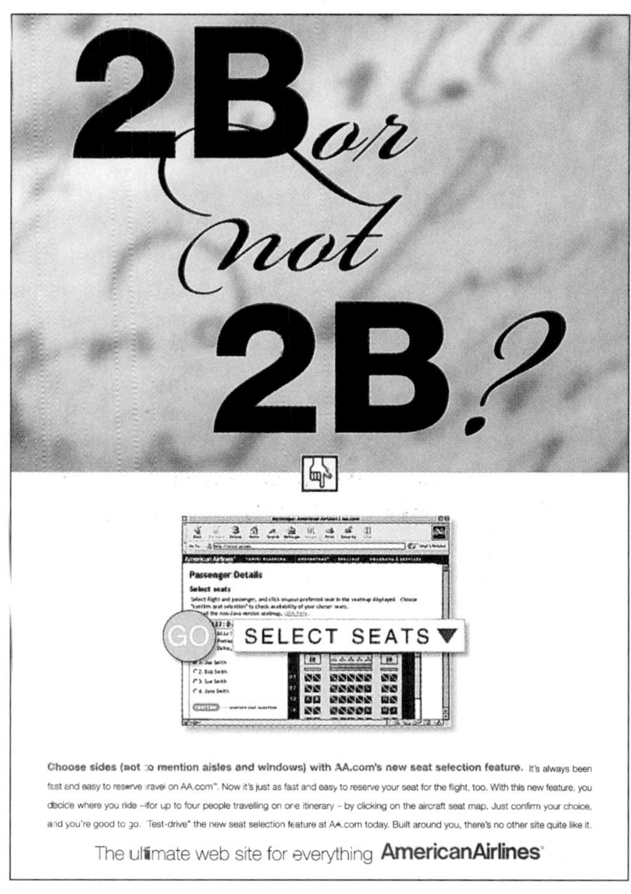

Exhibit 1–5 Travelers can use American Airlines' website to purchase tickets and reserve seats

Even as new technologies and formats create new ways for marketers to reach consumers, they are affecting the more traditional media. Television, radio, magazines, and newspapers are becoming more fragmented and reaching smaller and more selective audiences. A recent survey of leading U.S. advertising executives on trends that will shape the industry into the next century identified the segmentation of media audiences by new media technologies as the most important development.[19]

In addition to facing the decline in audience size for many media, marketers are facing the problem of consumers being less responsive to traditional advertising. They recognize that many consumers are turned off by advertising and tired of being bombarded with sales messages. These factors are prompting many marketers to look for alternative ways to communicate with their target audiences, such as making their selling messages part of popular culture. For example, marketers often hire product placement firms to get their brands into TV shows and movies. MGM/United Artists created special scenes in the recent James Bond movie *The World Is Not Enough* to feature BMW's new Z8 sports car. BMW used the movie tie-in to develop a full-scale promotional campaign to launch the new car.[20]

The integrated marketing communications movement is also being driven by changes in the ways companies market their products and services. A major reason for the growing importance of the IMC approach is the ongoing revolution that is changing the rules of marketing and the role of the traditional advertising agency.[21] Major characteristics of this marketing revolution include:

- *A shifting of marketing dollars from media advertising to other forms of promotion, particularly consumer and trade-oriented sales promotions.* Many marketers feel that traditional media advertising has become too expensive and is not cost-effective. Also, escalating price competition in many markets has resulted in marketers pouring more of their promotional budgets into price promotions rather than media advertising.
- *A movement away from relying on advertising-focused approaches, which emphasize mass media such as network television and national magazines, to solve communication problems.* Many companies are turning to lower-cost, more targeted communication tools such as event marketing and sponsorships, direct mail, sales promotion, and the Internet as they develop their marketing communication strategies.
- *A shift in marketplace power from manufacturers to retailers.* Due to consolidation in the retail industry, small local retailers are being replaced by regional, national, and international chains. These large retailers are using

their clout to demand larger promotional fees and allowances from manufacturers, a practice that often siphons money away from advertising. Moreover, new technologies such as checkout scanners give retailers information on the effectiveness of manufacturers' promotional programs. This is leading many marketers to shift their focus to promotional tools that can produce short-term results, such as sale promotion.

- *The rapid growth and development of database marketing.* Many companies are building databases containing customer names; geographic, demographic, and psychographic profiles; purchase patterns; media preferences; credit ratings; and other characteristics. Marketers are using this information to target consumers through a variety of direct-marketing methods such as telemarketing, direct mail, and direct-response advertising, rather than relying on mass media. Advocates of the approach argue that database marketing is critical to the development and practice of effective IMC.[22]
- *Demands for greater accountability from advertising agencies and changes in the way agencies are compensated.* Many companies are moving toward incentive-based systems whereby compensation of their ad agencies is based, at least in part, on objective measures such as sales, market share, and profitability. Demands for accountability are motivating many agencies to consider a variety of communication tools and less expensive alternatives to mass-media advertising.
- *The rapid growth of the Internet, which is changing the very nature of how companies do business and the ways they communicate and interact with consumers.* The Internet revolution is well under way, and the Internet audience is growing rapidly. The Internet is an *interactive* medium that is becoming an integral part of communications strategy, and even business strategy, for many companies.

This marketing revolution is affecting everyone involved in the marketing and promotional process. Companies are recognizing that they must change the ways they market and promote their products and services. They can no longer be tied to a specific communication tool (such as media advertising); rather, they should use whatever contact methods offer the best way of delivering the message to their target audiences. Ad agencies continue to reposition themselves as offering more than just advertising expertise and convince their clients that they can manage all or any part of their integrated communications needs. Most agencies recognize that their future success depends on their ability to understand all areas of promotion and help their clients develop and implement integrated marketing communications programs.

A successful IMC program requires that a firm find the right combination of promotional tools and techniques, define their role and the extent to which they can or should be used, and coordinate their use. To accomplish this, those responsible for the company's communications efforts must understand the role of promotion in the marketing program.

The Role of Promotion

Promotion has been defined as the coordination of all seller-initiated efforts to set up channels of information and persuasion to sell goods and services or promote an idea.[23] While implicit communication occurs through the various elements of the marketing mix, most of an organization's communications with the marketplace take place as part of a carefully planned and controlled promotional program. The basic tools used to accomplish an organization's communication objectives are often referred to as the **promotional mix** (Figure 1–1).

Traditionally the promotional mix has included four elements: advertising, sales promotion, publicity/public relations, and personal selling. However, in this text we view direct marketing as well as interactive media as major promotional-mix elements that modern-day marketers use to communicate with their target markets. Each element of the promotional mix is viewed as an integrated marketing commu-

Figure 1–1 Elements of the promotional mix

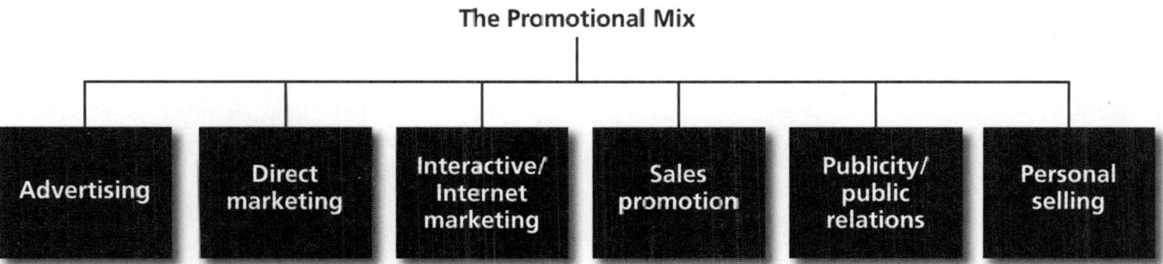

nications tool that plays a distinctive role in an IMC program. Each may take on a variety of forms. And each has certain advantages.

The Promotional Mix: The Tools for IMC

Advertising

Advertising is defined as any paid form of nonpersonal communication about an organization, product, service, or idea by an identified sponsor.[24] The *paid* aspect of this definition reflects the fact that the space or time for an advertising message generally must be bought. An occasional exception to this is the public service announcement (PSA), whose advertising space or time is donated by the media.

The *nonpersonal* component means advertising involves mass media (e.g., TV, radio, magazines, newspapers) that can transmit a message to large groups of individuals, often at the same time. The nonpersonal nature of advertising means there is generally no opportunity for immediate feedback from the message recipient (except in direct-response advertising). Therefore, before the message is sent, the advertiser must consider how the audience will interpret and respond to it.

Advertising is the best-known and most widely discussed form of promotion, probably because of its pervasiveness. It is also a very important promotional tool, particularly for companies whose products and services are targeted at mass consumer markets. More than 130 companies each spend over $100 million a year on advertising in the United States every year. Figure 1–2 shows the advertising expenditures of the 25 leading national advertisers in 1998.

There are several reasons why advertising is such an important part of many marketers' promotional mixes. First, it can be a very cost-effective method for communicating with large audiences. For example, during the 1999–2000 television season, the average 30-second spot on prime-time network television reached nearly 10 million households. The cost per thousand households reached was around $14.00.[25]

Advertising can be used to create brand images and symbolic appeals for a company or brand, a very important capability for companies selling products and services that are

Figure 1–2 25 leading advertisers in the United States in 1998

Rank	Advertiser	Ad Spending
1	General Motors Corp.	$2,940.4
2	Procter & Gamble Co.	2,650.3
3	Philip Morris Cos.	2,049.3
4	Daimler-Chrysler	1,646.7
5	Sears, Roebuck & Co.	1,578.3
6	Ford Motor Co.	1,520.7
7	AT&T Corp.	1,428.0
8	Walt Disney Co.	1,358.7
9	PepsiCo	1,263.4
10	Diageo	1,205.7
11	Warner-Lambert Co.	1,104.3
12	IBM Corp.	1,079.3
13	Time Warner	1,077.3
14	McDonald's Corp.	1,025.4
15	Unilever	1,015.0
16	J.C. Penney	991.9
17	MCI WorldComm	948.4
18	Toyota Motor Corp.	939.2
19	Bristol-Myers Squibb Co.	923.6
20	Sony Corp.	879.6
21	Viacom	825.9
22	Johnson & Johnson	816.5
23	L'Oreal	806.3
24	Federated Department Stores	794.2
25	U.S. government	792.0

Note: Figures are in millions of dollars.

Exhibit 1–6 Creative advertising has made Absolut the most popular brand of imported vodka in the United States

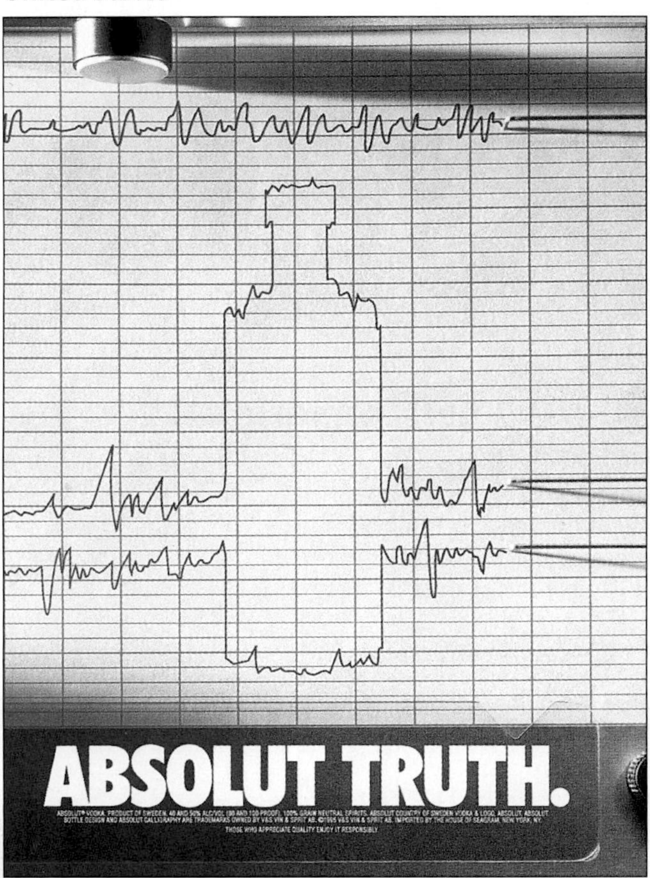

Exhibit 1–7 Eveready uses the popularity of its pink bunny campaign to generate support from retailers

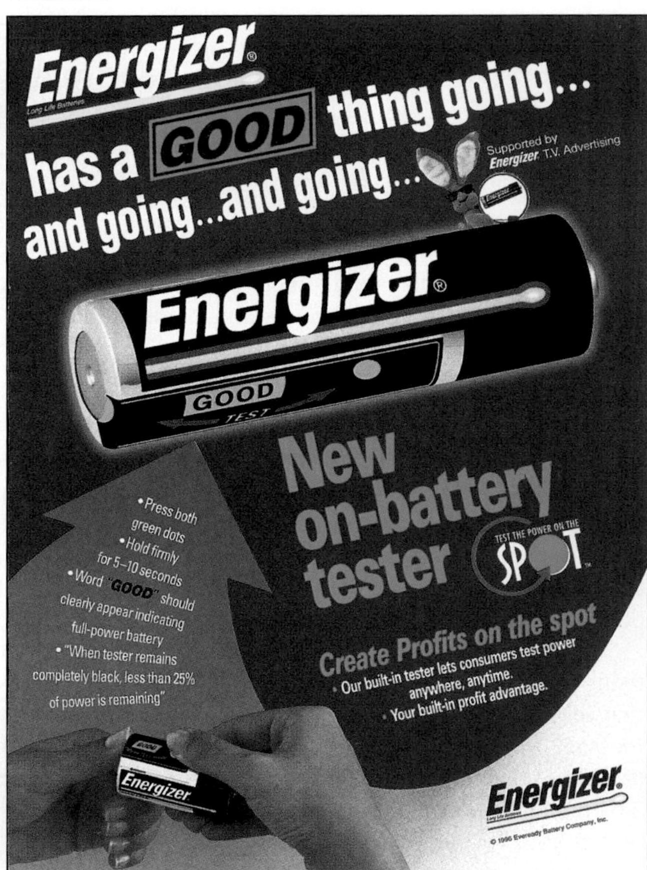

difficult to differentiate on functional attributes. For example, since 1980 Absolut has used creative advertising to position its vodka as an upscale, fashionable, sophisticated drink and differentiate it from other brands. The advertising strategy has been to focus attention on two unique aspects of the product: the Absolut name and the distinctive shape of the bottle (Exhibit 1–6). Most of the print ads used in this long-running campaign are specifically tailored for the magazine or region where they appear. The campaign, one of the most successful and recognizable in advertising history, has made the Absolut brand nearly synonymous with imported vodka. While all other spirits sales have declined by more than 40 percent over the past 15 years, Absolut sales have increased 10-fold and the various Absolut brands have a combined 70 percent market share.[26]

Another advantage of advertising is its ability to strike a responsive chord with consumers when differentiation across other elements of the marketing mix is difficult to achieve. Popular advertising campaigns attract consumers' attention and can help generate sales. These popular campaigns can also sometimes be leveraged into successful integrated marketing communications programs. For example, Eveready used the popularity of its Energizer Bunny campaign to generate support from retailers in the form of shelf space, promotional displays, and other merchandising activities (Exhibit 1–7). Consumer promotions such as in-store displays, premium offers, and sweepstakes feature the pink bunny. Pictures of the Energizer Bunny appear on Energizer packages to ensure brand identification and extend the campaign's impact to the point of purchase. Eveready has extended its integrated marketing efforts to include tie-ins with sports marketing and sponsorships.

The nature and purpose of advertising differ from one industry to another and/or across situations. The targets of an organization's advertising efforts often vary, as do its role and function in the marketing program. One advertiser may seek to generate immediate response or action from the customer; another may want to develop awareness or a positive image for its product or service over a longer period. For example, Exhibit 1–8 shows one of the ads from the popular "milk mustache" campaign. The goal of this campaign, which began in 1995, has been to change the image of milk and help reverse the decline in per-capita milk consumption in the United States.

Marketers advertise to the consumer market with national and retail/local advertising, which may stimulate primary or selective demand. For business/professional markets, they use business-to-business, professional, and trade advertising. Figure 1–3 describes the most common types of advertising.

Exhibit 1–8 The goals of the "milk mustache" campaign are to change the image of milk and increase sales of the product

Direct Marketing

One of the fastest-growing sectors of the U.S. economy is **direct marketing,** in which organizations communicate directly with target customers to generate a response and/or a transaction. Traditionally, direct marketing has not been considered an element of the promotional mix. However, because it has become such an integral part of the IMC program of many organizations and often involves separate objectives, budgets, and strategies, we view direct marketing as a component of the promotional mix.

Direct marketing is much more than direct mail and mail-order catalogs. It involves a variety of activities, including database management, direct selling, telemarketing, and direct-response ads through direct mail, the Internet, and various broadcast and print media. Some companies, such as Tupperware, Discovery Toys, and Amway, do not use any other distribution channels, relying on independent contractors to sell their products directly to consumers. Companies such as L.L. Bean, Lands' End, and J. Crew have been very successful in using direct marketing to sell their clothing products. Dell Computer and Gateway have experienced tremendous growth in the computer industry by selling a full line of personal computers through direct marketing.

One of the major tools of direct marketing is **direct-response advertising,** whereby a product is promoted through an ad that encourages the consumer to purchase directly from the manufacturer. Traditionally, direct mail has been the primary medium for direct-response advertising, although television and magazines have become increasingly important media. For example, Exhibit 1–9 shows a direct-response ad for the Bose Corporation's Acoustic Waveguide products. Direct-response advertising and other forms of direct marketing have become very popular over the past two decades, owing primarily to changing lifestyles, particularly the increase in two-income households. This has meant more discretionary income but less time for in-store shopping. The availability of credit cards and toll-free phone numbers has also facilitated the purchase of products from direct-response ads. More recently, the rapid growth of the Internet is fueling the growth of direct marketing. The convenience of shopping through catalogs or on a company's website and placing orders by mail, by phone, or online has led the tremendous growth of direct marketing.

Exhibit 1–9 The Bose Corporation uses direct-response advertising to promote its audio products

Figure 1–3 Classifications of advertising

ADVERTISING TO CONSUMER MARKETS

National Advertising
Advertising done by large companies on a nationwide basis or in most regions of the country. Most of the ads for well-known companies and brands that are seen on prime-time TV or in other major national or regional media are examples of national advertising. The goals of national advertisers are to inform or remind consumers of the company or brand and its features, benefits, advantages, or uses and to create or reinforce its image so consumers will be predisposed to purchase it.

Retail/Local Advertising
Advertising done by retailers or local merchants to encourage consumers to shop at a specific store, use a local service, or patronize a particular establishment. Retail or local advertising tends to emphasize specific patronage motives such as price, hours of operation, service, atmosphere, image, or merchandise assortment. Retailers are concerned with building store traffic, so their promotions often take the form of direct action advertising designed to produce immediate store traffic and sales.

Primary versus Selective Demand Advertising
Primary demand advertising is designed to stimulate demand for the general product class or entire industry. Selective demand advertising focuses on creating demand for a specific company's brands. Most advertising for various products and services is concerned with stimulating selective demand and emphasizes reasons for purchasing a particular brand.

An advertiser might concentrate on stimulating primary demand when, for example, its brand dominates a market and will benefit the most from overall market growth. Primary demand advertising is often used as part of a promotional strategy to help a new product gain market acceptance, since the challenge is to sell customers on the product concept as much as to sell a particular brand. Industry trade associations also try to stimulate primary demand for their members' products, among them cotton, milk, orange juice, pork, and beef.

ADVERTISING TO BUSINESS AND PROFESSIONAL MARKETS

Business-to-Business Advertising
Advertising targeted at individuals who buy or influence the purchase of industrial goods or services for their companies. Industrial goods are products that either become a physical part of another product (raw material or component parts), are used in manufacturing other goods (machinery), or are used to help a company conduct its business (e.g., office supplies, computers). Business services such as insurance, travel services, and health care are also included in this category.

Professional Advertising
Advertising targeted to professionals such as doctors, lawyers, dentists, engineers, or professors to encourage them to use a company's product in their business operations. It might also be used to encourage professionals to recommend or specify the use of a company's product by end-users.

Trade Advertising
Advertising targeted to marketing channel members such as wholesalers, distributors, and retailers. The goal is to encourage channel members to stock, promote, and resell the manufacturer's branded products to their customers.

Direct-marketing tools and techniques are also being used by companies that distribute their products through traditional distribution channels or have their own sales force. Direct marketing plays a big role in the integrated marketing communications programs of consumer-product companies and business-to-business marketers. These companies spend large amounts of money each year developing and maintaining databases containing the addresses and/or phone numbers of present and prospective customers. They use telemarketing to call customers directly and attempt to sell them products and services or qualify them as sales leads. Marketers also send out direct-mail pieces ranging from simple letters and flyers to detailed brochures, catalogs, and videotapes to give potential customers information about their products or services. Direct-marketing techniques are also used to distribute product samples or target users of a competing brand.

Interactive/Internet Marketing

As the new millennium begins, we are experiencing perhaps the most dynamic and revolutionary changes of any era in the history of marketing, as well as advertising and promotion. These changes are being driven by advances in technology and developments that have led to dramatic growth of communication through interactive media, particularly the Internet. **Interactive media** allow for a back-and-forth flow of information whereby users can participate in and modify the form and content of the information they receive in real time. Unlike traditional forms of marketing communications such as advertising, which are one-way in nature, these new media allow users to perform a variety of functions such as receive and alter information and images, make inquiries, respond to questions, and, of course, make purchases. In addition to the Internet, interactive media also include CD-ROMs, kiosks, and interactive television. However, the interactive medium that is having the greatest impact on marketing is the Internet, especially through the component known as the World Wide Web.

While the Internet is changing the ways companies design and implement their entire business and marketing strategies, it is also affecting their marketing communications programs. Thousands of companies, ranging from large multinational corporations to small local firms, have developed websites to promote their products and services, by providing current and potential customers with information, as well as to entertain and interact with consumers. Perhaps the most prevalent perspective on the Internet is that it is an advertising medium, as many marketers advertise their products and services on the websites of other companies and/or organizations. Actually, the Internet is a medium that can be used to execute all the elements of the promotional mix. In addition to advertising on the Web, marketers offer sales promotion incentives such as coupons, contests, and sweepstakes online, and they use the Internet to conduct direct marketing, personal selling, and public relations activities more effectively and efficiently. For example, Exhibit 1–10 shows an ad for Lands' End promoting the fact that consumers can now shop and purchase interactively through the company's website.

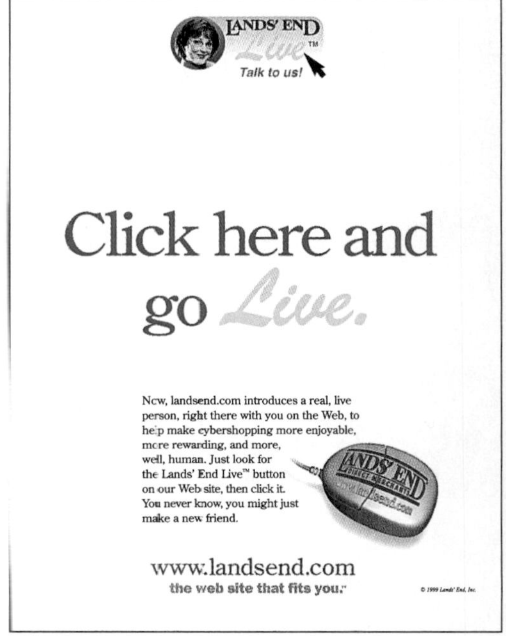

Exhibit 1–10 Lands' End uses its website as part of its direct-marketing efforts

While the Internet is a promotional medium, it can also be viewed as a marketing communications tool in its own right. Because of its interactive nature, it is a very effective way of communicating with customers. Many companies recognize the advantages of communicating via the Internet and are developing Web strategies and hiring interactive agencies specifically to develop their websites and make them part of their integrated marketing communications program. However, companies that are using the Internet effectively are integrating their Web strategies with other aspects of their IMC programs. As discussed in IMC Perspective 1–2, media advertising is becoming increasingly important as a way of driving consumers to websites.

IMC Perspective 1–2

Dot.coms Create an Ad Revenue Windfall for Traditional Media

The rapid growth of the Internet has led many experts to predict the demise of traditional print and broadcast media as more and more consumers go online. However, the old media are actually enjoying a windfall of ad spending from Internet companies that are racing to make their brands widely known outside cyberspace. Dot.coms and Web-related companies are pouring money into advertising as fast as investors pour it into the dot.coms. Many of these companies are paying heed to an old law of advertising that says share of mind leads to share of market. They are concerned that if they don't gain market share now, they are never going to get it. Dot.coms are expected to spend over $7 billion on media advertising in 2000. E-commerce firms such as job-hunting sites Monster.com and HotJobs.com, along with online trading companies such as E-Trade, bought nearly a quarter of the advertising time on the first Super Bowl of the new millennium and drove up the cost of a 30-second spot to nearly $3 million.

The biggest benefactors from the dot.com ad boom are traditional media as well as the advertising agencies that create the campaigns. Web companies want to imprint their names in as many minds as possible, and many are advertising on the major TV networks, which can deliver an audience of 18 million viewers in a prime-time hour. For the beleaguered networks, which have been losing viewers every year, the influx of new advertising comes at just the right time. The explosion of dot.com advertising has created a very tight market for commercial time and has helped push up ad rates 10 to 20 percent.

Pinhead Phil doesn't even know I'm leaving. hotjobs.com

Control who sees your resume with Hotblock. Only at the hottest hand on the web

Dot.com start-ups, most of which are desperate for name recognition, are also spending millions of dollars in good old low-tech radio. Radio ad revenues from Internet companies have been growing at 300 percent per year and are helping the medium experience its fastest advertising growth in history. Many of the Internet start-ups are turning to radio because they see it as a fast and relatively inexpensive way to build name recognition. Most of the dot.coms do not have time for carefully honed branding strategies and complicated media campaigns. Radio spots can be created in a few days, compared with a minimum of four weeks for a television commercial. Radio and TV are not the only media getting a windfall from the influx of dot.com ads. Many Internet start-ups are flocking to magazines and newspapers, particularly business publications such as *The Wall Street Journal, Fortune,* and *Business Week.*

Advertising agencies are also enjoying the skyrocketing demand for their services, and many are struggling to keep pace with it. The chief marketing officer of the TBWA/Chiat Day agency notes that her agency declined offers to handle well over 100 dot.com companies with prospective ad budgets of close to half a million dollars. Agencies that do take on dot.com clients are finding they must develop campaigns in Internet time where speed is crucial. Rather than having two or three months to develop an identity campaign, they are being asked to create attention-getting, edgy commercials in a few weeks. Many of the TV spots for the dot.coms use irreverent ads that rely on humor and shock value to get attention. Steve Hayden, president of brand services at the Ogilvy & Mather Worldwide agency, notes that most dot.com ads tend to have the same Generation X sensibility, a commonality that may have more to do with the age of the company founders than the sensibility of the audience. He predicts that the irreverent campaigns will give way to a more straightforward, "old-fashioned selling" approach.

It is difficult to fault the dot.coms for wanting to make a lot of noise and get the attention of consumers. Most experts predict there will be a dot.com shakeout as we enter the new millennium. For every dot.com that survives, hundreds of Internet start-ups will disappear and dot.com launches will be more select. Those that do survive will get stronger and have the marketing clout to leave weaker sites in the dust.com. Within a few years the windfall may end for the traditional media, as dot.com spending is expected to plateau once the winning companies take command of their markets. However, for the next few years, the traditional print and broadcast media are going to enjoy the dot.com spending spree until it goes kaboom.com.

Sources: Bradley Johnson, "Boom or Bust?" *Advertising Age's Interactive*, November 1, 1999, pp. 3, 52; Daniel Eisenberg, "The Net Loves Old Media," *Time*, November 1, 1999, pp. 60–61; Suein L. Hwang, "Old Media Get a Web Windfall," *The Wall Street Journal*, September 17, 1999, pp. B1, 3.

Sales Promotion

The next variable in the promotional mix is **sales promotion,** which is generally defined as those marketing activities that provide extra value or incentives to the sales force, distributors, or the ultimate consumer and can stimulate immediate sales. Sales promotion is generally broken into two major categories: consumer-oriented and trade-oriented activities.

Consumer-oriented sales promotion is targeted to the ultimate user of a product or service and includes couponing, sampling, premiums, rebates, contests, sweepstakes, and various point-of-purchase materials (Exhibit 1–11) These promotional tools encourage consumers to make an immediate purchase and thus can stimulate short-term sales. *Trade-oriented sales promotion* is targeted toward marketing intermediaries such as wholesalers, distributors, and retailers. Promotional and merchandising allowances, price deals, sales contests, and trade shows are some of the promotional tools used to encourage the trade to stock and promote a company's products.

Sales promotion expenditures in the United States exceeded $240 billion in 1999 and accounted for more promotional dollars than advertising.[27] Among many consumer package-goods companies, sales promotion is often 60 to 70 percent of the promotional budget.[28] In recent years many companies have shifted the emphasis of their promotional strategy from advertising to sales promotion. Reasons for the increased emphasis on sales promotion include declining brand loyalty and increased consumer sensitivity to promotional deals. Another major reason is that retailers have become larger and more powerful and are demanding more trade promotion support from companies.

Promotion and *sales promotion* are two terms that often create confusion in the advertising and marketing fields. As noted, promotion is an element of marketing by which firms communicate with their customers; it includes all the promotional-mix elements we have just discussed. However, many marketing and advertising

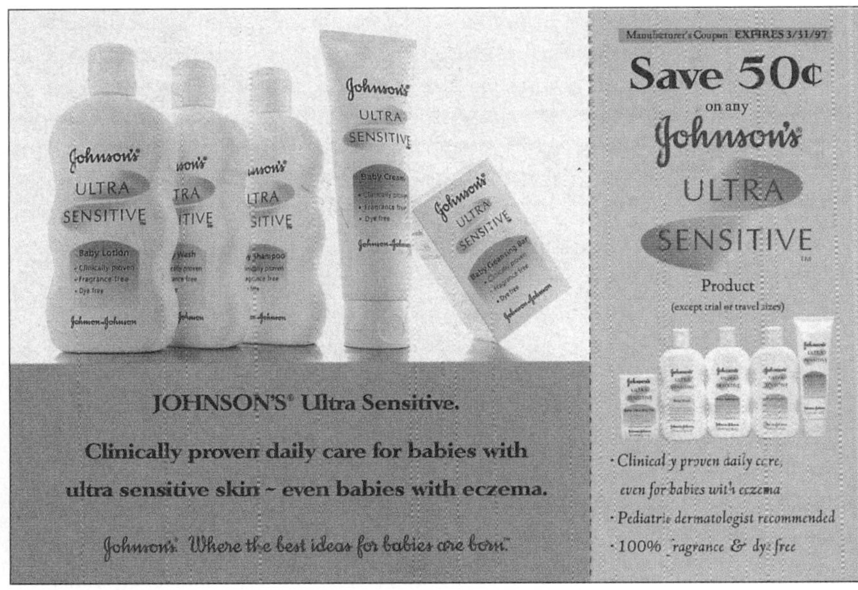

Exhibit 1–11 Coupons are a popular consumer-oriented sales promotion tool

practitioners use the term more narrowly to refer to sales promotion activities to either consumers or the trade (retailers, wholesalers). In this book, *promotion* is used in the broader sense to refer to the various marketing communications activities of an organization.

Publicity/Public Relations

Another important component of an organization's promotional mix is publicity/ public relations.

Publicity

Publicity refers to nonpersonal communications regarding an organization, product, service, or idea not directly paid for or run under identified sponsorship. It usually comes in the form of a news story, editorial, or announcement about an organization and/or its products and services. Like advertising, publicity involves nonpersonal communication to a mass audience, but unlike advertising, publicity is not directly paid for by the company. The company or organization attempts to get the media to cover or run a favorable story on a product, service, cause, or event to affect awareness, knowledge, opinions, and/or behavior. Techniques used to gain publicity include news releases, press conferences, feature articles, photographs, films, and videotapes.

An advantage of publicity over other forms of promotion is its credibility. Consumers generally tend to be less skeptical toward favorable information about a product or service when it comes from a source they perceive as unbiased. For example, the success (or failure) of a new movie is often determined by the reviews it receives from film critics, who are viewed by many moviegoers as objective evaluators. Another advantage of publicity is its low cost, since the company is not paying for time or space in a mass medium such as TV, radio, or newspapers. While an organization may incur some costs in developing publicity items or maintaining a staff to do so, these expenses will be far less than those for the other promotional programs.

Publicity is not always under the control of an organization and is sometimes unfavorable. Negative stories about a company and/or its products can be very damaging. For example, a few years ago negative stories about abdominal exercise machines appeared on ABC's "20/20" and NBC's "Dateline" newsmagazine TV shows. Before these stories aired, more than $3 million worth of the machines were being sold each week, primarily through infomercials. After the negative stories aired, sales of the machines dropped immediately; within a few months the product category was all but dead.[29] Ethical Perspective 1–3 discusses an example of how Metabolife tried to preempt negative publicity about one of its products.

Public Relations

It is important to recognize the distinction between publicity and public relations. When an organization systematically plans and distributes information in an attempt to control and manage its image and the nature of the publicity it receives, it is really engaging in a function known as public relations. **Public relations** is defined as "the management function which evaluates public attitudes, identifies the policies and procedures of an individual or organization with the public interest, and executes a program of action to earn public understanding and acceptance."[30] Public relations generally has a broader objective than publicity, as its purpose is to establish and maintain a positive image of the company among its various publics.

Public relations uses publicity and a variety of other tools—including special publications, participation in community activities, fund-raising, sponsorship of special events, and various public affairs activities—to enhance an organization's image. Organizations also use advertising as a public relations tool. For example, Exhibit 1–12 shows a corporate ad for DuPont, which shows how the company uses science to make life better.

Traditionally, publicity and public relations have been considered more supportive than primary to the marketing and promotional process. However, many firms have begun making PR an integral part of their predetermined marketing and

Ethical Perspective 1–3

Using the Internet to Preempt Negative Publicity

Marketers often find themselves in a situation where they must respond to negative publicity concerning their products. Companies usually fight back against bad press by issuing strong denials, running ads to present their side of the issue, and, occasionally, taking legal action against the news media after a story has been run. However, Metabolife, a company that makes diet pills and weight-loss supplement products, responded to negative publicity it was about to receive during a segment of ABC's "20/20" news program by utilizing the Internet to refute the story. In an unprecedented preemptive move, the company took the unusual step of posting the interview its chief executive, Michael Ellis, had given to "20/20" on its website before the interview actually aired.

Metabolife generates more than $1 billion in sales each year selling diet pills and weight-loss supplement products that it claims help people lose weight by speeding up the body's metabolism, using a combination of caffeine and the herbal stimulant ephedra. Two university studies have endorsed Metabolife's efficacy claims for weight loss. However, some scientists and doctors have expressed concern over the long-term safety of the company's product, arguing that extended use can have damaging side effects ranging from nervousness to strokes. The Food and Drug Administration has been unable to institute more stringent labeling and dosage rules for ephedrine dietary supplements such as Metabolife's products becuase it has limited powers to regulate herbal remedies.

Metabolife recently began receiving extensive media scrutiny regarding the efficacy and potentially dangerous side effects of its products. In September 1999 ABC's "20/20" correspondent Arnold Diaz taped an interview with Ellis in which concerns about Metabolife's products were discussed as well as the two university studies that the company says show the safety of the diet pills. However, to get Ellis to agree to the interview, ABC had to agree to tape the 70-minute session in front of an audience of several hundred Metabolife employees and allow the company to bring its own camera crew to record the session. An ABC spokesperson said ABC agreed to the unusual conditions because it was important to get the interview with Ellis.

Although ABC had not yet scheduled a broadcast date for the "20/20" story, Metabolife launched its preemptive strike a few weeks after the taping by posting the full, unedited interview with Ellis on a website (newsinterview.com). The company also took out full-page ads in *The New York Times* as well as other newspapers and ran ads on 600 radio stations nationwide directing people to the website. Metabolife noted that it posted the interview on its website because it was concerned that the "20/20" segment would not accurately reflect the facts and it wanted the public to see the entire interview as well as important supporting data it had supplied to ABC. ABC finally ran the story on a broadcast of "20/20" that aired in October 1999.

The posting of the interview on the Metabolife website was the first time that entire unedited and uncut footage of a TV news magazine interview was released by an independent source prior to the broadcast date. Many journalists have expressed concern that Metabolife's web campaign could set a dangerous precedent, encouraging subjects to air their interviews online or even give them to a rival news organization. Some television news executives have expressed concern that the episode could encourage sloppy journalism as reporters rush to get their stories out, and they are considering whether they should require subjects who tape interviews to sign an agreement not to distribute the material beforehand.

Metabolife has defended its actions by stating that it was concerned the "20/20" segment would not report the facts accurately and that it wanted consumers to be able to review the considerable amount of factual data and material available and be able to form their own opinions on the safety of its products. The company stated that it supports vigorous debate and scrutiny but it should be open and honest. It will be interesting to see if other companies follow the lead of Metabolife in taking steps to preempt negative publicity.

Sources: Daniel Eisenberg, "Defending a Diet Pill," *Time,* October 18, 1999, p. 80; Thomas Kupper, "Metabolife Rebuts TV Interview on Web Site," *San Diego Union-Tribune,* October 7, 1999, p. C1; "Metabolife Posts on Web Complete Unedited Footage of *20/20* Interview before the Show Airs," *PR Newswire,* October 6, 1999.

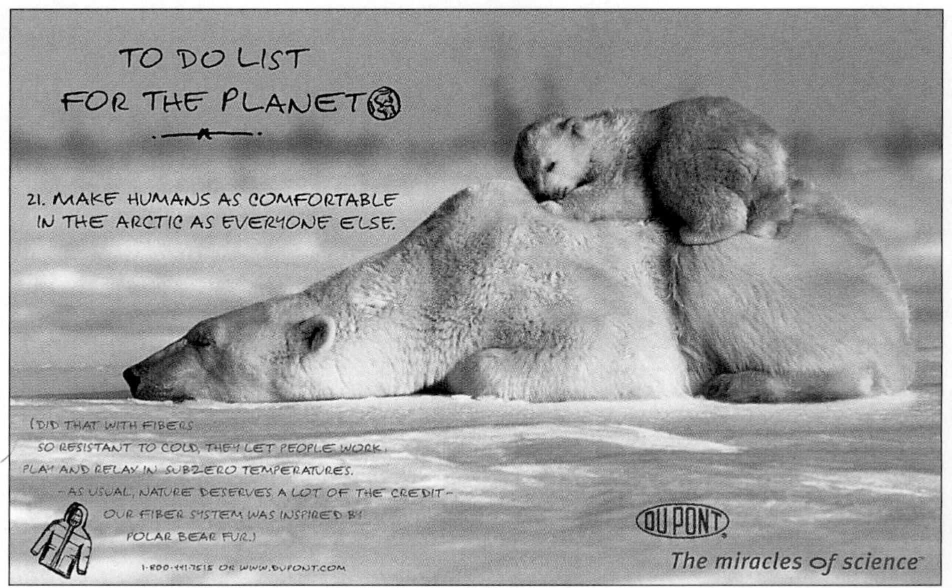

Exhibit 1–12 Advertising is often used to enhance companies' corporate images

promotional strategies. PR firms are increasingly touting public relations as a communications tool that can take over many of the functions of conventional advertising and marketing.[31]

Personal Selling

The final element of an organization's promotional mix is **personal selling,** a form of person-to-person communication in which a seller attempts to assist and/or persuade prospective buyers to purchase the company's product or service or to act on an idea. Unlike advertising, personal selling involves direct contact between buyer and seller, either face-to-face or through some form of telecommunications such as telephone sales. This interaction gives the marketer communication flexibility; the seller can see or hear the potential buyer's reactions and modify the message accordingly. The personal, individualized communication in personal selling allows the seller to tailor the message to the customer's specific needs or situation.

Personal selling also involves more immediate and precise feedback because the impact of the sales presentation can generally be assessed from the customer's reactions. If the feedback is unfavorable, the salesperson can modify the message. Personal selling efforts can also be targeted to specific markets and customer types that are the best prospects for the company's product or service.

Promotional Management

In developing a promotional strategy, a company combines the promotional mix elements, balancing the strengths and weaknesses of each, to produce an effective promotional campaign. **Promotional management** involves coordinating the promotional mix elements to develop a controlled, integrated program of effective marketing communications. The marketer must consider which promotional tools to use and how to combine them to achieve its marketing and promotional objectives. Companies also face the task of distributing the total promotional budget across the promotional mix elements. What percentage of the budget should they allocate to advertising, sales promotion, direct marketing, and personal selling?

Companies consider many factors in developing their promotional mixes, including the type of product, the target market, the buyer's decision process, the stage of the product life cycle, and the channels of distribution. Companies selling consumer products and services generally rely on advertising through mass media to communicate with ultimate consumers. Business-to-business marketers, who generally sell expensive, risky, and often complex products and services, more often use personal selling. Business-to-business marketers such as Honeywell do use advertising to perform important functions such as building awareness of the company and its products, generating leads for the sales force, and reassuring customers about the purchase they have made (see Exhibit 1–13).

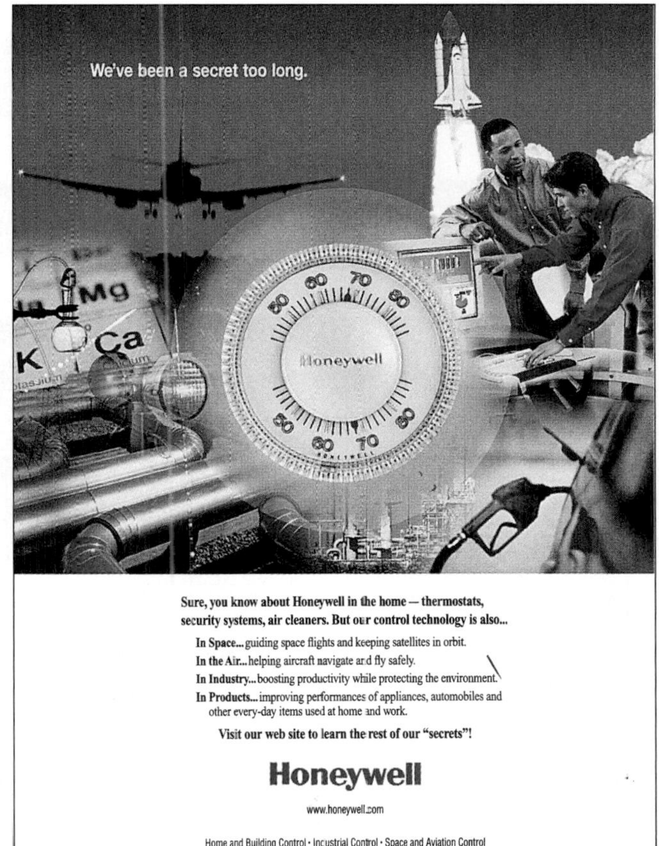

We've been a secret too long.
Honeywell
Sure, you know about Honeywell in the home — thermostats, security systems, air cleaners. But our control technology is also...
In Space... guiding space flights and keeping satellites in orbit.
In the Air... helping aircraft navigate and fly safely.
In Industry... boosting productivity while protecting the environment.
In Products... improving performances of appliances, automobiles and other every-day items used at home and work.
Visit our web site to learn the rest of our "secrets"!
Honeywell
www.honeywell.com
Home and Building Control · Industrial Control · Space and Aviation Control

Exhibit 1–13 Business-to-business marketers such as Honeywell use advertising to build awareness

Conversely, personal selling also plays an important role in consumer product marketing. A consumer-goods company retains a sales force to call on marketing intermediaries (wholesalers and retailers) that distribute the product or service to the final consumer. While the company sales reps do not communicate with the ultimate consumer, they make an important contribution to the marketing effort by gaining new distribution outlets for the company's product, securing shelf position and space for the brand, informing retailers about advertising and promotion efforts to users, and encouraging dealers to merchandise and promote the brand at the local market level.

Advertising and personal selling efforts vary depending on the type of market being sought, and even firms in the same industry may differ in the allocation of their promotional efforts. For example, in the cosmetics industry, Avon and Mary Kay Cosmetics concentrate on direct selling, whereas Revlon and Max Factor rely heavily on consumer advertising. Firms also differ in the relative emphasis they place on advertising and sales promotion. Companies selling high-quality brands use advertising to convince consumers of their superiority, justify their higher prices, and maintain their image. Brands of lower quality, or those that are hard to differentiate, often compete more on a price or "value for the money" basis and may rely more on sales promotion to the trade and/or to consumers.

The marketing communications program of an organization is generally developed with a specific purpose in mind and is the end product of a detailed marketing and promotional planning process. We will now look at a model of the promotional planning process that shows the sequence of decisions made in developing and implementing the IMC program.

The Promotional Planning Process

As with any business function, planning plays a fundamental role in the development and implementation of an effective promotional program. The individuals involved in promotion design a **promotional plan** that provides the framework for developing, implementing, and controlling the organization's integrated marketing communications programs and activities. Promotional planners must decide on the role and function of the specific elements of the promotional mix, develop strategies for each element, and implement the plan. Promotion is but one part of, and must be integrated into, the overall marketing plan and program.

A model of the IMC planning process is shown in Figure 1–4. The remainder of this chapter presents a brief overview of the various steps involved in this process.

Review of the Marketing Plan

The first step in the IMC planning process is to review the marketing plan and objectives. Before developing a promotional plan, marketers must understand where the company (or the brand) has been, its current position in the market, where it intends to go, and how it plans to get there. Most of this information should

Figure 1–4 An integrated marketing communications planning model

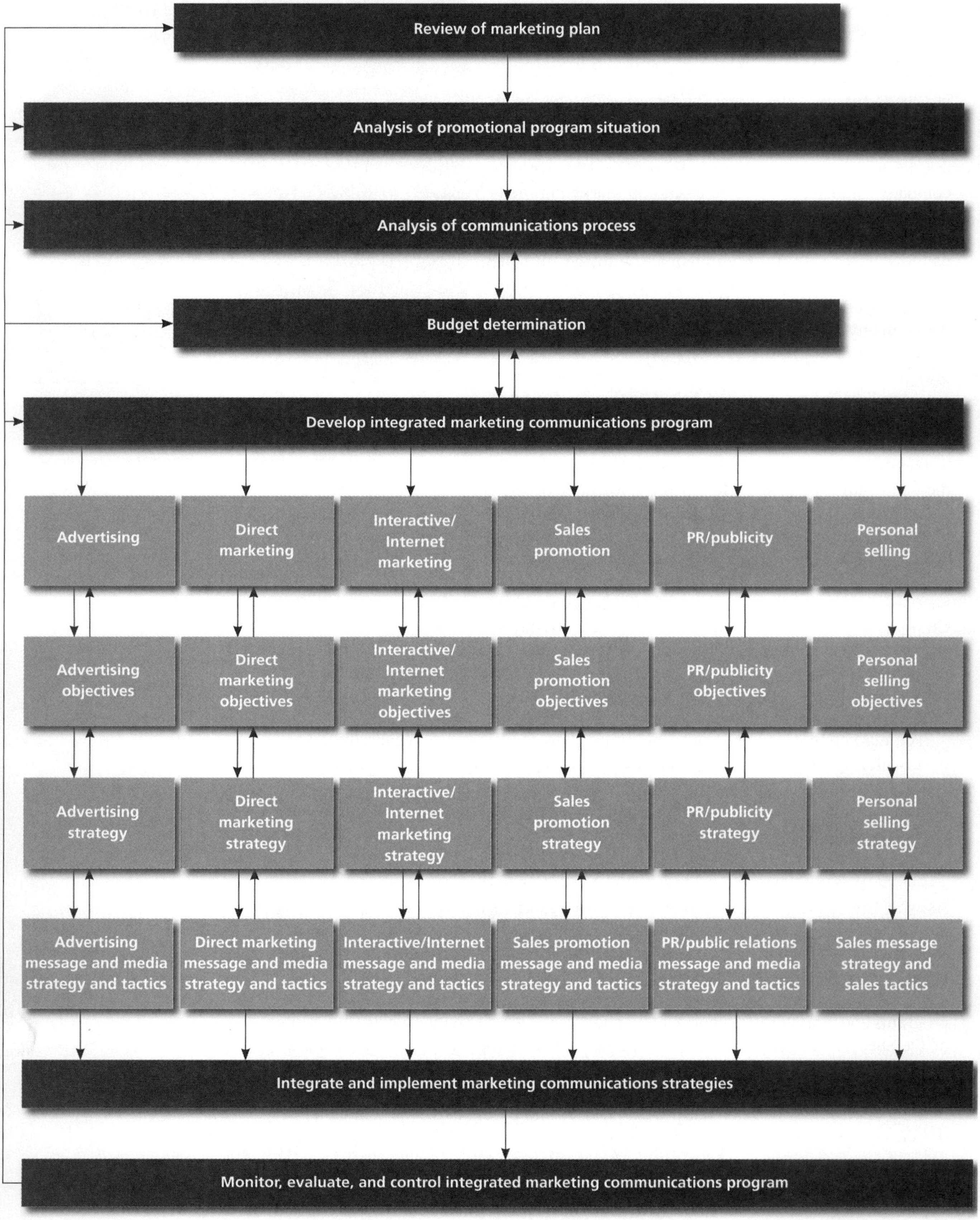

Review of marketing plan

Analysis of promotional program situation

Analysis of communications process

Budget determination

Develop integrated marketing communications program

Advertising	Direct marketing	Interactive/Internet marketing	Sales promotion	PR/publicity	Personal selling
Advertising objectives	Direct marketing objectives	Interactive/Internet marketing objectives	Sales promotion objectives	PR/publicity objectives	Personal selling objectives
Advertising strategy	Direct marketing strategy	Interactive/Internet marketing strategy	Sales promotion strategy	PR/publicity strategy	Personal selling strategy
Advertising message and media strategy and tactics	Direct marketing message and media strategy and tactics	Interactive/Internet message and media strategy and tactics	Sales promotion message and media strategy and tactics	PR/public relations message and media strategy and tactics	Sales message strategy and sales tactics

Integrate and implement marketing communications strategies

Monitor, evaluate, and control integrated marketing communications program

Figure 1–4 Concluded

Review of Marketing Plan
Examine overall marketing plan and objectives
Role of advertising and promotions
Competitive analysis
Assess environmental influences

Analysis of Promotional Program Situation

Internal analysis
- Promotional department organization
- Firm's ability to implement promotional program
- Agency evaluation and selection
- Review of previous program results

External analysis
- Consumer behavior analysis
- Market segmentation and target marketing
- Market positioning

Analysis of Communications Process
Analyze receiver's response processes
Analyze source, message, channel factors
Establish communications goals and objectives

Budget Determination
Set tentative marketing communications budget
Allocate tentative budget

Develop Integrated Marketing Communications Program

Advertising
- Set advertising objectives
- Determine advertising budget
- Develop advertising message
- Develop advertising media strategy

Direct marketing
- Set direct marketing objectives
- Determine direct marketing budget
- Develop direct marketing message
- Develop direct marketing media strategy

Interactive/Internet marketing
- Set interactive/Internet marketing objectives
- Determine interactive/Internet marketing budget
- Develop interactive/Internet message
- Develop interactive/Internet media strategy

Sales promotion
- Set sales promotion objectives
- Determine sales promotion budget
- Determine sales promotion tools and develop messages
- Develop sales promotion media strategy

Public relations/publicity
- Set PR/publicity objectives
- Determine PR/publicity budget
- Develop PR/publicity messages
- Develop PR/publicity media strategy

Personal selling
- Set personal selling and sales objectives
- Determine personal selling/sales budget
- Develop sales message
- Develop selling roles and responsibilities

Integrate and Implement Marketing Communications Strategies
Integrate promotional mix strategies
Create and produce ads
Purchase media time, space, etc.
Design and implement direct marketing programs
Design and distribute sales promotion materials
Design and implement public relations/publicity programs
Design and implement interactive/Internet marketing programs

Monitor, Evaluate, and Control Integrated Marketing Communications Program
Evaluate promotional program results/effectiveness
Take measures to control and adjust promotional strategies

be contained in the **marketing plan,** a written document that describes the overall marketing strategy and programs developed for an organization, a particular product line, or a brand. Marketing plans can take several forms but generally include five basic elements:

1. A detailed situation analysis that consists of an internal marketing audit and review and an external analysis of the market competition and environmental factors.
2. Specific marketing objectives that provide direction, a time frame for marketing activities, and a mechanism for measuring performance.
3. A marketing strategy and program that include selection of target market(s) and decisions and plans for the four elements of the marketing mix.
4. A program for implementing the marketing strategy, including determining specific tasks to be performed and responsibilities.
5. A process for monitoring and evaluating performance and providing feedback so that proper control can be maintained and any necessary changes can be made in the overall marketing strategy or tactics.

For most firms, the promotional plan is an integral part of the marketing strategy. Thus, the promotional planners must know the roles advertising and other promotional mix elements will play in the overall marketing program. The promotional plan is developed similarly to the marketing plan and often uses its detailed information. Promotional planners focus on information in the marketing plan that is relevant to the promotional strategy.

Promotional Program Situation Analysis

After the overall marketing plan is reviewed, the next step in developing a promotional plan is to conduct the situation analysis. In the IMC program, the situation analysis focuses on those factors that influence or are relevant to development of a promotional strategy. Like the overall marketing situation analysis, the promotional program situation analysis includes both an internal and an external analysis.

Internal Analysis

The **internal analysis** assesses relevant areas involving the product/service offering and the firm itself. The capabilities of the firm and its ability to develop and implement a successful promotional program, the organization of the promotional department, and the successes and failures of past programs should be reviewed. The analysis should study the relative advantages and disadvantages of performing the promotional functions in-house as opposed to hiring an external agency (or agencies). For example, the internal analysis may indicate the firm is not capable of planning, implementing, and managing certain areas of the promotional program. If this is the case, it would be wise to look for assistance from an advertising agency or some other promotional facilitator. If the organization is already using an ad agency, the focus will be on the quality of the agency's work and the results achieved by past and/or current campaigns.

This text will examine the functions ad agencies perform for their clients, the agency selection process, compensation, and considerations in evaluating agency performance. We will also discuss the role and function of other promotional facilitators such as sales promotion firms, direct-marketing companies, public relations agencies, and marketing and media research firms.

Another aspect of the internal analysis is assessing the strengths and weaknesses of the firm or the brand from an image perspective. Often the image the firm brings to the market will have a significant impact on the way it can advertise and promote itself as well as its various products and services. Companies or brands that are new to the market or those for whom perceptions are negative may have to concentrate on their images, not just the benefits or attributes of the specific product or service. On the other hand, a firm with a strong reputation and/or image is already a step ahead when it comes to marketing its products or services. For example, a recent nationwide survey found that the companies with the best overall reputations among American consumers are Johnson & Johnson, Coca-Cola, Hewlett-Packard, Intel, and Ben

& Jerry's.[32] Ben & Jerry's was rated the highest in the area of social responsibility, which involves perceptions of the company as a good citizen in its dealings with communities, employees, and the environment. Ben & Jerry's capitalizes on its image as a socially responsible company by supporting various community events (Exhibit 1–14).

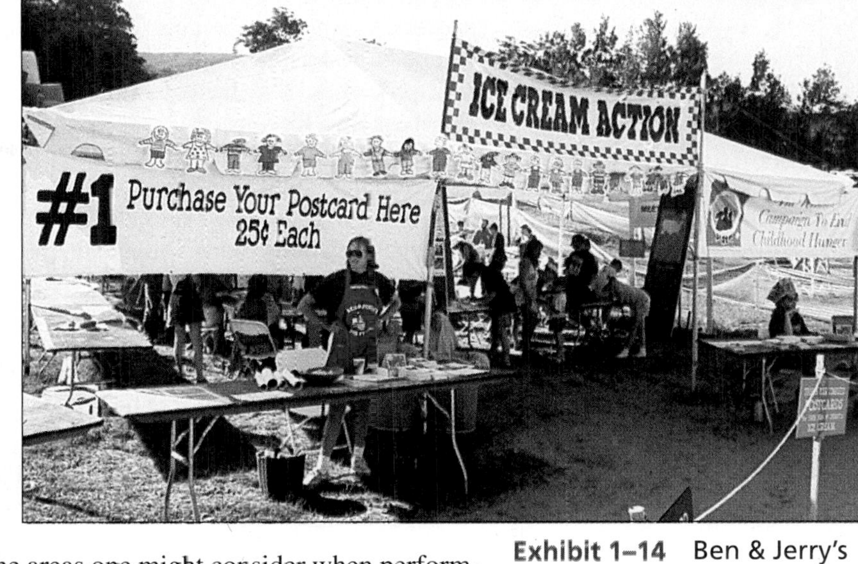

Exhibit 1–14 Ben & Jerry's has a very strong image and reputation as a socially responsible company

The internal analysis also assesses the relative strengths and weaknesses of the product or service; its advantages and disadvantages; any unique selling points or benefits it may have; its packaging, price, and design; and so on. This information is particularly important to the creative personnel who must develop the advertising message for the brand.

Figure 1–5 is a checklist of some of the areas one might consider when performing analyses for promotional planning purposes. Addressing internal areas may require information the company does not have available internally and must gather as part of the external analysis.

Figure 1–5 Areas covered in the situation analysis

Internal Factors	External Factors
Assessment of firm's promotional organization and capabilities	**Customer analysis**
Organization of promotional department	Who buys our product or service?
Capability of firm to develop and execute promotional programs	Who makes the decision to buy the product?
Determination of role and function of ad agency and other promotional facilitators	Who influences the decision to buy the product?
Review of firm's previous promotional programs and results	How is the purchase decision made? Who assumes what role?
Review previous promotional objectives	What does the customer buy? What needs must be satisfied?
Review previous promotional budgets and allocations	Why do customers buy a particular brand?
Review previous promotional mix strategies and programs	Where do they go or look to buy the product or service?
Review results of previous promotional programs	When do they buy? Any seasonality factors?
Assessment of firm or brand image and implications for promotion	What are customers' attitudes toward our product/service?
Assessment of relative strengths and weaknesses of product/service	What social factors might influence the purchase decision?
What are the strengths and weaknesses of product or service?	Do the customers' lifestyles influence their decisions?
What are its key benefits?	How is our product/service perceived by customers?
Does it have any unique selling points?	How do demographic factors influence the purchase decision?
Assessment of packaging/labeling/brand image	**Competitive analysis**
How does our product/service compare with competition?	Who are our direct and indirect competitors?
	What key benefits and positioning are used by our competitors?
	What is our position relative to the competition?
	How big are competitors' ad budgets?
	What message and media strategies are competitors using?
	Environmental analysis
	Are there any current trends or developments that might affect the promotional program?

External Analysis The **external analysis** focuses on factors such as characteristics of the firm's customers, market segments, positioning strategies, and competitors, as shown in Figure 1–5. An important part of the external analysis is a detailed consideration of customers' characteristics and buying patterns, their decision processes, and factors influencing their purchase decisions. Attention must also be given to consumers' perceptions and attitudes, lifestyles, and criteria for making purchase decisions. Often, marketing research studies are needed to answer some of these questions.

A key element of the external analysis is an assessment of the market. The attractiveness of various market segments must be evaluated and the segments to target identified. Once the target markets are chosen, the emphasis will be on determining how the product should be positioned. What image or place should it have in consumers' minds?

The external phase of the promotional program situation analysis also includes an in-depth examination of both direct and indirect competitors. While competitors were analyzed in the overall marketing situation analysis, even more attention is devoted to promotional aspects at this phase. Focus is on the firm's primary competitors: their specific strengths and weaknesses; their segmentation, targeting, and positioning strategies; and the promotional strategies they employ. The size and allocation of their promotional budgets, their media strategies, and the messages they are sending to the marketplace should all be considered.

Analysis of the Communications Process

This stage of the promotional planning process examines how the company can effectively communicate with consumers in its target markets. The promotional planner must think about the process consumers will go through in responding to marketing communications. The response process for products or services where consumer decision making is characterized by a high level of interest is often different from that for low-involvement or routine purchase decisions. These differences will influence the promotional strategy.

Communication decisions regarding the use of various source, message, and channel factors must also be considered. The promotional planner should recognize the different effects various types of advertising messages might have on consumers and whether they are appropriate for the product or brand. Issues such as whether a celebrity spokesperson should be used and at what cost may also be studied. Preliminary discussion of media mix options (print, TV, radio, newspaper, direct marketing) and their cost implications might also occur at this stage.

An important part of this stage of the promotional planning process is establishing communication goals and objectives. In this text, we stress the importance of distinguishing between communication and marketing objectives. **Marketing objectives** refer to what is to be accomplished by the overall marketing program. They are often stated in terms of sales, market share, or profitability.

Communication objectives refer to what the firm seeks to accomplish with its promotional program. They are often stated in terms of the nature of the message to be communicated or what specific communication effects are to be achieved. Communication objectives may include creating awareness or knowledge about a product and its attributes or benefits; creating an image; or developing favorable attitudes, preferences, or purchase intentions. Communication objectives should be the guiding force for development of the overall marketing communications strategy and of objectives for each promotional mix area.

Budget Determination

After the communication objectives are determined, attention turns to the promotional budget. Two basic questions are asked at this point: What will the promotional program cost? How will these monies be allocated? Ideally, the amount a firm needs to spend on promotion should be determined by what must be done to accomplish its communication objectives. In reality, promotional budgets are often determined using a more simplistic approach, such as how much money is available or a percentage of a company's or brand's sales revenue. At this stage, the budget is often tentative. It may not be finalized until specific promotional mix strategies are developed.

Developing the Integrated Marketing Communications Program

Developing the IMC program is generally the most involved and detailed step of the promotional planning process. As discussed earlier, each promotional mix element has certain advantages and limitations. At this stage of the planning process, decisions have to be made regarding the role and importance of each element and their coordination with one another. As Figure 1–4 shows, each promotional mix element has its own set of objectives and a budget and strategy for meeting them. Decisions must be made and activities performed to implement the promotional programs. Procedures must be developed for evaluating performance and making any necessary changes.

For example, the advertising program will have its own set of objectives, usually involving the communication of some message or appeal to a target audience. A budget will be determined, providing the advertising manager and the agency with some idea of how much money is available for developing the ad campaign and purchasing media to disseminate the ad message.

Two important aspects of the advertising program are development of the message and the media strategy. Message development, often referred to as *creative strategy,* involves determining the basic appeal and message the advertiser wishes to convey to the target audience. This process, along with the ads that result, is to many students the most fascinating aspect of promotion. *Media strategy* involves determining which communication channels will be used to deliver the advertising message to the target audience. Decisions must be made regarding which types of media will be used (e.g., newspapers, magazines, radio, TV, billboards) as well as specific media selections (e.g., a particular magazine or TV program). This task requires careful evaluation of the media options' advantages and limitations, costs, and ability to deliver the message effectively to the target market.

Once the message and media strategies have been determined, steps must be taken to implement them. Most large companies hire advertising agencies to plan and produce their messages and to evaluate and purchase the media that will carry their ads. However, most agencies work very closely with their clients as they develop the ads and select media, because it is the advertiser that ultimately approves (and pays for) the creative work and media plan.

A similar process takes place for the other elements of the IMC program as objectives are set, an overall strategy is developed, message and media strategies are determined, and steps are taken to implement them. While the marketer's advertising agencies may be used to perform some of the other IMC functions, they may also hire other communication specialists such as direct marketing and interactive and/or sales promotion agencies, as well as public relations firms.

Monitoring, Evaluation, and Control

The final stage of the promotional planning process is monitoring, evaluating, and controlling the promotional program. It is important to determine how well the promotional program is meeting communications objectives and helping the firm accomplish its overall marketing goals and objectives. The promotional planner wants to know not only how well the promotional program is doing but also why. For example, problems with the advertising program may lie in the nature of the message or in a media plan that does not reach the target market effectively. The manager must know the reasons for the results in order to take the right steps to correct the program.

This final stage of the process is designed to provide managers with continual feedback concerning the effectiveness of the promotional program, which in turn can be used as input into the planning process. As Figure 1–4 shows, information on the results achieved by the promotional program is used in subsequent promotional planning and strategy development.

Perspective and Organization of This Text

Traditional approaches to teaching advertising, promotional strategy, or marketing communications courses have often treated the various elements of the promotional mix as separate functions. As a result, many people who work in advertising, sales promotion, direct marketing, or public relations tend to approach marketing communications problems from the perspective of their particular specialty. An advertising person may believe marketing communications objectives are best met through the use of media advertising; a promotional specialist argues for a sales promotion program to motivate consumer response; a public relations person advocates a PR campaign to tackle the problem. These orientations are not surprising, since each person has been trained to view marketing communications problems primarily from one perspective.

In the contemporary business world, however, individuals working in marketing, advertising, and other promotional areas are expected to understand and use a variety of marketing communications tools, not just the one in which they specialize. Ad agencies no longer confine their services to the advertising area. Many are involved in sales promotion, public relations, direct marketing, event sponsorship, and other marketing communications areas. Individuals working on the client or advertiser side of the business, such as brand, product, or promotional managers, are developing marketing programs that use a variety of marketing communications methods.

This text views advertising and promotion from an integrated marketing communications perspective. We will examine all of the promotional mix elements and their roles in an organization's integrated marketing communications efforts. Although media advertising may be the most visible part of the communications program, understanding its role in contemporary marketing requires attention to other promotional areas such as the Internet and interactive marketing, direct marketing, sales promotion, public relations, and personal selling. Not all the promotional mix areas are under the direct control of the advertising or marketing communications manager. For example, personal selling is typically a specialized marketing function outside the control of the advertising or promotional department. Likewise, publicity/public relations is often assigned to a separate department. All of these departments should, however, communicate to coordinate all of the organization's marketing communications tools.

The purpose of this book is to provide you with a thorough understanding of the field of advertising and other elements of a firm's promotional mix and show how they are combined to form an integrated marketing communications program. To plan, develop, and implement an effective IMC program, those involved must understand marketing, consumer behavior, and the communications process. The first part of this book is designed to provide this foundation by examining the roles of advertising and other forms of promotion in the marketing process. We examine the process of market segmentation and positioning and consider their part in developing an IMC strategy. We also discuss how firms organize for IMC and make decisions regarding ad agencies and other firms that provide marketing and promotional services.

We then focus on consumer behavior considerations and analyze the communications process. We discuss various communications models of value to promotional planners in developing strategies and establishing goals and objectives for advertising and other forms of promotion. We also consider how firms determine and allocate their marketing communications budget.

After laying the foundation for the development of a promotional program, this text will follow the integrated marketing communications planning model presented in Figure 1–4. We examine each of the promotional mix variables, beginning with advertising. Our detailed examination of advertising includes a discussion of creative strategy and the process of developing the advertising message, an overview of media strategy, and an evaluation of the various media (print, broadcast, and support media). The discussion then turns to the other areas of the promotional mix: direct marketing, interactive/Internet marketing, sales promotion, public relations/publicity, and personal selling. Our examination of the IMC planning process concludes with a discussion of how the promotional program is monitored, evaluated, and controlled. Particular attention is given to measuring the effectiveness of advertising and other forms of promotion.

The final part of the text examines special topic areas and perspectives that have become increasingly important in contemporary marketing. We will examine the area of international advertising and promotion and the challenges companies face in developing IMC programs for global markets as well as various countries around the world. The text concludes with an examination of the environment in which integrated marketing communications operates, including the regulatory, social, and economic factors that influence, and in turn are influenced by, an organization's advertising and promotional program.

Summary

Advertising and other forms of promotion are an integral part of the marketing process in most organizations. Over the past decade, the amount of money spent on advertising, sales promotion, direct marketing, and other forms of marketing communication has increased tremendously, both in the United States and in foreign markets. To understand the role of advertising and promotion in a marketing program, one must understand the role and function of marketing in an organization. The basic task of marketing is to combine the four controllable elements, known as the marketing mix, into a comprehensive program that facilitates exchange with a target market. The elements of the marketing mix are the product or service, price, place (distribution), and promotion.

For many years, the promotional function in most companies was dominated by mass-media advertising. However, more and more companies are recognizing the importance of integrated marketing communications, coordinating the various marketing and promotional elements to achieve more efficient and effective communication programs. A number of factors underlie the move toward IMC by marketers as well as ad agencies and other promotional facilitators. Reasons for the growing importance of the integrated marketing communications perspective include a rapidly changing environment with respect to consumers, technology, and media. The IMC movement is also being driven by changes in the ways companies market their products and services. A shift in marketing dollars from advertising to sales promotion, the rapid growth and development of database marketing, and the fragmentation of media markets are among the key changes taking place.

Promotion is best viewed as the communication function of marketing. It is accomplished through a promotional mix that includes advertising, personal selling, publicity/public relations, sales promotion, direct marketing, and interactive/Internet marketing. The inherent advantages and disadvantages of each of these promotional mix elements influence the roles they play in the overall marketing program. In developing the promotional program, the marketer must decide which tools to use and how to combine them to achieve the organization's marketing and communication objectives.

Promotional management involves coordinating the promotional mix elements to develop an integrated program of effective marketing communication. The model of the IMC planning process in Figure 1–4 contains a number of steps: a review of the marketing plan; promotional program situation analysis; analysis of the communications process; budget determination; development of an integrated marketing communications program; integration and implementation of marketing communications strategies; and monitoring, evaluation, and control of the promotional program.

Key Terms

marketing, 8
exchange, 8
relationship marketing, 9
mass customization, 9
marketing mix, 10
integrated marketing communications (IMC), 10
promotion, 14
promotional mix, 14
advertising, 15
direct marketing, 17
direct-response advertising, 17
interactive media, 19
sales promotion, 21
publicity, 22
public relations, 22
personal selling, 24
promotional management, 24
promotional plan, 25
marketing plan, 28
internal analysis, 28
external analysis, 30
marketing objectives, 30
communication objectives, 30

Discussion Questions

1. Analyze the role of integrated marketing communications in the marketing of automobiles such as the Mazda Protegé. How is each element of the promotional mix used to market automobiles?

2. Discuss the role integrated marketing communications plays in relationship marketing. How might the mass customization of advertising and other forms of marketing communication be possible?

3. The communications-based marketing model developed by Tom Duncan and Sandra Moriarty emphasizes that an organization communicates with its customers at the corporate, marketing, and marketing communications levels. Select a company or organization and discuss how it communicates with its customer at each of these levels.

4. Discuss the various reasons why integrated marketing communications has become so popular among marketers over the past decade. Do you think the growth of IMC will continue? Why or why not?

5. The various classifications of advertising to consumer and business-to-business markets are shown in Figure 1–3. Choose one category of advertising to consumer markets and one to the business-to-business market, and find an ad that is an example of each. Discuss the specific goals and objectives each company might have for the ads you have chosen.

6. Discuss the role of direct marketing as an IMC tool, giving attention to the various forms of direct marketing.

7. Analyze the role of the Internet in the integrated marketing communications program of a company. Discuss how the Internet can be used to execute the various elements of the promotional mix.

8. IMC Perspective 1–2 discusses explosion in advertising being done by Internet-related companies. Discuss the role advertising and other forms of promotion might play in the marketing of a new online company. Find an example of advertising being done by a new dot.com company and analyze it. What are some of the reasons the advertising may or may not be effective in driving consumers to the company's website?

9. Ethical Perspective 1–3 discusses how Metabolife used the Internet to preempt negative publicity the company received from the ABC news show "20/20." Analyze Metabolife's posting of the full version of the "20/20" interview on its website and the use of advertising to encourage consumers to visit the site, as well as ABC's decision to let the company tape the interview. How might the developments in this case affect the reporting done by news organizations?

10. Why is it important for those who work in the field of advertising and promotion to understand and appreciate all various integrated marketing communications tools, not just the area in which they specialize?

Chapter Two

The Role of IMC in the Marketing Process

Chapter Objectives

- To understand the marketing process and the role of advertising and promotion in an organization's integrated marketing program.
- To know the various decision areas under each element of the marketing mix and how they influence and interact with advertising and promotional strategy.
- To understand the concept of target marketing in an integrated marketing communications program.
- To recognize the role of market segmentation and its use in an integrated marketing communications program.
- To understand the use of positioning and repositioning strategies.

Apparel Retailers Re-Dress Themselves

It seems that clothing retailers—like their customers—are very much into changing their styles. In some cases this means a complete makeover, while in others the changes may be much more subtle. One thing is certain, however, and that is—like fashions—nothing remains the same for very long these days. Some of the brands that you may be most familiar with—Gap, Eddie Bauer, Abercrombie & Fitch, and North Face—are just a few of the numerous clothing companies that have recently employed integrated marketing communications to change their images and/or target a different segment of the market.

Perhaps the most successful image change was achieved by the Gap. During the mid-1990s, Gap saw its sales fall and its inventory languish as a variety of competitors copied its products and even its store designs. Faced with a not-so-promising future, Gap decided to invest in integrated marketing and focus efforts on becoming a brand rather than just a retail operation. The makeover started with Gap's 262-store Old Navy division, which was given a significant increase in its advertising budget and the new positioning of "Shopping is fun again." In addition to traditional advertising, a variety of nontraditional ad forms were employed (ads on coffee cups and air fresheners), as were other IMC tools, including instant-win contests and giveaway promotions, promotional products, and sponsorships (an Indy 500 race team). Gap revitalized its Gap stores image as well. The budget was increased to $150 million (from $100 million). Television advertising was reinstated after a 12-year layoff, store windows and outdoor billboards took on a new image, and public relations, event marketing, and promotions were increased. An extremely successful e-commerce site was launched, and salespeople were retained to be more customer-oriented. The other offspring, BabyGap, and the more upscale Banana Republic (BR) stores adopted more of a Gap look, but differentiated themselves as well. For example, BR ran ads for its chino pants—Gap pushes khakis—on "Ally McBeal," "ER," and "The Practice." Store windows, print ads, and catalogs were used to promote suede—BR was one of the only retailers to

do so. The new image was complete and a huge success, with sales increases averaging in the 28 percent range and a new brand essence unrivaled by its competitors.

Another highly successful image change occurred at Abercrombie & Fitch (you may know it as simply Abercrombie). Unlike many of its competitors that tried to broaden their products' appeals to additional markets, Abercrombie pursued a more targeted approach, narrowing its market to the fastest-growing segment of the U.S. population—the 18- to 22-year-old segment. Pricing itself between the Gap and Banana Republic, Abercrombie transformed its image from an outdoor supply store to a college-oriented sorority and fraternity lifestyle position. With print ads laced with sexual undertones, its first television commercials ever, a "magalog" (enormous catalog) with a circulation of over 1 million (including 100,000 paid subscribers), and some controversial publicity, Abercrombie has become a key player in the college market. Limited clothing lines are now offered on its website as well.

Unfortunately, all repositioning strategies are not created equal, nor are their results as rewarding. Take the case of North Face. Long a favorite of the outdoor retailer and rugged hobbyists, North Face has attempted to broaden its appeal to a more mainstream America. The move is an attempt to position North Face in the $30 billion casual sportswear market, with less emphasis on the $5 billion specialty outdoor market. The brand has caught on with the Range Rover yuppie set and fashionable urban kids, but at the risk of alienating North Face's current customers and retailers. The company's fear is that the brand's image will be diluted. So far this seems to be right, as the stock has dropped from 26 to 9 and cash flows have been erratic. Still, North Face believes the outdoor market is hot, and it intends to cash in.

Another brand changing its colors—literally—is Eddie Bauer. After its strongest sales and profits year ever in 1996, the company projected more of the same for 1997 and increased its inventory. Unfortunately, not only did it expand the inventory, it also expanded the color selections, from its traditional hunter greens, burgundies, and navy blues to kiwi, electric blue, and (gads!) red, in an attempt to compete against Tommy Hilfiger and Nautica. When its loyal customer base (25-to-45-year-old nonurbans) balked at the new line, the company realized that it had walked away from its roots and its brand positioning. It quickly returned, and pursued a variety of marketing tactics to reclaim the brand image. Licensing (Eddie Bauer Ford Explorers and Giant Bicycles), increased direct marketing, point-of-purchase advertising, and store revamps have all been employed. The catalog has been redone, and a new focus on e-commerce will hopefully lead the brand back.

What these examples reflect is the necessity of a strong brand image. The more successful companies have focused on a specific image and have developed their IMC campaigns in support of that positioning. Those with difficulties have seemingly drifted from their core images in an attempt to broaden their appeal, resulting in less appeal to existing customers and potential confusion among others. Who will be next to join the list?

Sources: Teri Agins, "Banana Republic's Answer to Khaki Overdose: Chino," *Advertising Age*, March 28, 1999, pp. B1–4; Alice Z. Cuneo, "Abercrombie & Fitch Takes Its Ads to TV," *Advertising Age*, August 2, 1999, p. 1; Kathleen Morris, "A Slippery Slope for North Face," *Business Week*, December 7, 1998, pp. 66–68; Alice Z. Cuneo, "Revamped Colors Send Eddie Bauer Down Wrong Path," and "Abercrombie Helps Revive Moribund Brand via Frat Chic," *Advertising Age*, September 14, 1998, p. 30; Alice Z. Cuneo, "Marketer of the Year," *Advertising Age*, December 15, 1997, pp. 1, 18–20.

The above examples of retail apparel brand's image-creating strategies demonstrate a number of important marketing strategies that will be discussed in this chapter. These include the identification of market opportunities, market segmentation, target marketing and positioning, and marketing program development. The Gap's and Abercrombie's in-depth understanding of their markets and of the importance of a strong brand image coupled with a strong IMC program reflects the solid marketing orientation required to be successful in today's marketplace.

In this chapter, we take a closer look at how marketing strategies influence the role of promotion and how promotional decisions must be coordinated with other areas of the marketing mix. In turn, all elements of the marketing mix must be consistent in a strategic plan that results in an integrated marketing communications program. We use the model in Figure 2–1 as a framework for analyzing how promotion fits into an organization's marketing strategy and programs.

Figure 2–1 Marketing and promotions process model

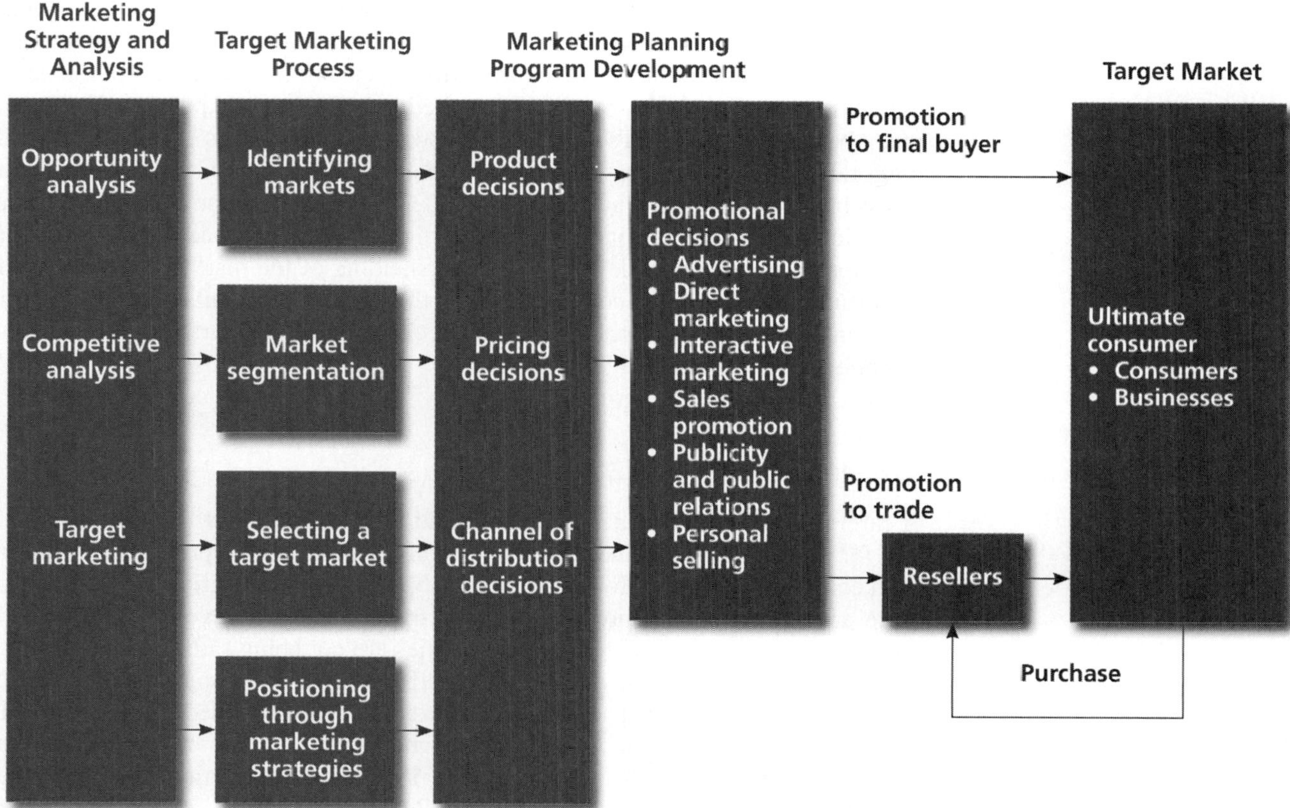

This model consists of four major components: the organization's marketing strategy and analysis, the target marketing process, the marketing planning program development (which includes the promotional mix), and the target market. As the model shows, the marketing process begins with the development of a marketing strategy and analysis in which the company decides the product or service areas and particular markets where it wants to compete. The company must then coordinate the various elements of the marketing mix into a cohesive marketing program that will reach the target market effectively. Note that a firm's promotion program is directed not only to the final buyer but also to the channel or "trade" members that distribute its products to the ultimate consumer. These channel members must be convinced there is a demand for the company's products so they will carry them and will aggressively merchandise and promote them to consumers. Promotions play an important role in the marketing program for building and maintaining demand not only among final consumers but among the trade as well, as evidenced by the North Face example.

As noted in Chapter 1, all elements of the marketing mix—price, product, distribution, and promotions—must be integrated to provide consistency and maximum communications impact. Development of a marketing plan is instrumental in achieving this goal.

As Figure 2–1 shows, development of a marketing program requires an in-depth analysis of the market. This analysis may make extensive use of marketing research as an input into the planning process. This input, in turn, provides the basis for the development of marketing strategies in regard to product, pricing, distribution, and promotion decisions. Each of these steps requires a detailed analysis, since this plan serves as the road map to follow in achieving marketing goals. Once the detailed market analysis has been completed and marketing objectives have been established, each element in the marketing mix must contribute to a comprehensive integrated marketing program. Of course, the promotional program element (the focus of this text) must be combined with all other program elements in such a way as to achieve maximum impact.

Marketing Strategy and Analysis

Any organization that wants to exchange its products or services in the marketplace successfully should have a **strategic marketing plan** to guide the allocation of its resources. A strategic marketing plan usually evolves from an organization's overall corporate strategy and serves as a guide for specific marketing programs and policies. For example, Abercrombie & Fitch's decision to reposition the brand is part of the overall corporate effort to attract a younger audience. As we noted earlier, marketing strategy is based on a situation analysis—a detailed assessment of the current marketing conditions facing the company, its product lines, or its individual brands. From this situation analysis, a firm develops an understanding of the market and the various opportunities it offers, the competition, and the **market segments** or target markets the company wishes to pursue. We examine each step of the marketing strategy and *planning* in this chapter.

Opportunity Analysis

A careful analysis of the marketplace should lead to alternative market opportunities for existing product lines in current or new markets, new products for current markets, or new products for new markets. **Market opportunities** are areas where there are favorable demand trends, where the company believes customer needs and opportunities are not being satisfied, and where it can compete effectively. For example, the number of people who exercise has increased tremendously in recent years, and the market for athletic shoes has reached over $7 billion.[1] Athletic-shoe companies such as Nike, Reebok, and others see the shoe market as an opportunity to broaden their customer base both domestically and internationally (Exhibit 2–1). To capitalize on this growth, New Balance increased its ad budget from $4 million to $13 million—advertising on television for the first time ever—and K-Swiss spent $17 million on its new campaign in 1999.[2] Adidas and Fila have also increased their expenditures.

Exhibit 2–1 L.A. Gear extends its market to France with this ad

A company usually identifies market opportunities by carefully examining the marketplace and noting demand trends and competition in various market segments. A market can rarely be viewed as one large homogeneous group of customers; rather, it consists of many heterogeneous groups, or segments. In recent years, many companies have recognized the importance of tailoring their marketing to meet the needs and demand trends of different market segments.[3]

For example, different market segments in the personal computer (PC) industry include the home, education, science, and business markets. These segments can be even further divided. The business market consists of both small companies and large corporations; the education market can range from elementary schools to colleges and universities. A company that is marketing its products in the PC industry must decide in which particular market segment or segments it wishes to compete. This decision depends on the amount and nature of competition the brand will face in a particular market. For example, Apple Computer is firmly entrenched in the education market. Now it is also targeting the business segment, where IBM and Compaq are strong competitors. IBM, in turn, has gained market share in the education segment. A competitive analysis is an important part of marketing strategy development and warrants further consideration.

Competitive Analysis

In developing the firm's marketing strategies and plans for its products and services, the manager must carefully analyze the competition to be faced in the marketplace. This may range from direct brand competition (which can also include its own brands) to more indirect forms of competition, such as product substitutes. For example, when Lay's introduced Baked Lay's low-fat chips, the product ended up taking away sales from the regular Lay's potato chip brand. At the same time, new consumers were gained from competing brands of potato chips.

In addition to having direct potato chip competitors, Lay's faces competition from other types of snack foods, such as pretzels and crackers. One might argue that other low-fat products also offer the consumer a choice and compete with Lay's as well (for example, fruits).

At a more general level, marketers must recognize they are competing for the consumer's discretionary income, so they must understand the various ways potential customers choose to spend their money. For example, sales of motorcycles in the United States had declined significantly in the late 1980s and early 1990s. This decline reflected shifting demographic patterns; aging baby boomers are less inclined to ride motorcycles, and the number of 18- to 34-year-old males has been declining. The drop in sales could also be attributed to the number of other options consumers could spend their discretionary income on, including Jet Skis, dirt bikes, home fitness equipment, spas, and home entertainment systems such as large-screen TVs and stereos. Thus, motorcycle marketers like Honda and Harley-Davidson had to convince potential buyers that a motorcycle was worth a sizable portion of their disposable income in comparison to other purchase options. Through successful marketing strategies, the industry was effective in reversing the downturn, increasing sales by over 25 percent by the late 1990s.[4]

An important aspect of marketing strategy development is the search for a **competitive advantage,** something special a firm does or has that gives it an edge over competitors. Ways to achieve a competitive advantage include having quality products that command a premium price, providing superior customer service, having the lowest production costs and lower prices, or dominating channels of distribution. Competitive advantage can also be achieved through advertising that creates and maintains product differentiation and brand equity, as shown by the long-running advertising campaign for Michelin tires, which stresses security as well as performance (Exhibit 2–2). For example, the strong brand images of Colgate toothpaste, Campbell's soup, Nike shoes, Kodak, and McDonald's give them a competitive advantage in their respective markets.

Exhibit 2–2 Michelin's campaign stresses safety and performance

Recently, there has been concern that some marketers have not been spending enough money on advertising to allow leading brands to sustain their competitive edge.[5] Advertising proponents have been calling for companies to protect their brand equity and franchises by investing more money in advertising instead of costly trade promotions. Some companies, recognizing the important competitive advantage strong brands provide, have been increasing their advertising investment in them. For example, Listerine increased its marketing budget to $114 million to support its brands,[6] and BMW expenditures increased to $73 million.[7] Sara Lee's ad budget increased from $3.4 million in 1996 to over $22 million in 1998.[8]

Companies must be concerned with the ever-changing competitive environment. Competitors' marketing programs have a major impact on the firm's marketing strategy, so they must be analyzed and monitored. The reactions of competitors to a company's marketing and promotional strategy are also very important. Competitors may cut price, increase promotional spending, develop new brands, or attack one another through comparative advertising. One of the more intense competitive rivalries is the battle between Coca-Cola and Pepsi. The latest round of the "cola wars" has gone international, as discussed in Global Perspective 2–1.

A final aspect of competition is the growing number of foreign companies penetrating the U.S. market and taking business from domestic firms. In products ranging from beer to cars to electronics, imports are becoming an increasingly strong form of competition with which U.S. firms must contend. As we move to a more global economy, U.S. companies must not only defend their domestic markets but also learn how to compete effectively in the international marketplace.

Target Market Selection

After evaluating the opportunities presented by various market segments, including a detailed competitive analysis, the company may select one, or more, as a target market. This target market becomes the focus of the firm's marketing effort, and goals and objectives are set according to where the company wants to be and what it hopes to accomplish in this market. As noted in Chapter 1, these goals and objectives are set in terms of specific performance variables such as sales, market share, and profitability. The selection of the target market (or markets) in which the firm will compete is an important part of its marketing strategy and has direct implications for its advertising and promotional efforts.

Recall from our discussion of the integrated marketing communications planning program that the situation analysis is conducted at the beginning of the promotional planning process. Specific objectives—both marketing and communications—are derived from the situation analysis, and the promotional mix strategies are developed to achieve these objectives. Marketers rarely go after the entire market with one product, brand, or service offering. Rather, they pursue a number of different strategies, breaking the market into segments and targeting one or more of these segments for marketing and promotional efforts. This means different objectives may be established, different budgets may be used, and the promotional mix strategies may vary, depending on the market approach used.

The Target Marketing Process

Because few, if any, products can satisfy the needs of all consumers, companies often develop different marketing strategies to satisfy different consumer needs. The process by which marketers do this (presented in Figure 2–2) is referred to as **target marketing** and involves four basic steps: identifying markets with unfulfilled needs, segmenting the market, targeting specific segments, and positioning one's product or service through marketing strategies.

Identifying Markets

When employing a target marketing strategy, the marketer identifies the specific needs of groups of people (or segments), selects one or more of these segments as a target, and develops marketing programs directed to each. This approach has found increased applicability in marketing for a number of reasons, including changes in the market (consumers are becoming much more diverse in their needs, attitudes, and lifestyles); increased use of segmentation by competitors; and the fact that more managers are trained in segmentation and realize the advantages associated

Figure 2–2 The target marketing process

Identifying markets with unfulfilled needs → Determining market segmentation → Selecting a market to target → Positioning through marketing strategies

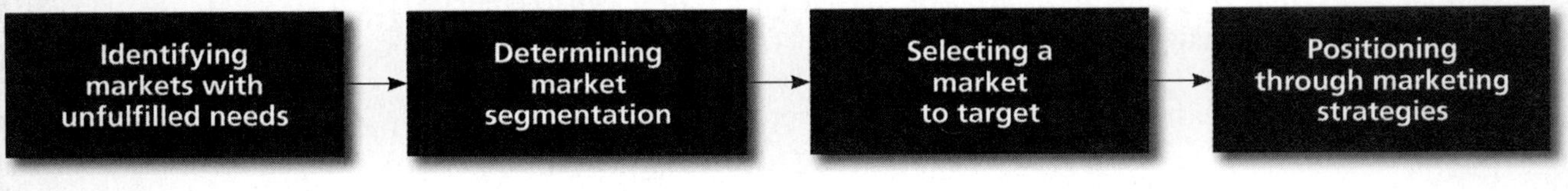

Global Perspective 2–1

Turning the World Coca-Cola Red

For more than two decades, The Coca-Cola Company and its archrival, PepsiCo, have been battling for control of the global soft-drink market. During the 1970s and 80s, most of the battles in the cola wars were fought in the U.S. market. In 1975 Pepsi launched its Pepsi Challenge, which showed consumers preferring the taste of Pepsi over Coke in blind taste tests, and by 1984 it had achieved a 2 percent market share lead over Coke in supermarket sales. Pepsi's success was a major factor in Coca-Cola's controversial decision to change the formula of its 99-year-old flagship brand and launch New Coke in 1985. Consumers loyal to the old formula protested, prompting the company to reintroduce the original Coke as Coca-Cola Classic.

Pepsi's success prompted its top executive, Roger Enrico, to write a book about the New Coke debacle titled *The Other Guy Blinked: How Pepsi Won the Cola Wars.* Pepsi continued to challenge Coke throughout the 1980s and into the 90s as the battle shifted to the fast-growing diet segment of the soft-drink market. Creative advertising such as the campaign for Diet Pepsi that featured Ray Charles singing "You've got the right one baby, uh-huh" seemed to give Pepsi the edge in advertising for a while. However, Enrico's proclamation of victory in the cola wars was premature. Coke has emerged the victor in both the U.S. and the worldwide markets in the most recent and fiercest battle yet of the cola titans.

Coca-Cola's assault on Pepsi actually began in 1993 when the company recognized that it needed to revitalize its advertising and overcome the perception that Pepsi is the hip soft drink for the youth market. The advertising for Coke Classic was turned over to the Hollywood talent firm Creative Artists Agency (CAA), which came up with the popular "Always Coca-Cola" campaign. Many analysts feel that commercials from the "Always" campaign, many of which were seen worldwide, were Coke's most successful advertising in over a decade. The new ad campaign helped The Coca-Cola Company expand its market share lead in the United States to 42 percent versus Pepsi's 31 percent, the largest in 20 years.

To go along with its gains in the United States, Coke also gained significant share in international markets. Coke overcame Pepsi's 10-year lead to become the market leader in Russia, and—through acquisitions—also became the leader in India and Venezuela (where it gained 80 percent market share overnight by convincing Pepsi's leading bottler to convert). Coke was also ahead of Pepsi in Mexico, Germany, Japan, and Brazil. But things do have a way of changing.

In Russia, sales of Coca-Cola quadrupled between 1991 and 1996, but by early 1999 that demand declined by one-third. Overall, in 1999 the bottling plants were operating at only 50 percent of capacity. Economic problems in Asia and South America also hurt the Atlanta-based company, to the point where net income dropped (by 14 percent) for the first time in a quarter of a century. Despite investing $1.4 billion in Brazil between 1995 and 1997, the company had lost 10 percent of the market by 1999. Demand was also declining in Venezuela, despite the billion-dollar acquisition, as Pepsi successfully fought back. A huge product recall in Europe in the spring of 1999 hurt Coke sales there and led to significant increases in marketing spending, though the company says that sales were just about at pre-crisis levels by the fall of 1999.

Things didn't go as well at home either. By the summer of 1999, according to *Beverage Digest,* Pepsi turned around a decade-long share loss to Coke, outperforming Coke in the first part of the year and gaining share. By midsummer, Pepsi had 31.4 percent of the market, while Coke held on to 44.5 percent.

In an attempt to turn around its slumping sales, Coca-Cola took on a new look in the late summer of 1999. While keeping the bottle to ensure its nostalgic image, a new label and presentation mode (cap off, soda fizzing out) were added to give the brand an "edgier" look. The "Always" slogan, adopted in 1993, was replaced in communications with "Enjoy." Bottle caps, stores signs, cans, bottles, and even the delivery trucks carried the new slogan. A new ad campaign was expected to follow.

Meanwhile, Pepsi was marketing a few changes of its own. The long-running "Generation Next" campaign was replaced by the tagline "The Joy of Cola"—reflecting a more mainstream appeal. (Management and the bottlers came to believe the old campaign was too narrowly focused on teens and too off-the-wall.) Aretha Franklin, Isaac Hayes, and Marlon Brando provided voice-overs for the new spots—quite a change from the 80s look featuring Michael Jackson and Madonna.

Pepsi also spun off its restaurant business and placed more emphasis on bottlers to strengthen its distribution system. A new package design—solid blue to differentiate it from Coke's red—also attempted to bolster the new image.

It's been an interesting battle between Coca-Cola and Pepsi. Like a football game, the field position is constantly changing. New plays are constantly being sent in, as are new players—both companies had significant management changes in the late 1990s. Keep watching; the score seems to change as well!

Sources: Nikhil Deogun, "Pepsi Unveils New Advertising Effort, Scraps 'Generation Next' Campaign," *The Wall Street Journal*, March 5, 1999, p. B5; Betsy McKay, "New Look for the Top Pop Aims to Infuse Some Fizz into a Nostalgic Image," *The Wall Street Journal*, October 13, 1999, p. B1; Nikhil Deogun, "Aggressive Push Abroad Dilutes Coke's Strength as Big Markets Stumble," *The Wall Street Journal*, February 8, 1999, p. A1; Patricia Sellers, "How Coke Is Kicking Pepsi's Can," *Fortune*, October 28, 1996, pp. 70–84.

with this strategy. Perhaps the best explanation, however, comes back to the basic premise that you must understand as much as possible about consumers to design marketing programs that meet their needs most effectively.

Target market identification isolates consumers with similar lifestyles, needs, and the like, and increases our knowledge of their specific requirements. The more marketers can establish this common ground with consumers, the more effective they will be in addressing these requirements in their communications programs and informing and/or persuading potential consumers that the product or service offering will meet their needs.

Let's use the beer industry as an example. Years ago, beer was just beer, with little differentiation, many local distributors, and few truly national brands. The industry began consolidating; many brands were assumed by the larger brewers or ceased to exist. As the number of competitors decreased, competition among the major brewers increased. To compete more effectively, brewers began to look at different tastes, lifestyles, and so on of beer drinkers and used this information in their marketing strategies. This process resulted in the identification of many market segments, each of which corresponds to different customers' needs, lifestyles, and other characteristics.

As you can see in Figure 2–3, the beer market has become quite segmented, offering superpremiums, premiums, populars (low price), imports, lights (low calorie),

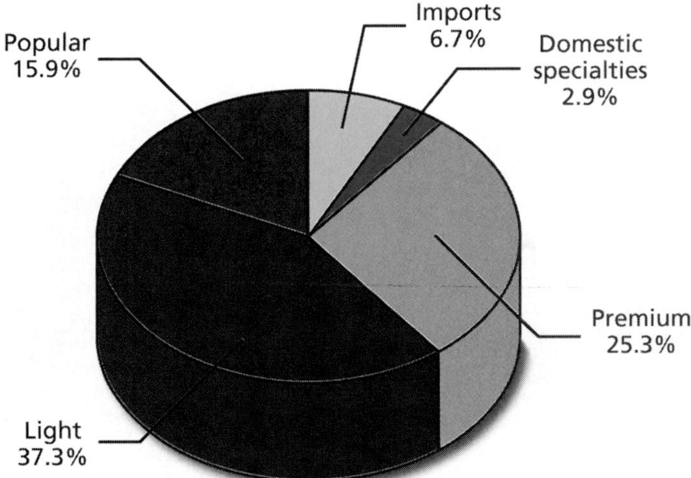

Figure 2–3 Market breakdown by product in the beer industry

and malts. Low-alcohol and nonalcoholic brands have also been introduced, as has draft beer in bottles and cans. And there are now imported lights, superpremium drafts, dry beers, and on and on. As you can see in Exhibit 2–3, to market to these various segments, Anheuser-Busch pursues a strategy whereby it offers a variety of products from which consumers can choose, varying the marketing mix for each. Each appeals to a different set of needs. Taste is certainly one; others include image, cost, and the size of one's waistline. A variety of other reasons for purchasing are also operating, including the consumer's social class, lifestyle, and economic status.

Marketers competing in nearly all product and service categories are constantly searching for ways to segment their markets in an attempt to better satisfy customers' needs. The remainder of this section discusses ways to approach this task.

Exhibit 2–3 Anheuser-Busch offers a variety of products to market

Market Segmentation

It is not possible to develop marketing strategies for every consumer. Rather, the marketer attempts to identify broad classes of buyers who have the same needs and will respond similarly to marketing actions. As noted by Eric N. Berkowitz, Roger A. Kerin, and William Rudelius, **market segmentation** is "dividing up a market into distinct groups that (1) have common needs and (2) will respond similarly to a marketing action."[9] The segmentation process involves five distinct steps:

1. Finding ways to group consumers according to their needs.
2. Finding ways to group the marketing actions—usually the products offered—available to the organization.
3. Developing a market-product grid to relate the market segments to the firm's products or actions.
4. Selecting the target segments toward which the firm directs its marketing actions.
5. Taking marketing actions to reach target segments.

The more marketers segment the market, the more precise is their understanding of it. But the more the market becomes divided, the fewer consumers are in each segment. Thus, a key decision is, How far should one go in the segmentation process? Where does the process stop? As you can see by the strategy taken in the beer industry, it can go far!

In planning the promotional effort, managers consider whether the target segment is substantial enough to support individualized strategies. More specifically, they consider whether this group is accessible. Can it be reached with a communications program? For example, you will see in Chapter 10 that in some instances there are no media that can be used to reach some targeted groups. Or the promotions manager may identify a number of segments but be unable to develop the required programs to reach them. The firm may have insufficient funds to develop the required advertising campaign, inadequate sales staff to cover all areas, or other promotional deficiencies. After determining that a segmentation strategy is in order, the marketer must establish the basis on which it will address the market. The following section discusses some of the bases for segmenting markets and demonstrates advertising and promotions applications.

Bases for Segmentation

As shown in Figure 2–4, several methods are available for segmenting markets. Marketers may use one of the segmentation variables or a combination of approaches. Consider the market segmentation strategy that might be employed to market snow skis. The consumer's lifestyle—active, fun-loving, enjoys outdoor sports—is certainly important. But so are other factors, such as age (participation in downhill skiing drops off significantly at about age 30) and income (Have you seen the price of a lift ticket lately?), as well as marital status. Let us review the bases for segmentation and examine some promotional strategies employed in each.

Figure 2–4 Some bases for market segmentation

Main Dimension	Segmentation Variables	Typical Breakdowns
A. Segmentation Variables and Breakdowns for Consumer Markets		
Customer Characteristics		
Geographic	Region	Pacific; Mountain; West North Central; West South Central; East North Central; East South Central; South Atlantic; Middle Atlantic; New England
	City or metropolitan statistical area (MSA) size	Under 5,000; 5,000 to 19,999; 20,000 to 49,999; 50,000 to 99,999; 100,000 to 249,999; 250,000 to 499,999; 500,000 to 999,999; 1,000,000 to 3,999,999; 4,000,000 or over
	Density	Urban; suburban; rural
	Climate	Northern; southern
Demographic	Age	Infant, under 6; 6 to 11; 12 to 17; 18 to 24; 25 to 34; 35 to 49; 50 to 64; 65 or over
	Sex	Male; female
	Family size	1 to 2; 3 to 4; 5 or over
	Stage of family life cycle	Young single; young married, no children; young married, youngest child under 6; young married, youngest child 6 or older; older married, with children; older married, no children under 18; older single; other older married, no children under 18
	Ages of children	No child under 18; youngest child 6 to 17; youngest child under 6
	Children under 18	0; 1; more than 1
	Income	Under $5,000; $5,000 to $14,999; $15,000 to $24,999; $25,000 to $34,999; $35,000 to $49,999; $50,000 or over
	Education	Grade school or less; some high school; high school graduate; some college; college graduate
	Race	Asian; black; Hispanic; white; other
	Homeownership	Own home; rent home
Psychographic	Personality	Gregarious; compulsive; extroverted; aggressive; ambitious
	Lifestyle	Use of one's time; values and importance; beliefs
Buying Situations		
Benefits sought	Product features	Situation specific; general
	Needs	Quality; service; economy
Usage	Rate of use	Light user; medium user; heavy user
	User states	Nonuser; ex-user; prospect; first-time user; regular user
Awareness and intentions	Readiness to buy	Unaware; aware; informed; interested; intending to buy
	Brand familiarity	Insistence; preference; recognition; nonrecognition; rejection
Buying condition	Type of buying activity	Minimum-effort buying; comparison buying; special-effort buying
	Kind of store	Convenience; wide breadth; specialty
B. Segmentation Variables and Breakdowns for Industrial Markets		
Customer Characteristics		
Geographic	Region	Pacific; Mountain; West North Central; West South Central; East North Central; East South Central; South Atlantic; Middle Atlantic; New England
	Location	In MSA; not in MSA
Demographic	SIC code	2-digit; 3-digit; 4-digit categories
	Number of employees	1 to 19; 20 to 99; 100 to 249; 250 or over
	Number of production workers	1 to 19; 20 to 99; 100 to 249; 250 or over
	Annual sales volume	Less than $1 million; $1 million to $10 million; $10 million to $100 million; over $100 million
	Number of establishments	With 1 to 19 employees; with 20 or more employees
Buying Situations		
Nature of good	Kind	Product or service
	Where used	Installation; component of final product; supplies
	Application	Office use; limited production use; heavy production use
Buying condition	Purchase location	Centralized; decentralized
	Who buys	Individual buyer; group
	Type of buy	New buy; modified rebuy; straight rebuy

Exhibit 2–4 Big Red markets to a specific geographic region

Geographic Segmentation In the **geographic segmentation** approach, markets are divided into different geographic units. These units may include nations, states, counties, or even neighborhoods. Consumers often have different buying habits depending on where they reside. For example, General Motors, among other car manufacturers, considers California a very different market from the rest of the United States and has developed specific marketing programs targeted to the consumers in that state. Other companies have developed programs targeted at specific regions. Exhibit 2–4 shows an ad for Big Red, just one of the regional soft-drink "cult" brands—along with Cheerwine (the Carolinas), Vernors (Michigan), and Moxie (New England)—that have found success by marketing in regional areas (in this case, Texas).

Demographic Segmentation Dividing the market on the basis of demographic variables such as age, sex, family size, education, income, and social class is called **demographic segmentation.** Secret deodorant and the Lady Schick shaver are products that have met with a great deal of success by using the demographic variable of sex as a basis for segmentation. iVillage, a website targeting women, may be one of the most successful websites on the Internet (Exhibit 2–5).

Although market segmentation on the basis of demographics may seem obvious, companies sometimes discover that they need to focus more attention on a specific demographic group. For example, Kodak and Procter & Gamble, among others, have had to redo their images for younger markets. And, as noted earlier, Abercrombie changed its image to reach the "echo boomer" (18- to 22-year-old) segment. The ad in Exhibit 2–6 is designed to give Nail Fetish a different look and increase its appeal to youth.

Other products that have successfully employed demographic segmentation include Virginia Slims cigarettes (sex), Doan's Pills (age), J.C. Penney Co. (race), Mercedes-Benz and BMW cars (income), and prepackaged dinners (family size).

While demographics may still be the most common method of segmenting markets, it is important to recognize that other factors may be the underlying basis for homogeneity and/or consumer behavior. The astute marketer will identify additional bases for segmenting and will recognize the limitations of demographics.

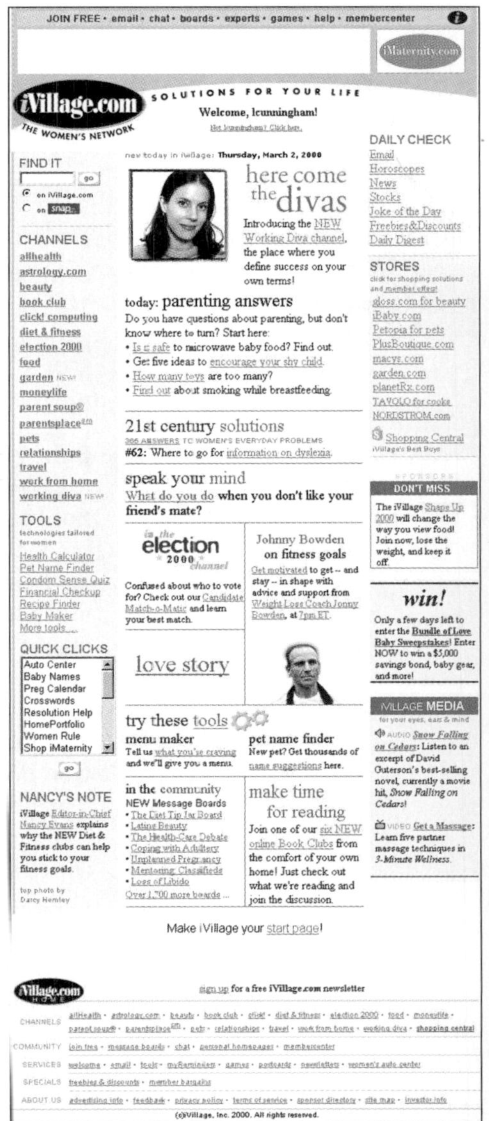

Exhibit 2–5 iVillage initiated a campaign targeted at women

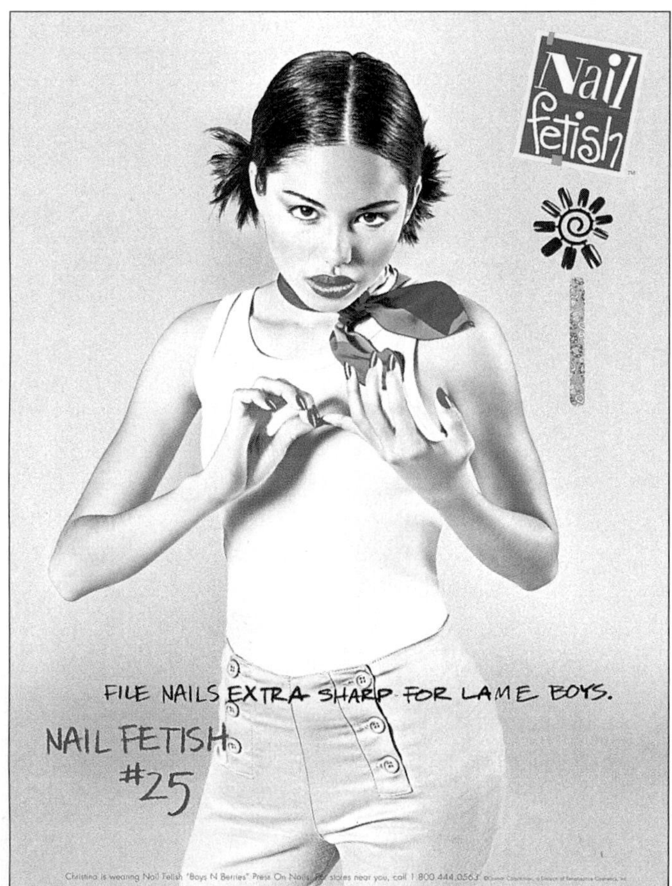

Nail fetish
FILE NAILS EXTRA SHARP FOR LAME BOYS.
NAIL FETISH #25

Exhibit 2–6 Nail Fetish changed its image to appeal to Generation X

Psychographic Segmentation Dividing the market on the basis of personality and/or lifestyles is referred to as **psychographic segmentation.** While there is some disagreement as to whether personality is a useful basis for segmentation, lifestyle factors have been used effectively. Many consider lifestyle the most effective criterion for segmentation.

The determination of lifestyles is usually based on an analysis of the activities, interests, and opinions (AIOs) of consumers. These lifestyles are then correlated with the consumers' product, brand, and/or media usage. For many products and/or services, lifestyles may be the best discriminator between use and nonuse, accounting for differences in food, clothing, and car selections, among numerous other consumer behaviors.[10] (See IMC Perspective 2–2.)

Psychographic segmentation has been increasingly accepted with the advent of the values and lifestyles (VALS) program. Although marketers employed lifestyle segmentation long before VALS and although a number of alternatives—for example, PRIZM—are available, VALS remains one of the more popular options. Developed by the Stanford Research Institute (SRI), VALS has become a very popular method for applying lifestyle segmentation. VALS 2 divides Americans into eight lifestyle segments that exhibit distinctive attitudes, behaviors, and decision-making patterns.[11] SRI believes that when combined with an estimate of the resources the consumer can draw on (education, income, health, energy level, self-confidence, and degree of consumerism), the VALS 2 system is an excellent predictor of consumer behaviors. A variety of companies, including Chevron, Mercedes, and Eastman Kodak, have employed the VALS 2 program. Campbell's Soup embarked on a new campaign in 2000 to position the soup as a "lifestyle" choice.

Behavioristic Segmentation Dividing consumers into groups according to their usage, loyalties, or buying responses to a product is **behavioristic segmentation.** For example, product or brand usage, degree of use (heavy versus light), and/or brand loyalty are combined with demographic and/or psychographic criteria to develop profiles of market segments. In the case of usage, the marketer assumes that nonpurchasers of a brand or product who have the same characteristics as purchasers hold greater potential for adoption than nonusers with different characteristics. A profile (demographic or psychographic) of the user is developed, which serves as the basis for promotional strategies designed to attract new users. For example, teenagers share certain similarities in their consumption behaviors. Those who do not currently own a Sony Discman are more likely to be potential buyers than people in other age groups.

Degree of use relates to the fact that a few consumers may buy a disproportionate amount of many products or brands. Industrial marketers refer to the **80–20 rule,** meaning 20 percent of their buyers account for 80 percent of their sales volume. Again, when the characteristics of these users are identified, targeting them allows for a much greater concentration of efforts and less wasted time and money. The same heavy-half strategy is possible in the consumer market as well. The majority of purchases of many products (for example, soaps and detergents, shampoos, cake mixes, beer, dog food, colas, bourbon, and toilet tissue—yes, toilet tissue!) are accounted for by a small proportion of the population. Perhaps you can think of some additional examples.

Benefit Segmentation In purchasing products, consumers are generally trying to satisfy specific needs and/or wants. They are looking for products that provide

IMC Perspective 2–2

Generation Y—Marketers May Have to Learn New Tricks

The 30 million–strong segment of 12- to 19-year-olds born between the years of 1979 and 1987 (some extend it to as late as 1994), known as Generation Y is three times the size of Generation X. Their spending is estimated to be somewhere between $97.3 billion and $141 billion annually, two-thirds of which goes to clothing, entertainment, and personal care. It seems that every marketer in the country—if not the world—wants part of their action. Unfortunately, it's not that easy.

According to Teen Research Unlimited, Generation Yers watch less TV than any other demographic group. Schoolwork, music, shopping, sports, and TV hold little interest. Levi's, Converse, and Nike are out of style, replaced by brands like Mudd, Paris Blues, and In Vitro—unknowns to their parents as well as many in the marketing world. Indeed, this group is very different. They are more radically diverse, 25 percent come from single-parent households, and three out of four have working mothers. They have been on the computer since nursery school.

Some Generations Yers will soon be out of school and into the working world, where their incomes will increase. No wonder marketers are so enamored of them. The problem is that marketers just can't figure them out! Brad Mehl, vice president of marketing at Bolt.com, thinks they are "jaded, a bit more skeptical." "Teens readily reject false images." Others consider them to be fickle, yet possessing a media savvy never seen before. While they are seemingly not accessible through traditional media, and spend more time on the Web than any other demographic group, no one has yet to find the right ingredients to capture their attention and interest. They can be extremely brand-loyal, yet they will drop a brand like a hot potato if they lose trust in it. Brand loyalty to them lasts six to eight months. Price is less relevant than quality and style.

Nike has learned about Generation Y the hard way. While the company is still quite popular with teens, its grip on this segment is slipping. Its image- and celebrity-laden ads, while a big hit with boomers, have not worked here. As one teen notes, "It doesn't matter to me that Michael Jordan has endorsed Nike." Overseas labor practices have also contributed to Nike's disfavor among this group. Levi's is experiencing the same problems. Its research has shown that their brand has lost popularity with this age group as well. In part, the problem stemmed from losing touch and attempting to apply traditional marketing tactics to a nontraditional segment.

So what does work? For one thing, different messages. Humor, irony, and truth are well received; obvious attempts to sell are not. Sprite's "Image is nothing. Obey your thirst" campaign is hugely successful, as is Penney's Arizona Jeans brand tagline "Just throw me the jeans." Pepsi's "Generation Next" was perceived as nothing more than an effort to sell. (Though Pepsi has been quite successful with its Mountain Dew brand.)

The media used may have to be different as well. As noted earlier, TV is not a popular medium, yet shows like *Dawson's Creek* and *Buffy the Vampire Slayer* are. The Internet is immensely popular and often accessed. (Both *Dawson's Creek* and *Buffy* have their own websites.) Successful companies are bolstering their ads with other IMC elements. Take the case of Tommy Hilfiger—the number-one brand among this group, according to research conducted by American Express. Unlike Levi's, to remain in touch, Hilfiger conducted research in music clubs to see how influentials wearing Hilfiger jeans wore the styles. It then supplemented its advertising with unusual promotions including having clothing giveaways to stars on VH1 and MTV, sponsoring Nintendo competitions, and placing popular Nintendo games in Hilfiger stores. Grassroots marketing—taking the product and the brand to the segment—works. As noted by Terri Lay, president of the Lee brand, "You need to go where they are, not just pick a fashion statement, put it on TV, and wait for them to come to you." The strategy has paid off for its Pipes brand.

As the members of Generation Y mature, the number and variety of marketers attempting to reach them will grow as well. Toyota has developed a new auto—the Echo—with low emissions and a lower price. GM has developed a Gen Y task force to gain understanding. Motorola and Apple are developing products targeted to this group as well—with Apple's iMac being extremely successful. There are many, many more trying to reach this segment. The big question is, Can they figure them out?

Sources: Kipp Cheng, "Setting Their Sites on Generation Y," *Brandweek,* August 9, 1999, pp. 38–39; Becky Ebencamp, "Tipping the Balance," *Brandweek,* May 10, 1999, pp. 4–7; Ellen Neuborne and Kathleen Kerwin, "Generation Y," *Business Week,* February 15, 1999, pp. 80–87.

specific benefits to satisfy these needs. The grouping of consumers on the basis of attributes sought in a product is known as **benefit segmentation** and is widely used.

Consider the purchase of a wristwatch. While you might buy a watch for particular benefits such as accuracy, water resistance, or stylishness, others may seek a different set of benefits. Watches are commonly given as gifts for birthdays, Christmas, and graduation. Certainly some of the same benefits are considered in the purchase of a gift, but the benefits the purchaser derives are different from those the user will obtain. Ads that portray watches as good gifts stress different criteria to consider in the purchase decision. The next time you see an ad or commercial for a watch, think about the basic appeal and the benefits it offers.

Another example of benefit segmentation can be seen in the toothpaste market. Some consumers want a product with fluoride (Crest, Colgate); others prefer one that freshens their breath (Close-Up, Aqua-Fresh). More recent benefit segments offer tartar control (Crest) and plaque reduction (Viadent). The Den-Mat Corp. introduced Rembrandt whitening toothpaste for consumers who want whiter teeth (Exhibit 2–7) and other brands followed with their own whitening attributes.

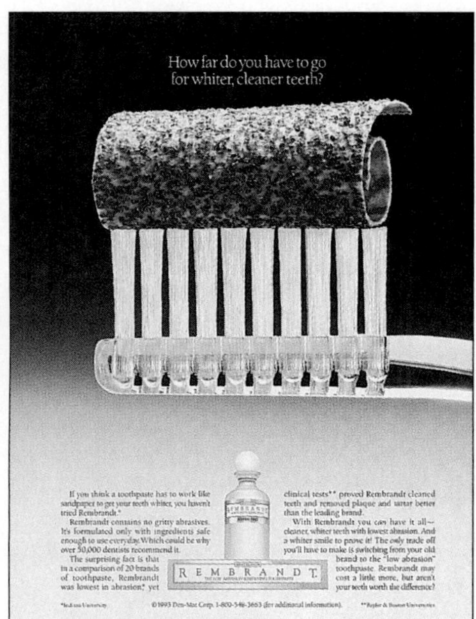

How far do you have to go
for whiter, cleaner teeth?
If you think a toothpaste has to work like sandpaper to get your teeth whiter, you haven't tried Rembrandt.*
Rembrandt contains no gritty abrasives. It's formulated only with ingredients safe enough to use everyday. Which could be why over 50,000 dentists recommend it.
The surprising fact is that in a comparison of 20 brands of toothpaste, Rembrandt was lowest in abrasion,* yet clinical tests** proved Rembrandt cleaned teeth and removed plaque and tartar better than the leading brand.
With Rembrandt you can have it all—cleaner, whiter teeth with lowest abrasion. And a whiter smile to prove it! The only trade off you'll have to make is switching from your old brand to the "low abrasion" toothpaste. Rembrandt may cost a little more, but aren't your teeth worth the difference?
REMBRANDT.
©1993 Den-Mat Corp. 1-800-548-3663 (for additional information).

Exhibit 2–7 Rembrandt toothpaste stresses the benefit of its superior whitening ability

The Process of Segmenting a Market The segmentation process develops over time and is an integral part of the situation analysis. It is in this stage that marketers attempt to determine as much as they can about the market: What needs are not being fulfilled? What benefits are being sought? What characteristics distinguish among the various groups seeking these products and services? A number of alternative segmentation strategies may be used. Each time a specific segment is identified, additional information is gathered to help the marketer understand this group.

For example, once a specific segment is identified on the basis of benefits sought, the marketer will examine lifestyle characteristics and demographics to help characterize this group and to further its understanding of this market. Behavioristic segmentation criteria will also be examined. In the purchase of ski boots, for example, specific benefits may be sought—flexibility or stiffness—depending on the type of skiing the buyer does. All this information will be combined to provide a complete profile of the skier.

A number of companies now offer research services to help marketing managers define their markets and develop strategies targeting them. The VALS and PRIZM systems discussed earlier are just a few of the services offered; others use demographic, socioeconomic, and geographic data to cluster consumer households into distinct "microgeographic" segments.

Whether these microunits meet the criteria for useful segmentation is determined by the user of the system. A national company might not attempt to define such small segments, but it could be useful for companies operating within one city or geographic area.

After completing the segmentation analysis, the marketer moves to the third phase shown in Figure 2–2: targeting a specific market.

Selecting a Target Market

The outcome of the segmentation analysis will reveal the market opportunities available. The next phase in the target marketing process involves two steps: (1) determining how many segments to enter and (2) determining which segments offer the most potential.

Determining How Many Segments to Enter Three market coverage alternatives are available. **Undifferentiated marketing** involves ignoring segment differences and offering just one product or service to the entire market.

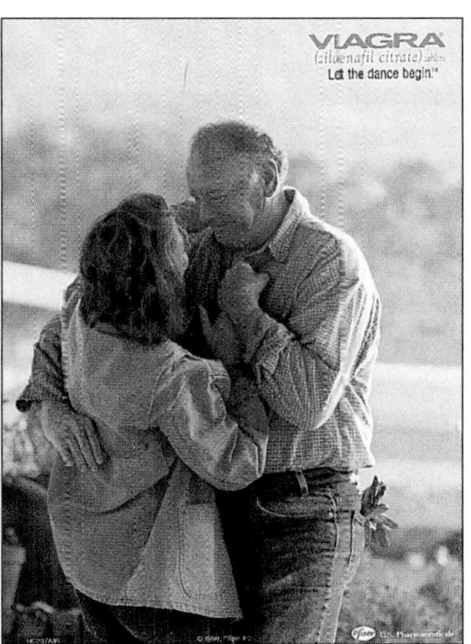

Exhibit 2–8 Viagra uses different appeals for the same product in different segments

For example, when Henry Ford brought out the first assembly-line automobile, all potential consumers were offered the same basic product: a black Ford. For many years, Coca-Cola offered only one product version. While this standardized strategy saves the company money, it does not allow the opportunity to offer different versions of the product to different markets.

Differentiated marketing involves marketing in a number of segments, developing separate marketing strategies for each. The Viagra ads in Exhibit 2–8 reflect this strategy. Notice how the two ads differ given alternate target markets and media.

While an undifferentiated strategy offers reduced costs through increased production, it does not allow for variety or tailoring to specific needs. Through differentiation, products—or advertising appeals—may be developed for the various segments, increasing the opportunity to satisfy the needs and wants of various groups.

The third alternative, **concentrated marketing**, is used when the firm selects one segment and attempts to capture a large share of this market. Volkswagen used this strategy in the 1950s when it was the only major automobile company competing in the economy-car segment in the United States. While Volkswagen has now assumed a more differentiated strategy, other companies have found the concentrated strategy effective. For example, Maxwell Business Systems has focused its business exclusively on providing software for job cost accounting/MIS systems for government contractors through its JAMIS product line (Exhibit 2–9).

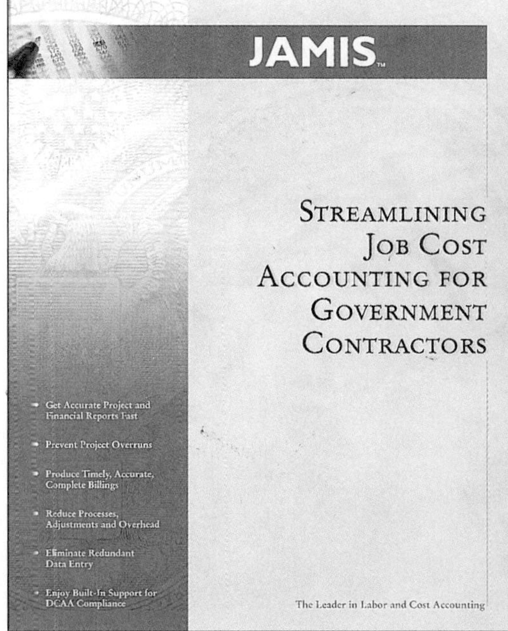

Exhibit 2–9 Maxwell Business Systems pursues a concentrated marketing strategy with JAMIS

Determining Which Segments Offer Potential

The second step in selecting a market involves determining the most attractive segment. The firm must examine the sales potential of the segment, the opportunities for growth, the competition, and its own ability to compete. Then it must decide whether it can market to this group. Stories abound of companies that have entered new markets only to find their lack of resources or expertise would not allow them to compete successfully. For example, Royal Crown (RC) Cola has often been quite successful in identifying new segment opportunities but because of limited resources has been less able to capitalize on them than Coke and Pepsi. RC was the first to bring to market diet colas and caffeine-free colas, but it has not been able to establish itself as a market leader in either market. After selecting the segments to target and determining that it can compete, the firm proceeds to the final step in Figure 2–2: the market positioning phase.

Market Positioning

Positioning has been defined as "the art and science of fitting the product or service to one or more segments of the broad market in such a way as to set it meaningfully apart from competition."[12] As you can see, the position of the product, service, or even store is the image that comes to mind and the attributes consumers perceive as related to it. This communication occurs through the message itself, which explains these benefits, as well as the media strategy employed to reach the target group. Take a few moments to think about how some products are positioned and how their positions are conveyed to you. For example, what comes to mind when your hear the name Mercedes, Dr. Pepper, or United Airlines? What about department stores such as Neiman-Marcus, Sears, and JCPenney? Now think of the ads for each of these products and companies. Are their approaches different from their competitors'? When and where are these ads shown?

Approaches to Positioning

Positioning strategies generally focus on either the consumer or the competition. While both approaches involve the association of product benefits with consumer needs, the former does so by linking the product with the benefits the consumer will derive or creating a favorable brand image, as shown in Exhibit 2–10. The latter approach positions the product by comparing it and the benefit it offers with the competition, as shown in Exhibit 2–11. Products like Scope mouthwash (positioning itself as better tasting than Listerine) and Now cigarettes (comparing their nicotine content to several other brands') have employed this strategy successfully.

Many advertising practitioners consider market positioning the most important factor in establishing a brand in the marketplace. David Aaker and John Myers note

Exhibit 2–10 Positioning that focuses on the consumer

Exhibit 2–11 Positioning that focuses on the competition

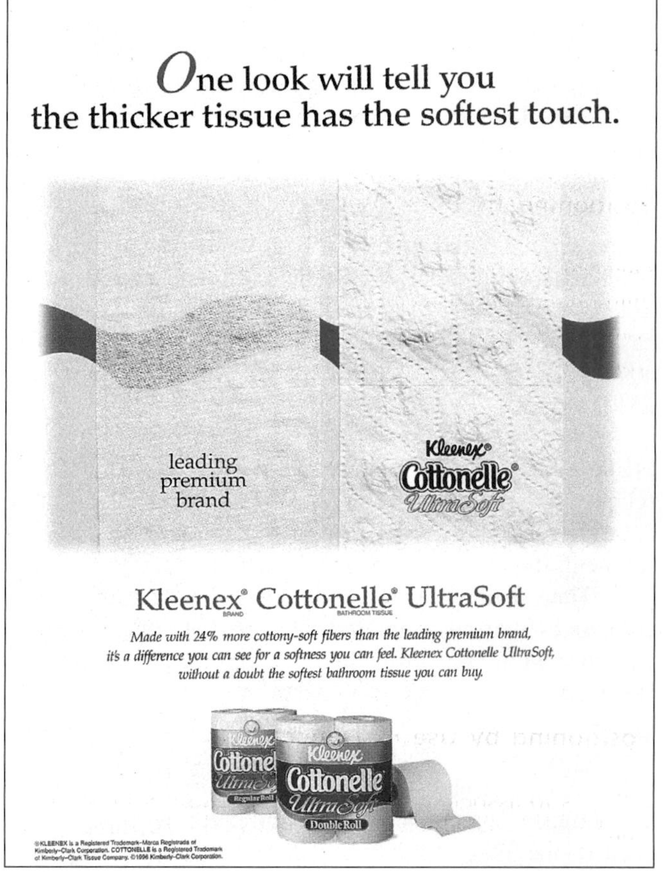

that the term position has recently been used to indicate the brand's or product's image in the marketplace.[13] Jack Trout and Al Ries suggest that this brand image must contrast with competitors'. They say, "In today's marketplace, the competitors' image is just as important as your own. Sometimes more important."[14] Thus, *positioning,* as used in this text, relates to the image of the product and or brand relative to competing products or brands. The position of the product or brand is the key factor in communicating the benefits it offers and differentiating it from the competition. Let us now turn to strategies marketers use to position a product.

Developing a Positioning Strategy

To create a position for a product or service, Trout and Ries suggest that managers ask themselves six basic questions:[15]

1. What position, if any, do we already have in the prospect's mind? (This information must come from the marketplace, not the managers' perceptions.)
2. What position do we want to own?
3. What companies must be outgunned if we are to establish that position?
4. Do we have enough marketing money to occupy and hold the position?
5. Do we have the guts to stick with one consistent positioning strategy?
6. Does our creative approach match our positioning strategy?

A number of positioning strategies might be employed in developing a promotional program. David Aaker and J. Gary Shansby discuss six such strategies: positioning by product attributes, price/quality, use, product class, users, and competitor.[16] Aaker and Myers add one more approach, positioning by cultural symbols.[17]

Positioning by Product Attributes and Benefits A common approach to positioning is setting the brand apart from competitors on the basis of the specific characteristics or benefits offered. Sometimes a product may be positioned on more than one product benefit. Marketers attempt to identify **salient attributes** (those that are important to consumers and are the basis for making a purchase decision). For example, when Apple first introduced its computers, the key benefit stressed was ease of use—an effective strategy, given the complexity of computers in the market at that time.

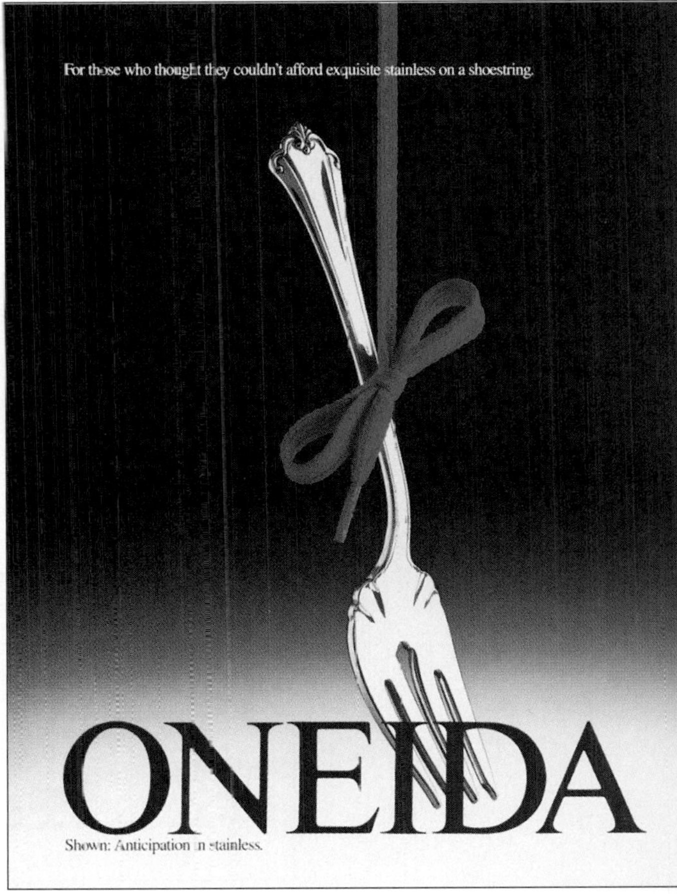

For those who thought they couldn't afford exquisite stainless on a shoestring.
ONEIDA
Shown: Anticipation in stainless.

Exhibit 2–12 Oneida positions its brand as having high quality for the right price

Positioning by Price/Quality Marketers often use price/quality characteristics to position their brands. One way they do it is with ads that reflect the image of a high-quality brand where cost, while not irrelevant, is considered secondary to the quality benefits derived from using the brand. Premium brands positioned at the high end of the market use this approach to positioning.

Another way to use price/quality characteristics for positioning is to focus on the quality or value offered by the brand at a very competitive price. For example, the Oneida ad shown in Exhibit 2–12 uses this strategy by suggesting that quality need not be unaffordable. Remember that although price is an important consideration, the product quality must be comparable to, or even better than, competing brands for the positioning strategy to be effective.

Positioning by Use or Application Another way to communicate a specific image or position for a brand is to associate it with a specific use or application. For example, Black & Decker introduced the SnakeLight as an innovative solution to the problem of

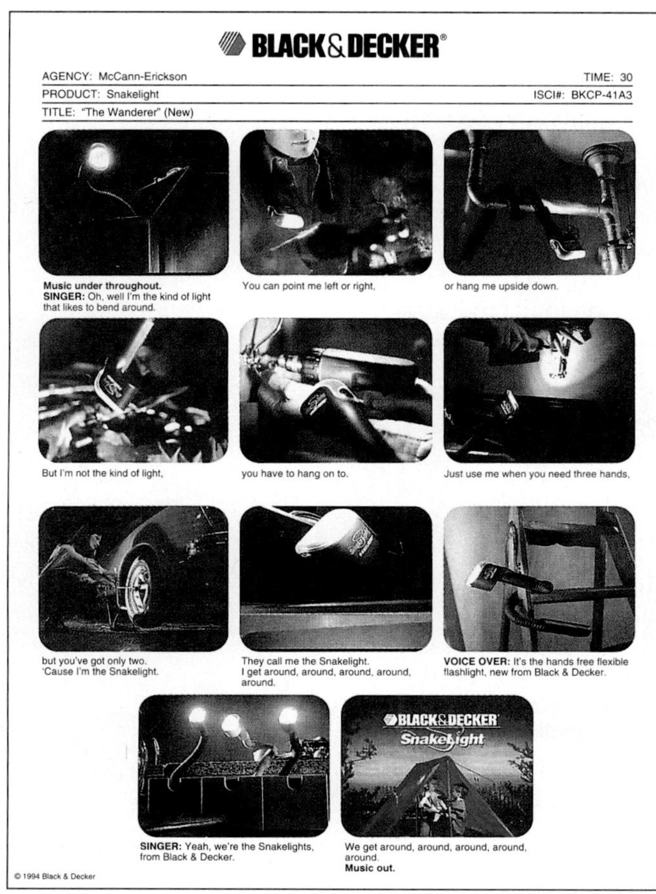

Exhibit 2–13 Black & Decker shows the various uses of the SnakeLight

trying to hold a flashlight while working. A TV commercial showed various uses for the product, while creative packaging and in-store displays were used to communicate the uses (Exhibit 2–13).

While this strategy is often used to enter a market based on a particular use or application, it is also an effective way to expand the usage of a product. For example, Arm & Hammer baking soda has been promoted for everything from baking to relieving heartburn to eliminating odors in carpets and refrigerators (Exhibit 2–14).

Positioning by Product Class Often the competition for a product comes from outside the product class. For example, airlines know that while they compete with other airlines, trains and buses are also viable alternatives. Amtrak has positioned itself as an alternative to airplanes, citing cost savings, enjoyment, and other advantages. Manufacturers of music CDs must compete with the cassette industry; many margarines position themselves against butter. Rather than positioning against another brand, an alternative strategy is to position oneself against another product category, as shown in Exhibit 2–15.

Positioning by Product User Positioning a product by associating it with a particular user or group of users is yet another approach. An example would be the Valvoline ad shown in Exhibit 2–16. This campaign emphasizes identification or association with a specific group, in this case, runners.

Positioning by Competitor Competitors may be as important to positioning strategy as a firm's own product or services. As Trout and Ries observe, the old strategy of ignoring one's competition no longer works.[18] (Advertisers used to think it was a cardinal sin to mention a competitor in their advertising.) In today's market,

Exhibit 2–14 Arm & Hammer baking soda demonstrates numerous product uses

Exhibit 2–15 An example of positioning by product class

Exhibit 2–16 Valvoline positions by product user

an effective positioning strategy for a product or brand may focus on specific competitors. This approach is similar to positioning by product class, although in this case the competition is within the same product category. Perhaps the best-known example of this strategy was Avis, which positioned itself against the car-rental leader, Hertz, by stating, "We're number two, so we try harder." The Kleenex ad shown earlier (Exhibit 2–11) is an example of positioning a brand against the competition. When positioning by competitor, a marketer must often employ another positioning strategy as well to differentiate the brand.

Positioning by Cultural Symbols Aaker and Myers include an additional positioning strategy in which cultural symbols are used to differentiate brands. Examples are the Jolly Green Giant, the Keebler elves, Speedy Alka-Seltzer, The Pillsbury Doughboy, Buster Brown, Ronald McDonald, Chiquita Banana, and Mr. Peanut. Each of these symbols has successfully differentiated the product it represents from competitors (Exhibit 2–17).

Exhibit 2–17 The Jolly Green Giant is a cultural symbol

Repositioning One final positioning strategy involves altering or changing a product's or brand's position. **Repositioning** a product usually occurs because of declining or stagnant sales or because of anticipated opportunities in other market positions. Repositioning is often difficult to accomplish because of entrenched perceptions about and attitudes toward the product or brand. Many companies' attempts to change their positions have met with little or no success. For example, Kmart (the store) and Aurora (the Oldsmobile) have both attempted to reposition themselves to a level of higher quality, appealing to younger and more well-to-do customers. Both have met with limited success. Sears has changed its positioning so often in recent years that consumers may not know exactly what image the company is trying to convey.

One extremely successful effort at repositioning was employed by *Rolling Stone* magazine. In an attempt to change advertisers' image of the type of person who reads *Rolling Stone,* the company embarked on

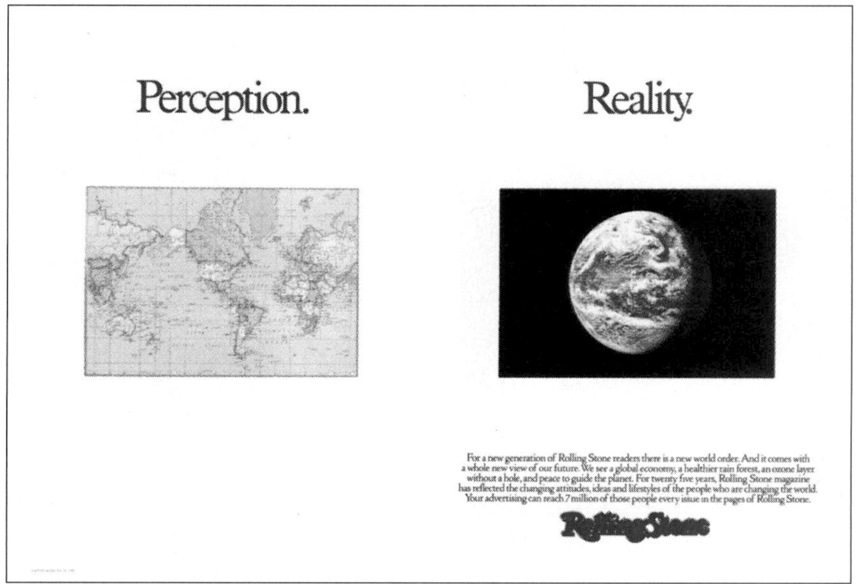

Perception.
Reality.
For a new generation of Rolling Stone readers there is a new world order. And it comes with
a whole new view of our future. We see a global economy, a healthier rain forest, an ozone layer
without a hole, and peace to guide the planet. For twenty five years, Rolling Stone magazine
has reflected the changing attitudes, ideas and lifestyles of the people who are changing the world.
Your advertising can reach 7 million of those people every issue in the pages of Rolling Stone.
Rolling Stone

Exhibit 2–18 This ad is one of a series used in the campaign to reposition *Rolling Stone* magazine

an extensive advertising campaign directed at potential advertisers. The ad shown in Exhibit 2–18 is just one example of how this strategy was successfully implemented.

IMC Perspective 2–3 describes how other companies have also been successful in their repositioning efforts.

Determining the Positioning Strategy

Having explored the alternative positioning strategies available, the marketer must determine which strategy is best suited for the firm or product and begin developing the positioning platform. As you remember from the promotional planning process in Chapter 1, the input into this stage will be derived from the situation analysis—specifically, the marketing research conducted therein. Essentially, the development of a positioning platform can be broken into a six-step process:[19]

1. *Identifying competitors.* This process requires broad thinking. Competitors may not be just those products and/or brands that fall into your product class or with which you compete directly. For example, a red wine competes with other red wines of various positions. It may also compete with white, sparkling, and nonalcoholic wines. Wine coolers provide an alternative, as do beer and other alcoholic drinks. Other nonalcoholic drinks may come into consideration at various times and/or situations. The marketer must consider all likely competitors, as well as the various effects of use and situations on the consumer.
2. *Assessing consumers' perceptions of competitors.* Once we define the competition, we must determine how they are perceived by consumers. Which attributes are important to consumers in evaluating a product and/or brand? As you might expect, for many products, they consider a wide variety of attributes or product benefits—most if not all of which are important. Much of marketing firms' research is directed at making such determinations. Consumers are asked to take part in focus groups and/or complete surveys indicating which attributes are important in their purchase decisions. For example, attributes considered important in the selection of a bank may include convenience, teller friendliness, financial security, and a host of other factors. This process establishes the basis for determining competitive positions.
3. *Determining competitors' positions.* After identifying the relevant attributes and their relative importance to consumers, we must determine how each competitor (including our own entry) is positioned with respect to each attribute. This will also show how the competitors are positioned relative to each other. Consumer research is required to make this assessment.
4. *Analyzing the consumers' preferences.* Our discussion of segmentation noted various factors that may distinguish among groups of consumers, including

IMC Perspective 2–3

Changing Images through Repositioning

There sometimes comes a point in a brand's life cycle where it is critical to decide between trying to compete with the existing image or trying to breathe new life into the brand by changing its position—that is, repositioning. While most marketers would agree that it is easier to create an image than to change an existing one, a number of companies have successfully repositioned themselves. Consider the following:

- *Sonic Corporation.* The number-five hamburger chain in the United States—with most of its 1,740 stores located in the South—had long been known for its drive-up service with roller-skating car hops and retro-style decor. The makeover, dubbed "Sonic 2000," changed the stores to a more "neon-intensive" look, along with making other upgrades. The new tagline, "New Look. Same great food," stressed the new image. Television ads continued to carry the Beach Boys music theme, but were changed to include a lead-in of the theme from the movie *2001: A Space Odyssey.* Aided by an increased advertising budget that rose from $15 million in 1993 to over $42 million in 1999, a broader media strategy resulted in increased brand awareness among existing and new customers. In addition, the redesigned stores showed an average sales increase of 8.1 percent over the previous year.
- *Miller Beer.* Miller Brewing Company, the longtime leader in the light-beer segment, saw its sales of the Miller Lite brand decline. The long-running position of Lite—"Tastes Great, Less Filling"—has been changed to reflect a "refreshing brew that drinkers crave," which was received favorably by wholesalers and consumers as well. A broader media schedule, which extended beyond the 21- to 28-year-old audience of the previous campaign, and more ethnic-oriented appeals also helped. In addition to changes in advertising, the packaging was changed on both bottles and cans, and the ad budget was increased by 12.2 percent. Lite's sales volume increased by 1.9 percent over the previous year—a sizable gain in a highly competitive market.
- *Volvo.* Considered by many to manufacture the safest cars in the world, Volvo had successfully captured the safety-minded auto buyer. Unfortunately, besides being perceived as safe, its autos were seen by consumers as being boxy—square, with little design—functional, and typical of a family with 2.4 kids and a dog. In 1998, Volvo decided to change all that. Showcasing two new cars—the C70 coupe and the convertible—Volvo set out to position the entire line as more stylish, emotional, and even sexy. The new "image cars" were supported by a $5 million budget for advertising which included spot TV and print, touting the new tagline "It will move you in ways Volvo never has." After seeing sales drop by 50 percent from 1986 to 1991, Volvo has very slowly regained market share. The new positioning promises to turn the turtle into a hare, however, as the new cars helped increase Volvo sales by 50 percent in the first six months after their introduction.
- *Wrigley's.* How can you reposition chewing gum? Ask Wrigley's. The marketer of the top-six chewing gum brands has created new images, pursued an integrated marketing communications approach, and successfully re-created many of Wrigley's brands. There was a successful campaign for Extra, the company's sugarless brand, and then for the old reliable Juicy Fruit. After declining sales, the company restored TV advertising under a new theme, "Gotta Have Sweet." In addition to being advertised via traditional media, the brand received its first Internet presence with the online promotion "The Juicy Fruit Scavenger Hunt," which encouraged teens to win prizes by searching for clues across a variety of websites including MTV.com, Sony.com, and Wrigley's own new site, juicyfruit.com. Next, Big Red, off the airwaves for over a year, initiated a $10 million campaign targeting 18- to 24-year-olds who are "primarily single, social and on-the-prowl in need of fresh breath." The old brand positioning of lasting a "little longer" was replaced. Two other brands, Spearmint and Doublemint, were next on the block to receive an image change. With the success of Juicy Fruit and Extra, Wrigley's is on its way to reversing the fortunes of its leading brands—all of which have declined in sales over the past few years.
- *U.S. News & World Report.* Among the most popular newsmagazines, *U.S. News & World Report* trails its rivals *Time* and *Newsweek* in the all-important

subscription-base category. Trailing *Newsweek* by 300 ad pages and *Time* by 500 through the first nine months of 1999, the company announced in late 1999 that the magazine would undergo an image change. The new positioning will extend the current "News you can use" positioning by focusing on previously popular content, such as rankings of colleges, graduate schools, and hospitals. The magazine will attempt to differentiate itself from its competitors by staying away from the entertainment and pop-culture coverage increasingly adopted by *Time* and *Newsweek* in favor of more business coverage. A new ad agency has been hired, and a complete redesign of the magazine is being undertaken. It's too early to tell what impact the change will have at this point, but keep watching to see if you can notice the difference.

As these examples indicate, it is often impossible to maintain a specific positioning over time. Times change, audiences change, and brands are often forced to change with them in order to survive. While not all repositioning efforts are successful, the examples above show that it can be done. Would it be fair to say in the case of *U.S. News & World Report* that only "*Time*" will tell?

Sources: Ann Marie Kerwin, "*U.S. News* Tries New Approaches to 'Focus' Future," *Ad Age,* October 25, 1999, p. 42; Stephanie Thompson, "Wrigley Readies New Ads to Freshen Sales," *Ad Age,* October 25, 1999, p. 4; Tara Weingarten and Leslie Kaufman, "Safe Sex Sells for Volvo," *Newsweek,* October 5, 1998, p. 61; Louise Kramer, "Sonic Pairs New TV Spot with Its Revamped Stores," *Ad Age,* April 6, 1998, p. 14; James B. Arnforfer, "Miller Freshens Creative for Lite, Genuine Draft," *Ad Age,* April 6, 1998, p. 4.

lifestyles, purchase motivations, and demographic differences. Each of these segments may have different purchase motivations and different attribute importance ratings. One way to determine these differences is to consider the *ideal brand* or *product,* defined as the object the consumer would prefer over all others, including objects that can be imagined but do not exist. Identifying the ideal product can help you identify different ideals among segments or identify segments with similar or the same ideal points.

5. *Making the positioning decision.* Going through the first four steps should let us decide which position to assume in the marketplace. Such a decision is not always clear and well defined, however, and research may provide only limited input. In that case, the marketing manager or groups of managers must make some subjective judgments. These judgments raise a number of questions:

- *Is the segmentation strategy appropriate?* Positioning usually entails a decision to segment the market. Consider whether the market segment sought will support an entry and whether it is in the best interests of the company to de-emphasize the remaining market. When a specific position is chosen, consumers may believe this is what the product is for. Those not looking for that specific benefit may not consider the brand. If the marketer decides on an undifferentiated strategy, it may be possible to be general in the positioning platform. For example, Mercury's slogan, "Imagine yourself in a Mercury," allows receivers to project themselves into a variety of situations, all of which (hopefully) involve a positive image of Mercury.
- *Are there sufficient resources available to communicate the position effectively?* It is very expensive to establish a position. One ad, or even a series of ads, is not likely to be enough. The marketer must commit to a long-range effort in all aspects of the marketing campaign to make sure the objectives sought are obtained. Too often, the firm abandons a position and/or advertising campaign long before it can establish a position successfully. The *Rolling Stone* repositioning discussed earlier is an excellent example of sticking with a campaign: The basic theme has been running for a number of years. In contrast, Sears has switched campaigns so often in the past few years it has been impossible to establish a distinct position in the consumer's mind. Further, once a successful position is attained, it is likely to attract competitors. It may become expensive to ward off me-too brands and continue to hold on to the brand distinction.

- *How strong is the competition?* The marketing manager must ask whether a position sought is likely to be maintained, given the strengths of the competition. For example, General Foods often makes it a practice not to be the first entry into a market. When competitors develop new markets with their entries, General Foods simply improves on the product and captures a large percentage of the market share. This leads to two basic questions: First, if our firm is first into the market, will we be able to maintain the position (in terms of quality, price, etc.)? Second, if a product is positioned as finest quality, it must be. If it is positioned as lowest cost, it has to be. Otherwise, the position claimed is sure to be lost.
- *Is the current positioning strategy working?* There is an old saying, "If it ain't broke, don't fix it." If current efforts are not working, it may be time to consider an alternative positioning strategy. But if they are working, a change is usually unwise. Sometimes executives become bored with a theme and decide it is time for a change, but this change causes confusion in the marketplace and weakens a brand's position. Unless there is strong reason to believe a change in positioning is necessary, stick with the current strategy.

6. *Monitoring the position.* Once a position has been established, we want to monitor how well it is being maintained in the marketplace. Tracking studies measure the image of the product or firm over time. Changes in consumers' perceptions can be determined, with any slippage immediately noted and reacted to. At the same time, the impact of competitors can be determined.

Before leaving this section, you might stop to think for a moment about the positioning (and repositioning) strategies pursued by different companies. Any successful product that comes to mind probably occupies a distinct market position.

Developing the Marketing Planning Program

The development of the marketing strategy and selection of a target market(s) tell the marketing department which customers to focus on and what needs to attempt to satisfy. The next stage of the marketing process involves combining the various elements of the marketing mix into a cohesive, effective marketing program. Each marketing mix element is multidimensional and includes a number of decision areas. Likewise, each must consider and contribute to the overall IMC program. We now examine product, price, and distribution channels and how each influences and interacts with the promotional program.

Product Decisions

An organization exists because it has some product, service, or idea to offer consumers, generally in exchange for money. This offering may come in the form of a physical product (such as a soft drink, pair of jeans, or car), a service (banking, airlines, or legal assistance), a cause (United Way, March of Dimes), or even a person (a political candidate). The product is anything that can be marketed and that, when used or supported, gives satisfaction to the individual.

A *product* is not just a physical object; it is a bundle of benefits or values that satisfies the needs of consumers. The needs may be purely functional, or they may include social and psychological benefits. For example, the ad for Michelin tires shown earlier stresses the quality built into Michelin tires (value) as well as their performance and durability (function). The term **product symbolism** refers to what a product or brand means to consumers and what they experience in purchasing and using it.[20] For many products, strong symbolic features and social and psychological meaning may be more important than functional utility.[21] For example, designer clothing such as Versace, Gucci, and Ferragamo is often purchased on the basis of its symbolic meaning and image, particularly by teenagers and young adults. Advertising plays an important role in developing and maintaining the image of these brands (Exhibit 2–19).

Exhibit 2–19 Advertising for designer clothing

Product planning involves decisions not only about the item itself, such as design and quality, but also about aspects such as service and warranties as well as brand name and package design. Consumers look beyond the reality of the product and its ingredients. The product's quality, branding, packaging, and even the company standing behind it all contribute to consumers' perceptions.[22] In an effective IMC program, advertising, branding, and packaging are all designed to portray the product as more than just a bundle of attributes. All are coordinated to present an image or positioning of the product that extends well beyond its physical attributes. Think for a minute about the ads for Nike; the product benefits and attributes are usually not even mentioned—yet information about the brand is communicated effectively.

Branding

Choosing a brand name for a product is important from a promotional perspective because brand names communicate attributes and meaning. Marketers search for brand names that can communicate product concepts and help position the product in customers' minds. Names such as Safeguard (soap), I Can't Believe It's Not Butter! (margarine), Easy-Off (oven cleaner), Arrid (antiperspirant), and Spic and Span (floor cleaner) all clearly communicate the benefits of using these products and at the same time create images extending beyond the names themselves.

One important role of advertising in respect to branding strategies is creating and maintaining **brand equity,** which can be thought of as an intangible asset of added value or goodwill that results from the favorable image, impressions of differentiation, and/or the strength of consumer attachment to a company name, brand name, or trademark. Brand equity allows a brand to earn greater sales volume and/or higher margins than it could without the name, providing the company with a competitive advantage. The strong equity position a company and/or its brand enjoys is often reinforced through advertising. For example, Rado watches command a premium price because of their high quality as well as the strong brand equity they have developed through advertising (Exhibit 2–20).

Exhibit 2–20 Rado creates strong brand equity through advertising

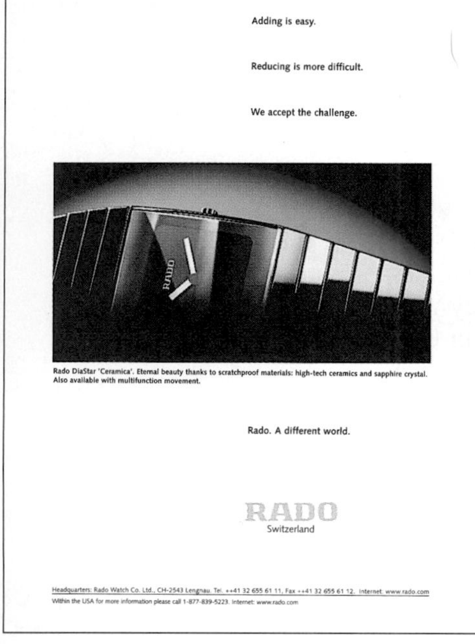

Packaging

Packaging is another aspect of product strategy that has become increasingly important. Traditionally, the package provided functional benefits such as economy, protection, and storage. However, the role and function of the package have changed because of the self-service emphasis of many stores and the fact that more and more buying decisions are made at the point of purchase. One study estimated that as many as two-thirds of all purchases made in the supermarket are

Exhibit 2–21 Duracell communicates through effective packaging

AT THE HEART OF A GREAT FRAGRANCE
is a scent that becomes yours alone.
It introduces you, compliments you, pleases you.
The classic fragrances of Tiffany.
TIFFANY
FOR
MEN
TRUESTE
TIFFANY
VISIT TIFFANY & CO. DAYTON'S HUDSON'S AND MARSHALL FIELD'S TO SAMPLE THE FRAGRANCES OF TIFFANY.
FOR OTHER LOCATIONS AND INQUIRIES PLEASE CALL 800-526-0649.

Exhibit 2–22 The packaging creates product image

unplanned. The package is often the consumer's first exposure to the product, so it must make a favorable first impression. A typical supermarket has more than 20,000 items competing for attention. Not only must a package attract and hold the consumer's attention, but it must also communicate information on how to use the product, divulge its composition and content, and satisfy any legal requirements regarding disclosure. Moreover, many firms design the package to carry a sales promotion message such as a contest, sweepstakes, or premium offer.

Many companies view the package as an important way to communicate with consumers and create an impression of the brand in their minds. Notice the effective use of the battery tester on the Duracell package shown in Exhibit 2–21. Besides offering value-added attributes beyond the product itself, the packaging gives Duracell a unique way to convey the claim that its batteries last longer. Design factors such as size, shape, color, and lettering all contribute to the appeal of a package and can be as important as a commercial in determining what goes from the store shelf to the consumer's shopping cart. Many products use packaging to create a distinctive brand image and identity. The next time you walk by a perfume counter, stop to look at the many unique package designs (see Exhibit 2–22). Packaging can also serve more functional purposes. For example, Tylenol's Safe-Ty-Lock bottle protects children from consuming the medicine when they shouldn't (Exhibit 2–23).

Price Decisions

The *price variable* refers to what the consumer must give up to purchase a product or service. While price is discussed in terms of the dollar amount exchanged for an item, the cost of a product to the consumer includes time, mental activity, and behavioral effort.[23] The marketing manager is usually concerned with establishing a price level, developing pricing policies, and monitoring competitors' and consumers' reactions to prices in the marketplace. A firm must consider a number of factors in determining the price it charges for its product or service, including costs, demand factors, competition, and perceived value. From an IMC perspective, the price must be consistent with the perceptions of the product, as well as the communications strategy. Higher prices, of course, will communicate a higher product quality, while

Exhibit 2–23 Packaging may also add product benefits

Exhibit 2–24 Some products compete on the basis of quality rather than price

lower prices reflect bargain or "value" perceptions (Exhibit 2–24). A product positioned as highest quality but carrying a lower price than competitors will only confuse consumers. In other words, the price, the advertising, and the distribution channels must present one unified voice speaking to the product's positioning.

Relating Price to Advertising and Promotion Factors such as product quality, competition, and advertising all interact in determining what price a firm can and should charge. The relationship among price, product quality, and advertising was examined in one study using information on 227 consumer businesses from the PIMS (Profit Impact of Marketing Strategies) project of the Strategic Planning Institute.[24] Several interesting findings concerning the interaction of these variables emerged from this study:

- Brands with high relative advertising budgets were able to charge premium prices, whereas brands that spent less than their competitors on advertising charged lower prices.
- Companies with high-quality products charged high relative prices for the extra quality, but businesses with high quality and high advertising levels obtained the highest prices. Conversely, businesses with low quality and low advertising charged the lowest prices.
- The positive relationship between high relative advertising and price levels was stronger for products in the late stage of the product life cycle, for market leaders, and for low-cost products (under $10).
- Companies with relatively high prices and high advertising expenditures showed a higher return on investment than companies with relatively low prices and high advertising budgets.

- Companies with high-quality products were hurt the most, in terms of return on investment, by inconsistent advertising and pricing strategies.

The study concluded that pricing and advertising strategies go together. High relative ad expenditures should accompany premium prices, and low relative ad expenditures should be tailored to low prices. These results obviously support the IMC perspective that one voice must be conveyed.

Distribution Channel Decisions

As consumers, we generally take for granted the role of marketing intermediaries or channel members. If we want a six-pack of soda or a box of detergent, we can buy it at a supermarket, a convenience store, or even a drugstore. Manufacturers understand the value and importance of these intermediaries.

One of a marketer's most important marketing decisions involves the way it makes its products and services available for purchase. A firm can have an excellent product at a great price, but it will be of little value unless it is available where the customer wants it, when the customer wants it, and with the proper support and service. **Marketing channels,** the place element of the marketing mix, are "sets of interdependent organizations involved in the process of making a product or service available for use or consumption."[25]

Channel decisions involve selecting, managing, and motivating intermediaries such as wholesalers, distributors, brokers, and retailers that help a firm make a product or service available to customers. These intermediaries, sometimes called **resellers,** are critical to the success of a company's marketing program.

The distribution strategy should also take into consideration the communication objectives and the impact that the channel strategy will have on the IMC program. Stewart and colleagues discuss the need for "integrated channel management," which "reflects the blurring of the boundaries of the communications and distribution functions."[26] Consistent with the product and pricing decisions, where the product is distributed will send a communications message. Does the fact that a product is sold at Nieman Marcus or Saks convey a different message regarding its image than if it were distributed at Kmart or Wal-Mart? If you think about it for a moment, the mere fact that the product is distributed in these channels communicates an image about it in your mind. Stewart gives examples of how channel elements contribute to communications—for example, grocery store displays, point-of-purchase merchandising, and shelf footage. The distribution channel in a well-integrated marketing program serves as a form of reminder advertising. The consumer sees the brand name and recalls the advertising. (Think about the last time you passed a McDonald's. Did it remind you of any of McDonald's ads?)

A company can choose not to use any channel intermediaries and sell to its customers through **direct channels.** This type of channel arrangement is sometimes used in the consumer market by firms using direct-selling programs, such as Avon, Tupperware, and Mary Kay, or firms that use direct-response advertising or telemarketing to sell their products. Direct channels are also frequently used by manufacturers of industrial products and services, which are often selling expensive and complex products that require extensive negotiations and sales efforts, as well as service and follow-up calls after the sale. The ad for Titleist putters reflect the higher cost and quality associated with the brand.

Chapter 15 provides a discussion of the role of the Internet in an IMC program. As will be seen, the Internet is relied upon by many companies as a direct channel of distribution, as they offer products and services for sale on their websites. Amazon.com and E-toys.com are just two of the many examples of such efforts.

Most consumer product companies distribute through **indirect channels,** usually using a network of wholesalers (institutions that sell to other resellers) and/or retailers (which sell primarily to the final consumer).

Developing Promotional Strategies: Push or Pull?

Most of you are aware of advertising and other forms of promotion directed toward ultimate consumers or business customers. We see these ads in the media and are often part of the target audience for the promotions. In addition to developing a consumer marketing mix, a company must have a program to motivate the channel members. Programs designed to persuade the trade to stock, merchandise, and promote a manufacturer's products are part of a **promotional push strategy.** The goal of this strategy is to push the product through the channels of distribution by aggressively selling and promoting the item to the resellers, or trade.

Promotion to the trade includes all the elements of the promotional mix. Company sales representatives call on resellers to explain the product, discuss the firm's plans for building demand among ultimate consumers, and describe special programs being offered to the trade, such as introductory discounts, promotional allowances, and cooperative ad programs. The company may use **trade advertising** to interest wholesalers and retailers and motivate them to purchase its products for resale to their customers. Trade advertising usually appears in publications that serve the particular industry.

A push strategy tries to convince resellers they can make a profit on a manufacturer's product and to encourage them to order the merchandise and push it through to their customers. Sometimes manufacturers face resistance from channel members who do not want to take on an additional product line or brand. In these cases, companies may turn to a **promotional pull strategy,** spending money on advertising and sales promotion efforts directed toward the ultimate consumer. The goal of a pull strategy is to create demand among consumers and encourage them to request the product from the retailer. Seeing the consumer demand, retailers will order the product from wholesalers (if they are used), which in turn will request it from the manufacturer. Thus, stimulating demand at the end-user level pulls the product through the channels of distribution.

Whether to emphasize a push or a pull strategy depends on a number of factors, including the company's relations with the trade, its promotional budget, and demand for the firm's products. Companies that have favorable channel relationships may prefer to use a push strategy and work closely with channel members to encourage them to stock and promote their products. A firm with a limited promotional budget may not have the funds for advertising and sales promotion that a pull strategy requires and may find it more cost effective to build distribution and demand by working closely with resellers. When the demand outlook for a product is favorable because it has unique benefits, is superior to competing brands, or is very popular among consumers, a pull strategy may be appropriate. Companies often use a combination of push and pull strategies, with the emphasis changing as the product moves through its life cycle.

The Role of Advertising and Promotion

As shown in the marketing model in Figure 2–1, the marketing program includes promotion both to the trade (channel members) and to the company's ultimate customers. And interactive marketers use the various promotional-mix elements—advertising, sales promotion, direct marketing, publicity/public relations, and personal selling—to inform consumers about their products, their prices, and places where the products are available. Each promotional-mix variable helps marketers achieve their promotional objectives, and all variables must work together to achieve an integrated marketing communications program.

To this point, we have discussed the various elements of the marketing plan that serves as the basis for the IMC program. The development and implementation of an IMC program is based on a strong foundation that includes market analysis, target marketing and positioning, and coordination of the various marketing mix elements. Throughout the following chapters of this text, we will explore the role of advertising and promotion in helping to achieve marketing objectives.

Summary

Promotion plays an important role in an organization's efforts to market its product, service, or ideas to its customers. Figure 2–1 shows a model for analyzing how promotions fit into a company's marketing program. The model includes a marketing strategy and analysis, target marketing, program development, and the target market. The marketing process begins with a marketing strategy that is based on a detailed situation analysis and guides for target market selection and development of the firm's marketing program.

In the planning process, the situation analysis requires that the marketing strategy be assumed. The promotional program is developed with this strategy as a guide. One of the key decisions to be made pertains to the target marketing process, which includes identifying, segmenting, target, and positioning to target markets. There are several bases for segmenting the market and various ways to position a product.

Once the target marketing process has been completed, marketing program decisions regarding product, price, distribution, and promotions must be made. All of these must be coordinated to provide an integrated marketing communications perspective, in which the positioning strategy is supported by one voice. Thus all product strategies, pricing strategies, and distribution choices must be made with the objective of contributing to the overall image of the product or brand. Advertising and promotion decisions, in turn, must be integrated with the other marketing mix decisions to accomplish this goal.

Key Terms

strategic marketing plan, 40
market segments, 40
market opportunities, 40
competitive advantage, 41
target marketing, 42
market segmentation, 45
geographic segmentation, 47
demographic segmentation, 47
psychographic segmentation, 48
behavioristic segmentation, 48
80-20 rule, 48
benefit segmentation, 50
undifferentiated marketing, 50
differentiated marketing, 51
concentrated marketing, 51
positioning, 52
salient attributes, 53
repositioning, 55
product symbolism, 59
brand equity, 60
marketing channels, 63
resellers, 63
direct channels, 63
indirect channels, 63
promotional push strategy, 64
trade advertising, 64
promotional pull strategy, 64

Discussion Questions

1. Some marketers contend that demographics is not really a basis for segmentation, but a descriptor of the segment. Discuss examples to support both positions.

2. It has been said that Generation Y is one of the more difficult segments to appeal to. Explain why this is so and cite examples of companies that have been successful in this endeavor.

3. Establishing brand image is often difficult for new companies. Explain what these companies must do to establish a strong brand image.

4. More and more business-to-business companies have gone away from purely trade advertising to advertising on consumer media. Is this likely to be a successful strategy? Why or why not?

5. A number of approaches to segmentation have been cited in the text. Provide examples of companies and/or brands that employ each.

6. Discuss the concept of competitive advantage. Pick three brands or products and discuss the specific competitive advantage that each stresses.

7. Describe how the positioning strategy adopted for a brand would need to be supported by all other elements of the marketing mix.

8. Discuss the concept of target marketing. Why is it so important to marketers?

9. What is meant by positioning? Discuss the various approaches to positioning and give examples of companies or brands that use each approach.

10. What factors would lead a marketer to the use of a repositioning strategy? Find a product or service that has been repositioned recently and analyze the strategy.

Chapter Three

Organizing for Advertising and Promotion: The Role of Ad Agencies and Other Marketing Communication Organizations

Chapter Objectives

- To understand how companies organize for advertising and other aspects of integrated marketing communications.
- To examine methods for selecting, compensating, and evaluating advertising agencies.
- To explain the role and functions of specialized marketing communications organizations.
- To examine various perspectives on the use of integrated services and responsibilities of advertisers versus agencies.

TBWA/Chiat/Day—The Agency That Thinks Different

The inaugural television commercial in Apple Computer's "Think different" campaign salutes the crazy ones, the rebels, the troublemakers, and the ones who see things differently. The voice-over in the spot says, "You can disagree with them. . . . The only thing you can't do is ignore them. They change things." Many in the advertising world feel these words could easily be used to describe TBWA/Chiat/Day, the advertising agency known for its popular cutting-edge creative work for Apple Computer as well as a number of other companies and products, including Absolut vodka, Taco Bell, Levi's jeans, Energizer batteries, Kinko's, Sony PlayStation, and Nissan and Infiniti automobiles.

Throughout the 1980s and into the 90s, New York–based TBWA and California–based Chiat/Day were widely recognized as two of the most dynamic and creative ad agencies in the world. *Advertising Age,* the ad industry's leading trade publication, named Chiat/Day the U.S. Agency of the Year in 1980 and 1988. In 1990 it was named Agency of the Decade, and its classic "1984" TV spot, used to introduce Apple's Macintosh personal computer, was chosen as the Commercial of the Decade. Many ad critics consider it the best commercial ever made. During the same period TBWA had also become well known for its outstanding creative work for clients such as Absolut vodka, Evian, and many others. In August 1995 the two agencies joined forces to form TBWA/Chiat/Day. Two years after the merger the combined agency was selected U.S. Agency of the Year by *Advertising Age, AdWeek, USA Today, Shoot Magazine,* and *Advertising Age's Creativity* magazine; the following year it was named Agency of the Year West by *AdWeek.* Today TBWA/Chiat/Day is part of the TBWA Worldwide agency, with combined billings of over $5 billion and 186 offices in over 65 countries worldwide.

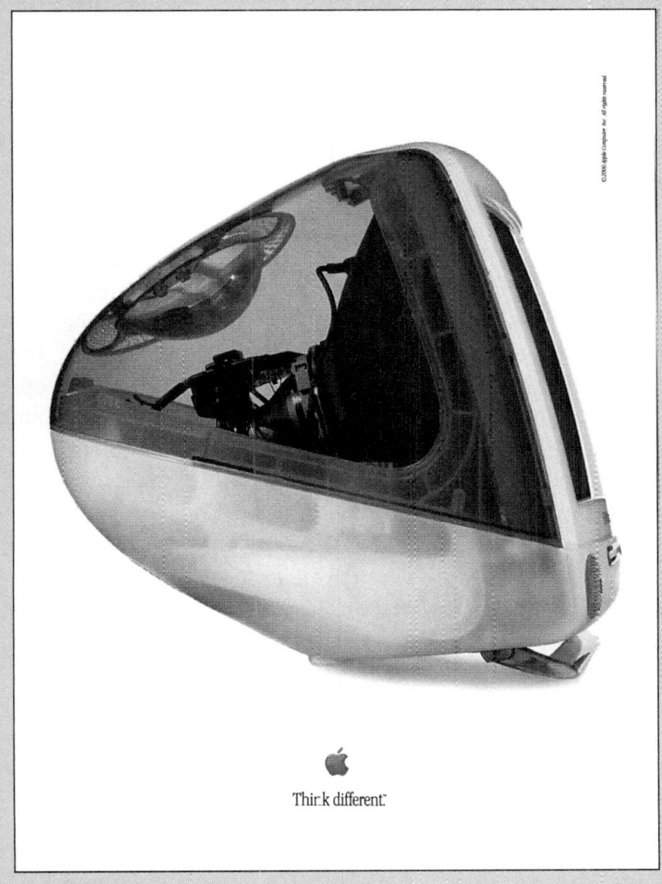

In 1997 Stephen Jobs, the founder and former CEO of Apple Computer, returned to the company to help revive the ailing personal computer market. One of the first calls he made was to Lee Clow, TBWA/Chiat/Day's legendary chairman and chief creative officer worldwide. Apple was considering a number of agencies at the time, but Jobs cut short the review process and awarded the business to TBWA/Chiat/Day, noting "I don't pick advertising agencies; I pick people." Clow and his staff responded by developing the "Think different" campaign, which honored people who changed this century for the better. The campaign helped change Apple for the better by restoring its image as an innovative leader in the personal computer industry. It also set the stage for Apple's highly successful launch of the iMac home computer.

When TBWA/Chiat/Day was competing for Levi Strauss & Co.'s core jeans account, the pitch team arrived at the client's headquarters in San Francisco three hours early in a large step van with a deejay aboard spinning hip-hop music at top volume. Once inside, they showed Levi executives an "idea video" that celebrated the jeans maker's history and place in American lore. The classic images included photographs of Western pioneers, factory workers, hippies at Woodstock, and Hollywood screen idols. It ended with an image of a pair of jeans flying high on a flagpole and the title "What's next?" What was next was TBWA/Chiat/Day winning the Levi's jeans account and the opportunity to restore the image of the iconic brand both to baby boomers and to their kids.

While perhaps best known for its creative work, TBWA/Chiat/Day is a well-balanced agency that is strong in all aspects of integrated marketing communications, including strategic thinking, account planning, and management, media strategy and planning, and the rapidly emerging area of interactive media. The agency has used its strategic marketing and account planning capabilities to help its clients better understand their markets and customers. To prepare for its work on the Levi's jeans account, Lee Clow hired a cultural anthropologist and interviewed former MTV employees to learn how cultural arbiters influence the fashion process.

After taking over the Taco Bell fast-food account, TBWA/Chiat/Day encouraged the company to better appreciate the brand's Mexican-food niche. The agency worked with Taco Bell to revitalize its marketing strategy and place more emphasis on teens and the brand's Mexican heritage. As part of the strategy the agency created a campaign for Taco Bell featuring a Spanish-speaking, taco-loving Chihuahua who is fast becoming an advertising icon. In one of the most popular spots in the campaign, he passes by a female dog for some Taco Bell food and in Spanish says, "Yo quiero Taco Bell" (I want Taco Bell). The campaign helped increase Taco Bell sales by three percent, which was the first increase in three years and is yet another example of why companies in need of creative marketing and advertising often say, "Yo quiero TBWA/Chiat/Day."

Sources: Angela Dawson, "True Blue Crew," *AdWeek,* January 25, 1999, pp. 74–77; Alice Z. Cuneo and Laura Petrecca, "The Best Agencies," *Advertising Age,* March 30, 1998, pp. S1–11

Developing and implementing an integrated marketing communications program is usually a complex and detailed process involving the efforts of many persons. As consumers, we generally give little thought to the individuals or organizations that create the clever advertisements that capture our attention or the contests or sweepstakes we hope to win. But for those involved in the marketing process, it is important to understand the nature of the industry and the structure and functions of the organizations involved. The advertising and promotions business is changing as marketers search for better ways to communicate with their customers. These changes are impacting the way marketers organize for marketing communications, as well as their relationships with advertising agencies and other communication specialists.

This chapter examines the various organizations that participate in the IMC process, their roles and responsibilities, and their relationship to one another. We discuss how companies organize internally for advertising and promotion. For most companies, advertising is planned and executed by an outside ad agency. Many large agencies offer a variety of other IMC capabilities, including public relations, sales promotion, and direct marketing. Thus, we will devote particular attention to the ad agency's role and the overall relationship between company and agency.

Other participants in the promotional process (such as direct-response, sales promotion, and interactive agencies and public relations firms) are becoming increasingly important as more companies take an integrated marketing communications approach to promotion. We examine the role of these specialized marketing communications organizations in the promotional process as well. The chapter concludes with a discussion of whether marketers are best served by using the integrated services of one large agency or the separate services of a variety of communications specialists.

Participants in the Integrated Marketing Communications Process: An Overview

Before discussing the specifics of the industry, we'll provide an overview of the entire system and identify some of the players. As shown in Figure 3–1, participants in the integrated marketing communications process can be divided into five major groups: the advertiser (or client), advertising agencies, media organizations, specialized communication services, and collateral services. Each group has specific roles in the promotional process.

The advertisers, or **clients,** are the key participants in the process. They have the products, services, or causes to be marketed, and they provide the funds that pay for advertising and promotions. The advertisers also assume major responsibility for developing the marketing program and making the final decisions regarding the advertising and promotional program to be employed. The organization may perform most of these efforts itself, either through its own advertising department or by setting up an in-house agency.

However, many organizations use an **advertising agency,** an outside firm that specializes in the creation, production, and/or placement of the communications message and that may provide other services to facilitate the marketing and promotions process. Many large advertisers retain the services of a number of agencies, particularly when they market a number of products. For example, Kraft Foods uses as many as 8 advertising agencies for its various brands, while Procter & Gamble uses 10 promotional agencies for its Canadian business alone. More and more, ad agencies are acting as partners with advertisers and assuming more responsibility for developing the marketing and promotional programs.

Media organizations are another major participant in the advertising and promotions process. The primary function of most media is to provide information or entertainment to their subscribers, viewers, or readers. But from the perspective of the promotional planner, the purpose of media is to provide an environment for the firm's marketing communications message. The media must have editorial or program content that attracts consumers so advertisers and their agencies will want to buy time or space with them. Exhibit 3–1 shows an ad run in advertising trade publications promoting the value of *Link* magazine as a media vehicle for reaching college students. While the media perform many other functions that help advertisers understand their markets and their customers, a medium's primary objective is to sell itself as a way for companies to reach their target markets with their messages effectively.

Figure 3–1 Participants in the integrated marketing communications process

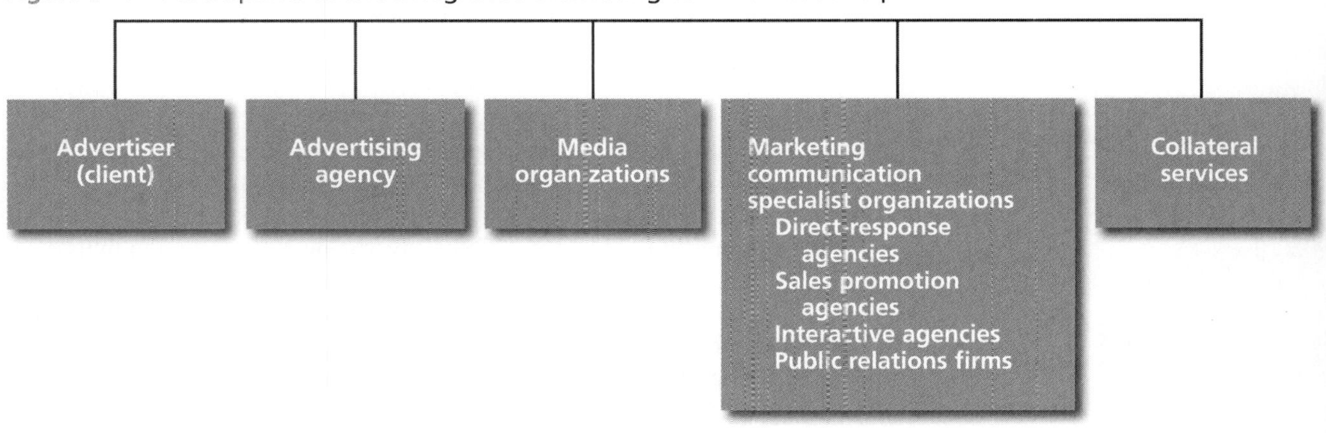

Exhibit 3–1 *Link* magazine advertises its value for reaching college students

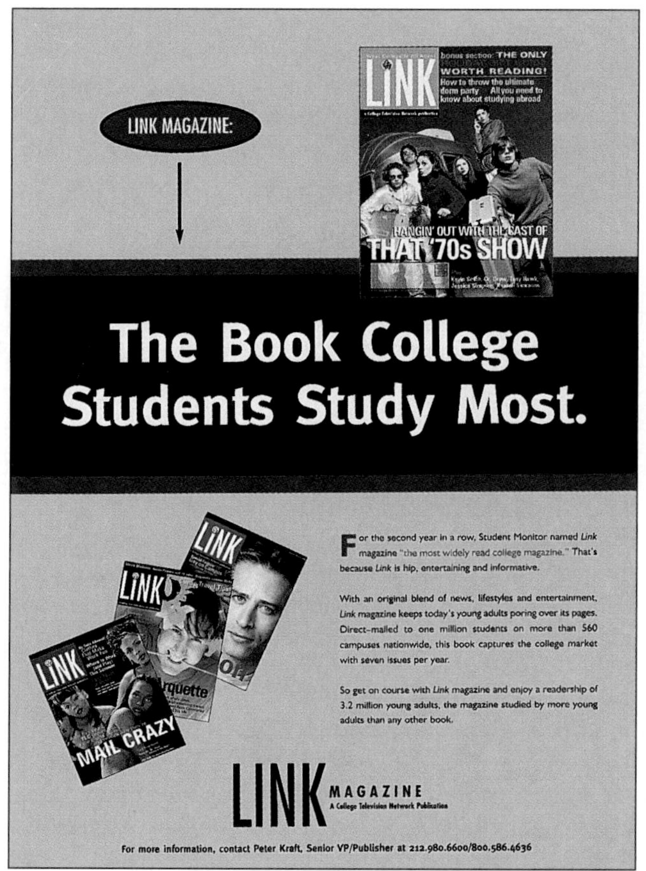

The next group of participants are organizations that provide **specialized marketing communications services.** They include direct marketing agencies, sales promotion agencies, interactive agencies, and public relations firms. These organizations provide services in their areas of expertise. A direct-response agency develops and implements direct marketing programs, while sales promotion agencies develop promotional programs such as contests and sweepstakes, premium offers, or sampling programs. Interactive agencies are being retained to develop websites for the Internet and help marketers as they move deeper into the realm of interactive media. Public relations firms are used to generate and manage publicity for a company and its products and services as well as to focus on its relationships and communications with its relevant publics.

The final participants shown in the promotions process of Figure 3–1 are those that provide **collateral services,** the wide range of support functions used by advertisers, agencies, media organizations, and specialized marketing communications firms. These individuals and companies perform specialized functions the other participants use in planning and executing advertising and other promotional functions. We will now examine the role of each participant in more detail. (Media organizations will be examined in Chapters 10 through 14.)

Organizing for Advertising and Promotion in the Firm: The Client's Role

Virtually every business organization uses some form of marketing communications. However, the way a company organizes for these efforts depends on several factors, including its size, the number of products it markets, the role of advertising and promotion in its marketing mix, the advertising and promotion budget, and its marketing organization structure. Many individuals throughout the organization may be involved in the promotions decision-making process. Marketing personnel have the most direct relationship with advertising and are often involved in many aspects of the decision process, such as providing input to the campaign plan, agency selection, and evaluation of proposed programs. Top management is usually interested in how the advertising program represents the firm, and this may also mean being involved in advertising decisions even when the decisions are not part of its day-to-day responsibilities.

While many people both inside and outside the organization have some input into the advertising and promotion process, direct responsibility for administering the program must be assumed by someone within the firm. Many companies have an advertising department headed by an advertising or communications manager operating under a marketing director. An alternative used by many large multiproduct firms is a decentralized marketing (brand management) system. A third option is to form a separate agency within the firm, an in-house agency. Each of these alternatives is examined in more detail in the following sections.

The Centralized System

In many organizations, marketing activities are divided along functional lines, with advertising placed alongside other marketing functions such as sales, marketing research, and product planning, as shown in Figure 3–2. The **advertising manager** is responsible for all promotions activities except sales. In the most common example of a **centralized system,** the advertising manager controls the entire promotions operation, including budgeting, coordinating creation and production of ads, planning media schedules, and monitoring and administering the sales promotions programs for all the company's products or services.

The specific duties of the advertising manager depend on the size of the firm and the importance it places on promotional programs. Basic functions the manager and staff perform include the following.

Planning and Budgeting

The advertising department is responsible for developing advertising and promotions plans that will be approved by management and recommending a promotions program based on the overall marketing plan, objectives, and budget. Formal plans are submitted annually or when a program is being changed significantly, as when a new campaign is developed. While the advertising department develops the promotional budget, the final decision on allocating funds is usually made by top management.

Administration and Execution

The manager must organize the advertising department and supervise and control its activities. The manager also supervises the execution of the plan by subordinates and/or the advertising agency. This requires working with such departments as production, media, art, copy, and sales promotion. If an outside agency is used, the advertising department is relieved of much of the executional responsibility; however, it must review and approve the agency's plans.

Figure 3–2 The advertising department under a centralized system

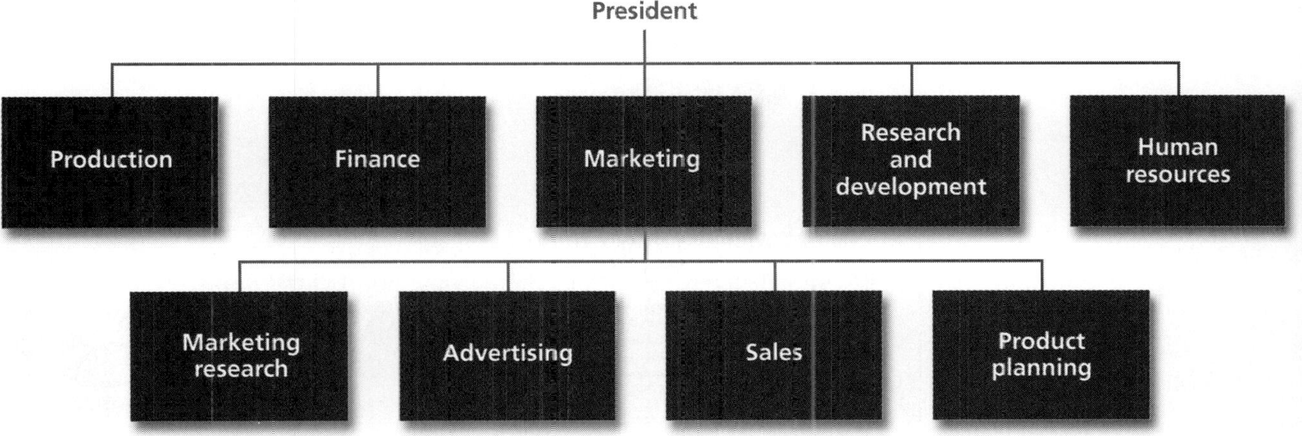

Coordination with Other Departments The manager must coordinate the advertising department's activities with those of other departments, particularly those involving other marketing functions. For example, the advertising department must communicate with marketing research and/or sales to determine which product features are important to customers and should be emphasized in the company's communications. Research may also provide profiles of product users and nonusers for the media department before it selects broadcast or print media. The advertising department may also be responsible for preparing material the sales force can use when calling on customers, such as sales promotion tools, advertising materials, and point-of-purchase displays.

Coordination with Outside Agencies and Services Many companies have an advertising department but still use many outside services. For example, companies may develop their advertising programs in-house while employing media buying services to place their ads and/or use collateral services agencies to develop brochures, point-of-purchase materials, and so on. The department serves as liaison between the company and any outside service providers and also determines which ones to use. Once outside services are retained, the manager will work with other marketing managers to coordinate their efforts and evaluate their performances.

A centralized organizational system is often used when companies do not have many different divisions, product or service lines, or brands to advertise. For example, airlines such as American and Continental have centralized advertising departments. Many companies prefer a centralized advertising department because developing and coordinating advertising programs from one central location facilitates communication regarding the promotions program, making it easier for top management to participate in decision making. A centralized system may also result in a more efficient operation because fewer people are involved in the program decisions, and as their experience in making such decisions increases, the process becomes easier.

At the same time, problems are inherent in a centralized operation. First, it is difficult for the advertising department to understand the overall marketing strategy for the brand. The department may also be slow in responding to specific needs and problems of a product or brand. As companies become larger and develop or acquire new products, brands, or even divisions, the centralized system may become impractical.

The Decentralized System

In large corporations with multiple divisions and many different products, it is very difficult to manage all the advertising, promotional, and other functions through a

Exhibit 3–2 Many of Procter & Gamble's brands compete against each other

centralized department. These types of companies generally have a **decentralized system,** with separate manufacturing, research and development, sales, and marketing departments for various divisions, product lines, or businesses. Many companies that use a decentralized system, such as Procter & Gamble, Gillette Co., and Nestlé, assign each product or brand to a **brand manager** who is responsible for the total management of the brand, including planning, budgeting, sales, and profit performance. (The term *product manager* is also used to describe this position.) The brand manager, who may have one or more assistant brand managers, is also responsible for the planning, implementation, and control of the marketing program.[1]

Under this system, the responsibilities and functions associated with advertising and promotions are transferred to the brand manager, who works closely with the outside advertising agency and other marketing communications specialists as they develop the promotional program.[2] In a multiproduct firm, each brand may have its own ad agency and may compete against other brands within the company, not just against outside competitors. For example, Exhibit 3–2 shows ads for Cheer and Tide, which are both Procter & Gamble products that compete for a share of the laundry detergent market.

As shown in Figure 3–3, the advertising department is part of marketing services and provides support for the brand managers. The role of marketing services is to

Figure 3–3 A decentralized brand management system

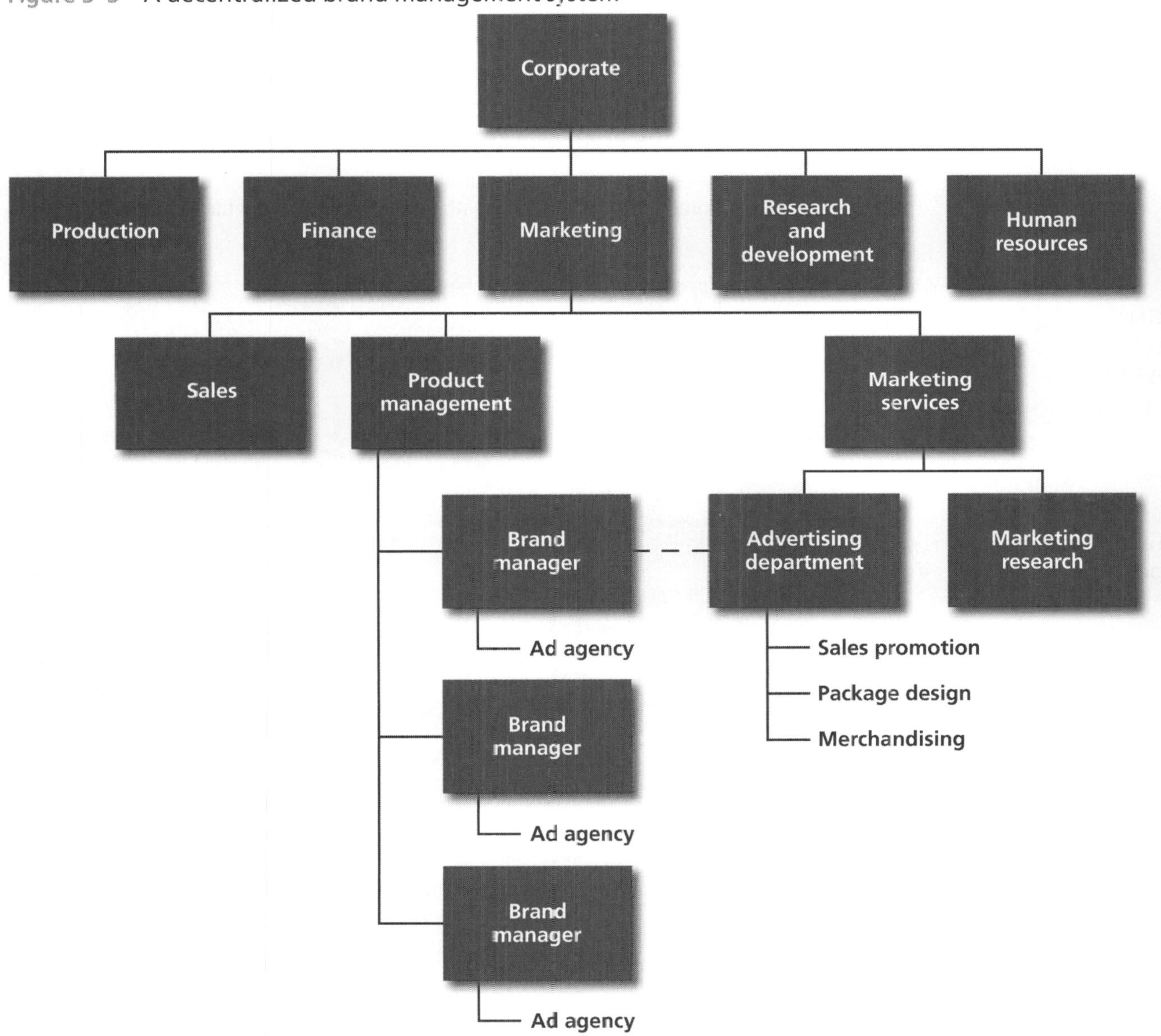

assist the brand managers in planning and coordinating the integrated marketing communications program. In some companies, the marketing services group may include sales promotion. The brand managers may work with sales promotion people to develop budgets, define strategies, and implement tactical executions for both trade and consumer promotions. Marketing services may also provide other types of support services, such as package design and merchandising.

Some companies may have an additional layer(s) of management above the brand managers to coordinate the efforts of all the brand managers handling a related group of products. An example is the organizational structure of Procter & Gamble, shown in Figure 3–4. This system—generally referred to as a **category management system**—includes category managers as well as brand and advertising managers. The category manager oversees management of the entire product category and focuses on the strategic role of the various brands in order to build profits and market share.[3]

The advertising manager may review and evaluate the various parts of the program and advise and consult with the brand managers. This person may have the authority to override the brand manager's decisions on advertising. In some multiproduct firms that spend a lot on advertising, the advertising manager may coordinate the work of the various agencies to obtain media discounts for the firm's large volume of media purchases.

An advantage of the decentralized system is that each brand receives concentrated managerial attention, resulting in faster response to both problems and opportunities. The brand manager system is also more flexible and makes it easier to adjust various aspects of the advertising and promotional program, such as creative platforms and media and sales promotion schedules.[4] IMC Perspective 3–1 discusses how General Motors is faring under a brand management system the company adopted at the end of the 90s.

There are some drawbacks to the decentralized approach. Brand managers often lack training and experience. The promotional strategy for a brand may be developed by a brand manager who does not really understand what advertising or sales

Figure 3–4 A Procter & Gamble division, using the category management system

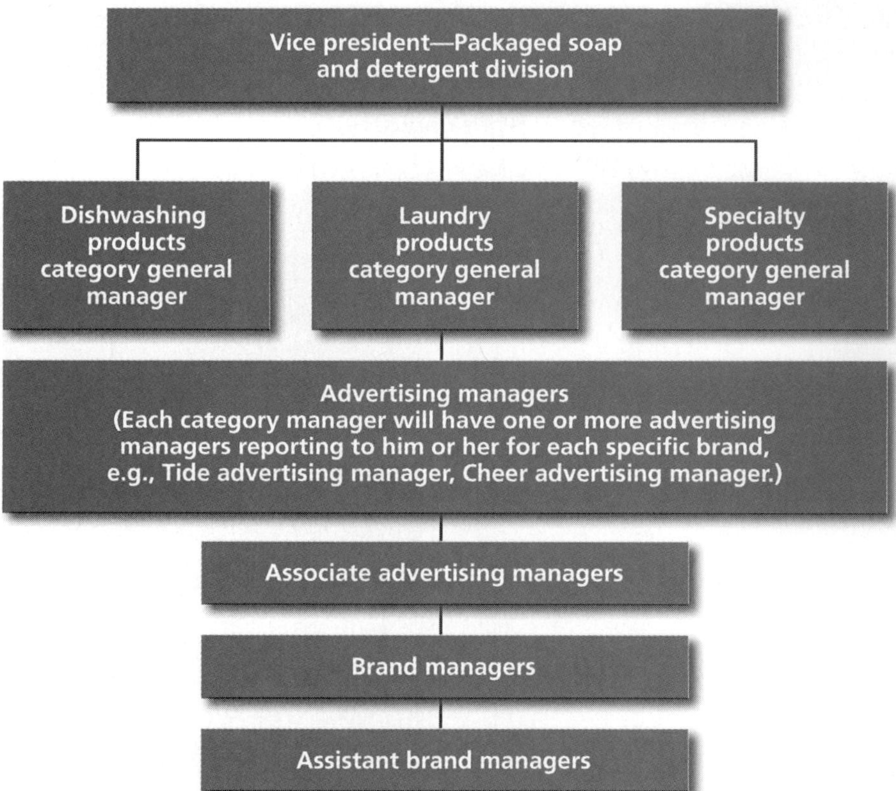

IMC Perspective 3–1

General Motors Drives the Brand Management Road

The use of a brand management organizational system has been around since 1927, when Procter & Gamble pioneered the concept by assigning a manager to work exclusively on Camay soap. Since then the practice of making a single manager a brand's internal champion with responsibility for all of its marketing has become commonplace in most large consumer, as well as industrial product, companies. However, General Motors (GM), the largest corporation in the United States, recently adopted the same brand management techniques used to sell cereal, toothpaste, soap, and thousands of other products in hopes of selling more cars.

The goal of General Motors founder Alfred P. Sloan was to "build a car for every purse and purpose," and for many years GM created some of the strongest brand names in the auto industry, including Cadillac, Pontiac, Chevrolet, Oldsmobile, and Buick. However, over the past few decades, fuzzy advertising and marketing as well as lookalike models from competing GM divisions helped blur the identity of many of these brands. The problem was compounded by a system where dozens of managers in marketing, sales, and planning would work on various aspects of marketing for many different models. Moreover, GM's traditional divisional managers had too many responsibilities and could not give enough attention to the individual brands.

To address these problems and once again create strong identities for its 40-plus brands of cars, trucks, minivans, and sport utility vehicles, GM appointed brand managers who work under the divisional general manager but are accountable for the sales success of individual brands such as the Chevrolet Malibu or Buick Century. The GM brand managers have full responsibility for marketing their vehicles, including pricing, advertising, and promotion. They are responsible for developing target markets as well as conceiving, implementing, and managing marketing campaigns that will differentiate their brands.

General Motors implemented its brand management system in 1996 and the new system has brought common processes, practices, and systems and has helped eliminate duplicated effort by its marketing divisions. And it has played a major role in increasing sales of GM models such as the Pontiac Grand Prix and Chevy Malibu.

One concern expressed over GM's brand management system is that it defines brands down too far, as every single model is a brand, and attention needs to be given to the image and positioning of divisions such as Oldsmobile and Cadillac. One GM division where GM is addressing this issue is Cadillac, which is striving to reclaim its luxury standard status.

At the end of 1999, Cadillac began a new advertising and positioning theme for the entire Cadillac division. The new ad campaign revolves around the design and technology theme, and signals a push for distinctive styling and technological innovation for all the Cadillac models. In the past, Cadillac models had their own advertising taglines. However, now advertising for various models such as Catera, Seville, and DeVille DTS will all use the theme "The Power of &," which signifies how Cadillac is combining design and technology in inspiring new ways. The campaign's goal is to build a uniform personality around the theme and in both print and TV ads an emphasis is placed on humanizing the image of Cadillac.

As one management consultant has noted, "The cornerstone of brand management is to stop chasing your competition and start chasing your customer. GM has gotten the message." GM's goal is for its brand management system to continue to create an array of well-defined brands that even Alfred Sloan would be proud of.

Sources: Tanya Irwin, "A Brand New Cadillac," *Adweek*, September 6, 1999, p. 30; Jean Halliday, "GM's Brand Management Report Card," *Advertising Age*, March 9, 1998, pp. 1, 26; Kathleen Kerwin, "GM Warms Up the Branding Iron," *Business Week*, September 23, 1996, pp. 153–54.

promotion can and cannot do and how each should be used. Brand managers may focus too much on short-run planning and administrative tasks, neglecting the development of long-term programs.

Another problem is that individual brand managers often end up competing for management attention, marketing dollars, and other resources, which can lead to unproductive rivalries and potential misallocation of funds. The manager's persuasiveness may become a bigger factor in determining budgets than the long-run profit potential of the brands. These types of problems were key factors in Procter & Gamble's decision to switch to a category management system.

Finally, the brand management system has been criticized for failing to provide brand managers with authority over the functions needed to implement and control the plans they develop.[5] Some companies have dealt with this problem by expanding the roles and responsibilities of the advertising and sales promotion managers and their staff of specialists. The staff specialists counsel the individual brand managers, and advertising or sales promotion decision making involves the advertising and/or sales promotion manager, the brand manager, and the marketing director.

In-House Agencies

Some companies, in an effort to reduce costs and maintain greater control over agency activities, have set up their own advertising agencies internally. An **in-house agency** is an advertising agency that is set up, owned, and operated by the advertiser. Some in-house agencies are little more than advertising departments, but in other companies they are given a separate identity and are responsible for the expenditure of large sums of advertising dollars. Large advertisers that use in-house agencies include Calvin Klein, Avon, Revlon, and Benetton. Many companies use in-house agencies exclusively; others combine in-house efforts with those of outside agencies. For example, No Fear handles most of its advertising in-house, but it does use an outside agency for some of its creative work (Exhibit 3–3). (The specific roles performed by in-house agencies will become clearer when we discuss the functions of outside agencies.)

A major reason for using an in-house agency is to reduce advertising and promotion costs. Companies with very large advertising budgets pay a substantial amount to outside agencies in the form of media commissions. With an internal structure, these commissions go to the in-house agency. An in-house agency can also provide related work such as sales presentations and sales force materials, package design,

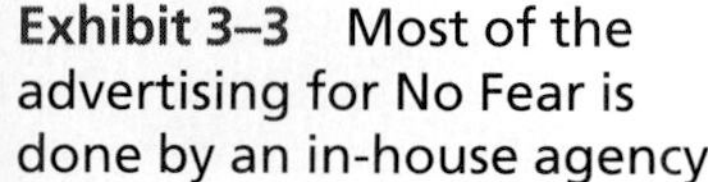
Exhibit 3–3 Most of the advertising for No Fear is done by an in-house agency

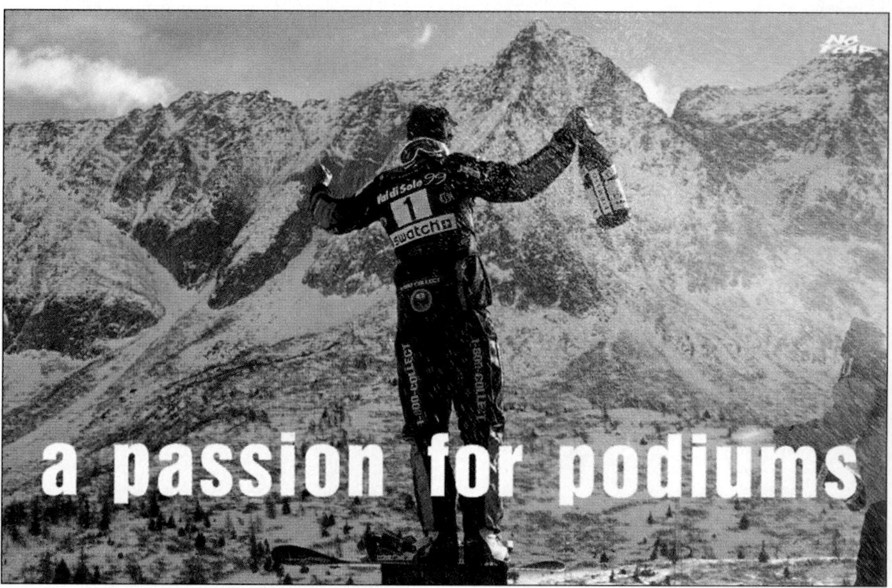

and public relations at a lower cost than outside agencies. A study by M. Louise Ripley found that creative and media services were the most likely functions to be performed outside, while merchandising and sales promotion were the most likely to be performed in-house.[6]

Saving money is not the only reason companies use in-house agencies. Time savings, bad experiences with outside agencies, and the increased knowledge and understanding of the market that come from working on advertising and promotion for the product or service day by day are also reasons. Companies can also maintain tighter control over the process and more easily coordinate promotions with the firm's overall marketing program. Some companies use an in-house agency simply because they believe it can do a better job than an outside agency could.[7]

Opponents of in-house agencies say they can give the advertiser neither the experience and objectivity of an outside agency nor the range of services. They argue that outside agencies have more highly skilled specialists and attract the best creative talent and that using an external firm gives a company a more varied perspective on its advertising problems and greater flexibility. In-house personnel may become narrow or grow stale while working on the same product line, but outside agencies may have different people with a variety of backgrounds and ideas working on the account. Flexibility is greater because an outside agency can be dismissed if the company is not satisfied, whereas changes in an in-house agency could be slower and more disruptive.

The cost savings of an in-house agency must be evaluated against these considerations. For many companies, high-quality advertising is critical to their marketing success and should be the major criterion in determining whether to use in-house services. Companies like Rockport and Redken Laboratories have moved their in-house work to outside agencies in recent years. Redken cited the need for a "fresh look" and objectivity as the reasons, noting that management gets too close to the product to come up with different creative ideas. Companies often hire outside agencies as they grow and their advertising budgets and needs increase. For example, the fast-growing personal computer company Gateway hired an outside agency a few years ago to handle all of its advertising.[8]

The ultimate decision as to which type of advertising organization to use depends on which arrangement works best for the company. The advantages and disadvantages of the three systems are summarized in Figure 3–5. We now turn our attention to the functions of outside agencies and their roles in the promotional process.

Figure 3–5 Comparison of advertising organization systems

Organizational system	Advantages	Disadvantages
Centralized	• Facilitated communications • Fewer personnel required • Continuity in staff • Allows for more top-management involvement	• Less involvement with and understanding of overall marketing goals • Longer response time • Inability to handle multiple product lines
Decentralized	• Concentrated managerial attention • Rapid response to problems and opportunities • Increased flexibility	• Ineffective decision making • Internal conflicts • Misallocation of funds • Lack of authority
In-house agencies	• Cost savings • More control • Increased coordination	• Less experience • Less objectivity • Less flexibility

Advertising Agencies

Many major companies use an advertising agency to assist them in developing, preparing, and executing their promotional programs. An ad agency is a service organization that specializes in planning and executing advertising programs for its clients. Over 10,000 agencies are listed in the *Standard Directory of Advertising Agencies* (the "Red Book"); however, most are individually owned small businesses employing fewer than five people. The U.S. ad agency business is highly concentrated. Nearly half of the domestic **billings** (the amount of client money agencies spend on media purchases and other equivalent activities) are handled by the top 500 agencies. In fact, just 10 U.S. agencies handle nearly 30 percent of the total volume of business done by the top 500 agencies in the United States. The top agencies also have foreign operations that generate substantial billings and income. The top 25 agencies, ranked by their U.S. gross incomes, are listed in Figure 3–6. The figure shows that the advertising business is also geographically concentrated, with 20 of the top 25 agencies headquartered in New York City. Nearly 40 percent of U.S. agency business is handled by New York-based agencies.[9] Other leading advertising centers in the United States include Boston, Chicago, Los Angeles, Detroit, San Francisco, and Minneapolis.

During the late 1980s and into the 90s, the advertising industry underwent major changes as large agencies merged with or acquired other agencies and support organizations to form large advertising organizations, or superagencies. These **superagencies** were formed so that agencies could provide clients with integrated marketing communications services worldwide. Some advertisers became disenchanted with the superagencies and moved to smaller agencies that were flexible and more responsive.[10] However, during the mid-90s the agency business went

Figure 3–6 Top 25 agencies ranked by U.S. gross income, 1998

Rank	Ad organization	Headquarters	Gross income ($ millions)
1	Grey Advertising	New York	$535.8
2	J. Walter Thompson	New York	496.2
3	McCann-Erickson Worldwide	New York	466.9
4	FCB Worldwide	New York	452.8
5	Leo Burnett USA	Chicago	396.8
6	Euro RSCG Worldwide	New York	378.4
7	Y & R Advertising	New York	365.1
8	BBDO Worldwide	New York	361.1
9	DDB Worldwide Communications	New York	342.8
10	Ogilvy & Mather Worldwide	New York	327.7
11	D'Arcy Masius Benton & Bowles	New York	260.0
12	TBWA/Chiat/Day	New York	247.4
13	Lowe Lintas & Partners Worldwide	New York	242.6
14	Saatchi & Saatchi	New York	205.6
15	Campbell-Ewald Co.	Warren, MI	185.7
16	Bates Worldwide	New York	170.5
17	CommonHealth	Parsippany, NJ	145.2
18	Nelson Communications	New York	134.9
19	Deutsch	New York	133.1
20	Hill, Holliday, Connors, Cosmopulos	Boston	124.0
21	Lowe Healthcare Worldwide	New York	122.8
22	Bernard Hordes Group	New York	114.9
23	Bozell Worldwide	New York	111.8
24	Arnold Communications	Boston	107.8
25	Publics	New York	107.3

through another wave of consolidation as a number of medium-size agencies were acquired and became part of large advertising organizations such as Omnicom Group, WPP Group, and the Interpublic Group of Cos. Many of the mid-size agencies were acquired by or forged alliances with larger agencies because their clients wanted an agency with international communications capabilities and their alignment with larger organizations gave them access to a network of agencies around the world.[11] For example, TBWA and Chiat/Day merged and became part of the TBWA Worldwide agency, which is part of the Omnicom Group, the world's largest agency holding company. The acquisition of mid-sized agencies by large advertising organizations has continued into the new millenium. In early 2000, Fallon McElligott, one of the largest and hottest independent U.S. ad agencies, was acquired by French advertising giant Publics. One of the reasons Fallon McElligott agreed to the deal was that it needed to become a global agency to serve its clients and with Publics' backing, the agency can expand into other major markets worldwide.[12]

Recently the merger and acquisition activity has moved in a new direction as many of the advertising organizations and major agencies have been acquiring companies specializing in areas such as interactive communications, direct marketing, and sales promotion so that they can offer their clients an ever-broader range of integrated marketing communication services.[13] For example, the Omnicom Group purchased a number of companies including Rapp Collins, a direct marketing company; Critical Mass, a Canadian-based interactive communications agency; and M/A/R/C, an integrated marketing services specialist.

The Ad Agency's Role

The functions performed by advertising agencies might be conducted by the clients themselves through one of the designs discussed earlier in this chapter, but most large companies use outside firms. This section discusses some reasons advertisers use external agencies.

Exhibit 3–4 Quill Communications specializes in creating ads for high-tech companies

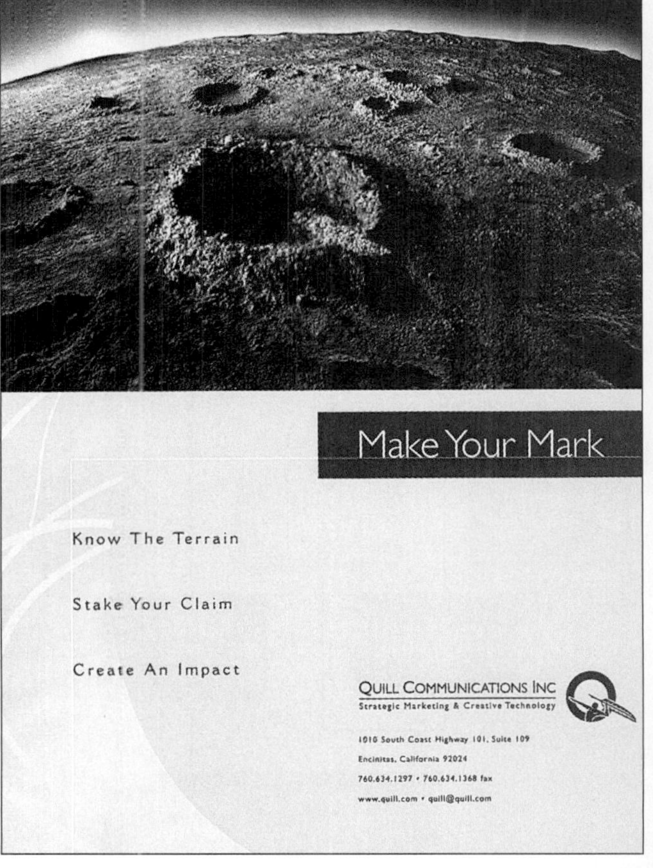

Reasons for Using an Agency

Probably the main reason outside agencies are used is that they provide the client with the services of highly skilled individuals who are specialists in their chosen fields. An advertising agency staff may include artists, writers, media analysts, researchers, and others with specific skills, knowledge, and experience who can help market the client's products or services. Many agencies specialize in a particular type of business and use their knowledge of the industry to assist their clients. For example, Quill Communications Inc. is an agency that specializes in developing advertising and communications for the high-technology and health care industries (Exhibit 3–4).

An outside agency can also provide an objective viewpoint of the market and its business that is not subject to internal company policies, biases, or other limitations. The agency can draw on the broad range of experience it has gained while working on a diverse set of marketing problems for various clients. For example, an ad agency that is handling a travel-related account may have individuals who have worked with airlines, cruise ship companies, travel agencies, hotels, and other travel-related industries. The agency may have experience in this area or may even have previously worked on the advertising account of one of the client's competitors. Thus, the agency can provide the client with insight into the industry (and, in some cases, the competition).

Types of Ad Agencies

Since ad agencies can range in size from a one- or two-person operation to large organizations with over 1,000 employees, the services offered and functions performed will vary. This section examines the different types of agencies, the services they perform for their clients, and how they are organized.

Full-Service Agencies

Many companies employ what is known as a **full-service agency,** which offers its clients a full range of marketing, communications, and promotions services, including planning, creating, and producing the advertising; performing research; and selecting media. A full-service agency may also offer nonadvertising services such as strategic market planning; sales promotions, direct marketing, and interactive capabilities; package design; and public relations and publicity.

The full-service agency is made up of departments that provide the activities needed to perform the various advertising functions and serve the client, as shown in Figure 3–7.

Account Services

Account services, or account management, is the link between the ad agency and its clients. Depending on the size of the client and its advertising budget, one or more account executives serve as liaison. The **account executive** is responsible for understanding the advertiser's marketing and promotions needs and interpreting them to agency personnel. He or she coordinates agency efforts in planning, creating, and producing ads. The account executive also presents agency recommendations and obtains client approval.

As the focal point of agency–client relationships, the account executive must know a great deal about the client's business and be able to communicate this to specialists in the agency working on the account.[14] The ideal account executive has a strong marketing background as well as a thorough understanding of all phases of the advertising process.

Figure 3–7 Full-service agency organizational chart

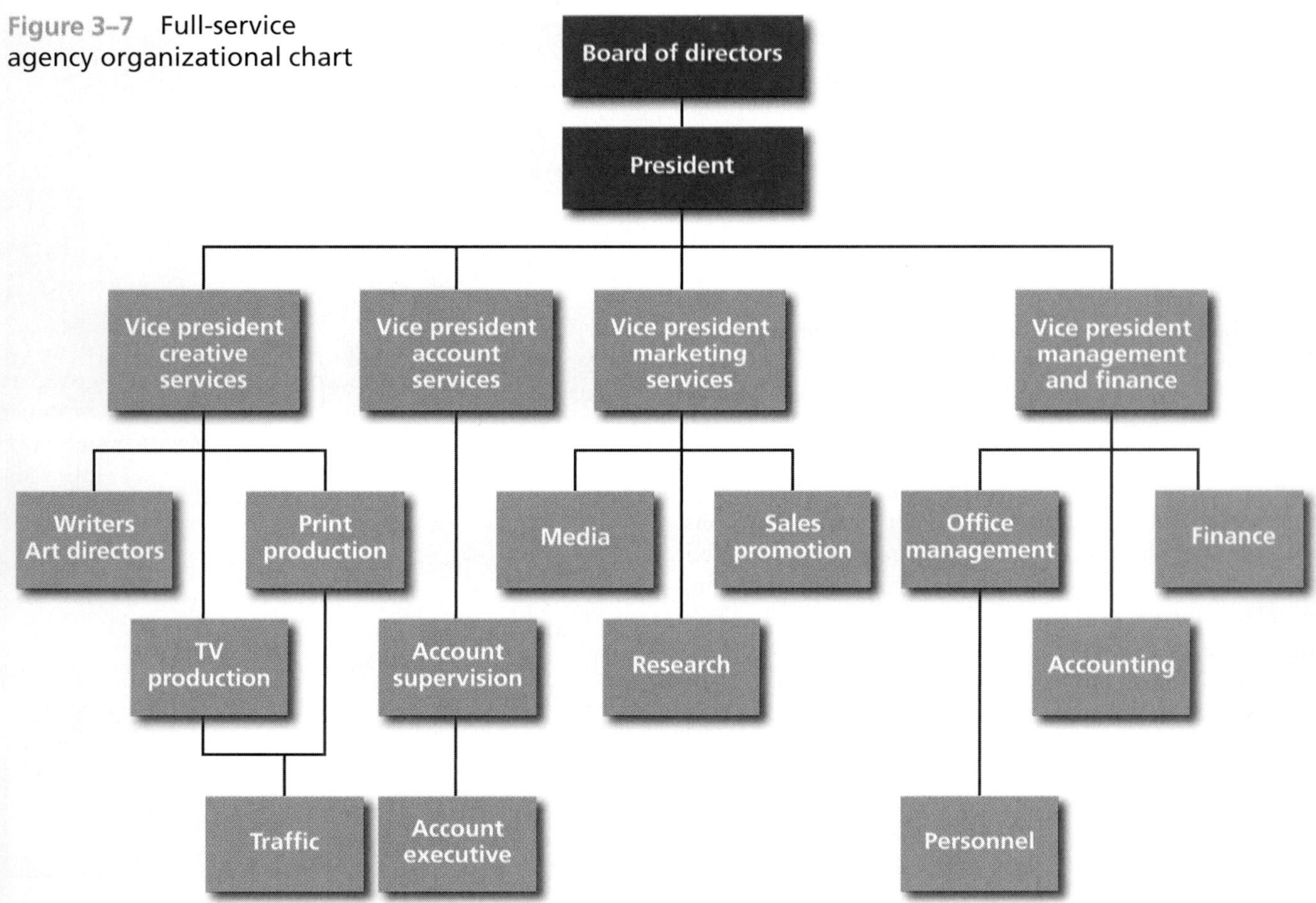

Career Profile

Jana Clayton

Assistant Account Executive at Doner Advertising

As a junior at Arizona State University (ASU), I decided to major in marketing since I felt this would provide me with the widest array of stimulating career opportunities. As part of my marketing program, I took a course in consumer behavior where we studied the mind of the consumer. This course peaked my interest in why people buy the things they do. One of the things I remember most from this class was our professor asking us to bring in a commercial and to give our personal "consumer" opinions on what we liked or disliked about the spot. Ironically, I chose a car commercial and remember liking it because it had a lot of pizzazz and evoked an emotional response. Little did I know that one day I'd be working on a major automotive account and helping develop the marketing strategies and creative concepts for TV commercials that are designed to connect with consumers on an emotional level.

"I feel that account management is definitely one of the most challenging jobs in the advertising business."

After graduating from ASU with my degree in marketing it was time to begin my career. As I began the job search in Orange County, California, "my destination of choice," I remembered learning about the concept of networking in college and other ways to discover exciting employment opportunities. However, I found my first job in advertising the old-fashioned way when I came across an ad in the local newspaper for an advertising job at the Doner agency and sent them my resume.

I accepted an entry-level position with Doner as an administrative assistant. Although I initially felt overqualified, the position actually provided me with a great opportunity to learn about the advertising industry and agency business. Within one year, I was promoted to an assistant account executive and was working on the Mazda account. Starting out as an administrative assistant really helped me become a more effective account person; I learned the basics of the agency and client side of the advertising business and this knowledge gave me the ability to seek a more challenging position in account management.

I feel that account management is definitely one of the most challenging jobs in the advertising business. As an account executive, you must develop and maintain relationships with the client, as well as work closely with various individuals within the agency to insure that each project is completed efficiently and effectively. I sometimes refer to myself as the *middleman* because I often find I communicate with and respond to individuals on the client side as well as within Doner.

The job responsibilities for my position vary from day to day, but one thing is certain—being flexible is definitely a must in advertising. Many times we are dealing with tight deadlines, which require excellent multitasking skills. What I enjoy most about my job is being an integral part of creating a piece of great advertising and then seeing the results. There is nothing more exciting than seeing the actual airing of a Mazda TV commercial or viewing a print ad that Doner created and saying to myself, "I helped make that happen."

One of the biggest challenges for our account management group is building and maintaining consumer awareness for the Mazda brands such as the Protegé. With so many automobile companies competing in the marketplace, it is a constant challenge to differentiate your product from the others, which is why Doner must stay on top of creating fresh and innovative ways to sell cars.

I had always imagined a job in advertising would be exciting and glamorous. I'm not sure about the glamorous part, but it is definitely exciting, interesting, and rewarding. With all that I've learned in advertising, I always remember a few key things: Be as flexible as possible. No idea is ever a dumb idea. And never take yourself too seriously.

Marketing Services Over the past two decades, use of marketing services has increased dramatically. One service gaining increased attention is research, as agencies realize that to communicate effectively with their clients' customers, they must have a good understanding of the target audience. As shown in Chapter 1, the advertising planning process begins with a thorough situation analysis, which is based on research and information about the target audience.

Most full-service agencies maintain a *research department* whose function is to gather, analyze, and interpret information that will be useful in developing advertising for their clients. This can be done through primary research—where a study is designed, executed, and interpreted by the research department—or through the use of secondary (previously published) sources of information. Sometimes the research department acquires studies conducted by independent syndicated research firms or consultants. The research staff then interprets these reports and passes on the information to other agency personnel working on that account.

The research department may also design and conduct research to pretest the effectiveness of advertising the agency is considering. For example, copy testing is often conducted to determine how messages developed by the creative specialists are likely to be interpreted by the receiving audience.

The *media department* of an agency analyzes, selects, and contracts for space or time in the media that will be used to deliver the client's advertising message. The media department is expected to develop a media plan that will reach the target market and effectively communicate the message. Since most of the client's ad budget is spent on media time and/or space, this department must develop a plan that both communicates with the right audience and is cost-effective.

Media specialists must know what audiences the media reach, their rates, and how well they match the client's target market. The media department reviews information on demographics, magazine and newspaper readership, radio listenership, and consumers' TV viewing patterns to develop an effective media plan. The media buyer implements the media plan by purchasing the actual time and space.

The media department is becoming an increasingly important part of the agency business as many large advertisers consolidate their media buying with one or a few agencies to save money and improve media efficiency. For example, for many years Nestlé had as many as 11 agencies purchasing media time for its products. Then Nestlé consolidated its media buying into one agency, which gave the company more clout in the media buying market and saved a considerable amount of money.[15] General Motors, Campbell Soup, and Coca-Cola are other large advertisers who have consolidated their media buying with one or two agencies.[16] An agency's strategic ability to negotiate prices and effectively use the vast array of media vehicles available is becoming as important as its ability to create ads.

The research and media departments perform most of the functions that full-service agencies need to plan and execute their clients' advertising programs. Some agencies offer additional marketing services to their clients to assist in other promotional areas. An agency may have a sales promotion department, or merchandising department, that specializes in developing contests, premiums, promotions, point-of-sale materials, and other sales materials. It may have direct-marketing specialists and package designers, as well as a PR/publicity department. Many agencies have developed interactive media departments to create websites for their clients. The growing popularity of integrated marketing communications has prompted many full-function agencies to develop capabilities and offer services in these other promotional areas. IMC Perspective 3–2 discusses how traditional advertising agencies are developing integrated marketing capabilities that extend beyond media advertising.

Creative Services The creative services department is responsible for the creation and execution of advertisements. The individuals who conceive the ideas for the ads and write the headlines, subheads, and body copy (the words constituting the message) are known as **copywriters.** They may also be involved in determining the basic appeal or theme of the ad campaign and often prepare a rough initial visual layout of the print ad or television commercial.

IMC Perspective 3–2

Agencies Learn That It's about More Than Advertising

During the late 1980s many of the world's largest advertising agencies recognized that their clients were shifting more and more of their promotional budgets away from traditional media advertising to other areas of marketing communication such as direct marketing, public relations, sales promotion, and event sponsorship. In response to this trend, many of these agencies began acquiring companies that were specialists in these areas and ended up turning them into profit-centered departments or subsidiaries that often ended up battling one another for a piece of their client's promotional budget. While the agencies could point to these specialists when touting their IMC capabilities, there was really little emphasis on integrating the various communication functions.

During the 90s some agencies began taking steps to place more of an emphasis on IMC by truly integrating it into all aspects of their operations. For example, the Leo Burnett agency brought in direct marketing, sales promotion, event marketing, and pubic relations professionals and dispersed them throughout the agency. Burnetters were expected to interact with clients not as advertising specialists who happened to know about sales promotion, direct marketing, or pubic relations but as generalists able to work with a variety of integrated marketing tools. Another agency that embraced IMC was Fallon McElligott, which hired a president of integrated marketing and expanded its capabilities in areas such as PR, events, and interactive advertising.

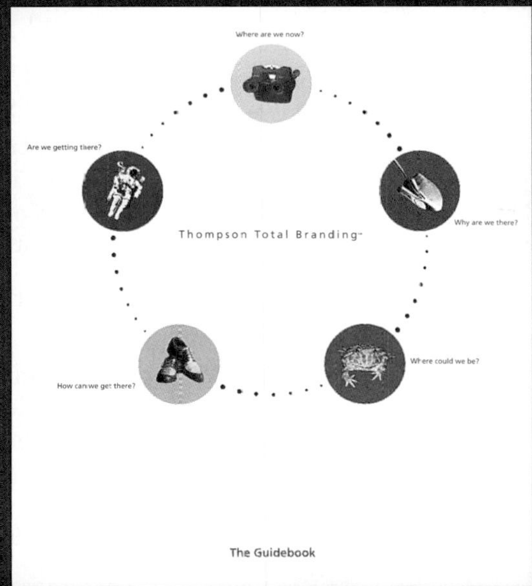

Where are we now?
Why are we there?
Where could we be?
How can we get there?
Are we getting there?
Thompson Total Branding™
The Guidebook

As we begin the new millennium, the shift toward IMC is taking place at a number of major ad agencies that are recognizing they must embrace a way of doing business that doesn't always involve advertising. Many companies are developing campaigns and strategies using event marketing, sponsorships, direct marketing, targeted radio, and the Internet with only peripheral use of print and TV advertising. The Internet poses a particular threat to traditional agencies as it is not well understood by many agency veterans and is taking yet another slice from the marketing communications budget pie.

A number of agencies are making the move toward more integrated approaches. DDB Needham Worldwide established Beyond DDB, a 140-person unit within its U.S. offices, which pursues new business using an IMC approach. The unit has won new business from companies such as U.S. Gypsum, the Cartoon Network, and Whirlpool. For U.S. Gypsum, DDB launched a "Rock Tour" promoting Gypsum's brand of wallboard, USG Sheetrock, to workers on construction sites in 110 cities nationwide. The promotion included a contest offering a chance to win a Chevy CK Rock Tour pickup truck and featured radio spots aired before dawn during "construction worker drive time."

At J. Walter Thompson, the agency's CEO, Chris Jones, has championed a program called Thompson Total Branding (TTB) that makes JWT the manager of a client's brand. TTB involves taking what the agency calls a "Branding Idea" and developing a total communications plan that helps decide which integrated marketing tools can most powerfully and persuasively communicate it. One of the company executives notes, "agencies are finally realizing that our job is creating branding solutions and, while those may involve advertising, it's not necessarily about advertising. That's a fundamental change in the way we operate." The ability to use various IMC tools has helped the agency secure new accounts such as Kimberly-Clark, Qwest, and Elizabeth Arden, and strengthen relationships with existing clients such as De Beers and Heinz Pet Products.

While traditional agencies have been preaching integrated marketing for years, many have not been really practicing it. However, these agencies are realizing they must alter their course if they plan to be competitive in the future. They are retraining their staffers in the use and best practices of various IMC tools and getting them, at long last, to focus on total communications solutions to their clients' businesses. The move toward integrated marketing communications appears to be for real this time around.

Sources: Ellen Nouborne, "Mad Ave: A Star Is Reborn," *Business Week,* July 26, 1999, pp. 54–64; Kate Fitzgerald, "Beyond Advertising," *Advertising Age,* August 3, 1998, pp. 1, 14.

While copywriters are responsible for what the message says, the *art department* is responsible for how the ad looks. For print ads, the art director and graphic designers prepare *layouts,* which are drawings that show what the ad will look like and from which the final artwork will be produced. For TV commercials, the layout is known as a *storyboard,* a sequence of frames or panels that depict the commercial in still form.

Members of the creative department work together to develop ads that will communicate the key points determined to be the basis of the creative strategy for the client's product or service. Writers and artists generally work under the direction of the agency's creative director, who oversees all the advertising produced by the organization. The director sets the creative philosophy of the department and may even become directly involved in creating ads for the agency's largest clients.

Once the copy, layout, illustrations, and mechanical specifications have been completed and approved, the ad is turned over to the *production department.* Most agencies do not actually produce finished ads; they hire printers, engravers, photographers, typographers, and other suppliers to complete the finished product. For broadcast production, the approved storyboard must be turned into a finished commercial. The production department may supervise the casting of people to appear in the ad and the setting for the scenes as well as choose an independent production studio. The department may hire an outside director to turn the creative concept into a commercial. For example, Nike has used film director Spike Lee to direct a number of its commercials; Airwalk shoes has used John Glen, who directed many of the James Bond films, for its TV spots. Copywriters, art directors, account managers, people from research and planning, and representatives from the client side may all participate in production decisions, particularly when large sums of money are involved.

Creating an advertisement often involves many people and takes several months. In large agencies with many clients, coordinating the creative and production processes can be a major problem. A *traffic department* coordinates all phases of production to see that the ads are completed on time and that all deadlines for submitting the ads to the media are met. The traffic department may be located in the creative services area of the agency, or be part of media or account management, or be separate.

Management and Finance

Like any other business, an advertising agency must be managed and perform basic operating and administrative functions such as accounting, finance, and human resources. It must also attempt to generate new business. Large agencies employ administrative, managerial, and clerical people to perform these functions. The bulk of an agency's income (approximately 64 percent) goes to salary and benefits for its employees. Thus, an agency must manage its personnel carefully and get maximum productivity from them.

Agency Organization and Structure

Full-function advertising agencies must develop an organizational structure that will meet their clients' needs and serve their own internal requirements. Most medium-size and large agencies are structured under either a departmental or a group system. Under the **departmental system,** each of the agency functions shown in Figure 3–7 is set up as a separate department and is called on as needed to perform its specialty and serve all of the agency's clients. Ad layout, writing, and production are done by the creative department, marketing services is responsible for any research or media selection and purchases, and the account services department handles client contact. Some agencies prefer the departmental system because it gives employees the opportunity to develop expertise in servicing a variety of accounts.

Many large agencies use the **group system,** in which individuals from each department work together in groups to service particular accounts. Each group is headed by an account executive or supervisor and has one or more media people, including media planners and buyers; a creative team, which includes copywriters, art directors, artists, and production personnel; and one or more account executives. The group may also include individuals from other departments such as marketing research, direct marketing, or sales promotion. The size and composition of the group varies depending on the client's billings and the importance of the account to the agency. For very important accounts, the group members may be assigned exclusively to one client. In some agencies, they may serve a number of smaller clients. Many agencies prefer the group system because employees become very knowledgeable about the client's business and there is continuity in servicing the account.

Other Types of Agencies and Services

Not every agency is a large full-service agency. Many smaller agencies expect their employees to handle a variety of jobs. For example, account executives may do their own research, work out their own media schedule, and coordinate the production of ads written and designed by the creative department. Many advertisers, including some large companies, are not interested in paying for the services of a full-service agency but are interested in some of the specific services agencies have to offer. Over the past few decades, several alternatives to full-service agencies have evolved, including creative boutiques and media buying services.

Creative Boutiques

A **creative boutique** is an agency that provides only creative services. These specialized companies have developed in response to some clients' desires to use only the creative talent of an outside provider while maintaining the other functions internally. The client may seek outside creative talent because it believes an extra creative effort is required or because its own employees do not have sufficient skills in this regard. Some advertisers have been bypassing traditional agencies and tapping into the movie industry for creative ideas for their commercials.[17] For example, a few years ago Coca-Cola entered into a joint venture with Disney and three former employees of Creative Artists Agency (CAA), a Hollywood talent agency, to create an in-house agency called Edge Creative. The agency created several commercials for Coca-Cola's flagship brand, including the popular polar bears spot (Exhibit 3–5).

Full-service agencies often subcontract work to creative boutiques when they are very busy or want to avoid adding full-time employees to their payrolls. Creative boutiques are usually founded by members of the creative departments of full-service agencies who leave the firm and take with them clients who want to retain their creative talents. These boutiques usually perform the creative function on a fee basis.

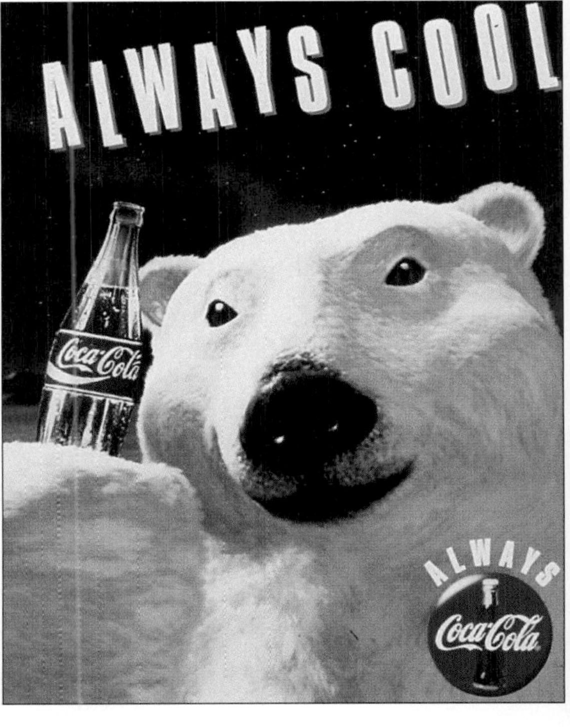

Exhibit 3–5 This popular Coca-Cola spot was done by the company's in-house creative boutique

Media Buying Services

Media buying services are independent companies that specialize in the buying of media, particularly radio and television time. The task of purchasing advertising media has grown more complex as specialized media proliferate, so media buying services have found a niche by specializing in the analysis and purchase of advertising time and space. Agencies and clients usually develop their own media strategies and hire the buying service to execute them. Some media buying services do help advertisers plan their media strategies. Because media buying services purchase such large

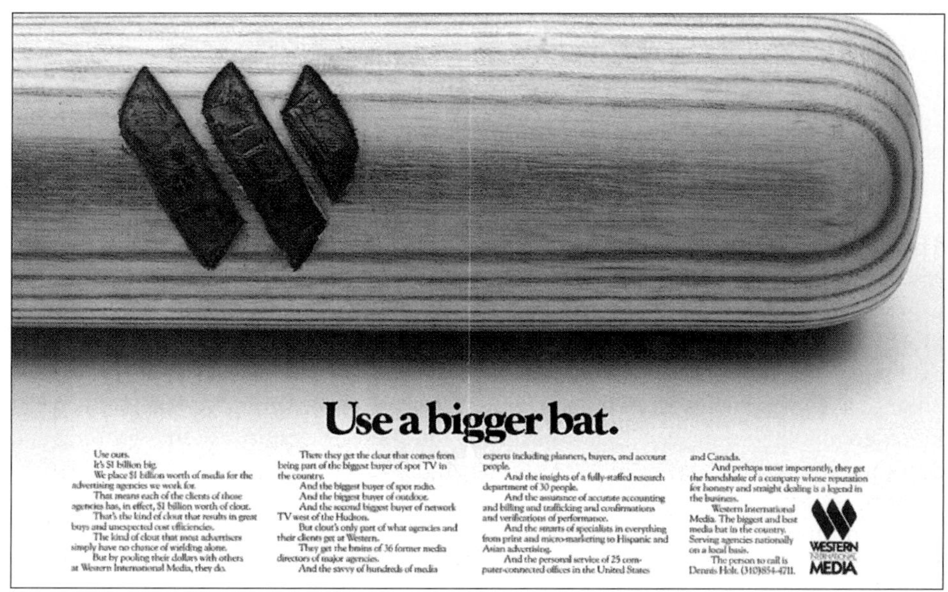

Exhibit 3–6 Western International Media is the leading independent media buying service

amounts of time and space, they receive large discounts and can save the small agency or client money on media purchases. Media buying services are paid a fee or commission for their work.

Media buying services have been experiencing strong growth in recent years as clients seek alternatives to full-service agency relationships. Many companies have been unbundling agency services and consolidating media buying to get more clout from their advertising budgets. Nike, Bugle Boy, and Pennzoil are among those that have switched some or all of their media buying from full-service agencies to independent media buyers. Exhibit 3–6 shows an ad promoting the services of Western International Media, the leading independent media buying company in the United States.

Agency Compensation

As you have seen, the type and amount of services an agency performs vary from one client to another. As a result, agencies use a variety of methods to get paid for their services. Agencies are typically compensated in three ways: commissions, some type of fee arrangement, or percentage charges.

Commissions from Media

The traditional method of compensating agencies is through a **commission system,** where the agency receives a specified commission (usually 15 percent) from the media on any advertising time or space it purchases for its client. (For outdoor advertising, the commission is $16\frac{2}{3}$ percent.) This system provides a simple method of determining payments, as shown in the following example.

Assume an agency prepares a full-page magazine ad and arranges to place the ad on the back cover of a magazine at a cost of $100,000. The agency places the order for the space and delivers the ad to the magazine. Once the ad is run, the magazine will bill the agency for $100,000, less the 15 percent ($15,000) commission. The media will also offer a 2 percent cash discount for early payment, which the agency may pass along to the client. The agency will bill the client $100,000 less the 2 percent cash discount on the net amount, or a total of $98,300, as shown in Figure 3–8. The $15,000 commission represents the agency's compensation for its services.

Appraisal of the Commission System

Use of the commission system to compensate agencies has been quite controversial for many years. A major problem centers on whether the 15 percent commission represents equitable compensa-

Media Bills Agency		Agency Bills Advertiser	
Costs for magazine space	$100,000	Costs for magazine space	$100,000
Less 15% commission	−15,000	Less 2% cash discount	−1,700
Cost of media space	85,000	Advertiser pays agency	$ 98,300
Less 2% cash discount	−1,700		
Agency pays media	$ 83,300	Agency income	$ 15,000

Figure 3–8 Example of commission system payment

tion for services performed. Two agencies may require the same amount of effort to create and produce an ad. However, one client may spend $200,000 on commissionable media, which results in a $30,000 agency income, while the other spends $2 million, generating $300,000 in commissions. Critics argue that the commission system encourages agencies to recommend high media expenditures to increase their commission level.

Another criticism of the commission system is that it ties agency compensation to media costs. In periods of media cost inflation, the agency is (according to the client) disproportionately rewarded. The commission system has also been criticized for encouraging agencies to ignore cost accounting systems to justify the expenses attributable to work on a particular account. Still others charge that this system tempts the agency to avoid noncommissionable media such as direct mail, sales promotions, or advertising specialties, unless they are requested by the client.

Defenders of the commission system argue that it is easy to administer and it keeps the emphasis in agency competition on nonprice factors such as the quality of the advertising developed. Proponents argue that agency services are proportional to the size of the commission, since more time and effort are devoted to the large accounts that generate high revenue for the agency. They also say the system is more flexible than it appears because agencies often perform other services for large clients at no extra charge, justifying such actions by the large commission they receive.

The commission system has been a highly debated topic among advertisers and agencies for years. Critics of the system have argued that it provides an incentive for agencies to do the wrong thing, such as recommending mass-media advertising when other forms of communication such as direct marketing or public relations might do a better job.[18] They argue that the commission system is outdated and must be changed. This does indeed appear to be happening. A recent study of agency compensation conducted by the Association of National Advertisers (ANA) indicates that agency compensation based on the traditional 15 percent commission is becoming rare.[19] The survey found that only 9 percent of clients use a 15 percent commission, and 75 percent said their agency compensation amounts to less than a 15 percent commission. However, nearly two-thirds of the companies indicated that they use the 15 percent commission as a benchmark to evaluate their current agency compensation agreements.

While the use of the 15 percent commission is on the wane, many advertisers still use some form of media commission to compensate their agencies. Many advertisers have gone to a **negotiated commission** system to compensate their agencies. This commission structure can take the form of reduced percentage rates, variable commission rates, and commissions with minimum and maximum profit rates. Negotiated commissions are designed to consider the needs of the clients as well as the time and effort exerted by the agency, thereby avoiding some of the problems inherent in the traditional 15 percent sytem. Some of the leading agencies now receive an average commission on media of 8 to 10 percent versus the traditional 15 percent.[20] Agencies are also relying less on media commissions for their income as their clients expand their integrated marketing communications programs to include other forms of promotion and cut back on mass-media advertising. The percentage of agency income from media commissions is declining, and a greater percentage is coming through other methods such as fees and performance incentives.

Fee, Cost, and Incentive-Based Systems

Since many believe the commission system is not equitable to all parties, many agencies and their clients have developed some type of fee arrangement or cost-plus agreement for agency compensation. Some are using incentive-based compensation, which is a combination of a commission and a fee system.

Fee Arrangement

There are two basic types of fee arrangement systems. In the straight or **fixed-fee method,** the agency charges a basic monthly fee for all of its services and credits to the client any media commissions earned. Agency and client agree on the specific work to be done and the amount the agency will be paid for it. Sometimes agencies are compensated through a **fee-commission combination,** in which the media commissions received by the agency are credited against the fee. If the commissions are less than the agreed-on fee, the client must make up the difference. If the agency does much work for the client in noncommissionable media, the fee may be charged over and above the commissions received.

Both types of fee arrangements require that the agency carefully assess its costs of serving the client for the specified period, or for the project, plus its desired profit margin. To avoid any later disagreement, a fee arrangement should specify exactly what services the agency is expected to perform for the client.

Cost-Plus Agreement

Under a **cost-plus system,** the client agrees to pay the agency a fee based on the costs of its work plus some agreed-on profit margin (often a percentage of total costs). This system requires that the agency keep detailed records of the costs it incurs in working on the client's account. Direct costs (personnel time and out-of-pocket expenses) plus an allocation for overhead and a markup for profits determine the amount the agency bills the client.

Fee agreements and cost-plus systems are commonly used in conjunction with a commission system. The fee-based system can be advantageous to both the client and the agency, depending on the size of the client, advertising budget, media used, and services required. Many clients prefer fee or cost-plus systems because they receive a detailed breakdown of where and how their advertising and promotion dollars are being spent. However, these arrangements can be difficult for the agency, as they require careful cost accounting and may be difficult to estimate when bidding for an advertiser's business. Agencies are also reluctant to let clients see their internal cost figures.

Incentive-Based Compensation

Many clients these days are demanding more accountability from their agencies and tying agency compensation to performance through some type of **incentive-based system.** While there are many variations, the basic idea is that the agency's ultimate compensation level will depend on how well it meets predetermined performance goals. These goals often include objective measures such as sales or market share as well as more subjective measures such as evaluations of the quality of the agency's creative work. Companies using incentive-based systems determine agency compensation through media commissions, fees, bonuses, or some combination of these methods. Some clients use a sliding scale whereby the agency's base compensation is less than the 15 percent commission but the agency can earn extra commissions or bonuses depending on how it meets sales or other performance goals.

Recognizing the movement toward incentive-based systems, some agencies have offered to tie their compensation to performance. For example, DDB Needham Worldwide began a guaranteed-results program a number of years ago whereby the agency receives a bonus in addition to agreed-upon compensation if its integrated marketing program improves the sales of the client's product. If sales do not improve, the agency rebates a substantial amount of its fees to the client. Young & Rubicam also has a performance-based arrangement with several of its clients, including Colgate, AT&T, and Kraft Foods.[21] Agency executives note that pay for performance works best when the agency has complete control over a campaign. Thus, if a campaign fails to help sell a product or service, the agency is willing to assume complete responsibility and take a reduction in compensation. On the other hand, if sales increase, the agency can receive greater compensation for its work.

Percentage Charges

Another way to compensate an agency is by adding a markup of **percentage charges** to various services the agency purchases from outside providers. These may include market research, artwork, printing, photography, and other services or materials. Markups usually range from 17.65 to 20 percent and are added to the client's overall bill. Since suppliers of these services do not allow the agency a commission, percentage charges cover administrative costs while allowing a reasonable profit for the agency's efforts. (A markup of 17.65 percent of costs added to the initial cost would yield a 15 percent commission. For example, research costs of $100,000 × 17.65% = $100,000 + $17,650 = $117,650. The $17,650 markup is about 15 percent of $117,650.)

The Future of Agency Compensation

As you can see, there is no one method of compensation to which everyone subscribes. Only a small percentage of advertisers are paying the traditional 15 percent commission. The recent ANA survey found that a compensation system based on commissions from media billings is used by only 35 percent of advertisers. One of the most significant findings from the ANA survey is the rapid rise in incentive-based compensation agreements. Thirty percent of the advertisers indicated that they are using some type of incentive program, with just over half of these programs including some kind of base fee to cover costs, plus various incentives. Other types of incentive programs use a fixed-percentage compensation rate when target objectives are met or offer sliding-scale incentive payments.

As more companies adopt IMC approaches, they are reducing their reliance on traditional media advertising, and this is leading to changes in agency compensation systems. For example, Procter & Gamble, which is a heavy user of television advertising and was one of the last major advertisers to pare back the standard 15 percent commission for its agencies, began testing a performance-based system for many of its brands in 1999. A P&G spokesperson noted that the company wants "to find a system that is 'media neutral.' That is, it wants a system without any inherent advantage for network TV at the expense of other media such as the Internet, billboards, magazines, and public-relations events, to name a few."[22] P&G joins a list of other major consumer products advertisers, such as Colgate-Palmolive, Unilever, and Campbell Soup, that have changed their systems to more closely link agency compensation to a product's performance in the market. Many automobile advertisers, including Nissan, Ford, BMW, and General Motors, are also using incentive-based systems.[23] GM made the change to encourage its agencies to look beyond traditional mass-media advertising and develop other ways of reaching consumers.[24]

Many companies are changing their compensation systems as they move away from traditional mass media and turn to a wider array of marketing communication tools. They are also trying to make their agencies more accountable and reduce agency compensation costs. However, advertisers must recognize that their compensation policies should provide agencies with a reasonable profit if they want quality work and the best results from their agencies.

Evaluating Agencies

Given the substantial amounts of money being spent on advertising and promotion, demand for accountability of the expenditures has increased. Regular reviews of the agency's performance are necessary. The agency evaluation process usually involves two types of assessments, one financial and operational and the other more qualitative. The **financial audit** focuses on how the agency conducts its business. It is designed to verify costs and expenses, the number of personnel hours charged to an account, and payments to media and outside suppliers. The **qualitative audit** focuses on the agency's efforts in planning, developing, and implementing the client's advertising programs and considers the results achieved.

The agency evaluation is often done on a subjective, informal basis, particularly in smaller companies where ad budgets are low or advertising is not seen as the most critical factor in the firm's marketing performance. Some companies have developed formal, systematic evaluation systems, particularly when budgets are large and the advertising function receives much emphasis. As advertising costs continue to rise, the top management of these companies wants to be sure money is being spent efficiently and effectively.

One example of a formal agency evaluation system is that used by Borden Foods Corporation, which markets a variety of consumer products. Borden's brand teams meet once a year with the company's agencies to review their performance. Brand management completes the advertising agency performance evaluation, part of which is shown in Exhibit 3–7. These reports are compiled and reviewed with the agency at each annual meeting. Borden's evaluation process covers eight areas of performance.

Borden and the agency develop an action plan to correct areas of deficiency. But some companies doubt whether advertising effectiveness can be directly related to sales and have developed their own evaluation procedures. R. J. Reynolds emphasizes creative development and execution, marketing counsel and ideas, promotion support, and cost controls, without any mention of sales figures. Sears focuses on the performance of the agency as a whole in an effort to establish a partnership between the agency and the client.

Exhibit 3–7 Borden's ad agency performance evaluation

IV. CREATIVE SERVICES

1. Agency regularly produces fresh ideas and original approaches

   Poor — Average — Excellent

   1 2 3 4 5 6 7 8 9 10
2. Creative executions are consistently on strategy

   1 2 3 4 5 6 7 8 9 10
3. Research is effectively used in strategic development and in pre- and post-testing of advertising

   1 2 3 4 5 6 7 8 9 10
4. Creative group is knowledgeable about Company's products, markets, and strategies

   1 2 3 4 5 6 7 8 9 10
5. Borden is encouraged to participate in creative development

   1 2 3 4 5 6 7 8 9 10
6. Creative group is concerned with good and consistent advertising communications, and develops campaigns/ads that exhibit this concern

   1 2 3 4 5 6 7 8 9 10
7. Creative group produces on time and submits for review in time to permit orderly revisions

   1 2 3 4 5 6 7 8 9 10
8. Creative group performs well under pressure

   1 2 3 4 5 6 7 8 9 10
9. Agency presentations are well-organized with sufficient examples of proposed executions

   1 2 3 4 5 6 7 8 9 10
10. Creative group participates in major campaign presentations

    1 2 3 4 5 6 7 8 9 10
11. Agency presents ideas and executions not requested but which they feel are good opportunities

    1 2 3 4 5 6 7 8 9 10
12. Creative group takes constructive criticism and redirection

    1 2 3 4 5 6 7 8 9 10
13. Creative group effectively controls costs

    1 2 3 4 5 6 7 8 9 10
14. Overall evaluation of creative services

    1 2 3 4 5 6 7 8 9 10

VI. MEDIA SERVICES

1. Media group actively explores new uses of the various media available

   Poor — Average — Excellent

   1 2 3 4 5 6 7 8 9 10
2. Agency media recommendations are objective and reflect sufficient knowledge of Company's markets, target consumers, services and objectives

   1 2 3 4 5 6 7 8 9 10
3. Agency exhibits a broad capability in media as opposed to specializing in one particular medium

   1 2 3 4 5 6 7 8 9 10
4. Agency keeps Client up-to-date on trends and developments in the field of media

   1 2 3 4 5 6 7 8 9 10
5. Agency subscribes to and makes use of available and applicable syndicated media services

   1 2 3 4 5 6 7 8 9 10
6. Agency engages in original research relating to the selection and use of media

   1 2 3 4 5 6 7 8 9 10
7. Agency provides Client with regular review and analysis of competition's media usage

   1 2 3 4 5 6 7 8 9 10
8. Agency media administrative practices are adequate, including coordination of media schedules, contracts, checking media to verify advertising has run, etc.

   1 2 3 4 5 6 7 8 9 10
9. Agency regularly conducts post-buy analysis on all media placements in a timely manner

   1 2 3 4 5 6 7 8 9 10
10. Agency is effective in media negotiations for best possible rates and position for Company advertising

    1 2 3 4 5 6 7 8 9 10
11. Media plans provide sufficient flexibility for opportunistic buys or other cost-saving strategies

    1 2 3 4 5 6 7 8 9 10
12. Agency communicates plan objectives and rationale effectively to brand management

    1 2 3 4 5 6 7 8 9 10
13. Media strategies establish specific and measurable goals for reach, frequency and other objectives

    1 2 3 4 5 6 7 8 9 10

These and other evaluation methods are being used more regularly by advertisers. As fiscal controls tighten, clients will require more accountability from their providers and adopt formal evaluation procedures.

Gaining and Losing Clients

The evaluation process described above provides valuable feedback to both the agency and the client, such as indicating changes that need to be made by the agency and/or the client to improve performance and make the relationship more productive. Many agencies have had very long-lasting relationships with their clients. For example, General Electric has been with the BBDO Worldwide agency for nearly 80 years. Other well-known companies or brands that have had long-lasting relationships include Marlboro/Leo Burnett (46 years), McDonald's/DDB Needham Worldwide (30 years), PepsiCo/BBDO (40 years), Frito-Lay/DDB Needham Worldwide (47 years), and Kellogg's/J. Walter Thompson (70 years). Exhibit 3–8 shows an ad run by Dr Pepper/Seven Up Inc. celebrating its long-term relationship with the Young & Rubicam agency.

While many successful client–agency relationships go on for a number of years, long-term relationships are becoming less common. A survey conducted a few years ago by the American Association of Advertising Agencies found that the average tenure of client–agency relationships declined from 7.2 years in 1984 to 5.3 years in 1996.[25] In recent years a number of long-standing client–agency relationships were terminated. Levi Strauss & Co. terminated its 68-year relationship with Foote, Cone & Belding, of San Francisco, in 1998 when it transferred its U.S. jeans account to TBWA/Chiat/Day.[26] Sprint recently ended its 18-year relationship with J. Walter Thompson and awarded its $150 million account to McCann-Erickson.[27]

There are a number of reasons clients switch agencies. Understanding these potential problems can help the agency avoid them.[28] In addition, it is important to understand the process agencies go through in trying to win new clients.

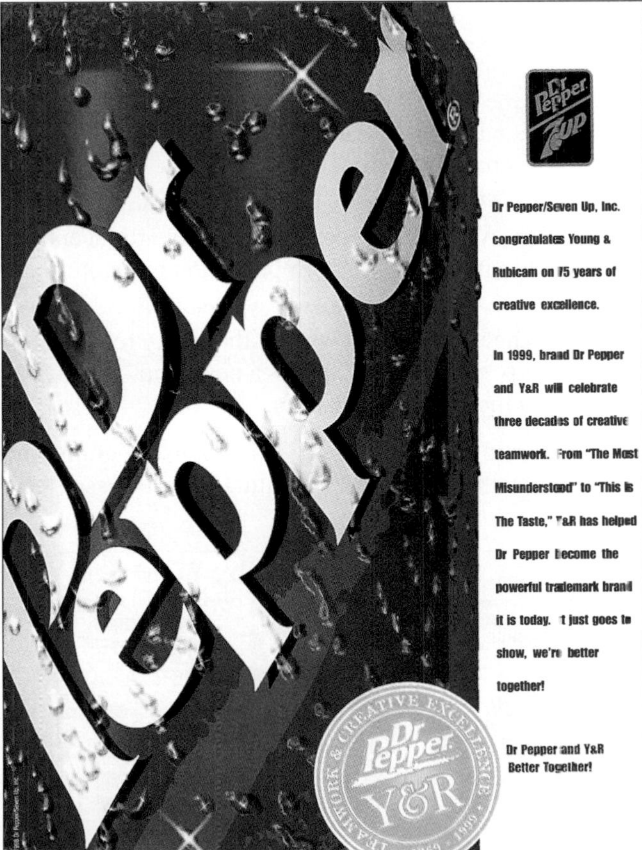

Dr Pepper
Dr Pepper 7Up
Dr Pepper/Seven Up, Inc. congratulates Young & Rubicam on 75 years of creative excellence.
In 1999, brand Dr Pepper and Y&R will celebrate three decades of creative teamwork. From "The Most Misunderstood" to "This is The Taste," Y&R has helped Dr Pepper become the powerful trademark brand it is today. It just goes to show, we're better together!
Dr Pepper and Y&R Better Together!
Teamwork & Creative Excellence
Dr Pepper Y&R
1969 · 1999

Exhibit 3–8 Young & Rubicam has been the agency for Dr Pepper for more than three decades

Why Agencies Lose Clients

Some of the more common reasons agencies lose clients follow:

- *Poor performance or service.* The client becomes dissatisfied with the quality of the advertising and/or the service provided by the agency.
- *Poor communication.* The client and agency personnel fail to develop or maintain the level of communication necessary to sustain a favorable working relationship.
- *Unrealistic demands by the client.* The client places demands on the agency that exceed the amount of compensation received and reduce the account's profitability.
- *Personality conflicts.* People working on the account on the client and agency sides do not have enough rapport to work well together.
- *Personnel changes.* A change in personnel at either the agency or the advertiser can create problems. New managers may wish to use an agency with which they have established ties. Agency personnel often take accounts with them when they switch agencies or start their own.
- *Changes in size of the client or agency.* The client may outgrow the agency or decide it needs a larger agency to handle its business. If the agency gets too large, the client may represent too small a percentage of its business to command attention.
- *Conflicts of interest.* A conflict may develop when an agency merges with another agency or when a client is part of an acquisition or merger. In the United States, an agency cannot handle two accounts that are in direct competition with each other. In some cases, even indirect competition will not be tolerated.
- *Changes in the client's corporate and/or marketing strategy.* A client may change its marketing strategy and think a new agency is needed to carry out the new program. For example, AT&T decided to change agencies following a major restructuring of the company that included the divestment of its NCR computer division and Lucent Technologies, its phone-equipment business. AT&T felt that a new agency was needed to develop a corporate image campaign that positions the company as a supplier of long-distance and other telecommunications services.[29]
- *Declining sales.* When sales of the client's product or service are stagnant or declining, advertising may be seen as contributing to the problem. A new agency may be sought for a new creative approach.
- *Conflicting compensation philosophies.* Disagreement may develop over the level or method of compensation. As more companies move toward incentive-based compensation systems, disagreement over compensation is becoming more commonplace.
- *Changes in policies.* Policy changes may result when either party reevaluates the importance of the relationship, the agency acquires a new (and larger) client, or either side undergoes a merger or acquisition.

If the agency recognizes these warning signs, it can try to adapt its programs and policies to make sure the client is satisfied. Some of the situations discussed here

are unavoidable, and others are beyond the agency's control. But to maintain the account, problems within the agency's control must be addressed.

The time may come when the agency decides it is no longer in its best interest to continue to work with the client. Personnel conflicts, changes in management philosophy, and/or insufficient financial incentives are just a few of the reasons for such a decision. Then the agency may terminate the account relationship.

How Agencies Gain Clients

Competition for accounts in the agency business is intense, since most companies have already organized for the advertising function and only a limited number of new businesses require such services each year. While small agencies may be willing to work with a new company and grow along with it, larger agencies often do not become interested in these firms until they are able to spend at least $1 million per year on advertising. Many of the top 15 agencies won't accept an account that spends less than $5 million per year. Once that expenditure level is reached, competition for the account intensifies.

In large agencies, most new business results from clients that already have an agency but decide to change their relationships. Thus, agencies must constantly search and compete for new clients. Some of the ways they do this follow.

Referrals Many good agencies obtain new clients as a result of referrals from existing clients, media representatives, and even other agencies. These agencies maintain good working relationships with their clients, the media, and outside parties that might provide business to them.

Solicitations One of the more common ways to gain new business is through direct solicitation. In smaller agencies, the president may solicit new accounts. In most large agencies, a new business development group seeks out and establishes contact with new clients. The group is responsible for writing solicitation letters, making cold calls, and following up on leads.

Presentations A basic goal of the new business development group is to receive an invitation from a company to make a presentation. This gives the agency the opportunity to sell itself—to describe its experience, personnel, capabilities, and operating procedures, as well as to demonstrate its previous work.

The agency may be asked to make a speculative presentation, in which it examines the client's marketing situation and proposes a tentative communications campaign. Because presentations require a great deal of time and preparation and may cost the agency a considerable amount of money without a guarantee of gaining the business, many firms refuse to participate in "creative shootouts." They argue that agencies should be selected on the basis of their experience and the services and programs they have provided for previous clients.[20] Nevertheless, most agencies do participate in this form of solicitation, either by choice or because they must do so to gain accounts.

Due in part to the emphasis on speculative presentations, a very important role has developed for *presentation consultants,* who specialize in helping clients choose ad agencies. Because their opinions are respected by clients, the entire agency review process may be structured according to their guidelines. As you might imagine, these consultants wield a great deal of power with both clients and agencies.

Public Relations Agencies also seek business through publicity/public relations efforts. They often participate in civic and social groups and work with charitable organizations pro bono (at cost, without pay) to earn respect in the community. Participation in professional associations such as the American Association of Advertising Agencies and the Advertising Research Foundation can also lead to new contacts. Successful agencies often receive free publicity throughout the industry as well as in the mass media.

Image and Reputation Perhaps the most effective way an agency can gain new business is through its reputation. Agencies that consistently develop excellent campaigns are often approached by clients. Agencies may enter their work in award

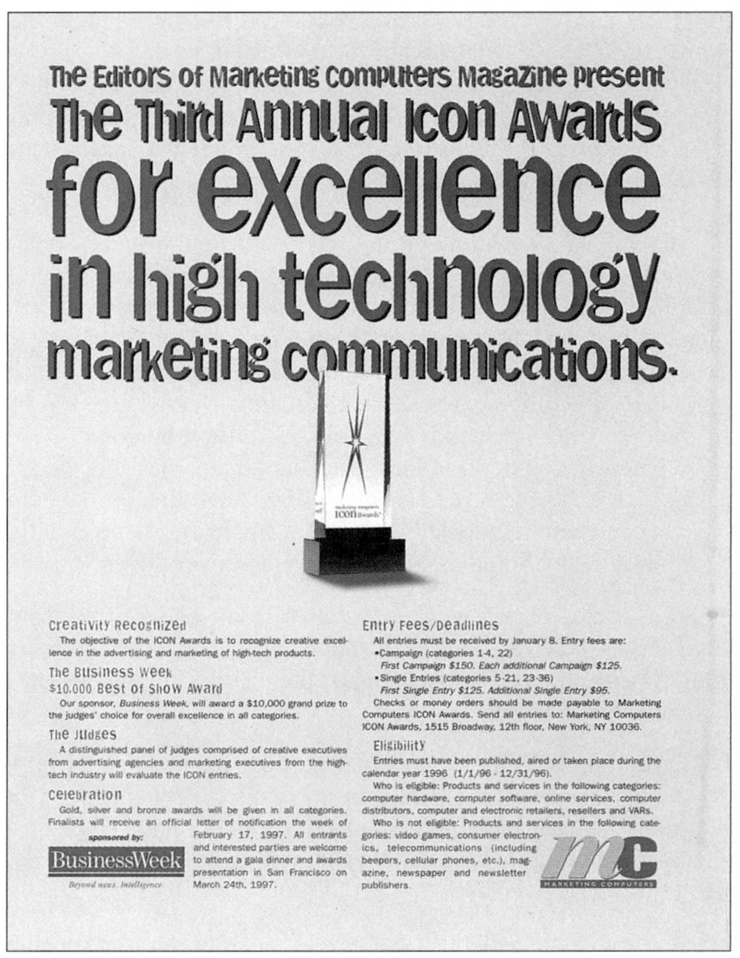

Exhibit 3–9 *Marketing Computers Magazine* holds an annual awards competition for advertisers in high technology marketing communications

competitions or advertise themselves to enhance their image in the marketing community (Exhibit 3–9).

Specialized Services

Many companies assign the development and implementation of their promotional programs to an advertising agency. But several other types of organizations provide specialized services that complement the efforts of ad agencies. Direct-response agencies, sales promotion agencies, and public relations firms are important to marketers in developing and executing IMC programs in the United States as well as international markets. Let us examine the functions these organizations perform.

Direct-Response Agencies

One of the fastest-growing areas of IMC is direct marketing, where companies communicate with consumers through telemarketing, direct mail, and other forms of direct-response advertising. As this industry has grown, numerous direct-response agencies have evolved that offer companies their specialized skills in both consumer and business markets. Figure 3–9 shows the top 10 direct-response agencies (several of which, including Ogilvy & Mather Direct, DraftDirect, and Grey Direct, are divisions or subsidiaries of large ad agencies).

Direct-response agencies provide a variety of services, including database management, direct mail, research, media services, and creative and production capabilities. While direct mail is their primary weapon, many direct-response agencies are expanding their services to include such areas as infomercial production and database management. Database development and management is becoming one of the most important services provided by direct-response agencies. Many

Rank	Agency, Headquarters	Revenue
1	Brann Worldwide, Deerfield, IL	$287,580
2	Draft Worldwide, Chicago	142,641
3	Rapp Collins Worldwide, New York	126,148
4	Bronnercom, Boston	124,200
5	Wunderman Cato Johnson, New York	120,495
6	Harte-Hanks/DiMark, Langhorne, PA	90,538
7	Grey Direct Marketing, New York	82,740
8	OgilvyOne Worldwide, New York	77,200
9	Carlson Marketing Group, Plymouth, MN	75,757
10	MRM/Gillespie, New York	48,600

Figure 3–9 Top 10 direct-marketing agencies

companies are using database marketing to pinpoint new customers and build relationships and loyalty among existing customers.[31]

A typical direct-response agency is divided into three main departments: account management, creative, and media. Some agencies also have a department whose function is to develop and manage databases for their clients. The account managers work with their clients to plan direct-marketing programs and determine their role in the overall integrated marketing communications process. The creative department consists of copywriters, artists, and producers. Creative is responsible for developing the direct-response message, while the media department is concerned with its placement.

Like advertising agencies, direct-response agencies must solicit new business and have their performance reviewed by their existing clients, often through formal assessment programs. Most direct-response agencies are compensated on a fee basis, although some large advertisers still prefer the commission system.

Sales Promotion Agencies

Developing and managing sales promotion programs such as contests, sweepstakes, refunds and rebates, premium and incentive offers, and sampling programs is a very complex task. Most companies use a **sales promotion agency** to develop and administer these programs. Some large ad agencies have created their own sales promotion department or acquired a sales promotion firm. However, most sales promotion agencies are independent companies that specialize in providing the services needed to plan, develop, and execute a variety of sales promotion programs.

Sales promotion agencies often work in conjunction with the client's advertising and/or direct-response agencies to coordinate their efforts with the advertising and direct-marketing programs. Services provided by large sales promotion agencies include promotional planning, creative, research, tie-in coordination, fulfillment, premium design and manufacturing, catalog production, and contest/sweepstakes management. Many sales promotion agencies are also developing direct/database marketing and telemarketing to expand their integrated marketing services capabilities. Sales promotion agencies are generally compensated on a fee basis. IMC Perspective 3–3 provides insight into how a successful promotional agency operates.

Public Relations Firms

Many large companies use both an advertising agency and a PR firm. The **public relations firm** develops and implements programs to manage the organization's publicity, image, and affairs with consumers and other relevant publics, including employees, suppliers, stockholders, government, labor groups, citizen action groups, and the general public. The PR firm analyzes the relationships between the client and these various publics, determines how the client's policies and actions relate to and

IMC Perspective 3–3

DVC—Promotional Agency of the Decade

During the 1990s the sales promotion industry experienced tremendous growth as promotional spending by marketers increased from $55 billion in 1991 to over $90 billion by the end of the decade. Promotional activities took root and flourished in a number of industries, including telecommunications, financial services, personal computers, and electronics, as well as the package-goods sectors. As the use of sales promotion increased, promotional agencies took their rightful seat next to advertising agencies at the branding and integrated marketing communications strategy sessions of their clients. One promotional agency that has been receiving invitations to IMC strategy sessions for a number of companies over the past decade is Dugan Valva Contess, or DVC, as it is now known. DVC, based in Morristown, New Jersey, was selected as Promotional Agency of the Decade by *PROMO Magazine,* the leading industry trade publication.

In 1991 DVC had only one major client and fewer than 20 employees (its account people often doubled as copywriters). Recognizing that many consumer package-goods companies were building in-house promotional staffs, DVC decided to pursue the telecommunications and pharmaceutical giants surrounding its New Jersey base. DVC got its first big break when personal relationships and an inside knowledge of its account-specific needs helped the agency win the AT&T account. DVC's first big program for AT&T was the International Hotel Program (IHOP), which used cooperative advertising created by the agency to help hotels fill their rooms. In return, hotels put placards in rooms telling guests how they could easily access AT&T long-distance service, and they included AT&T logos on card keys and complimentary newspapers and magazines. The campaign helped DVC develop its integrated marketing communications approach, as it required a variety of skills including database management, premium incentive merchandising, technology procurement, and advertising. In IHOP's first two years, the number of participating hotels grew from 300 to more than 4,000, and AT&T realized incremental long-distance revenue in the tens of millions of dollars. The program is working so well that it is still running today, six years after its launch.

DVC's success with AT&T helped the agency attract other clients such as Johnson & Johnson, Novus Financial, and Lucent Technologies, all of which insisted that DVC work with them as strategic partners, from planning through execution of their promotional programs. As the decade wore on, package-goods companies that had exhausted the creative capabilities of their internal promotional staffs came knocking on agency doors again. DVC's experience with its other clients served the agency well and helped it win several consumer-package-goods accounts from companies such as Coca-Cola, Pillsbury, Lever Brothers, and Fisher-Price.

DVC also proved that it could apply its expertise to the challenging health care area when it developed a unique promotional program for Intron A (an interferon drug marketed by Shering Oncology Biotech) that helped motivate cancer patients to take the drug and thus help cure themselves. Intron A keeps skin cancer from spreading to the lymph nodes and therefore helps patients avoid death. However, it must be taken daily for a year, costs $35,000, and makes patients feel as if they have the flu all the time. DVC developed the "Crossing Bridges" continuity program, which involved toll-free numbers staffed by medical professionals and patient "buddies," and sent out newsletters and letters of encouragement accompanied by premiums and coupons. The program raised Intron A compliance levels among melanoma patients from 50 to 66 percent in one year. It was chosen as one of the winners in the North American PRO Awards of Excellence competition, which recognizes outstanding promotional marketing. The selection was based on DVC's innovative use of promotional marketing in a category that has historically been averse to consumer-oriented promotions and marketing programs.

PROMO MAGAZINE

November 29, 1999

Mr. George Valva
Mr. Peter Dugan
Chief Executive Officers
DVC
10 Park Avenue
Morristown, NJ 07960

Dear George and Peter:

On behalf of the entire staff of PROMO, I extend to you our hearty congratulations on being named Agency of the Decade. Our selection process was rigorous and packed with debate, yet in the end the editors reached consensus that DVC was the ideal choice.

Your breathtaking growth, your pioneering work in non-packaged goods industries, your exploration of Internet marketing, and your corporate social consciousness all embodied the progress of the promotion discipline in the Nineties.

We look forward to continuing our dialog with DVC as you take on the challenges of a new decade, one that promises to be full of adventure and exciting opportunities for marketers.

Sincerely,

Al Urbanski
Editorial Director

THE MAGAZINE OF PROMOTION MARKETING
50 Washington Street • 8th Floor • Norwalk, CT 06854 • (203) 831-5400 • Fax (203) 831-5401
A publication of Cowles Business Media, Inc.

THANKS TO ALL DVC COLLEAGUES AND CLIENTS FOR MAKING THIS HONOR POSSIBLE.

DVC
Integrating Marketing, Communications & Technology
New York • Minneapolis/St. Paul • Atlanta

10 Park Avenue
Morristown, NJ 07960
t: 973-539-8880
f: 973-359-3401
e: gvalva@dvc.com
pdugan@dvc.com

To expand is integrated marketing capabilities in the rapidly developing Internet world, DVC recently acquired Muffin-Head Productions, a well-known Silicon Valley Web design firm, and Visient, a systems architecture and Internet technology developer. The acquisitions have helped DVC position itself as a promotional agency that provides fully integrated marketing communication and technology solutions for its clients and is uniquely qualified to help leading and emerging brands and companies drive their businesses and build relationships.

As the 90s came to a close, DVC was 20 times larger in size than it had been when the decade began. The agency believes that companies now compete in a world where every product is part service, every service is part product, and every business is becoming a convergence of many businesses. Companies need a promotional agency that is part marketing expert, part communication specialist, part business strategist, and part technologist. Sounds like they need DVC.

Source: Al Urbanski, "Agency of the Decade," *PROMO Magazine,* December 1999, pp. 67–69.

affect these publics, develops PR strategies and programs, implements these programs using various public relations tools, and evaluates their effectiveness.

The activities of a public relations firm include planning the PR strategy and program, generating publicity, conducting lobbying and public affairs efforts, becoming involved in community activities and events, preparing news releases and other communications, conducting research, promoting and managing special events, and managing crises. As companies adopt an IMC approach to promotional planning, they are coordinating their PR activities with advertising and other promotional areas. Many companies are integrating public relations and publicity into the marketing communications mix to increase message credibility and save media costs.[32] Public relations firms are generally compensated by retainer. We will examine their role in more detail in Chapter 17.

Interactive Agencies

With the rapid growth of the Internet and other forms of interactive media, a new type of specialized marketing communications organization has evolved—the interactive agency. Many marketers are using **interactive agencies** that specialize in the development and strategic use of various interactive marketing tools such as websites for the Internet, banner ads, CD-ROMs, and kiosks.[33] Many traditional advertising agencies have established interactive capabilities, ranging from a few specialists within the agency to an entire interactive division. For example, some of the largest interactive agencies such as Ogilvy Interactive, Grey Interactive, and Euro RSCG Interactive are affiliates of major agencies (see Figure 3–10). Ogilvy Interactive has developed websites and major interactive campaigns for a number of clients, including the award winning e-business campaign for IBM.

Figure 3–10 Top 10 U.S. interactive agencies

Rank	Agency	Headquarters
1	USWeb/CKS	Santa Clara, CA
2	iXL	Atlanta, GA
3	Agency.com	New York, NY
4	AppNet Systems	Bethesda, MD
5	Ogilvy Interactive	New York, NY
6	Cambridge Interactive	Cambridge, MA
7	Think New Ideas	New York, NY
8	Modem Medi-Poppe Tyson	Norwalk, CT
9	Proxicom	Reston, VA
10	Organic	San Francisco, CA

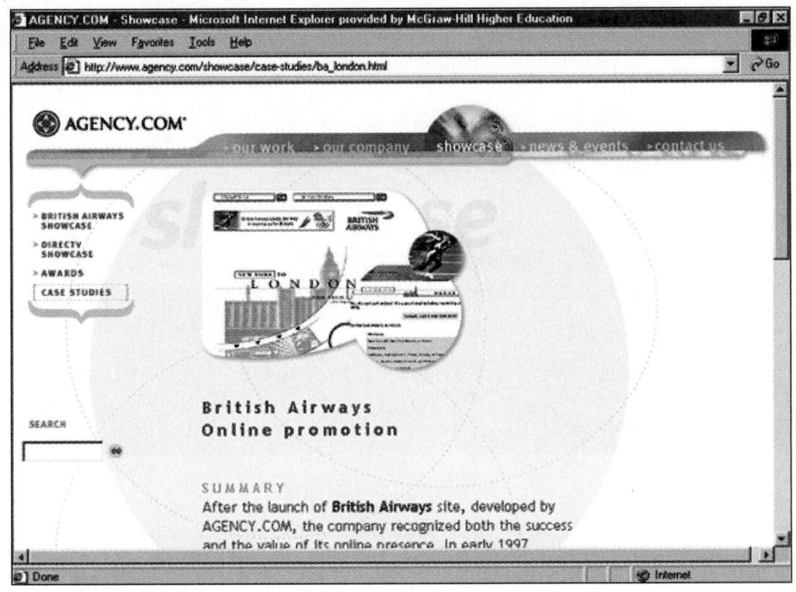

Exhibit 3–10 AGENCY.COM developed the website and various online promotions that support the global branding strategy for British Airways

While many agencies have or are developing interactive capabilities, a number of marketers are turning to more specialized interactive agencies to develop websites and interactive media. They feel these companies have more expertise in designing and developing websites as well as managing and supporting them. Interactive agencies range from smaller companies that specialize in website design and creation to full-service interactive agencies that provide all the elements needed for a successful Internet/interactive marketing program. These services include strategic consulting regarding the use of the Internet and online branding, technical knowledge, systems integration, and the development of electronic commerce capabilities.

Full-service interactive agencies, such as AGENCY.COM, have created successful Internet marketing programs for a number of companies, including Nike, MetLife, Ford Motor Company, McDonald's, and British Airways. For example, AGENCY.COM developed the website and various online promotions that support the new global brand positioning strategy for British Airways (Exhibit 3–10). As the Internet becomes an increasingly important marketing tool, more companies will be turning to interactive agencies to help them develop successful interactive marketing programs. The number of interactive agencies will continue to grow, as will their importance in the development and implementation of Internet-based strategies and initiatives.

Collateral Services

The final participants in the promotional process are those that provide various collateral services. They include marketing research companies, package design firms, consultants, media buying services, photographers, printers, video production houses, and event marketing services companies.

Marketing Research Companies

One of the more widely used collateral service organizations is the marketing research firm. Companies are increasingly turning to marketing research to help them understand their target audiences and to gather information that will be of value in designing and evaluating their advertising and promotions programs. Even companies with their own marketing research departments often hire outside research agencies to perform some services. Marketing research companies offer specialized services and can gather objective information that is valuable to the advertiser's promotional programs. They conduct *qualitative* research such as in-depth interviews and focus groups, as well as *quantitative* studies such as market surveys.

Integrated Marketing Communications Services

You have seen that marketers can choose from a variety of specialized organizations to assist them in planning, developing, and implementing an integrated marketing communications program. But companies must decide whether to use a different organization for each marketing communications function or consolidate them with a large advertising agency that offers all of these services under one roof.

As noted in Chapter 1, during the 1980s many of the large agencies realized that their clients were shifting their promotional dollars away from traditional advertising to other forms of promotion and began developing IMC capabilities. Some did this through mergers and acquisitions and became superagencies consisting of advertising, public relations, sales promotion, and direct-response agencies.

Many large agencies are continuing to expand their IMC capabilities by acquiring specialists in various fields. All the major agency holding companies either own or have substantial investments in interacative and direct-response agencies. For example, Interpublic Group, the world's third-largest advertising organization, recently purchased a stake in Icon Medialab International, a Swedish Internet-services company. Interpublic also retains a small stake in USWeb/CKS, which is the largest interactive agency.[34] A few years ago Interpublic also purchased DraftDirect Worldwide, one of the largest direct-response agencies. One of Interpublic's agencies, McCann-Erickson Worldwide, purchased Ad:vent, a leading specialist in the event marketing business, and merged the company with its existing event marketing operation, Momentum IMC.[35]

While some agencies are expanding their IMC capabilities by acquiring specialized firms and services, others are doing so internally. For example, Foote, Cone & Belding (FCB) recently reorganized and absorbed its sales promotion and direct marketing agencies into the general agency Marketing Drive, which is a global integrated marketing services company supporting all clients of FCB. FCB assigns individuals from various departments to "brand groups" that include account planning and creative members as well as staffers from the various IMC disciplines FCB handles for that client. The brand groups for whom FCB's primary responsibility is advertising, such as Coors, are led by ad staffers. A brand group for whom the agency's primary responsibility is sales promotion will be led by someone from Marketing Drive staff. Under this structure, brand building relies on a whole range of IMC tools rather than just advertising.[36] FCB has used the approach in successful brand building efforts for a number of clients such as Amazon.com, Dockers, and Taylor Made golf equipment (Exhibit 3–11).

The Foote, Cone & Belding approach to IMC is an example of what Ander Gronstedt and Esther Thorson call a *matrix organization design,* where an agency combines functional division and cross-functional task force teams.[37] In such an organization, planning and execution of integrated marketing communications programs are collaborative efforts by an interdepartmental account team. The members of the team come from different disciplines and bring a diversity of backgrounds, specialties, and perspectives that can be valuable in creating the IMC program for the client.

Exhibit 3–11 The Foote, Cone & Belding agency uses a variety of IMC tools to build brand identity for clients such as Taylor Made

Pros and Cons of Integrated Services

It has been argued that the concept of integrated marketing is nothing new, particularly in smaller companies and communication agencies that have been coordinating a variety of promotional tools for years. And larger advertising agencies have been trying to gain more of their clients' promotional business for over 20 years. However, in the past, the various services were run as separate profit centers. Each was motivated to push its own expertise and pursue its own goals rather than develop truly integrated marketing programs. Moreover, the creative specialists in many agencies resisted becoming involved in sales promotion or direct marketing. They preferred to concentrate on developing magazine ads or television commercials rather than designing coupons or direct-mail pieces.

Proponents of the integrated marketing services agency (the one-stop shop) contend that past problems are being solved and the various individuals in the agencies and subsidiaries are learning to work together to deliver a consistent message to the client's customers. They argue that maintaining control of the entire promotional process achieves greater synergy among each of the communications program elements. They also note that it is more convenient for the client to coordinate all of its marketing efforts—media advertising, direct mail, special events, sales promotions, and public relations—through one agency. An agency with integrated marketing capabilities can create a single image for the product or service and address everyone, from wholesalers to consumers, with one voice.

But not everyone wants to turn the entire IMC program over to one agency. Opponents say the providers become involved in political wrangling over budgets, do not communicate with each other as well and as often as they should, and do not achieve synergy. They also claim that agencies' efforts to control all aspects of the promotional program are nothing more than an attempt to hold on to business that might otherwise be lost to independent providers. They note that synergy and economies of scale, while nice in theory, have been difficult to achieve and competition and conflict among agency subsidiaries have been a major problem.[38]

Many companies use a variety of vendors for communication functions, choosing the specialist they believe is best suited for each promotional task, be it advertising, sales promotion, or public relations. Many marketers agree with the vice president of advertising at Reebok, who noted, "Why should I limit myself to one resource when there is a tremendous pool of fresh ideas available?"[39]

Responsibility for IMC: Agency versus Client

Surveys of advertisers and agency executives have shown that both groups believe integrated marketing is important to their organizations' success and that it will be even more important in the future.[40] However, marketers and agency executives have very different opinions regarding who should be in charge of the integrated marketing communications process. Many advertisers prefer to set strategy for and coordinate their own IMC campaigns, but most agency executives see this as their domain.

While agency executives believe their shops are capable of handling the various elements an integrated campaign requires, many marketers, particularly larger firms, disagree. Marketing executives say the biggest obstacle to implementing IMC is the lack of people with the broad perspective and skills to make it work. Agencies are felt to lack expertise in database marketing, marketing research, and information technology. Internal turf battles, agency egos, and fear of budget reductions are also cited as major barriers to successful integrated marketing campaigns.[41]

Many ad agencies are adding more resources to offer their clients a full line of services. They are expanding their agencies' capabilities in interactive and multimedia advertising, database management, direct marketing, public relations, and sales promotion. However, many marketers still want to set the strategy for their IMC campaigns and seek specialized expertise, more quality and creativity, and greater control and cost efficiency by using multiple providers.

Most marketers do recognize that ad agencies will no longer stick primarily to advertising and will continue to expand their IMC capabilities. There is an opportunity for agencies to broaden their services beyond advertising—but they will have to develop true expertise in a variety of integrated marketing communications areas. They will also have to create organizational structures that make it possible for individuals with expertise in a variety of communications areas to work well together both internally and externally. One thing is certain: as companies continue to shift their promotional dollars away from media advertising to other IMC tools, agencies will continue to explore ways to keep these monies under their roofs.

Summary

The development, execution, and administration of an advertising and promotions program involve the efforts of many individuals, both within the company and outside it. Participants in the integrated marketing communications process include the advertiser or client, ad agencies, media organizations, specialized marketing communications firms, and providers of collateral services.

Companies use three basic systems to organize internally for advertising and promotion. Centralized systems offer the advantages of facilitated communications, lower personnel requirements, continuity in staff, and more top-management involvement. Disadvantages include a lower involvement with overall marketing goals, longer response times, and difficulties in handling multiple product lines.

Decentralized systems offer the advantages of concentrated managerial attention, more rapid responses to problems, and increased flexibility, though they may be limited by ineffective decision making, internal conflicts, misallocation of funds, and a lack of authority. In-house agencies, while offering the advantages of cost savings, control, and increased coordination, have the disadvantage of less experience, objectivity, and flexibility.

Many firms use advertising agencies to help develop and execute their programs. These agencies may take on a variety of forms, including full-service agencies, creative boutiques, and media buying services. The first offers the client a full range of services (including creative, account, marketing, and financial and management services); the other two specialize in creative services and media buying, respectively. Agencies are compensated through commission systems, percentage charges, and fee- and cost-based systems. Recently, the emphasis on agency accountability has increased. Agencies are being evaluated on both financial and qualitative aspects, and some clients are using incentive-based compensation systems that tie agency compensation to performance measures such as sales and market share.

In addition to using ad agencies, marketers use the services of other marketing communication specialists, including direct marketing agencies, sales promotion agencies, public relations firms, and interactive agencies. A marketer must decide whether to use a different specialist for each promotional function or have all of its integrated marketing communications done by an advertising agency that offers all of these services under one roof.

Recent studies have found that most marketers believe it is their responsibility, not the ad agency's, to set strategy for and coordinate IMC campaigns. The lack of a broad perspective and specialized skills in nonadvertising areas is seen as the major barrier to agencies' increased involvement in integrated marketing communications.

Key Terms

clients, 69
advertising agency, 69
media organizations, 69
specialized marketing communications services, 70
collateral services, 70
advertising manager, 71
centralized system, 71
decentralized system, 73
brand manager, 73
category management system, 74
in-house agency, 76
billings, 78
superagencies, 78
full-service agency, 80
account executive, 80
copywriters, 82
departmental system, 84
group system, 85
creative boutique, 85
media buying services, 85
commission system, 86
negotiated commission, 87
fixed-fee method, 88
fee-commission combination, 88
cost-plus system, 88
incentive-based system, 88
percentage charges, 89
financial audit, 89
qualitative audit, 90
direct-response agency, 94
sales promotion agency, 95
public relations firm, 95
interactive agencies, 97

Discussion Questions

1. Identify the various organizations that participate in the integrated marketing communications process and briefly discuss their roles and responsibilities.

2. What are some of the specific responsibilities and duties of an advertising manager under a centralized advertising department structure? Why is an advertising manager needed if a company uses an outside agency?

3. What is a product or brand manager? Discuss how a brand manager would be involved with the integrated marketing communications program.

4. Discuss how the change to a brand management system helps General Motors in its efforts to create stronger brand identities and positioning platforms for its various models of cars, trucks, and sport utility vehicles. Do you agree with the strategy to use one advertising and positioning theme for the entire Cadillac division rather than giving each model its own advertising tagline?

5. Discuss the pros and cons of using an in-house advertising agency. What are some of the reasons why companies might change from using an in-house agency and hire an outside agency?

6. Discuss the various functions a full-service advertising agency performs for its clients. Might any one of these functions be more important than another?

7. Discuss the various methods by which advertising agencies are compensated. What factors will determine the type of compensation arrangement a company uses with an agency?

8. Why are many companies moving away from the traditional commission system and using incentive-based compensation for their advertising agencies? Why might an ad agency be reluctant to accept an incentive-based compensation system?

9. Discuss the various reasons why marketers often choose to switch advertising agencies. Find an example of a company that has recently changed advertising agencies and analyze the reasons given for the change.

10. What is an interactive agency? Discuss the reason why a marketer might choose to use an interactive agency rather than have a full-service agency develop its interactive marketing tools such as website design.

11. Discuss the reasons why a company might want to have all its integrated marketing communication activities performed versus having these activities performed by several different agencies who specialize in various areas of IMC.

Chapter Four

Perspectives on Consumer Behavior

Chapter Objectives

- To understand the role consumer behavior plays in the development and implementation of advertising and promotional programs.
- To understand the consumer decision-making process and how it varies for different types of purchases.
- To understand various internal psychological processes, their influence on consumer decision making, and implications for advertising and promotion.
- To recognize the various approaches to studying the consumer learning process and their implications for advertising and promotion.
- To recognize external factors such as culture, social class, group influences, and situational determinants and how they affect consumer behavior.
- To understand alternative approaches to studying consumer behavior.

Hypnotists, Medical Anthropologists, and Chinese Historians—Everyone Is Trying to Understand the Consumer

Whatever happened to asking consumers questions through traditional research techniques like surveys and interviews? These tried-and-true methods, while still used, are considered by some researchers to be too "old hat" or insufficient for gaining deep-seated insights into consumers' minds. Focus groups, combined with mood music, mind probing, and even hypnosis, are (at least to some) the tools of the day.

Take DaimlerChrysler, for example. In searching for a "breakthrough" car, the company shunned traditional marketing research techniques and instead employed an unconventional approach known as "archetype research." With billions of dollars of investments on the line, Chrysler recently shifted the bulk of its research to this methodology, which was developed by a French-born medical anthropologist, G. Clotaire Rapaille, whose previous work involved working with autistic children. To gain insights from deep inside consumers' minds, Rapaille conducted three-hour focus group sessions, in which—with lights dimmed and mood music in the background—consumers were asked to look at a prototype of the newly designed PT Cruiser and to go far back into their childhood to discuss what emotions were evoked, as well as to write stories about their feelings. After the sessions, Rapaille and a team of Chrysler employees read the stories, looking for what they refer to as "reptilian hot buttons," or nuggets of revealing emotions. According to Rapaille, remembering a new concept is dependent upon associating it with an emotion, and the more emotions evoked, the greater the likelihood of recall. The process led to significant design changes that resulted in a less-than-traditional-looking car, as can be seen in the picture here.

Emotional rescue.
2001 PT CRUISER
Can it be this obvious? Instead of therapy, is emotional fulfillment as simple as a commute? Only in this eye-catching retreat on wheels: the Chrysler PT Cruiser. Unique to its DNA with never-been-seen features like 26 seating configurations* and a nifty five-position shelf unit—not to mention the most original styling on the planet! And at a price from $16,000 to $19,395,** it's a clear antidote to the daily grind. 1.800.CHRYSLER or www.chrysler.com.
CHRYSLER

(By the way, Rapaille drives a black Porsche, a green Rolls Royce, and a white Chrysler minivan, if that tells you anything!)

Actually, Chrysler was not the first to employ archetype research. At least 10 years prior to Chrysler's use of the technique, Proctor & Gamble employed Rapaille to determine that aroma sells more coffee than taste because of the emotional ties to home. The Folger's coffee ad in which a young soldier returns home and brews a pot of coffee that causes his sleeping mother to wake up and sense that he has returned is a direct result of that research. General Motors has also used this research methodology.

In an equally unconventional approach, California wine maker Domain Chandon and its ad agency D'Arcy Masius Benton & Bowles of Los Angeles conducted focus groups of hypnotized consumers. In the groups, participants were asked to discuss their experiences and feelings about the first time they drank champagne and/or sparkling wine. According to Chandon and D'Arcy, traditional focus groups lead to "surface" discussions whereas drinking champagne involves more of an "inside"-driven and emotional response. By hypnotizing the participants, they felt they could get behind the barriers set up in conscious minds. The approach apparently worked; as noted by Diane Dreyer, senior VP at D'Arcy, some participants revealed romantic and sexual experiences that "I'm sure they wouldn't share in the waking state." The input from the groups was used in the development of a new advertising campaign that featured a sexual and passionate appeal, as well as a new logo. Essentially, the research led to a whole new positioning for the brand, with ads placed on billboards and in travel and epicurean magazines, as well as a move into e-commerce.

In his book *Why We Buy: The Science of Shopping,* retail consultant Paco Underhill attempts to explain why consumers buy. With a degree in Chinese history, Underhill shifted his emphasis to environmental psychology and, like Rapaille, found the consulting world much more lucrative. Equating the modern-day shopper with the "hunter-gatherer" mentality of the past, he sees men as shopping because of an obsession with a single item. Women, on the other hand, look upon shopping as a social occasion that provides a sense of liberation. At the mall they can escape their husbands and families, exercise their judgments, and see and be seen. Is this what women did in the caveman days?

Traditional or not, millions of dollars are now being invested in previously unheard-of techniques. Billions more are riding on the results. Are you willing to take the risk?

Sources: Alice Z. Cuneo, "Domain Chandon Looks beyond the Celebrations," *Advertising Age,* July 19, 1999, p. 9; Abigail Goldman, "Expert Offers Retailers Glimpse into Shoppers' Minds," *Los Angeles Times,* June 3, 1999, p. C5; Jeffrey Ball, "But How Does It Make You Feel?" *The Wall Street Journal,* May 3, 1999, p. B1.

The research examples described above reveal that the development of effective marketing communication programs begins with understanding why consumers behave as they do. Those who develop advertising and other promotional strategies begin by identifying relevant markets and then analyzing the relationship between target consumers and the product/service or brand. Often, in an attempt to gain insights, marketers will employ techniques borrowed from other disciplines. Research methods used in psychology, anthropology, and sociology are becoming more popular in businesses as managers attempt to explore consumers' purchasing motives. The motives for purchasing, attitudes, and lifestyles need to be understood before effective marketing strategies can be formulated.

These are just a few of the aspects of consumer behavior that promotional planners must consider in developing integrated marketing communication programs. As you will see, consumer choice is influenced by a variety of factors.

It is beyond the scope of this text to examine consumer behavior in depth. However, promotional planners need a basic understanding of consumer decision making, factors that influence it, and how this knowledge can be used in developing promotional strategies and programs. We begin with an overview of consumer behavior.

An Overview of Consumer Behavior

A challenge faced by all marketers is how to influence the purchase behavior of consumers in favor of the product or service they offer. For companies like American Express, this means getting consumers to charge more purchases on their AmEx cards. For BMW, it means getting them to purchase or lease a car; for business-to-business marketers like Canon or Ricoh, it means getting organizational buyers to purchase more of their copiers or fax machines. While their ultimate goal is to influence consumers' purchase behavior, most marketers understand that the actual purchase is only part of an overall process.

Consumer behavior can be defined as the process and activities people engage in when searching for, selecting, purchasing, using, evaluating, and disposing of products and services so as to satisfy their needs and desires. For many products and services, purchase decisions are the result of a long, detailed process that may include an extensive information search, brand comparisons and evaluations, and other activities. Other purchase decisions are more incidental and may result from little more than seeing a product prominently displayed at a discount price in a store. Think of how many times you have made impulse purchases in stores.

Marketers' success in influencing purchase behavior depends in large part on how well they understand consumer behavior. Marketers need to know the specific needs customers are attempting to satisfy and how they translate into purchase criteria. They need to understand how consumers gather information regarding various alternatives and use this information to select among competing brands. They need to understand how customers make purchase decisions. Where do they prefer to buy a product? How are they influenced by marketing stimuli at the point of purchase? Marketers also need to understand how the consumer decision process and reasons for purchase vary among different types of customers. For example, purchase decisions may be influenced by the personality or lifestyle of the consumer.[1] Notice how the ad shown in Exhibit 4–1 reflects the various roles in the life of the target audience member.

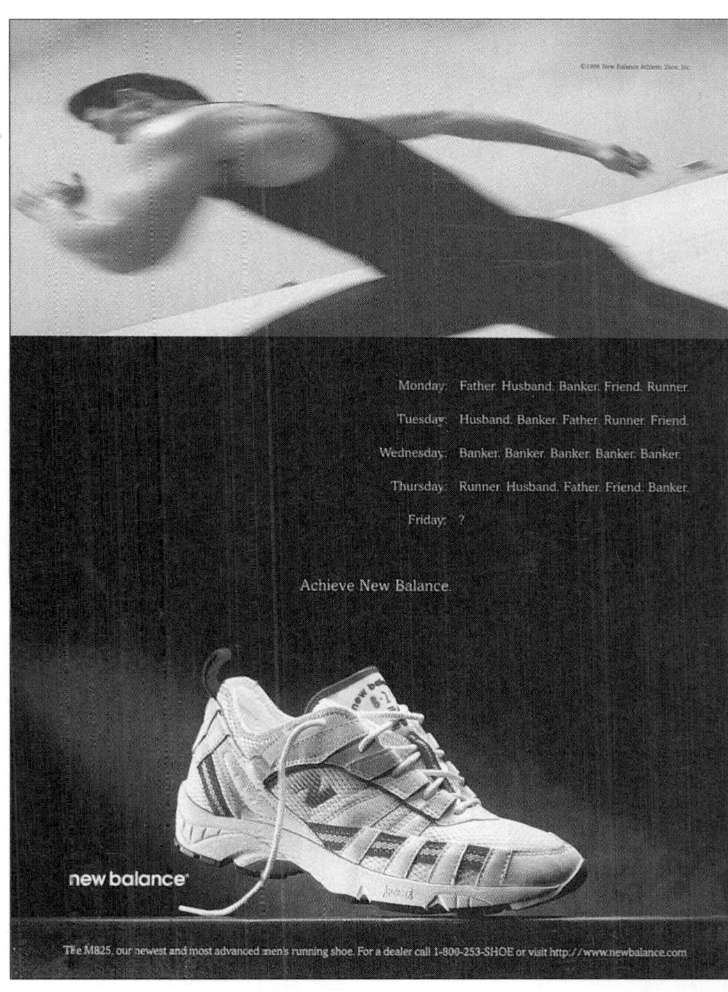

Exhibit 4–1 New Balance appeals to the active lifestyle

The conceptual model in Figure 4–1 will be used as a framework for analyzing the consumer decision process. We will discuss what occurs at the various stages of

Figure 4–1 A basic model of consumer decision making

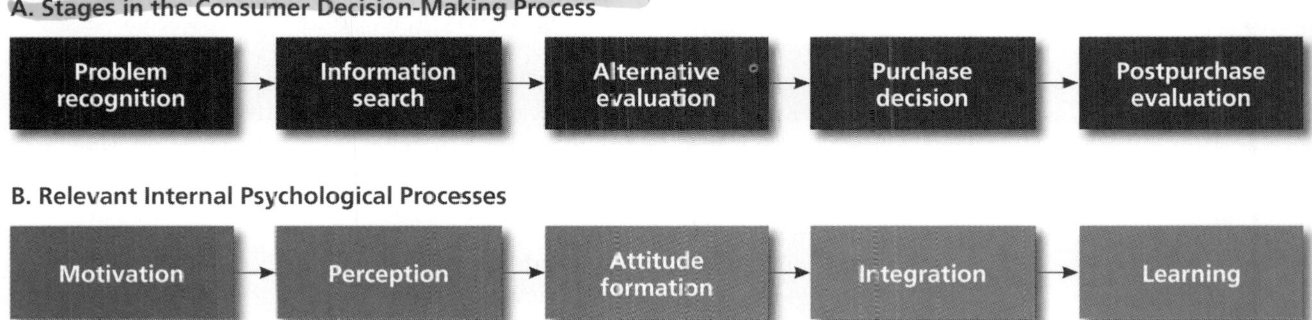

this model and how advertising and promotion can be used to influence decision making. We will also examine the influence of various psychological concepts, such as motivation, perception, attitudes, and integration processes. Variations in the consumer decision-making process will be explored, as will perspectives regarding consumer learning and external influences on the consumer decision process. The chapter concludes with a consideration of alternative means of studying consumer behavior.

The Consumer Decision-Making Process

As shown in Figure 4–1, the consumer's purchase decision process is generally viewed as consisting of stages through which the buyer passes in purchasing a product or service. This model shows that decision making involves a number of internal psychological processes. Motivation, perception, attitude formation, integration, and learning are important to promotional planners, since they influence the general decision-making process of the consumer. We will examine each stage of the purchase decision model and discuss how the various subprocesses influence what occurs at this phase of the consumer behavior process. We will also discuss how promotional planners can influence this process.

Problem Recognition

Figure 4–1 shows that the first stage in the consumer decision-making process is **problem recognition,** which occurs when the consumer perceives a need and becomes motivated to solve the problem. The problem recognition stage initiates the subsequent decision processes.

Problem recognition is caused by a difference between the consumer's *ideal state* and *actual state.* A discrepancy exists between what the consumer wants the situation to be like and what the situation is really like. (Note that *problem* does not always imply a negative state. A goal exists for the consumer, and this goal may be the attainment of a more positive situation.)

Exhibit 4–2 Rogaine helps women recognize hair loss problems

Sources of Problem Recognition The causes of problem recognition may be very simple or very complex and may result from changes in the consumer's current and/or desired state. These causes may be influenced by both internal and external factors.

Out of Stock Problem recognition occurs when consumers use their existing supply of a product and must replenish their stock. The purchase decision is usually simple and routine and is often resolved by choosing a familiar brand or one to which the consumer feels loyal.

Dissatisfaction Problem recognition is created by the consumer's dissatisfaction with the current state of affairs and/or the product or service being used. For example, a consumer may think her ski boots are no longer comfortable or stylish enough. Advertising may be used to help consumers recognize when they have a problem and/or need to make a purchase. The Rogaine ad shown in Exhibit 4–2 helps women realize that hair thinning is not just a man's problem.

New Needs/Wants Changes in consumers' lives often result in new needs and wants. For example, changes in one's financial situation, employment status, or lifestyle may create new needs and trigger problem recognition.

As you will see, when you graduate from college and begin your professional career, your new job may necessitate a change in your wardrobe. (Good-bye blue jeans and T-shirts, hello suits and ties.)

Not all product purchases are based on needs. Some products or services sought by consumers are not essential but are nonetheless desired. A **want** has been defined as a felt need that is shaped by a person's knowledge, culture, and personality.[2] Many products sold to consumers satisfy their wants rather than their basic needs.

Exhibit 4–3 This ad for Baby Orajel shows that baby teeth have special needs

Related Products/Purchases Problem recognition can also be stimulated by the purchase of a product. For example, the purchase of a new camera may lead to the recognition of a need for accessories, such as additional lenses or a carrying case. The purchase of a personal computer may prompt the need for software programs or upgrades.

Marketer-Induced Problem Recognition Another source of problem recognition is marketers' actions that encourage consumers not to be content with their current state or situation. Ads for personal hygiene products such as mouthwash, deodorant, and foot sprays may be designed to create insecurities that consumers can resolve through the use of these products. Marketers change fashions and clothing designs and create perceptions among consumers that their wardrobes are out of style. The Orajel ad in Exhibit 4–3 demonstrates the special needs of children's baby teeth to stimulate problem recognition.

Marketers also take advantage of consumers' tendency toward *novelty-seeking behavior,* which leads them to try different brands. Consumers often try new products or brands even when they are basically satisfied with their regular brand. Marketers encourage brand switching by introducing new brands into markets that are already saturated and by using advertising and sales promotion techniques such as free samples, introductory price offers, and coupons.

New Products Problem recognition can also occur when innovative products are introduced and brought to the attention of consumers. Marketers are constantly introducing new products and services and telling consumers about the types of problems they solve. For example, the Ericsson ad shown in Exhibit 4–4 introduces a new mobile phone that allows the businessperson to have a virtually wireless office.

Marketers' attempts to create problem recognition among consumers are not always successful. Consumers may not see a problem or need for the product the marketer is selling. A main reason many consumers were initially reluctant to purchase personal computers was that they failed to see what problems owning one would solve. One way PC manufacturers successfully activated problem recognition was by stressing how a computer helps children improve their academic skills and do better in school.

Exhibit 4–4 Ericsson introduces the wireless office

Examining Consumer Motivations

Marketers recognize that while problem recognition is often a basic, simple process, the way a consumer perceives a problem and becomes motivated to solve it will influence the remainder of the decision process. For example, one consumer may perceive the need to purchase a new watch from a functional perspective and focus on reliable, low-priced alternatives. Another consumer may see

Figure 4–2 Maslow's hierarchy of needs

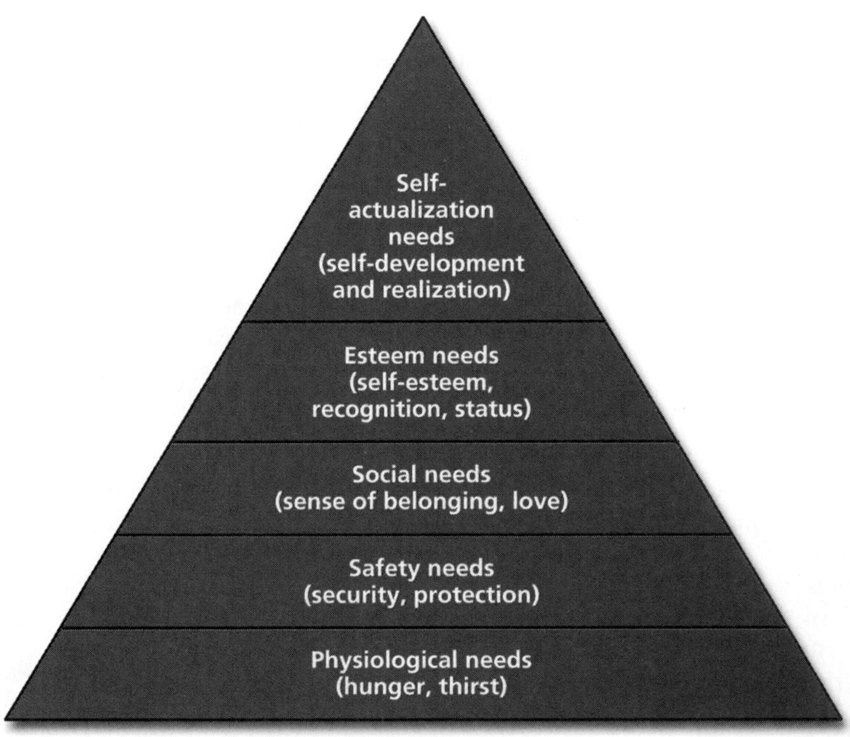

the purchase of a watch as more of a fashion statement and focus on the design and image of various brands. To better understand the reasons underlying consumer purchases, marketers devote considerable attention to examining **motives**—that is, those factors that compel a consumer to take a particular action.

Hierarchy of Needs One of the most popular approaches to understanding consumer motivations is based on the classic theory of human motivation popularized many years ago by psychologist Abraham Maslow.[3] His **hierarchy of needs** theory postulates five basic levels of human needs, arranged in a hierarchy based on their importance. As shown in Figure 4–2, the five needs are (1) *physiological*—the basic level of primary needs for things required to sustain life, such as food, shelter, clothing, and sex; (2) *safety*—the need for security and safety from physical harm; (3) *social/love and belonging*—the desire to have satisfying relationships with others and feel a sense of love, affection, belonging, and acceptance; (4) *esteem*—the need to feel a sense of accomplishment and gain recognition, status, and respect from others; and (5) *self-actualization*—the need for self-fulfillment and a desire to realize one's own potential.

Exhibit 4–5 Pampers appeals to needs for love and belonging in this ad

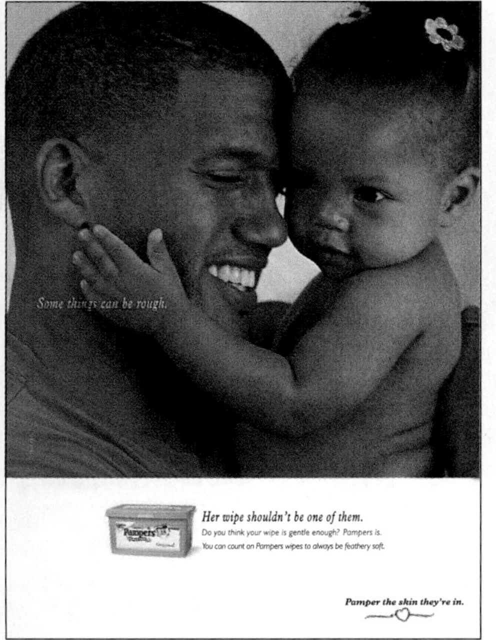

Her wipe shouldn't be one of them.
Do you think your wipe is gentle enough? Pampers is.
You can count on Pampers wipes to always be feathery soft.
Pamper the skin they're in.

According to Maslow's theory, the lower-level physiological and safety needs must be satisfied before the higher-order needs become meaningful. Once these basic needs are satisfied, the individual moves on to attempting to satisfy higher-order needs such as self-esteem. In reality, it is unlikely that people move through the needs hierarchy in a stairstep manner. Lower-level needs are an ongoing source of motivation for consumer purchase behavior. However, since basic physiological needs are met in most developed countries, marketers often sell products that fill basic physiological needs by appealing to consumers' higher-level needs. For example, in marketing its wipes, Pampers focuses on the love between parent and child (social needs) in addition to the gentleness of the product (Exhibit 4–5).

While Maslow's need hierarchy has flaws, it offers a framework for marketers to use in determining what needs they want their products and services to be shown satisfying. Advertising campaigns can then be designed to show how a brand can fulfill these needs. Marketers also recognize that different market segments emphasize different need levels.

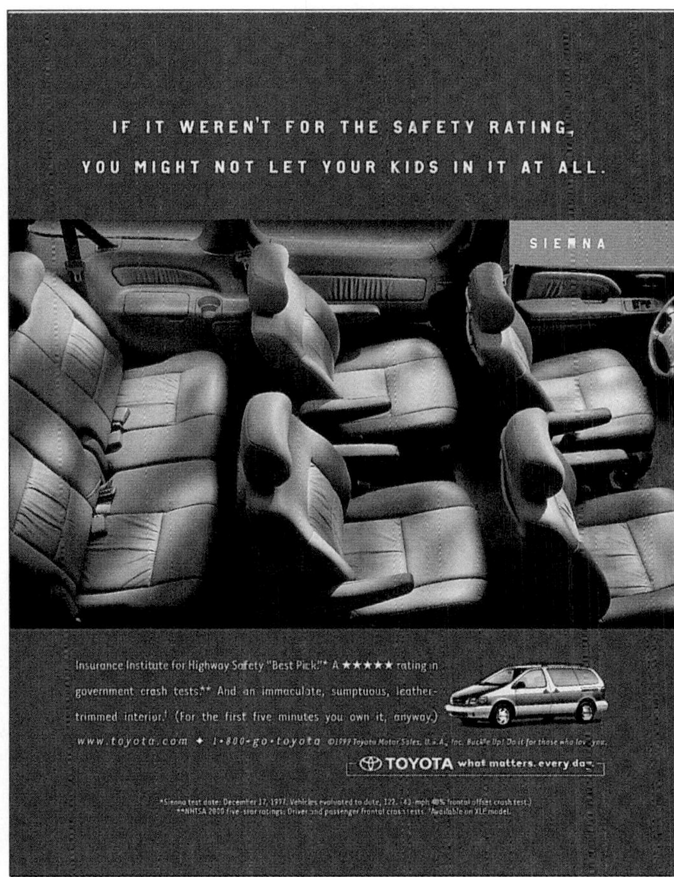

Exhibit 4–6 Toyota uses an appeal to safety needs

For example, a young single person may be attempting to satisfy social or self-esteem needs in purchasing a car, while a family with children will focus more on safety needs. Toyota used ads like the one in Exhibit 4–6 to position its cars as meeting the safety needs of consumers with children.

Psychoanalytic Theory A somewhat more controversial approach to the study of consumer motives is the **psychoanalytic theory** pioneered by Sigmund Freud.[4] Although his work dealt with the structure and development of personality, Freud also studied the underlying motivations for human behavior. Psychoanalytic theory had a strong influence on the development of modern psychology and on explanations of motivation and personality. It has also been applied to the study of consumer behavior by marketers interested in probing deeply rooted motives that may underlie purchase decisions.

Those who attempt to relate psychoanalytic theory to consumer behavior believe consumers' motivations for purchasing are often very complex and unclear to the casual observer—and to the consumers themselves. Many motives for purchase and/or consumption may be driven by deep motives one can determine only by probing the subconscious.

Among the first to conduct this type of research in marketing, Ernest Dichter and James Vicary were employed by a number of major corporations to use psychoanalytic techniques to determine consumers' purchase motivations. The work of these researchers and others who continue to use this approach assumed the title of **motivation research.**

Motivation Research in Marketing Motivation researchers use a variety of methodologies to gain insight into the underlying causes of consumer behavior. Methods employed include in-depth interviews, projective techniques, association tests, and focus groups in which consumers are encouraged to bring out associations related to products and brands (see Figure 4–3). As one might expect,

Figure 4–3 Some of the marketing research methods employed to probe the mind of the consumer

In-depth interviews
Face-to-face situations in which an interviewer asks a consumer to talk freely in an unstructured interview using specific questions designed to obtain insights into his or her motives, ideas, or opinions.

Projective techniques
Efforts designed to gain insights into consumers' values, motives, attitudes, or needs that are difficult to express or identify by having them project these internal states upon some external object.

Association tests
A technique in which an individual is asked to respond with the first thing that comes to mind when he or she is presented with a stimulus; the stimulus may be a word, picture, ad, and so on.

Focus groups
A small number of people with similar backgrounds and/or interests who are brought together to discuss a particular product, idea, or issue.

such associations often lead to interesting insights as to why people purchase. For example:

- Consumers prefer large cars because they believe such cars protect them from the "jungle" of everyday driving.[5]
- A man buys a convertible as a substitute mistress.
- Women like to bake cakes because they feel like they are giving birth to a baby.
- Women wear perfume to "attract a man" and "glorify their existence."
- Men like frankfurters better than women do because cooking them (frankfurters, not men!) makes women feel guilty. It's an admission of laziness.
- When people shower, their sins go down the drain with the soap as they rinse.[6]

As you can see from these examples, motivation research has led to some very interesting, albeit controversial, findings and to much skepticism from marketing managers. However, major corporations and advertising agencies continue to use motivation research to help them market their products.

Problems and Contributions of Psychoanalytic Theory and Motivation Research Psychoanalytic theory has been criticized as being too vague, unresponsive to the external environment, and too reliant on the early development of the individual. It also uses a small sample for drawing conclusions. Because of the emphasis on the unconscious, results are difficult if not impossible to verify, leading motivation research to be criticized for both the conclusions drawn and its lack of experimental validation. Since motivation research studies typically use so few participants, there is also concern that it really discovers the idiosyncracies of a few individuals and its findings are not generalizable to the whole population.

Still, it is difficult to ignore the psychoanalytic approach in furthering our understanding of consumer behavior. Its insights can often be used as a basis for advertising messages aimed at buyers' deeply rooted feelings, hopes, aspirations, and fears. Such strategies are often more effective than rationally based appeals.

Some corporations and advertising agencies have used motivation research to gain further insights into how consumers think. Examples include the following:[7]

- Chrysler had consumers sit on the floor, like children, and use scissors to cut words out of magazines to describe a car.[8]
- McCann-Erickson asked women to draw and describe how they felt about roaches. The agency concluded that many women associated roaches with men who had abandoned them and that this was why women preferred roach killers that let them see the roaches die.
- Saatchi & Saatchi used psychological probes to conclude that Ronald McDonald created a more nurturing mood than did the Burger King (who was perceived as more aggressive and distant).
- Foote, Cone & Belding gave consumers stacks of photographs of faces and asked them to associate the faces with the kinds of people who might use particular products.

While often criticized, motivation research has also contributed to the marketing discipline. The qualitative nature of the research is considered important in assessing how and why consumers buy. Focus groups and in-depth interviews are valuable methods for gaining insights into consumers' feelings, and projective techniques are often the only way to get around stereotypical or socially desirable responses. In addition, motivation research is the forerunner of psychographics (discussed in Chapter 2).

Finally, we know that buyers are sometimes motivated by symbolic as well as functional drives in their purchase decisions. At least one study has shown that two-thirds of all prime-time TV shows present an average of 5.2 scenes per hour that contain talk about sex. Thus, we see the use of sexual appeals and symbols in ads like Exhibit 4–7.

Exhibit 4–7 212 Men uses a sex appeal in its advertising

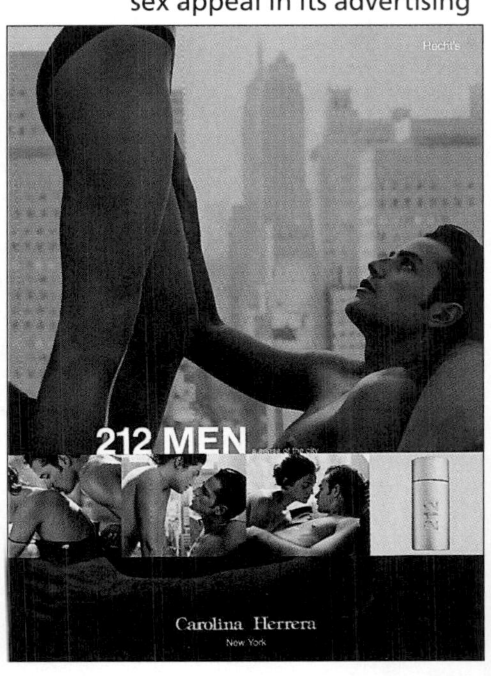

Information Search

The second stage in the consumer decision-making process is *information search.* Once consumers perceive a problem or need that can be satisfied by the purchase of a product or service, they begin to search for information needed to make a purchase decision. The initial search effort often consists of an attempt to scan information stored in memory to recall past experiences and/or knowledge regarding various purchase alternatives.[9] This information retrieval is referred to as **internal search.** For many routine, repetitive purchases, previously acquired information that is stored in memory (such as past performance or outcomes from using a brand) is sufficient for comparing alternatives and making a choice.

If the internal search does not yield enough information, the consumer will seek additional information by engaging in **external search.** External sources of information include:

- *Personal sources,* such as friends, relatives, or co-workers.
- *Marketer-controlled (commercial) sources,* such as information from advertising, salespeople, or point-of-purchase displays and the Internet.
- *Public sources,* including articles in magazines or newspapers and reports on TV.
- *Personal experience,* such as actually handling, examining, or testing the product.

Determining how much and which sources of external information to use involves several factors, including the importance of the purchase decision, the effort needed to acquire information, the amount of past experience relevant, the degree of perceived risk associated with the purchase, and the time available. For example, the selection of a movie to see on a Friday night might entail simply talking to a friend or checking the movie guide in the daily newspaper. A more complex purchase such as a new car might use a number of information sources—perhaps a review of *Road & Track, Motortrend,* or *Consumer Reports;* discussion with family members and friends; and test-driving of cars. At this point in the purchase decision, the information-providing aspects of advertising are extremely important.

Perception

Knowledge of how consumers acquire and use information from external sources is important to marketers in formulating communication strategies. Marketers are particularly interested in (1) how consumers sense external information, (2) how they select and attend to various sources of information, and (3) how this information is interpreted and given meaning. These processes are all part of **perception,** the process by which an individual receives, selects, organizes, and interprets information to create a meaningful picture of the world.[10] Perception is an individual process; it depends on internal factors such as a person's beliefs, experiences, needs, moods, and expectations. The perceptual process is also influenced by the characteristics of a stimulus (such as its size, color, and intensity) and the context in which it is seen or heard.

Sensation

Perception involves three distinct processes. **Sensation** is the immediate, direct response of the senses (taste, smell, sight, touch, and hearing) to a stimulus such as an ad, package, brand name, or point-of-purchase display. Perception uses these senses to create a representation of the stimulus. Marketers recognize that it is important to understand consumers' physiological reactions to marketing stimuli. For example, the visual elements of an ad or package design must attract consumers' favorable attention.

Marketers sometimes try to increase the level of sensory input so that their advertising messages will get noticed. For example, marketers of colognes and perfumes often use strong visuals as well as scent strips to appeal to multiple senses and attract the attention of magazine readers. Some advertisers have even inserted microcomputer chips into their print ads to play a song or deliver a message.

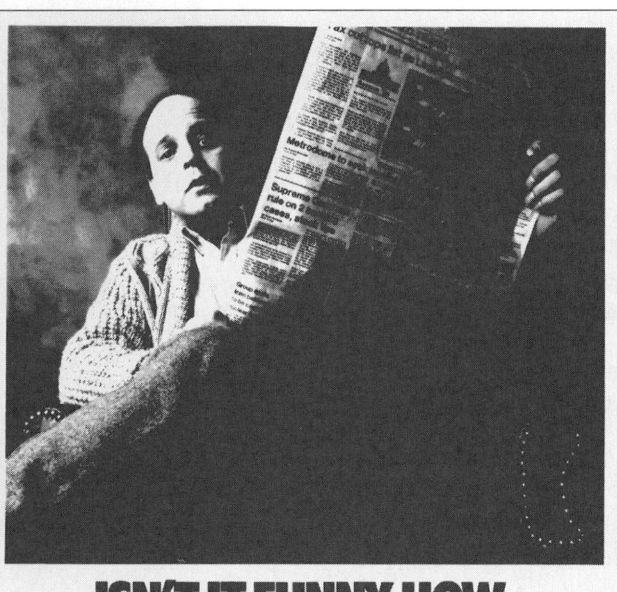

ISN'T IT FUNNY HOW
STEREO ADS ARE BORING
UNTIL YOU WANT A STEREO?
We admit it. There are times when advertising isn't especially interesting.
For instance, stereo ads when you're not looking for a new stereo. Or insurance ads when you're not looking for a new insurance company. Or detergent ads when you're not looking for a new detergent.
But suppose your stereo breaks down. Or your insurance rates go up. Or your laundry comes out gray.
All of a sudden, stereo ads, insurance ads and detergent ads start looking a lot more interesting.
It's one of the basic truths of advertising. We try to be entertaining, but that's not really our job. Our job is to help you make the right choices when you're in the market for any kind of product or service.
Of course, when you're not in the market, we recognize that advertising may seem beside the point. In that case, you're free to pretend it isn't there.
In fact, you're free to ignore advertising for as long as you choose.
Right up until your stereo breaks down.
ADVERTISING.
ANOTHER WORD FOR FREEDOM OF CHOICE.
American Association of Advertising Agencies

Exhibit 4–8 This ad reminds consumers of how advertising responds to their needs

Selecting Information

Sensory inputs are important but are only one part of the perceptual process. Other determinants of whether marketing stimuli will be attended to and how they will be interpreted include internal psychological factors such as the consumer's personality, needs, motives, expectations, and experiences. These psychological inputs explain why people focus attention on some things and ignore others. Two people may perceive the same stimuli in very different ways because they select, attend, and comprehend differently. An individual's perceptual processes usually focus on elements of the environment that are relevant to his or her needs and tune out irrelevant stimuli. Think about how much more attentive you are to advertising for personal computers, tires, or stereos when you are in the market for one of these products (a point that is made by the message from the American Association of Advertising Agencies in Exhibit 4–8).

Interpreting the Information

Once a consumer selects and attends to a stimulus, the perceptual process focuses on organizing, categorizing, and interpreting the incoming information. This stage of the perceptual process is very individualized and is influenced by internal psycho-

Figure 4–4 The selective perception process

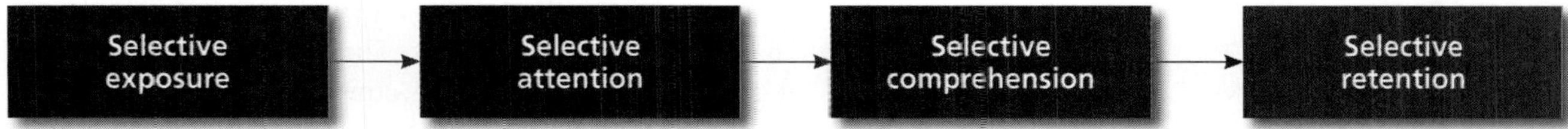

logical factors. The interpretation and meaning an individual assigns to an incoming stimulus also depend in part on the nature of the stimulus. For example, many ads are objective, and their message is clear and straightforward. Other ads are more ambiguous, and their meaning is strongly influenced by the consumer's individual interpretation.

Selectivity occurs throughout the various stages of the consumer's perceptual process. Perception may be viewed as a filtering process in which internal and external factors influence what is received and how it is processed and interpreted. The sheer number and complexity of the marketing stimuli a person is exposed to in any given day require that this filtering occur. **Selective perception** may occur at the exposure, attention, comprehension, or retention stage of perception, as shown in Figure 4–4.

Selective Perception

Selective exposure occurs as consumers choose whether or not to make themselves available to information. For example, a viewer of a television show may change channels or leave the room during commercial breaks.

Selective attention occurs when the consumer chooses to focus attention on certain stimuli while excluding others. One study of selective attention estimates the typical consumer is exposed to nearly 1,500 ads per day yet perceives only 76 of these messages.[11] Other estimates range as high as 3,000 exposures per day. This means advertisers must make considerable effort to get their messages noticed. Advertisers often use the creative aspects of their ads to gain consumers' attention. For example, some advertisers set their ads off from others by showing their products in color against a black-and-white background (Exhibit 4–9). This creative tactic has been used in advertising for many products, among them Cherry 7UP, Nuprin, and Pepto-Bismol.[12]

Exhibit 4–9 Tropicana attempts to create attention with this ad

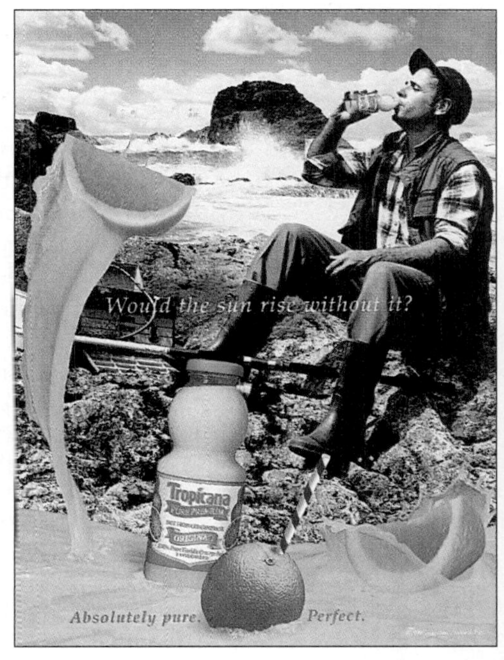

Even if the consumer does notice the advertiser's message, there is no guarantee it will be interpreted in the intended manner. Consumers may engage in **selective comprehension,** interpreting information on the basis of their own attitudes, beliefs, motives, and experiences. They often interpret information in a manner that supports their own position. For example, an ad that disparages a consumer's favorite brand may be seen as biased or untruthful, and its claims may not be accepted.

The final screening process shown in Figure 4–4 is **selective retention,** which means consumers do not remember all the information they see, hear, or read even after attending to and comprehending it. Advertisers attempt to make sure information will be retained in the consumer's memory so that it will be available when it is time to make a purchase. **Mnemonics** such as symbols, rhymes, associations, and images that assist in the learning and memory process are helpful. Many advertisers use telephone numbers that spell out the company name and are easy to remember. Eveready put pictures of its pink bunny on packages to remind consumers at the point of purchase of its creative advertising.

Subliminal Perception

Advertisers know consumers use selective perception to filter out irrelevant or unwanted advertising messages, so they employ various creative tactics to get their messages noticed. One controversial tactic advertisers have been accused of using is appealing to consumers' subconscious. **Subliminal perception** refers to the ability to perceive a stimulus that is below the level of conscious awareness. Psychologists generally agree it is possible to perceive things without being consciously aware of them.

As you might imagine, the possibility of using hidden persuaders such as subliminal audio messages or visual cues to influence consumers might be intriguing to advertisers but would not be welcomed by consumers. The idea of marketers influencing consumers at a subconscious level has strong ethical implications. Ethical Perspective 4–1 discusses researchers' mixed opinions as to whether subliminal messages are likely to be effective in influencing consumer behavior. The use of subliminal techniques is *not* a creative tactic we would recommend to advertisers.

Alternative Evaluation

After acquiring information during the information search stage of the decision process, the consumer moves to alternative evaluation. In this stage, the consumer compares the various brands or products and services he or she has identified as being capable of solving the consumption problem and satisfying the needs or motives that initiated the decision process. The various brands identified as purchase options to be considered during the alternative evaluation process are referred to as the consumer's *evoked set.*

The Evoked Set

The evoked set is generally only a subset of all the brands of which the consumer is aware. The consumer reduces the number of brands to be reviewed during the alternative evaluation stage to a manageable level. The exact size of the evoked set varies from one consumer to another and depends on such factors as the importance of the purchase and the amount of time and energy the consumer wants to spend comparing alternatives.

The goal of most advertising and promotional strategies is to increase the likelihood that a brand will be included in the consumer's evoked set and considered during alternative evaluation. Marketers use advertising to create *top-of-mind awareness* among consumers so that their brands are part of the evoked set of their target audiences. Popular brands with large advertising budgets use *reminder advertising* to maintain high awareness levels and increase the likelihood they will be considered by consumers in the market for the product. Marketers of new brands or those with a low market share need to gain awareness among consumers and break into their evoked sets. They can do this through methods such as comparative advertising, where their brand is compared to market leaders. The ad promoting Los Angeles as a better place to do business (Exhibit 4–10) shows this strategy being used in a different context from products and brands. The ad compares Los Angeles to four other cities and encourages prospective businesses to consider it in their evoked set of places to locate or relocate.

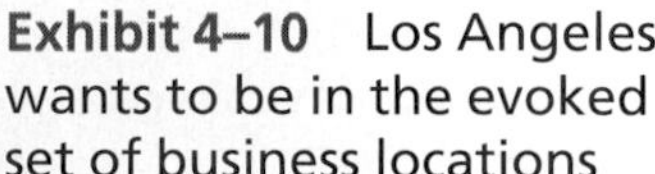
Exhibit 4–10 Los Angeles wants to be in the evoked set of business locations

Ethical Perspective 4–1

Subliminal Perception: It Just Won't Go Away

One of the most controversial topics in all of advertising is subliminal advertising. Rooted in psychoanalytic theory, subliminal advertising supposedly influences consumer behaviors by subconsciously altering perceptions or attitudes toward products without the knowledge—or consent—of the consumer. Marketers have promoted subliminal self-help audiotapes, weight-loss videos, and golf game improvement tapes. Studies have shown that the majority of American consumers believe that advertisers sometimes use subliminal advertising and that it works.

The concept of subliminal advertising was introduced in 1957 when James Vicary, a motivational researcher, reported that he increased the sales of popcorn and Coke by subliminally flashing "Eat popcorn" and "Drink Coca-Cola" across the screen during a movie in New Jersey. Since then, numerous books and research studies have been published regarding the effectiveness of this advertising form. Some of these have reported on the use of this technique by advertisers to manipulate consumers.

Numerous articles have reviewed the research in this area. In 1982, Timothy Moore reported that the effects of subliminal advertising are so weak that they pose serious difficulties for any marketing applications. In 1988, after additional research in this area, Moore said, "There continues to be no evidence that subliminal messages can influence motivation or complex behavior." Again in 1992, Moore concluded that "recent research in subliminal perception has provided very little evidence that stimuli below observers' subjective thresholds influence motives, attitudes, beliefs, or choices." Joel Saegart and Jack Haberstroh have supported Moore's conclusions in their studies. On the other hand, in 1994 Kathryn Theus concluded after an extensive review of the literature that "certain themes might be effectively applied by advertising or marketing specialists."

In more recent writings, opposite positions are again taken. In a study conducted in Australia by an ad agency and Mindtec (a consulting firm), 12 groups of television viewers were hypnotized and asked questions about specific commercials and programs. According to the study, 75 percent of the hypnotized subjects stated that sexy images were the main attraction for viewing, as opposed to only 22 percent of the nonhypnotized subjects. The researchers were surprised by the subliminal details that hypnotized participants were able to recall. In the ads, names and slogans that were visible only when the commercial was paused had high levels of recall, even when the brands recalled were not those being advertised. On the other hand, in his book, *Ice Cube Sex: The Truth about Subliminal Advertising,* Haberstroh reviews research and discussions with practitioners and concludes that subliminal advertising does not influence consumer behaviors, advertising recall, attitudes, or any other marketplace behavior.

When Haberstroh asked ad agency executives in 1984 if they had ever deliberately used subliminal advertising, 96 percent said no, 94 percent said they had never supervised the use of implants, and 91 percent denied knowing anyone who had ever used this technique. A study by Rogers and Seiler in 1994 supported these results, with over 90 percent denying any use of this subliminal implant.

Going even further, Haberstroh contends that subliminal advertising does not even exist except for a few pranksters playing around with artwork for fun. But not so fast! Fashion retailer French Connection is not only employing subliminal advertising but incorporating it into a tagline. Using print and posters, the tagline "subliminal advertising experiment" is arranged in such a way as to spell out the word *sex* if one reads vertically. Likewise, Master Lock has become the first company to run a one-second national print commercial. The goal of the ad is to reinforce the brand name. And, in upstate New York, a personal-injury lawyer is paying $35 each for one-second spots in an attempt to gain new clients. At this time, no one knows if any of these efforts have been successful.

Thus, while most consumers believe subliminal techniques are used and effective, researchers are divided as to their effects. It seems few people in the advertising world think subliminal advertising works and even fewer claim to use it, but there are still those who feel they are wrong. Will there ever be an end to this controversy?

Sources: "Hypnosis Reveals Ad Effects," *Adweek Asia,* January 29, 1999, p. 4; "Breaking French Connection," *Ad Age,* March 22, 1999, p. 52; "Blink of an Ad," *Time,* August 3, 1998, p. 51; Jack Haberstroh, *Ice Cube Sex: The Truth about Subliminal Advertising,* New York Times Publishing, 1996; Kathryn Theus, "Subliminal Advertising and the Psychology of Processing Unconscious Stimuli: A Review of Research," *Psychology & Marketing* 11, no. 3, 1994, pp. 271–90; Timothy Moore, "Subliminal Advertising: What You See Is What You Get," *Journal of Marketing* 46, no. 2 (Spring 1982), pp. 38–47; Timothy Moore, "The Case against Subliminal Manipulation," *Psychology and Marketing* 5, no. 4 (Winter 1988), pp. 297–316.

Advertising is a valuable promotional tool for creating and maintaining brand awareness and making sure a brand is included in the evoked set. However, marketers also work to promote their brands in the actual environment where purchase decisions are made. Point-of-purchase materials and promotional techniques such as in-store sampling, end-aisle displays, or shelf tags touting special prices encourage consumers to consider brands that may not have initially been in their evoked set.

Evaluative Criteria and Consequences

Once consumers have identified an evoked set and have a list of alternatives, they must evaluate the various brands. This involves comparing the choice alternatives on specific criteria important to the consumer. **Evaluative criteria** are the dimensions or attributes of a product or service that are used to compare different alternatives. Evaluative criteria can be objective or subjective. For example, in buying an automobile, consumers use objective attributes such as price, warranty, and fuel economy as well as subjective factors such as image, styling, and performance.

Evaluative criteria are usually viewed as product or service attributes. Many marketers view their products or services as *bundles of attributes,* but consumers tend to think about products or services in terms of their *consequences* instead. J. Paul Peter and Jerry Olson define consequences as specific events or outcomes that consumers experience when they purchase and/or consume a product or service.[13] They distinguish between two broad types of consequences. **Functional consequences** are concrete outcomes of product or service usage that are tangible and directly experienced by consumers. The taste of a soft drink or a potato chip, the acceleration of a car, and the clarity of a fax transmission are examples of functional consequences. **Psychosocial consequences** are abstract outcomes that are more intangible, subjective, and personal, such as how a product makes you feel or how you think others will view you for purchasing or using it.

Exhibit 4–11 This ad emphasizes the positive consequences of using the Top-Flite XL golf ball

Marketers should distinguish between product/service attributes and consequences, because the importance and meaning consumers assign to an attribute are usually determined by its consequences for them. Moreover, advertisers must be sure consumers understand the link between a particular attribute and a consequence. For example, the Top-Flite ad in Exhibit 4–11 focuses on the consequences of using the new Top-Flite XL golf ball, such as more distance and lower scores. Note how the highlighted scorecard is used to reinforce the point that the Top-Flite XL can help golfers achieve better scores.

Product/service attributes and the consequences or outcomes consumers think they will experience from a particular brand are very important, for they are often the basis on which consumers form attitudes and purchase intentions and decide among various choice alternatives. Two subprocesses are very important during the alternative evaluation stage: (1) the process by which consumer attitudes are created, reinforced, and changed and (2) the decision rules or integration strategies consumers use to compare brands and make purchase decisions. We will examine each of these processes in more detail.

Attitudes

Attitudes are one of the most heavily studied concepts in consumer behavior. According to Gordon Allport's classic definition, "attitudes are learned predispositions to respond to an object."[14] More recent perspectives view attitudes as a summary construct that represents an individual's overall feelings toward or evaluation of an object.[15] Consumers hold attitudes toward a variety of objects that are important to marketers, including individuals (celebrity endorsers such as Tiger Woods or Michael Jordan), brands (Cheerios, Kix), companies (Texaco, Microsoft), product categories (beef, pork, tuna), retail stores (Kmart, Sears), or even advertisements (the Energizer bunny ads).

Attitudes are important to marketers because they theoretically summarize a consumer's evaluation of an object (or brand or company) and represent positive or negative feelings and behavioral tendencies. Marketers' keen interest in attitudes is based on the assumption that they are related to consumers' purchase behavior. Considerable evidence supports the basic assumption of a relationship between attitudes and behavior.[16] The attitude-behavior link does not always hold; many other factors can affect behavior.[17] But attitudes are very important to marketers. Advertising and promotion are used to create favorable attitudes toward new products/services or brands, reinforce existing favorable attitudes, and/or change negative attitudes. An approach to studying and measuring attitudes that is particularly relevant to advertising is multiattribute attitude models.

Multiattribute Attitude Models

Consumer researchers and marketing practitioners have been using multiattribute attitude models to study consumer attitudes for two decades.[18] A **multiattribute attitude model** views an attitude object, such as a product or brand, as possessing a number of attributes that provide the basis on which consumers form their attitudes. According to this model, consumers have beliefs about specific brand attributes and attach different levels of importance to these attributes. Using this approach, an attitude toward a particular brand can be represented as

$$A_B = \sum_{i=1}^{n} B_i \times E_i$$

where A_B = attitude toward a brand

B_i = beliefs about the brand's performance on attribute i

E_i = importance attached to attribute i

n = number of attributes considered

For example, a consumer may have beliefs (B_i) about various brands of toothpaste on certain attributes. One brand may be perceived as having fluoride and thus preventing cavities, tasting good, and helping control tartar buildup. Another brand may not be perceived as having these attributes, but consumers may believe it performs well on other attributes such as freshening breath and whitening teeth.

To predict attitudes, one must know how much importance consumers attach to each of these attributes (E_i). For example, parents purchasing toothpaste for their children may prefer a brand that performs well on cavity prevention, a preference that leads to a more favorable attitude toward the first brand. Teenagers and young adults may prefer a brand that freshens their breath and makes their teeth white and thus prefer the second brand.

Consumers may hold a number of different beliefs about brands in any product or service category. However, not all of these beliefs are activated in forming an attitude. Beliefs concerning specific attributes or consequences that are activated and form the basis of an attitude are referred to as **salient beliefs.** Marketers should identify and understand these salient beliefs. They must also recognize that the saliency of beliefs varies among different market segments, over time, and across different consumption situations.

Attitude Change Strategies

Multiattribute models help marketers understand and diagnose the underlying basis of consumers' attitudes. By understanding the beliefs that underlie consumers' evaluations of a brand and the importance of various attributes or consequences, the marketer is better able to develop communication strategies for creating, changing, or reinforcing brand attitudes. The multiattribute model provides insight into several ways marketers can influence consumer attitudes, including:

- Increasing or changing the strength or belief rating of a brand on an important attribute.
- Changing consumers' perceptions of the importance or value of an attribute.
- Adding a new attribute to the attitude formation process.
- Changing perceptions of belief ratings for a competing brand.

The first strategy is commonly used by advertisers. They identify an attribute or consequence that is important and remind consumers how well their brand performs on this attribute. In situations where consumers do not perceive the marketer's brand as possessing an important attribute or the belief strength is low, advertising strategies may be targeted at changing the belief rating. Even when belief strength is high, advertising may be used to increase the rating of a brand on an important attribute. BMW's "The Ultimate Driving Machine" campaign is a good example of a strategy designed to create a belief and reinforce it through advertising.

Exhibit 4–12 Jeep adds a new attribute for consumers to consider

Marketers often attempt to influence consumer attitudes by changing the relative importance of a particular attribute. This second strategy involves getting consumers to attach more importance to the attribute in forming their attitude toward the brand. Marketers using this strategy want to increase the importance of an attribute their particular brand has.

The third strategy for influencing consumer attitudes is to add or emphasize a new attribute that consumers can use in evaluating a brand. Marketers often do this by improving their products or focusing on additional benefits or consequences associated with using the brand. Exhibit 4–12 shows how Jeep is introducing Quadra-Drive in an attempt to influence consumers' attitudes.

A final strategy marketers use is to change consumer beliefs about the attributes of competing brands or product categories. This strategy has become much more common with the increase in comparative advertising, where marketers compare their brands to competitors' on specific product attributes. An example of this is the Progresso ad shown in Exhibit 4–13, where the company compares what it has to offer to what Campbell's offers.

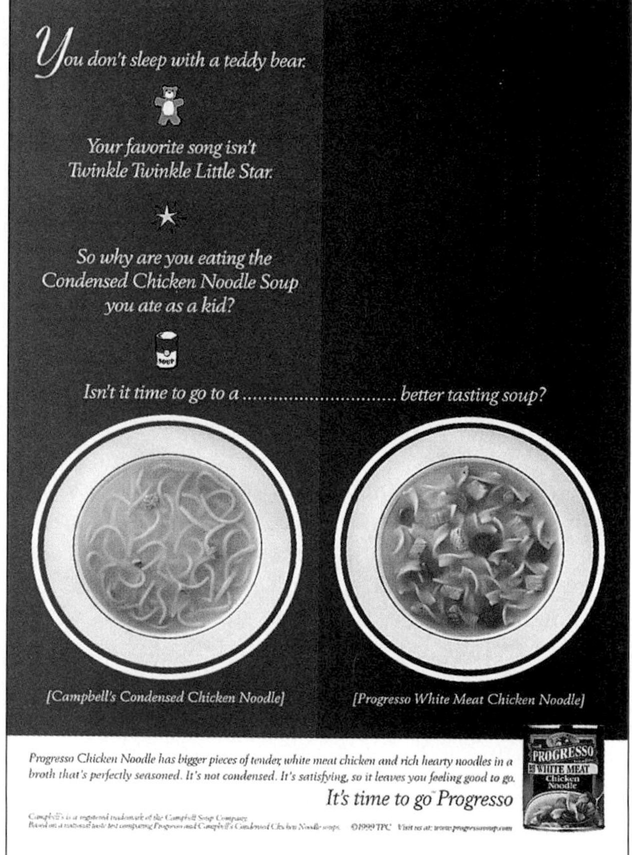

Exhibit 4–13 Progresso compares its products to those offered by Campbell's

Integration Processes and Decision Rules

Another important aspect of the alternative evaluation stage is the way consumers combine information about the characteristics of brands to arrive at a purchase decision. **Integration processes** are the way product knowledge, meanings, and beliefs are combined to evaluate two or more alternatives.[19] Analysis of the integration process focuses on the different types of *decision rules* or strategies consumers use to decide among purchase alternatives.

Consumers often make purchase selections by using formal integration strategies or decision rules that require examination and comparison of alternatives on specific attributes. This process involves a very deliberate evaluation of the alternatives, attribute by attribute. When consumers apply such formal decision rules, marketers need to know which attributes are being considered so as to provide the information the consumers require.

Sometimes consumers make their purchase decisions using more simplified decision rules known as **heuristics.** Peter and Olson note that heuristics are easy to use and are highly adaptive to specific environmental situations (such as a retail store).[20] For familiar products that are purchased frequently, consumers may use price-based heuristics (buy the least expensive brand) or promotion-based heuristics (choose the brand for which I can get a price reduction through a coupon, rebate, or special deal).

One type of heuristic is the **affect referral decision rule,**[21] in which consumers make a selection on the basis of an overall impression or summary evaluation of the various alternatives under consideration. This decision rule suggests that consumers have affective impressions of brands stored in memory that can be accessed at the time of purchase. How many times have you gone into a store and made purchases based on your overall impressions of the brands rather than going through detailed comparisons of the alternatives' specific attributes?

Marketers selling familiar and popular brands may appeal to an affect referral rule by stressing overall affective feelings or impressions about their products. Market leaders, whose products enjoy strong overall brand images, often use ads that promote the brand as the best overall. Coke's campaign "Enjoy Coke," Jeep's "There's only one," and Budweiser's "The king of beers" are all examples of this strategy (Exhibit 4–14).

Exhibit 4–14 Market leaders such as Budweiser can appeal to consumer affect

Purchase Decision

At some point in the buying process, the consumer must stop searching for and evaluating information about alternative brands in the evoked set and make a *purchase decision.* As an outcome of the alternative evaluation stage, the consumer may develop a **purchase intention** or predisposition to buy a certain brand. Purchase intentions are generally based on a matching of purchase motives with attributes or characteristics of brands under consideration. Their formation involves many of the personal subprocesses discussed in this chapter, including motivation, perception, attitude formation, and integration.

A purchase decision is not the same as an actual purchase. Once a consumer chooses which brand to buy, he or she must still implement the decision and make the actual purchase. Additional decisions may be needed, such as when to buy, where to buy, and how much money to spend. Often, there is a time delay between the formation of a purchase intention or decision and the actual purchase, particularly for highly involved and complex purchases such as automobiles, personal computers, and consumer durables.

For nondurable products, which include many low-involvement items such as consumer package goods, the time between the decision and the actual purchase may be short. Before leaving home, the consumer may make a shopping list that includes specific brand names because the consumer has developed **brand loyalty**—a preference for a particular brand that results in its repeated purchase.

Marketers strive to develop and maintain brand loyalty among consumers. They use reminder advertising to keep their brand names in front of consumers, maintain prominent shelf positions and displays in stores, and run periodic promotions to deter consumers from switching brands.

Maintaining consumers' brand loyalty is not easy. Competitors use many techniques to encourage consumers to try their brands, among them new product introductions and free samples. As Figure 4–5 shows, for many products fewer than 50 percent of consumers are loyal to one brand. Marketers must continually battle to maintain their loyal consumers while replacing those who switch brands.

Purchase decisions for nondurable, convenience items sometimes take place in the store, almost simultaneous with the purchase. Marketers must ensure that consumers have top-of-mind awareness of their brands so that they are quickly recognized and considered. These types of decisions are influenced at the actual point of purchase. Packaging, shelf displays, point-of-purchase materials, and promotional

Figure 4–5 Faithful or fickle? Percentage of users of these products who are loyal to one brand

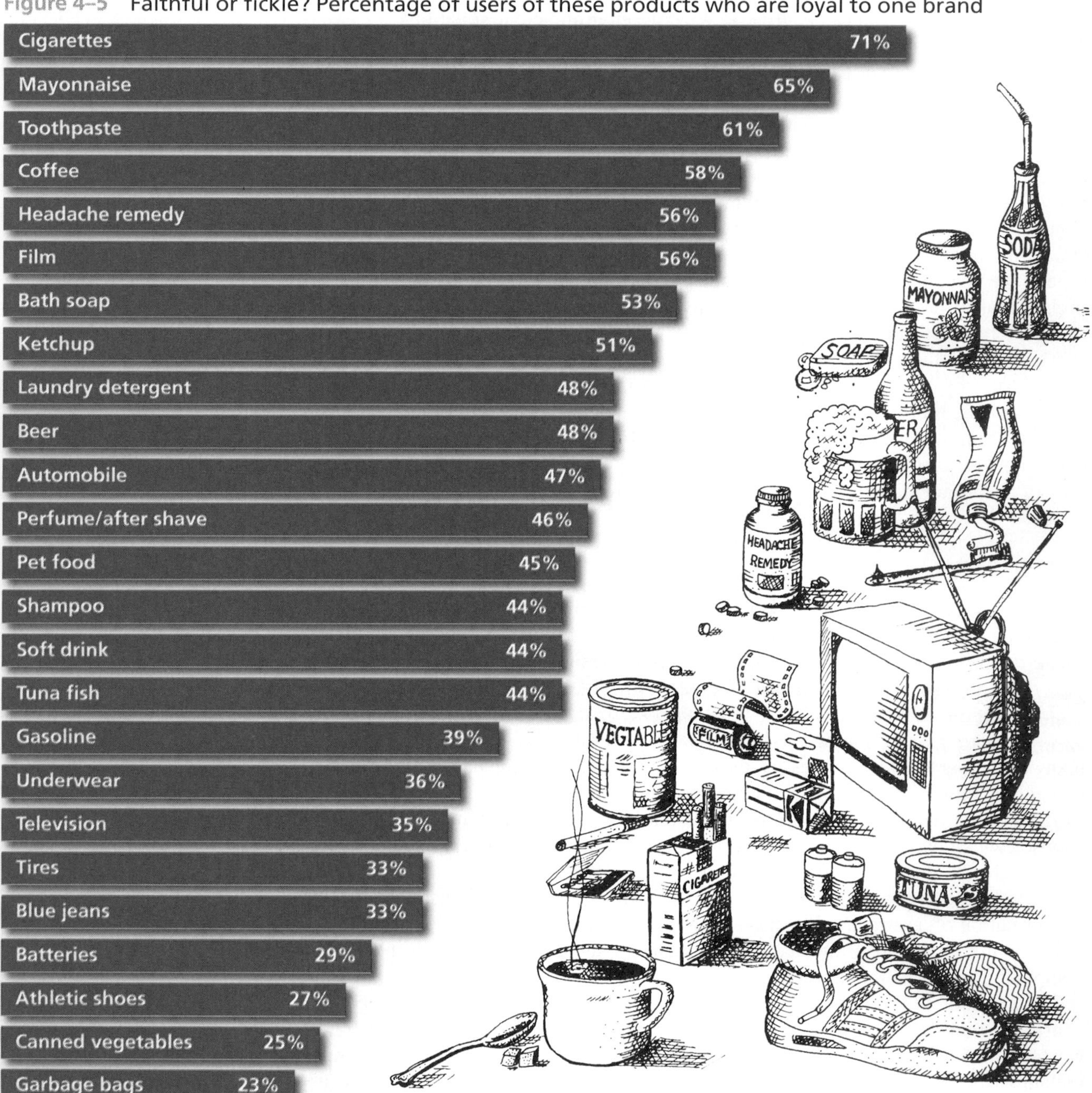

tools such as on-package coupons or premium offers can influence decisions made through constructive processes at the time of purchase.

Postpurchase Evaluation

The consumer decision process does not end with the purchase. After using the product or service, the consumer compares the level of performance with expectations and is either satisfied or dissatisfied. *Satisfaction* occurs when the consumer's expectations are either met or exceeded; *dissatisfaction* results when performance is below expectations. The postpurchase evaluation process is important because the feedback acquired from actual use of a product will influence the likelihood of future purchases. Positive performance means the brand is retained in the evoked set and increases the likelihood it will be purchased again. Unfavorable outcomes may lead the consumer to form negative attitudes toward the brand, lessening the likelihood it will be purchased again or even eliminating it from the consumer's evoked set.

Another possible outcome of purchase is **cognitive dissonance,** a feeling of psychological tension or postpurchase doubt that a consumer experiences after making a difficult purchase choice. Dissonance is more likely to occur in important decisions where the consumer must choose among close alternatives (especially if the unchosen alternative has unique or desirable features that the selected alternative does not have).

Consumers experiencing cognitive dissonance may use a number of strategies to attempt to reduce it. They may seek out reassurance and opinions from others to confirm the wisdom of their purchase decision, lower their attitudes or opinions of the unchosen alternative, deny or distort any information that does not support the choice they made, or look for information that does support their choice. An important source of supportive information is advertising; consumers tend to be more attentive to advertising for the brand they have chosen.[22] Thus, it may be important for companies to advertise to reinforce consumer decisions to purchase their brands.

Marketers must recognize the importance of the postpurchase evaluation stage. Dissatisfied consumers who experience dissonance not only are unlikely to repurchase the marketer's product but may also spread negative word-of-mouth information that deters others from purchasing the product or service. The best guarantee of favorable postpurchase evaluations is to provide consumers with a quality product or service that always meets their expectations. Marketers must be sure their advertising and other forms of promotion do not create unreasonable expectations their products cannot meet.

Marketers have come to realize that postpurchase communication is also important. Some companies send follow-up letters and brochures to reassure buyers and reinforce the wisdom of their decision. Many companies have set up toll-free numbers for consumers to call if they need information or have a question or complaint regarding a product. Marketers also offer liberalized return and refund policies and extended warranties and guarantees to ensure customer satisfaction. Some have used customers' postpurchase dissatisfaction as an opportunity for gaining new business, as is reflected in the ad for UUNET (Exhibit 4–15).

Exhibit 4–15 UUNET attempts to capitalize on consumer dissatisfaction

Variations in Consumer Decision Making

The preceding pages describe a general model of consumer decision making. But consumers do not always engage in all five steps of the purchase decision process or proceed in the sequence presented. They may minimize or even skip one or more stages if they have previous experience in purchasing the product or service or if the decision is of low personal, social, or economic significance. To develop effective promotional strategies and programs, marketers need some understanding of the problem-solving processes their target consumers use to make purchase decisions.[23]

Many of the purchase decisions we make as consumers are based on a habitual or routine choice process. For many low-priced, frequently purchased products, the decision process consists of little more than recognizing the problem, engaging in a quick internal search, and making the purchase. The consumer spends little or no effort engaging in external search or alternative evaluation.

Marketers of products characterized by a routine response purchase process need to get and/or keep their brands in the consumer's evoked set and avoid anything that may result in their removal from consideration. Established brands that have strong market share position are likely to be in the evoked set of most consumers. Marketers of these brands want consumers to follow a routine choice process and continue to purchase their products. This means maintaining high levels of brand awareness through reminder advertising, periodic promotions, and prominent shelf positions in retail stores.

Marketers of new brands or those with a low market share face a different challenge. They must find ways to disrupt consumers' routine choice process and get them to consider different alternatives. High levels of advertising may be used to encourage trial or brand switching, along with sales promotion efforts in the form of free samples, special price offers, high-value coupons, and the like.

A more complicated decision-making process may occur when consumers have limited experience in purchasing a particular product or service and little or no knowledge of the brands available and/or the criteria to use in making a purchase decision. They may have to learn what attributes or criteria should be used in making a purchase decision and how the various alternatives perform on these dimensions. For products or services characterized by problem solving, whether limited or extensive, marketers should make information available that will help consumers decide. Advertising that provides consumers with detailed information about a brand and how it can satisfy their purchase motives and goals is important. Marketers may also want to give consumers information at the point of purchase, through either displays or brochures. Distribution channels should have knowledgeable salespeople available to explain the features and benefits of the company's product or service and why it is superior to competing products.

The IBM ad in Exhibit 4–16 is a good example of how advertising can appeal to consumers who may be engaging in extended problem solving when considering corporate security. Notice how the ad communicates with consumers who know lit-

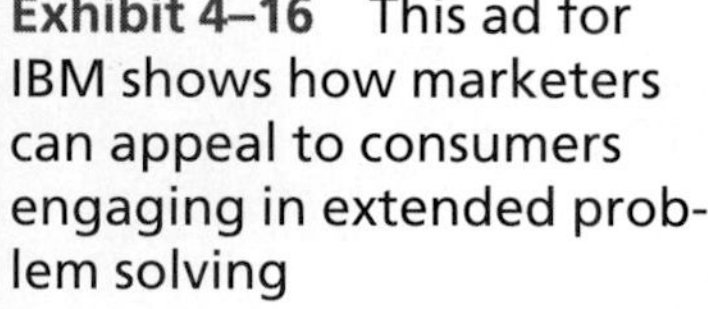

Exhibit 4–16 This ad for IBM shows how marketers can appeal to consumers engaging in extended problem solving

tle about how to purchase this product. The ad also makes more detailed information available by offering a toll-free number and a website.

The Consumer Learning Process

The discussion of the decision process shows that the way consumers make a purchase varies depending on a number of factors, including the nature of the product or service, the amount of experience they have with the product, and the importance of the purchase. One factor in the level of problem solving to be employed is the consumer's *involvement* with the product or brand. Chapter 5 examines the meaning of involvement, the difference between low- and high-involvement decision making, and the implications of involvement for developing advertising and promotional strategies.

Our examination of consumer behavior thus far has looked at the decision-making process from a *cognitive orientation*. The five-stage decision process model views the consumer as a problem solver and information processor who engages in a variety of mental processes to evaluate various alternatives and determine the degree to which they might satisfy needs or purchase motives. There are, however, other perspectives regarding how consumers acquire the knowledge and experience they use in making purchase decisions. To understand these perspectives, we examine various approaches to learning and their implications for advertising and promotion.

Consumer learning has been defined as "the process by which individuals acquire the purchase and consumption knowledge and experience they apply to future related behavior."[24] Two basic approaches to learning are the behavioral approach and cognitive learning theory.

Behavioral Learning Theory

Behavioral learning theories emphasize the role of external, environmental stimuli in causing behavior; they minimize the significance of internal psychological processes. Behavioral learning theories are based on the *stimulus–response orientation* (S–R), the premise that learning occurs as the result of responses to external stimuli in the environment. Behavioral learning theorists believe learning occurs through the connection between a stimulus and a response. We will examine the basic principles of two behavioral learning theory approaches: classical conditioning and operant conditioning.

Classical Conditioning

Classical conditioning assumes that learning is an *associative process* with an already existing relationship between a stimulus and a response. Probably the best-known example of this type of learning comes from the studies done with animals by the Russian psychologist Pavlov.[25] Pavlov noticed that at feeding times, his dogs would salivate at the sight of food. The connection between food and salivation is not taught; it is an innate reflex reaction. Because this relationship exists before the conditioning process, the food is referred to as an *unconditioned stimulus* and salivation is an *unconditioned response.* To see if salivation could be conditioned to occur in response to another neutral stimulus, Pavlov paired the ringing of a bell with the presentation of the food. After a number of trials, the dogs learned to salivate at the sound of the bell alone. Thus, the bell became a **conditioned stimulus** that elicited a **conditioned response** resembling the original unconditioned reaction.

Two factors are important for learning to occur through the associative process. The first is contiguity, which means the unconditioned stimulus and conditioned stimulus must be close in time and space. In Pavlov's experiment, the dog learns to associate the ringing of the bell with food because of the contiguous presentation of the two stimuli. The other important principle is *repetition,* or the frequency of the association. The more often the unconditioned and conditioned stimuli occur together, the stronger the association between them will be.

Figure 4–6 The classical conditioning process

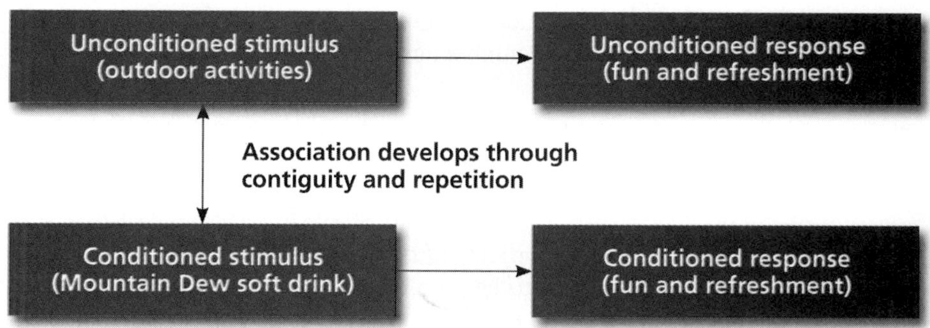

Applying Classical Conditioning Learning through classical conditioning plays an important role in marketing. Buyers can be conditioned to form favorable impressions and images of various brands through the associative process. Advertisers strive to associate their products and services with perceptions, images, and emotions known to evoke positive reactions from consumers. Many products are promoted through image advertising, in which the brand is shown with an unconditioned stimulus that elicits pleasant feelings. When the brand is presented simultaneously with this unconditioned stimulus, the brand itself becomes a conditioned stimulus that elicits the same favorable response.

Figure 4–6 provides a diagram of this process, and the ad for Brita in Exhibit 4–17 shows an application of this strategy. Notice how this ad associates Brita freshness with the freshness of a waterfall. The company's positioning plays off this association.

Exhibit 4–17 Brita associates itself with freshness

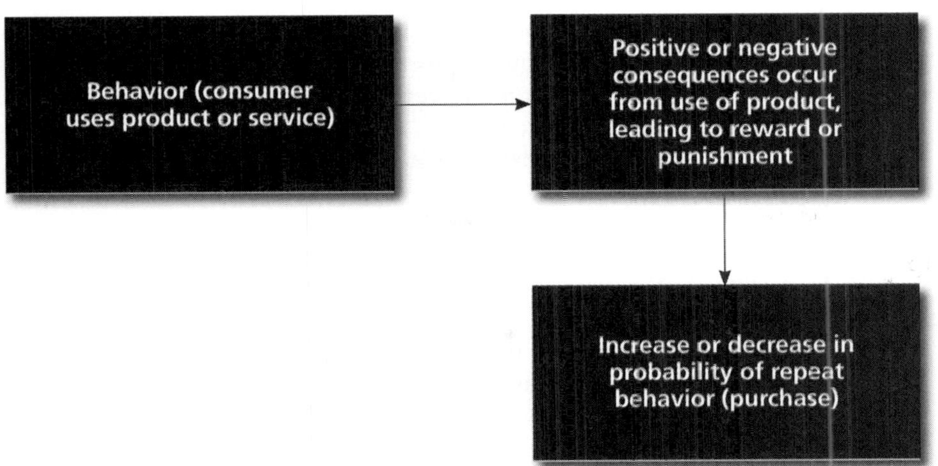

Behavior (consumer uses product or service)
Positive or negative consequences occur from use of product, leading to reward or punishment
Increase or decrease in probability of repeat behavior (purchase)

Figure 4–7 Instrumental conditioning in marketing

Classical conditioning can also associate a product or service with a favorable emotional state. A study by Gerald Gorn used this approach to examine how background music in ads influences product choice.[26] He found that subjects were more likely to choose a product when it was presented against a background of music they liked rather than music they disliked. These results suggest the emotions generated by a commercial are important because they may become associated with the advertised product through classical conditioning. Kellaris and colleagues also showed that music that was congruent with the message enhanced both ad recall and recognition.[27] Advertisers often attempt to pair a neutral product or service stimulus with an event or situation that arouses positive feelings, such as humor, an exciting sports event, or popular music.

Operant Conditioning

Classical conditioning views the individual as a passive participant in the learning process who simply receives stimuli. Conditioning occurs as a result of exposure to a stimulus that occurs before the response. In the **operant conditioning** approach, the individual must actively *operate* or act on some aspect of the environment for learning to occur. Operant conditioning is sometimes referred to as *instrumental conditioning* because the individual's response is instrumental in getting a positive reinforcement (reward) or negative reinforcement (punishment).

Reinforcement, the reward or favorable consequence associated with a particular response, is an important element of instrumental conditioning. Behavior that is reinforced strengthens the bond between a stimulus and a response. Thus, if a consumer buys a product in response to an ad and experiences a positive outcome, the likelihood that the consumer will use this product again increases. If the outcome is not favorable, the likelihood of buying the product again decreases.

The principles of operant conditioning can be applied to marketing, as shown in Figure 4–7. Companies attempt to provide their customers with products and services that satisfy their needs and reward them to reinforce the probability of repeat purchase. Reinforcement can also be implied in advertising; many ads emphasize the benefits or rewards a consumer will receive from using a product or service. Reinforcement also occurs when an ad encourages consumers to use a particular product or brand to avoid unpleasant consequences. For example, the ad for Energizer batteries in Exhibit 4–18 shows how using this product will help avoid negative consequences—that is, being without a working cell phone when you need it.

Two concepts that are particularly relevant to marketers in their use of reinforcement through promotional strategies are schedules of reinforcement and shaping. Different **schedules of reinforcement** result

Exhibit 4–18 Energizer batteries shows how to avoid negative consequences

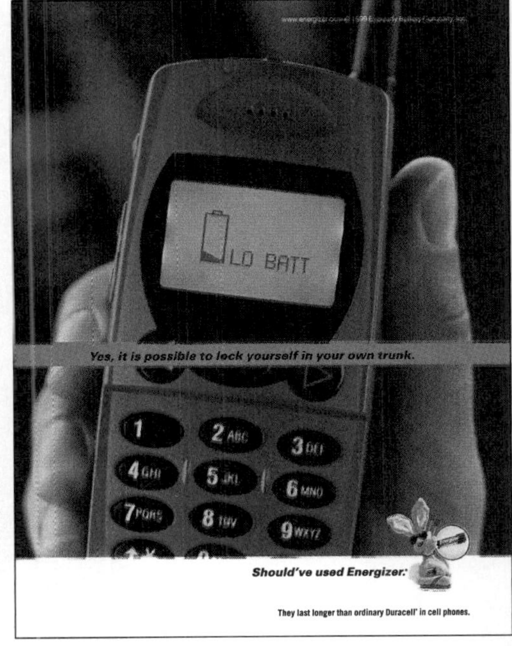

LO BATT
Yes, it is possible to lock yourself in your own trunk.
Should've used Energizer.
They last longer than ordinary Duracell in cell phones.

in varying patterns of learning and behavior. Learning occurs most rapidly under a *continuous reinforcement schedule,* in which every response is rewarded—but the behavior is likely to cease when the reinforcement stops. Marketers must provide continuous reinforcement to consumers or risk their switching to brands that do.

Learning occurs more slowly but lasts longer when a *partial* or *intermittent reinforcement schedule* is used and only some of the individual's responses are rewarded. Promotional programs have partial reinforcement schedules. A firm may offer consumers an incentive to use the company's product. The firm does not want to offer the incentive every time (continuous reinforcement), because consumers might become dependent on it and stop buying the brand when the incentive is withdrawn. A study that examined the effect of reinforcement on bus ridership found that discount coupons given as rewards for riding the bus were as effective when given on a partial schedule as when given on a continuous schedule.[28] The cost of giving the discount coupons under the partial schedule, however, was considerably less.

Reinforcement schedules can also be used to influence consumer learning and behavior through a process known as **shaping,** the reinforcement of successive acts that lead to a desired behavior pattern or response. Rothschild and Gaidis argue that shaping is a very useful concept for marketers:

> Shaping is an essential process in deriving new and complex behavior because a behavior cannot be rewarded unless it first occurs; a stimulus can only reinforce acts that already occur. New, complex behaviors rarely occur by chance in nature. If the only behavior to be rewarded were the final complex sought behavior, one would probably have to wait a long time for this to occur by chance. Instead, one can reward simpler existing behaviors; over time, more complex patterns evolve and these are rewarded. Thus the shaping process occurs by a method of successive approximations.[29]

In a promotional context, shaping procedures are used as part of the introductory program for new products. Figure 4–8 provides an example of how samples and discount coupons can be used to introduce a new product and take a consumer from trial to repeat purchase. Marketers must be careful in their use of shaping procedures: If they drop the incentives too soon, the consumer may not establish the desired behavior; but if they overuse them, the consumer's purchase may become contingent on the incentive rather than the product or service.

Figure 4–8 Application of shaping procedures in marketing

Terminal Goal: Repeat Purchase Behavior

Approximation Sequence	Shaping Procedure	Reinforcement Applied
Induce product trial	Free samples distributed; large discount coupon	Product performance; coupon
Induce purchase with little financial obligation	Discount coupon prompts purchase with little cost; coupon good for small discount on next purchase enclosed	Product performance; coupon
Induce purchase with moderate financial obligation	Small discount coupon prompts purchase with moderate cost	Product performance
Induce purchase with full financial obligation	Purchase occurs without coupon assistance	Product performance

Figure 4–9 The cognitive learning process

Cognitive Learning Theory

Behavioral learning theories have been criticized for assuming a mechanistic view of the consumer that puts too much emphasis on external stimulus factors. They ignore internal psychological processes such as motivation, thinking, and perception; they assume that the external stimulus environment will elicit fairly predictable responses. Many consumer researchers and marketers disagree with the simplified explanations of behavioral learning theories and are more interested in the complex mental processes that underlie consumer decision making. The cognitive approach to studying learning and decision making has dominated the field of consumer behavior in recent years. Figure 4–9 shows how cognitive theorists view the learning process.

Since consumer behavior typically involves choices and decision making, the cognitive perspective has particular appeal to marketers, especially those whose product/service calls for important and involved purchase decisions. Cognitive processes such as perception, formation of beliefs about brands, attitude development and change, and integration are important to understanding the decision-making process for many types of purchases. The subprocesses examined during our discussion of the five-stage decision process model are all relevant to a cognitive learning approach to consumer behavior.

Environmental Influences on Consumer Behavior

The consumer does not make purchase decisions in isolation. A number of external factors have been identified that may influence consumer decision making. They are shown in Figure 4–10 and examined in more detail in the next sections.

Culture

The broadest and most abstract of the external factors that influence consumer behavior is **culture,** or the complexity of learned meanings, values, norms, and customs shared by members of a society. Cultural norms and values offer direction and

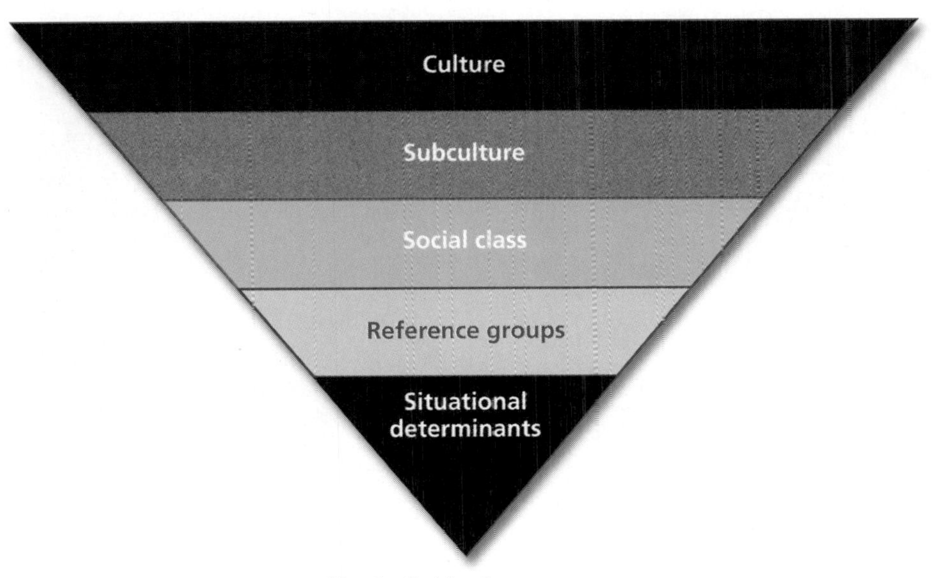

Figure 4–10 External influences on consumer behavior

guidance to members of a society in all aspects of their lives, including their consumption behavior. It is becoming increasingly important to study the impact of culture on consumer behavior as marketers expand their international marketing efforts. Each country has certain cultural traditions, customs, and values that marketers must understand as they develop marketing programs.

Marketers must also be aware of changes that may be occurring in a particular culture and the implications of these changes for their advertising and promotional strategies and programs. American culture continually goes through many changes that have direct implications for advertising. Marketing researchers monitor these changes and their impact on the ways companies market their products and services.

While marketers recognize that culture exerts a demonstrable influence on consumers, they often find it difficult to respond to cultural differences in different markets. The subtleties of various cultures are often difficult to understand and appreciate, but marketers must understand the cultural context in which consumer purchase decisions are made and adapt their advertising and promotional programs accordingly. Global Perspective 4–2 demonstrates differences in the way various cultures use the Internet.

Subcultures

Within a given culture are generally found smaller groups or segments whose beliefs, values, norms, and patterns of behavior set them apart from the larger cultural mainstream. These **subcultures** may be based on age, geographic, religious, racial, and/or ethnic differences. A number of subcultures exist within the United States. The three largest racial/ethnic subcultures are African-Americans, Hispanics, and various Asian groups. These racial/ethnic subcultures are important to marketers because of their size, growth, purchasing power, and distinct purchasing patterns. Marketers develop specific marketing programs for various products and services for these target markets. The ads in Exhibit 4–19 are just two of the many specifically designed to appeal to U.S. subcultures—in these cases, blacks and Hispanics. Many others can easily be found that target teens, Generations X and Y, the elderly, and so on.

Social Class

Virtually all societies exhibit some form of stratification whereby individuals can be assigned to a specific social category on the basis of criteria important to members of that society. **Social class** refers to relatively homogeneous divisions in a

Exhibit 4–19 Ads targeted to subcultures

Global Perspective 4–2

Consumer Behavior on the Internet—Not Really the World Wide Web?

It seems as if every day there is a new study reporting on the Internet shopper. Depending on what you read, the profile of such shoppers may vary, but in almost every case the profile is descriptive. Researchers know the consumers' gender and average age, their incomes, the number of times they get on the Net, and even how long they stay on once they are there. There is a wealth of information regarding users of the Internet—in the United States!

Although the commercial arm of the Internet is called the *World Wide Web,* much less is known about the consumer behaviors of users outside the United States. Some of the first studies regarding usage of the Net in other countries discussed habits in general terms and/or offered statistics relating to the number of people accessing the Web in different countries. Some even offered hypotheses as to why adoption of this new medium was different across cultures. Not much appeared, however, about consumer behaviors—even from a descriptive viewpoint—until two studies were reported in late 1999.

The first study, published by International Data Corporation (IDC), tabulated online survey responses from about 29,000 Internet users in over 100 countries. The researchers' conclusion was that buying behaviors on the Net differed substantially from country to country and even among neighboring countries. Here are some of the specific findings:

- Despite conventional belief, there are significant numbers of online customers in developing countries.
- Western Europe has the fastest Internet access, followed by the Asia-Pacific region, reporting the second-fastest links, and the United States, with the third-fastest.
- The U.S. user does more online purchasing than do users in any other country.
- The Japanese have the most access devices—25 percent report having three or more in their homes.
- Users are not necessarily "techies." All countries report a high number of users with little computer sophistication, including plumbers, teachers, and other people in nontechnical professions.

Media Metrix—one of the larger Internet research organizations—released what it calls the first detailed report on the surfing habits of Internet users in the United Kingdom, France, and Germany. The report's findings show that:

- German Web users spend the most time online, followed by the British and then the French.
- Germans spend about five hours a month, the British about four, and the French just three surfing the Web.
- In Germany and France, men outnumber women online by two to one; in the United Kingdom, as well as the United States, the numbers of men and women online are about equal.
- The most popular sites in France are Wanadoo, Yahoo, and Multimania. In Germany they are T-Online, Yahoo, and AOL; in the United Kingdom, Yahoo, Freeserve, and MSN. (In the United States, the most popular are About.com, Altavista, and Search services, followed by Amazon and Angelfire.)

Media Metrix obtained its results by monitoring Web usage in Europe on a real-time, click-by-click, page-by-page, minute-by-minute basis. While it did not report the number of persons monitored, the company says it currently has more than 50,000 people being measured in the United States alone.

So what does all this tell us? According to Mary Ann Packo, president of Media Metrix, the firm's research indicates that the Internet is truly a borderless medium and that, for the first time, companies now have access to research information on consumers outside the United States. John Gantz, chief research officer at IDC, notes: "The Web may be a global medium, but we found a lot of things about the way users behave in different countries that were counterintuitive to common perceptions about individual countries. . . . Some of the results we had will challenge the conventional wisdom about e-commerce in certain countries." According to Gantz, "Once you are on the Web you're immediately a global company—but you're not necessarily a success in every country."

While these studies certainly are not definitive, and are primarily descriptive, they are at least a start. Just as with marketing in the traditional marketplace, to be successful, Internet marketers will have to understand the consumers. They have started down this road—now let's see how far they go!

Sources: Tim Wilson, "Not a Global Village After All?—Consumer Behavior Varies Widely by Country, Study Says," *Internet Week,* December 6, 1999, p. 13; "Media Metrix European Web Surfing Figures Reveal All," Newsbytes.com, December 6, 1999.

"My darling child," said the Countess,
"tell a man you like his tie, and you will see his personality
unfold like a flower."
COUNTESS
MARA®
NECKWEAR

Exhibit 4–20 Countess Mara targets the upper classes

society into which people sharing similar lifestyles, values, norms, interests, and behaviors can be grouped. While a number of methods for determining social class exist, class structures in the United States are usually based on occupational status, educational attainment, and income. Sociologists generally agree there are three broad levels of social classes in the United States: the upper (14 percent), middle (70 percent), and lower (16 percent) classes.[30]

Social class is an important concept to marketers, since consumers within each social stratum often have similar values, lifestyles, and buying behavior. Thus, the various social class groups provide a natural basis for market segmentation. Consumers in the different social classes differ in the degree to which they use various products and services and in their leisure activities, shopping patterns, and media habits. Marketers respond to these differences through the positioning of their products and services, the media strategies they use to reach different social classes, and the types of advertising appeals they develop. The ad for Countess Mara in Exhibit 4–20 shows how a product attempts to appeal to the upper classes in both copy and illustration.

Reference Groups

Think about the last time you attended a party. As you dressed for the party, you probably asked yourself (or someone else) what others would be wearing. Your selection of attire may have been influenced by those likely to be present. This simple example reflects one form of impact that groups may exert on your behavior.

A group has been defined as "two or more individuals who share a set of norms, values, or beliefs and have certain implicitly or explicitly defined relationships to one another such that their behavior is interdependent."[31] Groups are one of the primary factors influencing learning and socialization, and group situations constitute many of our purchase decisions.

A **reference group** is "a group whose presumed perspectives or values are being used by an individual as the basis for his or her judgments, opinions, and actions." Consumers use reference groups as a guide to specific behaviors, even when the groups are not present.[32] In the party example, your peers—although not present—provided a standard of dress that you referred to in your clothing selection. Likewise, your college classmates, family, and co-workers, or even a group to which you aspire, may serve as referents, and your consumption patterns will typically conform to the expectations of the groups that are most important to you.

Marketers use reference group influences in developing advertisements and promotional strategies. The ads in Exhibit 4–21 are examples of *aspirational* reference groups (to which we might like to belong) and *disassociative* groups (to which we do not wish to belong), respectively.

Family Decision Making: An Example of Group Influences

In some instances, the group may be involved more directly than just as a referent. Family members may serve as referents to each other, or they may actually be involved in the purchase decision process—acting as an individual buying unit. As shown in Figure 4–11, family members may assume a variety of roles in the decision-making process.[33] Each role has implications for marketers.

First, the advertiser must determine who is responsible for the various roles in the decision-making process so messages can be targeted at that person (or those people). These roles will also dictate media strategies, since the appropriate magazines, newspapers, or TV or radio stations must be used. Second, understanding the decision-making process and the use of information by individual family members is critical to the design of messages and choice of promotional program elements. In sum, to create an effective promotional program, a marketer must have an overall understanding of how the decision process works and the role that each family member plays.

Exhibit 4–21 The ad on the left shows an aspirational reference group; the one on the right stresses a disassociative reference group

Situational Determinants

The final external factor is the purchase and usage situation. The specific situation in which consumers plan to use the product or brand directly affects their perceptions, preferences, and purchasing behaviors.[34] Three types of **situational determinants** may have an effect: the specific usage situation, the purchase situation, and the communications situation.

Figure 4–11 Roles in the family decision-making process

The initiator. The person responsible for initiating the purchase decision process; for example, the mother who determines she needs a new car.

The information provider. The individual responsible for gathering information to be used in making the decision; for example, the teenage car buff who knows where to find product information in specific magazines or collects it from dealers.

The influencer. The person who exerts influence as to what criteria will be used in the selection process. All members of the family may be involved. The mother may have her criteria, whereas others may each have their own input.

The decision maker(s). That person(s) who actually makes the decision. In our example, it may be the mother alone or in combination with another family member.

The purchasing agent. That individual who performs the physical act of making the purchase. In the case of a car, a husband and wife may decide to choose it together and sign the purchase agreement.

The consumer. The actual user of the product. In the case of a family car, all family members are consumers. For a private car, only the mother might be the consumer.

Usage refers to the circumstance in which the product will be used. For example, purchases made for private consumption may be thought of differently from those that will be obvious to the public. The *purchase* situation more directly involves the environment operating at the time of the purchase. Time constraints, store environments, and other factors may all have an impact. The *communications* situation is the condition in which an advertising exposure occurs (in a car listening to the radio, with friends, etc.). This may be most relevant to the development of promotional strategies, because the impact on the consumer will vary according to the particular situation. For example, a consumer may pay more attention to a commercial that is heard alone at home than to one heard in the presence of friends, at work, or anywhere distractions may be present. If advertisers can isolate a particular time when the listener is likely to be attentive, they will probably earn his or her undivided attention.

In sum, situational determinants may either enhance or detract from the potential success of a message. To the degree that advertisers can assess situational influences that may be operating, they will increase the likelihood of successfully communicating with their target audiences.

Alternative Approaches to Consumer Behavior

The preceding discussion of consumer behavior focused on consumer decision making as viewed from several psychological perspectives. However, in the past decade, a growing number of consumer researchers have examined this process from a different perspective, often referred to as *alternative, interpretive, postmodern,* or *postpositivist.* Regardless of the name, *alternative* ways of attempting to understand consumer behavior assume a cross-disciplinary approach. Consumer decision making is viewed from different perspectives and nonquantitative research methodologies are used to broaden the discipline from a sociopsychological focus. Multisensory, fantasy, and emotive aspects of consumer behavior are examined through research techniques such as individual interviews, ethnographic participant observer studies, and interpretative analyses commonly employed in disciplines outside the psychological arena (semiotics, literary criticism, philosophy, history). This orientation is shaped by research with roots in anthropological, sociological, and historical studies.

Those who conduct research from this perspective believe that consumers' decision-making processes do not occur in isolation. Rather, they view consumer decision making as influenced by cultural, linguistic, and historical factors. They use historical and situational contexts to add insights to our understanding of consumer behavior. In examining the significance of communications, they have adopted three perspectives:

- *Sociocultural.* Advertising and other forms of communication are viewed as both influencing and being influenced by culture. That is, consumers' interpretations of ads are shaped by their cultural values, and in turn, these ads will (over time) shape the culture themselves.
- *Structural.* Consumption behaviors are examined to discover underlying meanings. For example, the symbolic meanings of advertising are examined in regard to their association with the cultural stack of stories and myths.
- *Semiotic.* Products and ads are examined for their symbolic meanings to consumers—for example, the meanings of words. In addition, consumer "rituals" such as fashion codes, gift giving, and rumormongering are studied.

As you can see, the variety of titles assigned to this domain of consumer behavior research reflects the multidimensional perspectives from which consumers are viewed. Studies of how consumers make decisions and the impact of communications (both *on* the consumer and *by* the consumer) are shedding new light in consumer research.

Summary

This chapter introduced you to the field of consumer behavior and examined its relevance to promotional strategy. Consumer behavior is best viewed as the process and activities that people engage in when searching for, selecting, purchasing, using, evaluating, and disposing of products and services to satisfy their needs and desires. A five-stage model of the consumer decision-making process consists of problem recognition, information search, alternative evaluation, purchase, and postpurchase evaluation. Internal psychological processes that influence the consumer decision-making process include motivation, perception, attitude formation and change, and integration processes.

The decision process model views consumer behavior primarily from a cognitive orientation. The chapter considered other perspectives by examining various approaches to consumer learning and their implications for advertising and promotion. Behavioral learning theories such as classical conditioning and operant (instrumental) conditioning were discussed. Problems with behavioral learning theories were noted, and the alternative perspective of cognitive learning was discussed.

The chapter also examined relevant external factors that influence consumer decision making. Culture, subculture, social class, reference groups, and situational determinants were discussed, along with their implications for the development of promotional strategies and programs. The chapter concluded with an introduction to alternative perspectives on the study of consumer behavior (also called interpretive, postmodern, or postpositivist perspectives).

Key Terms

- consumer behavior, 107
- problem recognition, 108
- want, 109
- motives, 110
- hierarchy of needs, 110
- psychoanalytic theory, 111
- motivation research, 111
- internal search, 113
- external search, 113
- perception, 114
- sensation, 114
- selective perception, 115
- selective exposure, 115
- selective attention, 115
- selective comprehension, 115
- selective retention, 115
- mnemonics, 115
- subliminal perception, 115
- evaluative criteria, 118
- functional consequences, 118
- psychosocial consequences, 118
- multiattribute attitude model, 119
- salient beliefs, 119
- integration processes, 121
- heuristics, 121
- affect referral decision rule, 121
- purchase intention, 121
- brand loyalty, 121
- cognitive dissonance, 123
- classical conditioning, 125
- conditioned stimulus, 125
- conditioned response, 125
- operant conditioning, 127
- reinforcement, 127
- schedules of reinforcement, 127
- shaping, 128
- culture, 129
- subcultures, 130
- social class, 130
- reference group, 132
- situational determinants, 133

Discussion Questions

1. Psychoanalytic theory has been criticized for its problems with validity and reliability. How do the current methods discussed in the lead-in—for example, hypnosis—fare in regard to these criteria?

2. Explain how consumers might engage in each of the processes of selective perception described in the chapter. Provide examples.

3. Focusing on the multiattribute attitude model discussed in the chapter, discuss how marketers might change consumers' beliefs about a product or service. Also explain how attitude change might be achieved through changing the importance of these beliefs. Cite current examples.

4. Describe how cultural differences might impact viewers' perceptions of advertisements. Provide examples.

5. In the text it was indicated that families may influence the consumer decision-making process. Describe how various family members may assume the different roles described in Figure 4–11. Also explain how these roles might change depending upon the product under consideration.

6. The text discusses alternative approaches to studying consumer behavior. Explain how these approaches differ from those described earlier in the chapter.

7. Explain how the screening processes involved in selective perception might impact a viewer of television commercials.

8. What is subliminal perception? Describe how marketers are attempting to use this concept in the marketing of goods and services.

9. Discuss the three variations of the consumer decision-making process. What is the importance of communications in each type?

10. Postmodern research often involves a sociological perspective to understanding consumer behavior. Give examples of how sociology might impact purchase behaviors.

Chapter Five

The Communication Process

Chapter Objectives

- To understand the basic elements of the communication process and the role of communications in marketing.
- To examine various models of the communication process.
- To analyze the response processes of receivers of marketing communications, including alternative response hierarchies and their implications for promotional planning and strategy.
- To examine the nature of consumers' cognitive processing of marketing communications.

Inventing the New HP

The Hewlett-Packard Company was founded 60 years ago by Bill Hewlett and Dave Packard in a one-car garage in Palo Alto, California, with only $538 of combined personal capital. The company, which became known to most in the business world as "HP," is credited with spawning Silicon Valley, the region south of San Francisco where numerous high-technology companies began and are located today. HP's first commercial products were used for testing and measurement and led to HP's becoming the dominant company in this industry. HP later moved into the computer market and became the world's second-largest computing company. It then moved into the computer printer market and became the world's largest printing and imaging company. By the end of the 90s HP had grown to a $40 billion giant and was one of the best-known and most respected companies in the world. However, in 1999, after spinning off its test and measurement business, HP announced plans to reinvent itself as a computing and imaging company committed to making the Internet work for people.

While HP was well recognized, thanks in large part to its successful personal computer and printer business, it did not feel its image was consistent with the direction the company wanted to go in as part of its reinvention. HP had a powerful and positive brand image with customers as a company that was honest, well-respected, quality-minded, and that offered customers practical and useful solutions to their problems. However, it had developed a somewhat stodgy image as well, and there were misperceptions that the company was slow, not very responsive, and connected with the "old-guard" companies. Despite its size and history, HP was rarely seen as an innovative company, particularly in marketing fast-moving businesses such as the Internet.

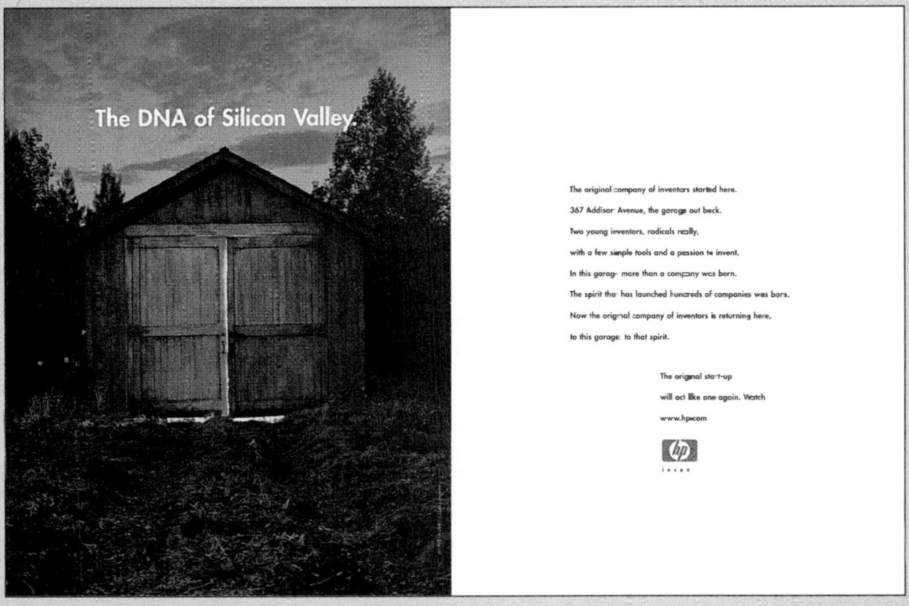

In late 1999, Carly Fiorina, HP's new president and chief executive officer, announced plans for a global branding campaign as part of her efforts to revitalize the company. The goal of the campaign is to build an image that reflects the type of company HP is today—dynamic, fast, inventive, committed, effective, and savvy. According to Fiorina, the intent is to remind employees, customers, and investors of HP's roots as a company started in a garage by David Packard and William Hewlett in 1939 and to rededicate the company to "inventive" ways of making unique products and helping customers solve problems. She notes, "Our new brand sends a 360-degree message. It starts with our employee audience and extends to everyone we work with and work for."

As one of the first steps in the campaign, Fiorina unveiled a new logo for HP during a keynote speech at COMDEX, the leading convention and trade show for the computer industry. The logo, which is designed to be more contemporary and convey a faster, more committed and invigorated company, features the HP initials without the name spelled out. The word *invent* underscores the logo, reflecting HP's roots as a company of inventors and one that has successfully reinvented itself many times to take advantage of new markets. The rationale behind the new logo is that the word *invent* lays the foundation for HP's future while leveraging HP's heritage as a company built on change and reinvention. Just as the brand name Coke is synonymous with refreshment and Nike is known for achievement, HP wants its customers to think of the word "inventiveness" when they think of the company.

The advertising campaign developed to support HP's new branding strategy began in December 1999 with "teaser" ads both in print and on television that use the original garage as a symbol of HP's enduring spirit of inventiveness. CEO Fiorina appears in and does the voice-over for two of the TV commercials in the campaign, which are called "Original Radicals" and "Wonderful Traveling Garage." Ms. Fiorina's participation was viewed as a way to show real commitment by her and HP. For example, in "Original Radicals" she describes HP's founders as radicals who launched their company in a garage with the mandate of inventing something useful and significant—an idea so simple that it was radical. She goes on to assert "The original start-up will act like one again . . . watch."

After running the teaser ads, HP shifted to TV spots and print messages that feature more specific descriptions of how the company plans to apply its ingenuity. HP began running the ads in international markets in 2000 and expected to spend about $200 million in the first year of the campaign to promote its new image. CEO Fiorina noted, "One of the things about HP is that we didn't used to talk about ourselves much. That's going to change." She views the new ad campaign as the first step in a multiyear journey that will enable HP to deliver on its brand promise and return to the "rules of the garage"—the original ideas that made the company great.

Sources: David P. Hamilton, "H-P to Relaunch Its Brand, Adopt New Logo," *The Wall Street Journal,* November 16, 1999, p. B8; Tom Quinlan, "Hewlett-Packard Launches Campaign to Energize Image," *San Jose Mercury News,* November 16, 1999; "HP CEO Fiorina Launches New Brand, New Logo," News Releases, www.hp.com, November 15, 1999.

The function of all elements of the integrated marketing communications program is to communicate. An organization's IMC strategy is implemented through the various communications it sends to current or prospective customers as well as other relevant publics. Organizations send communications and messages in a variety of ways, such as through advertisements, brand names, logos and graphic systems, websites, press releases, package designs, promotions, and visual images. Thus, those involved in the planning and implementation of an IMC program need to understand the communications process and how it occurs. As you can see from the opening vignette on the Hewlett-Packard Company, the way marketers communicate with their target audiences depends on many factors, including how much customers know and what they think about the company and the image it hopes to create. Developing an effective marketing communications program is far more complicated than just choosing a product feature or attribute to emphasize. Marketers must understand how consumers will perceive and interpret their messages and how these reactions will shape consumers' responses to the company and/or its product or service.

This chapter reviews the fundamentals of communication and examines various perspectives and models regarding how consumers respond to advertising and promotional messages. Our goal is to demonstrate how valuable an understanding of the communication process can be in planning, implementing, and evaluating the marketing communications program.

The Nature of Communication

Communication has been variously defined as the passing of information, the exchange of ideas, or the process of establishing a commonness or oneness of thought between a sender and a receiver.[1] These definitions suggest that for communication to occur, there must be some common thinking between two parties and information must be passed from one person to another (or from one group to another). As you will see in this chapter, establishing this commonality in thinking is not always as easy as it might seem; many attempts to communicate are unsuccessful.

The communication process is often very complex. Success depends on such factors as the nature of the message, the audience's interpretation of it, and the environment in which it is received. The receiver's perception of the source and the medium used to transmit the message may also affect the ability to communicate, as do many other factors. Words, pictures, sounds, and colors may have different meanings to different audiences, and people's perceptions and interpretations of them vary. For example, if you ask for a soda on the East Coast or West Coast, you'll receive a soft drink such as Coke or Pepsi. However, in parts of the Midwest and South, a soft drink is referred to as pop. If you ask for a soda, you may get a glass of pop with ice cream in it. Marketers must understand the meanings that words and symbols take on and how they influence consumers' interpretation of products and messages. This can be particularly challenging to companies marketing their products in foreign countries, as discussed in Global Perspective 5–1.

A Basic Model of Communication

Over the years, a basic model of the various elements of the communication process has evolved, as shown in Figure 5–1.[2] Two elements represent the major participants in the communication process, the sender and the receiver. Another two are the major communication tools, message and channel. Four others are the major communication functions and processes: encoding, decoding, response, and feedback. The last element, noise, refers to any extraneous factors in the system that can interfere with the process and work against effective communication.

Figure 5–1 A model of the communication process

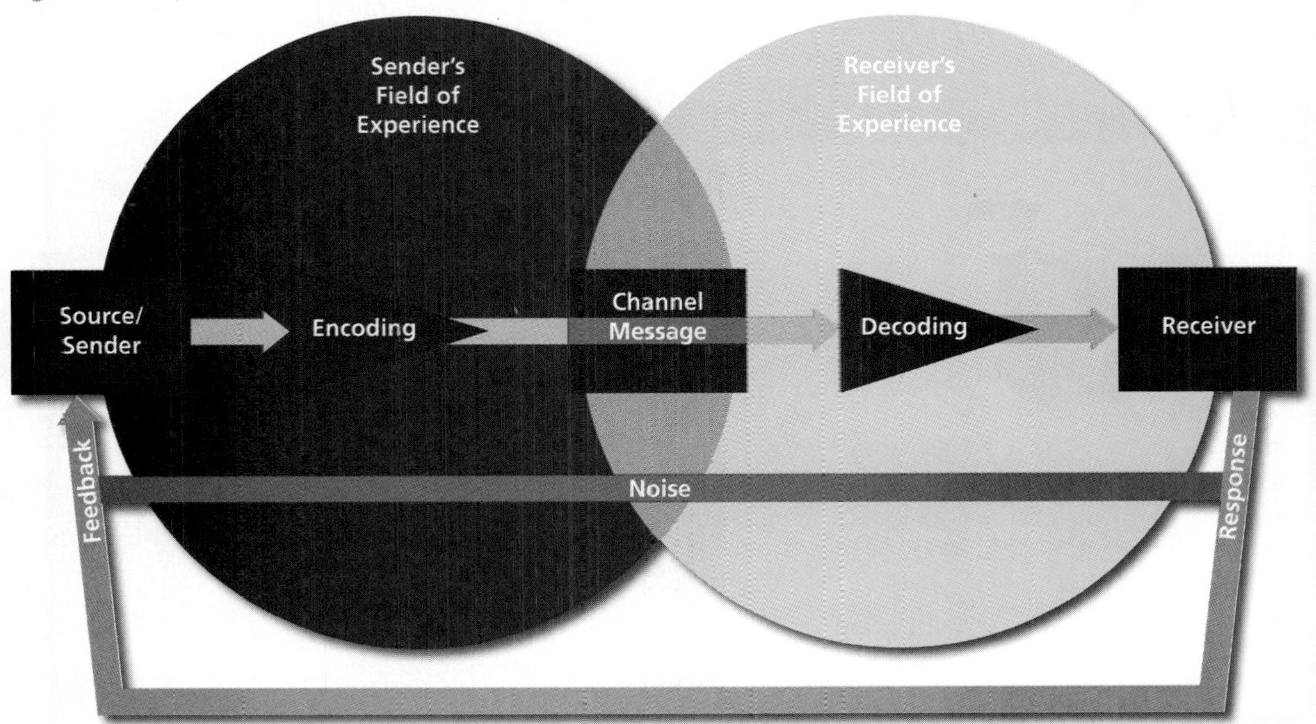

Global Perspective 5–1

Communication Problems in International Marketing

Communication is a major problem facing companies that market their products in foreign countries. Language is one of the main barriers to effective communication, as there are different languages in different countries, different languages or dialects within a single country, and more subtle problems of linguistic nuance and vernacular. International marketers must also be aware of the connotation of the words, signs, symbols, and expressions they use as brand names or logos or in various forms of promotion. Advertising copy, slogans, and symbols do not always transfer well into other languages. This not only impedes communication but also sometimes results in embarrassing blunders that can damage a company's or brand's credibility or image and cost it customers.

Mistranslations and faulty word choices have often created problems for firms engaging in international marketing. For example, the slogan "Come alive with Pepsi" translated too literally in some countries. The German translation was "Come out of the grave," while in Chinese it read, "Pepsi brings your ancestors back from the dead." A U.S. airline competing in Brazil advertised "rendezvous lounges" in its planes—until it discovered that in the Brazilian dialect of Portuguese this meant a place to make love. Budweiser's long-time slogan "The King of Beers" translates in Spanish as "Queen of Beers" because the noun *cerveza* (beer) has a feminine ending.

International marketers can also have linguistic problems with product and brand names and their meaning or pronunciation. China has many languages and dialects, with differences great enough that people from different regions of the country often cannot understand each other. Even among those who speak the same language, such as Mandarin, there often are substantial differences in the way the language is used. For example, *ji xuan ji* would be understood as "calculator" among Singaporean and Malaysian residents who speak Mandarin but as "computer" among many Chinese and Taiwanese Mandarin speakers. When Coca-Cola introduced its product to China, the Chinese characters sounded like *Coca-Cola* but meant "bite the wax tadpole." With the help of a language specialist, the company substituted four Mandarin characters that still sound like *Coca-Cola* but mean "can happy, mouth happy."

International marketers may also encounter problems with the way certain cultures interpret visual signs and symbols as well as nonverbal forms of communication. For example, signaling by making a circle with the thumb and forefinger has different meanings in various cultures. It means "OK" or "the best" to Americans and most Europeans, "money" to the Japanese, and "rudeness" to the Brazilians, while having a vulgar connotation in some Latin American countries. AT&T found that the thumbs-up in its "I plan" long-distance phone campaign presented a problem. Thumbs up signifies affirmation to most Americans, but to Russians and Poles, the fact that the person's palm was visible gave the ad an offensive meaning. AT&T hired a company that specialzies in translations to reshoot the graphic element in the ad so that only the back of the hand showed, conveying the intended meaning.

Company and brand names can also get lost in translation. Before launching *Good Housekeeping* magazine in Japan, the Hearst Corporation experimented with a number of Japanese translations of the title. The closest word in Japanese, *kaji,* means "domestic duties," which can be interpreted as work performed by servants. Hearst decided to retain the American name for the magazine but the word *Good* appears in much larger type on the front cover than the word *Housekeeping.*

самаЯ-самая
СамаЯ высокая степень сервиса, предоставляемого сегодня,
не предел для AT&T. Уже завтра, с помощью программы "Я План",
я смогу получить большее.
Как только я позвоню в AT&T по номеру 1 800 542-2025.
This advertisement was prepared by
YAR Communications, Inc.
Russian

The fast-food chain Wienerschnitzel (which in Germany means "breaded veal cutlet" rather than "hot dog") had to deal with the fact that its name is a mouthful, particularly for Spanish-speaking consumers. When the chain expanded into Mexico, its franchise shortened the name to Wieners so that people could pronounce it. Disc jockeys doing radio ads were told to read the name slowly and identify Wienerschnitzel as the place with the big red "W" on its sign.

Many multinational companies are trying to develop world brands that can be marketed internationally using the same brand name and advertising. However, they must be careful that brand names, advertising slogans, signs, symbols, and other forms of marketing communications don't lose something in the translation and are not misinterpreted by consumers in foreign countries.

Sources: Kevin Reagan, "In Asia, Think Globally, Communicate Locally," *Marketing News,* July 19, 1999, pp. 12, 14; Yumiko Ono, "Will *Good Housekeeping* Translate into Japanese?" *The Wall Street Journal,* December 30, 1997, p. B1; Greg Johnson, "Fast-Food Firms Learn Lessons of *El Mercado,*" *Los Angeles Times,* October 8, 1996, pp. A1, 16.

Source Encoding

The sender, or **source,** of a communication is the person or organization that has information to share with another person or group of people. The source may be an individual (say, a salesperson or hired spokesperson, such as a celebrity, who appears in a company's advertisements) or a nonpersonal entity (such as the corporation or organization itself). For example, the source of the ad shown in the opening vignette is the Hewlett-Packard Company, since no specific spokesperson or source is shown. However, in the ad shown in Exhibit 5–1, HP's CEO Carly Fiorina is also a source since she appears as a spokesperson for the company in the commercial.

Because the receiver's perceptions of the source influence how the communication is received, marketers must be careful to select a communicator the receiver believes is knowledgeable and trustworthy or with whom the receiver can identify or relate in some manner. (How these characteristics influence the receiver's responses is discussed further in Chapter 6.)

The communication process begins when the source selects words, symbols, pictures, and the like, to represent the message that will be delivered to the receiver(s). This process, known as **encoding,** involves putting thoughts, ideas, or information into a symbolic form. The sender's goal is to encode the message in such a way that it will be understood by the receiver. This means using words, signs, or symbols that are familiar to the target audience. Many symbols have universal meaning, such as the familiar circle with a line through it to denote no parking, no smoking, and so forth. Many companies also have highly recognizable symbols—such as McDonald's golden arches, Nike's swoosh, or the Coca-Cola trademark—that are known to consumers around the world.

Exhibit 5–1 Hewlett-Packard CEO Carly Fiorina appears as a spokesperson for the company in this commercial

Message

The encoding process leads to development of a **message** that contains the information or meaning the source hopes to convey. The message may be verbal or nonverbal, oral or written, or symbolic. Messages must be put into a transmittable form that is appropriate for the channel of communication being used. In advertising, this may range from simply writing some words or copy that will be read as a radio message to producing an expensive television commercial. For many products, it is not the actual words of the message that determine its communication effectiveness but rather the impression or image the ad creates. Notice how Spellbound perfume in Exhibit 5–2 uses only a picture to deliver its message. However, the product name and picture help communicate a feeling of attraction and fascination between the man and woman shown in the ad.

To better understand the symbolic meaning that might be conveyed in a communication, advertising and marketing researchers have begun focusing attention on **semiotics,** which studies the nature of meaning and asks how our reality—words, gestures, myths, signs, symbols, products/services, theories—acquire meaning.[3] Semiotics is important in marketing communications since products and brands acquire meaning through the way they are advertised and consumers use products and brands to express their social identities. Consumer researcher Michael Solomon notes: "From a semiotic perspective, every marketing message has three basic components: an object, a sign or symbol and an interpretant. The object is the product that is the focus of the message (e.g., Marlboro cigarettes). The sign is the sensory imagery that represents the intended meanings of the object (e.g., the Marlboro cowboy). The interpretant is the meaning derived (e.g., rugged, individualistic, American)."[4]

Marketers may use individuals trained in semiotics and related fields such as cultural anthropology to better understand the conscious and subconscious meanings the nonverbal signs and symbols in their ads transmit to consumers. For example, Levi Strauss & Co.'s agency, TBWA/Chiat/Day, hired a cultural anthropologist to help it better understand the image and meaning of clothing and fashion among young consumers. As part of the process, the agency research team recruited hip-looking young people in the streets of the East Village section of New York City, an area picked because they felt it is the best reflection of today's youth life. Those chosen were handed a piece of red cardboard and a white marker and asked to "write down something you believe in; something that's true about you or your world." The process provided the agency with insight into the teen market and was the impetus for an ad campaign featuring teenagers holding placards inscribed with their philosophical messages.[5] Exhibit 5–3 shows the thinking behind the various

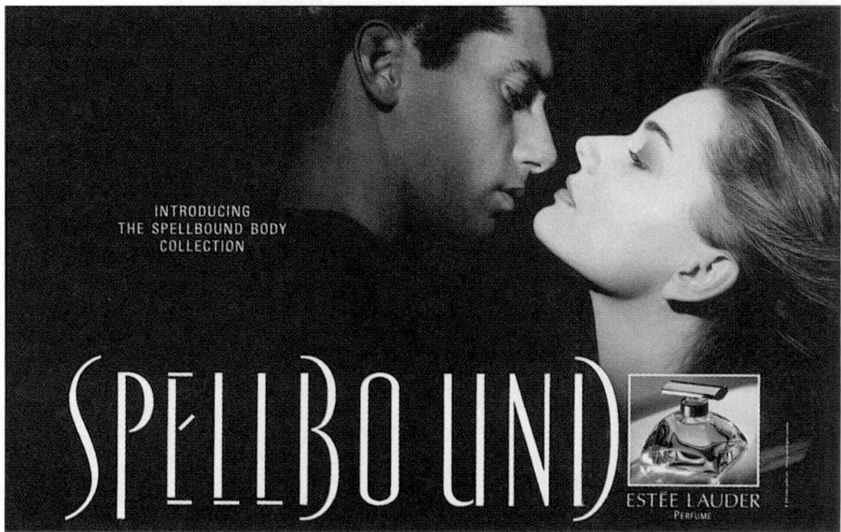

Exhibit 5–2 The image projected by an ad often communicates more than words

Exhibit 5–3 Semiotic analysis is used to describe the various elements of this Levi's ad

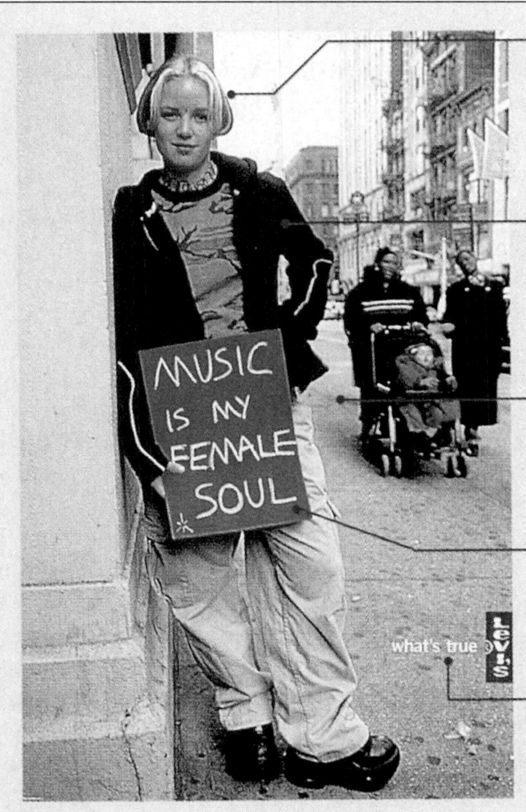

THE MODEL: A premed student at New York University
"We wanted people who are not defined by what they do but by what they are. We chose her because she looks like a Levi's type. She's young. She has her own point of view. She's sexy, but in an understated way. She's not trying too hard. She's definitely got something about her."

THE CLOTHES: Levi's cargo pants, her own T-shirt, zip-up sweatshirt, combat boots, and accessories
"It's important that she wore what she wanted. We're not trying to create a Levi's uniform; that wouldn't be very 'real.' We didn't use a professional stylist or a hairdresser; that wouldn't be real."

THE SETTING: Manhattan's East Village
"We picked New York City because it's the best reflection of today's youth life. We drove around the grittiest parts of the city. The people in the background [of this image] give it a street feel; it's obviously not staged in a studio."

THE STATEMENT: "Music is my female soul"
"It's hard for people to believe, but the [language] came totally from the kids; there was no prompting.... We liked the music theme [in this statement] because we do a lot to promote original music; we see music as being *the* voice of the young people."

THE TAG LINE: "What's true"
"The challenge with youth marketing these days is not to dictate to kids. This [line] is both a statement and a question. Is what we're saying true? Or is it a declaration? It works because it's provocative and ambiguous."

elements of one of the ads used in the campaign as explained by Sean Dee, the director of the Levi's brand.

Some advertising and marketing people are skeptical about the value of semiotics. They question whether social scientists read too much into advertising messages and are overly intellectual in interpreting them. However, the meaning of an advertising message or other form of marketing communication lies not in the message but with the people who see and interpret it. Moreover, consumers behave on the basis of meanings they ascribe to marketplace stimuli. Thus, marketers must consider the meanings consumers attach to the various signs and symbols. Semiotics may be helpful in analyzing how various aspects of the marketing program—such as advertising messages, packaging, brand names, and even the nonverbal communications of salespeople (gestures, mode of dress)—are interpreted by receivers.[6]

Channel

The **channel** is the method by which the communication travels from the source or sender to the receiver. At the broadest level, channels of communication are of two types, personal and nonpersonal. *Personal channels* of communication are direct interpersonal (face-to-face) contact with target individuals or groups. Salespeople serve as personal channels of communication when they deliver their sales message to a buyer or potential customer. Social channels of communication such as friends, neighbors, associates, co-workers, or family members are also personal channels. They often represent *word-of-mouth communication,* a powerful source of information for consumers.[7]

Nonpersonal channels of communication are those that carry a message without interpersonal contact between sender and receiver. Nonpersonal channels are generally referred to as the **mass media** or mass communications, since the message is sent to many individuals at one time. For example, a TV commercial broadcast on a prime-time show may be seen by 20 million households in a given evening. Nonpersonal channels of communication consist of two major types, print and broadcast. Print media include newspapers, magazines, direct mail, and billboards; broadcast media include radio and television.

Receiver/Decoding

The **receiver** is the person(s) with whom the sender shares thoughts or information. Generally, receivers are the consumers in the target market or audience who read, hear, and/or see the marketer's message and decode it. **Decoding** is the process of transforming the sender's message back into thought. This process is heavily influenced by the receiver's frame of reference or **field of experience,** which refers to the experiences, perceptions, attitudes, and values he or she brings to the communication situation.

For effective communication to occur, the message decoding process of the receiver must match the encoding of the sender. Simply put, this means the receiver understands and correctly interprets what the source is trying to communicate. As Figure 5–1 showed, the source and the receiver each have a frame of reference (the circle around each) that they bring to the communication situation. Effective communication is more likely when there is some *common ground* between the two parties. (This is represented by the overlapping of the two circles.) The more knowledge the sender has about the receivers, the better the sender can understand their needs, empathize with them, and communicate effectively.

While this notion of common ground between sender and receiver may sound basic, it often causes great difficulty in the advertising communications process. Marketing and advertising people often have very different fields of experience from the consumers who constitute the mass markets with whom they must communicate. Most advertising and marketing people are college-educated and work and/or reside in large urban areas such as New York, Chicago, or Los Angeles. Yet they are attempting to develop commercials that will effectively communicate with millions of consumers who have never attended college, work in blue-collar occupations, and live in rural areas or small towns. The executive creative director of a large advertising agency described how advertising executives become isolated from the cultural mainstream: "We pull them in and work them to death. And then they begin moving in sushi circles and lose touch with Velveeta and the people who eat it."[8]

Another factor that can lead to problems in establishing common ground between senders and receivers is age. IMC Perspective 5–2 discusses some interesting findings from a study that considered problems younger advertising professionals have in developing ads for older consumers.

Advertisers spend millions of dollars every year to understand the frames of reference of the target markets who receive their messages. They also spend much time and money pretesting messages to make sure consumers understand and decode them in the manner the advertiser intended.

Noise

Throughout the communication process, the message is subject to extraneous factors that can distort or interfere with its reception. This unplanned distortion or interference is known as **noise.** Errors or problems that occur in the encoding of the message, distortion in a radio or television signal, or distractions at the point of reception are examples of noise. When you are watching your favorite commercial on TV and a problem occurs in the signal transmission, it will obviously interfere with your reception, lessening the impact of the commercial.

Noise may also occur because the fields of experience of the sender and receiver don't overlap. Lack of common ground may result in improper encoding of the message—using a sign, symbol, or words that are unfamiliar or have different meaning to the receiver. The more common ground there is between the sender and the receiver, the less likely it is this type of noise will occur.

IMC Perspective 5–2

Is Ageism a Problem in Advertising?

It has often been argued that people who work in advertising are different from the typical consumers who represent the target markets for the clients' products and services. Some say advertising may better reflect those who work in the industry than the consuming public. Critics argue that most advertising is really about the people who create it, not about the consumers who actually buy the products being advertised.

A study conducted a few years ago on ageism in advertising considered potential problems that might arise because of age differences between agency personnel and older consumers. The study, which was conducted by High-Yield Marketing in conjunction with the Association of Advertising Agencies International, found that professionals who work in advertising agencies are much younger than the majority of the U.S. adult population. Nearly 40 percent of ad agency professionals are between the ages of 30 and 39, while only 20 percent of all adults are in their 30s.

While advertising agencies are largely staffed by young people, the youth bias is particularly evident in the creative departments. Agency employment drops like a rock after age 40, particularly among those involved in creating the ads. As a result, agencies rarely have creative professionals with a true understanding of life after age 40, not to mention life after 60 or 70. The report noted that "the majority of advertising agency professionals are in early adulthood, when empathic understanding for people of different generations is relatively unknown" and "most agency professionals are most comfortable advertising to younger consumers like themselves." Richard Lee, a principal of High-Yield Marketing, notes: "Most young agency staff, reflective of their life phase, are fixated on creating advertising that is hip, cool, impressive to their peers, and award-winning. This is more fulfilling than creating advertising for people with dated tastes who wouldn't know Smashing Pumpkins if they stepped on them."

Advertisers who are unable to connect with the so-called mature market may be squandering opportunities to reach a valuable market. People who are 50 or older and head a household account for 43 percent of the U.S. population and control more than 40 percent of discretionary income. Moreover, the number of Americans in their 50s will increase by 40 percent over the next 10 years. Many observers wonder why advertisers remain focused on consumers in their teens, 20s, and early 30s when spending power is becoming progressively more concentrated among those aged 50 and older. One reason may be that the conventional wisdom in marketing and advertising tells us that household formation is something that people do in their 20s and early 30s; so is buying homes, furniture, and appliances; so, especially, is buying clothing and supplies for babies and children; so is forming brand preferences that stick for life.

Another reason for the youth bias in advertising is the myths that persist about the older consumer, among both agencies and clients. Older people are stereotyped as unlikely to change brands and try something new and as less affluent than younger consumers. There is also the problem of advertisers not wanting to have their products and services perceived as being for older consumers for fear of damaging their brand images among younger consumers. The unfortunate result of these fallacies is that they can become a self-fulfilling prophecy. When older people see nothing directed at them, they gradually lose their sense of themselves as consumers, and this dampens their spending. Richard Lee notes that the youth bias in advertising is impeding the normal development of a healthy and profitable market of goods and services for people in their 50s and beyond.

Of course, not everyone in the advertising industry agrees with the findings of the ageism study. One agency executive calls the conclusions ridiculous, noting, "We have people of every age segment here." The president of the American Association of Advertising Agencies says, "Clearly in the case of the top 20 or 30 agencies, they have a balanced population that reflects the ages of the country's population. I'm not sure that is the case with smaller and mid-size agencies, nor with the new hotshot creative agencies simply because of who they would attract."

There has been some excellent advertising targeted at mature consumers over the past few years. Nike has run a series of ads featuring senior athletes, and Quaker Oats has been running ads featuring "George," a 60-something model who wears a muscle shirt revealing biceps that would be the envy of anyone 20 years younger. However, many believe that good ads targeted at older consumers are still too few and far between and that the youth bias in advertising is a major problem. They note that the best hope for the demise of the primary focus on youth in advertising is the marketing people who are growing and maturing themselves. Some feel that it has finally dawned on Madison Avenue, and on marketing people in general, that they ought to follow the green—which is quickly going gray. As one agency executive noted, "After all, Mick Jagger is in his 50s and is a grandfather."

Sources: Richard Lee, "The Youth Bias in Advertising," *American Demographics,* January 1997, pp. 47–50; Kevin Goldman, "Study Finds Agency Employees Favor Ads Directed at the Young," *The Wall Street Journal,* May 54, 1995, p. B8.

Response/Feedback

The receiver's set of reactions after seeing, hearing, or reading the message is known as a **response.** Receivers' responses can range from nonobservable actions such as storing information in memory to immediate action such as dialing a toll-free number to order a product advertised on television. Marketers are very interested in **feedback,** that part of the receiver's response that is communicated back to the sender. Feedback, which may take a variety of forms, closes the loop in the communications flow and lets the sender monitor how the intended message is being decoded and received.

For example, in a personal selling situation, customers may pose questions, comments, or objections or indicate their reactions through nonverbal responses such as gestures and frowns.[9] The salesperson has the advantage of receiving instant feedback through the customer's reactions. But this is generally not the case when mass media are used. Because advertisers are not in direct contact with the customers, they must use other means to determine how their messages have been received. While the ultimate form of feedback occurs through sales, it is often hard to show a direct relationship between advertising and purchase behavior. So marketers use other methods to obtain feedback, among them customer inquiries, store visits, coupon redemptions, and reply cards. Research-based feedback analyzes readership and recall of ads, message comprehension, attitude change, and other forms of response. With this information, the advertiser can determine reasons for success or failure in the communication process and make adjustments.

Successful communication is accomplished when the marketer selects an appropriate source, develops an effective message or appeal that is encoded properly, and then selects the channels or media that will best reach the target audience so that the message can be effectively decoded and delivered. In Chapter 6, we will examine the source, message, and channel decisions and see how promotional planners work with these controllable variables to develop communication strategies. Since these decisions must consider how the target audience will respond to the promotional message, the remainder of this chapter examines the receiver and the process by which consumers respond to advertising and other forms of marketing communications.

Analyzing the Receiver

To communicate effectively with their customers, marketers must understand who the target audience is, what (if anything) it knows or feels about the company's product or service, and how to communicate with the audience to influence its decision-making process. Marketers must also know how the market is likely to respond to various sources of communication or different types of messages. Before they make decisions regarding source, message, and channel variables, promotional planners must understand the potential effects associated with each of these factors. This section focuses on the receiver of the marketing communication. It examines how the audience is identified and the process it may go through in responding to a promotional message. This information serves as a foundation for evaluating the controllable communication variable decisions in the next chapter.

Identifying the Target Audience

The marketing communication process really begins with identifying the audience that will be the focus of the firm's advertising and promotional efforts. The target audience may consist of individuals, groups, niche markets, market segments, or a general public or mass audience (Figure 5–2). Marketers approach each of these audiences differently.

The target market may consist of *individuals* who have specific needs and for whom the communication must be specifically tailored. This often requires person-to-person communication and is generally accomplished through personal selling. Other forms of communication, such as advertising, may be used to attract the audience's attention to the firm, but the detailed message is carried by a salesperson who can respond to the specific needs of the individual customer. Life insurance, financial services, and real estate are examples of products and services promoted this way.

A second level of audience aggregation is represented by the *group.* Marketers often must communicate with a group of people who make or influence the purchase decision. For example, organizational purchasing often involves buying centers or committees that vary in size and composition. Companies marketing their products and services to other businesses or organizations must understand who is on the purchase committee, what aspect of the decision each individual influences, and the criteria each member uses to evaluate a product. Advertising may be directed at each member of the buying center, and multilevel personal selling may be necessary to reach those individuals who influence or actually make decisions.

Marketers look for customers who have similar needs and wants and thus represent some type of market segment that can be reached with the same basic communication strategy. Very small, well-defined groups of customers are often referred to as *market niches.* They can usually be reached through personal selling efforts or highly targeted media such as direct mail. The next level of audience aggregation is *market segments,* broader classes of buyers who have similar needs and can be reached with similar messages. As we saw in Chapter 2, there are various ways of segmenting markets and reaching the customers in these segments. As market segments get larger, marketers usually turn to broader-based media such as newspapers, magazines, and TV to reach them.

Marketers of most consumer products attempt to attract the attention of large numbers of present or potential customers (*mass markets*) through mass communication such as advertising or publicity. Mass communication is a one-way flow of information from the marketer to the consumer. Feedback on the audience's reactions to the message is generally indirect and difficult to measure.

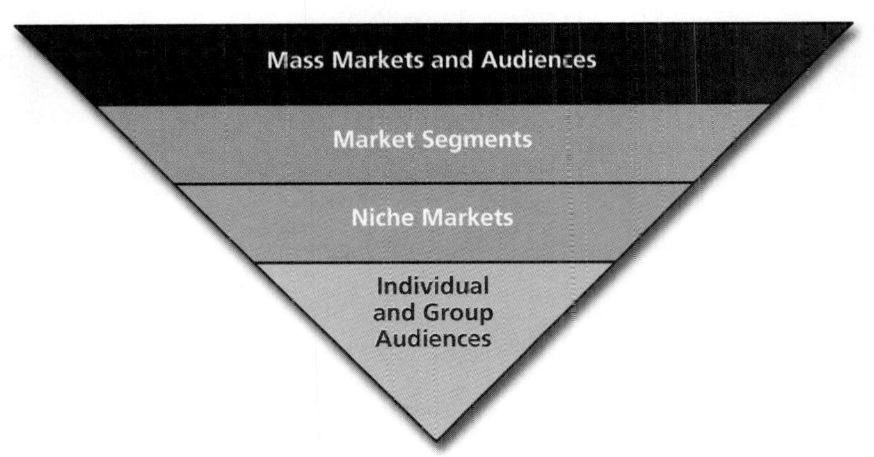

Figure 5–2 Levels of audience aggregation

TV advertising, for example, lets the marketer send a message to millions of consumers at the same time. But this does not mean effective communication has occurred. This may be only one of several hundred messages the consumer is exposed to that day. There is no guarantee the information will be attended to, processed, comprehended, or stored in memory for later retrieval. Even if the advertising message is processed, it may not interest consumers or may be misinterpreted by them. Studies by Jacob Jacoby and Wayne D. Hoyer have shown that nearly 20 percent of all print ads and even more TV commercials are miscomprehended by readers.[10]

Unlike personal or face-to-face communications, mass communications do not offer the marketer an opportunity to explain or clarify the message to make it more effective. The marketer must enter the communication situation with knowledge of the target audience and how it is likely to react to the message. This means the receiver's response process must be understood, along with its implications for promotional planning and strategy.

The Response Process

Perhaps the most important aspect of developing effective communication programs involves understanding the *response process* the receiver may go through in moving toward a specific behavior (like purchasing a product) and how the promotional efforts of the marketer influence consumer responses. In many instances, the marketer's only objective may be to create awareness of the company or brand name, which may trigger interest in the product. In other situations, the marketer may want to convey detailed information to change consumers' knowledge of and attitudes toward the brand and ultimately change their behavior.

Traditional Response Hierarchy Models

A number of models have been developed to depict the stages a consumer may pass through in moving from a state of not being aware of a company, product, or brand to actual purchase behavior. Figure 5–3 shows four of the best-known response hierarchy models. While these response models may appear similar, they were developed for different reasons.

Figure 5–3 Models of the response process

	Models			
Stages	**AIDA model[a]**	**Hierarchy of effects model[b]**	**Innovation adoption model[c]**	**Information processing model[d]**
Cognitive stage	Attention	Awareness Knowledge	Awareness	Presentation Attention Comprehension
Affective stage	Interest Desire	Liking Preference Conviction	Interest Evaluation	Yielding Retention
Behavioral stage	Action	Purchase	Trial Adoption	Behavior

The **AIDA model** was developed to represent the stages a salesperson must take a customer through in the personal selling process.[11] This model depicts the buyer as passing successively through attention, interest, desire, and action. The salesperson must first get the customer's attention and then arouse some interest in the company's product or service. Strong levels of interest should create desire to own or use the product. The action stage in the AIDA model involves getting the customer to make a purchase commitment and closing the sale. To the marketer, this is the most important stage in the selling process, but it can also be the most difficult. Companies train their sales reps in closing techniques to help them complete the selling process.

Perhaps the best known of these response hierarchies is the model developed by Robert Lavidge and Gary Steiner as a paradigm for setting and measuring advertising objectives.[12] Their **hierarchy of effects model** shows the process by which advertising works; it assumes a consumer passes through a series of steps in sequential order from initial awareness of a product or service to actual purchase. A basic premise of this model is that advertising effects occur over a period of time. Advertising communication may not lead to immediate behavioral response or purchase; rather, a series of effects must occur, with each step fulfilled before the consumer can move to the next stage in the hierarchy. As we will see in Chapter 7, the hierarchy of effects model has become the foundation for objective setting and measurement of advertising effects in many companies.

The **innovation adoption model** evolved from work on the diffusion of innovations.[13] This model represents the stages a consumer passes through in adopting a new product or service. Like the other models, it says potential adopters must be moved through a series of steps before taking some action (in this case, deciding to adopt a new product). The steps preceding adoption are awareness, interest, evaluation, and trial. The challenge facing companies introducing new products is to create awareness and interest among consumers and then get them to evaluate the product favorably. The best way to evaluate a new product is through actual use so that performance can be judged. Marketers often encourage trial by using demonstration or sampling programs or allowing consumers to use a product with minimal commitment (Exhibit 5–4). After trial, consumers either adopt the product or reject it.

The final hierarchy model shown in Figure 5–3 is the **information processing model** of advertising effects, developed by William McGuire.[14] This model assumes the receiver in a persuasive communication situation like advertising is an information processor or problem solver. McGuire suggests the series of steps a receiver goes through in being persuaded constitutes a response hierarchy. The stages of this model are similar to the hierarchy of effects sequence; attention and comprehension are similar to awareness and knowledge, and yielding is synonymous with liking. McGuire's model includes a stage not found in the other models: retention, or the receiver's ability to retain that portion of the comprehended information that he or she accepts as valid or relevant. This stage is important since most promotional campaigns are designed not to motivate consumers to take immediate action but rather to provide information they will use later when making a purchase decision.

Exhibit 5–4 Sampling or demonstration programs encourage trial of new products such as disposable contact lenses

Figure 5–4 Methods of obtaining feedback in the response hierarchy

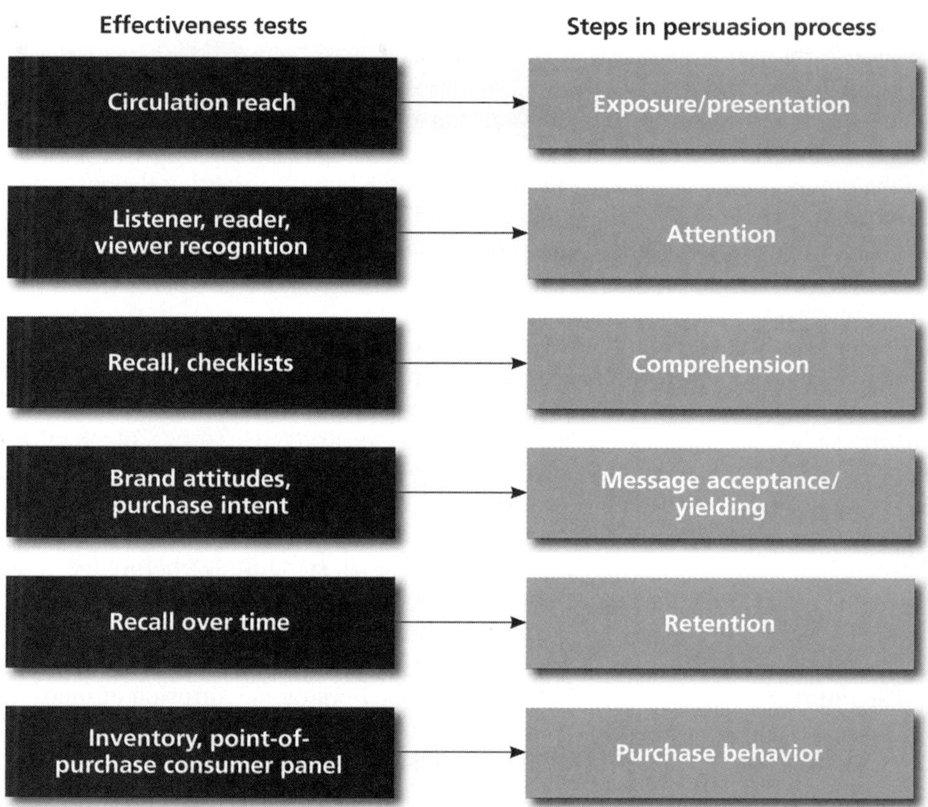

Exhibit 5–5 Advertising for innovative new products such as HDTV must make consumers aware of their features and benefits

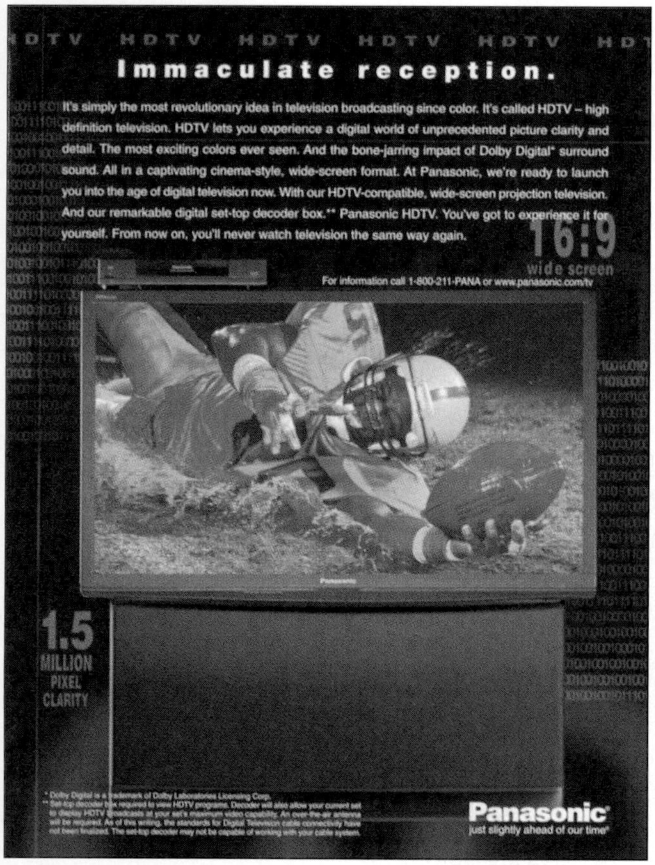

Each stage of the response hierarchy is a dependent variable that must be attained and that may serve as an objective of the communication process. As shown in Figure 5–4, each stage can be measured, providing the advertiser with feedback regarding the effectiveness of various strategies designed to move the consumer to purchase. The information processing model may be an effective framework for planning and evaluating the effects of a promotional campaign.

Implications of the Traditional Hierarchy Models

The hierarchy models of communication response are useful to promotional planners from several perspectives. First, they delineate the series of steps potential purchasers must be taken through to move them from unawareness of a product or service to readiness to purchase it. Second, potential buyers may be at different stages in the hierarchy, so the advertiser will face different sets of communication problems. For example, a company introducing an innovative product like Panasonic's high-definition television (HDTV) may need to devote considerable effort to making people aware of the product, how it works, and its benefits (Exhibit 5–5). Marketers of a mature brand that enjoys customer loyalty may need only supportive or reminder advertising to reinforce positive perceptions and maintain the awareness level for the brand.

The hierarchy models can also be useful as intermediate measures of communication effectiveness. The marketer needs to know where audience members are on the response hierarchy. For example, research may reveal that one target segment has low awareness of the advertiser's brand, whereas another is aware of the brand and its various attributes but has a low level of liking or brand preference.

For the first segment of the market, the communication task involves increasing the awareness level for the brand. The number of ads may be increased, or a product sampling program may be used. For the second segment, where awareness is already high but liking and preference are low, the advertiser must determine the reason for the negative feelings and then attempt to address this problem in future advertising.

When research or other evidence reveals a company is perceived favorably on a particular attribute or performance criterion, the company may want to take advantage of this in its advertising.

Evaluating Traditional Response Hierarchy Models As you saw in Figure 5–3, the four models presented all view the response process as consisting of movement through a sequence of three basic stages. The *cognitive stage* represents what the receiver knows or perceives about the particular product or brand. This stage includes awareness that the brand exists and knowledge, information, or comprehension about its attributes, characteristics, or benefits. The *affective stage* refers to the receiver's feelings or affect level (like or dislike) for the particular brand. This stage also includes stronger levels of affect such as desire, preference, or conviction. The *conative* or *behavioral stage* refers to the consumer's action toward the brand: trial, purchase, adoption, or rejection.

All four models assume a similar ordering of these three stages. Cognitive development precedes affective reactions, which precede behavior. One might assume that consumers become aware of and knowledgeable about a brand, develop feelings toward it, form a desire or preference, and then make a purchase. While this logical progression is often accurate, the response sequence does not always operate this way.

Over the past two decades, considerable research in marketing, social psychology, and communications has led to questioning of the traditional cognitive → affective → behavioral sequence of response. Several other configurations of the response hierarchy have been theorized.

Alternative Response Hierarchies

Michael Ray has developed a model of information processing that identifies three alternative orderings of the three stages based on perceived product differentiation and product involvement.[15] These alternative response hierarchies are the standard learning, dissonance/attribution, and low-involvement models (Figure 5–5).

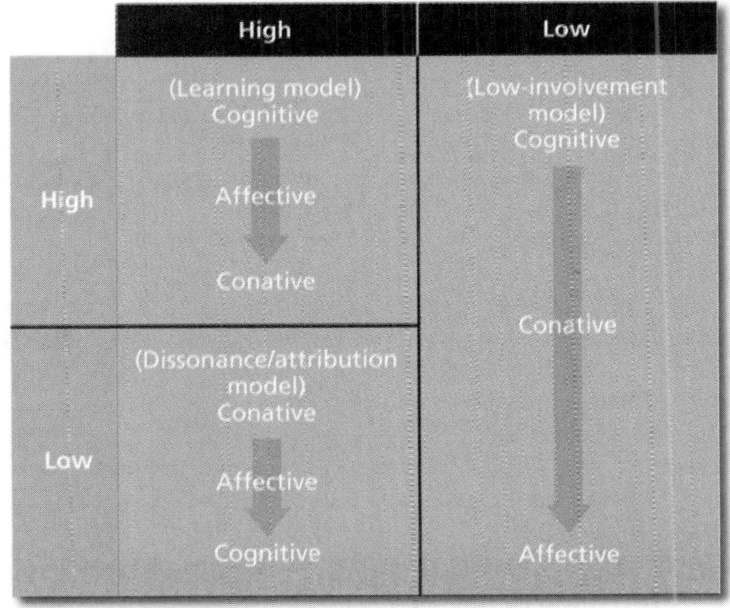

Figure 5–5 Alternative response hierarchies: the three-orders model of information processing

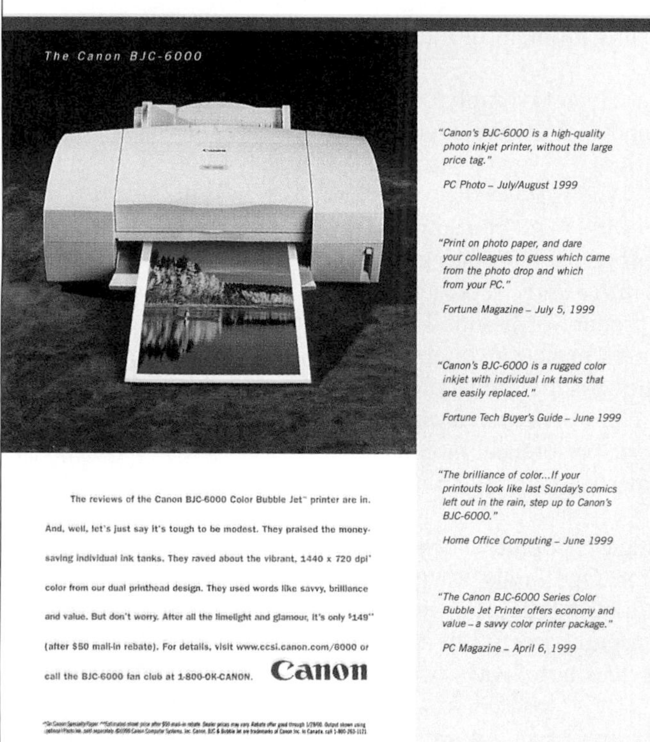

Don't worry. The fame hasn't gone to either of our dual printheads.
The Canon BJC-6000
"Canon's BJC-6000 is a high-quality photo inkjet printer, without the large price tag."
PC Photo – July/August 1999
"Print on photo paper, and dare your colleagues to guess which came from the photo drop and which from your PC."
Fortune Magazine – July 5, 1999
"Canon's BJC-6000 is a rugged color inkjet with individual ink tanks that are easily replaced."
Fortune Tech Buyer's Guide – June 1999
"The brilliance of color...If your printouts look like last Sunday's comics left out in the rain, step up to Canon's BJC-6000."
Home Office Computing – June 1999
"The Canon BJC-6000 Series Color Bubble Jet Printer offers economy and value – a savvy color printer package."
PC Magazine – April 6, 1999
The reviews of the Canon BJC-6000 Color Bubble Jet™ printer are in. And, well, let's just say it's tough to be modest. They praised the money-saving individual ink tanks. They raved about the vibrant, 1440 x 720 dpi* color from our dual printhead design. They used words like savvy, brilliance and value. But don't worry. After all the limelight and glamour, it's only $149** (after $50 mail-in rebate). For details, visit www.ccsi.canon.com/6000 or call the BJC-6000 fan club at 1-800-OK-CANON.
Canon

Exhibit 5–6 Ads for high-involvement products provide consumers with information to help them evaluate brands

The Standard Learning Hierarchy

In many purchase situations, the consumer will go through the response process in the sequence depicted by the traditional communication models. Ray terms this a **standard learning model,** which consists of a learn → feel → do sequence. Information and knowledge acquired or *learned* about the various brands are the basis for developing affect, or *feelings,* that guide what the consumer will *do* (e.g., actual trial or purchase). In this hierarchy, the consumer is viewed as an active participant in the communication process who gathers information through active learning.

Ray suggests the standard learning hierarchy is likely when the consumer is highly involved in the purchase process and there is much differentiation among competing brands. High-involvement purchase decisions such as those for industrial products and services and consumer durables like personal computers, printers, cameras, appliances, and cars are areas where a standard learning hierarchy response process is likely. Ads for products and services in these areas are usually very detailed and provide customers with information that can be used to evaluate brands and help them make a purchase decision (Exhibit 5–6).

The Dissonance/Attribution Hierarchy

A second response hierarchy proposed by Ray involves situations where consumers first behave, then develop attitudes or feelings as a result of that behavior, and then learn or process information that supports the behavior. This **dissonance/attribution model,** or do → feel → learn, occurs in situations where consumers must choose between two alternatives that are similar in quality but are complex and may have hidden or unknown attributes. The consumer may purchase the product on the basis of a recommendation by some nonmedia source and then attempt to support the decision by developing a positive attitude toward the brand and perhaps even developing negative feelings toward the rejected alternative(s). This reduces any *postpurchase dissonance* or anxiety the consumer may experience resulting from doubt over the purchase (as discussed in Chapter 4). Dissonance reduction involves *selective learning,* whereby the consumer seeks information that supports the choice made and avoids information that would raise doubts about the decision.

According to this model, marketers need to recognize that in some situations, attitudes develop *after* purchase, as does learning from the mass media. Ray suggests that in these situations the main effect of the mass media is not the promotion of original choice behavior and attitude change but rather the reduction of dissonance by reinforcing the wisdom of the purchase or providing supportive information. For example, the ad shown in Exhibit 5–7 reinforces consumers' decisions to purchase Michelin tires by showing the number of awards the brand has received for customer satisfaction.

As with the standard learning model, this response hierarchy is likely to occur when the consumer is involved in the purchase situation; it is particularly relevant for postpurchase situations. For example, a consumer may purchase tires recommended by a friend and then develop a favorable attitude toward the company and pay close attention to its ads to reduce dissonance.

Some marketers resist this view of the response hierarchy because they can't accept the notion that the mass media have no effect on the consumer's initial purchase decision. But the model doesn't claim the mass media have no effect—just that their major impact occurs after the purchase has been made. Marketing communications planners must be aware of the need for advertising and promotion

Exhibit 5–7 This ad reinforces the wisdom of the decision to purchase Michelin tires

efforts not just to encourage brand selection but to reinforce choices and ensure that a purchase pattern will continue.

The Low-Involvement Hierarchy

Perhaps the most intriguing of the three response hierarchies proposed by Ray is the **low-involvement hierarchy,** in which the receiver is viewed as passing from cognition to behavior to attitude change. This learn → do → feel sequence is thought to characterize situations of low consumer involvement in the purchase process. Ray suggests this hierarchy tends to occur when involvement in the purchase decision is low, there are minimal differences among brand alternatives, and mass-media (especially broadcast) advertising is important.

The notion of a low-involvement hierarchy is based in large part on Herbert Krugman's theory explaining the effects of television advertising.[16] Krugman wanted to find out why TV advertising produced a strong effect on brand awareness and recall but little change in consumers' attitudes toward the product. He hypothesized that TV is basically a low-involvement medium and the viewer's perceptual defenses are reduced or even absent during commercials. In a low-involvement situation, the consumer does not compare the message with previously acquired beliefs, needs, or past experiences. The commercial results in subtle changes in the consumer's knowledge structure, particularly with repeated exposure. This change in the consumer's knowledge does not result in attitude change but is related to learning something about the advertised brand, such as a brand name, ad theme, or slogan. According to Krugman, when the consumer enters a purchase situation, this information may be sufficient to trigger a purchase. The consumer will then form an attitude toward the purchased brand as a result of experience with it. Thus, in the low-involvement situation the response sequence is as follows:

Message exposure under low involvement →

Shift in cognitive structure → Purchase →

Positive or negative experience → Attitude formation

In the low-involvement hierarchy, the consumer engages in passive learning and random information catching rather than active information seeking. The advertiser must recognize that a passive, uninterested consumer may focus more on nonmessage elements such as music, characters, symbols, and slogans or jingles than actual message content. The advertiser might capitalize on this situation by developing a

Before.
After.
HEINZ
TOMATO
KETCHUP
HEINZ
TOMATO
KETCHUP
The best things in life never change.

Exhibit 5–8 Advertising promoting consistent quality has helped Heinz dominate the ketchup market

catchy jingle that is stored in the consumer's mind without any active cognitive processing and becomes salient when he or she enters the actual purchase situation.

Advertisers of low-involvement products also repeat simple product claims such as a key copy point or distinctive product benefit. A study by Scott Hawkins and Stephen Hoch found that under low-involvement conditions, repetition of simple product claims increased consumers' memory of and belief in those claims.[17] They concluded that advertisers of low-involvement products might find it more profitable to pursue a heavy repetition strategy than to reach larger audiences with lengthy, more detailed messages. For example, Heinz has dominated the ketchup market for over 20 years by repeatedly telling consumers that its brand is the thickest and richest. Heinz has used a variety of advertising campaigns over the years, but they all repeat the same basic theme and focus on the consistent quality of the brand (Exhibit 5–8).

Low-involvement advertising appeals prevail in much of the advertising we see for frequently purchased consumer products: Wrigley's Doublemint gum invites consumers to "Double your pleasure." Bounty paper towels claim to be the "quicker picker-upper." Oscar Mayer uses the catchy jingle, "I wish I were an Oscar Mayer wiener." Each of these appeals is designed to help consumers make an association without really attempting to formulate or change an attitude.

Another popular creative strategy used by advertisers of low-involvement products is what advertising analyst Harry McMahan calls *VIP,* or *visual image personality.*[18] Advertisers often use symbols like the Pillsbury doughboy, Morris the cat, Tony the tiger, Speedy Alka-Seltzer, and Mr. Clean to develop visual images that will lead consumers to identify and retain ads. IMC Perspective 5–3 discusses how the Taco Bell Chihuahua became a popular advertising VIP for the fast-food restaurant chain.

The Integrated Information Response Model

Advertising and consumer researchers recognize that not all response sequences and behaviors are explained adequately by either the traditional or the alternative response hierarchies. Advertising is just one source of information consumers use in forming attitudes and/or making purchase decisions. Moreover, for many consumers, purchase does not reflect commitment to a brand but is merely a way to obtain firsthand information from trial use of a product.

Robert Smith and William Swinyard developed a revised interpretation of the advertising response sequence.[19] Their **integrated information response model,** shown in Figure 5–6, integrates concepts from both the traditional and the low-involvement response hierarchy perspectives. It also accounts for the effects of direct experience and recognizes that different levels of belief strength result from advertising versus personal experience with a product.

The integrated information response model suggests several different response patterns that can result from advertising. For low-involvement purchases, a cognition → trial → affect → commitment response sequence may be operating. This can be seen in the top line of Figure 5–6. According to this sequence, advertising generally leads to low information acceptance, lower-order beliefs, and low-order affect. However, as repetitive advertising builds awareness, consumers become more likely to engage in a trial purchase to gather information. The direct experience that results from trial purchase leads to high information acceptance and higher-order beliefs and affect, which can result in commitment or brand loyalty.

Advertising generally leads only to lower-order beliefs and affect because it is seen as a biased source of interest, subject to much source and message discounting and/or rejection. But in some situations, such as when perceived risk and involvement are low, advertising may move consumers directly to purchase.

If consumers are involved with the product, they may seek additional information from other external sources (for example, more advertising, word of mouth,

IMC Perspective 5–3

Ay, Chihuahua! Move Over Morris

The use of animals and other creatures, both real and animated, as personality symbols for advertising products and services has been around for decades. Charlie the Tuna first began trying to trick fishermen into catching him in Starkist tuna commercials in 1961 and was recently brought back after a 10-year hiatus to help stimulate sales of the brand. Tony the Tiger has been saying Kellogg's Frosted Flakes are GRRReat for over three decades, while Quantas Airlines still occasionally uses Sydney the Koala, who began hating the airline for bringing too many tourists to Australia in the mid-60s. In the late 80s and early 90s Spuds MacKenzie, a bullterrier who was promoted as the "original party animal," appeared in ads for Bud Light and helped the brand become the leading brand of light beer. And of course one of the most enduring of all the spokes-animals is Morris, the finicky feline who has been appearing in commercials for 9-Lives cat food since 1969.

During the past decade several new creatures were introduced to consumers and have become advertising icons. Chiat/Day, the agency for Eveready, introduced the Energizer bunny in 1989 and he has helped keep sales of Energizer batteries going and going for over 10 years. A few years ago Anheuser-Busch introduced Frank and Louie, the two lizards whose edgy humor has helped make Budweiser commercials among the most popular on television.

The latest spokes-animal to achieve celebrity status in the advertising world is the Taco Bell® Chihuahua, a Spanish-speaking canine who loves the fast-food chain's tacos and burritos. Clay Williams, the creative director at the TBWA/Chiat/Day agency that created the campaign, said that the idea of using the little dog in the ads sprang from a lunch meeting when he and a fellow executive were surprised to see a Chihuahua with an attitude stroll past their table in a Venice Beach restaurant. The Chihuahua first delivered the now famous slogan "Yo quiero Taco Bell" in the summer of 1997 during an ad that ran only in the Northeastern states. The company's chief marketing officer notes that after running the ad, "Taco Bell was immediately on the map in those states that it wasn't before." Recognizing that consumers wanted to see more of the dog, Taco Bell quickly shifted the emphasis of the campaign to the Chihuahua.

Since appearing in the Taco Bell ads, the dog has become a pop-culture and advertising icon, attending the New York premiere of the movie *Godzilla* (the big-screen beast that the little dog referred to as a lizard in one popular TV spot), appearing on the cover of *TV Guide* magazine and being named to *Entertainment Weekly*'s 1998 list of the 100 most creative people in entertainment and *People* magazine's 25 most intriguing people of the year in 1999. Taco Bell has sold tens of millions of plush-toy versions of the dog and has developed a line of licensed merchandise emblazoned with his image. The campaign has generated the highest advertising awareness ever for Taco Bell. And most importantly, the Chihuahua has done what the agency promised it would do—burnish Taco Bell's image among teenagers and young adults as a hip place to eat.

The issue Taco Bell and TBWA/Chiat/Day now faces is determining how long the Chihuahua's appeal will last. The agency knows that just how long the dog can remain popular and continue to generate sales of tacos and burritos will depend on how well they handle its carefully crafted image and personality. Too much exposure among media-savvy teens could result in the dog's burning out before his time. While he still appears in the commercials, new spots are focusing more on the food than on the dog. Additionally, the company announced plans to drop the "Yo quiero Taco Bell" tagline and replace it with "Grande Taste, Loco Price. Only at Taco Bell." The company's new marketing chief has noted that while the dog has brought attention to Taco Bell, it needs to be used in such a way that it can do the same for the food.

The stars of commercials are usually the athletes, TV and movie stars, or other entertainers consumers admire. However, an ad character does not have to be human to help sell products. In the wonderful world of advertising, frogs and lizards can be croak-persons for beer, a bunny can drum up business for batteries, a finicky feline has his own fan club, and a miniscule dog with an attitude can get people to eat Mexican food. Ay Chihuahua!

Source: Kathryn Kranhold, "Taco Bell Ads to Focus on Food, Not Dog," *The Wall Street Journal,* October 11, 1999, p. B10; Greg Johnson, "Grooming an Icon for the Long Haul," *Los Angeles Times,* February 18, 1999, pp. C1, 5.

Figure 5–6 Integrated information response model

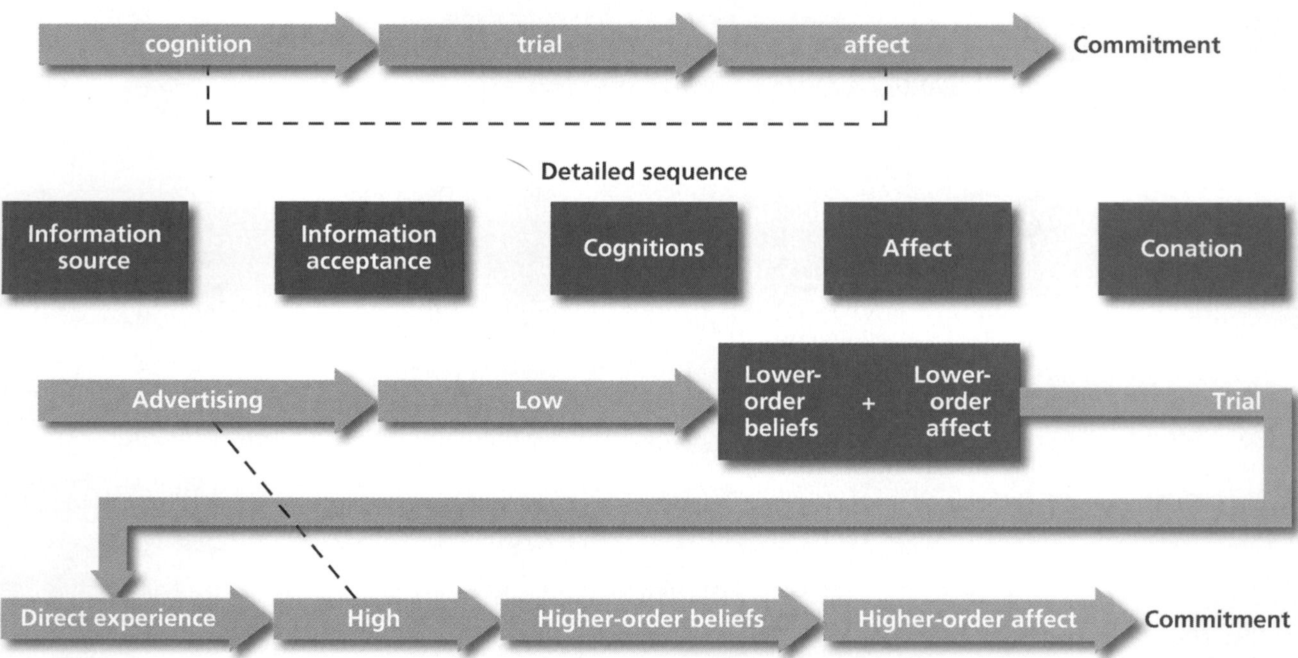

salespeople) and/or from direct experience. This means the response sequence is similar to the traditional hierarchy of effects model (cognition → affect → commitment). The higher-order response path (bottom line of Figure 5–6) shows that direct experience, and in some cases advertising, is accepted at higher-order magnitudes, resulting in higher-order beliefs and affect. This strong affect is more likely to result in preferences and committed purchases.

Smith and Swinyard discuss the implications of the integrated response model regarding promotional strategy for low- versus high-involvement products. For example, they recommend less enthusiastic promotional goals for low-involvement products, because advertising has a limited ability to form or change higher-order beliefs and affect:

> Low-involvement products, for example, could benefit from advertisements oriented to inducing trial by creating generally favorable lower order beliefs. This could be accomplished with campaigns designed to reduce perceived risk through repetition and familiarity, or those directly advocating a trial purchase. In addition, the integrated response model suggests that other marketing strategies designed to facilitate trial should be coupled with the advertising campaign. Free samples, coupons, price cuts, or effective point-of-purchase displays could all be integrated with media advertising to produce an environment highly conducive to trial. So too, because low-involvement products are frequently homogeneous, subsequent advertisements might be designed to reaffirm the positive aspects of trial. If successful, these efforts might generate brand loyalty based upon higher order beliefs and affect. This could be a major advantage for advertisers of low-involvement products where frequent brand switching may be based on the absence of antecedents for commitment (i.e., higher order beliefs and affect).[20]

For high-involvement products, more basic attitude change strategies are warranted. However, Smith and Swinyard note that the higher-order response sequence focuses attention on message acceptance as a prerequisite for affect development:

> In this instance, the advertising manager should attempt to isolate the conditions facilitating the formation of higher order beliefs. Factors influential in this process could include whether the message claims are easily verifiable (e.g., price) and/or demonstrable (e.g., styling), whether the individual knows the sponsoring company and its reputation/credibility, selection of a credible spokesperson to deliver the message, whether the message is consistent with already established beliefs, etc. It also is likely that interactions could exist

between acceptance factors, and that certain message configurations would be much more successful than others.[21]

Smith and Swinyard point out that communication strategies for high-involvement products may be difficult to implement since media advertising often has little effect on higher-order attitude formation or change. Thus, they suggest that marketing communications focus on achieving a product demonstration rather than a direct urge to purchase. Product demonstrations and information received from compelling personal communication sources, such as knowledgeable and well-trained in-store sales personnel, are more likely to change higher-order beliefs and affect and lead to purchase.

An important implication of the integrated information response model is that consumers are likely to integrate information from advertising, other sources, and direct experience in forming judgments about a brand. For example, in a recent study Robert Smith found that advertising can lessen the negative effects of an unfavorable trial experience on brand evaluations when the ad is processed before the trial. However, when a negative trial experience precedes exposure to an ad, cognitive evaluations of the ad are more negative.[22] Thus it is important to consider how consumers integrate advertising with other brand information sources, both before and after trial or purchase.

Implications of the Alternative Response Models The various response models offer an interesting perspective on the ways consumers respond to advertising and other forms of marketing communications. They also provide insight into promotional strategies marketers might pursue in different situations. A review of these alternative models of the response process shows that the traditional standard learning model does not always apply. The notion of a highly involved consumer who engages in active information processing and learning and acts on the basis of higher-order beliefs and a well-formed attitude may be inappropriate for some types of purchases. Sometimes consumers make a purchase decision on the basis of general awareness resulting from repetitive exposure to advertising, and attitude development occurs after the purchase, if at all. The integrated information response model suggests that the role of advertising and other forms of promotion may be to induce trial, so consumers can develop brand preferences primarily on the basis of their direct experience with the product.

From a promotional planning perspective, it is important that marketers examine the communication situation for their product or service and determine which type of response process is most likely to occur. They should analyze involvement levels and product/service differentiation as well as consumers' use of various information sources and their levels of experience with the product or service. Once the manager has determined which response sequence is most likely to operate, the integrated marketing communications program can be designed to influence the response process in favor of the company's product or service. Because this requires that marketers determine the involvement level of consumers in their target markets, we examine the concept of involvement in more detail.

Understanding Involvement

Over the past two decades, consumer behavior and advertising researchers have extensively studied the concept of involvement.[23] Involvement is viewed as a variable that can help explain how consumers process advertising information and how this information might affect message recipients. One problem that has plagued the study of involvement has been agreeing on how to define and measure it. Advertising managers must be able to determine targeted consumers' involvement levels with their products.

Some of the problems in conceptualizing and measuring involvement have been addressed in extensive review by Judith Zaichkowsky. She has noted that although there is no single precise definition of involvement, there is an underlying theme focusing on *personal relevance.*[24] Zaichkowsky developed an involvement construct

Figure 5–7 Involvement concept

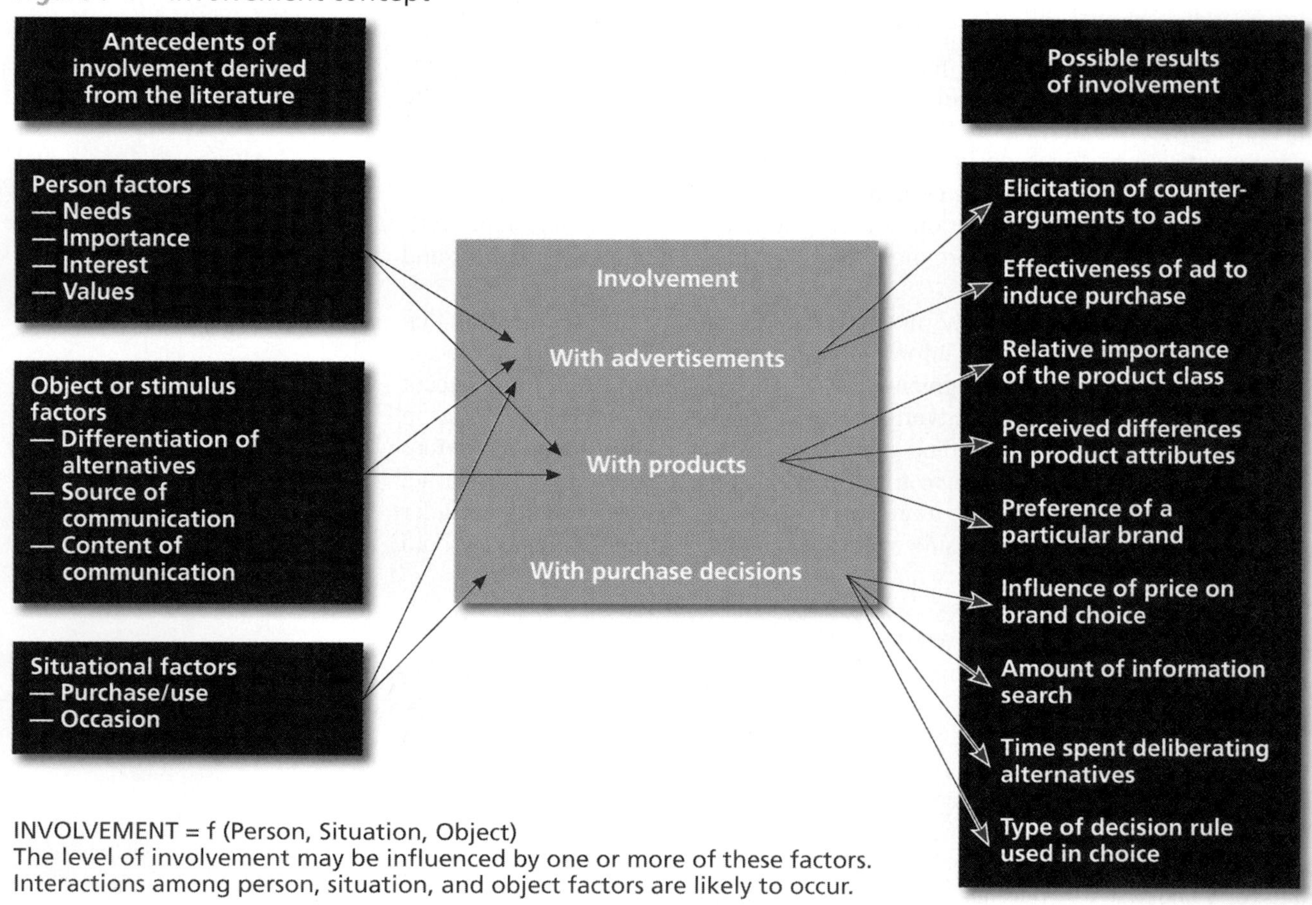

that includes three antecedents, or variables proposed to precede involvement (Figure 5–7). The first is traits of the person (value system, unique experiences, needs). The second factor is characteristics of the stimulus, or differences in type of media (TV, radio, or print), content of the communication, or product class variations. The third antecedent is situational factors, such as whether one is or is not in the market for a particular product.

The various antecedents can influence the consumer's level of involvement in several ways, including the way the consumer responds to the advertising, the products being advertised, and the actual purchase decision. This involvement theory shows that a variety of outcomes or behaviors can result from involvement with advertising, products, or purchase decisions.

Several other advertising planning grids have been developed that consider involvement levels as well as other factors, including response processes and motives that underlie attitude formation and subsequent brand choice.

The FCB Planning Model

An interesting approach to analyzing the communication situation comes from the work of Richard Vaughn of the Foote, Cone & Belding advertising agency. Vaughn and his associates developed an advertising planning model by building on traditional response theories such as the hierarchy of effects model and its variants and research on high and low involvement.[25] They added the dimension of thinking versus feeling processing at each involvement level by bringing in theories regarding brain specialization. The right/left brain theory suggests the left side of the brain is more capable of rational, cognitive thinking, while the right side is more visual and emotional and engages more in the affective (feeling) functions. Their model, which became known as the FCB grid, delineates four primary advertising planning strategies—informative, affective, habit formation, and satis-

	Thinking	Feeling
High involvement	**1. Informative (thinker)** Car–house–furnishings–new products model: Learn–feel–do (economic?) **Possible implications** Test: Recall, Diagnostics Media: Long copy format, Reflective vehicles Creative: Specific information, Demonstration	**2. Affective (feeler)** Jewelry–cosmetics–fashion apparel–motorcycles model: Feel–learn–do (psychological?) **Possible implications** Test: Attitude change, Emotional arousal Media: Large space, Image specials Creative: Executional, Impact
Low involvement	**3. Habit formation (doer)** Food–household items model: Do–learn–feel (responsive?) **Possible implications** Test: Sales Media: Small space ads, 10-second I.D.s, Radio; POS Creative: Reminder	**4. Self-satisfaction (reactor)** Cigarettes–liquor–candy model: Do–feel–learn (social?) **Possible implications** Test: Sales Media: Billboards, Newspapers, POS Creative: Attention

Figure 5–8 The Foote, Cone & Belding (FCB) grid

faction—along with the most appropriate variant of the alternative response hierarchies (Figure 5–8).

Vaughn suggests that the *informative strategy* is for highly involving products and services where rational thinking and economic considerations prevail and the standard learning hierarchy is the appropriate response model. The *affective strategy* is for highly involving/feeling purchases. For these types of products, advertising should stress psychological and emotional motives such as building self-esteem or enhancing one's ego or self-image.

The *habit formation strategy* is for low-involvement/thinking products with such routinized behavior patterns that learning occurs most often after a trial purchase. The response process for these products is consistent with a behavioristic learning-by-doing model (remember our discussion of operant conditioning in Chapter 4?). The *self-satisfaction strategy* is for low-involvement/feeling products where appeals to sensory pleasures and social motives are important. Again, the do → feel or do → learn hierarchy is operating, since product experience is an important part of the learning process. Vaughn acknowledges that some minimal level of awareness (passive learning) may precede purchase of both types of low-involvement products, but deeper, active learning is not necessary. This is consistent with the low-involvement hierarchy discussed earlier (learn → do → feel).

The FCB grid provides a useful way for those involved in the advertising planning process, such as creative specialists, to analyze consumer–product relationships and develop appropriate promotional strategies. Consumer research can be used to determine how consumers perceive products or brands on the involvement and thinking/feeling dimensions.[26] This information can then be used to develop effective creative options such as using rational versus emotional appeals, increasing involvement levels, or even getting consumers to evaluate a think-type product on the basis of feelings. The ad for the Kenmore Elite refrigerator in Exhibit 5–9 is an example of the latter strategy.

Exhibit 5–9 A think-type product is advertised by an appeal to feelings

Notice how it uses beautiful imagery to appeal to emotional concerns such as style and appearance. Appliances have traditionally been sold on the basis of more rational, functional motives.

Cognitive Processing of Communications

The hierarchical response models were for many years the primary focus of approaches for studying the receivers' responses to marketing communications. Attention centered on identifying relationships between specific controllable variables (such as source and message factors) and outcome or response variables (such as attention, comprehension, attitudes, and purchase intentions). This approach has been criticized on a number of fronts, including its black-box nature, since it can't explain what is causing these reactions.[27] In response to these concerns, researchers began trying to understand the nature of cognitive reactions to persuasive messages. Several approaches have been developed to examine the nature of consumers' cognitive processing of advertising messages.

The Cognitive Response Approach

One of the most widely used methods for examining consumers' cognitive processing of advertising messages is assessment of their **cognitive responses,** the thoughts that occur to them while reading, viewing, and/or hearing a communication.[28] These thoughts are generally measured by having consumers write down or verbally report their reactions to a message. The assumption is that these thoughts reflect the recipient's cognitive processes or reactions and help shape ultimate acceptance or rejection of the message.

The cognitive response approach has been widely used in research by both academicians and advertising practitioners. Its focus has been to determine the types of responses evoked by an advertising message and how these responses relate to attitudes toward the ad, brand attitudes, and purchase intentions. Figure 5–9 depicts the three basic categories of cognitive responses researchers have identified—product/message, source-oriented, and ad execution thoughts—and how they may relate to attitudes and intentions.

Product/Message Thoughts

The first category of thoughts comprises those directed at the product or service and/or the claims being made in the communication. Much attention has focused on two particular types of responses, counterarguments and support arguments.

Counterarguments are thoughts the recipient has that are opposed to the position taken in the message. For example, consider the ad for Ultra Tide shown in

Figure 5–9 A model of cognitive response

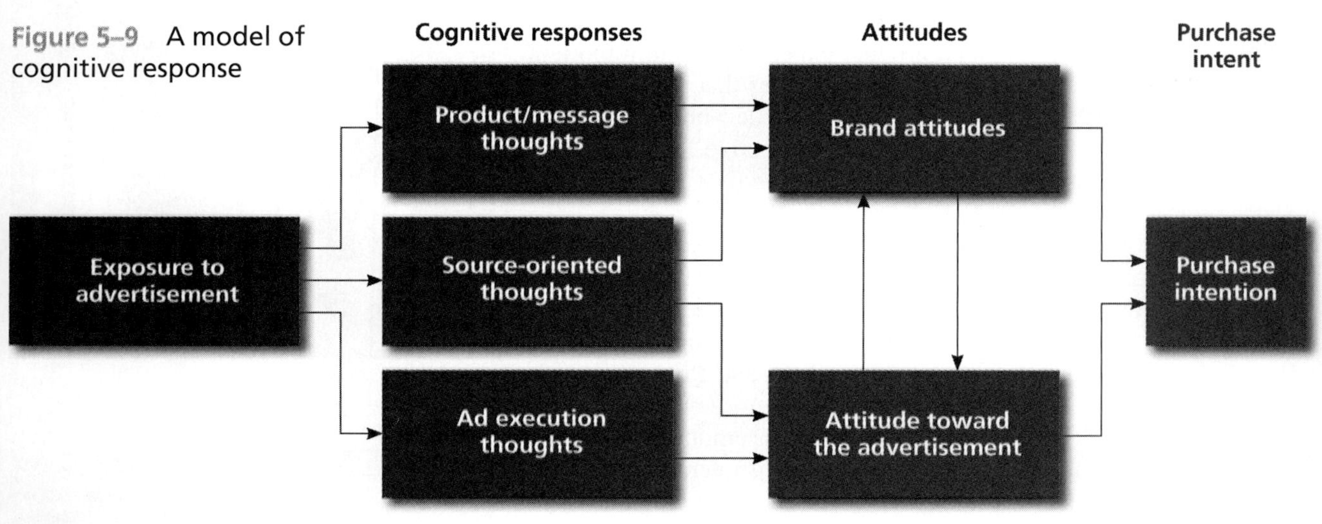

Exhibit 5–10. A consumer may express disbelief or disapproval of a claim made in an ad. ("I don't believe that any detergent could get that stain out!") Other consumers who see this ad may generate **support arguments,** or thoughts that affirm the claims made in the message. ("Ultra Tide looks like a really good product—I think I'll try it.")

The likelihood of counterarguing is greater when the message makes claims that oppose the receiver's beliefs. For example, a consumer viewing a commercial that attacks a favorite brand is likely to engage in counterarguing. Counterarguments relate negatively to message acceptance; the more the receiver counterargues, the less likely he or she is to accept the position advocated in the message.[29] Support arguments, on the other hand, relate positively to message acceptance. Thus, the marketer should develop ads or other promotional messages that minimize counterarguing and encourage support arguments.

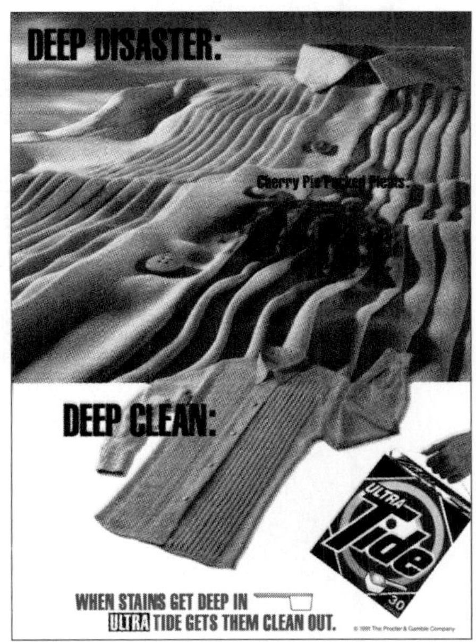

Exhibit 5–10 Consumers often generate support arguments in response to ads for quality products

Source-Oriented Thoughts

A second category of cognitive responses is directed at the source of the communication. One of the most important types of responses in this category is **source derogations,** or negative thoughts about the spokesperson or organization making the claims. Such thoughts generally lead to a reduction in message acceptance. If consumers find a particular spokesperson annoying or untrustworthy, they are less likely to accept what this source has to say.

Of course, source-related thoughts are not always negative. Receivers who react favorably to the source generate favorable thoughts, or **source bolsters.** As you would expect, most advertisers attempt to hire spokespeople their target audience likes so as to carry this effect over to the message. Considerations involved in choosing an appropriate source or spokesperson will be discussed in Chapter 6.

Ad Execution Thoughts

The third category of cognitive responses shown in Figure 5–9 consists of the individual's thoughts about the ad itself. Many of the thoughts receivers have when reading or viewing an ad do not concern the product and/or message claims directly. Rather, they are affective reactions representing the consumer's feelings toward the ad. These thoughts may include reactions to ad execution factors such as the creativity of the ad, the quality of the visual effects, colors, and voice tones. **Ad execution-related thoughts** can be either favorable or unfavorable. They are important because of their effect on attitudes toward the advertisement as well as the brand.

In recent years, much attention has focused on consumers' affective reactions to ads, especially TV commercials.[30] **Attitude toward the ad** ($A \rightarrow ad$) represents the receivers' feelings of favorability or unfavorability toward the ad. Advertisers are interested in consumers' reactions to the ad because they know that affective reactions are an important determinant of advertising effectiveness, since these reactions may be transferred to the brand itself or directly influence purchase intentions. One study found that people who enjoy a commercial are twice as likely as those who are neutral toward it to be convinced that the brand is the best.[31]

Consumers' feelings about the ad may be just as important as their attitudes toward the brand (if not more so) in determining an ad's effectiveness.[32] The importance of affective reactions and feelings generated by the ad depend on several factors, among them the nature of the ad and the type of processing engaged in by the receiver.[33] Many advertisers now use emotional ads designed to evoke feelings and affective reactions as the basis of their creative strategy. The success of this strategy depends in part on the consumers' involvement with the brand and their likelihood of attending to and processing the message.

We end our analysis of the receiver by examining a model that integrates some of the factors that may account for different types and levels of cognitive processing of a message.

The Elaboration Likelihood Model

Differences in the ways consumers process and respond to persuasive messages are addressed in the **elaboration likelihood model (ELM)** of persuasion, shown in Figure 5–10.[34] The ELM was devised by Richard Petty and John Cacioppo to explain the process by which persuasive communications (such as ads) lead to persuasion by influencing *attitudes.* According to this model, the attitude formation or change process depends on the amount and nature of *elaboration,* or processing, of relevant information that occurs in response to a persuasive message. High elaboration means the receiver engages in careful consideration, thinking, and evaluation of the information or arguments contained in the message. Low elaboration occurs when the receiver does not engage in active information processing or thinking but rather makes inferences about the position being advocated in the message on the basis of simple positive or negative cues.

The ELM shows that elaboration likelihood is a function of two elements, motivation and ability to process the message. *Motivation* to process the message depends on such factors as involvement, personal relevance, and individuals' needs and arousal levels. *Ability* depends on the individual's knowledge, intellectual

Figure 5–10 The elaboration likelihood model of persuasion

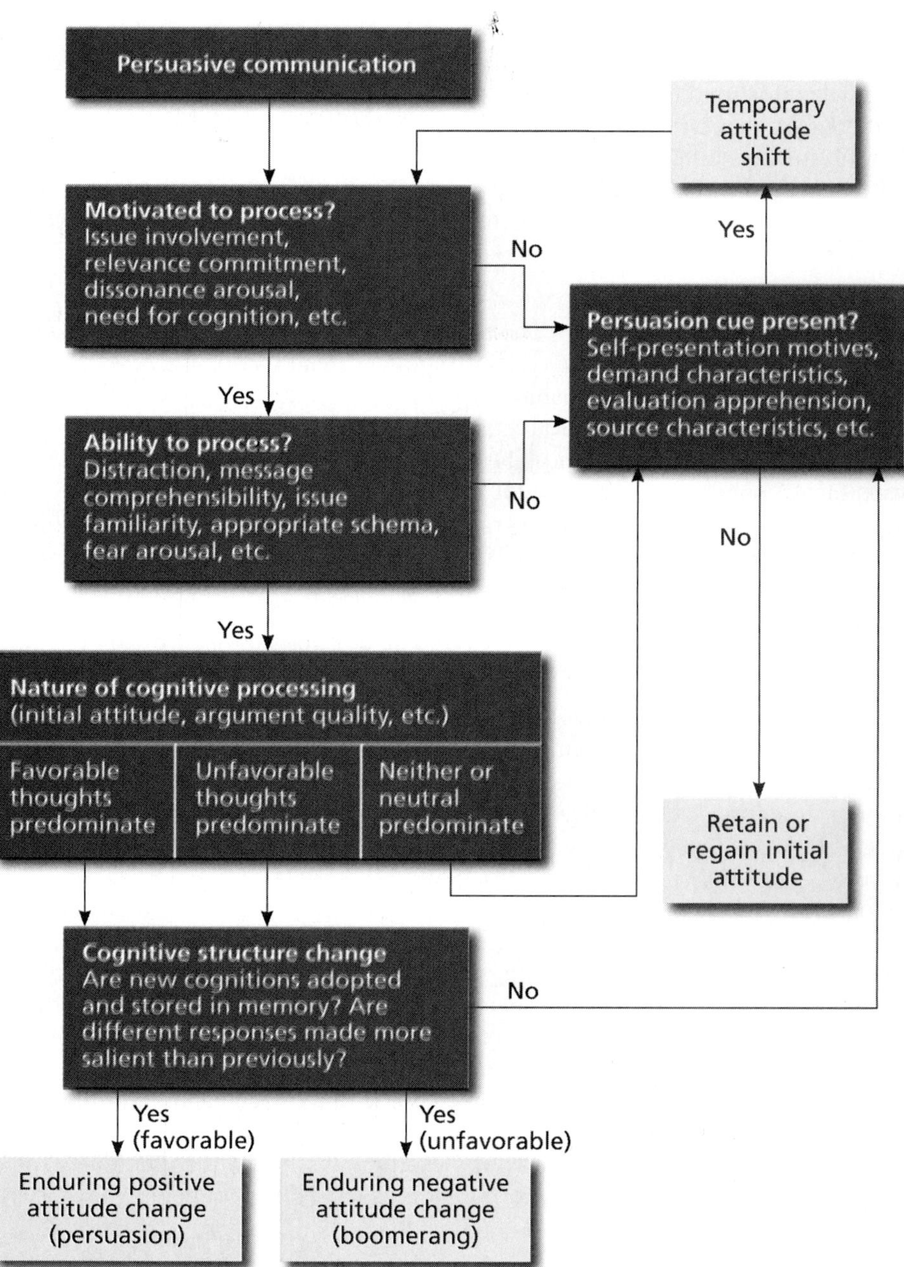

capacity, and opportunity to process the message. For example, an individual viewing a humorous commercial or one containing an attractive model may be distracted from processing the information about the product.

According to the ELM, there are two basic routes to persuasion or attitude change. Under the **central route to persuasion,** the receiver is viewed as a very active, involved participant in the communication process whose ability and motivation to attend, comprehend, and evaluate messages are high. When central processing of an advertising message occurs, the consumer pays close attention to message content and scrutinizes the message arguments. A high level of cognitive response activity or processing occurs, and the ad's ability to persuade the receiver depends primarily on the receiver's evaluation of the quality of the arguments presented. Predominantly favorable cognitive responses (support arguments and source bolsters) lead to favorable changes in cognitive structure, which lead to positive attitude change, or persuasion.

Conversely, if the cognitive processing is predominantly unfavorable and results in counterarguments and/or source derogations, the changes in cognitive structure are unfavorable and *boomerang,* or result in negative attitude change. Attitude change that occurs through central processing is relatively enduring and should resist subsequent efforts to change it.

Under the **peripheral route to persuasion,** shown on the right side of Figure 5–10, the receiver is viewed as lacking the motivation or ability to process information and is not likely to engage in detailed cognitive processing. Rather than evaluating the information presented in the message, the receiver relies on peripheral cues that may be incidental to the main arguments. The receiver's reaction to the message depends on how he or she evaluates these peripheral cues.

The consumer may use several types of peripheral cues or cognitive shortcuts rather than carefully evaluating the message arguments presented in an advertisement.[35] Favorable attitudes may be formed if the endorser in the ad is viewed as an expert or is attractive and/or likable or if the consumer likes certain executional aspects of the ad such as the way it is made, the music, or the imagery. Notice how the ad in Exhibit 5–11 for Right Guard Clear Stick and Clear Gel deodorant and antiperspirant contains several positive peripheral cues, including a popular celebrity endorser (basketball star Scottie Pippen) and excellent visual imagery. These cues might help consumers form a positive attitude toward the brand even if they do not process the message portion of the ad.

Exhibit 5–11 This ad contains peripheral cues, most notably a celebrity endorser

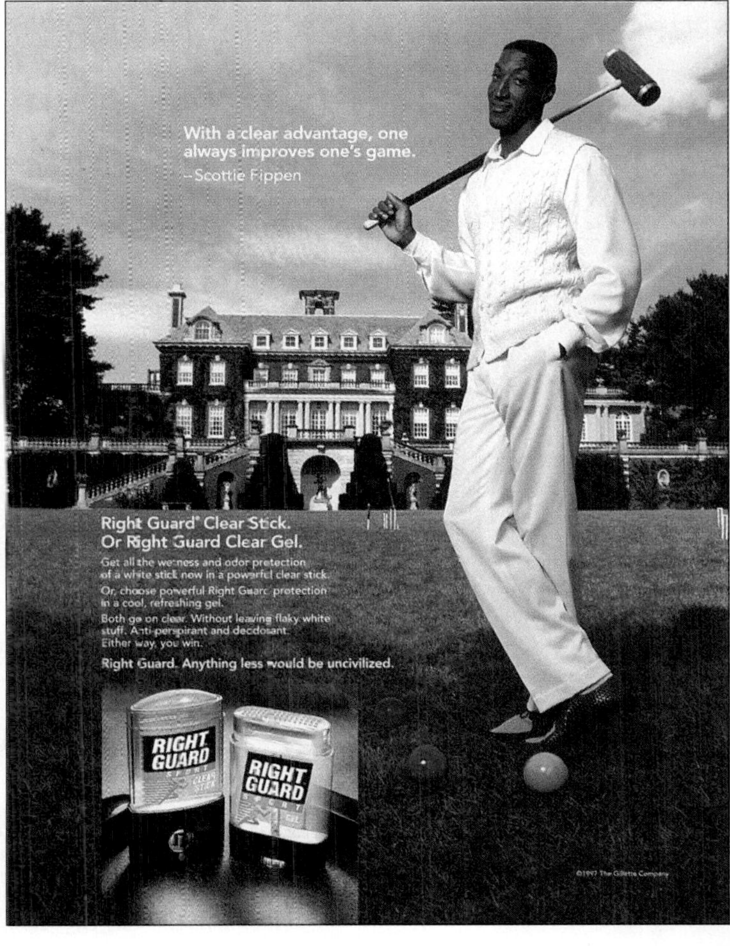

With a clear advantage, one always improves one's game.
–Scottie Pippen
Right Guard® Clear Stick.
Or Right Guard Clear Gel.
Get all the wetness and odor protection of a white stick now in a powerful clear stick.
Or, choose powerful Right Guard protection in a cool, refreshing gel.
Both go on clear. Without leaving flaky white stuff. Anti-perspirant and deodorant.
Either way, you win.
Right Guard. Anything less would be uncivilized.
RIGHT GUARD
RIGHT GUARD

Peripheral cues can also lead to rejection of a message. For example, ads that advocate extreme positions, use endorsers who are not well liked or have credibility problems, or are not executed well (such as low-budget ads for local retailers) may be rejected without any consideration of their information or message arguments. As shown in Figure 5–10, the ELM views attitudes resulting from peripheral processing as temporary. So favorable attitudes must be maintained by continual exposure to the peripheral cues, such as through repetitive advertising.

Implications of the ELM

The elaboration likelihood model has important implications for marketing communications, particularly with respect to involvement. For example, if the involvement level of consumers in the target audience is high, an ad or sales presentation should contain strong arguments that are difficult for the message recipient to refute or counterargue. If the involvement level of the target audience is low, peripheral cues may be more important than detailed message arguments.

An interesting test of the ELM showed that the effectiveness of a celebrity endorser in an ad depends on the receiver's involvement level.[36] When involvement was low, a celebrity endorser had a significant effect on attitudes. When the receiver's involvement was high, however, the use of a celebrity had no effect on brand attitudes; the quality of the arguments used in the ad was more important.

The explanation given for these findings was that a celebrity may serve as a peripheral cue in the low-involvement situation, allowing the receiver to develop favorable attitudes based on feelings toward the source rather than engaging in extensive processing of the message. A highly involved consumer, however, engages in more detailed central processing of the message content. The quality of the message claims becomes more important than the identity of the endorser.

The ELM suggests that the most effective type of message depends on the route to persuasion the consumer follows. Many marketers recognize that involvement levels are low for their product categories and consumers are not motivated to process advertising messages in any detail. That's why marketers of low-involvement products often rely on creative tactics that emphasize peripheral cues and use repetitive advertising to create and maintain favorable attitudes toward their brand.

Summarizing the Response Process and the Effects of Advertising

As you have seen from our analysis of the receiver, the process consumers go through in responding to marketing communications can be viewed from a number of perspectives. Vakratsas and Ambler recently reviewed more than 250 journal articles and books in an effort to better understand how advertising works and affects the consumer.[37] On the basis of their review of these studies, they concluded that although effects hierarchies have been actively employed for nearly 100 years, there is little support for the concept of a hierarchy of effects in the sense of temporal sequence. They note that in trying to understand the response process and the manner in which advertising works, there are three critical intermediate effects between advertising and purchase (Figure 5–11). These include *cognition,* the "thinking" dimension of a person's response; *affect,* the "feeling" dimension; and *experience,* which is a feedback dimension based on the outcomes of product purchasing and usage. They conclude that individual responses to advertising are

Figure 5–11 A framework for studying how advertising works

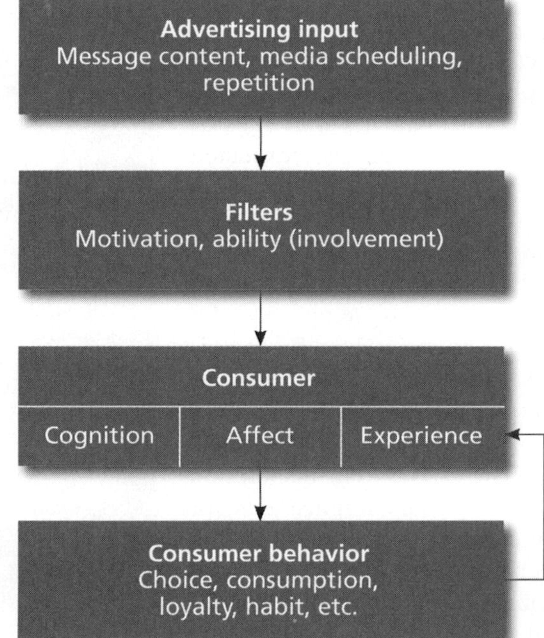

mediated or filtered by factors such as motivation and ability to process information, which can radically alter or change the individual's response to advertising. They suggest that the effects of advertising should be evaluated using these three dimensions, with some intermediate variables being more important than others, depending on factors such as the product category, stage of the product life cycle, target audience, competition, and impact of other marketing-mix components.

The implication is that marketers should focus on knowledge, liking, and trial as critical variables that advertising may affect. However, they should not assume a particular sequence of responses but rather engage in communications research and analysis to understand how advertising and other forms of promotion may affect these intermediate variables in various product/market situations. Those responsible for planning the IMC program need to learn as much as possible about their target market and how it may respond to advertising and other forms of marketing communications. The communication models presented in this chapter provide insight into how consumers may process and respond to persuasive messages and hopefully help marketers make better decisions in planning and implementing their promotional programs.

Summary

The function of all elements of the promotional mix is to communicate, so promotional planners must understand the communication process. This process can be very complex; successful marketing communications depend on a number of factors, including the nature of the message, the audience's interpretation of it, and the environment in which it is received. For effective communication to occur, the sender must encode a message in such a way that it will be decoded by the receiver in the intended manner. Feedback from the receiver helps the sender determine whether proper decoding has occurred or whether noise has interfered with the communication process.

Promotional planning begins with the receiver or target audience, as marketers must understand how the audience is likely to respond to various sources of communication or types of messages. For promotional planning, the receiver can be analyzed with respect to both its composition (i.e., individual, group, or mass audiences) and the response process it goes through. Different orderings of the traditional response hierarchy include the standard learning, dissonance/ attribution, and low-involvement models. The information response model integrates concepts from both the high- and low-involvement response hierarchy perspectives and recognizes the effects of direct experience with a product.

The cognitive response approach examines the thoughts evoked by a message and how they shape the receiver's ultimate acceptance or rejection of the communication. The elaboration likelihood model of attitude formation and change recognizes two forms of message processing, the central and peripheral routes to persuasion, which are a function of the receiver's motivation and ability to process a message. There are three critical intermediate effects between advertising and purchase including cognition, affect, and experience. Those responsible for planning the IMC program should learn as much as possible about their target audience and how it may respond to advertising and other forms of marketing communications.

Key Terms

communication, 139
source, 141
encoding, 141
message, 142
semiotics, 142
channel, 143
mass media, 143
receiver, 144
decoding, 144
field of experience, 144
noise, 144
response, 146
feedback, 146
AIDA model, 149
hierarchy of effects model, 149
innovation adoption model, 149
information processing model, 149
standard learning model, 152
dissonance/attribution model, 152
low-involvement hierarchy, 153
integrated information response model, 154
cognitive responses, 160
counterarguments, 160
support arguments, 161
source derogations, 161
source bolsters, 161
ad execution–related thoughts, 161
attitude toward the ad, 161
elaboration likelihood model (ELM) , 162
central route to persuasion, 163
peripheral route to persuasion, 163

Discussion Questions

1. Analyze the decision by Hewlett-Packard to develop a new branding campaign around the concept of *inventiveness.* What image is the company hoping to project to customer and other groups with this new branding campaign?

2. Discuss the various elements of the communications process. Find an example of an advertising campaign being used by a company and analyze this campaign in terms of these elements of the communications model.

3. How can companies marketing their products and services in a foreign country avoid some of the communications problems discussed in Global Perspective 5–1?

4. Discuss how semiotics can be of value to the field of integrated marketing communications. Select a marketing stimulus such as an advertisement, package, or other relevant marketing symbol and conduct a semiotic analysis of it such as the one shown in Exhibit 5–3.

5. The study discussed in IMC Perspective 5–2 suggests that ageism is a problem in the advertising business. Do you think young creative professionals can connect with and create ads that are effective for communicating with the mature market? What are some things that might be done to ensure that agencies do create ads that are relevant to older consumers?

6. Discuss the various forms feedback might take in the following situations:

- A salesman selling computer systems to large businesses has just made a sales presentation to a potential account.
- A consumer has just watched an infomercial for a revolutionary new exercise machine on late night television.
- An avid book reader has just logged onto the website of a company such as Amazon.com or Barnes & Noble.com.
- TV viewers watching the show "Friends" on a Thursday evening see a commercial for Calvin Klein jeans.

7. Explain how a company like Hewlett-Packard could use the four models of the response process shown in Figure 5–3 to develop IMC strategies for its various products.

8. Why do you think the Taco Bell advertising campaign featuring the Chihuahua has been so successful? How long do you think Taco Bell will be able to continue to use this campaign before it wears out and loses its impact?

9. An implication of the integrated information response model is that consumers are likely to take information from advertising and integrate it with direct experience to form judgments about a product. Explain how advertising could lessen the negative outcomes a consumer might experience when trying a brand.

10. What is meant by involvement in terms of advertising and consumer behavior? How might marketers determine the degree of involvement consumers have with their products and services?

11. Choose one of the four advertising planning strategies identified by the FCB grid shown in Figure 5–8. Find an example of an advertisement that you feel is a good example of this ad planning strategy.

12. Select an ad you think would be processed by a central route to persuasion and one where you think peripheral processing would occur. Show the ads to several people and ask them to write down the thoughts they have about each ad. Analyze their thoughts using the cognitive response categories discussed in the chapter.

Chapter Six

Source, Message, and Channel Factors

Chapter Objectives

- To study the major variables in the communication system and how they influence consumers' processing of promotional messages.
- To examine the considerations involved in selecting a source or communicator of a promotional message.
- To examine different types of message structures and appeals that can be used to develop a promotional message.
- To consider how the channel or medium used to deliver a promotional message influences the communication process.

Jenny Craig Takes a Chance with Monica Lewinsky

Marketers often use individuals who have achieved some form of celebrity status to serve as spokespersons for their companies. Most of the celebrities hired by companies to pitch their products or services are popular television and movie stars, entertainers, or athletes, although occasionally a politician or some other well-known public figure may be used. However, Jenny Craig, Inc., one of the world's largest weight management service companies, took the practice of hiring celebrity endorsers in a new direction recently with its decision to hire Monica Lewinsky as a spokeswoman. Lewinsky gained celebrity status as the former White House intern whose relationship with President Bill Clinton became a worldwide scandal that led to his impeachment trial.

Jenny Craig's Vice President for Marketing, Linell Killus, noted that Lewinsky was chosen as the spokeswoman for the company because she tried the program and it worked for her: "She's an example of a client success story, and obviously she's highly recognizable." When asked about Monica Lewinsky's appeal to Jenny Craig's target audience, mostly women age 25 to 54, Killus said: "She represents a busy active woman of today with a hectic lifestyle. And she has had weight issues and weight struggles for a long time. That represents a lot of women in America." Jenny Craig's president and chief operating officer, Patricia A. Larchett, explained the selection of the company's new spokeswoman by stating: "As many people recognize, Monica has struggled with her weight her whole life. We hope that, by sharing her story, we can reach countless others who struggle daily with eating and weight issues and demonstrate that, with Jenny Craig, it is possible to make positive, healthy changes in your life—on the outside and the inside."

The ads featuring Lewinsky began airing in January 2000 and promote a "low-carb option" to Jenny Craig's weight-loss regimen. She appears in two commercials, which include "before" pictures of her looking heavier. She talks of her previous attempts at dieting, saying: "I've tried every diet in the world. If it was stand on your head I've tried it. It it was eat only grapefruit, I've tried it. Magic diet pills, I've tried it." A more svelte "after" Lewinsky is then shown as flashbulbs go off in the background and she praises her new Jenny Craig diet. The commercials are part of a $7 million advertising campaign that includes a mixture of broadcast, cable, and Internet media running throughout the company's markets in the United States and Canada.

Officials at Jenny Craig believe the best way to communicate information about the benefits of its weight management program is by sharing the stories of successful clients. Rather than attempting to capitalize on the past, the company's ads positioned Lewinsky in the same way as other testimonials—as an example of a successful Jenny Craig client who had a compelling personal story to share. The company believes that, given the tremendous public interest in Monica Lewinsky, the campaign offers an opportunity to bring awareness of the Jenny Craig weight management program to more people than ever before. Linell Killus suggests: "She's someone who truly wants to change her life in a positive way and that's what Jenny Craig is all about." However, not everyone agrees with the decision to use Lewinsky. Some Jenny Craig franchisees have chosen to alternate advertisements from the new campaign rather than use the ads featuring Lewinsky because of her role in the impeachment scandal. Some industry analysts have expressed concern that the use of Lewinsky as a spokeswoman could be perceived as a publicity ploy and will draw negative reactions, particularly among women.

Jenny Craig is not the first company to use a celebrity whose fame is based on controversy. A few years ago Sarah Ferguson, the Duchess of York, sought a kind of public redemption and financial redress following her divorce from Prince Andrew by signing a lucrative deal with Weight Watchers International, another diet program. However, she was ultimately seen as a sympathetic figure because of her de facto banishment from the royal family. Whether the public sees Monica Lewinsky in the same light is questionable. It should be interesting to see if the use of Lewinsky as a spokesperson helps boost Jenny Craig's sales or backfires because of the negative reactions over the way she gained her celebrity status.

Sources: Constance L. Hays, "Monica Lewinsky Meets Jenny Craig, and a Spokeswoman Is Born," *The New York Times,* December 28, 1999, p. 1; Tony Fong, "Lewinsky to Debut in Jenny Craig Ad Campaign," *San Diego Union-Tribune,* December 29, 1999, pp. C1–2; "Jenny Craig Franchises Opt Out of Lewinsky Ads," Associated Press Newswires, January 6, 2000.

In this chapter, we analyze the major variables in the communication system: the source, the message, and the channel. We examine the characteristics of sources, how they influence reactions to promotional messages, and why one type of communicator is more effective than another. We then focus on the message itself and how structure and type of appeal influence its effectiveness. Finally, we consider how factors related to the channel or medium affect the communication process.

Promotional Planning through the Persuasion Matrix

To develop an effective advertising and promotional campaign, a firm must select the right spokesperson to deliver a compelling message through appropriate channels or media. Source, message, and channel factors are controllable elements in the communications model. The **persuasion matrix** (Figure 6–1) helps marketers see how each controllable element interacts with the consumer's response process.[1] The matrix has two sets of variables. *Independent variables* are the controllable components of the communication process, outlined in Chapter 5; *dependent variables* are the steps a receiver goes through in being persuaded. Marketers can choose the person or source who delivers the message, the type of message appeal used, and the channel or medium. And although they can't control the receiver, they can select their target audience. The destination variable is included because the initial message recipient may pass on information to others, such as friends or associates, through word of mouth.

Promotional planners need to know how decisions about each independent variable influence the stages of the response hierarchy so that they don't enhance one stage at the expense of another. A humorous message may gain attention but result

Figure 6–1 The persuasion matrix

Dependent variables: Steps in being persuaded	Independent variables: The communication components				
	Source	Message	Channel	Receiver	Destination
Message presentation			(2)		
Attention	(4)				
Comprehension				(1)	
Yielding		(3)			
Retention					
Behavior					

in decreased comprehension if consumers fail to process its content. Many ads that use humor, sexual appeals, or celebrities capture consumers' attention but result in poor recall of the brand name or message. The following examples, which correspond to the numbers in Figure 6–1, illustrate decisions that can be evaluated with the persuasion matrix.

1. *Receiver/comprehension: Can the receiver comprehend the ad?* Marketers must know their target market to make their messages clear and understandable. A less educated person may have more difficulty interpreting a complicated message. Jargon may be unfamiliar to some receivers. The more marketers know about the target market, the more they see which words, symbols, and expressions their customers understand.

2. *Channel/presentation: Which media will increase presentation?* A top-rated, prime-time TV program is seen by nearly 30 million households each week. *TV Guide* and *Reader's Digest* reach nearly 16 million homes with each issue. But the important point is how well they reach the marketer's target audience. CNN's "Moneyline" reaches only around a million viewers each weekday evening, but its audience consists mostly of upscale businesspeople who are prime prospects for expensive cars, financial services, and business-related products.

3. *Message/yielding: What type of message will create favorable attitudes or feelings?* Marketers generally try to create agreeable messages that lead to positive feelings toward the product or service. Humorous messages often put consumers in a good mood and evoke positive feelings that may become associated with the brand being advertised. Music adds emotion that makes consumers more receptive to the message. Many advertisers use explicit sexual appeals designed to arouse consumers or suggest they can enhance their attractiveness to the opposite sex. Some marketers compare their brands to the competition.

4. *Source/attention: Who will be effective in getting consumers' attention?* The large number of ads we are bombarded with every day makes it difficult for advertisers to break through the clutter. Marketers deal with this problem by using sources who will attract the target audience's attention—actors, athletes, rock stars, or attractive models. One positive aspect of Jenny Craig's use of Monica Lewinsky as a spokeswoman is that she is likely to capture the attention of consumers when they see her appearing in commercials for the company.

Source Factors

The source component is a multifaceted concept. When Michael Jordan appears in a commercial for Wheaties, is the source Jordan himself, the company (General Mills), or some combination of the two? And, of course, consumers get information from friends, relatives, and neighbors; in fact, personal sources may be the most influential factor in a purchase decision. Jim Beam appeals to personal sources and their ability to influence one another with its "Real Friends. Real Bourbon" campaign (Exhibit 6–1).

Exhibit 6–1 Jim Beam appeals to interpersonal influence with this ad

We use the term **source** to mean the person involved in communicating a marketing message, either directly or indirectly. A *direct source* is a spokesperson who delivers a message and/or demonstrates a product or service, like tennis star Andre Agassi who endorses Head tennis rackets in Exhibit 6–2. An *indirect source,* say, a model, doesn't actually deliver a message but draws attention to and/or enhances the appearance of the ad. Some ads use neither a direct nor an indirect source; the source is the organization with the message to communicate. Since most research focuses on individuals as a message source, our examination of source factors follows this approach.

Companies are very careful when selecting individuals to deliver their selling messages. Many firms spend huge sums of money for a specific person to endorse their product or company. They also spend millions recruiting, selecting, and training salespeople to represent the company and deliver sales presentations. They recognize that the characteristics of the source affect the sales and advertising message.

Marketers try to select individuals whose traits will maximize message influence. The source may be knowledgeable, popular, and/or physically attractive; typify the target audience; or have the power to reward or punish the receiver in some manner. Herbert Kelman developed three basic categories of source attributes: credibility, attractiveness, and power.[2] Each influences the recipient's attitude or behavior through a different process (see Figure 6–2).

Exhibit 6–2 Tennis star Andre Agassi serves as a spokesperson for Head

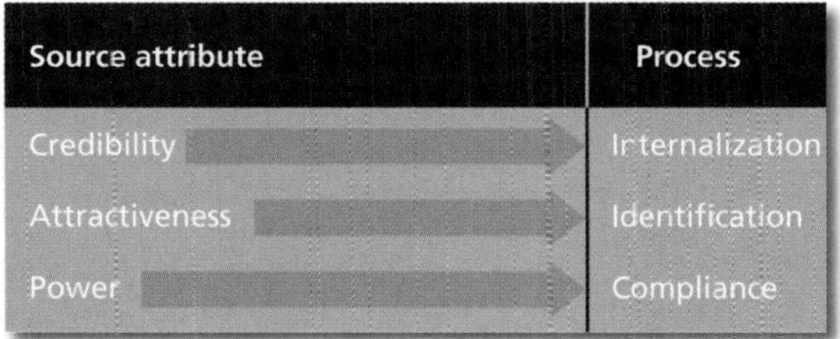

Figure 6–2 Source attributes and receiver processing modes

Source Credibility

Credibility is the extent to which the recipient sees the source as having relevant knowledge, skill, or experience and trusts the source to give unbiased, objective information. There are two important dimensions to credibility, expertise and trustworthiness.

A communicator seen as knowledgeable—someone with expertise—is more persuasive than one with less expertise. But the source also has to be trustworthy—honest, ethical, and believable. The influence of a knowledgeable source will be lessened if audience members think he or she is biased or has underlying personal motives for advocating a position (such as being paid to endorse a product).

One of the most reliable effects found in communications research is that expert and/or trustworthy sources are more persuasive than sources who are less expert or trustworthy.[3] Information from a credible source influences beliefs, opinions, attitudes, and/or behavior through a process known as **internalization,** which occurs when the receiver adopts the opinion of the credible communicator since he or she believes information from this source is accurate. Once the receiver internalizes an opinion or attitude, it becomes integrated into his or her belief system and may be maintained even after the source of the message is forgotten.

A highly credible communicator is particularly important when message recipients have a negative position toward the product, service, company, or issue being promoted, because the credible source is likely to inhibit counterarguments. As discussed in Chapter 5, reduced counterarguing should result in greater message acceptance and persuasion.

Applying Expertise

Because attitudes and opinions developed through an internalization process become part of the individual's belief system, marketers want to use communicators with high credibility. Companies use a variety of techniques to convey source expertise. Sales personnel are trained in the product line, which increases customers' perceptions of their expertise. Marketers of highly technical products recruit sales reps with specialized technical backgrounds in engineering, computer science, and other areas to ensure their expertise.

Spokespeople are often chosen because of their knowledge, experience, and expertise in a particular product or service area. Endorsements from individuals or groups recognized as experts, such as doctors or dentists, are also common in advertising (Exhibit 6–3). The importance of using expert sources was shown in a study by Roobina Ohanian, who found that the perceived expertise of celebrity endorsers was more important in explaining purchase intentions than their attractiveness or trustworthiness. She suggests that celebrity spokespeople are most effective when they are knowledgeable, experienced, and qualified to talk about the product they are endorsing.[4]

Exhibit 6–3 Dove promotes the fact that it is recommended by experts in skin care

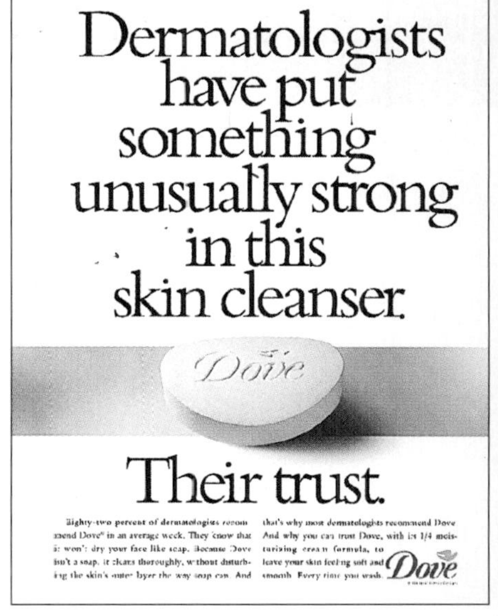

Dermatologists have put something unusually strong in this skin cleanser.
Dove
Their trust.
Dove

Applying Trustworthiness

While expertise is important, the target audience must also find the source believable. Finding celebrities or other figures with a trustworthy image is often difficult. Many trustworthy public figures hesitate to endorse products because of the potential impact on their reputation and image. It has been suggested that former CBS news anchor

Global Perspective 6–1

Selling Out, but Only Abroad

Many American celebrities make huge sums of money endorsing products and serving as advertising spokespeople. Some big stars won't do endorsements because they don't want fans to think they've sold out. But many stars who resist the temptation to cash in on their fame in the United States are only too happy to appear in ads in foreign countries.

Actress Kim Basinger has modeled hosiery in Italy; Woody Allen wrote and directed a series of commercials for the country's largest grocery chain, Co-op Italia, for several million dollars. Sharon Stone, who became a superstar with her sexy roles in movies like *Basic Instinct* and *Casino,* received between $1 million and $2 million to star in a racy ad for Pirelli Tires in Europe. An executive for the agency that did the ads says, "Pirelli's brand image is very Italian, quite sexy. We chose Sharon Stone because of who she is—very sexy, grown up, in control."

Nowhere are ads starring American celebrities more prevalent than in Japan. While the Japanese flood the United States with cars, TVs, and VCRs, the trade in celebrity endorsers flows the other way. Arnold Schwarzenegger pitches Nissin Cup Noodle and Chi Chin vitamin drink and can be seen straddling a rocket that blasts off and shoots him out of the frame in a commercial for Takeda Chemical Industries. Gene Hackman and Sylvester Stallone each received $1 million to represent Kirin beer. Bruce Willis appeared on Japanese television selling Subarus and Post Water, while his ex-wife, actress Demi Moore, pushes cosmetics. Japan's two major airlines have used Frank Sinatra and Richard Gere to fill seats. Actress Jodie Foster flirted with a group of men to the tune of the Fine Young Cannibals' "She Drives Me Crazy" in a Honda ad. Charlie Sheen praises Tokyo Gas, while Sigourney Weaver promotes the strengths of Nippon Steel.

Western celebrities are used to promote products in Japan for several reasons. Many Japanese identify with the Western style of life, and the celebrity endorsements give brands a certain international cachet. Also, Japanese advertising emphasizes style and mood rather than substance; consumers expect to be entertained by ads rather than bored by product testimonials. Because Japanese commercials commonly last only 15 seconds, advertisers find an instantly recognizable Western celebrity who can capture viewers' attention is well worth the money. According to an *Advertising Age* reporter, the movie studios also encourage celebrities to do ads in Japan because it boosts their visibility in the Far East. He says, "Increasingly the market for films is becoming global and the more recognizable the star, the better the picture will do in the Asian market." The studio and the celebrity benefit along with the marketer.

Many celebrities cashing in on foreign commercials try to protect their image at home. The stars commonly have nondisclosure clauses in their contracts, specifying that the ads cannot be shown—or sometimes even discussed (oops!)—outside the country for which they were intended. The worldwide head of commercials at the William Morris talent agency says that actors "believe that knowledge of that endorsement should stay within that country." Sorry about that.

Sources: Stephen Rae, "How Celebrities Make Killings on Commercials," *Cosmopolitan,* January 1997, pp. 164–67; Lauren David Peden, "Seen the One Where Arnold Sells Noodles?" *The New York Times,* June 20, 1993, p. 28; David Kilburn, "Japanese Airlines Tap U.S. Stars," *Advertising Age,* April 8, 1991.

Walter Cronkite, who has repeatedly been rated one of the most trusted people in America, could command millions of dollars as a product spokesperson. Global Perspective 6–1 discusses how some American celebrities protect their image by endorsing products abroad rather than in the United States.

Advertisers use various techniques to increase the perception that their sources are trustworthy. Hidden cameras are used to show that the consumer is not a paid spokesperson and is making an objective evaluation of the product. Disguised brands are compared. (Of course, the sponsor's brand always performs better than the consumer's regular brand, and he or she is always surprised.) Most consumers are skeptical of these techniques, so they may have limited value in enhancing perceptions of credibility.

Using Corporate Leaders as Spokespeople Another way of enhancing source credibility is to use the company president or chief executive officer as a spokesperson in the firm's advertising. Many companies believe the use of their president or CEO is the ultimate expression of the company's commitment to quality and customer service. In some cases, these ads have not only increased sales but also helped turn the company leaders into celebrities.[5] Lee Iacocca appeared in more than 60 commercials for Chrysler Corp. and became a national business hero for guiding the successful turnaround of the company. Another popular corporate spokesperson is Dave Thomas, the founder of Wendy's fast-food restaurants, who has been the company's pitchman since 1989 (Exhibit 6–4). Thomas has appeared in more than 500 Wendy's commercials and is widely credited with having helped increase the restaurant chain's sales.[6] Other well-known corporate leaders who sometimes appear in ads for their companies include Dell Computer founder and CEO, Michael Dell, and Southwest Airline's popular CEO Herb Kelleher.

Exhibit 6–4 Dave Thomas is a very effective spokesperson for Wendy's

Some research suggests the use of a company president or CEO can improve attitudes and increase the likelihood that consumers will inquire about the company's product or service.[7] It is becoming common for local retailers to use the owner or president in their ads. Companies are likely to continue using their top executives in their advertising, particularly when they have celebrity value that helps enhance the firms' image. However, there can be problems with this strategy. CEO spokespeople who become very popular may get more attention than their company's product/service or advertising message. And if a firm's image becomes too closely tied to a popular leader, there can be problems if that person leaves the company. IMC Perspective 6–2 discusses reasons why companies use CEOs and company owners as their advertising spokespersons.

Limitations of Credible Sources Several studies have shown that a high-credibility source is not always an asset, nor is a low-credibility source always a liability. High- and low-credibility sources are equally effective when they are arguing for a position opposing their own best interest.[8] A very credible source is more effective when message recipients are not in favor of the position advocated in the message.[9] However, a very credible source is less important when the audience has a neutral position, and such a source may even be less effective than a moderately credible source when the receiver's initial attitude is favorable.[10]

Another reason a low-credibility source may be as effective as a high-credibility source is the **sleeper effect,** whereby the persuasiveness of a message increases with the passage of time. The immediate impact of a persuasive message may be inhibited because of its association with a low-credibility source. But with time, the association of the message with the source diminishes and the receiver's attention focuses more on favorable information in the message, resulting in more support arguing. However, many studies have failed to demonstrate the presence of a sleeper effect.[11] Many advertisers hesitate to count on the sleeper effect, since exposure to a credible source is a more reliable strategy.[12]

Source Attractiveness

A source characteristic frequently used by advertisers is **attractiveness,** which encompasses similarity, familiarity, and likability.[13] *Similarity* is a supposed resemblance between the source and the receiver of the message, while *familiarity* refers to knowledge of the source through exposure. *Likability* is an affection for the source as a result of physical appearance, behavior, or other personal traits. Even when the sources are not athletes or movie stars, consumers often admire their physical appearance, talent, and/or personality.

IMC Perspective 6–2

Using the Owner to Pitch the Company

In 1971, the advertising agency for Perdue Farms, Inc. was developing a new ad campaign that would focus on the quality of Perdue chickens. The creative director suggested a novel strategy of featuring Frank Perdue, the tough-minded president of Perdue Farms, as the spokesperson for the company's advertising using a "tough man/tender chicken" theme. The company's sales soared as a result of the campaign, and Frank Perdue continued to pitch Perdue chicken in ads for more than 20 years, becoming a folk hero throughout the East in the process. Moreover, this campaign is often cited as setting the stage for the idea of using a company president, chief executive officer, or owner as an advertising spokesperson.

Over the past three decades, a number of major corporations have relied on their chief executive as an advertising spokesperson. Victor Kiam was a well-known spokesperson for Remington Products for many years with his familiar pitch "I liked the razor so much I bought the company." Lee Iacocca appeared in more than 60 TV commercials for Chrysler Corporation throughout the 1980s and early 90s, Orville Redenbacher pitched his brand of popcorn until he died, while Dave Thomas, the founder of Wendy's, continues to star in ads for the fast-food chain.

While these individuals are among the best known of the corporate leader spokespersons, the practice of using company presidents or owners in ads has an interesting history among small, local firms as well. In the early 1970s an auto dealer in Seattle became famous for demolishing a car with a sledgehammer during commercial breaks. "Crazy Eddie" Antar for years dressed up in a straightjacket and yelled "It's insane" on ads for a chain of stereo outlets in New York City. In Southern California, auto dealer Cal Worthington was long a staple on late-night TV with bits featuring him wing-walking on airplanes, and appearing with his dog Spot and other animals such as a giraffe, zebra, elephant, and hippopotamus to get attention.

"King" Stahlman
BAIL BONDS
"A Name You Can Trust"

Today, in markets around the country, TV viewers watching syndicated reruns, local sporting events, and late-night movies are likely to see commercials with local businesspeople hawking their companies, products, and/or services. For some small business owners, the decision to become quasi-actors has to do with advertising budgets too small to accommodate professional actors or announcers who may charge thousands of dollars to tape a few commercials. However, many marketing and advertising experts question the strategy of using company presidents or owners in ads and note that it is often egos rather than logic that results in their use. The experts suggest that businesspeople should only get in front of the camera if they exude credibility and possess the intangible quality of provoking a warm, fuzzy feeling in viewers. The general manager at one agency says: "If it's forced or purely an ego thing, forget it." He occasionally has been compelled to tell business owners bent on becoming TV personalities that they couldn't out-act a brick wall.

Some businesspeople do insist on appearing in commercials for their companies, which is one reason for the wide range in quality of the various owner-as-pitchman campaigns. One ad executive says: "They're content to stand stiffly in front of the camera reading the cue cards in monotone. They think they're helping the business. They don't realize until its too late that viewers are laughing at them."

However, many company owners are the ones doing the laughing—all the way to the bank—as a result of their ad campaigns. For example, George "King" Stahlman is a bail bondsman in San Diego and the star of dozens of his own TV commercials. He spends up to $15,000 a month saturating the local airways with his crusty visage and familiar tagline: "Let me help you out." Stahlman says about 75 percent of the people who walk into his office knows him from his television ads. For Stahlman, aligning his TV persona so strongly with the business has made him one of the few, if only, recognizable bail bondsmen in the public eye. Stahlman says: "Nobody knows the name of bail bondsmen, so when people go to the Yellow Pages, they pick my name because I've been on TV talking to them for years."

Some argue that the use of business owners in ads is an effective way of projecting an image of trust and honesty and, more important, the idea that the company isn't run by some faceless corporate monolith. As one expert notes: "These guys come into people's living rooms every night and, over the course of weeks and years, become like members of the family. It gets to the point that when you think of a certain product category, you think of the guy you see all the time on TV."

Even though not all CEOs and company owners are smooth in front of a camera, the practice of using corporate chieftains as advertising spokespeople is likely to continue. As one advertising executive notes: "It's a perk that's tougher to walk away from than a corporate jet."

Sources: Frank Green, "Masters of the Pitch," *The San Diego Union-Tribune,*" January 30, 2000, pp. I 1,6; and Joanne Lipman, "Chairmen Starring as Spokesmen May Eventually Lose their Luster," *The Wall Street Journal,* February 12, 1992, p. B6.

Source attractiveness leads to persuasion through a process of **identification,** whereby the receiver is motivated to seek some type of relationship with the source and thus adopts similar beliefs, attitudes, preferences, or behavior. Maintaining this position depends on the source's continued support for the position as well as the receiver's continued identification with the source. If the source changes position, the receiver may also change. Unlike internalization, identification does not usually integrate information from an attractive source into the receiver's belief system. The receiver may maintain the attitudinal position or behavior only as long as it is supported by the source or the source remains attractive.

Marketers recognize that receivers of persuasive communications are more likely to attend to and identify with people they find likable or similar to themselves. Similarity and likability are the two source characteristics marketers seek when choosing a communicator.

Applying Similarity

Marketers recognize that people are more likely to be influenced by a message coming from someone with whom they feel a sense of similarity.[14] If the communicator and receiver have similar needs, goals, interests, and lifestyles, the position advocated by the source is better understood and received. Similarity is used in various ways in marketing communications. Companies select salespeople whose characteristics match well with their customers'. A sales position for a particular region may be staffed by someone local who has background and interests in common with the customers. Global marketers often hire foreign nationals as salespeople so customers can relate more easily to them.

Companies may also try to recruit former athletes to sell sporting goods or beer, since their customers usually have a strong interest in sports. Several studies have shown that customers who perceive a salesperson as similar to themselves are more likely to be influenced by his or her message.[15]

Similarity is also used to create a situation where the consumer feels empathy for the person shown in the commercial. In a slice-of-life commercial, the advertiser usually starts by presenting a predicament with the hope of getting the consumer to think, "I can see myself in that situation." This can help establish a bond of similarity between the communicator and the receiver, increasing the source's level of persuasiveness. Many companies feel that the best way to connect with consumers is by using regular-looking, everyday people with whom the average person can easily identify. For example, Exhibit 6–5 shows Chris Dollard, a relatively unknown actor who is cast in many commercials because he is seen as "a regular Joe" whom consumers can relate to. Dollard has appeared in ads for a number of companies and products including JC Penney, MCI, Baked Tostitos, and Isuzu Rodeo.

Exhibit 6–5 Chris Dollard appears in many commercials because he looks like an everyday guy

Applying Likability: Using Celebrities

Advertisers recognize the value of using spokespeople who are admired: TV and movie stars, athletes, musicians, and other popular public figures. More than 20 percent of all TV commercials

Exhibit 6–6 Michael Jordan's many endorsements include Gatorade

feature celebrities, and advertisers pay hundreds of millions of dollars for their services. The top celebrity endorser is former basketball superstar Michael Jordan. Even though he retired in 1998, Jordan has an estimated $40 million a year in endorsement deals with companies such as MCI-WorldCom, Nike, Bijan Fragrances, Rayovac, Oakley, General Mills, and Quaker Oats (makers of Gatorade)[16] (Exhibit 6–6). One of the hottest new celebrity endorsers is golf phenom Tiger Woods, who has signed endorsement contracts worth more than $100 million with Nike, American Express, General Mills, and Buick (Exhibit 6–7).

Why do companies spend huge sums to have celebrities appear in their ads and endorse their products? They think celebrities have stopping power. That is, they draw attention to advertising messages in a very cluttered media environment. Marketers think a popular celebrity will favorably influence consumers' feelings, attitudes, and purchase behavior. And they believe celebrities can enhance the target audience's perceptions of the product in terms of image and/or performance. For example, a well-known athlete may convince potential buyers that the product will enhance their own performance.

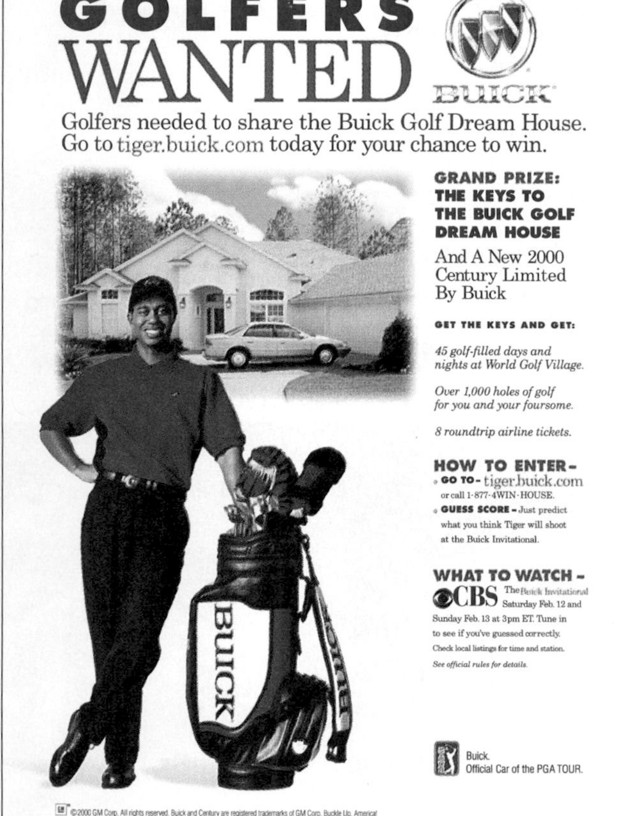

Exhibit 6–7 Tiger Woods has endorsement contracts with a number of companies including Buick

A number of factors must be considered when a company decides to use a celebrity spokesperson, including the dangers of overshadowing the product and being overexposed, the target audience's receptivity, and risks to the advertiser.

Overshadowing the Product How will the celebrity affect the target audience's processing of the advertising message? Consumers may focus their attention on the celebrity and fail to notice the brand. Advertisers should select a celebrity spokesperson who will attract attention and enhance the sales message, yet not overshadow the brand. For example, actress Lindsay Wagner was chosen as the spokeswoman for Ford Motor Co. dealers in Southern California because she brings a physical presence and star power to the advertising which attracts attention and makes it memorable. She is also very credible and accessible, which makes the advertising believable and likeable. And yet she never overshadows the brand, but rather enhances and humanizes it[17] (Exhibit 6–8).

Overexposure Consumers are often skeptical of endorsements because they know the celebrities are being paid.[18] This problem is particularly pronounced when a celebrity endorses too many products or companies and becomes overexposed. Advertisers can protect themselves against overexposure with an exclusivity clause limiting the number of products a celebrity can endorse. However, such clauses are usually expensive, and most celebrities agree not to endorse similar products anyway. Many celebrities, knowing their fame is fleeting, try to earn as much endorsement money as possible, yet they must be careful not to damage their credibility by endorsing too many products. For example, singer/actress Cher damaged her credibility as an advertising spokesperson by appearing in too many infomercials. When she realized that appearing in so many infomercials was devastating to her acting career as well, she ceased doing them.[19]

Exhibit 6–8 Lindsay Wagner is an effective endorser for Ford dealers because she does not overshadow the product

Target Audiences' Receptivity Consumers who are particularly knowledgeable about a product or service or have strongly established attitudes may be less influenced by a celebrity than those with little knowledge or neutral attitudes. One study found that college-age students were more likely to have a positive attitude toward a product endorsed by a celebrity than were older consumers.[20] The teenage market has generally been very receptive to celebrity endorsers, as evidenced by the frequent use of entertainers and athletes in ads targeted to this group for products such as apparel, cosmetics, and beverages. However, many marketers are finding that teenage consumers are more skeptical and cynical toward the use of celebrity endorsers and respond better to ads using humor, irony, and unvarnished truth.[21] Some marketers targeting teenagers have responded to this by no longer using celebrities in their campaigns or by poking fun at their use. For example, Sprite has developed a very effective campaign using ads that parody celebrity endorsers and carry the tagline "Image is nothing. Obey your thirst" (Exhibit 6–9).

CUT OUT AND PLACE OVER A PICTURE OF ANY MEDIOCRE ATHLETE HOLDING OUT FOR A $100 MILLION CONTRACT. SPRITE WON'T BE MORE REFRESHING, BUT IT'S CHEAPER THAN ACTUALLY PAYING THE BUM. IMAGE IS NOTHING. THIRST IS EVERYTHING. OBEY YOUR THIRST.
Sprite
"Does Sprite really refresh me? I don't know. Ask my agent."

Exhibit 6–9 Sprite parodies the use of celebrity endorsers in this ad

Some studies suggest that celebrity endorsements are becoming less important in influencing purchase decisions for a broad range of consumers.[22] In a survey of 30,000 consumers age 13 to 75 conducted by the Athletic Footwear Association, celebrity endorsements were the least important factor for buying a particular brand of shoe.

One company that believes celebrity endorsements are not worthwhile is New Balance, which has an across-the-board policy against them. The president of the company notes, "If you want the best shoe for yourself, you don't generally give a hoot if Michael Jordan wears it. We'd rather put the money into our factories than into the hands of celebrities."[23]

Risk to the Advertiser A celebrity's behavior may pose a risk to a company.[24] A number of entertainers and athletes have been involved in activities that could embarrass the companies whose products they endorsed. For example, Hertz used O. J. Simpson as its spokesperson for 20 years and lost all that equity when he was accused of murdering his ex-wife and her friend. Pepsi had a string of problems with celebrity endorsers; it severed ties with Mike Tyson, after his wife accused him of beating her, and with singer Michael Jackson, after he was accused of having sex with a 12-year-old boy. Pepsi dropped a TV commercial featuring Madonna when some religious groups and consumers objected to her "Like a Prayer" video and threatened to boycott Pepsi products. More recently, several companies including Pizza Hut and the Carl's Jr. fast-food chain terminated the endorsement contract with controversial basketball star Dennis Rodman because of his unpredictable behavior both on and off the court.[25]

To avoid these problems, companies often research a celebrity's personal life and background. Many endorsement contracts include a morals clause allowing the company to terminate the contract if a controversy arises. For example, in late 1999, Callaway Golf terminated its endorsement deal with well-known golfer John Daly on the grounds that he violated a clause in his contract prohibiting him from drinking or gambling.[26] However, marketers should remember that adding morals clauses to their endorsement contracts only gets them out of a problem; it does not prevent it.

Understanding the Meaning of Celebrity Endorsers

Advertisers must try to match the product or company's image, the characteristics of the target market, and the personality of the celebrity.[27] The image celebrities project to consumers can be just as important as their ability to attract attention. An interesting perspective on celebrity endorsement was developed by Grant McCracken.[28] He argues that credibility and attractiveness don't sufficiently explain how and why celebrity endorsements work and offers a model based on meaning transfer (Figure 6–3).

Figure 6–3 Meaning movement and the endorsement process

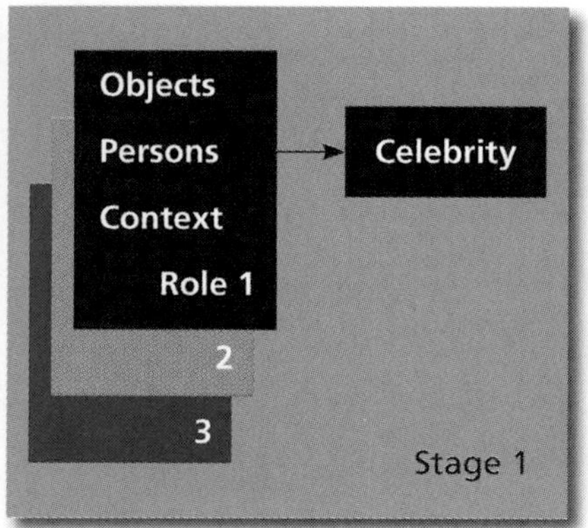

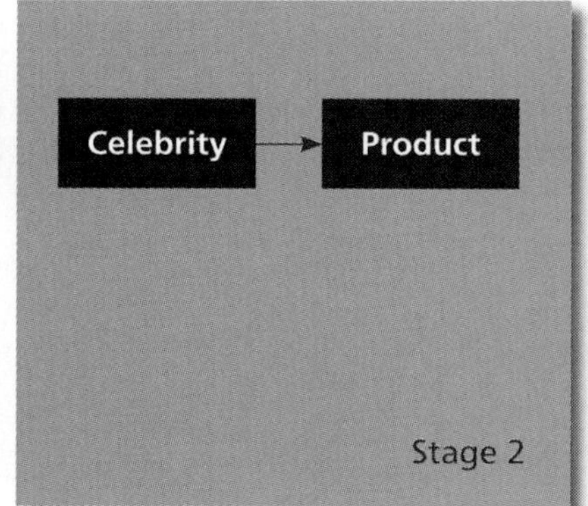

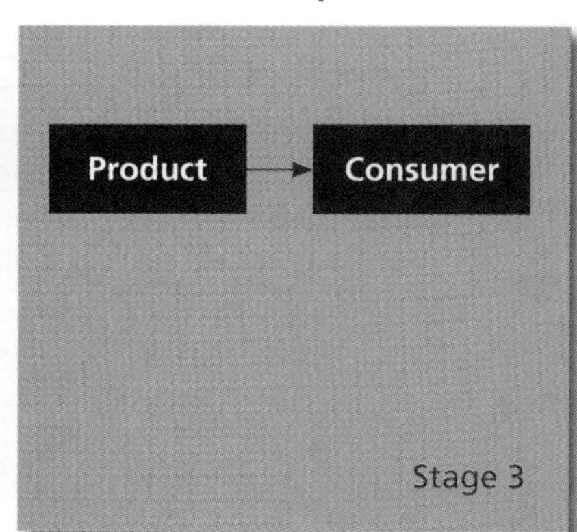

Key: → = Path of meaning movement

 = Stage of meaning movement

According to this model, a celebrity's effectiveness as an endorser depends on the culturally acquired meanings he or she brings to the endorsement process. Each celebrity contains many meanings, including status, class, gender, and age as well as personality and lifestyle. In explaining stage 1 of the meaning transfer process, McCracken notes:

> Celebrities draw these powerful meanings from the roles they assume in their television, movie, military, athletic, and other careers. Each new dramatic role brings the celebrity into contact with a range of objects, persons, and contexts. Out of these objects, persons, and contexts are transferred meanings that then reside in the celebrity.[29]

Examples of celebrities who have acquired meanings include actor Bill Cosby as the perfect father (from his role on "The Cosby Show"), tennis star Andre Agassi as the defiant tennis star (from his antics and performance on and off the court), and actor Jerry Seinfeld as the quirky comedian (from his role on the sitcom "Seinfeld").

McCracken suggests celebrity endorsers bring their meanings into the ad and transfer them to the product they are endorsing (stage 2 of the model in Figure 6–3). For example, Subaru's use of actor Paul Hogan as its spokesperson takes advantage of Hogan's image as a rugged, tough guy from the Australian outback which he developed from his roles in the *Crocodile Dundee* movies and other films. Subaru has done an excellent job of using Hogan in its ads for its Outback—a vehicle the company positions as the first sport utility wagon (Exhibit 6–10).

In the final stage of McCracken's model, the meanings the celebrity has given to the product are transferred to the consumer. Subaru touts the Outback as a vehicle that combines rough-terrain driving capability with the ride and comfort of a passenger car, and the use of Paul Hogan helps in creating this image. Subaru's vice president of marketing says, "A lot of sport utility shoppers are buying the rugged, go-anywhere image. Paul Hogan not only gives us a nice play on the Outback name but also a chance to help rugged-ize the Outback image."[30] McCracken notes that this final stage is complicated and difficult to achieve. The way consumers take pos-

Exhibit 6–10 Australian actor Paul Hogan helps position the Subaru Outback as a rugged, go-anywhere vehicle

session of the meaning the celebrity has transferred to a product is probably the least understood part of the process.

The meaning transfer model has some important implications for companies using celebrity endorsers. Marketers must first decide on the image or symbolic meanings important to the target audience for the particular product, service, or company. They must then determine which celebrity best represents the meaning or image to be projected. An advertising campaign must be designed that captures that meaning in the product and moves it to the consumer. Marketing and advertising personnel often rely on intuition in choosing celebrity endorsers for their companies or products, but some companies conduct research studies to determine consumers' perceptions of celebrities' meaning.

Marketers may also pretest ads to determine whether they transfer the proper meaning to the product. When celebrity endorsers are used, the marketer should track the campaign's effectiveness. Does the celebrity continue to be effective in communicating the proper meaning to the target audience? Celebrities who are no longer in the limelight may lose their ability to transfer any significant meanings to the product.

As we have seen, marketers must consider many factors when choosing a celebrity to serve as an advertising spokesperson for the company or a particular brand. IMC Perspective 6–3 discusses how marketers use research data to help in the choice of celebrity endorsers.

Applying Likability: Decorative Models

Advertisers often draw attention to their ads by featuring a physically attractive person who serves as a passive or decorative model rather than as an active communicator. Research suggests that physically attractive communicators generally have a positive impact and generate more favorable evaluations of both ads and products than less attractive models.[31] The gender appropriateness of the model for the product being advertised and his or her relevance to the product are also important considerations.[32] Products such as cosmetics or fashionable clothing are likely to benefit from the use of an attractive model, since physical appearance is very relevant in marketing these items. For example, Revlon uses supermodel Cindy Crawford in advertising for various cosmetics products such as its Fire & Ice fragrance (Exhibit 6–11).

Exhibit 6–11 Revlon makes effective use of supermodel Cindy Crawford in this ad

PLAY WITH FIRE.
SKATE ON THIN ICE.
REVLON
FIRE & ICE

Some models draw attention to the ad but not to the product or message. Studies show that an attractive model facilitates recognition of the ad but does not enhance copy readership or message recall.[33] Thus, advertisers must ensure that the consumer's attention will go beyond the model to the product and advertising message.

Source Power

The final characteristic in Kelman's classification scheme is **source power.** A source has power when he or she can actually administer rewards and punishments to the receiver. As a result of this power, the source may be able to induce another person(s) to respond to the request or position he or she is advocating. The power of the source depends on several factors. The source must be perceived as being able to administer positive or negative sanctions to the receiver *(perceived control)* and the receiver must think the source cares

IMC Perspective 6–3

Using *Q Ratings* to Help Choose a Celebrity Endorser

Obviously many marketers believe strongly in the value of celebrity spokespeople, as the amount of money they pay to celebrities continues to soar to record levels. Companies look for a celebrity who will attract viewers' attention and enhance the image of the company or brand. But how do they choose the right one? While some executives rely on their own intuition and gut feeling, many turn to research that measures a celebrity's appeal among the target audience.

To help select a celebrity endorser, many companies and their advertising agencies rely on *Q ratings* that are commercially available from a New York–based firm known as Marketing Evaluations, Inc. To determine its performer Q ratings for TV and movie actors and actresses and entertainers, the company surveys a representative national panel of 1,800 people twice a year and asks them to evaluate 1,500 performers. The sports personality Q ratings are based on a survey of 2,000 teens and adults that is conducted once a year and includes questions about approximately 450 active and retired players, coaches, managers, and sportscasters. In both studies respondents are asked to indicate whether they have ever seen or heard of the performer or sports personality and, if they have, to rate him or her on a scale that includes "one of my favorites," "very good," "good," "fair," and "poor." The *familiarity* score indicates what percentage of people have heard of the celebrity while the *one-of-my-favorites* score is an absolute measure of the celebrity's appeal or popularity. The well-known Q rating is calculated by dividing the percentage of respondents who indicated that a person is "one of my favorites" by the percentage of respondents who indicated that they have heard of that person. The Q rating thus answers the question: "How appealing is the person among those who do know him or her?"

Results from a 1999 survey by Marketing Evaluations found that Robin Williams was known by 88 percent of those surveyed and considered a favorite by 51 percent. Thus, his Q rating was 58 (51/88), which was the highest rating among all the performers measured. Other performers in the top 10, along with their Q ratings, were Tom Hanks (54), Harrison Ford (51), Bill Cosby (50), Mel Gibson (48), Michael Jordan (42), Della Reese (39), Ron Howard (39), Whoopi Goldberg (39), and Will Smith (39). The average Q score is around 18 for performers and 17 for sports personalities. Marketing Evaluations also breaks down the Q ratings on the basis of demographic criteria, such as respondent's age, income, occupation, education, and race, so that marketers have some idea of how a celebrity's popularity varies among different groups of consumers.

One of the problems facing advertisers is that some of the most popular movie stars do not endorse products or appear in commercials (at least in the United States). And although television has more channels than ever before, more prime-time shows than ever before, and, of course, more commercials than ever before, it seems to have smaller stars than it once had. For example, in 1990, the top 25 female TV performers averaged a 68 percent familiarity score, but by 1999 the number had fallen to just 50 percent. Among male performers, the top 25 TV stars had a familiarity score of 70 as recently as 1996, but it had declined to 58 by 1999. Reasons offered for the decline in the number of big TV stars include a decrease in the number of people watching network television as the TV viewing audience is spread over an increasing number of channels. While hit shows of the past reached 30 to 40 percent of the viewing audience, the same shows reach only 15 to 18 percent today. Other factors contributing to the decline in TV star power are the prevalence of newsmagazine shows, which take airtime away from star-driven shows; the increase in the number of animated shows; and the trend toward ensemble shows and away from single-star programs.

Many marketers are responding to decline in the number of big TV stars by using sports personalities to endorse a broader range of products. Sports celebrities aren't just selling sneakers and Gatorade anymore. Some of them can be seen in commercials for brokerage firms and even the staid New York Stock Exchange. For example, discount broker Charles Schwab is running a series of tongue-in-cheek ads in which athletes such as tennis player Anna Kournikova, football star Shannon Sharpe, and skier Picabo Street appear as savvy investors. The purpose of the campaign is to portray the athletes as people who trade stocks just like the everyday guy. There is one difference, however. The sports stars have higher Q ratings.

Sources: Marketing Evaluations, Inc., www.qscores.com; Dunstan Prial, "New Faces," *San Diego Union-Tribune*, December 22, 1999, pp. C1, 3; Bill Carter, "Stars Don't Shine as Brightly in an Expanding TV Universe," *Toronto Globe and Mail*, June 15, 1999, p. D1.

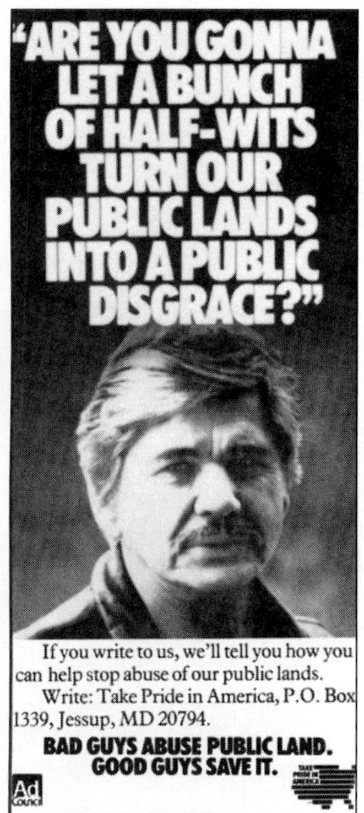

"ARE YOU GONNA LET A BUNCH OF HALF-WITS TURN OUR PUBLIC LANDS INTO A PUBLIC DISGRACE?"
If you write to us, we'll tell you how you can help stop abuse of our public lands.
Write: Take Pride in America, P.O. Box 1339, Jessup, MD 20794.
BAD GUYS ABUSE PUBLIC LAND. GOOD GUYS SAVE IT.
Ad Council

Exhibit 6–12 Actor Charles Bronson's authoritative image makes him an effective source

about whether or not the receiver conforms *(perceived concern).* The receiver's estimate of the source's ability to observe conformity is also important *(perceived scrutiny).*

When a receiver perceives a source as having power, the influence process occurs through a process known as **compliance.** The receiver accepts the persuasive influence of the source and acquiesces to his or her position in hopes of obtaining a favorable reaction or avoiding punishment. The receiver may show public agreement with the source's position but not have an internal or private commitment to this position. Persuasion induced through compliance may be superficial and last only as long as the receiver perceives that the source can administer some reward or punishment.

Power as a source characteristic is very difficult to apply in a nonpersonal influence situation such as advertising. A communicator in an ad generally cannot apply any sanctions to the receiver or determine whether compliance actually occurs. An indirect way of using power is by using an individual with an authoritative personality as a spokesperson. Actor Charles Bronson, who typifies this image, has appeared in public service campaigns commanding people not to pollute or damage our natural parks (Exhibit 6–12).

The use of source power applies more in situations involving personal communication and influence. For example, in a personal selling situation, the sales rep may have some power over a buyer if the latter anticipates receiving special rewards or favors for complying with the salesperson. Some companies provide their sales reps with large expense accounts to spend on customers for this very purpose. Representatives of companies whose product demand exceeds supply are often in a position of power; buyers may comply with their requests to ensure an adequate supply of the product. Sales reps must be very careful in their use of a power position, since abusing a power base to maximize short-term gains can damage long-term relationships with customers.

Message Factors

The way marketing communications are presented is very important in determining their effectiveness. Promotional managers must consider not only the content of their persuasive messages but also how this information will be structured for presentation and what type of message appeal will be used. Advertising, in all media except radio, relies heavily on visual as well as verbal information. Many options are available with respect to the design and presentation of a message. This section examines the structure of messages and considers the effects of different types of appeals used in advertising.

Message Structure

Marketing communications usually consist of a number of message points that the communicator wants to get across. An important aspect of message strategy is knowing the best way to communicate these points and overcome any opposing viewpoints audience members may hold. Extensive research has been conducted on how the structure of a persuasive message can influence its effectiveness, including order of presentation, conclusion drawing, message sidedness, refutation, and verbal versus visual message characteristics.

Order of Presentation

A basic consideration in the design of a persuasive message is the arguments' order of presentation. Should the most important message points be placed at the beginning of the message, in the middle, or at the end? Research on learning and memory generally indicates that items presented first and last are remembered better than those presented in the middle (see Figure 6–4).[34] This suggests that a communicator's strongest arguments should be presented early or late in the message but never in the middle.

Presenting the strongest arguments at the beginning of the message assumes a **primacy effect** is operating, whereby information presented first is most effective.

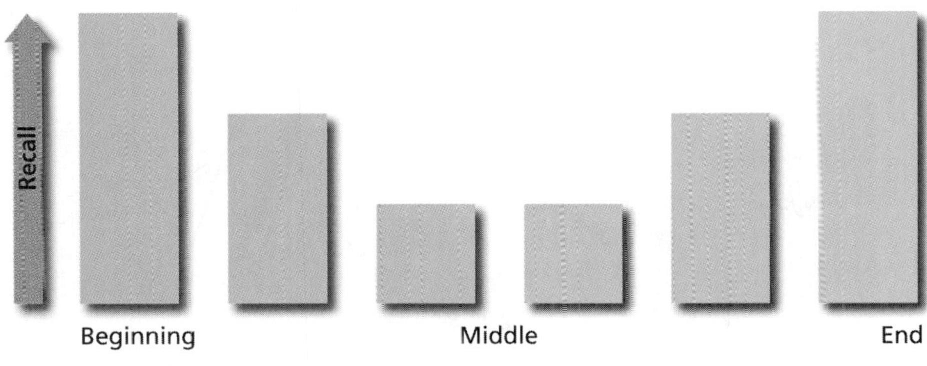

Figure 6–4 Ad message recall as a function of order of presentation

Putting the strong points at the end assumes a **recency effect,** whereby the last arguments presented are most persuasive.

Whether to place the strongest selling points at the beginning or the end of the message depends on several factors. If the target audience is opposed to the communicator's position, presenting strong points first can reduce the level of counterarguing. Putting weak arguments first might lead to such a high level of counterarguing that strong arguments that followed would not be believed. Strong arguments work best at the beginning of the message if the audience is not interested in the topic, so they can arouse interest in the message. When the target audience is predisposed toward the communicator's position or is highly interested in the issue or product, strong arguments can be saved for the end of the message. This may result in a more favorable opinion as well as better retention of the information.

The order of presentation can be critical when a long, detailed message with many arguments is being presented. Most effective sales presentations open and close with strong selling points and bury weaker arguments in the middle. For short communications, such as a 15- or 30-second TV or radio commercial, the order may be less critical. However, many product and service messages are received by consumers with low involvement and minimal interest. Thus, an advertiser may want to present the brand name and key selling points early in the message and repeat them at the end to enhance recall and retention.

Conclusion Drawing

Marketing communicators must decide whether their messages should explicitly draw a firm conclusion or allow receivers to draw their own conclusions. Research suggests that, in general, messages with explicit conclusions are more easily understood and effective in influencing attitudes. However, other studies have shown that the effectiveness of conclusion drawing may depend on the target audience, the type of issue or topic, and the nature of the situation.[35]

More highly educated people prefer to draw their own conclusions and may be annoyed at an attempt to explain the obvious or to draw an inference for them. But stating the conclusion may be necessary for a less educated audience, who may not draw any conclusion or may make an incorrect inference from the message. Marketers must also consider the audience's level of involvement in the topic. For highly personal or ego-involving issues, message recipients may want to make up their own minds and resent any attempts by the communicator to draw a conclusion. One study found that open-ended ads (without explicit conclusions) were more effective than closed-ended arguments that did include a specific conclusion—but only for involved audiences.[36]

Whether to draw a conclusion for the audience also depends on the complexity of the topic. Even a highly educated audience may need assistance if its knowledge level in a particular area is low. Does the marketer want the message to trigger immediate action or a more long-term effect? If immediate action is an objective, the message should draw a definite conclusion. This is a common strategy in political advertising, particularly for ads run close to election day. When immediate impact is not the objective and repeated exposure will give the audience members opportunities to draw their own conclusions, an open-ended message may be used.

Exhibit 6–13 Hewlett-Packard makes effective use of an open-ended approach

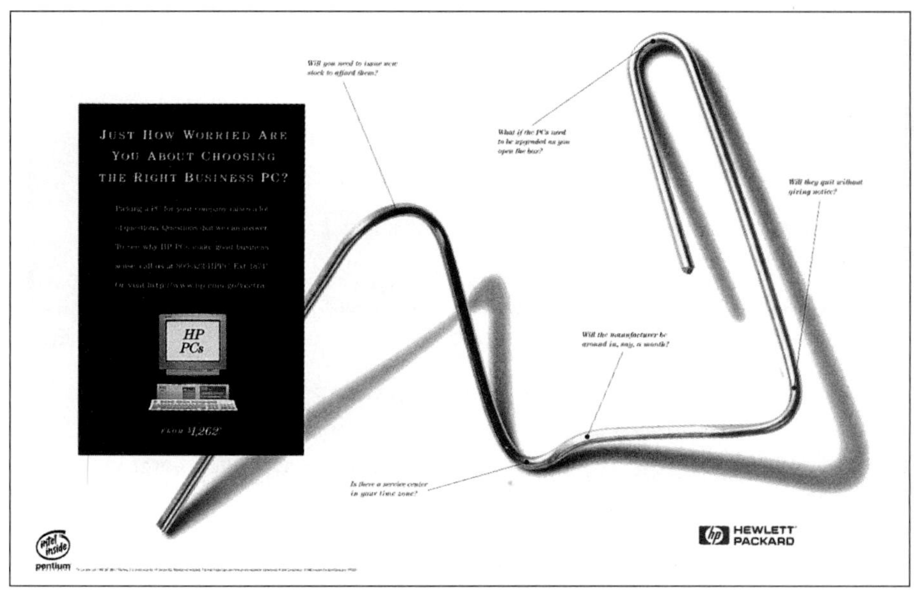

Drawing a conclusion in a message may make sure the target audience gets the point the marketer intended. But many advertisers believe that letting customers draw their own conclusions reinforces the points being made in the message. For example, a health services agency in Kentucky found that open-ended ads were more memorable and more effective in getting consumers to use health services than were ads stating a conclusion. Ads that posed questions about alcohol and drug abuse and left them unanswered resulted in more calls by teenagers to a help line for information than did a message offering a resolution to the problem.[37] The ad for Hewlett-Packard personal computers in Exhibit 6–13 is a very good example of an open-ended ad. The questions encourage individuals choosing a PC for their company to consider the benefits of purchasing from a well-known corporation like Hewlett-Packard rather than from a smaller, less reliable company.

Message Sidedness Another message structure decision facing the marketer involves message sidedness. A **one-sided message** mentions only positive attributes or benefits. A **two-sided message** presents both good and bad points. One-sided messages are most effective when the target audience already holds a favorable opinion about the topic. They also work better with a less educated audience.[38]

Two-sided messages are more effective when the target audience holds an opposing opinion or is highly educated. Two-sided messages may enhance the credibility of the source.[39] A better-educated audience usually knows there are opposing arguments, so a communicator who presents both sides of an issue is likely to be seen as less biased and more objective.

Most advertisers use one-sided messages. They are concerned about the negative effects of acknowledging a weakness in their brand or don't want to say anything positive about their competitors. There are exceptions, however. Sometimes advertisers compare brands on several attributes and do not show their product as being the best on every one.

In some situations marketers may focus on a negative attribute as a way of enhancing overall perceptions of the product. For example, W. K. Buckley Limited has become one of the leading brands of cough syrup in Canada by using a blunt two-sided slogan, "Buckley's Mixture. It tastes awful. And it works." Ads for the brand poke fun at the cough syrup's terrible taste but also suggest that the taste is a reason why the product is effective (Exhibit 6–14). Buckley's is using the humorous two-sided message strategy in its entry into the U.S. market.[40]

Refutation In a special type of two-sided message known as a **refutational appeal,** the communicator presents both sides of an issue and then refutes the opposing viewpoint. Since refutational appeals tend to "inoculate" the target audi-

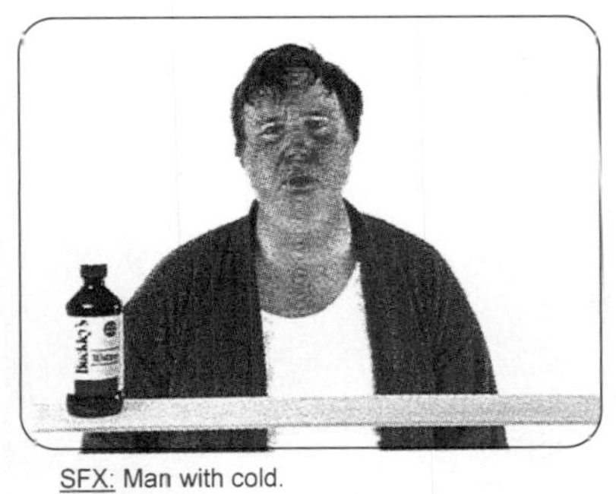

SFX: Man with cold.
ANNCR: You'll be amazed...

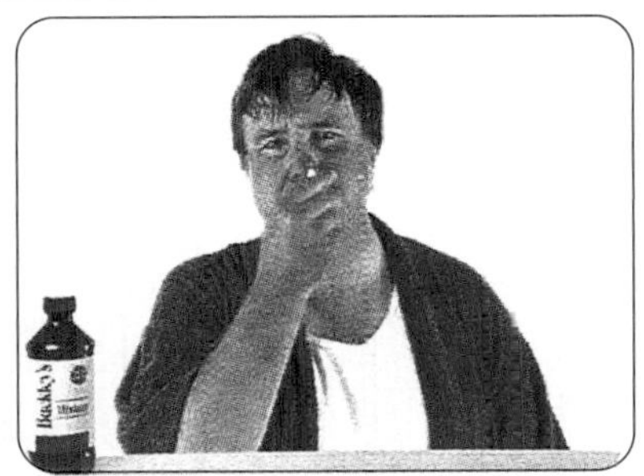

...at how quickly Buckley's Mixture relieves coughs due to colds.

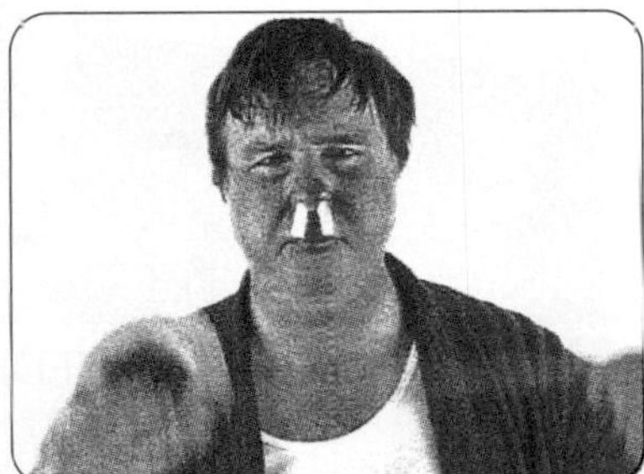

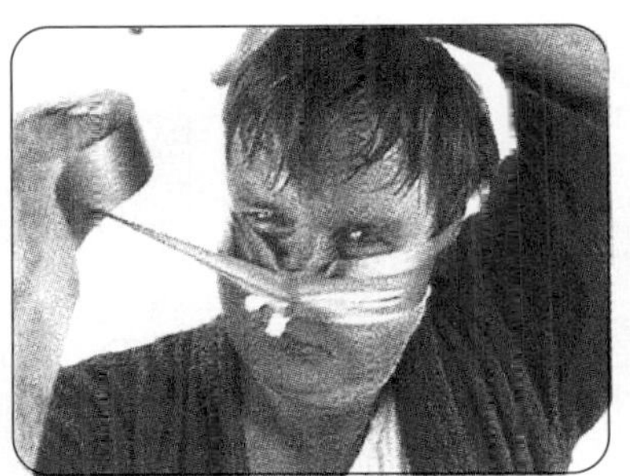

SFX: Duct tape rip.

ANNCR: You'll also be amazed...

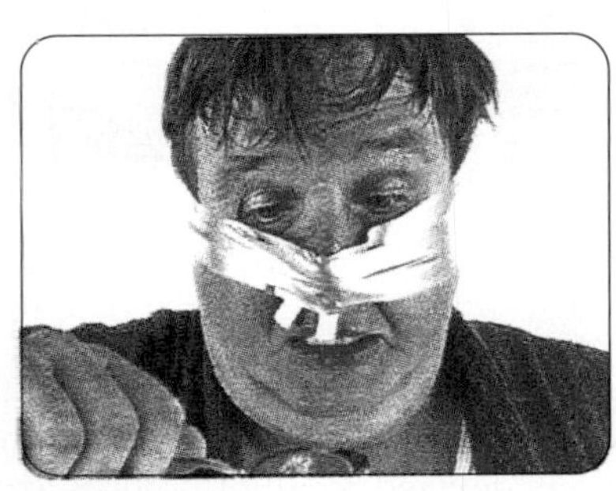

...at how it tastes.

Use as directed.
SFX: Scream.

Exhibit 6–14 Buckley's Cough Syrup uses a two-sided message to promote the product's effectiveness

ence against a competitor's counterclaims, they are more effective than one-sided messages in making consumers resistant to an opposing message.[41]

Refutational messages may be useful when marketers wish to build attitudes that resist change and must defend against attacks or criticism of their products or the company. For example, Exhibit 6–15 shows one of a series of ads from Apple Computer that were run a few years ago in response to negative publicity the company had been receiving regarding its long-term viability and position in the PC market. Market leaders, who are often the target of comparative messages, may find that acknowledging competitors' claims and then refuting them can help build resistant attitudes and customer loyalty.

Verbal versus Visual Messages

Thus far our discussion has focused on the information, or verbal, portion of the message. However, the nonverbal, visual elements of an ad are also very important. Many ads provide minimal amounts of information and rely on visual elements to communicate. Pictures are commonly used in advertising to convey information or reinforce copy or message claims.

Both the verbal and visual portions of an ad influence the way the advertising message is processed.[42] Consumers may develop images or impressions based on visual elements such as an illustration in an ad or the scenes in a TV commercial. In some cases, the visual portion of an ad may reduce its persuasiveness, since the processing stimulated by the picture may be less controlled and consequently less favorable than that stimulated by words.[43]

Exhibit 6–15 Apple used a refutational appeal to address concerns about the company

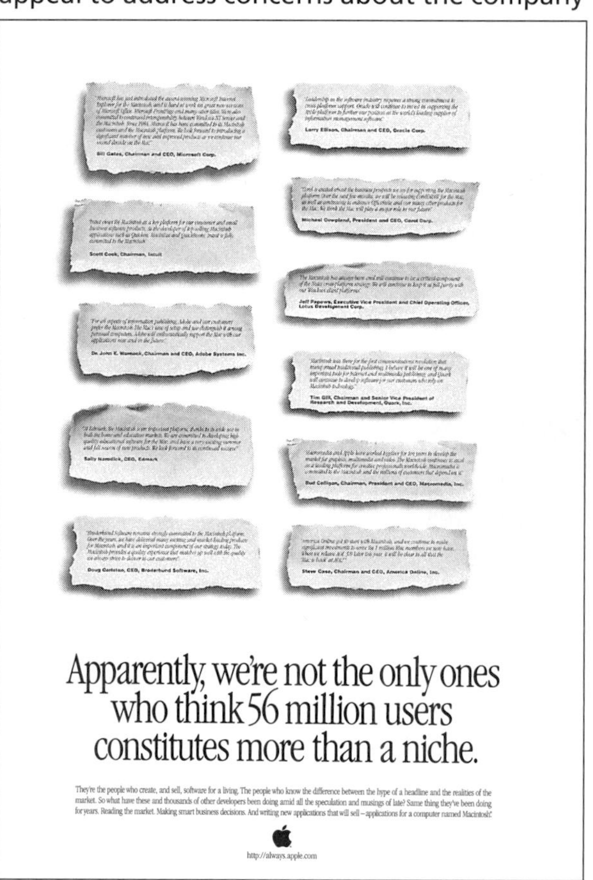

Doug Carlston, CEO, Broderbund Software, Inc.
Steve Case, Chairman and CEO, America Online, Inc.
Apparently, we're not the only ones who think 56 million users constitutes more than a niche.
They're the people who create, and sell, software for a living. The people who know the difference between the hype of a headline and the realities of the market. So what have these and thousands of other developers been doing amid all the speculation and musings of late? Same thing they've been doing for years. Reading the market. Making smart business decisions. And writing new applications that will sell – applications for a computer named Macintosh.
http://always.apple.com

Exhibit 6–16 Visual images are often designed to support verbal appeals

SCREAM
BY 2 PM YOUR BODY IS THIS PARCHED.
(YOUR PERFORMANCE IS DRYING UP, TOO.)
You've been on the slopes all morning. The last thing you remember is to drink H_2O. Sure you get thirsty. But by then, it's too late. Your performance is sliding, a headache is coming on and you're feeling the altitude. And you're not skiing at your peak.
Dehydration occurs quickly out there. The cold, high-altitude air is dry. You lose a lot of water just breathing. And since you're working hard and wearing lots of layers, you sweat a ton. We know that skiers who don't drink lose 1.5 liters of water in one morning.
That's where CamelBak® comes in. Convenient, Hands-Free Hydration™ provides enough water to keep your turns as sharp at 2 PM as they were at 9 AM.
For the scoop on all our products, call 800-767-8725 or hit our website at www.camelbak.com
You need 1.5 liters for a morning of skiing – we have a better way to carry it.
A CamelBak SnoBowl™ lets you drink easily throughout the day.
Our SnoBowl™ holds a 1.5 liter reservoir and easily fits under your jacket.
CAMELBAK
HYDRATE OR DIE®

Pictures affect the way consumers process accompanying copy. A recent study showed that when verbal information was low in imagery value, the use of pictures providing examples increased both immediate and delayed recall of product attributes.[44] However, when the verbal information was already high in imagery value, the addition of pictures did not increase recall. Advertisers often design ads where the visual image supports the verbal appeal to create a compelling impression in the consumer's mind. Notice how the ad for the CamelBak SnoBowl uses visual elements to support the claims made in the copy regarding the importance of being hydrated when skiing (Exhibit 6–16).

Sometimes advertisers use a different strategy; they design ads in which the visual portion is incongruent with or contradicts the verbal information presented. The logic behind this strategy is that the use of an unexpected picture or visual image will grab consumers' attention and get them to engage in more effortful or elaborative processing.[45] A number of studies have shown that the use of a visual that is inconsistent with the verbal content leads to more recall and greater processing of the information presented.[46]

Message Appeals

One of the advertiser's most important creative strategy decisions involves the choice of an appropriate appeal. Some ads are designed to appeal to the rational, logical aspect of the consumer's decision-making process; others appeal to feelings in an attempt to evoke some emotional reaction. Many believe that effective advertising combines the practical reasons for purchasing a product with emotional values. In this section we will examine several common types of message appeals, including comparative advertising, fear, and humor.

Comparative Advertising **Comparative advertising** is the practice of either directly or indirectly naming competitors in an ad and comparing one or more specific attributes.[47] This form of advertising became popular after the Federal Trade Commission (FTC) began advocating its use in 1972. The FTC reasoned that direct comparison of brands would provide better product information, giving consumers a more rational basis for making purchase decisions. Television networks cooperated with the FTC by lifting their ban on comparative ads, and the result was a flurry of comparative commercials.

Initially, the novelty of comparative ads resulted in greater attention. But since they have become so common, their attention-getting value has probably declined. Some studies show that recall is higher for comparative than noncomparative messages, but comparative ads are generally not more effective for other response variables, such as brand attitudes or purchase intentions.[48] Advertisers must also consider how comparative messages affect credibility. Users of the brand being attacked in a comparative message may be especially skeptical about the advertiser's claims.

Comparative advertising may be particularly useful for new brands, since it allows a new market entrant to position itself directly against the more established brands and to promote its distinctive advantages. Direct comparisons can help position a new brand in the evoked, or choice, set of brands the customer may be considering.

Comparative advertising is often used for brands with a small market share. They compare themselves to an established market leader in hopes of creating an association and tapping into the leader's market. Market leaders, on the other hand, often hesitate to use comparison ads, as most believe they have little to gain by featuring competitors' products in their ads. There are exceptions, of course; Coca-Cola resorted to comparative advertising in response to challenges made by Pepsi that were reducing Coke's market share. IMC Perspective 6–4 discusses how Savin Corp. has been using comparative ads to compete against Xerox in the copier market.

Fear Appeals Fear is an emotional response to a threat that expresses, or at least implies, some sort of danger. Ads sometimes use **fear appeals** to evoke this emotional response and arouse individuals to take steps to remove the threat. Some, like the antidrug ads used by the Partnership for a Drug-Free America, stress physical danger that can occur if behaviors are not altered. Others—like those for deodorant, mouthwash, or dandruff shampoos—threaten disapproval or social rejection.

How Fear Operates Before deciding to use a fear appeal–based message strategy, the advertiser should consider how fear operates, what level to use, and how different target audiences may respond. One theory suggests that the relationship between the level of fear in a message and acceptance or persuasion is curvilinear, as shown in Figure 6–5.[49] This means that message acceptance increases as the amount of fear used rises—to a point. Beyond that point, acceptance decreases as the level of fear rises.

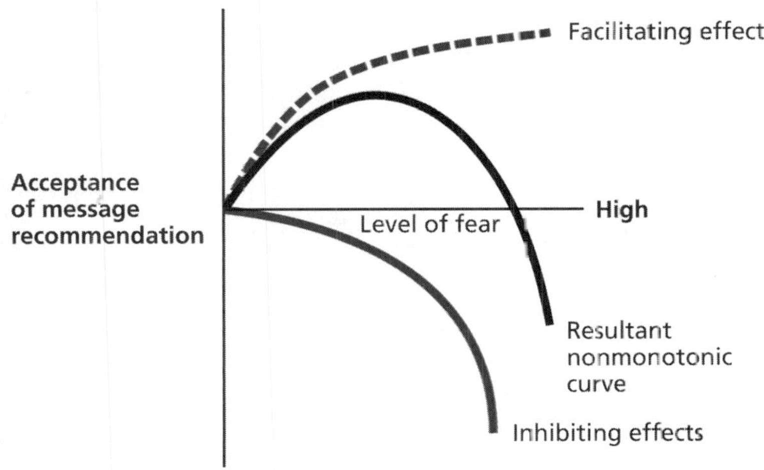

Figure 6–5 Relationship between fear levels and message acceptance

IMC Perspective 6–4

Savin Uses Comparative Ads to Take on Xerox—Again

In the late 1970s and early 80s Savin Corp. used a very effective comparative advertising campaign to overtake Xerox and become the top brand of office copiers in America. With the help of small, inexpensive copiers made by Ricoh Corporation of Japan but sold in the United States under the Savin brand, the company caught Xerox off guard by running advertisements comparing its products directly with those of the market leader. However, a decision to manufacture the copiers in-house at a new factory in Binghamton, New York, caused a severe financial crisis that ultimately led to Savin's filing for bankruptcy protection in 1992. A year after emerging from bankruptcy proceedings in 1994, Savin agreed to be acquired by Ricoh.

Since being acquired by Ricoh, Savin is getting back to what it did best: selling copiers made by Ricoh under its own name through its own network of branches that sell directly to companies. And as part of its new strategy for gaining market share, Savin has launched a comparative advertising campaign designed to re-create the old David versus Goliath battle. For the past several years, Savin has been running ads aimed directly at industry leader Xerox. The new ads alternate between piggybacking off Xerox's efforts to promote new digital copiers and mocking Xerox for wanting to be the "biggest" document company. Savin's comparative ads position the company as the "fastest, most responsive and easy to work with name in the business." As part of the campaign, Savin's longtime tagline, "We're going to win you over," has been refreshed to read, "We've got what it takes to win you over."

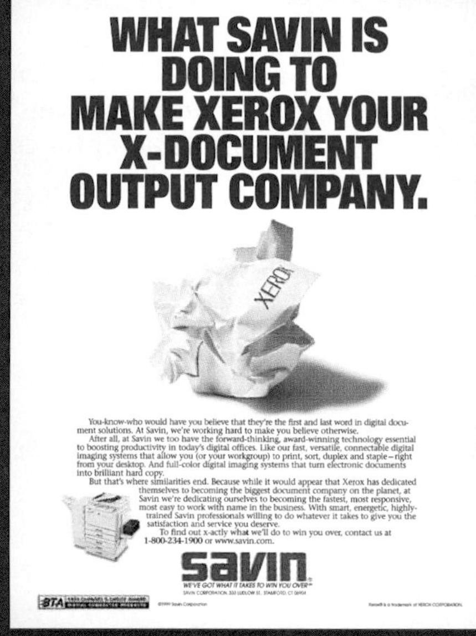

Savin's CEO, Jim Ivy, says that "going toe to toe with Xerox is part of our history. People remember Savin going after Xerox." And since many copier buyers tend to be middle-aged managers, Savin hopes the ad campaign will ring a bell with them. Ivy adds: "Even though we have been somewhat off the radar screen, a latent memory is easy to pull back again." To help jog the memory of copier buyers, Savin has tripled its advertising budget to more than $9 million and is running its new comparative ads in magazines such as *Time, Business Week,* and *Inc.,* as well as computer trade publications and in-flight magazines.

When the comparative campaign began in mid-1998, Savin had a small 2.9 percent share of the U.S. office-copier market, placing it a lowly 11th out of 14 brands, while Xerox led the industry with a 16.4 percent market share. Jim Ivy notes that with so many competitors, getting on customers' "short list" is important. Interestingly, Savin's ads ignore the eight or so brands that have higher market shares, such as Konica, Toshiba, Sharp, Canon, and Mita, and position the company right against Xerox. Xerox says it is not surprised by Savin's comparative campaign; according to a company spokesman: "The industry leader is always a target. We would prefer to let our technology, our products, our services and our market share speak for itself."

When asked about Savin's comparative advertising strategy, positioning guru Jack Trout notes: "When you are at the bottom, you should compare yourself to the top. But the issue is, do they have the credibility?" The answer appears to be a resounding yes, thanks in part to the comparative ad campaign and to new award-winning digital copiers that can also print. In 1998 and 1999 Savin's growth in sales outpaced that of all major providers of document output systems. The company increased its digital sales by 164 percent, and its digital share of the market (excluding personal copiers) rose to 12.5 percent, placing it fourth in the industry. CEO Ivy states, "Businesses of all sizes are responding positively to Savin's easy-to-do-business-with philosophy and our ability to provide one-stop shopping for output solutions." It appears that they are also responding to Savin's strategy of using comparative advertising to re-create the David versus Goliath imagery in the copier market.

Sources: Raju Narisetti, "Savin Hopes Campaign Will Boost Image," *The Wall Street Journal,* May 19, 1998, p. B10; "Savin Corp. Having Award-Winning Year," *Business Wire,* June 8, 1999.

This relationship between fear and persuasion can be explained by the fact that fear appeals have both facilitating and inhibiting effects.[50] A low level of fear can have facilitating effects; it attracts attention and interest in the message and may motivate the receiver to act to resolve the threat. Thus, increasing the level of fear in a message from low to moderate can result in increased persuasion. High levels of fear, however, can produce inhibiting effects; the receiver may emotionally block the message by tuning it out, perceiving it selectively, or denying its arguments outright. Figure 6–5 illustrates how these two countereffects operate to produce the curvilinear relationship between fear and persuasion.

A recent study by Anand-Keller and Block provides support for this perspective on how fear operates.[51] They examined the conditions under which low- and high-fear appeals urging people to stop smoking are likely to be effective. Their study indicated that a communication using a low level of fear may be ineffective because it results in insufficient motivation to elaborate on the harmful consequences of engaging in the destructive behavior (smoking). However, an appeal arousing high levels of fear was ineffective because it resulted in too much elaboration on the harmful consequences. This led to defensive tendencies such as message avoidance and interfered with processing of recommended solutions to the problem.

Another approach to the curvilinear explanation of fear is the protection motivation model.[52] According to this theory, four cognitive appraisal processes mediate the individual's response to the threat: appraising (1) the information available regarding the severity of the perceived threat, (2) the perceived probability that the threat will occur, (3) the perceived ability of a coping behavior to remove the threat, and (4) the individual's perceived ability to carry out the coping behavior.

This model suggests that both the cognitive appraisal of the information in a fear appeal message and the emotional response mediate persuasion. An audience is more likely to continue processing threat-related information, thereby increasing the likelihood that a coping behavior will occur.

The protection motivation model suggests that ads using fear appeals should give the target audience information about the severity of the threat, the probability of its occurrence, the effectiveness of a coping response, and the ease with which the response can be implemented.[53] For example, the Havrix ad in Exhibit 6–17 discusses how tourists can pick up hepatitis A when traveling to high-risk areas outside the United States and describes the severity of the problem. However, the ad reduces anxiety by offering a solution to the problem—a vaccination with Havrix.

Exhibit 6–17 This ad uses a mild fear appeal but reduces anxiety by offering a solution to a problem

It is also important to consider how the target audience may respond. Fear appeals are more effective when the message recipient is self-confident and prefers to cope with dangers rather than avoid them.[54] They are also more effective among nonusers of a product than among users. Thus, a fear appeal may be better at keeping nonsmokers from starting than persuading smokers to stop.

In reviewing research on fear appeals, Herbert Rotfeld has argued that some of the studies may be confusing different types of threats and the level of potential harm portrayed in the message with fear, which is an emotional response.[55] He concludes that the relationship between the emotional responses of fear or arousal and persuasion is not curvilinear but rather is monotonic and positive, meaning that higher levels of fear do result in greater persuasion. However, Rotfeld notes that not all fear messages are equally effective, because different people fear different things. Thus they will respond differently to the same threat, so the strongest threats are not always the most persuasive. This suggests that marketers using fear appeals must consider the emotional responses generated by the message and how they will affect reactions to the message.

Humor Appeals Humorous ads are often the best known and best remembered of all advertising messages. The humorous commercials for Miller Lite beer featuring ex-athletes and other celebrities were the basis of one of the most effective, longest-running ad campaigns ever developed. The company recently began using humorous messages for the brand once again. Many other advertisers, among them FedEx, Little Caesar's pizza, Pepsi, and Budweiser, have also used humor appeals effectively. Humor is usually presented through radio and TV commercials

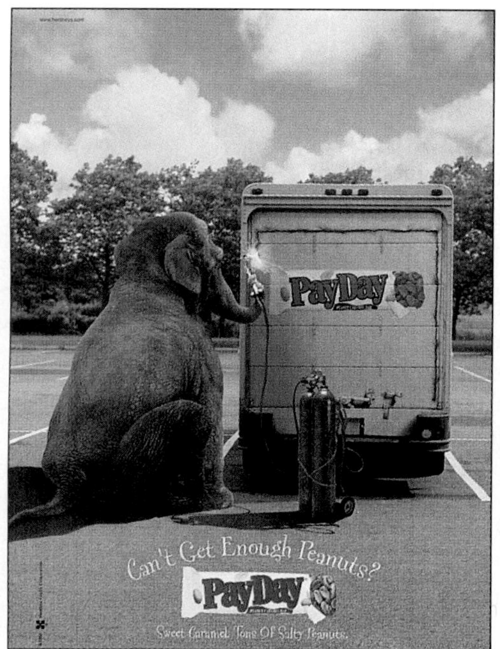

Exhibit 6–18 This clever ad is an example of how humor can be executed in print media

as these media lend themselves to the execution of humorous messages. However, humor is occasionally used in print ads as well. The clever PayDay ad shown in Exhibit 6–18 is an excellent example of how humor can be used to attract attention and convey a key selling point in a magazine ad.

Advertisers use humor for many reasons. Humorous messages attract and hold consumers' attention. They enhance effectiveness by putting consumers in a positive mood, increasing their liking of the ad itself and their feeling toward the product or service. And humor can distract the receiver from counterarguing against the message.[56]

Critics argue that funny ads draw people to the humorous situation but distract them from the brand and its attributes. Also, effective humor can be difficult to produce and some attempts are too subtle for mass audiences. And, as discussed in IMC Perspective 6–5, there is concern that humorous ads may wear out faster than serious appeals.

Clearly, there are valid reasons both for and against the use of humor in advertising. Not every product or service lends itself to a humorous approach. A number of studies have found that the effectiveness of humor depends on several factors, including the type of product and audience characteristics.[57] For example, humor has been more prevalent and more effective with low-involvement, feeling products than high-involvement, thinking products.[58] An interesting study surveyed the research and creative directors of the top 150 advertising agencies.[59] They were asked to name which communications objectives are facilitated through the appropriate situational use of humor in terms of media, product, and audience factors. The general conclusions of this study are as follows:

- Humor does aid awareness and attention, which are the objectives best achieved by its use.
  - Humor may harm recall and comprehension in general.
  - Humor may aid name and simple copy registration.
  - Humor may harm complex copy registration.
  - Humor may aid retention.
- Humor does not aid persuasion in general.
  - Humor may aid persuasion to switch brands.
  - Humor creates a positive mood that enhances persuasion.
- Humor does not aid source credibility.
- Humor is generally not very effective in bringing about action/sales.
- Creatives are more positive on the use of humor to fulfill all the above objectives than research directors are.
- Radio and TV are the best media in which to use humor; direct mail and newspapers are least suited.
- Consumer nondurables and business services are best suited to humor; corporate advertising and industrial products are least suited.
- Humor should be related to the product.
- Humor should not be used with sensitive goods or services.
- Audiences that are younger, better educated, upscale, male, and professional are best suited to humor; older, less educated, and downscale groups are least suited to humor appeals.

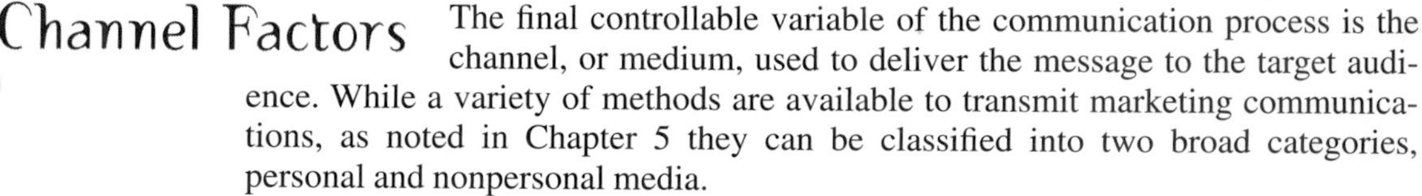

Channel Factors

The final controllable variable of the communication process is the channel, or medium, used to deliver the message to the target audience. While a variety of methods are available to transmit marketing communications, as noted in Chapter 5 they can be classified into two broad categories, personal and nonpersonal media.

IMC Perspective 6–5

Do Humorous Ads Wear Out Too Fast?

An issue of much concern to advertisers is the problem of commercial wearout, or the tendency of a message to lose its effectiveness when it is seen repeatedly. Wearout may occur for several reasons. One is inattention; consumers may no longer attend to an ad after several exposures, so the message loses its effectiveness. Another reason is that consumers may become annoyed at seeing an ad many times.

While wearout is a problem for any type of commercial, some advertising experts argue that humorous ads wear out much sooner than other formats because once the viewer gets the joke, the ad becomes boring. However, advocates of humor argue that ads filled with yuks are effective longer because consumers can tolerate a well-executed humorous commercial again and again.

Somewhere in the Gobi Desert...
(BKGD MUSIC)
DRILL SERGEANT #1 (BLOWS WHISTLE): And up the stairs! Down the stairs!
Bell, knocker, hand. Bell..,
DRILL SERGEANT #2: And one, two, three. (DELIVERY MEN IN TRAINING CLOSE CAR DOORS WITH FOOT.
DELIVERY GUY IN TRAINING: Pizza, pizza. (DRILL SERGEANT #1 GRABS GUY'S FACE) DRILL SERGEANT #1: Pizza, pizza. DELIVERY GUY: Pizza, pizza.
DRILL SERGEANT #2: Keep 'em steady!!
Go, go, go!! (SFX: MECHANICAL DOG CHASES DELIVERY GUY)
(SFX: TRAINING PROCESS CONTINUES)
DRILL SERGEANT #1: Pizza, pizza. MALE ANNCR: Little Caesars introduces...
delivery.
GUARANTEE
Now get two, top-of-the-line Little Caesars Pleasers delivered.
Little Caesars
(SFX: DOORBELL) LITTLE CAESAR: Pizza, pizza! (MUSIC ENDS)

So who is right? Well, a study conducted by Research Systems Corp. concludes that neither view is correct. Humorous ads wear out at the same rate as other types of ads, whether the commercials include comparative messages, celebrity spokespeople, or other approaches. According to the study, the average ad's effectiveness wears out within eight weeks.

Not everyone agrees with this study. Another research firm, Video Storyboard Tests, claims that humorous ads lose their effectiveness faster than other ads. Says the company's president, "The first time the ad is funny, the second time the ad is acceptable, and the third time it is a bore."

While individual humorous ads may get old fast, advertisers often get around this problem by using humorous campaigns consisting of many different commercials. For example, the Little Caesar's pizza chain has run more than 35 humorous ads in the past five years. FedEx, Energizer batteries, Pepsi, and Anheuser-Busch (Budweiser and Bud Light beer) have also made effective use of humor by constantly developing new commercials and working them into the ad rotation.

Some individual humorous commercials seem to have been immune to wearout. "Where's the beef?" which was used heavily by Wendy's in the mid-1980s, is a classic example of how to use humor to sell a product and not get in the way of the message.

One media consultant argues that it's quite simple to determine if a humorous spot or campaign is wearing out. "If the viewers laugh with you, you can be in it for the long haul. It's when they laugh at you that you're in trouble."

Sources: Dottie Enrico, "Humorous Touch Resonates with Consumers," *USA Today,* May 13, 1996, p. 3B; Kevin Goldman, "Ever Hear the One about the Funny Ad?" *The Wall Street Journal,* November 2, 1993, p. B11.

Personal versus Nonpersonal Channels

There are a number of basic differences between personal and nonpersonal communications channels. Information received from personal influence channels is generally more persuasive than information received via the mass media. Reasons for the differences are summarized in the following comparison of advertising and personal selling:

> From the standpoint of persuasion, a sales message is far more flexible, personal, and powerful than an advertisement. An advertisement is normally prepared by persons having minimal personal contact with customers. The message is designed to appeal to a large

number of persons. By contrast, the message in a good sales presentation is not determined in advance. The salesman has a tremendous store of knowledge about his product or service and selects appropriate items as the interview progresses. Thus, the salesman can adapt this to the thinking and needs of the customer or prospect at the time of the sales call. Furthermore, as objections arise and are voiced by the buyer, the salesman can treat the objections in an appropriate manner. This is not possible in advertising.[60]

Effects of Alternative Mass Media

The various mass media that advertisers use to transmit their messages differ in many ways, including the number and type of people they reach, costs, information processing requirements, and qualitative factors. The mass media's costs and efficiency in exposing a target audience to a communication will be evaluated in Chapters 10 through 12. However, we should recognize differences in how information is processed and how communications are influenced by context or environment.

Differences in Information Processing

There are basic differences in the manner and rate at which information from various forms of media is transmitted and can be processed. Information from ads in print media, such as newspapers, magazines, or direct mail, is *self-paced;* readers process the ad at their own rate and can study it as long as they desire. In contrast, information from the broadcast media of radio and television is *externally paced;* the transmission rate is controlled by the medium.

The difference in the processing rate for print and broadcast media has some obvious implications for advertisers. Self-paced print media make it easier for the message recipient to process a long, complex message. Advertisers often use print ads when they want to present a detailed message with a lot of information. Broadcast media are more effective for transmitting shorter messages or, in the case of TV, presenting pictorial information along with words.

While there are limits to the length and complexity of broadcast messages, advertisers can deal with this problem. One strategy is to use a radio or TV ad to get consumers' attention and direct them to specific print media for a more detailed message. For example, home builders use radio ads to draw attention to new developments and direct listeners to the real estate section of the newspaper for more details. Some advertisers develop broadcast and print versions of the same message. The copy portion is similar in both media, but the print ad can be processed at a rate comfortable to the receiver.

Effects of Context and Environment

Interpretation of an advertising message can be influenced by the context or environment in which the ad appears. Communication theorist Marshall McLuhan's thesis, "The medium is the message," implies that the medium communicates an image that is independent of any message it contains.[61] A **qualitative media effect** is the influence the medium has on a message. The image of the media vehicle can affect reactions to the message. For example, an ad for a high-quality men's clothing line might have more of an impact in a fashion magazine like *GQ* than in *Sports Afield.* Airlines, destination resorts, and travel-related services advertise in publications such as *Travel & Leisure* partly because the articles, pictures, and other ads help to excite readers about travel (Exhibit 6–19).

A media environment can also be created by the nature of the program in which a commercial appears. One study found that consumers reacted more positively to commercials seen during a happy TV program than a sad one.[62] Advertisers pay premium dollars to advertise on popular programs that create positive moods, like the Olympic Games and Christmas specials. Conversely, advertisers tend to avoid programs that create a negative mood among viewers or may be detrimental to the company or its products. Many companies won't advertise on programs with excessive violence or sexual content. As a corporate policy, Coca-Cola never advertises on TV

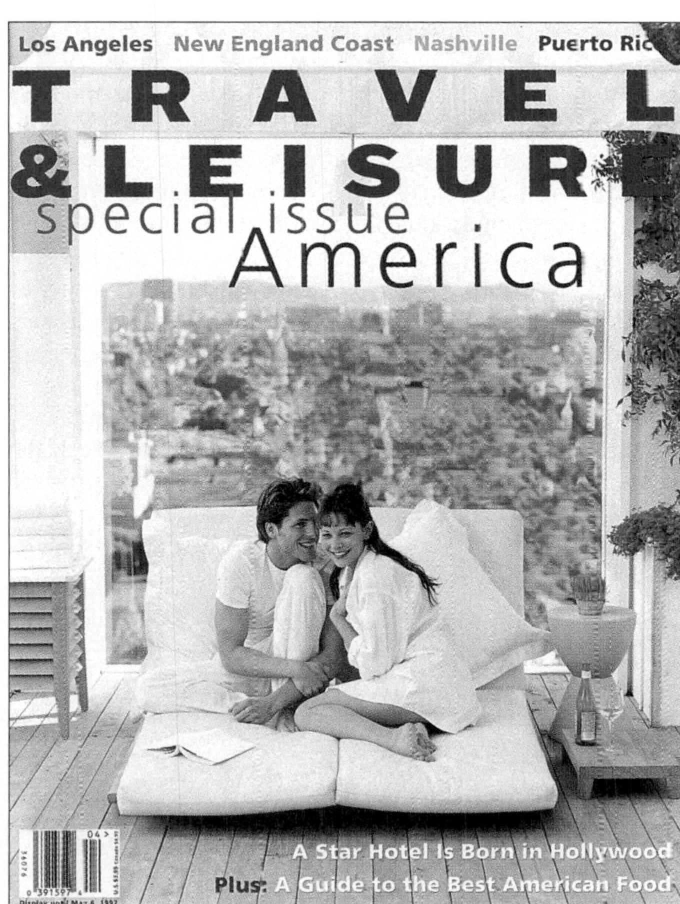

Exhibit 6–19 *Travel & Leisure* magazine creates an excellent reception environment for travel-related ads

news programs because it thinks bad news is inconsistent with Coke's image as an upbeat, fun product. A recent study by Andrew Aylesworth and Scott MacKenzie found that commercials placed in programs that induce negative moods are processed less systematically than ads placed in programs that put viewers in positive moods.[63] They suggest that media buyers might be well advised to follow the conventional wisdom of placing their ads during "feel-good" programming, especially if the message is intended to work through a central route to persuasion. However, messages intended to operate through a peripheral route to persuasion might be more effective if they are shown during more negative programs, where presumably viewers will not analyze the ad in detail because of their negative mood state.

Clutter

Another aspect of the media environment, which is important to advertisers, is the problem of **clutter,** which has been defined as the amount of advertising in a medium.[64] However, for television, clutter is often viewed as including all the nonprogram material that appears in the broadcast environment—commercials, promotional messages for shows, public service announcements (PSAs), and the like. Clutter is of increasing concern to advertisers since there are so many messages in various media competing for the consumer's attention. Half of the average magazine's pages contain ads and in some publications the ratio of ads to editorial content is even higher. On average, around a quarter of a broadcast hour on TV is devoted to commercials while most radio stations carry an average of 10 to 12 minutes of commercial time per hour. The high level of advertising often annoys consumers and makes it difficult for ads to communicate effectively.

Clutter has become a major concern among television advertisers as a result of increases in nonprogram time and the trend toward shorter commercials. While the 30-second commercial replaced 60-second spots as the industry standard in the

1970s, many advertisers are now using 15-second spots. The advertising industry continues to express concern over the highly cluttered viewing environment on TV. An industry-sponsored study found that the amount of clutter increased as much as 30 percent during the 1990s. The study, which was based on network programming during one-week periods in May and November 1999, found an average of close to 12 commercial minutes per prime-time hour. When nonprogramming time for PSAs and network promotions were included, the amount of clutter rose to an average of nearly 17 minutes during prime time and close to 21 minutes during daytime shows.[65] The problem is even greater during popular shows, to which the networks add more commercials because they can charge more. And, of course, advertisers and their agencies perpetuate the problem by pressuring the networks to squeeze their ads into top-rated shows with the largest audiences.

Advertisers and agencies want the networks to commit to a minimum amount of program time and then manage the nonprogram portion however they see fit. If the networks wanted to add more commercials, it would come out of their promos, PSAs, or program credit time. The problem is not likely to go away, however, and advertisers will continue to search for ways to break through the clutter, such as using humor, celebrity spokespeople, or novel, creative approaches.[66]

Summary

This chapter focused on the controllable variables that are part of the communication process—source, message, and channel factors. Decisions regarding each of these variables should consider their impact on the various steps of the response hierarchy the message receiver passes through. The persuasion matrix helps assess the effect of controllable communication decisions on the consumer's response process.

Selection of the appropriate source or communicator to deliver a message is an important aspect of communications strategy. Three important attributes are source credibility, attractiveness, and power. Marketers enhance message effectiveness by hiring communicators who are experts in a particular area and/or have a trustworthy image. The use of celebrities to deliver advertising messages has become very popular; advertisers hope they will catch the receivers' attention and influence their attitudes or behavior through an identification process. The chapter discusses the meaning a celebrity brings to the endorsement process and the importance of matching the image of the celebrity with that of the company or brand.

The design of the advertising message is a critical part of the communication process. There are various options regarding message structure, including order of presentation of message arguments, conclusion drawing, message sidedness, refutation, and verbal versus visual traits. The advantages and disadvantages of different message appeal strategies were considered, including comparative messages and emotional appeals such as fear and humor.

Finally, the channel or medium used to deliver the message was considered. Differences between personal and nonpersonal channels of communication were discussed. Alternative mass media can have an effect on the communication process as a result of information processing and qualitative factors. The context in which an ad appears and the reception environment are important factors to consider in the selection of mass media. Clutter has become a serious problem for advertisers, particularly on TV, where commercials have become shorter and more numerous.

Key Terms

persuasion matrix, 170
source, 172
credibility, 173
internalization, 173
sleeper effect, 175
attractiveness, 175
identification, 177
source power, 182
compliance, 184
primacy effect, 184
recency effect, 185
one-sided message, 186
two-sided message, 186
refutational appeal, 186
comparative advertising, 189
fear appeals, 189
qualitative media effect, 194
clutter, 195

Discussion Questions

1. The opening vignette discusses how Jenny Craig, Inc. is using Monica Lewinsky as a spokeswoman for the company. Discuss the pros and cons of the company's decision to use her as a spokeswoman. Do you think she will be an effective spokeswoman for Jenny Craig?

2. Choose a current print ad or TV commercial and use the persuasion matrix shown in Figure 6–1 to analyze how it might influence the various steps in the persuasion process.

3. Find examples of ads using some of the various source characteristics such as expertise, trustworthiness, attractiveness, and power. Discuss whether you feel the marketers are using these source factors effectively in their advertising.

4. IMC Perspective 6–2 discusses how some companies use their founder, president, or CEO as an advertising spokesperson. Discuss the pros and cons of this practice for both major corporations and smaller companies, such as a local retailer.

5. Former NBA basketball star Michael Jordan makes an estimated $40 million a year in endorsement deals even though he is retired and is no longer playing. Choose one of the companies or brands for which Jordan is the spokesperson and discuss whether he is still effective as endorser. How long do you think companies will continue to pay Jordan large sums of money to endorse their products and services?

6. Discuss the ethics of celebrities endorsing products in foreign countries but not in the United States to protect their image. Do you think celebrities hurt their reputations by endorsing products and appearing in ads? Why or why not?

7. Find a celebrity who is currently appearing in ads for a particular company or brand and analyze and use McCracken's meaning transfer model (shown in Figure 6–3) to analyze the use of the celebrity as a spokesperson.

8. What is meant by one-sided versus two-sided message? Discuss some of the reasons marketers may or may not want to use a two-sided message.

9. Discuss the pros and cons of using a comparative advertising message. Find an example of a current campaign where a marketer is using a comparative ad and evaluate the decision to do so.

10. Assume that you have been asked to consult for a government agency that wants to use a fear appeal message to encourage college students not to drink and drive. Explain how fear appeals might affect persuasion and what factors should be considered in developing the ads.

11. What is meant by a qualitative media effect? Choose a specific magazine and discuss the nature of the media environment in that publication.

12. What is meant by clutter in the broadcast media? What are some ways advertisers might deal with the increasing amount of clutter found on television?

Chapter Seven

Establishing Objectives and Budgeting for the Promotional Program

Chapter Objectives

- To recognize the importance and value of setting specific objectives for advertising and promotion.
- To understand the role objectives play in the IMC planning process and the relationship of promotional objectives to marketing objectives.
- To know the differences between sales and communications objectives and the issues regarding the use of each.
- To recognize some problems marketers encounter in setting objectives for their IMC programs.
- To understand the process of budgeting for IMC.
- To understand theoretical issues involved in budget setting.
- To know various methods of budget setting.

Australian for Beer Means Success for Foster's

After achieving double-digit growth in the flat import-beer market in the United States in 1990, Foster's Lager saw significant sales declines through 1993. Due to a number of factors, including increased competition, declining import sales, and the lowest share of voice in the category, things looked pretty dismal. In 1994, the Australian company decided that something significant had to be done. Marketing research indicated that the brand was still viable but that wholesaler support, consumer interest, and top-of-mind awareness would need to be improved for the company to survive. A new campaign—"Australian for Beer"—was developed in an attempt to reverse Foster's fortunes.

Unlike the traditional import beer, Foster's had a much broader base of customers, including not only traditional import-beer drinkers but also blue-collar domestic drinkers, most of whom consumed in heavier volumes. The brand was attractive due to its down-to-earth, less "stuffy and elite" image—the same image associated with its country of origin, Australia. Based on these strengths, the new campaign would position Foster's as the definitive Australian beer—unconventional, irreverent, fun, honest and not too serious. The use of authentic Australian words, phrases, and accents would reinforce the brand's lighthearted personality.

The objectives for the new campaign were to:

- Strengthen the brand's image.
- Maximize the brand's presence.
- Broaden its market base beyond the traditional import-beer drinker.

The creative objectives required that the messages carry the fun image but be simple and direct to differentiate Foster's from other imports while generating higher levels of consumption. With a budget that paled in comparison to the budgets of other imports, the campaign would have to create quite an impact to be successful.

Starting with billboards, the campaign developed into an integrated marketing communications program that involved marketing videos created to educate and motivate Foster's distributors, on- and off-premise promotions, and point-of-sale programs. Fifteen-second spot television commercials were added later. The goal was to maximize the effect of a limited media budget by making an impact and winning brand attention.

Did it work? Consider these results:

- Beer sales exceeded Foster's highest expectations, increasing by 12.1 percent in the first year.
- Performance in test markets indicated doubled sales growth over sales in nontest markets.
- Unaided brand awareness doubled.
- Trial and usage tripled.
- Brand awareness reached 73 percent, 40 percent higher than awareness for any other import brand, despite significantly lower spending.
- Specific recall of the advertising (90 percent) was twice that for any other beer brand—including non-imports Miller and Budweiser.
- Foster's advertising was the best liked in the industry.

The success continued in 1997 with 24 percent sales gains and into 1998 with 22 percent increases. The print ads "Dental Floss," "Fly Swatter," and "Preppy" and the TV ads "Salad" and "Witness Protection Program" continue to be considered some of the best beer ads ever developed for the U.S. market.

Meanwhile, success has not been limited to the United States. Foster's was the first Australian lager to be introduced in England and is still the brand leader. Again using the irreverent Australian image, the brand is considered to be England's beer of choice.

Sources: Howard Sherman, "Positioning a Brand for Long Term Growth," in *A Celebration of Effective Advertising: 30 Years of Winning EFFIE Awards* (New York: American Marketing Association, 1998), pp. 54–57; Andy Wood, "Campaign of the Week: Foster's Ice," *London, Marketing,* February 13, 1997, p. 12.

The Foster's lager example demonstrates how the setting of specific objectives for a brand can lead to effectiveness and sales growth even with a budget significantly smaller than competitors' budgets. Foster's success can be measured by both marketing and communications objectives. This chapter will examine how the goals for the integrated marketing communications program follow the company's overall marketing strategy and how these goals determine and are determined by the promotional budget.

Unfortunately, many companies have difficulty with the most critical step in the promotional planning process—setting realistic objectives that will guide the development of the IMC program. Complex marketing situations, conflicting perspectives regarding what advertising and other promotional mix elements are expected to accomplish, and uncertainty over resources make the setting of marketing communications objectives "a job of creating order out of chaos."[1] While the task of setting objectives can be complex and difficult, it must be done properly, because specific goals and objectives are the foundation on which all other promotional decisions are made. Budgeting for advertising and other promotional areas, as well as creative and media strategies and tactics, evolve from these objectives. They also provide a standard against which performance can be measured.

Setting specific objectives should be an integral part of the planning process. However, many companies either fail to use specific marketing communications objectives or set ones that are inadequate for guiding the development of the promotional plan or measuring its effectiveness. Many marketers are uncertain as to what integrated marketing communications should be expected to contribute to the marketing program. The goal of their company's advertising and promotional program is simple: to generate sales. They fail to recognize the specific tasks that advertising and other promotional mix variables must perform in preparing customers to buy a particular product or service.

As we know, advertising and promotion are not the only marketing activities involved in generating sales. Moreover, it is not always possible or necessary to measure the effects of advertising in terms of sales. For example, the Georgia-Pacific ad in Exhibit 7–1 is designed to promote the company's concern for the environment.

Exhibit 7–1 The objective of this ad is to promote Georgia-Pacific's concern for the environment

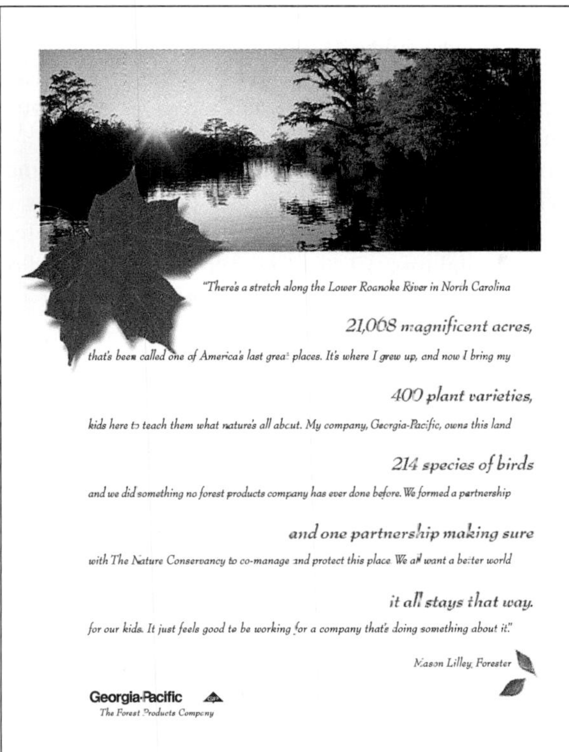

Exhibit 7–2 Ford's objectives for this ad may be other than sales

Consider the Ford ad shown in Exhibit 7–2. What objectives (other than generating sales) might the company have for this ad? How might its effectiveness be measured?

This chapter examines the nature and purpose of objectives and the role they play in guiding the development, implementation, and evaluation of an IMC program. Attention is given to the various types of objectives appropriate for different situations. We will also examine the budget-setting process and the interdependence of objective setting and budgeting.

The Value of Objectives

Perhaps one reason many companies fail to set specific objectives for their integrated marketing communications programs is that they don't recognize the value of doing so. Advertising and promotional objectives are needed for several reasons, including the functions they serve in communication, planning and decision making, and measurement and evaluation.

Communications

Specific objectives for the IMC program facilitate coordination of the various groups working on the campaign. Many people are involved in the planning and development of an integrated marketing communications program on the client side as well as in the various promotional agencies. The advertising and promotional program must be coordinated within the company, inside the ad agency, and between the two. Any other parties involved in the promotional campaign, such as public relations and/or sales promotion firms, research specialists, or media buying services, must also know what the company hopes to accomplish through its marketing communications program. Many problems can be avoided if all parties have written, approved objectives to guide their actions and serve as a common base for discussing issues related to the promotional program.

Planning and Decision Making

Specific promotional objectives also guide development of the integrated marketing communications plan. All phases of a firm's promotional strategy should be based on the established objectives, including budgeting, creative, and media decisions as well as supportive programs such as direct marketing, public relations/publicity, sales promotion, and/or reseller support.

Meaningful objectives can also be a useful guide for decision making. Promotional planners are often faced with a number of strategic and tactical options in terms of choosing creative options, selecting media, and allocating the budget among various elements of the promotional mix. Choices should be made based on how well a particular strategy matches the firm's promotional objectives.

Measurement and Evaluation of Results

An important reason for setting specific objectives is that they provide a benchmark against which the success or failure of the promotional campaign can be measured. Without specific objectives, it is extremely difficult to determine what the firm's advertising and promotion efforts accomplished. One characteristic of good objectives is that they are *measurable;* they specify a method and criteria for determining how well the promotional program is working. By setting specific and meaningful objectives, the promotional planner provides a measure(s) that can be used to evaluate the effectiveness of the marketing communications program. Most organizations are concerned about the return on their promotional investment, and comparing actual performance against measurable objectives is the best way to determine if the return justifies the expense.

Determining Promotional Objectives

Integrated marketing communications objectives should be based on a thorough situation analysis that identifies the marketing and promotional issues facing the company or a brand. The situation analysis is the foundation on which marketing objectives are determined and the marketing plan is developed. Promotional objectives evolve from the company's overall marketing plan and are rooted in its marketing objectives. Advertising and promotion objectives are not the same as marketing objectives (although many firms tend to treat them as synonymous).

Marketing versus Communications Objectives

Marketing objectives are generally stated in the firm's marketing plan and are statements of what is to be accomplished by the overall marketing program within a given time period. Marketing objectives are usually defined in terms of specific, measurable outcomes such as sales volume, market share, profits, or return on investment. Good marketing objectives are *quantifiable;* delineate the target market and note the time frame for accomplishing the goal (often one year). For example, a copy machine company may have as its marketing objective "to increase sales by 10 percent in the small-business segment of the market during the next 12 months." To be effective, objectives must also be *realistic* and *attainable.*

A company with a very high market share may seek to increase its sales volume by stimulating growth in the product category. It might accomplish this by increasing consumption by current users or encouraging nonusers to use the product. Some firms have as their marketing objectives expanding distribution and sales of their product in certain market areas. Companies often have secondary marketing objectives that are related to actions they must take to solve specific problems and thus achieve their primary objectives. For example, in the early 1990s San Antonio–based Pace Foods began a promotional campaign to expand its business beyond its traditional Texas base. To achieve this objective, its agency

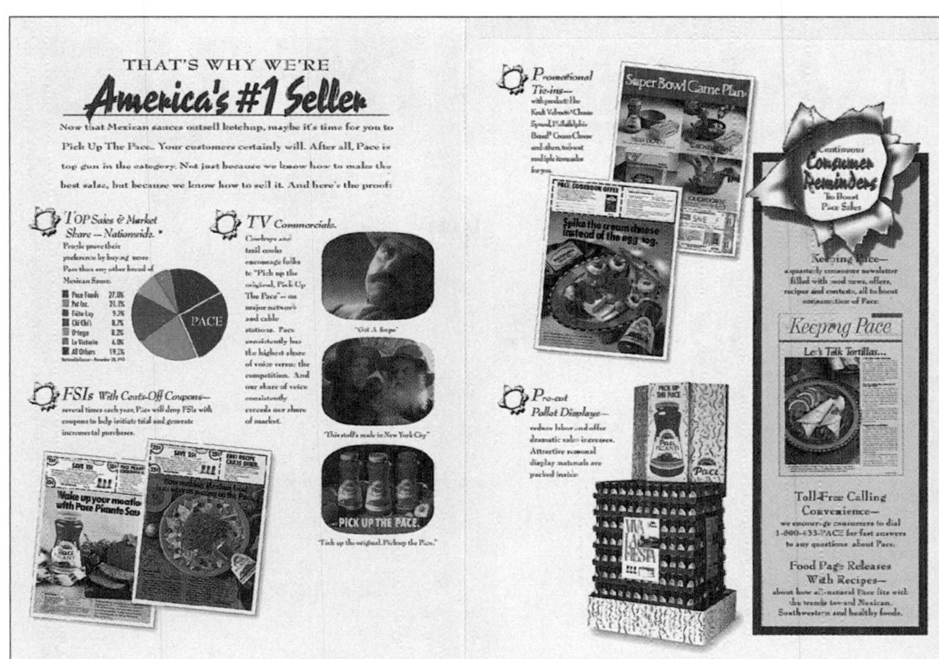

Exhibit 7–3 Pace Foods' New York City campaign has helped expand sales beyond the Texas market

set out to establish a position of authenticity and make Mexican food seem fun. An advertising campaign for Pace picante sauce poked fun at the New York City origins of a fictitious rival brand. Pace's vice president of sales and marketing said the idea behind the campaign was that Pace's sauce is created by people who live "where folks know what salsa should be." Pace also used various sales promotion tools such as coupons, promotional tie-ins, and point-of-purchase displays to generate sales (Exhibit 7–3). Sales of Pace picante sauce have tripled, and its 28 percent brand share makes it the market leader in a category that has surpassed ketchup.[2]

Once the marketing communications manager has reviewed the marketing plan, he or she should understand where the company hopes to go with its marketing program, how it intends to get there, and the role advertising and promotion will play. Marketing goals defined in terms of sales, profit, or market share increases are usually not appropriate promotional objectives. They are objectives for the entire marketing program, and achieving them depends on the proper coordination and execution of all the marketing mix elements, including not just promotion but product planning and production, pricing, and distribution.

Integrated marketing communications objectives are statements of what various aspects of the IMC program will accomplish. They should be based on the particular communications tasks required to deliver the appropriate messages to the target audience. Managers must be able to translate general marketing goals into communications goals and specific promotional objectives. Some guidance in doing this may be available from the marketing plan, as the situation analysis should provide important information on

- The market segments the firm wants to target and the target audience (demographics, psychographics, and purchase motives).
- The product and its main features, advantages, benefits, uses, and applications.
- The company's and competitors' brands (sales and market share in various segments, positioning, competitive strategies, promotional expenditures, creative and media strategies, and tactics).
- Ideas on how the brand should be positioned and specific behavioral responses being sought (trial, repurchase, brand switching, and increased usage).

Exhibit 7–4 These ads for Del Monte food products were part of a marketing strategy designed to increase sales and market share

For example, the ads for Del Monte stewed tomatoes and snack cups in Exhibit 7–4 were part of the company's marketing strategy to increase sales and market share for its various food products by targeting existing or lapsed users as well as new, younger customers. The 12-month, $20 million advertising campaign used a series of four-color ads featuring new recipe ideas and serving suggestions. All of the ads used the same graphic format to help build the overall franchise for Del Monte brands while promoting individual products. The campaign resulted in increased market share for all four of the advertised categories.

Sometimes companies do not have a formal marketing plan, and the information needed may not be readily available. In this case, the promotional planner must attempt to gather as much information as possible about the product and its markets from sources both inside and outside the company.

After reviewing all the information, the promotional planner should see how integrated marketing communications fits into the marketing program and what the firm hopes to achieve through advertising and other promotional elements. The next step is to set objectives in terms of specific communications goals or tasks.

Many promotional planners approach promotion from a communications perspective and believe the objective of advertising and other promotional mix elements is usually to communicate information or a selling message about a product or service. Other managers argue that sales or some related measure, such as market share, is the only meaningful goal for advertising and promotion and should be the basis for setting objectives. These two perspectives have been the topic of considerable debate and are worth examining further.

Sales versus Communications Objectives

Sales-Oriented Objectives

To many managers, the only meaningful objective for their promotional program is sales. They take the position that the basic reason a firm spends money on advertising and promotion is to sell its product or service. Promotional spending represents an investment of a firm's scarce resources that requires an economic justification. Rational managers generally compare investment options on a common financial basis, such as return on investment (ROI). As we'll discuss later in this chapter, determining the specific return on advertising and promotional dollars is often quite difficult. However, many managers believe that monies spent on advertising and other forms of promotion should produce measurable results, such as increasing sales volume by a certain percentage or dollar amount or increasing the brand's market share. They believe objectives (as well as the success or failure of the campaign) should be based on the achievement of sales results.

Some managers prefer sales-oriented objectives to make the individuals involved in advertising and promotion think in terms of how the promotional program will influence sales. Or they may confuse marketing objectives with advertising and promotional objectives. For example, as discussed in IMC Perspective 7–1, for Kellogg and Post the goal was to increase sales and market share versus store brands. This goal not only became the basis of the marketing plan but carried over as the primary objective of the promotional program. The success of the advertising and promotional campaign is judged only by attainment of these goals.

Problems with Sales Objectives Given Kellogg's and Post's failures to reverse their sales declines, does this mean the advertising and promotional program was ineffective? Or does it mean the price cuts didn't work? It might help to compare this situation to a football game and think of advertising as a quarterback. The quarterback is one of the most important players on the team but can be effective only with support from the other players. If the team loses, is it fair to blame the loss entirely on the quarterback? Of course not. Just as the quarterback is but one of the players on the football team, promotion is but one element of the marketing program, and there are many other reasons why the targeted sales level was not reached. The quarterback can lead his team to victory only if the linemen block, the receivers catch his passes, and the running backs help the offense establish a balanced attack of running and passing. Even if the quarterback plays an outstanding game, the team can still lose if the defense gives up too many points.

In the business world, poor sales results can be due to any of the other marketing mix variables, including product design or quality, packaging, distribution, or pricing. Advertising can make consumers aware of and interested in the brand, but it can't make them buy it, particularly if it is not readily available or is priced higher than a competing brand. As shown in Figure 7–1, sales are a function of many factors, not just advertising and promotion. There is an adage in marketing that states, "Nothing will kill a poor product faster than good advertising." Taken with the other factors shown in Figure 7–1, this adage demonstrates that all the marketing elements must work together if a successful plan is to be implemented.

Another problem with sales objectives is that the effects of advertising often occur over an extended period. Many experts recognize that advertising has a lagged or **carryover effect;** monies spent on advertising do not necessarily have an

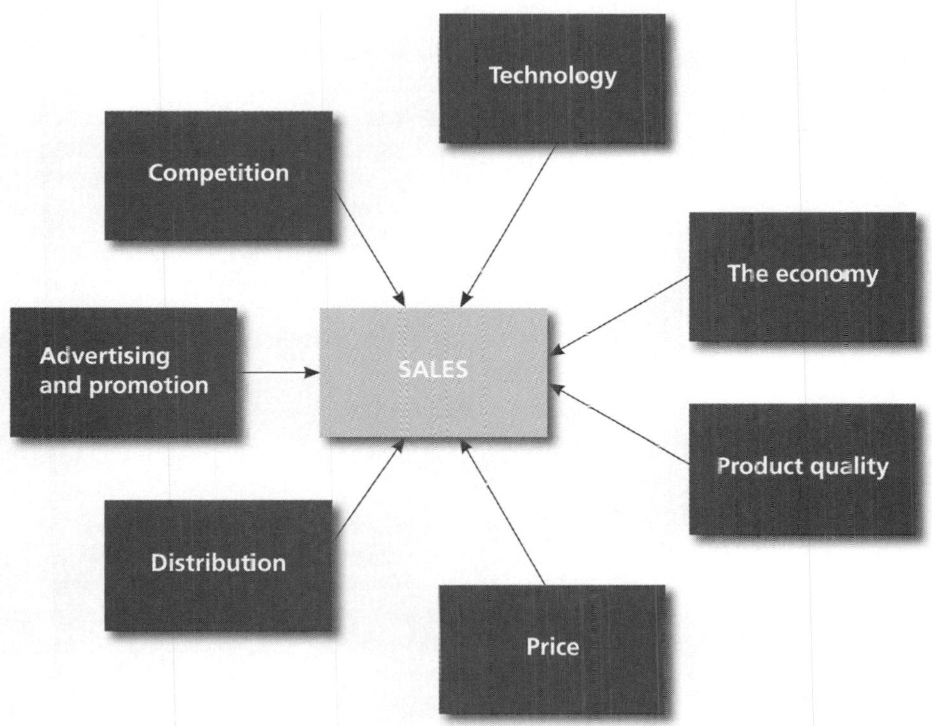

Figure 7–1 Factors influencing sales

IMC Perspective 7–1

Cereal Makers Change Objectives and Slash Budgets—without Much Success

A variety of factors can account for changes in the advertising and promotional budgets companies establish. One of the most common of these is a drop in sales. Take the cereal industry for example. In 1996, when Post Cereal found itself losing market share to the number 1 and 2 companies—Kellogg and General Mills, respectively—it tried to bring consumers back by slashing prices on its 22 cereal brands by an average of 20 percent (about a dollar). Kellogg immediately followed suit, as did General Mills (which had already announced a smaller price cut two years earlier).

How did these companies finance the lower prices? One way was by reducing advertising and promotional spending. As cereal prices continued to climb faster than the grocery price index in almost every year since 1983, much of the revenue was used to fund the advertising and promotions campaigns. (One estimate was that $1.02 of a $3.39 box of Kellogg's Corn Flakes went to advertising.) Once the revenues were reduced, the expenditures were reduced. Judann Pollack noted that if the cereal manufacturers maintained their price cuts for a year, advertising and promotional spending would decrease by $70 million (from $353 million) at Kellogg and $40 million (from $203 million) at Post.

But isn't it counterintuitive to decrease advertising and promotional spending when sales go down? Post didn't think so. The cuts were an attempt to make the name brands more price-competitive with store brands, which had experienced a 7 percent gain in market share from 1990 to 1997, due in part to the fact that they cost about a third as much as the Post and Kellogg offerings. Post attempted to follow the success its parent brand, Philip Morris, had when it employed the same strategy with Marlboro cigarettes. Brand managers considered the cuts a "return to rational marketing," noting that in the past price increases were often offset by heavy couponing and promotional incentives offered to dealers. These programs would be the first to feel the impact. Advertising would also feel it. Media spending on Kellogg's Frosted Flakes (over $51 million) and Frosted Mini-Wheats (approximately $49 million) also saw reductions.

Thomas Knowlton, Kellogg's North America president, claimed that the advertising and promotional spending cuts would be a short-term strategy. He said that with the price cuts, "we can't afford advertising that isn't working. We are going to be more demanding with our brands, and only proven ad campaigns will get full funding." More testing of ads and media would take place to help determine what was and was not working, said Knowlton.

So now, with the vision of hindsight, how did the strategy work? In the fall of 1998, Kellogg's announced a major layoff, and the chiefs of the North American and European Divisions quit. Earnings missed their targets in the previous two quarters of that year, and stock was down 30 percent for the year. Kellogg's share continued to fall, experiencing an 11 percent drop in the first half of the year and falling below General Mills in 1999. The cereal price cuts not only cut profits but, over recent years, resulted in $1.5 billion less in advertising outlays. A change in advertising agencies was initiated in the early fall, with six additional agencies asked to compete.

Information Resources, Inc., a research company that tracks sales using scanner data, announced that in the six-month period following the price cuts, Post's volume also fell, by 2.1 percent. Tim Callahan, general manager of cereals at Kraft (the parent company of Post Cereals), disagreed with these numbers, arguing that the strategy was a success and noting that other "intangibles" were not taken into consideration. Looking at these numbers he might have problems finding someone to agree with him.

Sources: "General Mills Outsells Kellogg's Cereals," *TulsaWorld,* Tulsa, OK, December 30, 1999, p. 2; Judann Pollack, "Price Cuts Unsettling to Cereal Business," *Advertising Age,* September 28, 1998, p. 510; "Kellogg Marketing Strategies under Revision," *PR Newswire,* September 4, 1998, p. 1087; John Greenwald, "Cereal Showdown," *Time,* April 29, 1996, pp. 60–61; Judann Pollack, "Cereals to Pare Ad Plans," *Advertising Age,* June 24, 1996, p. 1; Rance Crain, "Cereals Shouldn't Squeeze Ad Bucks," *Advertising Age,* July 1, 1996, p. 15.

immediate impact on sales.[3] Advertising may create awareness, interest, and/or favorable attitudes toward a brand, but these feelings will not result in an actual purchase until the consumer enters the market for the product, which may occur later. A review of econometric studies that examined the duration of cumulative advertising effects found that for mature, frequently purchased, low-priced products, advertising's effect on sales lasts up to nine months.[4] Models have been developed to account for the carryover effect of advertising and to help determine the long-term effect of advertising on sales.[5] The carryover effect adds to the difficulty of determining the precise relationship between advertising and sales.

Another problem with sales objectives is that they offer little guidance to those responsible for planning and developing the promotional program. The creative and media people working on the account need some direction as to the nature of the advertising message the company hopes to communicate, the intended audience, and the particular effect or response sought. As you will see shortly, communications objectives are recommended because they provide operational guidelines for those involved in planning, developing, and executing the advertising and promotional program.

Exhibit 7–5 Microsoft spent $200 million to launch Windows 95

Where Sales Objectives Are Appropriate

While there can be many problems in attempting to use sales as objectives for a promotional campaign, there are situations where sales objectives are appropriate. Certain types of promotion efforts are direct action in nature; they attempt to induce an immediate behavioral response from the prospective customer. A major objective of most sales promotion programs is to generate short-term increases in sales. When Microsoft introduced its Windows 95 operating system, it spent an estimated $200 million in the first year to create awareness and interest in the new product. A 30-minute "info-show," tie-in promotions with Cracker Jack, prelaunch parties and public relations activities around the world, point-of-sale displays, and millions of dollars in advertising were all part of the introduction. The success of Windows 95 was evidenced by the fact that customers lined up outside stores to purchase the product. Microsoft eventually achieved over 85 percent of the market and was taken to court for monopolizing the market (Exhibit 7–5).

Direct-response advertising is one type of advertising that evaluates its effectiveness on the basis of sales. Merchandise is advertised in material mailed to customers, in newspapers and magazines, or on television. The consumer purchases the merchandise by mail or by calling a toll-free number. The direct-response advertiser generally sets objectives and measures success in terms of the sales response generated by the ad. For example, objectives for and the evaluation of a direct-response ad on TV are based on the number of orders received each time a station broadcasts the commercial. Because advertising is really the only form of communication and promotion used in this situation and response is generally immediate, setting objectives in terms of sales is appropriate. The SkyTel interactive messaging system shown in Exhibit 7–6 is an example of a product sold through direct-response advertising.

Exhibit 7–6 Sales results are an appropriate objective for direct-response advertising

Retail advertising, which accounts for a significant percentage of all advertising expenditures, is another area where the advertiser often seeks a direct response, particularly when sales or special events are being promoted. The ad for Service Merchandise's Valentine's Day Sale shown in Exhibit 7–7 is designed to attract consumers to stores during the sales period (and to generate sales volume). Service Merchandise's management can determine the effectiveness of its promotional effort by analyzing store traffic and sales volume during sale days and comparing them to figures for nonsale days. But retailers may also allocate advertising and promotional dollars to image-building campaigns designed to create and enhance favorable perceptions of their stores. In this case, sales-oriented objectives would not be appropriate; the effectiveness of the campaign would be based on its ability to create or change consumers' image of the store.

Exhibit 7–7 Retail ads often seek sales objectives

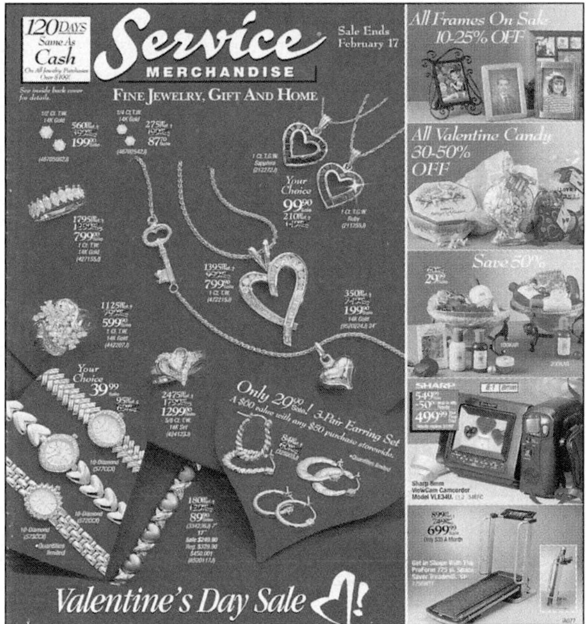

Sales-oriented objectives are also used when advertising plays a dominant role in a firm's marketing program and other factors are relatively stable. For example, many package-goods companies compete in mature markets with established channels of distribution, stable competitive prices and promotional budgets, and products of similar quality. They view advertising and sales promotion as the key determinants of a brand's sales or market share, so it may be possible to isolate the effects of these promotional mix variables.[6] Many companies have accumulated enough market knowledge with their advertising, sales promotion, and direct-marketing programs to have considerable insight into the sales levels that should result from their promotional efforts. Thus, they believe it is reasonable to set objectives and evaluate the success of their promotional efforts in terms of sales results. Established brands are often repositioned (as discussed in Chapter 2) with the goal of improving their sales or relative market share.

Advertising and promotional programs tend to be evaluated in terms of sales, particularly when expectations are not being met. Marketing and brand managers under pressure to show sales results often take a short-term perspective in evaluating advertising and sales promotion programs. They are often looking for a quick fix for declining sales or loss of market share. They ignore the pitfalls of making direct links between advertising and sales, and campaigns, as well as ad agencies, may be changed if sales expectations are not being met. As discussed in Chapter 3, many companies want their agencies to accept incentive-based compensation systems tied to sales performance. Thus, while sales may not be an appropriate objective in many advertising and promotional situations, managers are inclined to keep a close eye on sales and market share figures and make changes in the promotional program when these numbers become stagnant.

Communications Objectives

Some marketers do recognize the problems associated with sales-oriented objectives. They recognize that the primary role of an IMC program is to communicate and that planning should be based on communications objectives. Advertising and other promotional efforts are designed to achieve such communications as brand knowledge and interest, favorable attitudes and image, and purchase intentions. Consumers are not expected to respond immediately; rather, advertisers realize they must provide relevant information and create favorable predispositions toward the brand before purchase behavior will occur.

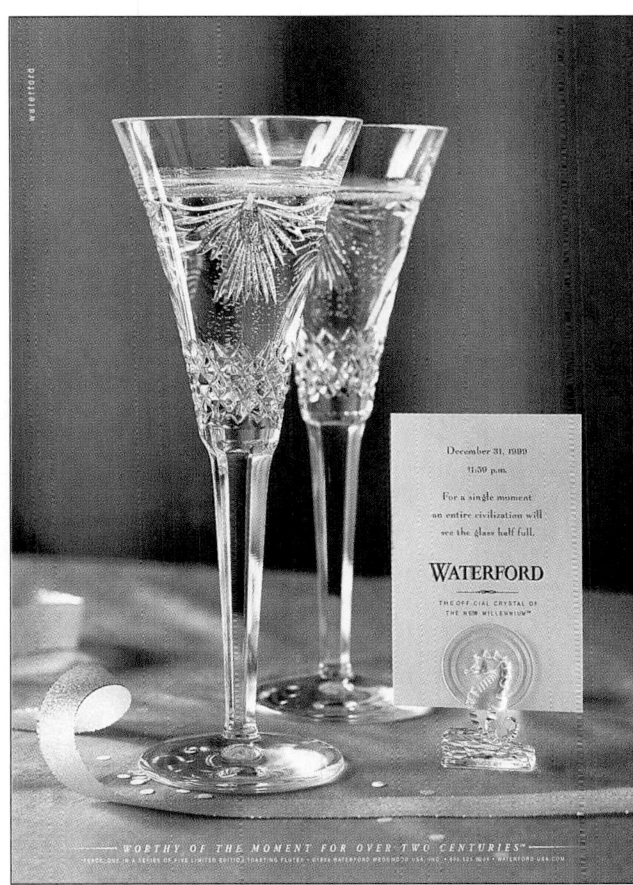

Exhibit 7–8 Waterford creates an image of quality products

For example, the ad for Waterford crystal in Exhibit 7–8 is designed to inform consumers of the product's tradition and craftsmanship. While there is no call for immediate action, the ad creates favorable impressions about the product so that consumers will consider it when they enter the market for crystal.

Advocates of communications-based objectives generally use some form of the hierarchical models discussed in Chapter 5 when setting advertising and promotion objectives. In all these models, consumers pass through three successive stages: cognitive, affective, and conative. As consumers proceed through the three stages, they move closer to making a purchase. Figure 7–2 shows the various steps in the Lavidge and Steiner hierarchy of effects model as the consumer moves from awareness to purchase, along with examples of types of promotion or advertising relevant to each step.

Communications Effects Pyramid Advertising and promotion perform communications tasks in the same way that a pyramid is built, by first accomplishing lower-level objectives such as awareness and knowledge or comprehension.[7] Subsequent tasks involve moving consumers who are aware of or knowledgeable about the product or service to higher levels in the pyramid (Figure 7–3). The initial stages, at the base of the pyramid, are easier to accomplish than those toward the top, such as trial and repurchase or regular use. Thus, the percentage of prospective customers will decline as they move up the pyramid. Figure 7–4 shows how a company introducing a new brand of shampoo targeted at 18- to 34-year-old females might set its IMC objectives using the communications effects pyramid.

The communications pyramid can also be used to determine promotional objectives for an established brand. The promotional planner must determine where the target audience lies with respect to the various blocks in the pyramid. If awareness levels for a brand and knowledge of its features and benefits are low, the communications objective should be to increase them. If these blocks of the pyramid are already in place, but liking or preference is low, the advertising goal may be to change the target markets' image of the brand and move consumers through to purchase.

Figure 7–2 Effect of advertising on consumers: movement from awareness to action

Related behavioral dimensions	Movement toward purchase	Example of types of promotion or advertising relevant to various steps
Conative The realm of motives. Ads stimulate or direct desires.	Purchase	Point-of-purchase Retail store ads Deals "Last-chance" offers Price appeals Testimonials
	Conviction	
Affective The realm of emotions. Ads change attitudes and feelings.	Preference	Competitive ads Argumentative copy
	Liking	"Image" copy Status, glamour appeals
Cognitive The realm of thoughts. Ads provide information and facts.	Knowledge	Announcements Descriptive copy Classified ads Slogans Jingles Skywriting
	Awareness	Teaser campaigns

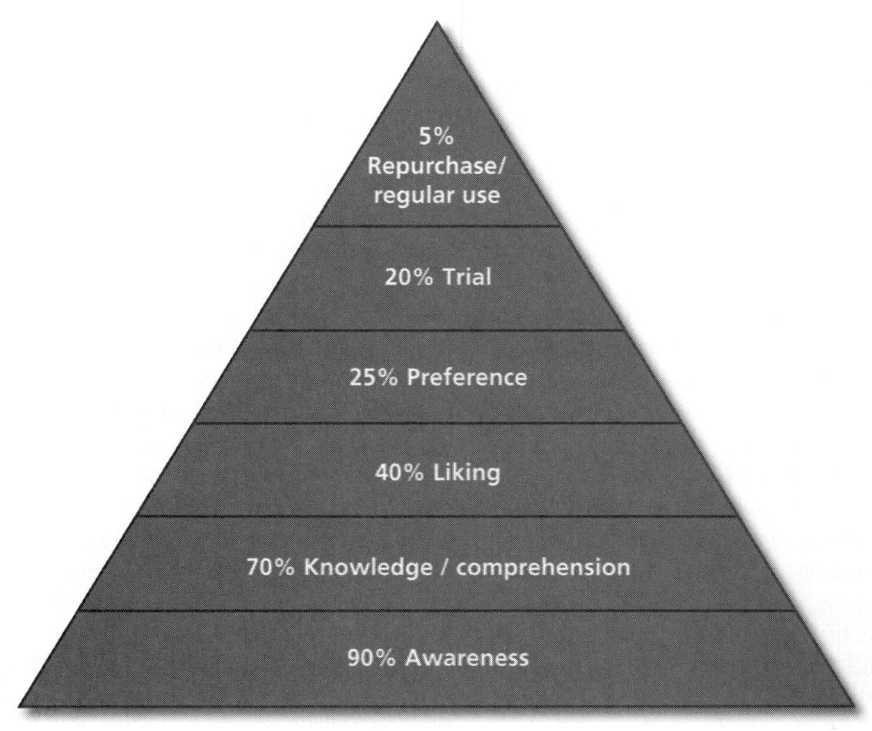

Figure 7–3 Communications effects pyramid

Product: Backstage Shampoo

Time period: Six months

Objective 1: Create awareness among 90 percent of target audience. Use repetitive advertising in newspapers, magazines, TV and radio programs. Simple message.

Objective 2: Create interest in the brand among 70 percent of target audience. Communicate information about the features and benefits of the brand—i.e., that it contains no soap and improves the texture of the hair

Objective 3: Create positive feelings about the brand among 40 percent and preference among 25 percent of the target audience. Create favorable attitudes by conveying information, promotions, sampling, etc.

Objective 4: Obtain trial among 20 percent of the target audience. Use sampling and cents-off coupons along with advertising and promotions.

Objective 5: Develop and maintain regular use of Backstage Shampoo among 5 percent of the target audience. Use continued reinforcement advertising, fewer coupons and promotions

Figure 7–4 Setting objectives using the communications effects pyramid

Problems with Communications Objectives Not all marketing and advertising managers accept communications objectives; some say it is too difficult to translate a sales goal into a specific communications objective. But at some point a sales goal must be transformed into a communications objective. If the marketing plan for an established brand has as an objective of increasing sales by 10 percent, the promotional planner will eventually have to think in terms of the message that will be communicated to the target audience to achieve this. Possible objectives include the following:

- Increasing the percentage of consumers in the target market who associate specific features, benefits, or advantages with our brand.
- Increasing the number of consumers in the target audience who prefer our product over the competition's.
- Encouraging current users of the product to use it more frequently or in more situations.
- Encouraging consumers who have never used our brand to try it.

In some situations, promotional planners may gain insight into communications objectives' relationship to sales from industry research. Evalucom, Inc., conducted a study of commercials for new products. Some succeeded in stimulating anticipated levels of sales; others did not. Figure 7–5 shows four factors the study identified that affect whether a commercial for a new product is successful in generating sales.

- **Communicating that something is different about the product.** Successful introductory commercials communicated some point of difference for the new product.
- **Positioning the brand difference in relation to the product category.** Successful commercials positioned their brand's difference within a specific product category. For example, a new breakfast product was positioned as the "crispiest cereal" and a new beverage as the "smoothest soft drink."
- **Communicating that the product difference is beneficial to consumers.** Nearly all of the successful commercials linked a benefit directly to the new product's difference.
- **Supporting the idea that something about the product is different and/or beneficial to consumers.** All the successful commercials communicated support for the product's difference claim or its relevance to consumers. Support took the form of demonstrations of performance, information supporting a uniqueness claim, endorsements, or testimonials.

Figure 7–5 Factors related to success of advertising for new products

In attempting to translate sales goals into specific communications objectives, promotional planners often are not sure what constitutes adequate levels of awareness, knowledge, liking, preference, or conviction. There are no formulas to provide this information. The promotional manager will have to use his or her personal experience and that of the brand or product managers, as well as the marketing history of this and similar brands. Average scores on various communications measures for this and similar products should be considered, along with the levels achieved by competitors' products. This information can be related to the amount of money and time spent building these levels as well as the resulting sales or market share figures.

At some point, sales-oriented objectives must be translated into what the company hopes to communicate and to whom it hopes to communicate it. For example, Milwaukee-based Midwest Express Airlines found itself in a situation where business travelers, its primary market, assumed that the airline's high level of service meant premium prices. To combat this perception, the "Best care. Same fare" campaign was developed. In the commercials, a man claimed Midwest's fares were higher, only to be told flatly by a female colleague that he was wrong. The conversations occurred in humorous settings, such as one where a man scrambles up a down escalator to keep up with a woman (Exhibit 7–9). Midwest was able to communicate its competitive fares and achieve its sales objective. The number of people who thought Midwest cost more than competitors declined by 17 percent within six months, while the airline's market share grew from 19 to 25 percent.[8]

Many marketing and promotional managers recognize the value of setting specific communications objectives and their important role as operational guidelines to the planning, execution, and evaluation of the promotional program. Communications objectives are the criteria used in the DAGMAR approach to setting advertising goals and objectives, which has become one of the most influential approaches to the advertising planning process.

Exhibit 7–9 Midwest Express increased its market share by advertising its competitive fares

DAGMAR: An Approach to Setting Objectives

In 1961, Russell Colley prepared a report for the Association of National Advertisers titled *Defining Advertising Goals for Measured Advertising Results* (DAGMAR).[9] In it, Colley developed a model for setting advertising objectives and measuring the results of an ad campaign. The major thesis of the **DAGMAR** model is that communications effects are the logical basis for advertising goals and objectives against which success or failure should be measured. Colley's rationale for communications-based objectives was as follows:

> Advertising's job, purely and simply, is to communicate to a defined audience information and a frame of mind that stimulates action. Advertising succeeds or fails depending on how well it communicates the desired information and attitudes to the right people at the right time and at the right cost.[10]

Under the DAGMAR approach, an advertising goal involves a **communications task** that is specific and measurable. A communications task, as opposed to a marketing task, can be performed by, and attributed to, advertising rather than to a combination of several marketing factors. Colley proposed that the communications task be based on a hierarchical model of the communications process with four stages:

- *Awareness*—making the consumer aware of the existence of the brand or company.
- *Comprehension*—developing an understanding of what the product is and what it will do for the consumer.
- *Conviction*—developing a mental disposition in the consumer to buy the product.
- *Action*—getting the consumer to purchase the product.

As discussed earlier, other hierarchical models of advertising effects can be used as a basis for analyzing the communications response process. Some advertising theorists prefer the Lavidge and Steiner hierarchy of effects model, since it is more specific and provides a better way to establish and measure results.[11]

While the hierarchical model of advertising effects was the basic model of the communications response process used in DAGMAR, Colley also studied other specific tasks that advertising might be expected to perform in leading to the ultimate objective of a sale. He developed a checklist of 52 advertising tasks to characterize the contribution of advertising and serve as a starting point for establishing objectives.

Characteristics of Objectives

A second major contribution of DAGMAR to the advertising planning process was its definition of what constitutes a good objective. Colley argued that advertising objectives should be stated in terms of concrete and measurable communications tasks, specify a target audience, indicate a benchmark starting point and the degree of change sought, and specify a time period for accomplishing the objective(s).

Concrete, Measurable Tasks The communications task specified in the objective should be a precise statement of what appeal or message the advertiser wants to communicate to the target audience. Advertisers generally use a copy platform to describe their basic message. The objective or copy platform statement should be specific and clear enough to guide the creative specialists who develop the advertising message. In the Midwest Express example, the objective was to combat the perception that its fares were higher than competitors'.

According to DAGMAR, the objective must also be measurable. There must be a way to determine whether the intended message has been communicated properly. Midwest Express measured its communications objective by asking airline travelers whether they thought Midwest's airfares were higher than those of competing airlines.

Target Audience Another important characteristic of good objectives is a well-defined target audience. The primary target audience for a company's product or service is described in the situation analysis. It may be based on descriptive variables such as geography, demographics, and psychographics (on which advertising media selection decisions are based) as well as on behavioral variables such as usage rate or benefits sought. IMC Perspective 7–2 demonstrates the objective-setting process involved in the launch of the new Subaru Outback. Notice how specifically the target audience was defined.

Benchmark and Degree of Change Sought To set objectives, one must know the target audience's present status concerning response hierarchy variables such as awareness, knowledge, image, attitudes, and intentions and then determine the degree to which consumers must be changed by the advertising campaign. Determining the target market's present position regarding the various response stages requires **benchmark measures.** Often a marketing research study must be conducted to determine prevailing levels of the response hierarchy. In the case of a new product or service, the starting conditions are generally at or near zero for all the variables, so no initial research is needed.

Establishing benchmark measures gives the promotional planner a basis for determining what communications tasks need to be accomplished and for specifying particular objectives. For example, a preliminary study for a brand may reveal that awareness is high but consumer perceptions and attitudes are negative. The objective for the advertising campaign must then be to change the target audience's perceptions of and attitudes toward the brand. In the case of Outback, the objectives were to generate high levels of awareness, given that existing levels were so low.

Quantitative benchmarks are not only valuable in establishing communications goals and objectives but essential for determining whether the campaign was successful. Objectives provide the standard against which the success or failure of a campaign is measured. An ad campaign that results in a 90 percent awareness level for a brand among its target audience cannot really be judged effective unless one knows what percentage of the consumers were aware of the brand before the campaign began. A 70 percent precampaign awareness level would lead to a different interpretation of the campaign's success than would a 30 percent level.

Specified Time Period A final consideration in setting advertising objectives is specifying the time period in which they must be accomplished. Appropriate time periods can range from a few days to a year or more. Most ad campaigns specify time periods from a few months to a year, depending on the situation facing the advertiser and the type of response being sought. For example, awareness levels for a brand can be created or increased fairly quickly through an intensive media schedule of widespread, repetitive advertising to the target audience. Repositioning of a product requires a change in consumers' perceptions and takes much more time. The repositioning of Marlboro cigarettes from a feminine brand to one with a masculine image, for instance, took several years.

Assessment of DAGMAR

The DAGMAR approach to setting objectives has had considerable influence on the advertising planning process. Many promotional planners use this model as a basis for setting objectives and assessing the effectiveness of their promotional campaigns. DAGMAR also focused advertisers' attention on the value of using communications-based rather than sales-based objectives to measure advertising effectiveness and encouraged the measurement of stages in the response hierarchy to assess a campaign's impact. Colley's work has led to improvements in the advertising and promotional planning process by providing a better understanding of the goals and objectives toward which planners' efforts should be directed. This usually results in less subjectivity and also leads to better communication and relationships between the client and its agency.

IMC Perspective 7–2

Subaru Outback—Uniquely Positioned to Boomers

The young professionals known as the baby boomer generation were responsible for the dramatic growth of the sports car segment including such vehicles as the Mazda RX7, Nissan Z cars, Toyota Supra, and Honda Prelude. As the boomers started families, however, the sports cars gave way to more practical family vehicles, particularly sport utility vehicles (SUVs) and specifically the Jeep Cherokee and Jeep Grand Cherokee. The rough and unstable ride and poor fuel economy were tolerated—though not appreciated—as a trade-off for the space for both cargo and people. As the families grew older, the level of tolerance decreased—though the love of the SUV remained.

Along came the Subaru Outback. Positioned as a hybrid with the versatility of an SUV but with a more comfortable ride and handling, the Outback was introduced in 1995 with very little fanfare—that is, no active marketing or advertising. The few who heard about the new vehicle received it with open arms, as did the dealers. With this optimism as a guide, Subaru conducted extensive research that led to significant model changes for the 1996 edition. The research also led to the positioning of the car as a "sports utility wagon" (so named by one of the participants in the research). The launch of the new SUW was supported by TV and print advertising, using Paul Hogan ("Crocodile Dundee") as the spokesperson and directly comparing the vehicle to competitive SUVs such as the Cherokee, Ford Explorer, and Chevy Blazer.

Targeting the married male, age 35 to 55, with a college degree, active lifestyle, and annual household income over $55,000, the Outback was positioned as having carlike qualities without sacrificing the attributes of the SUV. An extensive IMC program was developed, which included advertising, direct-marketing promotions, POP merchandising, public relations, and dealer motivation training and programs. Specific objectives were established, including: convince potential SUV buyers to consider the Outback rather than the SUV under consideration; generate high awareness through the use of Paul Hogan; generate high numbers of showroom visits; avoid discounts, while generating high sales volume and dealer profits; and attract at least 50 percent of sales from those intending to buy Ford, Chevy, or Jeep.

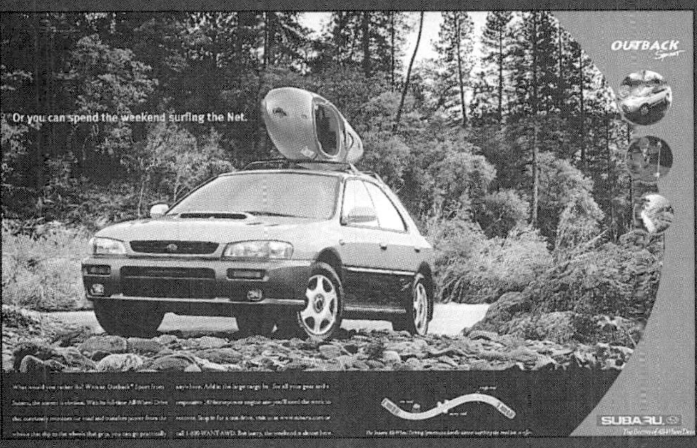

The media strategy linked the rugged imagery of Outback to active-lifestyle media: national cable TV (National Geographic Explorer, Discovery, and the Learning Channel); national print (*Backpacker, Outside, National Geographic, Smithsonian*); television (heavy schedules in prime time, local news, and sports); support media (outdoor and POP); and public relations (press kits and a PR campaign).

The only drawback to the IMC program was a lack of funding. Subaru knew that it would be highly outspent by its competitors and recognized that the launch would have to have high impact to be successful. How did Subaru do?

The launch was considered one of the most successful in the company's history, leading to the highest retail sales and most profits generated in any of the previous nine years. More specifically: recall increased from 33 to 38 percent in the first 60 days, reaching 50 percent by the end of the campaign—a 32.5 percent gain; dealer traffic increased by 15 to 20 percent; 55 percent of sales came from customers who had never owned a Subaru; the top three models traded in for the Outback were Jeep Grand Cherokee, Ford Explorer, and Chevy Blazer; the average transaction price increased by 12 percent; and sales increased by four times projections.

The total cost of the Outback launch was $17 million. To put this in perspective, Ford spent $120 million on the launch of the Taurus. Subaru increased its IMC budget, reaching $45 million for the 2000 model year, and continues to use Paul Hogan. As noted by *Ward's Auto World,* "You've got to hand it to Subaru for not simply dominating a corner of the market, but actually creating the niche."

Sources: Dave Guilford, "Subaru Backs Revamped Models with $45 million," *Advertising Age,* August 2, 1999, p. 46; Katherine Zachary, "Subaru Peaks Out," *Ward's Auto World,* October 1999, p. 55; Dennis Visich, www.Marketfiles.com, October 9, 1998.

Criticisms of DAGMAR

While DAGMAR has contributed to the advertising planning process, it has not been totally accepted by everyone in the advertising field. A number of problems have led to questions regarding its value as an advertising planning tool:[12]

- *Problems with the response hierarchy.* A major criticism of the DAGMAR approach is its reliance on the hierarchy of effects model. The fact that consumers do not always go through this sequence of communications effects before making a purchase has been recognized, and alternative response models have been developed.[13] DAGMAR MOD II recognizes that the appropriate response model depends on the situation and emphasizes identifying the sequence of decision-making steps that apply in a buying situation.[14]
- *Sales objectives.* Another objection to DAGMAR comes from those who argue that the only relevant measure of advertising objectives is sales. They have little tolerance for ad campaigns that achieve communications objectives but fail to increase sales. Advertising is seen as effective only if it induces consumers to make a purchase.[15] The problems with this logic were addressed in our discussion of communications objectives.
- *Practicality and costs.* Another criticism of DAGMAR concerns the difficulties involved in implementing it. Money must be spent on research to establish quantitative benchmarks and measure changes in the response hierarchy. This is costly and time-consuming and can lead to considerable disagreement over method, criteria, measures, and so forth. Many critics argue that DAGMAR is practical only for large companies with big advertising and research budgets. Many firms do not want to spend the money needed to use DAGMAR effectively.
- *Inhibition of creativity.* A final criticism of DAGMAR is that it inhibits advertising creativity by imposing too much structure on the people responsible for developing the advertising. Many creative personnel think the DAGMAR approach is too concerned with quantitative assessment of a campaign's impact on awareness, brand name recall, or specific persuasion measures. The emphasis is on passing the numbers test rather than developing a message that is truly creative and contributes to brand equity.

Problems in Setting Objectives

Although the DAGMAR model suggests a logical process for advertising and promotion planning, most advertisers and their agencies fail to follow these basic principles. They fail to set specific objectives for their campaigns and/or do not have the proper evidence to determine the success of their promotional programs. A classic study conducted by Stewart H. Britt examined problems with how advertisers set objectives and measure their accomplishment.[16] The study showed that most advertising agencies did not state appropriate objectives for determining success and thus could not demonstrate whether a supposedly successful campaign was really a success. Even though these campaigns may have been doing something right, they generally did not know what it was.

Although this study was conducted in 1969, the same problems exist in advertising today. A more recent study examined the advertising practices of business-to-business marketers to determine whether their ads used advertising objectives that met Colley's four DAGMAR criteria.[17] Entries from the annual Business/Professional Advertising Association Gold Key Awards competition, which solicits the best marketing communications efforts from business-to-business advertisers, were evaluated with respect to their campaigns' objectives and summaries of results. Most of these advertisers did not set concrete advertising objectives, specify objective tasks, measure results in terms of stages of a hierarchy of effects, or match objectives to evaluation measures. The authors concluded: "Advertising practitioners have only partially adopted the concepts and standards of objective setting and evaluation set forth 25 years ago."[18]

Improving Promotional Planners' Use of Objectives

As we have seen, it is important that advertisers and their agencies pay close attention to the objectives they set for their campaigns. They should strive to set specific and measurable objectives that not only guide promotional planning and decision making but also can be used as a standard for evaluating performance. Unfortunately, many companies do not set appropriate objectives for their integrated marketing communications programs.

Many companies fail to set appropriate objectives because top management has only an abstract idea of what the firm's IMC program is supposed to be doing. In a study by the American Business Press that measured the attitudes of chairs, presidents, and other senior managers of business-to-business advertising companies, more than half of the 427 respondents said they did not know whether their advertising was working and less than 10 percent thought it was working well.[19] This study showed overwhelmingly that top management did not even know what the company's advertising was supposed to do, much less how to measure it.

Few firms will set objectives that meet all the criteria set forth in DAGMAR. However, promotional planners should set objectives that are specific and measurable and go beyond basic sales goals. Even if specific communications response elements are not always measured, meeting the other criteria will sharpen the focus and improve the quality of the IMC planning process.

Setting Objectives for the IMC Program

One reason so much attention is given to advertising objectives is that for many companies advertising has traditionally been the major way of communicating with target audiences. Other promotional mix elements such as sales promotion, direct marketing, and publicity are used intermittently to support and complement the advertising program.

Another reason is that traditional advertising-based views of marketing communications planning, such as DAGMAR, have dominated the field for so long. These approaches are based on a hierarchical response model and consider how marketers can develop and disseminate advertising messages to move consumers along an effects path. This approach, shown in Figure 7–6, is what professor Don Schultz calls *inside-out planning.* He says, "It focuses on what the marketer wants to say, when the marketer wants to say it, about things the marketer believes are important about his or her brand, and in the media forms the marketer wants to use."[20]

Schultz advocates an *outside-in planning* process for IMC that starts with the customer and builds backward to the brand. This means that promotional planners

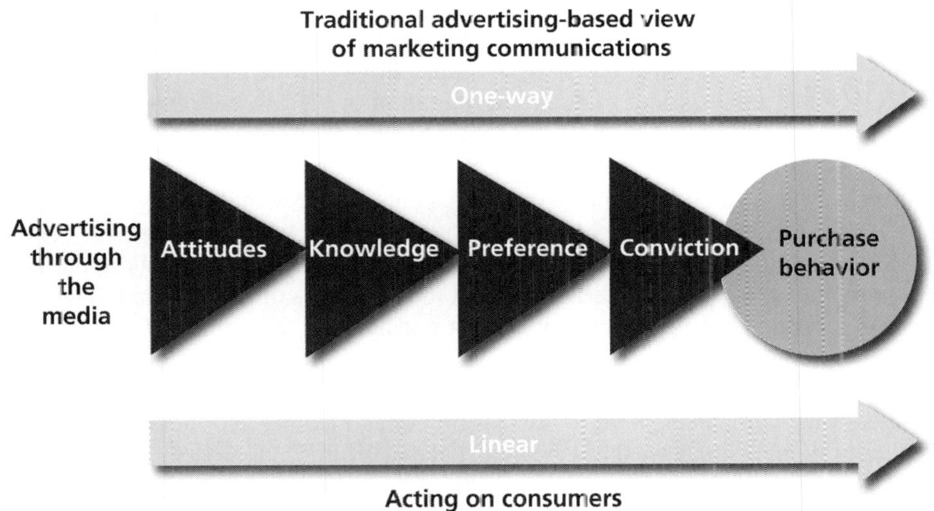

Figure 7–6 Traditional advertising-based view of marketing communications

study the various media customers and prospects use, when the marketer's messages might be most relevant to customers, and when they are likely to be most receptive to the message.

A similar approach is suggested by Professor Tom Duncan, who argues that IMC should use **zero-based communications planning,** which involves determining what tasks need to be done and which marketing communications functions should be used and to what extent.[21] This approach focuses on the task to be done and searches for the best ideas and media to accomplish it. Duncan notes that as with a traditional advertising campaign, the basis of an IMC campaign is a big idea. However, in IMC the big idea can be public relations, direct response, packaging, or sales promotion. Duncan suggests that an effective IMC program should lead with the marketing communications function that most effectively addresses the company's main problem or opportunity and should use a promotional mix that draws on the strengths of whichever communications functions relate best to the particular situation.

Exhibit 7–10 The San Diego Zoo attempts to attract visitors through advertising

Many of the considerations for determining advertising objectives are relevant to setting goals for other elements of the integrated marketing communications program. The promotional planner should determine what role various sales promotion techniques, publicity and public relations, direct marketing, and personal selling will play in the overall marketing program and how they will interact with advertising as well as with one another.

For example, the marketing communications program for the San Diego Zoological Society has a number of objectives. First, it must provide funding for the society's programs and maintain a large and powerful base of supporters for financial and political strength. The program must educate the public about the society's various programs and maintain a favorable image on a local, regional, national and even international level. A major objective of the IMC program is drawing visitors to the two attractions (Exhibit 7–10).

To achieve these objectives, the San Diego Zoological Society and its advertising agency developed an IMC program. As can be seen in Figure 7–7, this program employed a variety of integrated marketing communication tools. When setting objectives for these promotional elements, planners must consider what the firm hopes to communicate through the use of this element, among what target audience, and during what time period. As with advertising, results should be measured and evaluated against the original objectives, and attempts should be made to isolate the effects of each promotional element. Objectives for marketing communications elements other than advertising are discussed more thoroughly in Part Five of the text.

Establishing and Allocating the Promotional Budget

If you take a minute to look back at Figure 1–4 on page 26, you will see that while the arrows from the review of the marketing plan and the promotional situation analysis to analysis of the communications process are *unidirectional,* the flow between the communications analysis and budget determination is a *two-way interaction.* What this means is that while establishing objectives is an important part of the planning process, the limitations of the budget are important too. No organization has an unlimited budget, so objectives must be set with the budget in mind.

Often when we think of promotional expenditures of firms, we think only about the huge amounts being spent. We don't usually take the time to think about how these monies are being allocated and about the recipients of these dollars. The budgeting decisions have a significant impact not only on the firm itself but also on numerous others involved either directly or indirectly. The remainder of this chapter provides insight into some underlying theory with respect to budget setting, discusses how companies budget for promotional efforts, and demonstrates the inherent strengths and weaknesses associated with these approaches. Essentially, we focus on two primary budgeting decisions: establishing a budget amount and allocating the budget.

Figure 7–7 The San Diego Zoo sets objectives for various promotional elements

Advertising

Objectives:	Drive attendance to Zoo and Wild Animal Park. Uphold image and educate target audience and inform them of new attractions and special events and promotions.
Audience:	Members and nonmembers of Zoological Society. Households in primary and secondary geographic markets consisting of San Diego County and 5 other counties in southern California. Tertiary markets of 7 western states. Tourist and group sales markets.
Timing:	As allowed and determined by budget. Mostly timed to coincide with promotional efforts.
Tools/media:	Television, radio, newspaper, magazines, direct mail, outdoor, tourist media (television and magazine).

Sales Promotions

Objectives:	Use price, product, and other variables to drive attendance when it might not otherwise come.
Audience:	Targeted, depending on co-op partner, mostly to southern California market.
Timing:	To fit needs of Zoo and Wild Animal Park and cosponsoring partner.
Tools/media:	Coupons, sweepstakes, tours, broadcast tradeouts, direct mail: statement stuffers, fliers, postcards.

Public Relations

Objectives:	Inform, educate, create, and maintain image for Zoological Society and major attractions; reinforce advertising message.
Audience:	From local to international, depending on subject, scope, and timing.
Timing:	Ongoing, although often timed to coincide with promotions and other special events. Spur-of-the-moment animal news and information such as acquisitions, births, etc.
Tools/media:	Coverage by major news media, articles in local, regional, national and international newspapers, magazines and other publications such as visitors guides, tour books and guides, appearances by Zoo spokesperson Joanne Embery on talk shows (such as "The Tonight Show").

Cause Marketing/Corporate Sponsorships/Events Underwriting

Objectives:	To provide funding for Zoological Society programs and promote special programs and events done in cooperation with corporate sponsor. Must be win-win business partnership for Society and partner.
Audience:	Supporters of both the Zoological Society and the corporate or product/service partner.
Timing:	Coincides with needs of both partners, and seasonal attendance generation needs of Zoo and Wild Animal Park.
Tools:	May involve advertising, publicity, discount co-op promotions, ticket trades, hospitality centers. Exposure is directly proportional to amount of underwriting by corporate sponsor, both in scope and duration.

Direct Marketing

Objectives:	Maintain large powerful base of supporters for financial and political strength.
Audience:	Local, regional, national and international. Includes children's program (Koala Club), seniors (60+), couples, single memberships, and incremental donor levels.
Timing:	Ongoing, year-round promotion of memberships.
Tools:	Direct mail and on-grounds visibility.

Group Sales

Objectives:	Maximize group traffic and revenue by selling group tours to Zoo and Wild Animal Park.
Audience:	Conventions, incentive groups, bus tours, associations, youth, scouts, schools, camps, seniors, clubs, military, organizations, domestic and foreign travel groups.
Timing:	Targeted to drive attendance in peak seasons or at most probable times such as convention season.
Tools:	Travel and tourism trade shows, telemarketing, direct mail, trade publication advertising.

Establishing the Budget

The size of a firm's advertising and promotions budget can vary from a few thousand dollars to more than a billion. When companies like Procter & Gamble and General Motors spend over a billion dollars per year to promote their products, they expect such expenditures to accomplish their stated objectives. The budget decision is no less critical to a firm spending only a few thousand dollars; its ultimate success or failure may depend on the monies spent. One of the most critical decisions facing the marketing manager is how much to spend on the promotional effort.

Unfortunately, many managers fail to realize the value of advertising and promotion. They treat the communications budget as an expense rather than an investment. Instead of viewing the dollars spent as contributing to additional sales and market share, they see budget expenses as cutting into profits. As a result, when times get tough, the advertising and promotional budget is the first to be cut—even though there is strong evidence that exactly the opposite should occur, as Exhibit 7–11 argues. Moreover, the decision is not a one-time responsibility. A new budget is formulated every year, each time a new product is introduced, or when either internal or external factors necessitate a change to maintain competitiveness.

While it is one of the most critical decisions, budgeting has perhaps been the most resistant to change. A comparison of advertising and promotional texts over the past 10 years would reveal the same methods for establishing budgets. The theoretical basis for this process remains rooted in economic theory and marginal analysis. (Advertisers also use an approach based on **contribution margin**—the difference between the total revenue generated by a brand and its total variable costs. But, as Robert Steiner says, *marginal analysis* and *contribution margin* are essentially synonymous terms.)[22] We begin our discussion of budgeting with an examination of these theoretical approaches.

Exhibit 7–11 The AAAA promotes the continued use of advertising in a recession

IN A RECESSION, THE BEST DEFENSE IS A GOOD OFFENSE.

It's a recession. Your instincts demand that you cut the ad budget. But, as the McGraw-Hill Research[1] analysis of business-to-business advertising expenditures during the 1981-82 recession shows, it's those with the courage to maintain or increase advertising in a recession who reap a major sales advantage over their competitors who panic and fall back into a defensive posture. And this advantage continues to expand long after the recession is over.

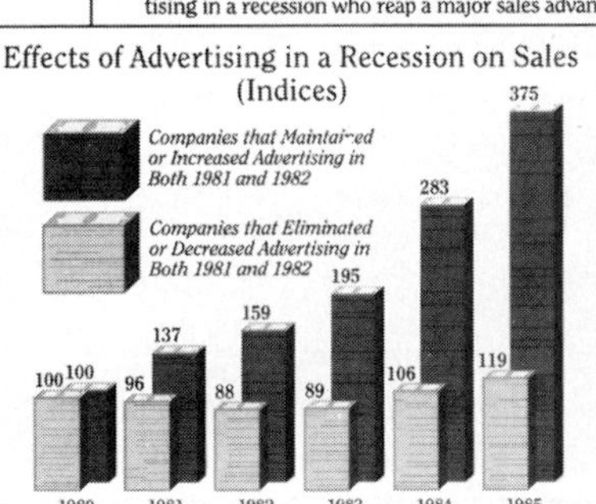

McGraw-Hill Research, 1986.

Recessions last an average of 11 months, but any advertising decision made during one can have permanent repercussions. The McGraw-Hill study demonstrates that nervous advertisers lose ground to the brave and can't gain it back. In 1980, according to the chart seen here, sales indices were identical, but by 1985 the brave had racked up a 3.2 to 1 sales advantage. A similar study done by McGraw-Hill during the 1974-75 recession corroborates the 1980's research.

A recession is the single greatest period in which to make short- and long-term gains. And, surprisingly, increasing advertising modestly during one has much the same effect on your profits as cutting advertising does. According to The Center for Research & Development's October 1990 study of consumer advertising during a recession, advertisers who yield "to the natural inclination to cut spending in an effort to increase profits in a recession find that it doesn't work."[2] This study, relying on the PIMS[3] database, also uncovered that aggressive recessionary advertisers picked up 4.5 *times* as much market share gain as their overcautious competitors, leaving them in a far better position to exploit the inevitable recovery and expansion.

Chevrolet countered its competitors during the 1974-75 recession by aggressively beefing up its ad spending and attained a two percent market share increase. Today, two share points in the automotive industry are worth over $4 billion. Delta Airlines and Revlon also boosted ad spending in the 1974-75 recession and achieved similar results.

Continuous advertising sustains market leadership. And it's far easier to sustain momentum than it is to start it up again. Consider this list of market category leaders: Campbell's, Coca-Cola, Ivory, Kellogg, Kodak, Lipton and Wrigley. This is the leadership list for 1925. And 1990. These marketers have maintained a relentless commitment to their brands in both good times and bad. Kellogg had the guts to pump up its ad spending during the Great Depression and cemented a market leadership it has yet to relinquish.

These are the success stories. Space and diplomacy don't allow the mention of the names of those who lacked gusto and chose to cut their ad spending in recessionary times.

But if you would like to learn more about how advertising can help make the worst of times the best of times, please write to Department C, American Association of Advertising Agencies, 666 Third Avenue, New York, New York 10017, enclosing a check for five dollars. You will receive a booklet covering the pertinent research done on all the U.S. recessions since 1923. Please allow 4 to 6 weeks for delivery.

[1] McGraw-Hill Research, 1986. [2] The Center for Research and Development ©1990.
[3] Profit Impact of Market Strategies, The Strategic Planning Institute, Cambridge, MA.

AAAA

Theoretical Issues in Budget Setting Most of the models used to establish advertising budgets can be categorized as taking an economic or a sales response perspective.

Marginal Analysis Figure 7–8 graphically represents the concept of **marginal analysis.** As advertising/promotional expenditures increase, sales and gross margins also increase to a point, but then they level off. Profits are shown to be a result of the gross margin minus advertising expenditures. Using this theory to establish its budget, a firm would continue to spend advertising/promotional dollars as long as the marginal revenues created by these expenditures exceeded the incremental advertising/promotional costs. As shown on the graph, the optimal expenditure level is the point where marginal costs equal the marginal revenues they generate (point *A*). If the sum of the advertising/promotional expenditures exceeded the revenues they generated, one would conclude the appropriations were too high and scale down the budget. If revenues were higher, a higher budget might be in order. (We will see later in this chapter that this approach can also be applied to the allocation decision.)

While marginal analysis seems logical intuitively, certain weaknesses limit its usefulness. These weaknesses include the assumptions that (1) sales are a direct result of advertising and promotional expenditures and this effect can be measured and (2) advertising and promotion are solely responsible for sales. Let us examine each of these assumptions in more detail.

1. *Assumption that sales are a direct measure of advertising and promotions efforts.* Earlier in this chapter we discussed the fact that the advertiser needs to set communications objectives that contribute to accomplishing overall marketing objectives but at the same time are separate. One reason for this strategy is that it is often difficult, if not impossible, to demonstrate the effects of advertising and promotions on sales. In studies using sales as a direct measure, it has been almost impossible to establish the contribution of advertising and promotion. As noted by Frank Bass, "There is no more difficult, complex, or controversial problem in marketing than measuring the influence of advertising on sales."[23] In the words of David Aaker and James Carman, "Looking for the relationship between advertising and sales is somewhat worse than looking for a needle in a haystack."[24] Thus, to try to show that the size of the budget will directly affect sales of the product is misleading. A more logical approach would be to examine the impact of various budgets on the attainment of communications objectives.

As we saw in the discussion of communications objectives, sales are not the only goal of the promotional effort. Awareness, interest, attitude change, and other communications objectives are often sought, and while the bottom line may be to sell the product, these objectives may serve as the basis on which the promotional program is developed.

2. *Assumption that sales are determined solely by advertising and promotion.* This assumption ignores the remaining elements of the marketing mix—price, product,

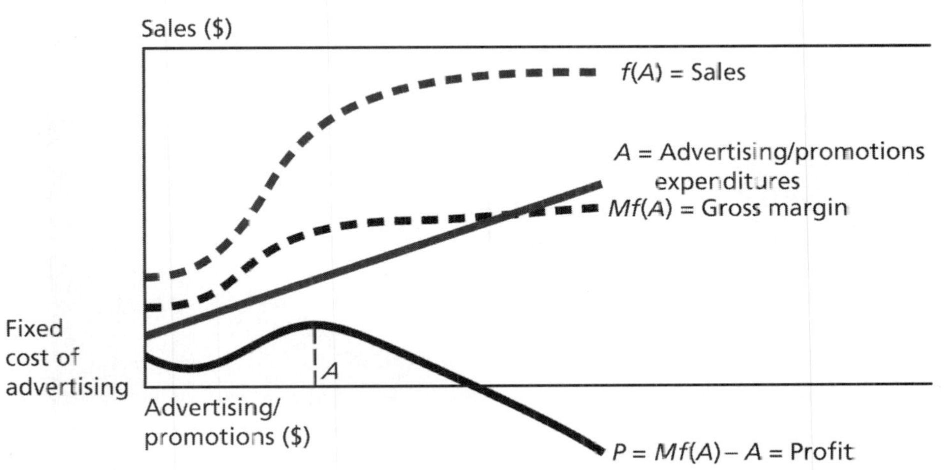

Figure 7–8 Marginal analysis

and distribution—which do contribute to a company's success. Environmental factors may also affect the promotional program, leading the marketing manager to assume the advertising was or was not effective when some other factor may have helped or hindered the accomplishment of the desired objectives.

Overall, you can see that while the economic approach to the budgeting process is a logical one, the difficulties associated with determining the effects of the promotional effort on sales and revenues limit its applicability. Marginal analysis is seldom used as a basis for budgeting (except for direct-response advertising).

Sales Response Models You may have wondered why the sales curve in Figure 7–8 shows sales leveling off even though advertising and promotions efforts continue to increase. The relationship between advertising and sales has been the topic of much research and discussion designed to determine the shape of the response curve.

Almost all advertisers subscribe to one of two models of the advertising/sales response function: the concave-downward function or the S-shaped response curve.

- *The concave-downward function.* After reviewing more than 100 studies of the effects of advertising on sales, Julian Simon and Johan Arndt concluded that the effects of advertising budgets follow the microeconomic law of diminishing returns.[25] That is, as the amount of advertising increases, its incremental value decreases. The logic is that those with the greatest potential to buy will likely act on the first (or earliest) exposures, while those less likely to buy are not likely to change as a result of the advertising. For those who may be potential buyers, each additional ad will supply little or no new information that will affect their decision. Thus, according to the **concave-downward function model,** the effects of advertising quickly begin to diminish, as shown in Figure 7–9A. Budgeting under this model suggests that fewer advertising dollars may be needed to create the optimal influence on sales.
- *The S-shaped response function.* Many advertising managers assume the **S-shaped response curve** (Figure 7–9B), which projects an S-shaped response function to the budget outlay (again measured in sales). Initial outlays of the advertising budget have little impact (as indicated by the essentially flat sales curve in range A). After a certain budget level has been reached (the beginning of range B), advertising and promotional efforts begin to have an effect, as additional increments of expenditures result in increased sales. This incremental gain continues only to a point, however, because at the beginning of range C additional expenditures begin to return little or nothing in the way of sales. This model suggests a small advertising budget is likely to have no impact beyond the sales that may have been generated through other means (for example, word of mouth). At the other extreme, more does not necessarily mean better: Additional dollars spent beyond range B have no additional

Figure 7–9 Advertising sales/response functions

A. The Concave-Downward Response Curve

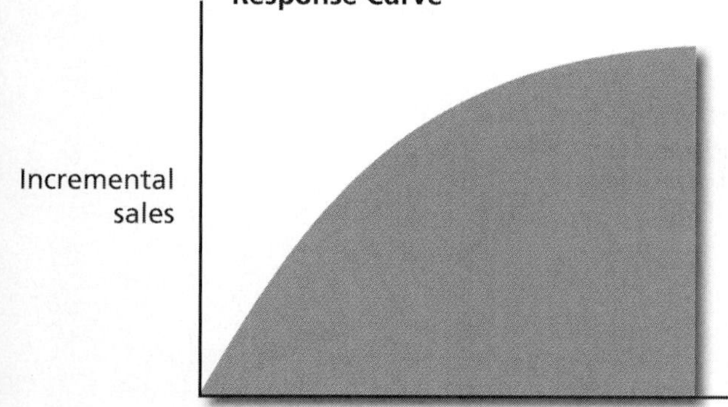

B. The S-Shaped Response Function

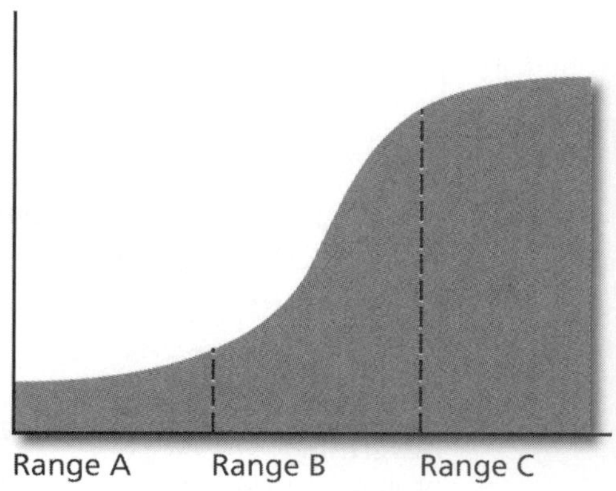

impact on sales and for the most part can be considered wasted. As with marginal analysis, one would attempt to operate at that point on the curve in area B where the maximum return for the money is attained.

Weaknesses in these sales response models render them of limited use to practitioners for direct applications. Many of the problems seen earlier—the use of sales as a dependent variable, measurement problems, and so on—limit the usefulness of these models. At the same time, keep in mind the purpose of discussing such models. Even though marginal analysis and the sales response curves may not apply directly, they give managers some insight into a theoretical basis of how the budgeting process should work. Some empirical evidence indicates the models may have validity. One study, based on industry experience, has provided support for the S-shaped response curve; the results indicate that a minimum amount of advertising dollars must be spent before there is a noticeable effect on sales.[26]

The studies discussed in earlier chapters on learning and the hierarchy of effects also demonstrate the importance of repetition on gaining awareness and on subsequent higher-order objectives such as adoption. Thus, while these models may not provide a tool for setting the advertising and promotional budget directly, we can use them to guide our appropriations strategy from a theoretical basis. As you will see later in this chapter, such a theoretical basis has advantages over many of the methods currently being used for budget setting and allocation.

Additional Factors in Budget Setting While the theoretical bases just discussed should be considered in establishing the budget appropriation, a number of other issues must also be considered. A weakness in attempting to use sales as a *direct* measure of response to advertising is that various situational factors may have an effect. In one comprehensive study, 20 variables were shown to affect the advertising/sales ratio. Figure 7–10 lists these factors and their relationships.[27] For

Figure 7–10 Factors influencing advertising budgets

Factor	Relationship of Advertising/Sales	Factor	Relationship of Advertising/Sales
Product Factors		***Customer Factors***	
Basis for differentiation	+	Industrial products users	—
Hidden product qualities	+	Concentration of users	+
Emotional buying motives	+	***Strategy Factors***	
Durability	—	Regional markets	—
Large dollar purchase	—	Early stage of brand life cycle	+
Purchase frequency	Curvilinear	High margins in channels	—
Market Factors		Long channels of distribution	+
Stage of product life cycle		High prices	+
Introductory	+	High quality	+
Growth	+	***Cost Factors***	
Maturity	—	High profit margins	+
Decline	—		
Inelastic demand	+		
Market share	—		
Competition			
Active	+		
Concentrated	+		
Pioneer in market	—		

Note: + relationship means the factor leads to a positive effect of advertising on sales; — relationship indicates little or no effect of advertising on sales.

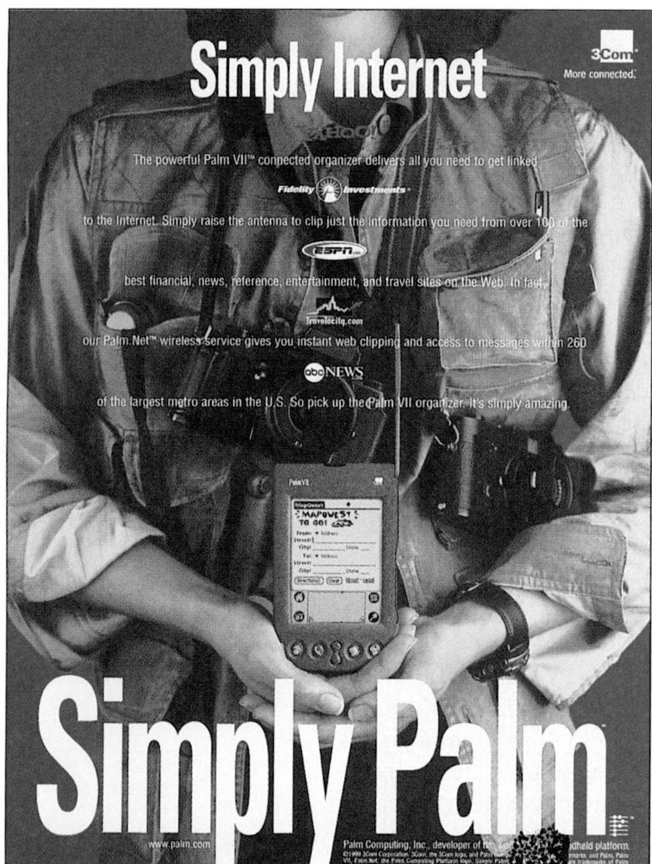

Exhibit 7–12 A strong basis for differentiation could show a noticeable effect of advertising on sales (Courtesy Palm, Inc. Photography by Timothy Greenfield-Sanders.)

a product characterized by emotional buying motives, hidden product qualities, and/or a strong basis for differentiation, advertising would have a noticeable impact on sales (see Exhibit 7–12). Products characterized as large dollar purchases and those in the maturity or decline stages of the product would be less likely to benefit. The study showed that other factors involving the market, customer, costs, and strategies employed have different effects.

The results of this study are interesting but limited, since they relate primarily to the percentage of sales dollars allocated to advertising and the factors influencing these ratios. As we will see later in this chapter, the percentage-of-sales method of budgeting has inherent weaknesses in that the advertising and sales effects may be reversed. So we cannot be sure whether the situation actually led to the advertising/sales relationship or vice versa. Thus, while these factors should be considered in the budget appropriation decision, they should not be the sole determinants of where and when to increase or decrease expenditures.

The *Advertising Age* Editorial Sounding Board consists of 92 executives of the top 200 advertising companies in the United States (representing the client side) and 130 executives of the 200 largest advertising agencies and 11 advertising consultants (representing the agency side). A survey of the board yielded the factors shown in Figure 7–11 that are gaining and losing importance in budget setting. Clearly, there is little consensus. While clients most commonly cite intended changes in advertising strategy and/or creative approaches as important in setting the ad budget, those on the agency side are more likely to cite *profit contribution goals* or other financial targets of the client as growing in importance.

Figure 7–11 Importance of factors in budget setting

Advertisers—Referring to Own Companies	
Increasing in Importance	
Intended changes in advertising strategy and/or creative approach	51%
Competitive activity and/or spending levels	47
Profit contribution goal or other financial target	43
Decreasing in Importance	
Level of previous year's spending, with adjustment	17
Senior management dollar allocation or set limit	11
Volume share projections	8

Agencies—Referring to Client Companies	
Increasing in Importance	
Profit contribution goal or other financial target	56%
Competitive activity and/or spending levels	43
Intended changes in advertising strategy and/or creative approach	37
Decreasing in Importance	
Projections/assumptions on media cost increases	25
Level of previous year's spending, with adjustment	24
Modifications in media strategy and/or buying techniques	17

Regarding which factors are decreasing in importance, only the level of the previous year's spending is a key factor to both groups.

Overall, the responses of these two groups reflect in part their perceptions as to how budgets are set. To understand the differences in the relative importance of these factors, it is important to understand the approaches currently employed in budget setting. The next section examines these approaches.

Budgeting Approaches

The theoretical approaches to establishing the promotional budget are seldom employed. In smaller firms, they may never be used. Instead, a number of methods developed through practice and experience are implemented. This section reviews some of the more traditional methods of setting budgets and the relative advantages and disadvantages of each. First, you must understand two things: (1) Many firms employ more than one method, and (2) budgeting approaches vary according to the size and sophistication of the firm.

Top-Down Approaches

The approaches discussed in this section may be referred to as **top-down approaches** because a budgetary amount is established (usually at an executive level) and then the monies are passed down to the various departments (as shown in Figure 7–12). These budgets are essentially predetermined and have no true theoretical basis. Top-down methods include the affordable method, arbitrary allocation, percentage of sales, competitive parity, and return on investment (ROI).

The Affordable Method In the **affordable method** (often referred to as the "all-you-can-afford method"), the firm determines the amount to be spent in various areas such as production and operations. Then it allocates what's left to advertising and promotion, considering this to be the amount it can afford. The task to be performed by the advertising/promotions function is not considered, and the likelihood of under- or overspending is high, as no guidelines for measuring the effects of various budgets are established.

Strange as it may seem, this approach is common among small firms. Unfortunately, it is also used in large firms, particularly those that are not marketing-driven and do not understand the role of advertising and promotion. For example, many high-tech firms focus on new product development and engineering and assume

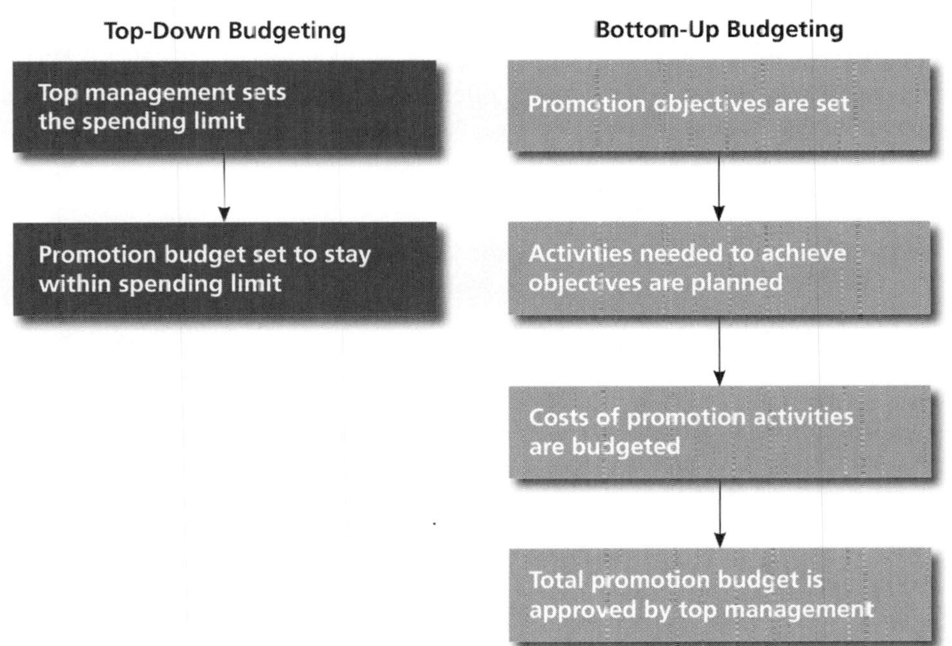

Top-Down Budgeting
Top management sets the spending limit
Promotion budget set to stay within spending limit
Bottom-Up Budgeting
Promotion objectives are set
Activities needed to achieve objectives are planned
Costs of promotion activities are budgeted
Total promotion budget is approved by top management

Figure 7–12 Top-down versus bottom-up approaches to budget setting

that the product, if good enough, will sell itself. In these companies, little money may be left for performing the advertising and promotions tasks.

The logic for this approach stems from "We can't be hurt with this method" thinking. That is, if we know what we can afford and we do not exceed it, we will not get into financial problems. While this may be true in a strictly accounting sense, it does not reflect sound managerial decision making from a marketing perspective. Often this method does not allocate enough money to get the product off the ground and into the market. In terms of the S-shaped sales response model, the firm is operating in range A. Or the firm may be spending more than necessary, operating in range C. When the market gets tough and sales and/or profits begin to fall, this method is likely to lead to budget cuts at a time when the budget should be increased.

Arbitrary Allocation Perhaps an even weaker method than the affordable method for establishing a budget is **arbitrary allocation,** in which virtually no theoretical basis is considered and the budgetary amount is often set by fiat. That is, the budget is determined by management solely on the basis of what is felt to be necessary. In a discussion of how managers set advertising budgets, Melvin Salveson reported that these decisions may reflect "as much upon the managers' psychological profile as they do economic criteria."[28] While Salveson was referring to larger corporations, the approach is no less common in small firms and nonprofit organizations.

The arbitrary allocation approach has no obvious advantages. No systematic thinking has occurred, no objectives have been budgeted for, and the concept and purpose of advertising and promotion have been largely ignored. Other than the fact that the manager believes some monies must be spent on advertising and promotion and then picks a number, there is no good explanation why this approach continues to be used. Yet budgets continue to be set this way, and our purpose in discussing this method is to point out only that it is used—not recommended.

Percentage of Sales Perhaps the most commonly used method for budget setting (particularly in large firms) is the **percentage-of-sales method,** in which the advertising and promotions budget is based on sales of the product. Management determines the amount by either (1) taking a percentage of the sales dollars or (2) assigning a fixed amount of the unit product cost to promotion and multiplying this amount by the number of units sold. These two methods are shown in Figure 7–13.

A variation on the percentage-of-sales method uses a percentage of projected future sales as a base. This method also uses either a straight percentage of projected sales or a unit cost projection. In the straight-percentage method, sales are projected for the coming year based on the marketing manager's estimates. The budget is a percentage of these sales, often an industry standard percentage like those presented in Figure 7–14.

Figure 7–13 Alternative methods for computing percentage of sales for Eve Cologne

Method 1: Straight Percentage of Sales		
2000	Total dollar sales	$1,000,000
	Straight % of sales at 10%	$100,000
2001	Advertising budget	$100,000
Method 2: Percentage of Unit Cost		
2000	Cost per bottle to manufacturer	$4.00
	Unit cost allocated to advertising	1.00
2001	Forecasted sales, 100,000 units	
2001	Advertising budget (100,000 × $1)	$100,000

Figure 7–14 1999 advertising-to-sales ratios for the 200 largest ad-spending industries

Industry	SIC Code	Ad Dollars: As % of Sales	Ad Dollars: As % of Margin	Annual Ad Growth Rate (%)
Accident & health insurance	6321	0.9%	10.6%	11.3%
Advertising	7310	4.5	10.6	30.8
Agricultural chemicals	2870	8.1	25.8	16.6
Agriculture production-crops	100	2.1	8.2	3.0
Air courier services	4513	1.5	12.2	56.7
Air transport, scheduled	4512	1.2	7.8	2.7
Air cond., heating, refrig. equipment	3585	1.4	5.3	6.1
Amusement & recreation svcs	7900	5.1	20.9	23.1
Apparel & other finished products	2300	5.5	15.3	1.6
Apparel and accessory stores	5600	6.3	14.2	9.6
Auto and home supply stores	5531	1.1	2.7	8.1
Auto dealers, gas stations	5500	1.7	10.1	29.6
Auto rent & lease, no drivers	7510	2.7	6.0	14.4
Bakery products	2050	1.4	2.7	5.0
Beverage	2080	7.4	12.1	–6.4
Biological pds. except diagnostics	2836	2.4	5.2	10.2
Blankbooks, binders, bookbind	2780	4.2	7.1	–0.4
Bldg matl, hardwr, garden-retl	5200	2.6	6.8	5.9
Books: pubg, pubg & printing	2731	8.5	19.0	5.4
Btld & can soft drinks, water	2086	5.3	10.9	11.7
Business services, nec	7389	0.5	1.6	5.6
Cable and other pay TV svcs	4841	1.3	2.8	–1.6
Can, frozn, presrv fruit & veg	2030	4.7	10.7	5.0
Catalog, mail-order houses	5961	8.4	27.8	10.6
Chemicals & allied products	2800	1.9	4.4	1.7
Cigarettes	2111	3.9	6.8	–8.7
Cmp and cmp software stores	5734	1.1	7.2	–2.2
Cmp integrated sys design	7373	0.7	2.4	7.6
Cmp processing, data prep svc	7374	1.1	2.4	3.2
Cmp programming, data process	7370	6.8	16.7	5.3
Communications equip, nec	3669	1.3	3.4	5.3
Communications services, nec	4899	3.4	6.0	29.4
Computer & office equipment	3570	1.6	5.3	1.8
Computer communication equip	3576	2.7	4.5	15.1
Computer peripheral equip. nec	3577	2.2	4.6	7.7
Computer storage devices	3572	1.8	6.1	12.7
Computers & software-whsl	5045	0.3	3.8	13.1
Construction machinery & equip	3531	0.5	1.4	7.9
Construction-special trade	1700	3.2	8.4	10.6
Convenience stores	5412	1.2	3.0	–5.3
Cnvrt papr, paprbrd, except boxes	2670	3.8	8.0	4.8
Cookies and crackers	2052	3.5	6.2	10.0
Cutlery, hand tools, gen hrdwr	3420	11.8	24.1	10.6
Dairy products	2020	0.9	34.5	20.7
Dental equipment & supplies	3843	1.6	2.9	9.1
Department stores	5311	3.7	13.0	5.3
Distilled and blended liquor	2085	4.3	33.1	10.8
Dolls and stuffed toys	3942	15.2	29.5	11.2
Drawng, insulatng nonfer wire	3357	0.8	2.0	2.2
Drug & proprietary stores	5912	0.9	3.2	18.2
Drugs and proprietary-whsl	5122	2.6	28.9	11.6
Eating and drinking places	5810	3.8	27.9	5.7
Eating places	5812	4.2	16.4	6.6
Educational services	6200	4.2	10.2	9.3
Elec meas & test instruments	3825	2.9	6.1	7.2
Electr, oth elec eq, ex cmp	3600	1.3	5.3	–5.7

Industry	SIC Code	Ad Dollars: As % of Sales	Ad Dollars: As % of Margin	Annual Ad Growth Rate (%)
Electric housewares and fans	3634	6.4%	18.3%	6.9%
Electric lighting, wiring eq	3640	1.9	5.0	1.5
Electrical indi apparatus	3620	2.3	6.7	8.0
Electromedical apparatus	3845	1.3	2.1	10.1
Electronic comp, accessories	3670	2.2	5.4	1.6
Electronic computers	3571	1.5	4.4	10.5
Engines and turbines	3510	2.4	8.2	9.5
Engr, acct, research, mgmt. rel svcs	8700	1.7	5.7	22.2
Equip rental & leasing, nec	7359	2.0	3.4	9.4
Fabricated plate work	3443	2.7	13.8	12.9
Fabricated rubber products, nec	3060	1.8	5.8	11.7
Family clothing stores	5651	3.7	10.0	14.1
Farm machinery and equipment	3523	1.1	3.8	4.6
Food and kindred products	2000	10.2	24.0	–0.4
Food stores	5400	4.0	12.6	15.2
Footwear, except rubber	3140	4.5	11.2	10.1
Furniture stores	5712	6.9	17.4	9.4
Games, toys, chld. veh, except dolls	3944	12.0	21.1	4.3
General indi mach & equip, nec	3569	0.9	2.3	13.9
Grain mill products	2040	7.5	15.0	–5.6
Greeting cards	2771	3.5	5.1	1.5
Groceries & related products-whsl	5140	2.2	14.7	5.5
Grocery stores	5411	1.1	3.8	8.6
Hardwr, plumb, heat equip-whsl	5070	4.1	27.5	9.6
Health services	8000	8.7	21.1	20.8
Heating equip, plumbing fixture	3430	6.6	15.4	–11.8
Help supply services	7363	0.8	3.8	19.5
Hobby, toy and games shops	5945	3.0	11.3	1.0
Home furniture & equip store	5700	3.0	7.3	10.3
Hospital & medical svc plans	6324	0.4	2.6	10.2
Hotels and motels	7011	2.7	11.4	–1.8
Household appliances	3630	3.0	10.3	6.0
Household audio & video equip	3651	4.2	12.3	8.8
Household furniture	2510	7.6	24.0	12.6
Ice cream & frozen desserts	2024	2.0	7.6	–6.6
In vitro, in vivo diagnostics	2835	1.1	2.6	–6.9
Indi inorganic chemicals	2810	1.1	2.6	3.2
Indi trucks, tractors, trailers	3537	1.7	7.0	6.6
Industrial measurement instr	3823	0.8	1.8	7.7
Industrial organic chemicals	2860	1.1	3.2	–3.1
Investment advice	6282	5.4	16.1	10.5
Jewelry stores	5944	4.6	10.3	9.4
Knit outerwear mills	2253	2.9	10.4	3.5
Knitting mills	2250	3.6	12.5	–2.5
Lab analytical instruments	3826	1.7	3.2	11.6
Leather and leather products	3100	8.8	15.5	12.2
Lumber & oth bldg matl-retl	5211	0.7	2.3	8.4
Malt beverages	2082	7.5	16.2	–1.5
Management services	8741	1.0	6.6	10.0
Manifold business forms	2761	9.7	26.5	7.5
Meat-packing plants	2011	7.8	26.0	7.2
Membership sport & rec clubs	7997	5.6	13.5	–2.5
Men's, boys' frnsh, work clthng	2320	3.0	7.0	11.6
Metal forgings and stampings	3460	1.7	8.1	47.5
Metalworking machinery & equip	3540	4.5	11.5	1.7
Millwork, veneer, plywood	2430	3.5	9.9	12.8

Figure 7–14 Concluded

Industry	SIC Code	Ad Dollars As % of Sales	Ad Dollars As % of Margin	Annual Ad Growth Rate (%)	Industry	SIC Code	Ad Dollars As % of Sales	Ad Dollars As % of Margin	Annual Ad Growth Rate (%)
Misc amusement & rec service	7990	3.7%	8.9%	18.0%	Plastics, resins, elastomers	2821	0.5%	1.8%	−31.1%
Misc business services	7380	1.3	2.4	12.4	Poultry slaughter & process	2015	3.4	18.4	9.4
Misc durable goods-whsl	5090	3.5	14.5	25.6	Prefab wood bldgs, components	2452	1.8	6.1	22.3
Misc elec machy, equip, supplies	3690	4.2	12.3	4.4	Prepackaged software	7372	3.7	5.1	12.2
Misc fabricated textile products	2390	1.0	3.8	14.4	Prof & coml eq & supply-whsl	5040	1.3	3.8	8.7
Misc food preps, kindred products	2090	3.0	7.7	17.8	Racing, incl track operations	7948	2.5	5.8	14.0
Misc furniture and fixtures	2590	2.3	6.4	10.2	Radio broadcasting stations	4832	6.3	18.6	31.1
Misc general mdse stores	5399	4.5	19.5	−4.5	Radio, TV broadcast, comm equip	3663	0.4	1.2	8.1
Misc manufacturing industries	3990	4.2	7.9	9.7	Radio, TV, cons electr stores	5731	3.9	15.5	6.8
Misc nondurable goods-whsl	5190	0.5	2.3	−17.9	Radiotelephone communication	4812	4.6	8.4	21.9
Misc shopping goods stores	5940	3.2	11.0	12.7	Real estate dealers	6532	3.9	5.4	17.2
Misc transportation equip	3790	5.3	17.3	3.0	Real estate investment trust	6798	3.8	12.2	30.6
Miscellaneous publishing	2741	27.1	41.0	18.2	Record and tape stores	5735	1.4	3.7	7.0
Miscellaneous retail	5900	0.7	2.3	0.4	Refrig & service ind machine	3580	2.0	6.4	12.9
Mortgage bankers & loan corr	6162	4.9	10.5	16.7	Retail stores, nec	5990	3.7	9.9	15.1
Motion pict, videotape prodtn	7812	8.0	25.4	2.8	Rubber and plastics footwear	3021	10.4	27.8	12.5
Motion pict, videotape distr	7822	5.6	14.3	−1.3	Scrap & waste materials-whsl	5093	4.7	48.5	28.1
Motion picture theaters	7830	2.8	15.8	10.4	Security brokers & dealers	6211	1.1	1.8	9.1
Motor veh supply, new pts-whsl	5013	0.4	1.5	−1.7	Semiconductor, related device	3674	3.2	5.6	14.9
Motor vehicle part, accessory	3714	0.9	3.3	10.9	Shoe stores	5661	3.0	7.8	8.4
Motor vehicles & car bodies	3711	2.7	10.9	6.8	Soap, detergent, toilet preps	2840	10.7	21.9	4.4
Motorcycles, bicycles & parts	3751	1.7	4.9	9.6	Spec outpatient facility, nec	8093	0.9	2.7	17.6
Motors and generators	3621	0.9	3.2	6.4	Special clean, polish props	2842	12.8	22.1	7.9
Newspaper: pubg, pubg & print	2711	2.2	5.0	2.5	Special industry machinery	3550	2.1	6.0	9.6
Office furniture, except wood	2522	1.0	2.5	16.2	Special industry machy, nec	3559	1.2	2.9	2.7
Operative builders	1531	1.0	8.1	11.9	Sporting & athletic gds, nec	3949	5.6	14.8	13.9
Ophthalmic goods	3851	7.8	11.4	16.4	Steel works & blast furnaces	3312	1.9	21.0	17.0
Ordnance and accessories	3480	2.1	7.2	2.2	Structural clay products	3250	2.7	5.9	10.2
Ortho, prosth, surg appl, supply	3842	2.1	3.8	4.1	Subdivide, dev, except cemetery	6552	6.9	20.2	8.8
Paints, varnishes, lacquers	2851	3.1	7.3	11.1	Sugar & confectionery prods	2060	12.7	32.6	3.8
Paper & paper products-whsl	5110	0.4	1.9	12.1	Surgical, med instr, apparatus	3841	1.7	2.6	12.2
Paper mills	2621	1.8	4.3	−1.4	Tele & telegraph apparatus	3661	1.0	2.8	−2.2
Patent owners and lessors	6794	7.5	11.8	−34.3	TV broadcast station	4833	5.6	13.8	12.8
Pens, pencils, oth artist matl	3950	8.1	19.3	−0.2	Tires and inner tubes	3011	1.8	5.8	2.0
Perfume, cosmetic, toilet prep	2844	11.9	19.0	4.8	Tobacco products	2100	3.9	5.7	7.2
Periodical: pubg, pubg & print	2721	6.0	12.6	6.5	Trucking, courier svc, except air	4210	0.6	9.9	10.7
Personal credit institutions	6141	2.5	5.0	25.3	Variety stores	5331	1.1	5.0	4.7
Personal services	7200	2.4	7.1	6.1	Watches, clocks and parts	3873	13.7	23.3	17.4
Petroleum refining	2911	0.7	3.4	2.8	Water transportation	4400	7.3	18.5	15.6
Pharmaceutical preparation	2834	5.8	8.2	3.1	Wine, brandy & brandy spirits	2084	11.3	19.2	10.5
Phone comm except radiotelephone	4813	3.0	6.5	9.9	Wmns, miss, chld, infnt undgrmt	2340	5.4	15.0	9.4
Phono records, audiotape, disk	3652	13.4	37.8	15.1	Women's clothing stores	5621	4.7	12.3	6.8
Photographic equip & supply	3861	4.3	8.7	−1.5	Women's, misses, jrs outerwear	2330	3.7	12.6	7.5
Plastics products, nec	3089	5.1	15.0	5.7	Wood hshld furn, except upholsrd	2511	3.5	11.6	7.4

One advantage of using future sales as a base is that the budget is not based on last year's sales. As the market changes, management must factor the effect of these changes on sales into next year's forecast rather than relying on past data. The resulting budget is more likely to reflect current conditions and be more appropriate.

Figure 7–14 reveals that the percentage allocated varies from one industry to the next. Some firms budget a very small percentage (for example, 0.7 percent in lumber and wood products), and others spend a much higher proportional amount (12.0 percent in the games and toy industry). Actual dollar amounts spent vary markedly according to the company's total sales figure. Thus, a smaller percentage of sales in the construction machinery industry may actually result in significantly more advertising dollars being spent.

Proponents of the percentage-of-sales method cite a number of advantages. It is financially safe and keeps ad spending within reasonable limits, as it bases spending on the past year's sales or what the firm expects to sell in the upcoming year. Thus, there will be sufficient monies to cover this budget, with increases in sales leading to budget increases and sales decreases resulting in advertising decreases. The percentage-of-sales method is simple, straightforward, and easy to implement. Regardless of which basis—past or future sales—is employed, the calculations used to arrive at a budget are not difficult. Finally, this budgeting approach is generally stable. While the budget may vary with increases and decreases in sales, as long as these changes are not drastic the manager will have a reasonable idea of the parameters of the budget.

At the same time, the percentage-of-sales method has some serious disadvantages, including the basic premise on which the budget is established: sales. Letting the level of sales determine the amount of advertising and promotions dollars to be spent reverses the cause-and-effect relationship between advertising and sales. It treats advertising as an expense associated with making a sale rather than an investment. As discussed in IMC Perspective 7–3, companies that consider promotional expenditures an investment reap the rewards.

A second problem with this approach was actually cited as an advantage earlier: stability. Proponents say that if all firms use a similar percentage, that will bring stability to the marketplace. But what happens if someone varies from this standard percentage? The problem is that this method does not allow for changes in strategy either internally or from competitors. An aggressive firm may wish to allocate more monies to the advertising and promotions budget, a strategy that is not possible with a percentage-of-sales method unless the manager is willing to deviate from industry standards.

The percentage-of-sales method of budgeting may result in severe misappropriation of funds. If advertising and promotion have a role to perform in marketing a product, then allocating more monies to advertising will, as shown in the S-shaped curve, generate incremental sales (to a point). If products with low sales have smaller promotion budgets, this will hinder sales progress. At the other extreme, very successful products may have excess budgets, some of which may be better appropriated elsewhere.

The percentage-of-sales method is also difficult to employ for new product introductions. If no sales histories are available, there is no basis for establishing the budget. Projections of future sales may be difficult, particularly if the product is highly innovative and/or has fluctuating sales patterns.

Finally, if the budget is contingent on sales, decreases in sales will lead to decreases in budgets when they most need to be increased. Continuing to cut the advertising and promotion budgets may just add impetus to the downward sales trend. On the other hand, some of the more successful companies have allocated additional funds during hard times or downturns in the cycle of sales. Companies that maintain or increase their ad expenditures during recessions achieve increased visibility and higher growth in both sales and market share (compared to those that reduce advertising outlays). For example, Sunkist can attribute at least some of its success in maintaining its strong image to the fact that it has maintained consistent levels of advertising expenditures over 80 years, despite recessions.[29]

While the percentage-of-future-sales method has been proposed as a remedy for some of the problems discussed here, the reality is that problems with forecasting, cyclical growth, and uncontrollable factors limit its effectiveness.

Competitive Parity If you asked marketing managers if they ever set their advertising and promotions budgets on the basis of what their competitors allocate, they would probably deny it. Yet if you examined the advertising expenditures of these companies, both as a percentage of sales and in respect to the media where they are allocated, you would see little variation in the percentage-of-sales figures for firms

IMC Perspective 7–3

Investing in Advertising and Promotions

Many marketers think of advertising and promotions as an expense of making a sale. When it comes time to cut costs, the promotional budget often takes the big hit. More astute companies take a different perspective. They consider advertising and promotion an investment that will pay off in the long run—sometimes years later (see chart). Consider the following examples:

- *Xerox.* The leading copier maker doubled its advertising and promotions budget to $200 million in 1999 to promote its digital products. In addition to increasing its media budget, the company announced plans to invest more in marketing research, increase new product announcements, and more clearly and specifically define its market. By the end of 1999, Xerox had generated more revenue from its digital products and services than from its traditional analog copiers to which it is more closely associated.
- *Kia.* Once a struggling firm, almost a nonentity in the U.S. automobile market, Kia has invested heavily in advertising since 1994. After Kia came out of bankruptcy in 1998, its advertising budget for that year reached $75 million, climbed to $80 million in 1999, and is projected to hit $100 million by 2001. The reason? Kia sales are skyrocketing. After increasing sales by 61 percent in 1999, the company is forecasting its U.S. sales to increase another 29 percent in 2000. The once-bankrupt company expects its profits to triple in 2000.
- *Charles Schwab.* In an attempt to change the way people purchase mutual funds, Charles Schwab initiated an advertising campaign designed to show existing and potential companies the fees that they might pay at other brokerage houses. The campaign generated over 140,000 mail leads and increased assets to over $2 billion during a three-month period. OneSource mutual fund holders increased by 34 percent and assets by 54 percent.
- *Residence Inn by Marriott.* Marriott ran an IMC campaign that proved so successful in the first three months that it continued for two years. A single print ad, reminder postcards targeted to existing customers, direct-mail pitches, and point-of-purchase displays led to a 12 percent increase in occupancy rates during the time period.
- *Philip Morris.* Introduced in the 1920s, Marlboro cigarettes had only a 1 percent brand share 30 years later. In 1954, the company invested in a distinctive brand image (the cowboy) that it has maintained into the present. Marlboro now holds a 60 to 70 percent brand share among young smokers in the United States, and the cowboy image is recognized around the world.

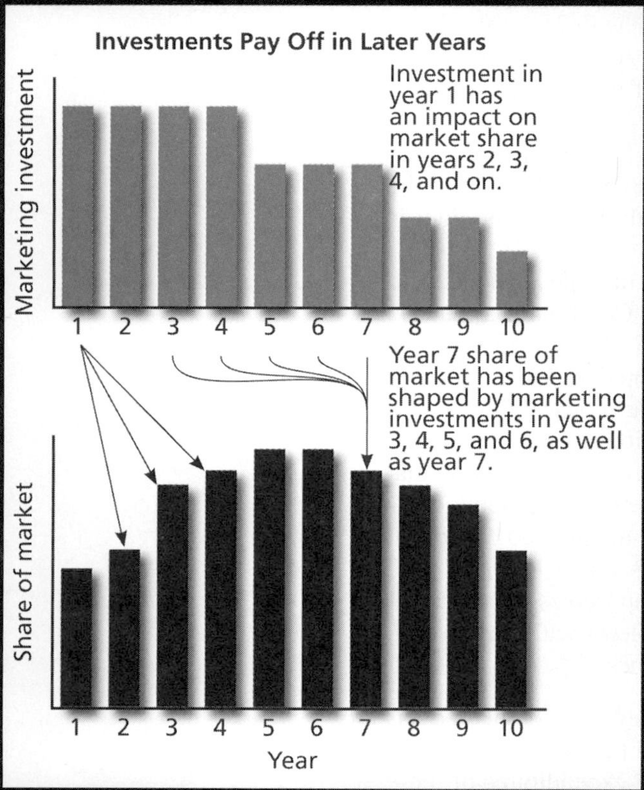

Investments Pay Off in Later Years

Derrith Lambka, corporate advertising manager for Hewlett-Packard, says there is more and more pressure on marketing departments to prove that advertising and promotions are a good investment. He says managers are looking at spending to receive the "greatest return possible." If they are patient and look at the investment strategies of the companies mentioned above, they just may find that spending more on advertising and promotions fit the bill.

Sources: John O'Dell, "Kia Motors Ousts Agency in Surprise Move after Praising Its Humorous Ad Campaign," *Los Angeles Times,* November 18, 1999, p. 4; "Hyundai, Kia Target Sale of 2.77 Mil. Cars in 2000," *Korea Herald,* December 22, 1999, p. 1; "Xerox Decides to Double 1999 Advertising Budget," *Reuters,* October 6, 1998; Adrian J. Slywotzky and Benson P. Shapiro, "Leveraging to Beat the Odds: The New Marketing Mind-Set," *Harvard Business Review,* September/October 1993, pp. 97–107.

within a given industry. Such results do not happen by chance alone. Companies that provide competitive advertising information, trade associations, and other advertising industry periodicals are sources for competitors' expenditures. Larger corporations often subscribe to services such as Competitive Media Reporting, which estimates the top 1,000 companies' advertising in 10 media and in total. Smaller companies often use a **clipping service,** which clips competitors' ads from local print media, allowing the company to work backward to determine the cumulative costs of the ads placed.

In the **competitive parity method,** managers establish budget amounts by matching the competition's percentage-of-sales expenditures. The argument is that setting budgets in this fashion takes advantage of the collective wisdom of the industry. It also takes the competition into consideration, which leads to stability in the marketplace by minimizing marketing warfare. If companies know that competitors are unlikely to match their increases in promotional spending, they are less likely to take an aggressive posture to attempt to gain market share. This minimizes unusual or unrealistic ad expenditures.

The competitive parity method has a number of disadvantages, however. For one, it ignores the fact that advertising and promotions are designed to accomplish specific objectives by addressing certain problems and opportunities. Second, it assumes that because firms have similar expenditures, their programs will be equally effective. This assumption ignores the contributions of creative executions and/or media allocations, as well as the success or failure of various promotions. Further, it ignores possible advantages of the firm itself; some companies simply make better products than others.

Also, there is no guarantee that competitors will continue to pursue their existing strategies. Since competitive parity figures are determined by examination of competitors' previous years' promotional expenditures (short of corporate espionage), changes in market emphasis and/or spending may not be recognized until the competition has already established an advantage. Further, there is no guarantee that a competitor will not increase or decrease its own expenditures, regardless of what other companies do. Finally, competitive parity may not avoid promotional wars. Coke versus Pepsi and Anheuser-Busch versus Miller have been notorious for their spending wars, each responding to the other's increased outlays.

In summary, few firms employ the competitive parity method as a sole means of establishing the promotional budget. This method is typically used in conjunction with the percentage-of-sales or other methods. It is never wise to ignore the competition; managers must always be aware of what competitors are doing. But they should not just emulate them in setting goals and developing strategies.

Return on Investment (ROI) In the percentage-of-sales method, sales dictate the level of advertising appropriations. But advertising causes sales. In the marginal analysis and S-shaped curve approaches, incremental investments in advertising and promotions lead to increases in sales. The key word here is *investment.* In the **ROI budgeting method,** advertising and promotions are considered investments, like plant and equipment. Thus, the budgetary appropriation (investment) leads to certain returns. Like other aspects of the firm's efforts, advertising and promotion are expected to earn a certain return.

While the ROI method looks good on paper, the reality is that it is rarely possible to assess the returns provided by the promotional effort—at least as long as sales continue to be the basis for evaluation. Thus, while managers are certain to ask how much return they are getting for such expenditures, the question remains unanswered, and ROI remains a virtually unused method of budgeting.

Summary of Top-Down Budgeting Methods You are probably asking yourself why we even discussed these budgeting methods if they are not recommended for use or have severe disadvantages that limit their effectiveness. But you must understand the various methods used in order to recognize their limitations, especially since these flawed methods are commonly employed by marketers throughout the United States, Europe, and Canada, as demonstrated in the results of a

Figure 7–15 Comparison of methods for budgeting

Study	San Augustine and Foley (1975)	Patti and Blasko (1981)	Lancaster and Stern (1983)	Blasko and Patti (1984)	Hung and West (1991)
Population	Large Consumer/ Industrial Advertisers	Large Consumer/ Services Advertisers	Large Consumer Advertisers	Large Industrial Advertisers	Large & Medium Advertisers in U.K., U.S., & Canada
Sample	50/50	54	60	64	100
Methods					
Quantitative models	2/4	51	20	3	NA
Objective and task	6/10	63	80	74	61
Percent anticipated sales	50/28	53	53	16	32
Unit anticipated sales	8/10	22	28	NA	9
Percent past year's sales	14/16	20	20	23	10
Unit past year's sales	6/4	NA	15	2	NA
Affordable	30/26	20	13	33	41
Arbitrary	12/34	4	NA	13	NA
Competitive parity	NA	24	33	21	25
Previous budget	NA	NA	3	NA	NA
Share of voice	NA	NA	5	NA	NA
Others	26/10	NA	12	NA	NA

Note: Figures exceed 100% due to multiple responses. NA = No answer.

number of research studies shown in Figure 7–15. Tradition and top management's desire for control are probably the major reasons why top-down methods continue to be popular.

As shown in Figure 7–15, the use of percentage-of-sales methods remains high, particularly the method based on anticipated sales. Unfortunately, the affordable method appears to be on the increase. On the decrease are two methods not yet discussed: quantitative models and the objective and task method. Let us now turn our discussion to these methods as well as one other, payout planning.

Build-Up Approaches

The major flaw associated with the top-down methods is that these judgmental approaches lead to predetermined budget appropriations often not linked to objectives and the strategies designed to accomplish them. A more effective budgeting strategy would be to consider the firm's communications objectives and budget what is deemed necessary to attain these goals. As noted earlier, the promotional planning model shows the budget decision as an interactive process, with the communications objectives on one hand and the promotional mix alternatives on the other. The idea is to budget so these promotional mix strategies can be implemented to achieve the stated objectives.

Objective and Task Method It is important that objective setting and budgeting go hand in hand rather than sequentially. It is difficult to establish a budget without specific objectives in mind, and setting objectives without regard to how much money is available makes no sense. For example, a company may wish to create awareness among X percent of its target market. A minimal budget amount will be required to accomplish this goal, and the firm must be willing to spend this amount.

The **objective and task method** of budget setting uses a **buildup approach** consisting of three steps: (1) defining the communications objectives to be accomplished, (2) determining the specific strategies and tasks needed to attain them, and (3) estimating the costs associated with performance of these strategies and tasks. The total budget is based on the accumulation of these costs.

Implementing the objective and task approach is somewhat more involved. The manager must monitor this process throughout and change strategies depending on how well objectives are attained. As shown in Figure 7–16, this process involves several steps:

1. *Isolate objectives.* When the promotional planning model is presented, a company will have two sets of objectives to accomplish—the marketing objectives for the product and the communications objectives. After the former are established, the task involves determining what specific communications objectives will be designed to accomplish these goals. Communications objectives must be specific, attainable, and measurable, as well as time limited.
2. *Determine tasks required.* A number of elements are involved in the strategic plan designed to attain the objectives established. (These strategies constitute the remaining chapters in this text.) These tasks may include advertising in various media, sales promotions, and/or other elements of the promotional mix, each with its own role to perform.
3. *Estimate required expenditures.* Buildup analysis requires determining the estimated costs associated with the tasks developed in the previous step. For example, it involves costs for developing awareness through advertising, trial through sampling, and so forth.
4. *Monitor.* As you will see in Chapter 19 on measuring effectiveness, there are ways to determine how well one is attaining established objectives. Performance should be monitored and evaluated in light of the budget appropriated.
5. *Reevaluate objectives.* Once specific objectives have been attained, monies may be better spent on new goals. Thus, if one has achieved the level of consumer awareness sought, the budget should be altered to stress a higher-order objective such as evaluation or trial.

The major advantage of the objective and task method is that the budget is driven by the objectives to be attained. The managers closest to the marketing effort will have specific strategies and input into the budget-setting process.

The major disadvantage of this method is the difficulty of determining which tasks will be required and the costs associated with each. For example, specifically what tasks are needed to attain awareness among 50 percent of the target market?

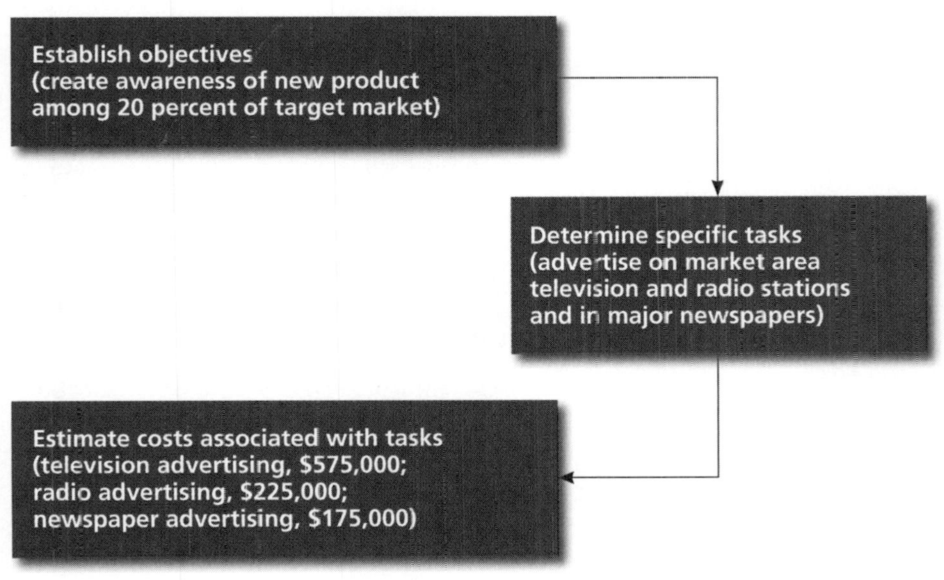

Figure 7–16 The objective and task method

How much will it cost to perform these tasks? While these decisions are easier to determine for certain objectives—for example, estimating the costs of sampling required to stimulate trial in a defined market area—it is not always possible to know exactly what is required and/or how much it will cost to complete the job. This process is easier if there is past experience to use as a guide, with either the existing product or a similar one in the same product category. But it is especially difficult for new product introductions. As a result, budget setting using this method is not as easy to perform or as stable as some of the methods discussed earlier. Given this disadvantage, many marketing managers have stayed with those top-down approaches for setting the total expenditure amount.

The objective and task method offers advantages over methods discussed earlier but is more difficult to implement when there is no track record for the product. The following section addresses the problem of budgeting for new product introductions.

Payout Planning The first months of a new product's introduction typically require heavier-than-normal advertising and promotion appropriations to stimulate higher levels of awareness and subsequent trial. After studying more than 40 years of Nielsen figures, James O. Peckham estimated that the average share of advertising to sales ratio necessary to launch a new product successfully is approximately 1.5:2.0.[30] This means that a new entry should be spending at approximately twice the desired market share, as shown in the two examples in Figure 7–17. For example, in the food industry, brand 101 gained a 12.6 percent market share by spending

Figure 7–17 Share of advertising/sales relationship (two-year summary)

A. New Brands of Food Products

Brand	Average share of advertising	Attained share of sales	Ratio of share of advertising to share of sales
101	34%	12.6%	2.7
102	16	10.0	1.6
103	8	7.6	1.1
104	4	2.6	1.5
105	3	2.1	1.4

B. New Brands of Toiletry Products

Brand	Average share of advertising	Attained share of sales	Ratio of share of advertising to share of sales
401	30%	19.5%	1.5
402	25	16.5	1.5
403	20	16.2	1.2
404	12	9.4	1.3
405	16	8.7	1.8
406	19	7.3	2.6
407	14	7.2	1.9
408	10	6.0	1.7
409	7	6.0	1.2
410	6	5.9	1.0
411	10	5.9	1.7
412	6	5.2	1.2

34 percent of the total advertising dollars in this category. Likewise, brand 401 in the toiletry industry had a 30 percent share of advertising dollars to gain 19.5 percent of sales.

To determine how much to spend, marketers often develop a **payout plan** that determines the investment value of the advertising and promotion appropriation. The basic idea is to project the revenues the product will generate, as well as the costs it will incur, over two to three years. Based on an expected rate of return, the payout plan will assist in determining how much advertising and promotions expenditure will be necessary when the return might be expected. A three-year payout plan is shown in Figure 7–18. The product would lose money in year 1, almost break even in year 2, and finally begin to show substantial profits by the end of year 3.

The advertising and promotion figures are highest in year 1 and decline in years 2 and 3. This appropriation is consistent with Peckham's findings and reflects the additional outlays needed to make as rapid an impact as possible. (Keep in mind that shelf space is limited, and store owners are not likely to wait around for a product to become successful.) The budget also reflects the firm's guidelines for new product expenditures, since companies generally have established deadlines by which the product must begin to show a profit. Finally, keep in mind that building market share may be more difficult than maintaining it—thus the substantial dropoff in expenditures in later years.

While the payout plan is not always perfect, it does guide the manager in establishing the budget. When used in conjunction with the objective and task method, it provides a much more logical approach to budget setting than the top-down approaches previously discussed. Yet on the basis of the studies reported on in Figure 7–15, payout planning does not seem to be a widely employed method.

Quantitative Models Attempts to apply *quantitative models* to budgeting have met with limited success. For the most part, these methods employ **computer simulation models** involving statistical techniques such as multiple regression analysis to determine the relative contribution of the advertising budget to sales. Because of problems associated with these methods, their acceptance has been limited, as demonstrated in the figures reported earlier in Figure 7–15. Quantitative models have yet to reach their potential. As computers continue to find their way into the advertising domain, better models may be forthcoming. Specific discussion of these models is beyond the scope of this text, however. Such methods do have merit but may need more refinement before achieving widespread success.

Summary of Budgeting Methods

There is no universally accepted method of setting a budget figure. Weaknesses in each method may make it unfeasible or inappropriate. As Figure 7–15 shows, the use of the objective and task method continues to increase, whereas less sophisticated methods are declining in favor. More advertisers are also employing the payout planning approach.

In a more recent study of how managers make decisions regarding advertising and promotion budgeting decisions, George Low and Jakki Mohr interviewed 21 managers in eight consumer-product firms. Their research focused on the decision processes and procedures used to set spending levels on the factors that influence the allocation of advertising and promotion dollars.

	Year 1	Year 2	Year 3
Product sales	15.0	35.50	60.75
Profit contribution (@ $0.50/case)	7.5	17.75	30.38
Advertising/promotions	15.0	10.50	8.50
Profit (loss)	(7.5)	7.25	21.88
Cumulative profit (loss)	(7.5)	(0.25)	21.63

Figure 7–18 Example of three-year payout plan ($ millions)

Figure 7–19 How advertising and promotions budgets are set

The Nature of the Decision Process
• Managers develop overall marketing objectives for the brand. • Financial projections are made on the basis of the objectives and forecasts. • Advertising and promotions budgets are set on the basis of quantitative models and managerial judgment. • The budget is presented to senior management, which approves and adjusts the budgets. • The plan is implemented (changes are often made during implementation). • The plan is evaluated by comparing the achieved results with objectives.
Factors Affecting Budget Allocations
• The extent to which risk taking is encouraged and/or tolerated. • Sophistication regarding the use of marketing information. • Managerial judgment. • Use of quantitative tools. • Brand differentiation strategies. • Brand equity. • The strength of the creative message. • Retailer power. • Short- versus long-term focus. • Top-down influences. • Political sales force influences. • Historical inertia. • Ad hoc changes.

On the basis of their results (shown in Figure 7–19), the authors concluded that the budget-setting process is still a perplexing issue to many managers and that institutional pressures led to a greater proportion of dollars being spent on sales promotions than managers would have preferred. In addition, the authors concluded that to successfully develop and implement the budget, managers must (1) employ a comprehensive strategy to guide the process, avoiding the piecemeal approach often employed, (2) develop a strategic planning framework that employs an integrated marketing communications philosophy, (3) build in contingency plans, (4) focus on long-term objectives, and (5) consistently evaluate the effectiveness of programs.[31]

By using these approaches in combination with the percentage-of-sales methods, these advertisers are likely to arrive at a more useful, accurate budget. For example, many firms now start the budgeting process by establishing the objectives they need to accomplish and then limit the budget by applying a percentage-of-sales or another method to decide whether or not it is affordable. Competitors' budgets may also influence this decision.

Allocating the Budget

Once the budget has been appropriated, the next step is to allocate it. The allocation decision involves determining which markets, products, and/or promotional elements will receive which amounts of the funds appropriated.

Allocating to Advertising and Promotion Elements

As noted earlier, advertisers have begun to shift some of their budget dollars away from traditional advertising media and into sales promotions targeted at both the consumer and the trade. Direct marketing, the Internet, and other promotional tools are also receiving increased attention and competing for more of the promotional budget. The advantage of more target selectivity has led to an increased emphasis on direct marketing, while a variety of new media have given marketers new ways to reach prospective customers. Rapidly rising media costs, the ability of sales promotions to motivate trial, maturing of the product and/or brand, and the need for more aggressive promotional tools have also led to shifts in strategy.[32] (We will discuss consumer and trade promotions and the reasons for some of these changes in Chapter 16.)

Some marketers have also used the allocation decision to stretch their advertising dollar and get more impact from the same amount of money. For example, General Motors recently reevaluated its advertising and promotional expenditures and made significant shifts in allocations by both media and product.[33] Other companies have reevaluated as well, including Procter & Gamble, Apple Computer, and Dow Chemical.

Client/Agency Policies Another factor that may influence budget allocation is the individual policy of the company or the advertising agency. The agency may discourage the allocation of monies to sales promotion, preferring to spend them on the advertising area. The agency position is that promotional monies are harder to track in terms of effectiveness and may be used improperly if not under its control. (In many cases commissions are not made on this area, and this fact may contribute to the agency's reluctance.)[34]

The orientation of the agency or the firm may also directly influence where monies are spent. Many ad agencies are managed by officers who have ascended through the creative ranks and are inclined to emphasize the creative budget. Others may have preferences for specific media. For example, BBDO Worldwide, one of the largest advertising agencies in the United States, has positioned itself as an expert in cable TV programming and often spends more client money in this medium. McCann-Erickson is spending more monies on the Internet. Both the agency and the client may favor certain aspects of the promotional program, perhaps on the basis of past successes, that will substantially influence where dollars are spent.

Market Size While the budget should be allocated according to the specific promotional tools needed to accomplish the stated objectives, the *size* of the market will affect the decision. In smaller markets, it is often easier and less expensive to reach the target market. Too much of an expenditure in these markets will lead to saturation and a lack of effective spending. In larger markets, the target group may be more dispersed and thus more expensive to reach. Think about the cost of purchasing media in Chicago or New York City versus a smaller market like Columbus, Ohio, or Birmingham, Alabama. The former would be much more costly and would require a higher budget appropriation.

Market Potential For a variety of reasons, some markets hold more potential than others. Marketers of snow skis would find greater returns on their expenditures in Denver, Colorado, than in Fort Lauderdale, Florida. Imported Mexican beers sell better in the border states (Texas, Arizona, California) than in the Midwest. A disproportionate number of imported cars are sold in California and New England. When particular markets hold higher potential, the marketing manager may decide to allocate additional monies to them. (Keep in mind that just because a market does not have high sales does not mean it should be ignored. The key is *potential*—and a market with low sales but high potential may be a candidate for additional appropriations.)

There are several methods for estimating marketing potential. Many marketers conduct research studies to forecast demand and/or use secondary sources of information such as those provided by government agencies or syndicated services like Dun & Bradstreet, A. C. Nielsen, and Audits and Surveys. One source for consumer goods information is the *Survey of Buying Power,* published annually by *Sales & Marketing Management* magazine. The survey contains population, income, and retail sales data for states, counties, metropolitan statistical areas, and cities in the United States and Canada with populations of 40,000 or more.

Market Share Goals Two recent studies in the *Harvard Business Review* discussed advertising spending with the goal of maintaining and increasing market share.[35] John Jones compared the brand's share of market with its share of advertising voice (the total value of the main media exposure in the product category). Jones classified the brands as "profit taking brands, or underspenders" and "investment brands, those whose share of voice is clearly above their share of market." His study indicated that for those brands with small market shares, profit takers are in the minority; however, as the brands increase their market share, nearly three out of five have a proportionately smaller share of voice.

Jones noted that three factors can be cited to explain this change. First, new brands generally receive higher-than-average advertising support. Second, older, more mature brands are often "milked"—that is, when they reach the maturity stage, advertising support is reduced. Third, there's an advertising economy of scale whereby advertising works harder for well-established brands, so a lower expenditure is required. Jones concluded that for larger brands, it may be possible to reduce advertising expenditures and still maintain market share. Smaller brands, on the other hand, have to continue to maintain a large share of voice.

James Schroer addressed the advertising budget in a situation where the marketer wishes to increase market share. His analysis suggests that marketers should:

- Segment markets, focusing on those markets where competition is weak and/or underspending instead of on a national advertising effort.
- Determine their competitors' cost positions (how long the competition can continue to spend at the current or increased rate).
- Resist the lure of short-term profits that result from ad budget cuts.
- Consider niching strategies as opposed to long-term wars.

Figure 7–20 shows Schroer's suggestions for spending priorities in various markets.

Economies of Scale in Advertising Some studies have presented evidence that firms and/or brands maintaining a large share of the market have an advantage over smaller competitors and thus can spend less money on advertising and realize a better return.[36] Larger advertisers can maintain advertising shares that are smaller than their market shares because they get better advertising rates, have declining average costs of production, and accrue the advantages of advertising several products jointly. In addition, they are likely to enjoy more favorable time and space positions, cooperation of middlepeople, and favorable publicity. These advantages are known as **economies of scale.**

Reviewing the studies in support of this position and then conducting research over a variety of small package products, Kent Lancaster found that this situation did not hold true and that in fact larger brand share products might actually be at a disadvantage.[37] His results indicated that leading brands spend an average of 2.5

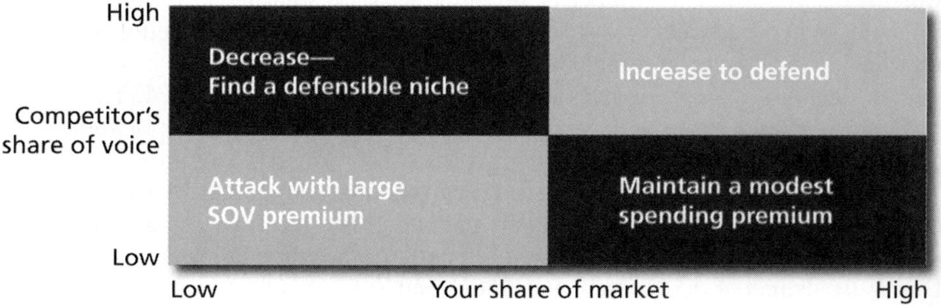

Figure 7–20 The share of voice (SOV) effect and ad spending: priorities in individual markets

percentage points more than their brand share on advertising. More specifically, his study concluded:

1. There is no evidence that larger firms can support their brands with lower relative advertising costs than smaller firms.
2. There is no evidence that the leading brand in a product group enjoys lower advertising costs per sales dollar than do other brands.
3. There is no evidence of a static relationship between advertising costs per dollar of sales and the size of the advertiser.

The results of this and other studies suggest there really are no economies of scale to be accrued from the size of the firm or the market share of the brand.[38]

Organizational Characteristics In a review of the literature on how allocation decisions are made between advertising and sales promotion, George Low and Jakki Mohr concluded that organizational factors play an important role in determining how communications dollars are spent.[39] The authors note that the following factors influence the allocation decision. These factors vary from one organization to another, and each influences the relative amounts assigned to advertising and promotion:

- The organization's structure—centralized versus decentralized, formalization, and complexity.
- Power and politics in the organizational hierarchy.
- The use of expert opinions (for example, consultants).
- Characteristics of the decision maker (preferences and experience).
- Approval and negotiation channels.
- Pressure on senior managers to arrive at the optimal budget.

One example of how these factors might influence allocations relates to the level of interaction between marketing and other functional departments, such as accounting and operations. The authors note that the relative importance of advertising versus sales promotion might vary from department to department. Accountants, being dollars-and-cents minded, would argue for the sales impact of promotions, while operations would argue against sales promotions because the sudden surges in demand that might result would throw off production schedules. The marketing department might be influenced by the thinking of either of these groups in making its decision.

The use of outside consultants to provide expert opinions might also affect the allocation decision. Trade journals, academic journals, and even books might also be valuable inputs into the decision maker's thinking. In sum, it seems obvious that many factors must be taken into account in the budget allocation decision. Market size and potential, specific objectives sought, and previous company and/or agency policies and preferences all influence this decision.

Summary

This chapter has examined the role of objectives in the planning and evaluation of the IMC program and how firms budget in an attempt to achieve these objectives. Specific objectives are needed to guide the development of the promotional program, as well as to provide a benchmark against which performance can be measured and evaluated. Objectives serve important functions as communications devices, as a guide to planning the IMC program and deciding on various alternatives, and for measurement and evaluation.

Objectives for IMC evolve from the organization's overall marketing plan and are based on the roles various promotional mix elements play in the marketing program. Many managers use sales or a related measure such as market share as the basis for setting objectives.

However, many promotional planners believe the role of advertising and other promotional mix elements is to communicate because of the various problems associated with sales-based objectives. They use communications-based objectives like those in the response hierarchy as the basis for setting goals.

Much of the emphasis in setting objectives has been on traditional advertising-based views of marketing communications. However, many companies are moving toward zero-based communications planning, which focuses on what tasks need to be done, which marketing communication functions should be used, and to what extent. Many of the principles used in setting advertising objectives can be applied to other elements in the promotional mix.

As you have probably concluded, the budget decision is not typically based on supporting experiences or strong theoretical foundations. Nor is it one of the more soundly established elements of the promotional program. The budgeting methods used now have some major problems. Economic models are limited, often try to demonstrate the effects on sales directly, and ignore other elements of the marketing mix. Some of the methods discussed have no theoretical basis and ignore the roles advertising and promotion are meant to perform.

One possible way to improve the budget appropriation is to tie the measures of effectiveness to communications objectives rather than to the broader-based marketing objectives. Using the objective and task approach with communications objectives may not be the ultimate solution to the budgeting problem, but it is an improvement over the top-down methods. Marketers often find it advantageous to employ a combination of methods.

As with determining the budget, managers must consider a number of factors when allocating advertising and promotions dollars. Market size and potential, agency policies, and the preferences of management itself may influence the allocation decision.

Key Terms

marketing objectives, 202
integrated marketing communications objectives, 203
carryover effect, 205
DAGMAR, 213
communications task, 213
benchmark measures, 214
zero-based communications planning, 218
contribution margin, 220
marginal analysis, 221
concave-downward function model, 222
S-shaped response curve, 222
top-down approaches, 225
affordable method, 225
arbitrary allocation, 226
percentage-of-sales method, 226
clipping service, 231
competitive parity method, 231
ROI budgeting method, 231
objective and task method, 233
buildup approach, 233
payout plan, 235
computer simulation models, 235
economies of scale, 238

Discussion Questions

1. Critics of the percentage-of-sales method of budget setting contend that this method "reverses the advertising and sales relationship," and that it "treats advertising as an expense rather than an investment." Explain what these arguments mean and discuss their merits.

2. In meeting with your new boss, he informs you that the only goal of advertising and promotion is to generate sales. Present your argument as to why communications objectives must also be considered.

3. Discuss some of the reasons managers continue to set budgets using "top-down" budgeting methods.

4. What are some of the organizational characteristics that influence the budgeting decision? Give examples of each.

5. In Figure 7–19, Low and Mohr list a number of factors that affect the budget allocation decision. Describe and provide examples of each.

6. Discuss the value of setting objectives for the integrated marketing communications program. What important functions do objectives serve?

7. What are some of the problems associated with using sales objectives?

8. Explain the difference between investing in advertising and spending. Cite examples of companies that have successfully invested.

9. Discuss how you would explain to a small-business owner why he or she needs to budget a larger amount to advertising and promotion. Base your argument on the S-shaped response function.

10. Some advertisers believe economies of scale are accrued in the advertising process. Discuss their reasons for taking this position. Does research evidence support it?

Chapter Eight

Creative Strategy: Planning and Development

Chapter Objectives

- To discuss what is meant by advertising creativity and examine the role of creative strategy in advertising.
- To examine creative strategy development and the roles of various client and agency personnel involved in it.
- To consider the process that guides the creation of advertising messages and the research inputs into the stages of the creative process.
- To examine various approaches used for determining major selling ideas that form the basis of an advertising campaign.

The Perpetual Debate: Creative versus Hard-Sell Advertising

For decades there has been a perpetual battle over the role of advertising in the marketing process. The war for the soul of advertising has been endlessly fought between those who believe ads should move people and those who just want to move products. On one side are the "suits" or "rationalists," who argue that advertising must sell the product or service and that the more selling points or information in an ad, the better its chance of moving the consumer to purchase. On the other side are the "poets" or proponents of creativity, who argue that advertising has to build an emotional bond between consumers and brands or companies that goes beyond product advertising. The debate over the effectiveness of creative or arty advertising is not new. The rationalists have taken great delight in pointing to long lists of creative and award-winning campaigns over the years that have failed in the marketplace, such as the humorous commercials for Alka-Seltzer from the 1960s and 70s, the Joe Isuzu spokes-liar ads from the late 80s, and the Subaru "What to drive?" spots from the early 90s.

There are also several recent examples of creative campaigns that moved consumers' emotions but were terminated because they failed to move the sales needle and they put accounts and reputations on the line. Levi Strauss & Co. terminated Foote, Cone & Belding, of San Francisco, from its Levi's jean account after 67 years because of declining sales, even though the agency had consistently earned rave reviews and awards for its creative work. Nissan asked TBWA/Chiat/Day to change from the image-oriented "Enjoy the ride" campaign, which sought to make an icon of the mysterious "Mr. K," an elderly, smiling Japanese man who represented the founder of the company's North American subsidiary and appeared at the end of each commercial with a jack terrier. Though the ads were entertaining and critically acclaimed, they left Nissan dealers complaining that they didn't sell cars.

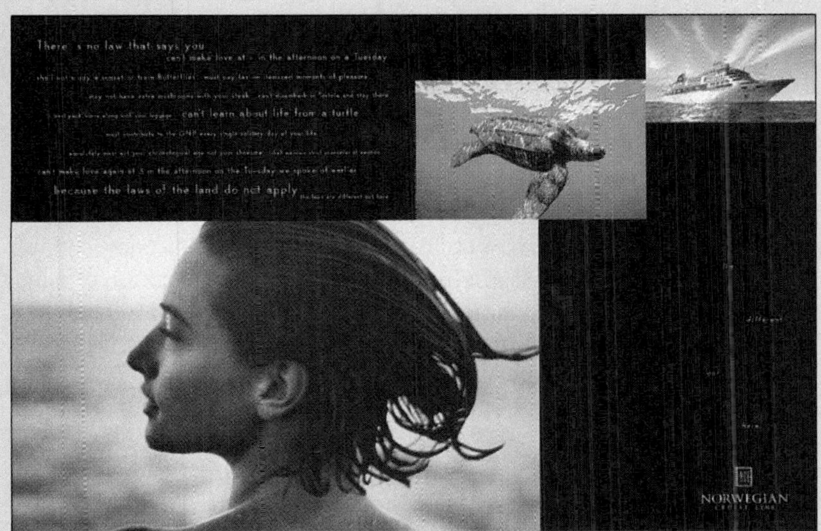

Another company that had differences of opinion with its agency over artsy versus more hard-sell advertising is Norwegian Cruise

Lines. The company's marketing director, Nina Cohen, felt that the sensual "It's different out here" campaign produced by Goodby, Silverstein & Partners was gorgeous but irrelevant. She said, "Every frame of those ads was frameable, but we're not in the framing business." Cohen added that while "there are some creative icons out there who feel they have some higher voice to answer to, as clients, we're the ones you have to answer to." However, co-creative director Jeff Goodby considered his agency's creative work for Norwegian both beautiful and effective and argues that the impact of creative and entertaining advertising on sales isn't always quantifiable for good reason. He notes: "It's where the magic happens in advertising, and you can never predict that. It's dangerous to be suspicious of that."

Many of the "poets" on the creative side agree with Jeff Goodby and like to cite the teaching of legendary adman Bill Bernbach, who preached that persuasion is an art, not a science, and its success is dependent on a complex mix of intangible human qualities than can be neither measured nor predicted. Bob Kuperman, president and CEO of TBWA/Chiat/Day North America, which is the agency for Nissan and a shop that is passionately on the side of ads that move people, argues: "Before you can be believed, you have to be liked. If we use this belief in the way we conduct our daily lives, what makes us think consumers don't use that process in the decisions they make?" Steve Hayden, creative director on the IBM account at Ogilvy & Mather Worldwide, believes that most consumer buying decisions are made using irrational processes and says, "When anything like Nissan's Mr. K works, people become upset because it is totally irrational."

The culture clash over whether ads that can entertain and provoke can also work as ads that sell is increasing as businesses face more pressure to produce measurable results and costs skyrocket for producing commercials and media time. Veteran brand marketing and positioning consultant Jack Trout explains the debate by noting that most clients are driven by results: "Their lives revolve around how they're doing out there. They don't care about winning awards, and when their advertising doesn't work they get all bent out of shape. Given the current costs of media and production, the adage about not knowing which half of your ad budget is wasted takes on an ominous new meaning. Even half a budget is a ton of money these days."

Most of the "poets" who support advertising that connects on an emotional level insist that selling products is as much a priority for them as it is for those on the rational side of the debate. Bob Kuperman argues, "We've proven that this kind of advertising works, otherwise we wouldn't be in business, us or the agencies that practice the craft at this level." And Jeff Goodby argues that those involved in the debate should not lose sight of the fact that advertising alone doesn't make a sale—the product and the marketer also have to deliver on promises.

It is unlikely there will ever be peace between the warring factions as long as there are rationalists and poets who make a point of arguing over which approach works best. Steve Hayden says, "It's the ad industry's reflection of the essential Platonic/Aristotelian split in the world, pitting two groups of people against each other who usually can't agree which end is up." However, Nina Cohen, who has worked on both the agency and the client sides of the business, is bewildered by the intense opinions held by people on each side and asks, "Aren't we all here to do the same thing?" meaning to build brands and business. While the answer is, of course, yes, the debate over how to do it is likely to continue.

Sources: Anthony Vagnoni, "Creative Differences," *Advertising Age*, November 17, 1997, pp. 1, 28, 30; Robert L. Simison, "Nissan Drafts a Designer to Do the Talking," *The Wall Street Journal*, April 9, 1999, p. B6.

One of the most important components of an integrated marketing communications program is the advertising message. While the fundamental role of an advertising message is to communicate information, it does much more. The commercials we watch on TV or hear on radio and the print ads we see in magazines and newspapers are a source of entertainment, motivation, fascination, fantasy, and sometimes irritation as well as information. Ads and commercials appeal to, and often create or shape, consumers' problems, desires, and goals. From the marketer's perspective, the advertising message is a way to tell consumers how the product or service can solve a problem or help satisfy desires or achieve goals. Advertising can also be used to create images or associations and position a brand in the consumer's mind

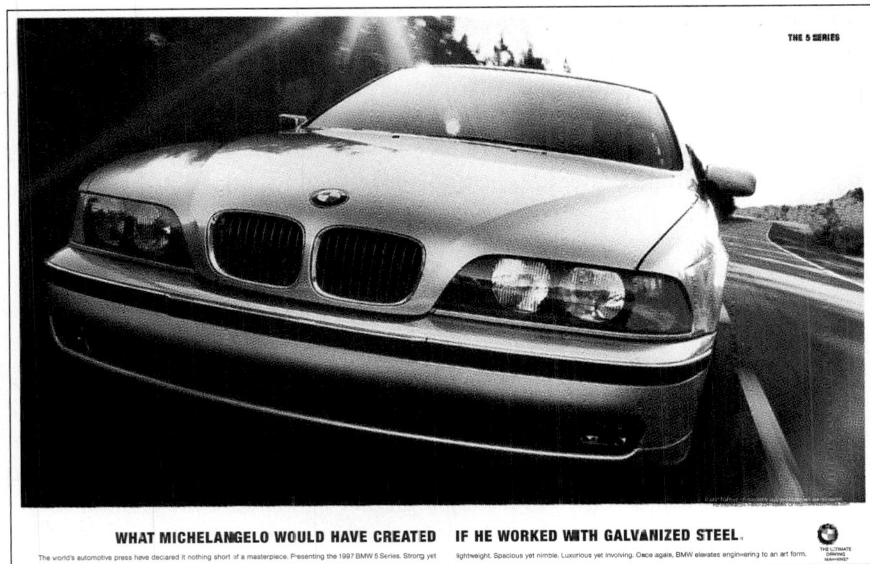

Exhibit 8–1 Excellent advertising helps create an image for BMW automobiles as "the ultimate driving machine"

as well as transform the experience of buying and/or using a product or service. Many consumers who have never driven or even ridden in a BMW perceive it as "the ultimate driving machine" (Exhibit 8–1). Many people feel good about sending Hallmark greeting cards because they have internalized the company's advertising theme, "when you care enough to send the very best."

One need only watch an evening of commercials or peruse a few magazines to realize there are a myriad of ways to convey an advertising message. Underlying all of these messages, however, are a **creative strategy** that determines what the advertising message will say or communicate and **creative tactics** for how the message strategy will be executed. In this chapter, we focus on advertising creative strategy. We consider what is meant by creativity, particularly as it relates to advertising, and examine a well-known approach to creativity in advertising.

We also examine the creative strategy development process and various approaches to determining the *big idea* that will be used as the central theme of the advertising campaign and translated into attention-getting, distinctive, and memorable messages. Creative specialists are finding it more and more difficult to come up with big ideas that will break through the clutter and still satisfy the concerns of their risk-averse clients. Yet their clients are continually challenging them to find the creative message that will strike a responsive chord with their target audience.

Some of you may not be directly involved in the design and creation of ads; you may choose to work in another agency department or on the client side of the business. However, because creative strategy is often so crucial to the success of the firm's promotional effort, everyone involved in the promotional process should understand the creative strategy and tactics that underlie the development of advertising campaigns and messages, as well as the creative options available to the advertiser. Also, individuals on the client side as well as agency people outside the creative department must work with the creative specialists in developing the advertising campaign, implementing it, and evaluating its effectiveness. Thus, marketing and product managers, account representatives, researchers, and media personnel must appreciate the creative process and develop a productive relationship with creative personnel.

The Importance of Creativity in Advertising

For many students, as well as many advertising and marketing practitioners, the most interesting aspect of advertising is the creative side. We have all at one time or another been intrigued by an ad and admired the creative insight that went into it. A great ad is a joy to behold and often an epic to create, as the cost of producing a TV commercial can exceed $1 million. Many companies see this as money well spent. They realize that

the manner in which the advertising message is developed and executed is often critical to the success of the promotional program, which in turn can influence the effectiveness of the entire marketing program. Procter & Gamble, Levi Strauss, Nissan, Compaq, Coke, Pepsi, Nike, McDonald's, and many other companies spend millions of dollars each year to produce advertising messages and hundreds of millions more to purchase media time and space to run them. While these companies make excellent products, they realize creative advertising is also an important part of their marketing success.

Good creative strategy and execution can often be central to determining the success of a product or service or reversing the fortunes of a struggling brand. Conversely, an advertising campaign that is poorly conceived or executed can be a liability. Many companies have solid marketing and promotional plans and spend substantial amounts of money on advertising, yet have difficulty coming up with a creative campaign that will differentiate them from their competitors. For example, Burger King changed its advertising theme 19 times in the past 25 years and changed agencies 7 times in search of a campaign that would give the chain a strong identity in the fast-food market. During many of these campaigns, market share dropped and franchisees were unhappy with the company's inability to come up with an effective campaign.[1] Recently Burger King returned to its original positioning of "Have it your way" but is seeking to extend beyond the simple customization of toppings and into the customer service dimension with a new campaign theme, "Going the distance," which began running in late 1999[2] (Figure 8–1).

Just because an ad or commercial is creative or popular does not mean it will increase sales or revive a declining brand. Many ads have won awards for creativity but failed to increase sales. In some instances, the failure to generate sales has cost the agency the account. For example, many advertising people believe some of the best ads of all time were those done for Alka-Seltzer years ago, including the classic "Mama Mia! That's a spicy meatball!" and "I can't believe I ate the whole thing." While the commercials won numerous creative awards, Alka-Seltzer sales still declined and the agencies lost the account.[3] As discussed in the chapter's open-

Figure 8–1 Burger King advertising campaign themes

- Burger King dismisses BBDO, creator of its most famous slogan, "Have it your way," and hires J. Walter Thompson, New York (Aug. 1976)
- "America loves burgers, and we're America's Burger King" (Nov. 1977–Feb. 1978)
- "Who's got the best darn burger?" (Feb. 1978–Jan. 1980)
- "Make it special. Make it Burger King" (Jan. 1980–Jan. 1982)
- "Aren't you hungry for Burger King now?" (Jan. 1982–Sept. 1982)
- "Battle of the burgers" (Sept. 1982–Mar. 1983)
- "Broiling vs. frying" campaign tied to "Aren't you hungry?" (Mar. 1983–Sept. 1983)
- "The big switch" campaign (Sept. 1983–Nov. 1985)
- "Search for Herb" campaign (Nov. 1985–June 1986)
- "This is a Burger King town" (June 1986–Jan. 1987)
- "The best food for fast times" (Jan. 1987–Oct. 1987)
- BK hires NW Ayer, New York, and fires JWT (Oct. 1987)
- "We do it like you'd do it" (Apr. 1988–May 1989)
- BK hires D'Arcy Masius Benton & Bowles, and Saatchi & Saatchi, New York, firing Ayer (May 1989)
- "Sometimes you gotta break the rules" (Oct. 1989–Apr. 1991)
- "Your way. Right away" (April 1991–Oct. 1992)
- "BK Tee Vee: I love this place!" (Oct. 1992–1994)
- "Get your burger's worth" (1994–1998)
- "It just tastes better" (1998–1999)
- "Go the distance" (1999–)

Exhibit 8–2 In Nissan's new ads, the cars are once again the stars

ing vignette, when its sales declined, Nissan asked its agency to replace the popular and amusing "Enjoy the ride" campaign with ads featuring the cars and, in some cases, comparisons with the competition[4] (Exhibit 8–2).

Many advertising and marketing people have become ambivalent toward, and in some cases even critical of, advertising awards.[5] They argue that agency creative people are often more concerned with creating ads that win awards than ones that sell their clients' products. Other advertising people believe awards are a good way to recognize creativity that often does result in effective advertising. Global Perspective 8–1 discusses how the emphasis on creative awards has shifted to the international arena with awards like the Cannes Gold Lion trophies.

As we saw in Chapter 7, the success of an ad campaign cannot always be judged in terms of sales. However, many advertising and marketing personnel, particularly those on the client side, believe advertising must ultimately lead the consumer to purchase the product or service. Finding a balance between creative advertising and effective advertising is difficult. To better understand this dilemma, we turn to the issue of creativity and its role in advertising.

Advertising Creativity

What Is Creativity?

Creativity is probably one of the most commonly used terms in advertising. Ads are often called creative. The people who develop ads and commercials are known as creative types. And advertising agencies develop reputations for their creativity. Perhaps so much attention is focused on the concept of creativity because many people view the specific challenge given to those who develop an advertising message as being creative. It is their job to turn all of the information regarding product features and benefits, marketing plans, consumer research, and communication objectives into a creative concept that will bring the advertising message to life. This begs the question: What is meant by *creativity* in advertising?

Different Perspectives on Advertising Creativity

Perspectives on what constitutes creativity in advertising differ. At one extreme are people who argue that advertising is creative only if it sells the product. An advertising message's or campaign's impact on sales counts more than whether it is innovative or wins awards. At the other end of the continuum are those who judge the creativity of an ad in terms of its artistic or aesthetic value and originality. They contend creative ads can break through the competitive clutter, grab the consumer's attention, and have some impact.

Global Perspective 8–1

Cannes Lions Continue to Be Advertising's International Status Symbol

For many years the most coveted prize for creativity in advertising was a Clio Award. However, the Clios lost much of their prestige after financial problems resulted in cancellation of the 1992 awards ceremony. And even though they still sponsor an annual awards competition, the Clios have never regained their former status as the advertising industry's premier award for creative excellence. However, there are a number of other popular and well-recognized U.S.-based advertising award competitions that recognize outstanding creative work. These include the Kelley Awards, given by the Magazine Publishers of America; the Best Awards, sponsored by *Advertising Age;* the One Show, sponsored by the One Club for Art and Copy; and the Effies, which are given each year by the New York American Marketing Association.

While these contests remain very popular in the United States, on a global level the Cannes International Advertising Film Festival is now widely considered the most prestigious advertising award competition. The Cannes competition receives entries from agencies around the world hoping to win Lions (the name of the award) in each of the major categories—television; print and poster; online (cyber) advertising, which was added in 1998; and media buying and planning, which was awarded for the first time in 1999. Many of the top U.S. agencies do not enter the print and poster contest, which is usually dominated by agencies from the United Kingdom, whose style of advertising is considered more popular among the Cannes jury.

Agencies from the United States generally focus their entries on the TV part of the competition, where they fare much better than they do in the print category. Such was the case in the 1999 Cannes competition as U.S. agencies failed to win any Gold Lions in the print and poster competition. However, they dominated the TV awards, winning six Gold Lions, seven Silver Lions, and nine bronzes. The U.S. new-media agencies also swept the second annual Cyber Lions competition, as Ogilvy-Interactive won the Grand Prix Award and two other Lions for its online "e-business" campaign for IBM, which customized IBM's online ads to areas of interest for its different clients. U.S. gold winners for TV included Wieden & Kennedy, which picked up two Gold Lions for a series of Nike shoes and apparel spots; J. Walter Thompson, New York, for the Kellogg's Raisin Bran Crunch spot "Slackers"; Cliff Freeman & Partners' "Don" spot for Video Rental Store; and DDB, Chicago, for two Anheuser-Busch Budweiser spots, including "On the Road Again" and "Open Road."

The other U.S.-agency Gold Lion TV winner was the much-talked-about but controversial Outpost.com commercials from Cliff Freeman & Partners, New York, which were infamous for tattooing the company name on children's foreheads and firing gerbils out of cannons. The Outpost.com ads were beaten out for the International Advertising Festival's Grand Prix Award for the best overall TV commercial by a spot done for the U.K. newspaper *The Independent;* called "Litany," it was created by the Lowe Howard-Spink London agency. The black-and-white spot features quick cuts of people and rapid-fire orders not to talk, smoke, drink, do drugs, and the like. Then, as a bundle of *Independent* newspapers drops to the street, the final, pointedly ironic admonition appears, "Don't buy. Don't read." The message is that the *Independent*'s readers have minds of their own, and the commercial sets up the paper as a defender of the freedom not to be cowed by fear and small-mindedness. International Advertising Festival jury president Keith Reinhard, chairman and CEO of DDB Worldwide, said the choice of "Litany" was "an arrow" to the industry. He said, "The jury felt a special responsibility as the last jury of the 1990s to point the industry in a direction that was perhaps a little more aspirational and reflected qualities we think are important." He added that there was a sensitivity among the jurors to the body of violence in commercials and the Outpost.com spot was considered too violent.

Another U.K. agency, TBWA Simmons Palmer GGT, London, captured the print and poster Grand Prix for a Sony PlayStation ad called "Nipples." The copyless ad depicts a young boy and girl whose nipples strain against their shirts, forming the symbols

+, –, 0—the key icons on video game controls. The PlayStation ad narrowly beat out another U.K. ad, called "Wedding," which was part of a low-price campaign for the Volkswagen Polo automobile.

While many advertising people are critical of creative awards, the Cannes competition attracts over 4,000 entries each year in the print and TV categories, so someone must think such awards are important. And don't try to downplay their importance to DM9, DDB, Sao Paulo, as the Brazilian shop won Agency of the Year for picking up the most Lions overall in the TV, print, cyber, and media competitions. Agencies like DM9 know that the prestige of a Cannes Gold Lion Award enhances their image and helps attract new business.

Sources: Laurel Wentz, "Grand Prix Ad Winners Reflect 'Aspirational' Direction," *Advertising Age,* June 28, 1999, pp. 1, 66; Bob Garfield, "Savor the Paradox, Delicious Difference," *Advertising Age,* June 28, 1999, p. 67.

As you might expect, perspectives on advertising creativity often depend on one's role. A study by Elizabeth Hirschman examined the perceptions of various individuals involved in the creation and production of TV commercials, including management types (brand managers and account executives) and creatives (art director, copywriter, commercial director, and producer).[6] She found that product managers and account executives view ads as promotional tools whose primary purpose is to communicate favorable impressions to the marketplace. They believe a commercial should be evaluated in terms of whether it fulfills the client's marketing and communicative objectives. The perspective of those on the creative side was much more self-serving, as Hirschman noted:

> In direct contrast to this client orientation, the art director, copywriter, and commercial director viewed the advertisement as a communication vehicle for promoting their own aesthetic viewpoints and personal career objectives. Both the copywriter and art director made this point explicitly, noting that a desirable commercial from their standpoint was one which communicated their unique creative talents and thereby permitted them to obtain "better" jobs at an increased salary.[7]

In her interviews, Hirschman also found that brand managers were much more risk-averse and wanted a more conservative commercial than the creative people, who wanted to maximize the impact of the message.

What constitutes creativity in advertising is probably somewhere between the two extremes. To break through the clutter and make an impression on the target audience, an ad often must be unique and entertaining. As noted in Chapter 5, research has shown that a major determinant of whether a commercial will be successful in changing brand preferences is its "likability," or the viewer's overall reaction.[8] TV commercials and print ads that are well designed and executed and generate emotional responses can create positive feelings that are transferred to the product or service being advertised. Many creative people believe this type of advertising can come about only if they are given considerable latitude in developing advertising messages. But ads that are creative only for the sake of being creative often fail to communicate a relevant or meaningful message that will lead consumers to purchase the product or service.

Everyone involved in planning and developing an advertising campaign must understand the importance of balancing the "it's not creative unless it sells" perspective with the novelty/uniqueness and impact position. Marketing and brand managers or account executives must recognize that imposing too many sales- and marketing-oriented communications objectives on the creative team can result in mediocre advertising, which is often ineffective in today's competitive, cluttered media environment. At the same time, the creative specialists must recognize that the goal of advertising is to assist in selling the product or service and good advertising must communicate in a manner that helps the client achieve this goal.

Advertising creativity is the ability to generate fresh, unique, and appropriate ideas that can be used as solutions to communications problems. To be *appropriate* and effective, a creative idea must be relevant to the target audience. Many ad agencies recognize the importance of developing advertising that is creative and different yet communicates relevant information to the target audience. Figure 8–2 shows the

Figure 8–2 D'Arcy, Masius Benton & Bowles's universal advertising standards

1. *Does this advertising position the product simply and with unmistakable clarity?*

   The target audience for the advertised product or service must be able to see and sense in a flash *what* the product is for, *whom* it is for, and *why* they should be interested in it.

   Creating this clear vision of how the product or service fits into their lives is the first job of advertising. Without a simple, clear, focused positioning, no creative work can begin.

2. *Does this advertising bolt the brand to a clinching benefit?*

   Our advertising should be built on the most compelling and persuasive consumer benefit—not some unique-but-insignificant peripheral feature.

   Before you worry about how to say it, you must be sure you are saying *the right thing*. If you don't know what the most compelling benefit is, you've got to find out before you do anything else.

3. *Does this advertising contain a Power Idea?*

   The Power Idea is the vehicle that transforms the strategy into a dynamic, creative communications concept. It is the core creative idea that sets the stage for brilliant executions to come. The ideal Power Idea should:

   - Be describable in a simple word, phrase, or sentence without reference to any final execution.
   - Be likely to attract the prospect's attention.
   - Revolve around the clinching benefit.
   - Allow you to brand the advertising.
   - Make it easy for the prospect to vividly experience our client's product or service.

4. *Does this advertising design in Brand Personality?*

   The great brands tend to have something in common: the extra edge of having a Brand Personality. This is something beyond merely identifying what the brand does for the consumer; all brands *do* something, but the great brands also *are* something.

   A brand can be whatever its designers want it to be—and it can be so from day one.

5. *Is this advertising unexpected?*

   Why should our clients pay good money to wind up with advertising that looks and sounds like everybody else's in the category? They shouldn't.

   We must dare to be different, because sameness is suicide. We can't be outstanding unless we first stand out.

   The thing is not to *emulate* the competition but to *annihilate* them.

6. *Is this advertising single-minded?*

   If you have determined the right thing to say and have created a way to say it uncommonly well, why waste time saying anything else?

   If we want people to remember one big thing from a given piece of advertising, let's not make it more difficult than it already is in an overcommunicated world.

   The advertising should be all about that one big thing.

7. *Does this advertising reward the prospect?*

   Let's give our audience something that makes it easy—even pleasurable—for our message to penetrate: a tear, a smile, a laugh. An emotional stimulus is that special something that makes them want to see the advertising again and again.

8. *Is this advertising visually arresting?*

   Great advertising you remember—and can play back in your mind—is unusual to look at: compelling, riveting, a nourishing feast for the eyes. If you need a reason to strive for arresting work, go no further than Webster: "Catching or holding the attention, thought, or feelings. Gripping. Striking. Interesting."

9. *Does this advertising exhibit painstaking craftsmanship?*

   You want writing that is really written. Visuals that are designed. Music that is composed.

   Lighting, casting, wardrobe, direction—all the components of the art of advertising are every bit as important as the science of it. It is a sin to nickel-and-dime a great advertising idea to death.

   Why settle for good, when there's great? We should go for the absolute best in concept, design, and execution.

   This is our craft—the work should sparkle.

   "Our creative standards are not a gimmick," Steve emphasizes. "They're not even revolutionary. Instead, they are an explicit articulation of a fundamental refocusing on our company's only reason for being.

   "D'Arcy's universal advertising standards are the operating link between our vision today—and its coming reality."

perspective on creativity that the D'Arcy, Masius Benton & Bowles agency developed to guide its creative efforts and help achieve superior creativity consistently. The agency views a creative advertising message as one that is built around a creative core or power idea and uses excellent design and execution to communicate information that interests the target audience. It has used these principles in doing outstanding creative work for Procter & Gamble's Charmin and Pampers brands, Norelco, and many other popular brands.

Advertising creativity is not the exclusive domain of those who work on the creative side of advertising. The nature of the business requires creative thinking from everyone involved in the promotional planning process. Agency people, such as account executives, media planners, researchers, and attorneys, as well as those on the client side, such as marketing and brand managers, must all seek creative solutions to problems encountered in planning, developing, and executing an advertising campaign. An excellent example of creative synergy between the media and creative departments of an agency, as well as with the client, is seen in the TBWA/Chiat/Day agency and its relationship with Absolut vodka. As discussed in Chapter 1, the creative strategy for the brand plays off the distinctive shape of its bottle and depicts it with visual puns and witty headlines that play off the Absolut name. The agency and client recognized they could carry the advertising campaign further by tailoring the print ads for the magazines or regions where they appear. Absolut's media schedule includes over 100 magazines, among them various consumer and business publications. The creative and media departments work together selecting magazines and deciding on the ads that will appeal to the readers of each publication. The creative department is often asked to create media-specific ads to run in a particular publication. Exhibit 8–3 shows an Absolut ad that was developed specifically for *Los Angeles Magazine.*

Exhibit 8–3 Absolut vodka creates ads specifically for the publication in which they appear, such as this one for *Los Angeles Magazine*

The Creative Challenge

Those who work on the creative side of advertising often face a real challenge. They must take all the research, creative briefs, strategy statements, communications objectives, and other input and transform them into an advertising message. Their job is to write copy, design layouts and illustrations, or produce commercials that effectively communicate the central theme on which the campaign is based. Rather than simply stating the features or benefits of a product or service, they must put the advertising message into a form that will engage the audience's interest and make the ads memorable.[9]

The job of the creative team is challenging because every marketing situation is different and each campaign or advertisement may require a different creative approach. Numerous guidelines have been developed for creating effective advertising,[10] but there is no magic formula. As copywriter Hank Sneiden notes in his book *Advertising Pure and Simple:*

> Rules lead to dull stereotyped advertising, and they stifle creativity, inspiration, initiative, and progress. The only hard and fast rule that I know of in advertising is that there are no rules. No formulas. No right way. Given the same problem, a dozen creative talents would solve it a dozen different ways. If there were a sure-fire formula for successful advertising, everyone would use it. Then there'd be no need for creative people. We would simply program robots to create our ads and commercials and they'd sell loads of product—to other robots.[11]

Taking Creative Risks

Many creative people follow proven formulas when creating ads because they are safe. Clients often feel uncomfortable with advertising that is too different. Bill Tragos, former chair of TBWA, the advertising agency noted for its excellent creative work for Absolut vodka, Evian, and many other clients, says, "Very few clients realize that the reason that their work is so bad is that they are the ones who commandeered it and directed it to be that way. I think that at least 50 percent of an agency's successful work resides in the client."[12]

Many creative people say it is important for clients to take some risks if they want breakthrough advertising that gets noticed. One agency that has been successful in getting its clients to take risks is Wieden & Kennedy, best known for its excellent creative work for companies such as Nike, Microsoft, and ESPN. The agency's founders believe a key element in its success has been a steadfast belief in taking risks when most agencies and their clients have been retrenching and becoming more conservative.[13] The agency can develop great advertising partly because clients like Nike are willing to take risks and go along with the agency's priority system, which places the creative work first and the client–agency relationship second. The agency has even terminated relationships with large clients like Gallo when they interfered too much with the creative process.

An example of a company that has been taking creative risks with its advertising is Crunch Fitness, a trendy health club chain that has become known for quirky commercials that are part of its "No judgments" campaign. While traditional health club advertising touts flat stomachs and bulging biceps to drive memberships, Crunch differentiates itself from the fitness fray with offbeat humor and a message of self-acceptance. The commercials, which target young, educated, urban professionals, depict average people engaged in everyday rituals. One of the spots shows a business stiff who notices coffee on his clean white shirt. He picks up a bottle of correction fluid and spreads it over the stain as the copyline on the screen reads: "Creativity . . . often goes unnoticed" (Exhibit 8–4). The creative director for Mad Dogs & Englishmen, the agency that developed the campaign, says: "The spots are little thoughts to live by. We wanted to take the idea of 'no judgments'—anyone can come here—and develop it into 'Stop judging yourself.' That's the Crunch philosophy." Crunch Fitness president and CEO Doug Levine supports the offbeat campaign, noting, "I think it's more important to say it's a gym with a different attitude."[14]

Not all companies or agencies agree that advertising has to be risky to be effective, however. Many marketing managers are more comfortable with advertising that simply communicates product or service features and benefits and gives the consumer a reason to buy. They see their ad campaigns as multimillion-dollar investments whose goal is to sell the product rather than finance the whims of their agency's creative staff. They argue that some creative people have lost sight of advertising's bottom line: Does it sell?

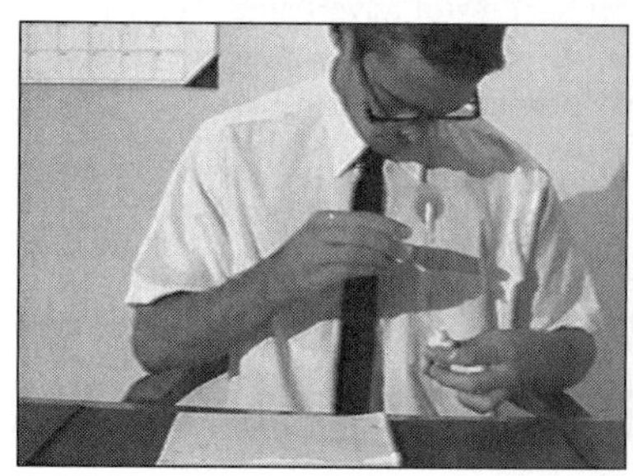

Exhibit 8–4 Crunch Fitness takes a creative risk with its quirky commercials

The issue of how much latitude creative people should be given and how much risk the client should be willing to take is open to considerable debate. However, clients and agency personnel generally agree that the ability to develop novel yet appropriate approaches to communicating with the customer makes the creative specialist valuable—and often hard to find.

Creative Personnel

The image of the creative advertising person perpetuated in novels, movies, and TV shows is often one of a freewheeling, freethinking, eccentric personality. The educational background of creative personnel is often in nonbusiness areas such as art, literature, music, humanities, or journalism, so their interests and perspectives tend to differ from those of managers with a business education or background. Creative people tend to be more abstract and less structured, organized, or conventional in their approach to a problem, relying on intuition more often than logic.

Advertising creatives are sometimes stereotyped as odd, perhaps because they dress differently and do not always work the conventional 9-to-5 schedule. Of course, from the perspective of the creatives, it is the marketing or brand managers and account executives (the "suits") who are strange. In many agencies, you can't tell the creative personnel from the executives by their dress or demeanor. Yet the differences between creative and managerial personalities and perspectives must be recognized and tolerated so creative people can do their best work and all those involved in the advertising process can cooperate.

Most agencies thrive on creativity, for it is the major component in the product they produce. Thus, they must create an environment that fosters the development of creative thinking and creative advertising. Clients must also understand the differences between the perspectives of the creative personnel and marketing and product managers. While the client has ultimate approval of the advertising, the opinions of creative specialists must be respected when advertising ideas and content are evaluated. (Evaluation of the creative's ideas and work is discussed in more detail in Chapter 9.)

The Creative Process

Some advertising people say creativity in advertising is best viewed as a process and creative success is most likely when some organized approach is followed. This does not mean there is an infallible blueprint to follow to create effective advertising; as we saw earlier, many advertising people reject attempts to standardize creativity or develop rules. However, most do follow a process when developing an ad.

One of the most popular approaches to creativity in advertising was developed by James Webb Young, a former creative vice president at the J. Walter Thompson agency. Young said, "The production of ideas is just as definite a process as the production of Fords; the production of ideas, too, runs an assembly line; in this production the mind follows an operative technique which can be learned and controlled; and that its effective use is just as much a matter of practice in the technique as in the effective use of any tool."[15] Young's model of the creative process contains five steps:

1. *Immersion.* Gathering raw material and information through background research and immersing yourself in the problem.
2. *Digestion.* Taking the information, working it over, and wrestling with it in the mind.
3. *Incubation.* Putting the problems out of your conscious mind and turning the information over to the subconscious to do the work.
4. *Illumination.* The birth of an idea—the "Eureka! I have it!" phenomenon.
5. *Reality or verification.* Studying the idea to see if it still looks good or solves the problem; then shaping the idea to practical usefulness.

Young's process of creativity is similar to a four-step approach outlined much earlier by English sociologist Graham Wallas:

1. *Preparation.* Gathering background information needed to solve the problem through research and study.
2. *Incubation.* Getting away and letting ideas develop.
3. *Illumination.* Seeing the light or solution.
4. *Verification.* Refining and polishing the idea and seeing if it is an appropriate solution.

Models of the creative process are valuable to those working in the creative area of advertising, since they offer an organized way to approach an advertising problem. Preparation or gathering of background information is the first step in the creative process. As we saw in earlier chapters, the advertiser and agency start by developing a thorough understanding of the product or service, the target market, and the competition. They also focus on the role of advertising in the marketing and promotional program.

These models do not say much about how this information will be synthesized and used by the creative specialist because this part of the process is unique to the individual. In many ways, it's what sets apart the great creative minds and strategists in advertising. However, many agencies are now using a process called *account planning* to gather information and help creative specialists as they go through the creative process of developing advertising.

Account Planning

To facilitate the creative process, many agencies now use **account planning,** which is a process that involves conducting research and gathering all relevant information about a client's product or service, brand, and consumers in the target audience. Account planning began in Great Britain during the 1960s and 70s and has spread to agencies in the United States as well as throughout Europe and Asia. The concept has become very popular in recent years as many agencies have seen the successful campaigns developed by agencies that are strong advocates of account planning.[16] One such agency is Goodby, Silverstein & Partners, which has used account planning to develop highly successful campaigns for clients such as Polaroid, Hewlett-Packard, Sega, and Nike as well as the popular "Got milk?" ads for the California Milk Processor Board.

Jon Steel, vice president and director of account planning at the agency's San Francisco office, has written an excellent book on the process titled *Truth, Lies & Advertising: The Art of Account Planning.*[17] He notes that the account planner's job is to provide the key decision makers with all the information they require to make an intelligent decision. According to Steel, "Planners may have to work very hard to influence the way that the advertising turns out, carefully laying out a strategic foundation with the client, handing over tidbits of information to creative people when, in their judgment, that information will have the greatest impact, giving feedback on ideas, and hopefully adding some ideas of their own."

Account planning plays an important role during creative strategy development by driving the process from the customers' point of view. Planners will work with the client as well as other agency personnel, such as the creative team and media specialists. They discuss how the knowledge and information they have gathered can be used in the development of the creative strategy as well as other aspects of the advertising campaign. Account planners are usually responsible for all the research (both qualitative and quantitative) conducted during the creative strategy development process. In the following section we examine how various types of research and information can provide input to the creative process of advertising. This information can be gathered by account planners or others whose job it is to provide input to the process.

Inputs to the Creative Process: Preparation, Incubation, Illumination

Background Research Only the most foolish creative person or team would approach an assignment without first learning as much as possible about the client's product or service, the target market, the competition, and any other relevant background information. The creative specialist should also be knowledgeable about general trends, conditions, and developments in the marketplace, as well as research on specific advertising approaches or techniques that might be effective. The creative specialist can acquire background information in numerous ways. Some informal fact-finding techniques have been noted by Sandra Moriarty:

- Reading anything related to the product or market—books, trade publications, general interest articles, research reports, and the like.
- Asking everyone involved with the product for information—designers, engineers, salespeople, and consumers.
- Listening to what people are talking about. Visits to stores, malls, restaurants, and even the agency cafeteria can be informative. Listening to the client can be particularly valuable, since he or she often knows the product and market best.
- Using the product or service and becoming familiar with it. The more you use a product, the more you know and can say about it.
- Working in and learning about the client's business to understand better the people you're trying to reach.[18]

To assist in the preparation, incubation, and illumination stages, many agencies provide creative people with both general and product-specific preplanning input. **General preplanning input** can include books, periodicals, trade publications, scholarly journals, pictures, and clipping services, which gather and organize magazine and newspaper articles on the product, the market, and the competition, including the latter's ads. This input can also come from research studies conducted by the client, the agency, the media, or other sources.

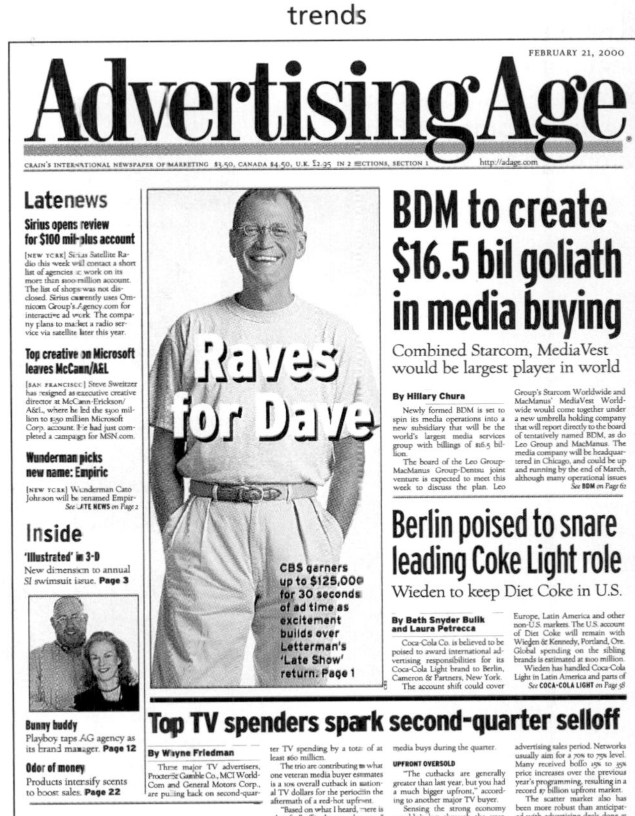

FEBRUARY 21, 2000

AdvertisingAge

CRAIN'S INTERNATIONAL NEWSPAPER OF MARKETING $3.50, CANADA $4.50, U.K. £2.95 IN 2 SECTIONS, SECTION 1 http://adage.com

Latenews

Sirius opens review for $100 mil-plus account

[NEW YORK] Sirius Satellite Radio this week will contact a short list of agencies to work on its more than $100 million account. The list of shops was not disclosed. Sirius currently uses Omnicom Group's Agency.com for interactive ad work. The company plans to market a radio service via satellite later this year.

Top creative on Microsoft leaves McCann/A&L

[SAN FRANCISCO] Steve Sweitzer has resigned as executive creative director at McCann-Erickson/A&L, where he led the $300 million to $350 million Microsoft Corp. account. He had just completed a campaign for MSN.com.

Wunderman picks new name: Empiric

[NEW YORK] Wunderman Cato Johnson will be renamed Empir-

See LATE NEWS on Page 2

Inside

'Illustrated' in 3-D

New dimension to annual SI swimsuit issue. **Page 3**

Bunny buddy

Playboy taps AG agency as its brand manager. **Page 12**

Odor of money

Products intensify scents to boost sales. **Page 22**

Raves for Dave

CBS garners up to $125,000 for 30 seconds of ad time as excitement builds over Letterman's 'Late Show' return. Page 1

CBS

BDM to create $16.5 bil goliath in media buying

Combined Starcom, MediaVest would be largest player in world

By Hillary Chura

Newly formed BDM is set to spin its media operations into a new subsidiary that will be the world's largest media services group with billings of $16.5 billion.

The board of the Leo Group-MacManus Group-Dentsu joint venture is expected to meet this week to discuss the plan. Leo Group's Starcom Worldwide and MacManus' MediaVest Worldwide would come together under a new umbrella holding company that will report directly to the board of tentatively named BDM, as do Leo Group and MacManus. The media company will be headquartered in Chicago, and could be up and running by the end of March, although many operational issues

See BDM on Page 62

Berlin poised to snare leading Coke Light role

Wieden to keep Diet Coke in U.S.

By Beth Snyder Bulik and Laura Petrecca

Coca-Cola Co. is believed to be poised to award international advertising responsibilities for its Coca-Cola Light brand to Berlin, Cameron & Partners, New York.

The account shift could cover Europe, Latin America and other non-U.S. markets. The U.S. account of Diet Coke will remain with Wieden & Kennedy, Portland, Ore. Global spending on the sibling brands is estimated at $100 million.

Wieden has handled Coca-Cola Light in Latin America and parts of

See COCA-COLA LIGHT on Page 58

Top TV spenders spark second-quarter selloff

By Wayne Friedman

Three major TV advertisers, Procter & Gamble Co., MCI WorldCom and General Motors Corp., are pulling back on second-quarter TV spending by a total of at least $60 million.

The trio are contributing to what one veteran media buyer estimates is a 10% overall cutback in national TV dollars for the period in the aftermath of a red-hot upfront.

"Based on what I heard, there is a lot of sell-off in the second quarter," said a New York media executive. "We have a bunch of people seeking relief." Networks usually allow advertisers to trim 50% of their media buys during the quarter.

UPFRONT OVERSOLD

"The cutbacks are generally greater than last year, but you had a much bigger upfront," according to another major TV buyer.

Sensing the strong economy wouldn't last through the year, many networks oversold much of their inventory—believed to be 80% to 85% of total supply of commercial time—in the last upfront advertising sales period. Networks usually aim for a 70% to 75% level. Many received boffo 15% to 35% price increases over the previous year's programming, resulting in a record $7 billion upfront market.

The scatter market also has been more robust than anticipated with advertising deals done at double-digit percent price increases over upfront pricing.

"It's still a strong market," said

See NETWORKS on Page 58

NEWSPAPER

To Subscribe Call 888-288-5900

Exhibit 8–5 Industry publications like *Advertising Age* are excellent sources of information on market trends

Another useful general preplanning input concerns trends, developments, and happenings in the marketplace. Information is available from a variety of sources, including local, state, and federal governments, secondary research suppliers, and various industry trade associations, as well as advertising and media organizations. For example, advertising industry groups like the American Association of Advertising Agencies and media organizations like the National Association of Broadcasters (NAB) and Magazine Publishers of America (MPA) publish research reports and newsletters that provide information on market trends and developments and how they might affect consumers. Those involved in developing creative strategy can also gather relevant and timely information by reading publications like *Adweek, Advertising Age, Brand Week,* and *The Wall Street Journal* (Exhibit 8–5).

Product/Service-Specific Research In addition to getting general background research and preplanning input, creative people receive **product/service-specific preplanning input.** This information generally comes in the form of specific studies conducted on the product or service, the target audience, or a combination of the two. Quantitative and qualitative consumer research such as attitude studies, market structure and positioning studies such as perceptual mapping and lifestyle research, focus group interviews, and demographic and psychographic profiles of users of a particular product, service, or brand are examples of product-specific preplanning input.

Many product- or service-specific studies helpful to the creative team are conducted by the client or the agency. A number of years ago, the BBDO ad agency developed an approach called **problem detection**[19] for finding ideas around which creative strategies could be based. This research technique involves asking consumers familiar with a product (or service) to generate an exhaustive list of things that bother them or problems they encounter when using it. The consumers rate these problems in order of importance and evaluate various brands in terms of their association with each problem. A problem detection study can provide valuable input for product improvements, reformulations, or new products. It can also give the creative people ideas regarding attributes or features to emphasize and guidelines for positioning new or existing brands.

Some agencies conduct psychographic studies annually and construct detailed psychographic or lifestyle profiles of product or service users. DDB Needham conducts a large-scale psychographic study each year using a sample of 4,000 U.S. adults. The agency's Life Style Study provides its creative teams with a better understanding of the target audience for whom they are developing ads.

For example, information from its Life Style Study was used by DDB Needham's creative department in developing a recent advertising campaign for Westin. The agency's Life Style Study showed that the younger business travelers the luxury hotel chain was targeting are highly confident, intelligent, assertive, and classy and considered themselves to be a "winner." Rather than using the traditional images that feature buildings and golf courses, the creative team decided to "brand the user" by playing to their ego and reinforcing their strong self-image. The ad campaign used the tagline "Who is he/she sleeping with? Westin. Choose your travel partner wisely" (Exhibit 8–6).

Exhibit 8–6 DDB Needham's Life Style Study provided valuable input in the development of this campaign for Westin

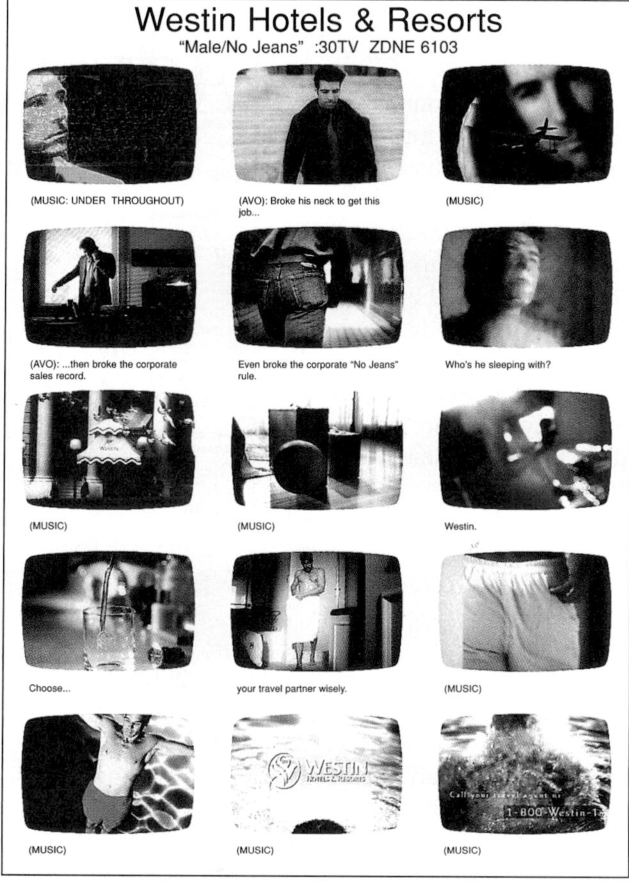

Recently a number of advertising agencies have been conducting branding research to help better identify clients' customers and how they connect to their brands. Young & Rubicam has been using its "Brand Asset Valuator" research tool for several years, while the Leo Burnett agency recently unveiled a new brand research technique called "Brand Stock." DDB Worldwide has also begun providing clients with branding research conducted through a global marketing study consisting of 14,000 consumer interviews about 500 brands. The proprietary research called "Brand Capital" is designed to give DDB and its clients an in-depth look at consumers' preferences for various products and their beliefs on numerous subjects and issues. Agencies use this research to determine how a brand is perceived among consumers and these insights, in turn, are used to develop more effective advertising campaigns.[20]

Qualitative Research Input Many agencies, particularly larger ones with strong research departments, have their own research programs and specific techniques they use to assist in the development of creative strategy and provide input to the creative process. In addition to the various quantitative research studies, qualitative research techniques such as in-depth interviews or focus groups can provide the creative team with valuable insight at the early stages of the creative process. **Focus groups** are a research method whereby consumers (usually 10 to 12 people) from the target market are led through a discussion regarding a particular topic. Focus groups give insight as to why and how consumers use a product or service, what is important to them in choosing a particular brand, what they like and don't like about various products or services, and any special needs they might have that aren't being satisfied. A focus group session might also include a discussion of types of ad appeals to use or evaluate the advertising of various companies.

Focus group interviews bring the creative people and others involved in creative strategy development into contact with the customers. Listening to a focus group gives copywriters, art directors, and other creative specialists a better sense of who the target audience is, what the audience is like, and who the creatives need to write, design, or direct to in creating an advertising message. Focus groups can also be used to evaluate the viability of different creative approaches under consideration and suggest the best direction to pursue.[21]

Generally, creative people are open to any research or information that will help them understand the client's target market better and assist in generating creative ideas. The advertising industry is recognizing the importance of using research to guide the creative process. The Advertising Research Foundation recently initiated the David Ogilvy Awards, named after the advertising legend who founded Ogilvy & Mather. These awards are presented to teams of advertising agencies, client companies, and research companies in recognition of research that has been used successfully to determine the strategy and effectiveness of ad campaigns. IMC Perspective 8–2 discusses how the California Milk Processor Board, which is a past winner of the David Ogilvy Award, used both quantitative and qualitative research in developing the popular "Got milk?" advertising campaign.

Inputs to the Creative Process: Verification, Revision

The verification and revision stage of the creative process evaluates ideas generated during the illumination stage, rejects inappropriate ones, refines and polishes those that remain, and gives them final expression. Techniques used at this stage include directed focus groups to evaluate creative concepts, ideas, or themes; message communication studies; portfolio tests; and evaluation measures such as viewer reaction profiles.

At this stage of the creative process, members of the target audience may be asked to evaluate rough creative layouts and to indicate what meaning they get

IMC Perspective 8–2

Using Research to Understand Why People Drink It Is Key to "Got Milk?" Campaign

If you are like most consumers, when you need to quench a thirst you probably reach for a soft drink, a glass of juice, iced tea, or just a plain glass of water. However, if you have a peanut-butter-and-jelly sandwich, a chocolate-chip cookie, or a brownie in front of you, or are about to have a bowl of cereal, there is really only one choice: milk. Nothing else will do. That is the idea behind the "Got milk?" advertising campaign created by Goodby, Silverstein & Partners, San Francisco, for the California Milk Processor Board. The popular campaign, which began in 1994, has expanded beyond California and is now being used on a national level. It is an excellent example of how marketing research can be a valuable input to the creative process.

When Jeff Manning was hired as executive director of the California Milk Processor Board in 1993, milk consumption had been declining across the country for nearly three decades. The decline was particularly bad in California, where overall consumption fell an average of 2 to 3 percent per year between the late 1980s and early 90s. Manning was given a mandate to develop a marketing program that would stop the decline of milk consumption in the state and increase sales. When he hired Goody, Silverstein, he made it clear that the goal of the ad campaign was increased sales, not image enhancement.

Manning had a strong hunch that would prove to be very valuable to the development of the ad campaign. While previous ads showed milk as a beverage that was consumed alone, Manning felt that most people drink milk in combination with other foods: "If you ask people when milk is critical, they'll tell you it's when they have cereal in the bowl or cookies in their mouth. The driver is not the milk. It's the food." Manning's hypothesis became a guiding force for the qualitative and quantitative research conducted to develop the campaign. A telephone survey of Californians found that 88 percent of milk is consumed at home and it is usually accompanied by other foods, most frequently cereal. The survey was valuable in identifying other companion foods, which include cookies, pastries, brownies, and peanut-butter-and-jelly sandwiches. However, the agency wanted to determine which situations prompt a strong desire for milk and how people feel when they are deprived of it.

To observe the effects of "milk deprivation," the agency added a unique twist to its focus groups. In return for extra payment, people agreed to not drink any milk for a week before the focus groups and to keep a diary of everything they ate or drank in that time. The participants found that going without milk was easier said than done. One man described his usual pattern of waking up bleary-eyed and pouring a bowl of cereal, only to find no milk in the fridge. One participant said, "It's so bad, you'd even steal milk from your kid." Another respondent noted, "Never mind your kid. You're so desperate, you'd even steal it from your cat." The focus group stories formed the basis for a series of humorous TV commercials emphasizing the agony that awaits those who run out of milk.

In 1999, Manning and the agency once again used marketing research to take the milk deprivation strategy behind the campaign in a slightly different direction by adding a health message. Although Manning had been resisting using the health message, new market research convinced

him otherwise. National research found that if a mother drinks milk, her children drink twice as much milk as the children of non-milk-drinking mothers. One of the new spots developed by the agency shows a mother urging her children to drink milk with their meal. The children say they want soda and argue that their neighbor, Mr. Miller, tells them he doesn't need to drink milk. Just then, the children look out the window and see Mr. Miller gardening, but when he tries to push a wheelbarrow, his arms fall off. The children are then seen slurping down large glasses of milk. Another spot features a TV chef who shows off by eating a habanero, planning to immediately drink a glass of milk because it has elements to counteract the hot pepper. However, a stagehand has swiped the milk, and in the last scene the chef appears to have gone up in smoke.

Although television advertising is the largest and most visible part of the campaign, an entire integrated marketing strategy has been built around the "Got milk?" theme. Radio ads remind people to stop for milk on their way home. Billboards are strategically placed near shopping malls and grocery and convenience stores. Point-of-purchase reminders and coupons are used in aisles containing cookies, cereals, cake mixes, and other companion foods. There have also been joint promotions with companion food companies as well as the Girl Scouts of America and their annual cookie drive.

The "Got milk?" campaign is widely recognized for its creative excellence and has met Jeff Manning's goal of stopping the decline in milk sales. Despite increasing milk prices in some parts of the state, per capita milk consumption has remained steady at about 23 gallons. The campaign has also been extended to the rest of the country. Dairy Management Inc., a group of dairy-product producers, has licensed many of the earlier TV spots for national airing and is also planning on using the new health benefit ads as well.

Sources: Alice Z. Cuneo, "New 'Got Milk?' Tactic: Got Health?" *Advertising Age,* April 19, 1999, p. 32; Paula Mergenhagen, "How 'Got Milk?' Got Sales," *Marketing Tools,* September 1996, pp. 4–7.

from the ad, what they think of its execution, or how they react to a slogan or theme. The creative team can gain insight into how a TV commercial might communicate its message by having members of the target market evaluate the ad in storyboard form. A **storyboard** is a series of drawings used to present the visual plan or layout of a proposed commercial. It contains a series of sketches of key frames or scenes along with the copy or audio portion for each scene (Exhibit 8–7).

Testing a commercial in storyboard form can be difficult because storyboards are too abstract for many consumers to understand. To make the creative layout more realistic and easier to evaluate, the agency may produce an **aniamatic,** a videotape of the storyboard along with an audio soundtrack. Storyboards and aniamatics are useful for research purposes as well as for presenting the creative idea to other agency personnel or to the client for discussion and approval.

At this stage of the process, the creative team is attempting to find the best creative approach or execution style before moving ahead with the campaign themes and going into actual production of the ad. The verification/revision process may include more formal, extensive pretesting of the ad before a final decision is made. Pretesting and related procedures are examined in detail in Chapter 19.

Advertising Campaigns

Most ads are part of a series of messages that make up an IMC or **advertising campaign,** which is a set of interrelated and coordinated marketing communication activities that center on a single theme or idea that appears in different media across a specified time period. Determining the unifying theme around which the campaign will be built is a critical part of the creative process, as it sets the tone for the individual ads and other forms of marketing communications that will be used. A **campaign theme** should be a strong idea, as it is the central message that will be communicated in all the advertising and other promotional activities.

Exhibit 8–7 Marketers can gain insight into consumers' reactions to a commercial by showing them a storyboard

SFX: CAR AND FOOT TRAFFIC AMBIENCE
VO: Why did the chicken cross the road? To open a 7/24 Savings Plan at San Diego Trust.
Because with $500 in savings . . . he can avoid getting henpecked by monthly charges on a checking account.
What's more, he can access his nest egg through our huge ATM network . . .
SFX: BANK AMBIENCE
. . . and round-the-clock phone service.
VO: And of course, the interest he'll earn on savings isn't just chicken feed.
So open a 7/24 Savings Plan at San Diego Trust
And give yourself a good reason to . . .
SFX: COCKA DOODLE DOO

Advertising campaign plans are short-term in nature and, like marketing and IMC plans, are done on an annual basis. However, the campaign themes are usually developed with the intention of being used for a longer time period. Unfortunately, many campaign themes last only a short time, usually because they are ineffective or market conditions and/or competitive developments in the marketplace change. IMC Perspective 8–3 discusses the problems companies and brands such as United Airlines, 7Up, and Miller Lite beer have been having in trying to develop effective ad campaigns.

IMC Perspective 8–3

Searching for the Right Campaign Theme

Some of the most memorable and successful advertising campaign themes of all times were those developed for 7Up, United Airlines, and Miller Lite beer. However, for various reasons such as changing consumer trends, competitive developments, market conditions, and other factors, these marketers decided to change their advertising themes, but they are finding that it is not easy coming up with new campaigns that are just as successful.

In the 1970s and 80s 7Up used the "Un-cola" theme, which positioned the brand as an alternative to market leaders Coke and Pepsi and helped make 7Up the third most popular soft drink in the United States for many years. However, as more noncola soft drinks entered the market, the "Un-cola" segment of the market became more crowded and competitive and the theme was not felt to be effective in differentiating 7Up from brands such as Sprite, Mt. Dew, Slice, Sunkist, and others. Cadbury Schweppes, which owns the brand, has tried a number of tactics to revive 7Up, from tweaking its taste to bringing back a version of the "Un" slogan by using the tagline "Are You an Un?" The campaign portrayed hip teens unmoved by an evil syndicate that wants to control their purchasing behavior and featured commercials asking "Are U an Un?" Many 7Up bottlers felt the ads were too edgy and took too long for consumers to understand, and the campaign was dropped after a year. In late 1999 7Up began running a new campaign built around the tagline "Make 7Up Yours" and starring comedian Orlando Jones. The new ads jauntily play on the "up yours" part of the slogan and show Jones as an enthusiastic 7Up marketer pulling out all the stops to boost the brand's popularity; for example, Jones projects the familiar red dot logo onto the moon, which then blows up.

In 1996 United Airlines changed agencies and abandoned its long-running "Fly the Friendly Skies" campaign theme. United's new agency, Fallon McElligott, developed a new campaign theme, "Rising," which focused on the problems airline travelers must endure and promised that United would rise above the hassles. While other airlines copied the mea culpa flavor of the "Rising" theme, the message was confusing to many United customers. Moreover, the company's employees, who own a majority of parent UAL Corp., didn't like it either, since it implicitly blamed them for travel problems. In late 1999 United asked Fallon to come up with something new that plays to the business traveler and touts United's product and service improvements. However, the client also wanted something more in line with its blockbuster "Friendly Skies" campaign of the past. In early 2000, the "Rising" theme was replaced with a nostalgic campaign built around the theme "United for a better journey." The emotional ads emphasize the theme of bringing people together and, at the same time, give a bow to the airline's employees for working to create a better journey. The ads will also highlight specific product or service enhancements such as the carrier's expanded leg room in economy class and its upgraded website.

In 1991, when its beer sales slowed, Miller Brewing dumped the two-decade-old "Tastes great/less filling" campaign, which featured famous ex-athletes and other celebrities arguing over whether the brand's main appeal was its great taste or the fact that it was less filling. What followed was an eight-year odyssey of advertising flip-flops that included adolescent humor and far-out wit to chase young male beer drinkers. Spots featuring cowboys singing good-bye to their beer on the way to the bathroom didn't help sell a lot of Miller Lite. During the later half of the 90s there were four different ad campaigns in five years for Lite. In 1999 Miller tried a version of an ad theme used for the brand 25 years ago with a campaign pitting celebrities against one another in mock arguments over the beer's merits. This campaign lasted less than a year as Miller switched agencies as well as ad themes. The latest campaign revives the 29-year-old "Miller Time" tagline that was used in the 1970s for the Miller High Life brand. The new ads from the Ogilvy & Mather agency use the theme "Grab a Miller Lite. It's Miller Time" and feature guys bonding over beer, sexy women, and humorous vignettes. They show friends doing things and enjoying their time together and center on the ritual and camaraderie of having a beer. The agency's creative director says: "When we get down to the heart and soul of the brand, it's always been about the occasion and the time guys spend together—the banter and the real talk."

It should be interesting to see if the new campaigns help 7Up sell more soft drinks, help Miller Lite sell more beer, and get more travelers to seek a better journey on United. If these campaigns are not successful, you can be certain the companies will send their ad agencies back to the drawing board to find ones that do move the sales needle.

Sources: Susan Carey, "United Grounds Its 'Rising' Campaign," *The Wall Street Journal*, January 7, 2000, p. B2; Betsy McKay, "7Up Drops 'Un' for a New Ad Campaign," *The Wall Street Journal*, September 15, 1999, p. B8; Kathryn Kranhold, "Looks Like It's Miller Time Again As the Brewer Goes Back to Basics," *The Wall Street Journal*, March 6, 2000, p. B10.

Figure 8–3 Examples of successful long-running advertising campaigns

Company or Brand	Campaign Theme
Nike	"Just do it."
Allstate Insurance	"You're in good hands with Allstate."
Hallmark cards	"When you care enough to send the very best."
De Beers	"A diamond is forever."
Intel	"Intel inside."
State Farm Insurance	"Like a good neighbor, State Farm is there."
Timex watches	"It takes a licking and keeps on ticking."
Dial soap	"Aren't you glad you use Dial? Don't you wish everyone did?"

While some marketers change their campaign themes often, a successful campaign theme may last for years. Philip Morris has been using the "Marlboro country" campaign for nearly 40 years, General Mills has positioned Wheaties cereal as the "Breakfast of Champions" for decades, and BMW has used the "ultimate driving machine" theme since 1974. Even though BMW has changed agencies several times over the past three decades, the classic tagline has been retained. Figure 8–3 lists some of the more enduring ad campaign themes.

Like any other area of the marketing and promotional process, the creative aspect of advertising and the development of the campaign theme is guided by specific goals and objectives. A creative strategy that focuses on what must be communicated will guide the selection of the campaign theme and the development of all messages used in the ad campaign. The creative strategy is based on several factors, including identification of the target audience; the basic problem, issue, or opportunity the advertising must address; the major selling idea or key benefit the message needs to communicate; and any supportive information that needs to be included in the ad. Once these factors are determined, a creative strategy statement should describe the message appeal and execution style that will be used. Many ad agencies outline these elements in a document known as the copy or creative platform.

Copy Platform

The written **copy platform** specifies the basic elements of the creative strategy. Different agencies may call this document a creative platform or work plan, creative brief, creative blueprint, or creative contract. The account representative or manager assigned to the account usually prepares the copy platform. In larger agencies, an individual from research or the strategic account planning department may write it. People from the agency team or group assigned to the account, including creative personnel as well as representatives from media and research, have input. The advertising manager and/or the marketing and brand managers from the client side ultimately approve the copy platform. Figure 8–4 shows a sample copy-platform outline that can be used to guide the creative process. Just as there are differ-

Figure 8–4 Copy platform outline

1. Basic problem or issue the advertising must address.
2. Advertising and communications objectives.
3. Target audience.
4. Major selling idea or key benefits to communicate.
5. Creative strategy statement (campaign theme, appeal, and execution technique to be used).
6. Supporting information and requirements.

ent names for the copy platform, there are variations in the outline and format used and in the level of detail included.

Several components of the copy platform were discussed in previous chapters. For example, Chapter 7 examined the DAGMAR model and showed how the setting of advertising objectives requires specifying a well-defined target audience and developing a communication task statement that spells out what message must be communicated to this audience. Determining what problem the product or service will solve or what issue must be addressed in the ad helps in establishing communication objectives for the campaign to accomplish. For example, in developing a campaign for Polaroid a few years ago, Goodby, Silverstein & Partners was faced with the challenge of redefining the relevancy of instant photography and bringing Polaroid cameras out of the closet and back into everyday use. Working with Polaroid's marketing personnel, the agency came up with the idea of focusing on an instant picture as a solution to a problem, an instant tool or "catalyst" to make something happen. The advertising message is designed to give people ideas about how to use their forgotten Polaroid cameras.

Two critical components of the copy platform are the development of the major selling idea and creative strategy development. These two steps are often the responsibility of the creative team or specialist and form the basis of the advertising campaign theme. For Polaroid, the major selling idea was "the picture is only the beginning," and the resulting campaign theme built around this idea was "See what develops." The creative strategy was to have each ad in the campaign tell a story in which a Polaroid camera sets off a chain reaction. For example, one of the TV commercials featured a harried architect in a meeting telling his wife on the phone that he can't possibly come home for lunch. But in a sultry voice she tells him to look in his briefcase, saying "I left you something this morning." He pulls out a Polaroid photo, his eyes widen, and he says, "I'll be there in 10 minutes." Another humorous spot from the campaign shows a dog, wrongfully being scolded for upsetting the trash while an evil-looking cat sneers from the other side of the kitchen. The owner leaves, and the cat goes for the trash once again. However, this time the dog takes a Polaroid snapshot of the cat, astride the trash with a chicken bone in its mouth, and then patiently waits, incriminating photo in mouth, as the door opens and the owner returns. "Oh dear," we hear as the picture fades (Exhibit 8–8).

Many copy platforms also include supporting information and requirements (brand identifications, disclaimers, and the like) that should appear in any advertising

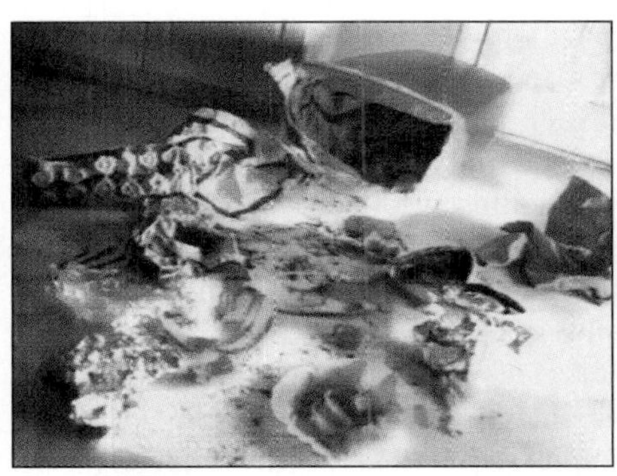

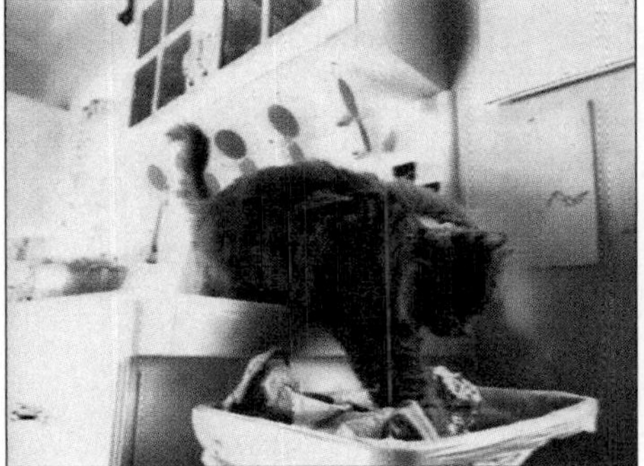

Exhibit 8–8 The major selling idea behind this Polaroid commercial is that the picture is only the beginning of the story

message. This information may be important in ensuring uniformity across various executions of the ads used in a campaign or in meeting any legal requirements. One of the major challenges for the creative team is determining the major selling idea that will be used as the basis of the campaign. We examine below some approaches often used for determining the major selling idea and campaign theme.

The Search for the Major Selling Idea

An important part of creative strategy is determining the central theme that will become the **major selling idea** of the ad campaign. As A. Jerome Jeweler states in his book *Creative Strategy in Advertising:*

> The major selling idea should emerge as the strongest singular thing you can say about your product or service. This should be the claim with the broadest and most meaningful appeal to your target audience. Once you determine this message, be certain you can live with it; be sure it stands strong enough to remain the central issue in every ad and commercial in the campaign.[22]

Some advertising experts argue that for an ad campaign to be effective it must contain a big idea that attracts the consumer's attention, gets a reaction, and sets the advertiser's product or service apart from the competition's. Well-known adman John O'Toole describes the *big idea* as "that flash of insight that synthesizes the purpose of the strategy, joins the product benefit with consumer desire in a fresh, involving way, brings the subject to life, and makes the reader or audience stop, look, and listen."[23]

Of course, the real challenge to the creative team is coming up with the big idea to use in the ad. Many products and services offer virtually nothing unique, and it can be difficult to find something interesting to say about them. David Ogilvy, generally considered one of the most creative advertising copywriters ever to work in the business, has stated:

> I doubt if more than one campaign in a hundred contains a big idea. I am supposed to be one of the more fertile inventors of big ideas, but in my long career as a copywriter I have not had more than 20, if that.[24]

While really great ideas in advertising are difficult to come by, there are many big ideas that became the basis of very creative, successful advertising campaigns. Classic examples include "We try harder," which positioned Avis as the underdog car-rental company that provided better service than Hertz; the "Pepsi generation" theme and subsequent variations like "the taste of a new generation" and "GenerationNext"; the "Be all you can be" theme used in recruitment ads for the U.S. Army; and Wendy's "Where's the beef?" which featured the late, gravelly voiced Clara Peller delivering the classic line that helped make the fast-food chain a household name. More recent big ideas that have resulted in effective advertising campaigns include the "Intel inside" campaign for Intel microprocessors that go in personal computers; Nike's "Just do it"; the "It keeps going and going" theme for Energizer batteries, featuring the pink bunny; and the "Like a rock" theme for Chevrolet trucks.

Big ideas are important in business-to-business advertising as well. For example, Beacon Manufacturing Co. was unimpressed with the way blankets were advertised and wanted to do something different to get the attention of retail stores' buyers and merchandise managers. Beacon and its agency, Easterby & Associates, leveraged the popularity of the company's vice president of sales, Ted Smith, into an advertising campaign. "Adventures of Teddy" elevated Smith into an Everyman willing to go the extra mile to prove his product's superiority. The ads have shown Smith being tossed in the air by a Beacon blanket, hanging from a helicopter with a Beacon blanket, using one as a parachute, and keeping sharks at bay with one. The idea resulted in great advertising that has helped Beacon increase sales three times the industry average (Exhibit 8–9).

It is difficult to pinpoint the inspiration for a big idea or to teach advertising people how to find one. However, several approaches can guide the creative team's

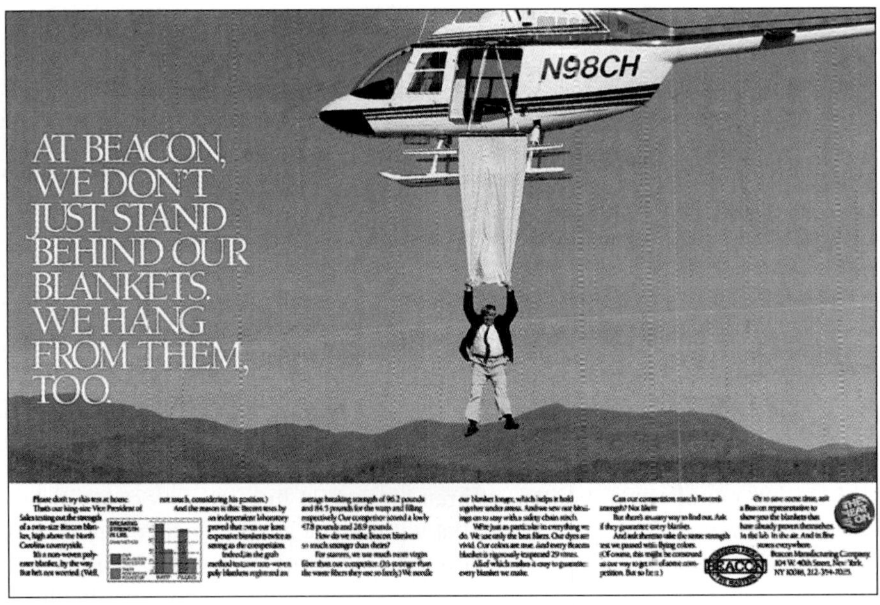

N98CH
AT BEACON, WE DON'T JUST STAND BEHIND OUR BLANKETS. WE HANG FROM THEM, TOO.
BEACON

Exhibit 8–9 The "Adventures of Teddy" campaign for Beacon blankets is an excellent example of a big idea in business-to-business advertising

search for a major selling idea and offer solutions for developing effective advertising. Some of the best-known approaches follow:

- Using a unique selling proposition.
- Creating a brand image.
- Finding the inherent drama.
- Positioning.

Unique Selling Proposition

The concept of the **unique selling proposition (USP)** was developed by Rosser Reeves, former chair of the Ted Bates agency, and is described in his influential book *Reality in Advertising.* Reeves noted three characteristics of unique selling propositions:

1. Each advertisement must make a proposition to the consumer. Not just words, not just product puffery, not just show-window advertising. Each advertisement must say to each reader: "Buy this product and you will get this benefit."
2. The proposition must be one that the competition either cannot or does not offer. It must be unique either in the brand or in the claim.
3. The proposition must be strong enough to move the mass millions, that is, pull over new customers to your brand.[25]

Reeves said the attribute claim or benefit that forms the basis of the USP should dominate the ad and be emphasized through repetitive advertising. An example of advertising based on a USP is the campaign for Colgate's new Total toothpaste (Exhibit 8–10).The brand's unique ingredients make it the only toothpaste that provides long-lasting protection and has been proved effective in fighting cavities between brushings.

For Reeves's approach to work, there must be a truly unique product or service attribute, benefit, or inherent advantage that can be used in the claim. The approach may require considerable research on the product and consumers, not only to determine the USP but also to document the claim. As we shall see in Chapter 21, the Federal Trade Commission objects to advertisers' making claims of superiority or uniqueness without providing supporting data. Also, some companies have sued their competitors for making unsubstantiated uniqueness claims.[26]

Advertisers must also consider whether the unique selling proposition affords them a *sustainable competitive advantage* that competitors

Exhibit 8–10 This Colgate Total ad uses a unique selling proposition

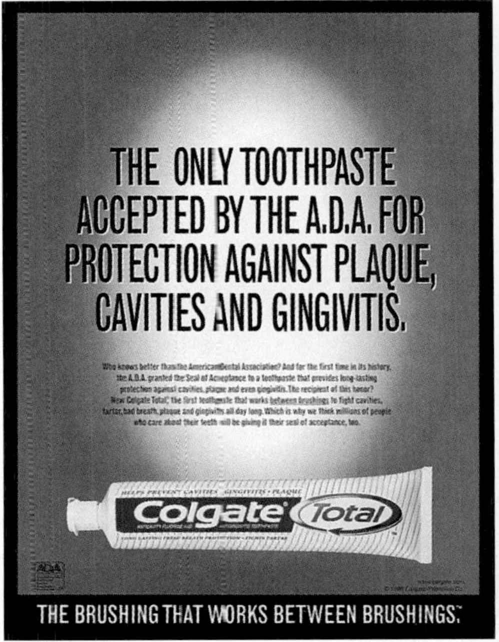

THE ONLY TOOTHPASTE ACCEPTED BY THE A.D.A. FOR PROTECTION AGAINST PLAQUE, CAVITIES AND GINGIVITIS.
Colgate Total
THE BRUSHING THAT WORKS BETWEEN BRUSHINGS.

cannot easily copy. In the package-goods field in particular, companies quickly match a brand feature for feature, so advertising based on USPs becomes obsolete. For example, a few years ago Procter & Gamble invented a combination shampoo and conditioner to rejuvenate its struggling Pert brand. The reformulated brand was called Pert Plus and its market share rose from 2 to 12 percent, making it the leading shampoo. But competing brands like Revlon and Suave quickly launched their own two-in-one formula products.[27]

Creating a Brand Image

In many product and service categories, competing brands are so similar that it is very difficult to find or create a unique attribute or benefit to use as the major selling idea. Many of the package-goods products that account for most of the advertising dollars spent in the United States are difficult to differentiate on a functional or performance basis. The creative strategy used to sell these products is based on the development of a strong, memorable identity for the brand through **image advertising.**

David Ogilvy popularized the idea of brand image in his famous book *Confessions of an Advertising Man.* Ogilvy said that with image advertising, "every advertisement should be thought of as a contribution to the complex symbol which is the brand image." He argued that the image or personality of the brand is particularly important when brands are similar:

> The greater the similarity between brands, the less part reason plays in brand selection. There isn't any significant difference between the various brands of whiskey, or cigarettes, or beer. They are all about the same. And so are the cake mixes and the detergents and the margarines. The manufacturer who dedicates his advertising to building the most sharply defined personality for his brand will get the largest share of the market at the highest profit. By the same token, the manufacturers who will find themselves up the creek are those shortsighted opportunists who siphon off their advertising funds for promotions.[28]

Image advertising has become increasingly popular and is used as the main selling idea for a variety of products and services, including soft drinks, liquor, cigarettes, cars, airlines, financial services, perfume/colognes, and clothing. Many consumers wear designer jeans or Ralph Lauren polo shirts or drink certain brands of beer or soft drinks because of the image of these brands. The key to successful image advertising is developing an image that will appeal to product users. For example, the sports apparel company No Fear uses this type of advertising to create a unique image for the brand as representing the outer limits of human performance. Ads like the one in Exhibit 8–11 have helped create this image for No Fear.

Exhibit 8–11 Advertising for No Fear creates a unique image for the brand as representing the outer limits of human performance

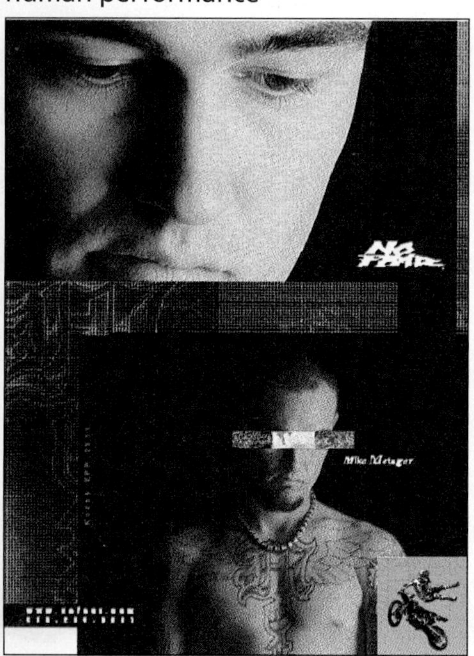

Finding the Inherent Drama

Another approach to determining the major selling idea is finding the **inherent drama** or characteristic of the product that makes the consumer purchase it. The inherent drama approach expresses the advertising philosophy of Leo Burnett, founder of the Leo Burnett agency in Chicago. Burnett said inherent drama "is often hard to find but it is always there, and once found it is the most interesting and believable of all advertising appeals."[29] He believed advertising should be based on a foundation of consumer benefits with an emphasis on the dramatic element in expressing those benefits.

Burnett advocated a down-home type of advertising that presents the message in a warm and realistic way. Some of the more famous ads developed by his agency using the inherent drama approach are for McDonald's, Maytag appliances, Kellogg's cereals, and Hallmark cards. Notice how the Hallmark commercial shown in Exhibit 8–12 uses this approach to deliver a poignant message.

Positioning

The concept of *positioning* as a basis for advertising strategy was introduced by Jack Trout and Al Ries in the early 1970s and has become a popular basis of creative development.[30] The basic idea is that advertising is used to establish or "position" the product or service in a particular place in the consumer's mind. Positioning is done for

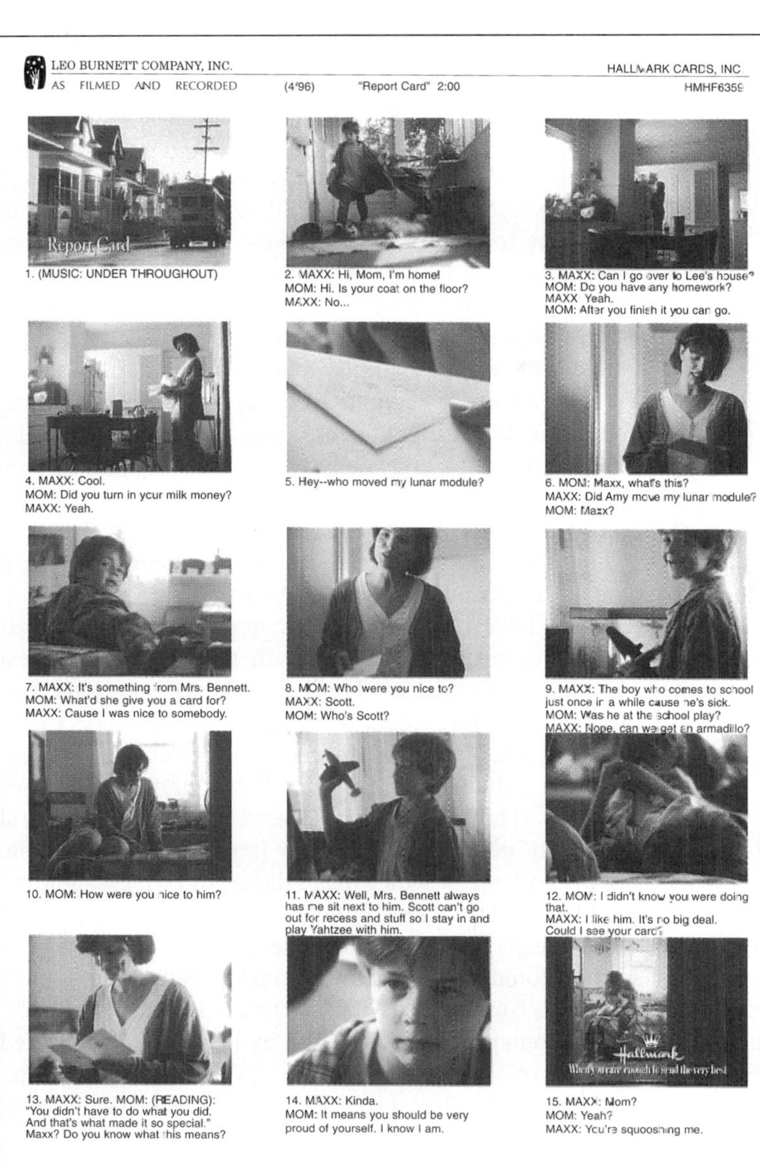

Exhibit 8–12 This Hallmark commercial uses an inherent drama approach

companies as well as for brands. For example, the ad shown in Exhibit 8–13 is part of a campaign designed to reinforce 3M's image and position as an innovative company.

Trout and Ries originally described positioning as the image consumers had of the brand in relation to competing brands in the product or service category, but the concept has been expanded beyond direct competitive positioning. As discussed in Chapter 2, products can be positioned on the basis of product attributes, price/quality, usage or application, product users, or product class. Any of these can spark a major selling idea that becomes the basis of the creative strategy and results in the brand's occupying a particular place in the minds of the target audience. Since positioning can be done on the basis of a distinctive attribute, the positioning and unique selling proposition approaches can overlap. Positioning approaches have been used as the foundation for a number of successful creative strategies.

Positioning is often the basis of a firm's creative strategy when it has multiple brands competing in the same market. For example, Procter & Gamble markets more than 10 brands of laundry detergent—and positions each one differently, as shown in Figure 8–5.

The USP, brand image, inherent drama, and positioning approaches are often used as the basis of the creative strategy for ad campaigns. These creative styles have become associated with some of the most successful creative minds in advertising and their agencies.[31] However, many other creative approaches are available.

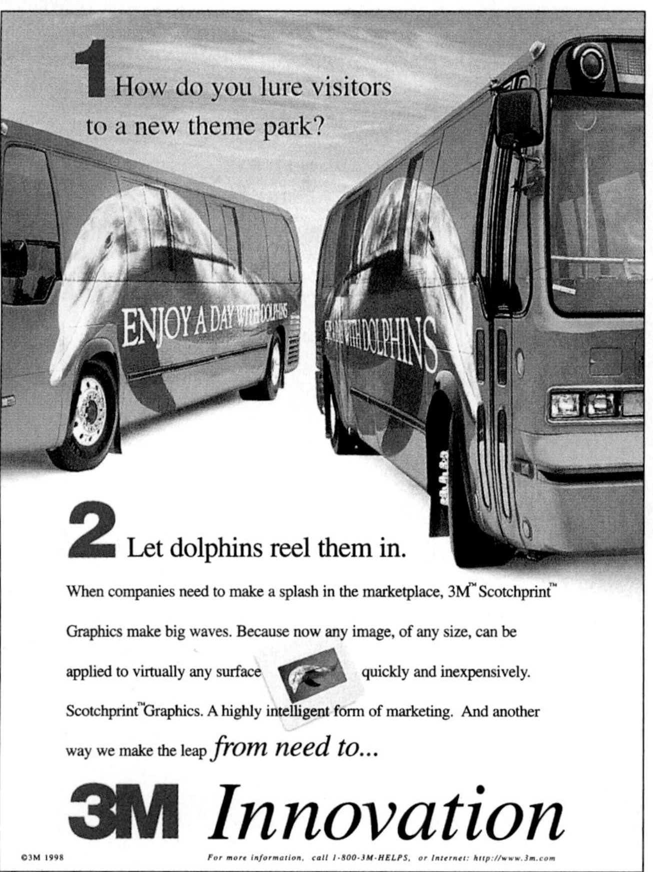

1 How do you lure visitors to a new theme park?
2 Let dolphins reel them in.
When companies need to make a splash in the marketplace, 3M™ Scotchprint™ Graphics make big waves. Because now any image, of any size, can be applied to virtually any surface quickly and inexpensively.
Scotchprint™ Graphics. A highly intelligent form of marketing. And another way we make the leap *from need to...*
3M Innovation
©3M 1998
For more information, call 1-800-3M-HELPS, or Internet: http://www.3m.com

Exhibit 8–13 This ad positions 3M as an innovative company

Some of the more contemporary advertising visionaries who have had a major influence on modern-day advertising include Hal Riney of Hal Riney & Partners, Lee Clow and Jay Chiat of TBWA/Chiat/Day, Dan Wieden of Wieden & Kennedy, and Jeff Goodby and Rich Silverstein of Goodby, Silverstein & Partners. In describing today's creative leaders, Anthony Vagnoni of *Advertising Age* writes: "The modern creative kings don't write books, rarely give interviews or lay out their theories on advertising. They've endorsed no set of rules, professed no simple maxims like Mr. Ogilvy's famous "When you don't have anything to say, sing it." If pronouncements and books are out the window, what's replaced them is a conscious desire to lift the intelligence level of advertising. Today's leaders see advertising as an uplifting social force, as a way to inspire and entertain."[32]

Goodby and Silverstein note: "Advertising works best when it sneaks into people's lives, when it doesn't look or feel like advertising. It's about treating people at their best, as opposed to dealing with them at their lowest common denominator." They describe their creative formula as doing intelligent work that the public likes to see and that, at the same time, has a sales pitch.[33] Lee Clow says: "No rule book will tell you how to target the masses anymore. The best of us understand the sociocultural realities of people and how they interact with the media. If we didn't, we couldn't make the kinds of messages that people would be able to connect with."[34]

Specific agencies are by no means limited to any one creative approach. For example, the famous "Marlboro country" campaign, a classic example of image advertising, was developed by Leo Burnett Co. Many different agencies have followed the unique selling proposition approach advocated by Rosser Reeves at Ted Bates. The challenge to the creative specialist or team is to find a major selling idea—whether it is based on a unique selling proposition, brand image, inherent drama, position in the market, or some other approach—and use it as a guide in developing an effective creative strategy.

In their search for a big idea, advertisers consider many different creative options that might grab consumers' attention. However, as discussed in Ethical Perspective 8–4, many people believe some advertisers are going too far in their efforts to break through the advertising clutter and have an impact on consumers.

Figure 8–5 A P&G detergent for every washday need

Brand	Positioning
Tide	Tough, powerful cleaner
Cheer	Tough cleaner and color protection
Bold	Detergent plus fabric softener
Gain	Sunshine scent and odor-removing formula
Era	Stain pretreatment and stain removal
Dash	Value brand
Oxydol	Bleach-boosted formula, whitening
Solo	Detergent and fabric softener in liquid form
Dreft	Outstanding cleaning for baby clothes, safe for tender skin
Ivory Snow	Fabric and skin safety on baby clothes and fine washables
Ariel	Tough cleaner, aimed at Hispanics

Ethical Perspective 8–4

Calvin Klein and Benetton Continue to Create Controversies with Shock Ads

Many creative people complain that advertising has become bland and boring because marketers are too concerned about offending someone and restrict themselves to ads that are politically correct. However, not all advertisers are worried about their ads offending consumers; some are even deliberately creating controversial ads. Critics call this genre *shock advertising* and claim that its intent is to elicit attention for a brand name by jolting consumers.

Two companies best known for using shock ads are Calvin Klein and Benetton, both of which do their advertising in-house. For Calvin Klein, shock tactics and controversy go hand in hand. In 1980, Klein caused an outcry with two of its jeans commercials: "The Feminist," featuring a teenage Brook Shields saying, "Nothing comes between me and my Calvins," and a spot called "The Teenager," in which a young model proclaims, "If my jeans could talk, I'd be ruined." Although some TV stations banned the ads, a spokesperson for Klein noted that "jeans are about sex" and continued using shocking ads.

In 1995 Klein pushed the envelope too far and created one of the greatest furors in the history of American advertising with the "kiddy porn" campaign for CK jeans, which featured young models who appeared to be around 15 years old in provocative poses. Public outcry, led by the American Family Association, led to an investigation whether Klein and its in-house agency, CRK, had violated child pornography laws. The Justice Department found no evidence of wrongdoing. However, Klein still had to contend with threats of consumer boycotts of stores where CK Jeans were sold, retailers who refused to stock the brand, and intense criticism from the media. In their book *Under the Radar: Talking to Today's Cynical Consumer,* Jonathan Bond and Richard Kirshenbaum criticize the campaign and write: "The kiddy porn ads vaulted right over the edge and into an abyss that made even the trendsetters feel uncomfortable. . . . Klein entered the land of taboo, which elicited responses that ranged from anger to outrage. The juxtaposition of children and sex is a subject of such angst and moral disgrace with most Americans that we are just not willing to accept it as a vehicle for anything commercial. We are offended by not only the poor taste displayed in using underage models, but by the almost instant recognition that Calvin Klein was tapping this vein purely for publicity reasons." Although the campaign was canceled not long after it first aired, it was still considered a sales success and Calvin Klein continues to push the shock envelope with many of its ads.

Benetton, the Italian-based clothing manufacturer whose ads are well known worldwide for their shock value, says it has a different reason for using this type of advertising. Benetton's creative director, Oliviero Toscani, says the controversial images are designed to raise public awareness of social issues and position the company as a cutting-edge, socially conscious marketer.

Benetton has been regarded as a renegade of the advertising world since 1989, when it ran a print ad featuring a black woman nursing a white baby. Other shock ads have featured such images as a black man's hand handcuffed to a white man's, a priest kissing a nun, an AIDS patient and his family moments before his death, and the blood-soaked uniform of a young soldier killed in the war in Bosnia. In its latest shock campaign, Benetton joined Italy's offensive against the death penalty with ads that show piercing portraits of American death-row inmates in prison uniforms staring into the camera over the words "Sentenced to Death." The prisoner's name, date of birth, crime, and expected method of execution follow. Toscani visited prisons across the United States for over two years to create the series, called "Life on Death Row." He said the goal of the campaign, which began running on billboards worldwide in early 2000, is to foster debate on capital punishment, even at the cost of losing American customers.

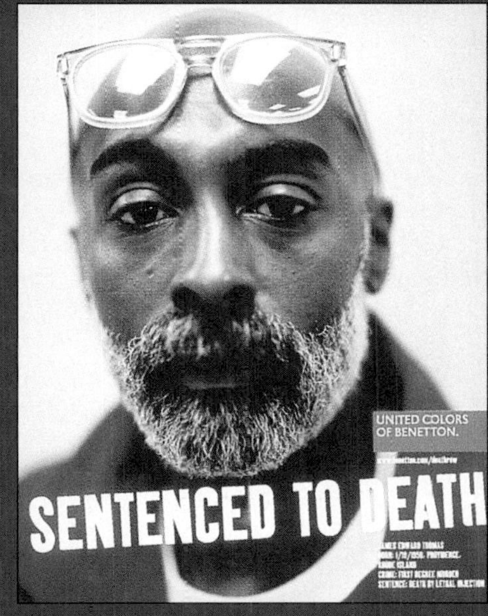

Critics argue that the real goal of the Benetton ads is to generate publicity. Some accuse Benetton of exploiting human suffering to sell its clothing. The Benetton ads are controversial even in more liberal European countries, and advertising self-regulatory bodies in Britain, France, and Spain have condemned some of the ads and urged magazines in these countries to reject them. A Benetton spokesman has stated: "Yes, we mean to shock some people with our ads. But people who are shocked by this have been living in a cocoon. They need to be shocked into seeing what's going on in the world."

It is likely that Benetton will continue breaking the rules and shocking people with its advertising. Of course, it may also get them to think about some of the world's problems in the process.

Sources: Elizabeth Greenspan, "Ads Take on Capital Punishment," *San Diego Union-Tribune*, January 9, 2000; Jonathan Bond and Richard Kirshenbaum, *Under the Radar: Talking to Today's Cynical Consumer* (New York: Wiley, 1998); Robert Gustafson, Johan Yssel, and Lea Witta, "Ad Agency Employees Give View on Calvin Klein, Benetton Ads," *Marketing News*, September 23, 1996, p. 16.

Summary

The creative development and execution of the advertising message are a crucial part of a firm's integrated marketing communications program and are often the key to the success of a marketing campaign. Marketers generally turn to ad agencies to develop, prepare, and implement their creative strategy since these agencies are specialists in the creative function of advertising. The creative specialist or team is responsible for developing an effective way to communicate the marketer's message to the customer. Other individuals on both the client and the agency sides work with the creative specialists to develop the creative strategy, implement it, and evaluate its effectiveness.

The challenge facing the writers, artists, and others who develop ads is to be creative and come up with fresh, unique, and appropriate ideas that can be used as solutions to communications problems. Creativity in advertising is a process of several stages, including preparation, incubation, illumination, verification, and revision. Various sources of information are available to help the creative specialists determine the best campaign theme, appeal, or execution style.

Creative strategy development is guided by specific goals and objectives and is based on a number of factors, including the target audience, the basic problem the advertising must address, the objectives the message seeks to accomplish, and the major selling idea or key benefit the advertiser wants to communicate. These factors are generally stated in a copy platform, which is a work plan used to guide development of the ad campaign. An important part of creative strategy is determining the major selling idea that will become the central theme of the campaign. There are several approaches to doing this, including using a unique selling proposition, creating a brand image, looking for inherent drama in the brand, and positioning.

Key Terms

creative strategy, 245
creative tactics, 245
advertising creativity, 249
account planning, 254
general preplanning input, 255
product/service-specific preplanning input, 255
problem detection, 256
focus groups, 257
storyboard, 259
aniamatic, 259
advertising campaign, 259
campaign theme, 259
copy platform, 262
major selling idea, 264
unique selling proposition (USP), 265
image advertising, 266
inherent drama, 266

Discussion Questions

1. The opening vignette to the chapter discusses the debate over creative versus hard-sell advertising. Discuss the arguments for and against each perspective. Which do you support?

2. Discuss the role of creativity in advertising. Who should be responsible for judging it—clients or agency creative personnel?

3. Explain what is meant by creative strategy and creative tactics. Find an example of an advertising campaign and evaluate the creative strategy and tactics used in the ads.

4. Review the various advertising campaign themes used by Burger King that are shown in Figure 8–1. Why do you think Burger King has had such a difficult time finding an effective campaign theme? What is your opinion of the "Going the Distance" theme which began running in late 1999?

5. What is your opinion of advertising awards, such as the Cannes Lions, that are based solely on creativity? If you were a marketer looking for an agency, would you take these creative awards into consideration in your agency evaluation process? Why or why not?

6. Find an example of a print ad that you think is very creative and an ad you feel is dull and boring. Evaluate each ad from a creative perspective. What makes one ad creative and the other bland?

7. Assume you have been assigned to work on the advertising campaign for a new soft drink. Describe the various types of general and product-specific preplanning input you might provide to the creative team.

8. Find an example of an advertising campaign theme that has been used for a long time. Why do you think the advertiser has been able to use this theme so long?

9. IMC Perspective 8–3 discusses the problems 7Up, United Airlines and Miller Lite beer have had in developing successful advertising campaigns. Choose one of these companies or brands and evaluate the various ad campaigns that have been used for it. Find an example of an ad from the current campaign and evaluate it.

10. Find an example of an ad or campaign that you think reflects one of the approaches used to develop a major selling idea such as unique selling proposition, brand image, inherent drama, or positioning. Discuss how the major selling idea is used in this ad or campaign.

11. Evaluate the use of shock advertising by companies such as Calvin Klein and Benetton. Why do you think these companies use this type of advertising?

12. What is your opinion of Benetton's latest advertising campaign that features portraits of death-row inmates? Do you agree with Benetton's position that it is trying to raise social consciousness of controversial issues such as the death penalty or do you feel that the campaign is being used to generate publicity for the company?

Chapter Nine

Creative Strategy: Implementation and Evaluation

Chapter Objectives

- To analyze various types of appeals that can be used in the development and implementation of an advertising message.
- To analyze the various creative execution styles that advertisers can use and the advertising situations where they are most appropriate.
- To analyze various tactical issues involved in the creation of print advertising and TV commercials.
- To consider how clients evaluate the creative work of their agencies and discuss guidelines for the evaluation and approval process.

Jack's Back and So Are Jack in the Box Sales

Jack in the Box, Inc., operates and franchises more than 1,550 fast-food restaurants in 14 states in the West, Southwest, and Southeast, and is the nation's fifth largest hamburger chain. In January 1993, an outbreak of food-related illness was traced to some Jack in the Box locations in Seattle; it resulted in hundreds of people becoming ill and the death of four children. Although the real source of the problem was a meat supplier, the crisis and publicity surrounding it nearly ruined the company. Sales slumped following the outbreak and Jack in the Box reported a loss for nine consecutive quarters. The company, which was known as Foodmaker, Inc., at the time, responded by instituting a stringent food-safety program that is now considered the best in the industry. However, the company was also looking for a way to reverse its declining sales and return to profitability.

In 1994, following a management restructuring and growing competitive pressure from national and regional fast-food chains, Foodmaker dropped its agency of eight years, which had been running advertising that was narrowly focused on specific products and promotions and gave little attention to brand image. Four agencies were invited to pitch the account, and TBWA/Chiat/Day prevailed. While preparing for its presentation, the agency worked closely with Jack in the Box's vice president of marketing communications to define its strategy. The research the agency conducted among fast-food patrons showed that consumers really did not understand what Jack in the Box stood for as a brand, and the product- and promotion-focused advertising made this even less clear. The consumer research revealed that many Jack in the Box customers yearned for the good old days, when a large, colorful, plastic clown head welcomed them to the restaurant's drive-throughs and asked, "Can I take your order?" The research also

showed that consumers remembered a 1980 commercial in which the clown icon was literally blown up in an effort to signal a move away from the company's youth-oriented image and a focus on menu items that appealed to adult tastes.

Jack in the Box and its new agency decided that they needed to metaphorically hang an "Under New Management" sign on the company in order to win back consumer confidence. Chiat's creative director, Dick Sittig, conceived the idea of bringing a revamped Jack in the Box clown character back to life with the return of Jack, the company's founder. Sittig drew up a creative strategy for a new campaign, "Jack's Back and he's going to make Jack in the Box better than ever." Jack would be an irreverent CEO spokesperson who would represent change, reinstill consumer confidence, and be more in tune with the 18- to 34-year-old heavy fast-food users' sense of humor.

Foodmaker launched the "Jack's Back" campaign with a commercial in which Jack returns to the company's headquarters and blows up the boardroom. Jack, who is nearly 7 feet tall and usually clad in business attire, has an oversized Ping-Pong ball for a head, capped with a pointed yellow hat, and a permanent smile from ear to ear. The campaign was an instant success, and Jack has become a cultural icon with the target audience of 18- to 34-year-old males and with women and children as well. The company established an 800 number so that consumers could talk to Jack and purchase "Jack's Back" T-shirts and other items. In one of the ads, Jack-head antenna balls were brought to life to help push the grilled sourdough burger. Consumers bought more than a million of the antenna balls at over $1 each, and the balls sold out at many restaurants in a few days. Greg Joumas, the company's new vice president of marketing communications, says people think Jack is a real person. "As in magic, we've attained a suspension of disbelief."

In 1997, TBWA/Chiat/Day resigned from the Jack in the Box account to take over the advertising for one of the company's fast-food competitors, Taco Bell. However, Dick Sittig formed a new agency, Kowloon Wholesale Seafood Co., and took the creative and account portions of the business with him. Sittig is a one-man creative powerhouse for Jack in the Box. Not only does he serve as the sole copywriter, art director, and director of the campaign, but he's the voice of Jack. His ads have won many awards including gold and silver Lions at Cannes, Clios, and New York Art Directors Pencils. Jack has been used in a variety of situations, from new product intros and pricing ads to image and branding-focused messages. Sittig says, "Since Jack is a character and not a real person, he's not confined to the restaurant. That lets us keep him fresh, and it keeps the audience guessing."

Since the campaign began, Foodmaker has reported 18 consecutive quarters of growth and record profits. Consumer research confirms that Jack has created brand awareness and increased the brand's appeal. The campaign has been so successful in creating brand identity that in late 1999 parent company Foodmaker decided to change its corporate name to Jack in the Box Inc. The company received a tremendous amount of publicity with the name change, and Jack even rang the closing bell on the New York Stock Exchange the day the company's new ticker symbol appeared. Jack in the Box plans to open more than 500 new restaurants in the next five years, many of them in new markets in the Southeast, and ultimately to become a national chain. As the company moves into new markets such as Nashville, Charlotte, and Baton Rouge, the challenge will be introducing the Jack character where he is completely unknown. Sittig says he has scouted the new markets for ideas unique to each one and promises "Jack will be hanging with the locals."

Sources: Angela Dawson, "Hitting the Jackpot," *Adweek,* October 4, 1999, pp. 20–22; Frank Green, "Foodmaker's New Name Has Familiar Ring," *San Diego Union Tribune,* July 20, 1999, pp. C1, 3.

In Chapter 8, we discussed the importance of advertising creativity and examined the various steps in the creative process. We focused on determining what the advertising message should communicate. This chapter focuses on *how* the message will be executed. It examines various appeals and execution styles that can be used to develop the ad and tactical issues involved in the design and production of effective advertising messages. We conclude by presenting some guidelines clients can use to evaluate the creative work of their agencies.

Appeals and Execution Styles

The **advertising appeal** refers to the approach used to attract the attention of consumers and/or to influence their feelings toward the product, service, or cause. An advertising appeal can also be viewed as "something that moves people, speaks to their wants or needs, and excites their interest."[1] The **creative execution style** is the way a particular appeal is turned into an advertising message presented to the consumer. According to William Weilbacher:

> The appeal can be said to form the underlying content of the advertisement, and the execution the way in which that content is presented. Advertising appeals and executions are usually independent of each other; that is, a particular appeal can be executed in a variety of ways and a particular means of execution can be applied to a variety of advertising appeals. Advertising appeals tend to adapt themselves to all media, whereas some kinds of executional devices are more adaptable to some media than others.[2]

Advertising Appeals

Hundreds of different appeals can be used as the basis for advertising messages. At the broadest level, these approaches are generally broken into two categories: informational/rational appeals and emotional appeals. In this section, we focus on ways to use rational and emotional appeals as part of a creative strategy. We also consider how rational and emotional appeals can be combined in developing the advertising message.

Informational/Rational Appeals

Informational/rational appeals focus on the consumer's practical, functional, or utilitarian need for the product or service and emphasize features of a product or service and/or the benefits or reasons for owning or using a particular brand. The content of these messages emphasizes facts, learning, and the logic of persuasion.[3] Rational-based appeals tend to be informative, and advertisers using them generally attempt to convince consumers that their product or service has a particular attribute(s) or provides a specific benefit that satisfies their needs. Their objective is to persuade the target audience to buy the brand because it is the best available or does a better job of meeting consumers' needs. For example, the Quaker Oats company uses a rational appeal in noting how fiber from oatmeal may help reduce the risk of heart disease (Exhibit 9–1).

Exhibit 9–1 Quaker Oatmeal uses a rational appeal to promote the health benefits of oatmeal

Now he has another reason to smile!

Heart healthy news announced by the FDA.
Soluble fiber from oatmeal, as part of a low saturated fat, low cholesterol diet, may reduce the risk of heart disease.

QUAKER OATMEAL

QUAKER OATS

Quick'n Hearty

Quaker Oatmeal. Oh, what those Oats can do.™
©1997 QOC
http://www.quakeroatmeal.com

Many rational motives can be used as the basis for advertising appeals, including comfort, convenience, economy, health, and sensory benefits such as touch, taste, and smell. Other rational motives or purchase criteria commonly used in advertising include quality, dependability, durability, efficiency, efficacy, and performance. The particular features, benefits, or evaluative criteria that are important to consumers and can serve as the basis of an informational/rational appeal vary from one product or service category to another as well as among various market segments.

Weilbacher identified several types of advertising appeals that fall under the category of rational approaches, among them feature, competitive advantage, favorable price, news, and product/service popularity appeals.

Ads that use a *feature appeal* focus on the dominant traits of the product or service. These ads tend to be highly informative and present the customer with a number of important product attributes or features that will lead to favorable attitudes and can be used

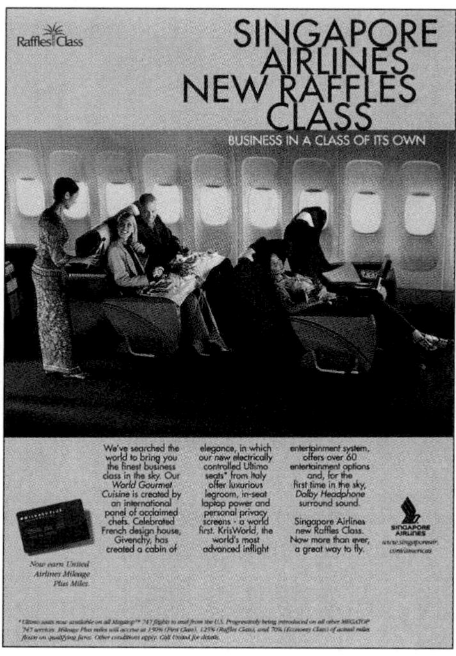

Exhibit 9–2 Singapore Airlines uses a feature appeal ad to promote its new Raffles class

Exhibit 9–3 A price appeal is used to promote Denny's breakfast deals

as the basis for a rational purchase decision. Technical and high-involvement products often use this advertising approach. This type of appeal can also be used for a service. Notice how the Singapore Airlines ad in Exhibit 9–2 focuses on the various features of its new Raffles class of service.

When a *competitive advantage appeal* is used, the advertiser makes either a direct or an indirect comparison to another brand (or brands) and usually claims superiority on one or more attributes. This type of appeal was discussed in Chapter 6 under comparative advertising.

A *favorable price appeal* makes the price offer the dominant point of the message. Price appeal advertising is used most often by retailers to announce sales, special offers, or low everyday prices. Price appeal ads are often used by national advertisers during recessionary times. Many fast-food chains have made price an important part of their marketing strategy through promotional deals and "value menus" or lower overall prices, and their advertising strategy is designed to communicate this. Many other types of advertisers use price appeals as well. In Exhibit 9–3, Denny's restaurants use a price appeal to promote big breakfast deals.

News appeals are those in which some type of news or announcement about the product, service, or company dominates the ad. This type of appeal can be used for a new product or service or to inform consumers of significant modifications or improvements. This appeal works best when a company has important news it wants to communicate to its target market. The Quaker Oatmeal ad shown in Exhibit 9–1, which announced the news from the Food and Drug Administration regarding the health benefits of eating oatmeal, is an example of a news appeal.

Product/service popularity appeals stress the popularity of a product or service by pointing out the number of consumers who use the brand, the number who have switched to it, the number of experts who recommend it, or its leadership position in the market. The main point of this advertising appeal is that the wide use of the brand proves its quality or value and other customers should consider using it. The Excedrin ad in Exhibit 9–4 uses this type of advertising appeal.

Exhibit 9–4 This ad promotes the popularity of Excedrin among doctors

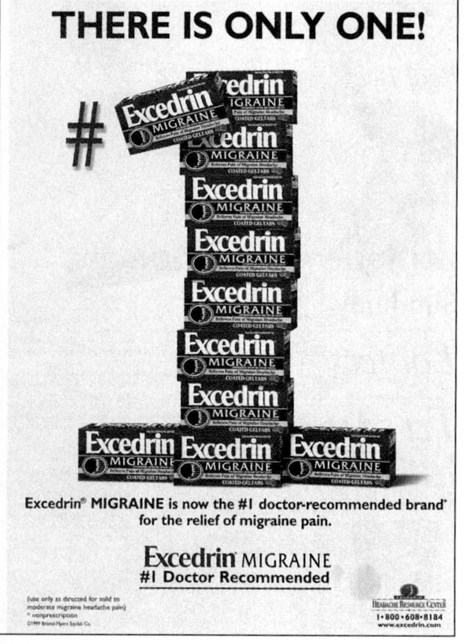

Emotional Appeals

Emotional appeals relate to the customers' social and/or psychological needs for purchasing a product or service. Many of consumers' motives for their purchase decisions are emotional, and their feelings about a brand can be more important than knowledge of its features or attributes. Advertisers for many products and services view rational, information-based appeals as dull. Many advertisers believe appeals to consumers' emotions work better at selling brands that do not differ markedly from competing brands, since rational differentiation of them is difficult.[4]

Many feelings or needs can serve as the basis for advertising appeals designed to influence consumers on an emotional level, as shown in Figure 9–1. These appeals are based on the psychological states or feelings directed to the self (such as pleasure or excitement), as well as those with a more social orientation (such as status or recognition).

Advertisers can use emotional appeals in many ways in their creative strategy. Kamp and Macinnis note that commercials often rely on the concept of *emotional integration,* whereby they portray the characters in the ad as experiencing an emotional benefit or outcome from using a product or service.[5] Ads using humor, sex, and other appeals that are very entertaining, arousing, upbeat, and/or exciting can affect the emotions of consumers and put them in a favorable frame of mind. Many TV advertisers use poignant ads that bring a lump to viewers' throats. Hallmark, AT&T, Kodak, and Oscar Mayer often create commercials that evoke feelings of warmth, nostalgia, and/or sentiment.

Marketers use emotional appeals in hopes that the positive feeling they evoke will transfer to the brand and/or company. Research shows that positive mood states and feelings created by advertising can have a favorable effect on consumers' evaluations of a brand.[6] Studies also show that emotional advertising is better remembered than nonemotional messages.[7]

McDonald's changed its advertising strategy recently and is putting more emotion in its commercials to evoke a feel-good connection with consumers. The company's senior vice president of marketing explained the change by stating, "Over the last couple of years, we had been very good on the humor side but we really hadn't done a lot to reach and touch people with heart-warming or wholesome or romantic or heart-tugging emotions."[8] One of the heart-tugging commercials, called "New Math," shows a big sister teaching her brother how to count as

Figure 9–1 Bases for emotional appeals

Personal States or Feelings	Social-Based Feelings
Safety	Recognition
Security	Status
Fear	Respect
Love	Involvement
Affection	Embarrassment
Happiness	Affiliation/belonging
Joy	Rejection
Nostalgia	Acceptance
Sentiment	Approval
Excitement	
Arousal/stimulation	
Sorrow/grief	
Pride	
Achievement/accomplishment	
Self-esteem	
Actualization	
Pleasure	
Ambition	
Comfort	

only an older sibling can. Using McDonald's french fries as an aid, while her mother isn't watching, she methodically counts out a big pile for herself and a small one for her increasingly distressed brother. McDonald's and its agencies feel the new ads take advantage of the chain's unique bond with consumers, which is a significant point of differentiation in the highly competitive fast-food business.

Another reason for using emotional appeals is to influence consumers' interpretations of their product usage experience. One way of doing this is through what is known as transformational advertising. A **transformational ad** is defined as "one which associates the experience of using (consuming) the advertised brand with a unique set of psychological characteristics which would not typically be associated with the brand experience to the same degree without exposure to the advertisement."[9]

Transformational ads create feelings, images, meanings, and beliefs about the product or service that may be activated when consumers use it, transforming their interpretation of the usage experience. Christopher Puto and William Wells note that a transformational ad has two characteristics:

1. It must make the experience of using the product richer, warmer, more exciting, and/or more enjoyable than that obtained solely from an objective description of the advertised brand.
2. It must connect the experience of the advertisement so tightly with the experience of using the brand that consumers cannot remember the brand without recalling the experience generated by the advertisement.[10]

Transformational advertising can differentiate a product or service by making the consumption experience more enjoyable. The "reach out and touch someone" campaign used by AT&T for many years to encourage consumers to keep in touch with family and friends by phone is an example of the successful use of transformational advertising. McDonald's has also used transformational advertising very effectively to position itself as the fast-food chain where parents (or grandparents) can enjoy a warm, happy experience with their children. Norwegian Cruise Lines uses transformational advertising to create a unique image of the cruise experience and differentiate itself from competitors with its "As far from the everyday as a ship can take you. That's the Norwegian Way" campaign. The goal of the campaign is to demonstrate how Norwegian provides each guest with a unique reprieve from the mundane routines of everyday life. Both the dramatic visuals and ad copy depict the vast array of experiences and activities to be enjoyed during one individual day on a Norwegian Cruise Line's voyage (Exhibit 9–5).

Exhibit 9–5 Norwegian Cruise Lines uses transformational advertising to create a unique image of the cruise experience

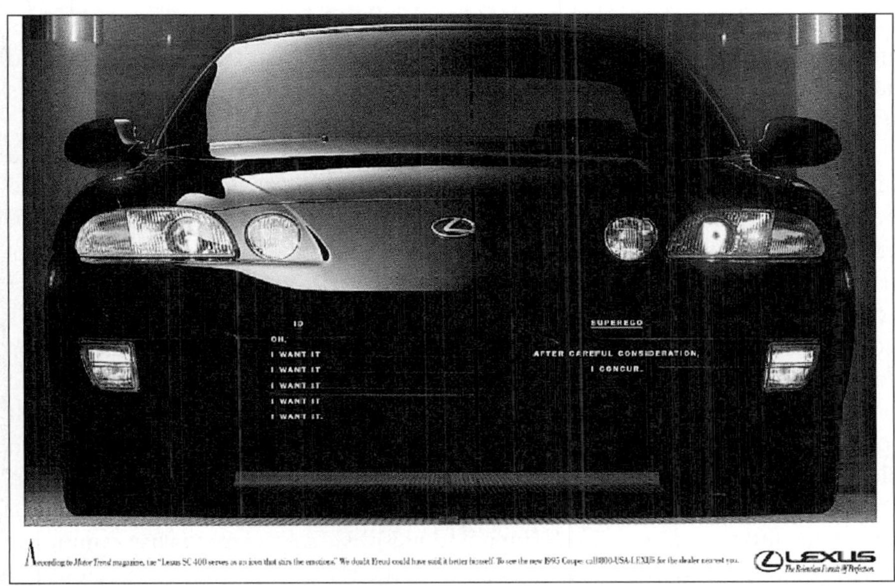

Exhibit 9–6 Lexus addresses both rational and emotional appeals in this clever ad

Combining Rational and Emotional Appeals In many advertising situations, the decision facing the creative specialist is not whether to choose an emotional or a rational appeal but rather determining how to combine the two approaches. As noted copywriters David Ogilvy and Joel Raphaelson have stated:

> Few purchases of any kind are made for entirely rational reasons. Even a purely functional product such as laundry detergent may offer what is now called an emotional benefit—say, the satisfaction of seeing one's children in bright clean clothes. In some product categories the rational element is small. These include soft drinks, beer, cosmetics, certain personal care products, and most old-fashioned products. And who hasn't experienced the surge of joy that accompanies the purchase of a new car?[11]

Consumer purchase decisions are often made on the basis of both emotional and rational motives, and attention must be given to both elements in developing effective advertising. Exhibit 9–6 shows a very clever ad that uses the Freudian concepts of id and superego to suggest that there are both emotional and rational reasons for purchasing the Lexus SC 400 coupe.

Advertising researchers and agencies have given considerable thought to the relationship between rational and emotional motives in consumer decision making and how advertising influences both. McCann-Erickson Worldwide, in conjunction with advertising professor Michael Ray, developed a proprietary research technique known as *emotional bonding.* This technique evaluates how consumers feel about brands and the nature of any emotional rapport they have with a brand compared to the ideal emotional state they associate with the product category.[12]

The basic concept of emotional bonding is that consumers develop three levels of relationships with brands, as shown in Figure 9–2. The most basic relationship

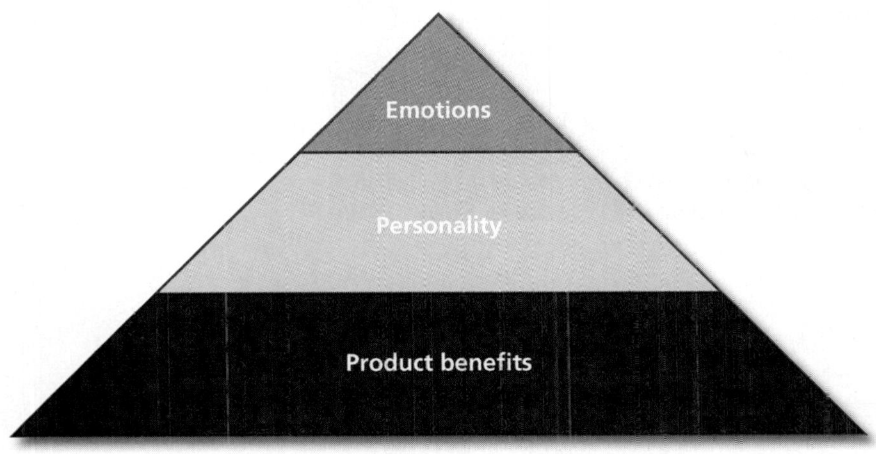

Figure 9–2 Levels of relationships with brands

indicates how consumers *think* about brands in respect to product benefits. This occurs, for the most part, through a rational learning process and can be measured by how well advertising communicates product information. Consumers at this stage are not very brand loyal, and brand switching is common.

At the next stage, the consumer assigns a *personality* to a brand. For example, a brand may be thought of as self-assured, aggressive, and adventurous, as opposed to compliant and timid. The consumer's judgment of the brand has moved beyond its attributes or delivery of product/service benefits. In most instances, consumers judge the personality of a brand on the basis of an assessment of overt or covert cues found in its advertising.

McCann-Erickson researchers believe the strongest relationship that develops between a brand and the consumer is based on feelings or emotional attachments to the brand. Consumers develop *emotional bonds* with certain brands, which result in positive psychological movement toward them. The marketer's goal is to develop the greatest emotional linkage between its brand and the consumer. McCann-Erickson believes advertising can develop and enrich emotional bonding between consumers and brands. McCann and its subsidiary agencies use emotional bonding research to provide strategic input into the creative process and determine how well advertising is communicating with consumers. McCann-Erickson used emotional bonding research as the basis for its award-winning "Priceless" campaign for MasterCard International. When the agency took over the account a few years ago, MasterCard was perceived as an ordinary credit card you keep in your wallet. The challenge was to create an emotional bond between consumers and MasterCard without losing the brand's functional appeal. McCann-Erickson developed a sentimental campaign that uses ads that take the sum total of an experience and declare that it has no price tag. Each commercial and print ad ends with the theme "There are some things money can't buy. For everything else there's MasterCard" (Exhibit 9–7).

Additional Types of Appeals

Not every ad fits neatly into the categories of rational or emotional appeals. For example, ads for some brands can be classified as **reminder advertising,** which has the objective of building brand awareness

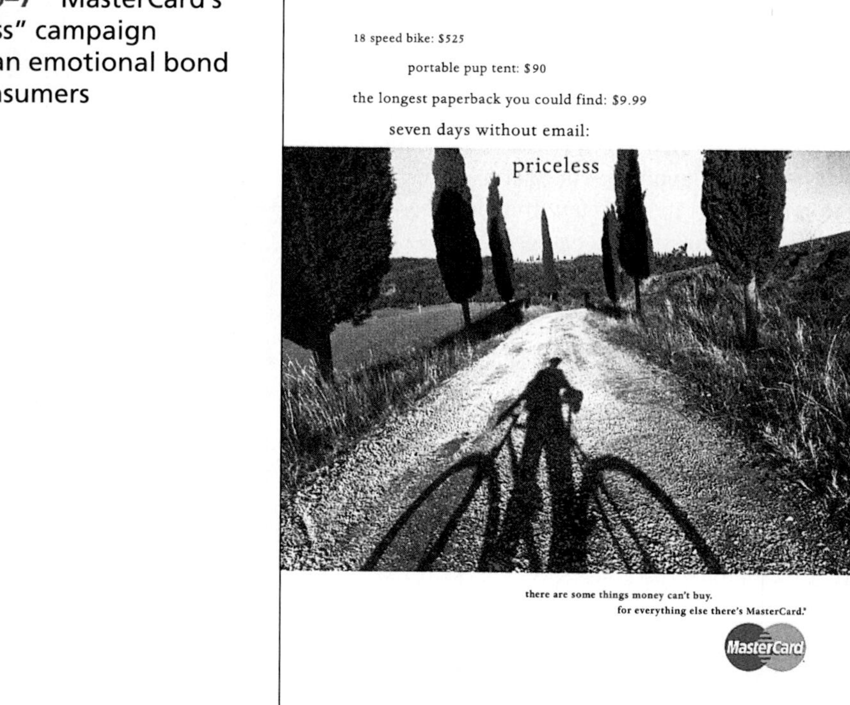

18 speed bike: $525
portable pup tent: $90
the longest paperback you could find: $9.99
seven days without email:
priceless
there are some things money can't buy.
for everything else there's MasterCard.
MasterCard
www.mastercard.com

Exhibit 9–7 MasterCard's "Priceless" campaign creates an emotional bond with consumers

and/or keeping the brand name in front of consumers. Well-known brands and market leaders often use reminder advertising. For example, Altoids breath mints runs reminder ads to build national brand awareness and communicate its quirky "curiously strong" message to consumers (Exhibit 9–8). Products and services that have a seasonal pattern to their consumption also use reminder advertising, particularly around the appropriate period. For example, marketers of candy products often increase their media budgets and run reminder advertising around Halloween, Valentine's Day, Christmas, and Easter.

Advertisers introducing a new product often use **teaser advertising,** which is designed to build curiosity, interest, and/or excitement about a product or brand by talking about it but not actually showing it. Teasers, or *mystery ads* as they are sometimes called, are also used by marketers to draw attention to upcoming advertising campaigns and generate interest and publicity for them. For example, Lee Jeans used teaser ads as part of its successful "Can't bust 'em" campaign for its new Dungarees line that features the Buddy Lee doll (Exhibit 9–9). The denim-dressed doll, which was used in Lee's promotional displays from the 1920s through the 50s, was brought back and billed as a "Man of Action." Lee's agency, Fallon McElligott, introduced Buddy with a "phantom campaign" designed to intrigue influential trendsetters among the 17- to 22-year-old target market. Posters of Buddy Lee, unidentified and unbranded, were wild-posted in "cool" areas of 15 markets to generate curiosity. The agency then produced a six-minute film, *The Buddy Lee Story,* that was run on "graveyard cable," 2 A.M. slots on Comedy Central and other cable channels. Again, the product was never mentioned, but the film did associate Buddy with the Lee Company and its "Can't bust 'em" spirit.

Exhibit 9–8 Altoids uses reminder advertising to build brand awareness

The goal of the teaser campaign was to let the trendsetters discover Buddy and spread the news about him. The teaser campaign was successful in generating word of mouth and helped accelerate the popularity of the brand as subsequent advertising featuring Buddy hawking the Dungarees line was introduced. The campaign helped make initial sales of the Dungaree's line four times higher than anticipated and resulted in a 3 percent increase in market share for Lee even though overall denim sales were flat.[13]

Teaser ads are often used for new movies or TV shows and for major product launches. They are especially popular among automotive advertisers for introducing a new model or announcing significant changes in a vehicle. For example,

Exhibit 9–9 Lee Jeans used a successful teaser campaign featuring Buddy Lee to help introduce its Dungarees line

Chrysler has used teaser ads to introduce its Neon subcompact and new models of the Jeep Grand Cherokee.

Teaser campaigns can generate interest in a new product, but advertisers must be careful not to extend them too long or they will lose their effectiveness.[14] Many advertising experts thought the teaser campaign used by Infiniti to introduce its cars to the U.S. market in 1989 ran too long and created confusion among consumers.[15] As one advertising executive says, "Contrary to what we think, consumers don't hold seminars about advertising. You have to give consumers enough information about the product in teaser ads to make them feel they're in on the joke."[16]

Many ads are not designed to sell a product or service but rather to enhance the image of the company or meet other corporate goals such as soliciting investment or recruiting employees. These are generally referred to as corporate image advertising and are discussed in detail in Chapter 17.

Advertising Execution

Once the specific advertising appeal that will be used as the basis for the advertising message has been determined, the creative specialist or team begins its execution. *Creative execution* is the way an advertising appeal is presented. While it is obviously important for an ad to have a meaningful appeal or message to communicate to the consumer, the manner in which the ad is executed is also important.

One of the best-known advocates of the importance of creative execution in advertising was William Bernbach, founder of the Doyle Dane Bernbach agency. In his famous book on the advertising industry, *Madison Avenue,* Martin Mayer notes Bernbach's reply to David Ogilvy's rule for copywriters that "what you say in advertising is more important than how you say it." Bernbach replied, "Execution can become content, it can be just as important as what you say. A sick guy can utter some words and nothing happens; a healthy vital guy says them and they rock the world."[17] Bernbach was one of the revolutionaries of his time who changed advertising creativity on a fundamental level by redefining how headlines and visuals were used, how art directors and copywriters worked together, and how advertising could be used to arouse feelings and emotions. IMC Perspective 9–1 discusses how the emergence of the Internet and advertising for Web-based companies may be leading to a new creative revolution in advertising.

An advertising message can be presented or executed in numerous ways:

- Straight sell or factual message
- Scientific/technical evidence
- Demonstration
- Comparison
- Testimonial
- Slice of life
- Animation
- Personality symbol
- Fantasy
- Dramatization
- Humor
- Combinations

We now examine these formats and considerations involved in their use.

Exhibit 9–10 Castrol uses a straight-sell execution style in this ad

Straight Sell or Factual Message

One of the most basic types of creative executions is the straight sell or factual message. This type of ad relies on a straightforward presentation of information concerning the product or service. This execution is often used with informational/rational appeals, where the focus of the message is the product or service and its specific attributes and/or benefits.

Straight-sell executions are commonly used in print ads. A picture of the product or service occupies part of the ad, and the factual copy takes up the rest of the space. (See the ad for Castrol Syntec motor oil in Exhibit 9–10.) They are also used in TV advertising, with an announcer generally delivering the sales message while the product/service is shown on the screen. Ads for high-involvement consumer products as well as industrial and other business-to-business products generally use this format.

IMC Perspective 9–1

Will the Internet and Dot.com Advertising Drive the New Creative Revolution?

"I'm always hoping that one day some young man will come into my office and say, 'Your 96 rules for creating good ads are for the birds. They're all based on research that is out of date and irrelevant. Here are 96 new rules based on new research. Throw yours out the window.... You're an old dodo, living in the past. Move over, I have written a new dogma, a new dialectic, and I am the prophet of the future.'"

This appeal for someone to lead a new creative revolution in advertising was written by legendary adman David Ogilvy in his classic book, *The Art of Writing Advertising,* which was published in 1965. In the 60s, revolutionaries such as Ogilvy, Bill Bernbach, Leo Burnett, and Rosser Reeves turned advertising creativity on its head. Marty Cooke, executive creative director at M&C Saatchi, New York, describes the state of advertising creativity before these revolutionaries came along as follows: "It was the Dark Ages, manufacturers shouting out of the factory window. There was no emotional connection. It was basically what the client wanted you to say. The creative revolution was about finding a way to talk to people. It was like finding perspective."

The creative revolution that occurred during the 60s was in many ways inspired by the emergence of television as a dominant medium for advertising. Now the Internet is the new technology invading homes in the United States as well as other countries, and many advertising people feel it is driving a new creative revolution in advertising that is sorely needed. Madison Avenue has never seen a boom as explosive, spectacular, and sudden as the "great dot.com ad boom" of 1999. Ads for Internet companies such as portals and e-commerce sites are everywhere. And as these companies compete for consumers' attention and a piece of their mind-set, they are producing a new type of advertising whose style is as daring and unconventional as the entrepreneurs who built the online companies. Many feel that these Web pioneers boast an unbridled spirit that encourages and nurtures creativity.

Many of those who work in advertising feel that creativity had come to a standstill in recent years. However, a torrent of rebellious dot.com advertising has instilled a renewed faith in the creative spirit of the advertising community. With its unconventional agency hiring procedures and speedy turnaround demands, the fast-paced, rough-and-tumble dot.com world is dramatically altering the way the advertising business is conducted. Veteran commercial director Joe Pytka says, "A lot of traditional advertising is looking hugely old fashioned," and notes that the most interesting campaigns he has worked on recently are for dot.com companies such as Stamps.com and AltaVista.

Some of the most creative and popular ads for a Web company are part of the campaign created for the online trading firm Ameritrade and feature Stuart, the young, ponytailed, red-headed trader. In one of the most popular spots from the campaign he is seen squeezing his face inside the office photocopier, making invitations for a big weekend party. When his supervisor summons him to his office, it appears as though Stuart is in trouble, but he's really there to get the boss's Ameritrade account running. The spot features classic lines, which Stuart delivers with a lack of deference to his boss, such as "Let's light this candle!" and "You're riding the wave of the future, my man!" As the boss becomes excited over his newfound online trading skills, Stuart performs an unforgettable gyrating, semispastic victory dance.

While many of the ads for online companies are very creative and fun to watch, some experts feel that most of the dot.com ads are very weak with not much to say. Critics argue that the dot.coms want superfantastic branding campaigns delivered on *Internet time,* which means immediately. In some cases ad agencies must turn around national print, radio, and TV campaigns in as little as three weeks rather than the months this normally takes. The president of one agency jokes, "We call it McBranding." All the dot.coms want their advertising to be the funniest or most outrageous and portray them as the most "Internetty" company on the block. However, in the

888 590 7003

end, all the dot.com advertising starts to look the same and even boring.

Many in the advertising community believe that the real creative revolution will come not from ads for Internet companies but from the medium itself. They feel that the skills of the creative community will really be unleashed as technological limitations that handcuff Web creativity, such as bandwidth problems, are solved and the Internet converges with other traditional media such as television and print. It does appear that a new creative revolution is under way courtesy of the Internet. John Hegarty, chairman of Bartle Bogle Hegarty, sums up the feeling of many creative people when he says, "I can't think of a more exciting time to be in the advertising business."

Sources: Eleftheria Parpis, "You Say You Want a Revolution," *Adweek,* December 13, 1999, pp. 29–36; Amy Kover, "Dot-com Time Bomb on Madison Avenue," *Fortune,* December 6, 1999, pp. 235–36; Anthony Vagnoni, "They Might Be Giants," *Advertising Age,* April 27, 1998, pp. 1, 20, 24.

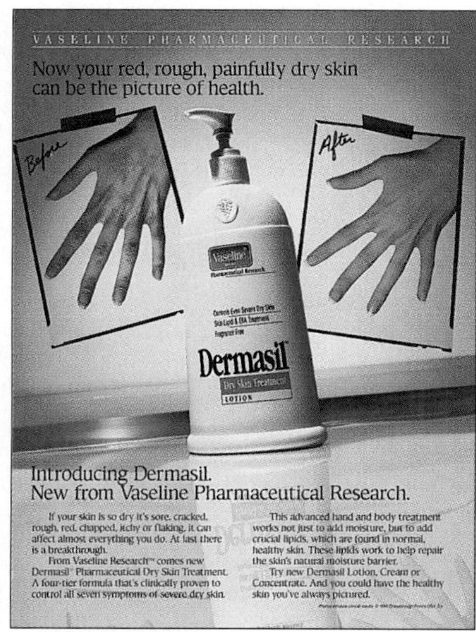

Exhibit 9–11 This Dermasil ad cites a scientific study

Scientific/Technical Evidence

In a variation of the straight sell, scientific or technical evidence is presented in the ad. Advertisers often cite technical information, results of scientific or laboratory studies, or endorsements by scientific bodies or agencies to support their advertising claims. For example, an endorsement from the American Council on Dental Therapeutics on how fluoride helps prevent cavities was the basis of the campaign that made Crest the leading brand on the market. The ad for Dermasil Pharmaceutical Dry Skin Treatment shown in Exhibit 9–11 uses this execution style to emphasize the breakthrough from Vaseline Research.

Demonstration

Demonstration advertising is designed to illustrate the key advantages of the product/service by showing it in actual use or in some staged situation. Demonstration executions can be very effective in convincing consumers of a product's utility or quality and of the benefits of owning or using the brand. TV is particularly well suited for demonstration executions, since the benefits or advantages of the product can be shown right on the screen. Although perhaps a little less dramatic than TV, demonstration ads can also work in print, as shown in the ad for Du Pont's Teflon® Bakeware Liners (Exhibit 9–12).

Comparison

Brand comparisons can also be the basis for the advertising execution. The comparison execution approach is increasingly popular among advertisers, since it offers a direct way of communicating a brand's particular advantage over its competitors or positioning a new or lesser-known brand with industry leaders. Comparison executions are often used to execute competitive advantage appeals, as discussed earlier.

Testimonial

Many advertisers prefer to have their messages presented by way of a testimonial, where a person praises the product or service on the basis of his or her personal experience with it (Exhibit 9–13). Testimonial executions can have ordinary satisfied customers discuss their own experiences with the brand and the benefits of using it. This approach can be very effective when the person delivering the testimonial is someone with whom the target audience can identify or who has an interesting story to tell. The testimonial must be based on actual use of the product or service to avoid legal problems, and the spokesperson must be credible.

Testimonials can be particularly effective when they come from a recognizable or popular source. Ultra Slim-Fast has used a variety of celebrities, including former Los Angeles Dodgers manager Tommy Lasorda, talk-show host Kathie Lee Gifford, and her husband, sportscaster Frank Gifford, to deliver testimonials on its effectiveness in weight loss. The company has also used actress Brooke Shields to reach a younger market.

A related execution technique is the endorsement, where a well-known or respected individual such as a celebrity or expert in the product or service area speaks on behalf of the company or the brand. When endorsers promote a company

Exhibit 9–12 This ad demonstrates the benefits of Du Pont's Teflon® Bakeware Liners

Exhibit 9–13 This ad uses a testimonial execution effectively

or its products or services, the message is not necessarily based on their personal experiences.

Slice of Life A widely used advertising format, particularly for package-goods products, is the slice-of-life execution, which is generally based on a problem/solution approach. This type of ad portrays a problem or conflict that consumers might face in their daily lives. The ad then shows how the advertiser's product or service can resolve the problem.

Slice-of-life executions are often criticized for being unrealistic and irritating to watch because they are often used to remind consumers of problems of a personal nature, such as dandruff, bad breath, body odor, and laundry problems. Often these ads come across as contrived, silly, phony, or even offensive to consumers. However, many advertisers still prefer this style because they believe it is effective at presenting a situation to which most consumers can relate and at registering the product feature or benefit that helps sell the brand.

For many years, Procter & Gamble was known for its reliance on slice-of-life advertising executions. In 1980, two-thirds of the company's commercials used either the slice-of-life or testimonial format. However, P&G has begun using humor, animation, and other less traditional execution styles. Now only one in four of the company's ads relies on slice-of-life or testimonials.[13]

Slice-of-life or problem/solution execution approaches are not limited to consumer-product advertising. Many business-to-business marketers use this type of advertising to demonstrate how their products and services can be used to solve business problems. For example, AT&T used this approach in executing the "It's all within your reach" campaign that promoted a broad array of the company's

Exhibit 9–14 AT&T uses a slice-of-life execution to advertise its wireless services

offerings. The ads in the campaign used emotionally charged moments to demonstrate how AT&T understands and helps individuals reach their goals by offering the most relevant solutions to the challenges of working and living in today's fast-paced world and managing one's personal life and business pressures.

An award-winning commercial from the campaign was a spot called "Beaches," which focused on a working mother and her very busy life (Exhibit 9–14). The ad addressed the problem facing many working parents: They would like to spend more time with their children but need to go to work and kids don't always understand why. This situation, and the frustration often associated with it, is captured in the ad when the little girl says to her mother, "Mom, when can I be a client?" Thanks to AT&T Wireless Services, the mother is able to take the kids to the beach and still conduct her important conference call as scheduled.[19]

Some business-to-business marketers use a variation of the problem/solution execution that is sometimes referred to as *slice-of-death advertising.*[20] This execution style is used in conjunction with a fear appeal, as the focus is on the negative consequences that result when businesspeople make the wrong decision in choosing a supplier or service provider. For example, FedEx has used this type of advertising for nearly three decades through humorous, but to-the-point, commercials that show what might happen when important packages and documents aren't received on time.

Animation An advertising execution approach that has become popular in recent years is animation. With this technique, animated scenes are drawn by artists or created on the computer, and cartoons, puppets, or other types of fictional characters may be used. Cartoon animation is especially popular for commercials targeted at children.

Animated cartoon characters have also been used successfully by the Leo Burnett agency in campaigns for Green Giant vegetables (the Jolly Green Giant) and Keebler cookies (the Keebler elves). Another successful example of animation execution was the ad campaign developed for the California Raisin Advisory Board. A technique called Claymation was used to create the dancing raisin characters used in these ads.

The use of animation as an execution style may increase as creative specialists discover the possibilities of computer-generated graphics and other technological innovations.[21] Exhibit 9–15 shows an ad for Stagg Chili that uses computer-generated graphics and animation.

Some advertisers have begun using Roger Rabbit–style ads that mix animation with real people. Nike has used this technique to develop several creative, entertaining commercials. One featured Michael Jordan and Bugs Bunny trouncing a foursome of bullies on the basketball court and was the inspiration for the movie *Space Jam.* Commercials featuring Jordan and animated characters are also used by MCI WorldCom.

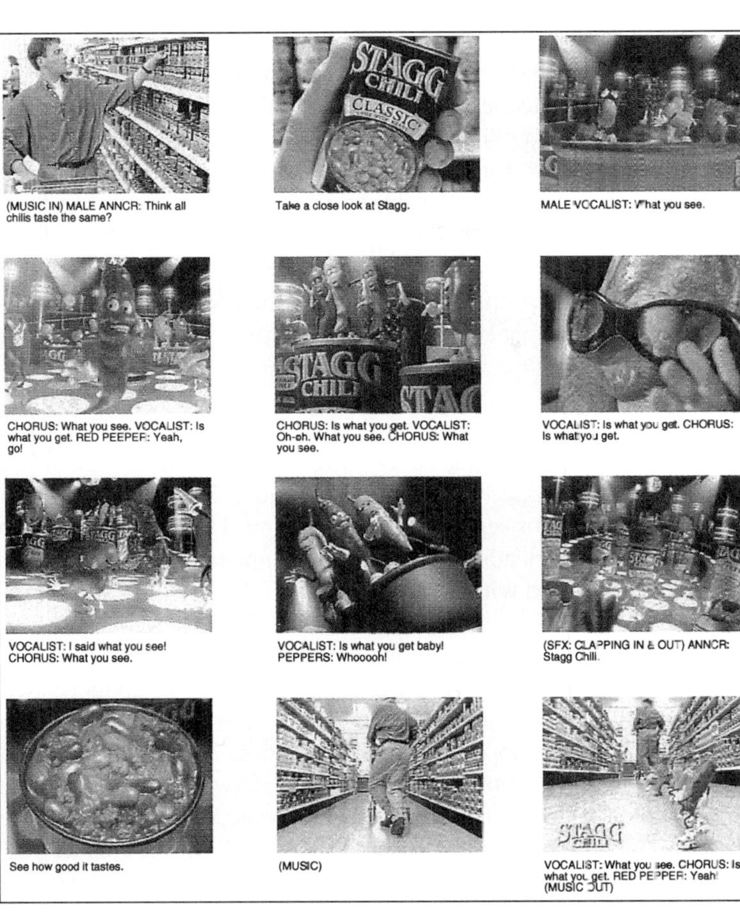

STAGG CHILI CLASSIC
(MUSIC IN) MALE ANNCR: Think all chilis taste the same?
Take a close look at Stagg.
MALE VOCALIST: What you see.
STAGG CHILI
CHORUS: What you see. VOCALIST: Is what you get. RED PEEPER: Yeah, go!
CHORUS: Is what you get. VOCALIST: Oh-oh. What you see. CHORUS: What you see.
VOCALIST: Is what you get. CHORUS: Is what you get.
VOCALIST: I said what you see! CHORUS: What you see.
VOCALIST: Is what you get baby! PEPPERS: Whooooh!
(SFX: CLAPPING IN & OUT) ANNCR: Stagg Chili.
See how good it tastes.
(MUSIC)
STAGG CHILI
VOCALIST: What you see. CHORUS: Is what you get. RED PEPPER: Yeah! (MUSIC OUT)

Exhibit 9–15 This ad for Stagg Chili uses an animation execution

Exhibit 9–16 The Maytag repairman is an example of an advertising personality symbol

Personality Symbol Another type of advertising execution involves developing a central character or personality symbol that can deliver the advertising message and with which the product or service can be identified. This character can be a person, like Mr. Whipple, who asked shoppers, "Please don't squeeze the Charmin," or the Maytag repairman, who sits anxiously by the phone but is never needed because the company's appliances are so reliable (Exhibit 9–16). The campaign for the Jack in the Box fast-food chain, which was discussed in the opening vignette to this chapter, uses "Jack" as a personality symbol to deliver the company's advertising message.

Personality figures can also be built around animated characters and animals. As discussed in Chapter 5, visual image personalities (VIPs) such as Morris the Cat and Tony the Tiger have been used for decades to promote 9-Lives cat food and Kellogg's Frosted Flakes, respectively. H. J. Heinz Co. began using Charlie the Tuna to promote Star-Kist tuna in 1961 and recently brought the character out of retirement to appear in a national ad campaign for the brand (Exhibit 9–17). While the old "Sorry Charlie" commercials portrayed Charlie as not being good enough for Star-Kist, the new ads use the spokesfish in a different way, such as giving a courtroom address saying all tunas are not created equal and asking jurors to judge for themselves. The tagline for the new spots featuring Charlie is "Our best quality, best tasting tuna ever."[22]

Exhibit 9–17 H. J. Heinz has brought back Charlie the tuna in ads for Star-Kist

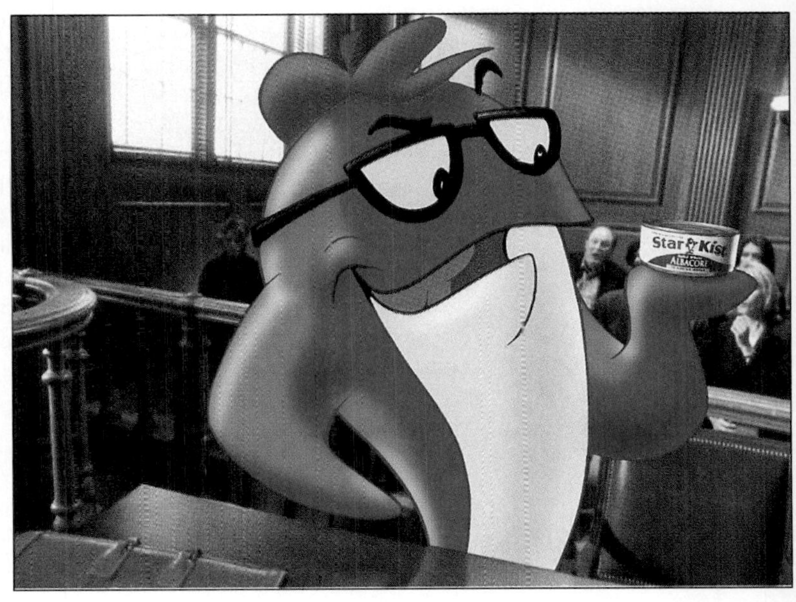

Anheuser-Busch has created popular personality symbols in the talking lizards, Frank

and Louie, who have been appearing in ads for Budweiser beer for the past five years. However, the company has had to deal with complaints from some consumer groups who argue that the animated characters are popular among children and might encourage underage drinking. The company strongly denies that it is using the characters to target minors and argues that the ads do not have any effect on children or encourage underage drinking.[23] Actually the controversy over the Budweiser lizards has been mild compared to the furor that was created by R. J. Reynolds' use of Old Joe Camel, the cartoon character used in ads for Camel cigarettes for many years. Ethical Perspective 9–2 discusses the controversy this campaign created and what has happened since RJR stopped using the "smooth character" in its advertising.

Fantasy An execution technique that is popular for emotional types of appeals such as image advertising is fantasy. Fantasy executions are particularly well suited for television, as the commercial can become a 30-second escape for the viewer into another lifestyle. The product or service becomes a central part of the situation created by the advertiser. Cosmetics ads often use fantasy appeals to create images and symbols that become associated with the brand.

Dramatization Another execution technique particularly well suited to television is dramatization, where the focus is on telling a short story with the product or service as the star. Dramatization is somewhat akin to slice-of-life execution in that it often relies on the problem/solution approach, but it uses more excitement and suspense in telling the story. The purpose of using drama is to draw the viewer into the action it portrays. Advocates of drama note that when it is successful, the audience becomes lost in the story and experiences the concerns and feelings of the characters.[24] According to Sandra Moriarty, there are five basic steps in a dramatic commercial:

> First is exposition, where the stage is set for the upcoming action. Next comes conflict, which is a technique for identifying the problem. The middle of the dramatic form is a period of rising action where the story builds, the conflict intensifies, the suspense thickens. The fourth step is the climax, where the problem is solved. The last part of a drama is the resolution, where the wrap-up is presented. In advertising that includes product identification and call to action.[25]

Exhibit 9–18 This Zerex ad uses a dramatization execution

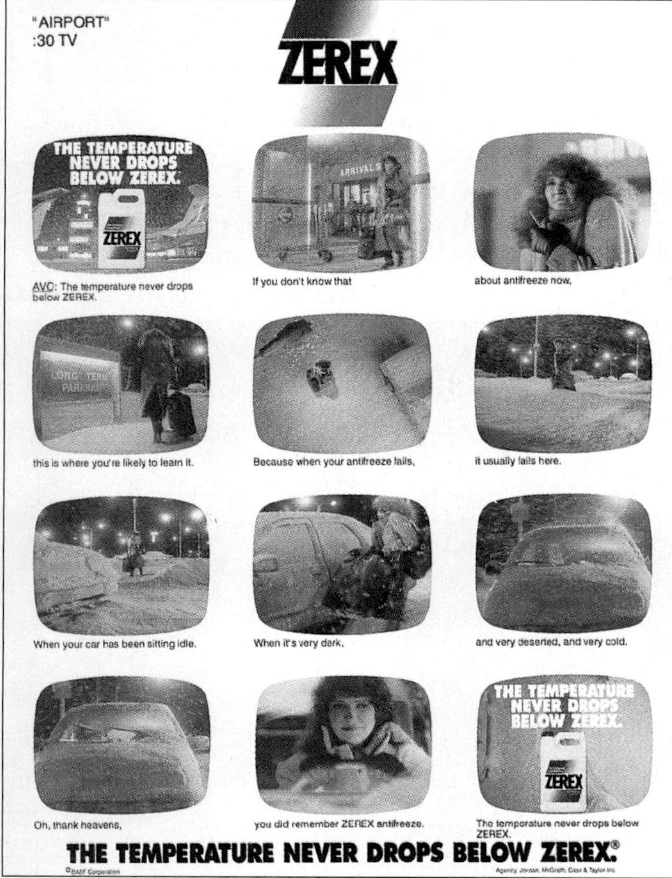

The real challenge facing the creative team is how to encompass all these elements in a 30-second commercial. A good example of the dramatization execution technique is the ad for Zerex antifreeze in Exhibit 9–18, which shows a woman's sense of relief when her car starts at the airport on a cold winter night. The ad concludes with a strong identification slogan, "The temperature never drops below Zerex," that connects the brand name to its product benefit.

Humor Like comparisons, humor was discussed in Chapter 6 as a type of advertising appeal, but this technique can also be used as a way of presenting other advertising appeals. Humorous executions are particularly well suited to television or radio, although some print ads attempt to use this style. The pros and cons of using humor as an executional technique are similar to those associated with its use as an advertising appeal.

Combinations Many of the execution techniques can be combined to present the advertising message. For example, animation is often used to create personality symbols or present a fantasy. Slice-of-life ads are

Ethical Perspective 9–2

Camel Looks for a New Campaign after Retiring Joe Camel

In late 1987, RJR Nabisco launched the "smooth character" advertising campaign featuring Old Joe, a cartoon camel. The campaign was soon criticized as an effort by RJR to reposition the Camel brand to appeal to young people. Critics argued that ads showing Old Joe accompanied by beautiful women, race cars, jet airplanes, and other appealing images were particularly intriguing to children. They also argued that the campaign was another example of the tobacco industry's efforts to sustain sales by attracting teenagers, since 90 percent of smokers start before they reach the age of 21.

The controversy surrounding the campaign heated up in 1991, when three studies published in the *Journal of the American Medical Association* concluded the smooth-character ads were more successful at marketing Camels to children than to adults. These findings led a powerful coalition of health groups—formed by the American Medical Association, the American Cancer Society, and the American Lung Association—to petition the Federal Trade Commission (FTC) to take action to stop RJR's use of the smooth-characters ads. In 1993, FTC staff recommended an outright ban of the campaign on the grounds that it entices minors to smoke. However, in 1994, the FTC voted 3–2 not to ban the Joe Camel ads.

Despite all the criticism, RJR continued using the campaign, arguing that its responsibility was to its shareholders and it would be wrong to stop it solely because of criticism from antismokers. However, while the Joe Camel campaign was increasing Camel sales, it was also continuing to create problems for RJR. In May 1997 the FTC filed an unfair-advertising complaint against the company, charging that the campaign caused substantial injury to children, and sought an irrevocable guarantee that the ads would never be used again. In June 1997, the federal government negotiated a landmark settlement with the tobacco industry that called for banning the use of the cartoon character in cigarette ads. As part of the settlement, the tobacco industry also agreed to eliminate all outdoor advertising and some magazines with large numbers of youth readers from its media schedules. A month later RJR announced that it was phasing out the Joe Camel ads and would begin a new campaign using the theme "What you're looking for." RJR insisted that scrapping Joe Camel was entirely a marketing decision that was not affected by the tobacco industry's settlement agreement or the FTC investigation.

By late 1997 RJR stopped running all Camel ads featuring Old Joe and began a new campaign using the theme "What you're looking for." However, the new campaign was short-lived, and RJR has tried several different approaches over the past two years. One of its efforts used the theme "Mighty tasty!" which was crammed with jarring, surrealistic images by photographer David La Chappelle, such as bare-chested men sitting in a hot tub with a bevy of admiring women. However, according to Camel's vice president of marketing, the new campaign didn't translate in the "postsettlement environment" where the images could not be used on billboards or in many magazines.

In late 1999 Camel began a new repositioning campaign that taps into the brand's mystical Turkish roots and image. The theme of the new campaign is "Pleasure to burn," and it uses print ads with images of a Sam Spade–like man and a pinup-style woman. Camel's new marketing push also includes a program to build relationships with its customers through a custom quarterly publication called *CML,* which will be mailed to age-restricted smokers in 30 states. *CML* aims to capture the brand's essence with articles on exotic topics such as the French Foreign Legion and a serial soap opera called "Rebecca's Revenge." The magazine will also offer merchandise ranging from cigarette lighters to Turkish coffee and specially blended Camel Exotic blends, a series of four types of cigarettes offered for the superpremium price of $6 per pack and available via mail order only. Ads within the magazine are initially confined to Camel, although RJR may consider running ads from other products that fit the *CML* image.

Although Camel's advertising has been shifting like desert sands, the brand's sales and market share have remained steady at just under 5 percent since the heyday of the Joe Camel campaign in 1996. One branding consultant credits Camel's strong brand image for its ability to retain its market share, noting that Camel has never strayed too far from that mystical, Turkish image. He notes that with its new campaign, "it's returning to its brand soul." Many antismoking advocates are happy that RJR is not returning to Old Joe Camel.

Sources: Judann Pollack, "Camel Explores Exotic Route in New Campaign," *Advertising Age,* November 22, 1999, p. 4; Yumiko Ono and Bruce Ingersoll, "RJR Retires Joe Camel, Adds Sexy Smokers," *The Wall Street Journal,* July 11, 1997, pp. B1, 5; Ira Teinowitz, "Joe Camel Is No Tony Tiger to Kids," *Advertising Age,* February 21, 1994, p. 36.

often used to demonstrate a product or service. Comparisons are sometimes made using a humorous approach. FedEx uses humorous executions of the slice-of-death genre depicting businesspeople experiencing dire consequences when they use another delivery service and an important document doesn't arrive on time. It is the responsibility of the creative specialist(s) to determine whether more than one execution style should be used in creating the ad.

Creative Tactics

Our discussion thus far has focused on the development of creative strategy and various appeals and execution styles that can be used for the advertising message. Once the creative approach, type of appeal, and execution style have been determined, attention turns to creating the actual advertisement. The design and production of advertising messages involve a number of activities, among them writing copy, developing illustrations and other visual elements of the ad, and bringing all of the pieces together to create an effective message. In this section, we examine the verbal and visual elements of an ad and discuss tactical considerations in creating print ads and TV commercials.

Creative Tactics for Print Advertising

The basic components of a print ad are the headline, the body copy, the visual or illustrations, and the layout (the way they all fit together). The headline and body copy portions of the ad are the responsibility of the copywriters; artists, often working under the direction of an art director, are responsible for the visual presentation. Art directors also work with the copywriters to develop a layout, or arrangement of the various components of the ad: headlines, subheads, body copy, illustrations, captions, logos, and the like. We briefly examine the three components of a print ad and how they are coordinated.

Headlines

The **headline** is the words in the leading position of the ad—the words that will be read first or are positioned to draw the most attention.[26] Headlines are usually set in larger, darker type and are often set apart from the body copy or text portion of the ad to give them prominence. Most advertising people consider the headline the most important part of a print ad.

The most important function of a headline is attracting readers' attention and interesting them in the rest of the message. While the visual portion of an ad is obviously important, the headline often shoulders most of the responsibility of attracting readers' attention. Research has shown the headline is generally the first thing people look at in a print ad, followed by the illustration. Only 20 percent of readers go beyond the headline and read the body copy.[27] So in addition to attracting attention, the headline must give the reader good reason to read the copy portion of the ad, which contains more detailed and persuasive information about the product or service. To do this, the headline must put forth the main theme, appeal, or proposition of the ad in a few words. Some print ads contain little if any body copy, so the headline must work with the illustration to communicate the entire advertising message.

Exhibit 9–19 The headline of this ad catches the attention of young consumers

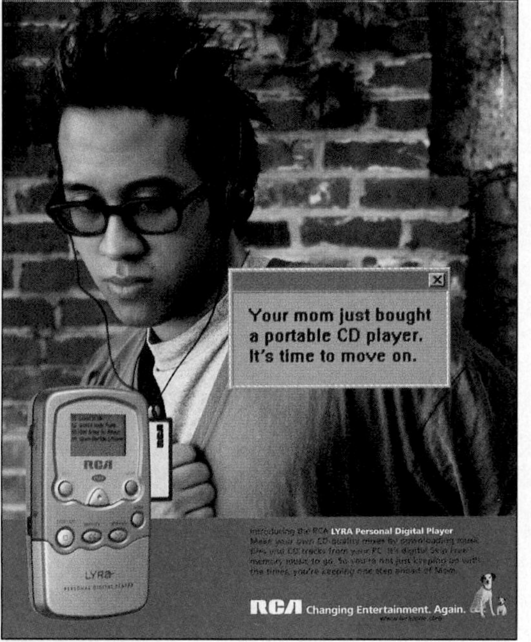

Headlines also perform a segmentation function by engaging the attention and interest of consumers who are most likely to buy a particular product or service. Advertisers begin the segmentation process by choosing to advertise in certain types of publications (e.g., a travel, general interest, or fashion magazine). An effective headline goes even further in selecting good prospects for the product by addressing their specific needs, wants, or interests. For example, the headline in the ad for RCA's LYRA personal digital player shown in Exhibit 9–19 catches the attention of consumers who want the latest technology in audio products.

Types of Headlines There are numerous headline possibilities. The type used depends on several factors, including the creative strategy, the particular advertising situation (e.g., product type, media vehicle(s) being used, timeliness), and its relationship to other components of the ad, such as the illustration or body copy. Headlines can be categorized as direct and indirect. **Direct headlines** are straightforward and informative in terms of the message they are presenting and the target audience they are directed toward. Common types of direct headlines include those offering a specific benefit, making a promise, or announcing a reason the reader should be interested in the product or service.

Indirect headlines are not straightforward about identifying the product or service or getting to the point. But they are often more effective at attracting readers' attention and interest because they provoke curiosity and lure readers into the body copy to learn an answer or get an explanation. Techniques for writing indirect headlines include using questions, provocations, how-to statements, and challenges.

Indirect headlines rely on their ability to generate curiosity or intrigue so as to motivate readers to become involved with the ad and read the body copy to find out the point of the message. This can be risky if the headline is not provocative enough to get the readers' interest. Advertisers deal with this problem by using a visual appeal that helps attract attention and offers another reason for reading more of the message. For example, in Exhibit 9–20, the headline is accompanied by an amusing illustration that entices travelers to read the message to learn more about the Fresca® World Ski Card and how to get it. Do you think this ad would have been as effective with a more traditional illustration such as a skier?

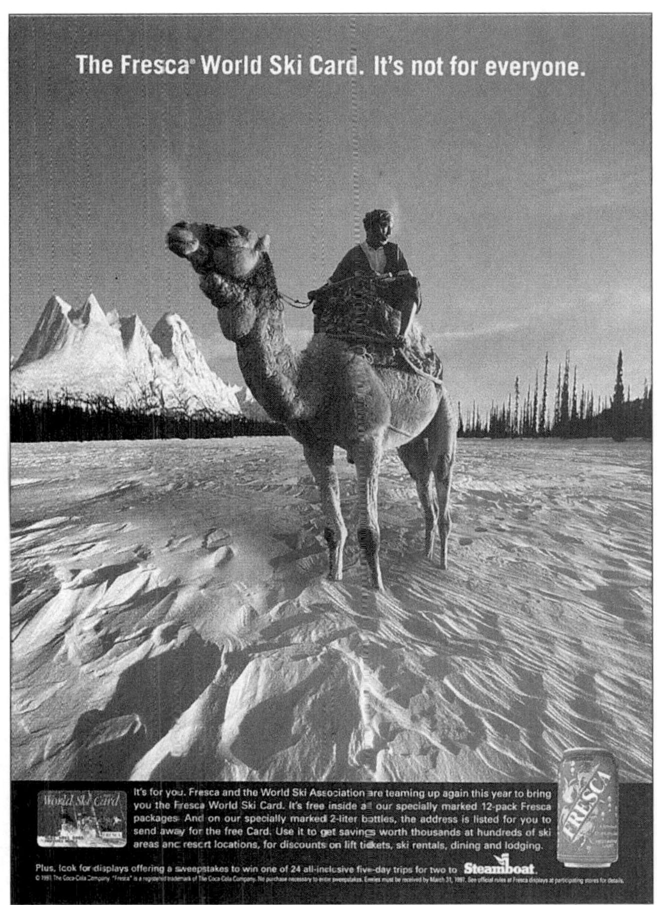

Exhibit 9–20 This ad combines an indirect headline with an amusing illustration to attract readers' attention

Subheads While many ads have only one headline, it is also common to see print ads containing the main head and one or more secondary heads, or **subheads.** Subheads are usually smaller than the main headline but larger than the body copy. They may appear above or below the main headline or within the body copy. The AT&T ad shown in Exhibit 9–21 uses subheads within the body copy.

Subheads are often used to enhance the readability of the message by breaking up large amounts of body copy and highlighting key sales points. Their content reinforces the headline and advertising slogan or theme.

Exhibit 9–21 This ad uses subheads to make the copy easier to read

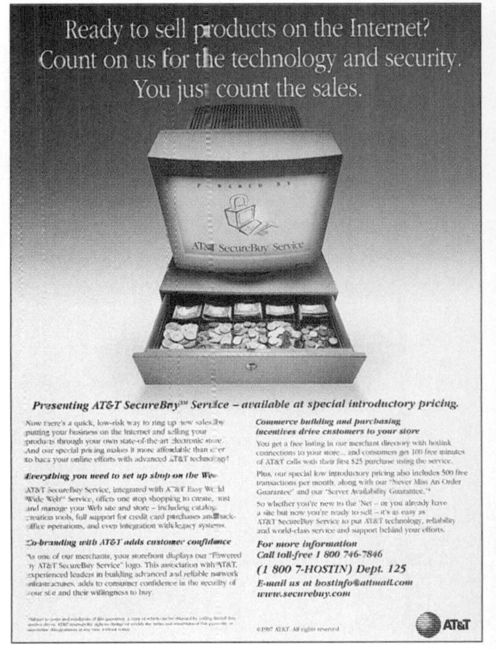

Body Copy

The main text portion of a print ad is referred to as the **body copy** (or sometimes just *copy*). While the body copy is usually the heart of the advertising message, getting the target audience to read it is often difficult. The copywriter faces a dilemma: The body copy must be long enough to communicate the advertiser's message yet short enough to hold readers' interest.

Body copy content often flows from the points made in the headline or various subheads, but the specific content depends on the type of advertising appeal and/or execution style being used. For example, straight-sell copy that presents relevant information, product features and benefits, or competitive advantages is often used with the various types of rational appeals discussed earlier in the chapter. Emotional appeals often use narrative copy that tells a story or provides an interesting account of a problem or situation involving the product.

Advertising body copy can be written to go along with various types of creative appeals and executions—comparisons, price appeals, demonstrations, humor, dramatizations, and the like. Copywriters choose a copy style that is appropriate for the type of appeal being used and effective for executing the creative strategy and communicating the advertiser's message to the target audience.

Visual Elements

The third major component of a print ad is the visual element. The illustration is often a dominant part of a print ad and plays an important role in determining its effectiveness. The visual portion of an ad must attract attention, communicate an idea or image, and work in a synergistic fashion with the headline and body copy to produce an effective message. In some print ads, the visual portion of the ad is essentially the message and thus must convey a strong and meaningful image. For example, the award-winning ad for Sims Snowboards shown in Exhibit 9–22 uses a powerful visual image. In a scene reminiscent of the protestor blocking military vehicles in Beijing's Tiananmen Square during the 1989 student uprising, a snowboarder stands in the path of snow-grooming machines (which pack the snow, to the distress of snowboarders). The single line of copy, "In a courageous act of solidarity, a lone snowboarder stands up for freedom," reinforces the message presented by the visual image.

Many decisions have to be made regarding the visual portion of the ad: what identification marks should be included (brand name, company or trade name, trademarks, logos); whether to use photos or hand-drawn or painted illustrations; what colors to use (or even perhaps black and white or just a splash of color); and what the focus of the visual should be.

Layout

While each individual component of a print ad is important, the key factor is how these elements are blended into a finished advertisement. A **layout** is the physical arrangement of the various parts of the ad, including the headline, subheads, body copy, illustrations, and any identifying marks. The layout shows where each part of the ad will be placed and gives guidelines to the people working on the ad. For example, the layout helps the copywriter determine how much space he or she has to work with and how much copy should be written. The layout can also guide the art director in determining the size and type of photos. In the ad for Sims Snowboards shown in Exhibit 9–22, the layout is designed to make the ad look like it was reprinted from a newspaper page. Notice how this theme is carried through in the copy, which reads like a newspaper photo caption and ends with "Story on 2C." Layouts are often done in rough form and presented to the client so that the advertiser can visualize what the ad will look like before giving preliminary approval.

Exhibit 9–22 This ad for Sims Snowboards uses a strong visual image and a layout that resembles a newspaper page

The agency should get client approval of the layout before moving on to the more costly stages of print production.

Creative Tactics for Television

As consumers, we see so many TV commercials that it's easy to take for granted the time, effort, and money that go into making them. Creating and producing commercials that break through the clutter on TV and communicate effectively is a detailed, expensive process. On a cost-per-minute basis, commercials are the most expensive productions seen on television.

TV is a unique and powerful advertising medium because it contains the elements of sight, sound, and motion, which can be combined to create a variety of advertising appeals and executions. Unlike print, the viewer does not control the rate at which the message is presented, so there is no opportunity to review points of interest or reread things that are not communicated clearly. As with any form of advertising, one of the first goals in creating TV commercials is to get the viewers' attention and then maintain it. This can be particularly challenging because of the clutter and because people often view TV commercials while doing other things (reading a book or magazine, talking).

Like print ads, TV commercials have several components. The video and audio must work together to create the right impact and communicate the advertiser's message.

Video

The video elements of a commercial are what is seen on the TV screen. The visual portion generally dominates the commercial, so it must attract viewers' attention and communicate an idea, message, and/or image. A number of visual elements may have to be coordinated to produce a successful ad. Decisions have to be made regarding the product, the presenter, action sequences, demonstrations, and the like, as well as the setting(s), the talent or characters who will appear in the commercial, and such other factors as lighting, graphics, color, and identifying symbols.

Audio

The audio portion of a commercial includes voices, music, and sound effects. Voices are used in different ways in commercials. They may be heard through the direct presentation of a spokesperson or as a conversation among various people appearing in the commercial. A common method for presenting the audio portion of a commercial is through a **voiceover,** where the message is delivered or action on the screen is narrated or described by an announcer who is not visible. A trend among major advertisers is to have celebrities with distinctive voices do the voiceovers for their commercials.[28] Actor Richard Dreyfuss does the voiceovers in some Honda commercials, Adam Arkin is the voice in Subway ads, Jeff Goldblum does Apple Computers, and William Shatner does Priceline.com.

Music is also an important part of many TV commercials and can play a variety of roles.[29] In many commercials, the music provides a pleasant background or helps create the appropriate mood. Advertisers often use **needledrop,** which Linda Scott describes as follows:

> Needledrop is an occupational term common to advertising agencies and the music industry. It refers to music that is prefabricated, multipurpose, and highly conventional. It is, in that sense, the musical equivalent of stock photos, clip art, or canned copy. Needledrop is an inexpensive substitute for original music; paid for on a one-time basis, it is dropped into a commercial or film when a particular normative effect is desired.[30]

In some commercials, music is much more central to the advertising message. It can be used to get attention, break through the advertising clutter, communicate a key selling point, help establish an image or position, or add feeling.[31] For example, music can work through a classical conditioning process to create positive emotions that become associated with the advertised product or service. Music can also create a positive mood that makes the consumer more receptive toward the advertising message.[32] IMC Perspective 9–3 discusses the important role music plays in the "Like a Rock" campaign for Chevy trucks.

Because music can play such an important role in the creative strategy, many companies have paid large sums for the rights to use popular songs in their commercials. For example, Microsoft paid a reported $4 million to use the Rolling Stones' classic "Start Me Up" to introduce the advertising campaign for Windows 95.[33] Nortel Networks licensed the rights to use the classic Beatles' song "Come Together" (although it is performed by a different group) as the central theme in the company's new global advertising campaign.[34]

Another important musical element in both TV and radio commercials is **jingles,** catchy songs about a product or service that usually carry the advertising theme and a simple message. For example, Doublemint gum has used the well-known "Double your pleasure, double your fun with Doublemint, Doublemint gum" for years. The jingle is very memorable and serves as a good reminder of the product's minty flavor. Oscar Mayer has used the popular jingles for some of its products, such as the bologna song ("My bologna has a first name/ It's O-S-C-A-R") and the Oscar Mayer wiener song ("I'd love to be an Oscar Mayer wiener"), as the basis of integrated marketing programs. The company's fleet of wienermobiles travel the country as part of the Oscar Mayer Talent Search, where local auditions are held in search of children who will continue the 30-year tradition of singing the catchy bologna and wiener jingles.[35]

Exhibit 9–23 Volkswagen's award-winning commercials are some of the most popular in recent years

Jingles can be used by themselves as the basis for a musical commercial. Diet Coke brought back its old slogan "Just for the taste of it," set it to a luxurious musical score, and made it the basis of a multimillion-dollar ad campaign. In some commercials, jingles are used more as a form of product identification and appear at the end of the message. Jingles are often composed by companies that specialize in writing commercial music for advertising. These jingle houses work with the creative team to determine the role music will play in the commercial and the message that needs to be communicated.

Planning and Production of TV Commercials

One of the first decisions that has to be made in planning a TV commercial is the type of appeal and execution style that will be used. Television is well suited to both rational and emotional advertising appeals or combinations of the two. Various execution styles used with rational appeals, such as a straight sell or announcement, demonstration, testimonial, or comparison, work well on TV.

Advertisers recognize that they need to do more than talk about, demonstrate, or compare their products or services. Their commercials have to break through the clutter and grab viewers' attention; they must often appeal to emotional, as well as rational, buying motives. Television is essentially an entertainment medium, and many advertisers recognize that their commercials are most successful when they entertain as well as inform. Many of the most popular advertising campaigns are characterized by commercials with strong entertainment value, like the Budweiser spots featuring the talking lizards, the humorous "Got milk?" ads discussed in Chapter 8, and the musical spots for the Gap. Some of the most popular commercials recently have been those created for Volkswagen's "Drivers wanted" campaign, which explores drivers' life experiences with their VWs[36] (Exhibit 9–23). TV is particularly well suited to drama; no other advertising medium can touch emotions as well. Various emotional appeals such as humor, fear, and fantasy work well on TV, as do dramatizations and slice-of-life executions.

Planning the Commercial

The various elements of a TV commercial are brought together in a **script,** a written version of a commercial that provides a detailed description of its video and audio content. The script shows the various audio components of the commercial—the copy to be spoken by voices, the music, and sound effects. The video portion of the script provides the visual plan of the commercial—camera actions and angles, scenes,

IMC Perspective 9–3

Chevy Trucks Find a Rock-Solid Advertising Theme

In 1990 the Chevrolet truck line was in a battle for survival. Sales were down; factories were closing. R. M. "Mac" Whisner, manager of Chevy truck advertising, and Don Gould of Campbell-Ewald Advertising knew they had to find a way to bolster the Chevy truck line, which accounts for well over half of all Chevrolet sales. The marketing research showed that Chevy trucks performed well and were viewed as good-looking, but they were also perceived as least dependable, least durable, and wimpy. These perceptions had to be changed.

Gould and his colleagues had two campaigns ready to test, but he didn't like either one. Desperate, he spent a weekend hunting through his music collection looking for inspiration and noticed an old tape of Bob Seger's. Gould recalls, "Right on the cover it said 'Like a Rock,' and I thought, 'That is *exactly* what we need.'" He patched together a mock-up commercial using old videotape with the song and rushed it to California for a focus group test.

One of the participants in the focus group was a carpenter named Fred. In the taped interviews before the presentation, Fred described himself as the most vocal critic of American trucks. He considered them shoddy. However, after viewing the mock-up commercial, Fred was a changed man. "You got me!" he shouted. He and the rest of the group said there was no way they could ever buy another truck without at least looking at a Chevy. Gould says, "Good old Fred sold this. When he talked about goosebumps, we knew we had a hit." They got the same response from every focus group test they did. They didn't just have a great commercial; they had one that was making audiences stand up and cheer.

There was still one problem, however. Chevrolet did not have the rights to air it. In the rush to put the test commercial together, there had been no time to acquire the rights to use the lyrics from Seger, and when they asked, he turned them down. For six months Seger kept saying no, as he did not want to do any commercials. Gould finally convinced Seger's manager, Punch Andrews, to watch the ad. After 15 seconds Andrews was convinced. Seger, a workaday rocker with blue-collar Michigan roots, recalls Andrews telling him: "I know I've been bringing you these commercials for years and you have always said no. But this one makes sense. This is trucks. You drive them. It's very American." Seger adds, "There was this feeling that the Japanese were running us off our heels and maybe we could help."

But Seger was not swayed until one night when he was dining with his wife at a restaurant in Detroit. An autoworker came up to the table and politely asked him to do something to help the auto industry. Seger had just read that GM had lost over $1 billion in a single quarter and decided that if he could do something to help, he would. The next day he called Andrews and told him to accept (but not before first checking to make sure the autoworker was legitimate and not working for the ad agency).

The "Like a Rock" song has propelled one of the most successful and long-lasting campaigns in automotive advertising and has become a three-word mission statement for the entire Chevrolet truck division. The manager for Chevy trucks says, "It is not just a marketing campaign. It captures the soul of the brand. It is how to build a truck, it is how to run a company."

It is also the foundation of a great ad campaign for selling trucks. General Motors has been producing Chevy trucks at or near capacity for several years. Chevy has become a strong number-two truck brand in the United States and annual sales have increased 33 percent since 1991. Marketing and strategy consultant Jack Trout says of the campaign, "There is a handful of brilliant positioning ideas in the auto business—Volvo and safety, BMW and driving—and this is one of them: Chevy trucks, like a rock. I would never change it."

Sources: Joe Urschel, "Three Words That Evolved into a Corporate Hymn," *USA Today,* January 5, 1996, pp. 1, 2A; Dottie Enrico, "Chevy Campaign Is Solid 'Like a Rock,'" *USA Today,* February 19, 1996, p. 5B.

transitions, and other important descriptions. The script also shows how the video corresponds to the audio portion of the commercial.

Once the basic script has been conceived, the writer and art director get together to produce a storyboard, a series of drawings used to present the visual plan or layout of a proposed commercial. The storyboard contains still drawings of the video scenes and descriptions of the audio that accompanies each scene. Like layouts for print ads, storyboards provide those involved in the production and approval of the commercial with a good approximation of what the final commercial will look like. In some cases an aniamatic (a videotape of the storyboard along with the soundtrack) may be produced if a more finished form of the commercial is needed for client presentations or pretesting.

Production Once the storyboard or aniamatic of the commercial is approved, it is ready to move to the production phase, which involves three stages:

1. *Preproduction*—all the work and activities that occur before the actual shooting/recording of the commercial.
2. *Production*—the period during which the commercial is filmed or videotaped and recorded.
3. *Postproduction*—activities and work that occur after the commercial has been filmed and recorded.

The various activities of each phase are shown in Figure 9–3. Before the final production process begins, the client must usually review and approve the creative strategy and the various tactics that will be used in creating the advertising message.

Client Evaluation and Approval of Creative Work

While the creative specialists have much responsibility for determining the advertising appeal and execution style to be used in a campaign, the client must evaluate and approve the creative approach before any ads are produced. A number of people on the client side may be involved in evaluating the creative work of the agency, including the advertising or communications manager, product or brand managers, marketing director or vice president, representatives from the legal department, and sometimes even the president or chief executive officer (CEO) of the company or the board of directors.

The amount of input each of these individuals has in the creative evaluation and approval process varies depending on the company's policies, the importance of the product to the company, the role of advertising in the marketing program, and the advertising approach being recommended. IMC Perspective 9–4 discusses how Chiat/Day had to convince Apple's board of directors to air the "1984" commercial used to introduce the Macintosh personal computer and recently chosen as the greatest TV commercial of all time.

Figure 9–3 The three phases of production for commercials

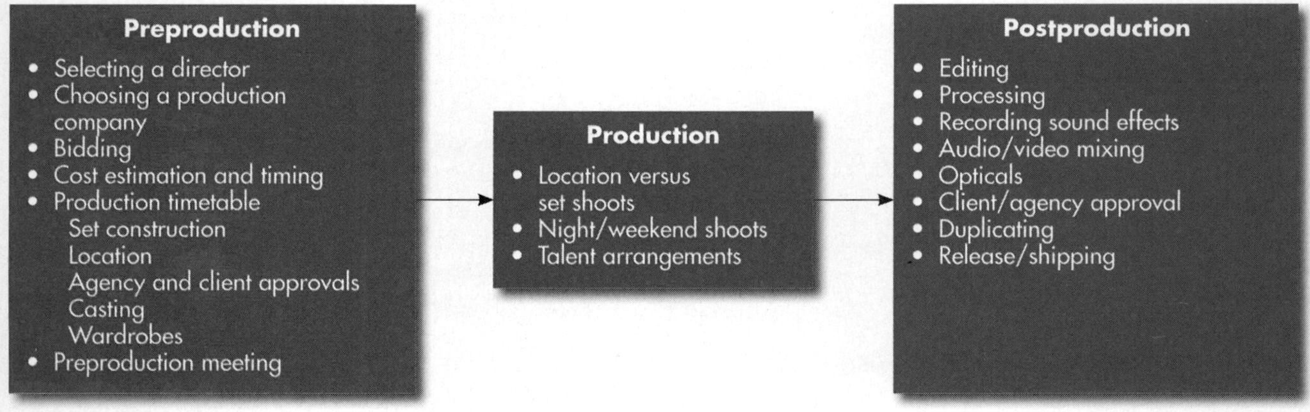

IMC Perspective 9–4

The Greatest Commercial of All Time—and Why We Almost Didn't See It

In 1983, Apple Computer was planning the introduction of its line of Macintosh personal computers, designed to take on its main competitor, corporate giant IBM. Apple had just lost its lead in the PC market to IBM and its previous product introduction, the $10,000 Lisa, had not been very successful. Some analysts suggested that the survival of Apple might depend on the market's response to the Mac.

Apple's marketing strategy called for the introduction of the Macintosh to be a major event that would generate immediate support for the new product. The advertising agency, Chiat/Day, was given the creative challenge of coming up with a blockbuster idea that would result in a dramatic commercial to introduce the Mac. Chiat/Day's creative team developed a commercial based on the concept of Big Brother (purportedly symbolizing IBM) from George Orwell's classic novel *1984.* The ad used stark images of Orwell's dystopia and a dramatic scene of a young woman throwing a mallet through a movie screen to destroy the controlling force. More than $500,000 was spent to produce the "1984" commercial, which was filmed in London by well-known film director Ridley Scott and contained a cast of more than 200.

When the commercial was first shown at Apple's annual sales meeting in October 1983, there was stunned silence followed by a 15-minute standing ovation. Apple was ready to showcase the 60-second commercial in two spots during the 1984 Super Bowl that would cost $500,000 each. But there was still one problem—getting approval from Apple's board of directors for the avant-garde ad and the million-dollar media purchase.

The board thought the commercial was too controversial and might be detrimental to Apple's image, particularly in the business market. The cost-conscious board also thought the Super Bowl rates were too expensive and directed the agency to sell off the two spots. The agency began working to sell off the media time while simultaneously lobbying Apple not to cancel the ad. The agency did manage to sell one of the 60-second spots but could not attract a reasonable offer for the other. Two days before the game, the Apple board reluctantly approved airing the commercial.

The Super Bowl showing of "1984" was the only time it ever appeared as a commercial spot on network TV. The impact of the ad was tremendous. It was the focus of attention in the media and the talk of the advertising and marketing industries. Perhaps most important, the ad helped Apple achieve a very ambitious sales goal. Apple projected sales of 50,000 Macs in the first 100 days; actual sales surpassed 72,000 units.

Over time the "1984" spot became one of the most talked-about commercials ever. In 1990, *Advertising Age,* the ad industry's leading trade publication, chose it as the commercial of the decade and named Chiat/Day agency of the decade. Ten years after the commercial first ran, it was still receiving numerous accolades. In January 1994, *Advertising Age* published a feature story that said the "1984" spot had changed the nature of advertising forever. It helped turn the Super Bowl from a mere football game into advertising's superevent of the year. And it ushered in the era of advertising as news: The three major TV networks replayed parts or all of the spot as a story on nightly news programs. John O'Toole, president of the American Association of Advertising Agencies, said "1984" was the beginning of a new era of integrated marketing communications as event marketing, with sales promotion and PR built in.

Many view the Macintosh PC as one of the most significant new products ever introduced, since it

revolutionized personal computing and transformed the production of graphics around the world. The "computer for the rest of us" is also credited with helping to bring computing power to the people. As *Advertising Age* critic Bob Garfield said, "This is what happens when breakthrough technology is given the benefit of the greatest TV commercial ever made." He is not alone in his praise of the spot. In 1999 *TV Guide* named the "1984" spot the greatest TV commercial of all time. And to think that the ad came close to never running!

Sources: Dottie Enrico, "The Best Ads Keep Going and...Going," *TV Guide,* July 2–9, 1999, pp. 2–6+; Bradley Johnson, "10 Years after '1984': The Commercial and the Product That Changed Advertising," *Advertising Age,* June 1994, pp. 1, 12–14; Bob Garfield, "Breakthrough Product Gets Greatest TV Spot," *Advertising Age,* January 10, 1994, p. 14; Cleveland Horton, "Apple's Bold '1984' Scores on All Fronts," *Advertising Age,* January 1, 1990, p. 12. Reprinted with permission from the June 1994, January 10, 1994, and January 1, 1990, issues of *Advertising Age.* Copyright Crain Communications, Inc. 1990, 1994.

Earlier in this chapter, we noted that Procter & Gamble has been moving away from testimonials and slice-of-life advertising executions to somewhat riskier and more lively forms of advertising. But the company remains conservative and has been slow to adopt the avant-garde ads used by many of its competitors. Agencies that do the advertising for various P&G brands recognize that quirky executions that challenge the company's subdued corporate culture are not likely to be approved.[37]

In many cases, top management is involved in selecting an ad agency and must approve the theme and creative strategy for the campaign. Evaluation and approval of the individual ads proposed by the agency often rest with the advertising and product managers who are primarily responsible for the brand. The account executive and a member of the creative team present the creative concept to the client's advertising and product and/or marketing managers for their approval before beginning production. A careful evaluation should be made before the ad actually enters production, since this stage requires considerable time and money as suppliers are hired to perform the various functions required to produce the actual ad.

The client's evaluation of the print layout or commercial storyboard can be difficult, since the advertising or brand manager is generally not a creative expert and must be careful not to reject viable creative approaches or accept ideas that will result in inferior advertising. However, personnel on the client side can use the guidelines discussed next to judge the efficacy of creative approaches suggested by the agency.

Guidelines for Evaluating Creative Output

Advertisers use numerous criteria to evaluate the creative approach suggested by the ad agency. In some instances, the client may want to have the rough layout or storyboard pretested to get quantitative information to assist in the evaluation. However, the evaluation process is usually more subjective; the advertising or brand manager relies on qualitative considerations. Basic criteria for evaluating creative approaches are discussed next:

- *Is the creative approach consistent with the brand's marketing and advertising objectives?* One of the most important factors the client must consider is whether the creative appeal and execution style recommended by the agency are consistent with the marketing strategy for the brand and the role advertising and promotion have been assigned in the overall marketing program. This means the creative approach must be compatible with the image of the brand and the way it is positioned in the marketplace and should contribute to the marketing and advertising objectives.
- *Is the creative approach consistent with the creative strategy and objectives? Does it communicate what it is supposed to?* The advertising appeal and execution must meet the communications objectives laid out in the copy platform, and the ad must say what the advertising strategy calls for it to say. Creative specialists can lose sight of what the advertising message is supposed to be and come up with an approach that fails to execute the advertising strategy. Individuals responsible for approving the ad should ask the creative spe-

cialists to explain how the appeal or execution style adheres to the creative strategy and helps meet communications objectives.

- *Is the creative approach appropriate for the target audience?* Generally, much time has been spent defining, locating, and attempting to understand the target audience for the advertiser's product or service. Careful consideration should be given to whether the ad appeal or execution recommended will appeal to, be understood by, and communicate effectively with the target audience. This involves studying all elements of the ad and how the audience will respond to them. Advertisers do not want to approve advertising that they believe will receive a negative reaction from the target audience. For example, it has been suggested that advertising targeted to older consumers should use models who are 10 years younger than the average age of the target audience, since most people feel younger than their chronological age.[38] Advertisers also face a considerable challenge developing ads for the teen market because teenagers' styles, fashions, language, and values change so rapidly. They may find they are using an advertising approach, a spokesperson, or even an expression that is no longer popular among teens.
- *Does the creative approach communicate a clear and convincing message to the customer?* Most ads are supposed to communicate a message that will help sell the brand. Many ads fail to communicate a clear and convincing message that motivates consumers to use a brand. While creativity is important in advertising, it is also important that the advertising communicate information attributes, features and benefits, and/or images that give consumers a reason to buy the brand.
- *Does the creative execution keep from overwhelming the message?* A common criticism of advertising, and TV commercials in particular, is that so much emphasis is placed on creative execution that the advertiser's message gets overshadowed. Many creative, entertaining commercials have failed to register the brand name and/or selling points effectively.

  For example, a few years ago the agency for North American Philips Lighting Corp. developed an award-winning campaign that focused on the humorous results when lightbulbs fail at just the wrong time. The spots included a woman who appears to accidentally vacuum up her screeching cat after a lightbulb blows out and an elderly couple using Philips Pastel bulbs to create a romantic mood (Exhibit 9–24). While the purpose of the campaign was to help Philips make inroads into General Electric's dominance in the lightbulb market, many consumers did not notice the Philips brand name. A Video Storyboard survey showed that many viewers thought the ads were for GE lightbulbs. Surveys taken a year later by the agency that created the campaign showed that brand awareness and sales had increased considerably, but some advertising people still think the ads were so creative and entertaining that they overwhelmed the message.[39]

  With the increasing amount of clutter in most advertising media, it may be necessary to use a novel creative approach to gain the viewer's or reader's attention. However, the creative execution cannot overwhelm the message. Clients must walk a fine line: Make sure the sales message is not lost, but be careful not to stifle the efforts of the creative specialists and force them into producing dull, boring advertising.
- *Is the creative approach appropriate for the media environment in which it is likely to be seen?* Each media vehicle has its own specific climate that results from the nature of its editorial content, the type of reader or viewer it attracts, and the nature of the ads it contains. Consideration should be given to how well the ad fits into the media environment in which it will be shown. For example, the Super Bowl has become a showcase for commercials. People who care very little about advertising know how much a 30-second commercial costs and pay as much attention to the ads as to the game itself, so many advertisers feel compelled to develop new ads for the Super Bowl or to save new commercials for the game.

Exhibit 9–24 Some advertising experts think these Philips Lighting commercials may have been too creative and overwhelmed the message

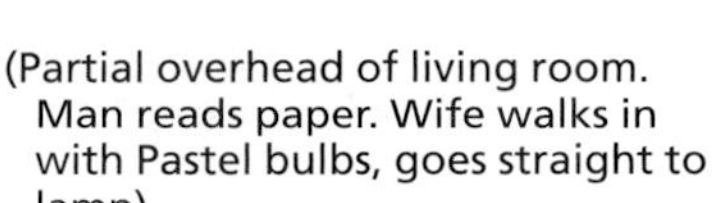

(Partial overhead of living room. Man reads paper. Wife walks in with Pastel bulbs, goes straight to lamp).
ANNCR: For a change of mood, (Wife turns off lamp, as husband ignores her).
ANNCR: Change to Philips Softone Pastel light bulbs. (Woman switches on lamp. It now gives a warm peach hue to the whole room).
MUSIC. (Piano riff) (Shot over piano as man sings).

MAN: I'm in the mood for love. Simply because…
(Woman slides into frame with bottle of champagne).
MAN: (Singing) you're near me. (Suddenly, the cork pops out and flies at the man).
MAN: Funny but when you're
SFX: Cork pop. (Cork hits man on forehead, leaving a little impression).
SFX: Bop! (He's stunned into silence for a brief moment. He launches back into the song with great enthusiasm).

MAN: near me.
(Woman puts bottle in bucket at left of piano and slides next to him).
MAN: I'm in the mood for love.
ANNCR: Make everything seem more beautiful…
(All the colors are represented. Each bulb lights up in sequence from left to right. "Philips" clicks on)…
ANNCR: With new Softone Pastels. It's time to change your bulb to Philips.

- *Is the ad truthful and tasteful?* Marketers also have to consider whether an ad is truthful, as well as whether it might offend consumers. For example, the Just For Feet athletic footwear chain ran a commercial on the 1999 Super Bowl that featured a Kenyan runner who was tracked like an animal by white mercenaries, drugged unconscious, and fit with a pair of running shoes—which goes against centuries of Kenyan tradition. The spot led to charges of neocolonialism and racism from outraged consumers and the media and created a major public relations problem for the company. Just For Feet had to pull the spot after running it only one time and ended up suing its ad agency.[40] The ultimate responsibility for determining whether an ad deceives or offends the target audience lies with the client. It is the job of the advertising or brand manager to evaluate the approach suggested by the creative specialists against company standards. The firm's legal department may be asked to review the ad to determine whether the creative appeal, message content, or execution could cause any problems for the company. It is much better to catch any potential legal problems before the ad is shown to the public.

The advertising manager, brand manager, or other personnel on the client side can use these basic guidelines in reviewing, evaluating, and approving the ideas offered by the creative specialists. There may be other factors specific to the firm's advertising and marketing situation. Also, there may be situations where it is acceptable to deviate from the standards the firm usually uses in judging creative output. As we shall see in Chapter 19, the client may want to move beyond these subjective criteria and use more sophisticated pretesting methods to determine the effectiveness of a particular approach suggested by the creative specialist or team.

Summary

In this chapter, we examined how the advertising message is implemented and executed. Once the creative strategy that will guide the ad campaign has been determined, attention turns to the specific type of advertising appeal and execution format to carry out the creative plan. The appeal is the central message used in the ad to elicit some response from consumers or influence their feelings. Appeals can be broken into two broad categories, rational and emotional. Rational appeals focus on consumers' practical, functional, or utilitarian need for the product or service; emotional appeals relate to social and/or psychological reasons for purchasing a product or service. Numerous types of appeals are available to advertisers within each category.

The creative execution style is the way the advertising appeal is presented in the message. A number of common execution techniques were examined in the chapter, along with considerations for their use. Attention was also given to tactical issues involved in creating print and TV advertising. The components of a print ad include headlines, body copy, illustrations, and layout. We also examined the video and audio components of TV commercials and various considerations involved in the planning and production of commercials.

Creative specialists are responsible for determining the advertising appeal and execution style as well as the tactical aspects of creating ads. However, the client must review, evaluate, and approve the creative approach before any ads are produced or run. A number of criteria can be used by advertising, product, or brand managers and others involved in the promotional process to evaluate the advertising messages before approving final production.

Key Terms

advertising appeal, 275
creative execution style, 275
informational/rational appeals, 275
emotional appeals, 276
transformational ad, 278
reminder advertising, 280
teaser advertising, 281
headline, 290
direct headlines, 291
indirect headlines, 291
subheads, 291
body copy, 291
layout, 292
voiceover, 293
needledrop, 293
jingles, 294
script, 294

Discussion Questions

1. Analyze the Jack in the Box campaign discussed in the opening vignette to the chapter. Why do you think this campaign has been so successful?

2. Discuss the difference between an advertising appeal and a creative execution style. Find several ads and analyze the particular appeal and execution style used in each.

3. Discuss the various motives that can be used as the basis of rational advertising appeals. Find examples of ads that use some of these rational motives as the basis for their advertising appeal.

4. Discuss some of the various social and psychological states or needs that might be used as the basis for emotional advertising appeals. Find examples of ads that use social and psychological needs as the basis for their advertising appeals.

5. What is meant by transformational advertising? Analyze the ad for Norwegian Cruise Lines shown in Exhibit 9–5 from a transformational advertising perspective.

6. Describe the use of dramatization as an advertising execution technique. Discuss a product or service for which dramatization might be an effective form of execution.

7. IMC Perspective 9–1 discusses the idea that the Internet and advertising for online companies is leading to a new creative revolution in advertising. Do you feel advertising for various dot.com and online companies is leading to a new creative revolution in advertising? Why or why not?

8. Why do consumer packaged-goods advertisers such as Procter & Gamble often use slice-of-life executions? Can this advertising technique be used for business-to-business products as well?

9. Discuss the role of headlines and subheads in print advertisements. Find examples of print ads that use various types of direct and indirect headlines.

10. Analyze the "Like a Rock" campaign for Chevrolet trucks discussed in IMC Perspective 9–3. Why do you think this campaign has been so successful in striking a responsive chord with truck buyers? How long do you think Chevrolet trucks can use this campaign theme?

11. Discuss the role of music in advertising. Why might companies such as Microsoft and Nortel Networks pay large sums of money for the rights to use popular songs in their commercials?

Chapter Ten

Media Planning and Strategy

Chapter Objectives

- To understand the key terminology used in media planning.
- To know how a media plan is developed.
- To know the process of developing and implementing media strategies.
- To be familiar with sources of media information and characteristics of media.

A Media Marriage: The Internet Marries an Older Partner

Imagine that your college team is playing an away game and that you want to see it. Unfortunately, it is not on TV, but you can listen to the game because it is being broadcast through the Internet. As you listen, you think how nice it would be to be able to watch the game—even if it was just on your computer screen. Then you start to fantasize about being able to communicate with your friends in other parts of the country who are watching the game (without the cost of phone calls every time something happens) and about having instant access to statistics on the teams and players. Well dream no more—it is about to happen, and sooner than you think, as a result of a few recent "media marriages." AOL has married Time Warner, and ACTV and CatchTV have tied the knot.

The marriage between AOL and Time Warner has been touted in the media as "evolutionary," "the start of a new era," and "tearing down the Berlin Wall between broadcast video and the Internet." AOL, America's largest web portal with over 22 million subscribers, purchased Time Warner, owner of TimeLife magazines (including *Sports Illustrated, Fortune,* and *People*), CNN, Turner Broadcasting (TBS), HBO, Atlantic Records, Warner Brothers TV Network, and Warner Brothers Records and movies, to name a few! It's the new merging with the traditional.

Why would one of the hottest Internet companies be interested in a traditional media provider—especially one that is debt-ridden? The answer is *content.* Internet companies know that to grow they must provide interesting content to their viewers, and what they have right now is not enough. Time Warner can provide, among other things, digital WB movies on demand, the ability to download music from WB labels, TV shows like "ER," "Friends," and "Buffy the Vampire Slayer," and the Cartoon Network. In addition, the merger will allow for improved video quality, digital photography, and three-dimensional features—all at a much faster pace than is typical today. Current Internet content, interestingly

enough, is often compared to TV in the early days—"repurposed" from one medium to another (in the old days, it was radio to TV). Many claim that there is nothing novel about the Internet content and not enough developed specifically for the Internet. AOL believes that younger audiences are particularly interested in the interactive capabilities of media due to their desire to multi-task. Many experts feel that the acquisition will provide AOL with the foundation to deliver mass interactive content over the Internet.

And what about Time Warner? What does it get out of the deal? Besides receiving new money, it will acquire access to AOL's millions of subscribers—a nice database with which to start cross-promoting, cross-marketing, and product tie-in efforts. In addition, Time Warner becomes portable, able to present content through laptops and eventually even through hand-held products like Palm Pilots. Equally appealing is the opportunity to go direct—consider the attraction of not having to produce or ship CDs or go through wholesalers and retailers to get them distributed. All consumers have to do to hear Madonna or Faith Hill is download the recording from the Internet (for a fee).

And what about that other marriage? ACTV, through its product "HyperTV," synchronizes the delivery of content on the Web with TV programming. To use HyperTV, the viewer must watch TV while online. For example, you can purchase an enhanced version of the pay-per-view airing of *Austin Powers: The Spy Who Shagged Me* which includes added content and information online as well as e-commerce interactively. CatchTV created and patented digital "bookmarking," which enables users to save addresses of Web pages related to TV programming or advertising and then view the pages before, during, and after the TV program has aired. The marriage allows for more and easier access to content. ACTV has also signed deals with the Box Music Network (part of MTV's interactive division) and Showtime Networks.

It seems the Internet just can't get enough content these days. While ACTV married someone its own age, AOL sought an older, more traditional partner. The question now is will the marriage last?

Sources: William J. Holstein and Fred Vogelstein, "You've Got a Deal," *U.S. News & World Report,* January 24, 2000, pp. 33–44; Daniel Okrent, "Happily Ever After?" *Time,* January 24, 2000, pp. 39–43; Kipp Cheng, "ACTV to Expand with CatchTV Acquisition," *Adweek,* November 22, 1999, p. 40.

The AOL–Time Warner and ACTV-CatchTV mergers described in this chapter's opening vignette are just two of the many changes taking place in the media environment. Perhaps at no other time in history have so many changes taken place that significantly alter the media decision process. As you will see in the following chapters, these changes offer the marketer opportunities not previously available, but they also require in-depth knowledge of all the alternatives. Integrated marketing communications programs are no longer a luxury; they are a necessity. Media planners must now consider new options as well as recognize the changes that are occurring in traditional sources. New and evolving media contribute to the already difficult task of media planning. Planning when, where, and how the advertising message will be delivered is a complex and involved process. The primary objective of the media plan is to develop a framework that will deliver the message to the target audience in the most efficient, cost-effective manner possible—that will communicate what the product, brand, and/ or service can do.

This chapter presents the various methods of message delivery available to marketers, examines some key considerations in making media decisions, and discusses the development of media strategies and plans. Later chapters will explore the relative advantages and disadvantages of the various media and examine each in more detail.

An Overview of Media Planning

The media planning process is not an easy one. Options include mass media such as television, newspapers, radio, and magazines (and the choices available within each of these categories) as well as out-of-the-home media such as outdoor advertising, transit advertising, and electronic billboards. A variety of support media such as direct marketing, interactive media, promotional products advertising, and in-store point-of-purchase options must also be considered.

While at first glance the choices among these alternatives might seem relatively straightforward, this is rarely the case. Part of the reason media selection becomes so involved is the nature of the media themselves. TV combines both sight and sound, an advantage not offered by other media. Magazines can convey more information and may keep the message available to the potential buyer for a much longer time. Newspapers also offer their own advantages, as do outdoor, direct media, and each of the others. The Internet offers many of the advantages of other media but is also limited in its capabilities. The characteristics of each alternative must be considered, along with many other factors. This process becomes even more complicated when the manager has to choose between alternatives within the same medium—for example, between *Time* and *Newsweek* or between "The Practice" and "Friends."

The potential for achieving effective communications through a well-designed media strategy warrants the added attention. The power of an effective media strategy was demonstrated by PC Flowers, at one time the smallest of the 25,000 members in the Florists' Transworld Delivery Association. The company then started to advertise its services on Prodigy, the interactive computer service. Within four months, PC Flowers moved into the top 10; now it consistently ranks as one of the top two FTD members in the world.[1] Likewise, MCI, the number-two long-distance company, was losing market share to AT&T until it began blitzing the market with promotions and other ad messages. In one year, MCI ran more than 50 different TV commercials in addition to specialized spots on Chinese, Hispanic, and Russian television. The company effectively stemmed the market share erosion.[2]

The product and/or service being advertised affects the media planning process. As demonstrated in Figure 10–1, firms have found some media more useful than others in conveying their messages to specific target audiences. For example, GM and Procter & Gamble tend to rely more heavily on broadcast media, while others like JCPenney and Federated Department Stores (not shown) place more emphasis on print media. The result is placement of advertising dollars in these preferred media—and significantly different media strategies.

Some Basic Terms and Concepts

Before beginning our discussion of media planning, we review some basic terms and concepts used in the media planning and strategy process.

Media planning is the series of decisions involved in delivering the promotional message to the prospective purchasers and/or users of the product or brand. Media planning is a process, which means a number of decisions are made, each of which may be altered or abandoned as the plan develops.

The media plan is the guide for media selection. It requires development of specific **media objectives** and specific **media strategies** (plans of action) designed to

Figure 10–1 Leaders by U.S. advertising spending

Rank		Total U.S. Ad Spending	Magazine and Newspaper	TV, Cable, and Radio	Outdoor, Yellow Pages, International
1	General Motors Corp.	$2,940.4	$643.2	$1,454.8	$56.2
2	Procter & Gamble Co.	2,650.3	412.6	1,304.8	11.9
3	Philip Morris Co.	2,049.3	389.5	804.7	70.2
4	DaimlerChrysler	1,646.7	424.8	946.4	28.5
5	Sears, Roebuck & Co.	1,578.3	298.2	422.1	21.6
6	Ford Motor Co.	1,520.7	446.4	694.5	39.1
7	AT&T Corp.	1,428.0	180.5	410.1	23.5
8	Walt Disney Co.	1,358.7	216.1	577.9	21.2
9	PepsiCo	1,263.4	38.6	293.1	8.2
10	Diageo	1,205.7	86.6	560.4	16.1

attain these objectives. Once the decisions have been made and the objectives and strategies formulated, this information is organized into the media plan.

The **medium** is the general category of available delivery systems, which includes broadcast media (like TV and radio), print media (like newspapers and magazines), direct mail, outdoor advertising, and other support media. The **media vehicle** is the specific carrier within a medium category. For example, *Time* and *Newsweek* are print vehicles; "20/20" and "60 Minutes" are broadcast vehicles. As you will see in later chapters, each vehicle has its own characteristics as well as its own relative advantages and disadvantages. Specific decisions must be made as to the value of each in delivering the message.

Reach is a measure of the number of different audience members exposed at least once to a media vehicle in a given period of time. **Coverage** refers to the potential audience that might receive the message through a vehicle. Coverage relates to potential audience; reach refers to the actual audience delivered. (The importance of this distinction will become clearer later in this chapter.) Finally, **frequency** refers to the number of times the receiver is exposed to the media vehicle in a specified period.

The Media Plan

The media plan determines the best way to get the advertiser's message to the market. In a basic sense, the goal of the media plan is to find that combination of media that enables the marketer to communicate the message in the most effective manner to the largest number of potential customers at the lowest cost.

The activities involved in developing the media plan and the purposes of each are presented in Figure 10–2. As you can see, a number of decisions must be made throughout this process. As the plan evolves, events may occur that necessitate changes. Many advertisers find it necessary to alter and update their objectives and strategies frequently.

Problems in Media Planning

Unfortunately, the media strategy decision has not become a standardized task. A number of problems contribute to the difficulty of establishing the plan and reduce its effectiveness. These problems include insufficient information, inconsistent terminologies, time pressures, and difficulty measuring effectiveness.

Insufficient Information

While a great deal of information about markets and the media exists, media planners often require more than is available. Some data are just not measured, either because they cannot be or because measuring them would be too expensive. For example, continuous measures of radio listenership exist, but only periodic listenership studies are reported due to sample size and cost constraints. There are problems with some measures of audience size in TV and print as well, as demonstrated by IMC Perspective 10–1.

The timing of measurements is also a problem; some audience measures are taken only at specific times of the year. (For example, **sweeps periods** in February, May, July, and November are used for measuring TV audiences and setting advertising rates.) This information is then generalized to succeeding months, so future planning decisions must be made on past data that may not reflect current behaviors. Think about planning for TV advertising for the fall season. There are no data on the audiences of new shows, and audience information taken on existing programs during the summer may not indicate how these programs will do in the fall because summer viewership is generally much lower. While the advertisers can review these programs before they air, they do not have actual audience figures.

The lack of information is even more of a problem for small advertisers, who may not be able to afford to purchase the information they require. As a result, their decisions are based on limited or out-of-date data that was provided by the media themselves, or no data at all.

Figure 10–2 Activities involved in developing the media plan

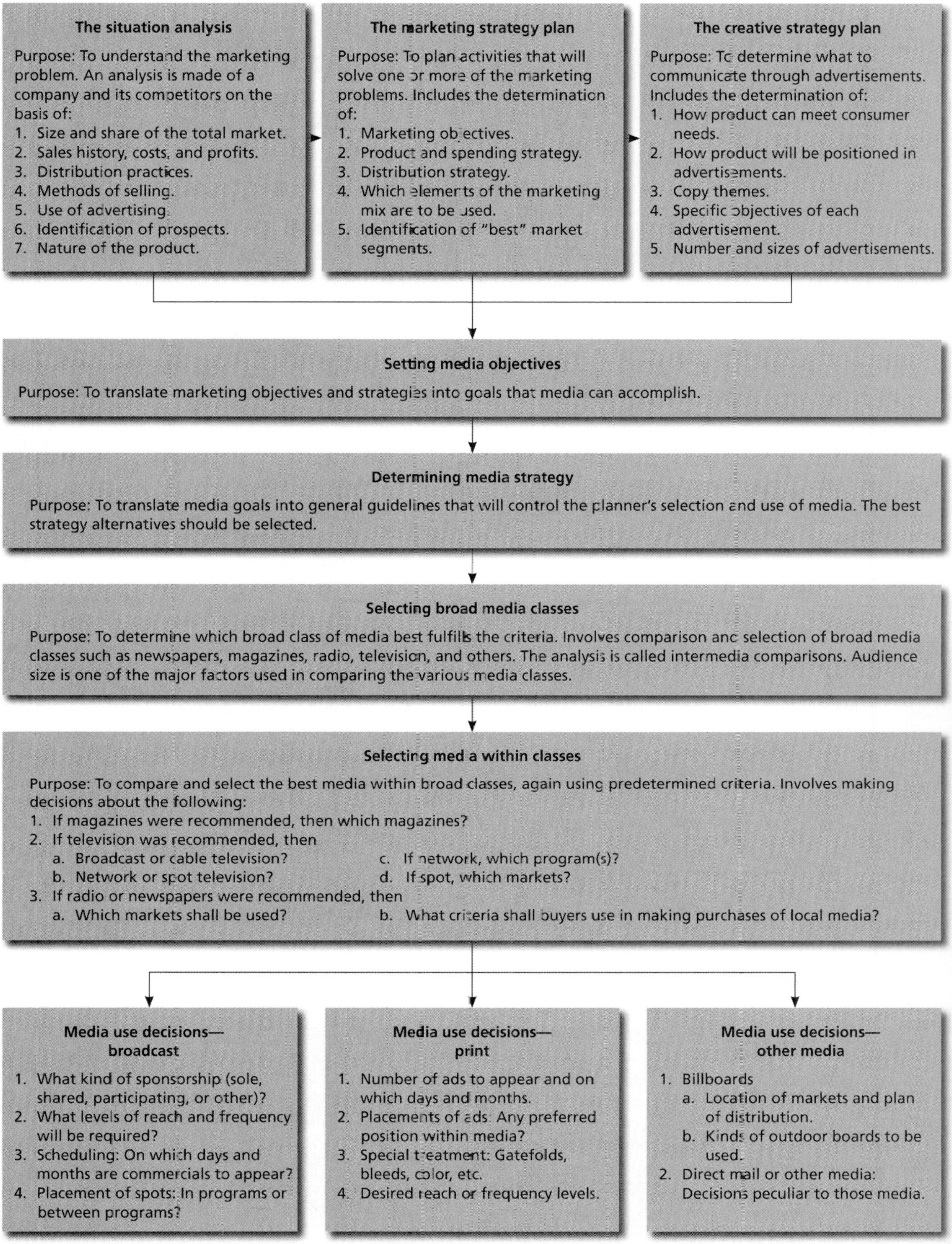

The situation analysis

Purpose: To understand the marketing problem. An analysis is made of a company and its competitors on the basis of:
1. Size and share of the total market.
2. Sales history, costs, and profits.
3. Distribution practices.
4. Methods of selling.
5. Use of advertising.
6. Identification of prospects.
7. Nature of the product.

The marketing strategy plan

Purpose: To plan activities that will solve one or more of the marketing problems. Includes the determination of:
1. Marketing objectives.
2. Product and spending strategy.
3. Distribution strategy.
4. Which elements of the marketing mix are to be used.
5. Identification of "best" market segments.

The creative strategy plan

Purpose: To determine what to communicate through advertisements. Includes the determination of:
1. How product can meet consumer needs.
2. How product will be positioned in advertisements.
3. Copy themes.
4. Specific objectives of each advertisement.
5. Number and sizes of advertisements.

Setting media objectives

Purpose: To translate marketing objectives and strategies into goals that media can accomplish.

Determining media strategy

Purpose: To translate media goals into general guidelines that will control the planner's selection and use of media. The best strategy alternatives should be selected.

Selecting broad media classes

Purpose: To determine which broad class of media best fulfills the criteria. Involves comparison and selection of broad media classes such as newspapers, magazines, radio, television, and others. The analysis is called intermedia comparisons. Audience size is one of the major factors used in comparing the various media classes.

Selecting media within classes

Purpose: To compare and select the best media within broad classes, again using predetermined criteria. Involves making decisions about the following:
1. If magazines were recommended, then which magazines?
2. If television was recommended, then
   a. Broadcast or cable television?
   b. Network or spot television?
   c. If network, which program(s)?
   d. If spot, which markets?
3. If radio or newspapers were recommended, then
   a. Which markets shall be used?
   b. What criteria shall buyers use in making purchases of local media?

Media use decisions—broadcast

1. What kind of sponsorship (sole, shared, participating, or other)?
2. What levels of reach and frequency will be required?
3. Scheduling: On which days and months are commercials to appear?
4. Placement of spots: In programs or between programs?

Media use decisions—print

1. Number of ads to appear and on which days and months.
2. Placements of ads: Any preferred position within media?
3. Special treatment: Gatefolds, bleeds, color, etc.
4. Desired reach or frequency levels.

Media use decisions—other media

1. Billboards
   a. Location of markets and plan of distribution.
   b. Kinds of outdoor boards to be used.
2. Direct mail or other media: Decisions peculiar to those media.

IMC Perspective 10–1

Media Services Companies under Attack

Advertising costs are determined by how many people can be reached through the medium. In print media, such costs are based on circulation and readership figures; in broadcast, the basis is ratings. As in any industry, firms compete directly to provide advertisers with these audience numbers. Because so many billions of dollars are spent on advertising each year, the figures the services provide are critical. One would expect that competing firms' information would be valid and consistent. Those in the magazine and newspaper industries believe that it isn't, and they are unhappy about it.

The two primary providers of information on magazine readership are Mediamark Research Inc. (MRI) and Simmons Market Research Bureau (SMRB). Because of the importance media buyers place on the figures, they have become crucial to individual publications. As the vice president of one top ad agency noted, "If the readership numbers shift just a hair, there is a big shift in the number of ad pages." Yet MRI's and SMRB's numbers rarely agree, causing many to question their validity.

One such dispute involved *USA Today, The Wall Street Journal,* and MRI. The MRI readership survey showed dramatic gains in audience counts for both newspapers. But MRI, citing problems associated with its new measurement system, discarded the new results, calling them "statistically unbalanced." It said it would return to the old measurement methodology. The newspapers sent a joint letter of protest noting that they were "alarmed" over this "arbitrary decision." A comparison of the MRI and SMRB numbers added to the controversy. According to SMRB, the *Journal*'s adult readership was 4.8 million—29 percent higher than MRI's 3.4 million. *USA Today* had 5.9 million adult readers according to Simmons, but 34 percent fewer according to MRI (3.9 million).

SMRB was also under attack. Hearst, Times Mirror, and Condé Nast refused to use the audience measuring company, citing methodology problems. The Magazine Publishers of America research committee noticed what appeared to be illogical numbers in the SMRB research materials. Like MRI, SMRB said it would change its research methods—to those previously employed by MRI.

One of the biggest complaints involved the research methodology employed, particularly as it related to response rates. Simmons problems were apparently perceived as worse than MRI's, as MRI became the market leader, with SMRB relegated to a backup role. Then, in mid-1999, SMRB realized that it had to fight back and announced a new method for data collection. Since using a phone survey was resulting in only about a 20 percent cooperation rate among the 100,000 people contacted, Simmons adopted the approach used by MRI—face-to-face interviews. MRI claims to knock on 32,000 doors and attain a 70 percent cooperation rate on the preliminary personal interview, with 60 percent of those interviewed completing a media habits booklet yielding a 42 percent response rate. Simmons now samples 28,000 households door-to-door and includes special booklets for kids and teens. SMRB expects to double its response rate to 40 percent making it more competitive with MRI.

Meanwhile, MRI announced that it is introducing a new, diary-driven sampling technique to more efficiently measure magazine audience accumulation. MRI claims that the move is necessary, as broadcast media audience information has become more sophisticated, making magazines less competitive. While some buyers are encouraged (Condé Nast has committed to buying the study, while Hearst is supportive but taking a wait-and-see attitude), others are not so sure. Because the new method tracks only 46 magazines, too many generalizations will need to be made, according to a media director at one of the top agencies.

Almost everyone in the industry knows there are problems with print audience measurement. However, it appears that no one has a better solution. *USA Today* and *The Wall Street Journal* have argued with MRI. Hearst, Condé Nast, and Times Mirror dropped SMRB (though some of their magazines recently resubscribed). To MRI's and SMRB's credit, both are responding to their customers' demands and attempting to improve their products. But a solution does not seem to be around the corner. Says Alan Jurmain, executive director of media services at Lowe & Partners/SMS, "There are flaws with both Simmons and MRI . . . but until someone comes up with something better—well, it's better to be partially right than precisely wrong." So it will apparently be business as usual for the foreseeable future.

Sources: "Magazines: A Better Read on Readers," *Mediaweek Online,* November 8, 1999, pp. 1–3; Lisa Granastein, "A New Read on Readers," *Mediaweek Online,* March 23, 1998, pp. 1–4; Keith J. Kelly, "New Player, New Idea in Readership Fray," *Advertising Age,* April 29, 1996, p. 51; Keith J. Kelly, "Simmons Research Repairs Reputation," *Advertising Age,* October 2, 1996, p. 46; Keith J. Kelly, "*USA Today, Journal,* Fume at MRI," *Advertising Age,* March 25, 1996, p. 1.

Inconsistent Terminologies Problems arise because the cost bases used by different media often vary and the standards of measurement used to establish these costs are not always consistent. For example, print media may present cost data in terms of the cost to reach a thousand people (cost per thousand, or CPM), broadcast media use the cost per ratings point (CPRP), and outdoor media use the number of showings. Audience information that is used as a basis for these costs has also been collected by different methods. Finally, terms that actually mean something different (such as *reach* and *coverage*) may be used synonymously, adding to the confusion.

Time Pressures It seems that advertisers are always in a hurry—sometimes because they need to be, other times because they think they need to be. Actions by a competitor—for example, the cutting of airfares by one carrier—require immediate response. But sometimes a false sense of urgency dictates time pressures. In either situation, media selection decisions may be made without proper planning and analyses of the markets and/or media.

Difficulty Measuring Effectiveness Because it is so hard to measure the effectiveness of advertising and promotions in general, it is also difficult to determine the relative effectiveness of various media or media vehicles. While progress is being made in this regard (particularly in the area of direct-response advertising), the media planner must usually guess at the impact of these alternatives.

Because of these problems, not all media decisions are quantitatively determined. Sometimes managers have to assume the image of a medium in a market with which they are not familiar, anticipate the impact of recent events, or make judgments without full knowledge of all the available alternatives.

While these problems complicate the media decision process, they do not render it an entirely subjective exercise. The remainder of this chapter explores in more detail how media strategies are developed and ways to increase their effectiveness.

Developing the Media Plan

The promotional planning model in Chapter 1 discussed the process of identifying target markets, establishing objectives, and formulating strategies for attaining them. The development of the media plan and strategies follows a similar path, except that the focus is more specifically keyed to determining the best way to deliver the message. The process, shown in Figure 10–3, involves a series of stages: (1) market analysis, (2) establishment of media objectives, (3) media strategy development and implementation, and (4) evaluation and follow-up. Each of these is discussed in turn, with specific examples. Appendix B to this chapter is an actual media plan, which we refer to throughout the remainder of the chapter to exemplify each phase further.

Market Analysis and Target Market Identification

The situation analysis stage of the overall promotional planning process involves a complete review of internal and external factors, competitive strategies, and the like. In the development of a media strategy, a market analysis is again performed, although this time the focus is on the media and delivering the message. The key questions at this stage are these: To whom shall we advertise (who is the target market)? What internal and external factors may influence the media plan? Where (geographically) and when should we focus our efforts?

Figure 10–3 Developing the media plan

Market analysis → Establishment of media objectives → Media strategy development and implementation → Evaluation and follow-up

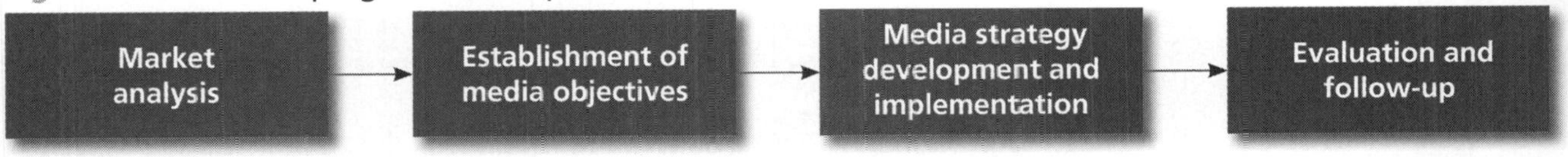

To Whom Shall We Advertise?

While a number of target markets might be derived from the situation analysis, to decide which specific groups to go after, the media planner may work with the client, account representative, marketing department, and creative directors. A variety of factors can assist media planners in this decision. Some will require primary research, whereas others will be available from published (secondary) sources.

The Simmons Market Research Bureau (SMRB) provides secondary information: syndicated data on audience size and composition for approximately 100 publications, as well as broadcast exposure and data on usage of over 800 consumer products and services. This information comes in the form of raw numbers, percentages, and indexes. As seen in Figure 10–4, information is given on

Figure 10–4 Market research profile of cola users

	TOTAL U.S. '000	ALL USERS A '000	B % DOWN	C % ACROSS	D INDX	HEAVY USERS EIGHT OR MORE A '000	B % DOWN	C % ACROSS	D INDX	BOTTLED A '000	B % DOWN	C % ACROSS	D INDX	CANNED A '000	B % DOWN	C % ACROSS	D INDX
TOTAL ADULTS	182456	107986	100.0	59.2	100	34162	100.0	18.7	100	64427	100.0	35.3	100	77735	100.0	42.6	100
MALES	87118	57364	53.1	65.8	111	19037	55.7	21.9	117	33966	52.7	39.0	110	41533	53.4	47.7	112
FEMALES	95338	50622	46.9	53.1	90	15125	44.3	15.9	85	30461	47.3	32.0	90	36202	46.6	38.0	89
18-24	25530	17961	16.6	70.4	119	7633	22.3	29.9	160	11523	17.9	45.1	128	13715	17.6	53.7	126
25-34	44118	29093	26.9	65.9	111	10646	31.2	24.1	129	17994	27.9	40.8	116	22039	28.4	50.0	117
35-44	37521	23183	21.5	61.8	104	6716	19.7	17.9	96	13883	21.5	37.0	105	17172	22.1	45.8	107
45-54	25346	14302	13.2	56.4	95	4240	12.4	16.7	89	8281	12.9	32.7	93	9798	12.6	38.7	91
55-64	21009	11029	10.2	52.5	89	2655	7.8	12.6	67	5946	9.2	28.3	80	7563	9.7	36.0	84
65 OR OLDER	28934	12419	11.5	42.9	73	2271	6.6	7.8	42	6801	10.6	23.5	67	7449	9.6	25.7	60
18-34	69647	47054	43.6	67.6	114	18279	53.5	26.2	140	29517	45.8	42.4	120	35754	46.0	51.3	120
18-49	120585	78177	72.4	64.8	110	27394	80.2	22.7	121	48074	74.6	39.9	113	58377	75.1	48.4	114
25-54	106984	66577	61.7	62.2	105	21603	63.2	20.2	108	40158	62.3	37.5	106	49009	63.0	45.8	108
35-49	50938	31123	28.8	61.1	103	9115	26.7	17.9	96	18557	28.8	36.4	103	22623	29.1	44.4	104
50 OR OLDER	61871	29810	27.6	48.2	81	6768	19.8	10.9	58	16353	25.4	26.4	75	19358	24.9	31.3	73
GRADUATED COLLEGE	35347	18823	17.4	53.3	90	4256	12.5	12.0	64	10728	16.7	30.4	86	13919	17.9	39.4	92
ATTENDED COLLEGE	35167	20303	18.8	57.7	98	6323	18.5	18.0	96	11597	18.0	33.0	93	15374	19.8	43.7	103
GRADUATED HIGH SCHOOL	70823	43928	40.7	62.0	105	15062	44.1	21.3	114	26676	41.4	37.7	107	31808	40.9	44.9	105
DID NOT GRADUATE HIGH SCHOOL	41119	24932	23.1	60.6	102	8521	24.9	20.7	111	15426	23.9	37.5	106	16634	21.4	40.5	95
EMPLOYED MALES	67846	46006	42.6	67.8	115	15993	46.8	23.6	126	27566	42.8	40.6	115	33752	43.4	49.7	117
EMPLOYED FEMALES	57394	30497	28.2	53.1	90	9317	27.3	16.2	87	18245	28.3	31.8	90	22414	28.8	39.1	92
EMPLOYED FULL-TIME	112285	69201	64.1	61.6	104	22930	67.1	20.4	109	41409	64.3	36.9	104	50475	64.9	45.0	106
EMPLOYED PART-TIME	12955	7302	6.8	56.4	95	2380	7.0	18.4	98	4402	6.8	34.0	96	5692	7.3	43.9	103
NOT EMPLOYED	57216	31483	29.2	55.0	93	8852	25.9	15.5	83	18616	28.9	32.5	92	21569	27.7	37.7	88
PROFESSIONAL/MANAGER	31819	17101	15.8	53.7	91	4515	13.2	14.2	76	10036	15.6	31.5	89	12604	16.2	39.6	93
TECHNICAL/CLERICAL/SALES	39581	22672	21.0	57.3	97	7008	20.5	17.7	95	13089	20.3	33.1	94	16905	21.7	42.7	100
PRECISION/CRAFT	14839	10235	9.5	69.0	117	4012	11.7	27.0	144	6535	10.1	44.0	125	7470	9.6	50.3	118
OTHER EMPLOYED	39001	26494	24.5	67.9	115	9775	28.6	25.1	134	16151	25.1	41.4	117	19187	24.7	49.2	115
SINGLE	40179	26098	24.2	65.0	110	10217	29.9	25.4	136	16252	25.2	40.4	115	19644	25.3	48.9	115
MARRIED	108808	64055	59.3	58.9	99	18481	54.1	17.0	91	37570	58.3	34.5	98	45904	59.1	42.2	99
DIVORCED/SEPARATED/WIDOWED	33469	17834	16.5	53.3	90	5464	16.0	16.3	87	10606	16.5	31.7	90	12188	15.7	36.4	85
PARENTS	60855	40631	37.6	66.8	113	13482	39.5	22.2	118	25180	39.1	41.4	117	30061	38.7	49.4	116
WHITE	156458	90780	84.1	58.0	98	28116	82.3	18.0	96	53093	82.4	33.9	96	65803	84.7	42.1	99
BLACK	20509	13774	12.8	67.2	113	5160	15.1	25.2	134	9041	14.0	44.1	125	9432	12.1	46.0	108
OTHER	5489	3432	3.2	62.5	106	885	2.6	16.1	86	2293	3.6	41.8	118	2500	3.2	45.5	107
NORTHEAST-CENSUS	38593	22160	20.5	57.4	97	5368	15.7	13.9	74	16028	24.9	41.5	118	14293	18.4	37.0	87
MIDWEST	44281	24898	23.1	56.2	95	7327	21.4	16.5	88	12677	19.7	28.6	81	19201	24.7	43.4	102
SOUTH	62591	39118	36.2	62.5	106	14519	42.5	23.2	124	24320	37.7	38.9	110	26905	34.6	43.0	101
WEST	36991	21811	20.2	59.0	100	6947	20.3	18.8	100	11402	17.7	30.8	87	17337	22.3	46.9	110
COUNTY SIZE A	75891	43359	40.2	57.1	97	12309	36.0	16.2	87	26324	40.9	34.7	98	30712	39.5	40.5	95
COUNTY SIZE B	54708	33119	30.7	60.5	102	10665	31.2	19.5	104	19543	30.3	35.7	101	24116	31.0	44.1	103
COUNTY SIZE C	27729	16793	15.6	60.6	102	5938	17.4	21.4	114	9674	15.0	34.9	99	12452	16.0	44.9	105
COUNTY SIZE D	24127	14715	13.6	61.0	103	5250	15.4	21.8	116	8886	13.8	36.8	104	10456	13.5	43.3	102
METRO CENTRAL CITY	57518	35162	32.6	61.1	103	11223	32.9	19.5	104	19989	31.0	34.8	98	26734	34.4	46.5	109
METRO SUBURBAN	85780	49004	45.4	57.1	97	14390	42.1	16.8	90	29956	46.5	34.9	99	34168	44.0	39.8	93
NON METRO	39158	23820	22.1	60.8	103	8549	25.0	21.8	117	14482	22.5	37.0	105	16834	21.7	43.0	101
TOP 5 ADI'S	40412	23079	21.4	57.1	96	6233	18.2	15.4	82	15097	23.4	37.4	106	15727	20.2	38.9	91
TOP 10 ADI'S	57709	32644	30.2	56.6	96	9067	26.5	15.7	84	21381	33.2	37.0	105	22081	28.4	38.3	90
TOP 20 ADI'S	83116	47625	44.1	57.3	97	13722	40.2	16.5	88	29571	45.9	35.6	101	33506	43.1	40.3	95
HSHLD. INC. $75,000 OR MORE	21409	11472	10.6	53.6	91	3137	9.2	14.7	78	6677	10.4	31.2	88	8465	10.9	39.5	93
$60,000 OR MORE	36836	20296	18.8	55.1	93	5450	16.0	14.8	79	11854	18.4	32.2	91	14883	19.1	40.4	95
$50,000 OR MORE	53155	29435	27.3	55.4	94	8401	24.6	15.8	84	17518	27.2	33.0	93	21230	27.3	39.9	94
$40,000 OR MORE	75291	42438	39.3	56.4	95	12102	35.4	16.1	86	24710	38.4	32.8	93	31064	40.0	41.3	97
$30,000 OR MORE	102396	59510	55.1	58.1	98	17769	52.0	17.4	93	35324	54.8	34.5	98	43174	55.5	42.2	99
$30,000 - $39,999	27105	17072	15.8	63.0	106	5667	16.6	20.9	112	10614	16.5	39.2	111	12111	15.6	44.7	105
$20,000 - $29,999	30317	18768	17.4	61.9	105	6373	18.7	21.0	112	10822	16.8	35.7	101	13883	17.9	45.8	107
$10,000 - $19,999	29855	18353	17.0	61.5	104	6479	19.0	21.7	116	11297	17.5	37.8	107	13108	16.9	43.9	103
UNDER $10,000	19888	11355	10.5	57.1	96	3541	10.4	17.8	95	6985	10.8	35.1	99	7571	9.7	38.1	89
HOUSEHOLD OF 1 PERSON	23383	11336	10.5	48.5	82	2915	8.5	12.5	67	6621	10.3	28.3	80	7727	9.9	33.0	78
2 PEOPLE	59547	31809	29.5	53.4	90	9263	27.1	15.6	83	17730	27.5	29.8	84	22690	29.2	38.1	89
3 OR 4 PEOPLE	72643	46028	42.6	63.4	107	15192	44.5	20.9	112	28128	43.7	38.7	110	33353	42.9	45.9	108
5 OR MORE PEOPLE	26884	18813	17.4	70.0	118	6793	19.9	25.3	135	11948	18.5	44.4	126	13965	18.0	51.9	122
NO CHILD IN HSHLD.	109702	59165	54.8	53.9	91	17626	51.6	16.1	86	33808	52.5	30.8	87	41560	53.5	37.9	89
CHILD(REN) UNDER 2 YEARS	15048	10548	9.8	70.1	118	4030	11.8	26.8	143	6875	10.7	45.7	129	7752	10.0	51.5	121
2 - 5 YEARS	25473	17985	16.7	70.6	119	6250	18.3	24.5	131	11774	18.3	46.2	131	13493	17.4	53.0	124
6 - 11 YEARS	34011	23085	21.4	67.9	115	7433	21.8	21.9	117	14221	22.1	41.8	118	17375	22.4	51.1	120
12 - 17 YEARS	33774	22170	20.5	65.6	111	7394	21.6	21.9	117	13733	21.3	40.7	115	16230	20.9	48.1	113
RESIDENCE OWNED	124747	69384	64.3	55.6	94	19886	58.2	15.9	85	40350	62.6	32.3	92	49466	63.6	39.7	93
VALUE: $70,000 OR MORE	69554	36947	34.2	53.1	90	9297	27.2	13.4	71	21652	33.6	31.1	88	26509	34.1	38.1	89
VALUE: UNDER $70,000	55193	32437	30.0	58.8	99	10588	31.0	19.2	102	18699	29.0	33.9	96	22957	29.5	41.6	98

(1) the number of adults in the United States by each category under consideration; (2) the number of users; (3) the percentage of users falling into each category (for example, the percentage who are female); (4) the percentage of each category that uses the product (for example, the percentage of all females using); (5) an index number; and (6) the same information classified by heavy, medium, and light users. Both Simmons and its major competitor, Mediamark Research Inc. (MRI), also provide lifestyle information and media usage characteristics of the population.

Media planners are often more concerned with the percentage figures and index numbers than with the raw numbers. This is largely due to the fact that they may have their own data from other sources, both primary and secondary; the numbers provided may not be specific enough for their needs; or they question the numbers provided because of the methods by which they were collected. (See IMC Perspective 10–1.) The total (raw) numbers provided by Simmons and MRI are used in combination with the media planner's own figures.

On the other hand, the **index number** is considered a good indicator of the potential of the market. This number is derived from the formula

$$\text{Index} = \frac{\text{Percentage of users in a demographic segment}}{\text{Percentage of population in the same segment}} \times 100$$

An index number over 100 means use of the product is proportionately greater in that segment than in one that is average (100) or less than 100. For example, the MRI data in Figure 10–5 show that people in the age groups 45–54, 35–44, and 25–34, respectively, are more likely to purchase cellular phones than those in the other age segments, as are those with a household income of $40,000 or more. Most occupation groups are users, though executives/managers and professionals are more likely to be. College graduates also have a high index. Depending on their overall strategy, marketers may wish to use this information to determine which groups are now using the product and target them or to identify a group that is currently using the product less and attempt to develop that segment.

While the index is helpful, it should not be used alone. Percentages and product usage figures are also needed to get an accurate picture of the market. Just because the index for a particular segment of the population is very high, that doesn't always mean it is an attractive segment to target. The high index may be a result of a low denominator (a very small proportion of the population in this segment). In Figure 10–6, the 18- to 24-year-old age segment has the highest index, but it also has both the lowest product usage and the lowest population percentage. A marketer who relied solely on the index would be ignoring a full 82 percent of product users.

Keep in mind that while Simmons and MRI provide demographic, geographic, and psychographic information, other factors may be more useful in defining specific markets.

What Internal and External Factors Are Operating?

Media strategies are influenced by both internal and external factors operating at any given time. *Internal factors* may involve the size of the media budget, managerial and administrative capabilities, or the organization of the agency, as demonstrated in Figure 10–7. *External factors* may include the economy (the rising costs of media), changes in technology (the availability of new media), competitive factors, and the like. While some of this information may require primary research, much information is available through secondary sources, including magazines, syndicated services, and even the daily newspaper.

One service's competitive information was shown in Figure 10–1. The Competitive Media Reporting Service provides media spending figures for various brands competing in the same market. Competitive information is also available from many other sources, as shown in Appendix A to this chapter.

Figure 10–5 Cellular phones purchased in the past year—MRI report

3.1% of all adults purchased a cellular phone in the past year. Of this group, women account for 51.1%; 36.4% graduated from college; 26.0% are ages 25-34; 15.1% have $50,000–$59,999 household income and members of this group are 62% more likely than average adults to have purchased a cellular phone in the past year.		
Base: All adults	Population (000) 5,863 Percent of Target	Percent of Base 3.1% Index
Men	48.9	102
Women	51.1	98
Household heads	54.3	89
Homemakers	58.9	95
Graduated college	36.4	176
Attended college	29.8	112
Graduated high school	26.7	79
Did not graduate high school	7.2	38
18–24	11.9	92
25–34	26.0	117
35–44	27.7	128
45–54	20.5	132
55–64	9.2	82
65 or over	4.6	28
18–34	37.9	108
18–49	78.1	119
25–54	74.3	125
Employed full-time	74.8	137
Employed part-time	10.8	112
Sole wage earner	15.3	87
Not employed	14.4	40
Professional	16.1	166
Executive/admin/managerial	15.5	172
Clerical/sales/technical	26.6	141
Precision/crafts/repair	9.4	132
Other employed	18.0	92
H/D income $75,000 or more	38.5	239
H/D income $60,000–$74,999	15.7	162
H/D income $50,000–$59,999	15.1	162
H/D income $40,000–$49,999	13.5	119
H/D income $30,000–$39,999	8.5	62
H/D income $20,000–$29,999	5.0	33
H/D income $10,000–19,999	3.2	22
H/D income less than $10,000	0.4	4

Figure 10–6 How high indexes can be misleading

Age Segment	Population in Segment (percent)	Product Use in Segment (percent)	Index
18–24	15.1	18.0	119
25–34	25.1	25.0	100
35–44	20.6	21.0	102
45+	39.3	36.0	91

Figure 10–7 Organizing the media buying department

While various firms and ad agencies have different ways of organizing the media buying department, three seem to be the most common. The first form employs a product/media focus, the second places more emphasis on the market itself, and the third organizes around media classes alone:

- **Form 1** In this organizational arrangement, the media buyers and assistant media buyers are responsible for a product or group of products and/or brands. Their media planner both plans and buys for these products/brands in whichever geographic areas they are marketed. For example, if the agency is responsible for the advertising of Hart skis, the media planners determine the appropriate media in each area for placing the ads for these skis. The logic underlying this approach is that the planner knows the product and will identify the best media and vehicles for promoting it.
- **Form 2** In this approach, the market is the focal point of attention. Media planners become "experts" in a particular market area and are responsible for planning and buying for all products/brands the firm and/or agency markets in those areas. For example, a planner may be responsible for the Memphis, Tennessee, market. If the agency has more than one client who wishes to market in this area, media selection for all of the brands/products is the responsibility of the same person. The logic is that his or her knowledge of the media and vehicles in the area allows for a more informed media choice. The nonquantitative characteristics of the media get more attention under this approach.
- **Form 3** Organizing around a specific class of media—for example, print or broadcast—is a third alternative. The purchasing and development unit handles all the agency print or broadcast business. Members of the media department become specialists who are brought in very early in the promotional planning process. Planners perform only planning functions, while buyers are responsible for all purchases. The buying function itself may be specialized with specific responsibilities for specialty advertising, national buys, local buys, and so on. Knowledge of the media and the audience each serves is considered a major benefit. Also, people who handle all the media buys can negotiate better deals.

As to which strategy works best, who's to say? Each has been in use for some time. The second approach requires that the agency be big enough and have enough clients to support the geographic assignment. The third alternative seems to be the most common design.

Where to Promote?

The question of where to promote relates to geographic considerations. As noted in Chapter 7, companies often find that sales are stronger in one area of the country or the world than another and may allocate advertising expenditures according to the market potential of an area (see Figure 10–8). For years, Whirlpool has had a much greater brand share of the appliance market in the East and Midwest than in the Southeast and West. The question is, where will the ad dollars be more wisely spent? Should Whirlpool allocate additional promotional monies to those markets where the brand is already the leader to maintain market share, or does more potential exist in those markets where the firm is not doing as well and there is more room to grow? Perhaps the best answer is that the firm should spend advertising and promotion dollars where they will be the most effective—that is, in those markets where they will achieve the desired objectives. Unfortunately, as we have seen so often, it is not always possible to measure directly the impact of promotional efforts. At the same time, certain tactics can assist the planner in making this determination.

Figure 10–8 Companies allocation of media dollars—U.S. and international

		Media Spending ($ millions)								
Rank	Advertiser	Outside U.S.	U.S.	World-wide	Africa	Asia	Europe	Latin America	Middle East	Canada
1	P&G Co.	$3,018.2	$1,729.3	$4,747.6	$ 0.6	$627.4	$1,847.3	$430.1	$57.7	$55.3
2	Unilever	2,737.3	691.2	3,423.5	43.4	643.2	1,629.3	373.3	20	28.2
3	Nestlé	1,559.3	273.8	1,833	11.1	299.4	1,016	209.2	17.5	6
4	Volkswagen	1,070.4	255.4	1,325.8	0	29	871.7	140.8	5.4	23.5
5	Ford Motor Co.	1,049.5	1,180	2,229.5	0	64.9	706.3	151.7	12.4	114.6

Figure 10–9 Survey of buying power index

Rhode Island

POPULATION

S&MM ESTIMATES: 12/31/90

METRO AREA / County / City	Total Population (Thousands)	% Of U.S.	Median Age Of Pop.	% of Population by Age Group: 18-24 Years	25-34 Years	35-49 Years	50 & Over	Households (Thousands)
PROVIDENCE–PAWTUCKET–								
WOONSOCKET	**921.4**	**.3674**	**34.1**	**11.8**	**17.0**	**20.1**	**28.4**	**347.2**
Bristol	49.0	.0196	35.9	10.9	15.5	20.9	30.5	17.6
Kent	162.1	.0646	35.9	8.9	16.9	22.3	29.2	62.4
Warwick	85.9	.0342	36.9	8.7	16.7	21.4	31.5	33.6
Providence	598.9	.2388	33.8	12.2	17.3	19.2	28.7	227.4
Cranston	76.4	.0305	37.3	9.5	17.5	20.7	32.8	29.5
East Providence	50.6	.0202	36.9	9.1	16.9	19.4	33.3	20.0
• Pawtucket	73.0	.0291	33.7	10.2	19.1	17.8	29.7	29.9
• Providence	161.4	.0644	29.6	18.0	17.6	16.5	24.0	59.1
• Woonsocket	44.1	.0176	33.3	10.9	17.9	17.9	28.9	17.7
Washington	111.4	.0444	32.6	14.2	16.2	21.9	24.3	39.8
SUBURBAN TOTAL	642.9	.2563	35.5	10.5	16.6	21.4	29.3	240.5
OTHER COUNTIES								
Newport	87.5	.0349	33.8	11.8	17.6	22.3	25.5	32.8
TOTAL METRO COUNTIES	**921.4**	**.3674**	**34.1**	**11.8**	**17.0**	**20.1**	**28.4**	**347.2**
TOTAL STATE	**1,008.9**	**.4023**	**34.1**	**11.8**	**17.0**	**20.3**	**28.1**	**380.0**

RETAIL SALES BY STORE GROUP

METRO AREA / County / City	Total Retail Sales ($000)	Food ($000)	Eating & Drinking Places ($000)	General Mdse. ($000)	Furniture/ Furnish. Appliance ($000)	Automotive ($000)	Drug ($000)
PROVIDENCE–PAWTUCKET–							
WOONSOCKET	**6,621,140**	**1,390,972**	**740,007**	**750,465**	**291,612**	**1,175,964**	**301,155**
Bristol	239,949	66,787	27,747	2,630	6,814	53,545	13,682
Kent	1,687,207	275,155	168,616	307,478	55,278	301,666	58,221
Warwick	1,241,231	159,242	114,017	300,202	47,168	189,376	34,648
Providence	3,832,852	814,370	442,223	400,598	197,994	690,435	198,710
Cranston	513,493	116,552	55,772	21,447	43,116	94,507	34,699
East Providence	405,889	72,226	38,188	22,368	20,077	130,818	20,625
• Pawtucket	514,684	105,502	42,451	110,785	21,226	73,536	34,132
• Providence	931,996	174,406	126,906	59,502	63,388	169,702	39,520
• Woonsocket	292,009	70,461	20,413	36,712	12,715	72,514	14,174
Washington	861,132	234,660	101,421	39,759	31,526	130,318	30,542
SUBURBAN TOTAL	4,882,451	1,040,603	550,237	543,466	194,283	860,212	213,329
OTHER COUNTIES							
Newport	703,842	121,062	118,031	34,174	29,726	176,816	18,994
TOTAL METRO COUNTIES	**6,621,140**	**1,390,972**	**740,007**	**750,465**	**291,612**	**1,175,964**	**301,155**
TOTAL STATE	**7,324,982**	**1,512,034**	**858,038**	**784,639**	**321,338**	**1,352,780**	**320,149**

EFFECTIVE BUYING INCOME

S&MM ESTIMATES: 12/31/90

% of Hslds. by EBI Group: (A) $10,000-$19,999 (B) $20,000-$34,999 (C) $35,000-$49,999 (D) $50,000 & Over

METRO AREA / County / City	Total EBI ($000)	Median Hsld. EBI	A	B	C	D	Buying Power Index
PROVIDENCE–PAWTUCKET–							
WOONSOCKET	**13,161,017**	**28,441**	**19.4**	**25.5**	**18.6**	**20.9**	**.3714**
Bristol	727,359	30,275	19.2	26.8	17.6	23.9	.0182
Kent	2,422,662	30,869	17.0	27.8	21.2	21.1	.0756
Warwick	1,322,227	31,519	16.5	27.6	21.5	21.8	.0463
Providence	8,427,416	27,115	20.2	24.4	17.8	20.3	.2319
Cranston	1,237,230	31,764	17.7	24.6	19.9	25.2	.0323
East Providence	777,080	30,763	18.3	25.3	21.5	22.1	.0219
• Pawtucket	997,942	25,377	21.5	26.0	17.8	16.3	.0286
• Providence	1,924,178	20,802	24.2	23.5	13.4	14.8	.0558
• Woonsocket	566,843	23,811	22.3	24.4	16.8	15.5	.0165
Washington	1,583,580	30,461	18.6	28.1	19.4	22.3	.0457
SUBURBAN TOTAL	9,672,054	31,087	17.8	26.1	20.0	23.3	.2705
OTHER COUNTIES							
Newport	1,414,978	31,746	17.5	24.8	19.4	25.8	.0388
TOTAL METRO COUNTIES	**13,161,017**	**28,441**	**19.4**	**25.5**	**18.6**	**20.9**	**.3714**
TOTAL STATE	**14,575,995**	**28,696**	**19.2**	**25.5**	**18.6**	**21.3**	**.4102**

Using Indexes to Determine Where to Promote In addition to the indexes from Simmons and MRI, three other indexes may also be useful:

1. **The Survey of Buying Power Index,** published annually by *Sales and Marketing Management* magazine, is conducted for every major metropolitan market in the United States and is based on a number of factors, including population, effective buying income, and total retail sales in the area. Each of these factors is individually weighted to drive a buying power index that charts the potential of a particular metro area, county, or city relative to the United States as a whole. The resulting index gives media planners insight into the relative value of that market, as shown in Figure 10–9. When used in combination with other market information, the survey of buying power index helps the marketer determine which geographic areas to target.

2. **The Brand Development Index (BDI)** helps marketers factor the rate of product usage by geographic area into the decision process.

$$\text{BDI} = \frac{\text{Percentage of brand to total U.S. sales in the market}}{\text{Percentage of total U.S. population in the market}} \times 100$$

The BDI compares the percentage of the brand's total U.S. sales in a given market area with the percentage of the total population in the market to determine the sales potential for that brand in that market area. An example of this calculation is shown in Figure 10–10. The higher the index number, the more market potential

Figure 10–10 Calculating BDI

$$\text{BDI} = \frac{\text{Percentage of brand sales in South Atlantic region}}{\text{Percentage of U.S. population in South Atlantic region}} \times 100$$

$$= \frac{50\%}{16\%} \times 100$$

$$= 312$$

$$\text{CDI} = \frac{\text{Percentage of product category sales in Utah/Idaho}}{\text{Percentage of total U.S. population in Utah/Idaho}} \times 100$$

$$= \frac{1\%}{1\%} \times 100$$

$$= 100$$

$$\text{BDI} = \frac{\text{Percentage of total brand sales in Utah/Idaho}}{\text{Percentage of total U.S. population in Utah/Idaho}} \times 100$$

$$= \frac{2\%}{1\%} \times 100$$

$$= 200$$

Figure 10–11 Using CDI and BDI to determine market potential

exists. In this case, the index number indicates this market has high potential for brand development (see Appendix B for targeted cities).

3. **The Category Development Index (CDI)** is computed in the same manner as the BDI, except it uses information regarding the product category (as opposed to the brand) in the numerator:

$$\text{CDI} = \frac{\text{Percentage of product category total sales in market}}{\text{Percentage of total U.S. population in market}} \times 100$$

The CDI provides information on the potential for development of the total product category rather than specific brands. When this information is combined with the BDI, a much more insightful promotional strategy may be developed. For example, consider the market potential for coffee in the United States. One might first look at how well the product category does in a specific market area. In Utah and Idaho, for example, the category potential is low (see Figure 10–11). The marketer analyzes the BDI to find how the brand is doing relative to other brands in this area. This information can then be used in determining how well a particular product category and a particular brand are performing and figuring what media weight (or quantity of advertising) would be required to gain additional market share, as shown in Figure 10–12.

While these indexes provide important insights into the market potential for the firm's products and/or brands, this information is supplemental to the overall strategy determined earlier in the promotional decision-making process. In fact, much of this information may have already been provided to the media planner. Since it

	High BDI	Low BDI
High CDI	High market share Good market potential	Low market share Good market potential
Low CDI	High market share Monitor for sales decline	Low market share Poor market potential

High BDI and high CDI	This market usually represents good sales potential for both the product category and the brand.
High BDI and low CDI	The category is not selling well, but the brand is; probably a good market to advertise in but should be monitored for declining sales.
Low BDI and high CDI	The product category shows high potential but the brand is not doing well; the reasons should be determined.
Low BDI and low CDI	Both the product category and the brand are doing poorly; not likely to be a good place for advertising.

Figure 10–12 Using BDI and CDI indexes

may be used more specifically to determine the media weights to assign to each area, this decision ultimately affects the budget allocated to each area as well as other factors such as reach, frequency, and scheduling.

Establishing Media Objectives

Just as the situation analysis leads to establishment of marketing and communications objectives, the media situation analysis should lead to determination of specific media objectives. The media objectives are not ends in themselves. Rather, they are designed to lead to the attainment of communications and marketing objectives. Media objectives are the goals for the media program and should be limited to those that can be accomplished through media strategies. An example of media objectives is this: Create awareness in the target market through the following:

- Use broadcast media to provide coverage of 80 percent of the target market over a six-month period.
- Reach 60 percent of the target audience at least three times over the same six-month period.
- Concentrate heaviest advertising in winter and spring, with lighter emphasis in summer and fall.

Developing and Implementing Media Strategies

Having determined what is to be accomplished, media planners consider how to achieve these objectives. That is, they develop and implement media strategies, which evolve directly from the actions required to meet objectives and involve the criteria in Figure 10–13.

The Media Mix

A wide variety of media and media vehicles are available to advertisers. While it is possible that only one medium and/or vehicle might be employed, it is much more likely that a number of alternatives will be used. The objectives sought, the characteristics of the product or service, the size of the budget, and individual preferences are just some of the factors that determine what combination of media will be used.

As an example, consider a promotional situation in which a product requires a visual demonstration to be communicated effectively. In this case, TV may be the most effective medium. If the promotional strategy calls for coupons to stimulate trial, print media may be necessary. For in-depth information, the Internet may be best.

By employing a media mix, advertisers can add more versatility to their media strategies, since each medium contributes its own distinct advantages (as demonstrated in later chapters). By combining media, marketers can increase coverage, reach, and frequency levels while improving the likelihood of achieving overall communications and marketing goals.

Figure 10–13 Criteria considered in the development of media plans

- The media mix
- Target market coverage
- Geographic coverage
- Scheduling
- Reach versus frequency
- Creative aspects and mood
- Flexibility
- Budget considerations

Target Market Coverage

The media planner determines which target markets should receive the most media emphasis. (In the media plan for Bumble Bee Tuna in Appendix B, this was determined to be women 25–54 and geographic markets.) Developing media strategies involves matching the most appropriate media to this market by asking, "Through which media and media vehicles can I best get my message to prospective buyers?" The issue here is to get coverage of the market, as shown in Figure 10–14. The optimal goal is full market coverage, shown in the second pie chart. But this is a very optimistic scenario. More realistically, conditions shown in the third and fourth charts are most likely to occur. In the third chart, the coverage of the media does not allow for coverage of the entire market, leaving some potential customers without exposure to the message. In the fourth chart, the marketer is faced with a problem of overexposure (also called **waste coverage**), in which the media coverage

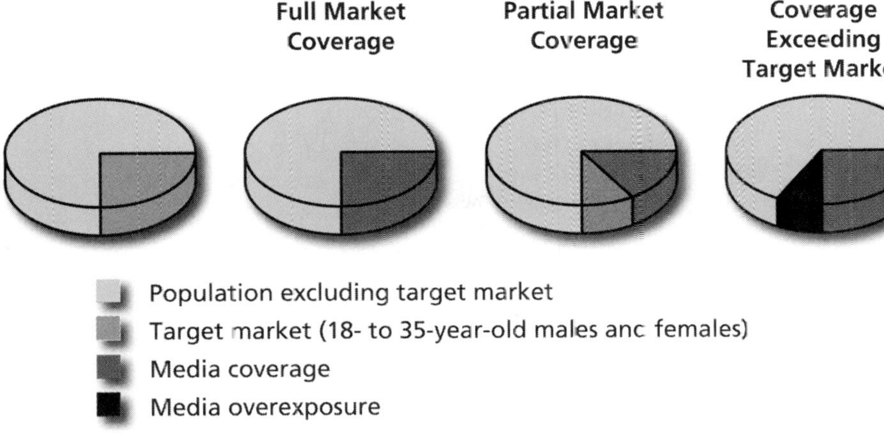

Figure 10–14 Marketing coverage possibilities

exceeds the targeted audience. If media coverage reaches people who are not sought as buyers and are not potential users, then it is wasted. (This term is used for coverage that reaches people who are not potential buyers and/or users. Consumers may not be part of the intended target market but may still be considered as potential—for example, those who buy the product as a gift for someone else.)

The goal of the media planner is to extend media coverage to as many of the members of the target audience as possible while minimizing the amount of waste coverage. The situation usually involves trade-offs. Sometimes one has to live with less coverage than desired; other times, the most effective media expose people not sought. In this instance, waste coverage is justified because the media employed are likely to be the most effective means of delivery available and the cost of the waste coverage is exceeded by the value gained from their use.

When watching football games on TV, you may have noticed commercials for stock brokerage firms such as Charles Schwab and Merrill Lynch. Not all viewers are candidates for stock market services, but a very high percentage of potential customers can be reached with this strategy. So the program is considered a good media buy because the ability to generate market coverage outweighs the disadvantages of high waste coverage.

Figure 10–15 shows how information provided by Simmons can be used to match media to target markets. It profiles magazines read and TV shows watched

Figure 10–15 Magazines purchased by people who do aerobics

		AEROBICS				20 OR MORE DAYS			
	TOTAL U.S. '000	A '000	B % ACROSS DOWN	C %	D INDX	A '000	B % ACROSS DOWN	C %	D INDX
REDBOOK	10533	1074	9.1	10.2	157	760	10.1	7.2	174
ROAD & TRACK	3838	*133	1.1	3.5	53	**55	0.7	1.4	35
ROLLING STONE	6154	496	4.2	8.1	124	317	4.2	5.2	124
SCIENTIFIC AMERICAN	1835	*137	1.2	7.5	115	**57	0.8	3.1	75
SELF	2957	594	5.0	20.1	310	466	6.2	15.8	381
SESAME STREET MAGAZINE	3606	444	3.8	12.3	190	292	3.9	8.1	196
SEVENTEEN	3532	259	2.2	7.3	113	*165	2.2	4.7	113
SHAPE	1664	252	2.1	15.1	234	*185	2.4	11.1	269
SKI	1764	*176	1.5	10.0	154	**102	1.4	5.8	140
SKIING	1535	*161	1.4	10.5	162	**86	1.1	5.6	135
SMITHSONIAN	6299	464	3.9	7.4	114	219	2.9	3.5	84
SOAP OPERA DIGEST	6437	756	6.4	11.7	181	433	5.7	6.7	162
SOUTHERN LIVING	7213	675	5.7	9.4	144	506	6.7	7.0	169
SPORT	3012	**153	1.3	5.1	78	**67	0.9	2.2	54
THE SPORTING NEWS	3348	*179	1.5	5.3	82	**128	1.7	3.8	92
SPORTS AFIELD	3370	**91	0.8	2.7	42	**37	0.5	1.1	27
SPORTS ILLUSTRATED	21035	1002	8.5	4.8	73	611	8.1	2.9	70
STAR	10704	814	6.9	7.6	117	470	6.2	4.4	106
SUNDAY MAGAZINE NETWORK	34831	2761	23.3	7.9	122	1828	24.2	5.2	127
SUNSET	3255	269	2.3	8.3	127	185	2.4	5.7	137
TV GUIDE	39127	2620	22.1	6.7	103	1565	20.7	4.0	97
TENNIS	1548	**102	0.9	6.6	102	**82	1.1	5.3	128
TIME	24413	1734	14.7	7.1	110	1165	15.4	4.8	115
TRAVEL & LEISURE	2520	189	1.6	7.5	116	*144	1.9	5.7	138
TRUE STORY	3060	*312	2.6	10.2	157	**234	3.1	7.6	185
USA TODAY	6199	459	3.9	7.4	114	328	4.3	5.3	128
USA WEEKEND	34618	2192	18.5	6.3	98	1369	18.1	4.0	96
U.S. NEWS & WORLD REPORT	13465	830	7.0	6.2	95	596	7.9	4.4	107
US	4059	453	3.8	11.2	172	311	4.1	7.7	185
VANITY FAIR	1974	292	2.5	14.3	228	*173	2.3	8.8	212

by people who do aerobics. (You can practice using index numbers here.) From Figure 10–15, you can see that *Shape, Self,* and *Vanity Fair* magazines would likely be wise selections for aerobics ads, whereas *Road and Track, Sports Afield,* or *Sport* would be less likely to lead to the desired exposures.

Geographic Coverage

Snow skiing is much more popular in some areas of the country than in others. It would not be the wisest of strategies to promote skis in those areas where interest is not high, unless you could generate an increase in interest. It may be possible to promote an interest in skiing in the Southeast, but a notable increase in sales of ski equipment is not very likely, given the market's distance from snow. The objective of weighting certain geographic areas more than others makes sense, and the strategy of exerting more promotional efforts and dollars in those areas follows naturally. (The Bumble Bee Tuna media plan emphasizes five primary cities and six secondary cities.)

Scheduling

Obviously, companies would like to keep their advertising in front of consumers at all times as a constant reminder of the product and/or brand name. In reality, this is not possible for a variety of reasons (not the least of which is the budget). Nor is it necessary. The primary objective of *scheduling* is to time promotional efforts so that they will coincide with the highest potential buying times. For some products these times are not easy to identify; for others they are very obvious. Three scheduling methods available to the media planner—continuity, flighting, and pulsing—are shown in Figure 10–16.

Continuity refers to a continuous pattern of advertising, which may mean every day, every week, or every month. The key is that a regular (continuous) pattern is developed without gaps or nonadvertising periods. Such strategies might be used for advertising for food products, laundry detergents, or other products consumed on an ongoing basis without regard for seasonality.

A second method, **flighting,** employs a less regular schedule, with intermittent periods of advertising and nonadvertising. At some time periods there are heavier promotional expenditures, and at others there may be no advertising. Many banks, for example, spend no money on advertising in the summer but maintain advertising throughout the rest of the year. Snow skis are advertised heavily between October and April; less in May, August, and September; and not at all in June and July.

Pulsing is actually a combination of the first two methods. In a pulsing strategy, continuity is maintained, but at certain times promotional efforts are stepped up. In the automobile industry, advertising continues throughout the year but may increase in April (income-tax refund time), September (when new models are brought out), and the end of the model year. The scheduling strategy depends on the objectives, buying cycles, and the budget, among other factors. There are certain advantages and disadvantages to each scheduling method, as shown in Figure 10–17. (Notice that in the Bumble Bee Tuna media plan in Appendix B, flighting is recommended for all markets.) One very recent and comprehensive study

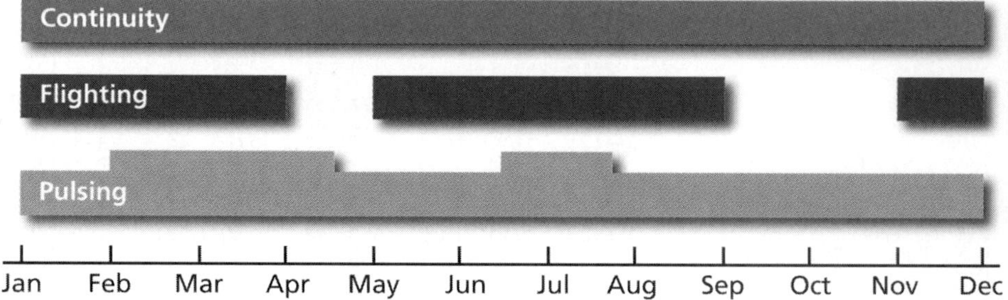

Figure 10–16 Three methods of promotional scheduling

	Continuity
Advantages	Serves as a constant reminder to the consumer
	Covers the entire buying cycle
	Allows for media priorities (quantity discounts, preferred locations, etc.)
Disadvantages	Higher costs
	Potential for overexposure
	Limited media allocation possible

	Flighting
Advantages	Cost efficiency of advertising only during purchase cycles
	May allow for inclusion of more than one medium or vehicle with limited budgets
Disadvantages	Weighting may offer more exposure and advantage over competitors
	Increased likelihood of wearout
	Lack of awareness, interest, retention of promotional message during nonscheduled times
	Vulnerability to competitive efforts during nonscheduled periods

	Pulsing
Advantages	All of the same as the previous two methods
Disadvantages	Not required for seasonal products (or other cyclical products)

Figure 10–17 Characteristics of scheduling methods

(acclaimed by many in the TV research community as "the most comprehensive study ever to shed light on scheduling") indicates that continuity is more effective than flighting. On the basis of the idea that it is important to get exposure to the message as close as possible to when the consumer is going to make the purchase, the study concludes that advertisers should continue weekly schedules as long as possible.[3] The key here may be the "as long as possible" qualification. Given a significant budget, continuity may be more of an option than it is for those with more limited budgets.

Reach versus Frequency

Since advertisers have a variety of objectives and face budget constraints, they usually must trade off reach and frequency. They must decide whether to have the message be seen or heard by more people (reach) or by fewer people more often (frequency).

How Much Reach Is Necessary? Thinking back to the hierarchies discussed in Chapter 5, you will recall that the first stage of each model requires awareness of the product and/or brand. The more people are aware, the more are likely to move to each subsequent stage. Achieving awareness requires reach—that is, exposing potential buyers to the message. New brands or products need a very high level of reach, since the objective is to make all potential buyers aware of the new entry. High reach is also desired at later stages of the hierarchy. For example, at the trial stage of the adoption hierarchy, a promotional strategy might use cents-off coupons or free samples. An objective of the marketer is to reach a larger number of people with these samples, in an attempt to make them learn of the product, try it, and develop favorable attitudes toward it. (In turn, these attitudes may lead to purchase.)

The problem arises because there is no known way of determining how much reach is required to achieve levels of awareness, attitude change, or buying intentions, nor can we be sure an ad placed in a vehicle will actually reach the intended audience. (There has been some research on the first problem, which will be discussed in the section below on effective reach.)

If you buy advertising time on "60 Minutes," will everyone who is tuned to the program see the ad? No. Many viewers will leave the room, be distracted during the commercial, and so on, as shown in Figure 10–18 (which also provides a good example of the difference between reach and coverage). If I expose everyone in my target group to the message once, will this be sufficient to create a 100 percent level of awareness? The answer again is no. This leads to the next question: What frequency of exposure is necessary for the ad to be seen and to have an impact?

What Frequency Level Is Needed? With respect to media planning, *frequency* carries a slightly different meaning. (Remember when we said one of the problems in media planning is that terms often take on different meanings?) Here frequency is the number of times one is exposed to the media vehicle, not necessarily to the ad itself. While one study has estimated the actual audience for a commercial may be as much as 30 percent lower than that for the program, not all researchers agree.[4] Figure 10–18 demonstrates that depending on the program, this number may range from 12 percent to 40 percent.

Most advertisers do agree that a 1:1 exposure ratio does not exist. So while your ad may be placed in a certain vehicle, the fact that a consumer has been exposed to that vehicle does not ensure that your ad has been seen. As a result, the frequency level expressed in the media plan overstates the actual level of exposure to the ad. This overstatement has led some media buyers to refer to the reach of the media vehicle as "opportunities to see" an ad rather than actual exposure to it.

Because the advertiser has no sure way of knowing whether exposure to a vehicle results in exposure to the ad, the media and advertisers have adopted a compromise: One exposure to the vehicle constitutes reach, given that this exposure must occur for the viewer even to have an opportunity to see the ad. Thus, the exposure figure is used to calculate reach and frequency levels. But this compromise does not help determine the frequency required to make an impact. The creativity of the ad, the involvement of the receiver, noise, and many other intervening factors confound any attempts to make a precise determination.

At this point, you may be thinking, "If nobody knows this stuff, how do they make these decisions?" That's a good question, and the truth is that the decisions

Figure 10–18 Who's still there to watch the ads?
How many viewers actually watch a commercial? R. D. Percy & Co. reports that its advanced people meters, equipped with heat sensors that detect viewers present, indicate that spots retain, on average, 82 percent of the average-minute ratings for the quarter hour. During early morning news programs, "commercial efficiency" (as Percy calls it) is lower because so many people are bustling about, out of the room (blue), but the rate rises at night.

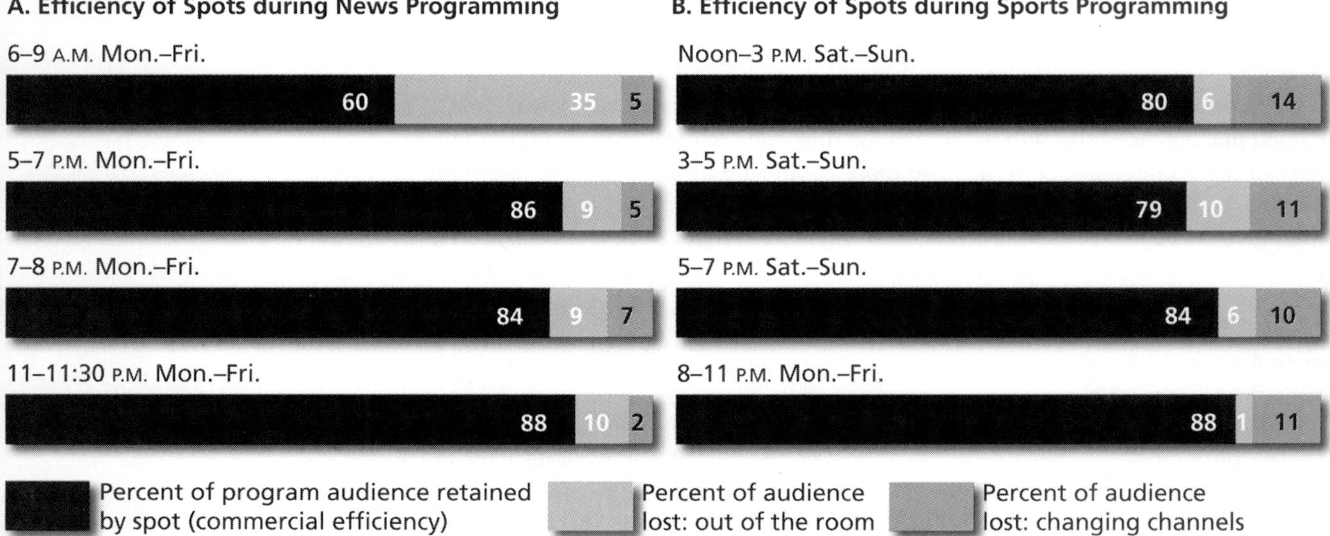

are not always made on hard data. Says Joseph Ostrow, executive vice president/director of communications services with Young and Rubicam, "Establishing frequency goals for an advertising campaign is a mix of art and science but with a definite bias toward art."[5] Let us first examine the process involved in setting reach and frequency objectives and then discuss the logic of each.

Establishing Reach and Frequency Objectives

It is possible to be exposed to more than one media vehicle with an ad, resulting in repetition (frequency). If one ad is placed on one TV show one time, the number of people exposed is the reach. If the ad is placed on two shows, the total number exposed once is **unduplicated reach.** Some people will see the ad twice. The reach of the two shows, as depicted in Figure 10–19, includes a number of people who were reached by both shows (C). This overlap is referred to as **duplicated reach.**

Both unduplicated and duplicated reach figures are important. Unduplicated reach indicates potential new exposures, while duplicated reach provides an estimate of frequency. Most media buys include both forms of reach. Let us consider an example.

A measure of potential reach in the broadcast industry is the TV (or radio) **program rating.** This number is expressed as a percentage. For an estimate of the total number of homes reached, multiply this percentage times the number of homes with TV sets. For example, if there are 100.8 million homes with TV sets in the United States and the program has a rating of 30, then the calculation is 0.30 times 100.8, or 30.24 million homes. (We go into much more detail on ratings and other broadcast terms in Chapter 11.)

Using Gross Ratings Points

The media buyer typically uses a numerical indicator to know how many potential audience members may be exposed to a series of commercials. A summary measure that combines the program rating and the average number of times the home is reached during this period (frequency of exposure) is a commonly used reference point known as **gross ratings points (GRP):**

$$\text{GRP} = \text{Reach} \times \text{Frequency}$$

GRPs are based on the total audience the media schedule may reach; they use a duplicated reach estimate. **Target ratings points (TRP)** refer to the number of people in the primary target audience the media buy will reach—and the number of times. Unlike GRP, TRP does not include waste coverage.

A. Reach of One TV Program

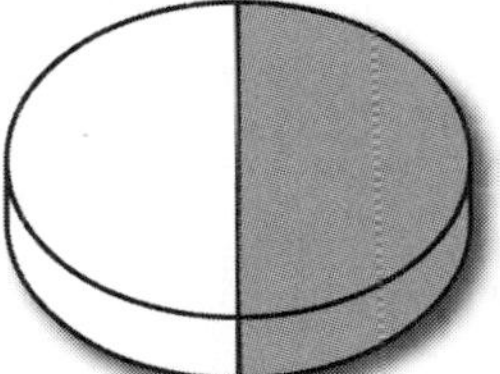

Total market audience reached

B. Reach of Two Programs

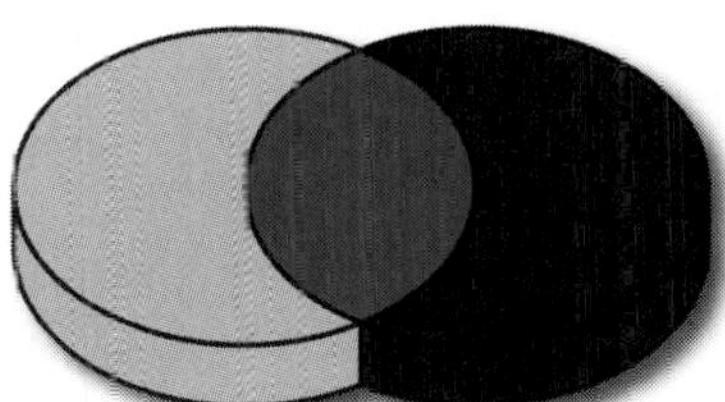

Total market audience reached

C. Duplicated Reach

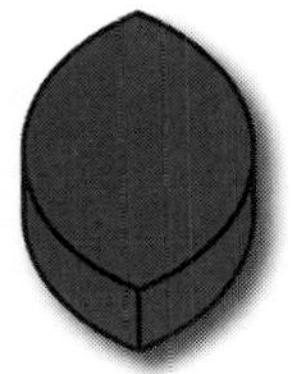

Total market reached with both shows

D. Unduplicated Reach

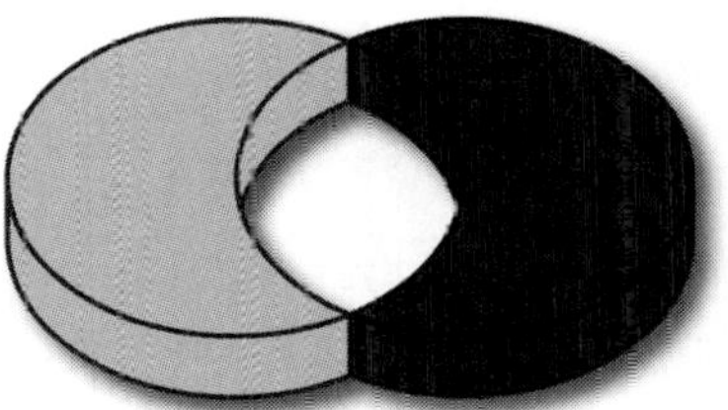

Total reach less duplicated reach

Figure 10–19 Representation of reach and frequency

Given that GRPs do not measure actual reach, the advertiser must ask: How many GRPs are needed to attain a certain reach? How do these GRPs translate into effective reach? For example, how many GRPs must one purchase to attain an unduplicated reach of 50 percent, and what frequency of exposure will this schedule deliver? The following example may help you to understand how this process works.

First you must know what these ratings points represent. A purchase of 100 GRPs could mean 100 percent of the market is exposed once or 50 percent of the market is exposed twice or 25 percent of the market is exposed four times, and so on. As you can see, this information must be more specific for the marketer to use it effectively. To know how many GRPs are necessary, the manager needs to know how many members of the intended audience the schedule actually reaches. The chart in Figure 10–20 helps make this determination.

In Figure 10–20, a purchase of 100 TRPs on one network would yield an estimated reach of 32 percent of the total households in the target market. This figure would climb to 37.2 percent if two networks were used and 44.5 percent with three. Working backward through the formula for GRPs, the estimate of frequency of exposure—3.125, 2.688, and 2.247, respectively—demonstrates the trade-off between reach and frequency.

As an example of a media buy, Denny's purchased 1,300 GRPs in a 10-week period to introduce a new Grand Slam promotion. This purchase employed TV spots in 28 markets and was estimated to reach 40 percent of the target audience an average of 17 times. To determine if this was a wise media buy, we need to know whether this was an effective reach figure. Certainly, reaching 40 percent of the target market is attractive. But why was the frequency level so high? And was it likely to be effective? In other words, does this level of GRPs affect awareness, attitudes, and purchase intentions?

A number of researchers have explored this issue. David Berger, vice president and director of research at Foote, Cone & Belding, has determined that 2,500 GRPs are likely to lead to roughly a 70 percent probability of high awareness, 1,000 to 2,500 would yield about a 33 percent probability, and less than 1,000 would probably result in almost no awareness.[6] David Olson obtained similar results and further showed that as awareness increased, trial of the product would also increase, although at a significantly slower rate.[7] In both cases, it was evident that high numbers of GRPs were required to make an impact.

Figure 10–21 summarizes the effects that can be expected at different levels of exposure, on the basis of research in this area. A number of factors may be operating, and direct relationships may be difficult to establish.[8] In addition to the results shown in Figure 10–21, Joseph Ostrow has shown that while the number of repetitions increases awareness rapidly, it has much less impact on attitudinal and behavioral responses.[9]

You can imagine how expensive it was for Denny's to purchase 1,300 gross ratings points on TV. Now that you have additional information, we will ask again, "Was this a good buy?"

Figure 10–20 Estimates of reach for network TRPs

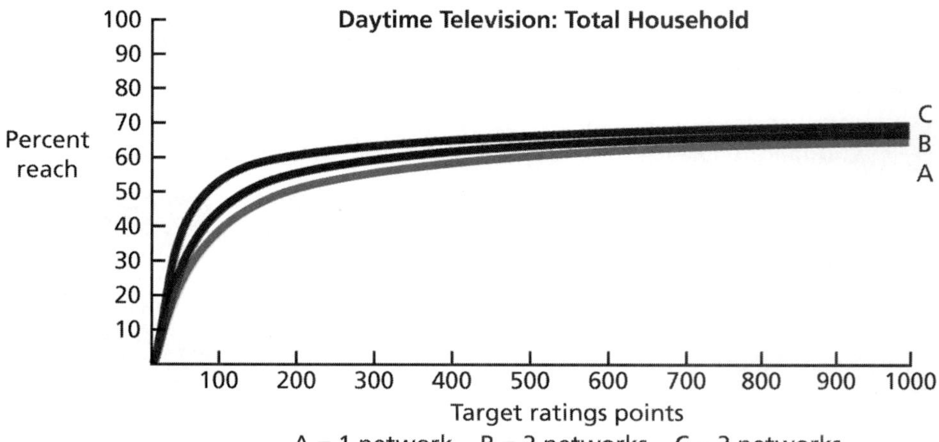

1. One exposure of an ad to a target group within a purchase cycle has little or no effect in most circumstances.
2. Since one exposure is usually ineffective, the central goal of productive media planning should be to enhance frequency rather than reach.
3. The evidence suggests strongly that an exposure frequency of two within a purchase cycle is an effective level.
4. Beyond three exposures within a brand purchase cycle or over a period of four or even eight weeks, increasing frequency continues to build advertising effectiveness at a decreasing rate but with no evidence of decline.
5. Although there are general principles with respect to frequency of exposure and its relationship to advertising effectiveness, differential effects by brand are equally important.
6. Nothing we have seen suggests that frequency response principles or generalizations vary by medium.
7. The data strongly suggest that wearout is not a function of too much frequency; it is more of a creative or copy problem.

Figure 10–21 The effects of reach and frequency

Determining Effective Reach Since marketers have budget constraints, they must decide whether to increase reach at the expense of frequency or increase the frequency of exposure but to a smaller audience. A number of factors influence this decision. For example, a new product or brand introduction will attempt to maximize reach, particularly unduplicated reach, to create awareness in as many people as possible as quickly as possible. At the same time, for a high-involvement product or one whose benefits are not obvious, a certain level of frequency is needed to achieve effective reach.

Effective reach represents the percentage of a vehicle's audience reached at each effective frequency increment. This concept is based on the assumption that one exposure to an ad may not be enough to convey the desired message. As we saw earlier, no one knows the exact number of exposures necessary for an ad to make an impact, although advertisers have settled on three as the minimum. Effective reach (exposure) is shown in the shaded area in Figure 10–22 in the range of 3 to 10 exposures. Fewer than 3 exposures is considered insufficient reach, while more than 10 is considered overexposure and thus ineffective reach. This exposure level is no guarantee of effective communication; different messages may require more or fewer exposures. For example, Jack Myers, president of Myers Reports, argues that the three-exposure theory was valid in the 1970s when consumers were exposed to approximately 1,000 ads per day. Now that they are exposed to 3,000 to 5,000 per day, three exposures may not be enough. Adding in the fragmentation of

Figure 10–22 Graph of effective reach

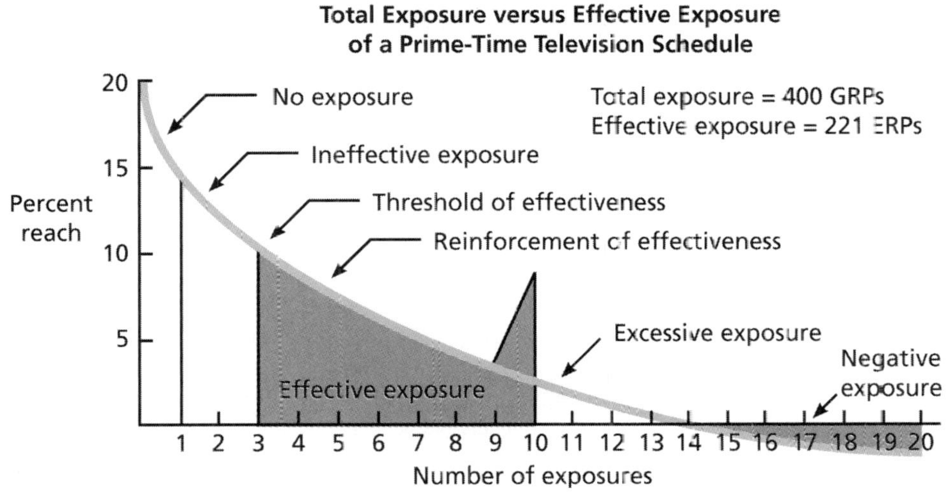

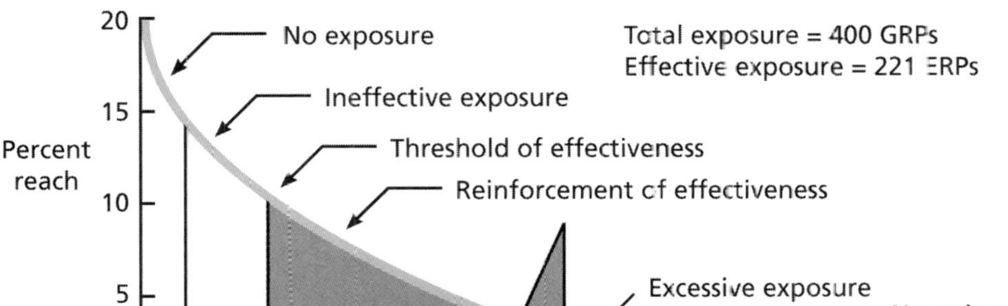

GRPs = Gross rating points
ERPs = Effective rating points

television, the proliferation of magazines, and the advent of a variety of alternative media leads Myers to believe that 12 exposures may be the *minimum* level of frequency required. Also, Jim Surmanek, vice president of International Communications Group, contends that the complexity of the message, message length, and recency of exposure also impact this figure.[10]

Since they do not know how many times the viewer will actually be exposed, advertisers typically purchase GRPs that lead to more than three exposures to increase the likelihood of effective reach and frequency.

Determining effective reach is further complicated by the fact that when calculating GRPs, advertisers use a figure that they call **average frequency,** or the average number of times the target audience reached by a media schedule is exposed to the vehicle over a specified period. The problem with this figure is revealed in the following scenario:

Consider a media buy in which:

50 percent of audience is reached 1 time.

30 percent of audience is reached 5 times.

20 percent of audience is reached 10 times.

Average frequency = 4

In this media buy, the average frequency is 4, which is slightly more than the number established as effective. Yet a full 50 percent of the audience receives only one exposure. Thus, the average frequency number can be misleading, and using it to calculate GRPs might result in underexposing the audience.

Although GRPs have their problems, they can provide useful information to the marketer. A certain level of GRPs is necessary to achieve awareness, and increases in GRPs are likely to lead to more exposures and/or more repetitions—both of which are necessary to have an effect on higher-order objectives. Perhaps the best advice for purchasing GRPs is offered by Ostrow, who recommends the following strategies:[11]

1. Instead of using average frequency, the marketer should decide what minimum frequency goal is needed to reach the advertising objectives effectively and then maximize reach at that frequency level.
2. To determine effective frequency, one must consider marketing factors, message factors, and media factors. (See Figure 10–23.)

In summary, the reach-versus-frequency decision, while critical, is very difficult to make. A number of factors must be considered, and concrete rules do not always apply. The decision is often more of an art than a science.

Creative Aspects and Mood

The context of the medium in which the ad is placed may also affect viewers' perceptions. A specific creative strategy may require certain media. Because TV provides both sight and sound, it may be more effective in generating emotions than other media; magazines may create different perceptions from newspapers. In developing a media strategy, marketers must consider both creativity and mood factors. Let us examine each in more detail.

Creative Aspects

It is possible to increase the success of a product significantly through a strong creative campaign. But to implement this creativity, you must employ a medium that will support such a strategy. For example, the campaign for 212 cologne shown in Chapter 4 used print media to communicate the message effectively. Kodak and McDonald's, among many others, have effectively used TV to create emotional appeals. In some situations, the media strategy to be pursued may be the driving force behind the creative strategy, as the media and creative departments work closely together to achieve the greatest impact with the audience of the specific media.

Figure 10–23 Factors important in determining frequency levels

Marketing Factors

- *Brand history.* Is the brand new or established? New brands generally require higher frequency levels.
- *Brand share.* An inverse relationship exists between brand share and frequency. The higher the brand share, the lower the frequency level required.
- *Brand loyalty.* An inverse relationship exists between loyalty and frequency. The higher the loyalty, the lower the frequency level required.
- *Purchase cycles.* Shorter purchasing cycles require higher frequency levels to maintain top-of-mind awareness.
- *Usage cycle.* Products used daily or more often need to be replaced quickly, so a higher level of frequency is desired.
- *Competitive share of voice.* Higher frequency levels are required when a lot of competitive noise exists and when the goal is to meet or beat competitors.
- *Target group.* The ability of the target group to learn and to retain messages has a direct effect on frequency.

Message or Creative Factors

- *Message complexity.* The simpler the message, the less frequency required.
- *Message uniqueness.* The more unique the message, the lower the frequency level required.
- *New versus continuing campaigns.* New campaigns require higher levels of frequency to register the message.
- *Image versus product sell.* Creating an image requires higher levels of frequency than does a specific product sell.
- *Message variation.* A single message requires less frequency; a variety of messages requires more.
- *Wearout.* Higher frequency may lead to wearout. This effect must be tracked and used to evaluate frequency levels.
- *Advertising units.* Larger units of advertising require less frequency than smaller ones to get the message across.

Media Factors

- *Clutter.* The more advertising that appears in the media used, the more frequency is needed to break through the clutter.
- *Editorial environment.* The more consistent the ad is with the editorial environment, the less frequency is needed.
- *Attentiveness.* The higher the level of attention achieved by the media vehicle, the less frequency is required. Low-attention-getting media require more repetitions.
- *Scheduling.* Continuous scheduling requires less frequency than does flighting or pulsing.
- *Number of media used.* The fewer media used, the lower the level of frequency required.
- *Repeat exposures.* Media that allow for more repeat exposures (for example, monthly magazines) require less frequency.

Mood Certain media enhance the creativity of a message because they create a mood that carries over to the communication. For example, think about the moods created by the following magazines: *Gourmet, Skiing, Travel,* and *House Beautiful.* Each of these special-interest vehicles puts the reader in a particular mood. The promotion of fine wines, ski boots, luggage, and home products is enhanced by this mood. What different images might be created for your product if you advertised it in the following media?

The New York Times versus the *National Enquirer*

Architectural Digest versus *Reader's Digest*

A highly rated prime-time TV show versus an old rerun

The message may require a specific medium and a certain media vehicle to achieve its objectives. Likewise, certain media and vehicles have images that may carry over to the perceptions of messages placed within them.

Flexibility

An effective media strategy requires a degree of flexibility. Because of the rapidly changing marketing environment, strategies may need to be modified. If the plan has not built in some flexibility, opportunities may be lost and/or the company may not be able to address new threats. Flexibility may be needed to address the following:

1. *Market opportunities.* Sometimes a market opportunity arises that the advertiser wishes to take advantage of. For example, the development of a new advertising medium may offer an opportunity that was not previously available.
2. *Market threats.* Internal or external factors may pose a threat to the firm, and a change in media strategy is dictated. For example, a competitor may alter its media strategy to gain an edge. Failure to respond to this challenge could create problems for the firm.
3. *Availability of media.* Sometimes a desired medium (or vehicle) is not available to the marketer. Perhaps the medium does not reach a particular target segment or has no time or space available. There are still some geographic areas that certain media do not reach. Even when the media are available, limited advertising time or space may have already been sold or cutoff dates for entry may have passed. Alternative vehicles or media must then be considered.
4. *Changes in media or media vehicles.* A change in the medium or in a particular vehicle may require a change in the media strategy. For example, the advent of cable TV opened up new opportunities for message delivery, as will the introduction of interactive media. The Internet has led many consumer companies to adopt this medium, while for business-to-business marketers the Web has almost become a requirement to succeed. Likewise, a drop in ratings or a change in editorial format may lead the advertiser to use different programs or print alternatives.

Fluctuations in these factors mean the media strategy must be developed with enough flexibility to allow the manager to adapt to specific market situations.

Budget Considerations

One of the more important decisions in the development of media strategy is cost estimating. The value of any strategy can be determined by how well it delivers the message to the audience with the lowest cost and the least waste. We have already explored a number of factors, such as reach, frequency, and availability, that affect this decision. The marketer tries to arrive at the optimal delivery by balancing cost with each of these. (Again, the Bumble Bee Tuna plan in Appendix B, p. 339, demonstrates how this issue is addressed.) As the following discussion shows, understanding cost figures may not be as easy as it seems.

Advertising and promotional costs can be categorized in two ways. The **absolute cost** of the medium or vehicle is the actual total cost required to place the message. For example, a full-page four-color ad in *Newsweek* magazine costs about $144,000. **Relative cost** refers to the relationship between the price paid for advertising time or space and the size of the audience delivered; it is used to compare media vehicles. Relative costs are important because the manager must try to optimize audience delivery within budget constraints. Since a number of alternatives are available for delivering the message, the advertiser must evaluate the relative costs associated with these choices. The way media costs are provided and problems in comparing these costs across media often make such evaluations difficult.

Determining Relative Costs of Media

To evaluate alternatives, advertisers must compare the relative costs of media as well as vehicles within these media. Unfortunately, the broadcast, print, and out-of-home media do not always provide the same cost breakdowns, nor necessarily do vehicles within the print media. Following are the cost bases used:

1. **Cost per thousand (CPM).** For years the magazine industry has provided cost breakdowns on the basis of cost per thousand people reached. The formula for this computation is

$$\text{CPM} = \frac{\text{Cost of ad space (absolute cost)}}{\text{Circulation}} \times 1{,}000$$

Figure 10–24 provides an example of this computation for two vehicles in the same medium—*Time* and *Newsweek*—and shows that (all other things being equal) *Time* is a more cost-effective buy, even though its absolute cost is higher. (We will come back to "all other things being equal" in a moment.)

2. **Cost per ratings point (CPRP).** The broadcast media provide a different comparative cost figure, referred to as cost per ratings point or *cost per point (CPP),* based on the following formula:

$$\text{CPRP} = \frac{\text{Cost of commercial time}}{\text{Program rating}}$$

An example of this calculation for a spot ad in a local TV market is shown in Figure 10–25. It indicates that "ER" would be more cost-effective than "Who Wants to be a Millionaire."

3. **Daily inch rate.** For newspapers, cost effectiveness is based on the daily inch rate, which is the cost per column inch of the paper. Like magazines, newspapers now use the cost-per-thousand formula discussed earlier to determine relative costs. As shown in Figure 10–26, the *Boston Globe* costs significantly more to advertise in than does the *Boston Herald* (again, all other things being equal).

As you can see, it is difficult to make comparisons across various media. What is the broadcast equivalent of cost per thousand or the column inch rate? In an attempt

	Time	*Newsweek*
Per-page cost	\$156,000	\$144,000
Circulation	4.0 million	3.1 million
Calculation of CPM	$\frac{156{,}000 \times 1{,}000}{4{,}000{,}000}$	$\frac{144{,}000 \times 1{,}000}{3{,}100{,}000}$
CPM	\$39.00	\$46.45

Figure 10–24 Cost per thousand computations: *Time* versus *Newsweek*

	"Who Wants to Be a Millionaire"	"ER"
Cost per spot ad	\$3,500	\$4,000
Rating	11	15
Reach (households)	109,000	135,000
Calculation	\$3,500/11	\$4,000/15
CPRP (CPP)	\$318.18	\$266.67

Figure 10–25 Comparison of cost per ratings point: "Who Wants to Be a Millionaire" versus "ER" in a local TV market

Figure 10–26 Comparative costs in newspaper advertising

	Boston Globe	Boston Herald
Cost per page	\$32,205	\$15,135
Cost per inch	\$268.60	\$216.50
Circulation	499,000	308,000
Calculation	$\text{CPM} = \dfrac{\text{Page cost} \times 1{,}000}{\text{Circulation}}$	
	$= \dfrac{\$32{,}205 \times 1{,}000}{499{,}000}$	$\dfrac{\$15{,}135 \times 1{,}000}{308{,}000}$
	\$64.54	\$49.14

to standardize relative costing procedures, the broadcast and newspaper media have begun to provide costs per thousand, using the following formulas:

$$\text{Television: } \frac{\text{Cost of 1 unit of time} \times 1{,}000}{\text{Program rating}} \qquad \text{Newspapers: } \frac{\text{Cost of ad space} \times 1{,}000}{\text{Circulation}}$$

While the comparison of media on a cost-per-thousand basis is important, intermedia comparisons can be misleading. The ability of TV to provide both sight and sound, the longevity of magazines, and other characteristics of each medium make direct comparisons difficult. The media planner should use the cost-per-thousand numbers but must also consider the specific characteristics of each medium and each media vehicle in the decision.

The cost per thousand may overestimate or underestimate the actual cost effectiveness. Consider a situation where some waste coverage is inevitable. The circulation (using the *Time* magazine figures to demonstrate our point) exceeds the target market. If the people reached by this message are not potential buyers of the product, then having to pay to reach them results in too low a cost per thousand, as shown in scenario A of Figure 10–27. We must use the potential reach to the target market—the destination sought—rather than the overall circulation figure. A

Figure 10–27 Cost per thousand estimates

Scenario A: Overestimation of Efficiency

Target market	18–49
Magazine circulation	4,000,000
Circulation to target market	65% (2,600,000)
Cost per page	\$156,000

$$\text{CPM} = \frac{\$156{,}000 \times 1{,}000}{4{,}000{,}000} = \$39$$

$$\text{CPM (actual target audience)} = \frac{\$156{,}000 \times 1{,}000}{2{,}600{,}000} = \$60$$

Scenario B: Underestimation of Efficiency

Target market	All age groups, male and female
Magazine circulation	4,000,000
Cost per page	\$156,000
Pass-along rate	3* (33% of households)

$$\text{CPM (based on readers per copy)} = \frac{\text{Page cost} \times 1{,}000}{\text{Circulation} + 3(1{,}320{,}000)} = \frac{\$156{,}000 \times 1{,}000}{7{,}960{,}000}$$

$$= \$19.60$$

*Assuming pass-along was valid.

medium with a much higher cost per thousand may be a wiser buy if it is reaching more potential receivers. (Most media buyers rely on **target CPM (TCPM),** which calculates CPMs based on the target audience, not the overall audience.)

CPM may also underestimate cost efficiency. Magazine advertising space sellers have argued for years that because more than one person may read an issue, the actual reach is underestimated. They want to use the number of **readers per copy** as the true circulation. This would include a **pass-along rate,** estimating the number of people who read the magazine without buying it. Scenario B in Figure 10–27 shows how this underestimates cost efficiency. Consider a family in which a father, mother, and two teenagers read each issue of *Time*. Assume such families constitute 33 percent of *Time*'s circulation base. While the circulation figure includes only one magazine, in reality there are four potential exposures in these households, increasing the total reach to 7.96 million.

While the number of readers per copy makes intuitive sense, it has the potential to be extremely inaccurate. The actual number of times the magazine changes hands is difficult to determine. How many people in a fraternity read each issue of *Sports Illustrated* or *Playboy* that is delivered? How many people in a sorority or on a dorm floor read each issue of *Cosmopolitan* or *Allure*? How many of either group read each issue of *Business Week*? While research is conducted to make these determinations, pass-along estimates are very subjective and using them to estimate reach is speculative. These figures are regularly provided by the media, but managers are selective about using them. At the same time, the art of media buying enters, for many magazines' managers have a good idea how much greater the reach is than their circulation figures provided.

In addition to the potential for over- or underestimation of cost efficiencies, CPMs are limited in that they make only *quantitative* estimates of the value of media. While they may be good for comparing very similar vehicles (such as *Time* and *Newsweek*), they are less valuable in making intermedia comparisons. We have already noted some differences among media that preclude direct comparisons.

You can see that the development of a media strategy involves many factors. Ostrow may be right when he calls this process an art rather than a science, as so much of it requires going beyond the numbers. IMC Perspective 10–2 discusses some of the ways effective media planners are successful.

Evaluation and Follow-Up

All plans require some evaluation to assess their performance. The media plan is no exception.

In outlining the planning process, we stated that objectives are established and strategies developed for them. Having implemented these strategies, marketers need to know whether or not they were successful. Measures of effectiveness must consider two factors: (1) How well did these strategies achieve the media objectives? (2) How well did this media plan contribute to attaining the overall marketing and communications objectives? If the strategies were successful, they should be used in future plans. If not, their flaws should be analyzed.

The problem with measuring the effectiveness of media strategies is probably obvious to you at this point. At the outset of this chapter, we suggested the planning process was limited by problems with measurements and lack of consistent terminology (among others). While these problems limit the degree to which we can assess the relative effectiveness of various strategies, it is not impossible to make such determinations. Sometimes it is possible to show that a plan has worked. Even if the evaluation procedure is not foolproof, it is better than no attempt.

Computers in Media Planning

Attempts to improve on the media buying process through the use of computers have received a great deal of attention. While advanced planning models have been around since at least 1963, for the most part these models have met with limited success. Programs based on linear programming, simulation, and iteration have been adopted by a number of agencies, but there remains a great deal of skepticism regarding their practicality.[12]

IMC Perspective 10–2
What Makes Media Planners Successful?

Every year *Adweek,* a trade magazine for advertisers, picks its "Media All-Stars." The awards are given to media directors in different categories, including print, broadcast, and new media, and a Media Director of the Year is selected. How does one win such an honor? Here's how:

Media Planning: Peter Gardiner, Bozell, New York. As director of media planning for Bozell, Gardiner is in charge of a staff of 60 and nearly a billion dollars in media spending. Currently he spends his time developing plans for *The New York Times,* Bell Atlantic Mobile, Lycos, Unisys, Sara Lee, Mutual of Omaha, and numerous other clients. When Gardiner came to Bozell, he transformed a staid and traditional media department to a dynamic, innovative, and distinctly nontraditional one. Because of his background in integrated marketing communications, Gardiner was able to land the Pharmaceutical Manufacturers and Research Association account ($25 million), Bank of America ($80 million), Datek Online ($80 million), and IKON Office Solutions ($30 million), among others.

Gardiner's success is attributed to his notion that media and marketing programs must be fully merged. IMC, he says, requires dissolving the barriers between media and mixing and matching them into a "crazy-quilt" and distinctly unique marketing plan. He notes, "The benefits are enormous, because consumers are approached in fresh ways, and clutter can be minimized," but purchasing media is a difficult challenge because of their still traditional selling methods. To solve the problem, Gardiner occasionally allows intuition to take precedence over research.

Gardiner learned integrated marketing at Time, Inc., but really demonstrated it effectively at Bozell, where he changed the media department to assume an IMC orientation. His center-stage client was the Dairy Management and Milk Processor Education Program (MilkPEP) and the "Milk Mustache" campaign. The media team developed dozens of plans, including the development of *The Best of Nickelodeon Magazine,* which was targeted to kids and funded solely by MilkPEP; a milk-sponsored TV show, *The Sports Illustrated for Kids Good Sport Awards Presented by Milk;* and a partnership with iVillage to provide information about the benefits of calcium. In addition, there are dozens of cross-corporate programs like the one between Nickelodeon and ESPN. His biggest challenge? "Finding and keeping the right people."

Out of Home: Jennifer Sparks, Colby, Effer & Partners, Los Angeles. As media supervisor for the California Pizza Kitchen (CPK) account, Jennifer never dreamed she would start a billboard war over pizza. But one 14- by 48-foot billboard above the 99 Cent Store in Los Angeles was the first shot. The board carried the message "If They Sold a Tandori Chicken Pizza for Under a Buck, Then They'd Have Something," followed by an arrow pointing into the discount store. The owners of the store fought back with their own board with an arrow pointing back up and stating, "If You Want a Tandori Chicken Pizza for $9.99 You Can Go There—Or You Can Come In Here and Get A Plain Cheese Pizza for 99 Cents." The friendly battle got major play in the local TV and print media, including articles in *The Wall Street Journal, Adweek, The Los Angeles Times,* and the *Los Angeles Daily News.* The successful pairing of creativity with media placement led to a variety of other locations, with signs over palm reader shops, dry cleaners, florists, and dental office buildings, to mention a few. Some of the billboard locations were near car washes, which afforded CPK the opportunity to give away free pizza to waiting customers.

The $250,000, three-month campaign (not counting the publicity gained through other media) led to increased traffic in CPK restaurants and "a quantum leap in awareness" for CPK's menu items. Beyond using creativity and good placement, Sparks had to "arm-wrestle, prod and coddle" outdoor companies to secure the location-specific signage.

Media Director of the Year: Mark Stewart, Universal McCann, New York. Ira Carlin, chairman of Universal McCann, in describing Mark Stewart notes that he is smart. But, he notes, so are a lot of other media directors. What makes Mark so smart is his "lateral thinking" and incredible imagination that leads to "off the wall stuff." Mark responds by saying that he doesn't know what "lateral thinking" is but that he has good insights and ideas that he gets from looking beyond the numbers and the basic tools. "It's not about the media; it's about understanding the consumer: how they think and act and why, how they interact with the client's product. Then, and only then, can you begin to think about harnessing media."

Over the past two years Stewart has helped his agency attract approximately $1.7 billion in new business including such clients as General Motors, Johnson & Johnson, Sprint, and Microsoft. Stewart's approach to understanding the consumer has meant a new way of media buying at McCann. It means media and creative personnel working closely together, and the media plan being part of an overall strategic marketing plan. It means listening to the consumer and moving away from the traditional media seller–media buyer relationship—one that Stewart considers the worst possible scenario!

As you can see from the above, a variety of factors and approaches can lead to success. At the same time, there are consistencies that exist across all these cases. Understanding the consumer and delivering the message through an integrated marketing program seem to be the essentials for successful media planning.

Sources: Michael Freeman, "Media All-Stars: Jennifer Sparks," *Adweek*, December 6, 1999, pp. 60–64; Verne Gray, "Media All-Stars: Peter Gardiner," *Adweek*, December 6, 1999, pp. 12–18; Eric Schmuckler, "Media All-Stars: Mark Stewart," *Adweek*, December 6, 1999, pp. 4–10.

Computers have been used, however, to automate each of the four steps involved in planning and strategy development. While the art of media strategy has not been mechanized, advances in the quantitative side have significantly improved managers' decision-making capabilities while saving substantial time and effort. Let us briefly examine some of these methods.

Computers in Market Analysis

Earlier in this chapter, we provided examples of Simmons and MRI data. In Chapter 2, we reviewed the information in Prizm and VALS, as well as other such systems. All these data can be accessed either through an interactive system or on the agency's own PC. For example, MRI offers its clients interactive capabilities with its mainframe or its MEMRI software database that can be used on a PC to cross-tabulate media and demographic data, estimate reach and frequency, and rank costs, in addition to numerous other applications. The databases can also interface with Prizm and VALS data. Simmons also allows access to Prizm, VALS, and others.

Other market analysis programs are also available. Nelson and Scarborough provide demographic, geographic, psychographic, and product and media use information that can be used for media planning (Exhibit 10–1). Census tract information and socioeconomic data are also accessible. These systems are linked to Nielsen data for scheduling and targeting to specific groups.

Analyses of these data can help planners determine which markets and which groups should be targeted for advertising and promotions. By using this information along with other data, the marketer can also define media objectives.

Exhibit 10–1 Scarborough Reports provide valuable information to media planners

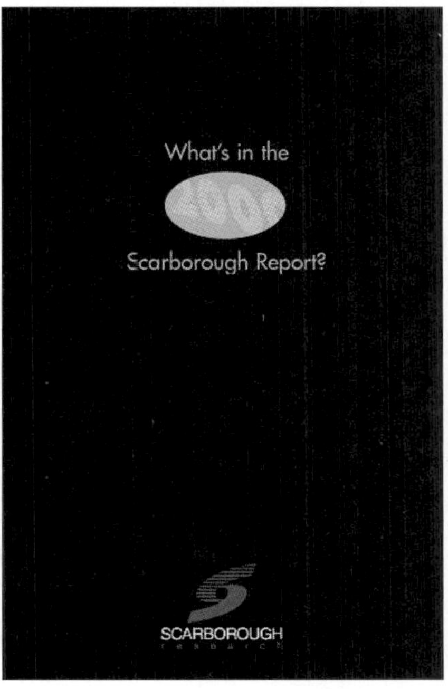

Computers in Media Strategy Development

In the section on strategy development, we discussed the need to make decisions regarding coverage, scheduling, costs, and the trade-off between reach and frequency, among others. Of primary benefit to media planners are the programs that assist in development of these strategies. While there are far too many of these programs to review here, we will provide a small sampling to demonstrate our point.

Reach and Frequency Analyses on the Computer

Figure 10–28 demonstrates how software programs are being used to determine reach and frequency levels and assist in deciding which alternative is best. The Telmar program computes various media mixes for TV and radio at different

Figure 10–28 Telmar media plan for a local bank

Media Mix (A 25–54)	Reach Frequency (%/X)	3+ Level (%)	1st Quarter Weekly Cost
TV (125)	84/4.5	51	$21,480
TV (125) R (125)	91/8.2	71	29,450
TV (125) R (150)*	92/9.0	73	31,045
TV (150)	86/5.2	57	25,660
TV (150) R (125)	92/9.0	73	33,625
TV (150) R (150)	92/9.8	74	35,220
TV (175)	89/5.9	61	29,930
TV (175) R (125)	93/9.7	75	37,900
TV (175) R (150)	93/10.5	76	39,490
TV (200)	90/6.7	65	34,255
TV (200) R (125)	93/10.5	76	42,225
TV (200) R (150)	93/11.3	78	43,820

Note: Based on a three-week flight.

*Recommended.

TRPs, with reach and frequency estimates, the number of people reached three or more times, and the costs. The program has determined that a mix of 125 TRPs on TV and 150 TRPs on radio would result in the best buy. Keep in mind that this recommendation considers only the most efficient combination of quantifiable factors and does not allow for the art of media buying.

Figure 10–28 shows just one of the many examples of how computer programs are being used in media strategy development. Other computer-based media planning programs are available; the following list is just a small sample:

- **ADplus** provides for media planning, reach and frequency analysis, media mix information, budgeting, and more.
- **Adware** provides Arbitron and Nielsen information, calculates media costs, projects GRPs, and more.
- **DSI (Datatrak Systems, Inc.)** provides integrated systems for a full range of agency functions, from media and production to planning, buying, billing, and traffic. Software programs include Spot Media Datatrak, Network Media Datatrak, Print Media Datatrak, and Print Analysis Datatrak.
- **IMS** offers a fully integrated suite of software that performs market analysis, target identification, print and broadcast planning, and more. It also provides access to over 600 databases, including syndicated and proprietary, media and marketing, consumer, trade, domestic, and international data.
- **Marketing Resources, Inc.** ranks stations in each market according to delivery potential and costs and calculates projected ratings.
- **Media Plan, Inc.,** offers multimedia planning, reach and frequency, and flowchart tools. Software includes Manas (flowchart), MultiReach, and MediaPlan RollUp.
- **Media Control by Control G Software** has a Print Media Control Module and Broadcast Media Control. The software packages help to manage media planning by controlling deadlines, station and spot mix, contract usage, and much more.
- **Neilsen SAVIE** (formerly AdExpress) provides a full picture of cable TV alternatives and the value of each by using multiple databases, such as product purchasing data, customer preference cluster data, Neilsen audience data, and specific systems data.

- **Strata Marketing, Inc.** provides Windows-based TV and radio prebuy and postbuy software systems. Programs include StrataView Radio, StrataView TV, StrataView Buy Management System, and Q-View.
- **Tapscan** uses syndicated data useful in radio media planning, including ratings data and reach and frequency analysis.
- **MRI+** contains MRI research, rate card data, and ABC and BPA figures for 5,700 consumer and trade magazines.
- **Telmar** allows planners to analyze media data, devise media plans, and create flowcharts. It is linked to major syndicated data services.
- **TVscan** provides information like Tapscan's for TV.
- **TV Conquest** combines Nielsen, Donnelley, and Simmons data to provide demographic, product usage, and ratings information.

In addition to these, media models have been developed to show the effects of media selection on advertising responses:

1. *Evaluation models* are exposure distribution models that estimate the reach and frequency of media vehicles on the basis of probability theories.
2. *Allocation models* are comprehensive models used to optimize advertising budget allocation.
3. *Interaction models* consider the interaction effects between copy and media selection in predicting advertising effects.

Unfortunately, these models also have weaknesses that limit their adoption.[13]

The one area where computers have not yet provided a direct benefit is in the evaluation stage of the media plan. While these programs do generate what they consider to be optimal TRP, GRP, and media mixes and allow for pre- and postbuy analyses, the true test is what happens when the plan is implemented. We reserve our discussion of the evaluation process for Chapter 19 on measuring effectiveness.

Optimizers

In recent years the U.S. market has been introduced to computer programs designed to maximize the reach of the media buy or minimize the cost. These programs, known as **optimizers,** were developed in the United Kingdom and brought to the United States and linked to Nielsen data. Originally cost-prohibitive, programs such as SuperMidas, Xpert, and Spot-On have now become affordable to most agencies and buyers.

Optimizers use cost, reach, and target points to provide the media buyer with either the highest reach or the lowest cost available on the basis of Nielsen respondent data, not a formula. As shown in Figure 10–29, the buyer specifies whether he or she wants to achieve highest reach or lowest cost. One is specified, the second is optimized, and the result (target points) is a function of the two. As an example, the buyer may dictate a specified budget, and the program will yield the optimal reach. Alternatively, one may start with a defined reach goal, and the budget will be optimized.

Optimizers have met with both great acceptance and criticism in the television industry. Supporters believe that these programs will provide the long-sought solution to optimizing reach and cost trade-offs. They cite the success of optimizers in Britain to support their position. Others are not so sure. Erwin Ephron of Ephron, Papazian & Ephron advertising in New York notes that the programs may be more

Figure 10–29 Optimization

	Optimized: Cost	Optimized: Reach
Cost		Lowest cost per reach point
Reach	Highest reach per dollar	

suited to the controlled markets of the United Kingdom than those of the United States. He cautions that optimization should not be considered a substitute for media planning and that the programs base all decisions on CPMs rather than taking into consideration the value of viewers reached. Given the short time optimizers have been used in the United States, it is difficult to determine their value at this point.[14]

Characteristics of Media

To this point, we have discussed the elements involved in the development of media strategy. One of the most basic elements in this process is the matching of media to markets. In the following chapters, you will see that each medium has its own characteristics that make it better or worse for attaining specific objectives. First, Figure 10–30 provides an overall comparison of media and some of the characteristics by which they are evaluated. This is a very general comparison, and the various media options must be analyzed for each situation. Nevertheless, it is a good starting point and serves as a lead-in to subsequent chapters.

Figure 10–30 Media characteristics

Media	Advantages	Disadvantages
Television	Mass coverage High reach Impact of sight, sound, and motion High prestige Low cost per exposure Attention getting Favorable image	Low selectivity Short message life High absolute cost High production costs Clutter
Radio	Local coverage Low cost High frequency Flexible Low production costs Well-segmented audiences	Audio only Clutter Low attention getting Fleeting message
Magazines	Segmentation potential Quality reproduction High information content Longevity Multiple readers	Long lead time for ad placement Visual only Lack of flexibility
Newspapers	High coverage Low cost Short lead time for placing ads Ads can be placed in interest sections Timely (current ads) Reader controls exposure Can be used for coupons	Short life Clutter Low attention-getting capabilities Poor reproduction quality Selective reader exposure
Outdoor	Location specific High repetition Easily noticed	Short exposure time requires short ad Poor image Local restrictions
Direct mail	High selectivity Reader controls exposure High information content Opportunities for repeat exposures	High cost/contact Poor image (junk mail) Clutter
Internet and interactive media	User selects product information User attention and involvement Interactive relationship Direct selling potential Flexible message platform	Limited creative capabilities Websnarl (crowded access) Technology limitations Few valid measurement techniques Limited reach

Summary

This chapter has presented an overview of the determination of media objectives, development of the media strategy, and formalization of objectives and strategy in the form of a media plan. Sources of media information, characteristics of media, and an actual plan were also provided.

The media strategy must be designed to supplement and support the overall marketing and communications objectives. The objectives of this plan are designed to deliver the message the program has developed.

The basic task involved in the development of media strategy is to determine the best matching of media to the target market, given the constraints of the budget. The media planner attempts to balance reach and frequency and to deliver the message to the intended audience with a minimum of waste coverage. At the same time, a number of additional factors affect the media decision. Media strategy development has been called more of an art than a science because while many quantitative data are available, the planner also relies on creativity and nonquantifiable factors.

This chapter discussed many factors, including developing a proper media mix, determining target market and geographic coverage, scheduling, and balancing reach and frequency. Creative aspects, budget considerations, the need for flexibility in the schedule, and the use of computers in the media planning process were also considered.

The chapter also introduced a number of resources available to the media planner. A summary chart of advantages and disadvantages of various media was provided, as was an example of a media plan.

Key Terms

media planning, 305
media objectives, 305
media strategies, 305
medium, 306
media vehicle, 306
reach, 306
coverage, 306
frequency, 306
sweeps periods, 306
index number, 311
waste coverage, 316
continuity, 318
flighting, 318
pulsing, 318
unduplicated reach, 321
duplicated reach, 321
program rating, 321
gross ratings points (GRP), 321
target ratings points (TRP), 321
effective reach, 323
average frequency, 324
absolute cost, 326
relative cost, 326
cost per thousand (CPM), 327
cost per ratings point (CPRP), 327
daily inch rate, 327
target CPM (TCPM), 329
readers per copy, 329
pass-along rate, 329
optimizers, 333

Discussion Questions

1. The text lists both internal and external factors that might impact the media strategy. Provide examples of each and discuss how they might impact the media plan.

2. Using the BDI and CDI indices, explain the least desirable market situation for marketers. Provide an example. Then do the same for the most desirable situation.

3. Discuss the role of optimizers in media planning.

4. Media planning involves a trade-off between reach and frequency. Explain what this means and give examples of when reach should be emphasized over frequency and vice versa.

5. What is meant by readers per copy? Explain the advantages and disadvantages associated with the use of this figure.

6. One long-time advertising agency executive noted that buying media is both an art and a science, with a leaning toward art. Explain what this means and provide examples.

7. Explain the difference between CPM and TCPM. Which would be of more relevance to the marketer?

8. Discuss some of the factors that are important in determining frequency levels. Give examples of each factor.

9. Describe the four stages of developing the media plan. Briefly describe what occurs at each stage.

10. Explain why more media are now presenting their relative cost figures as CPM. Discuss advantages and disadvantages of this.

Appendixes

Appendix A

Sources of Media Information

Cross-reference guide to advertising media sources

	General Information	Competitive Activities	Market Information (Geographic)	Audience Information (Target Groups)	Advertising Rates
Nonmedia information (general marketing)	1, 10, 15, 16, 20, 21, 22	1	10, 11, 15, 16, 18, 19, 21, 24	15, 16, 20	
Multimedia or intermedia	1, 15, 16, 20	1, 13	18	2, 24	2
Daily newspapers				5, 15, 16, 20	2, 23
Weekly newspapers					23
Consumer magazines	14	13		15, 16, 20	2, 23
Farm publications				5, 25	2, 23
Business publications			6, 8	6, 25	2, 23
Network television		7, 13		4, 15, 16, 17, 20	2
Spot television		7, 13		4, 15, 16, 17, 20	2, 23
Network radio		7		12, 15, 16, 17, 20, 26	2
Spot radio				4, 5, 12, 17, 20	2, 23
Direct mail					2, 23
Outdoor		13			2, 9
Transit					2

1. *Advertising Age*
2. Advertising agency media estimating guides
3. American Business Press, Inc. (ABP)
4. Arbitron Ratings Company
5. Audit Bureau of Circulations (ABC)
6. Business/Professional Advertising Association (B/PAA) Media Data
7. Broadcast Advertisers Reports (BAR)
8. Business Publications Audit of Circulation (BPA)
9. *Buyer's Guide to Outdoor Advertising*
10. *State and Metropolitan Area Data Book*
11. *Editor & Publisher Market Guide*
12. Survey of World Advertising Expenditures, Stach/Inra/Hooper
13. Competitive Media Reporting
14. Magazine Publishers Association of America (MPA)
15. Mediamark Research, Inc. (MRI)
16. Mendelsohn Media Research, Inc. (MMR)
17. Nielsen Media Research Company
18. Prizm
19. *Sales and Marketing Management Survey of Buying Power*
20. Simmons Market Research Bureau: *Study of Media and Markets*
21. *Standard Directory of Advertisers*
22. *Standard Directory of Advertising Agencies*
23. Standard Rate and Data Service
24. Telmar
25. Verified Audit Circulation Corporation (VAC)

Appendix B

Media Plan for Bumble Bee Tuna

Bumble Bee Tuna
Media Plan
Phillips-Ramsey

Communications Objectives

- Increase expansion strategies into 11 markets, with primary emphasis on 5 key markets (Group A) and 6 secondary markets (Group B).
- Develop media strategies to create high awareness in new product intro markets.
- Develop media strategies to sustain achieved awareness levels.

Media Overview

Media Objectives

- Achieve the following combined TV/Print minimum average four-week TRP levels:
  - Bumble Bee Introduction 700
  - Sustaining #1 200
  - New Product Introduction 400
  - Sustaining #2 200
- As budget permits, incorporate the following expansion strategies:
  1. Run the complete TV plan—24 weeks—in all five markets.
  2. Beef up the New Product Introduction to 500 TRPs/four weeks.
  3. Increase the Sustaining #2 levels to 250 TRPs/four weeks.

Market Groups

- Top five: 45% category white meat (WM) volume and 51% Bumble Bee (BB) white meat (WM) volume.
- Remaining six: 18% category WM volume and 17% BB WM volume.

Media Details

Television

- Schedule length: On-air weeks total 24 in all Top Five markets.
- Weight levels: TRPs vary by campaign period in order to achieve the combined TV/Print Media Objectives.

Print

- Regional editions of publications selected for ad flexibility and CPM.
- Will provide May–December continuity coverage in all eleven markets.

Out-of-Home: New York

- Subway posters: 1,000+ per month for 5 months.
- Bus shelters: 60+ per month for 3 months.

Media Plan Summary

Markets

	Group A	Group B	Combined
# markets	5	6	11
% BB WM volume	51.0	17.4	68.4
% category WM volume	44.7	17.8	62.5
% U.S. TV HH	14.2	11.9	26.1

Media Strategy

Develop a media mix, where required and affordable, as follows:

- **Television:** Deliver designated weekly TRP levels over a maximum of three periods: 2nd Q, 3rd Q, and 4th Q, depending upon market importance and TV costs.
- **Out-of-home:** Bus shelters/subway signs in NY; posters in selective markets.
- **Magazine:** Regional editions rather than local-market editions due to lower cost and CPMs.

Select the media emphasis by market based on:

1. High BB and category WM volume.
2. BB strength vis-a-vis the category and competitors.
3. Opportunity for BB share increase.
4. Targeted media availability and cost.
5. Total available media budget.

Note: *All* markets receive magazine ad support.

Local Media Selection Rationale

New York: Protect highest volume = TV in 2nd and 3rd Qtrs; shelters and subway signs.

Boston: Share-increase opportunity = TV in all three Qtrs; posters in 2nd Q.

Miami: BB dominant in share = TV in 2nd Q; posters in 2nd Q.

Hartford: BB strongest, protect share = TV in 2nd and 3rd Qtrs.

Philadelphia: Share-increase opportunity = TV in all three Qtrs.

Tampa: Protect share = TV in 2nd and 3rd Qtrs.

Detroit: Share-increase opportunity = TV in all three Qtrs.

Baltimore: Strong BB share = Media too costly [print only].

Washington: BB highest share = Media too costly [print only].

Los Angeles: Share-increase opportunity in #3 category market = TV in 3rd Q.

Albany: Mid-range share, volume potential law = Print only.

Market BDIs

Market	% BB WM Volume Per mkt	% BB WM Volume Cume	% Category WM Per mkt	% Category WM Cume	WM: CDI	WM: BDIs BB	WM: BDIs COS	WM: BDIs SK	% U.S. TV HH Per mkt	% U.S. TV HH Cume
New York	26.8	26.8	20.2	20.2	297	395	260	256	6.9	6.9
Boston	7.7	34.5	10.4	30.6	372	275	349	246	2.22	9.12
Miami	7.6	42.1	4.4	35	236	407	111	182	1.42	10.54
Hartford/ New Haven	3.8	45.9	3.4	38.4	300	315	219	247	0.94	11.48
Philadelphia	5.1	51	6.3	44.7	199	160	215	202	2.72	142

BB: Bumble Bee
COS: Chicken of the Sea
SK: Starkist

IMS Model Summary Report

Target: women 25–54

Media/ Calculations	A	B	C	D
Better Homes & Gardens	0	2	2	1
Parade	3	0	0	0
People	2	2	2	1
USA Weekend	2	3	0	1
Family Circle	0	3	2	1
Total inserts	7	10	6	4
Gross rating points	223	241	156	99
Reach percent	77.6	75.1	65.8	63.1
Effective reach percent 3+	45.8	41.7	24.0	7.7
Average frequency	2.88	3.21	2.37	1.57
Median frequency	2.77	2.80	2.09	1.39

Schedule Key:
A = Qtr. AMJ
B = Qtr. JAS
C = Qtr. OND
D = "Avg." 4-week

Combined Media Delivery: TV + Print

Average 4-week

GRPs	Reach %	Avg Freq	Eff Rch 3+ %
405	86.3%	4.69	50.1%

Source: 1997 MRI Fall.

Market Mate—TV Market Report (March 12, 1998)

Report demo: Females 25–54 Schedule: A (4 weeks) Budget $(000): 0.0

Market	Bumble Bee Introduction: May				
	Total GRPs	Reach %	Avg Freq	Gr Imps (000)	3+ Reach %
Boston	700	62.7	11.16	9181	44.6
Hartford & New Haven	700	64.6	10.83	3834	48.2
Miami–Ft. Lauderdale	700	68.0	10.30	5427	48.7
New York	700	65.1	10.75	30473	45.5
Philadelphia	700	54.7	10.83	11237	45.2

Report demo: Females 25–54 Schedule: B (4 weeks) Budget $(000): 0.0

Market	Sustaining Period: June/July/Aug				
	Total GRPs	Reach %	Avg Freq	Gr Imps (000)	3+ Reach %
Boston	200	47.5	4.21	2623	24.3
Hartford & New Haven	200	48.8	4.10	1096	24.8
Miami–Ft. Lauderdale	200	49.7	4.02	1551	25.1
New York	200	47.6	4.20	8707	24.4
Philadelphia	200	48.5	4.13	3211	24.7

Report demo: Females 25–54 Schedule: C (4 weeks) Budget $(000): 0.0

Market	"New Product" Introduction: Aug/Sept				
	Total GRPs	Reach %	Avg Freq	Gr Imps (000)	3+ Reach %
Boston	400	56.3	7.11	5246	35.8
Hartford & New Haven	400	58.0	6.90	2191	36.9
Miami–Ft. Lauderdale	400	59.5	6.72	3101	37.7
New York	400	56.5	7.07	17413	36.0
Philadelphia	400	52.0	7.70	6421	33.3

Report demo: Females 25–54 Schedule: D (4 weeks) Budget $(000): 0.0

Market	Sustaining Period: Sept/Oct/Nov/Dec				
	Total GRPs	Reach %	Avg Freq	Gr Imps (000)	3+ Reach %
Boston	200	46.0	4.34	2623	23.8
Hartford & New Haven	200	48.8	4.10	1096	24.8
Miami–Ft. Lauderdale	200	51.9	3.85	1551	25.8
New York	200	51.0	3.83	8707	25.5
Philadelphia	200	48.3	4.14	3211	24.7

Market Mate—TV Schedule Comparison Report (March 12, 1998)

Market: BOSTON
Report demo: Females 25–54
Pop (000): 1311.6

Calculation	A	B	C	D
GRPs	700	200	400	200
Reach %	62.7	47.5	56.3	48.0
Avg Freq	11.16	4.21	7.11	4.34
Gr Imps (000)	9181	2623	5246	2823
Eff Reach % 3+	44.6	24.3	35.8	23.8

Market: HARTFORD & NEW HAVEN
Report demo: Females 25–54
Pop (000): 547.7

Calculation	A	B	C	D
GRPs	700	200	400	200
Reach %	64.6	48.8	58.0	48.8
Avg Freq	10.83	4.10	6.90	4.10
Gr Imps (000)	3834	1095	2191	1096
Eff Reach % 3+	46.2	24.8	35.9	24.8

Market: MIAMI–FT. LAUDERDALE
Report Demo: Females 25–54
Pop (000): 775.3

Calculation	A	B	C	D
GRPs	700	200	400	200
Reach %	68.0	49.7	59.5	51.9
Avg Freq	10.30	4.02	6.72	3.85
Gr Imps (000)	5427	1551	3101	1551
Eff Reach % 3+	48.7	25.1	37.7	25.8

Market: NEW YORK
Report demo: Females 25–54
Pop (000): 4363.3

Calculation	A	B	C	D
GRPs	700	200	400	200
Reach %	65.1	47.6	56.6	51.0
Avg Freq	10.75	4.20	7.07	3.93
Gr Imps (000)	30473	8707	17413	8707
Eff Reach % 3+	48.5	24.4	38.0	25.5

Market: PHILADELPHIA
Report Demo: Females 25–54
Pop (000): 1605.3

Calculation	A	B	C	D
GRPs	700	200	400	200
Reach %	64.7	48.5	52.0	48.3
Avg Freq	10.83	4.13	7.70	4.14
Gr Imps (000)	11237	3211	6421	3211
Eff Reach % 3–	46.2	24.7	33.3	24.7

Average Four-Week TV Delivery
A = Bumble Bee Intro: May
B = Sustaining Period: June/July/August
C = New Product Intro: August/Sept
D = Sustaining Period: Sept/Oct/Nov/Dec

Media Plans by Market

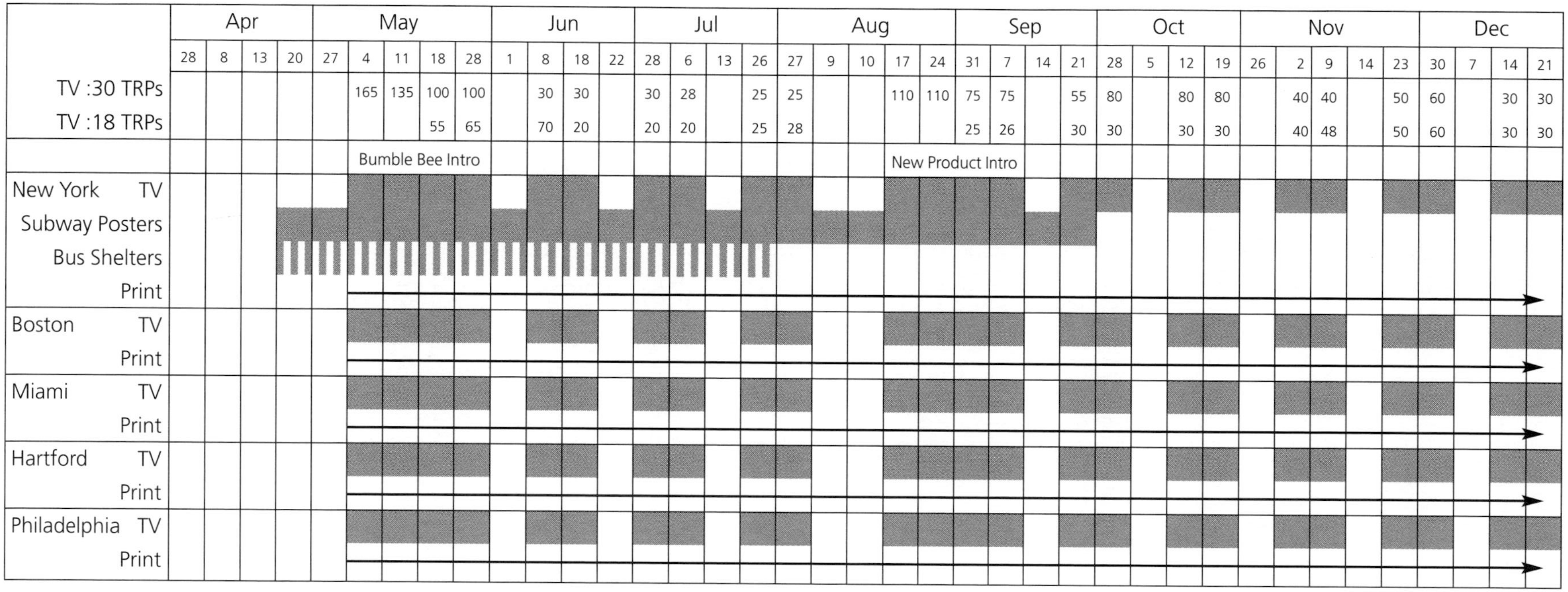

	Apr				May					Jun				Jul				Aug					Sep				Oct				Nov					Dec			
	28	8	13	20	27	4	11	18	28	1	8	18	22	28	6	13	26	27	9	10	17	24	31	7	14	21	28	5	12	19	26	2	9	14	23	30	7	14	21
TV :30 TRPs						165	135	100	100		30	30		30	28		25	25			110	110	75	75		55	80		80	80		40	40		50	60		30	30
TV :18 TRPs								55	65		70	20		20	20		25	28					25	26		30	30		30	30		40	48		50	60		30	30
						Bumble Bee Intro															New Product Intro																		
New York TV																																							
Subway Posters																																							
Bus Shelters																																							
Print																																							
Boston TV																																							
Print																																							
Miami TV																																							
Print																																							
Hartford TV																																							
Print																																							
Philadelphia TV																																							
Print																																							

Avg. 4 week delivery	Intro	Sustaining	Intro	Sustaining
TRPs	794	214	406	346
Net reach %	88.2	81.5	87.0	72.8
Average frequency	7.10	2.56	5.80	3.37
3+ reach %	62%	38.6	53.8	33%

TV Plan

	Apr				May					Jun				Jul				Aug					Sep				Oct				Nov					Dec			
	28	8	13	20	27	4	11	18	28	1	8	18	22	28	6	13	26	27	9	10	17	24	31	7	14	21	28	5	12	19	26	2	9	14	23	30	7	14	21
						Bumble Bee Intro															New Product Intro																		
:30 TRPs						155	155	160	160		30	30		30	28		25	25			110	110	75	75		55	80		80	80		40	40		50	60		30	30
:18 TRPs								55	65		70	20		20	20		25	28					25	26		30	30		30	30		40	48		50	60		30	30
New York																																							
Boston																																							
Miami																																							
Hartford																																							
Philadelphia																																							

Regional Print Plan—All Markets

	Apr				May					Jun				Jul				Aug					Sep				Oct				Nov					Dec				First Key Dates	
	28	8	13	20	27	4	11	18	28	1	8	18	22	28	6	13	26	27	9	10	17	24	31	7	14	21	28	5	12	19	26	2	9	14	23	30	7	14	21	Issue	Closing
Parade									X			X			X																									May 24	Apr 10
USA Weekend							X			X				X			X					X																		May 17	Apr 10
People								→				→						→		→								→		→										May 18	Mar 30
Better Homes & Gardens														—	—	—	→	—	—	—	—	→					—	—	—	→	—	—	—	—	→					July	Apr 16
Family Circle													—	—	→	—	—	→	—	—	—	→				—	—	→				—	→							June 23	Mar 20

Market Media Plan: New York

TV info:

6.90% U.S. TV households

7.45% U.S. women 25–54

Food sales:

73% by chains

Top chains:

A&P, Grand Union, Pathmark, Waldbaum, Edwards, King Kullen, Acme, Food Emporium, ShopRite

Brand data:

26.8% BB WM volume

WM CDI = 297

BB BDI = 395

COS BDI = 250

SK BDI = 255

Local Media Plans

Television

19 weeks on-air.

	2nd Q	3rd Q	4th Q	Total
$(000) by Q:	269.0	247.2	-0-	516.2

"Political Protection Period" = Aug. 1–Sept. 14

Out-of-Home

1,140 subway signs @ $24K/month* × 6 months.
107 bus shelters @ $100K/month** × 3 months.
*NY metro. **NY metro, Long Is., Westchester.

	2nd Q	3rd Q	4th Q	Total
$(000) by Q:	372.0	72.0	-0-	444.0

Magazine

	# inserts
Parade	3
USA Weekend	5
People	6
Better Homes & Gardens	4
Family Circle	5

Market Media Plan: Boston

TV info:

2.22% U.S. TV households

2.27% U.S. women 25–54

Food sales:

77% by chains

Top chains:

Stop & Shop, Demoulas, Shaws, Star, Shop N Save

Brand data:

7.7% BB WM volume

WM CDI = 372

BB BDI = 275

COS BDI = 349

SK BDI = 246

Local Media Plans

Television

Full 26 weeks on-air.

	2nd Q	3rd Q	4th Q	Total
$(000) by Q:	125.7	115.9	68.0	309.6

"Political Protection Periods" = Aug. 1–Sept. 14 [state].
Sept. 4–Nov. 2 [federal].

Out-of-Home

70 posters @ $51K/month × 3 months.

	2nd Q	3rd Q	4th Q	Total
$(000) by Q:	153.0	-0-	-0-	153.0

Magazine

	# inserts
Parade	3
USA Weekend	5
People	6
Better Homes & Gardens	4
Family Circle	5

Market Media Plan: Miami

TV info:
- 1.42% U.S. TV households
- 1.37% U.S. women 25–54

Food sales:
- 73% by chains

Top chains:
- Publix, Winn Dixie, Sedanos

Brand data:
- 7.6% BB WM volume
- WM CDI = 236
- BB BDI = 407
- COS BDI = 111
- SK BDI = 182

Local Media Plans

Television

9 weeks on-air.

	2nd Q	3rd Q	4th Q	Total
$(000) by Q:	112.8	-0-	-0-	112.8

Out-of-Home

55 posters @ $40K/month × 4 months.

	2nd Q	3rd Q	4th Q	Total
$(000) by Q:	120.0	40.0	-0-	160.0

Magazine

	# inserts
Parade	3
People	6
Better Homes & Gardens	4
Family Circle	5

[*USA Weekend* dropped due to minimal coverage at high cost.]

Market Media Plan: Hartford/ New Haven

TV info:
- .94% U.S. TV households
- .93% U.S. women 25–54

Food sales:
- 61% by chains

Top chains:
- Stop & Shop, Waldbaums, Big Y, Shaws

Brand data:
- 3.8% BB WM volume
- WM CDI = 300
- BB BDI = 315
- COS BDI = 219
- SK BDI = 247

Local Media Plans

Television

19 weeks on-air.

	2nd Q	3rd Q	4th Q	Total
$(000) by Q:	56.6	53.1	-0-	109.7

"Political Protection Period" = Aug. 1–Sept. 14.

Out-of-Home

[not recommended].

	2nd Q	3rd Q	4th Q	Total
$(000) by Q:				-0-

Magazine

	# inserts
Parade	3
USA Weekend	5
People	6
Better Homes & Gardens	4
Family Circle	5

Market Media Plan: Philadelphia

TV info:

2.72% U.S. TV households

2.74% U.S. women 25–54

Food sales:

69% by chains

Top chains:

Acme, Super Fresh, Pathmark, Genuardi, Food Lion, Giant Martins

Brand data:

5.1% BB WM volume

WM CDI = 199

BB BDI = 160

COS BDI = 215

SK BDI = 202

Local Media Plans

Television

Full 26 weeks on-air.

	2nd Q	3rd Q	4th Q	Total
$(000) by Q:	167.6	156.8	90.6	415.0

"Political Protection Periods" = Aug. 1–Sept. 14 [state].
Sept. 4–Nov. 2 [federal].

Out-of-Home

[not recommended].

	2nd Q	3rd Q	4th Q	Total
$(000) by Q:				-0-

Magazine

	# inserts
Parade	3
USA Weekend	5
People	6
Better Homes & Gardens	4
Family Circle	5

Chapter Eleven

Evaluation of Broadcast Media

Chapter Objectives

- To examine the structure of the television and radio industries and the role of each medium in the advertising program.
- To consider the advantages and limitations of TV and radio as advertising media.
- To explain how advertising time is purchased for the broadcast media, how audiences are measured, and how rates are determined.
- To consider future trends in TV and radio and how they will influence the use of these media in advertising.

"Who Wants to Be a Millionaire": ABC's Final Answer to the Ratings Race

During the summer of 1999, the ABC television network was looking for programming to plug a hole in its summer schedule. The network decided to try a knockoff of a quiz show that was popular in Britain called "Who Wants to Be a Millionaire," where a contestant wins up to a million dollars by answering a series of multiple-choice questions that become progressively more difficult. The new show's popularity took ABC, as well as the other networks, by surprise, as it was number 1 in the TV ratings for several weeks during the summer. "Millionaire" was not part of ABC's prime-time fall schedule. However, network programmers decided to add the show to their evening schedule to see if it could repeat its summer ratings success.

"Who Wants to Be a Millionaire" returned to prime time in November and quickly became the most watched program of the season, dethroning NBC's "ER," which had been the number-1 show for the past several years. By midseason "Millionaire" had become more than just a hit show; it was a certifiable phenomenon. ABC began airing the quiz show during prime time on three nights: Sunday, Tuesday, and Thursday. By late January, the Thursday edition of "Who Wants to Be a Millionaire" was the most watched show of the year, averaging over 30 million viewers each week. And the next two highest-rated shows were the "Millionaire" Sunday and Tuesday night telecasts. A Tuesday night airing of the show in late January was watched by more than 35 million viewers, making it the most watched TV show of the season. No other network show had attracted so many viewers in the Tuesday 8 P.M. time slot since 1996 when NBC aired the Summer Olympics during prime time.

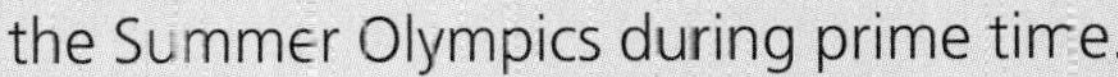

For ABC, "Who Wants to Be a Millionaire" has created both a ratings and a financial windfall. The show doubled and, in some cases, tripled the number of ABC's viewers, compared with the shows it replaced. Moreover, the shows that follow "Millionaire" have benefited from its popularity, as it has funneled additional viewers to them. For example, the sitcom "Dharma & Greg" had its highest audience ever following a telecast of "Millionaire," and the quiz show's big start to the evening has also helped programs such as "NYPD Blue" get higher ratings. Thanks to the popularity of "Who Wants to Be a Millionaire," many media experts were correct when they predicted that ABC would be the most watched network for the entire season. This was the first time ABC won the ratings crown since 1994–95 and only the second time the network has finished first in 20 years.

The success of "Who Wants to Be a Millionaire" has not gone unnoticed by the other networks. Since ABC struck ratings gold with "Millionaire," each of the other networks has rushed its own quiz shows into its prime-time schedule. Fox countered with "Greed: The Series," NBC with "Twenty-One," and CBS with another British import called "Winning Lines." However, thus far none of the imitators has even come close to matching the audience size of "Who Wants to Be a Millionaire."

Several reasons have been mentioned for the success of "Millionaire," such as the deceptive brilliance of its simplicity and the drama it generates, the viewing public's deep-seated craving for big money in the era of dot.com millionaires, and the popularity of the show's host, Regis Philbin. Another reason for the success of the show is that it has revived the concept of families watching TV together (at least for an hour), as the show's popularity transcends demographic groups. According to Nielsen Media Research, during January 2000, the quiz show was among the four favorite programs of children between the ages of 2 and 11, adults over 55, and every demographic group in between. The show has been criticized for its simple early-round questions by some who see it as the "dumbing down" of America. However, according to executive producer Michael Davies, that is one of the secrets to the show's success. He notes, "The questions are deliberately easy in the beginning, because you want to get everybody into the show."

"Who Wants to Be a Millionaire" has been hailed as the most important breakthrough for network television in years. However, television critics are also wondering just how long the phenomenon can continue, and some predict the show will have only a two- or three-year run. By the time you read this, the excitement over "Who Wants to Be a Millionaire" may have subsided, its ratings may have dropped, and it may have had to use a few of its "life lines" to survive. On the other hand, we may all still be watching "Who Wants to Be a Millionaire" and cheering for the contestants as they respond to Regis Philbin's question that has become part of pop culture: "Is that your final answer?"

Sources: Richard Huff, "ABC Is Doing A-OK in Heated Television Ratings Race," *New York Daily News,* January 28, 2000, p. E10; Joanne Ostrow, "Quiz Craze 'Millionaire' Ratings Success Stuns Experts, Sends Network Programmers into Overtime Thinking Up Copycat Shows," *Denver Post,* January 24, 2000, p. E1; Joel Stein, "Going Millionaire Crazy," *Time,* January 17, 2000, pp. 80–83.

Popular shows such as "Who Wants to Be a Millionaire" are very important to marketers because they are part of our primary form of entertainment, television. TV has virtually saturated households throughout the United States and most other countries and has become a mainstay in the lives of most people. The average American household watches over seven hours of TV a day, and the tube has become the predominant source of news and entertainment for many people. Nearly 85 percent of the TV households in the United States have a VCR, and many people have entertainment centers with big-screen TVs, VCRs, and stereos. On any given evening during the prime-time hours of 8 to 11 P.M., more than 90 million people are watching TV. Popular shows like "Friends" and "ER" may have more than 30 million viewers. The large numbers of people who watch television are important to the TV networks and stations because they can sell time on these programs to marketers who want to reach that audience with their advertising messages. Moreover, the qualities that make TV a great medium for news and entertainment also encourage creative ads that can have a strong impact on customers.

Radio is also an integral part of our lives. Many of us wake up to clock radios in the morning and rely on radio programs to inform and/or entertain us while we drive to work or school. For many people, radio is a constant companion in their cars, at home, even at work. The average American listens to the radio more than three hours each day.[1] Like TV viewers, radio listeners are an important audience for marketers.

In this chapter, we examine the broadcast media of TV and radio, including the general characteristics of each as well as their specific advantages and disadvantages. We examine how advertisers use TV and radio as part of their advertising and media strategies, how they buy TV and radio time, and how audiences are measured and evaluated for each medium. We also examine the factors that are changing the role of TV and radio as advertising media.

Television

It has often been said that television is the ideal advertising medium. Its ability to combine visual images, sound, motion, and color presents the advertiser with the opportunity to develop the most creative and imaginative appeals of any medium. However, TV does have certain problems that limit or even prevent its use by many advertisers.

Advantages of Television

TV has numerous advantages over other media, including creativity and impact, coverage and cost effectiveness, captivity and attention, and selectivity and flexibility.

Creativity and Impact

Perhaps the greatest advantage of TV is the opportunity it provides for presenting the advertising message. The interaction of sight and sound offers tremendous creative flexibility and makes possible dramatic, lifelike representations of products and services. TV commercials can be used to convey a mood or image for a brand as well as to develop emotional or entertaining appeals that help make a dull product appear interesting.

Television is also an excellent medium for demonstrating a product or service. For example, print ads are effective for showing a car and communicating information regarding its features, but only a TV commercial can put you in the driver's seat and give you the sense of actually driving, as shown by the Porsche commercial in Exhibit 11–1.

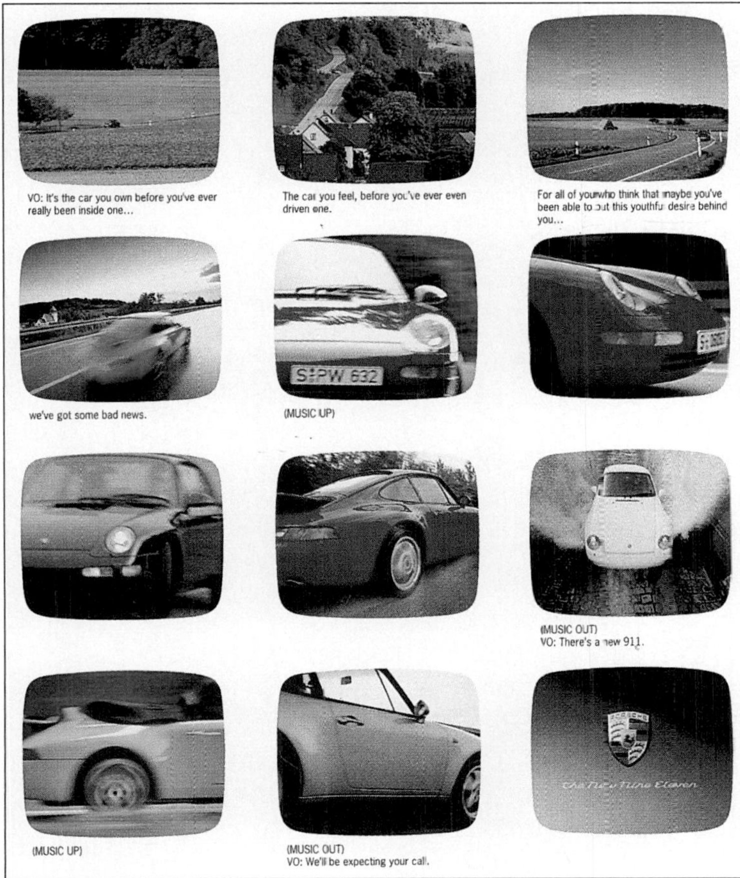

Exhibit 11–1 This TV commercial helps viewers feel the sensation of driving a sports car

Coverage and Cost Effectiveness Television advertising makes it possible to reach large audiences. Nearly everyone, regardless of age, sex, income, or educational level, watches at least some TV. Most people do so on a regular basis. According to Nielsen estimates, nearly 260 million people, 77 percent of whom are 18 or older, are in TV households.[2]

Marketers selling products and services that appeal to broad target audiences find that TV lets them reach mass markets, often very cost efficiently. The average prime-time TV show reaches 7 million homes; a top-rated show like "ER" may reach nearly 20 million homes and perhaps twice that many viewers. In 1999, the average cost per thousand (CPM) homes reached was around $14 for network evening shows and $4.00 for daytime weekly shows.[3]

Because of its ability to reach large audiences in a cost-efficient manner, TV is a popular medium among companies selling mass-consumption products. Companies with widespread distribution and availability of their products and services use TV to reach the mass market and deliver their advertising messages at a very low cost per thousand. Television has become indispensable to large consumer package-goods companies, carmakers, and major retailers. Companies like Procter & Gamble and Coca-Cola spend more than 80 percent of their media advertising budget on various forms of TV—network, spot, cable, and syndicated programs. Figure 11–1 shows the top 25 network TV advertisers and their expenditures.

Captivity and Attention Television is basically intrusive in that commercials impose themselves on viewers as they watch their favorite programs. Unless

Figure 11–1 Top 25 network TV advertisers, 1999

Rank	Company	Measured Advertising ($ millions)
1	General Motors Corp.	$887.7
2	Procter & Gamble Co.	621.5
3	Johnson & Johnson	438.4
4	Philip Morris Cos.	383.2
5	Ford Motor Co.	359.2
6	McDonald's Corp.	296.8
7	Tricon Global Restaurants	287.9
8	DaimlerChrysler	286.5
9	MCI WorldCom	274.4
10	Diageo	270.0
11	AT&T Corp.	259.2
12	Warner-Lambert Co.	245.0
13	Walt Disney Co.	228.0
14	Toyota Motor Sales USA	227.5
15	Unilever	223.4
16	Anheuser-Busch	210.6
17	L'Oreal	209.9
18	Sprint Corp.	205.2
19	Time Warner	189.9
20	PepsiCo	189.0
21	Sears, Roebuck & Co.	186.9
22	US Government	180.1
23	Visa USA	168.8
24	American Home Products Corp.	166.0
25	Nissan Motor Corp. USA	163.9

we make a special effort to avoid commercials, most of us are exposed to thousands of them each year. The increase in viewing options and the penetration of VCRs, remote controls, and other automatic devices have made it easier for TV viewers to avoid commercial messages. Studies of consumers' viewing habits found that as much as a third of program audiences may be lost during commercial breaks.[4] However, the remaining viewers are likely to devote some attention to many advertising messages. As discussed in Chapter 5, the low-involvement nature of consumer learning and response processes may mean TV ads have an effect on consumers simply through heavy repetition and exposure to catchy slogans and jingles.

Selectivity and Flexibility Television has often been criticized for being a nonselective medium, since it is difficult to reach a precisely defined market segment through the use of TV advertising. But some selectivity is possible due to variations in the composition of audiences as a result of program content, broadcast time, and geographic coverage. For example, Saturday morning TV caters to children; Saturday and Sunday afternoon programs are geared to the sports-oriented male; and weekday daytime shows appeal heavily to homemakers.

With the growth of cable TV, advertisers refine their coverage further by appealing to groups with specific interests such as sports, news, history, the arts, or music. Exhibit 11–2 shows an ad promoting Animal Planet, a new cable network launched by the Discovery Channel, that focuses solely on animals.

Advertisers can also adjust their media strategies to take advantage of different geographic markets through local or spot ads in specific market areas. Ads can be scheduled to run repeatedly or to take advantage of special occasions. For example, companies such as Anheuser-Busch and Gillette are often major sponsors during baseball's World Series, which allows them to advertise heavily to men who constitute the primary market for their products.

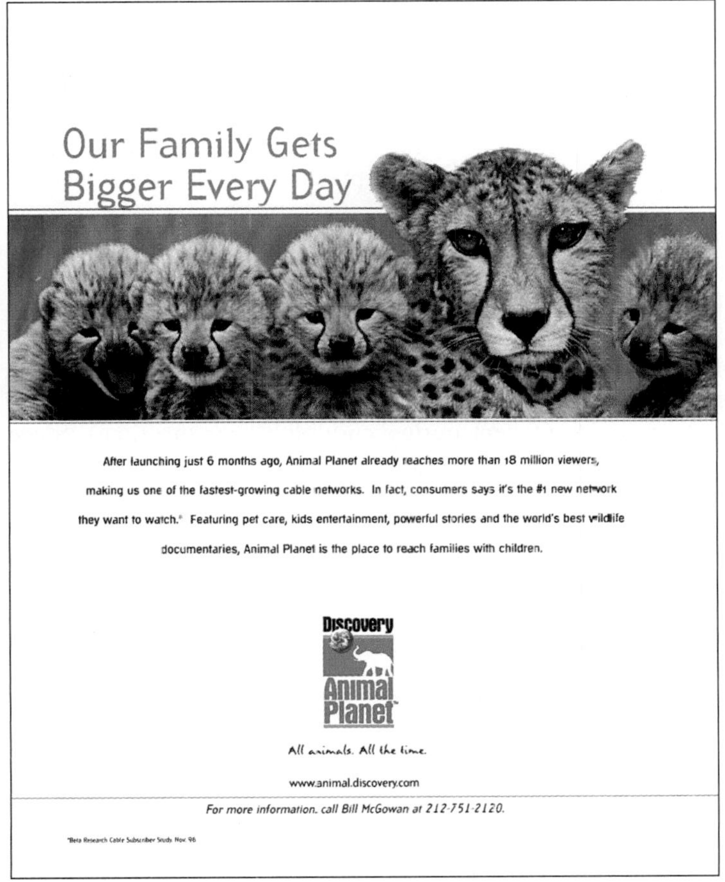

Exhibit 11–2 Animal Planet is a new cable network that focuses entirely on animals

Limitations of Television

Although television is unsurpassed from a creative perspective, the medium has several disadvantages that limit or preclude its use by many advertisers. These problems include high costs, the lack of selectivity, the fleeting nature of a television message, commercial clutter, limited viewer attention, and distrust of TV ads.

Costs

Despite the efficiency of TV in reaching large audiences, it is an expensive medium in which to advertise. The high cost of TV stems not only from the expense of buying airtime but also from the costs of producing a quality commercial. Production costs for a national brand 30-second spot average nearly $300,000 and can reach over a million for more elaborate commercials.[5] Many advertisers such as Burger King, Coca-Cola, and others develop commercials specifically for certain ethnic markets such as African-Americans and Hispanics.[6] More advertisers are using media-driven creative strategies that require production of a variety of commercials, which drive up their costs. Even local ads can be expensive to produce and often are not of high quality. The high costs of producing and airing commercials often price small- and medium-size advertisers out of the market. However, IMC Perspective 11–1 discusses how a number of small dot.com companies have been taking a chance by advertising on the Super Bowl, which has the most expensive ad rates of any TV program.

Lack of Selectivity

Some selectivity is available in television through variations in programs and cable TV. But advertisers who are seeking a very specific, often small, target audience find the coverage of TV often extends beyond their market, reducing its cost effectiveness (as discussed in Chapter 10). Geographic selectivity can be a problem for local advertisers such as retailers, since a station bases its rates on the total market area it reaches. For example, stations in Pittsburgh, Pennsylvania, reach viewers in western and central Pennsylvania, eastern Ohio, northern West Virginia, and even parts of Maryland. The small company whose market is limited to the immediate Pittsburgh area may find TV an inefficient media buy, since the stations cover a larger geographic area than the merchant's trade area.

Audience selectivity is improving as advertisers target certain groups of consumers through the type of program or day and/or time when they choose to advertise. However, TV still does not offer as much audience selectivity as radio, magazines, newspapers, or direct mail for reaching precise segments of the market.

Fleeting Message

TV commercials usually last only 30 seconds or less and leave nothing tangible for the viewer to examine or consider. Commercials have become shorter and shorter as the demand for a limited amount of broadcast time has intensified and advertisers try to get more impressions from their media budgets. As shown in Figure 11–2, 30-second commercials became the norm in the mid-1970s. In September 1986, the three networks began accepting 15-second spots across their full schedules (except during children's viewing time). Since 1987, these shorter spots have been accounting for about a third of all network commercials.

Figure 11–2 Changes in percentage of network commercials by length

Commercial Length	1965	1975	1980	1985	1987	1988	1989	1990	1994	1995	1997	1998
15	—	—	—	10	31	36	38	35	30	32	30	31
30	23	93	96	84	65	61	57	60	66	65	67	63
60	77	6	2	2	2	2	2	2	2	1	1	3
All others	—	1	2	4	2	1	3	3	2	2	2	3

IMC Perspective 11–1

Advertising on the Super Bowl: It's Not Just for Big Companies Anymore

Americans love their football, and Super Bowl Sunday has become an unofficial national holiday. The game nearly always draws the largest TV audience of the year, and its appeal spans various age groups, sexes, and regions of the country. The Super Bowl has even developed a global appeal, as it is now seen in more than 60 countries. While most consumers think about the Super Bowl as the biggest football game of the year, many marketers view it as the premier marketing event as well. The Super Bowl has become the most important advertising showcase of the year, particularly for companies willing to spend more than $2 million for a 30-second commercial.

Many advertising historians note that the frenzy over Super Bowl advertising began when Apple Computer ran its highly publicized "1984" spot (discussed in IMC Perspective 9–4). That commercial demonstrated to marketers how advertising to one of the largest worldwide audiences in a single TV event could be leveraged to make a statement with tremendous impact. It was the inspiration for "advertising as an event," and since then many marketers have used the big game to introduce new ad campaigns and marketing programs.

For many years the high costs of advertising on the Super Bowl limited the roster of advertisers to large companies with deep pockets, such as Coca-Cola, Frito Lay, Anheuser-Busch, and others. One of the few exceptions was Master Lock, a relatively small company that used nearly all its advertising budget every year from 1974 to 1996 to run an ad on the Super Bowl. However, recently there has been a dramatic change in the lineup of advertisers for Super Sunday as a number of dot.com companies have been buying time on the big game to pitch their websites. While members of America's corporate elite such as Anheuser-Busch, Pepsi-Cola, Motorola, and Visa USA shell out millions of dollars to run multiple ads during the game, they are now being joined by a blitz of dot.coms, many of which are spending their entire ad budgets to run one ad on the Super Bowl. In some cases, these dot.coms are betting their entire company on the idea that advertising on the Super Bowl will drive consumers to their websites and generate future revenue or help them raise venture capital.

Two of the first dot.com companies to take a chance on Super Bowl ads were the job-hunting sites HotJobs.com and Monster.com. HotJobs.com spent $2 million to produce and run an ad on the 1999 Super Bowl even though the company's total revenue was only $4 million at the time. According to CEO Richard Johnson, the gamble paid off: "As the result of this windfall of publicity, we became a brand overnight. When we went to do our fund-raising, everybody had heard of us." Monster.com also gambled and won by advertising on the 1999 Super Bowl with a critically acclaimed spot featuring children talking cynically about what they want to be when they grow up. Both companies returned for their second Super Bowl appearances during the 2000 game.

After seeing the success of Hotjobs.com and Monster.com, a rash of other Web companies hoped to make a big splash by advertising on the first Super Bowl of the new century. A dozen other dot.coms joined the two job-hunting sites, making viewers of the game feel like they just watched a long promotion for unknown websites interspersed with a bit of football. Among the dot.com rookies on the 2000 advertising roster were Computer.com, Autotrader.com, pet-supply

This is the worst commercial on the Super Bowl.

www.lifeminders.com

seller Pets.com, E*Trade, and another job site, Kforce. One company, the e-mail marketing firm LifeMinders.com, tried to grab viewers with a desperation play. The agency it hired did not have enough time to produce a spot for the game, so the company created the ad themselves. The spot consisted of big black letters on a yellow background proclaiming, "This is the worst commercial on the Super Bowl."

OurBeginnings.com, which sells stationery for weddings and such, is yet another example of a Web company that took a major risk by advertising on the Super Bowl. The company paid more than $3 million to run four pregame spots and an ad during the third quarter of the 2000 game even though it had only a little over $1 million in revenue. The company used an interactive twist to its Super Bowl ads by letting visitors to its website vote on whether the ads should be "warm and fuzzy," "over the edge," or "hysterically funny." The decision was to use a funny spot that featured brides angry over a botched wedding engaged in a slapstick brawl.

Many companies feel that advertising on the Super Bowl is worth the millions of dollars it costs because of the enormous viewing audience it delivers. They also note that the Super Bowl is one occasion where as much attention is paid to the commercials as to the program and the spots receive an enormous amount of hype and publicity. Some media planners argue that the cost of advertising on the big game has become too high and that companies would be better off spreading the millions of dollars they spend for one Super Bowl ad over a longer time period. However, it is likely that companies, both large and small, will continue to want to be part of advertising's biggest showcase.

Sources: Kathryn Kranhold, "The Real Action: Ad Bowl XXXIV," *The Wall Street Journal,* January 28, 2000, pp. B1, 4; Jay Schulberg, "Super Bowl Ads No Longer Score for Advertisers," *Advertising Age,* January 19, 2000, p. 28; Greg Farrell, "Advertising's Super Day Ruled by the Dot," *USA Today,* September 7, 1999, p. B1.

An important factor in the decline in commercial length has been the spiraling inflation in media costs over the past decade. With the average cost of a prime-time spot reaching over $100,000, many advertisers see shorter commercials as the only way to keep their media costs in line. A 15-second spot typically sells for half the price of a 30-second spot. By using 15- or even 10-second commercials, advertisers think they can run additional spots to reinforce the message or reach a larger audience. Many advertisers believe shorter commercials can deliver a message just as effectively as longer spots for much less money.

Several years ago, many advertising people predicted 15-second spots would become the dominant commercial unit by the early 1990s. However, the growth in the use of 15-second commercials peaked at 38 percent in 1989 and has recently declined to around 30 percent. The decline may be due to several factors, including creative considerations, lower prices for network time, and a desire by the networks to restrict clutter.[7]

Clutter The problems of fleeting messages and shorter commercials are compounded by the fact that the advertiser's message is only one of many spots and other nonprogramming material seen during a commercial break, so it may have trouble being noticed. One of advertisers' greatest concerns with TV advertising is the potential decline in effectiveness because of such *clutter.*

The next time you watch TV, count the number of commercials, promotions for the news or upcoming programs, or public service announcements that appear during a station break and you will appreciate why clutter is a major concern. A recent study sponsored by the advertising industry found a record level of clutter during prime-time television broadcasts on the major networks. The study analyzed one week of broadcasts during May and November of 1999 and found that the four major networks averaged 16 minutes and 43 seconds of nonprogramming content. The hour-long police drama "NYPD Blue" had the most clutter of any prime-time show with one episode having nearly 18 minutes of clutter.[8] With all of these messages competing for our attention, it is easy to understand why the viewer comes away confused or even annoyed and unable to remember or properly identify the product or service advertised.

One cause of clutter is the use of shorter commercials and **split-30s,** 30-second spots in which the advertiser promotes two different products with separate messages. Clutter also results when the networks and individual stations run promotional announcements for their shows, make more time available for commercials, and redistribute time to popular programs. For many years, the amount of time available for commercials was restricted by the Code Authority of the National Association of Broadcasters to 9.5 minutes per hour during prime time and 12 minutes during nonprime time. The Justice Department suspended the code in 1982 on the grounds that it violated antitrust law. At first the networks did not alter their time standards, but in recent years they have increased the number of commercial minutes in their schedules. The networks argue that they must increase commercial inventory or raise their already steep rates. Advertisers and agencies have been pressuring the networks to cut back on the commercials and other sources of clutter.

Limited Viewer Attention

When advertisers buy time on a TV program, they are not purchasing guaranteed exposure but rather the opportunity to communicate a message to large numbers of consumers. But there is increasing evidence that the size of the viewing audience shrinks during a commercial break. People leave the room to go to the bathroom or to get something to eat or drink, or they are distracted in some other way during commercials.

Getting consumers to pay attention to commercials has become an even greater challenge in recent years. The increased presence of VCRs and remote controls has led to the problems of zipping and zapping. **Zipping** occurs when customers fast-forward through commercials as they play back a previously recorded program. A study by Nielsen Media Research found that while 80 percent of recorded shows are actually played back, viewers zip past more than half of the commercials.[9] Another study found that most viewers fully or partially zipped commercials when watching a prerecorded program.[10]

Zapping refers to changing channels to avoid commercials. Over three-quarters of homes in the United States now have television sets with remote controls, which enable viewers to switch channels easily. An observational study conducted by John Cronin found as much as a third of program audiences may be lost to electronic zapping when commercials appear.[11] The Nielsen study found that most commercial zapping occurs at the beginning and, to a lesser extent, the end of a program. Zapping at these points is likely to occur because commercial breaks are so long and predictable. Zapping has also been fueled by the emergence of 24-hour continuous-format programming on cable channels such as CNN, MTV, and ESPN. Viewers can switch over for a few news headlines, sports scores, or a music video and then switch back to the program. Research shows that young adults zap more than older adults, and men are more likely to zap than women.[12]

How to inhibit zapping? The networks use certain tactics to hold viewers' attention, such as previews of the next week's show or short closing scenes at the end of a program. Some programs start with action sequences before the opening credits and commercials. A few years ago, Anheuser-Busch began using the Bud Frame, in which the ad frames live coverage of a sporting event. Some advertisers believe that producing different executions of a campaign theme is one way to maintain viewers' attention. Others think the ultimate way to zap-proof commercials is to produce creative advertising messages that will attract and hold viewers' attention. However, this is easier said than done, as many consumers just do not want to watch commercials. As more viewers gain access to remote controls and the number of channels increases, the zapping problem is likely to continue.

A recent study on zapping among viewers of the five major commercial channels in the Netherlands was conducted by Lex van Meurs.[13] He found that during commercial breaks, 29 percent of the audience stopped watching television or switched away to another channel. This loss of viewers was partially compensated for by an average increase of 7 percent of new viewers who zapped in from another channel. The study also found that people stop viewing TV during a commercial break because they have a reason to stop watching television altogether or they want to find out what is being shown on other channels. The number of people zapping in and out during breaks was not caused by the type of products being advertised or by specific characteristics of the commercials.

IMC Perspective 11–2

Is Television Advertising Doomed?

How much would you be willing to pay to never have to watch another TV commercial, be able to automatically record shows with your favorite actor, or record more than one show at a time? How about being able to leave the room in the middle of an exciting football game to answer the door or go to the bathroom and, when you return, being able to resume watching the game from the point where you left? These capabilities are no longer the dreams of TV viewers. They are now realities thanks to new consumer electronic devices called *personal video recorders*, or *PVRs* (also called digital video recorders) that have recently hit the market.

Two companies, Replay Networks and TiVo, have developed the new digital TV-recording devices, which save programs to a massive multigigabyte internal hard drive that can hold 10 to 30 hours of programming. Using a phone line, the PVRs download program schedules that pop up on the screen, and with some simple programming through a remote control, consumers can click on shows they want to watch rather than punching in times and channels. The devices also allow users to create "channels" based on their own search criteria, such as types of shows or names of entertainers. The TiVo device even makes recommendations on the basis of how users have rated other programs.

PVRs also allow users to rewind or pause in the middle of a live broadcast while the device keeps recording, resume watching from the point where they stopped, and then skip ahead to catch up to the live broadcast. And among the player's most anticipated, and controversial, features are buttons that allow users to skip past commercials at superhigh speeds. Replay Networks and TiVo hope that these features, along with the ease of using their devices, will win over consumers, many of whom have given up trying to master their VCRs. And if consumers do embrace the new technology, the result will be TV on demand, which will have a dramatic impact on television advertising.

Television shows have always belonged in time slots, and viewers watch whatever is on at that particular time. Moreover, advertisers are used to this world of synchronous viewing and buy ad time based on Nielsen ratings, which measure how many people are watching a show at a given moment. However, the digital PVRs make it very easy for TV viewers to watch shows on their own time.

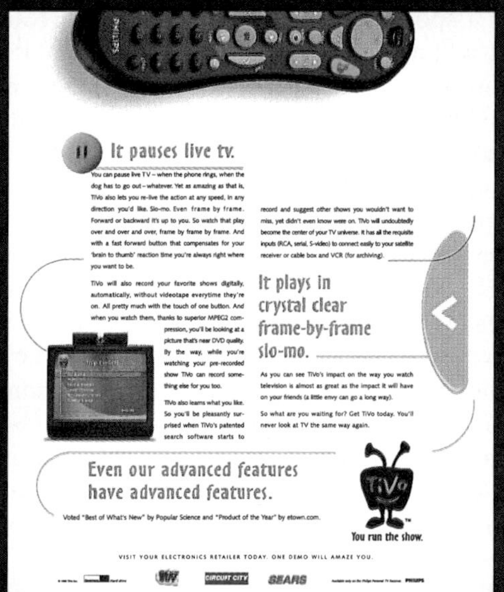

Watching TV will be more like surfing the Web than viewing a movie. This may reduce the influence of the Nielsen ratings and bring the one-to-one world of the Internet to television. PVRs will also make it much easier for content providers to push programming directly to end-users, potentially on a pay-per-view, commercial-free basis.

The PVR companies note that rather than fearing their new technology, advertisers should be embracing it, since the marriage of TV and online will make possible interactive advertising and the ability to purchase products right off of the television screen. PVR companies could take certain commercials out of a program and replace them with ads that are of more interest to specific types of TV viewers or ads that include contests or other incentives that will encourage consumers not to skip them. Moreover, the CEO of Replay Networks notes that the company is not out to kill the television networks, because its business relies on the programming they provide. Without commercials, there would be no money to pay for new programming, which would mean the supply of new shows could end unless other means of funding were found.

Both Replay Networks and TiVo have begun marketing their new PVRs and personal television service. However, experts predict that it will take at least a few years before the new PVR technology reaches enough homes to become a major threat to TV advertising's traditional business model. Television will remain a passive medium, and network TV will thrive for years to come as companies continue to pay millions of dollars to hawk their products and services on the air. However, it appears that changes are under way that may revolutionize the way we watch television and make the traditional TV advertising business model obsolete. In the future, TV viewers may not have to sit through all those ads for paper towels, toothpaste, and automobiles. On the other hand, would TV really be as much fun without the commercials?

Sources: Thomas Kupper, "TV Ads May Be Doomed, Expert Says," *San Diego Union-Tribune*, November 3, 1999, pp. C1, 4; James Poniewozik, "Here Come PVRs, Is Network TV Doomed?" *Time*, September 27, 1999, pp. 62–63; J. William Gurley, "How the Web Will Warp Advertising," *Fortune*, November 9, 1998, pp. 119–120.

Advances in technology are likely to continue to lead to changes in television viewing habits, which will impact the number of consumers who watch TV commercials. IMC Perspective 11–2 discusses how a new type of digital recording device, known as the personal video recorder (PVR), will affect the way consumers watch TV and impact television's business model.

Distrust and Negative Evaluation

To many critics of advertising, TV commercials personify everything that is wrong with the industry. Critics often single out TV commercials because of their pervasiveness and the intrusive nature of the medium. Consumers are seen as defenseless against the barrage of TV ads, since they cannot control the transmission of the message and what appears on their screens. Viewers dislike TV advertising when they believe it is offensive, uninformative, or shown too frequently or when they do not like its content.[14] Studies have shown that of the various forms of advertising, distrust is generally the highest for TV commercials.[15] Also, concern has been raised about the effects of TV advertising on specific groups, such as children or the elderly.[16]

Buying Television Time

A number of options are available to advertisers that choose to use TV as part of their media mix. They can purchase time in a variety of program formats that appeal to various types and sizes of audiences. They can purchase time on a national, regional, or local basis. Or they can sponsor an entire program, participate in the sponsorship, or use spot announcements during or between programs.

The purchase of TV advertising time is a highly specialized phase of the advertising business, particularly for large companies spending huge sums of money. Large advertisers that do a lot of TV advertising generally use agency media specialists or specialized media buying services to arrange the media schedule and purchase TV time. Decisions have to be made regarding national or network versus local or spot purchases, selection of specific stations, sponsorship versus participation, different classes of time, and appropriate programs. Local advertisers may not have to deal with the first decision, but they do face all the others.

Network versus Spot

A basic decision for all advertisers is allocating their TV media budget to network versus local or spot announcements. Most national advertisers use network schedules to provide national coverage and supplement this with regional or local spot purchases to reach markets where additional coverage is desired.

Network Advertising

A common way advertisers disseminate their messages is by purchasing airtime from a **television network.** A network assembles a series of affiliated local TV stations, or **affiliates,** to which it supplies programming and services. These affiliates, most of which are independently owned, contractually agree to preempt time during specified hours for programming provided by the networks and to carry the national advertising within the program. The networks share the advertising revenue they receive during these time periods with the affiliates. The affiliates are also free to sell commercial time in nonnetwork periods and during station breaks in the preempted periods to both national and local advertisers.

The three traditional major networks are NBC, ABC, and CBS. The Fox Broadcasting Co. broadcasts its programs over a group of affiliated independent stations and has become the fourth major network. A number of Fox's prime-time programs, such as "Ally McBeal," "Malcom in the Middle," and "The X-Files," have become very popular, particularly among the 18-to-49 age group that is often targeted by advertisers. Fox has also become a major player in sports programming with its contracts to broadcast sporting events such as NFL football and Major League Baseball.

Exhibit 11–3 UPN is one of the newest television networks

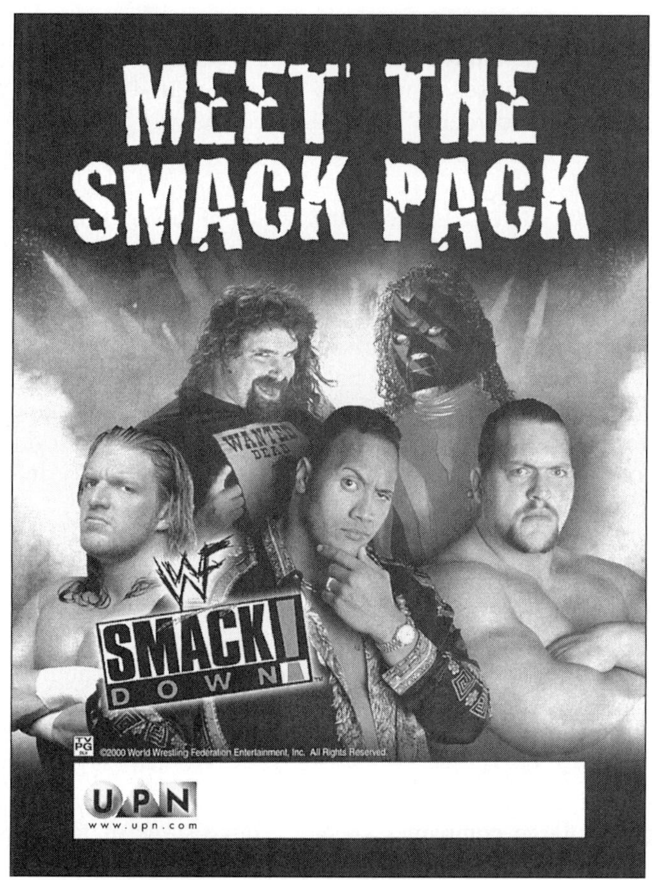

Two additional competitors in network television have emerged over the past five years. WB is a network that was originally financed by Time Warner and, following the merger with AOL, is now part of the AOL–Time Warner media conglomerate. WB reaches a national audience through its affiliates, and its programming includes popular shows such as "Felicity," "Dawson's Creek," and "Buffy, the Vampire Slayer." The other new network is United Paramount Network (UPN), which has more than 100 affiliates and now has five nights a week of prime-time programming that includes shows such as "Star Trek: Voyager" and "WWF Smackdown" (Exhibit 11–3).

The networks have affiliates throughout the nation for almost complete national coverage. When an advertiser purchases airtime from one of these four national networks, the commercial is transmitted across the nation through the affiliate station network. Network advertising truly represents a mass medium, as the advertiser can broadcast its message simultaneously throughout the country.

A major advantage of network advertising is the simplification of the purchase process. The advertiser has to deal with only one party or media representative to air a commercial nationwide. The networks also offer the most popular programs and generally control prime-time programming. Advertisers interested in reaching huge nationwide audiences generally buy network time during the prime viewing hours of 8 to 11 P.M. eastern time.

The major drawback is the high cost of network time. Figure 11–3 shows cost estimates for a 30-second spot on the three networks' prime-time shows during the 1999–2000 television season.[17] Many of the popular prime-time shows charge $300,000 or more for a 30-second spot; the highest-rated shows, like "Friends" and "ER," can command half a million dollars. Thus, only advertisers with large budgets can afford to use network advertising on a regular basis.

Availability of time can also be a problem as more advertisers turn to network advertising to reach mass markets. Traditionally, most prime-time commercial spots, particularly on the popular shows, are sold during the **up-front market,** a buying period that occurs before the TV season begins. Advertisers hoping to use

Figure 11–3 What TV shows cost: estimated price of a 30-second spot on the major networks

1999-2000 network TV price estimates

Prices for ad time take a dip among the strongest-performing series on network TV.

SUNDAY	7 p.m. (ET)		8 p.m.		9 p.m.	10 p.m.
ABC	Wonderful World of Disney $95,000				Snoops $105,000	The Practice $250,000
CBS	60 Minutes $240,000		Touched by An Angel $290,000		CBS Sunday Night Movie $212,000	
NBC	Dateline NBC $89,000		Third Watch $160,000		NBC Sunday Night Movie $112,000	
FOX	TBA TK	King of the Hill $138,000	The Simpsons $229,000	Futurama $200,000	The X-Files $300,000	No Fox programming
WB	7th Heaven: Beginnings $21,000		Felicity $57,000		Jack & Jill $40,000	No WB programming

MONDAY	8 p.m.		9 p.m.		10 p.m.
ABC	20/20 $119,000		Monday Night Football $380,000		
CBS	King of Queens $220,000	Ladies' Man $210,000	Raymond $312,000	Becker $245,000	Family Law $185,000
NBC	Suddenly Susan $135,000	Veronica's Closet $130,000	Law & Order: Special Victims Unit $148,000		Dateline NBC $128,000
FOX	Time of Your Life $165,000		Ally McBeal $300,000		No Fox programming
UPN	Moesha $25,000	The Parkers $20,000	The Grown Ups $20,000	Malcolm & Eddie $17,000	No UPN programming
WB	7th Heaven $72,000		Safe Harbor $39,000		No WB programming

TUESDAY	8 p.m.		9 p.m.		10 p.m.
ABC	Spin City $220,000	It's Like, You Know $175,000	Dharma & Greg $315,000	Sports Night $210,000	Once & Again/NYPD Blue* $210,000/$220,000
CBS	JAG $210,000		60 Minutes II $196,000		Judging Amy $120,000
NBC	Just Shoot Me $250,000	3rd Rock $130,000	Will & Grace $225,000	Mike O'Malley $149,000	Dateline NBC $138,000
FOX	Ally $159,000	That '70s Show $127,000	Party of Five $185,000		No Fox programming
UPN	Dilbert $20,000	Shasta McNasty $15,000	Secret Agent Man $15,000		No UPN programming
WB	Buffy, the Vampire Slayer $82,000		Angel $73,000		No WB programming

WED.	8 p.m.		9 p.m.		10 p.m.
ABC	Two Guys, a Girl $210,000	The Norm Show $180,000	Drew Carey $370,000	Oh Grow Up $230,000	20/20 $160,000
CBS	Cosby $130,000	Work With Me $163,000	CBS Wednesday Movie $130,000		
NBC	Dateline NBC $101,000		The West Wing $183,000		Law & Order $172,000
FOX	Beverly Hills, 90210 $164,000		Get Real $120,000		No Fox programming
UPN	Seven Days $22,000		Stak Trek: Voyager $86,000		No UPN programming
WB	Dawson's Creek $86,000		Roswell $85,000		No WB programming

THURSDAY	8 p.m.		9 p.m.		10 p.m.
ABC	Whose Line? $130,000	Whose Line? $75,000	Wasteland $80,000		20/20 $85,000
CBS	Diagnosis Murder $105,000		Chicago Hope $124,000		48 Hours $90,000
NBC	Friends $510,000	Jesse $336,000	Frasier $466,000	Stark Raving Mad $336,000	ER $545,000
FOX	Manchester Prep $87,000		Family Guy $121,000	Action $121,000	No Fox programming
UPN	WWF Smackdown! $40,000				No UPN programming
WB	Popular $34,000		Charmed $51,000		No WB programming

FRIDAY	8 p.m.		9 p.m.		10 p.m.
ABC	The Hughleys $100,000	Boy Meets World $115,000	Sabrina $140,000	Odd Man Out $115,000	20/20 $148,000
CBS	Kids Say Darndest $115,000	Love or Money $123,000	Now & Again $82,000		Nash Bridges $168,000
NBC	Providence $160,000		Dateline NBC $100,000		Cold Feet $103,000
FOX	Ryan Caulfield $83,000		Harsh Realm $78,000		No Fox programming
UPN	Blockbuster Video's Shockwave Cinema $12,000				No UPN programming
WB	Steve Harvey $23,000	For Your Love $24,000	Mission Hill $26,000	Jamie Foxx $27,000	No WB programming

SATURDAY	8 p.m.		9 p.m.	10 p.m.
ABC	ABC Saturday Night Movie $75,000			
CBS	Early Edition $119,000		Martial Law $110,000	Walker, Texas Ranger $121,000
NBC	Freaks & Geeks $90,000		The Pretender $101,000	Profiler $101,000
FOX	Cops $70,000	Cops $80,000	America's Most Wanted $75,000	No Fox programming

*Until 'NYPD Blue' premieres. Source: Averages compiled from estimates of advertising agencies and media buying companies.

prime-time network advertising must plan their media schedules and often purchase TV time as much as a year in advance. Demands from large clients who are heavy TV advertisers force the biggest agencies to participate in the up-front market. However, TV time is also purchased during the **scatter market** that runs through the TV season. Some key incentives for buying up front, such as cancellation options and lower prices, are becoming more available in the quarterly scatter market. Network TV can also be purchased on a regional basis, so an advertiser's message can be aired in certain sections of the country with one media purchase.

Spot and Local Advertising

Spot advertising refers to commercials shown on local TV stations, with time negotiated and purchased directly from the individual stations. All nonnetwork advertising done by a national advertiser is known as **national spot advertising;** airtime sold to local firms such as retailers, restaurants, banks, and auto dealers is known as **local advertising.** Local advertisers want media whose coverage is limited to the geographic markets in which they do business. This may be difficult to accomplish with TV, but many local businesses are large enough to make efficient use of TV advertising.

Spot advertising offers the national advertiser flexibility in adjusting to local market conditions. The advertiser can concentrate commercials in areas where market potential is greatest or where additional support is needed. This appeals to advertisers with uneven distribution or limited advertising budgets, as well as those interested in test marketing or introducing a product in limited market areas. National advertisers often use spot television advertising through local retailers or dealers as part of their cooperative advertising programs and to provide local dealer support.

A major problem for national advertisers is that spot advertising can be more difficult to acquire, since the time must be purchased from a number of local stations. Moreover, there are more variations in the pricing policies and discount structure of individual stations than of the networks. However, this problem has been reduced somewhat by the use of **station reps,** individuals who act as sales representatives for a number of local stations in dealings with national advertisers.

Spot ads are subject to more commercial clutter, since local stations can sell time on network-originated shows only during station breaks between programs, except when network advertisers have not purchased all the available time. Viewership generally declines during station breaks, as people may leave the room, zap to another channel, attend to other tasks, or stop watching TV.

While spot advertising is mostly confined to station breaks between programs on network-originated shows, local stations sell time on their own programs, which consist of news, movies, syndicated shows, or locally originated programs. Most cities have independent stations that spot advertisers use. Local advertisers find the independent stations attractive because they generally have lower rates than the major network affiliates.

The decision facing most national advertisers is how to combine network and spot advertising to make effective use of their TV advertising budget. Another factor that makes spot advertising attractive to national advertisers is the growth in syndication.

Syndication

Advertisers may also reach TV viewers by advertising on **syndicated programs,** shows that are sold or distributed on a station-by-station, market-by-market basis. A syndicator seeks to sell its program to one station in every market. There are several types of syndicated programming. *Off-network syndication* refers to reruns of network shows that are bought by individual stations. Shows that are popular in off-network syndication include "Seinfeld," "The Drew Carey Show," and "Friends." The FCC prime-time access rule forbids large-market network affiliates from carrying these shows from 7 to 8 P.M., but independent stations are not affected by this restriction. A show must have a minimum number of episodes before it is eligible for syndication, and there are limits on network involvement in the financing or production of syndicated shows.

Off-network syndication shows are very important to local stations because they provide quality programming with an established audience. The syndication market is also very important to the studios that produce programs and sell them to the networks. Most prime-time network shows initially lose money for the studios, since the licensing fee paid by the networks does not cover production costs. Over four years (the time it takes to produce the 88 episodes needed to break into syndication), half-hour situation comedies often run up a deficit of millions, and losses on a one-hour drama show are even higher. However, the producers recoup their money when they sell the show to syndication.

First-run syndication refers to shows produced specifically for the syndication market. The first-run syndication market is made up of a variety of shows, including some that did not make it as network shows and are moved into syndication while new episodes are being produced. Examples of popular first-run syndication shows include talk shows like "Live with Regis & Kathie Lee," "Jerry Springer," and "The Rosie O"Donnell Show" and dramas such as "Star Trek: Voyager" and "Highlander."

Advertiser-supported or *barter syndication* is the practice of selling shows to stations in return for a portion of the commercial time in the show, rather than (or in addition to) cash. The commercial time from all stations carrying the show is packaged into national units and sold to national advertisers. The station sells the remaining time to local and spot advertisers. Both off-network and first-run syndicated programs are offered through barter syndication. Usually, more than half of the advertising time is presold, and the remainder is available for sale by the local advertiser. Barter syndication allows national advertisers to participate in the syndication market with the convenience of a network-type media buy, while local stations get free programming and can sell the remainder of the time to local or spot advertisers. Recently, the straight barter deal has given way to more barter/cash arrangements, where the station pays for a program at a reduced rate and accepts a number of preplaced bartered ads. Top-rated barter syndicated programs include "Wheel of Fortune," "Jeopardy," and "The Oprah Winfrey Show."

Syndication now accounts for more than a third of the national broadcast audience and has become a very big business, generating ad revenue comparable to any of the big three networks. Syndicated shows have become more popular than network shows in certain dayparts, such as daytime, early prime time, and late fringe. In some markets, syndicated shows like "Wheel of Fortune" draw a larger audience than the network news.

Many national advertisers use syndicated shows to broaden their reach, save money, and target certain audiences. For example, "Baywatch" is one of the most popular shows in syndication because it reaches the highly sought after, and often difficult to reach, young adult audience (ages 18 to 34) and is more cost-effective than network shows (Exhibit 11–4). Figure 11–4 shows the top 10 syndicated programs in 1999.

Syndication has certain disadvantages, such as more commercial time and thus more clutter. The audience for syndicated shows is often older and more rural, and syndicators do not supply as much research information as the networks do. Syndication also creates more problems for media buyers, since a syndicated show may not be seen in a particular market or may be aired during an undesirable time period. Thus, media buyers have to look at each market and check airtimes and other factors to put together a syndication schedule.

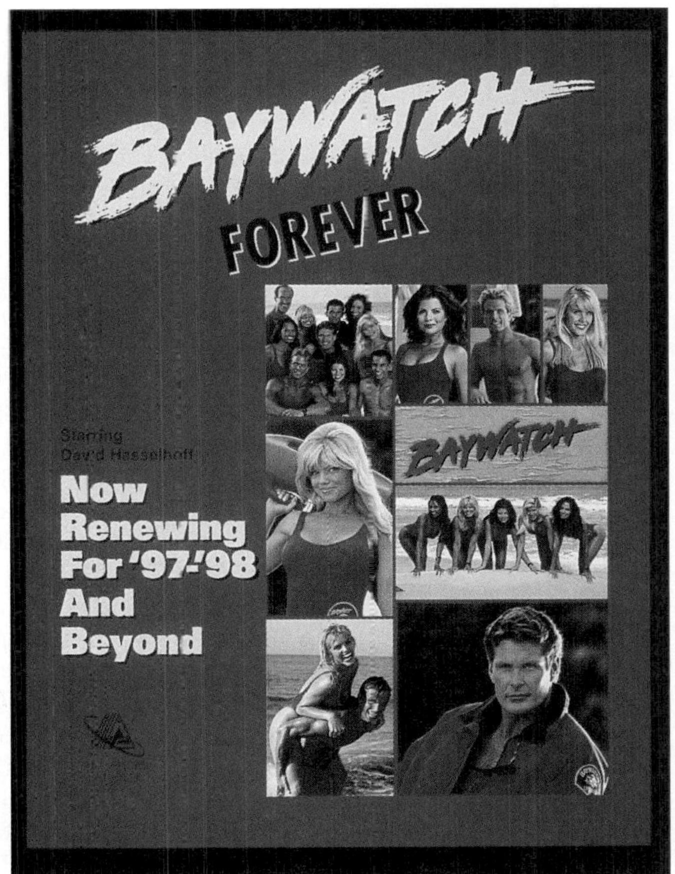

Exhibit 11–4 Baywatch is a popular syndicated show for reaching young adults

Methods of Buying Time

In addition to deciding whether to use network versus spot advertising, advertisers must decide whether to sponsor an entire program, participate in a program, or use spot announcements between programs. Sponsorship of a program and participations are available on either a network or a local market basis, whereas spot announcements are available only from local stations.

Rank	Program	Rating %
1	Wheel of Fortune	10.6
2	Jeopardy	8.9
3	Judge Judy	6.8
4	Oprah Winfrey Show	6.5
5	Friends	6.3
6	Jerry Springer	6.3
7	Seinfeld	5.8
8	Entertainment Tonight	5.5
9	Frasier	5.0
10	X-Files	5.0

Figure 11–4 Top 10 regularly scheduled syndicated programs

Sponsorship Under a **sponsorship** arrangement, an advertiser assumes responsibility for the production and usually the content of the program as well as the advertising that appears within it. In the early days of TV, most programs were produced and sponsored by corporations and were identified by their name, for example, "Texaco Star Theater" and "The Colgate Comedy Hour." Today most shows are produced by either the networks or independent production companies that sell them to a network.

Some companies are becoming more involved in the production business. For example, Procter & Gamble, which has been producing soap operas since 1950, entered into an agreement with Paramount Television Groups to develop shows for network TV and first-run syndication. A consortium of nine major advertisers—AT&T, Campbell Soup, General Motors, Coca-Cola, Sears, McDonald's, Clorox, Coors, and Reebok—joined Television Production Partners, a new venture to develop movies, specials, and limited-run series. Each company chooses which programs it wants to be involved with and takes a portion of the commercial spots.[18]

Several major companies have been sponsoring special programs for many years, such as the Kraft Masterpiece Theater and Hallmark Hall of Fame dramatic series. In 1994 Hallmark acquired RHI Entertainment Inc., the company that produces its wholesome Hall of Fame productions as well as TV miniseries and movies. Sole sponsorship of programs is usually limited to specials and has been declining. However, some companies, including Ford, AT&T, General Electric, IBM, and Chrysler, do still use program sponsorships occasionally.

A company might choose to sponsor a program for several reasons. Sponsorship allows the firm to capitalize on the prestige of a high-quality program, enhancing the image of the company and its products. For example, the Ford Motor Company received a great deal of favorable publicity when it sponsored the commercial-free television debut of the Holocaust movie *Schindler's List.* Companies also sponsor programs to gain more control over the shows carrying their commercials. For example, Wendy's International has been involved in sponsorship of family-oriented programs.

Another reason is that the sponsor has control over the number, placement, and content of its commercials. Commercials can be of any length as long as the total amount of commercial time does not exceed network or station regulations. Advertisers introducing a new product line often sponsor a program and run commercials that are several minutes long to introduce and explain the product. IBM used this strategy to introduce new generations of products. While these factors make sponsorship attractive to some companies, the high costs of sole sponsorship limit this option to large firms. Most commercial time is purchased through other methods, such as participations.

Participations Most advertisers either cannot afford the costs of sponsorship or want greater flexibility than sole sponsorship permits. Nearly 90 percent of network advertising time is sold as **participations,** with several advertisers buying commercial time or spots on a particular program. An advertiser can participate in a certain program once or several times on a regular or irregular basis. Participating advertisers have no financial responsibility for production of the program; this is assumed by the network or individual station that sells and controls the commercial time.

There are several advantages to participations. First, the advertiser has no long-term commitment to a program, and expenditures can be adjusted to buy whatever number of participation spots fits within the budget. This is particularly important to small advertisers with a limited budget. The second advantage is that the TV budget can be spread over a number of programs, thereby providing for greater reach in the media schedule.

The disadvantage of participations is that the advertiser has little control over the placement of ads, and there may also be problems with availability. Preference is given to advertisers willing to commit to numerous spots, and the firm trying to buy single spots in more than one program may find that time is unavailable in certain shows, especially during prime time.

Spot Announcements

As discussed earlier, spot announcements are bought from the local stations and generally appear during time periods adjacent to network programs (hence the term **adjacencies**), rather than within them. Spot announcements are most often used by purely local advertisers but are also bought by companies with no network schedule (because of spotty or limited distribution) and by large advertisers that use both network and spot advertising.

Selecting Time Periods and Programs

Another consideration in buying TV time is selecting the right period and program for the advertiser's commercial messages. The cost of TV advertising time varies depending on the time of day and the particular program, since audience size varies as a function of these two factors. TV time periods are divided into **dayparts,** which are specific segments of a broadcast day.

The time segments that make up the programming day vary from station to station. However, a typical classification of dayparts for a weekday is shown in Figure 11–5. The various daypart segments attract different audiences in both size and nature, so advertising rates vary accordingly. Prime-time draws the largest audiences, with 8:30 to 9 P.M. being the most watched half-hour time period and Sunday the most popular night for television. Since firms that advertise during prime time must pay premium rates, this daypart is dominated by the large national advertisers.

The various dayparts are important to advertisers since they attract different demographic groups. For example, daytime TV generally attracts women; early morning attracts women and children. The late-fringe (late-night) daypart period has become popular among advertisers trying to reach young adults who tune into "The Late Show with David Letterman" on CBS and NBC's "The Tonight Show with Jay Leno." Audience size and demographic composition also vary depending on the type of program. Situation comedies attract the largest prime-time audiences, with women 18 to 34 comprising the greatest segment of the audience. Feature films rank second, followed by general drama shows. Women 55 and older are the largest audience segment for these programs.

Cable Television

The Growth of Cable

Perhaps the most significant development in the broadcast media has been the expansion of **cable television.** Cable, or CATV (community antenna television), which delivers TV signals through fiber or coaxial wire rather than the airways, was developed to provide reception to remote areas that couldn't receive broadcast signals. Cable then expanded to metropolitan areas and grew rapidly due to the improved reception and wider selection of stations it offered subscribers. Cable has experienced substantial growth during the past two decades. In 1975, only 13 percent of TV households had cable. By 2000, cable penetration reached 68 percent of the nation's 100 million households.[19] Cable programming also reaches another 10 percent of U.S. homes through alternative delivery systems such as direct broadcast satellite (DBS).

Morning	7:00 A.M.–9:00 A.M., Monday through Friday
Daytime	9:00 A.M.–4:30 P.M., Monday through Friday
Early fringe	4:30 P.M.–7:30 P.M., Monday through Friday
Prime-time access	7:30 P.M.–8:00 P.M., Sunday through Saturday
Prime time	8:00 P.M.–11:00 P.M., Monday through Saturday, and 7:00 P.M.–11 P.M., Sunday
Late news	11:00–11:30 P.M., Monday through Friday
Late fringe	11:30–1:00 A.M., Monday through Friday

Figure 11–5 Common television dayparts

Cable subscribers pay a monthly fee for which they receive an average of more than 60 channels, including the local network affiliates and independent stations, various cable networks, superstations, and local cable system channels. Cable networks and channels have a dual revenue stream; they are supported by both subscriber fees and ad revenue. Cable operators also offer programming that is not supported by commercial sponsorship and is available only to households willing to pay a fee beyond the monthly subscription charge. These premium channels include HBO, Showtime, and The Movie Channel.

Cable TV broadens the program options available to the viewer as well as the advertiser by offering specialty channels, including all-news, pop music, country music, sports, weather, educational, and cultural channels as well as children's programming. Figure 11–6 shows the most popular cable channels along with the types of programming they carry and their number of subscribers. Many cable systems also carry **superstations,** independent local stations that send their signals nationally via satellite to cable operators to make their programs available to subscribers. Programming on superstations such as TBS and WGN generally consists of sports, movies, and reruns of network shows. The superstations do carry national advertising and are a relatively inexpensive option for cable households across the country.

Cable has had a considerable influence on the nature of television as an advertising medium. First, the expanded viewing options have led to considerable audience fragmentation. Much of the growth in cable audiences has come at the expense of the three major networks. Cable channels now have about 32 percent of the prime-time viewing audience, while the total share of the three networks has declined to around 50 percent. Many cable stations have become very popular among consumers, leading advertisers to reevaluate their media plans and the prices they are willing to pay for network and spot commercials on network affiliate stations. The networks, recognizing the growing popularity of cable, have become involved with the cable industry. ABC purchased ESPN, while NBC started two cable channels in the early 90s—the Consumer News and Business Channel (CNBC) and Sports Channel America—and in 1996 entered in a joint venture with Microsoft to launch MSNBC, a 24-hour news channel.[20]

Advertising on Cable

Cable advertising revenues have increased steadily since the mid-1980s and exceeded $11 billion in 1999. Much of this growth has come from advertising on the national cable networks such as CNN, ESPN, USA, and MTV. However, many national advertisers have been shifting some of their advertising budgets to spot cable and purchasing through local operators as well as the national cable networks. Over the past four years, spot cable revenues have averaged 20 percent annual growth, reaching nearly $2.5 billion in 1999.

Like broadcast TV, cable time can be purchased on a national, regional, or local (spot) level. Many large marketers advertise on cable networks to reach large numbers of viewers across the country with a single media buy. Regional advertising on cable is available primarily through sports and news channels that cover a certain geographic area.

Many national advertisers are turning to spot advertising on local cable systems to reach specific geographic markets. Spot cable affords them more precision in reaching specific markets, and they can save money by using a number of small, targeted media purchases rather than making one network buy. The growth in spot cable advertising is also being facilitated by the use of **interconnects,** where a number of cable systems in a geographic area are joined for advertising purposes. These interconnects increase the size of the audience an advertiser can reach with a spot cable buy. For example, Chicago Cable Interconnect reaches more than 1.7 million subscribers in the greater Chicago metropolitan area; the ADLINK Digital Interconnect delivers 3 million cable subscribers in Los Angeles and four surrounding counties. More sophisticated interconnect systems are developing that will pool large numbers of cable systems and allow spot advertisers to reach more viewers. These new systems will also allow local advertisers to make more selective cable buys, since they can purchase the entire interconnect or one of several zones within the system.

Network	Estimated Coverage*	Type of Programming
USA Network	79.5	Entertainment/movies/sports
TBS	78.6	Entertainment/movies/sports
The Discovery Channel	78.0	Family/health/technology/science
CNN	77.4	News/information
Nickelodeon/Nick At Nite	76.3	Youth interest/comedy/cartoons/game shows
ESPN	76.0	Sports
TNN	76.0	General entertainment/sports/movies/outdoors programming
Fox Family Channel	76.0	Family/general/original
TNT	75.3	Movies/general entertainment/sports
Lifetime	75.0	News/information/women's interests
A&E Network	73.7	Biographies/mysteries/movies/documentaries
MTV	73.3	Music video/entertainment
The Weather Channel	73.0	National/regional/local weather
CNN Headline News	73.0	News/information
The Learning Channel (TLC)	73.0	Science/history/lifestyle/real-life adventure/behavior
CNBC	71.0	Financial and business news/interviews and discussions
American Movie Classics	71.0	Movies/documentaries
VH-1	68.9	Music videos/movies/concerts
E! Entertainment	65.0	Entertainment/celebrities/pop culture
Sci-Fi Channel	64.5	Science fiction programming
Comedy Central	64.0	Comedy
ESPN2	62.0	Sports
Cartoon Network	60.0	Cartoons
History Channel	60.0	Historical documentaries/movies
Home and Garden TV	59.0	Home/gardening/crafts
BET Networks	58.0	Entertainment/information for African Americans
Animal Planet	55.0	Wildlife documentaries/pet care/children's entertainment
FX Networks	52.0	General entertainment
Court TV	48.0	Court/legal
MSNBC	47.0	News/information
Fox News Channel	46.0	News/information
Food Network	45.0	Food/health/nutrition
Bravo	43.0	Film and arts
CMT: Country Music Television	40.3	Country music (video)
The Travel Channel	35.0	Travel-related programming
The Golf Channel	30.0	Golf

*Millions of U.S. households reached.

Figure 11–6 Major cable networks

Career Profile

Kristin Longley

Research Specialist at Cox CableRep Gulf Coast

I always knew that I wanted to work in television and broadcast journalism. To prepare for a career in these fields, I attended the prestigious University of Missouri School of Journalism where I majored in the broadcast sequence and graduated with honors. Following graduation I took a job with the NBC-owned and operated affiliate in San Diego where I worked for three years as a programming assistant before being promoted to Promotion Coordinator. While working at the station I attended graduate school and received a Masters degree in Mass Communications and Telecommunications from San Diego State University in 1998. I worked for a short time as an adjunct professor of Broadcast Journalism and Business Communications at the University of West Florida before returning to the television industry as a research specialist for Cox CableRep Gulf Coast.

"Working in the media industry is exciting because things are changing so quickly."

Cox CableRep is the advertising division of Cox Communications, which serves approximately six million customers nationwide and is the nation's fifth largest cable television company. Cox offers an array of services beyond cable and digital television, including local and long distance telephone and high-speed Internet access, and has been honored as the most innovative cable company by Inter@ctive Week for two consecutive years. Cox CableRep Gulf Coast is based in Pensacola, Florida, and serves nearly 300,000 households in markets such as Gulf Shores, Alabama and Pensacola, Fort Walton, and Panama City, Florida. As a research specialist I do client and market specific studies and presentations for over 50 clients each year that help advertisers understand their markets and make better media buying decisions.

I am known at CableRep for my ability to strategically position cable advertising in a very competitive media environment. In my first year as a research specialist, I provided the company with marketing research that helped generate over $1 million in new revenue, most of which was captured from broadcast affiliates in the Gulf Coast market. The great thing about cable is that we are able to target an advertiser's message, both geographically and demographically. Broadcast TV is an inefficient media buy for many local companies because they are reaching viewers living as far as 250 miles from their business in the far reaches of a Designated Market Area. However with cable, we use a digital signal to insert commercials in 14 different geographic zones that allows us to target an advertising campaign to meet the needs of local businesses.

The great thing about my job is providing both large and small clients with research that helps them in their media planning. For national clients, I provide cable ratings and share information. Many national agencies base their media buys on cost per rating point (CPP) or cost per thousand (CPM), so I use special software that pulls ratings for all 34 cable networks. For local advertisers, we use a qualitative database from Arbitron to help us demographically target which networks are best for a specific client. For example, an automobile dealer may want to know what prospective car buyers watch on cable while an investment company or interior decorator may want to know the best way to reach upscale adults over the age of 35. Our local data allows us to provide very rich marketing information to nearly all of our clients.

An important part of my job is using detailed quantitative and qualitative software and presenting it in a format that makes sense and has value to clients. Market statistics are just numbers unless they are presented in a way that makes sense and has value to clients. I also have to separate myself from the role of account executive or salesperson. I try to show comparable media comparisons, even though many of the media are different in nature. Having a good relationship with others in research roles definitely helps, as is having strong and trusting relationships with clients.

Working in the media industry is exciting because things are changing so quickly. We always have new technologies, new products, new networks, and new shows. If you want to succeed in this industry it is important to be able to adapt to this constantly changing environment. Internships are a great way to get your foot in the door and gain valuable experience if you are interested in pursuing a career in this fast-paced and dynamic business.

While spot cable is becoming very popular among national advertisers, it has some of the same problems as spot advertising on broadcast TV. The purchasing process is very complicated and time consuming; media buyers must contact hundreds of cable systems to put together a media schedule consisting of spot cable buys. Local cable systems also do not provide advertisers with strong support or much information on demographics, lifestyle, or viewership patterns.

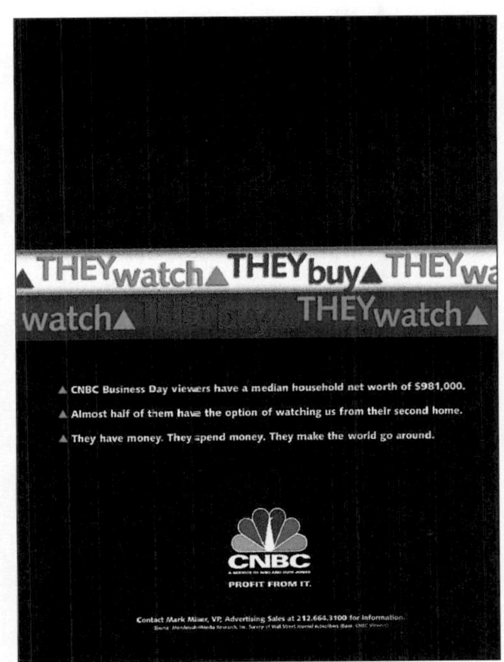

Exhibit 11–5 CNBC has become the leader in business news and has a very affluent viewing audience

Advantages of Cable

Cable TV has experienced tremendous growth as an advertising medium because it has some important advantages. A primary one is selectivity. Cable subscribers tend to be younger, more affluent, and better educated than nonsubscribers and have greater purchasing power. Moreover, the specialized programming on the various cable networks reaches very specific target markets.

Many advertisers have turned to cable because of the opportunities it offers for **narrowcasting,** or reaching very specialized markets. For example, MTV is used by advertisers in the United States and many other countries to reach teenagers and young adults. CNBC is now the worldwide leader in business news and reaches a highly educated and affluent audience (Exhibit 11–5). As discussed in IMC Perspective 11–3, ESPN has become synonymous with sports and is very popular among advertisers who want to target men of all ages.

Advertisers are also interested in cable because of its low cost and flexibility. Advertising rates on cable programs are much lower than those for the shows on the major networks. Advertising time on network shows can cost two to three times as much on a cost-per-thousand basis in some time periods.[21] Spot advertising is also considerably cheaper on most cable stations, while local cable is the most affordable television advertising vehicle available. This makes TV a much more viable media option for smaller advertisers with limited budgets and those interested in targeting their commercials to a well-defined target audience. Also, cable advertisers generally do not have to make the large up-front commitments, which may be as much as a year in advance, the networks require.

In addition to costing less, cable gives advertisers much greater flexibility in the type of commercials that can be used. While most network commercials are 30- or 15-second spots, commercials on cable are often longer. **Infomercials,** commercials that range from 3 to 30 minutes in length, are common on cable. Direct-response advertisers often use these longer ads to describe their products or services and encourage consumers to call in their orders during the commercial. The use of infomercials by direct-response advertisers is discussed in Chapter 14.

The low costs of cable make it a very popular advertising medium among local advertisers. Car dealers, furniture stores, restaurants, and many other merchants are switching advertising spending from traditional media such as radio, newspapers, and even magazines to take advantage of the low rates of local cable channels. Local cable advertising is one of the fastest-growing segments of the advertising market, and cable systems are increasing the percentage of revenue they earn from local advertising.

Limitations of Cable

While cable has become increasingly popular among national, regional, and local advertisers, it still has a number of drawbacks. One major problem is that cable is overshadowed by the major networks, as households with basic cable service still watch considerably more network and syndicated programming than cable shows. This stems from the fact that cable generally has less desirable programming than broadcast TV.

Another drawback of cable is audience fragmentation. Although cable's share of the TV viewing audience has increased significantly, the viewers are spread out among the large number of channels available to cable subscribers. The number of viewers who watch any one cable channel is generally quite low. Even MTV, ESPN, and CNN have prime-time ratings of only about 1 or 2. The large number of cable stations has fragmented audiences and made buying procedures more difficult, since

IMC Perspective 11–3

ESPN—The Sports Franchise

For many years, TV sports programming consisted primarily of football, baseball, and, to a lesser extent, basketball. When ESPN, the first cable network devoted entirely to sports programming, was launched in 1979 the critics declared that "all the good sports are already on the three networks." They ridiculed the network for broadcasting sports like stock-car racing, which was described as "two hours of left turns." No one is laughing at ESPN today. It is now one of the top cable networks, with nearly 75 million subscribers, and televises more than 4,900 live or original hours of sports programming that includes over 65 different sports. It has spawned two other U.S. sports networks—ESPN2, a combination of traditional and emerging sports, and ESPNEWS. There are also the ESPN Radio Network, ESPN SportsZone website, one of the most visited in cyberspace with over 20 million hits a week, and *ESPN the Magazine,* which was launched in 1998.

The success of the ESPN franchise is largely responsible for the current explosion in sports programming. Fans' hunger for all types of televised sports shows no signs of abating, and sports programming has become the key to the growth plans of most big media companies, including the Walt Disney Co. (which owns ABC and ESPN), AOL–Time Warner Inc., and News Corp.'s Fox Broadcasting Co.

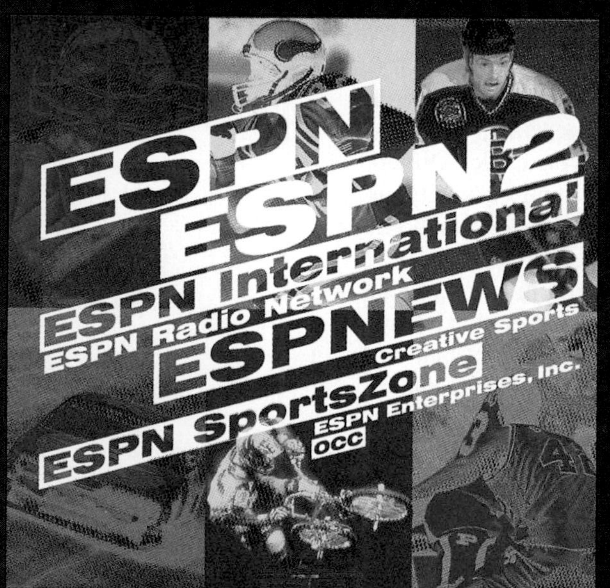

One of the most popular and best-known features of ESPN's programming is "SportsCenter," the one-hour sports news show that is aired numerous times throughout the day and night. "SportsCenter" is more than a part of ESPN's programming; it is emblematic of the entire network and has helped position the network as the place for the ultimate sports fan, not just another cable channel showing sports. One of the factors that has contributed to the popularity and image of "SportsCenter" is the award-winning "Behind the Scenes" advertising campaign developed by the Wieden & Kennedy agency. The humorous ads purport to give viewers a behind-the-scenes look at the production of "SportsCenter" and feature various ESPN personalities as well as popular athletes. The campaign has been instrumental in helping create a brand identity for "SportsCenter" that has carried over to the entire network.

In addition to being popular among sports fans, ESPN has also become one of Madison Avenue's favorite television networks. Media experts argue that ESPN delivers more pure value per advertising impression than any other program on television. ESPN is watched by more men between the ages of 18 and 24 than any other ad-supported cable network. The network is particularly good at delivering large concentrations of young, male sports fans, a group that is difficult to reach but highly coveted by marketers.

ESPN is now much more than just the number-1 cable network. It is an entire brand franchise that has become synonymous with sports in America as well as many other countries.

Sources: Joe Mandese, "Matching Ratings to Ad $$, ESPN Comes Out Tops," *Advertising Age,* April 12, 1999, p. S2; Noreen O'Leary, "Top 20 Ad Campaigns," *Adweek,* November 9, 1998, p. 188; and Jeff Jensen, "Cable TV Marketer of the Year," *Advertising Age,* December 9, 1996, pp. S1–2.

numerous stations must be contacted to reach the majority of the cable audience in a market. There are also problems with the quality and availability of local ratings for cable stations as well as research on audience characteristics.

Cable also still lacks total penetration, especially in the major markets. As of late 1999, cable penetration was 74 percent in the New York City designated market area, and 65 percent in Los Angeles, and 60 percent in Chicago. While cable programming now penetrates 78 percent of all U.S. television households, this still means that nearly a quarter of the market cannot be reached by advertising on cable.

The Future of Cable Cable TV should continue to experience strong growth as its audience share increases and advertisers spend more money to reach cable viewers. However, the cable industry faces several challenges: increases in the number of channels, leading to fragmentation of the audience, changes in government regulations, and competition in the programming distribution business from other telecommunications companies and direct broadcast satellite services. Advances in technology such as digital video compression and fiber optics, coupled with massive investments in system upgrades, are making it possible for cable operators to offer more channels and thus subject existing cable channels to greater competition. In 1999, over 42 million U.S. homes could receive at least 54 channels. An average 95 percent of cable subscribers could receive 30 channels or more. Increases in the number of channels available lead to further fragmentation of the cable audience and make it more difficult for cable networks to charge the ad rates needed to finance original programming. Some of the growth in cable channels will come from **multiplexing,** or transmitting multiple channels from one network. Several major cable networks, including ESPN, the Nashville Network, and the Discovery Channel, own several channels.

The cable industry has also been affected by changes in government regulation. In the early 90s, concerns over poor service and high rates led to a revolt against the cable industry. As a result, Congress passed legislation in 1993 that rolled back the provisions of the Cable Television Act of 1984, allowed local governments to regulate basic cable rates, and forced cable operators to pay licensing fees for local broadcast programming they used to retransmit for free. The Telecommunications Act of 1996 allows local phone companies to offer cable service. However, as part of this act, federal regulation of the cable industry expired on April 1, 1999, and cable rates are now deregulated.[22]

One of the biggest threats facing the cable industry is competition from **direct broadcast satellite (DBS) services,** which use a system whereby TV and radio programs are sent directly from a satellite to homes equipped with a small dish. DBS companies such as DirecTV and EchoStar now have nearly 10 million subscribers, many of whom have come to them at the expense of cable companies. DBS companies have been aggressively marketing their service, superior picture quality, and greater channel choice as subscribers receive as many as 200 channels that include news, music, and sports in crisp, digital video and CD-quality sound. A major competitive restriction to DBS services was removed in late 1999 when the federal government passed legislation allowing satellite TV companies to carry local broadcast signals in most major markets.[23]

The future of cable as an advertising medium will ultimately depend on the size and quality of the audiences cable stations can reach with their programs. This in turn will depend on cable's ability to offer programs that attract viewers and subscribers. Cable's image as a stepchild in program development and acquisition has changed. Cable networks such as VH1, E!, TBS, and others have been creating original films, documentaries, and other programs that draw significant ratings (Exhibit 11–6). Networks like A&E, the Discovery Channel, and the Learning Channel provide outstanding cultural and educational programming.

Cable TV will continue to be a popular source of sports programming and is very important to advertisers interested in reaching the male market. There are over 11 regional cable sports networks, and with companies such as Fox Sports, advertisers can buy multiple regions with one media buy. Cable networks are also paying large sums for the rights to sports programming.

Exhibit 11–6 VH1 promotes its investment in movies and other programming

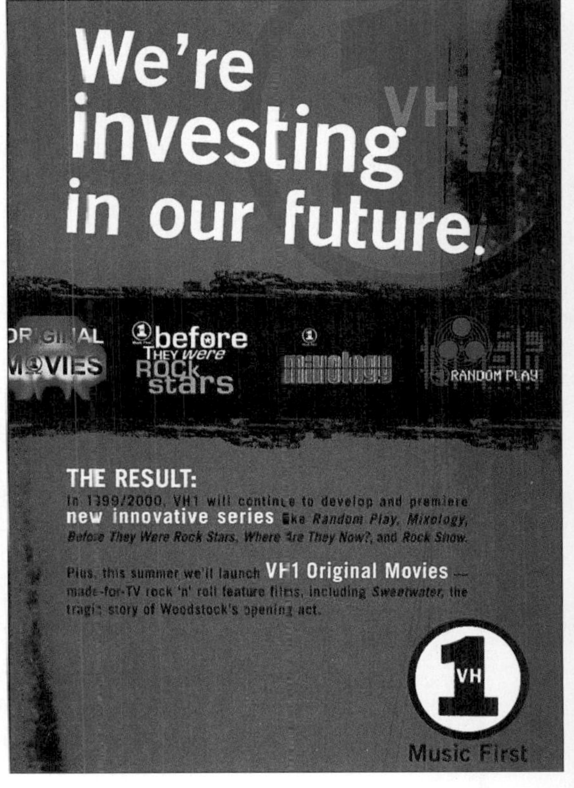

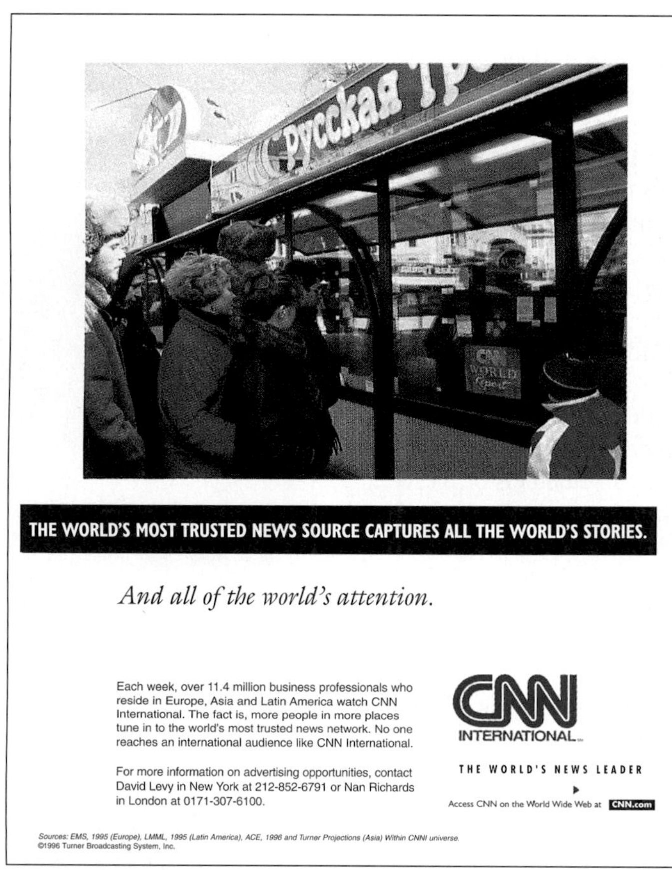

Русская
CNN WORLD Report
THE WORLD'S MOST TRUSTED NEWS SOURCE CAPTURES ALL THE WORLD'S STORIES.
And all of the world's attention.
Each week, over 11.4 million business professionals who reside in Europe, Asia and Latin America watch CNN International. The fact is, more people in more places tune in to the world's most trusted news network. No one reaches an international audience like CNN International.
For more information on advertising opportunities, contact David Levy in New York at 212-852-6791 or Nan Richards in London at 0171-307-6100.
CNN INTERNATIONAL
THE WORLD'S NEWS LEADER
Access CNN on the World Wide Web at CNN.com
Sources: EMS, 1995 (Europe), LMML, 1995 (Latin America), ACE, 1996 and Turner Projections (Asia) Within CNNI universe.
©1996 Turner Broadcasting System, Inc.

Exhibit 11–7 CNN International is the authoritative source for news throughout the world

Deals by ESPN for exclusive Sunday night coverage of National Football League and Major League Baseball games have proved that cable networks can compete with the major networks in a sports bidding war.

As cable penetration increases, its programming improves, and more advertisers discover its efficiency and ability to reach targeted market segments, cable's popularity as an advertising medium should continue to grow. Many agencies have developed specialists to examine the use of cable in their clients' media schedules. Cable networks are also looking to international markets as a source of future growth. Both ESPN and MTV have expanded into South America, Europe, and Asia, while TV viewers throughout the world tune to CNN International for news (Exhibit 11–7). Global Perspective 11–4 discusses how MTV has become the major way of reaching young consumers around the globe.

Measuring the TV Audience

One of the most important considerations in TV advertising is the size and composition of the viewing audience. Audience measurement is critical to advertisers as well as to the networks and stations. Advertisers want to know the size and characteristics of the audience they are reaching when they purchase time on a particular program. And since the rates they pay are a function of audience size, advertisers want to be sure audience measurements are accurate.

Audience size and composition are also important to the network or station, since they determine the amount it can charge for commercial time. Shows are frequently canceled because they fail to attract enough viewers to make their commercial time attractive to potential advertisers. Determining audience size is not an exact science and has been the subject of considerable controversy through the years. In this section, we examine how audiences are measured and how advertisers use this information in planning their media schedules.

Audience Measures

The size and composition of television audiences are measured by ratings services. The sole source of network TV and local audience information is the A. C. Nielsen Co. For many years local audience information was also available from the Arbitron Co., but Arbitron exited the local TV ratings business at the end of 1993 due to steep financial losses.[24] Nielsen gathers viewership information from a sample of TV homes and then projects this information to the total viewing area. The techniques used to gather audience measurement information include diaries, electronic meters or recorders, and personal interviews. Nielsen provides various types of information that can be used to measure and evaluate a station's audience. These measures are important to media planners as they weigh the value of buying commercial time on a program.

Television Households The number of households in the market that own a TV is sometimes referred to as the *universe estimate* (UE). Nielsen estimates that 100.8 million U.S. households owned at least one TV set as of January 2000. Since over 98 percent of U.S. households own a TV set, **television households** generally correspond to the number of households in a given market.

Program Rating Probably the best known of all audience measurement figures is the **program rating,** the percentage of TV households in an area that are tuned to a specific program during a specific time period. The program rating is calculated by

Global Perspective 11–4

MTV Goes Global—but with a Local Touch

MTV (Music Television) Network was launched in the United States in 1981 as a joint venture between American Express and Warner Communications. Almost from the outset, the pioneering 24-hour music video cable channel put young viewers in a trance, influencing how they looked, talked, and shopped. The outfit that all but invented the rock video has become perhaps the biggest force in the music world. It is also the premiere platform for marketers trying to woo young consumers in 136 countries and 310 million households around the world. Every week nearly 188 million people watch their MTV—and 80 percent of them tune in outside the U.S.

In 1986, Viacom International purchased MTV and a year later launched its first overseas channel in Europe. MTV's first international venture got off to a wobbly start, piping a single feed across Europe, with English-speaking veejays. MTV learned the hard way that, while Europe's youth agreed with the slogan "I want my MTV!" they didn't want a homogeneous version as their tastes vary by country. Local copycats cropped up and stole MTV's viewers and sponsors, and the network suffered as a result. In 1995 MTV changed its strategy and broke Europe into regional feeds. It now has five feeds in on the Continent: one for the United Kingdom and Ireland; another for Germany, Austria, and Switzerland; one for Scandinavia; a broader broadcast for Belgium, Greece, France, and Israel; and one just for Italy alone.

Viacom is also pushing MTV ever deeper into markets in Asia. Its first Chinese channel was launched in 1995 and since then it has boosted distribution dramatically with a mix of cable, direct-satellite, and broadcast TV. From its base in Singapore, MTV Asia operates an English-Hindi channel for India, separate Mandarin feeds for China and Taiwan, English and local channels across Southeast Asia, and a Korean outlet for South Korea. China now gets MTV up to 6 hours a day in 47 million cable homes and 300 million Chinese households got the chance to see a Chinese version of MTV's video awards. MTV's coverage is unmatched in reaching Asia's vast ranks of young consumers. Nearly two-thirds of Asia's three billion people are under the age of 35. The middle class is expanding and splashy Western-brands products, from Procter & Gamble personal products to Nokia cell phones, are symbols of making it among consumers.

In Europe and Asia, digital and satellite technology have made localization of programming easier and less expensive as six feeds can be beamed off of one satellite transponder. While some of the programming shown in various countries can originate from the U.S., MTV channels worldwide air more locally produced and programmed content. MTV devotes airtime overseas to popular U.S. stars like Mariah Carey, Britney Spears, and the Backstreet Boys. However, in most markets, 70 percent of the video fare is local music, as more and more countries have their own popular music and local stars who sing in their own language. The president of MTV's international networks says: "People root for the home team, culturally and musically. Local repertoire is a worldwide trend. There are fewer global megastars."

Going local offers political benefits as well. MTV must constantly fight the perception that it is trying to take an American version of what is popular and trying to implant it globally. MTV executives note that the company is always trying to fight the stereotype that MTV channels in various countries are importing American culture. Viacom's chairman, Sumner Redstone, denies the charge and says to do so would be a kind of cultural imperialism. Instead, he says, MTV is "cultivating and nurturing local artists and shows." For example, MTV India produces 21 homegrown shows hosted by local veejays who speak Hinglish, a kind of hip, city-bred blend of Hindi and English. The country also has a very vibrant and rapidly expanding movie and music scene and most of the music on MTV India comes from Hindi movies.

In all, MTV now airs 23 different feeds around the world, all tailored for their respective markets.

RESEARCH PROVES THAT
YOUNG ADULTS
IN ASIA HAVE
ONLY ONE
THING ON THEIR
MINDS! (It's something we've known all along... But now it's official.)

Asia's Most Wanted Music Channel

Localized feeds and programming make it easier to sell commercials overseas, because the advertising budgets of multinational companies tend to be local rather than regional. MTV's advertising revenues continue to rise as more marketers are recognizing that young people trust MTV, and they trust what is shown on MTV. Music is a common language that travels, and MTV has a formula that entrances young people around the globe.

Sources: Brett Pulley and Andrew Tanzer, "Sumner's Gemstone," *Forbes,* February 21, 2000, pp. 106–11; Sally Beatty and Carol Hymowitz, "How MTV Stays Tuned In to Teens," *The Wall Street Journal,* March 21, 2000, pp. B1, 4.

dividing the number of households tuned to a particular show by the total number of households in the area. For example, if 12 million households (HH) watched "NYPD Blue," the national rating would be 11.9, calculated as follows:

$$\text{Rating} = \frac{\text{HH tuned to show}}{\text{Total U.S. HH}} = \frac{12{,}000{,}000}{100{,}800{,}000} = 11.9$$

A **ratings point** represents 1 percent of all the television households in a particular area tuned to a specific program. On a national level, 1 ratings point represents 1,008,000 households. Thus, a top-rated program like "ER" which has an average rating of 19, reaches 19.1 million households each week ($19 \times 1{,}008{,}000$).

The program rating is the key number to the stations, since the amount of money they can charge for commercial time is based on it. Ratings points are very important to the networks as well as to individual stations. A 1 percent change in a program's ratings over the course of a viewing season can gain or lose millions of dollars in advertising revenue. Advertisers also follow ratings closely, since they are the key measure for audience size and commercial rates.

Households Using Television The percentage of homes in a given area where TV is being watched during a specific time period is called **households using television (HUT).** This figure, sometimes referred to as sets in use, is always expressed as a percentage. For example, if 60 million of the U.S. TV households have their sets turned on at 10 P.M. on a Thursday night, the HUT figure is 59.5 percent (60 million out of 100.8 million). Television usage varies widely depending on the time of day and season of the year.

Share of Audience Another important audience measurement figure is the **share of audience,** which is the percentage of households using TV in a specified time period that are tuned to a specific program. This figure considers variations in the number of sets in use and the total size of the potential audience, since it is based only on those households that have their sets turned on. Audience share is calculated by dividing the number of households (HH) tuned to a show by the number of households using television (HUT). Thus, if 60 million U.S. households had their sets turned on during the 10 P.M. time slot when "NYPD Blue" is shown, the share of audience would be 20, calculated as follows:

$$\text{Share} = \frac{\text{HH tuned to show}}{\text{U.S. households using TV}} = \frac{12{,}000{,}000}{60{,}000{,}000} = 20$$

Audience share is always higher than the program rating unless all the households have their sets turned on (in which case they would be equal). Share figures are important since they reveal how well a program does with the available viewing audience. For example, late at night the size of the viewing audience drops substantially, so the best way to assess the popularity of a late-night program is to examine the share of the available audience it attracts relative to competing programs.

Ratings services also provide an audience statistic known as **total audience,** the total number of homes viewing any five-minute part of a telecast. This number can be broken down to provide audience composition figures that are based on the distribution of the audience into demographic categories.

Network Audience Information

Nielsen Television Index The source of national and network TV audience information is the Nielsen Television Index (NTI), which provides daily and weekly estimates of TV viewing and national sponsored network and major cable program audiences. For more than 25 years, Nielsen provided this information using a two-pronged system consisting of a national sample of metered households along with a separate sample of diary households. In the metered households, an electronic measurement device known as the **audimeter** (audience meter) was hooked up to the TV set to continuously measure the channels to which the set was tuned. Network viewing for the country (the famous Nielsen ratings) was based on the results provided by audimeters placed in a national sample of homes carefully selected to represent the population of U.S. households. The metered households were supported by a separate panel of households that recorded viewing information in diaries. Since the audimeter could measure only the channel to which the set was tuned, the diary panel was used to gather demographic data on the viewing audience.

For many years, the television and advertising industries expressed concern over the audimeter/diary system. The information from diaries was not available to the network and advertising analysts for several weeks, and studies indicated the method was overstating the size of some key demographic audiences. Cooperation rates among diary keepers declined, and often the person who kept a household's diary did not note what other family members watched when he or she wasn't home. The complex new video environment and explosion in viewing options also made it difficult for diary keepers to maintain accurate viewing records.

As a result of these problems, and in response to competitive pressure from an audience measurement company from England, AGB, in 1987 Nielsen made the people meter the sole basis of its national rating system and eliminated the use of the diary panel.

The People Meter The **people meter** is an electronic measuring device that incorporates the technology of the old-style audimeter in a system that records not only what is being watched but also by whom in 5,000 homes. The actual device is a small box with eight buttons—six for the family and two for visitors—that can be placed on the top of the TV set (Exhibit 11–8). A remote control unit permits electronic entries from anywhere in the room. Each member of the sample household is assigned a button that indicates his or her presence as a viewer. The device is also equipped with a sonar sensor to remind viewers entering or leaving the room to log in or out on the meter.

The viewership information the people meter collects from the household is stored in the home system until it is retrieved by Nielsen's computers. Data collected include when the set is turned on, which channel is viewed, when the channel is changed, and when the set is off, in addition to who is viewing. The demographic characteristics of the viewers are also in the system, and viewership can be matched to these traits. Nielsen's operation center processes all this information each week for release to the TV and advertising industries. Nielsen uses a sample of metered households in the nation's largest markets (New York, Los Angeles, and Chicago) to provide overnight viewing results.

Exhibit 11–8 Nielsen uses the people meter to measure national TV audiences

Local Audience Information

Information on local audiences is important to both local advertisers and firms making national spot buys. The Nielsen Station Index (NSI) measures TV station audiences in 210 local markets known as **designated market areas (DMA).** DMAs are nonoverlapping areas used for planning, buying, and evaluating TV audiences and are generally a group of counties in which stations located in a metropolitan or central area achieve the largest audience share. NSI reports information on viewing by time periods and programs and includes audience size and estimates of viewing over a range of demographic categories for each DMA.

Nielsen measures viewing audiences in every television market at least four times a year. The major markets (New York, Chicago, Los Angeles) are covered six times a year. The ratings periods when all 210 DMAs are surveyed are known as

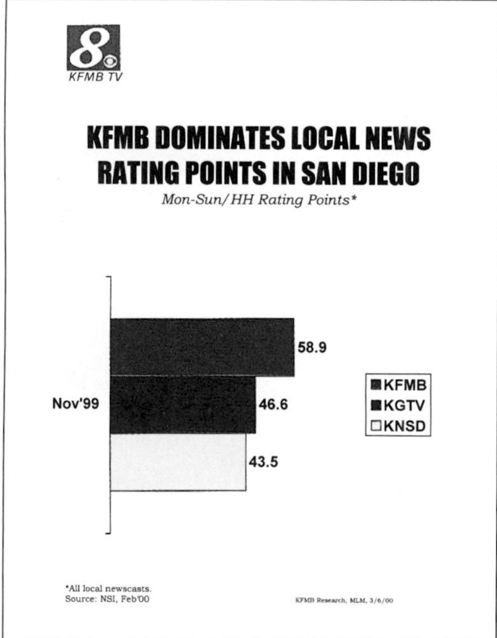

Exhibit 11–9 KFMB promotes its dominance of the sweeps rating period for local news

sweeps. The networks and local stations use numbers gathered during the sweeps rating periods in selling TV time. Exhibit 11–9 shows how KFMB, the CBS affiliate in San Diego, promotes its dominance of the sweeps ratings for local news.

However, as discussed in IMC Perspective 11–5, many advertising professionals believe the audience estimates gathered during the sweeps are overestimated because of special programming and promotions that occur during these periods.

Developments in Audience Measurement

For years the advertising industry has been calling for changes in the way TV viewing audiences are measured, at both the national and local levels.[25] Many people believe people meters are only the first step in improving the way audiences are measured. While the people meter is seen as an improvement over the diary method, it still requires cooperation on an ongoing basis from people in the metered homes. Viewers in the Nielsen households, including young children, must punch a preassigned number on the remote control device each time they start or stop watching. Media researchers argue that kids forget and adults tire of the task over the two years they are in the Nielsen sample. Nielsen has been trying to develop passive measurement systems that require less involvement by people in metered homes and can produce more accurate measures of the viewing audience. However, such a system does not appear to be forthcoming in the near future.

Much of the concern over the Nielsen measurements involves the diary system used to measure viewing in the 210 local markets. This system requires that every 15 minutes viewers write down station call letters, channel numbers, programs, and who is watching. Many homes do not return completed diaries, and many of those that are returned are often not filled out correctly. Nielsen executives acknowledge the problems with its measurement system for local markets and is trying to correct them. The company is testing new diaries, sending out more of them, and working to improve the response rates.[26] Nielsen is also considering switching to a continuous measurement system for local markets rather than relying solely on the sweeps measurement system.[27] (See IMC Perspective 11–5.)

Recently a number of advertisers and ad agencies increased their criticism of Nielsen's local diary system, saying the handwritten method used to measure viewing audiences and gather demographic data in local audiences is antiquated. They argue that people meters are a far more accurate measurement system and should be used in local markets as well as on a national level. Nielsen has begun exploring the possibility of expanding the use of people meters to local markets. However, issues such as who will bear the cost of installing the people meters and how they would add to the cost of Nielsen's services are still major factors that have to be addressed.[28] In late 1999 Nielsen began talking to TV stations and cable operators in the Boston area about installing 600 people meters. This would make Boston, the nation's sixth largest TV market, the first to use people meters for local audience measurement.[29]

Nielsen has been battling with the networks, local TV stations, and ad agencies for years over the accuracy of its numbers. Many in the industry suspect that Nielsen is not moving fast enough to improve its audience measurement systems because it has a virtual monopoly in both the national and the local ratings business. They would like to see some competition.

The major networks, advertisers, and agencies have explored alternatives to Nielsen Media Research. The most recent effort to develop an alternative to Nielsen was a system developed by Statistical Research Inc. (SRI) called Smart-TV, which was initially funded by the three major networks and big advertisers such as Procter & Gamble, AT&T, and General Motors.[30] SRI claimed its Smart-TV system had many advantages over Nielsen's people meter and tested the system in Philadelphia in 1998. However, in May 1999 SRI canceled a national rollout of the new measurement system due to a lack of funding.[31] The failure of Smart-TV has led many in the advertising community to question whether an alternative to the Nielsen sys-

IMC Perspective 11–5

Is It Time to Do Away with Sweeps Ratings?

The cornerstone of selling local television time is the sweeps rating periods, which are held in November, February, May, and, to a lesser extent, August by Nielsen Media Research to determine what stations and shows are being watched. The numbers gathered during the sweeps periods are used as guideposts in the buying and selling of TV ad time during the rest of the year. However, many people in the advertising industry are enraged over the TV stations' practice of artificially bolstering their ratings during sweeps periods with special programming and contests, games, and other nontypical promotions. They argue that ratings taken during these periods are not indicative of what can be expected the other 36 weeks of the year, when networks run their regular programming and promotions are not used to boost local viewing audiences.

Advertisers and their agencies have become accustomed to the usual tactics used to beef up program schedules during the sweeps months, from blockbuster network programming to lurid sensationalism in local newscasts. Of much greater concern, however, is the blatant use of ratings grabbers such as big-prize sweepstakes, contests, and giveaways during sweeps. Nielsen Media Research says the number of unusual sweeps-period station promotions—most often giveaway contests on local newscasts—is growing faster than ever. For example, during a recent sweeps period, a Houston station conducted a watch-and-win contest offering $2,000 each day to viewers of its 5 P.M., 6 P.M., and 10 P.M. newscasts. Nielsen's research has confirmed that giveaway promotions can substantially affect a TV station's audience share. However, while ratings spike during these promotions, they generally drop back to precontest levels when the cash giveaway stops.

Nielsen is working with the advertising industry to solve the sweeps problem. It provides red flags in its printed reports if stations use special promotions to bump up their ratings. However, the tapes that are fed into the agencies' media department computers contain only the ratings. Alert buyers can spot unusual blips in continuously metered TV markets, but in other markets the sweeps-period numbers are the only numbers available and they have no benchmark. One proposal made by Nielsen is that the computer tape used by many agencies be highlighted in some way so that media buyers know which stations are running the contests and when.

Advertisers, agencies, and the major TV networks argue that the long-term solution to the problem is for Nielsen to switch to continuous measurement, 13-week averages reported four times a year, rather than relying on the artificially hyped numbers from the sweeps periods. However, Nielsen argues that such a service would be costly and the TV and advertising industries would have to be willing to pay a higher price for ratings information. There may also be some resistance from the local stations that have grown accustomed to getting higher ad rates year-round from the sweeps numbers. They also save money by compressing the bulk of their promotional spending into a few specific sweeps periods.

The CBS television network recently proposed a "checkerboard" plan in which the sweeps measurements would be spread over two months instead of one. To keep costs down, Nielsen would do local diary measurements every other week during that two-month period. CBS contends that networks and local stations will have a more difficult time maintaining the special programming and promotions for two months instead of one.

Additional proposals have been put forth to solve the problem of the get-viewers-quick schemes that distort the accuracy of measures taken during the sweeps. However, the key issue is whether the television industry will take some action to try to solve the problem.

Sources: Allen Banks, "Close the Book on Sweeps," *Advertising Age*, March 15, 1999, p. 33; "Passing Buck on the Sweeps," *Advertising Age*, March 8, 1999, p. 32; Erwin Ephron, "How to Curb TV's Sweeps Ratings Game," *Advertising Age*, February 3, 1997, p. 30.

tem will ever be developed. However, as new delivery systems for TV are developed, such as digital signals through set-top boxes, there is hope that other measurement methods will emerge as well.[32]

Many advertising professionals hope that a focus of new technology for measuring viewing audiences will be on developing rating systems for commercials, not just for programs. The Nielsen system measures the audiences for the programs surrounding the commercials rather than the commercials themselves. But with zipping, zapping, people leaving the room, and people being distracted from the TV during commercial breaks, there is a need to develop accurate ratings of more than just program audience viewing.

For over 50 years consumers passively received TV programming and commercials. This is changing rapidly, however, as the major cable operators, telecommunications companies, and others bring various entertainment, information, and interactive services into homes via television. Researchers argue that the Nielsen system is being overwhelmed by the explosion in the number of TV sets, delivery systems, and program options available. These developments must be carefully monitored by advertisers and media planners as well as by people in the TV industry, as they can have a profound impact on audience size and composition and on the way advertisers use and pay for the use of TV as an advertising medium. Improvements in measurement technology are needed to accommodate these developments.

Radio

Television has often been referred to as the ideal advertising medium, and to many people it personifies the glamour and excitement of the industry. Radio, on the other hand, has been called the Rodney Dangerfield of media because it gets no respect from many advertisers. Dominated by network programming and national advertisers before the growth of TV, radio has evolved into a primarily local advertising medium. Network advertising generally accounts for less than 5 percent of radio's revenue.[33] Radio has also become a medium characterized by highly specialized programming appealing to very narrow segments of the population.

The importance of radio is best demonstrated by the numbers. There are more than 11,000 radio stations in this country, including 4,784 commercial AM stations and 5,720 commercial FM stations. There are over 576 million radios in use in the United States, an average of 5.6 per household. Radio reaches 75 percent of all Americans over the age of 12 each day and has grown into a ubiquitous background to many activities, among them reading, driving, running, working, and socializing. The average American listens to radio 3 hours and 12 minutes every weekday and nearly $5^1/_2$ hours every weekend.[34] The pervasiveness of this medium has not gone unnoticed by advertisers; radio advertising revenue grew from $8.8 billion in 1990 to over $17 billion in 1999.

Radio has survived and flourished as an advertising medium because it offers advertisers certain advantages for communicating messages to their potential customers. However, radio has inherent limitations that affect its role in the advertiser's media strategy.

Advantages of Radio

Radio has many advantages over other media, including cost and efficiency, selectivity, flexibility, mental imagery, and integrated marketing opportunities.

Cost and Efficiency

One of the main strengths of radio as an advertising medium is its low cost. Radio commercials are very inexpensive to produce. They require only a script of the commercial to be read by the radio announcer or a copy of a prerecorded message that can be broadcast by the station. The cost for radio time is also low. A minute on network radio may cost only $5,000, which translates into a cost per thousand of only $3 to $4. Local advertising on radio stations costs about $6 per thousand households, compared to more than $20 for local TV advertising. The low relative costs of radio make it one of the most efficient of all advertising media, and the low absolute cost means the budget needed for an effective radio campaign is often lower than that for other media.

The low cost of radio means advertisers can build more reach and frequency into their media schedule within a certain budget. They can use different stations to broaden the reach of their messages and multiple spots to ensure adequate frequency. For example, a number of Internet start-ups have been heavy users of radio in their efforts to build brand awareness. Companies such as More.com, which sells drugstore items on the Internet, see radio as a fast and relatively inexpensive way to get their names known. Radio commercials can be produced more quickly than TV spots, and the companies can run them more often[35] Many national advertisers also recognize the cost efficiency of radio and use it as part of their media strategy. IMC Perspective 11–6 discusses the important role radio advertising has played in the marketing campaign for the Motel 6 chain.

Selectivity Another major advantage of radio is the high degree of audience selectivity available through the various program formats and geographic coverage of the numerous stations. Radio lets companies focus their advertising on specialized audiences such as certain demographic and lifestyle groups. Most areas have radio stations with formats such as adult contemporary, easy listening, classical music, country, news/talk shows, jazz, and all news, to name a few. Figure 11–7 shows the percentage of the radio listening audience captured by various radio formats. For

Figure 11–7 There's a radio format for everyone

Format	18–24	Format	25–34
Top 40	18.5	Adult contemporary (AC)	16.6
Urban	17.5	Album rock	12.1
Adult contemporary (AC)	13.6	Top 40	10.7
Album rock	10.9	Urban	9.8
Modern rock	8.9	News/talk	9.3
Country	8.0	Country	9.1
Spanish	6.9	Spanish	7.7
Classic rock	4.1	Modern rock	6.7
News/talk	3.5	Classic rock	6.0
Urban AC	2.8	Urban AC	4.0
Oldies	2.1	Oldies	2.4
Religious	1.0	NAC/smooth jazz	2.0
NAC/smooth jazz	0.9	Religious	1.7
Remaining formats	0.9	Remaining formats	1.0
Classical	0.3	Classical	0.6
MOR/big band	0.1	MOR/big band	0.2

Format	35–44	Format	45–54
Adult contemporary (AC)	16.6	News/talk	19.6
News/talk	13.9	Adult contemporary (AC)	16.9
Country	9.8	Oldies	12.3
Album rock	9.4	Country	10.8
Classic rock	8.1	Spanish	5.6
Top 40	6.6	NAC/smooth jazz	5.3
Spanish	6.4	Urban AC	4.6
Urban	6.2	Classic rock	4.4
Oldies	5.8	Urban	4.2
Urban AC	5.0	Album rock	4.1
NAC/smooth jazz	4.1	Top 40	3.4
Modern rock	3.1	Religious	2.8
Religious	2.4	Classical	2.2
Remaining formats	1.1	MOR/big band	1.7
Classical	1.0	Modern rock	1.2
MOR/big band	0.6	Remaining formats	1.0

Note: Read as The Top-40 format captures an 18.5% share of radio listening among persons 18 to 24 years old.

IMC Perspective 11–6

Motel 6 Wants Travelers to "See the Light"

One of the largest and fastest-growing portions of the U.S. lodging market is the economy or budget segment, which is dominated by Motel 6 (the "6" originally stood for $6-a-night rooms when the company was founded in 1962). Prior to 1986 Motel 6 had no marketing department, never had an advertising campaign, charged guests to have their television sets connected, and did not even provide telephones in its rooms.

In 1986, Motel 6 hit bottom as it lost $18.7 million and its occupancy rate dropped to 66 percent. This prompted the investment company that bought the chain to take steps to turn it around. Phones were installed in every room; rooms were refurbished; and a number of new motels were built. By 1988, Motel 6 had earnings of over $5 million and occupancy was up to over 73 percent. While these changes were important in Motel 6's turnaround, the company's top executives agree that such a rapid reversal would not have been possible without a pervasive radio campaign featuring Tom Bodett, who was a contractor-turned-writer, as spokesperson for the company. Bodett has remained the star of the chain's radio ads since 1986 and also does the voice-over in most of its TV spots as well.

Motel 6 originally went with radio in the late 80s because it had a limited ad budget of just over $1 million and believed radio was the best way to reach travelers, most of whom arrived by car or truck without a reservation. The goal of this phase of Motel 6's advertising was to position the company as "the lowest priced of any national chain." Bodett would deliver down-home humorous messages telling travelers it is OK to be cheap, and the ads would end with the tagline "We'll leave the light on for you." It has been suggested that his country-style voice and delivery have been very effective on radio because they project a variety of faces to listeners.

In the early 1990s Motel 6 entered what it calls its "second phase," with ads featuring Bodett talking about the motel's amenities such as cable TV, free phone calls, and a reservation system. Several of the spots also poked fun at the frivolous amenities offered by expensive hotels. In 1994 the company ran its first TV commercial, which was called "Blank Screen." The visual consisted of only a black screen with the Motel 6 logo on the bottom. The voice-over featured Tom Bodett telling viewers: "This is what one of our rooms looks like when you're sleeping and you know, it looks just like one of those big fancy hotels. The only difference is that ours won't cost you as much money." From 1997 to 1999 the company's advertising entered its third phase, with ads focused on the $600 million the company spent to upgrade the facilities and renovate its rooms.

In 1999 Motel 6 began what it is calling the "fourth phase" of Tom Bodett's advertising for the chain. The new campaign uses a new tagline, "When did you first see the light?" and is designed to dispel any notions that Motel 6 attracts disreputable guests because it is an economy-class hotel. The chain's vice president of marketing, Carol Kirby, says: "Many people really weren't sure who they'd meet at a Motel 6. We wanted people to understand that Motel 6 was for people like them. It's a huge cross-section of middle class America." Rod Underhill, a principal at the Richards group, says that the goal of the campaign is to let travelers know that they won't just be comfortable in the rooms but will also be comfortable with the people next door. Underhill notes that the chain's research indicates there are still people who are a little worried that an undesirable person may be next door. He argues that this is the last hurdle Motel 6 needs to overcome.

The new campaign will include five new 15-second TV commercials showing the type of people who stay at a Motel 6, including a construction worker who travels to jobs "on my own dime"; a middle-aged couple who

Sample Motel 6 radio spot

"Hi. Tom Bodett for Motel 6 with a plan for anyone whose kids are on their own now. Take a drive, see some of the country and visit a few relatives. Like your sister Helen and her husband Bob. They're wonderful folks and always happy to pull the hide-a-bed out for you, but somehow the smell of mothballs just isn't conducive to gettin' a good night's sleep. And since Bob gets up at 5:30, well that means you do too. So here's the plan. Check into Motel 6. 'Cause for around 22 bucks, the lowest prices of any national chain, you'll get a clean, comfortable room, and Helen and Bob'll think you're mighty considerate. Well you are, but maybe more important, you can sleep late and not have to wonder if the towels in their bathroom are just for decoration. My rule of thumb is, if they match the tank and seat cover, you better leave 'em alone. Just call 505-891-6161 for reservations. I'm Tom Bodett for Motel 6. Give my best to Helen and Bob and we'll leave the light on for you."

One of the 100-plus radio spots for Motel 6 created by The Richards Group.

found Motel 6 while touring the South; and a father and son who stay there on fishing trips. Motel 6 also is continuing to spend heavily on radio advertising, with about 40 percent of the media budget being allocated to radio spots featuring Bodett.

Over the past 14 years, the advertising campaign for Motel 6 has been extremely effective. A study conducted in fall 1999 found that the company's advertising awareness was the highest in its category, as nearly 60 percent of consumers recognized Motel 6's advertising. Radio advertising has played a major role in the success of the campaign and has resulted in Motel 6 leaving a lot of lights on for travelers. The new user campaign should be just as effective in showing travelers the light about the chain's clientele.

Sources: David Goetzl, "Motel 6 Ads Seek to Reassure Public About Its Clientele," *Advertising Age,* April 19, 1999, p. 12; "Motel 6 Grabs Top Awareness Spot," *Adweek Southwest,* October 25, 1999; "King of the Road," *Marketing and Media Decisions,* March 1989, pp. 80–86.

example, among 18- to 24-year olds, the most popular radio format is top 40, while those between the ages of 45 and 54 prefer news/talk. Elusive consumers like teenagers, college students, and working adults can be reached more easily through radio than most other media.

Radio can reach consumers other media can't. Light television viewers spend considerably more time with radio than with TV and are generally an upscale market in terms of income and education level. Light readers of magazines and newspapers also spend more time listening to radio. Radio has become a popular way to reach specific non-English-speaking ethnic markets. Los Angeles, New York City, Dallas, and Miami have several radio stations that broadcast in Spanish and reach these areas' large Hispanic markets. As mass marketing gives way to market segmentation and regional marketing, radio will continue to grow in importance.

Flexibility

Radio is probably the most flexible of all the advertising media because it has a very short closing period, which means advertisers can change their message almost up to the time it goes on the air. Radio commercials can usually be produced and scheduled on very short notice. Radio advertisers can easily adjust their messages to local market conditions and marketing situations.

Mental Imagery

A potential advantage of radio that is often overlooked is that it encourages listeners to use their imagination when processing a commercial message. While the creative options of radio are limited, many advertisers take advantage of the absence of a visual element to let consumers create their own picture of what is happening in a radio message.

Radio may also reinforce television messages through a technique called **image transfer,** where the images of a TV commercial are implanted into a radio spot.[36] First the marketer establishes the video image of a TV commercial. Then it uses a similar, or even the same, audio portion (spoken words and/or jingle) as the basis for the radio counterpart. The idea is that when consumers hear the radio message, they will make the connection to the TV commercial, reinforcing its video images. Image transfer offers advertisers a way to make radio and TV ads work together synergistically. This promotional piece put out by the Radio Advertising Bureau shows how the image transfer process works (Exhibit 11–10).

Integrated Marketing Opportunities

Radio provides marketers with a variety of integrated marketing opportunities. Radio stations become an integral part of

Exhibit 11–10 The Radio Advertising Bureau promotes the concept of imagery transfer

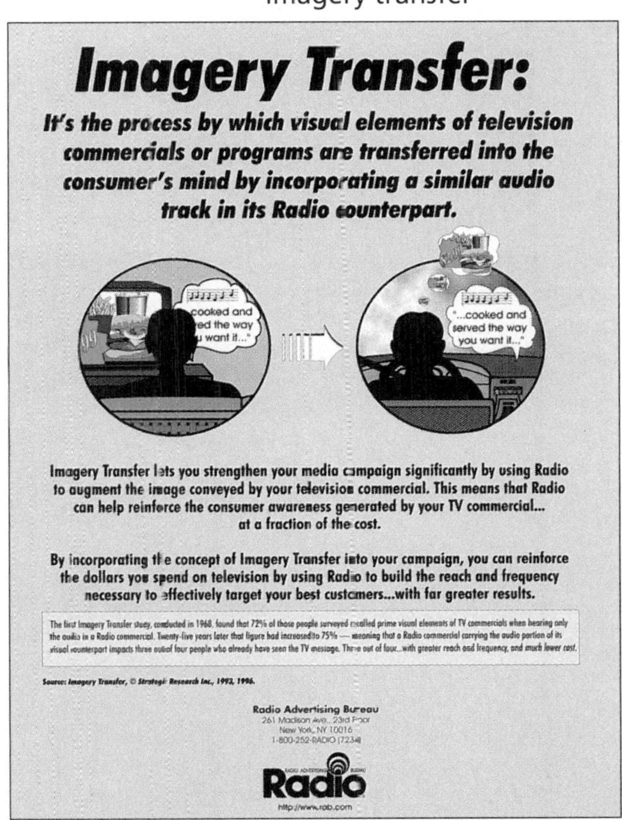

many communities, and the deejays and program hosts may become popular figures. Advertisers often use radio stations and personalities to enhance their involvement with a local market and to gain influence with local retailers. Radio also works very effectively in conjunction with place-based/point-of-purchase promotions. Retailers often use on-site radio broadcasts combined with special sales or promotions to attract consumers to their stores and get them to make a purchase. Live radio broadcasts are also used in conjunction with event marketing. For example, Banana Boat Suncare often sponsors live broadcast promotions at beaches, sporting events, and festivals, setting up product booths for sampling and giveaways (Exhibit 11–11).

Limitations of Radio

Several factors limit the effectiveness of radio as an advertising medium, among them creative limitations, fragmentation, chaotic buying procedures, limited research data, limited listener attention, and clutter. The media planner must consider them in determining the role the medium will play in the advertising program.

Creative Limitations

A major drawback of radio as an advertising medium is the absence of a visual image. The radio advertiser cannot show the product, demonstrate it, or use any type of visual appeal or information. A radio commercial is, like a TV ad, a short-lived and fleeting message that is externally paced and does not allow the receiver to control the rate at which it is processed. Because of these creative limitations many companies tend to ignore radio, and agencies often assign junior people to the development of radio commercials.

Fragmentation

Another problem with radio is the high level of audience fragmentation due to the large number of stations. The percentage of the market tuned to any particular station is usually very small. The top-rated radio station in many major metropolitan areas with a number of AM and FM stations may attract less than 10 percent of the total listening audience. Advertisers that want a broad reach in their radio advertising media schedule have to buy time on a number of stations to cover even a local market.

Chaotic Buying Procedures

It should be readily apparent how chaotic the media planning and purchasing process can become for the advertiser that wants to use radio on a nationwide spot basis. Acquiring information and evaluating and contracting for time with even a fraction of the 10,500 commercial stations that

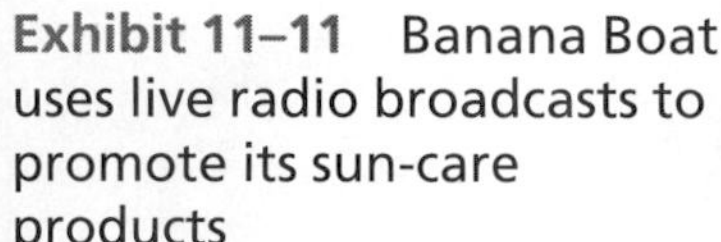
Exhibit 11–11 Banana Boat uses live radio broadcasts to promote its sun-care products

operate across the country can be very difficult and time-consuming. This problem has diminished somewhat in recent years as the number of radio networks and of syndicated programs offering a package of several hundred stations increases.

Limited Research Data Audience research data on radio are often limited, particularly compared with TV, magazines, or newspapers. Most radio stations are small operations and lack the revenue to support detailed studies of their audiences. And most users of radio are local companies that cannot support research on radio listenership in their markets. Thus, media planners do not have as much audience information available to guide them in their purchase of radio time as they do with other media.

Limited Listener Attention Another problem that plagues radio is that it is difficult to retain listener attention to commercials. Radio programming, particularly music, is often the background to some other activity and may not receive the listeners' full attention. Thus they may miss all or some of the commercials. One environment where radio has a more captive audience is in cars. But getting listeners to pay attention to commercials can still be difficult. Most people preprogram their car radio and change stations during commercial breaks. A study by Avery Abernethy found large differences between exposure to radio programs versus advertising for listeners in cars. They were exposed to only half of the advertising broadcast and changed stations frequently to avoid commercials.[37] Another factor that is detracting from radio listening in motor vehicles is the rapid growth of cellular phones. A recent study found that half of commuters surveyed who own a cell phone reported listening to less radio than they did a year earlier.[38]

Clutter Clutter is just as much a problem with radio as with other advertising media. Most radio stations carry an average of nearly 10 minutes of commercials every hour. During the popular morning and evening rush hours, the amount of commercial time may exceed 12 minutes. Advertisers must create commercials that break through the clutter or use heavy repetition to make sure their messages reach consumers. In a study of radio listeners conducted by Edison Research, perceptions of increased ad clutter were cited by participants as a reason for spending less time listening to radio.[39]

Another factor that may contribute to the problem of commercial clutter on radio is a new technological system called Cash, developed by the Prime Image Company.[40] The machine momentarily stores the broadcast of a live show, creating an imperceptible delay. When the rebroadcast airs seconds later, the Cash system has reduced the pauses between words and shortened long syllables in order to add more space for commercials. This allows stations to add up to six minutes of extra airtime per hour, which may mean as many as 12 more 30-second commercials. Unlike the case with previous systems that compressed broadcasts and replayed them at a faster pace, listeners cannot recognize the effect. However, they are very likely to recognize the increased number of commercials, which will only compound the clutter problem.

Buying Radio Time

The purchase of radio time is similar to that of television, as advertisers can make either network, spot, or local buys. Since these options were reviewed in the section on buying TV time, they are discussed here only briefly.

Network Radio Advertising time on radio can be purchased on a network basis using one of the national networks. There are currently three major national radio networks, Westwood One, ABC, and Premier. There are also more than 100 regional radio networks across the country. Using networks minimizes the amount of negotiation and administrative work needed to get national or regional coverage, and the costs are lower than those for individual stations. However, the number of

Exhibit 11–12 Rush Limbaugh's talk radio show is syndicated nationally

affiliated stations on the network roster and the types of audiences they reach can vary considerably, so the use of network radio reduces advertisers' flexibility in selecting stations.

An important trend in radio is the increasing number of radio networks and syndicated programs that offer advertisers a package of several hundred stations. For example, conservative Rush Limbaugh's radio show is syndicated nationally and is carried by more than 500 stations, reaching more than 11 million people weekly (Exhibit 11–12). Syndication reduces audience fragmentation and purchasing problems and increases radio's appeal to national advertisers.

Spot Radio

National advertisers can also use spot radio to purchase airtime on individual stations in various markets. The purchase of spot radio provides greater flexibility in selecting markets, individual stations, and airtime and adjusting the message for local market conditions. Spot radio accounts for about 20 percent of radio time sold. Figure 11–8 shows the top 20 national advertisers and how they allocate their radio budgets between network and spot radio.

Local Radio

By far the heaviest users of radio are local advertisers; nearly 79 percent of radio advertising time is purchased from individual stations by local companies. Auto dealers, retailers, restaurants, and financial institutions are among the heaviest users of local radio advertising. But a number of radio advertisers are

Figure 11–8 Radio's Top 20 National Network and Spot Advertisers

Rank	National Advertiser	Total*	Network*	Spot*
1	MCI WorldCom	$47.4	$1.6	$45.8
2	Chattem Inc. (Phisoderm, Gold Bond, Sunsource, etc.)	40.9	40.8	0.1
3	Warner-Lambert Co. (Listerine, Rolaids, Benadryl, etc.)	40.6	39.5	1.1
4	Political issues	39.7	—	39.7
5	News Corp. Ltd. (Fox TV/20th Century Fox, etc.)	37.5	1.7	35.8
6	AT&T Corp.	37.2	8.7	28.5
7	Procter & Gamble (Folgers, Pringles, Tide, etc.)	32.4	25.4	7.0
8	Berkshire Hathaway (GEICO, Dairy Queen, etc.)	32.3	14.1	18.2
9	Kmart Corp.	31.4	9.0	22.4
10	Daimler-Chrysler Dealer Assn.	29.8	—	29.8
11	GTE Corp.	29.8	—	29.8
12	General Motors Corp.	29.6	7.2	22.4
13	JCPenney Co., Inc.	28.1	18.7	9.4
14	CompUSA, Inc.	27.7	—	27.7
15	National Amusements, Inc. (Comedy Central, Blockbuster, UPN, etc.)	27.5	4.0	23.5
16	Allstate Corp.	27.1	11.3	15.8
17	U.S. Government	26.7	11.6	15.1
18	Time Warner (HBO, Time, Turner Broadcasting, etc.)	26.4	3.4	23.0
19	SBC Communications (Southwestern Bell)	26.3	—	26.3
20	Diageo PLC (Burger King, various alcoholic beverages)	24.7	0.5	24.2

*All revenue figures are in millions of dollars.

switching to local cable TV because the rates are comparable and there is the added advantage of TV's visual impact.

Time Classifications

As with television, the broadcast day for radio is divided into various time periods or dayparts, as shown in Figure 11–9. The size of the radio listening audience varies widely across the dayparts, and advertising rates follow accordingly. The largest radio audiences (and thus the highest rates) occur during the early morning and late afternoon drive times. Radio rates also vary according to the number of spots or type of audience plan purchased, the supply and demand of time available in the local market, and the ratings of the individual station. Rate information is available directly from the stations and is summarized in Standard Rate and Data Service's (SRDS) Spot Radio Rates and Data for both local stations and radio networks. Some stations issue rate cards like the one shown in Figure 11–10. But many stations do not adhere strictly to rate cards and the rates published in SRDS. Their rates are negotiable and depend on factors such as availability, time period, and number of spots purchased.

Audience Information

One problem with radio is the lack of audience information. Because there are so many radio stations and thus many small, fragmented audiences, the stations cannot support the expense of detailed audience measurement. Also, owing to the nature of

Morning drive time	6:00–10:00 A.M.
Daytime	10:00 A.M. –3:00 P.M.
Afternoon/evening drive time	3:00–7:00 P.M.
Nighttime	7:00 P.M. –12:00 A.M.
All night	12:00–6:00 A.M.

Figure 11–9 Dayparts for radio

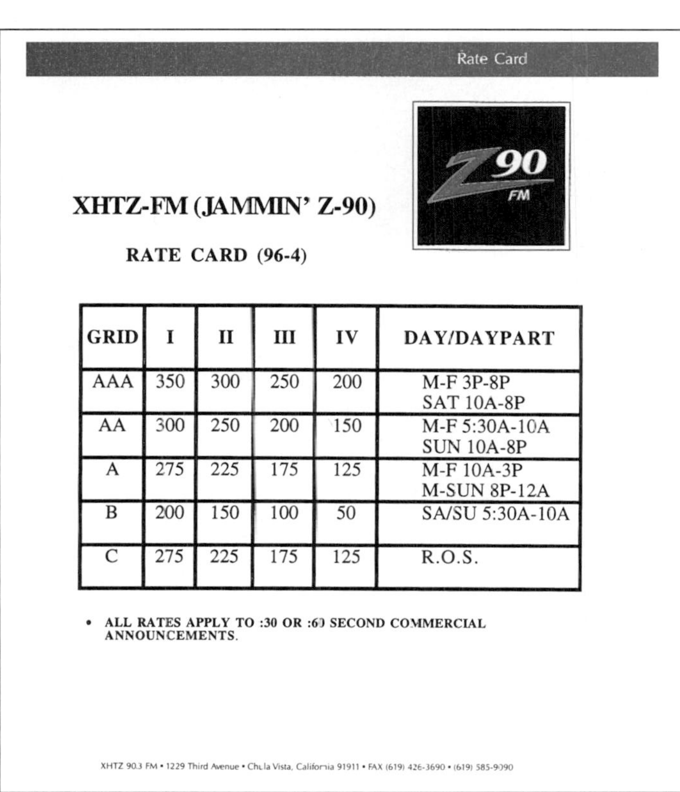
Rate Card

XHTZ-FM (JAMMIN' Z-90)

RATE CARD (96-4)

GRID	I	II	III	IV	DAY/DAYPART
AAA	350	300	250	200	M-F 3P-8P SAT 10A-8P
AA	300	250	200	150	M-F 5:30A-10A SUN 10A-8P
A	275	225	175	125	M-F 10A-3P M-SUN 8P-12A
B	200	150	100	50	SA/SU 5:30A-10A
C	275	225	175	125	R.O.S.

- ALL RATES APPLY TO :30 OR :60 SECOND COMMERCIAL ANNOUNCEMENTS.

XHTZ 90.3 FM • 1229 Third Avenue • Chula Vista, California 91911 • FAX (619) 426-3690 • (619) 585-9090

Figure 11–10 Sample radio rate card

radio as incidental or background entertainment, it is difficult to develop precise measures of who listens at various time periods and for how long. There are now two major radio ratings services: Arbitron is the primary supplier of audience information for local stations, and RADAR (Radio's All-Dimension Audience Research) studies supply information on network audiences.

Arbitron Arbitron covers 260 local radio markets with one to four ratings reports per year. Arbitron has a sample of representative listeners in each market maintain a diary of their radio listening for seven days. Audience estimates for the market are based on these diary records and reported by time period and selected demographics in the Arbitron Ratings/Radio book, to which clients subscribe. Figure 11–11 provides a sample page from the Arbitron ratings report for people in the 18-to-49 age target audience across the various dayparts. The three basic estimates in the Arbitron report are

- Person estimates—the estimated number of people listening.
- Rating—the percentage of listeners in the survey area population.
- Share—the percentage of the total estimated listening audience.

These three estimates are further defined by using quarter-hour and cume figures. The **average quarter-hour (AQH) figure** expresses the average number of people estimated to have listened to a station for a minimum of five minutes during any quarter-hour in a time period. For example, station KCBQ has an average quarter-hour listenership of 2,500 during the weekday 6–10 A.M. daypart. This means that any weekday, for any 15-minute period during this time period, an average of 2,500 people between the ages of 18 and 49 are tuned to this station. This figure helps to determine the audience and cost of a spot schedule within a particular time period.

Cume stands for cumulative audience, the estimated total number of different people who listened to a station for at least five minutes in a quarter-hour period within a reported daypart. In Figure 11–11, the cumulative audience of people 18 to 49 for station KCBQ during the weekday morning daypart is 26,300. Cume estimates the reach potential of a radio station.

The **average quarter-hour rating (AQH RTG)** expresses the estimated number of listeners as a percentage of the survey area population. The **average quarter-hour share (AQH SHR)** is the percentage of the total listening audience tuned to each sta-

Figure 11–11 Partial sample page from Arbitron radio ratings report

Target Audience, Persons 18–49								
	Monday–Friday 6–10 A.M.				Monday–Friday 10 A.M.–3 P.M.			
	AQH (00)	CUME (00)	AQH RTG	AQH SHR	AQH (00)	CUME (00)	AQH RTG	AQH SHR
KCBQ								
METRO	25	263	.2	.8	40	365	.3	1.3
TSA	25	263			40	365		
KCBQ-FM								
METRO	101	684	.7	3.1	117	768	.9	3.7
TSA	101	684			117	768		
KCEO								
METRO	11	110	.1	.3	8	81	.1	.3
TSA	11	110			8	81		
KFMB								
METRO	171	790	1.3	5.3	106	678	.8	3.3
TSA	171	790			106	678		

tion. It shows the share of listeners each station captures out of the total listening audience in the survey area. The average quarter-hour rating of station KCBQ during the weekday 6–10 A.M. daypart is 0.2, while the average quarter-hour share is 0.8.

While Arbitron focuses primarily on local audience measurement, the company has made several proposals to the major radio networks to begin tracking network radio audiences. In early 1999 Arbitron indicated that it planned to compete with Statistical Research Inc.'s RADAR report (discussed below) as a source for national ratings numbers.[41] Arbitron is proposing to offer more frequent reports and base its ratings on the 1.4 million diaries it collects each year versus the 12,000 interviews done by RADAR.

Arbitron also recently began measuring listenership to webcasts.[42] In December 1999 the company released the first-ever rating data for webcasts of radio stations in its new monthly *InfoStream* report. This report provides monthly cume ratings and "time spent tuning" for 236 radio stations that are streaming their signals on the Web. Arbitron's research has found that 30 percent of online users have listened to Internet radio stations and the number continues to grow. This will make the measurement of radio listening over the Internet a very important area in the future.

RADAR Another rating service is Statistical Research Inc.'s RADAR (Radio's All-Dimension Audience Research) studies, which are sponsored by the major radio networks. Audience estimates are collected twice a year on the basis of 12,000 daily telephone interviews covering seven days of radio listening behavior. Each listener is called daily for a week and asked about radio usage from the day before until that moment. RADAR provides network audience measures, along with estimates of audience size for all stations and various segments. The audience estimates are time-period measurements for the various dayparts. RADAR also provides estimates of network audiences for all commercials and commercials within various programs. The research is conducted year-round and is published annually in *Radio Usage and Network Radio Audiences.*

As with TV, media planners must use the audience measurement information to evaluate the value of various radio stations in reaching the advertiser's target audience and their relative cost. The media buyer responsible for the purchase of radio time works with information on target audience coverage, rates, time schedules, and availability to optimize the advertiser's radio media budget.

Target Audience, Persons 18–49												
	Monday–Friday 3–7 P.M.				Monday–Friday 7 P.M. –Mid				Weekend 10 A.M. –7 P.M.			
	AQH (00)	CUME (00)	AQH RTG	AQH SHR	AQH (00)	CUME (00)	AQH RTG	AQH SHR	AQH (00)	CUME (00)	AQH RTG	AQH SHR
KCBQ												
METRO	36	340	.3	1.4	6	138		.5	51	356	.4	2.4
TSA	36	340			6	138			51	356		
KCBQ-FM												
METRO	83	736	.6	3.2	23	354	.2	2.1	67	616	.5	3.2
TSA	83	736			23	354			67	616		
KCEO												
METRO	10	95	.1	.4		8			1	8		
TSA	10	95				8			1	8		
KFMB												
METRO	141	1092	1.0	5.4	87	827	.6	7.9	92	567	.7	4.4
TSA	141	1092			87	827			92	567		

Summary

Television and radio, or the broadcast media, are the most pervasive media in most consumers' daily lives and offer advertisers the opportunity to reach vast audiences. Both broadcast media are time rather than space oriented and organized similarly in that they use a system of affiliated stations belonging to a network, as well as individual stations, to broadcast their programs and commercial messages. Advertising on radio or TV can be done on national or regional network programs or purchased in spots from local stations.

TV has grown faster than any other advertising medium in history and has become the leading medium for national advertisers. No other medium offers its creative capabilities; the combination of sight, sound, and movement give the advertiser a vast number of options for presenting a commercial message with high impact. Television also offers advertisers mass coverage at a low relative cost. Variations in programming and audience composition, along with the growth of cable, are helping TV offer more audience selectivity to advertisers. While television is often viewed as the ultimate advertising medium, it has several limitations, including the high cost of producing and airing commercials, a lack of selectivity relative to other media, the fleeting nature of the message, and the problem of commercial clutter. The latter two problems have been compounded in recent years by the trend toward shorter commercials.

Information regarding the size and composition of national and local TV audiences is provided by the A. C. Nielsen Co. The amount of money networks or stations can charge for commercial time on their programs is based on its audience measurement figures. This information is also important to media planners, as it is used to determine the combination of shows needed to attain specific levels of reach and frequency with the advertiser's target market.

Future trends in television include the continued growth of cable, competition to local cable operators from direct broadcast satellite systems, and a resulting increase in channels available to television households. Changes are also likely to occur in the measurement of viewing audiences—for example, continuous measurement of audiences.

The role of radio as an entertainment and advertising medium has changed with the rapid growth of television. Radio has evolved into a primarily local advertising medium that offers highly specialized programming appealing to narrow segments of the market. Radio offers advertisers the opportunity to build high reach and frequency into their media schedules and to reach selective audiences at a very efficient cost. It also offers opportunities for integrated marketing programs such as place-based promotions and event sponsorships.

The major drawback of radio is its creative limitations owing to the absence of a visual image. The short and fleeting nature of the radio commercial, the highly fragmented nature of the radio audience, and clutter are also problems.

As with TV, the rate structure for radio advertising time varies with the size of the audience delivered. The primary sources of information are Arbitron for local radio audiences and RADAR studies for network audiences.

Key Terms

split-30s, 360
zipping, 361
zapping, 361
television network, 363
affiliates, 363
up-front market, 364
scatter market, 365
spot advertising, 365
national spot advertising, 365
local advertising, 365
station reps, 366
syndicated programs, 366
sponsorship, 368
participations, 368
adjacencies, 369
dayparts, 369
cable television, 369
superstations, 370
interconnects, 370
narrowcasting, 373
infomercials, 373
multiplexing, 375
direct broadcast satellite (DBS) services, 375
television households, 376
program rating, 376
ratings point, 378
households using television (HUT), 378
share of audience, 378
total audience, 378
audimeter, 379
people meter, 379
designated market areas (DMAs), 379
sweeps, 380
image transfer, 385
average quarter-hour (AQH) figure, 390
cume, 390
average quarter-hour rating, 390
average quarter-hour share, 390

Discussion Questions

1. The opening vignette discusses the tremendous popularity of the ABC television game show "Who Wants to Be a Millionaire." Why do you think this show has been so popular among TV viewers? Discuss the financial impact of the show's popularity for ABC.

2. Discuss the advantages of television as an advertising medium and the importance of these factors to major advertisers such as automobile companies or packaged goods marketers.

3. Television is often described as a mass medium that offers little selectivity to advertisers. Do you agree with this statement? What are some of the ways selectivity can be achieved through TV advertising?

4. IMC Perspective 11–1 discusses how many dot.com companies have been spending large amounts of money to advertise on recent Super Bowls. Do you think it makes sense for these Internet marketers to spend such large amounts of money to advertise on a single television event such as the Super Bowl? Defend your position.

5. Choose a particular television daypart other than prime time and analyze the products and services advertised during this period. Why do you think these companies have chosen to advertise during this daypart?

6. Discuss how technological developments are likely to affect the way viewers watch television in the near future. What are the implications for TV advertising?

7. Discuss the advantages and limitation of advertising on cable TV. Discuss how both large national advertisers and small local companies might use cable TV effectively in their media plans.

8. Discuss the methods used to measure network and local TV viewing audiences. Do you think the measurement methods used for each are producing reliable and valid estimates of the viewing audiences? How might they be improved?

9. What are the advantages and disadvantages of advertising on radio? What types of advertisers are most likely to use radio?

10. What is meant by imagery transfer in radio advertising? Find an example of a radio campaign that is using this concept and evaluate it.

11. Discuss some of the factors that media buyers should take into consideration when buying advertising time on radio.

Chapter Twelve

Evaluation of Print Media

Chapter Objectives

- To examine the structure of the magazine and newspaper industries and the role of each medium in the advertising program.
- To analyze the advantages and limitations of magazines and newspapers as advertising media.
- To examine the various types of magazines and newspapers and the value of each as an advertising medium.
- To discuss how advertising space is purchased in magazines and newspapers, how readership is measured, and how rates are determined.
- To consider future developments in magazines and newspapers and how these trends will influence their use as advertising media.

Fast Company—the New Model for Business Magazines

Thousands of new magazines have been introduced over the past decade, each with high hopes of attracting large numbers of readers and in turn attracting the ad revenue needed to survive and prosper. Many of these magazines failed to survive, and others are struggling to keep their circulation base and number of ad pages high enough to stay out of the red. However, those whose editorial platform appeals to the needs, interests, and lifestyles of certain groups are finding success. And one relatively new publication that is doing this particularly well is the new economy of works style magazine, *Fast Company.*

Fast Company was founded in 1993 by former *Harvard Business Review* editors Alan Webber and William Taylor. After raising money and developing a prototype, they shopped the concept around to a number of publishers and found financial backing from Mort Zuckerman and Fred Drasner, the publishers of *U.S. News & World Report.* The idea behind *Fast Company* was that it would be a different kind of business magazine, one that would give people the tools they need to succeed in today's world of work. While most business magazines are observational, *Fast Company* is about real people and real ideas that they can use. The idea of a "work style" magazine was based on the observation that in the 90s, work was more personal than ever before, and more professionals defined themselves through their work rather than through the company that employed them.

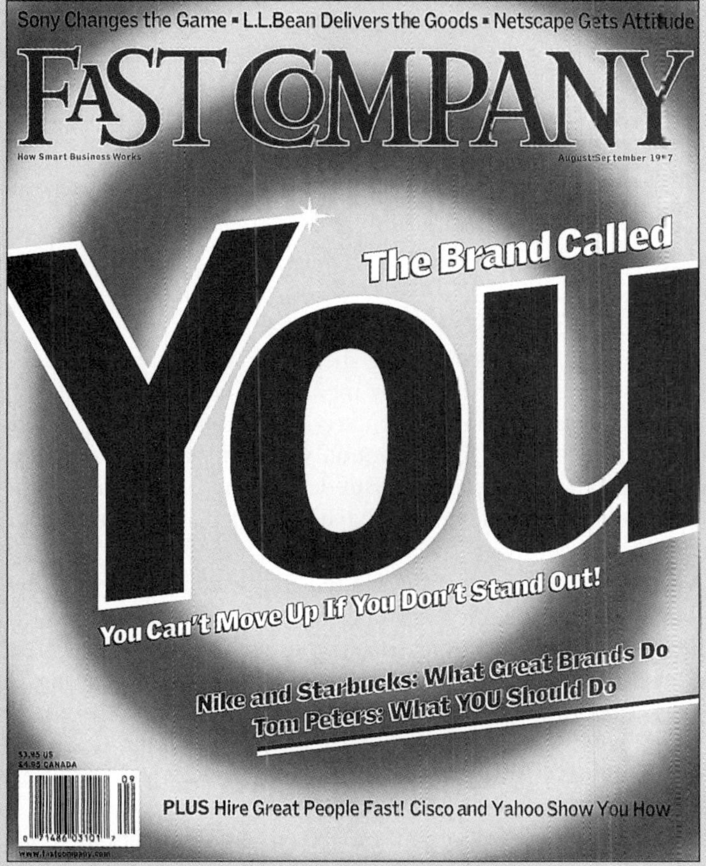

Fast Company debuted in November 1995, as the business world was shifting emphasis from top-down management to a bottom-up view of problem solving. The new magazine caught the wave of the new economy before it crested and has been riding it ever since. By being just slightly ahead, the magazine has named business trends as they surfaced. Ideas such as professionals charting their own careers and even opting for self-employment were chronicled in often-quoted cover stories "Free Agent Nation" and "The Brand Called You." The theme of one issue was "I Gotta Get a Life" and discussed emotions and values and drove the point home with an article called "Work Is Crazy—Get Sane!" In the new world order, where e-mail and voicemail blur the lines between work and home, where conventional management rules no longer apply, *Fast Company* provides its readers with a resource, a lifeline of sorts. William Taylor notes, "People come to us not only to learn about what's going on today, but what could be going on tomorrow. They want us to help them set some goals and paint a picture of what business could be like if we all made it that way."

One of the reasons for the success of *Fast Company* is the passion it evokes from readers. It is one of the few magazines that stirs its readers into a cult-like frenzy. It has fan clubs, first organized by individual readers, dubbed "Company of Friends," that meet in some 115 locations worldwide to exchange management and career advice and to discuss personal fulfillment issues. About 25,000 *Fast Company* readers have signed on to the Company of Friends website, creating a worldwide network that runs from New Zealand to Boston. As its founding editors are quick to note, *Fast Company* is as much a movement as it is a magazine. What *Martha Stewart Living* is to homebodies, *Fast Company* is to the average Dilbert. Alan Webber says, "We understood when we created this magazine there was a community of people that needed to be introduced to each other. We gave them a badge of belonging, an identifier."

Workers are not the only ones embracing *Fast Company;* advertisers recognize that the magazine is an excellent way to reach the new breed of professionals who are more likely to wear blue jeans than pin stripes. A diverse group of advertisers such as Saturn, Donna Karan, American Express, BMW, Volkswagen, and other companies show up regularly in *Fast Company's* pages. The magazine's total number of advertising pages has been increasing at nearly 50 percent a year as advertisers recognize that it is an excellent vehicle for reaching both men and women who are in the prime of their working careers and have a great deal of discretionary income.

Fast Company has fast-tracked its way to success even more quickly than most of the business professionals who read it. Since being launched as a bimonthly with a circulation of 100,000, it is now published 12 times a year and its paid circulation is expected to reach over half a million by the end of 2000. The magazine has already exceeded its business plan and has won numerous design awards. In 1996, it was selected as *Adweek*'s "Startup of the Year" and *Advertising Age's* "Launch of the Year." *Fast Company* was named "Magazine of the Year" by *Advertising Age* in 1999 and also was awarded an Ellie for general excellence by the National Magazine Awards. In 2000 Allan Webber and Bill Taylor were named "Editor of The Year" by *Mediaweek* magazine. It appears that *Fast Company* has fashioned a new model for business magazines that sets it apart from the rest of the pack.

Sources: Kitty Bowe Hearty, "The A-Ha! Moment," *Adweek,* March 6, 2000, pp. M56-M60; Lisa Granatstein, "In the 'Company' of Ellie," *Mediaweek,* May 3, 1999, pp. 14–15; Ann Marie Kerwin, "Magazine of the Year," *Advertising Age,* March 8, 1999, pp. S1, 18.

Magazines and newspapers have been advertising media for more than two centuries; for many years, they were the only major media available to advertisers. With the growth of the broadcast media, particularly television, reading habits declined. More consumers turned to TV viewing not only as their primary source of entertainment but also for news and information. But despite the competition from the broadcast media, newspapers and magazines have remained important media vehicles to both consumers and advertisers.

Thousands of magazines are published in the United States and throughout the world. They appeal to nearly every specific consumer interest and lifestyle, as well as to thousands of businesses and occupations. By becoming a highly specialized medium that reaches specific target audiences, the magazine industry has prospered. Newspapers are still the primary advertising medium in terms of both ad revenue and number of advertisers. Newspapers are particularly important as a local advertising medium for hundreds of thousands of retail businesses and are often used by large national advertisers as well.

Magazines and newspapers are an important part of our lives. For many consumers, newspapers are their primary source of product information. They would not think of going shopping without checking to see who is having a sale or clipping coupons from the weekly food section or Sunday inserts. Many people read a number of different magazines each week or month to become better informed or simply entertained. Individuals employed in various occupations rely on business magazines to keep them current about trends and developments in their industries as well as in business in general.

While most of us are very involved with the print media, it is important to keep in mind that few newspapers or magazines could survive without the support of advertising revenue. Consumer magazines generate an average of 47 percent of their revenues from advertising; business publications receive nearly 73 percent. Newspapers generate 70 percent of their total revenue from advertising. In many cities, the number of daily newspapers has declined because they could not attract enough advertising revenue to support their operations. The print media must be able to attract large numbers of readers or a very specialized audience to be of interest to advertisers.

The Role of Magazines and Newspapers

The role of magazines and newspapers in the advertiser's media plan differs from that of the broadcast media because they allow the presentation of detailed information that can be processed at the reader's own pace. The print media are not intrusive like radio and TV, and they generally require some effort on the part of the reader for the advertising message to have an impact. For this reason, newspapers and magazines are often referred to as *high-involvement media*.[1] Over 80 percent of U.S. households subscribe to or purchase magazines, while the average household buys six different magazines each year.[2]

Newspapers are received in nearly two-thirds of American households daily. Most magazines, however, reach a very selective audience. Like radio, they can be valuable in reaching specific types of consumers and market segments. While both magazines and newspapers are print media, the advantages and disadvantages of the two are quite different, as are the types of advertising each attracts. This chapter focuses on these two major forms of print media. It examines the specific advantages and limitations of each, along with factors that are important in determining when and how to use newspapers and magazines in the media plan.

Magazines

Over the past several decades, magazines have grown rapidly to serve the educational, informational, and entertainment needs of a wide range of readers in both the consumer and business markets. Magazines are the most specialized of all advertising media. While some magazines—such as *Reader's Digest, Time,* and *TV Guide*—are general mass-appeal publications, most are targeted to a very specific audience. There is a magazine designed to appeal to nearly every type of consumer in terms of demographics, lifestyle, activities, interests, or fascination. Numerous magazines are targeted toward specific businesses and industries as well as toward individuals engaged in various professions (Exhibit 12–1).

The wide variety makes magazines an appealing medium to a vast number of advertisers. Although TV accounts for the largest dollar amount of advertising expenditures among national advertisers, more companies advertise in magazines than in any other medium. Users of magazines range from large consumer products companies such as Procter & Gamble and General Motors, which spend over $400 million a year on magazine advertising, to a small company advertising scuba equipment in *Skin Diver* magazine.

Classifications of Magazines

To gain some perspective on the various types of magazines available and the advertisers that use them, consider the way magazines are generally classified. Standard Rate and Data Service (SRDS), the primary reference source on periodicals for media planners, divides magazines into three broad categories based on the audience to which

Exhibit 12–1 Magazines targeted to a specific industry or profession

they are directed: consumer, farm, and business publications. Each category is then further classified according to the magazine's editorial content and audience appeal.

Consumer Magazines Consumer magazines are bought by the general public for information and/or entertainment. SRDS divides 2,700 domestic consumer magazines into 51 classifications, among them general interest, sports, travel, and women's. Another way of classifying consumer magazines is by distribution: They can be sold through subscription or circulation, store distribution, or both. *Time* and *Newsweek* are sold both through subscription and in stores; *Woman's World* is sold only through stores. *People* magazine was originally sold only through stores but then added subscription sales as it gained in popularity. Figure 12–1 shows the top 10 magazines in terms of subscriptions and single-copy sales, respectively. Magazines can also be classified by frequency; weekly, monthly, and bimonthly are the most common.

Figure 12–1 Top magazines by subscriptions and single-copy sales

By Subscriptions		By Single-Copy Sales	
1. *Reader's Digest*	11,840,910	1. *Cosmopolitan*	2,003,438
2. *TV Guide*	9,234,198	2. *TV Guide*	1,881,982
3. *National Geographic*	8,227,858	3. *Family Circle*	1,847,557
4. *Better Homes & Gardens*	7,220,023	4. *National Enquirer*	1,786,241
5. *Ladies' Home Journal*	4,088,789	5. *Woman's Day*	1,744,625
6. *Time*	3,890,058	6. *Star*	1,518,077
7. *McCall's*	3,744,988	7. *People*	1,437,037
8. *Good Housekeeping*	3,378,069	8. *First For Women*	1,339,222
9. *Home & Away*	3,236,821	9. *Good Housekeeping*	1,171,906
10. *Sports Illustrated*	3,161,821	10. *Glamour*	1,139,418

Note: Figures are for six months ended December 31, 1999.

Consumer magazines represent the major portion of the magazine industry, accounting for nearly two-thirds of all advertising dollars spent in magazines. The distribution of advertising revenue in consumer magazines is highly concentrated; the top 25 magazines receive more than 70 percent of total consumer magazine advertising. Consumer magazines are best suited to marketers interested in reaching general consumers of products and services as well as to companies trying to reach a specific target market. The most frequently advertised categories in consumer magazines are automotive, direct response, toiletries and cosmetics, computers, office equipment and stationery, and business and consumer services. Marketers of tobacco products spend much of their media budget in magazines, since they are prohibited from advertising in the broadcast media.

While large national advertisers tend to dominate consumer magazine advertising in terms of expenditures, the more than 2,000 consumer magazines are also important to smaller companies selling products that appeal to specialized markets. Special-interest magazines assemble consumers with similar lifestyles or interests and offer marketers an efficient way to reach these people with little wasted coverage or circulation. For example, a manufacturer of ski equipment such as Nordica, Rossignol, or Salomon might find *Powder* the best vehicle for advertising to serious skiers.

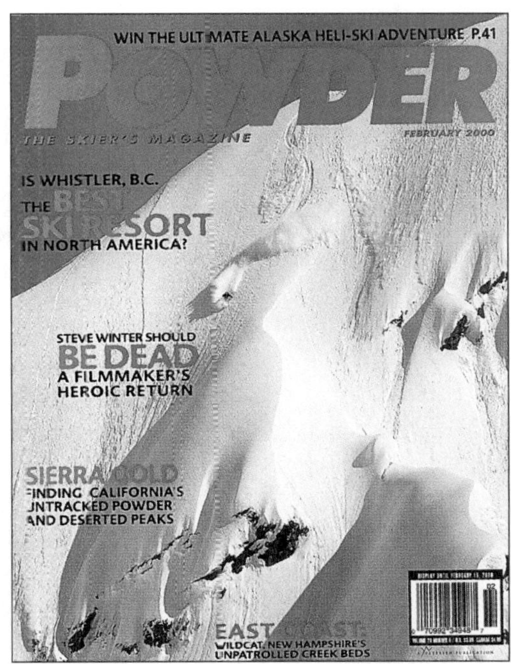

Exhibit 12–2 *Powder* magazine is an excellent medium for reaching the serious skier

Not only are these specialty magazines of value to firms interested in reaching a specific market segment, but their editorial content often creates a very favorable advertising environment for relevant products and services. For example, avid skiers cannot wait for the first snowfall after reading the season's first issues of *Powder* or *Skiing* magazine and may be quite receptive to the ads they carry for skiing products and destination ski resorts (Exhibit 12–2).

Farm Publications

The second major SRDS category consists of all the magazines directed to farmers and their families. About 300 publications are tailored to nearly every possible type of farming or agricultural interest. Standard Rate and Data Service breaks farm publications into 11 classifications, ranging from general-interest magazines aimed at all types of farmers (e.g., *Farm Journal, Successful Farming, Progressive Farmer*) to those in specialized agricultural areas such as poultry (*Gobbles*), hog farming (*National Hog Farmer*), or cattle raising (*Beef*—see Exhibit 12–3). A number of farm publications are directed at farmers in specific states or regions, such as *Nebraska Farmer* or *Montana Farmer Stockman.* Farm publications are not classified with business publications because historically farms were not perceived as businesses.

Exhibit 12–3 *Beef* magazine is read by many cattle ranchers

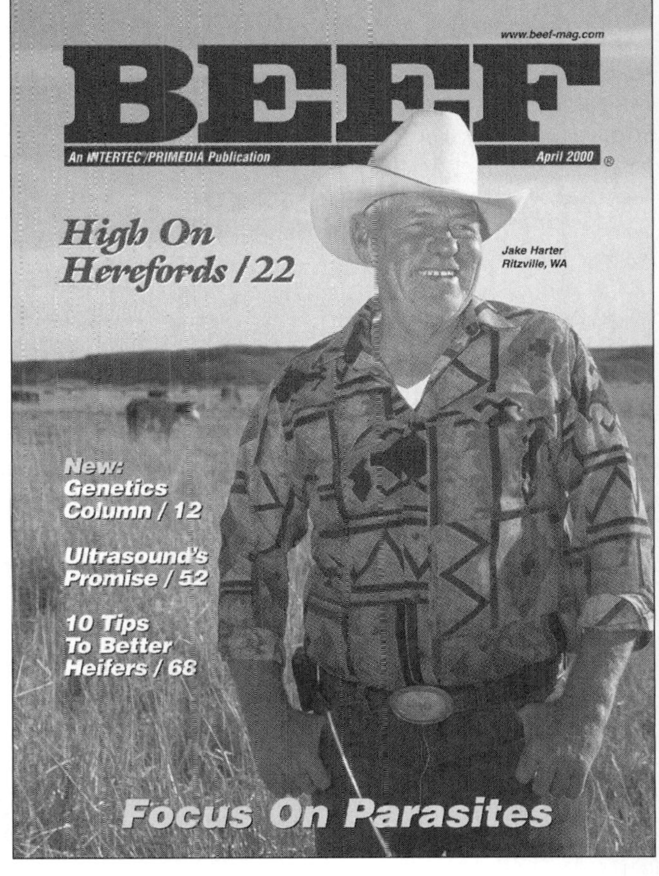

Business Publications

Business publications are those magazines or trade journals published for specific businesses, industries, or occupations. Standard Rate and Data Service breaks down over 7,500 U.S. magazines and trade journals into 186 categories. The major categories include

1. Magazines directed at specific professional groups, such as *National Law Review* for lawyers and *Architectural Forum* for architects.
2. Industrial magazines directed at businesspeople in various manufacturing and production industries—for example, *Iron Age, Chemical Week,* and *Industrial Engineering.*

3. Trade magazines targeted to wholesalers, dealers, distributors, and retailers, among them *Progressive Grocer, Drug Store News, Women's Wear Daily,* and *Restaurant Business.*
4. General business magazines aimed at executives in all areas of business, such as *Forbes, Fortune,* and *Business Week.* (General business publications are also included in SRDS's consumer publications edition.)

The numerous business publications reach specific types of professional people with particular interests and give them important information relevant to their industry, occupation, and/or careers. Business publications are important to advertisers because they provide an efficient way of reaching the specific types of individuals who constitute their target market. Much marketing occurs at the trade and business-to-business level, where one company sells its products or services directly to another.

Advantages of Magazines

Magazines have a number of characteristics that make them attractive as an advertising medium. Strengths of magazines include their selectivity, excellent reproduction quality, creative flexibility, permanence, prestige, readers' high receptivity and involvement, and services they offer to advertisers.

Selectivity

One of the main advantages of using magazines as an advertising medium is their **selectivity,** or ability to reach a specific target audience. Magazines are the most selective of all media except direct mail. Most magazines are published for special-interest groups. The thousands of magazines published in the United States reach all types of consumers and businesses and allow advertisers to target their advertising to segments of the population who buy their products. For example, *Modern Photography* is targeted toward camera buffs, *Stereo Review* reaches those with an avid interest in music, and *Ebony* focuses on the upscale African-American market. Many new magazines are introduced each year targeting new interests and trends. According to Samir Husni, who has been tracking magazine launches since 1985, the category with the greatest number of new magazines during the past 15 years is sports.[3] Nearly 1,000 new titles have been introduced into the crowded sports magazine field, with many of these launches occurring in recent years. Many of the new magazines are targeted at nontraditional sports, such as skateboarding, snowboarding, wrestling, and weight lifting. For example, *Muscle & Fitness Hers* is a new magazine that targets women who are into serious fitness training and weight lifting (Exhibit 12–4). Weider Publications launched the magazine in response to the dramatic increase in strength training by women during the 1990s.[4]

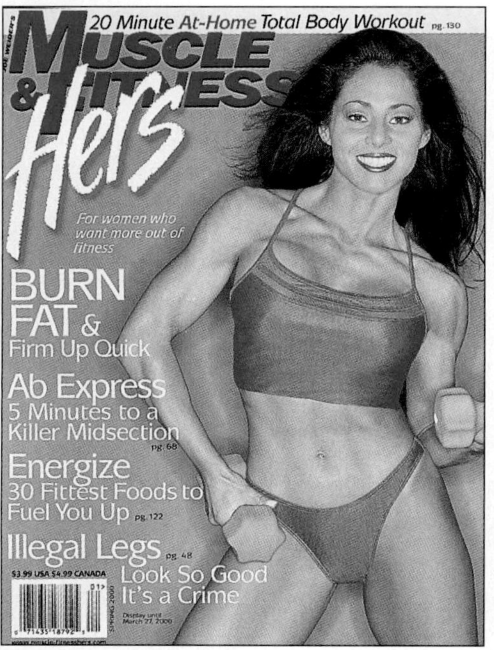

Exhibit 12–4 *Muscle & Fitness Hers* is one of the many magazines launched in the sports category in recent years

In addition to providing selectivity based on interests, magazines can provide advertisers with high demographic and geographic selectivity. *Demographic selectivity,* or the ability to reach specific demographic groups, is available in two ways. First, most magazines are, as a result of editorial content, aimed at fairly well-defined demographic segments. *Ladies' Home Journal, Ms., Self,* and *Cosmopolitan* are read predominantly by women; *Esquire, Playboy,* and *Sports Illustrated* are read mostly by men. Older consumers can be reached through publications like *Modern Maturity.* IMC Perspective 12–1 discusses how publishers have been introducing new magazines targeted at teens in an effort to reach this elusive, but important, market segment.

A second way magazines offer demographic selectivity is through special editions. Even magazines that appeal to broader audiences, such as *Reader's Digest, Time,* or *Newsweek,* can provide a high degree of demographic selectivity through their special demographic editions. Most of the top consumer magazines publish different editions targeted at different demographic markets.

IMC Perspective 12–1

Magazine Publishers Seek the Most Elusive Readers of All—Teenagers

Teenagers are one of the fastest-growing market segments in America. There are nearly 31 million teen boys and girls in the United States, and according to Teenage Research Unlimited, a market research firm that specializes on teenagers, they either spend, or encourage their parents to spend, over $122 billion a year. While their numbers and purchasing power make teens a very attractive segment for marketers, they are also a difficult market to reach, particularly through magazines. Teenagers spend a lot more time listening to radio, watching TV, and surfing the Internet than reading magazines.

There are a number of magazines that have been targeting teenage girls for years. For example, *Seventeen* was first published in 1944 and has been helping teens grow up for 56 years. *Teen* magazine and *YM* have also been popular with young girls for decades. All three magazines have been experiencing strong growth recently, particularly in single-copy sales through newsstands. In fact, the entire teen publishing market has been growing fast over the past few years, and a number of new titles aimed at teenage girls have been introduced, such as *CosmoGirl.* However, the new title that is having the most impact on the teen magazine market is *Teen People,* a junior version of the popular *People* magazine that is published by Time, Inc.

Teen People was launched in 1997 and after only one year reached a circulation of over 1.2 million, prompting one circulation expert to note, "I've been in the business for 30 years, and I don't remember anything like *Teen People.*" Like its namesake older sibling, the magazine is heavy on celebrity fare. However, managing editor Christina Ferrari notes that the magazine also focuses on beauty, fashion, relationships, and serious issues such as drunk driving and drug abuse. One of the reasons for the magazine's success is that it stays on the cutting edge of what is important and relevant to teens. The magazine keeps a group of 4,000 teen trend-spotters on call, encouraging them to help hone story ideas and inviting them to regional sales offices for pizza and focus group discussions about what's cool and what's not. Sometimes the teens are given $100 and instructions to buy certain types of products and then explain their purchases. All this information is compiled carefully and presented to advertisers.

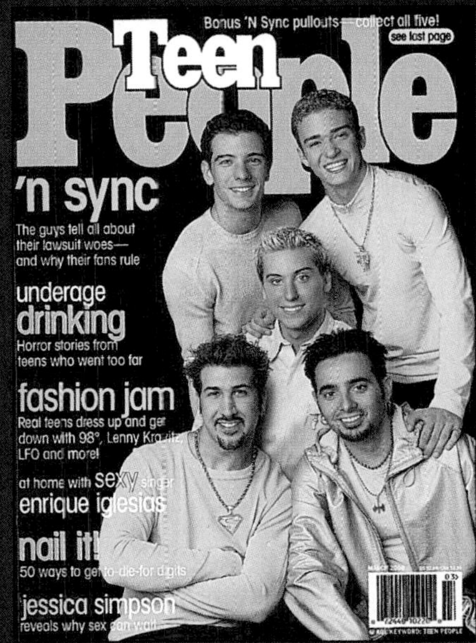

While *Teen People* manages to reach a dual sex audience, females account for nearly 80 percent of its readers; like other publications, it has found that teenage boys are the most elusive of all magazine readers. However, another publisher, Times Mirror Magazines, which publishes *Field & Stream* and *Popular Science,* believes it has found a formula to attract the elusive teenage male. The publisher's TransWorld Media division, which publishes niche magazines such as *Skateboarding, Snowboarding,* and *Surf,* recently introduced *TransWorld's Stance,* a lifestyle publication built around extreme sports. The general-interest magazine covers all parts of the extreme-sports culture—interests typically embraced by males between the ages of 14 and 21.

According to the CEO of TransWorld Media, the common denominators for teenage boys are videogames, music, shoes, girls, and cars. He notes, "The concept of *Stance* is to take the culture of male teens as we know it through our vertical titles and create a broad spectrum that cuts across sports." The new publication's editorial director says: "There is a whole sort of culture that exists in the youth sector that can be summed up as California extreme-sports guy meets New York street culture. That hasn't really been introduced into the mainstream. We think the time is right to do that."

The new magazine, which debuted in February 2000, features articles and product information on clothes, sneakers, videos, music, cars, computers, and sports equipment. It also profiles celebrities, especially those prominent in the extreme-sports world and, according to the editorial director, includes "some girls in there for the guys to look at." The magazine is published every other month and sold at newsstands as well as through TransWorld's network of music, skateboarding, surf, and snowboarding shops.

Marketers will be keeping a close watch on *Stance* and other new magazines that target the elusive teen market. *Teen People* has already proved that it can attract teen readers, particularly females, and advertisers have flocked to the magazine—it carried nearly a thousand pages of advertising in 1999. An advertising executive at Procter & Gamble notes: "Anything we can do to reach these consumers, we are going to do. And magazines targeted toward teens do a good job."

Sources: Ann Marie Kerwin, "Times Mirror Takes X-treme 'Stance,'" *Advertising Age,* November 8, 1999, p. 42; Wendy Bounds, "Teen-Magazine Boom: Beauty, Fashion, Stars and Sex," *The Wall Street Journal,* December 7, 1998, pp. B1, 4.

Geographic selectivity lets an advertiser focus ads in certain cities or regions. One way to achieve geographic selectivity is by using a magazine that is targeted toward a particular area. Magazines devoted to regional interests include *Yankee* (New England), *Southern Living* (South), *Sunset* (West), and *Texas Monthly* (guess where?), among many others. One of the more successful media developments of recent years has been the growth of city magazines in most major American cities. *Los Angeles Magazine, Philadelphia,* and *Denver,* to name a few, provide residents of these areas with articles concerning lifestyle, events, and the like, in these cities and their surrounding metropolitan areas (Exhibit 12–5).

Another way to achieve geographic selectivity in magazines is through purchasing ad space in specific geographic editions of national or regional magazines. A number of publications divide their circulation into groupings based on regions or major metropolitan areas and offer advertisers the option of concentrating their ads in these editions. For example, *Newsweek* breaks the United States into 11 geographic areas and offers regional editions for each, as shown in Exhibit 12–6. *Newsweek* also offers advertisers their choice of editions directed to the top 40, 20, or 10 metropolitan areas. Many magazines allow advertisers to combine regional or metropolitan editions to best match the geographic market of interest to them.

Standard Rate and Data Service lists over 350 consumer magazines offering geographic and/or demographic editions. Regional advertisers can purchase space in editions that reach only areas where they have distribution, yet still enjoy the

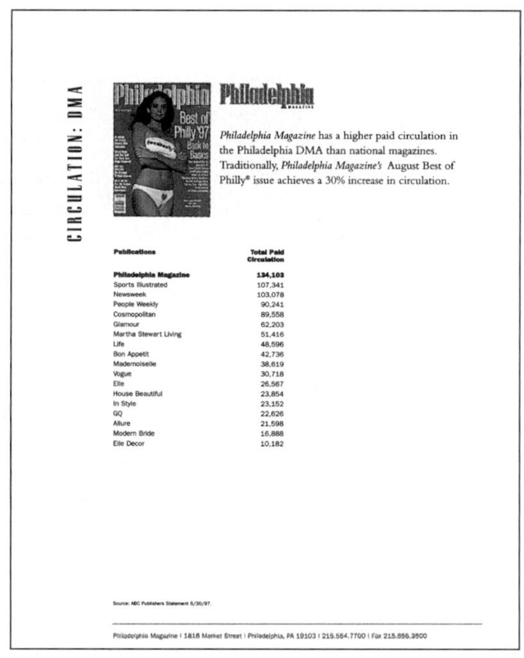

Philadelphia Magazine has a higher paid circulation in the Philadelphia DMA than national magazines. Traditionally, *Philadelphia Magazine's* August Best of Philly® issue achieves a 30% increase in circulation.

Publications	Total Paid Circulation
Philadelphia Magazine	**134,103**
Sports Illustrated	107,341
Newsweek	103,078
People Weekly	90,241
Cosmopolitan	89,558
Glamour	62,203
Martha Stewart Living	51,416
Life	48,596
Bon Appetit	42,736
Mademoiselle	38,619
Vogue	30,718
Elle	26,567
House Beautiful	23,854
In Style	23,152
GQ	22,626
Allure	21,598
Modern Bride	16,888
Elle Decor	10,182

Source: ABC Publishers Statement 6/30/97.

Philadelphia Magazine | 1818 Market Street | Philadelphia, PA 19103 | 215.564.7700 | Fax 215.656.3500

Exhibit 12–5 City magazines such as *Philadelphia* offer advertisers high geographic selectivity

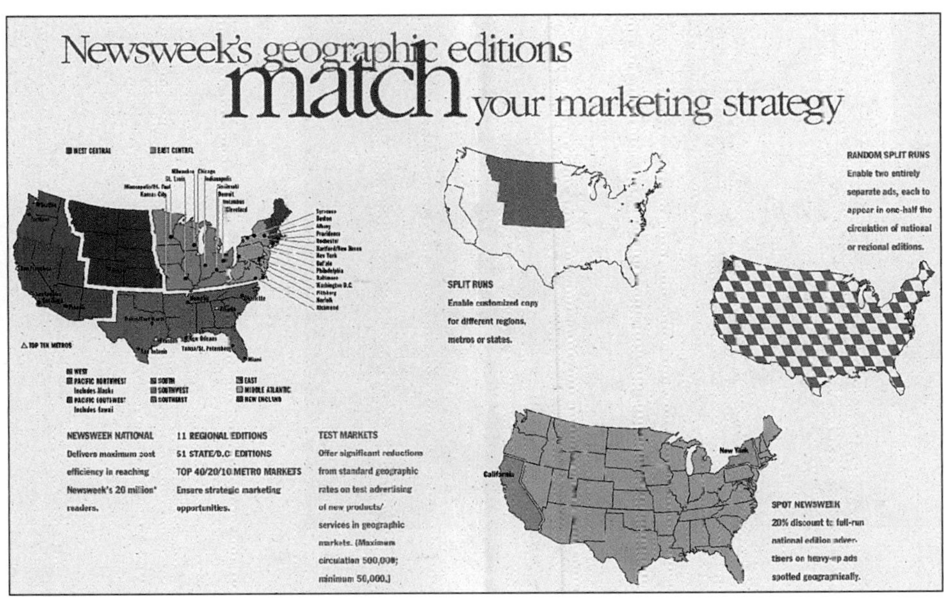

Exhibit 12–6 Geographic editions of *Newsweek* magazine

prestige of advertising in a major national magazine. National advertisers can use the geographic editions to focus their advertising on areas with the greatest potential or those needing more promotional support. They can also use regional editions to test-market products or alternative promotional campaigns in various regions of the country.

Ads in regional editions can also list the names of retailers or distributors in various markets, thus encouraging greater local support from the trade. The trend toward regional marketing is increasing the importance of having regional media available to marketers. The availability of regional and demographic editions can also reduce the cost per thousand for reaching desired audiences.

Reproduction Quality

One of the most valued attributes of magazine advertising is the reproduction quality of the ads. Magazines are generally printed on high-quality paper stock and use printing processes that provide excellent reproduction in black and white or color. Since magazines are a visual medium where illustrations are often a dominant part of an ad, this is a very important property. The reproduction quality of most magazines is far superior to that offered by the other major print medium of newspapers, particularly when color is needed. The use of color has become a virtual necessity in most product categories, and more than two-thirds of all magazine ads now use color.

Creative Flexibility

In addition to their excellent reproduction capabilities, magazines also offer advertisers a great deal of flexibility in terms of the type, size, and placement of the advertising material. Some magazines offer (often at extra charge) a variety of special options that can enhance the creative appeal of the ad and increase attention and readership. Examples include gatefolds, bleed pages, inserts, and creative space buys.

Gatefolds enable an advertiser to make a striking presentation by using a third page that folds out and gives the ad an extra-large spread. Gatefolds are often found at the inside cover of large consumer magazines or on some inside pages. Advertisers use gatefolds to make a very strong impression, especially on special occasions such as the introduction of a new product or brand. For example, automobile advertisers often use gatefolds to introduce new versions of their cars each model year. Not all magazines offer gatefolds, however, and they must be reserved well in advance and are sold at a premium.

Bleed pages are those where the advertisement extends all the way to the end of the page, with no margin of white space around the ad Bleeds give the ad an impression of being larger and make a more dramatic impact. Many magazines charge an extra 10 to 20 percent for bleeds.

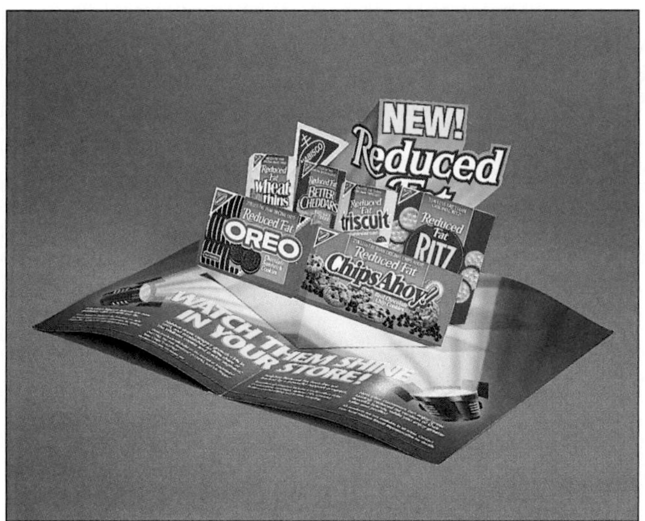

Exhibit 12–7 Nabisco used a pop-up ad to get the attention of trade magazine readers

In addition to gatefolds and bleed pages, creative options available through magazines include unusual page sizes and shapes. Some advertisers have grabbed readers' attention by developing three-dimensional pop-up ads that jump off the page. Exhibit 12–7 shows a pop-up ad that Nabisco used in several trade magazines to promote its Reduced Fat cracker and cookie products.

Various other *inserts* are used in many magazines. These include return cards, recipe booklets, coupons, records, and even product samples. Cosmetic companies use scratch-and-sniff inserts to introduce new fragrances, and some companies use them to promote deodorants, laundry detergents, or other products whose scent is important. Inserts are also used in conjunction with direct-response ads and as part of sales promotion strategies.

Scented ads, pop-ups, singing ads, and other techniques are ways to break through the clutter in magazines and capture consumers' attention. However, there recently has been some backlash against various types of *printaculars.* Critics argue that they alter the appearance and feel of a magazine and the reader's relationship to it. Advertisers do not want to run regular ads that have to compete against heavy inserts, pop-ups, talking ads, or other distractions. Some advertisers and agencies are even asking publishers to notify them when they plan to run any spectacular inserts so that they can decide whether to pull their regular ads from the issue.[5]

Creative space buys are another option of magazines. Some magazines let advertisers purchase space units in certain combinations to increase the impact of their media budget. For example, WD-40, an all-purpose lubrication product, uses half- or quarter-page ads on consecutive pages of several magazines, mentioning a different use for the product on each page, as shown in Exhibit 12–8. This strategy gives the company greater impact for its media dollars and is helpful in promoting the product's variety of uses.

Permanence

Another distinctive advantage offered by magazines is their long life span. TV and radio are characterized by fleeting messages that have a very short life span; newspapers are generally discarded soon after being read. Magazines, however, are generally read over several days and are often kept for reference. They are retained in the home longer than any other medium and are generally referred to on several occasions. A study of magazine audiences found that readers devote nearly an hour over a period of two or three days to reading an average magazine.[6] Studies have also found that nearly 75 percent of consumers retain magazines for future reference.[7] One benefit of the longer life of magazines is that reading occurs at a less hurried pace and there is more opportunity to examine ads in considerable detail. This means ads can use longer and more detailed copy, which can be very important for high-involvement and complex products or

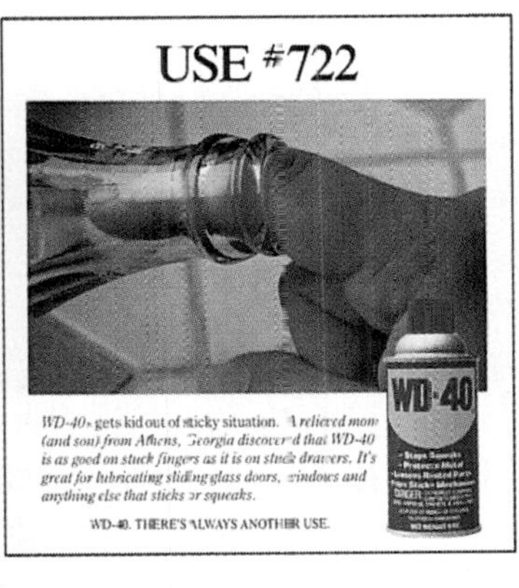

Exhibit 12–8 WD-40 uses quarter-page ads to get greater impact from its media budget

services. The permanence of magazines also means readers can be exposed to ads on multiple occasions and can pass magazines along to other readers.

Prestige Another positive feature of magazine advertising is the prestige the product or service may gain from advertising in publications with a favorable image. Companies whose products rely heavily on perceived quality, reputation, and/or image often buy space in prestigious publications with high-quality editorial content whose consumers have a high level of interest in the advertising pages. For example, *Esquire* and *GQ* cover men's fashions in a very favorable environment, and a clothing manufacturer may advertise its products in these magazines to enhance the prestige of its lines. *Architectural Digest* provides an impressive editorial environment that includes high-quality photography and artwork. The magazine's upscale readers are likely to have a favorable image of the publication that may transfer to the products advertised on its pages. *Good Housekeeping* provides a unique consumer's refund or replacement policy for products that bear the limited warranty seal or advertise in the magazine. This can increase a consumer's confidence in a particular brand and reduce the amount of perceived risk associated with a purchase.

While most media planners recognize that the environment created by a publication is important, it can be difficult to determine the image a magazine provides. Subjective estimates based on media planners' experience are often used to assess a magazine's prestige, as are objective measures such as reader opinion surveys.[8]

Consumer Receptivity and Involvement With the exception of newspapers, consumers are more receptive to advertising in magazines than in any other medium. Magazines are generally purchased because the information they contain interests the reader, and ads provide additional information that may be of value in making a purchase decision. The Study of Media Involvement conducted for the Magazine Publishers of America (MPA) found that magazines are the medium

Figure 12–2 Magazines are the premier source of consumer knowledge

The Study of Media Involvement, conducted by Beta Research, an independent research firm, reports that magazines are the medium turned to most by consumers for knowledge, information, and usable ideas. In fact, 95 percent of U.S. adults cite magazines as their premier source of insight and ideas. This is also true when consumers seek information about specific topics affecting their lives—ranging from automobiles to fashion to personal finance.

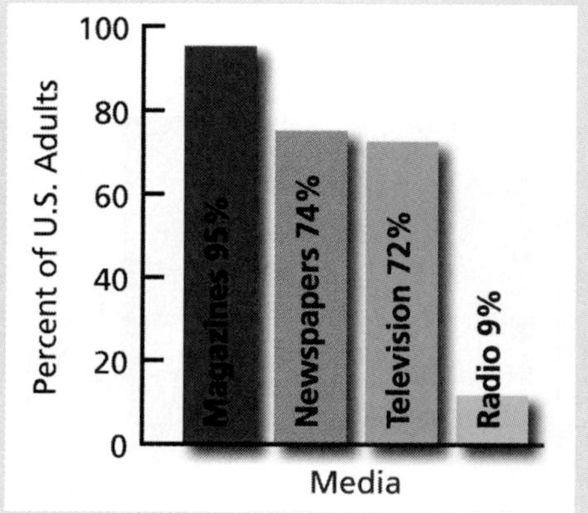

Note: Based on net of 12 measured product categories. Multiple responses.

	Percent of Adults Referring to:			
Area of Interest	Magazines	TV	Newspapers	Radio
Automobiles	39%	21%	29%	1%
Beauty and grooming	63	20	5	0
Clothing and fashion	58	18	15	0
Computers: hardware and software	54	14	11	0
Food	50	19	22	1
Fitness and exercise	49	36	6	1
Financial planning	45	11	31	2
Home repair/decorating	69	13	11	0
Sports: equipment/performance	49	24	7	1
Travel: personal and business	42	16	29	2

turned to most by consumers for knowledge, information, and usable ideas (see Figure 12–2). The study found that magazines are consumers' primary source of information for a variety of products and services, including automobiles, beauty and grooming, clothing and fashion, financial planning, and personal and business travel.[9] The MPA cites consumers' involvement with print ads as part of its "Magazines. Where Great Brands Begin" campaign that promotes the value of magazines in successful marketing programs and in brand building (Exhibit 12–9).

In addition to their relevance, magazine ads are likely to be received favorably by consumers because, unlike broadcast ads, they are nonintrusive and can easily be ignored. Studies show that the majority of magazine readers welcome ads; only a small percentage have negative attitudes toward magazine advertising.[10] Some magazines, such as bridal or fashion publications, are purchased as much for their advertising as for their editorial content. MPA-sponsored studies have shown that magazine readers are more likely to attend to and recall ads than are TV viewers.

Services A final advantage of magazines is the special services some publications offer advertisers. Some magazines have merchandising staffs that call on trade intermediaries like retailers to let them know a product is being advertised in their publication and to encourage them to display or promote the item. Another service offered by magazines (usually the larger ones) is research studies that they conduct on consumers. These studies may deal with general consumer trends, changing purchase patterns, and media usage or may be relevant to a specific product or industry.

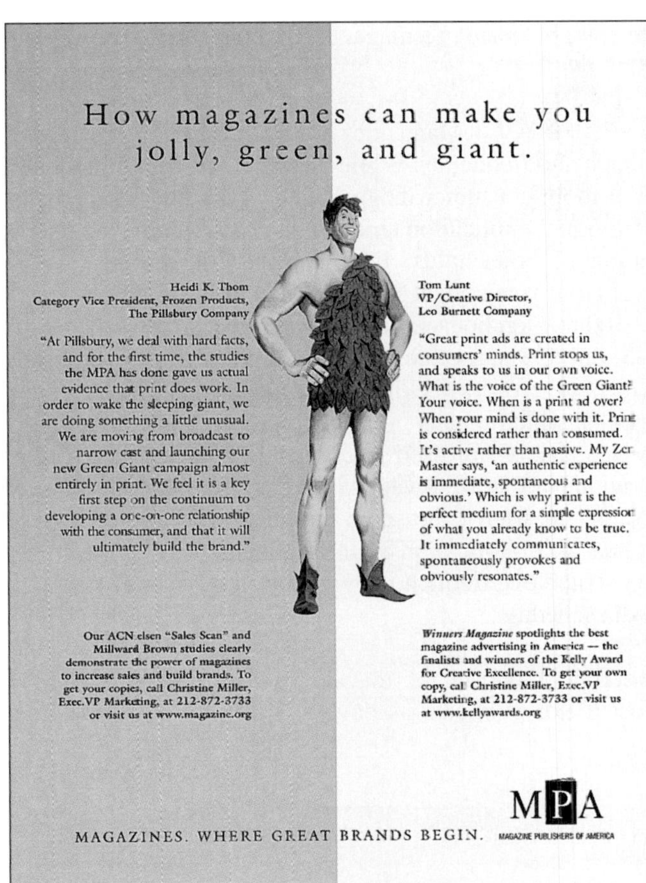

Exhibit 12–9 This ad is part of a campaign by the Magazine Publishers of America promoting the value of magazine advertising

An important service offered by some magazines is **split runs,** where two or more versions of an ad are printed in alternate copies of a particular issue of a magazine. This service is used to conduct a split-run test, which allows the advertiser to determine which ad generates the most responses or inquiries, providing some evidence as to their effectiveness.

Disadvantages of Magazines

Although the advantages offered by magazines are considerable, they have certain drawbacks too. These include the costs of advertising, their limited reach and frequency, the long lead time required in placing an ad, and the problem of clutter and heavy advertising competition.

Costs The costs of advertising in magazines vary according to the size of the audience they reach and their selectivity. Advertising in large mass-circulation magazines like *TV Guide, Time,* or *Reader's Digest* can be very expensive. For example, a full-page, four-color ad in *Time* magazine's national edition (circulation 4.1 million) cost $183,000 as of January 1, 2000. Popular positions such as the back cover cost even more. By contrast, a full-page, four-color ad in *Tennis* (circulation 707,884) cost $57,550.

Like any medium, magazines must be considered not only from an absolute cost perspective but also in terms of relative costs. Most magazines emphasize their effectiveness in reaching specific target audiences at a low cost per thousand. Also, an increasing number of magazines are offering demographic and geographic editions, which helps lower their costs. Media planners generally focus on the relative costs of a publication in reaching their target audience. However, they may recommend a magazine with a high cost per thousand because of its ability to reach a small, specialized market segment. Of course, advertisers with limited budgets will be interested in the absolute costs of space in a magazine and the costs of producing quality ads for these publications.

Limited Reach and Frequency

Magazines are generally not as effective as other media in offering reach and frequency. While nearly 90 percent of adults in the United States read one or more consumer magazines each month, the percentage of adults reading any individual publication tends to be much smaller, so magazines have a thin penetration of households. For example, *TV Guide* has the second-highest circulation of any magazine, at just over 11 million, but this represents only 11 percent of the 100 million households in the United States.

As shown in Figure 12–3, only 33 magazines had a paid circulation over 2 million at the end of 1999. Thus, advertisers seeking broad reach must make media buys in a number of magazines, which means more negotiations and transactions. For a broad reach strategy, magazines are used in conjunction with other media. Since most magazines are monthly or at best weekly publications, the opportunity for building frequency through the use of the same publication is limited. Using multiple ads in the same issue of a publication is an inefficient way to build frequency. Most advertisers try to achieve frequency by adding other magazines with similar audiences to the media schedule.

Long Lead Time

Another drawback of magazines is the long lead time needed to place an ad. Most major publications have a 30- to 90-day lead time,

Figure 12–3 Top 50 magazines in paid circulation

Rank	Publication	Circulation	Rank	Publication	Circulation
1.	*Reader's Digest*	12,556,410	26.	*YM*	2,262,532
2.	*TV Guide*	11,116,180	27.	*Redbook*	2,250,262
3.	*National Geographic Magazine*	8,514,274	28.	*Glamour*	2,200,304
4.	*Better Homes & Gardens*	7,611,023	29.	*U.S. News & World Report*	2,195,668
5.	*Family Circle*	5,002,875	30.	*National Enquirer*	2,136,539
6.	*Good Housekeeping*	4,549,975	31.	*'Teen*	2,126,567
7.	*Ladies' Home Journal*	4,525,455	32.	*AAA Going Places*	2,056,289
8.	*Woman's Day*	4,280,909	33.	*Smithsonian*	2,027,759
9.	*McCall's*	4,208,988	34.	*Money*	1,929,347
10.	*Time*	4,122,699	35.	*V.F.W. Magazine*	1,853,350
11.	*People*	3,543,856	36.	*Parents**	1,806,806
12.	*Sports Illustrated*	3,251,117	37.	*Field & Stream*	1,790,251
13.	*Home & Away*	3,236,821	38.	*Star*	1,752,557
14.	*Playboy*	3,151,512	39.	*Ebony*	1,720,378
15.	*Newsweek*	3,147,497	40.	*Country Living*	1,690,255
16.	*React*	3,140,366	41.	*Teen People*	1,665,974
17.	*Medizine**	3,091,219	42.	*Maxim*	1,663,686
18.	*The Cable Guide*	3,084,559	43.	*Life*	1,619,761
19.	*Prevention*	3,037,457	44.	*Men's Health*	1,606,221
20.	*Cosmopolitan*	2,854,511	45.	*Woman's World*	1,579,085
21.	*The American Legion Magazine*	2,658,561	46.	*Golf Digest*	1,559,853
22.	*Via Magazine*	2,568,006	47.	*First For Women*	1,557,717
23.	*Southern Living*	2,535,930	48.	*Popular Science*	1,552,076
24.	*Seventeen*	2,392,562	49.	*Shape*	1,519,787
25.	*Martha Stewart Living*	2,363,785	50.	*Entertainment Weekly*	1,464,345

Note: Figures are averages for six months ended December 31, 1999.

which means space must be purchased and the ad must be prepared well in advance of the actual publication date. No changes in the art or copy of the ad can be made after the closing date. This long lead time means magazine ads cannot be as timely as other media, such as radio or newspapers, in responding to current events or changing market conditions.

Clutter and Competition

While the problem of advertising clutter is generally discussed in reference to the broadcast media, magazines also have this drawback. The clutter problem for magazines is something of a paradox: The more successful a magazine becomes, the more advertising pages it attracts, and this leads to greater clutter. In fact, magazines generally gauge their success in terms of the number of advertising pages they sell.

Magazine publishers do attempt to control the clutter problem by maintaining a reasonable balance of editorial pages to advertising. According to the Magazine Publishers of America, the average consumer magazine contains 48 percent advertising and 52 percent editorial.[11] However, many magazines contain ads on more than half of their pages. This clutter makes it difficult for an advertiser to gain readers' attention and draw them into the ad. Thus, many print ads use strong visual images, catchy headlines, or some of the creative techniques discussed earlier to grab the interest of magazine readers. Some advertisers create their own custom magazines to sidestep the advertising clutter problem as well as to have control over editorial content. A number of companies have also been publishing their own magazines to build relationships with their customers. For example, Farmer's Insurance sends its customers a magazine called *The Friendly Review* that contains useful articles on a variety of topics. Federal Express publishes *Via FedEx,* a free magazine full of career and office management tips for some of its most important customers, professional secretaries.

A recent trend among some companies is to enter into joint agreement with traditional publishers to produce custom magazines that they sell to their customers. For example, Swedish retailer IKEA has partnered with John Brown Contract Publishing to custom-publish a magazine titled *space.*[12] *space* is both a showcase for IKEA merchandise and a magazine that contains informative articles about home furnishings, modern design, and lifestyle trends. *space* is sold at IKEA stores, and on newsstands, throughout North America. The custom-publishing division of Hachette Filapacchi publishes a magazine for Ray-Ban Sunglasses called *Sun* and one for Sony that doubles as a catalog called *Sony Style* (Exhibit 12–10). Custom-published magazines have also become very popular among tobacco companies, such as Philip Morris, which direct-mail them to their customer base.[13]

Clutter is not as serious an issue for the print media as for radio or TV, since consumers tend to be more receptive and tolerant of print advertising. They can also control their exposure to a magazine ad simply by turning the page.

Exhibit 12–10 *Sun* is a magazine custom-published for Ray-Ban

Magazine Circulation and Readership

Two of the most important considerations in deciding whether to use a magazine in the advertising media plan are the size and characteristics of the audience it reaches. Media buyers evaluate magazines on the basis of their ability to deliver the advertiser's message to as many people as possible in the target audience. To do this, they must consider the circulation of the publication as well as its total readership and match these figures against the audience they are attempting to reach.

Circulation

Circulation figures represent the number of individuals who receive a publication through either subscription or store purchase. The number of copies distributed to these original subscribers or purchasers is known as *primary circulation* and is the basis for the magazine's rate structure. Circulation fluctuates from issue to issue, particularly for magazines that rely heavily on retail or newsstand sales. Many publications base their rates on *guaranteed circulation* and give advertisers a rebate if the number of delivered magazines falls below the guarantee. To minimize rebating, most guaranteed circulation figures are conservative; that is, they are set safely below the average actual delivered circulation. Advertisers are not charged for any excess circulation.

Many publishers became unhappy with the guaranteed circulation concept, since it requires them to provide refunds if guarantees are not met but results in a bonus for advertisers when circulation exceeds the guarantee. Thus, many publications have gone to a circulation rate base system. Rates are based on a set average circulation that is nearly always below the actual circulation delivered by a given issue but carries no guarantee. However, circulation is unlikely to fall below the rate base, since this would reflect negatively on the publication and make it difficult to attract advertisers at prevailing rates.

Circulation Verification Given that circulation figures are the basis for a magazine's advertising rates and one of the primary considerations in selecting a publication, the credibility of circulation figures is important. Most major publications are audited by one of the circulation verification services. Consumer magazines and farm publications are audited by the Audit Bureau of Circulations (ABC), which was organized in 1914 and is sponsored by advertisers, agencies, and publishers. ABC collects and evaluates information regarding the subscriptions and sales of magazines and newspapers to verify their circulation figures. Only publications with 70 percent or more paid circulation (which means the purchaser paid at least half the magazine's established base price) are eligible for verification audits by ABC. Certain business publications are audited by the Business Publications Audit (BPA) of Circulation. Many of these are published on a **controlled-circulation basis,** meaning copies are sent (usually free) to individuals the publisher believes can influence the company's purchases.

Circulation verification services provide media planners with reliable figures regarding the size and distribution of a magazine's circulation that help them evaluate its worth as a media vehicle. The ABC statement also provides other important information. It shows how a magazine is distributed by state and size, as well as percentage of the circulation sold at less than full value and percentage arrears (how many subscriptions are being given away). Many advertisers believe that subscribers who pay for a magazine are more likely to read it than are those who get it at a discount or for free.

Media buyers are generally skeptical about publications whose circulation figures are not audited by one of the verification services, and some companies will not advertise in unaudited publications. Circulation data, along with the auditing source, are available from Standard Rate and Data Service or from the publication itself. Exhibit 12–11 shows a sample magazine publisher's statement, which is subject to audit by Audit Bureau of Circulations.

Readership and Total Audience Advertisers are often interested in the number of people a publication reaches as a result of secondary, or pass-along, readership. **Pass-along readership** can occur when the primary subscriber or purchaser gives a magazine to another person or when the publication is read in doctors' waiting rooms or beauty salons, on airplanes, and so forth.

Advertisers generally attach greater value to the primary in-home reader than the pass-along reader or out-of-home reader, as the former generally spends more time with the publication, picks it up more often, and receives greater satisfaction from it. Thus, this reader is more likely to be attentive and responsive to ads. However, the value of pass-along readers should not be discounted. They can greatly expand a magazine's readership. *People* magazine commissioned a media research study to determine that its out-of-home audience spends as much time reading the publication as do its primary in-home readers.

You can calculate the **total audience,** or **readership,** of a magazine by multiplying the readers per copy (the total number of primary and pass-along readers) by the circulation of an average issue. For example, a magazine that has a circulation of 1 million and 3.5 readers per copy has a total audience of 3.5 million. However, rate

Career Profile

Mary Beth Gaik

Sales Representative at *Newsweek* Magazine

I think I was destined for a career in media. As a high school student I was inspired by authors Carl Woodward and Bob Bernstein and by writing for the school paper. I chose journalism as a major at the University of Wisconsin–Madison where I focused on public relations classes, as helping companies communicate with the public appealed to me. In my senior year, I won an internship promoting films on campus for Columbia Pictures. A typical project meant hauling around a giant terrarium filled with Tootsie Rolls to promote *Tootsie* or filling the student union with two inches of sand in January to get students psyched about the movie *Spring Break.*

After college I headed for Hollywood where I thought I had found my dream career—motion picture publicity. It was a blast working on movies, meeting stars, and going to the Academy Awards, but eventually I tired of the egos and the subterfuge of the ruthless entertainment industry. I took a job in ad sales at *Daily Variety,* the major trade paper to the entertainment industry. Once I started selling advertising, I realized I had been selling something to someone ever since I was a little kid. Didn't I always sell more cookies than any other Girl Scout? Who always won the Polaroid camera in the church magazine fundraiser?

"The most exciting part of my job is creatively solving a client's marketing challenges."

Advertising sales is about providing information, solving problems, and creating a win-win situation for both the client and the publication. While selling national advertising is very strategic and sophisticated, it is still about selling. We often react negatively to the word "salesman," but everything we do requires some selling skills and ability. You will have to sell yourself to get into graduate school or get a job after graduation. Being a good salesperson requires an innate comfort level with pitching new business and hearing the word "no." If you find sales about as appealing as a tetanus shot, then go the client side. But if you do like selling, consider the benefits: great pay, flexible hours, tangible performance achievements, and power over your income.

Once I honed my sales skills, I wanted a more challenging position. After spending three months researching industries, I decided I wanted to stay in advertising sales, but at a major magazine. I chose *Newsweek* because of the quality of its journalism and its credibility. Selling adverting space for a large circulation magazine like *Newsweek* also meant calling on marketers with large advertising budgets, providing greater flexibility and more opportunities to be creative for the client.

National magazine publishing sales is not just about selling pages. Managing a major account like E-Toys or Paramount Home Video requires coming up with big ideas to extend the value of the client's advertising budget beyond their pages in the magazine. The most exciting part of my job is creatively solving a client's marketing challenges, which often results in selling more pages. When Suzuki was launching its new Grand Vitara midsize SUV, they needed to reach young, very active singles and couples. Research showed the target market for this vehicle ran marathons and competed in other outdoor activities. Suzuki asked for *Newsweek*'s help in promoting the vehicle immediately after its launch in one of the seven key markets they had identified. I worked with our marketing department and presented six different ideas to Suzuki. They were ecstatic over the opportunity to be the title sponsor of the Seattle Marathon. The big idea sold the program and *Newsweek* won the Suzuki business over many other worthy magazines.

I feel I am well suited for advertising sales on a national magazine because I love to win and this job constantly provides me the opportunities to do so. I work with advertisers in a variety of industries and each account provides a new opportunity to be inventive. And the perks are awesome! This past winter I took my best clients skiing in Aspen. I often dine at the finest restaurants in Los Angeles and have season tickets to the theater. And yes, that was me in the front row with my Apple Computer clients at the Beck concert!

Exhibit 12–11 Example of an Audit Bureau of Circulations publisher's statement

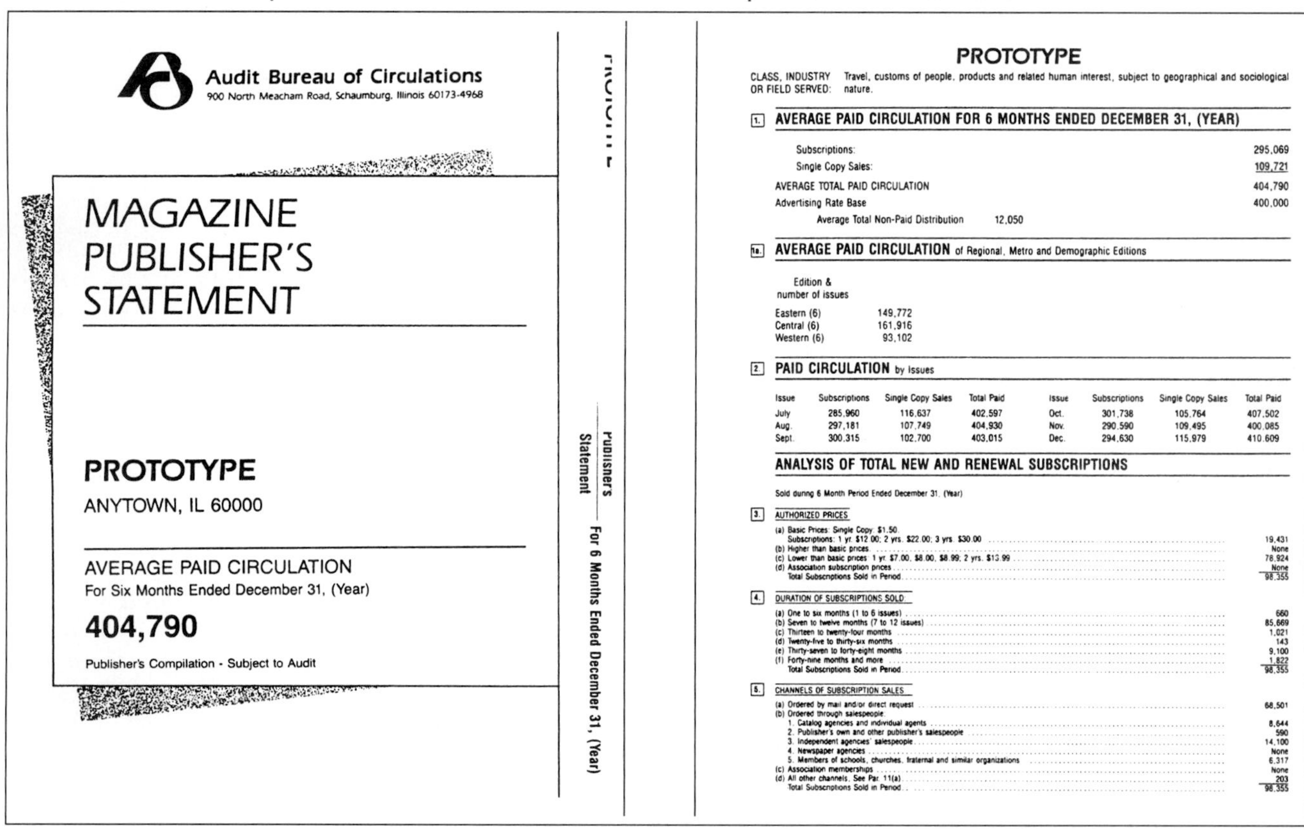

Audit Bureau of Circulations
900 North Meacham Road, Schaumburg, Illinois 60173-4968

MAGAZINE PUBLISHER'S STATEMENT

PROTOTYPE
ANYTOWN, IL 60000

AVERAGE PAID CIRCULATION
For Six Months Ended December 31, (Year)

404,790

Publisher's Compilation - Subject to Audit

Publisher's Statement — For 6 Months Ended December 31, (Year)

PROTOTYPE

CLASS, INDUSTRY OR FIELD SERVED: Travel, customs of people, products and related human interest, subject to geographical and sociological nature.

1. AVERAGE PAID CIRCULATION FOR 6 MONTHS ENDED DECEMBER 31, (YEAR)

Subscriptions:	295,069
Single Copy Sales:	109,721
AVERAGE TOTAL PAID CIRCULATION	404,790
Advertising Rate Base	400,000
Average Total Non-Paid Distribution 12,050	

1a. AVERAGE PAID CIRCULATION of Regional, Metro and Demographic Editions

Edition & number of issues	
Eastern (6)	149,772
Central (6)	161,916
Western (6)	93,102

2. PAID CIRCULATION by Issues

Issue	Subscriptions	Single Copy Sales	Total Paid	Issue	Subscriptions	Single Copy Sales	Total Paid
July	285,960	116,637	402,597	Oct.	301,738	105,764	407,502
Aug.	297,181	107,749	404,930	Nov.	290,590	109,495	400,085
Sept.	300,315	102,700	403,015	Dec.	294,630	115,979	410,609

ANALYSIS OF TOTAL NEW AND RENEWAL SUBSCRIPTIONS

Sold during 6 Month Period Ended December 31, (Year)

3. AUTHORIZED PRICES

(a) Basic Prices: Single Copy: $1.50. Subscriptions: 1 yr. $12.00; 2 yrs. $22.00; 3 yrs. $30.00	19,431
(b) Higher than basic prices	None
(c) Lower than basic prices: 1 yr. $7.00, $8.00, $8.99; 2 yrs. $13.99	78,924
(d) Association subscription prices	None
Total Subscriptions Sold in Period	98,355

4. DURATION OF SUBSCRIPTIONS SOLD:

(a) One to six months (1 to 6 issues)	660
(b) Seven to twelve months (7 to 12 issues)	85,669
(c) Thirteen to twenty-four months	1,021
(d) Twenty-five to thirty-six months	143
(e) Thirty-seven to forty-eight months	9,100
(f) Forty-nine months and more	1,822
Total Subscriptions Sold in Period	98,355

5. CHANNELS OF SUBSCRIPTION SALES

(a) Ordered by mail and/or direct request	68,501
(b) Ordered through salespeople:	
1. Catalog agencies and individual agents	8,644
2. Publisher's own and other publisher's salespeople	590
3. Independent agencies' salespeople	14,100
4. Newspaper agencies	None
5. Members of schools, churches, fraternal and similar organizations	6,317
(c) Association memberships	None
(d) All other channels, See Par. 11(a)	203
Total Subscriptions Sold in Period	98,355

structures are generally based on the more verifiable primary circulation figures, and many media planners devalue pass-along readers by as much as 50 percent. Total readership estimates are reported by major syndicated magazine research services (discussed next), but media buyers view these numbers with suspicion.

Audience Research for Magazines

While circulation and total audience size are important in selecting a media vehicle, the media planner is also interested in the match between the magazine's readers and the advertiser's target audience. Information on readers is available from several sources, including the publication's own research and syndicated studies. Most magazines provide media planners with reports detailing readers' demographics, financial profile, lifestyle, and product usage characteristics. The larger the publication, the more detailed and comprehensive the information it usually can supply about its readers. For example, Exhibit 12–12 shows information *Newsweek* provides to media buyers on readership of the magazine by upscale women.

Syndicated research studies are also available. For consumer magazines, primary sources of information are Simmons Market Research Bureau's *Study of Media and Markets* and the studies of Mediamark Research Inc. (MRI). These studies provide a broad range of information on the audiences of major national and regional magazines, including demographics, lifestyle characteristics, and product purchase and usage data. Most large ad agencies and media buying services also conduct ongoing research on the media habits of consumers. All this information helps determine the value of various magazines in reaching particular types of product users.

Audience information is generally more limited for business publications than for consumer magazines. The widely dispersed readership and nature of business publication readers make audience research more difficult. Media planners generally rely on information provided by the publication or by sources such as Standard Rate and Data Service. SRDS's Business Publication Advertising Source provides

WOMEN AUDIENCE

UPSCALE WOMEN ON THE RISE

CONTEMPORARY CAREER WOMEN

More women than ever before are building successful careers. They are essential breadwinners for their families...and they have become an increasingly important target for marketers of a wide range of consumer products and services.

UPWARDLY MOBILE

Why do professional/managerial women choose Newsweek over the traditional "women's" publications? Today, women's worlds encompass more than their homes, and Newsweek provides these upscale and educated women with the information they need to succeed in business and in life.

An Exclusive Audience

Percentage of Newsweek readers who do NOT read. .

Working Woman	91.3%
Vanity Fair	90.4
Redbook	80.7
Elle	94.7
McCall's	79.1
Ladies' Home Journal	76.0

Base: Professional/Managerial Women

PURCHASING POWER PLUS

Newsweek enables you to target your message to more women with more spending power than those reached in traditional women's magazines and the business books.

Women, Individual Employment Income $50,000+
(Population = 4,786,000)

	Audience	%Cov.
Newsweek	867,000	18.1
Ladies' Home Journal	588,000	12.3
McCall's	448,000	9.4
Redbook	397,000	8.3
Vanity Fair	367,000	7.7
Fortune	367,000	7.7
Wrkg Woman*	303,000	6.3
Bus. Week	300,000	6.3
Forbes*	273,000	5.7
Elle*	240,000	5.0

Source: 1998 Fall MRI
**Projections relatively unstable*

Newsweek

Exhibit 12–12 *Newsweek* provides media buyers with information on readership of the magazine by upscale women

the titles of individuals who receive the publication and the type of industry in which they work. This information can be of value in understanding the audiences reached by various business magazines.

Purchasing Magazine Advertising Space

Cost Elements Magazine rates are primarily a function of circulation. Other variables include the size of the ad, its position in the publication, the particular editions (geographic, demographic) chosen, any special mechanical or production requirements, and the number and frequency of insertions.

Advertising space is generally sold on the basis of space units such as full page, half page, and quarter page, although some publications quote rates on the basis of column inches. The larger the ad, the greater the cost. However, many advertisers use full-page ads since they result in more attention and readership. Studies have found that full-page ads generated 36 percent more readership than half-page ads.[14]

Ads can be produced or run using black and white, black and white plus one color, or four colors. The more color used in the ad, the greater the expense because of the increased printing costs. On average, a four-color ad costs 30 percent more than a black-and-white ad. Advertisers generally prefer color ads because they have greater visual impact and are superior for attracting and holding attention.[15] Starch INRA Hooper, Inc., analyzed the effect of various factors on the readership of magazine ads. The "noted" scores (the percentage of readers who remember seeing the ad in a publication they read) are 45 percent higher for a four-color full-page ad than for a black-and-white ad. A four-color spread (two facing pages) outperforms a black-and-white spread by 53 percent.[16] Ads requiring special mechanical production such as bleed pages or inserts may also cost extra.

Rates for magazine ad space can also vary according to the number of times an ad runs and the amount of money spent during a specific period. The more often an advertiser contracts to run an ad, the lower are the space charges. Volume discounts are based on the total space purchased within a contract year, measured in dollars.

Exhibit 12–13 Advertisers can reach alumni of Dartmouth and other Ivy schools through the Ivy League Network

Advertisers can also save money by purchasing advertising in magazine combinations, or networks.

Magazine networks offer the advertiser the opportunity to buy space in a group of publications as a package deal. The publisher usually has a variety of magazines that reach audiences with similar characteristics. Networks can also be publishers of a group of magazines with diversified audiences or independent networks that sell space in groups of magazines published by different companies. For example, the News Network sells space in a group of news-oriented publications such as *Time, Newsweek,* and *U.S. News & World Report.* The Ivy League Network is a consortium of alumni magazines of Ivy League schools and one non-Ivy, Stanford University. Advertisers can purchase ad space and reach the well-educated, affluent alumni of all eight schools with one media purchase through the network (Exhibit 12–13).

The Future for Magazines

The magazine industry has experienced strong growth over the past several years, and magazine advertising revenue and total ad pages reached record levels in 1999.[17] A strong economy led to significant gains in most of the major advertising categories, with increases in automotive advertising leading the way. Like other major media, the magazine industry is benefiting from the boom in advertising by Internet companies as the dot-coms have become a major source of ad revenue for both consumer and business publications.[18]

While advertising revenue for magazines has been experiencing strong growth, there are still some major issues facing the industry. The cost of paper and ink continues to rise, and the industry is facing the possibility of a 15 percent increase in second-class postage rates in 2001, which would have a dramatic impact on publishers' cost structure.[19] And while magazine advertising revenue has been increasing, publishers' second revenue stream, circulation, has been declining, leaving many publications vulnerable to an economic downturn. Magazines are also facing strong competition from other media such as television, the Internet, and direct mail; and, as discussed in IMC Perspective 12–2, they are being asked to demonstrate that they can build brand awareness and help increase sales. Publishers are looking at a number of ways to improve their position—including stronger editorial platforms, better circulation management, cross-magazine and media deals, database marketing, technological advances, and electronic delivery methods—to make advertising in magazines more appealing to marketers.

Exhibit 12–14 *Yahoo! Internet Life* is a successful new magazine

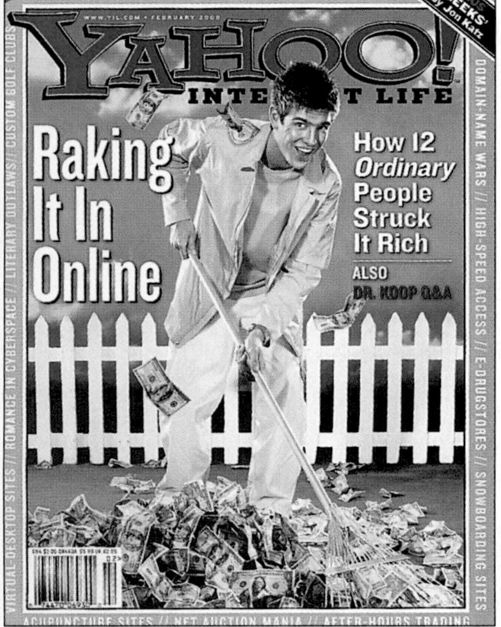

Stronger Editorial Platforms

Magazines with strong editorial platforms that appeal to the interests, lifestyles, and changing demographics of consumers as well as business and market trends in the new millennium are in the best position to attract readers and advertisers. For example, the opening vignette discussed how *Fast Company* has been successful by developing a different type of business magazine that provides readers with information and ideas for succeeding in the modern workplace. Another successful new magazine is *Yahoo! Internet Life,* whose editorial content focuses on the Internet but does so as a general-interest consumer publication[20] (Exhibit12–14).

Circulation Management

One of the major challenges facing magazine publishers is trying to increase or even maintain their circulation bases. Circulation is the second major source of revenue for most publications, and publishers must carefully manage the costs of attracting and maintaining additional readers or subscribers. The cost of acquiring subscriptions has increased dramatically over the past decade, from $337 to mail 1,000 subscription offers in 1990 to $430 in 1998. At the same time, there has been a decline in the prices consumers pay for subscriptions. In

IMC Perspective 11–2

Proving That Magazine Ads Work

For years magazine publishers focused most of their attention on selling ads in their magazines and devoted less attention to proving the ads were effective. At many magazines, efforts at measuring effectiveness were often limited to tracking consumer response to 800 numbers that appeared in print ads. However, the carefree days are over as many new advertising media have emerged, such as niche-oriented cable TV networks, narrowly targeted radio stations, and the Internet. Moreover, there are more than twice as many magazines competing for media dollars as there were a decade ago. With so many media options available, marketers now want tangible proof that magazine advertising is effective and can build brand awareness, help position a brand, or actually deliver sales.

Magazines have typically promised advertisers *exposure* or access to a well-defined audience such as fashion-conscious young women, sports-obsessed men, or automotive buffs. However, advertisers want evidence of more than exposure. They want proof that seeing an ad for Calvin Klein jeans in *Cosmo* makes readers more likely to spend $80 to buy them or that placing an ad for a Volkswagen Jetta in *Rolling Stone* helps the brand stick in consumers' minds long enough to influence their next auto purchase. The executive vice president of Conde Naste Publications, Inc., which publishes popular titles such as *Vogue, GQ, Glamour,* and *Vanity Fair,* says: "Twenty years ago, our only obligation to advertisers was to gather people who would see the ad. Now we must prove the ad actually does something. Sometimes, that's possible; sometimes it's not."

Magazines increasingly have to compete against media that can provide evidence that their ads do indeed do something. For example, the Internet can show accountability instantly because consumers' movements and purchases can be tracked through their mouse clicks. And with new digital technology, television sets will soon become transactional tools, allowing consumers to order information and goods right from their sofas with a remote control. Magazines can ill afford to wait any longer to prove that they work. For example, General Motors, the nation's largest advertiser, spent only 21 percent of its advertising budget on consumer magazines in 1998, down from 27 percent just four years earlier. GM's top marketing executive argues that magazines spend too much time in a self-congratulatory mode. He notes: "The only thing we've learned at GM about magazines is through our own proprietary research. There's so much upside potential, but they need to reposition themselves in the new world."

The magazine industry is taking steps to address the accountability issue. The industry's lead trade group, Magazine Publishers of America (MPA), recently spent half a million dollars investigating ways to prove magazine effectiveness. One of the group's studies found that boosting ad spending in magazines increased short-term sales of products and also generated more sales over time. Sales increased among magazine-exposed households for 8 of the 10 brands measured. Individual magazines are also trying to prove how advertising in their pages can help build a brand or move the sales needle. Some magazines are finding ways to mesh the print side of their business with the e-commerce potential of the Internet. For example, print ads in Meredith Corp.'s *Wood* magazine will direct readers to Wood's website, where they will be able to buy wood tools and equipment in a virtual mall. The magazine's publisher feels that the print ads will drive traffic to the website that it would not normally get. In turn, the magazine expects to attract more print advertising because it will offer the additional e-commerce component.

Magazines are taking other steps to demonstrate the efficacy of print ads. Some are forging closer alliances with advertising agencies, which are also under strong pressure to exhibit accountability to their clients. Other publishers are opening up their subscriber databases to advertisers. For example, at the American Express Co. publishing division, which prints upscale titles such as *Travel & Leisure* and *Food & Wine,* the magazines often make use of the database the parent company gleans from its 19 million credit-card holders. For some advertisers, American Express magazines track credit-card activity to help determine whether sales of a specific product increased during a particular magazine promotion.

Consumers' loyalty to magazines and their willingness to spend uninterrupted, focused time with them has always been a powerful selling point for the medium. Now, however, magazines must prove that their connection with readers will generate sales for the companies that advertise in them. As Chris Miller, the MPA's head of marketing, notes: "One of the most important questions for this industry is the bottom-line question—does it drive sales?"

Source: Wendy Bounds, "Magazines Seek to Demonstrate Efficacy of Ads," *The Wall Street Journal,* April 12, 1999, pp. B1, 3.

1990 the average magazine subscription rate was $26.90. In 1998 it was $22.57. Thus, publishers have to pay more to maintain their rate bases (the circulation level guaranteed to advertisers), but they make less money on each subscription sold.[21]

Publishers are also facing a drop in sweepstakes-generated circulation as a result of the controversy that developed over consumer confidence in the sweepstakes-related subscription offers. Agents such as Publishers Clearing House and American Family Enterprises have been going through changes, both self-imposed and externally dictated, that have greatly reduced the number of subscriptions they generate for publishers.[22] To compensate for losses from sweepstakes agents, publishers are looking to other methods of generating subscribers, such as making subscriptions available through websites, offering free trial copies online, conducting special promotions, or using other agents such as school-related subscription services.[23]

Many magazines are also focusing more attention on managing their circulation bases. For many years, magazines focused on increasing their circulation under the assumption that higher circulation meant higher advertising rates. However, publishers are now realizing that the cost of attracting and maintaining the last 10 to 15 percent of their circulation base is often greater than the additional revenue generated, since these subscribers require numerous direct-mail solicitations, premium offers, or discount subscriptions.

A number of magazines have reduced their circulation base in recent years. Many publishers believe they can pass on price increases more easily to their core readers or subscribers and offer advertisers a more loyal and focused audience. Many advertisers welcome the improvement in circulation management. They would rather reach a few hundred thousand fewer subscribers than pay for inefficient circulation and be hit with advertising rate increases each year. Many magazines are also using the monies saved on the circulation side to improve the editorial content of their publications, which should attract more readers—and advertisers.

Cross-Magazine and Media Deals

Another important development involves the way ad space is sold; there will be more cross- or multimagazine and cross-media ad packages. **Multimagazine deals** involve two or more publishers offering their magazines to an advertiser as one package. For example, *Newsweek* offers cross-magazine deals with several other publishers, including Meredith and Times Mirror. Many magazines are also making **cross-media advertising** deals that include several different media opportunities from a single company or a partnership of media providers. For example, with the recent merger of America Online (AOL) and Time Warner, it is likely that the new company will offer advertisers the opportunity for cross-media deals whereby they can advertise in magazines owned by the media conglomerate, such as *Time, Sports Illustrated, People,* and *Fortune;* on its TV stations, such as CNN, TNT, TBS, and the WB Network; and through AOL and other websites.[24]

Database Marketing

Many advertisers are increasingly turning to magazines as a cost-efficient way of reaching specialized audiences. As marketers continue to move toward greater market segmentation, market niche strategies, and regional marketing, they are making greater use of magazines because of their high selectivity and ability to avoid wasted coverage or circulation. Magazines are using advances in technology and *database marketing* to divide their audiences on the basis of demographics, psychographics, or regions and to deliver more personalized advertising messages. Database marketing lets advertisers personalize their advertising by merging their own databases with those of a magazine. By selectively accessing information from a magazine's database, advertisers can choose from an array of information on consumers, such as product usage or purchase intention data. Marketers will increasingly advertise in magazines that are targeted specifically to narrow groups of subscribers.[25]

Advances in Technology

Two important technological developments are making it possible for advertisers to deliver personalized messages to tightly targeted audiences: selective binding technology and ink-jet imaging. **Selective bind-**

ing is a computerized production process that allows the creation of hundreds of copies of a magazine in one continuous sequence. Selective binding enables magazines to target and address specific groups within a magazine's circulation base. They can then send different editorial or advertising messages to various groups of subscribers within the same issue of a publication. **Ink-jet imaging** reproduces a message by projecting ink onto paper rather than using mechanical plates. This process makes it possible to personalize an advertising message. Many publishers believe selective binding and ink-jet imaging will let advertisers target their messages more finely and let magazines compete more effectively with direct mail and other direct-marketing vehicles. Exhibit 12–15 shows how *Newsweek* promotes the capabilities of ink-jet imaging for targeting advertising messages.

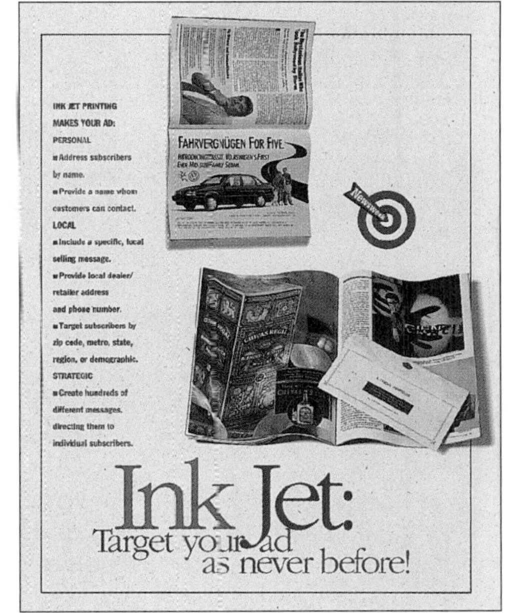

Exhibit 12–15 *Newsweek* promotes the value of ink-jet imaging

Publishers are also developing new technologies that will enhance the creative opportunities available to magazine advertisers. Advertisers use a variety of techniques in print ads to capture readers' attention, including sound, scents, moving images, and pop-up ads. Current technologies are being refined and made more cost effective, and a number of new technologies will be incorporated into print ads soon. These include anaglyphic images (three-dimensional materials that are viewed with colored glasses); lenticular (color) images printed on finely corrugated plastic that seem to move when tilted; and pressure- or heat-sensitive inks that change color on contact. These new technologies will give advertisers ways to break through the advertising clutter. However, these new print technologies can be very costly. Moreover, many advertisers and agencies are concerned that ads that use these new technologies may do so at the expense of other ads in the magazine, so they may pressure publishers to control their use. Some creative people have also expressed concern that these new technologies are gimmicks being substituted for creative advertising ideas.[26]

Online Delivery Methods

Many magazines are keeping pace with the digital revolution and the continuing consumer interest in technology by making their publications available online. As of late 1999 there were nearly 300 magazines with online versions, and many more are becoming available each month. Online versions of magazines such as *Business Week* offer the many advantages of the Internet to publishers and subscribers (Exhibit 12–16). They also provide advertisers with

Exhibit 12–16 Magazines such as *Business Week* are now available online

the opportunity for sponsorships as well as banner ads and promotions on the online versions of the magazines. However, it remains to be seen whether people will want their magazines delivered online or prefer to read them in more traditional form. As the presence of magazines online grows, the industry will also have to address important issues regarding audience measurement and how to determine consumers' exposure to and interactions with online advertising. Advertising on the Internet is discussed in Chapter 15.

Newspapers

Newspapers, the second major form of print media, are the largest of all advertising media in terms of total dollar volume. In 1999 more than $46 billion was spent on newspaper advertising, or about 22 percent of the total advertising expenditures in the United States. Newspapers are an especially important advertising medium to local advertisers, particularly retailers. However, newspapers are also valuable to national advertisers. Many of the advertising dollars spent by local retailers are actually provided by national advertisers through cooperative advertising programs (discussed in Chapter 16). Newspapers vary in terms of their characteristics and their role as an advertising medium.

Types of Newspapers

The traditional role of newspapers has been to deliver prompt, detailed coverage of news as well as to supply other information and features that appeal to readers. The vast majority of newspapers are daily publications serving a local community. However, weekly, national, and special-audience newspapers have special characteristics that can be valuable to advertisers.

Daily Newspapers Daily newspapers, which are published each weekday, are found in cities and larger towns across the country. Many areas have more than one daily paper. Daily newspapers are read by nearly 60 percent of adults each weekday and by 68 percent on Sundays.[27] They provide detailed coverage of news, events, and issues concerning the local area as well as business, sports, and other relevant information and entertainment. Daily newspapers can further be classified as morning, evening, or Sunday publications. In 1999, there were 1,489 daily newspapers in the United States; of these, 52 percent were evening papers and 48 percent morning. There were also 897 Sunday newspapers, most of which were published by daily newspapers.

Weekly Newspapers Most weekly newspapers originate in small towns or suburbs where the volume of news and advertising cannot support a daily newspaper. These papers focus primarily on news, sports, and events relevant to the local area and usually ignore national and world news, sports, and financial and business news. Weeklies are the fastest-growing class of newspapers; in 1999, there were nearly 8,000 in the United States. Weeklies appeal primarily to local advertisers because of their geographic focus and lower absolute cost. Most national advertisers avoid weekly newspapers because of their duplicate circulation with daily or Sunday papers in the large metropolitan areas and problems in contracting for and placing ads in these publications. However, the contracting and scheduling problems associated with these papers have been reduced by the emergence of syndicates that publish them in a number of areas and sell ad space in all of their local newspapers through one office.

National Newspapers Newspapers in the United States with national circulation include *USA Today, The Wall Street Journal,* and *The Christian Science Monitor.* All three are daily publications and have editorial content with a nationwide appeal. *USA Today,* which positions itself as "the nation's newspaper," has the largest circulation of any newspaper in the country, at 2.3 million copies a day. *The Wall Street Journal* sells over 1.7 million copies a day and is an excellent means of reaching businesspeople. National newspapers appeal primarily to large national advertisers and to regional advertisers that use specific geographic editions of these publications. For example, *The Wall Street Journal* has three geographic editions covering 18 regions in which ads can be placed, while *USA Today* offers advertisers the opportunity to run ads in its national edition or any of 25 regionals.

Recently *The New York Times* was classified as a national newspaper rather than a regional publication by Competitive Media Reporting, which has developed a new policy on how it defines national newspapers.[28] This policy states that a paper must publish at least five times a week and have no more than 67 percent of its distribution in any one area. More than 33 percent of its display advertising must come from national advertising categories, and more than 50 percent of its advertising must come from national advertisers. Designation as a national newspaper is important to major newspapers in attracting national advertisers.[29] Exhibit 12–17 shows an ad run by *The New York Times* informing advertisers of its classification as a national newspaper.

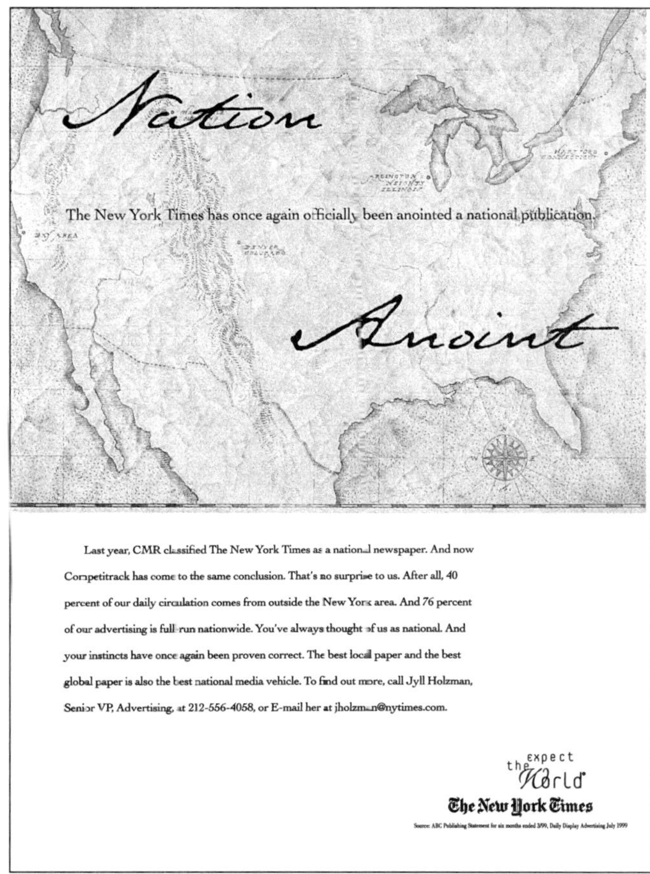

Nation
The New York Times has once again officially been anointed a national publication.
Anoint
Last year, CMR classified The New York Times as a national newspaper. And now Competitrack has come to the same conclusion. That's no surprise to us. After all, 40 percent of our daily circulation comes from outside the New York area. And 76 percent of our advertising is full-run nationwide. You've always thought of us as national. And your instincts have once again been proven correct. The best local paper and the best global paper is also the best national media vehicle. To find out more, call Jyll Holzman, Senior VP, Advertising, at 212-556-4058, or E-mail her at jholzman@nytimes.com.
expect the World
The New York Times

Exhibit 12–17 *The New York Times* promotes its classification as a national newspaper

Special-Audience Newspapers A variety of papers offer specialized editorial content and are published for particular groups, including labor unions, professional organizations, industries, and hobbyists. Many people working in advertising read *Advertising Age,* while those in the marketing area read *Marketing News.* Specialized newspapers are also published in areas with large foreign-language-speaking ethnic groups, among them Polish, Chinese, Hispanics, Vietnamese, and Filipinos. In the United States, there are newspapers printed in more than 40 languages.

Newspapers targeted at various religious groups compose another large class of special-interest papers. For example, more than 140 Catholic newspapers are published across the United States. Another type of special-audience newspaper is one most of you probably read regularly during the school year, the college newspaper. More than 1,300 colleges and universities publish newspapers that offer advertisers an excellent medium for reaching college students (Exhibit 12–18).

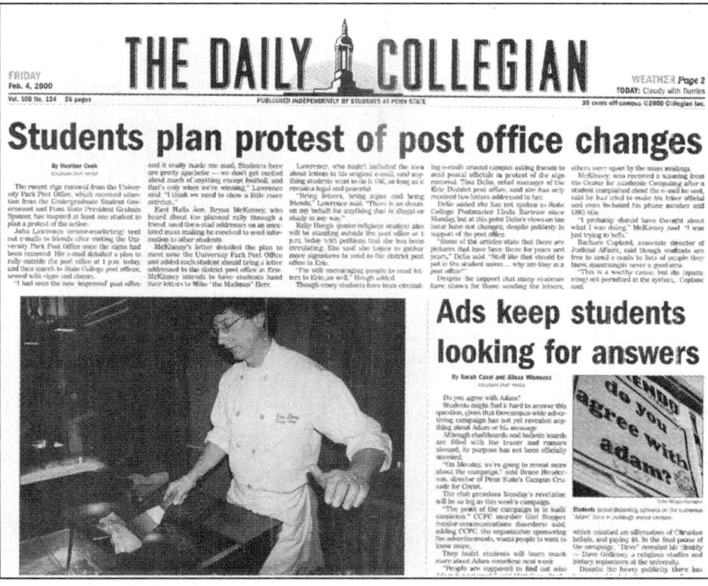

Exhibit 12–18 College newspapers such as *The Daily Collegian* are an excellent way to reach students

Newspaper Supplements

Although not a category of newspapers per se, many papers include magazine-type supplements, primarily in their Sunday editions. Sunday supplements have been part of most newspapers for many years and come in various forms. One type is the syndicated Sunday magazine, such as *Parade* or *USA Weekend,* distributed in hundreds of papers throughout the country. *Parade* has a circulation of over 37 million; *USA Weekend* is carried by more than 350 newspapers with a combined circulation of over 20 million. These publications are similar to national magazines and carry both national and regional advertising.

Some large newspapers publish local Sunday supplements distributed by the parent paper. These supplements contain stories of more local interest, and both local and national advertisers buy ad space. The *New York Times Sunday Magazine* is the best-known local supplement. The *Washington Post, San Francisco Examiner,* and *Los Angeles Times* have their own Sunday magazines.

In some areas, papers have begun carrying regional supplements as well as specialized weekday supplements that cover specific topics such as food, sports, or entertainment. Supplements are valuable to advertisers that want to use the newspaper yet get four-color reproduction quality in their ads.

Types of Newspaper Advertising

The ads appearing in newspapers can also be divided into different categories. The major types of newspaper advertising are display and classified. Other special types of ads and preprinted inserts also appear in newspapers.

Display Advertising

Display advertising is found throughout the newspaper and generally uses illustrations, headlines, white space, and other visual devices in addition to the copy text. Display ads account for approximately 70 percent of the advertising revenue of the average newspaper. The two types of display advertising in newspapers are local and national (general).

Local advertising refers to ads placed by local organizations, businesses, and individuals who want to communicate with consumers in the market area served by the newspaper. Supermarkets and department stores are among the leading local display advertisers, along with numerous other retailers and service operations such as banks and travel agents. Local advertising is sometimes referred to as retail advertising because retailers account for 85 percent of local display ads.

National or *general advertising* refers to newspaper display advertising done by marketers of branded products or services that are sold on a national or regional level. These ads are designed to create and maintain demand for a company's product or service and to complement the efforts of local retailers that stock and promote the advertiser's products. Major retail chains, automakers, and airlines are heavy users of newspaper advertising.

Classified Advertising

Classified advertising also provides newspapers with a substantial amount of revenue. These ads are arranged under subheads according to the product, service, or offering being advertised. Employment, real estate, and automotive are the three major categories of classified advertising. While most classified ads are just text set in small type, some newspapers also accept classified display advertising. These ads are run in the classified section of the paper but use illustrations, larger type sizes, white space, borders, and even color to stand out.

Special Ads and Inserts

Special advertisements in newspapers include a variety of government and financial reports and notices and public notices of changes in business and personal relationships. Other types of advertising in newspapers include political or special-interest ads promoting a particular candidate, issue, or cause. **Preprinted inserts** are another type of advertising distributed through newspapers. These ads do not appear in the paper itself; they are printed by the advertiser and then taken to the newspaper to be inserted before delivery. Many retailers use inserts such as circulars, catalogs, or brochures in specific circulation zones to reach shoppers in their particular trade areas.

Advantages of Newspapers

Newspapers have a number of characteristics that make them popular among both local and national advertisers. These include their extensive penetration of local markets, flexibility, geographic selectivity, reader involvement, and special services.

Extensive Penetration

One of the primary advantages of newspapers is the high degree of market coverage, or penetration, they offer an advertiser. In most areas, 60 percent or more of households read a daily newspaper, and the reach figure may exceed 70 percent among households with higher incomes and education levels. Most areas are served by one or two daily newspapers, and often the same company owns both, publishing a morning and an evening edition. By making one space buy, the advertiser can achieve a high level of overall reach in a particular market.

The extensive penetration of newspapers makes them a truly mass medium and provides advertisers with an excellent opportunity for reaching all segments of the population with their message. Also, since many newspapers are published and read daily, the advertiser can build a high level of frequency into the media schedule.

Flexibility

Another advantage of newspapers is the flexibility they offer advertisers. First, they are flexible in terms of requirements for producing and running the ads. Newspaper ads can be written, laid out, and prepared in a matter of hours. For most dailies, the closing time by which the ad must be received is usually only 24 hours before publication (although closing dates for special ads, such as those using color, and Sunday supplements are longer). The short production time and closing dates make newspapers an excellent medium for responding to current events or presenting timely information to consumers. For example, Chevrolet Trucks ran a newspaper ad congratulating major league baseball star Cal Ripken, Jr. the day after he got his 3,000th career hit. Ripken is a spokesperson for the Chevy Truck line and the newspaper ad was a very timely salute to his reaching this great milestone (Exhibit 12–19).

A second dimension of newspapers' flexibility stems from the creative options they make available to advertisers. Newspaper ads can be produced and run in various sizes, shapes, and formats; they can use color or special inserts to gain the interest of readers. Ads can be run in Sunday magazines or other supplements, and a variety of scheduling options are possible, depending on the advertiser's purpose.

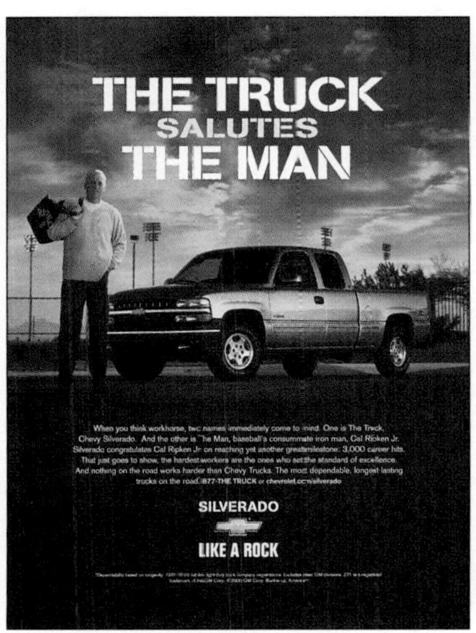

Exhibit 12–19 Chevy Trucks used a newspaper ad for a timely salute to Cal Ripken

Geographic Selectivity Newspapers generally offer advertisers more geographic or territorial selectivity than any other medium except direct mail. Advertisers can vary their coverage by choosing a paper—or combination of papers—that reaches the areas with the greatest sales potential. National advertisers take advantage of the geographic selectivity of newspapers to concentrate their advertising in specific areas they can't reach with other media or to take advantage of strong sales potential in a particular area. For example, BMW, Mercedes, and Volvo use heavy newspaper media schedules in California and New York/New Jersey to capitalize on the high sales potential for luxury import cars in these markets.

A number of companies, including General Motors, AT&T, and Campbell, use newspapers in their regional marketing strategies. Newspaper advertising lets them feature products on a market-by-market basis, respond and adapt campaigns to local market conditions, and tie into more retailer promotions, fostering more support from the trade.

Local advertisers like retailers are interested in geographic selectivity or flexibility within a specific market or trade area. Their media goal is to concentrate their advertising on the areas where most of their customers are. Many newspapers now offer advertisers various geographic areas or zones for this purpose. For example, the *Chicago Tribune* offers combinations of the 95 zip zones shown in Exhibit 12–20.

Reader Involvement and Acceptance Another important feature of newspapers is consumers' level of acceptance and involvement with papers and the ads they contain. The typical daily newspaper reader spends time each day reading the weekday newspaper and even more time reading the Sunday paper. Most consumers rely heavily on newspapers not only for news, information, and entertainment but also for assistance with consumption decisions.

Many consumers actually purchase a newspaper *because* of the advertising it contains. Consumers use retail ads to determine product prices and availability and to see who is having a sale. One aspect of newspapers that is helpful to advertisers

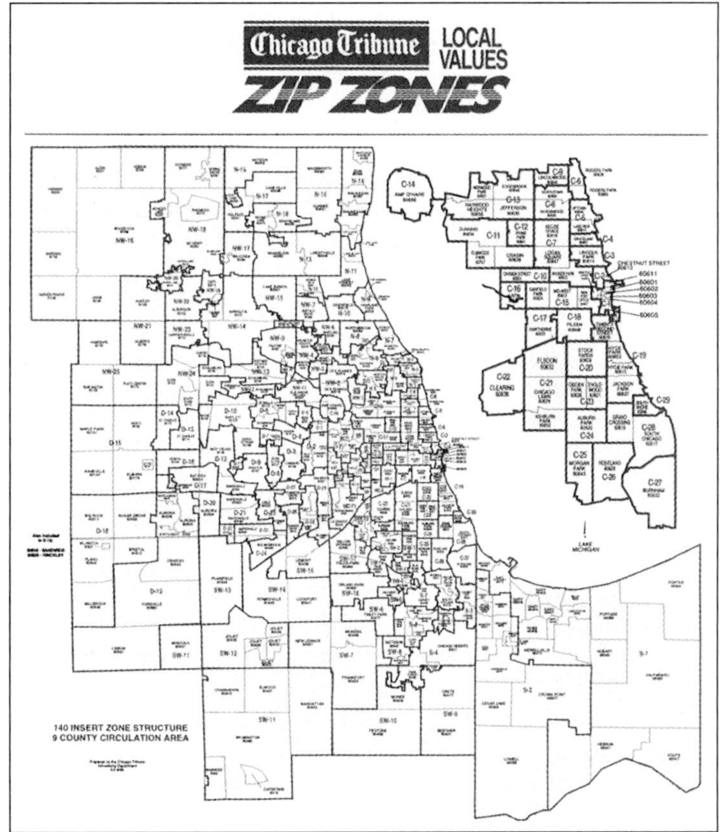

Exhibit 12–20 The *Chicago Tribune* offers advertisers combinations of 95 different zip zones

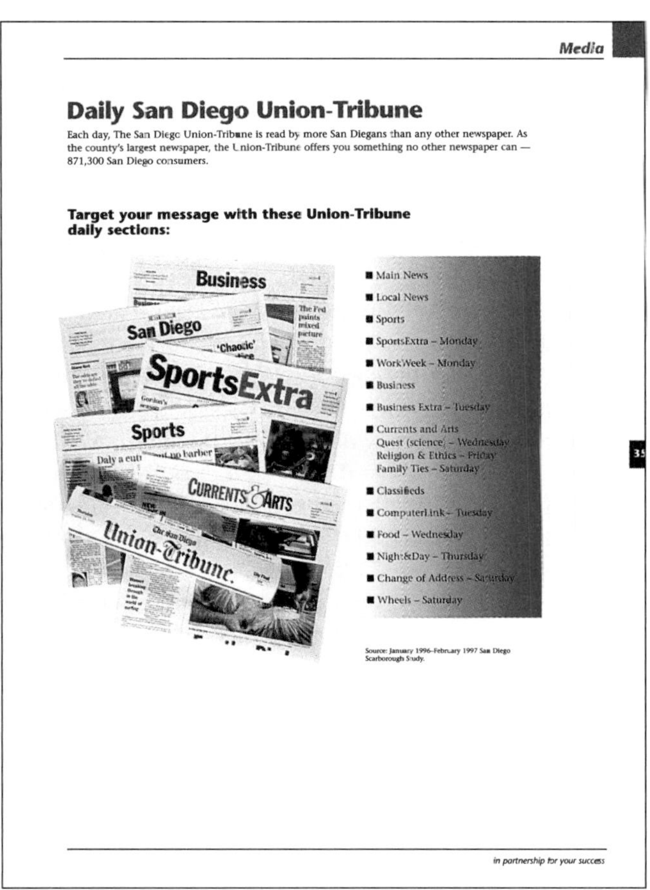

Media

Daily San Diego Union-Tribune

Each day, The San Diego Union-Tribune is read by more San Diegans than any other newspaper. As the county's largest newspaper, the Union-Tribune offers you something no other newspaper can — 871,300 San Diego consumers.

Target your message with these Union-Tribune daily sections:

- Main News
- Local News
- Sports
- SportsExtra – Monday
- WorkWeek – Monday
- Business
- Business Extra – Tuesday
- Currents and Arts
  Quest (science) – Wednesday
  Religion & Ethics – Friday
  Family Ties – Saturday
- Classifieds
- ComputerLink – Tuesday
- Food – Wednesday
- Night&Day – Thursday
- Change of Address – Saturday
- Wheels – Saturday

Source: January 1996–February 1997 San Diego Scarborough Study.

in partnership for your success

Exhibit 12–21 Ads can be run in various sections of most newspapers

is readers' knowledge about particular sections of the paper. Most of us know that ads for automotive products and sporting goods are generally found in the sports section, while ads for financial services are found in the business section. The weekly food section in many newspapers is popular for recipe and menu ideas as well as for the grocery store ads and coupons offered by many stores and companies. Exhibit 12–21 shows how the *San Diego Union-Tribune* promotes various sections of the paper to potential advertisers.

The value of newspaper advertising as a source of information has been shown in several studies. One study found that consumers look forward to ads in newspapers more than in other media. In another study, 80 percent of consumers said newspaper ads were most helpful to them in doing their weekly shopping. Newspaper advertising has also been rated the most believable form of advertising in numerous studies.

Services Offered The special services newspapers offer can be valuable to advertisers. For example, many newspapers offer merchandising services and programs to manufacturers that make the trade aware of ads being run for the company's product and help convince local retailers they should stock, display, and promote the item.

Many newspapers are also excellent sources of local market information through their knowledge of market conditions and research like readership studies and consumer surveys. For example, the publisher of the *San Diego Union-Tribune,* the major daily newspaper in San Diego, provides information on the local market through reports such as the Marketbook (Exhibit 12–22).

Newspapers can also assist small companies through free copywriting and art services. Small advertisers without an agency or advertising department often rely on the newspaper to help them write and produce their ads.

Exhibit 12–22 Newspaper publishers are often an excellent source for information on local markets

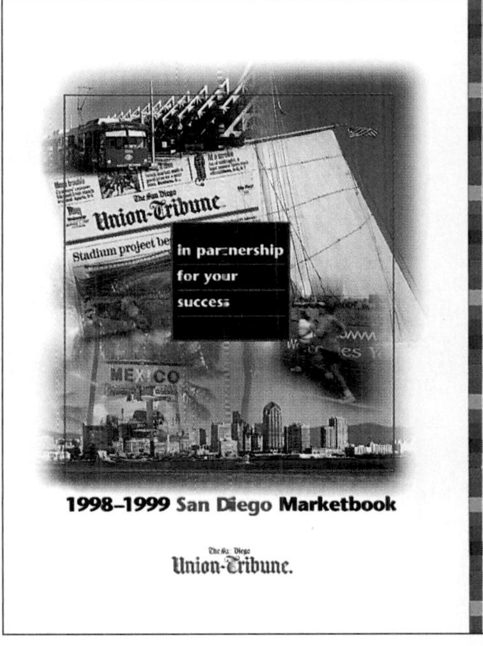

Limitations of Newspapers

While newspapers have many advantages, like all media they also have disadvantages that media planners must consider. The limitations of newspapers include their reproduction problems, short life span, lack of selectivity, and clutter.

Poor Reproduction One of the greatest limitations of newspapers as an advertising medium is their poor reproduction quality. The coarse paper stock used for newspapers, the absence of color, and the lack of time papers have available to achieve high-quality reproduction limits the quality of most newspaper ads. Newspapers have improved their reproduction quality in recent years, and color reproduction has become more available. Also, advertisers desiring high-quality color in newspaper ads can turn to such alternatives as freestanding inserts or Sunday supplements. However, these are more costly and may not be desirable to many advertisers. As a general rule, if the visual appearance of the product is important, the advertiser will not rely on newspaper ads. Ads for food products and fashions generally use magazines to capitalize on their superior reproduction quality and color.

Short Life Span Unlike magazines, which may be retained around the house for several weeks, a daily newspaper is generally kept less than a day. So an ad is unlikely to have any impact beyond the day of publication, and repeat exposure is very unlikely. Compounding this problem are the short amount of time many consumers spend with the newspaper and the possibility they may not even open certain sections of the paper. Media planners can offset these problems somewhat by using high frequency in the newspaper schedule and advertising in a section where consumers who are in the market for a particular product or service are likely to look. Figure 12–4 shows readership figures for various sections of newspapers by gender and ethnic background.

Lack of Selectivity While newspapers can offer advertisers geographic selectivity, they are not a selective medium in terms of demographics or lifestyle characteristics. Most newspapers reach broad and very diverse groups of consumers, which makes it difficult for marketers to focus on narrowly defined market segments. For example, manufacturers of fishing rods and reels will find newspapers very inefficient because of the wasted circulation that results from reaching all the newspaper readers who don't fish. Thus, they are more likely to use special-interest magazines such as *Field & Stream* or *Fishing World.* Any newspaper ads for their products will be done through cooperative plans whereby retailers share the costs or spread them over a number of sporting goods featured in the ad.

Figure 12–4 Weekday newspaper pages or sections generally read

	Percentage of Weekday Audience					
Section Readership	Adults	Men	Women	White	Black	Spanish/ Hispanic
Business pages/section	62	67	56	63	52	50
Classified advertising	55	57	54	55	60	56
Comics	59	60	58	60	55	51
Entertainment (movies, theater, etc.)	68	63	73	68	67	64
Food pages/section	56	48	65	58	49	46
Main news section	90	89	91	91	86	83
Sports pages/section	62	76	47	62	59	60
TV or radio listings	54	54	55	55	52	48

Note: Spanish/Hispanic defined as "of Spanish or Hispanic origin." Base = Top 50 designated market areas.

Clutter Newspapers, like most other advertising media, suffer from clutter. Because 64 percent of the average daily newspaper in the United States is devoted to advertising, the advertiser's message must compete with numerous other ads for consumers' attention and interest. Moreover, the creative options in newspapers are limited by the fact that most ads are black and white. Thus, it can be difficult for a newspaper advertiser to break through the clutter without using costly measures such as large space buys or color. Some advertisers use creative techniques like *island ads*—ads surrounded by editorial material. Island ads are found in the middle of the stock market quotes on the financial pages of many newspapers. Exhibit 12–23 shows an island ad for Cathay Pacific Airways that targets business travelers to Hong Kong and other Asian destinations.

Exhibit 12–23 Island ads are a way to break through the clutter in newspaper advertising

The Newspaper Audience

As with any medium, the media planner must understand the nature and size of the audience reached by a newspaper in considering its value in the media plan. Since newspapers as a class of media do an excellent job of penetrating their market, the typical daily newspaper gives advertisers the opportunity to reach most of the households in a market. But, while local advertisers aim to cover a particular market or trade area, national advertisers want to reach broad regions or even the entire country. They must purchase space in a number of papers to achieve the desired level of coverage.

The basic sources of information concerning the audience size of newspapers come from the circulation figures available through rate cards, publishers' statements, or Standard Rate and Data Service's *Newspaper Rates and Data.* Circulation figures for many newspapers are verified by the Audit Bureau of Circulation which was discussed earlier. Advertisers that use a number of papers in their media plan generally find SRDS the most convenient source.

Newspaper circulation figures are generally broken down into three categories: the city zone, the retail trading zone, and all other areas. The **city zone** is a market area composed of the city where the paper is published and contiguous areas similar in character to the city. The **retail trading zone** is the market outside the city zone whose residents regularly trade with merchants within the city zone. The "all other" category covers all circulation not included in the city or retail trade zone.

Sometimes circulation figures are provided only for the primary market, which is the city and retail trade zones combined, and the other area. Both local and national advertisers consider the circulation patterns across the various categories in evaluating and selecting newspapers.

National advertisers often buy newspapers on the basis of the size of the market area they cover. For example, General Motors might decide to purchase advertising in the top 10 markets, the top 50 markets, the top 100 markets, and so on. A national advertiser gets different levels of market coverage depending on the number of market areas purchased.

Audience Information Circulation figures provide the media planner with the basic data for assessing the value of newspapers and their ability to cover various market areas. However, the media planner also wants to match the characteristics of a newspaper's readers with those of the advertiser's target audience. Data on newspaper audience size and characteristics are available from commercial research services and from studies conducted by the papers.

Commercial studies providing readership information for the top 100 or so major markets are supplied by Simmons Market Research Bureau, Scarbough Research, and Mediamark Research, Inc. (MRI). These studies cover more than 150 daily newspapers and provide reach and frequency estimates for various demographic groups. Their audience information is valuable for comparing newspapers with other media vehicles, for which similar data are generally available. Many ad executives and media planners believe the newspaper industry must expand the amount of audience research data available or risk losing more advertising dollars to magazines and television.

Many newspapers commission their own audience studies to provide current and potential advertisers with information on readership and characteristics of readers such as demographics, shopping habits, and lifestyles. These studies are often designed to promote the effectiveness of the newspaper in reaching various types of consumers. Since they are sponsored by the paper itself, many advertisers are skeptical of their results. Careful attention must be given to the research methods used and conclusions drawn by these studies.

Purchasing Newspaper Space

Advertisers are faced with a number of options and pricing structures when purchasing newspaper space. The cost of advertising space depends not only on the newspaper's circulation but also on factors such as premium charges for color or special sections as well as discounts available. The purchase process and the rates paid for newspaper space differ for national and local advertisers.

National versus Local Rates

The rates paid by national advertisers are, on average, 75 percent higher than those paid by local advertisers. Newspaper publishers claim the rate differential is justified for several reasons. First, they argue it costs more to handle national advertising since ad agencies get a 15 percent commission and commissions must also be paid to the independent sales reps who solicit nonlocal advertising. Second, they note that national advertising is less dependable than local advertising; national advertisers usually don't use newspapers on a continual basis like local advertisers do. Finally, newspaper publishers contend that demand for national advertising is inelastic—it will not increase if rates are lowered or decrease if rates are raised. This means there is no incentive to lower the national advertisers' rates.

National advertisers do not view these arguments as valid justification for the rate differential. They argue that the costs are not greater for handling national advertising than for local business and that many national advertisers use newspapers on a regular basis. Since they use an agency to prepare their ads, national advertisers are less likely to request special services. The large and costly staff maintained by many newspapers to assist in the design and preparation of advertising is used mostly by local advertisers.

Exhibit 12–24 The Newspaper National Network encourages national advertisers to run their ads in newspapers

The differential rate structure for national versus local advertising has been the source of considerable controversy. Some newspapers are making efforts to narrow the rate differential, as is the Newspaper Association of America (NAA). In 1993, the NAA created the Newspaper National Network (NNN) to target national advertisers in six low-use categories: automotive, cosmetics and toiletries, food, household products, liquor and beverages, and drugs and remedies.[30] The network's goal is to attract more advertising dollars from national advertisers in these categories by promoting the strategic use of newspapers and facilitating the purchase of newspaper space with their one order/one bill model. Exhibit 12–24 shows an ad encouraging national advertisers to place their ads in newspapers through the NNN.

Many marketers sidestep the national advertiser label and the higher rates by channeling their newspaper ads through special category plans, cooperative advertising deals with retailers, and local dealers and distributors that pay local rates. However, the rate differential does keep many national advertisers from making newspapers a larger part of their media mix.

Newspaper Rates

Traditionally, newspaper space for national advertisers has been sold by the agate line. The problem is that newspapers use columns of varying width. Some have six columns per page, while others have eight or nine, which affects the size, shape, and costs of an ad. This results in a complicated production and buying process for national advertisers purchasing space in a number of newspapers.

To address this problem and make newspapers more comparable to other media that sell space and time in standard units, the newspaper industry switched to **standard advertising units (SAU)** in 1984. All newspapers under this system use column widths 2 [1/16] inches wide, with tabloid-size papers five columns wide and standard or broadcast papers six columns. The column inch is the unit of measurement to create the 57 standard units or format sizes shown in Figure 12–5.

A national advertiser can prepare one ad in a particular SAU, and it will fit every newspaper in the country that accepts SAUs. Rates are quoted on that basis. Since over 1,400 (about 90 percent) of daily newspapers use the SAU system, the purchase and production process has been simplified tremendously for national advertisers.

Newspaper rates for local advertisers continue to be based on the column inch, which is 1 inch deep by 1 column wide. Advertising rates for local advertisers are quoted per column inch, and media planners calculate total space costs by multiplying the ad's number of column inches by the cost per inch.

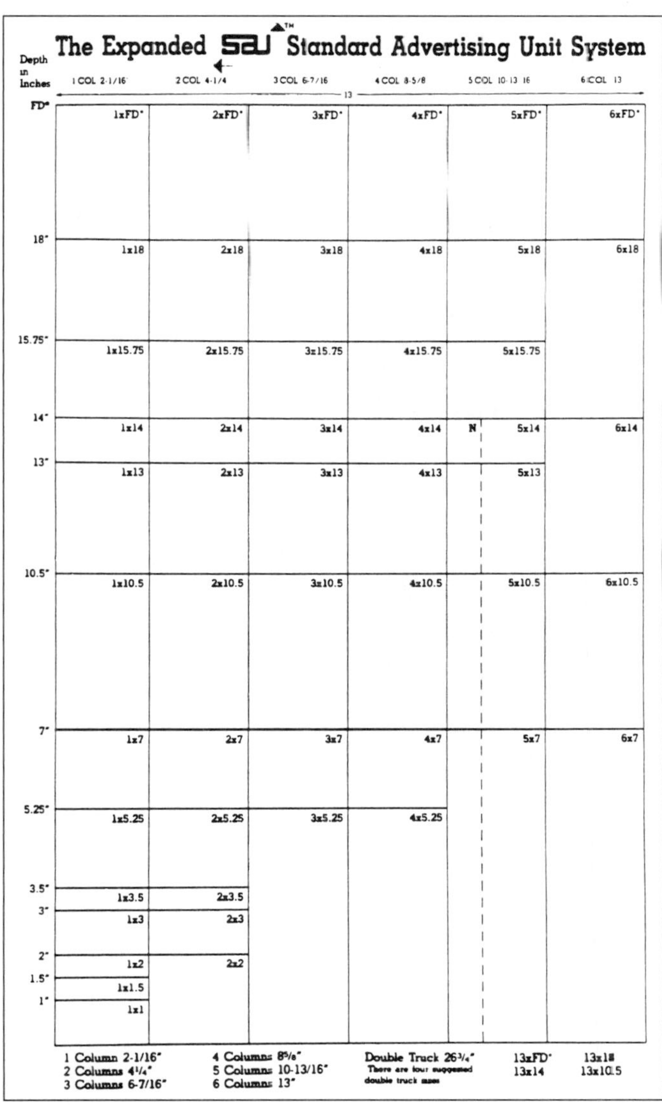

Figure 12–5 The standard advertising unit system

Rate Structures While the column inch and SAU are used to determine basic newspaper advertising rates, the media planner must consider other options and factors. Many newspapers charge **flat rates,** which means they offer no discount for quantity or repeated space buys. Others have an **open-rate structure,** which means various discounts are available. These discounts are generally based on frequency or bulk purchases of space and depend on the number of column inches purchased in a year.

Newspaper space rates also vary with an advertiser's special requests, such as preferred position or color. The basic rates quoted by a newspaper are **run of paper (ROP),** which means the paper can place the ad on any page or in any position it desires. While most newspapers try to place an ad in a requested position, the advertiser can ensure a specific section and/or position on a page by paying a higher **preferred position rate.** Color advertising is also available in many newspapers on an ROP basis or through preprinted inserts or Sunday supplements.

Advertisers can also buy newspaper space based on **combination rates,** where they get a discount for using several newspapers as a group. Typically, a combination rate occurs when a publisher owns both a morning and an evening newspaper in a market and offers a reduced single rate for running the same ad in both newspapers, generally within a 24-hour period. Combination discounts are also available when the advertiser buys space in several newspapers owned by the publisher in a number of markets or in multiple newspapers affiliated in a syndicate or newspaper group. Exhibit 12–25 shows an ad promoting the three newspapers published by the *Miami Herald* in the south Florida market.

The Future for Newspapers

Newspapers remain the largest advertising medium in terms of total advertising volume. Since 1991 newspapers have maintained year-to-year gains in advertising business and are expected to reach a record $50 million in 2000.[31] Newspapers'

Exhibit 12–25 Marketers can advertise in the three newspapers published by the *Miami Herald*

largest advertising category is retail, and consolidation among department stores and grocery chains is likely to lead to a slight decline in ad volume. National advertising in newspapers is growing as major advertisers such as Procter & Gamble, Kraft, Nestlé, and General Motors use the medium more. However, newspapers have fallen behind TV and magazines as a medium for national advertisers; they accounted for only 4.5 percent of the $126 million spent by national advertisers in 1999.[32]

Newspapers' major strength lies in their role as a medium that can be used effectively by local advertisers on a continual basis. It is unlikely that newspapers' importance to local advertisers will change in the near future. However, there are a number of problems and issues newspapers must address to maintain their strong position as a dominant local advertising medium and to gain more national advertising. These include competition from other advertising media, maintaining and managing circulation, cross-media opportunities, and declining readership

Competition from Other Media The newspaper industry's battle to increase its share of national advertising volume has been difficult. In addition to the problems of reproduction quality and rate differentials, newspapers face competition from other media for both national and local advertisers' budgets. The newspaper industry is particularly concerned about the *bypass,* or loss of advertisers to direct marketing and telemarketing.

To deal with this problem, many newspapers will have to gear up to compete as direct marketers. Many papers are already building databases by collecting information from readers that potential advertisers can use to target specific groups or for direct marketing. Newspapers already have a distribution system that can reach nearly every household in a market every day. It is likely that many newspapers will find ways to make their extensive databases and distribution systems available to marketers that want to target consumers with direct-marketing efforts. By supplementing newspaper advertising with direct mail, marketers can be encouraged to invest more of their advertising dollars with newspaper publishers.

The intermedia battle that newspapers find themselves involved in is no longer limited to national advertising. Many companies are investigating the Internet as a marketing tool and a place to invest advertising dollars that might otherwise go to newspapers. Local radio and TV stations (particularly cable stations), as well as the expanding number of Yellow Pages publishers, are aggressively pursuing local advertisers. Newspapers will have to fight harder to retain those advertisers. Many newspapers have expanded their marketing capabilities and are making efforts to develop and sustain relationships with their advertisers. Some have created sophisticated databases and direct-mail capabilities, which they offer as value-added services. Others are increasing their marketing research departments, preparing comprehensive market studies for major customers, and, in some cases, serving as media advisors and marketing partners.[33]

Circulation Like magazines, many newspapers are taking a closer look at their circulation and analyzing whether the cost of getting additional circulation is justified by the advertising revenue it generates. Many papers are raising newsstand and home delivery rates and circulation revenue is accounting for more of their total revenue.

Several major metropolitan newspapers have found that advertisers use newspapers to reach consumers within specific geographic areas and do not want to pay for readers in outlying areas. Thus, some papers are eliminating what has been called "ego circulation" and focusing more on regional editions in their immediate trade area.

Cross-Media Buys Another area where newspapers may be following the lead of magazines is cross-newspaper and media buys. Newspapers within, as well as across, various regions are banding together to offer national advertisers a package of newspapers so they won't have to purchase space in individual papers. A number of newspaper networks are being formed to help newspapers compete for more of the media expenditures of national advertisers.

Cross-media buys involving newspapers with other media vehicles are also likely to become more prevalent. For example, the *Washington Post* has been involved in a cross-media deal with *Newsweek,* while large companies that own newspapers, magazines, and broadcast media are also offering cross-media packages to advertisers (Exhibit 12–26).

Attracting and Retaining Readers The growth of newspapers as an advertising medium may be limited by the reduced popularity of the medium itself. Newspaper readership has been on a steady decline for the past two decades. The percentage of the adult population reading a newspaper on the average weekday has declined from 78 percent in 1970 to 58 percent today. The percentage of U.S. households receiving a daily newspaper has declined from 77 percent in 1980 to 60 percent. The decline in newspaper readership can be attributed to several factors, including the fast-paced, time-poor lifestyle of the modern dual-income household and the continued growth, popularity, and viewing options of TV.

A number of newspapers have been redesigned to be more interesting and easier and faster to read. Changes include the increased use of color and graphics as well as expanded coverage of sports and entertainment. Some papers have begun providing short summaries of articles in each section of the paper so readers can skim them and decide what they want to read.

Of particular concern to publishers is the decline in newspaper readership among important market segments such as women and young adults. Surveys show the percentage of women who read a newspaper on a typical day declined from 67 percent in 1981 to 53 percent in 1999.[34] Newspapers and advertisers are concerned because women are far more likely than men to make buying decisions. Many newspapers are introducing new women's sections and revising old ones to make them more appealing to modern women. This means including articles on such issues as health, parenting, and careers—for example, how women with children and jobs manage their time.

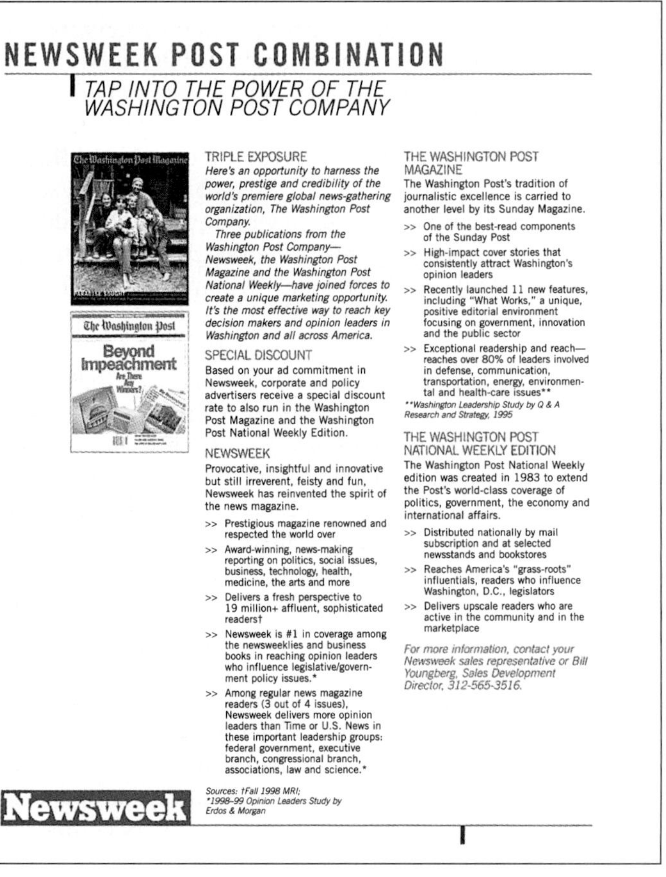

Exhibit 12–26 *Newsweek* and the *Washington Post* offer advertisers a cross-media opportunity

Newspapers are also concerned about where their future readers will come from, since many young people are heavy TV viewers and also are spending more and more time surfing the Internet. However, as discussed in IMC Perspective 12–3, a recent study found that newspaper readership is high among teens, and many papers are making special efforts to attract teenagers in hopes they will become and remain regular readers. The newspaper industry is also taking steps to maintain readership among young people. For example, the Newspaper Association of America (NAA) developed an advertising campaign using the theme "It all starts with newspapers" that encourages young people to read the newspaper every day. The ads ask parents to "encourage your child to read a newspaper every day" and feature celebrities such as musician Jon Bon Jovi, basketball star Grant Hill, and actress Meryl Streep promoting newspapers as literacy tools. Exhibit 12–27 shows one of the ads from that campaign, featuring pop-music star Brandy.[35]

The newspaper industry faces a major challenge. To increase circulation and readership and continue to attract advertising revenue, it must make newspapers more interesting to readers by targeting specific groups and expanding services to encourage advertisers to continue using newspapers. In 1999 the newspaper industry launched a comprehensive program to address some of these issues. Called the Newspaper Readership Initiative, this program seeks to reverse the decline in newspaper readership and circulation and make newspapers a part of every advertiser's media plan.[36]

The growth of the Internet and online services is another factor that may erode newspaper readership. As penetration of the Internet into households increases, newspapers and magazines are among the most threatened of the major media. A survey conducted for *Advertising Age* found that consumers with home Internet access are less likely to use magazines or newspapers as a primary information source when shopping for a car, financial services, travel, or fashion. The study also found that consumers from teens to seniors are comfortable with the idea of using the Internet in the future to read books, magazines, and newspapers.[37]

Newspaper publishers are addressing this threat by making their papers available online. Nearly every major newspaper has established a website, and many publishers now make their papers available online. The number of U.S. newspapers available online increased from less than 100 in 1995 to more than 900 in 1999. Many papers are also developing innovative programs for advertisers to attract their online advertising dollars. Networks are forming to help local newspapers go online and to facilitate the sale and purchase of banner ads and sponsorships. But as with magazines, audience measurement and user involvement are making it difficult for newspapers to attract advertisers and are issues that must be addressed.

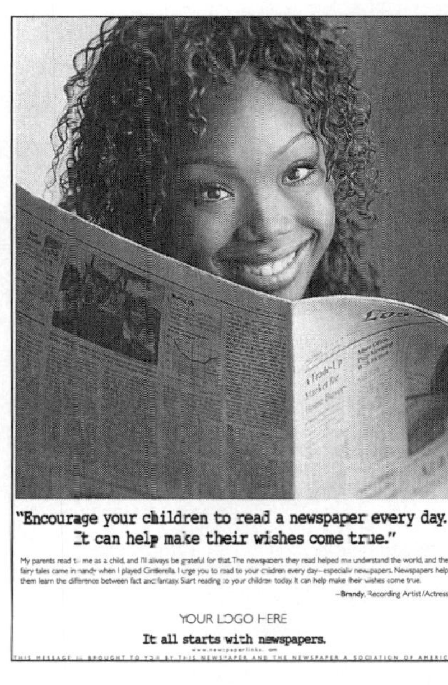

Exhibit 12–27 This ad is part of a campaign encouraging young people to read newspapers

IMC Perspective 12–3

Newspapers Go after Teenage Readers

As discussed in IMC Perspective 12–1, their numbers and purchasing power make teens a very attractive segment for marketers but one that can be difficult to reach through the print media. Teenagers are the darlings of the marketing world, and, as a result, they are being showered with movies, TV shows, websites, and magazines created just for them. They are also a generation that has learned to get their daily news and information from 24-hour TV news channels and the Internet. Like other media, newspapers want to reach teens, and doing so will in turn help them attract advertisers and ensure the industry's future readership strength. The good news for the newspaper industry is that despite the myriad of other media competing for teens' attention, the majority of teenagers are still reading newspapers.

A recent study of 12,000 teens conducted by Teenage Research Unlimited for the Newspaper Association of America found that nearly 70 percent of young people (age 12 to 17) read a newspaper in the last week and 40 percent of them read or looked at a local daily paper in the past day. Among older teens, age 15 to 17, 75 percent read a daily newspaper in the past week. For Sunday newspapers, 72 percent of teens read or looked at a Sunday newspaper in the past month, and the figure jumps to 78 percent for older teens. Not surprisingly, the sports and comic sections are read most frequently by teens (59 percent and 43 percent, respectively), although 40 percent say they read the front page as well.

The teens surveyed said newspapers do the best job in educating them about the local community, providing detail in stories, being accurate and believable, and providing them with helpful information. When asked about the media they most rely on for news, more than two-thirds of teens look to newspapers for local community news, 63 percent rely on newspapers for high school and youth sports news, and just over half count on newspapers for information about local politics and government news. For overall news and information content, newspapers were cited by 47 percent of teens, compared to 32 percent who cited second-ranked television. Newspapers were cited as the second most preferred media by teens for advertising information; they like TV for awareness of new products, but rely on newspapers for pricing information, for local availability of products, and for classified advertising.

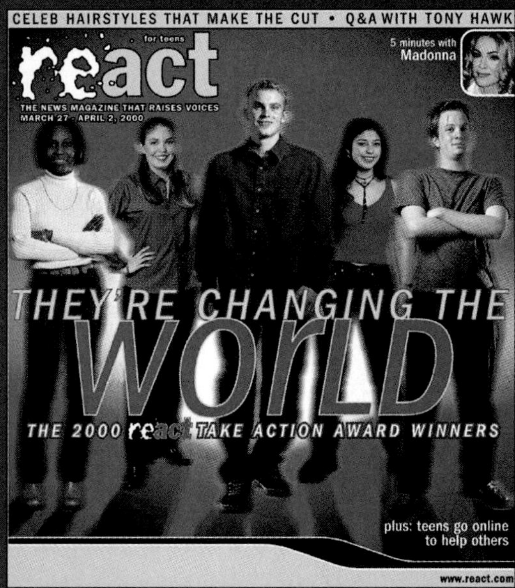

The results of the study bode well for newspapers. However, looking to ensure its future, the newspaper industry is working hard to convince teens they should continue to read the paper. Lee Kravitz, editor of *React,* a weekly newspaper supplement and website published by Parade Publications, notes: "There's a lesson that we've learned from the world of marketing, and that is branding young is important. If you want them to read the paper when they're 30, 40 or 50, you have to get them to read now when they're teens."

Publishers are putting more resources behind teen and youth pages, with some issuing monthly tabloid-style supplements and others using weekly or monthly broadsheet pages aimed directly at teens. For example, Parade developed *React* specifically because newspaper publishers wanted to reach out to teens. Scholastic, Inc., and *The New York Times* entered into a joint venture to develop *The New York Times Upfront,* a magazine supplement targeting teens. Some papers, such as the Minneapolis *Star Tribune,* which features a Minnesota Youth News page, are using teen writers and photographers working alongside adults to bring a young perspective to the newspaper. Many publishers are also developing websites to go along with their teen sections and supplements. *React*'s website is a popular destination for teens and *Upfront* includes a website as well.

Some media buyers are skeptical about the newspaper industry's stamina in continuing efforts to reach teen readers. However, finding advertisers interested in marketing to teens is not very difficult. The pages of *React* contain ads for brands such as Procter & Gamble's Secret deodorant, Coty teen fragrances, Nintendo, and Reebok. Many advertising executives feel that teens are reading more newspapers today than they did 10 years ago because the papers make it more fun and interesting for them and are making newspapers a part of their lifestyle. However, the president of a teen-oriented ad agency notes that if newspapers don't embrace teens, the Internet will eclipse them as a source of news and information. It appears that many papers are taking steps to ensure that this doesn't happen.

Sources: Laurie Freeman, "Teen-agers Turn Heartthrobs for Eager Publishers," *Advertising Age,* April 29, 1999, p. S8; "Teens Read and Rely on Newspapers, According to New NAA Study," *Newspaper Association of America,* February 16, 1999.

Summary

Magazines and newspapers, the two major forms of print media, play an important role in the media plans and strategy of many advertisers. Magazines are a very selective medium and are very valuable for reaching specific types of customers and market segments. The three broad categories of magazines are consumer, farm, and business publications. Each of these categories can be further classified according to the publication's editorial content and audience appeal.

In addition to their selectivity, the advantages of magazines include their excellent reproduction quality, creative flexibility, long life, prestige, and readers' high receptivity to magazine advertising, as well as the services they offer to advertisers. Disadvantages of magazines include their high cost, limited reach and frequency, long lead time, and the advertising clutter in most publications.

Advertising space rates in magazines vary according to a number of factors, among them the size of the ad, position in the publication, particular editions purchased, use of color, and number and frequency of insertions. Rates for magazines are compared on the basis of the cost per thousand, although other factors such as the editorial content of the publication and its ability to reach specific target audiences must also be considered.

Newspapers represent the largest advertising medium in terms of total volume, receiving nearly a fourth of all advertising dollars. Newspapers are a very important medium to local advertisers, especially retailers. They are also used by national advertisers, although the differential rate structure for national versus local advertisers is a source of controversy. Newspapers are a broad-based medium that reaches a large percentage of households in a particular area. Newspapers' other advantages include flexibility, geographic selectivity, reader involvement, and special services. Drawbacks of newspapers include their lack of high-quality ad reproduction, short life span, lack of audience selectivity, and clutter.

Trends toward market segmentation and regional marketing are prompting many advertisers to make more use of newspapers and magazines. However, both magazines and newspapers face increasing competition from such other media as radio, cable TV, direct marketing, and the Internet. Both magazines and newspapers are working to improve the quality of their circulation bases, offer database marketing services, and initiate cross-media deals. Rising costs and declining readership are problems for many magazines and newspapers. Both magazines and newspapers are making their publications available online, but problems with audience measurement and interactions with ads are important issues that must be resolved.

Key Terms

selectivity, 400
gatefolds, 403
bleed pages, 403
split runs, 407
controlled-circulation basis, 410
pass-along readership, 410
total audience/readership, 410
magazine networks, 414
multimagazine deals, 416
cross-media advertising, 416
selective binding, 416–17
ink-jet imaging, 417
display advertising, 420
classified advertising, 420
preprinted inserts, 420
city zone, 425
retail trading zone, 425
standard advertising units (SAU), 427
flat rates, 428
open-rate structure, 428
run of paper (ROP), 428
preferred position rate, 428
combination rates, 428

Discussion Questions

1. The vignette at the beginning of the chapter discusses the success of the magazine *Fast Company.* Discuss the reasons why this new magazine has been so successful. Find a copy of *Fast Company* and analyze the types of companies who are advertising in the magazine.

2. Discuss the advantages and disadvantages of magazines as an advertising medium. How do magazines differ from television and radio as advertising media?

3. Describe what is meant by selectivity with regard to the purchase of advertising media and discuss some of the ways magazines provide selectivity to advertisers.

4. Explain why advertisers of products such as cosmetics or women's clothing would choose to advertise in magazines such as *Vogue* or *Elle* which devote most of their pages to advertising rather than articles.

5. Discuss how circulation figures are used in evaluating magazines and newspapers as part of a media plan and setting advertising rates.

6. If you were purchasing magazine ad space for a manufacturer of snowboarding equipment, what factors would you consider? Would your selection of magazines be limited to snowboarding publications? Why or why not?

7. Discuss the advantages and disadvantages of newspapers as an advertising medium. How might the decision to use newspapers in a media plan differ for national versus local advertisers?

8. Discuss the reasons why most newspapers charge national advertisers higher rates than local advertisers. Do you think the rate differential for national versus local advertisers is justified?

9. Why do you think newspaper readership in the U.S. has been declining over the past decade? Do you think campaigns such as NAA's "It all starts with newspapers" can help reverse the decline in newspaper readership?

10. Discuss the challenges and opportunities magazines and newspapers are facing from the growth of the Internet.

Chapter Thirteen

Support Media

Chapter Objectives

- To recognize the various support media available to the marketer in developing an IMC program.
- To develop an understanding of the advantages and disadvantages of support media.
- To know how audiences for support media are measured.

How Can They Change the Ads on the Backstops between Innings?—It's "Virtually" Possible

Next time you watch a Major League Baseball game, watch the advertisements appearing on the backstop behind the batter. At the top of the inning, you will see an ad for one company—let's say Yahoo.com—between innings you may see one for Office Depot, and at the bottom of the inning you may see Toyota's message. Or perhaps you were watching a college football game on ESPN and you saw different ads appearing between the goalposts every time an extra point or field goal was kicked. Did you ever wonder how they could change those ads so quickly? Actually they don't. What you are seeing is a new technology called *virtual advertising,* in which the ads are digitally entered onto your screen. While you are seeing the ads on your screen, people at the stadium are seeing a blank wall.

Virtual advertising has been around for a few years, with the San Francisco Giants baseball team being the first to test the medium in the summer of 1996. The San Diego Padres and Philadelphia Phillies started using it in 1997, and the Seattle Mariners tested it in one game that same year. Fox Sports has used virtual advertising on a regional basis, and ESPN has placed virtual ads on its Sunday night football games aired nationally. The new advertising form is catching on so quickly that the San Diego Padres sold out all their virtual spots for the 1999 baseball season at a 25 percent rate increase over 1998, and a number of other teams are expected to begin to offer them in the 2000 season.

In virtual advertising, ad messages are inserted into a TV picture so that they appear to be part of the stadium scene. The advertiser can pay the same price for the virtual placement as it would

for a 30-second spot on the same game telecast. The cost can range from as low as $8,000 to as much as $25,000 on an ESPN national telecast. In baseball, the ads last as long as the half inning—typically 4 to 8 minutes. Other sports events using virtual advertising include football, arena football, and tennis. Exposure times, of course, are calculated differently for each sport.

Advertisers like the new virtual capabilities for a number of reasons. First, the ads are shown while the event is still active, rather than during commercial slots, increasing the likelihood of viewer attention. Second, the format allows for a large number of companies to participate (the three mentioned above all appeared in a single Padres game), and since the ads are digitally created, there are few production difficulties and little inventory to contend with. The same game shown in two different markets can carry different ads for each market.

Before you begin to think that this technology is limited to sports, consider this: In a 1999 episode of the prime-time entertainment show "Seven Days," virtual product placements appeared for the first time in such programming. After the program had been produced and put on the air, Princeton Video Image created the placements in a syndicated rerun, with a Wells Fargo bank sign, Kenneth Cole shopping bags, and bottles of Coca-Cola and Evian appearing on the screen. The products, bags, and signs never existed in the actual episode. The Mexican TV network Televisa is also inserting visual product placements in entertainment shows in Mexico. Televisa charges $1,000 per insertion. The potential seems endless, as almost any product can be placed in a syndicated show, in almost any scene—creating a bonanza for advertisers.

Not everyone is so happy about the new medium, however. Some industry experts are concerned that the potential for virtual advertising and product placements may lead to oversaturation, becoming offensive and in poor taste. They note that product placement buyers will seek prominent placements, at key parts of the program, and that actors and actresses will become unknowing (and even unwilling) endorsers. (Imagine Ally McBeal carrying a Prada purse even though she never actually had one in the performance!) Equally important, they contend, is the potential for crass commercialism, with ads and placements getting in the way of program content—again irritating the viewer. Finally, and no less important, what about the actual sponsor or advertiser in a commercial break of the program? If Pepsi buys a regular ad on the program, and Coke, or even Evian, is allowed to appear as a product placement, what impact does that have on Pepsi's commercial? If General Motors sponsors college football games, and a virtual ad for Toyota appears every time a field goal or extra point is kicked, is that fair?

At this point, virtual advertising and product placements are in the infancy stage. But who knows how quickly the medium will catch on? The next time you watch "I Love Lucy," Lucy may be drinking a Diet Coke, while Ricky takes Viagra. Or the UCLA placekicker—whose team is sponsored by Adidas—may be kicking into a Nike ad. Who knows how things will change?

Sources: Stuart Elliott, "A Video Process Allows the Insertion of Brand-Name Products in TV Shows Already on Film," *New York Times,* March 29, 1999, p. 11; John Consoli, "Virtual Ads Set to Pitch," *Mediaweek,* March 22, 1999, mediaweek.com; "Virtual Ads, Real Problems," *Advertising Age,* March 24, 1999, p. 30; "Virtual Signage Breaks into Prime Time," *Mediaweek,* March 29, 1999, mediaweek.com.

Virtual ads and product placements are just a few of the many different ways that companies and organizations get their messages out. Ads have also appeared on manhole covers, inside restroom stalls, even on beepers. In this chapter, we review a number of support media, some that are new to the marketplace and others that have been around a while. We discuss the relative advantages and disadvantages, cost information, and audience measurement of each. We refer to them as **support media** because the media described in the previous chapters dominate the media strategies of large advertisers, particularly national advertisers. Support media are used to reach those people in the target market the primary media may not have reached and to reinforce, or support, their messages.

You may be surprised at how many different ways there are to deliver the message and how often you are exposed to them. Let's begin by examining the scope of the support media industry and some of the many alternatives available to marketers.

The Scope of the Support Media Industry

Support media are referred to by several titles, among them **alternative media, nonmeasured media,** and **nontraditional media.** These terms describe a vast variety of channels used to deliver communications and to promote products and services. In this chapter we will discuss many of these media (though, as you might imagine, it would be impossible for us to discuss them all).

Many advertisers, as well as the top 100 advertising agencies, have increased their use of nontraditional support media, and as new alternatives are developed, this use will continue to grow. Figures for nontraditional media do not include some of the most popular support media, such as out-of-home advertising, specialty advertising, and advertising in the Yellow Pages. Let us examine some of these in more detail.

Out-of-Home Media

Out-of-home advertising encompasses many advertising forms, including outdoor (billboards and signs), transit (both inside and outside the vehicle), skywriting, and a variety of other media. While outdoor advertising is used most often, as shown in Figure 13–1, the others are also increasing in use.

Outdoor Advertising

Outdoor advertising has probably existed since the days of cave dwellers. Both the Egyptians and the Greeks used it as early as 5,000 years ago. Outdoor is certainly one of the more pervasive communication forms, particularly if you live in an urban or suburban area.

Even though outdoor accounts for only about 2.3 percent of all advertising expenditures and the number of billboards has decreased, the medium has grown steadily in terms of dollars billed. In 1982, approximately $888 million was spent in this area; by 1995 this figure had risen to about $2.1 billion. The 1999 figures rose by 9.7 percent over that of 1998, to 4.8 billion.[1] As the medium was once dominated by

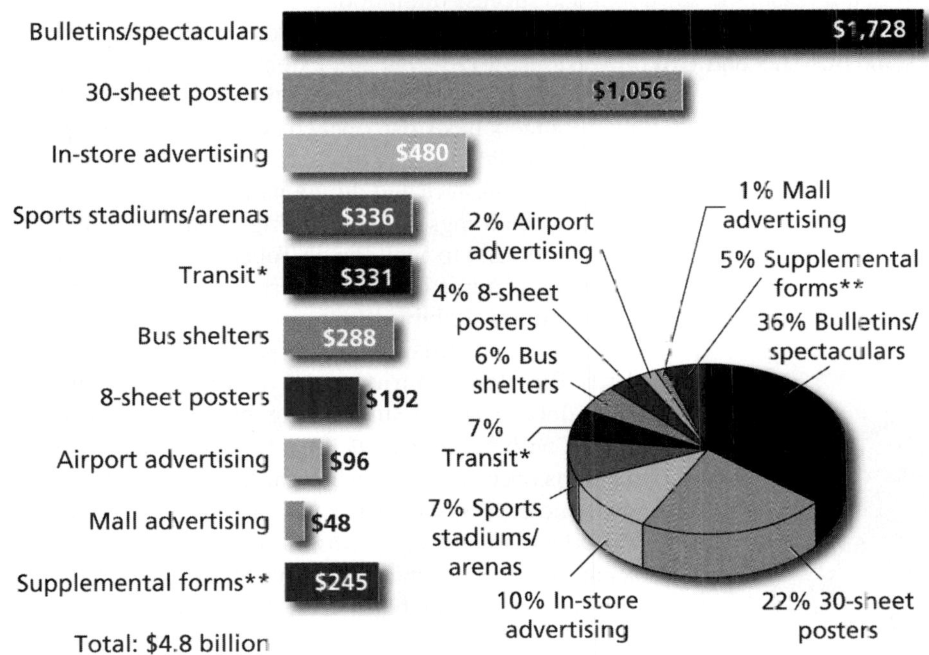

Figure 13–1 Estimated gross billings by media category show that outdoor ads are still the most popular

Figure 13–2 Outdoor advertising expenditures ranked by percent of total 1999 revenues

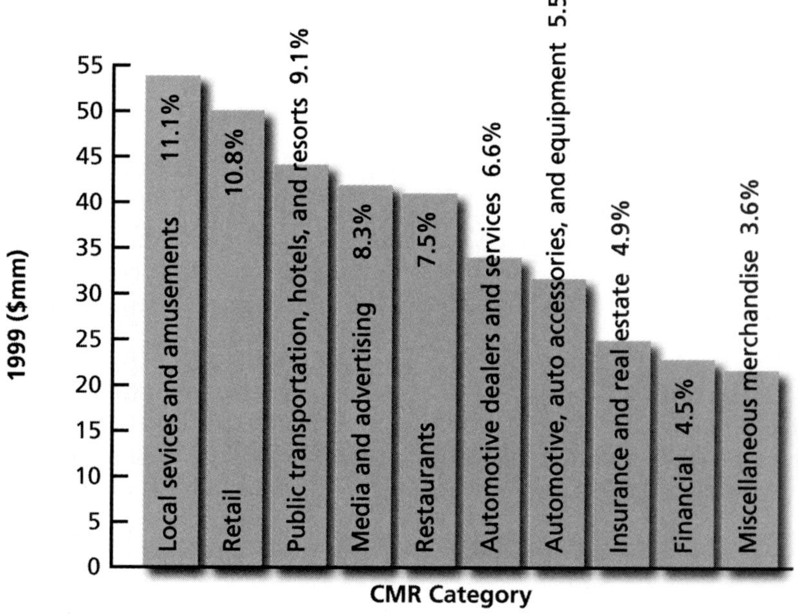

tobacco advertisers (25 percent of its $1.5 billion revenue came from cigarette advertising in 1991), there were concerns in the industry when an agreement was reached with 46 states in November 1998 to ban all cigarette ads. Increased expenditures from automotive, retail, and financial companies and from new advertisers such as the "dot-coms" have more than made up for the losses. Companies like the Gap, Universal Pictures, and Airtouch Communications are just a few employing this medium. As shown in Figure 13–2, outdoor continues to be used by a broad client base, a demonstration of its continued acceptance in the industry. The increase in the number of women in the work force has led to more advertising of products targeted to this segment, and the increases in the number of vehicles on the road and the number of miles driven have led to increased expenditures by gas companies and food and lodging providers.

A major reason for the continued success of outdoor is its ability to remain innovative through technology. As Exhibit 13–1 shows, billboards are no longer limited to standard sizes and two dimensions; 3-D forms and extensions are now used to attract attention. Electronic billboards and inflatables, like the one in Exhibit 13–2 that was used to promote Power Rangers have also opened new markets. You probably have been exposed to either signboards or electronic billboards at sports stadiums, in supermarkets, in the campus bookstore and dining halls, in shopping malls, on the freeways, or on the sides of buildings, from neon signs on skyscrapers in New York City to Mail Pouch Tobacco signs painted on the sides of barns in the Midwest. This is truly a pervasive medium (Exhibit 13–3).

Exhibit 13–1 Outdoor advertising goes beyond two dimensions

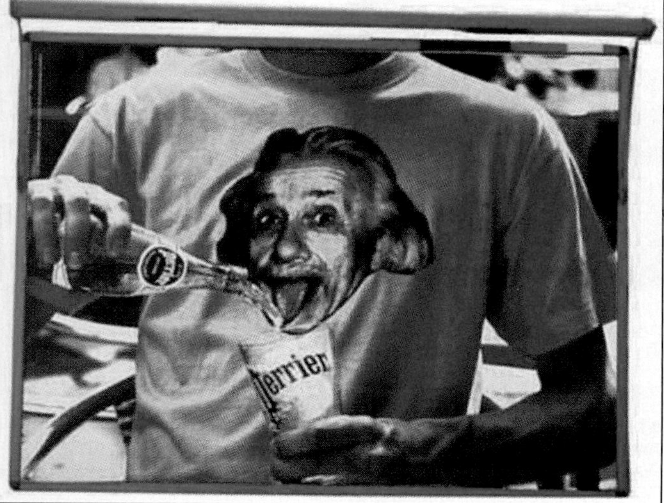

Outdoor advertising does have its critics. Ever since Lady Bird Johnson tried to rid the interstate highways of billboard advertising during her husband's presidency with the Highway Beautification Act of 1965, there has been controversy regarding its use. As previously noted, legislation has passed in 46 states banning the advertising of cigarettes on billboards. In addition, a number of cities and states have considered extending the ban to alcoholic beverages.[2] Consumers themselves seem to have mixed emotions about the medium. In a Maritz AmeriPoll asking consumers about their opinions of billboards, 62 percent of the respondents said they thought billboards should not be banned, while 52 percent said they should be strictly regulated. When asked if billboards were entertaining, 80 percent of

Exhibit 13–2 Inflatables bring new meaning to outdoor advertising

Exhibit 13–3 Most desirable out-of-home advertising locations

Bright lights, big cities

The most expensive and desirable locations for out-of-home advertising, based on an informal poll of more than a dozen top outdoor media company executives, agency media buyers and Wall Street observers, conducted by *Advertising Age.*

Location	Price/month
Times Square New York City	$50,000-$150,000
Sunset Strip Los Angeles	$30,000-$100,000
Lincoln Tunnel New York City/Weehawken, N.J.	$25,000-$60,000
Long Island Expressway (outside Midtown Tunnel) Long Island City, N.Y.	$25,000-$60,000
Union Square San Francisco	$20,000-$50,000
101N Freeway (toward Bay Bridge) San Francisco	$20,000-$40,000
Kennedy Expressway Chicago	$20,000-$30,000
Eisenhower Expressway Chicago	$15,000-$30,000
I-95 (at Biscayne heading toward South Beach) Miami	$10,000-$20,000
I-94 Detroit	$10,000-$20,000
Southwest Freeway (outside Galleria) Houston	$10,000-$20,000
Intersection of Stemmons & LBJ freeways Dallas	$10,000-$20,000
West side of L.A. (Hollywood, Santa Monica)	$10,000-$15,000

those surveyed said no, and when asked if billboards could be beautiful, only 27 percent said yes.[3]

Media buyers have not completely adopted outdoor, partially because of image problems and because of the belief that it is difficult to buy. (Approximately 80 percent of outdoor advertising is purchased by local merchants and companies.) Let us examine some of the advantages and disadvantages of the medium in more detail.

Advantages and Disadvantages of Outdoor Advertising

Outdoor advertising offers a number of advantages:

1. *Wide coverage of local markets.* With proper placement, a broad base of exposure is possible in local markets, with both day and night presence. A 100 GRP **showing** (the percentage of duplicated audience exposed to an outdoor poster daily) could yield exposure to an equivalent of 100 percent of the marketplace daily, or 3,000 GRPs over a month. This level of coverage is likely to yield high levels of reach.

2. *Frequency.* Because purchase cycles are typically for 30-day periods, consumers are usually exposed a number of times, resulting in high levels of frequency.

3. *Geographic flexibility.* Outdoor can be placed along highways, near stores, or on mobile billboards, almost anywhere that laws permit. Local, regional, or even national markets may be covered.

4. *Creativity.* As shown in Exhibit 13–1, outdoor ads can be very creative. Large print, colors, and other elements attract attention.

5. *Ability to create awareness.* Because of its impact (and the need for a simple message), outdoor can lead to a high level of awareness.

6. *Efficiency.* Outdoor usually has a very competitive CPM when compared to other media. The average CPM of outdoor is less than that of radio, TV, magazines, and newspapers.

7. *Effectiveness.* Outdoor advertising can often lead to sales, as demonstrated in Figure 13–3. In a study reported by BBDO advertising, 35 percent of consumers surveyed said they had called a phone number they saw on an out-of-home ad.[4] A study reported by Mukesh Bhargava and Naveen Donthu showed that outdoor advertising can have a significant effect on sales, particularly when combined with a promotion.[5]

8. *Production capabilities.* Modern technologies have reduced production times for outdoor advertising to allow for rapid turnaround time.

At the same time, however, there are limitations to outdoor, many of them related to its advantages:

1. *Waste coverage.* While it is possible to reach very specific audiences, in many cases the purchase of outdoor results in a high degree of waste coverage. It is not likely that everyone driving past a billboard is part of the target market.

Figure 13–3 Higher sales from outdoor advertising

Brand	Outdoor Used	Results
Hormel chili	#25 poster showing	Sales increased 8.5% Share grew 4.6%
Slice beverage	33 posters in Chicago positioned near Jewel stores	Sales at Jewel stores increased 18%
Neon automobile	#50 showing in 23 markets	60% of year one production sold out in 4 months
Shoney's Restaurants	47 posters in Nashville	Dessert sales up 27%
NFL on Fox network	Bulletins in 14 markets	Ratings up . . . no make-goods necessary

2. *Limited message capabilities.* Because of the speed with which most people pass by outdoor ads, exposure time is short, so messages are limited to a few words and/or an illustration. Lengthy appeals are not likely to be effective.

3. *Wearout.* Because of the high frequency of exposures, outdoor may lead to a quick wearout. People are likely to get tired of seeing the same ad every day.

4. *Cost.* Because of the decreasing signage available and the higher cost associated with inflatables, outdoor advertising can be expensive in both an absolute and a relative sense.

5. *Measurement problems.* One of the more difficult problems of outdoor advertising lies in the accuracy of measuring reach, frequency, and other effects. (As you will see in the measurement discussion, this problem is currently being addressed, though it has not been resolved.)

6. *Image problems.* Outdoor advertising has suffered some image problems as well as some disregard among consumers.

In sum, outdoor advertising has both advantages and disadvantages for marketers. Some of these problems can be avoided with other forms of out-of-home advertising.

Additional Out-of-Home Media

Several other forms of outdoor advertising are also available. As you read about them, keep in mind the advantages and disadvantages of outdoor in general mentioned earlier and consider whether these alternatives have the same advantages and/or provide a possible solution to the disadvantages.

Aerial Advertising

Airplanes pulling banners, skywriting (in letters as high as 1,200 feet), and blimps all constitute another form of outdoor advertising available to the marketer: **aerial advertising.** Generally these media are not expensive in absolute terms and can be useful for reaching specific target markets. For example, Coppertone has often used skywriting over beach areas to promote its tanning lotions, Gallo used skywriting to promote its wine coolers (Bartles & Jaymes), and local advertisers promote special events, sales, and the like. Exhibit 13–4 shows one of the many products, services, and/or events that have used this medium. Perhaps one of the more interesting examples of aerial advertising is that shown in Exhibit 13–5. Pizza Hut paid about $1 million to have a 30-foot version of its new logo on an unmanned Russian Proton rocket. The logo was visible for only a few seconds, but Pizza Hut felt the exposure was well worth the investment. (The company also put pizza on the Space Shuttle for those assembling the orbiting space platform.)

Mobile Billboards

Another outdoor medium is **mobile billboards** (see Exhibit 13–6). Some companies paint Volkswagen Beetles with ads called Beetleboards; others paint trucks and vans. Still others put ads on small billboards, mount them on trailers, and drive around and/or park in the geographic areas being tar-

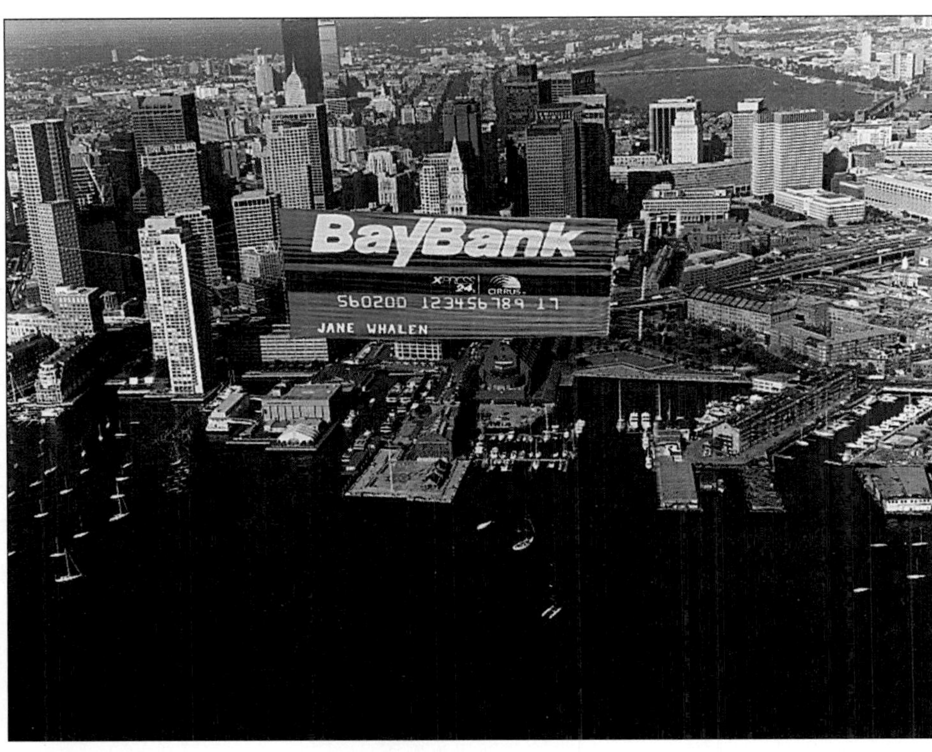

Exhibit 13–4 Aerial advertising is used by a variety of marketers

Exhibit 13–5 Pizza Hut takes aerial advertising to new heights

geted (Exhibit 13–6). Costs depend on the area and the mobile board company's fees, though even small and large organizations have found the medium affordable. One small company in California found that its five mobile cars account for 25 percent of its earnings, and a study conducted jointly by 3M and the American Trucking Association estimated that one truck traveling about 60,000 miles a year would create about 10 million viewer impressions of the ad placed on it.[6] In December 1999, the Traffic Audit Bureau (TAB) announced a new tracking methodology. In its first audit, the bureau estimated that three trucks with a Seiko watch ad on them were seen by an average of 121,755 people per day in the Chicago area.[7] Pennzoil, E-Bay, and America Online are a few advertisers that have used this medium (Exhibit 13–6).

In-Store Media

Advertisers spend an estimated $17 billion to promote their products in supermarkets and other stores with untypical media like displays, banners, and shelf signs. These point-of-purchase materials include video displays on shopping carts, kiosks

Exhibit 13–6
An interesting and unusual example of a mobile billboard

Trucks often serve as mobile billboards

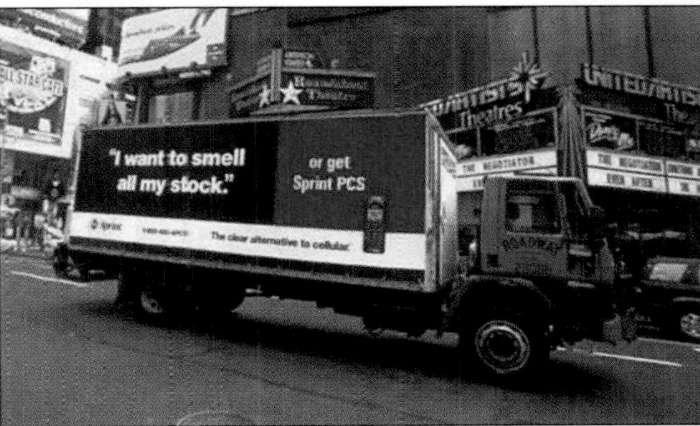

that provide recipes and beauty tips, and coupons at counters and cash registers, LED (light-emitting diode) boards, and ads that broadcast over in-house screens. IBM spends an estimated $15 million per year in this area. At one time, Miller Brewing Co. used 30 to 40 agencies to provide these services (it now uses 10). Figure 13–4 lists a few of the many **in-store media** options.

Much of the attraction of point-of-purchase media is based on figures from the Point of Purchase Advertising Institute (POPAI) that state approximately two-thirds of consumers' purchase decisions are made in the store; some impulse categories demonstrate an 80 percent rate.[8] Many advertisers are spending more of

Figure 13–4 In-store media options

Company/Program	Medium
ActMedia	
Act Now	Co-op couponing/sampling
Aisle Vision	Ad posters inserted in stores' directory signs
Carts	Ad placed on frame inside/outside shopping cart
Impact	Customized in-store promotion events
Instant Coupon Machine	Coupon dispensers mounted in shelf channels
Act Radio	Live format in-store radio network
Shelf Take-One	Two-sided take-one offers in plastic see-thru cartridges placed at shelf
Shelf Talk	Plastic frames on shelf near product
Addvantage Media Group	Shopping cart calculators
Advanced Promotion Technologies	
Vision System	Scanner-driven, card-based promotion system using audio/video at checkout
Alpine Promotions	"Adsticks" dividers that separate food at grocery store checkout
Audits and Surveys Worldwide	Tracks in-store sales using scanner data
Catalina Marketing	
Checkout Coupon	Scanner-driven coupon program that generates coupons at checkout
Checkout Message	Targeted ad messages delivered at checkout
Save Now	Instant electronic discounts
Donnelly Marketing	
Convert	Solo/customized promotion events
In-Store Advertising	Two-sided LED display units that hang above five high-traffic areas
Innova Marketing	In-store actresses and actors providing product demonstrations
Time In-Store	In-store couponing
Valassis In-Store	In-store couponing
SPAR Marketing Force	In-store demos and customized events
Media One, Inc.	
SuperAd	Backlit ads placed in checkout lanes
Stratmar Systems	
Field Services	In-store demos and customized events
StratMedia	Shopping cart ad program
Supermarket Communications Systems	
Good Neighbor Direct	Bulletin board distribution center

their dollars where decisions are made now that they can reach consumers at the point of purchase, providing additional product information while reducing their own efforts.

Miscellaneous Outdoor Media

As shown in Figure 13–5, there are numerous outdoor media available, adding to the pervasiveness of this medium. The next time you are out, take a few moments to observe how many different forms of outdoor advertising you are exposed to.

Audience Measurement in Out-of-Home Media

A number of sources of audience measurement and other information are available:

- Competitive Media Reports (formerly BAR/LNA) provides information on expenditures on outdoor media by major advertisers.
- Simmons Market Research Bureau conducts research annually for the Institute of Outdoor Advertising, providing demographic data, exposures, and the like. Mediamark Research Inc. (MRI) provides similar data.
- Standard Rate & Data Service provides a sourcebook on rate information, production requirements, closing dates, etc.
- Eight-Sheet Outdoor Advertising Association provides a buyers' guide containing facts and figures regarding outdoor advertising.
- Shelter Advertising Association provides a buyers' guide containing facts and figures regarding shelter advertising.
- Audience Measurement by Market for Outdoor (AMMO) audience estimates are provided by Marketmath, Inc., for outdoor showings in over 500 markets. Published annually, the reports are based on a series of local market travel studies and circulation audits and provide demographic characteristics of audiences.
- The Institute of Outdoor Advertising is a trade organization of the outdoor advertising industry. It gathers cost data and statistical information for outdoor advertising space purchases.

Figure 13–5 Out-of-home advertising faces/vehicles

Medium	1999 Estimate
30-sheet posters	210,000 posters
8-sheet posters	140,000 posters
Bulletins	56,000 bulletins
Buses	37,600 buses*
Commuter rail/subways	13,000 cars
Bus shelters	34,000**
Airports	100 airports
Shopping malls	1,200 malls
Grocery store displays	24,000 stores
Drugstores	10,000 stores
Convenience stores	10,000 stores
Professional sports stadiums/arenas	77 facilities

There are well over 30 types of out-of-home media vehcles in active use by advertisers today (many of which did not exist in 1970). The following media forms are also now available in various markets around the country:

- Painted walls
- Truck advertising
- Catering trucks
- Displays on college campuses
- Displays on military bases
- Air banner towing
- Movie theater advertising
- Kiosks
- Doctor's offices/waiting rooms
- Health clubs
- Jumbo Trons
- Golf course signage
- Ski resort signage
- Taxi signage
- Truck-stop advertising

*The United States has a total of 60,000 buses; 37,600 carry advertising.
**Includes shelter-size displays in parking lots/garages, approximately 1,500 in number.

- Harris-Donovan Media Systems employs a mathematical model using data supplied by the Traffic Audit Bureau and segmented by time period and billboard size. The data provide audience figures in the top 50 metropolitan areas and are available to subscribers on any IBM-compatible computer.
- The Point of Purchase Advertising Institute is a trade organization of point-of-purchase advertisers collecting statistical and other market information on POP advertising.
- The Outdoor Advertising Association of America (OAAA) is the primary trade association of the industry. It assists members with research, creative ideas, and more effective use of the medium and has a website at www.oaa.org.
- The Media Market Guide (MMG) provides physical dimensions, population characteristics, and media opportunities for the top 100 media markets.
- The Traffic Audit Bureau (TAB) is the auditing arm of the industry. TAB conducts traffic counts on which the published rates are based.
- The Traffic Audit Bureau for Media Measurement provides data regarding exposures to a variety of out-of-home media, including bus shelters, aerial banners, in-store media, and billboards. This organization was formed in response to complaints that current methodologies might overstate the reach provided by these media.
- Scarborough publishes local market studies providing demographic data, product usage, and outdoor media usage.
- Computer packages like Telmar, Donnelly, TAPSCAN, and IMS also provide information comparing outdoor with other media.

One of the weaknesses associated with outdoor advertising is audience measurement. Space rates are usually based on the number of desired showings, as shown in Figure 13–6. For example, a 100 showing would theoretically provide coverage to the entire market. In San Diego, this would mean coverage of approximately 2 million people for a monthly rate of $30,600 to $37,200. Along with rate information, the companies offering outdoor billboards provide reach and frequency estimates—but there is no valid way to verify that the showings are performing as promised. The buyer is somewhat at the mercy of the selling agent.

In response to criticism, the industry has implemented a gross ratings point system similar to that used in the television industry. While the system has helped, problems associated with the use of GRPs (discussed earlier in this text) limit the usefulness of this information. Many experts think the new service provided by Harris Media Systems is a significant improvement over the AMMO system, resulting in more credible information.[9]

Transit Advertising

Another form of out-of-home advertising is **transit advertising.** While similar to outdoor in the sense that it uses billboards and electronic messages, transit is targeted at the millions of people who are exposed to commercial transportation

Figure 13–6 Posting space rates, San Diego market (per-month basis)

Showing Size	1 Month	3 Months	6 Months	12 Months
#25 (15 posters)	$10,650	$10,350	$10,050	$ 9,750
#50 (30 posters)	21,300	20,700	20,100	19,500
#75 (45 posters)	31,950	31,050	30,150	29,250
#100 (60 posters)	37,200	35,700	33,000	30,600

facilities, including buses, taxis, commuter trains, elevators, trolleys, airplanes, and subways.

Transit advertising has been around for a long time, but recent years have seen a renewed interest in this medium. Due in part to the increased number of women in the work force (they can be reached on their way to work more easily than at home), audience segmentation, and the rising cost of TV advertising, yearly transit ad spending increased from $43 million in 1972 to over $300 million in 1998.[10] Much of this spending has come from package-goods companies such as Colgate, H. J. Heinz, Kraft–General Foods, and Weight Watchers, which like transit's lower costs and improved frequency of exposures. Other retailers, movie studios, and business-to-business companies have also increased expenditures in this area.

Types of Transit Advertising

There are actually three forms of transit advertising: (1) inside cards, (2) outside posters, and (3) station, platform, or terminal posters.

Inside Cards If you have ever ridden a commuter bus, you have probably noticed the inside cards placed above the seats and luggage area advertising restaurants, TV or radio stations, or a myriad of other products and services. An innovation is the electronic message boards that carry current advertising information. The ability to change the message and the visibility provide the advertiser with a more attention-getting medium.

Transit cards can be controversial. For example, in the New York subway system, many of the ads for chewing gum, soup, and Smokey the Bear have given way to public service announcements about AIDS, unwanted pregnancies, rape, and infant mortality. While subway riders may agree that such issues are important, many of them complain that the ads are depressing and intrusive.

A variation on inside transit advertising is shown in Exhibit 13–7. The airline ticket holder is a very effective form of advertising communication. It takes advantage of a captive audience and keeps the message in front of the passenger the whole time he or she is holding the ticket.

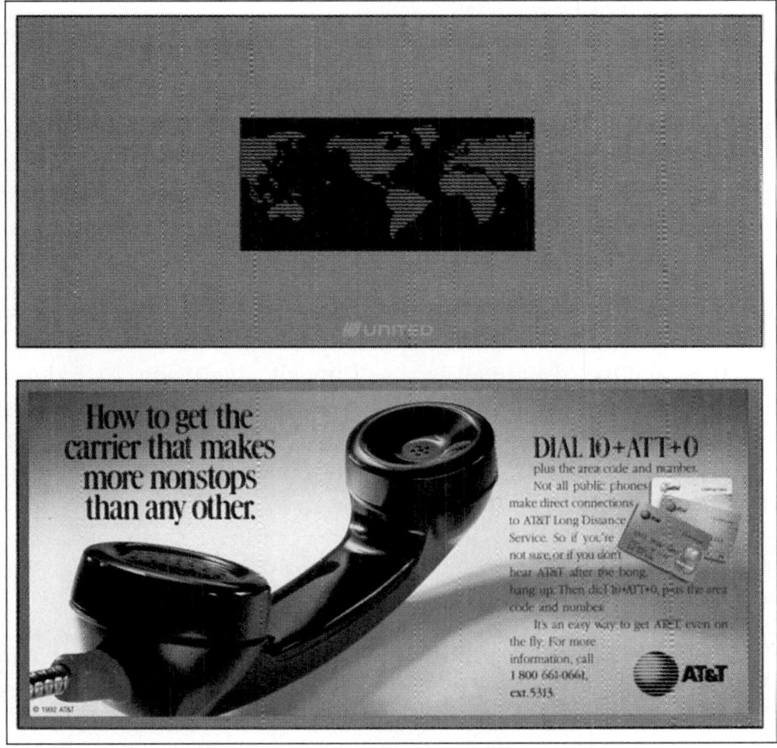

Exhibit 13–7 Airline ticket holders are used to promote a variety of products

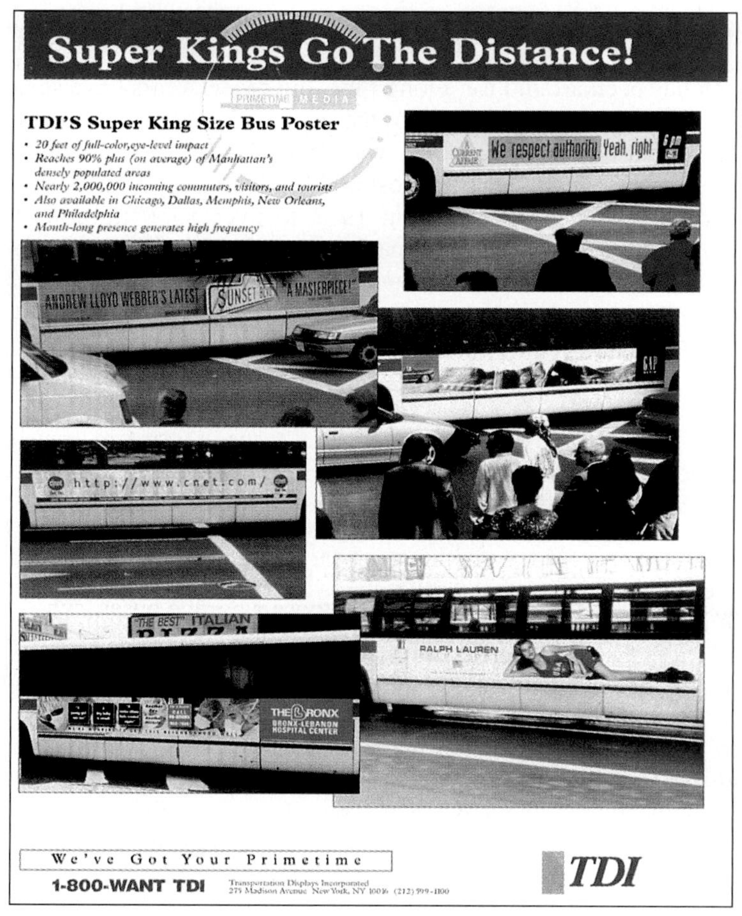

Exhibit 13–8 Outside posters often appear on buses

Outside Posters Advertisers use various forms of outdoor transit posters to promote products and services. These **outside posters** may appear on the sides, backs, and/or roofs of buses, taxis, trains, and subway and trolley cars. An example is shown in the TDI ad in Exhibit 13–8.

The increased sophistication of this medium was demonstrated in a test market in Barcelona, Spain, during the 1992 Summer Olympics. Viatex—a joint venture among Atlanta-based Bevilaqua International (a sports marketing company), Saatchi & Saatchi Lifestyle Group, and Warrec Co., a Connecticut-based international business firm—mounted electronic billboards on the sides of buses. These monitors flashed Olympic news and ads that could change at scheduled times. Electronic beacons located throughout the city were activated as the buses drove by to change the message for the various locations.

Station, Platform, and Terminal Posters Floor displays, island showcases, electronic signs, and other forms of advertising that appear in train or subway stations, airline terminals, and the like are all forms of transit advertising. As Exhibit 13–9 shows, **terminal posters** can be very attractive and attention getting. Bus shelters often provide the advertiser with expanded coverage where other outdoor boards may be restricted. Gannett Transit recently introduced electronic signs on subway platforms in New York.

Advantages and Disadvantages of Transit Advertising

Advantages of using transit advertising include the following:

1. *Exposure.* Long length of exposure to an ad is one major advantage of indoor forms. The average ride on mass transit is 30 to 44 minutes, allowing for plenty of exposure time.[11] As with airline tickets, the audience is essentially a captive one, with nowhere else to go and nothing much to do. As a result, riders are likely to

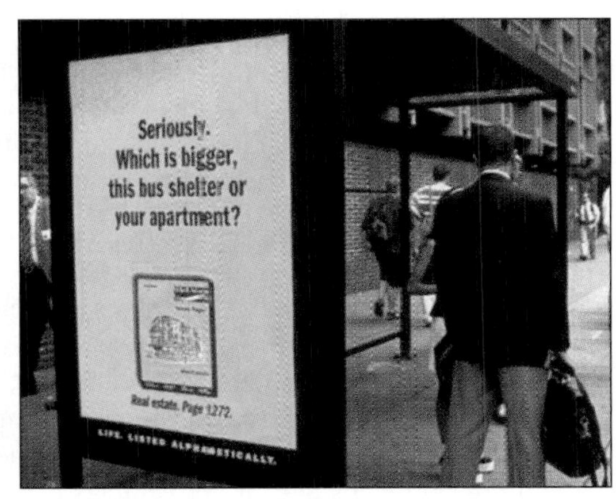

Exhibit 13–9 Terminal posters can be used to attract attention

read the ads—more than once. A second form of exposure transit advertising provides is the absolute number of people exposed. About 9 million people ride mass transit every week, providing a substantial number of potential viewers.[12]

2. *Frequency.* Because our daily routines are standard, those who ride buses, subways, and the like are exposed to the ads repeatedly. If you rode the same subway to work and back every day, in one month you would have the opportunity to see the ad 20 to 40 times. The locations of station and shelter signs also afford high frequency of exposure.

3. *Timeliness.* Many shoppers get to stores on mass transit. An ad promoting a product or service at a particular shopping area could be a very timely communication.

4. *Geographic selectivity.* For local advertisers in particular, transit advertising provides an opportunity to reach a very select segment of the population. A purchase of a location in a certain neighborhood will lead to exposure to people of specific ethnic backgrounds, demographic characteristics, and so on.

5. *Cost.* Transit advertising tends to be one of the least expensive media in terms of both absolute and relative costs. An ad on the side of a bus can be purchased for a very reasonable CPM.

Some disadvantages are also associated with transit:

1. *Image factors.* To many advertisers, transit advertising does not carry the image they would like to represent their products or services. Some advertisers may think having their name on the side of a bus or on a bus stop bench does not reflect well on the firm.

2. *Reach.* While an advantage of transit advertising is the ability to provide exposure to a large number of people, this audience may have certain lifestyles and/or behavioral characteristics that are not true of the target market as a whole. For example, in rural or suburban areas, mass transit is limited or nonexistent, so the medium is not very effective for reaching these people.

3. *Waste coverage.* While geographic selectivity may be an advantage, not everyone who rides a transportation vehicle or is exposed to transit advertising is a potential customer. For products that do not have specific geographic segments, this form of advertising incurs a good deal of waste coverage.

Another problem is that the same bus may not run the same route every day. To save wear and tear on the vehicles, some companies alternate city routes (with much stop and go) with longer suburban routes. Thus, a bus may go downtown one day and reach the desired target group but spend the next day in the suburbs, where there may be little market potential.

4. *Copy and creative limitations.* It may be very difficult to place colorful, attractive ads on cards or benches. And while much copy can be provided on inside cards, on the outside of buses and taxis the message is fleeting and short copy points are necessary.

5. *Mood of the audience.* Sitting or standing on a crowded subway may not be conducive to reading advertising, let alone experiencing the mood the advertiser would like to create. Controversial ad messages may contribute to this less than positive feeling. Likewise, hurrying through an airport may create anxieties that limit the effectiveness of the ads placed there.

In summary, an advantage for one product or service advertiser may be a disadvantage for another. Transit advertising can be an effective medium, but one must understand its strengths and weaknesses to use it properly.

Audience Measurement in Transit Advertising

As with outdoor advertising, the cost basis for transit is the number of showings. In transit advertising, a 100 showing means one ad appears on or in each vehicle in the system; a showing of 50 means half of the vehicles carry the ad. If you are placing such ads on taxicabs, it may be impossible to determine who is being exposed to them.

Rate information comes from the sellers of transit advertising, and audience information is very limited. So much of the information marketers need to purchase transit ads does not come from purely objective sources.

Promotional Products Marketing

According to the Promotional Products Association International (PPA), **promotional products marketing** is "the advertising or promotional medium or method that uses promotional products, such as ad specialties, premiums, business gifts, awards, prizes, or commemoratives." Promotional products marketing is the more up-to-date name for what used to be called specialty advertising. **Specialty advertising** has now been provided with a new definition:

> A medium of advertising, sales promotion, and motivational communication employing imprinted, useful, or decorative products called advertising specialties, a subset of promotional products.
>
> Unlike premiums, with which they are sometimes confused (called advertising specialties), these articles are always distributed free—recipients don't have to earn the specialty by making a purchase or contribution.[13]

Exhibit 13–10 Promotional products can be a valuable contributor to the IMC program

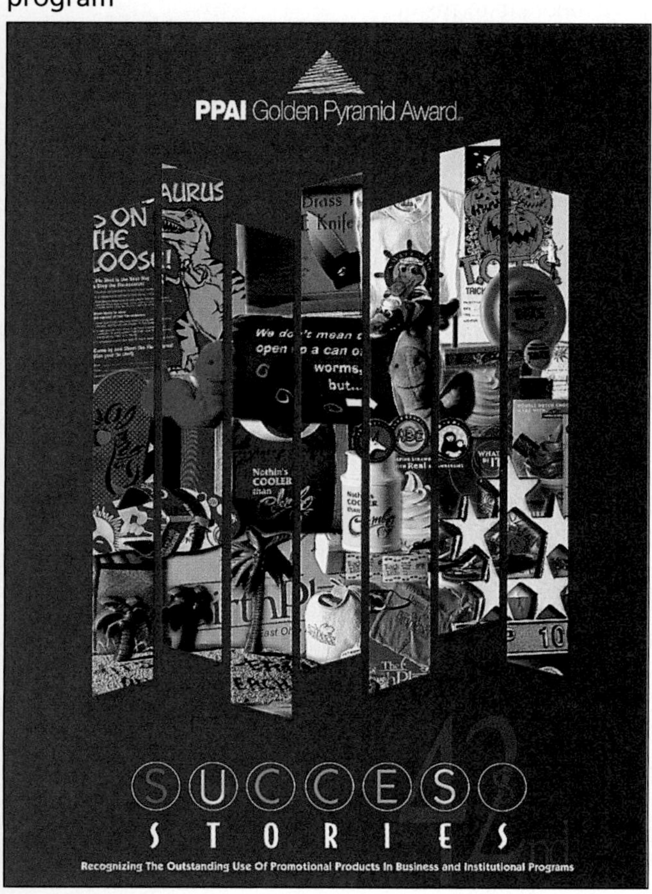

As you can see from these descriptions, specialty advertising is often considered both an advertising and a sales promotion medium. In our discussion, we treat it as a supportive advertising medium, in the IMC program (Exhibit 13–10).

There are over 15,000 *advertising specialty* items, including ballpoint pens, coffee mugs, key rings, calendars, T-shirts, and matchbooks. Unconventional specialties such as plant holders, wall plaques, and gloves with the advertiser's name printed on them are also used to promote a company or its product; so are glassware, trophies, awards, and vinyl products. In fact, advertisers spend over $13.1 billion per year on specialty advertising items. The increased use of this medium makes it the fastest-growing of all advertising or sales promotion media.[14]

If you stop reading for a moment and look around your desk (or bed or beach blanket), you'll probably find some specialty advertising item nearby. It may be the pen you are using, a matchbook, or even a book cover with the campus bookstore name on it. (Figure 13–7 shows the percentage of sales by product category.) Specialty items are used for many promotional purposes: to thank a customer for patronage, keep the name of the company in front of consumers, introduce new products, or reinforce

Figure 13–7 Sales of promotional products by category (numbers in parentheses indicate sales by product category)

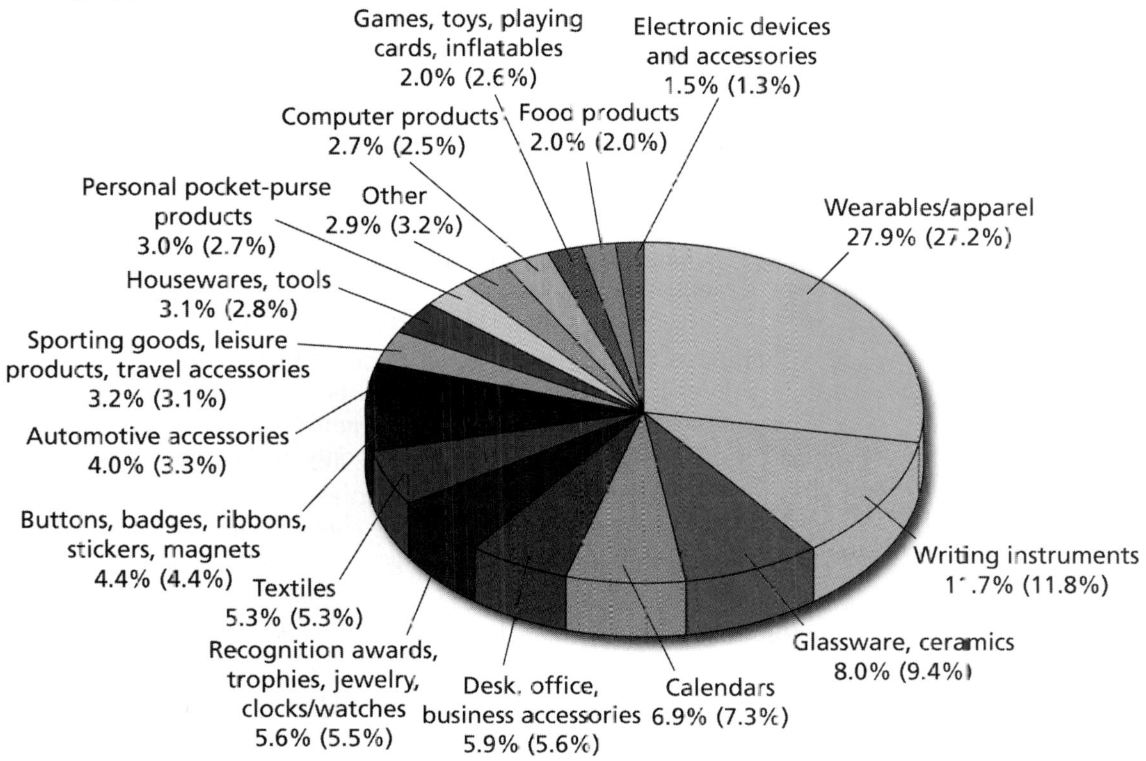

Product Category	Items Included
Wearables/apparel	Aprons, uniforms, blazers, caps, headbands, jackets, neckwear, footwear, etc.
Writing instruments	Pens, pencils, markets, highlighters, etc.
Glassware/ceramics	China, crystal, mugs, figurines, etc.
Calendars	Wall and wallet calendars, desk diaries, pocket secretaries, etc.
Desk/office/business accessories	Briefcases, folders, desk pen sets, calculators, cubed paper, etc.
Recognition awards/trophies/ emblematic jewelry/clocks and watches	Plaques, certificates, etc.
Textiles	Totebags, flags, towels, umbrellas, pennants, throws, blankets, etc.
Buttons/badges/ribbons/ stickers/magnets	Decals, transfers, signs, banners, etc.
Automotive accessories	Key tags, bumper strips, road maps, floormats, window shades, etc.
Sporting goods/leisure products/ travel accessories	Picnic/party products, camping equipment, barbecue items, bar products, plastic cups, binoculars, luggage, passport cases, etc.
Houseware/tools	Measuring devices, kitchen products, picture frames, household decorations, ornaments, tool kits, first aid kits, furniture, flashlights, cutlery, weather instruments, etc.
Personal/pocket-purse products	Pocket knives, grooming aids, lighters, matches, sunglasses, wallets, etc.
Computer products	Mouse pads, monitor frames, disk carriers, wrist pads, software, etc.
Games/toys/playing cards/ inflatables	Kites, balls, puzzles, stuffed animals, etc.
Food gifts	Candy, nuts, gourmet meat, spices, etc.
Electronic devices and accessories	Radios, TVs, videotapes, music CDs, phone cards, etc.

the name of an existing company, product, or service. Advertising specialties are often used to support other forms of product promotions.

Advantages and Disadvantages of Promotional Products Marketing

Like any other advertising medium, promotional products marketing offers the marketer both advantages and disadvantages. Advantages include the following:

1. *Selectivity.* Because specialty advertising items are generally distributed directly to target customers, the medium offers a high degree of selectivity. The communication is distributed to the desired recipient, reducing waste coverage.

2. *Flexibility.* As the variety of specialty items in Figure 13–7 demonstrates, this medium offers a high degree of flexibility. A message as simple as a logo or as long as is necessary can be distributed through a number of means. Both small and large companies can employ this medium, limited only by their own creativity.

3. *Frequency.* Most forms of specialty advertising are designed for retention. Key chains, calendars, and pens remain with the potential customer for a long time, providing repeat exposures to the advertising message at no additional cost.

4. *Cost.* Some specialty items are rather expensive (for example, leather goods), but most are affordable to almost any size organization. While they are costly on a CPM basis when compared with other media, the high number of repeat exposures drives down the relative cost per exposure of this advertising medium

5. *Goodwill.* Promotional products are perhaps the only medium that generates goodwill in the receiver. Because people like to receive gifts and many of the products are functional (key chains, calendars, etc.), consumers are grateful to receive them. In a recent study of users of promotional products, goodwill was cited as the number 1 reason for use.

6. *Supplementing other media.* A major advantage of promotional products marketing is its ability to supplement other media. Because of its low cost and repeat exposures, the simplest message can reinforce the appeal or information provided through other forms. For example, the Cartoon Network, which includes two of the world's largest animated film libraries, used specialty products to target 500 cable TV stations featuring "Wile E. Coyote and the Roadrunner." It delivered a crowbar and a brown box whose lid read "One ACME Launch Assistance Tool" to each station. The crates contained promotional launch items such as ad slicks, literature, videos, and audiotapes describing the new network. Of the 500 networks, 480 signed up for the new program.

Promotional products have also been used to support trade shows, motivate dealers, recognize employees, and promote consumer and sales force contests.

Disadvantages of promotional products marketing include the following:

1. *Image.* While most forms of specialty advertising are received as friendly reminders of the store or company name, the firm must be careful choosing the specialty item. The company image may be cheapened by a chintzy or poorly designed advertising form.

2. *Saturation.* With so many organizations now using this advertising medium, the marketplace may become saturated. While you can always use another ballpoint pen or book of matches, the value to the receiver declines if replacement is too easy, and the likelihood that you will retain the item or even notice the message is reduced. The more unusual the specialty, the more value it is likely to have to the receiver.

3. *Lead time.* The lead time required to put together a promotional products message is significantly longer than that for most other media.

Even with its disadvantages promotional products can be an effective medium, as demonstrated in IMC Perspective 13–1.

IMC Perspective 13–1

Successfully Promoting Everything from Lungs to Plastic News

Each year the Promotional Products Association International (PPAI) holds a meeting to honor its Golden Pyramid Award winners. These awards are given to those companies that have successfully and creatively used Promotional Products to achieve their communications and/or marketing goals. Categories include goodwill programs, consumer promotions, business-to-business promotions, sales incentive programs, and not-for-profit. As can be seen by some of the winning examples that follow, these programs can achieve some very interesting results:

American Lung Association of Florida. The objective of the promotional campaign was to encourage participation and commitment to a nonsmoking program involving 1,200 high school students and to recognize their adult facilitators. The American Lung Association of Florida conducted a study of 57 Florida high schools to examine students' smoking habits and develop effective stop-smoking programs. At each of the eight sessions in the 10-week study, students were given a series of promotional products incentives carrying the "N-O-T" (Not on Tobacco) logo. Each item promoted the theme—for example, wallets reflected how much money could be saved, stress balls gave quitters something to do with their hands on "quit day," and locker mirrors reflected how good they would look after they quit smoking. Of the 1,000 students who began the program, more than 90 percent consistently attended the sessions and a substantial number quit smoking.

Plastics News. The trade publication's objective was to sell ads in their show issue and promote attendance at a House of Blues awards presentation party. Positioning themselves as the best resource for information on the plastics industry, *Plastics News* and *Plastics News on the Web* used a play on words to dub themselves as the "News Brothers" (see the photo). The campaign mailed a blues CD to 2,000 prospects, accounts, and agencies in the plastics industry. Two follow-up mailings were sent eight weeks prior to the plastics trade show to promote visiting the booth and attending an awards party at the House of Blues. At the party, attendees received "News Brothers" masks and at the trade show they were handed scratch-off cards, with winners receiving sunglasses and harmonica key chains. The promotion resulted in a 25 percent increase in advertising space sold, booth traffic and visits to the website increased dramatically, and 150 new paid subscriptions were gained.

Ingalls Employees Credit Union. The credit union had an objective of teaching children the importance of saving and increasing credit union memberships in the target market of children 10 years of age and younger. Using a spin-off of its slogan "Your Family's Financial Navigator," the promotional products campaign used a "Nawi-Gator" alligator mascot to appeal to the kids. Nawi was featured in the credit union's quarterly newsletter, radio spots, and public appearances. Nawi-Gator posters were placed in all branches to get attention, as were balloons. Kids who signed up received a membership that included a Nawi-Gator magnet frame, and those who deposited money into savings received incentive bucks that could be redeemed to purchase insulated lunch sacks, sport packs, T-shirts, stuffed alligators, nylon wallets, and knapsacks. In a one-year period, the Nawi-Gator Saver Club grew from 369 to 1,000 members and deposits in the first 60 days reached $30,000—doubling the goal of $15,000.

As you can see, promotional products can be used in a variety of ways by a variety of companies. What you probably didn't know is that every one of the Pyramid winners cited above paid less than $10 per contact to achieve its goal. Now that is a success story!

Sources: "PPAI Golden Pyramid Award Success Stories," Promotional Products Association International, 1999; "Golden Pyramid Competition," Promotional Products Association International, 1998.

Audience Measurement in Promotional Products Marketing

Owing to the nature of the industry, specialty advertising has no established ongoing audience measurement system. Research has been conducted in an attempt to determine the impact of this medium, however, including the following reports.

A study by Schreiber and Associates indicated 39 percent of people receiving advertising specialties could recall the name of the company as long as six months later, and a study conducted by A. C. Nielsen found that 31 percent of respondents were still using at least one specialty they had received a year or more earlier.[15]

A study by Gould/Pace University found the inclusion of a specialty item in a direct-mail piece generated a greater response rate and 321 percent greater dollar purchases per sale than mail pieces without such items.[16] Studies at Baylor University showed that including an ad specialty item in a thank-you letter can improve customers' attitudes toward a company's sales reps by as much as 34 percent and toward the company itself by as much as 52 percent.[17] Finally, Richard Manville Research reported the average household had almost four calendars; if they had not been given such items free, two-thirds of the respondents said they would purchase one, an indication of the desirability of this particular specialty item.[18] Figure 13–8 demonstrates how promotional products can be used effectively in an IMC program.

The Promotional Products Association International (www.ppai.org) is the trade organization of the field. The PPAI helps marketers develop and use specialty advertising forms. It also provides promotional and public relations support for specialty advertising and disseminates statistical and educational information.

Yellow Pages Advertising

When we think of advertising media, many of us overlook one of the most popular forms in existence—the **Yellow Pages.** While most of us use the Yellow Pages frequently, we tend to forget they are advertising. Over 200 publishers produce more than 6,500 Yellow Pages throughout the United States, generating $12.1 billion in advertising expenditures. This makes the Yellow Pages the fifth-largest medium (just behind radio).[19]

More than 90 percent of the industry's ad revenues are accounted for by nine big operators: the seven regional Bell companies, the Donnelley Directory, and GTE Directories.[20] Local advertisers constitute the bulk of the ads in these directories (about 90 percent), though national advertisers such as U-Haul, Sears, and General Motors use them as well.[21]

Figure 13–8 The Impact of promotional products in an IMC program

Combining Promotional Products with:	Effect
Advertising	Including direct mail with a promotional product increased response to a print ad to 4.2%, versus 2.3% with direct mail only and .7% with an ad only.
Personal selling	Customers receiving a promotional product expressed more goodwill toward the company than did those receiving a letter. They rated the company more positively in 52% of the cases and rated the salespeople more proficient (34%) and more capable (16%). Business-to-business customers receiving a promotional product were 14% more likely to provide leads, while salespersons who gave gifts to customers received 22% more leads than those who did not.
Trade shows	Responses to invitations to visit a booth were higher when a promotional product was enclosed.
Direct	Responses to direct-mail sales pieces were 1.9% with only a letter but 3.3% with a promotional product (75% higher). Other studies have shown increases of 50 to 66%.

Interestingly, there are several forms of Yellow Pages. (Because AT&T never copyrighted the term, any publisher can use it.) They include the following:

- *Specialized directories.* Directories are targeted at select markets such as Hispanics, blacks, Asians, and women. Also included in this category are toll-free directories, Christian directories, and many others.
- *Audiotex.* The "talking Yellow Pages" offer oral information on advertisers.
- *Interactive.* Consumers search the database for specific types of information. Advertisers can update their listings frequently.
- *Internet directories.* As of 1998 there were 907 websites that provided some form of Internet-based Yellow Pages (see www.kelseygroup.com). These directories include national directories which provide a nationwide database of business listings; local and regional directories, which provide information on a local or regional basis; and "shared" directories, in which local companies join together to form a national database.
- *Other services.* Some Yellow Pages directories offer coupons and freestanding inserts. In Orange County, California, telephone subscribers received samples of Golden Grahams and Cinnamon Toast Crunch cereals when their Yellow Pages were delivered.

The Yellow Pages are often referred to as a **directional medium** because the ads do not create awareness or demand for products or services; rather, once consumers have decided to buy, the Yellow Pages point them in the direction where their purchases can be made.[22] The Yellow Pages are thus considered the final link in the buying cycle, as shown in Exhibit 13–11.

Advantages and Disadvantages of Yellow Pages

The Yellow Pages offer the following advantages to advertisers:

1. *Wide availability.* A variety of directories are published. According to the Yellow Pages Publishers Association, consumers refer to the Yellow Pages more than 19.4 billion times yearly.[23]
2. *Action orientation.* Consumers use the Yellow Pages when they are considering, or have decided to take, action.
3. *Costs.* Ad space and production costs are relatively low compared to other media.
4. *Frequency.* Because of their longevity (Yellow Pages are published yearly), consumers return to the directories time and again. The average adult refers to the Yellow Pages about twice a week,[24] and 60 percent of U.S. households use the Yellow Pages weekly.[25]
5. *Nonintrusiveness.* Because consumers choose to use the Yellow Pages, they are not considered an intrusion. Studies show that most consumers rate the Yellow Pages very favorably.[26]

Disadvantages of the Yellow Pages include the following:

1. *Market fragmentation.* Since Yellow Pages are essentially local media, they tend to be very localized. Add to this the increasing number of specialized directories, and the net result is a very specific offering.
2. *Timeliness.* Because Yellow Pages are printed only once a year, they become outdated. Companies may relocate, go out of business, or change phone numbers in the period between editions.
3. *Lack of creativity.* While the Yellow Pages are somewhat flexible, their creative aspects are limited.

Exhibit 13–11 The Yellow Pages are the final link in the buying cycle

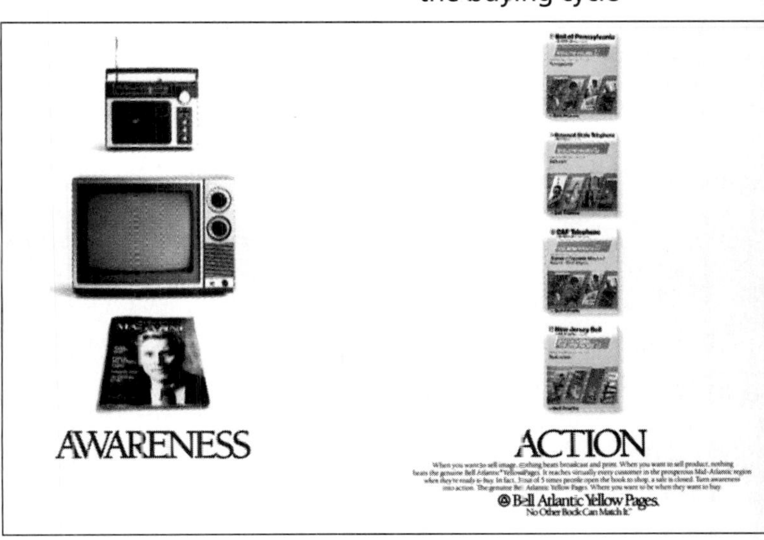

4. *Lead times.* Printing schedules require that ads be placed a long time before the publications appear. It is impossible to get an ad in after the deadline, and advertisers need to wait a long time before the next edition.

5. *Clutter.* A recent study by Avery Abernethy indicates that the Yellow Pages (like other media) experience problems with clutter.

Audience Measurement in the Yellow Pages Two forms of audience measurement are employed in the Yellow Pages industry. As with other print media, *circulation* is counted as the number of either individuals or households possessing a particular directory. But Yellow Pages advertisers have resisted the use of circulation figures for evaluating audience size, arguing that this number represents only *potential* exposures to an ad.[27] Given that households may possess more than one directory, advertisers argued for a figure based on *usage.* The National Yellow Pages Monitor (NYPM) now provides Yellow Pages directory ratings and usage behavior by market. Using a diary method similar to that used for broadcast media, this ratings method allows advertisers to determine both the absolute and relative costs of advertising in different directories (see Figure 13–9). Statistical Research Inc. (SRI) conducts national studies to measure Yellow Pages usage. Simmons and MRI provide demographic and usage information.

The trade association for the Yellow Pages, the Yellow Pages Publishers Association (www.yppa.org), provides industry information, rates, educational materials, and assistance to advertisers and potential advertisers. The YPPA also disseminates educational and statistical information.

Other Media

There are numerous other nontraditional ways to promote products. Some are reviewed here.

Advertising in Movie Theaters and Videos

Two methods of delivering the message that are increasing quickly (to the dismay of many) are the use of movie theaters and video rentals to promote products and/or services. Commercials shown before the film and previews, with both local and national sponsorships, have almost replaced cartoons. For example, Coca-Cola Co. has frequently advertised the Coke Classic brand in movie theaters and promoted Fruitopia with a 60-second spot in this medium. Sears, Gap, and Target have also employed this medium, as have over 50 other companies. McDonald's and Outback Steak Houses are prime users. On videos, companies place ads before the movies as well as on the cartons they come in. Pepsi advertises on the video of *Casper.* Disney often promotes its upcoming movies as well as Disney World (10 minutes of advertising preceded *The Lion King* on video).[28] (If you have ever rented a Disney movie, you are well aware of this!) The Canadian government has shown "stay in school" spots, knowing that the movies are a good way to reach 12- to 17-year-olds. Dozens of other advertisers have also used this medium, including Sega, AT&T, and DeBeers.

Figure 13–9 The Yellow Pages use a usage rating system

CPM Based on Directory Circulation

Directory	Circulation	Cost for a Full-Page Ad	CPM
A	509,000	$28,000	$55.01
B	505,000	$21,000	$41.58

CPM Based on Directory Usage (Ratings)

Directory	Total References per Year	Share of References	Cost for a Full-Page Ad	CPM
A	58,400,000	76.9%	$28,000	$ .48
B	17,500,000	23.1%	$21,000	$1.20

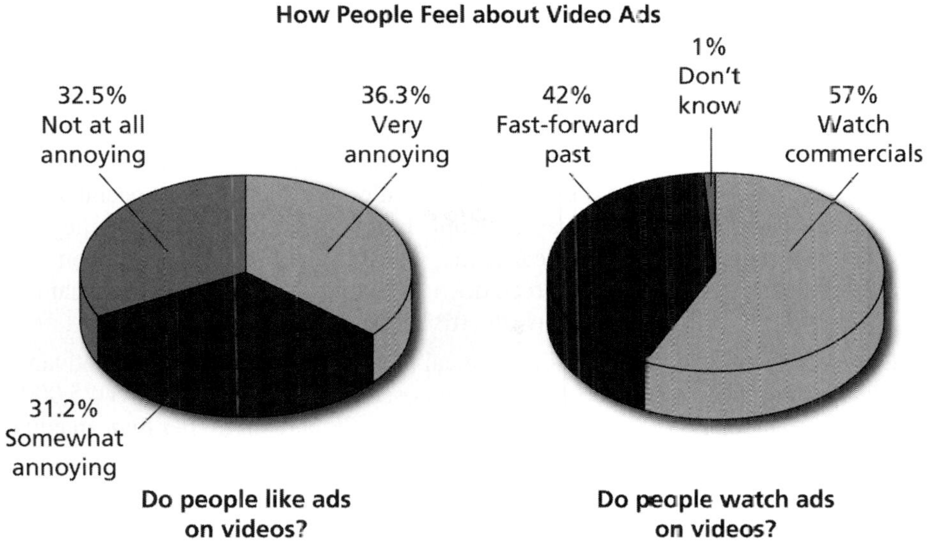

How People Feel about Video Ads

32.5% Not at all annoying | 36.3% Very annoying | 31.2% Somewhat annoying

Do people like ads on videos?

42% Fast-forward past | 1% Don't know | 57% Watch commercials

Do people watch ads on videos?

Figure 13–10 Consumer opinions about ads on video

Consumer reaction to ads in movie theaters and on videos is mixed. As shown in Figure 13–10, most people think ads on videos are annoying or very annoying (67.5 percent). But the same survey showed that as many as 57 percent watch these commercials. The same seems to hold true for advertising in movie theaters. In an *Advertising Age*/Gallup national sample of moviegoers, 35 percent were against a ban on ads in movie theaters and another 21 percent were unsure whether such a ban should be enacted.[29] The survey was taken after Walt Disney Co. announced it would stop showing its movies in any theater that runs on-screen advertising along with the films. While advertisers were infuriated, Disney claimed its surveys showed customers were extremely irritated by such ads and as a result might quit coming to the theaters.[30]

Adam Snyder, writing in *Brandweek* magazine, believes that pushing movies is acceptable but beyond that consumers are likely to react negatively.[31] Nevertheless, Blake Thomas, marketing vice president for MGM/UA Home Entertainment, claims "We could conceivably sell as much air time as we want, since advertisers cannot resist the temptation of reaching tens of millions of viewers."[32]

Advantages of Movie and Video Advertising

Both movies and videos provide a number of advantages to advertisers, including the following:

1. *Exposure.* The number of people attending movies is substantial; ticket sales are over $5 billion per year,[33] and attendance continues to climb. At the same time, the number of households using VCRs is increasing. These growth figures mean that more people are likely to be exposed to the ads. These viewers constitute a captive audience who are also known to watch less television than the average.[34]

2. *Mood.* If viewers like the movie, the mood can carry over to the product advertised. For example, when BMW placed its Z3 in the movie *GoldenEye,* it hoped viewers' excitement and good feelings toward the movie would carry over to the car—it did.

3. *Cost.* The cost of advertising in a theater varies from one setting to the next. However, it is low in terms of both absolute and relative costs per exposure.

4. *Recall.* Research indicates that the next day about 87 percent of viewers can recall the ads they saw in a movie theater. This compares with a 20 percent recall rate for television.[35]

5. *Clutter.* Lack of clutter is another advantage offered by advertising in movie theaters. Most theaters limit the number of ads.

6. *Proximity.* Since many theaters are located in or adjacent to shopping malls, potential customers are "right next door."

Disadvantages of Movie and Video Advertising

Some of the disadvantages associated with movies and videos as advertising media follow:

1. *Irritation.* Perhaps the major disadvantage is that many people do not wish to see advertising in these media. A number of studies suggest these ads may create a high degree of annoyance.[36] This dissatisfaction may carry over to the product itself, to the movies, or to the theaters. Mike Stimler, president of the specialty video label Water Bearer Films, says, "People boo in movie theaters when they see product advertising."[37] Anne-Marie Marcus, vice president of sales for Screen Vision, contends that the furor has died down, though the T. J. Maxx retail chain says it is unlikely to use this form of advertising again.[38]
2. *Cost.* While the cost of advertising in local theaters has been cited as an advantage because of the low rates charged, ads exposed nationally cost up to $425,000 per minute to reach 25 million viewers. This rate is 20 percent higher than an equal exposure on television. CPMs also tend to be higher than in other media.

While only two disadvantages of theater advertising have been mentioned, the first is a strong one. Many people who have paid to see a movie (or rent a video) perceive advertising as an intrusion. In a study by Michael Belch and Don Sciglimpaglia, many moviegoers stated that not only would they not buy the product advertised, but they would consider boycotting it. So advertisers should be cautious in their use of this medium. If they want to use movies, they might consider an alternative—placing products in the movies.

Product Placements in Movies and TV

An increasingly common way to promote a product is by showing the actual product or an ad for it as part of a movie or TV show. While such **product placement** does not constitute a major segment of the advertising and promotions business, it has proved effective for some companies. (Note: Like specialty advertising, product placement is sometimes considered a promotion rather than an advertising form. This distinction is not a critical one, and we have decided to treat product placement as a form of advertising.)

A number of companies pay to have their products used in movies and music videos. For example, in the movie *Austin Powers,* the villain Dr. Evil's spacecraft was in the shape of a "Big Boy" from the Big Boy restaurant chain. In *The Spy Who Shagged Me,* Starbucks was prominently featured. Exhibit 13–12 shows how BMW was able to get its product featured in the movie *The World Is Not Enough.* Avis, Ericcson, and BMW were all in the James Bond movie *Tomorrow Never Dies.* The movie had its own website with links to the companies with placements, and the companies, in turn, had links on their websites to the movie site. Essentially, this

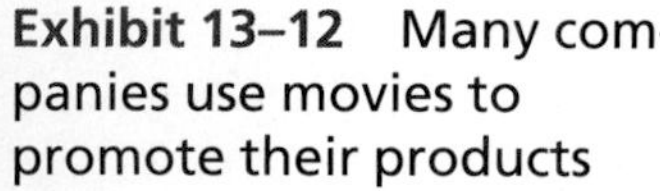
Exhibit 13–12 Many companies use movies to promote their products

form is advertising without an advertising medium. The audience doesn't realize a product promotion is going on. Viewers tend to see brand names in films as lending realism to the story. Yet the impact on the buying public is real. For example, when Reese's Pieces were used in the movie *E.T.,* sales rose 70 percent and the candies were added to the concessions of 800 movie theaters where they had previously not been sold.[39] Sales of Ray-Ban Wayfarer sunglasses tripled after Tom Cruise wore them in the movie *Risky Business,* and Ray-Ban Aviator sales increased 40 percent after he wore them in *Top Gun.*[40]

The move to place products on TV programs is also on the increase. In 1988, CBS broke its long-standing tradition of not mentioning brand names in its programs. The use of product placements has also been on the increase in foreign markets, as shown in Global Perspective 13–2.

Advantages of Product Placements

A number of advantages of product tie-ins have been suggested:

1. *Exposure.* A large number of people see movies each year (over 1 billion admissions per year). The average film is estimated to have a life span of three and one-half years (with 75 million exposures), and most of these moviegoers are very attentive audience members. When this is combined with the increasing home video rental market and network and cable TV (for example, HBO, Showtime, the Movie Channel), the potential exposure for a product placed in a movie is enormous. And this form of exposure is not subject to zapping, at least not in the theater.

   High exposure numbers are also offered for TV tie-ins, based on the ratings and (at least in the case of soaps) the possibility to direct the ad to a defined target market.

2. *Frequency.* Depending on how the product is used in the movie (or program), there may be ample opportunity for repeated exposures (many, for those who like to watch a program or movie more than once). For example, if you are a regular watcher of the new CBS program "Survivors," you will be exposed to the products placed therein a number of times.

3. *Support for other media.* Ad placements may support other promotional tools. For example, Mirage Resorts ran four minutes of commercials promoting its Treasure Island Resort on an NBC special titled "Treasure Island: The Adventure Begins," a story about a boy's adventures at the Treasure Island Resort. Kimberly-Clark Corp. created a sweepstakes, coupon offer, and TV-based ad around its Huggies diapers, featured in the movie *Baby Boom.*

4. *Source association.* In Chapter 6, we discussed the advantages of source identification. When consumers see their favorite movie star wearing Keds, drinking Gatorade, or driving a Mercedes, this association may lead to a favorable product image. The purple dinosaur Barney achieved tremendous sales success as a result of its PBS show, "Barney & Friends." Thomas the Tank Engine never used paid commercials, yet it rivaled the sales of Teenage Mutant Ninja Turtles and G.I. Joe, thanks to its appearance on PBS.[41]

5. *Cost.* While the cost of placing a product may range from free samples to $1 million, these are extremes. The CPM for this form of advertising can be very low, owing to the high volume of exposures it generates.

6. *Recall.* A number of firms have measured the impact of product placements on next-day recall. Results ranged from Johnson's Baby Shampoo registering 20 percent to Kellogg's Corn Flakes registering 67 percent (in the movie *Raising Arizona*). Average recall is approximately 38 percent. Again, these scores are better than those reported for TV viewing. A study provided by Pola Gupta and Kenneth Lord showed that prominently displayed placements led to strong recall.[42]

7. *Bypassing regulations.* In the United States as well as many foreign countries, some products are not permitted to advertise on television or to specific market segments. Product placements have allowed the cigarette and liquor industries to have their products exposed, circumventing these restrictions.

Global Perspective 13–2

Product Placements Go International

By now you are certainly aware of product placements in movies and on television. (If you are not, you haven't been paying attention!) While product placements have been around in movies for quite some time, their popularity and growth really started with the movie *E.T.,* in which the space creature who visits earth eats Reese's Pieces. Subsequent successes led to significant growth in the industry and eventually the move to television programming. Now it is quite common to see product placements in almost every movie and numerous television shows.

If you are a Warren Miller ski fan, you may have noticed the product placements in many of the company's adventure ski films. These 90-minute films feature skiers and snowboarders navigating the steepest terrain in the world while performing unbelievable stunts. The films, which attract about a half-million enthusiasts per release, follow a simple formula: some of the world's best skiers and riders challenging the most dangerous and beautiful mountains on virtually every continent, with numerous and humorous scenes and product placements for companies like Salomon, Burton, Rossignol, and nonendemic companies like Nissan, Motorola, and Ocean Spray interspersed. The films have a strong U.S. and international following.

While Salomon and Ocean Spray go skiing, Pedigree dog food and McDonald's (among others) reach the "stay at home" crowd through product placements on a Spanish-language television show known as "Sabado Gigante" (Gigantic Saturday) aired by Univision. Originating in Chile, the takeoff on the U.S.'s "NewlyWed Game" not only shows products but actively engages the audience in promoting them. For example, on one show, the host had the audience sing the jingle for sponsor Payless Shoe Source to thank the company for providing money for the contestants. The sponsors couldn't be more pleased.

But the product-placement nirvana may have recently been uncovered in yet another foreign market—China. The world's most populated country has recently opened up its doors to foreign companies, which are enamored by the sales potential. However, the government-controlled television stations keep a close watch on what is allowed to be shown, as well as on who will be permitted to advertise. Because advertisements are in 10-minute blocks, it is usually difficult for the advertiser to attract attention—thus the popularity of product placements for getting one's products noticed. For example, in the popular show "Love Talks," star Q Ying (a young business professional) rushes to work and then realizes that she has left an important folder at home. The camera zeros in on the folder, which just happens to be next to a tube of Pond's Vaseline Intensive Care lotion. In another scene she borrows a Motorola cell phone from a stranger. The show, also seen throughout Asia, is sold on video in Canada and the United States, and is being followed by a sequel called "Home"—another young-professional-themed program.

The cost to sponsor a product on "Love Talks" ranges from $240,000 to $360,000, reaping quite a profit for the show's producer United Media—a Hong Kong–based company. Those placing the products love the show as well, as the plugs are quite obvious and just about any product can be scripted into the show—with little or no concern for pretext. In addition, exposure is not limited to television. United Media manages and promotes the show's stars and features them in promotions on its website. Just about anything (and any product) goes, except for Viagra, cigarettes, and condoms.

The companies mentioned above are just a few of the many taking their product placements international. Giant advertising agencies like Saatchi & Saatchi and McCann-Erikson are increasing their efforts in this area, primarily because of the ability to get products noticed. While traditional advertising methods are certainly still used, many viewers are tuning them out. But when you have to sing along with the sponsor's commercial jingle—well, that makes the sponsor a little harder to ignore!

Sources: Peter Wonacott, "Chinese TV Is an Eager Medium for (Lots of) Product Placement," *The Wall Street Journal,* January 26, 2000, p. B12; Bob Ortega, "Extreme Skiing Meets Extreme Product Placement," *The Wall Street Journal,* December 28, 1998, p. B1.

8. *Acceptance.* A study by Pola Gupta and Stephen Gould indicated that viewers are accepting of promotional products and in general evaluate them positively, though some products (alcohol, guns, cigarettes) are perceived as less acceptable.[43]

Disadvantages of Product Placements

Some disadvantages are also associated with product placements:

1. *High absolute cost.* While the CPM may be very low for product placement in movies, the absolute cost of placing the product may be very high, pricing some advertisers out of the market. For example in the Disney film *Mr. Destiny,* it cost $20,000 to have a product seen in the film, $40,000 for an actor to mention the product, and $60,000 for the actor to actually use it.[44]
2. *Time of exposure.* While the way some products are exposed to the audience has an impact, there is no guarantee viewers will notice the product. Some product placements are more conspicuous than others. When the product is not featured prominently, the advertiser runs the risk of not being seen (although, of course, the same risk is present in all forms of media advertising).
3. *Limited appeal.* The appeal that can be made in this media form is limited. There is no potential for discussing product benefits or providing detailed information. Rather, appeals are limited to source association, use, and enjoyment. The endorsement of the product is indirect, and the flexibility for product demonstration is subject to its use in the film.
4. *Lack of control.* In many movies, the advertiser has no say over when and how often the product will be shown. Sony, as noted, found its placement in the movie *Last Action Hero* did not work as well as expected. Fabergé developed an entire Christmas campaign around its Brut cologne and its movie placement, only to find the movie was delayed until February.
5. *Public reaction.* Many TV viewers and moviegoers are incensed at the idea of placing ads in programs or movies. These viewers want to maintain the barrier between program content and commercials. If the placement is too intrusive, they may develop negative attitudes toward the brand. The FTC has explored options for limiting placements without consumer notification.
6. *Competition.* The appeal of product placements has led to increased competition to get one's product placed. BMW was originally placed in the movie *The Firm*—only to be ousted when Mercedes offered a higher bid. In *Wall Street,* Michael Douglas refers to *Fortune* magazine as the financial bible rather than *Forbes* because the former offered more money.[45] The result of this competition is higher prices and no guarantee that one's product will be placed.
7. *Negative placements.* Some products may appear in movie scenes that are disliked by the audience or create a less than favorable mood. For example, in the movie *Missing,* a very good, loyal father takes comfort in a bottle of Coke, while a Pepsi machine appears in a stadium where torturing and murders take place—not a good placement for Pepsi.

Audience Measurement for Product Placements

To date, no audience measurement is available except from the providers. Potential advertisers often have to make decisions based on their own creative insights or rely on the credibility of the source. However, at least two studies have demonstrated the potential effectiveness of product placements.

In addition to the studies reported earlier, research by Eva Steortz showed that viewers had an average recall for placements of 38 percent.[46] And Damon Darlin has provided evidence that an aura of glamour is added to products associated with celebrities.[47] Research companies like PR Data Systems (mentioned earlier) compare the amount of time a product is exposed in the program/movie to the cost of an equivalent ad spot to measure value. (As you will see in Chapter 19, however, we have problems with this measure of effectiveness.)

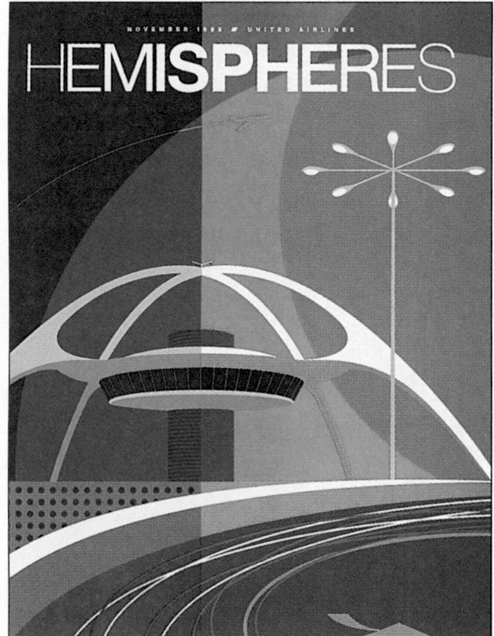

Exhibit 13–13 In-flight magazines are available on most carriers

In-Flight Advertising

Another rapidly growing medium is **in-flight advertising.** As the number of flying passengers increases (to over 5 million per month on American, United, and Delta alone), so too does the attractiveness of this medium. In-flight advertising includes three forms:

- *In-flight magazines.* Free magazines (like the one shown in Exhibit 13–13) published by the airlines are offered on almost every plane in the air. United Airlines distributes over 1 million of its *Hemispheres* magazines each month and estimates potential exposures at 1.7 million.[48]
- *In-flight videos.* In-flight videos have been common on international flights for some time and are now being used on domestic flights. Commercials were not originally included in these videos. Now about $18 million in commercials is booked on flights per year ($12 million on international flights).[49] While not all airlines offer in-flight commercials, companies like Japan Air Lines, Delta, TWA, and British Airways are participating. Some of these commercial messages are as long as three minutes. For example, SKY-TV has features on United, TWA, and US Airways, with a bonus feature on broadcast.com included (Exhibit 13–14).
- *In-flight radio. USA Today*'s in-flight radio is run by the same people responsible for publishing its newspaper.

Advantages and Disadvantages of In-Flight Advertising

Advantages of in-flight advertising include the following:

1. *A desirable audience.* The average traveler is 45 years old and has a household income over $83,700. Both business and tourist travelers tend to be upscale, an attractive audience to companies targeting these groups. Many of these passengers hold top management positions in their firms. *Hemispheres* reaches over 4 percent of business professionals and estimates that almost 71 percent of the magazine's readership are professionals. Other demographics are favorable as well (see Figure 13–11).[50]

2. *A captive audience.* As noted in the discussion about ticket covers, the audience in an airplane cannot leave the room. Particularly on long flights, many passengers

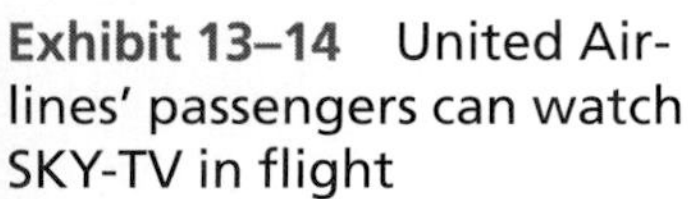
Exhibit 13–14 United Airlines' passengers can watch SKY-TV in flight

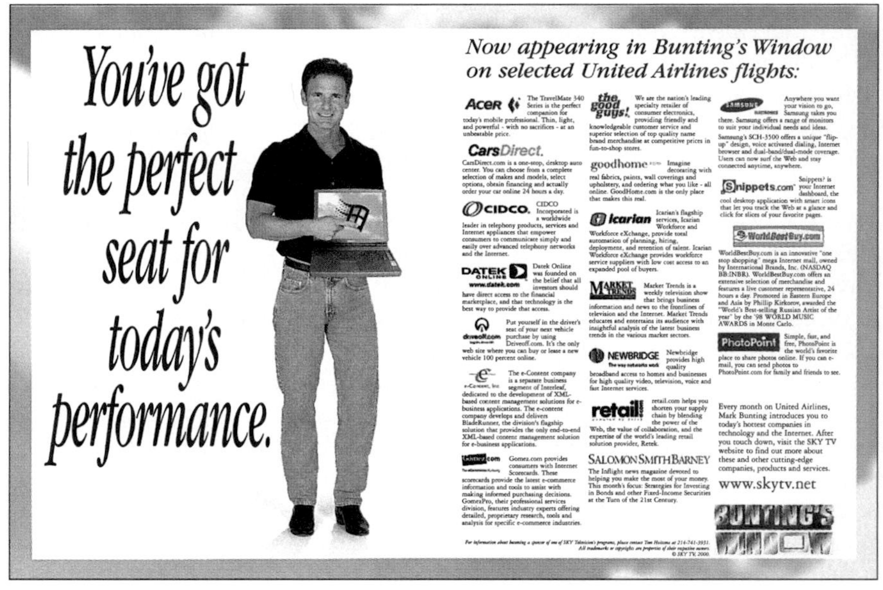

Figure 13–11 In-flight media reach a desirable target audience

Upwardly Employed

Base: Adults
Target market: Professional/managerial

	(000)	Percent Coverage	Percent Composition	Index	Rank
Harvard Business Review	370	1.4	76.9	141	1
Attache	868	3.2	75.2	137	2
ABA Journal	356	1.3	74.0	135	3
Robb Report	233	0.9	71.9	131	4
Cigar Aficionado	548	2.0	71.7	131	5
Hemispheres	1133	4.1	70.9	130	6

Corporate Influentials

Base: Adults
Target market: Top management

	(000)	Percent Coverage	Percent Composition	Index	Rank
Departures	203	2.3	42.6	242	1
Harvard Business Review	201	2.3	41.8	237	2
Robb Report	124	1.4	38.3	217	3
The Wall Street Journal	1754	19.9	35.5	201	4
Hemispheres	541	6.1	33.9	192	5
ABA Journal	160	1.8	33.3	189	6

Business Travelers

Base: Adults
Target market: Spent 7+ nights in hotels for business during the past year

	(000)	Percent Coverage	Percent Composition	Index	Rank
Hemispheres	1108	7.3	69.4	227	1
Attache	780	5.1	67.5	221	2
American Way 2-issue	1649	10.8	65.4	214	3
SW Airlines Spirit	965	6.3	64.2	211	4
Sky Magazine	1574	10.3	64.2	210	5
NW Air World Traveler	785	5.1	63.1	207	6

are willing (and even happy) to have in-flight magazines to read, news to listen to, and even commercials to watch.

3. *Cost.* The cost of in-flight commercials is lower than that of business print media. A 30-second commercial on United Airlines that offers exposure to 3,500,000 passengers costs approximately $27,500. A four-color spread in *Forbes* and *Fortune* would cost double that amount. The SKY-TV videos mentioned earlier cost less than a half-page ad in *The Wall Street Journal.*

4. *Segmentation capabilities.* In-flight allows the advertiser to reach specific demographic groups, as well as travelers to a specific destination. For example, Martell cognac targeted only first-class passengers on JAL's New York to Tokyo route.[51]

Disadvantages of in-flight advertising include the following:

1. *Irritation.* Many consumers are not pleased with the idea of ads in general and believe they are already too intrusive. In-flight commercials are just one more place, they think, where advertisers are intruding.

2. *Limited availability.* Many airlines limit the amount of time they allow for in-flight commercials. Japan Air Lines, for example, allows a mere 220 seconds per flight.

3. *Lack of attention.* Many passengers may decide to tune out the ads, not purchase the headsets required to get the volume, or simply ignore the commercials.

4. *Wearout.* Given projections for significant increases in the number of in-flight ads being shown, airline passengers may soon be inundated by these commercials.

Miscellaneous Other Media

As noted earlier in this chapter, the variety of advertising support media continues to increase, and discussing or even mentioning all is beyond the scope of this text. However, the following are provided just to demonstrate a few of the many options:

- *Place-based media.* The idea of bringing the advertising medium to the consumers wherever they may be underlies the strategy behind place-based media. TV monitors and magazine racks have appeared in classrooms, doctors' offices, and health clubs, among a variety of other locations. After an initial introduction and failure by Whittle Communications, K-III Communications acquired Channel One. As shown in Figure 13–12, place-based media have become a profitable venture for K-III and an attractive alternative for media buyers. Many advertisers, like Vans, Paramount Pictures, and Disney, support and use this medium in the classroom, arguing that both the sponsor and the "cash-strapped" schools benefit. But some observers, like the Consumers Union and consumer advocate Ralph Nader, denounce it as "crass commercialism."[52]
- *Kiosks.* The growth of interactive kiosks was briefly mentioned in Chapter 10. Advertisers pay rates ranging from $1,000 to $2,500 a month for signage and interactive ads on kiosks that are placed in malls, movie theaters, and other high-traffic areas. Additional charges may accrue for more complex interactive programs. Companies like Ameritech and North Communications have increased their involvement in this medium. Intel has deployed over 1,000 kiosks in computer stores to give consumers immediate access to the Internet.[53]
- *Others.* Just a few other examples of the use of support media: Motorola is advertising on pagers; Muzak, a provider of background music, has teamed with Tyme ATMs to broadcast ads at bank ATM sites; movie companies are advertising on popcorn bags in theaters; and MCI has offered Swedish phone customers free long-distance calling if they agree to listen to a commercial every 10 seconds. There are many other examples, as is well demonstrated in Exhibit 13–15 (at least he earned something from the fight!).

Figure 13–12 Place-based media make a comeback

Venture	Venue	Reach	Costs
Channel One	Secondary schools	350,000 classrooms; 8 million teens/day	$175–200K/unit CPM: $25 vs. teens
CNN Airport Network	Airports	25 airports, 1,100 gates; 9 million viewers/month	CPM: $30 vs. men 25–54
Channel M	Video arcades	100 mall arcades; 2 million kids age 7–24/month	$55K/unit CPM: N.A.
Cafe USA	Mall food courts	40 malls* 4 million people/month	$3K/mall/mo. CPM: $20 vs. women 18–49

Exhibit 13–15 Ads often appear in the strangest places

Summary

This chapter introduced you to the vast number of support media available to marketers. These media, also referred to as nontraditional or alternative media, are just a few of the many ways advertisers attempt to reach their target markets. We have barely scratched the surface here. Support media include out-of-home advertising (outdoor, in-store, and transit), promotional products, product placements in movies and TV, and in-flight advertising, among many others.

Support media offer a variety of advantages. Cost, ability to reach the target market, and flexibility are just a few of those cited in this chapter. In addition, many of the media discussed here have effectively demonstrated the power of their specific medium to get results.

But each of these support media has disadvantages. Perhaps the major weakness with most is the lack of audience measurement and verification. Unlike many of the media discussed earlier in this text, most nontraditional media do not provide audience measurement figures. So the advertiser is forced to make decisions without hard data or based on information provided by the media.

As the number and variety of support media continue to grow, it is likely the major weaknesses will be overcome. When that occurs, these media may no longer be considered nontraditional or alternative.

Key Terms

support media, 438
alternative media, 439
nonmeasured media, 439
nontraditional media, 439
out-of-home advertising, 439
showing, 441
aerial advertising, 442
mobile billboards, 442
in-store media, 444
transit advertising, 446
inside cards, 447
outside posters, 448
terminal posters, 448
promotional products marketing, 450
specialty advertising, 450
Yellow Pages, 454
directional medium, 455
product placement, 458
in-flight advertising, 462

Discussion Questions

1. Some advertisers claim that virtual ads are bad for the advertising industry in general. Explain some of the reasons why they feel this way. Are these reasons valid?

2. What are promotional products? List some of the advantages and disadvantages of this medium. Provide examples where the use of this medium would be appropriate.

3. Discuss some of the merits of in-flight advertising. What types of products might most effectively use this medium?

4. Support media have also been called alternative media, nonmeasured media, and nontraditional media. Why has the medium been assigned these titles?

5. Explain how various support media might be used as part of an IMC program. Take any three of the media discussed in the chapter and explain how they might be used in an IMC program for automobiles, cellular telephones, and Internet services.

6. A prevalent strategy among advertisers is to get themselves into television shows and movies. Discuss the possible advantages and disadvantages that might result from such exposures.

7. The YPPA has recently gone to the diary method for collecting information regarding Yellow Pages usage. Discuss some of the problems that might be associated with this methodology.

8. The Yellow Pages has been proven to be an extremely effective advertising medium for some firms. Explain why the Yellow Pages are so effective. Are there any limitations associated with this medium? If so, what are they?

9. Discuss advantages and disadvantages associated with advertising in movie theaters and on videotapes. For what types of products and/or services might these media be most effective?

10. What are place-based media? Explain what type of advertisers would most benefit from their use.

Chapter Fourteen

Direct Marketing

Chapter Objectives

- To recognize the area of direct marketing as a communications tool.
- To know the strategies and tactics involved in direct marketing.
- To demonstrate the use of direct-marketing media.
- To determine the scope and effectiveness of direct marketing.

Business Marketers Go Digitally Direct

If you watch much television, you are probably aware of the Flowbee (a haircutter that attaches to your vacuum), the Rotato potato peeler, slicer, chopper and dicer, and numerous psychic networks. You are probably also aware of the Culinare Rocket Chef, George Forman Barbeque, and Aeor's "Bed in a Minute." But are you familiar with Novartis Seeds or Boise Cascade Office Products? How about Millipore (maker of purification products)? What do these companies have in common, you ask? All of them have found success through direct marketing, and most of them have now begun to market their products directly on the Internet.

You may or may not be aware that Novartis, Boise Cascade, and Millipore are business-to-business marketers. Like hundreds of other business-to-business companies, they have found that they can market directly to their customers through the Internet. So many b-to-b companies have begun to alter their ways of marketing from traditional methods (sales forces, etc.) to direct marketing that at least one consultant (Tracy Emerick) of Receptive Marketing believes that the term *direct marketing* may disappear as a separate category. Emerick notes, "People who historically sold through sales forces, whether it's product catalogs, direct sales calls or direct mailings, are finding that many of these functions are able to be done online." He goes on to note that direct human-to-human contact will be redefined in the future. The numbers may bear him out. In a survey conducted among direct marketers in late 1999, 95 percent of them said that they are now using the Net for sales and marketing applications. In another survey, b-to-b sales on the Internet were projected to reach $7.1 billion in 1999.

H. Robert Wientzen, president and CEO of the Direct Marketing Association, says that the Internet has accelerated the growth of direct marketing overall, as successful companies have taken traditional direct-marketing strategies and applied them to the Web. Millipore has taken its 250-page catalog and shifted it to the Internet and has been able to do so in several languages. Cisco Connection Online—another b-to-b site—is selling $11 million a day ($4 billion/year) online, and Mintaka Technology Group, a startup, has been extremely successful in direct one-to-one selling.

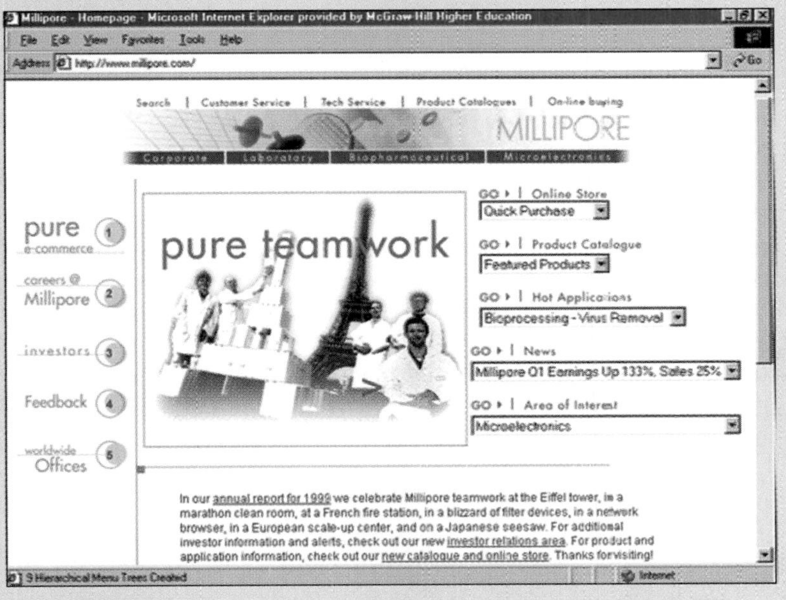

Does all this success on the Internet mean trouble for direct marketing as we now know it? And what about the sales force? If the Net is so effective, will business-to-business companies even need a sales force in the future? Tracy Emerick notes that the companies that increase marketing efforts online are going to have to streamline the traditional customer service and personal selling efforts and change the way a customer wishes to buy a product and the way the company wants to sell it. Somehow, they are going to have to figure out how to take all the advantages personal selling now has to offer and put them on the Internet—a daunting, if not impossible, task.

Years ago, when catalogs were first introduced, many people thought retail stores would become a thing of the past. When television was introduced, there were those who said that radio and print were dead. Neither of these predictions came true; in fact, radio and print are doing quite well, and the marriage between retail and direct marketing has never been better (as evidenced by the number of retail stores that have emerged as a result of successful direct marketing and the number of retailers now engaged in direct marketing both through the mail and on the Internet). Jeffrey Jurick, president and CEO of Fala Group, a major direct-marketing production house, contends that the Internet and other direct-marketing tools are actually more complementary than they are competitive. Other experts agree, noting that with the advent of the digital world, business as usual is what is dead. Direct marketers are going to have to evolve, changing the way they do business and adopting the Internet as another direct-marketing tool. But, says Ruth Stevens, former director of direct marketing for the IBM Software Group, "The way a direct marketer sees the Internet is that it's the greatest direct marketing medium to ever come down the pike. For those direct marketers who want to continue what they're doing, the medium offers an abundance of opportunities." Once again, a threat becomes an opportunity—at least in the world of business-to-business marketing.

Sources: Laurie Freeman, "Digital Direct," *Business Marketing,* October 1999, pp. 21–25; Philip Clark, "Internet Fuels Rapid B-to-B Growth," *Business Marketing,* November 1999, p. 16; Geoffrey Brewer, "Planting the Seeds of Marketing Success," *Sales & Marketing Management,* August 1998, p. 73.

It seems that you can hardly pick up a newspaper, turn on the television, or read a magazine these days without seeing something about the Internet. The Internet has become an extremely powerful communications tool. But when we think of the Internet, we usually think about consumer companies, without realizing how extensively it is used by business-to-business marketers. As the lead-in to this chapter shows, the Internet has already become a powerful direct-marketing tool. But it is also important to realize that the Internet, like advertising and direct mail, is but one of the tools used by direct marketers.

Direct Marketing

While most companies continue to rely primarily on the other promotional mix elements to move their products and services through intermediaries, an increasing number are going directly to the consumer. These companies believe that while the traditional promotional mix tools such as advertising, sales promotion, and personal selling are effective in creating brand image, conveying information, and/or creating awareness, going direct with these same tools can generate an immediate behavioral response. Direct marketing is a valuable tool in the integrated communications program, though it seeks somewhat different objectives.

In this chapter, we discuss direct marketing and its role as a communications tool. Direct marketing is one of the fastest-growing forms of promotion in terms of dollar expenditures, and for many marketers it is rapidly becoming the medium of choice for reaching consumers. Stan Rapp and Thomas Collins, in their book *Maximarketing,* propose that direct marketing be the driving force behind the overall marketing program.[1] They present a nine-step model that includes creating a database, reaching prospects, developing the sale, and developing the relationship. We begin by defining direct marketing and then examine direct-marketing media and their use in the overall communications strategy. The section concludes with a basis for evaluating the direct-marketing program and a discussion of the advantages and disadvantages of this marketing tool.

Defining Direct Marketing

As noted in Chapter 1, **direct marketing** is a system of marketing by which organizations communicate directly with target customers to generate a response or transaction. This response may take the form of an inquiry, a purchase, or even a vote. In his *Dictionary of Marketing Terms,* Peter Bennett defines direct marketing as:

> The total of activities by which the seller, in effecting the exchange of goods and services with the buyer, directs efforts to a target audience using one or more media (direct selling, direct mail, telemarketing, direct-action advertising, catalogue selling, cable TV selling, etc.) for the purpose of soliciting a response by phone, mail, or personal visit from a prospect or customer.[2]

First we must distinguish between direct marketing and direct-marketing media. As you can see in Figure 14–1, direct marketing is an aspect of total marketing—that is, it involves marketing research, segmentation, evaluation, and the like, just as our planning model in Chapter 1 did. Direct marketing uses a set of **direct-response media,** including direct mail, telemarketing, interactive TV, print, the Internet, and other media. These media are the tools by which direct marketers implement the communications process.

The purchases of products and services through direct-response advertising currently exceed $1.5 trillion and are projected to reach $2.3 trillion by the year 2004.[3] Firms that use this marketing method range from major retailers such as Montgomery Ward and Victoria's Secret to publishing companies to computer retailers to financial services. Business-to-business and industrial marketers have also significantly increased their direct-marketing efforts, as noted earlier.

The Growth of Direct Marketing

Direct marketing has been around since the invention of the printing press in the 15th century. Ben Franklin was a very successful direct marketer in the early 1700s, and Warren Sears and Montgomery Ward (you may have heard of these guys) were using this medium in the 1880s.

The major impetus behind the growth of direct marketing may have been the development and expansion of the U.S. Postal Service, which made catalogs available to both urban and rural dwellers. Catalogs revolutionized America's buying habits; consumers could now shop without ever leaving their homes.

But catalogs alone do not account for the rapid growth of direct marketing. A number of factors in American society have led to the increased attractiveness of this medium for both buyer and seller:

- *Consumer credit cards.* There are now over 1 billion credit cards—bank, oil company, retail, and so on—in circulation in the United States. This makes it feasible for consumers to purchase both low- and high-ticket items through direct-response channels and assures sellers that they will be paid. It is projected that over $882 billion will be charged on credit cards in the year 2000.[4] Of course, not all of this will be through direct marketing, but a high percentage of direct purchases do use this method of payment, and companies such as American Express, Diners Club, MasterCard, and Visa are among the heaviest direct advertisers.
- *Direct-marketing syndicates.* Companies specializing in list development, statement inserts, catalogs, and sweepstakes have opened many new opportunities to marketers. The number of these companies continues to expand, creating even more new users.

Figure 14–1 Direct marketing flowchart

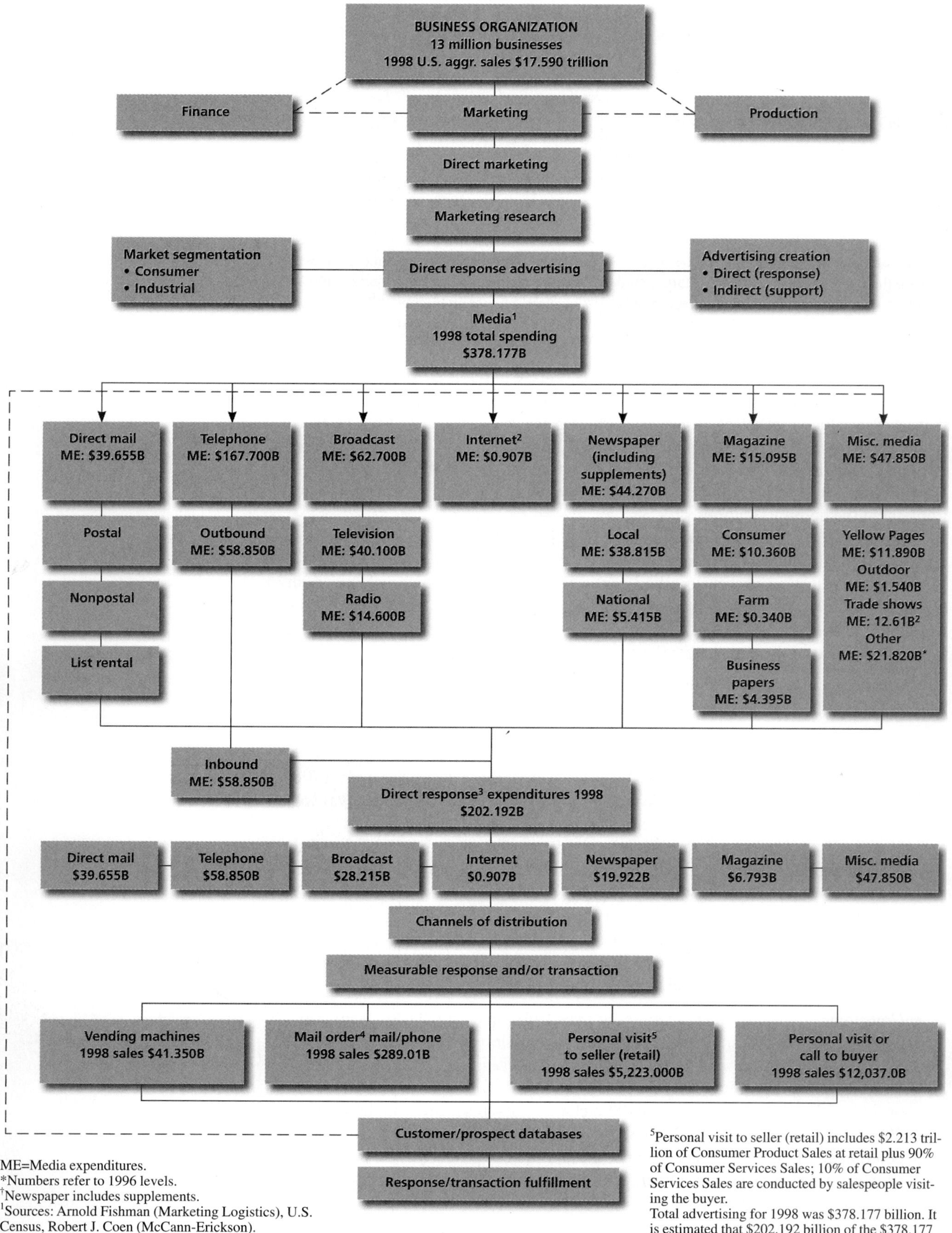

ME=Media expenditures.
*Numbers refer to 1996 levels.
†Newspaper includes supplements.
[1]Sources: Arnold Fishman (Marketing Logistics), U.S. Census, Robert J. Coen (McCann-Erickson).
[2]*Business Marketing,* May 1999. Figure based on companies with sales/revenues of $50 million and up.
[3]Direct Response Expenditures are calculated as a percentage of total expenditures in each medium: Direct Mail (100%), Telephone (50%), Broadcast (45%), Yellow Pages (100%), Newspaper (45%), Magazine (45%), Misc. (100%), Internet (100%).
[4]The Mail Order Sales Figure excludes $69.810 billion of charitable mail order contributions which are not included in the $17.590 trillion of U.S. Aggregate Sales.
[5]Personal visit to seller (retail) includes $2.213 trillion of Consumer Product Sales at retail plus 90% of Consumer Services Sales; 10% of Consumer Services Sales are conducted by salespeople visiting the buyer.

Total advertising for 1998 was $378.177 billion. It is estimated that $202.192 billion of the $378.177 billion, or 53% of this volume, is direct response advertising. New section of the Flow Chart reports direct response components of overall media advertising expenditures. A growing percentage of Broadcast, Newspaper and Magazine advertising dollars can be categorized as direct response advertising. The percentage is growing rapidly as marketers learn the efficiency of measuring advertising performance.

- *The changing structure of American society and the market.* One of the major factors contributing to the success of direct marketing is that so many Americans are now "money-rich and time-poor."[5] The rapid increase in dual-income families (in 1999 an estimated 60 percent of women were in the work force) has meant more income.[6] At the same time, the increased popularity of physical fitness, do-it-yourself crafts and repairs, and home entertainment have reduced the time available for shopping and have increased the attractiveness of direct purchases.
- *Technological advances.* The rapid technological advancement of the electronic media and of computers has made it easier for consumers to shop and for marketers to be successful in reaching the desired target markets. Well over 110 million television homes receive home shopping programs, and home channel purchases are projected to reach $15.6 billion by 2006.[7]
- *Miscellaneous factors.* A number of other factors have contributed to the increased effectiveness of direct marketing, including changing values, more sophisticated marketing techniques, and the industry's improved image. These factors will also ensure the success of direct marketing in the future. The variety of companies employing direct marketing (see Figure 14–2) demonstrates its potential.

While some organizations rely on direct marketing solely to generate consumer response, in many others direct marketing is an integral part of the IMC program. They use direct marketing to achieve other than sales goals and integrate it with other program elements. We first examine the role of direct marketing in the IMC program and then consider its more *traditional* role.

The Role of Direct Marketing in the IMC Program

Long the stepchild of the promotional mix, direct marketing is now becoming an important component in the integrated marketing programs of many organizations. In fact, direct-marketing activities support and are supported by other elements of the promotional mix.

Combining Direct Marketing with Advertising

Obviously, direct marketing is in itself a form of advertising. Whether through mail, print, or TV, the direct-response offer is an ad. It usually contains an 800 or 900 number or a form that requests mailing information. Sometimes the ad supports the direct selling effort. For example, Victoria's Secret runs image ads to support its store and catalog sales. Both Marlboro and Benson & Hedges advertise their cigarettes,

Figure 14–2 Top 10 direct-marketing industries ($ billions)

Industry	1999 ($)	Compound Annual Growth 1994–1999
1. Nonstore retailers	$115.2	8.7%
2. Real estate	55.2	5.7
3. General-merchandise stores	50.4	9.2
4. Auto dealers/service stations	47.3	10.1
5. Membership organizations	40.6	8.3
6. Insurance carriers/agents	39.3	9.4
7. Food and kindred products	35.3	3.5
8. Health services	34.9	9.0
9. Depository institutions	29.4	4.6
10. Entertainment	28.8	12.5

achieving a carryover effect of their image to their direct-response merchandise catalogs. Direct-response ads or infomercials are also referred to in retail outlet displays.

Combining Direct Marketing with Public Relations As you will see later in this text, public relations activities often employ direct-response techniques. Private companies may use telemarketing activities to solicit funds for charities or cosponsor charities that use these and other direct response techniques to solicit funds. Likewise, corporations and/or organizations engaging in public relations activities may include 800 or website numbers in their ads or promotional materials.

Combining Direct Marketing with Personal Selling Telemarketing and direct selling are two methods of personal selling (others will be discussed in Chapter 18). Nonprofit organizations like charities often use telemarketing to solicit funds. As you will see in Chapter 18, for-profit companies are also using telemarketing with much greater frequency to screen and qualify prospects (which reduces selling costs) and to generate leads. Direct-mail pieces are often used to invite prospective customers to visit auto showrooms to test-drive new cars; the salesperson then assumes responsibility for the selling effort.

Combining Direct Marketing with Sales Promotions How many times have you received a direct-mail piece notifying you of a sales promotion or event or inviting you to participate in a contest or sweepstakes? Ski shops regularly mail announcements of special end-of-season sales. Airlines send out mailers announcing promotional airfares. Nordstom and other retail outlets call their existing customers to notify them of special sales promotions. Each of these is an example of a company using direct-marketing tools to inform customers of sales promotions. In turn, the sales promotion event may support the direct-marketing effort. Databases are often built from the names and addresses acquired from a promotion, and direct mail and/or telemarketing calls follow. Carol Wright, one of the nation's leading direct mailers of coupons, participated with ABC's Daytime Emmy Awards Show in all major markets to mail coupons to 30 million households promoting the awards show and major programs. The joint venture promoted Carol Wright as well as local radio station affiliates, while offering consumers a chance to win valuable prizes including a trip to the awards ceremony. (See Exhibit 14–1.)[8]

To successfully implement direct-marketing programs, companies must make a number of decisions. As in other marketing programs, they must determine (1) what the program's objectives will be; (2) which markets to target (through the use of a list or marketing database); (3) what direct-marketing strategies will be employed; and (4) how to evaluate the effectiveness of the program.

Exhibit 14–1 Direct marketers cross-promote with sales promotions

Direct-Marketing Objectives

The direct marketer seeks a direct response. The objectives of the program are normally behaviors—for example, test drives, votes, contributions, and/or sales. A typical objective is defined through a set response, perhaps a 2 to 3 percent response rate.

Not all direct marketing seeks a behavioral response, however. Many organizations use direct marketing to build an image, maintain customer satisfaction, and inform and/or educate customers in an attempt to lead to future actions. Exhibit 14–2 shows how the state of Texas uses direct mail to encourage travel.

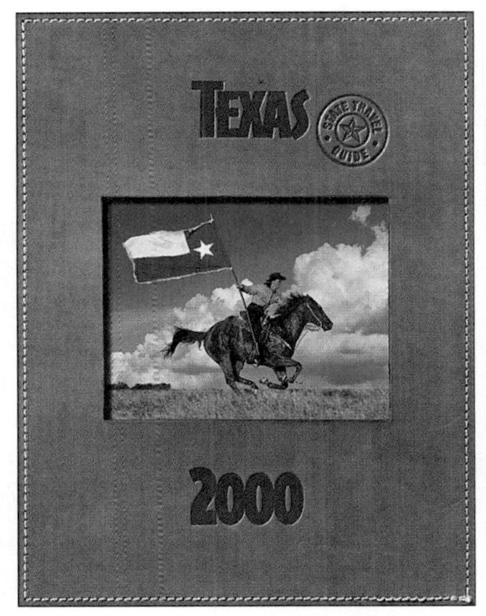

Exhibit 14–2 Texas encourages visits through direct mail

Developing a Database

As we have discussed throughout this text, market segmentation and targeting are critical components of any promotional program. Direct-marketing programs employ these principles even more than others, since the success of a direct-marketing program is in large part tied to the ability to do *one-to-one marketing*. Research by the U.S. Postal Service showed that 65 percent of the companies surveyed rely on their internal databases for marketing purposes.[9] To segment and target their markets, direct marketers use a **database,** a listing of customers and/or potential customers. This database is a tool for **database marketing**—the use of specific information about individual customers and/or prospects to implement more effective and efficient marketing communications.[10]

Figure 14–3 demonstrates how database marketing works. As you can see, the database marketing effort must be an integral part of the overall IMC program. At the very least, this list contains names, addresses, and Zip codes; more sophisticated databases include information on demographics and psychographics, purchase transactions and payments, personal facts, neighborhood data, and even credit histories (see Figure 14–4). This database serves as the foundation from which the direct-marketing programs evolve. Databases are used to perform the following functions:[11]

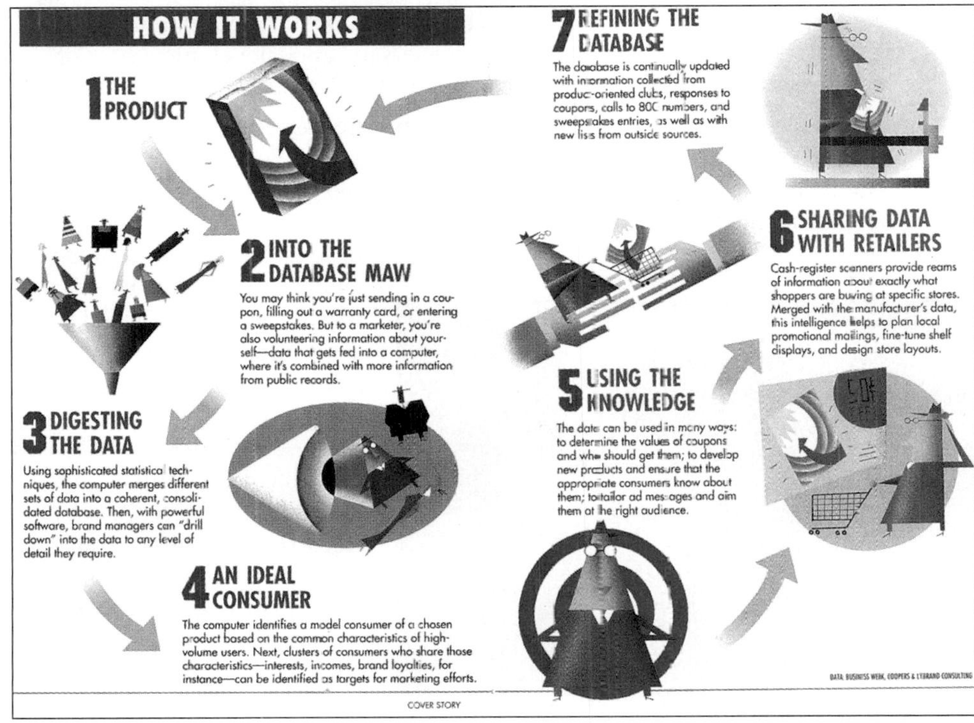

Figure 14–3 How database marketing works

Figure 14–4 Contents for a comprehensive database

Consumer Database	Business-to-Business Database
Name	Name of company/contact/decision maker(s)
Address/Zip code	Title of contact
Telephone number	Telephone number
Length of residence	Source of order/inquiry or referral
Age	Credit history
Gender	Industrial classification
Marital status	Size of business
Family data (number of children, etc.)	Revenues
Education	Number of employees
Income	Time in business
Occupation	Headquarters location
Transaction history	Multiple locations
Promotion history	Purchase history
Inquiring history	Promotion history
Unique identifier	Inquiry history
	Unique identifier

- *Improving the selection of market segments.* Some consumers are more likely to be potential purchasers, users, voters, and so on than others. By analyzing the characteristics of the database, a marketer can target a greater potential audience. For example, catalog companies have become very specialized. Companies such as Lands' End, Lilly's Kids, and Johnson & Murphy have culled their lists and become much more efficient, targeting only those who are most likely to purchase their products.
- *Stimulate repeat purchases.* Once a purchase has been made, the customer's name and other information are entered into the database. These people are proven direct-marketing users who offer high potential for repurchase. Magazines, for example, routinely send out renewal letters and/or call subscribers before the expiration date. Blockbuster Entertainment helps its video-rental customers select movies and locate additional Blockbuster locations. Companies from window cleaners to carpet cleaners to car dealers build a base of customers and contact them when they are "due" to repurchase.
- *Cross-sell.* Customers who demonstrate a specific interest also constitute strong potential for other products of the same nature. For example, the National Geographic Society has successfully sold globes, maps, videos, travel magazines, and an assortment of other products to subscribers who obviously have an interest in geography and/or travel. Likewise, Victoria's Secret has expanded its clothing lines primarily through sales to existing customers, and Kraft–GF has successfully cross-sold products in its varied food line. Upon responding to the direct-mail piece sent by Hertz (Exhibit 14–3), you are asked for your permission for Hertz to provide your name to its parent company, Ford, and others, and to allow Hertz to send you information on other products and services.

Exhibit 14–3 Hertz seeks permission to use receivers' names

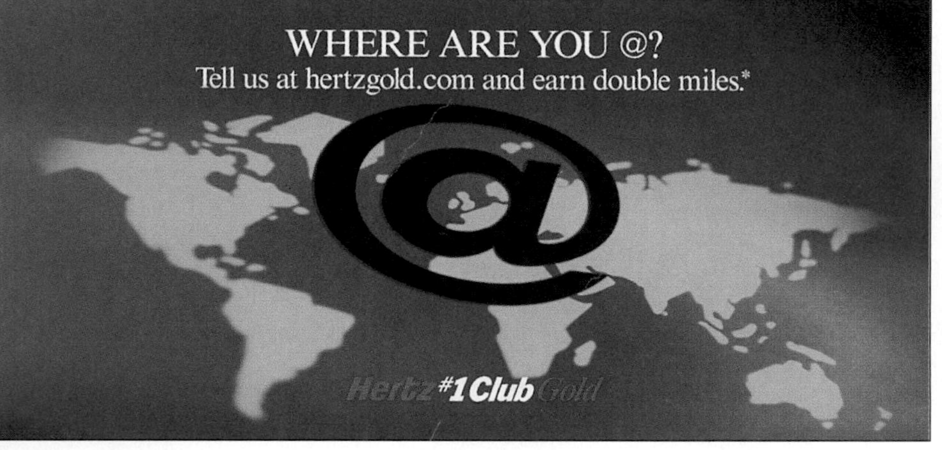

WHERE ARE YOU @?
Tell us at hertzgold.com and earn double miles.*
Hertz #1 Club Gold

Numerous other companies have established comprehensive databases on existing and potential customers both in the United States and internationally. Database marketing has become so ubiquitous that many people are concerned about invasion of privacy. Direct marketers are concerned as well. The Direct Marketing Association (DMA), the trade association for direct marketers, has asked its members to adhere to ethical rules of conduct in their marketing efforts. It points out that if the industry does not police itself, the government will.

Sources of Database Information

There are many sources of information for direct-marketing databases:

- *The U.S. Census Bureau.* Census data provide information on almost every household in the United States. Data include household size, demographics, income, and other information.
- *The U.S. Postal Service.* Postal Zip codes and the extended four-digit code provide information on both household and business locations.
- *List services.* Many providers of lists are available. The accuracy and timeliness of the lists vary.
- *Standard Rate and Data Service.* SRDS provides information regarding both consumer and business lists. Published in two volumes, *Direct Mail List Rates and Data* contains over 50,000 list selections in hundreds of classifications.
- *Simmons Market Research Bureau.* SMRB conducts an annual study of customers who buy at home via mail or telephone (see Figure 14–5). It compiles information on total orders placed, types of products purchased, demographics, and purchase satisfaction, among others.
- *Direct Marketing Association.* The direct marketers' trade organization promotes direct marketing and provides statistical information on direct-marketing use. The DMA's *Fact Book of Direct Marketing* contains information regarding use, attitudes toward direct marketing, rules and regulations, and so forth.

Consumer-goods manufacturers, banks, credit bureaus, retailers, charitable organizations, and other business operations also sell lists and other selected information. Companies can build their own databases through completed warranty cards, surveys, and so on.

Determining the Effectiveness of the Database

While many companies maintain a database, many do not use them effectively. Collecting names and information is not enough; the list must be kept current, purged of old and/or inactive customers, and updated frequently. The more information about customers that can be contained in the database, the more effective it will be. The Postal Service recommends an **RFM scoring method** for this purpose.[12] RFM stands for the recency, frequency, and monetary transactions between the company and the customer. More specifically, data need to be entered each time there is a transaction so the company can track how recently purchases have been made, how often they are made, and what amounts of money are being spent. In addition, tracking which products and/or services are used increases the ability to conduct the activities previously mentioned on page 476. By analyzing the database on a regular basis, the company or organization can identify trends and buying patterns that will help it establish a better relationship with its customers by more effectively meeting their needs.

Direct-Marketing Strategies and Media

As with all other communications programs discussed in this text, marketers must decide the message to be conveyed, the size of the budget, and so on. Perhaps the major difference between direct-marketing programs and other promotional mix programs regards the use of media.

As shown in Figure 14–1, direct marketing employs a number of media, including direct mail, telemarketing, direct-response broadcasting, the Internet, and print.

Figure 14–5 SMRB provides information on consumers who ordered merchandise by mail or phone

	Total US 000	Ordered by Mail or Phone A 000	B % Down	C Across %	D Indx
Total adults	185,822	97,715	100.0	52.6	100
Males	88,956	42,488	43.5	47.8	91
Females	96,866	55,227	56.5	57.0	108
Principal shoppers	112,018	60,697	62.1	54.2	103
18–24	23,965	9,846	10.1	41.1	78
25–34	42,832	22,434	23.0	52.4	100
35–44	39,908	23,902	24.5	59.9	114
45–54	27,327	16,047	16.4	58.7	112
55–64	21,238	10,939	11.2	51.5	98
65 or older	30,552	14,547	14.9	47.6	91
18–34	66,798	32,280	33.0	48.3	92
18–49	121,918	65,339	66.9	53.6	102
25–54	110,067	62,383	63.8	56.7	108
35–49	55,120	33,059	33.8	60.0	114
50 or older	63,905	32,376	33.1	50.7	96
Graduated college	36,463	23,374	23.9	64.1	122
Attended college	44,294	24,904	25.5	56.2	107
Graduated high school	66,741	34,408	35.2	51.6	98
Did not graduate high school	38,324	15,028	15.4	39.2	75
Employed males	65,500	32,228	33.0	49.2	94
Employed females	55,910	34,804	35.6	62.3	118
Employed full-time	110,363	60,402	61.8	54.7	104
Employed part-time	11,047	6,630	6.8	60.0	114
Not employed	64,412	30,682	31.4	47.6	91
Professional/manager	31,718	19,851	20.3	62.6	119
Technical/clerical/sales	37,895	22,703	23.2	59.9	114
Precision/craft	13,954	6,930	7.1	49.7	94
Other employed	37,843	17,548	18.0	46.4	88
Single	41,284	17,744	18.2	43.0	82
Married	109,023	62,594	64.1	57.4	109
Divorced/separated/widowed	35,515	17,376	17.8	48.9	93
Parents	62,342	35,701	36.5	57.3	109
White	158,841	87,327	89.4	55.0	105
Black	21,122	7,896	8.1	37.4	71
Other	5,859	2,492	2.6	42.5	81
Household income					
$75,000 or more	24,165	14,731	15.1	61.0	116
$60,000 or more	40,979	24,220	24.8	59.1	112
$50,000 or more	57,996	34,185	35.0	58.9	112
$40,000 or more	80,078	47,018	48.1	58.7	112
$30,000 or more	106,838	62,069	63.5	58.1	110
$30,000–$39,000	26,759	15,051	15.4	56.2	107
$20,000–$29,000	30,669	15,147	15.5	49.4	94
$10,000–$19,999	29,083	13,069	13.4	44.9	85
Under $10,000	19,232	7,430	7.6	38.6	73

Each medium is used to perform specific functions, although they generally follow a one- or two-step approach.

In the **one-step approach,** the medium is used directly to obtain an order. You've probably seen TV commercials for products like wrench sets, workout equipment, or magazine subscriptions in which the viewer is urged to phone a toll-free number to place an order immediately. Usually these ads accept credit cards or cash on delivery and give an address. Their goal is to generate an immediate sale when the ad is shown.

The **two-step approach** may involve the use of more than one medium. The first effort is designed to screen, or qualify, potential buyers. The second effort generates the response. For example, many companies use telemarketing to screen on the basis of interest, then follow up to interested parties with more information designed to achieve an order or use personal selling to close the sale.

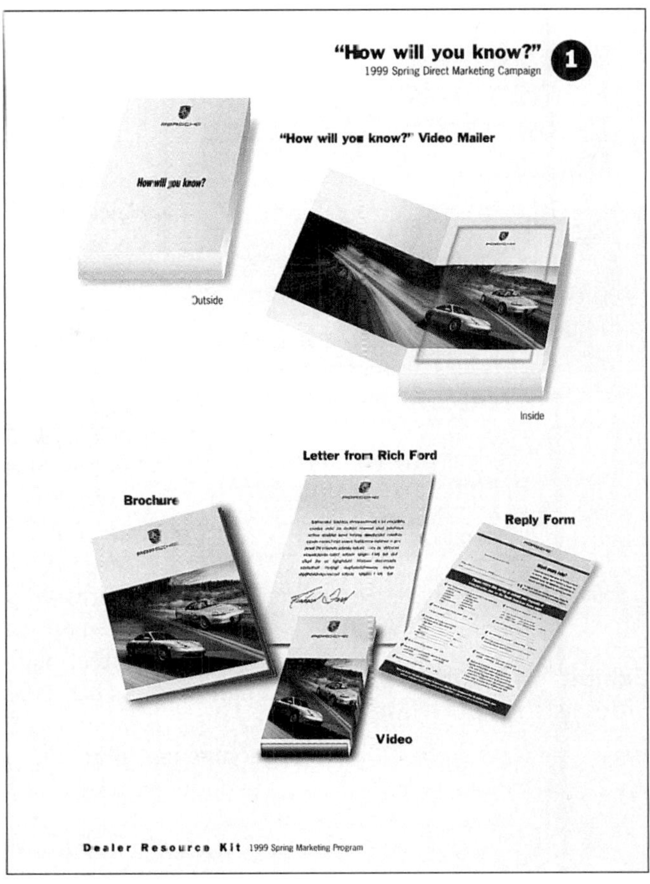

Exhibit 14–4 Porsche targets direct mail to upscale audiences

Direct Mail Direct mail is often called junk mail—the unsolicited mail you receive. More advertising dollars continue to be spent in direct mail than in almost any other advertising medium—an estimated $42.2 billion in 1999.[13] Mail-order sales exceeded $479 billion in 1999 ($297 billion in the consumer market).[14] Direct mail is not restricted to small companies seeking our business. Respected large companies such as General Electric, American Express, and Citicorp have increased their expenditures in this area, as have many others. Sales through direct mail in the business-to-business market are expected to reach over $430 billion by the year 2004.[15]

Many advertisers shied away from direct mail in the past, fearful of the image it might create or harboring the belief that direct mail was useful only for low-cost products. But this is no longer the case. For example, Porsche Cars North America, Inc., uses direct mail to target high-income, upscale consumers who are most likely to purchase its expensive sports cars (Exhibit 14–4). In one example, Porsche developed a direct-mail piece that was sent to a precisely defined target market: physicians in specialties with the highest income levels. This list was screened to match the demographics of Porsche buyers and narrowed further to specific geographic areas. The direct-mail piece was an x-ray of a Porsche 911 Carrera 4 written in the language of the medical audience. This creative campaign generated one of the highest response rates of any mailing Porsche has done in recent years.[16] The materials shown in Exhibit 14–5 are just some of the ones sent by Mercedes to introduce its new sports utility vehicle. Hyundai significantly increased its use of direct mail in 1999, sending out 320,000 mailers to consumers in 31 markets, offering them a $50 American Express Gift Cheque if they would test-drive the new Sonata.[17]

Exhibit 14–5 Mercedes used direct mail to introduce its new SUV

Keys to the success of direct mail are the **mailing list,** which constitutes the database from which names are generated, and the ability to segment markets. Lists have become more current and more selective, eliminating waste coverage. Segmentation

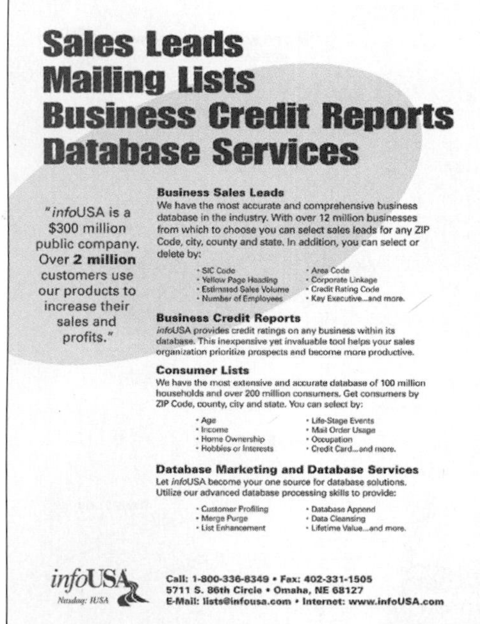

Exhibit 14–6 InfoUSA provides lists for purchase

on the basis of geography (usually through Zip codes), demographics, and lifestyles has led to increased effectiveness. The most commonly used lists are of individuals who have already purchased direct-mail products.

The importance of the list has led to a business of its own. It has been estimated that there are over 38 billion names on lists, and many companies have found it profitable to sell the names of purchasers of their products and/or services to list firms. Companies like A. B. Zeller and Metromail provide such lists on a national level, and in most metropolitan areas there are firms providing the same service locally (Exhibit 14–6).

While direct-mail continues to be a favorite medium of many advertisers, and projections are that the market will continue to grow at approximately 6.2 percent through 2004, this medium has been seriously threatened by the Internet. Between 1994 and 1999 direct-mail expenditures rose at the rate of 7.4 percent per year while Internet expenditures increased at the rate of 160 percent. Internet projections are for a 45.7 percent growth rate through 2004.[18] Interestingly, the Internet is both a threat and an opportunity, as Internet companies have increased their expenditures in direct mail to drive potential customers to their sites. For example, VisualCities.com mailed over 100,000 direct-mail pieces to attract users to its site. Nevertheless, the direct-mail business has experienced lower response rates from customers than in the past and has seen many advertisers shift dollars from this medium to the Net.[19] Many companies, particularly in the business-to-business market, have shifted from print to online catalogs, and legal problems have also hurt the industry.

Catalogs Major participants in the direct-marketing business include catalog companies. The number of catalogs mailed and the number of catalog shoppers have increased significantly since 1984, with sales growing by an average of 5.5 percent each year between 1990 and 1995. Catalog sales are expected to reach $93 billion in 1999.[20]

Many companies use catalogs in conjunction with their more traditional sales and promotional strategies. For example, companies like Pottery Barn, Nordstrom, and JCPenney sell directly through catalogs but also use them to inform consumers of product offerings available in the stores. Some companies (for example, Fingerhut and Alloy) rely solely on catalog sales. Others that started out exclusively as catalog companies have branched into retail outlets, among them The Sharper Image, Lands' End, and Banana Republic. L.L. Bean recently opened a superstore on the East Coast (Exhibit 14–7). As you can see by the following examples, the products being offered through this medium have reached new heights as well:

Exhibit 14–7 Lands' End is one of many successful catalog companies

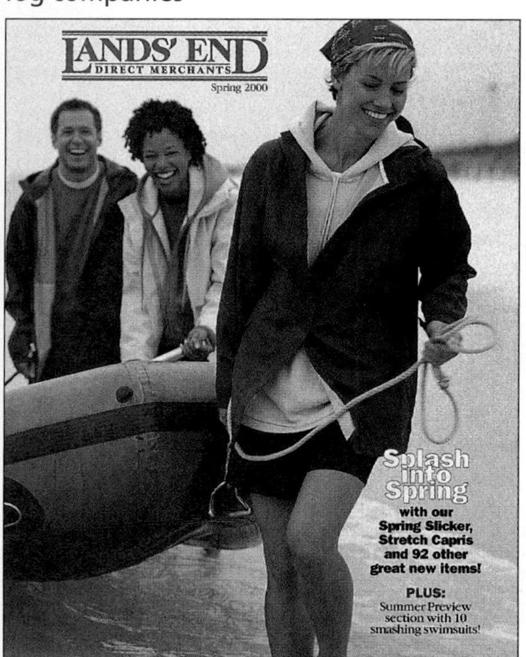

- Victoria's Secret featured a $1 million Miracle Bra in its Christmas catalog. Modeled by supermodel Claudia Schiffer, the bra contained over 100 carats of real diamonds as well as hundreds of semiprecious stones.
- Saks' Holding Co., a division of Saks Fifth Avenue, offered a pair of Mercedes-Benz convertibles in a catalog, with bidding to start at $50,000.
- Hammacher Schlemmer featured a $43,000 taxicab and a $34,000 train set in its Christmas catalog.
- The Sharper Image offered a $375,000 silver saddle in its catalog (though it didn't sell any).

In addition to the traditional hard copies, catalogs are now available on the Internet for both consumer and business-to-business customers. In some instances in the consumer market the catalog merchandise is available in retail stores as well. In others, the catalog and retail divisions are treated as separate entities. For example, if you purchase through the Eddie Bauer catalog, you can exchange or return the merchandise to the retail stores. Victoria's Secret products must be returned to the catalog department. At the Gap, the catalog is used to supplement the inventory in stock, and phone orders for different sizes and so on can be made from the store and shipped for free.

Broadcast Media The success of direct marketing in the broadcast industry has been truly remarkable; over 77 percent of the U.S. population report that they have viewed a direct-response appeal on TV.[21] Direct-response TV is estimated to have generated more than $63.2 billion in sales in 1999—with projections of $92.5 billion by 2004. However, failure by interactive TV, less triers, and alternative technologies such as the Internet have led to forecasts of slower growth in the next few years.[22]

Two broadcast media are available to direct marketers: television and radio. While radio was used quite extensively in the 1950s, its use and effectiveness have dwindled substantially in recent years. Thus, the majority of direct-marketing broadcast advertising now occurs on TV, which receives the bulk of our attention here. It should be pointed out, however, that the two-step approach is still very common on the radio, particularly with local companies.

Direct marketing in the broadcast industry involves both direct-response advertising and support advertising. In **direct-response advertising,** the product or service is offered and a sales response is solicited, through either the one- or two-step approach previously discussed. Examples include ads for magazine subscriptions, CDs and tapes, and tips on football or basketball betting. Toll-free phone numbers are included so that the receiver can immediately call to order. **Support advertising** is designed to do exactly that—support other forms of advertising. Ads for Publishers Clearing House or *Reader's Digest* or other companies telling you to look in your mailbox for a sweepstakes entry are examples of support advertising.

Direct-response TV encompasses a number of media, including direct-response TV spots like those just mentioned, infomercials, and home shopping shows (teleshopping). And as noted in Chapter 10, Internet -TV has recently been introduced.

Infomercials The lower cost of commercials on cable and satellite channels has led advertisers to a new form of advertising. An **infomercial** is a long commercial that ranges from 3 to 60 minutes. (Most are 30 minutes long, though the five-minute format is gaining in popularity.) Many infomercials are produced by the advertisers and are designed to be viewed as regular TV shows. Consumers dial a toll-free 800 or 900 number to place an order. Programs such as "Liquid Luster," "Amazing Discoveries," and "Stainerator" (the so-called miracle-product shows) were the most common form of infomercial in the 1980s. While this form of show is still popular, the infomercial industry has been adopted by many big, mainstream marketers (Exhibit 14–8). Apple Computer, Microsoft, Sony, Volvo, and Philips Electronics are just some of the many others now employing this method of communication (Exhibit 14–9). Infomercials were used by both parties in the 2000 presidential race.

Exhibit 14–8 Dirt Devil uses infomercials to sell its products

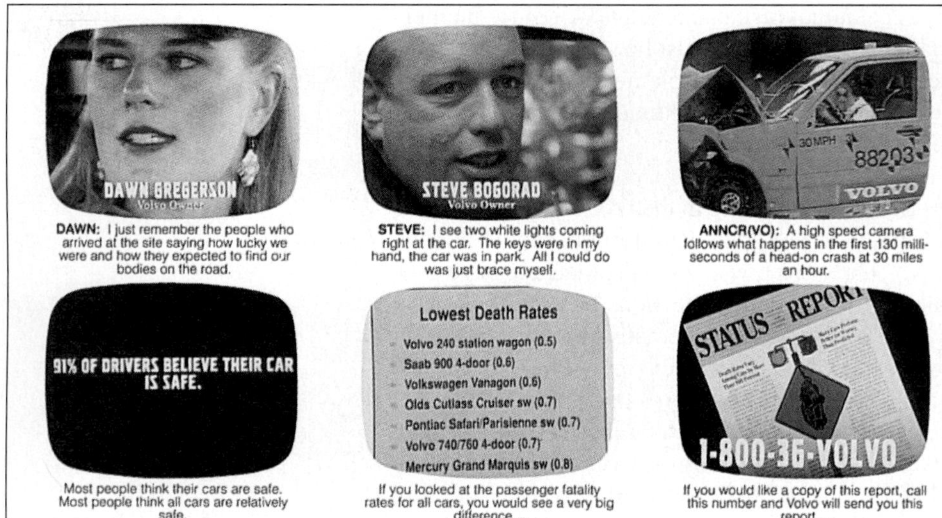

Exhibit 14–9 Volvo uses an infomercial to attract buyers

As to their effectiveness, studies indicate that infomercials get watched and sell products. Figure 14–6 shows the results of a study by Naveen Donthu and David Gilliland profiling infomercial viewers and buyers. It demonstrates that this advertising medium is indeed effective with a broad demographic base, not significantly different from the infomercial nonshopper in age, education, income, or gender. There are also a number of differences between infomercial shoppers and nonshoppers, as this figure shows. Infomercial sales in the year 2000 were expected to exceed $20 billion, three times the amount spent in 1995.[23] Retail stores are benefiting from infomercials as well, as brand awareness leads to increased in-store purchases.[24] IMC Perspective 14–1 discusses more examples of companies using infomercials.

However, some people are not sold on the idea of ads disguised as programs. For example, infomercials disguised as "ultrahip" TV shows have been targeted at teenagers, raising fears that kids under the age of 13 will be susceptible to their lure. Consumer complaints are on the rise, and the FTC has already levied fines for

Figure 14–6 Here's who's watching (and buying from) infomercials

Hypothesis Number: Construct	Infomercial Shopper (n = 84)	Infomercial Nonshopper (n = 284)	Difference Significant at the 0.05 Level?
H1: Age[a]	2.6	2.8	N
H1: Education[b]	2.4	2.2	N
H1: Income[c]	2.8	2.7	N
H1: Gender[d]	1.4	1.5	N
H2: Importance of convenience	4.2	2.8	Y[e]
H3: Brand consciousness	3.5	3.0	Y[e]
H4: Price consciousness	4.1	3.6	Y
H5: Variety-seeking propensity	3.9	3.0	Y
H6: Impulsiveness	3.2	2.6	Y
H7: Innovativeness	3.8	3.0	Y
H8: Number of hours per week spent watching television	20	14	Y
H9: Risk aversion	2.1	3.5	Y
H10: Attitude toward shopping	1.8	3.1	Y
H11: Attitude toward direct marketing	3.1	2.1	Y
H12: Attitude toward advertising	3.5	2.9	Y

[a]Age: 1 = <20; 2 = 20–35; 3 = 36–50; 4 = 51–65; 5 = >65.
[b]Education: 1 = some school; 2 = high school diploma; 3 = some college; 4 = college degree; 5 = postgraduate degree.
[c]Income: 1 = <$15K; 2 = $15–30K; 3 = $31–45K; 4 = $46–60K; 5 = >$60K.
[d]Gender: 1 = female; 2 = male.
[e]Significant in opposite direction as hypothesized.

IMC Perspective 14–1

From Sobakawa Pillows to Volvos—Infomercials Go Prime Time

It's three o'clock in the morning; you just got in and you turn on the TV set. On the TV is actress Jenilee Harrison ("Three's Company," "Dallas") and a doctor of Oriental medicine demonstrating a pillow full of buckwheat husks. Not really interested in buckwheat pillows, you switch the channel, and you see "Creating Wealth," informing you about how to get rich. Changing again you see Dionne Warwick's "Psychic Friends." One last chance, you think to yourself as you change the channel, and there it is—a commercial for Lexus. Finally, a real TV program. But wait, it's not really a commercial at all; it's another one-hour program designed to inform you about, and sell you, a product.

What you are seeing are *infomercials*—program-length commercials designed to sell you anything from fitness equipment to health programs to products and services. And they work! Infomercials are usually shown in the late night and early morning or at other times when regular program ratings are low—for example, Sunday mornings or Saturdays when there is no sports programming. Given the low cost of media time and low production costs, informercials have reached enough of an audience to rake in millions of dollars of profits. They have also attracted the attention of many companies hoping to cash in on this means of selling.

But now the infomercial has gone big time! Consider this list of companies that are using infomercials: America Online, Discover Card, DirectTV, MGM, and the New England Patriots, not to mention Hoover, Magnavox, and the Arthritis Foundation. Volkswagen was the first auto company to introduce a new model (Golf) via infomercial in Europe. Volvo ran a 28-minute commercial 13 times on cable channels, offering an 800 number to call for a 100-page publication about the car. The program generated 4,000 calls (and leads) to the auto company. In addition, Volvo was able to track which channel the call came from, at what time of day, and the potential for sales. Volvo followed up with a second mailing, and planned to do a second flight shortly thereafter.

General Motors (GM) used infomercials to introduce its 1999 Chevrolet Silverado. The 30-minute program discussed development of the truck and featured baseball star Cal Ripkin Jr. Like Volvo, GM conducted tracking research and was quite pleased with the results. Hewlett-Packard introduced its first commercial in 1998—a 28.5 minute program promoting its new greeting-card kits.

But not all infomercials are shown in the off hours, and not all are so successful. Rising costs and lower response rates have caused infomercial sponsors to consider new tactics—for example, requiring that the consumer call in for the price or promoting a low-cost item and then cross-selling more expensive ones. In 1998, CBS was the first of the major networks to replace regularly syndicated programs with infomercials on company-owned stations. Fourteen of the stations aired infomercials for Feed the Children and for Time-Life's Heartland Music. Unfortunately, thousands of irate viewers called in demanding that "Hollywood Squares" and "Entertainment Tonight" be put back on. ("Hollywood Squares" was actually shown at a later time slot.) The share points for CBS dropped significantly compared to those for the regular programming. You can be sure those viewers didn't buy anything!

One of the pioneers of the informercial has also fallen upon hard times. You may remember Nordictrack—the successful marketer of cross-country ski machines. At one time (1993), Nordictrack saturated the overnight airwaves, with sales approaching $500 million per year. By 1999, the company was in chapter 11 (bankrupt), with three straight years of operating losses totaling $217 million. A multitude of competitors, higher costs and prices, and some errors in product designs led to the demise. Interestingly, so did product quality. The original Nordictrack machines were made so well and so durable that they almost never needed to be replaced. Thus, when the market hit maturity, Nordictrack had to develop a replacement, unfortunately with much less success.

One of the problems with the marketing of "fad items" through infomercials is that the fads typically have a short life span. The company has to make it quick or may not make it at all. Whether this holds true for the bigger guys (Volvo, Lexus, etc.) remains to be seen. Right now, they don't think so.

Sources: Jean Halliday, "Volvo Ready to Act on Leads after Infomercial Success," *Advertising Age,* January 25, 1999, p. 61; "HP Airs First Infomercial," *Advertising Age,* October 23, 1998; Jay Weiner, "How Nordictrack Lost Its Footing," *Business Week,* December 14, 1998; Michael Freeman, "Pay for Play on CBS O & O's," *Mediaweek,* December 14, 1998, p. 96.

deceptive endorsements against infomercial sponsors. Four consumer groups (the Consumer Federation of America, Center for the Study of Commercialism, Center for Media Education, and Telecommunications Research and Action Center) have asked the FCC to require all infomercials to display a symbol that indicates a "paid ad" or "sponsored by" so viewers won't confuse them with regular programming.

TV Advertorials In 1999, Peugot took its first step into TV programming by developing a series of **advertorials** to show the public its entire model range. Peugeot is the first auto manufacturer to use TV advertorials. The company developed eight 5-minute films positioning the autos as "The Drive of Your Life" while providing comprehensive information on test drives, technical specifications, and demonstrations. In addition, the auto company developed advertorials for its website, with each advertorial targeted to different target audiences.[25]

Teleshopping The development of toll-free telephone numbers, combined with the widespread use of credit cards, has led to a dramatic increase in the number of people who shop via their TV sets. Jewelry, kitchenware, fitness products, insurance, compact discs, and a variety of items are now promoted (and sold) this way. The two major shopping channels in the United States [QVC and the Home Shopping Network (HSN)], account for over $3.4 billion worth of sales, though there are indications that this medium may have reached maturity. As industry studies project only a 5 percent growth rate, to $15.6 billion, by 2006.[26] Sales at HSN are declining, while the sales of the others are increasing less than forecasted. In a national research study, 55 percent of Americans stated that they had never purchased through TV shopping and do not intend to start. Another 65 percent said that they are buying less. A number of reasons for the maturing of this market have been offered; many believe that the primary cause is a shift of existing customers to the World Wide Web and limited success in attracting new audiences.[27] To address this latter problem, QVC is pursuing international markets (including the United Kingdom, Canada, and Latin America) to follow up on its successes in Germany and Japan, partnerships (United signed on as official airline of the "Quest for America's Best" program), and sponsorships (for example, Geoff Bodine on the Nascar circuit).

Exhibit 14–10 A direct-response print ad

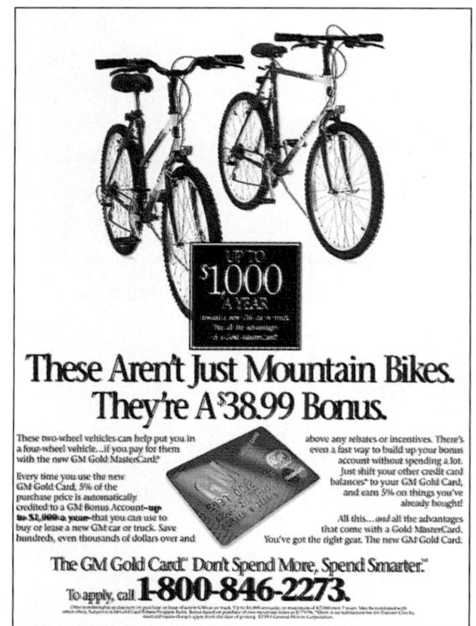

Print Media Magazines and newspapers are difficult media to use for direct marketing. Because these ads have to compete with the clutter of other ads and because the space is relatively expensive, response rates and profits may be lower than in other media. This does not mean these media are not used (as evidenced by the fact that expenditures total over $8.9 billion).[28] Exhibit 14–10 shows a direct ad that appeared in *Time* magazine. You can find many more in specific interest areas like financial newspapers or sports, sex, or hobby magazines.

Telemarketing If you have a telephone, you probably do not have to be told about the rapid increase in the use of **telemarketing,** or sales by telephone. Both profit and charitable organizations have employed this medium effectively in both one- and two-step approaches. Combined telemarketing sales (consumer and business-to-business) totaled over $538 billion in 1999—with $230 billion in the consumer market.[29] Telemarketing is a very big industry and still growing. Consider these facts:

- Over 5.4 million people are now employed in the telemarketing industry.[30]
- Telemarketing accounts for 71 percent of all b-to-b marketing sales.[31]
- Marketers spend an estimated $66.9 billion a year on outbound telemarketing calls.[32]

Business-to-business marketers like Adobe Systems, Kaiser Permanente, and Hewlett-Packard are just a few of the many companies that use this direct-marketing medium effectively.

As telemarketing continues to expand in scope, a new dimension referred to as **audiotex** or **telemedia** has evolved. Tom Eisenhart defines telemedia as the "use of telephone and voice information services (900, 800, and 976 numbers) to market, advertise, promote, entertain, and inform."[33] Many telemedia programs are interactive. While many people still think of 900 and 976 numbers as rip-offs or "sex, lies, and phone lines," over 7,000 programs are carried on 900 numbers alone, including Tele-Lawyer, a legal information services organization; Bally's Health & Tennis Corp., the nation's largest health-club chain; and NutraSweet. Figure 14–7 shows more specifically how 800/900 numbers are used as marketing tools.[34]

Problems associated with telemarketing include its potential for fraud and deception and its potential for annoyance. (Doesn't it seem as if every time you sit down to dinner you receive a phone call from someone trying to sell you something or asking for a donation?)

Those in the telemarketing and telemedia industry have responded to public criticisms. Dial-a-Porn and its ilk hold a diminishing share of 800, 900, and 976 offerings. As more and more large companies use telemedia, its tarnished image will likely brighten up.

Electronic Teleshopping Unlike infomercials and home shopping channels, which have relied on broadcast or cable TV, **electronic teleshopping** is an online shopping and information retrieval service accessed through personal computers. While we will discuss e-commerce in detail in the next chapter, it is important to reiterate that Internet shopping is a direct-response medium that traditional direct marketers are adding to their businesses as well. For example, QVC, the

Figure 14–7 The use of 800, 900, and 976 numbers in marketing

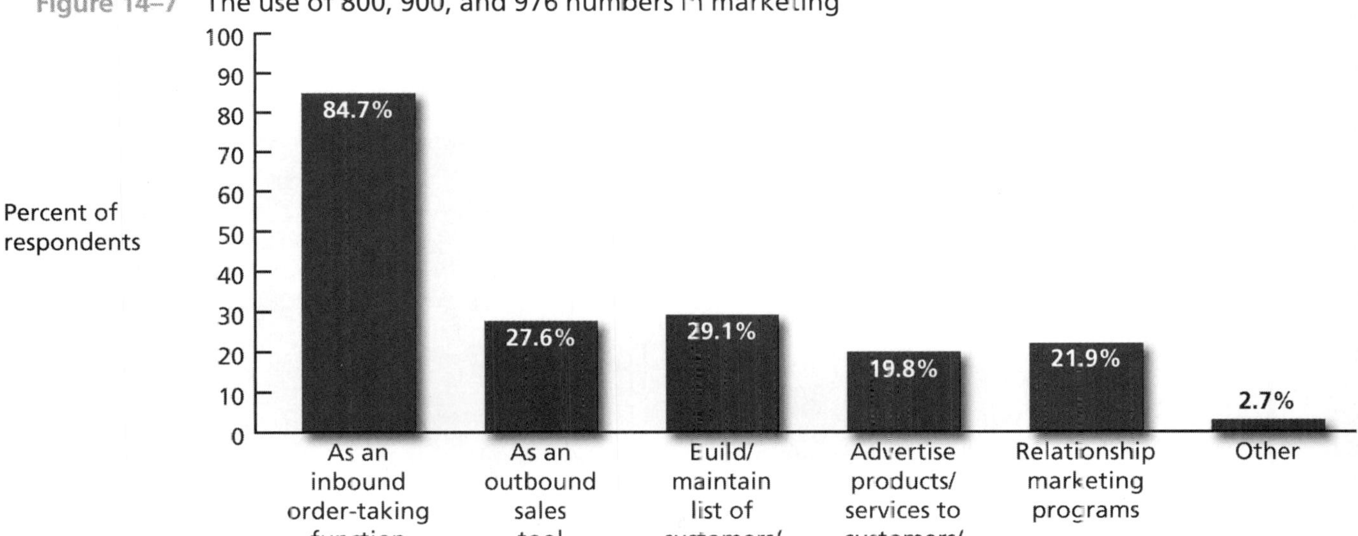

Note: *Direct* forecast survey was conducted by Jacobson Consulting Applications. The firms mailed a four-page questionnaire to direct-marketing executives, on an *n*th name basis from *Direct*'s circulation list. There were 565 responses.

home shopping channel, has started iQVC, an Internet home shopping channel that complements its cable TV channel and adds incremental sales (the cable channel drives customers to the website). The company was one of the first "Web department stores" to turn a profit.[35] Other direct marketers have met with less success, finding out the hard way that selling on the Internet requires different strategies. One such company, K-Tel, Inc., a highly successful direct-response TV marketer (Top 40 music, Veg-o-matic), has had much less success in adapting its traditional methods to the Web.[36]

Direct Selling

An additional element of the direct-marketing program is **direct selling,** the direct, personal presentation, demonstration, and sales of products and services to consumers in their homes. Avon, Amway, Mary Kay Inc., and Tupperware are some of the best-known direct-selling companies in the United States and are now extending these programs overseas (Exhibit 14–11). Close to 9.7 million people engage in direct selling throughout the world; 99 percent of them are independent contractors (not employees of the firm they represent). These 9.7 million generate approximately $23.7 billion in sales.[37]

The three forms of direct selling are

1. *Repetitive person-to-person selling.* The salesperson visits the buyer's home, job site, or other location to sell frequently purchased products or services (for example, Amway).
2. *Nonrepetitive person-to-person selling.* The salesperson visits the buyer's home, job site, or other location to sell infrequently purchased products or services (for example, Encyclopaedia Britannica).
3. *Party plans.* The salesperson offers products or services to groups of people through home or office parties and demonstrations (for example, Tupperware and PartyLite Gifts).

While a number of products and services are sold through direct selling, home and family care products (32.2 percent) and personal care products (25.9 percent) are the most popular. The "typical" direct-selling representative is female (73 percent) and married (77 percent) and 43 years of age (Figure 14–8). For most of the representatives, direct selling is not a full-time job, but an opportunity to earn additional income and a way to get the product at a discount for themselves. Over half of those employed in this industry spend less than 10 hours a week selling, and 90 percent spend less than 30 hours a week.

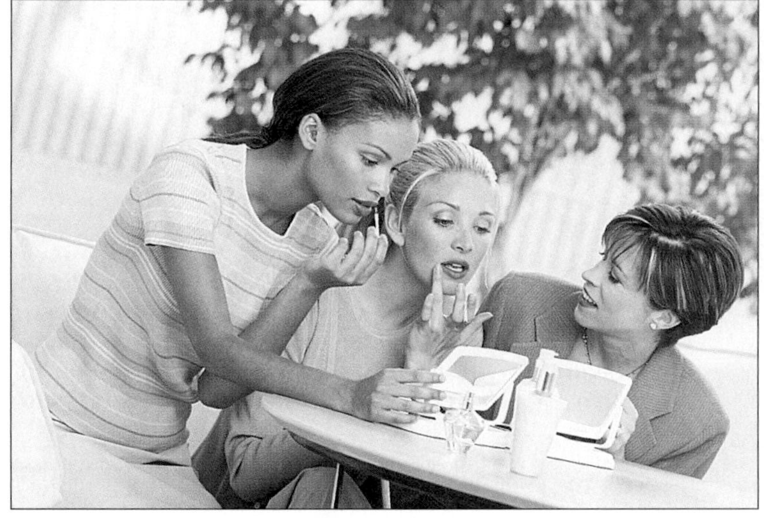

Exhibit 14–11 Mary Kay is one of the many companies that use direct selling to market their products

Figure 14–8 1998 direct sales force demographics

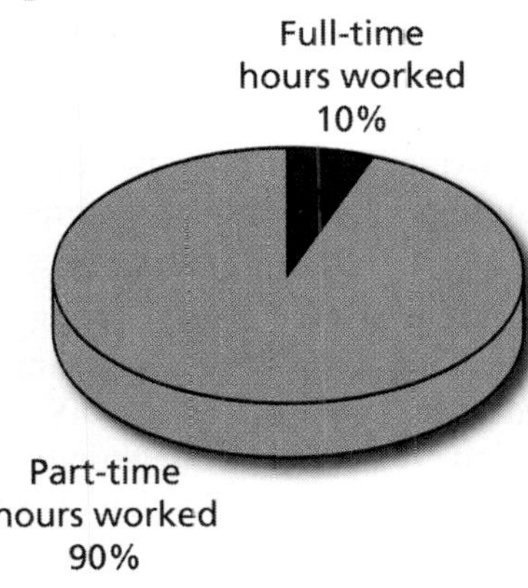

Demographics of Direct Salespeople	
Independent contractors	99.8%
Employees	0.2
Female	73
Male	27*
Less than 30 hours per week	90
30–39 hours per week	4
40 or more hours per week	6

*From DSA's 1999 National Salesforce Survey.

Evaluating the Effectiveness of Direct Marketing

Because they generate a direct response, measuring the effectiveness of direct-marketing programs is not difficult. Using the **cost per order (CPO),** advertisers can evaluate the relative effectiveness of an ad in only a few minutes based on the number of calls generated. By running the same ad on different stations, a direct marketer can determine the relative effectiveness of the medium itself. For example, if the advertiser targets a $5 return per order and a broadcast commercial (production and print) costs $2,500, the ad is considered effective if it generates 500 orders. Similar measures have been developed for print and direct-mail ads.

For direct-marketing programs that do not have an objective of generating a behavioral response, traditional measures of effectiveness can be applied. (We discuss these measures in Chapter 19.)

Advantages and Disadvantages of Direct Marketing

Many of the advantages of direct marketing have already been presented. A review of these and some additions follow:

1. *Selective reach.* Direct marketing lets the advertiser reach a large number of people and reduces or eliminates waste coverage. Intensive coverage may be obtained through broadcast advertising or through the mail. While not everyone drives on highways where there are billboards or pays attention to TV commercials, virtually everyone receives mail. A good list allows for minimal waste, as only those consumers with the highest potential are targeted. For example, a political candidate can direct a message at a very select group of people (those living in a certain Zip code or members of the Sierra Club, say); a music club can target recent purchasers of CD players.

2. *Segmentation capabilities.* Marketers can purchase lists of recent product purchasers, car buyers, bank-card holders, and so on. These lists may allow segmentation on the basis of geographic area, occupation, demographics, and job title, to mention a few. Combining this information with the geocoding capabilities of Prizm or VALS (discussed in Chapter 2), marketers can develop effective segmentation strategies.

3. *Frequency.* Depending on the medium used, it may be possible to build frequency levels. The program vehicles used for direct-response TV advertising are usually the most inexpensive available, so the marketer can afford to purchase repeat times. Frequency may not be so easily accomplished through the mail, since consumers may be annoyed to receive the same mail repeatedly.

4. *Flexibility.* Direct marketing can take on a variety of creative forms. For example, the Discovery Network sent 17-inch TV sets to media buyers through the mail. The only message accompanying the TV sets was one on the cord that said "Plug

me in" and another on a videotape that read "Play me." Upon doing so, the recipient was greeted with a seven-minute promotional video. Direct-mail pieces also allow for detailed copy that provides a great deal of information. The targeted mailing of videotapes containing product information has increased dramatically, as companies have found this a very effective way to provide potential buyers with product information. Black & Decker, Steamboat Springs Ski Resort, and a variety of auto companies have successfully employed this medium.

5. *Timing.* While many media require long-range planning and have long closing dates, direct-response advertising can be much more timely. Direct mail, for example, can be put together very quickly and distributed to the target population. TV programs typically used for direct-response advertising are older, less sought programs that are likely to appear on the station's list of available spots. Another common strategy is to purchase available time at the last possible moment to get the best price.

6. *Personalization.* No other advertising medium can personalize the message as well as direct media. Parents with children at different age levels can be approached, with their child's name included in the appeal. Car owners are mailed letters congratulating them on their new purchase and offering accessories. Computer purchasers are sent software solicitations. Graduating college students receive very personalized information that recognizes their specific needs and offers solutions (such as credit cards).

7. *Costs.* While the CPM for direct mail may be very high on an absolute and a relative basis, its ability to specifically target the audience and eliminate waste coverage reduces the actual CPM. The ads used on TV are often among the lowest-priced available, and a video can be delivered for less than $1 (including postage).

A second factor contributing to the cost effectiveness of direct-response advertising is the cost per customer purchasing. Because of the low cost of media, each sale generated is very inexpensive.

8. *Measures of effectiveness.* No other medium can measure the effectiveness of its advertising efforts as well as direct response. Feedback is often immediate and always accurate.

Disadvantages of direct marketing include the following:

1. *Image factors.* As we noted earlier, the mail segment of this industry is often referred to as junk mail. Many people believe unsolicited mail promotes junk products, and others dislike being solicited. Even some senders of direct mail, including Motorola, GM, and Air Products & Chemicals, say they throw out most of the junk mail they receive. This problem is particularly relevant given the increased volume of mail being sent. (One study estimates the typical American receives 14 pieces of junk mail per week.)[38] In 1999 over 201.6 billion pieces of mail were sent in the United States alone.[39]

Likewise, direct-response ads on TV are often low-budget ads for lower-priced products, which contributes to the image that something less than the best products are marketed in this way. (Some of this image is being overcome by the home shopping channels, which promote some very expensive products.) As you can see in Ethical Perspective 14–2, other factors have also created image problems for the direct-marketing industry.

2. *Accuracy.* One of the advantages cited for direct mail and telemarketing was targeting potential customers specifically. But the effectiveness of these methods depends on the accuracy of the lists used. People move, change occupations, and so on, and if the lists are not kept current, selectivity will decrease. Computerization has greatly improved the currency of lists and reduced the incidence of bad names; however, the ability to generate lists is becoming a problem.[40]

3. *Content support.* In our discussion of media strategy objectives in Chapter 10, we said the ability of magazines to create mood contributes to the overall effectiveness of the ads they carry. In direct-response advertising, mood creation is limited to the surrounding program and/or editorial content. Direct mail and online services are unlikely to create a desirable mood.

Ethical Perspective 14–2

Sweepstakes Blues—Direct Marketers May Not Be a Winner

Dick Clark and Ed McMahon have been TV celebrities for decades. Now they are being sued by the attorneys general of six states. Where did they go wrong?

Clark and McMahon are spokesmen for American Family Publishers (AFP), one of the "big four" direct-mail magazine sweepstakes companies (the others are Time-Life, Inc., Readers' Digest, and Publishers' Clearing House. Unfortunately for them, an AFP mailer sent to 200 million people contained a message, by name, that stated: "If you have the winning number, please be advised: It's down to a two-person race for $11,000,000—you and one other person in (state) were issued the winning number. Whoever returns it first wins all!" Alongside the message were pictures of the two celebrities with a "personal" message encouraging a fast response. Believing that only 100 people throughout the US were left in the sweepstakes, many hopefuls sent their returns by overnight mail. Some (about 20) even flew to AFP headquarters in Tampa, Florida, to claim their winnings. One wrote million-dollar checks to his kids. A woman in Baltimore borrowed $1,500 for airfare to fly to Tampa to collect her prize. Unfortunately, they hadn't won anything.

Enter the attorneys general, who felt that the company had finally stepped over the line and had deceived the public. After AFP negotiated a settlement with 32 states, 6 of the states filed a civil action suit against McMahon and Clark personally. Calling the contest a "scam," "ripoff," and "bold and blatantly fraudulent," they accused the celebrities of "flat-out lying" to the public.

But AFP is not alone. Thousands of complaints have been filed by outraged consumers who felt they were deceived by sweepstakes companies. Many, believing that they will increase their chances of winning, purchase products they don't want. Others invest family savings, and at least one man committed suicide over the humiliation he felt once he determined he had been deceived. Seeing this, the attorneys general determined that something had to be done to clean up the industry.

The big four send out over 1 billion contest mailers a year, reaching approximately 8 of every 10 households. These "stamp sheet" sellers account for approximately 12 percent of the $7 billion-per-year magazine subscription market, but a strong economy coupled with state lotteries and legalized gambling has led to a 30 percent decline in sales over the past five years, resulting in more aggressive marketing tactics.

Other direct-marketing industries have been criticized as well. In 1998, consumer advocate Ralph Nader organized a group called Commercial Alert to help parents and communities defend themselves against intrusive marketing campaigns. The group's initial action asked Congress and state legislatures to establish "family hours" between 6 and 9 P.M. as a time in which telemarketers would not be permitted to phone. A number of states have cracked down on the "booze-by-mail" business—the shipping of alcohol purchased through direct mail or on the Internet directly to the consumer. The National Advertising Division of the Council of Better Business Bureaus has increased its policing of deceptive advertising, paying very close attention to infomercials. The Good Housekeeping Institute has also become involved, rating infomercials on the basis of a combination of performance, price, and accuracy of their TV claims.

The impact of all this has not gone unnoticed in the direct-marketing industry. The bad publicity over the sweepstakes company has resulted in as much as 30 to 70 percent declines in subscriptions. The Direct Marketing Association (DMA) has suggested proposals that will require marketers using sweepstakes to decrease the potential for deception. The DMA also promised Congress that it would rewrite its ethics code and enforce it more vigorously. But it may be too late.

Sources: "Institute's Testers Affix Rating Stars to Infomercial Fare," *Arizona Republic,* November 13, 1999, p. B4; Patricia Barry, "Sweepstakes on Trial," *AARP Bulletin,* June 1999, pp. 3–22; Greg Jaffe, "Sweepstakes Industry May Not Be a Winner!" *The Wall Street Journal,* February 18, 1998, p. B1.

Summary

This chapter introduced you to the rapidly growing field of direct marketing, which involves a variety of methods and media beyond direct mail and telemarketing. The versatility of direct marketing offers many different types of companies and organizations a powerful promotional and selling tool.

Direct marketing continues to outpace other advertising and promotional areas in growth; many of the Fortune 500 companies now use sophisticated direct-marketing strategies. Database marketing has become a critical component of many marketing programs.

Advantages of direct marketing include its selective reach, segmentation, frequency, flexibility, and timing. Personalized and custom messages, low costs, and the ability to measure program effectiveness are also advantages of direct-marketing programs.

At the same time, a number of disadvantages are associated with the use of direct marketing. Image problems, the proliferating sale and use of databases (some of them based on inaccurate lists), lack of content support, and the intrusive nature of the medium make some marketers hesitant to use direct-marketing tools. However, self-policing of the industry and involvement by large, sophisticated companies have led to significant improvements. As a result, the use of direct marketing will continue to increase.

Key Terms

direct marketing, 471
direct-response media, 471
database, 475
database marketing, 475
RFM scoring method, 477
one-step approach, 479
two-step approach, 479
mailing list, 479
direct-response advertising, 481
support advertising, 481
infomercial, 481
advertorial, 484
telemarketing, 484
audiotex, 485
telemedia, 485
electronic teleshopping, 485
direct selling, 486
cost per order (CPO), 487

Discussion Questions

1. Identify some of the factors that have contributed to the growth of direct marketing. Do you see these factors being as relevant today? Discuss why or why not, and the impact they will have on direct marketing in the future.

2. Explain how a consumer goods company might employ database marketing. A business-to-business company? A service company?

3. The catalog has become an important part of the shopping lives of many consumers. Describe different groups that you think might find catalogs useful in the consumer market, and explain what aspects of catalogs would attract them to this medium.

4. Direct selling has seen rapid adoption in foreign markets, particularly in areas like Eastern Europe. Explain why direct selling might be more rapidly adopted in these markets.

5. Most of the methods for measuring effectiveness of direct marketing have to do with behaviors like sales, cost-per-order, etc. Explain how the adoption model discussed in Chapter 5 might also be employed to measure effectiveness.

6. One of the disadvantages associated with direct-marketing media is the high cost per exposure. Some marketers feel that this cost is not really as much of a disadvantage as is claimed. Argue for or against this position.

7. Why have companies like Volvo, Cadillac, and General Motors increased their use of infomercials? Is this a wise strategy?

8. Give an example of how companies might use direct marketing as part of an IMC program. Provide examples of both consumer and business marketers.

9. Direct marketing has been beset by a number of problems that have tarnished its image. Discuss some of these and what might be done to improve direct marketing's image.

10. How might business-to-business marketers use telemarketing effectively?

Chapter Fifteen

The Internet and Interactive Media

Chapter Objectives

- To understand the different ways the Internet is used to communicate.
- To know the advantages and disadvantages of the Internet and interactive media.
- To know the role of the Internet and interactive media in an IMC program.
- To understand how to evaluate the effectiveness of communications through the Internet.

Everyone's On as the Internet Turns 30!

Thirty years ago, Stanford University and UCLA connected the first two computers to begin something called the "Internet" by logging in with the word *log.* Well, at least they tried to begin it. The first message that actually came through was "I.O. Crash." That "crash" message is just about the only thing that today's Internet has in common with the initial version. Born on September 2, 1969, on a room-size computer at UCLA, the Internet at that time was named ARPANET (Advanced Research Project Agency), by the U.S. Department of Defense, which developed the network as a way to connect research agencies across the nation. Only about 15 people were there to witness the first connection—far fewer than today, when as many as 90 million are connected. When e-mail—which allowed person-to-person connections rather than just computer-to-computer ones—was added in 1972, the Internet began to catch on. In 1991, when the World Wide Web enabled businesses and consumers to connect to the network, the Internet really began to grow up. And grow up it did! No one could possibly have imagined how large it would become.

At the start of the 21st century, it seems as though everyone is on the Internet. In the business-to-business market, almost every company has a site. You would be hard-pressed to find a Fortune 1000 company—business-to-business or consumer—that doesn't have its own site, and individuals from movie stars to teenagers have their own home pages. There are sites for Porsche owners, Peugot 606 owners, doctors, pet owners, travel destinations, and fan clubs. By 1998, there were more e-mails (9.4 billion per day) sent in the United States than there were first-class-mail pieces. Consider some of the following:

- *www.talentmarket.monster.com.* You may be familiar with www.monster.com, the site that helps people find full-time jobs. You are probably less familiar with the company's site for "free agents," that is, independent professionals who auction off their services

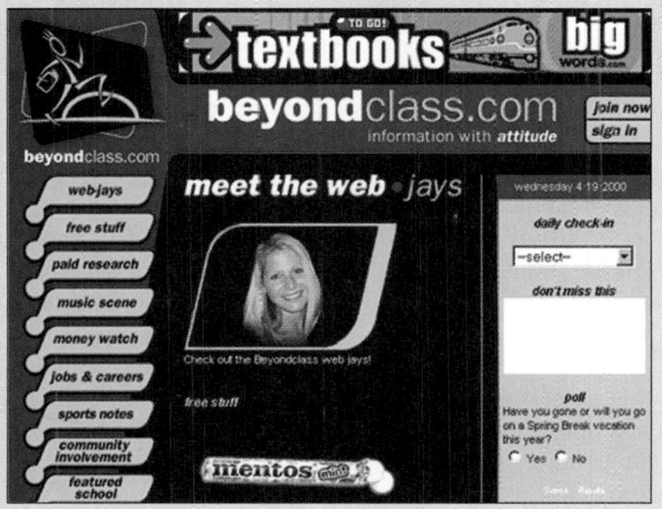

- *www.wine.com.* This is an e-commerce site that sells wine.
- *www.disney.com.* This is the Walt Disney Company's Disneyland on the Web.
- *www.e-centives.com.* This site delivers personalized incentives to customers online on the basis of their unique shopping profiles and interests.

- *www.beyondclass.com.* Targeted to college students, this site provides information regarding careers, finances, and so on, while giving students the opportunity to earn money through research and to win free prizes.
- *www.espanol.lycos.com.* This Lycos portal contains 14 sites targeting Hispanics in the United States and South America.

And this is just a sampling. There are literally thousands of sites out there selling automobiles, pet supplies, loans, and just about anything else you might want to buy. In addition, government agencies have discovered the Web: the city of Ferndale, Michigan, used eBay (the online auction site) to auction off surplus stop signs it had acquired for use in the event of a Y2K power outage; Pennsylvania officials auctioned off a state construction project, saving taxpayers an estimated $500,000; a Riverside County, California, tax collector auctioned off tax-delinquent properties in an attempt to collect $100,000 in back taxes; and Oregon officials sold surplus and confiscated property ranging from street signs to a white leather halter top (it sold for $50).

By the end of 1999, there were so many websites that, according to most estimates, major portals like Yahoo! and Lycos contain only about 16 percent of the total number of sites. There has been such a flood of registrations for domain names that ".com" listings are extremely difficult to get and the ".net" ones are in limited supply as well. Because so many companies have similar names, confusion and fraud are rampant. A number of companies have changed their names to avoid confusion, while others have changed them to more accurately express what they do. For example, InfoSeek became Go.com; computer site Onsale bought Egghead and then changed its name to Egghead.com; and the Mining Co. search engine became About.com. Companies like TradeZone.com and GreatDomains.com have developed successful businesses by specializing in the selling of domain names. Some entrepreneurial types have purchased domain names with the idea of auctioning them off. For example, the owner of www.GeorgeBush.com bought the name and then tried to sell it to the presidential candidate. The George Bush, Jr., campaign later purchased every name it could that might be close to the candidate's name to ensure that those logging on would find him.

When will the Internet stop growing? Not very soon, according to the experts. No one could have predicted way back in the era of Woodstock (the first one) that the Internet would be where it is today. And no one knows where it will be 30 years from now.

Sources: Julie Tamaki, "Taxman Is Latest to Jump into Internet Auction Craze," *Los Angeles Times,* February 7, 2000, p. A3; Bradley Johnson, "Internet Turns the Big 30," *Advertising Age,* August 30, 1999, p. 28; Laurie Freeman, "Domain-Name Dilemma Worsens," *Advertising Age,* November 8, 1999, p. 100.

By now you probably don't have to be told about the incredible variety of websites that are on the Internet offering anything from advice to products or services that are given away or sold. As the lead-in to this chapter indicates, the World Wide Web (WWW) has become the most popular component of the Internet, and its growth shows no signs of slowing. Sources estimate that 85 percent of all college students use the Internet, with over 40 percent accessing it on a daily basis.[1] For many students, it has become their first source of information for everything from school research to travel planning. Interestingly, not everyone has been able to capitalize on the market potential of the Internet, including some of the more successful "brick and mortar" companies. Procter & Gamble, for example, has experienced problems with establishing a brand identity for its products on the Web, and Levi's recently abandoned its attempt to sell its jeans through the Internet. Companies have learned that merely putting up a homepage does not guarantee success and that the strategies that have worked effectively in traditional markets do not necessarily transfer well to the Internet.

In this chapter we will discuss the Internet, marketers' objectives for using the Net, and ways to measure the effectiveness of this new medium. As you will see, the Internet is a valuable component of the integrated marketing communications program and, like other components, is most effective when used in conjunction with other program elements.

Defining the Internet

Before beginning our discussion, it may be useful to establish some common ground. While all of us are familiar with the Internet, the degree to which we are familiar varies. Understanding the material presented in this chapter will be easier if you are familiar with the terms used in the discussion.

The **Internet** is a worldwide means of exchanging information and communicating through a series of interconnected computers. As noted, it was started as a U.S. Defense Department project, but it is now accessible to anyone with a computer and a modem. While the most popular component of the Internet is the **World Wide Web (WWW),** there are other features as well, as shown in Figure 15–1. For marketers, a number of these features offer potential, but it is the Web that has developed as the commercial component. For that reason, the following discussion will focus on using the Web as a communications and sales tool. Before reading further, however, please take a few minutes to examine Figure 15–2, to familiarize yourself with some of the terms that we will be using. In reality, there are many more words that have been added to our language as a result of the growth of the Internet (you can actually purchase a dictionary of Internet terms), but space permits only a small inclusion here. Thus, we have stayed away from the technical jargon, concentrating primarily on marketing communications terms. If you are not familiar with terms like *URL, backbone, browser,* and so on, you may wish to consult another source before continuing.

Developing an Internet Program

As with other media discussed earlier in this text, using the Internet requires the development of a plan. This plan should consider target audiences (users of the Net), specific objectives and strategies, and methods for measuring effectiveness.

Web Participants

The Web, like all other media, has both customers (users) and those trying to reach these users (advertisers, sponsors, e-commerce). As with other media, there are sites that are targeted to consumers and sites in the business-to-business (b-to-b) market. Let's start our discussion with the users—the target markets.

Figure 15–1 Features of the Internet

Feature	Use
Electronic mail (e-mail)	Allows users to send electronic mail anywhere in the world
Usenet	Discussion groups, newsgroups, and electronic bulletin boards, similar to those offered by online services
Telnet	Online databases, library catalogs, and electronic journals at hundreds of colleges and public libraries
File transfer protocol (ftp) or hypertext transfer protocol (http)	The ability to transfer files from one mainframe computer to another
Client server	Allows for the transfer of files from one mainframe computer to another
Gopher	A document retrieval system used to search for information
Wide Area Information Server (WAIS)	Enables one to use keywords in specific databases and retrieve full text information
World Wide Web (WWW)	Does much the same thing as gopher and WAIS, but combines sound, graphic images, video, and hypertext on a single page; the commercial arm of the Internet

Figure 15–2 Internet terminology

Term	Definition
Ad clicks	Number of times users click on an ad banner.
Ad click rate	Often referred to as "click-through," the percentage of ad views that result in an ad click.
Ad views (impressions)	Number of times an ad banner is downloaded (and presumably seen by viewers).
Banner	An ad on a Web page that may be "hot-linked" to the advertiser's site.
Button	An advertisement smaller than a traditional banner ad. Buttons are usually square in shape and located down the left or right side of the site; sometimes referred to as "tiles."
CPC	Cost per click—a marketing formula used to price ad banners. Some advertisers pay on the basis of the number of clicks a specific ad banner gets.
CPM	Cost per thousand for a site.
Domain name	The unique name of an Internet site. There are six domains widely used in the U.S.: .com (commercial), .edu (education), .net (network operations), .gov (U.S. government), .mil (U.S. military), and .org (organization). Additional two letter domains specify a country, for example, .sp for Spain.
Hit	Each instance in which a server sends a file to a browser. Hits are used to measure the traffic on a site.
Interstitial	An advertisement that appears in a window on your screen while you are waiting for a Web page to load.
Link	An electronic connection between two websites.
Opt-in-e-mail	List of Internet users who have voluntarily signed up to receive commercial e-mail about topics of interest.
Page views	Number of times a user requests a page that contains a particular ad; used to indicate the number of times an ad was potentially seen, or "gross impressions."
Rich media	Advanced technology used in Internet ads, such as streaming video, which allows interaction and special effects.
Sponsorships	The sponsoring of a site's content by an advertiser.
Unique users	Number of different individuals who visit a site within a specific time period.
Valid hits	Number of hits that deliver all the information to a user (excludes error messages, redirects, etc.)
Visits	A sequence of requests made by one user at one site.

Users: Consumer Market As noted in the lead-in, the growth of the Internet has been phenomenal. As of 1995, there were an estimated 14.9 million households using the Net. By 1998 the number had grown to 54 million in the United States and 95 million worldwide, with projections that it will increase to 282 million by the end of 2002[2]—and the projections are constantly being altered as more and more users come aboard. As shown in Figure 15–3, the adoption curve of the Internet greatly outpaces that of any other medium. A number of reasons have been offered to explain this rapid adoption. A long period of economic prosperity, Internet innovation, heavy investments by companies, and (as noted in the previous chapter) changing lifestyles of the American consumer (consumers are now "money rich and time poor") have all contributed.

Figure 15–3 Adoption curves for various media—the Web is ramping fast

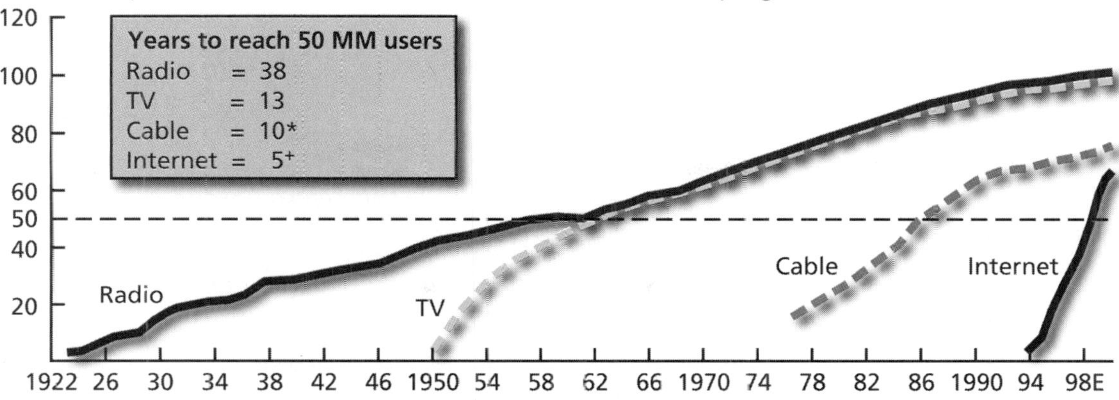

* The launch of HBO in 1976 was used to estimate the beginning of cable as an entertainment/advertising medium. Though cable technology was developed in the late 1940s, its initial use was primarily for the improvement of reception in remote areas. It was not until HBO began to distribute its pay-TV movie service via satellite in 1976 that the medium became a distinct content and advertising alternate to broadcast television.

+ Morgan Stanley Technology Research Estimate

The demographic profile of Internet users has changed as well. Whereas in 1996, the Web was clearly a male-dominated medium (82 percent male versus 18 percent female), by 2000 the numbers reflected an even 50-50 usage. The average age of Internet users is now 34.9 years, with more than 65 percent having household incomes of $50,000 or more. The average household income of users in 1999 was $60,800. More than 75 percent of users have attended college (as opposed to 46 percent of the overall U.S. population).[3] Besides their being more wealthy and educated, a recent study by Scarborough Research indicates that Web users have active lifestyles, leading them to adopt the medium for convenience and time management purposes.[4] Whereas in the past the average user of the Internet tended to be a "techie," today's user reflects the U.S. population more closely, as can be seen in Figures 15–4 and 15–5. Figure 15–4 shows the reasons given for accessing the

Figure 15–4 What users do online

What do you do when you go online?	1998	1997
Gather news or info	91.2%	87.8%
Send e-mail	88.2	83.2
Conduct research	79.4	80.5
Surf various sites	68.5	75.3
Shop	26.8	17.8
Post to bb's	22.7	30.0
Play games	21.8	33.7
Participate in chats	18.4	30.8
None of these	1.2	1.9
Have you purchased anything online in the past year?		
Yes	28.3%	23.5%
Have you used a credit card online?		
Yes	29.1%	

Figure 15–5 Products purchased on the Internet; rating frequency of online buying

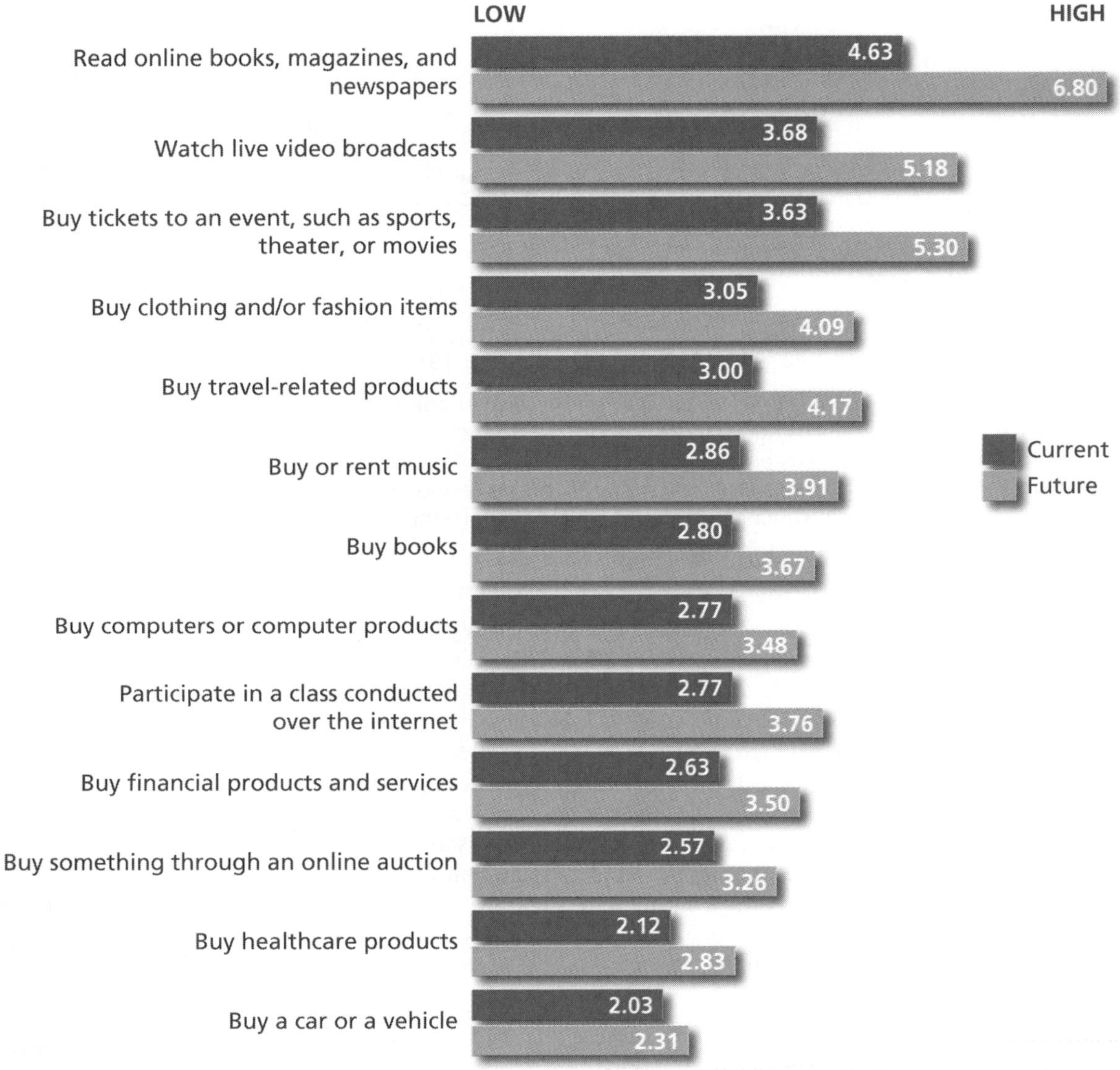

LOW — HIGH

	Current	Future
Read online books, magazines, and newspapers	4.63	6.80
Watch live video broadcasts	3.68	5.18
Buy tickets to an event, such as sports, theater, or movies	3.63	5.30
Buy clothing and/or fashion items	3.05	4.09
Buy travel-related products	3.00	4.17
Buy or rent music	2.86	3.91
Buy books	2.80	3.67
Buy computers or computer products	2.77	3.48
Participate in a class conducted over the internet	2.77	3.76
Buy financial products and services	2.63	3.50
Buy something through an online auction	2.57	3.26
Buy healthcare products	2.12	2.83
Buy a car or a vehicle	2.03	2.31

Internet, while Figure 15–5 shows the types of products and services most frequently purchased.

Shoppers While Figures 15–4 and 15–5 reflect the profile of Internet users and their primary reasons for using the Net, the profile of Internet shoppers is slightly different. The Scarborough study found that Internet users can be segmented into two distinct groups: (1) those 18 and over who shop on the Web, and (2) the "wired but wary"—those who use the Internet but do not shop there. As shown in Figure 15–6, those most prone to shop—who constitute approximately 25 percent of Internet users—are very upscale and have diverse Internet usage patterns. As noted by Bob Cohen, president of Scarborough Research, "E-shoppers clearly evidence a rich, active, and diverse lifestyle. The shoppers travel, attend sporting events, and engage in a variety of activities including swimming, biking, and photography. Because of their active lifestyles, they are attracted to the convenience offered by e-shopping."[5] People in the wired-but-wary segment also have active lives, and they tend to be more upscale than nonusers. Their characteristics are similar to those of the shoppers but not as pronounced. Their Internet usage is less diversified, and their primary motivation for using it is e-mail.

While most predictions are that the use of the Internet will continue to grow at an astounding pace, not all studies agree. A 1999 study of 1,000 users and 1,000

Lifestyle Activities	E-Shoppers	Wired but Wary	Unwired
Bicycling	40%	37%	23%
Camping	24	22	17
Swimming	52	46	31
Hiking/backpacking	20	17	8
Photography	34	26	18
Saw 3+ movies in past month	36	31	20
Attended pro sporting event	45	41	28
Belong to health/exercise club	24	20	9
Used ATM card	75	65	41
Made foreign trip in last three years	54	49	34
Belong to frequent flyer program	37	28	11
Household owns cell phone	64	59	36
10+ times fast food in past month	31	24	20
Bought from TV shopping show	19	12	11
Bought from direct mail	75	61	56

Figure 15–6 Internet shopper profiles

nonusers by Cyber Dialogue suggests that the growth of the Internet audience has slowed and, in fact, is reaching maturity. The study concludes that the decline in growth can be explained by a number of factors:[6]

- A demographic "digital divide" between consumers who can afford PCs and online access and those who cannot.
- Adults who feel that they have no need for the Internet.
- People who have tried the Internet and discontinued using it because it doesn't meet their needs.

The last of these groups has tripled in number, between 1997 and 1999, to approximately 28 million adults, according to Cyber Dialogue. If the numbers are correct, they are indicative of a growth rate decline. (The number of users will continue to grow but at a slower pace.) Another study, conducted by eMarketer, projects a slowdown in online advertising spending over the period 1999–2004. While total expenditures will increase, the rate of growth is expected to slow, according to the study's data.[7]

Whether the growth in Internet usage and e-commerce will slow or continue to grow at its current pace, it will account for a substantial amount of consumer spending. In 1999, consumer expenditures on the Internet reached approximately $20 billion, with expectations of $184 billion by 2004.[8] These numbers make the Internet a medium to be reckoned with, and they offer strong potential to marketers.

Users: Business to Business The consumer market figures may seem astronomical enough, but they pale in comparison to the figures on business-to-business marketing. While some consumer companies feel that a website is of little value, most business marketers consider it a necessity. A number of studies place the percentage of businesses (large and small) that have or soon will have websites at over 90 percent. The number of businesses online reached 6.3 million in 1999 and is expected to rise to 8.3 million by 2004, with over 100 million business-to-business decision makers online.[9] The revenue generated by these business sites is much higher than that generated in the consumer market—$4.7 billion in 1999, with projections of $2.7 trillion by the year 2004 (yes, that is a *t*!).[10] Businesses in the computer and electronics, shipping and warehousing, and utilities industries expect that by 2004 they will conduct over 70 percent of their transactions over the Internet. (So-called heavy industries like aerospace and defense are expected to transact less than 50 percent through this medium.)

Business-to-business marketers use the Internet in a variety of ways. Hewlett-Packard has budgeted over $100 million to target b-to-b users of its equipment.[11] Cisco and Dell use the Web to track and distribute sales leads in real time, while others like Scientific International train their sales representatives and host sales meetings via the web as well as sell.[12] Cisco estimates that it saves $1 million per month by having sales meetings on the Web.[13] One of the main benefits for business-to-business marketers is the ability to acquire information about products and services. In today's Internet world, a company can immediately pull up the product and service offerings of a provider, without having to make a phone call or wait for a salesperson to visit. In turn, the same company can reach thousands of potential customers that it would not have been possible to reach without a website—at a significantly reduced cost. Ford and Delta Airlines may have started a new trend when they announced that all of their 350,000 and 72,000 employees, respectively, would be given free PCs for their home use. The reason? To allow them to connect to the Internet and to facilitate communications in their work as well as with other employees.[14]

Web Objectives

When major corporations first began to conduct business on the Internet, they put up websites primarily for information purposes. Companies like United Airlines and Maytag had sites that were really not much more than online catalogs designed for information purposes only. The role of the website quickly changed, however; sites have become much more creative, offering promotions, chat rooms, and even products and services for sale. With the introduction of Java in 1995, it became possible to create fancier graphics, audio, and animation online. This resulted in marketers' utilizing the Internet in an entirely new way, moving beyond the purely informational role. As you will see, the objective of disseminating information still remains, but additional communications and sales objectives are now being pursued.

Developing and Maintaining a Website

Before we discuss marketers' Web objectives in detail, it is important that you understand the role of the **website**—the place where information is made available to users of the Internet by the provider. Developing and maintaining a successful website requires significant time and effort. To attract visitors to the site and have them return to it requires a combination of creativity, effective marketing, and continual updating of the site. As the number of sites continues to increase, the demand for service providers such as site developers and webmasters escalates as well. Developing and maintaining a website now requires an expensive and time intensive commitment.

Exhibit 15–1 demonstrates what makes a website work. Making a site work and having one work successfully are not the same thing, however, and whether a site is effective is determined by what it is that management hopes to achieve through the site. As already noted, some sites are offered for informational purposes only (this tends to be more common in the business-to-business market than the consumer market), while others approach the market much more aggressively. For example, Kimberly-Clark Corporation, the manufacturer of Huggies brand (diapers, Pull-Ups training pants, and Little Swimmers swim pants) has been extremely successful in its Internet marketing efforts. The Huggies homepage (Exhibit 15–2) goes well beyond providing information. The site has additional objectives, such as developing a relationship with parents, establishing a brand image for the products through online campaigns, and supporting sales. For example, one campaign designed to develop one-on-one relationships offered a free sample to anyone who sent in his or her name, address, and e-mail address. Thousands of people responded to the offer, providing Kimberly-Clark with an enormous database useful for future marketing efforts. Another targeted parents visiting other websites such as CTW.org (Children's Television Workshop—producer of "Sesame Street"),

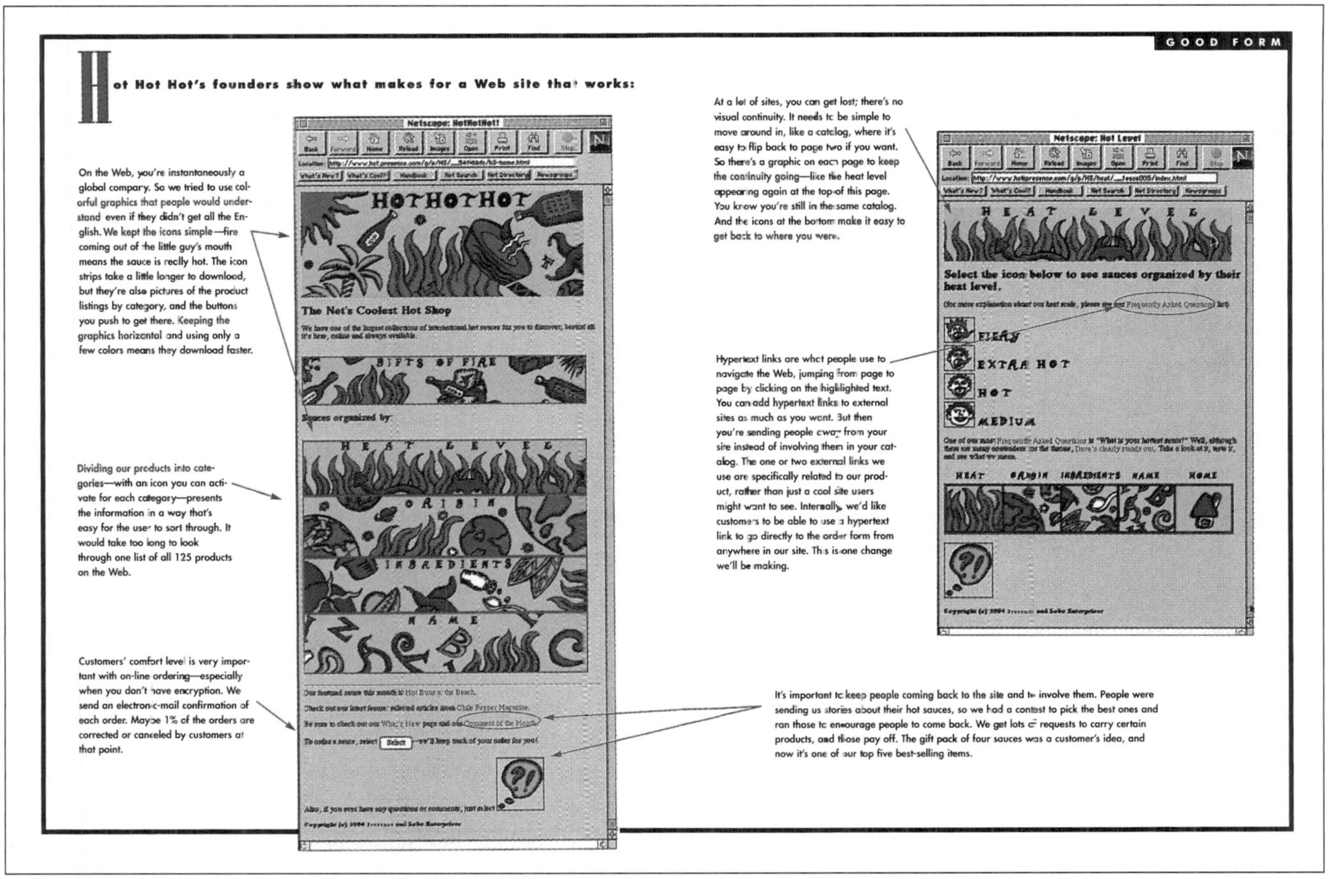

GOOD FORM
Hot Hot Hot's founders show what makes for a Web site that works:
On the Web, you're instantaneously a global company. So we tried to use colorful graphics that people would understand even if they didn't get all the English. We kept the icons simple—fire coming out of the little guy's mouth means the sauce is really hot. The icon strips take a little longer to download, but they're also pictures of the product listings by category, and the buttons you push to get there. Keeping the graphics horizontal and using only a few colors means they download faster.
Dividing our products into categories—with an icon you can activate for each category—presents the information in a way that's easy for the user to sort through. It would take too long to look through one list of all 125 products on the Web.
Customers' comfort level is very important with on-line ordering—especially when you don't have encryption. We send an electronic-mail confirmation of each order. Maybe 1% of the orders are corrected or canceled by customers at that point.
At a lot of sites, you can get lost; there's no visual continuity. It needs to be simple to move around in, like a catalog, where it's easy to flip back to page two if you want. So there's a graphic on each page to keep the continuity going—like the heat level appearing again at the top of this page. You know you're still in the same catalog. And the icons at the bottom make it easy to get back to where you were.
Hypertext links are what people use to navigate the Web, jumping from page to page by clicking on the highlighted text. You can add hypertext links to external sites as much as you want. But then you're sending people away from your site instead of involving them in your catalog. The one or two external links we use are specifically related to our product, rather than just a cool site users might want to see. Internally, we'd like customers to be able to use a hypertext link to go directly to the order form from anywhere in our site. This is one change we'll be making.
It's important to keep people coming back to the site and to involve them. People were sending us stories about their hot sauces, so we had a contest to pick the best ones and ran those to encourage people to come back. We get lots of requests to carry certain products, and those pay off. The gift pack of four sauces was a customer's idea, and now it's one of our top five best-selling items.
Netscape: HotHotHot!
HOTHOTHOT
The Net's Coolest Hot Shop
GIFTS OF FIRE
Sauces organized by:
HEAT LEVEL
ORIGIN
INGREDIENTS
NAME
Netscape: Hot Level
Select the icon below to see sauces organized by their heat level.
FIERY
EXTRA HOT
HOT
MEDIUM

Exhibit 15–1 Hot Hot Hot founders demonstrate what makes a website work

Women.com, iVillage.com, and BabyZone.com. In addition, anyone typing in the keywords *diapers* or *infant care* on portals Lycos and Excite was greeted with a Huggies banner ad. To bring visitors to the site, Huggies provided tips on baby care, chat with other parents, access to other baby links, and additional information about Huggies products. Finally, to support sales, the site directed customers to the nearest retail store that sells Huggies brands.

The Huggies Disposable Diapers and Baby Wipes Site - Microsoft Internet Explorer provided by McGraw Hill Higher Education
http://www.huggies.com/
Explore HUGGIES World
parentstages.com
The best of the web, for every parenting stage.
click here
Baby Smart
• Expert Advice • Information For all of baby's stages
Parenting Community
• The Discussion Place - New! • Parents' Picks • Conferences
Happy Baby
• Songs • Games • Recipes
HUGGIES Diapers & Wipes
• Information • Offers • Sweepstakes • FAQs
HUGGIES Boutique
What's New
Audio This Week

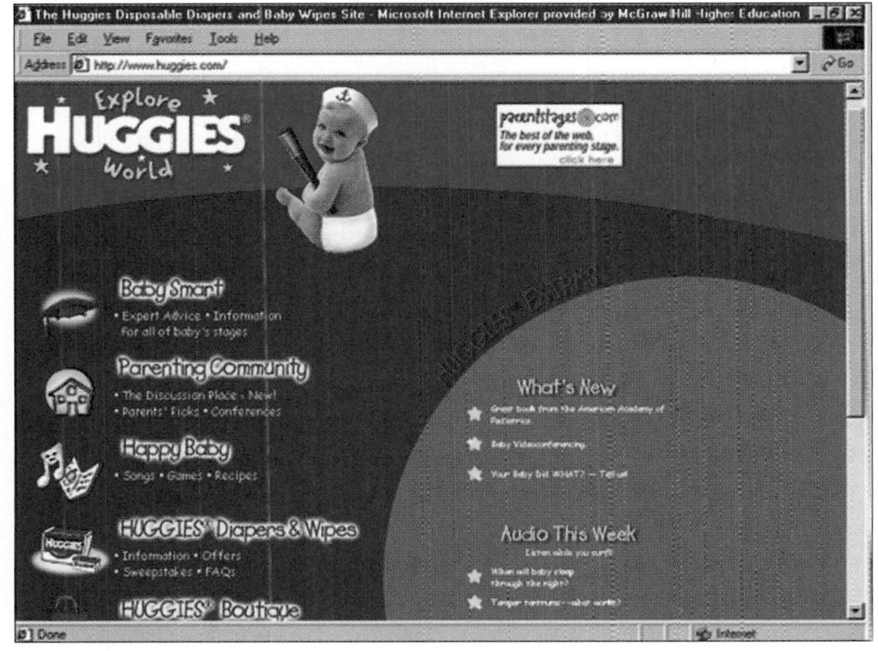

Exhibit 15–2 Huggies homepage

As the Huggies example demonstrates, a website can be an effective tool for the marketer. Depending on the nature of one's business and one's marketing objectives for the Internet, a website can range from being a very simple source of information about the company and its products to being a powerful tool for developing a brand image, sampling, and even generating sales. Following are some of the objectives sought by those marketing on the Internet.

Communications Objectives

Unlike other media discussed thus far in the text, the Internet is actually a hybrid of media. In part, it is a communications medium, allowing companies to create awareness, provide information, and influence attitudes, as well as pursue other communications objectives. But it is also in part a direct-response medium, allowing the user to both purchase and sell products through e-commerce. Thus, we will discuss two sets of objectives pursued by companies that use the Internet. Let's first look at some of the communications objectives these companies want to achieve.

Disseminate Information

One of the primary objectives for using the Web is to provide in-depth information about a company's products and services. In business-to-business markets, having a website has become a necessity, as more and more buyers expect that a company will have a site providing them with detailed information about its offerings. In the government sector, contracts are often put out to bid on the Internet. Information regarding requirements, specifications, submission dates, and so on, is disseminated much quicker, to more potential candidates, and at a much lower cost via the Net than it is through other media. For many consumer companies, their websites serve as a means of communicating more information about their products and services. The Huggies site discussed earlier shows how a website can facilitate this objective, while the Cheerios® box shown in Exhibit 15–3 demonstrates how General Mills refers users to its site for additional information.

Exhibit 15–3 Cheerios® uses their package to send users to their homepage

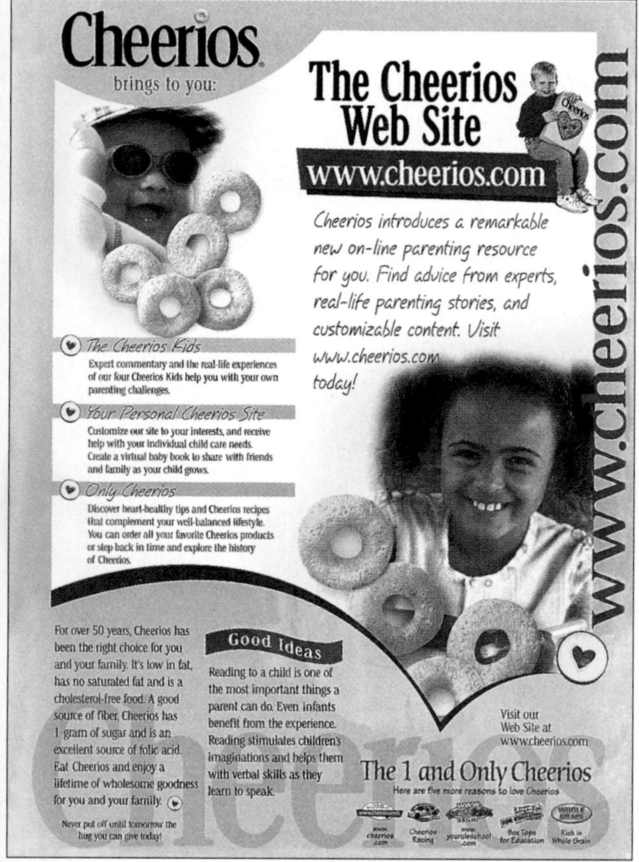

Create Awareness

Advertising on the Web can be useful in creating awareness of an organization as well as its specific product and service offerings. For small companies with limited budgets, the Web offers the opportunity to create awareness well beyond what might be achieved through traditional media. For example, a company in Los Angeles that distributed paper to business-to-business firms in the local market now conducts 80 percent of its business internationally as a result of posting its website.

Gather Research Information

The Web has been used by marketers to gain audience profile information. Companies use it to establish and maintain relationships with their clients, to research the marketplace, and to gather competitive information. The amount of information collected about consumers—often without their knowledge—has become an issue for concern among many consumer and government groups, as discussed in Ethical Perspective 15–1.

Create an Image

Many websites are designed to reflect the image a company wants to portray. For example, when you have a few minutes to spare, check out the consumer site at www.kennethcole.com or the business-to-business site at www.Xerox.com. Both of these are excellent examples of websites used for image building

Ethical Perspective 15–1

Big Brother May Be Here—Does the Internet Know Too Much?

Imagine you went to a restaurant with a date, had a burger, paid with a cedit card, and left. The next time you go there, the waiter or waitress, armed with your profile data, greets you with, "Hey Joe, how are you? Mary is over there in the seat you sat in last time. Would you like to join her for dinner again?" Then you find out that your burger has been cooked and your drink is on the table. Forget the fact that you are with another date and are on a diet that doesn't include burgers. Sound a little bizarre? To some, this is the restaurant equivalent of the Internet. The Net's ability to profile you through your visits to and interactions at websites provides marketers with an enormous amount of data on you—some of which you may not want them to have.

Are you aware that almost every time you access a website you get a "cookie"? Unfortunately, its not the Mrs. Field's type. A *cookie* on the Internet is a computer code sent by the site to your computer—usually without your knowledge. During the entire period of time that you are at the site, the cookie is collecting information about your interaction, including where you visit, how long you stay there, how frequently you return to certain pages, and even your electronic address. Fill out a survey to collect free information or samples, and marketers know even more about you—like your name, address, and any other information you provide. While this may sound scary enough, cookies aren't even the latest in technology. A new system called I-librarian Alexa—named for the legendary third century B.C. library in Alexandria, Egypt—does even more. While cookies track what you are doing at one site, Alexa collects data on all your Web activity, such as which sites you visit next, how long you stay there, whether you click on ads, etc. All this information is available to marketers, who use it to market more effectively to you. Not only do you not get paid for providing the information; you probably don't even know that you are giving it.

Until recently, Internet marketers claimed that they never linked electronic information to names and addresses. Cookies could tell where the site was accessed from but could provide the user's name and personal information only if this data was volunteered. But many companies never told you that your completion of the registration form to receive that free sample gave them the opportunity to make the link. Now, they don't even need your completion of a form—they can get the information electronically. Intel's new Pentium chip has an identifying code that makes it possible to track your surfing habits.

Why are Internet marketers so desperate to get your profile? According to them, it's to improve their marketing programs and to tailor the information more specifically to your needs. For example, DoubleClick, which places banner ads on 11,500 websites and has a database of 100 million files (mostly anonymous) of Web users—most acquired without the users' knowledge—purchased Abacus Direct, a direct-marketing organization with 90 million names, addresses, and phone numbers. Linking the two databases will undoubtedly lead to the loss of anonymity for online users. This, in turn, could lead to a flood of direct-mail pieces, telemarketing calls, and so on, as the information is sold to other Internet marketers.

But the problem doesn't stop there. With just a name and a social security number, individuals can access your private credit information and use it without your knowledge. They can also access marriage licenses, property records, motor vehicle information, and even health information—until they get caught. For you, the situation could end up being a nightmare of paperwork to get your name and credit cleared. Elementary and high schools are building databases with everything from your DNA to your report cards in them.

While many consumers are less concerned about their personal information being accessed than their credit cards and legal or health information, a significant number are concerned enough to warrant the attention of self-regulating and government agencies. For example, the Internet Engineering Task Force—a standards policy body for the Internet—is considering new regulations on the use of cookies. (Companies defend their actions saying that consumers can "opt out" of providing profile information, but this option is typically buried in the third or fourth line of the site's privacy statement, which very few people read.) The Federal Trade Commission (FTC) is also getting involved, exploring privacy policies, kids' websites, and the marketing of alcohol to teenagers through the Internet, among other issues. Companies are also getting involved. IBM announced that it will pull all advertising from websites that do not have an explicit privacy policy.

Consumers are getting personally involved as well. In a study conducted by Louis Harris and Associates, 82 percent of these respondents complained that they felt they had lost all control over how their personal information is being used. Three out of four said businesses asked for too much information. Two-thirds said they are not willing at all to provide personal and financial information to websites in exchange for more personal targeting. The problem is, they don't know they are giving this information away every time they access the Web!

Sources: Will Rodger, "Surfer Beware: Advertiser's on Your Trail," *USA Today,* January 26, 2000, p. B1; Deward C. Baig, Marcia Stepanek, and Neil Gross, "The Internet Wants Your Personal Info. What's in It for You?" *Businessweek Online,* April 5, 1999; Noble Sprayberry, "Confronting the Cookie Monster," *Los Angeles Times,* August 22, 1999, p. I-9.

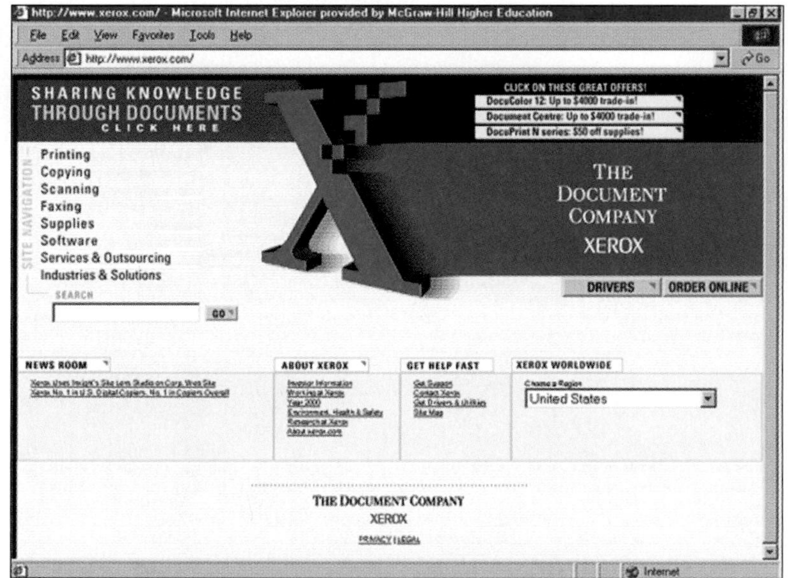

Exhibit 15–4 Xerox uses the Web to enhance their image

(Exhibit 15–4). Interestingly, one of the difficulties traditional marketers have experienced is that of creating a brand image on the Internet. While some of these companies have been successful, others have not fared as well and have come to realize that branding and image-creating strategies must be specifically adapted to this medium.

Stimulate Trial Some websites offer electronic coupons in an attempt to stimulate trial of their products. Others, just through the frequency of their ads on the Web, encourage visits to their sites—for example, "Amazon.com" seems to appear on almost any page you access on a site (Exhibit 15–5). The ease of trying a site merely by clicking on a link is attractive to time-starved users, and items like CDs and books have become big sellers as a result of this technique.

Improve Customer Service By providing information, answering inquiries, and offering an opportunity to register complaints, many companies have found websites useful for improving customer service and building relationships. Some high-technology companies are now using their websites to present information that previously was provided in instruction manuals and by technicians at toll-free phone numbers.

Exhibit 15–5 Amazon.com seems to appear everywhere on the Web

Buy Books!
amazon.com.
· Buy Books HERE
· Christian Books
· *SEARCH AMAZON

Increase Distribution While some companies use their sites to promote e-commerce (sales through the Internet), others use them to distribute coupons and samples. Through **affiliations**—relationships among websites in which companies cross-promote one another's products and each is credited for sales that accrue through its site—companies have increased their exposure base by linking to other sites for purposes of creating awareness as well as distributing product. For example, some sites sell products for other companies without ever taking physical possession of the goods.

E-Commerce

The Internet also offers the opportunity to sell directly to customers in both the consumer market and the business-to-business market. This direct selling of goods and services has been labeled **e-commerce.** As already noted, in 1999 e-commerce generated over $20 billion in sales in the United States, with projections of $184 billion by 2004. Over 33 percent of all college students say they have shopped online, with an average purchase being $38.[15]

As noted earlier, many companies maintain their existing "brick and mortar" stores while also selling through the Internet. Consumer-targeted companies like Eddie Bauer, Gap, and Barnes and Noble are a few examples. Others like Amazon.com, eBay.com, and E-toys.com maintain Internet sites only (Exhibit 15–6). At least one company, Egghead.com, based in Portland, Oregon, closed its 40 retail outlets and now sells products only on the Internet or by phone. Still other companies adopt a hybrid approach. Many auto dealers, finding that they were losing sales to the Internet, have founded organizations and networks online. On these systems, potential buyers can go directly to the network to gather information about automobiles. Once they have decided on a make and model they prefer, the system directs them to the nearest participating dealer. Other industries have begun to adopt this model as well, having seen the success of the auto industry.

Exhibit 15–6 eBay is a very popular Internet site

We will discuss more about e-commerce and strategies employed in this area a little later in the chapter. Before we do, let's have a look at how the Internet can be used as part of an IMC program.

The Internet and Integrated Marketing Communications

"Rumors of my demise are greatly exaggerated." This famous quote of Mark Twain can be used to describe the relationship between the Internet and traditional media quite well. As the Internet boom took off, a number of prognosticators predicted that the Internet would constitute "the end of traditional media" and "the death blow to advertisers"; they suggested that traditional media would suffer greatly as marketers moved their communications dollars to the Internet. Others suggested a moratorium on building retail stores and shopping malls, predicting that e-commerce would replace in-person shopping. In fact, the Internet may be one of the strongest arguments yet for companies to adopt an integrated marketing communications perspective. Rather than hurting traditional media and reducing the expenditures therein, the Internet both complements and relies on other media in an effective IMC program. With this in mind, let's discuss how the Internet and other IMC program elements work together.

Advertising

The Internet both supports advertising and relies on advertising for its own success. In 1999, $4 billion was spent by advertisers on the Internet to promote and sell their products.[16] At the same time, Internet companies have been a boon to traditional media, spending over $1 billion in these media to promote their sites.[17] As can be seen in Figure 15–7, most of these monies were spent on television, with magazines also receiving significant amounts of the expenditures. On the January 2000 Superbowl broadcast, 50 percent of the advertisements were for "dot-com" companies that paid as much as $2 million per spot to promote themselves.[18]

Advertising on the Internet Like broadcast or print, the Internet is an advertising medium. Companies and organizations working to promote their products

Figure 15–7 Dot-com spending by media

Rank	Measured Media	Jan.–Sept. 1999	Jan.–Sept. 1998	Percent Change
1	Network television	$278,275,800	$60,184,500	362.4%
2	Magazines	265,085,100	91,401,600	190.0
3	Cable TV	202,627,000	43,471,900	366.1
4	Spot television	166,928,300	44,120,000	278.4
5	National spot radio	154,621,400	27,400,800	464.3
6	National newspapers	148,659,900	41,404,000	259.0
7	Newspapers	69,392,900	17,522,500	296.0
8	Network radio	43,137,500	17,172,200	151.2
9	Outdoor	24,640,300	3,972,400	520.3
10	Sunday magazine	6,978,300	581,000	1,101.1
11	Syndication	5,715,200	1,910,700	199.1

and services must consider this medium as they would television, magazines, outdoor, and so on. Advertising on the Internet employs a variety of forms.

Banners The most common form of advertising on the Web is **banner ads** (Exhibit 15–7), accounting for approximately 53 percent of advertising expenditures. Banner ads may be used for creating awareness or recognition or for direct-marketing objectives. Initially banner ads constituted the vast majority of advertising on the Net, but studies indicating their questionable effectiveness have led to a decline in usage. However, recent studies have shown that banner ads do have an impact, and this finding may lead to increased use of this method of advertising in the future.[19]

Sponsorships The second most common form of advertising is **sponsorships,** which account for approximately 30 percent of total advertising expenditures. There are two types of sponsorships. *Regular sponsorships* occur when a company pays to sponsor a section of a site, for example, Clairol's sponsorship of a page on GirlsOn.com and Intuit's Turbo Tax sponsorship of a page on Netscape's financial section. A more involved agreement is the **content sponsorship,** in which the sponsor not only provides dollars in return for name association but participates in providing the content itself. In some cases, the site is responsible for providing content and having it approved by the sponsor; in other instances, the sponsor may contribute all or part of the content. Due in part to the decline in the effectiveness of banner ads and to the desire for more enrollment and exposure, sponsorships have been increasing in popularity. (For an excellent example of content sponsorship, see Ford's Auto Center on the iVillage website.)

Pop-Ups When you access the Internet, have you ever seen a small window appear on Netscape advertising AOL's "Instant Messenger"? Such windows are known as **pop-ups,** and they often appear when you access a certain site. Pop-ups are usually larger than a banner ad but smaller than a full screen.

Interstitials **Interstitials** are ads that appear on your screen while you are waiting for a site's content to download. Although some advertisers believe that interstitials are irritating and more of a nuisance than a benefit, a study conducted by Grey

Exhibit 15–7 Banner advertising on the Net

Think
Click to see the new ThinkPad 380.
IBM

Advertising found that only 15 percent of those surveyed felt that the ads were irritating (versus 9 percent for banner ads) and that 47 percent liked the ads (versus 38 percent for banners). Perhaps more importantly, while ad recall of banner ads was approximately 51 percent, recall of interstitials was much higher, at 76 percent. Pop-ups and interstitials account for approximately 6 percent of all advertising on the Internet.[20]

Push Technologies **Push technologies,** or **webcasting** technologies, allow companies to "push" a message to consumers rather than waiting for them to find it. Push technologies dispatch web pages and news updates and may have sound and video geared to specific audiences and even individuals. For example, a manager whose job responsibilities involve corporate finance might log on to his or her computer and find new stories are automatically there on the economy, stock updates, or a summary of a speech by Alan Greenspan. Companies like Pointcast provide screen savers that automatically "hook" the viewer to their sites for sports, news, weather reports, and/or other information that the viewer has specified. Users can use **personalization**—that is, they can personalize their sites to request the kinds of specific information they are most interested in viewing. For example, if you are into college sports, you can have updates sent to you through sites providing college sports information. The service is paid for by advertisers who flash their messages on the screen.

Links While considered by some as not a type of advertising, **links** serve many of the same purposes as are served by the types discussed above. For example, a visitor to one site may click on a link that provides additional information and/or related materials at another site. Thus someone on ESPN.com might link to Nike.com and find information on sports-related products.

Other forms of advertising, such as ads placed in chat rooms, are also available. Given the limited use of many of these alternatives, we suggest the reader consult additional resources for more information.

Advertising by Internet Companies

It's almost impossible to turn on the television, listen to the radio, or read a magazine these days without being exposed to a dot-com ad. As more and more advertisers use the Internet as a medium to promote their goods and services, the sites that they advertise on, as well as the search engines and portals that host these sites, continue to increase their advertising expenditures in traditional media. In fact, Internet advertisers have become the category of advertisers accounting for the most expenditures on local television stations. Magazines, newspapers, and outdoor have also benefited from their expenditures. In addition, a number of new print media have developed as trade magazines for the industry.

One of the primary reasons for the use of traditional media is the number of people whom these media impact. With close to a hundred million viewers turned to the Superbowl and millions more tuned in to regular programming, television provides exposure that the Internet could never provide on its own. Likewise, magazines also provide excellent reach while offering the advantage of targeting special interests. For example, *Sports Illustrated* is an excellent medium for websites like www.ESPN.com, Yahoo! Sports, or www.CBSsportsLineFootball.com (Exhibit 15–8). Financial magazines are useful for promoting sites like www.eTrade.com, as are those with an

Exhibit 15–8 Yahoo! Sports may use *Sports Illustrated* to promote its site

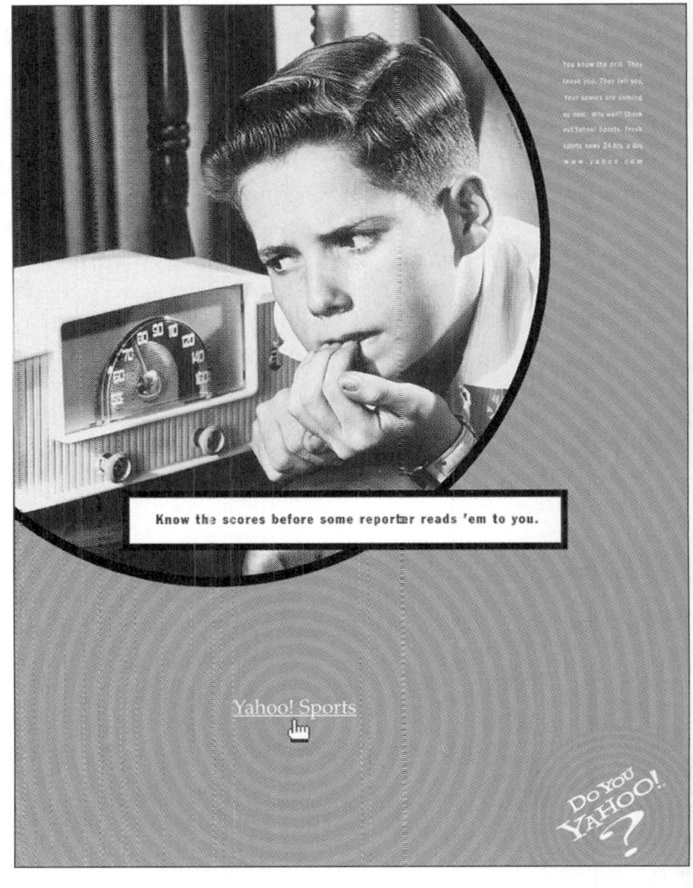

upscale demographic audience. Special-interest magazines like *Brill's Content* are excellent media for sites like www.thestreet.com. The exposure provided by direct marketing and outdoor makes them effective media for Internet advertisers that want to gain awareness of their sites.

Sales Promotion on the Internet

The next time you log on to a website, take a minute to notice how the site attempts to get you to come back. Sales promotion has become the most frequently used (overused?) method of encouraging repeat visits. Repeat visits are one measure of audience size used to determine the price a site is able to charge advertisers and sponsors; therefore, one of the primary objectives of a site is to get you to come back. Notice on the homepage of www.beyondclass.com, shown in the lead-in to this chapter, the section of the site titled "free stuff," which encourages students to come back to the site in an attempt to win prizes. Sites offer everything from free e-mail to instant messaging to telephone services. They also offer sweepstakes. At the Virgin Atlantic Airways site, CEO Richard Branson appears and asks you to enter a sweepstakes. Visit www.BMW.com and enter a contest for a free BMW, or go to the Brita water site and get a chance to win $500,000—and the list goes on (Exhibit 15–9). Procter and Gamble's successful use of integrated marketing discussed in IMC Perspective 15–2 is just one example of how effective sales promotions can be incorporated into the Web effectively.

Exhibit 15–9 Sweepstakes and contests are commonly employed on the Internet

As you will see in Chapter 16, delivering coupons on the Net is another rapidly growing use of sales promotion. Excite and e-centives.com (a provider of sales promotions for Internet applications) have entered a marketing alliance that gives Excite users access to an online couponing system very similar to that in the real world. At www.coolsavings.com, marketers can access the site directly to update their promotion offers and to promote various products and services. In exchange for the free coupons, consumers provide valuable database information when they complete a short survey to qualify. Each of the coupons is assigned a unique number and bar code so that when it is redeemed, the marketer can track the effectiveness of the offer. Other companies, like www.hotcoupons.com, provide coupon distribution as well. A study for NPD Online Research indicated that 30 percent of the Web user respondents had used online coupons in 1999 and that the number of users continues to increase. The study also indicated that consumers' awareness of online coupons is nearly 80 percent (among Web users).[21] Webstakes.com has taken its online sweepstakes and promotions to Japan, the United Kingdom, Ireland, Australia, and New Zealand.[22]

Personal Selling on the Internet

The Internet has been both a benefit and a detriment to many of those involved in personal selling—particularly those in the business-to-business market. For some, the Internet has been a threat that might take away job opportunities. Companies have found that they can remain effective—even increase effectiveness—by building a strong Web presence. The high-cost and poor-reach disadvantages of personal selling are allowing these companies to reduce new hires and even cut back on their existing sales forces.

On the positive side, websites have been used quite effectively to enhance and support the selling effort. As noted earlier, the Web has become a primary source of infor-

IMC Perspective 15–2

A Tale of Website Strategies, Denim Disasters, and "Perty" Good Promotions

Levi Strauss and Procter & Gamble—you have heard of these guys—have been two traditionally successful "brick and mortar" marketers. You would think that being successful in the traditional world of marketing would ensure, or at least improve, the probability of success on the Internet. Well, that's not necessarily so.

Take the case of Levi's. The company's decision in late 1999 to stop selling clothes through the Internet came as a complete surprise to many marketers. One of the Internet pioneers, Levi's launched its first site in 1994 and poured over $8 million into site development and enhancement before calling it quits. Levi's management said the site was just not affordable; costs were continuing to rise and the company could not continue to support the effort. Still, the potential must have been there, so what happened? According to those in the industry, Levi's made a number of mistakes. At the outset, management deliberated and failed to commit for four years before deciding to carry inventory. When the managers did finally decide, they didn't carry the flagship 401 jeans, fearing a backlash from European and Asian customers, who couldn't buy online and thus would be paying more for the product. The managers were also fearful of retaliation from their retailers, which account for Levi's $4 billion yearly sales. Poor sales by the company in 1998 led to budget cuts that hit the e-commerce site particularly hard, as all Web advertising, including a planned TV campaign, was curtailed. The lack of advertising support kept necessary visitors away, and in Nielsen ratings surveys, the site ranked well below sites of competitors Gap, Eddie Bauer, and J. Crew. As might be expected, key personnel left Levi's to work at other sites—some of which were direct competitors. Retailers, which at first wanted Levi's to stay offline, now wanted their own opportunity to sell Levi's products through their Internet sites. When Levi's refused, the retailers increased pressures to get permission. In the fall of 1998, Levi's gave in and granted JCPenney's and Macy's permission to offer its products online. Penney's promotion and sales of "plus-size" Levi's jeans may have been the final stake in Levi's website heart, as well as in its attempts to reconnect with younger consumers.

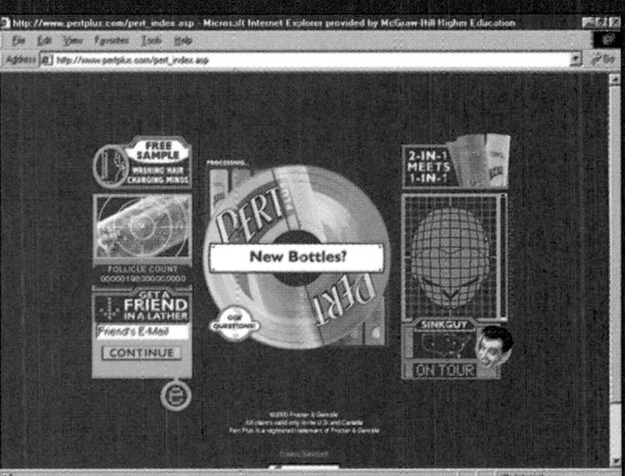

P&G, on the other hand, has done "Perty" good. P&G brand manager Kevin Burke decided that a website would contemporize the ailing shampoo brand Pert and serve as a useful outlet for distributing samples. Burke also felt the site would effectively complement the new $20 million ad campaign in which a goofy "sink guy" runs around Miami Beach offering to wash people's hair with reformulated PertPlus. Even Burke would likely admit that he could hardly have expected or even hoped for the success that the site achieved. Three specific objectives were given for the website: (1) generate awareness for the reformulation of the shampoo, (2) get customers to try it, and (3) gather data about Web users. The relatively small, 10-page site devoted only 2 pages to describing the product, with other pages devoted to gathering data, offering samples, and providing visitors with the opportunity to enter a sweepstakes to win a trip to Miami Beach. Visitors could also click on a link to instantly send an e-mail to a friend, encouraging them to visit the site to obtain a free sample of their own. There was also a page that cross-referenced the three entertainment sites that P&G advertised on: Sony Station, MTV online, and E! online. In addition, banner ads were run on 13 other sites, and sponsorships generated 40.5 million impressions. As can be seen on the " Pert Plus Stats" shown here, the campaign was incredibly successful.

So what's the moral of these two tales? Simply put, they tell us one thing. If you want your site to be successful, you must believe in it and commit to it. Most importantly, you have to market it. Just ask Kevin Burke!

Sources: Luisa Kroll, "Denim Disaster," *Forbes,* November 29, 1999, p. 181; Cindy Waxer, "501 Blues," *Business 2.0,* January 2000, pp. 53–56; Debra Aho Williamson, "P&G's Reformulated Pert Plus Builds Consumer Relationships," *Advertising Age,* June 28, 1999, p. 52.

mation for millions of customers in the consumer and business-to-business markets. Visitors to websites can gain volumes of information about a company's products and services. In return, the visitors become a valuable resource for leads that both internal and external salespersons can follow up, and they become part of a prospect database. Not only can potential customers learn about the company's offerings, but the selling organization can serve and qualify prospects more cost-effectively.

The Web can also be used to stimulate trial. For many companies, personal salespersons can reach only a fraction of the potential customer base. Through trial demonstrations and/or samples offered online, customers can determine if the offering satisfies their needs and if so request a personal sales call. In such cases both parties benefit from time and cost savings.

Some companies have used the Internet to improve their one-on-one relationships with customers. By providing more information in a more timely and efficient manner, a company enables customers to learn more about what it has to offer. This increases the opportunity for cross-selling and customer retention. For example, Neoforma.com links hospitals and medical supply vendors with listings of 300,000 medical products, with pages describing separate product categories.[23] For those interested in medical products, the site has become a one-stop shopping center. In addition, by providing a website, companies can improve their response times to inquiries as well as complaints, thereby improving customer service.

Yet another use of the Internet is for sales conferences. A number of companies, including Cisco and Scientific American, have used Internet video to hold sales conferences, saving the salespeople important time and the companies millions of dollars.

In a well-designed IMC program, the Internet and personal selling are designed to be complementary tools—working together to increase sales. It appears that more and more companies are coming to this realization.

Public Relations on the Internet

As with other media, the Internet is a useful medium for conducting public relations activities. Many sites devote a portion of their content to public relations activities, including the provision of information about the company, its philanthropic activities, annual reports, and so on. Shel Holtz, in his book *Public Relations on the Internet,* notes that the public relations industry has been slow to adopt the Internet. Some of the more traditional public relations organizations do not use the Net at all, while most others use it primarily as a tool for disseminating information. Holtz notes that the Web offers a number of opportunities to public relations practitioners, including: (1) the development of media relations websites, (2) the ability to provide customized information dissemination, and (3) the development of positive e-mail relationships.

One example of the use of public relations on the Internet is provided by Chrysler. Working with reporters, Chrysler developed a one-stop information source for the media (the public could also use the site, but reporters would have to register to use the "newsroom"). News stories and other forms of content, photo images, and cross-references to other sites or media were included on the site, as were press kits and a calender of upcoming events (Exhibit 15–10). The objective of the site was to improve relations with the press, and Chrysler was quite effective in doing so.

Other examples of effective use of public relations activities on the Internet are also available, as you will see in the chapter on public relations. The Web is a useful medium for conducting public relations activities, and its use for this function is on the increase.

At the same time, many philanthropic and nonprofit organizations have found the Internet to be a useful way to generate funds. Several sites have developed to perform the functions that are required in traditional fund-raising programs. For example, in just one month in 1999 during the war between Serbia and Kosovo, the American Red Cross was able to raise $1 million for aid to Kosovo citizens through its website.[24] Other sites have been formed to handle public relations activities for

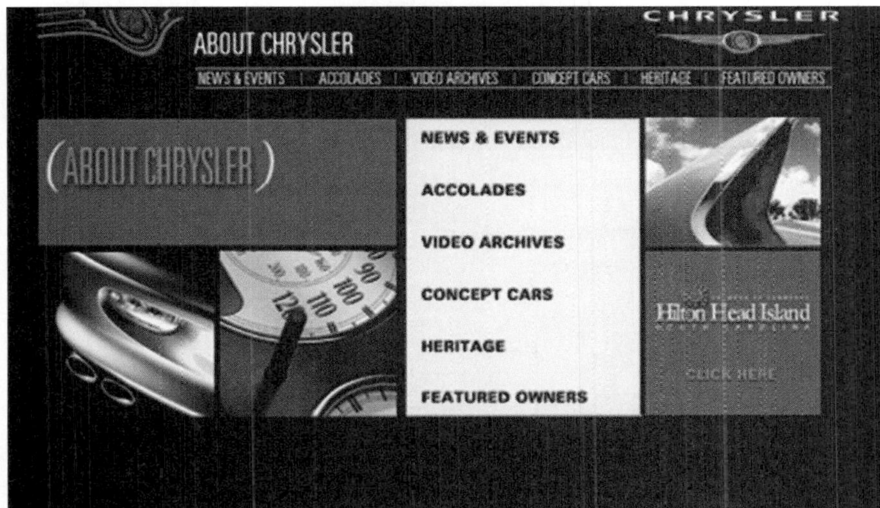

Exhibit 15–10 Chrysler provides public relations information on its site

charitable organizations, provide information regarding the causes the charity supports, collect contributions, and so on.

Direct Marketing on the Internet

Our discussion of direct marketing and the Internet will approach the topic from two perspectives: the use of direct-marketing tools for communications objectives (as discussed in Chapter 14), and e-commerce. As we stated previously, many direct-marketing tools like direct mail, infomercials, and the like, have been adapted to the Internet, as you will see. At the same time, e-commerce—selling directly to the consumer via the Internet—has become an industry of its own.

Direct Mail

Direct mail on the Internet is essentially an electronic version of regular mail. Like regular mail it is highly targeted, relies heavily on lists, and attempts to reach consumers with specific needs through targeted messages. As we discussed earlier under personalization, consumers can opt to have specific types of e-mail sent to them and other types not sent. For example, if you permit, *The New York Times* will e-mail you information about specific promotions, articles that will appear, books on sale, and other items that you might purchase from it, as will American Express.

Sometimes users may also receive less targeted and unwanted e-mails. The electronic equivalent of junk mail, these messages are referred to as **SPAM.** Because of the high volumes of SPAM that have been sent, and the fact that many consumers consider it a nuisance, the U.S. government has passed laws regulating its use.

Catalog-oriented companies like Lands' End have also increased their use of the electronic media. The company recently aired television commercials to promote the ease and efficiency of using its online catalog, and sent customers in its existing database direct-mail pieces informing them of the same.

While many consumers don't like SPAM or other forms of e-mail, at least one study has shown the effectiveness of e-mails. In a survey of 667 online consumers, conducted by E-Buyersguide.com, 63 percent of the respondents said they first found their "e-tailers" by responding to e-mail promotions.[25]

Database Marketing

A number of database services exist on the Internet. For example, EDGAR (Electronic Data Gathering and Retrieval) contains all the documents that companies are required to file electronically with the Securities and Exchange Commission. This information includes key financials, management personnel, and so on. Hundreds of other databases exist as well. Some companies have established successful database marketing businesses on the Web. One such company, Freelotto, has a 10 million–member database available to marketers (at a price) who may want to target all types of customers, including credit card users,

Exhibit 15–11 Amazon.com offers more than just books

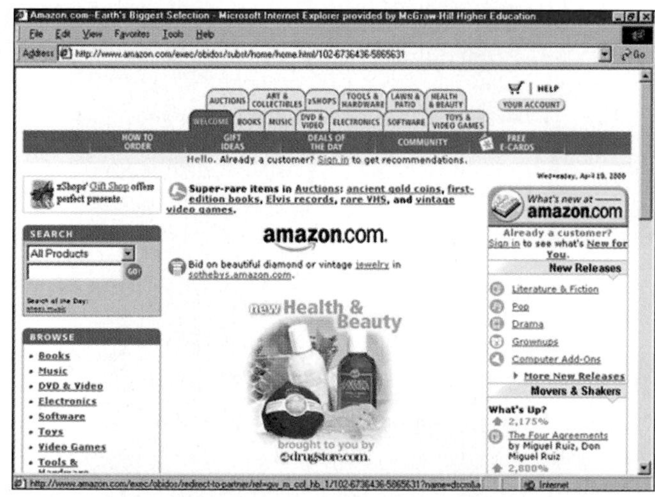

gardeners, and computer users, among others. The company offers a "one-stop" service that collects the names and addresses, qualifies the prospects, and e-mails the seller's messages. Many companies have developed electronic databases to be used in the same way, as described in Chapter 14.

Infomercials Yes, even the infomercial has discovered the Net. The same people who brought you "Amazing Discoveries" infomercials on television now produce infomercials for the Internet (and they are not alone). One such infomercial, by iMall, a company based in Provo, Utah, runs marketing seminars on how to make money on the Internet. Other companies are expected to follow. Does this mean we will soon see FlowBees on the Web?

E-Commerce E-commerce, or direct sales on the Internet, has truly taken off. A study by Harris Interactive Surveys revealed that 33 percent of online users expected to purchase at least one item over the Internet during the 1999 holiday season. If they did, the results would be some $9.5 billion in expenditures in that very short time period.[26]

All indications are that this number will continue to increase in the future. While CDs, books, and travel account for most Internet purchases, a number of other items are finding their way there as well. Clothing, automobiles, and stocks and bonds are now regularly purchased through the Internet. Amazon.com, most known for its book sales, now offers a variety of other products for sale—including pharmaceuticals (Exhibit 15–11).

While more and more consumers buy online, consumer sales are only about one-sixth of those by business-to-business marketers. Cisco systems alone did $9.5 billion of e-commerce in 1999, more than 75 percent of its total sales.[27] Other business-to-business companies like Applied Industrial Technologies, National SemiConductor, and Xerox have also found success in the world of e-commerce.

Perhaps the best way to end our discussion of how the Internet fits into an IMC program is with an example. IMC Perspective 15–3 details how IBM successfully employed an IMC program effectively utilizing the Internet.

Measuring Effectiveness of the Internet

Companies measuring the effectiveness of the Internet employ a variety of methods, most of which can be done electronically. As you will see in a moment, a number of companies provide Internet measures as part of a package; that is, they provide audience measurement information (demographics, psychographics, etc.) as "up-front' information, as well as some of the effectiveness measures described below. First, we will discuss some of the measures used to determine the effectiveness of a website. Then, we will discuss some of the companies providing these measures.

IMC Perspective 15–3

IBM's B-to-B IMC Program Taps the Internet

These days it's hard to miss IBM's "Self-service Web sites from IBM service customers better" advertising campaign on TV. It's also hard to miss it if you pick up a magazine or newspaper around the world. What you may not have seen is the IBM campaign running on the Internet—but you should. The message promoted in the traditional media is that IBM is a solutions provider. On the Internet, the ads specifically show how.

The IMC campaign actually was developed back in 1997 and was a bit of a departure from IBM's typical way of advertising. In the past, separate advertisements might be run in a variety of media, with little or no connection between them. When the company initiated the e-business solutions campaign, it recognized that a more integrated campaign would be required, employing a variety of media but maintaining consistency across the channels and in the positioning. More importantly, the media play different and complementary roles. For example, teaser ads are run in print and on TV with the objective of gaining exposure and attention and driving the receiver to the Internet for more information. The timing of the humorous TV vignettes is simultaneous with the print ads in *The New York Times, The Wall Street Journal, USA Today, The Washington Post, Financial Times, Forbes, Business Week,* and *Information Week,* which provide more detail on how IBM helped its customers solve an e-business problem. The print ads then direct the reader to the website to acquire even more information.

In addition to using the traditional media, IBM places a high degree of emphasis on the Internet. An *e* rather than an *a* inside of the "@" mark was used for branding IBM as an Internet company. Every IBM customer could use the mark on his or her website, and IBM carried the logo on all its communications. Banner ads were placed on portals as well as other sites. Clicking on the banner took the viewer to a rich-medium "minisite" that showed how IBM helped a company solve its specific problem. Newer ads promoting its server products also use TV and print to drive viewers to the Net. Once there, they will see banner ads with Java script, which allows users to participate in the processes being advertised. For example, an ad for eSeeds.com, an online vendor of seeds, allows the user to sow seeds and then water them by holding the mouse button down. The flowers then grow while the user watches. The message explains that eSeeds is building its business on an IBM AS/400 server.

In 1998 IBM spent $45 million on Internet ads—7 percent of the total $600 million budget. By 1999 10 percent, or $60 million, will be allocated to the Net. This makes IBM the largest single online advertiser in the world. But the question is, "Is it working?"

In 1994, *Financial Times* rated IBM at the bottom of its brand value list—assigning a value of a negative $50 million to IBM due to the myriad of directions the company was going in with no apparent cohesion. The new IMC campaign was designed with three goals in mind: (1) to alert the world to the fact that e-business was transforming the way IBM would do business in the future; (2) to establish a strong brand association between IBM and e-business solutions; and (3) to convince its own 300,000 employees in 160 countries that IBM was itself a player in the e-business world. The company and its advertising agency, Ogilvy & Mather, believed that a more cohesive and integrated approach was necessary. They were right!

Sources: Peter T. Leach, "The Blue Period," *Critical Mass,* Fall 1999, pp. 86–92; "IBM E-Business," *1999 Effie Awards* (American Marketing Association, 1999), p. 24.

Measures of Effectiveness

You will see that there are some problems with these measures that must be considered when employing them. Let's start off with a description of some of the effectiveness measures commonly employed on the Internet:

- *Hits.* The number of times that a specific component of a site is requested. Hits could represent 100 people making one request or one person making 100 requests. As a result, hits have been criticized. The primary value of hits is to let the website owner know which part(s) of the site are most and least popular.
- *Viewers.* The number of viewers to a site.
- *Unique visitors.* The number of different visitors to a site within a specified period of time.
- *Clicks (click-throughs).* The number of visitors to a site that click onto a banner ad to retrieve more information. Some companies bill clients on the number of clicks their ad generates, contending that this is the most effective way of providing value for the expenditure. Others, like P&G, have found clicks to be less than accurate and place less emphasis on this measure.
- *Click-through rate.* The ratio of click-throughs from an ad to a page within the advertiser's website. For example, a successful ad might entice 2 percent of those who see it to click to acquire more information.
- *Impressions/page views.* The number of times viewers view a page.

The above-mentioned measures are perhaps the most commonly used measures. While useful, they provide information only on users' interactions with a site. For the most part, this information is most useful for determining navigation and content analysis. The information is typically collected by a **cookie,** an electronic device attached to your file (usually without your knowing it) that collects information on where you visit, how many times you visit, where you click, and the like. Due in part to weaknesses in these measures and advertisers' desire for additional information, a number of other measures are now being employed, including the ones discussed below.

Online Measuring A joint venture between Flycast Communications and Millward Brown has led to a research tool employing online measuring that collects information regarding demographics, psychographics, location of Web access, media usage, and buying habits. Clients can determine who saw their ads, determine reach, and ascertain whether the right target audience was reached. Advertisers can test the impact of their messages, receiving a report detailing impressions and clicks by time of day and day of the week.

In 1999, Amazon.com paid $250 million in stock to acquire Alexa, a little-known service. The service tracks what sites are on the Internet and where, as well as who, goes to them. The appeal of Alexa is that it goes beyond "cookies," which don't track a user's other Web visits. Alexa collects data on all Web activity by any user who signs up for it. Measures as to how much traffic a site gets, whether users like the site, and where they go next are all reported (see Ethical Perspective 15–1). The database is already twice the size of all the printed matter in the Library of Congress.[28]

Recall and Retention Ipsos-ASI performs 20,000 continuous daily interviews with Web users to determine recall and whether viewers remember the ads they see, as well as whether there is a "halo-effect" among ads.

Nonresponse A company named MatchLogic is developing a measure to determine where consumers go once they have been exposed to an advertisement but decide not to click on it.

Surveys Survey research, conducted both online and through traditional methods, is employed to determine everything from site usage to attitudes toward a site.

Panels Adapting traditional research methods, PCData has formed a panel of 100,000 online users. The company's research provides information on demographics, unique users, frequency of visitors, pages viewed, and how long a viewer stays at a site ("stickiness"). Nielsen Media Research offers panel data as well.

Sales Of course, for the e-commerce marketers, a prime indicator of effectiveness is the number of sales generated. Adding information regarding demographics, user behaviors, and so on, can increase the effectiveness of this measure.

Tracking Some companies now provide information regarding site performance (downtime, speed, etc.) as well as analyze shopping patterns, tying demographic information to site activities, frequency of hits, number of repeat visitors, and the like, over time to assist advertisers in developing more targeted and effective messages. The information can also be used to measure the effectiveness of site content by determining how many visitors access the content, how long they stay there, and how many pages are read.

The above measures reveal that the Internet has its own set of criteria for measuring effectiveness and is also borrowing from traditional measures—for example, brand recall is becoming a major area of focus.[29] Many of the companies that provide research information in traditional media (Nielsen, Ipsos-ASI) are now extending their reach into the Internet world. Others (MediaMetrics, Jupiter, Forrester) have developed measures specifically for online users. Academics are also beginning to publish articles related to measuring effectiveness on the Internet. Studies on consumers' attitudes toward a site, response variations in e-mail surveys, and similarities between brick-and-mortar retailing and e-commerce are just a few of the many articles being published in academic journals to advance the measurement of the Internet.[30]

Unfortunately, not all of the methods used to measure Internet activity and effectiveness are accurate. We discuss some of these later in this chapter, under disadvantages of the Internet.

Sources of Measurement Data

The number of sources available that provide information about the Internet is enormous. Below we provide a partial list just to give you some indication of the types of information available. Most of the companies listed are the largest and/or most cited sources, and the list is by no means intended to be exhaustive:

- *Arbitron.* Arbitron provides demographic, media usage, and lifestyle data on users of the Internet as well as other interactive media.
- *MRI* and *SMRB.* Both of these companies (discussed in Chapter 10) now provide information regarding viewership profiles for the Internet and other interactive media. Nielsen offers similar data.
- *Audit Bureau of Circulations.* This print agency is developing a product called WebFacts to certify web counts.
- *Internet Advertising Bureau (IAB).* A trade organization of the Internet, IAB provides information on statistics, usage, and strategies regarding the Internet.
- *iVALS.* The same VALS discussed in Chapter 2, iVALS provides value and lifestyle information about Internet users.
- *PC-Meter.* This is a metering service that measures how much time computer users spend at their machines, what software and services they access, and how long they spend online.

- *eMarketer.* This company publishes comparative data from various research sources and explains the different methods used to arrive at the projections. It also publishes its own projections.
- *eAdvertiser.* A joint venture between eMarketer and *Advertising Age,* eAdvertiser publishes a series of reports combining the former's projections but geared more specifically to the advertising community.
- *DoubleClick.* DoubleClick is a seller of advertising space on websites and a provider of tracking and reporting for advertisers. It purchased NetGravity, a provider of in-house ad tracking software, so that it could offer advertisers a more complete package.
- *24/7.* This firm provides many of the services offered by DoubleClick, such as the ability to place an advertiser's ad on a variety of sites, targeted or run-of-site.
- *Jupiter, Forrester,* and *MediaMetrics.* These are three of the largest providers of statistics and website information, including data on users, projections, trends, and so on.
- Business 2.0, The Industry Standard, *and* Fast Company. Each of these business-to-business magazines targets those interested in the Internet, from both a technological as well as a business perspective, with emphasis on the latter.
- *Internet Advertising Report* and *Individual.com.* Both these organizations provide an online newsletter containing information on trends, statistics, and other articles of interest to Internet users in the business community.

Advantages and Disadvantages of the Internet

A number of advantages of the Internet can be cited:

1. *Target marketing.* A major advantage of the Web is the ability to target very specific groups of individuals with a minimum of waste coverage. For those in the business-to-business market, the Internet resembles a combination trade magazine and trade show, as only those most interested in the products and/or services a site has to offer will visit the site (others have little or no reason to do so). In the consumer market, through personalization and other targeting techniques, sites are becoming more tailored to meet one's needs and wants.

2. *Message tailoring.* As a result of precise targeting, messages can be designed to appeal to the specific needs and wants of the target audience. The interactive capabilities of the Net make it possible to carry on one-to-one marketing with increased success in both the business and the consumer markets.

3. *Interactive capabilities.* Because the Internet is interactive, it provides strong potential for increasing customer involvement and satisfaction and almost immediate feedback for buyers and sellers. A study of online users found that 24 percent watched the 2000 Superbowl while multitasking online.[31] As multitasking increases, the interactive capabilities of the Internet will make this medium even more attractive.

4. *Information access.* Perhaps the greatest advantage of the Internet is its availability as an information source. Internet users can find a plethora of information about almost any topic of their choosing merely by conducting a search through one of the search engines. Once they have visited a particular site, users can garner a wealth of information regarding product specifications, costs, purchase information, and so on. Links will direct them to even more information if it is desired.

5. *Sales potential.* The numbers provided earlier in this chapter demonstrate the incredible sales numbers being generated in both the business-to-business and the consumer segments. Forecasts are for almost exponential growth in the future.

6. *Creativity.* Creatively designed sites can enhance a company's image, lead to repeat visits, and positively position the company or organization in the consumer's mind.

7. *Exposure.* For many smaller companies, with limited budgets, the World Wide Web enables them to gain exposure to potential customers that heretofore would have been impossible. For a fraction of the investment that would be required using traditional media, companies can gain national and even international exposure in a timely manner.

8. *Speed.* For those requesting information on a company, its products, and/or its service offerings, the Internet is the quickest means of acquiring this information.

While it is a potentially effective medium, the Internet also has its disadvantages:

1. *Measurement problems.* One of the greatest disadvantages of the Internet is the lack of reliability of the research numbers generated. A quick review of forecasts, audience profiles, and other statistics offered by research providers will demonstrate a great deal of variance—leading to a serious lack of validity and reliability. One company mentioned earlier, eMarketer, has attempted to reconcile such differences and explain the reasoning for the discrepancies (differences in methodologies employed), but the problem still exists. One of the industry's largest and most cited trade publications has written an exposé of a heavily cited Internet research company, referring to the numbers it provides as "scary."[32] Others have stressed concerns over the fact that most site's figures are not audited, which may lead to rampant cheating in respect to the numbers reported.[33]

2. *Audience characteristics.* Due in part to the accelerating growth of the Net, audience characteristics change quickly. Numbers reported may be outdated quickly and often vary from one provider to the next.

3. *Websnarl.* At times, downloading information from the Net takes a long time. When there are a number of users, the time increases and some sites may be inaccessible due to too many visitors. For many users who expect speed, this is a major disadvantage.

4. *Clutter.* As the number of ads proliferates, the likelihood of one ad's being noticed drops accordingly. The result is that some ads may not get noticed, and some consumers may become irritated by the clutter. Some studies already show that banner ads may be losing effectiveness for this very reason.

5. *Potential for deception.* The Center for Media Education has referred to the Web as "a web of deceit" in regard to attempts of advertisers to target children with subtle advertising messages. The Center, among others, has asked the government to regulate the Internet. In addition, data collection without consumers' knowledge and permission, hackers, and credit card theft are a number of problems confronting the Internet.

6. *Costs.* The costs of doing business on the Internet continue to increase. While it is possible to establish a site inexpensively, establishing a good site and maintaining it is becoming more and more costly. As noted earlier, Levi's found the cost of maintaining a site it considered "world-class" was prohibitive and one of the reasons for abandoning its e-commerce efforts. Likewise, the CPMs of advertising on the Internet are often higher than some traditional media, as shown in Figure 15–8.

Medium	Vehicle	Cost	Reach	CPM
TV	:30 network prime time	$120,000	10 million households	$12
Consumer magazine	Page, 4-color in *Cosmopolitan*	$86,155	2.5 million paid readers	35
Online service	Banner on CompuServe major-topic page	$10,000 per month	750,000 visitors	13
Website	Banner on Infoseek	$10,000 per month	500,000 page views per month	20

Figure 15–8 Ad rate comparison across major media

7. *Limited production quality.* Although it is improving, net advertising does not offer the capabilities of many competitive media from a production standpoint. While the advent of advanced technologies and rich media is narrowing the gap, the Net still lags behind some traditional media in this area.

8. *Poor reach.* While the Internet numbers are growing in leaps and bounds, its reach is still far behind that of television. As a result, as discussed earlier, Internet companies have turned to traditional media to achieve reach and awareness goals. In addition, statistics show that only a small percentage of sites on the Internet are captured by search engines and that the top 50 sites listed account for 95 percent of the sites visited.[34]

Overall, the Internet offers marketers some very definite advantages over traditional media. At the same time, disadvantages and limitations render this medium as less than a one-stop solution. However, as part of an IMC program, the Internet is a very valuable tool.

Additional Interactive Media

While the Internet has captured most of the attention of marketers, additional interactive media are also available and can be used as a contributor to an IMC program. Interactive CD-ROMs, kiosks, and interactive phones have been used by marketers to provide information to their audiences. Interactive television advertising was recently introduced to Manhattan, New York, by Time Warner. While others have tested interactive TV ads, this venture is considered a milestone as nearly 150,000 New Yorkers will have access to the interactive ads.[35] The agency executives stated that the most important capability of these media was their ability to be linked with traditional marketing projects.

One of the more attention getting and promising of the new interactive media is WebTV. A wholly owned subsidiary of Microsoft, WebTV had more than 1 million subscribers in 2000[36] (Exhibit 15–12). Another interactive TV company, OpenTV, has over 300,000 subscribers.[37] Many marketers are betting on the fact that future computer users will access the Internet through their television sets. As noted earlier, multitasking will allow television viewers to watch an event—for example, a football game—and pull up information on players, history of the matchups between the teams, and other statistics without ever leaving the couch or the game. (The numbers will appear in a window.) Or suppose you are watching the TV show "Friends" and like the sweater Rachel is wearing. You simply drag your mouse over to Rachel and click on her sweater, and a window will appear providing you with information regarding colors, materials, sizes, and costs. You may then ask to see

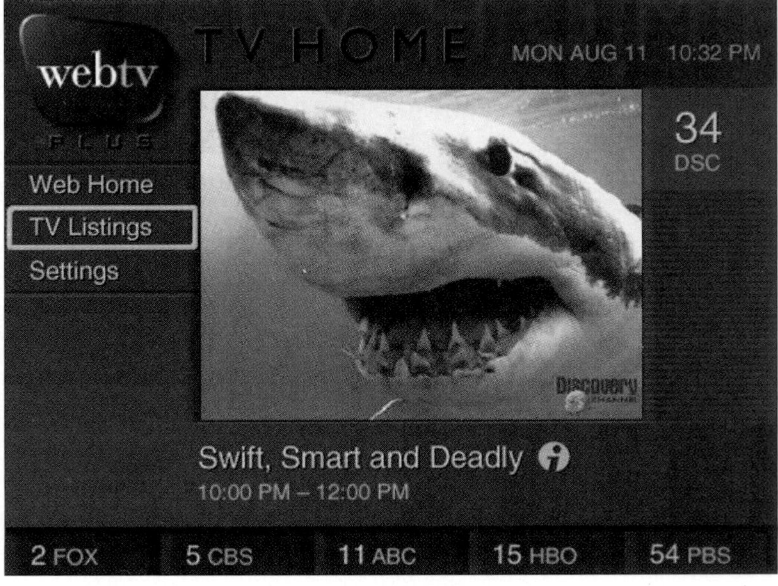

Exhibit 15–12 WebTV offers many services

other garments to mix and match with the sweater. You may then be asked if you wish to order and what shipping arrangements you prefer. If you have previously ordered, you are done, as your information has been stored in a database. If not, this first time you will be asked for personal information, including credit card number. You have ordered without leaving the couch or missing a minute of programming. WebTV's "Personal TV" service allows viewers complete control over what they watch and when they watch it. In addition, viewers can pause the live program, digital video record, and instant replay. The service also allows for fast forwarding, rewinding, skipping ahead, and/or searching for one's favorite scene.

While interactive TV sounds like the future, so far the results have not been as encouraging as marketers had hoped for. Two of the test markets for the concept have proven to be failures, and the major content providers like General Electric (NBC) and Walt Disney Company (ABC) have expressed less interest in the concept than had been expected. It may just be that when the viewer is watching TV they just want to watch TV—we will wait to see.

Summary

This chapter introduced you to the Internet and interactive media. It explained some of the objectives for these media and how they can be used in an IMC program.

The discussion of the Internet focused on understanding the key terms used in the industry, the objectives sought when using the Internet, and Internet communications strategies. In addition, the role of the Internet in an IMC program was discussed, with an explanation of how all the IMC program elements can be used with the Internet. Advantages of the Internet—including the ability to target markets, interactive capabilities, and relationship building—were discussed. In addition, disadvantages—including high costs, unreliable measurements and statistics, and relatively low reach (compared to that of traditional media)—were reviewed. Sources of Internet measurement data were also provided.

The Internet has been the most rapidly adopted medium of our time. It holds great potential for both business-to-business and consumer marketers. However, contrary to popular belief, the Internet is not a stand-alone medium. Its role in an integrated marketing communications program strengthens the overall program as well as the effectiveness of the Internet itself.

Interactive media, particularly WebTV, has not yet fulfilled its promise. While still in its infancy, the medium has not received the acceptance and use expected. Test market indications are that the medium still needs improvements—particularly in content—before reaching mass acceptance.

Key Terms

Internet, 495
World Wide Web (WWW), 495
website, 500
affiliations, 504
e-commerce, 505
banner ads, 506
sponsorships, 506
content sponsorship, 506
pop-ups, 506
interstitials, 506
push technologies, 507
webcasting, 507
personalization, 507
links, 507
SPAM, 511
cookie, 514

Discussion Questions

1. While some believe that the Internet poses a threat to traditional media, others disagree, arguing that it is just another medium to marketers. Explain some of the arguments on both sides. What is your conclusion?

2. The Internet is growing at an extemely rapid pace. At the same time there are indications that this growth will slow. Discuss some factors that may lead to decreased growth of the use of this medium.

3. Discuss the objectives marketers may be seeking in their use of the Internet. Which is the Internet best suited for?

4. Explain the different forms that advertisers might use to advertise on the Internet. Discuss some of the advantages and disadvantages associated with each.

5. What is meant by personalization? Give an example of how a consumer company might use personalization.

6. A number of Internet marketers have been criticized as engaging in unethical practices. Discuss some of the practices that might be considered unethical. What should be done to curtail these practices?

7. Discuss some of the ways that marketers attempt to measure the effectiveness of their programs on the Internet. How do these measures relate to more traditional measures? Describe the advantages and disadvantages of traditional versus Internet measures.

8. Discuss some of the advantages of using the Internet. For which types of companies is the Internet best suited? Why?

9. What is interactive TV? Explain how interactive television differs from traditional television. Give an example of how a company might employ this medium.

10. Many marketers feel that the Internet offers much more potential to business-to-business marketers than it does to consumer marketers. Detail some of the reasons they feel this way and draw a conclusion as to the merits of this argument.

Chapter Sixteen

Sales Promotion

Chapter Objectives

- To understand the role of sales promotion in a company's integrated marketing communications program and to examine why it is increasingly important.
- To examine the various objectives of sales promotion programs.
- To examine the types of consumer- and trade-oriented sales promotion tools and the factors to consider in using them.
- To understand how sales promotion is coordinated with advertising.
- To consider potential problems and abuse by companies in their use of sales promotion.

The Real Action These Days Is below the Line

For years many marketers viewed advertising as the crown jewel of communication and the primary tool for brand building. However, more marketers are recognizing that brands are the sum total of all marketing communications and that no single IMC tool is capable of building brand image, sales, and relationships with consumers, as well as the trade, at the same time. While Coca-Cola spends over $700 million a year on media advertising, the soft drink giant also allocates several hundred million dollars to promotions. During the past two summers, Coca-Cola has committed over $50 million of its marketing budget to promotions that reward consumers with cash prizes for finding ATM cards in 2.2 million packages of soda. Its summer ad campaigns tell consumers how to use Coca-Cola Cards to get discounts at local restaurants and movie theaters.

When Taco Bell was introducing its new Gorditas, the fast-food chain used a promotional tie-in with the movie *Godzilla* that was designed to encourage trial of the new menu item. The "Find Godzilla and Win" instant-win game played off of the central theme of the movie, in which hoards of people scurry around New York City looking for a 200-foot monster. A game piece with an innovative decoder screen was attached to every medium and large drink cup and to Gorditas wrappers. Consumers could peel off the game piece and use the decoder to hunt for a hidden image of Godzilla to win instantly, or they could collect individual letters to spell out Godzilla and win a million dollars. The promotion was supported by clever TV spots showing the tiny Taco Bell chihuahua mascot looking for Godzilla while crooning "Here lizard, lizard." When a huge reptilian shadow falls over him he quips, "I think I need a bigger box."

Many marketers are realizing they need to get a bigger box as well, and it needs to contain more than just 30-second TV commercials and print ads. A variety of companies from package goods, fast food, and automotive to consumer electronic and financial services are making branding the core of their marketing strategies. In the process, they are recognizing that a solid branding strategy requires true integration of all the

various marketing communication tools. Moreover, many are discovering that sales promotion is the engine that drives the sales numbers.

Brand managers and marketing executives generally agree that advertising is essential in positioning a brand and building its promise, personality, and image. However, today's consumers are concerned about more than a promise or brand image; they want image to be accompanied by an offer or extra incentive. Other so-called below-the-line IMC discipline areas such as event marketing and sales promotion are being used to build customer equity and are taking center stage alongside advertising. The new mandate is to deliver experiences that deepen each consumer's relationship with the brand. The California Milk Advisory Board learned that teenage girls were wallpapering their bedrooms with milk mustache ads, so the board gave away trading cards and screen savers featuring the ads at fairs and summer events and through websites.

In the past sales promotion specialists would be brought in *after* key strategic branding decisions were made. They were viewed primarily as tacticians whose role was to develop a promotional program such as a contest or sweepstakes coupon or sampling program that would create a short-term spike in sales. However, many companies are now making promotion specialists part of the strategic brand-building team. For example, at the Chicago-based Foote, Cone & Belding agency, a recent reorganization created a new division known as Marketing Drive, which puts sales promotion and direct marketing on a par with the traditional advertising function. Its staff is assigned to brand groups for clients such as Wendy's, Nestlés, and Coors beer that include account planning and creative specialists. FCB's president, Brian Williams, notes, "Rather than be identified as promotions experts, we want Impact to be identified as branding experts within the discipline of promotion." He insists that brand groups be "media neutral" or unbiased about the right promotional mix for each client. They are asked to consider whatever promotional tool is necessary to target segments and build short-term business and long-term reputation.

More and more companies are realizing that much of the real action in marketing these days is happening below the line. There is pressure to build brand image *and* sales that comes from serving Wall Street and consumers. The financial community wants to see sales and profits, while consumers love their brands but also want some extra incentive to buy them. As one promotional expert notes, "These days, marketing is about using a call to action to get consumers into the habit of using your brand." And for many companies, sales promotion is the call to action being used to move consumers and to connect with them.

Sources: Betsy Spethmann, "Sudden Impact," *Promo Magazine,* April 1999, pp. 42–48, and "Is Advertising Dead," *Promo Magazine,* September 1998, pp. 32–36, 159–62.

As discussed in the opening vignette, marketers have come to recognize that advertising alone is not always enough to move their products off store shelves and into the hands of consumers. Companies also use sales promotion methods targeted at both consumers and the wholesalers and retailers that distribute their products to stimulate demand. Most companies' integrated marketing communications programs include consumer and trade promotions that are coordinated with advertising, direct marketing, and publicity/public relations campaigns as well as sales force efforts.

This chapter focuses on the role of sales promotion in a firm's IMC program. We examine how marketers use both consumer- and trade-oriented promotions to influence the purchase behavior of consumers as well as wholesalers and retailers. We explore the objectives of sales promotion programs and the various types of sales promotion tools that can be used at both the consumer and trade level. We also consider how sales promotion can be integrated with other elements of the promotional mix and look at problems that can arise when marketers become overly dependent on consumer and trade promotions, especially the latter.

The Scope and Role of Sales Promotion

Sales promotion has been defined as "a direct inducement that offers an extra value or incentive for the product to the sales force, distributors, or the ultimate consumer with the primary objective of creating an immediate sale."[1] Keep in mind several important aspects of sales promotion as you read this chapter.

First, sales promotion involves some type of inducement that provides an *extra incentive* to buy. This incentive is usually the key element in a promotional program; it may be a coupon or price reduction, the opportunity to enter a contest or sweepstakes, a money-back refund or rebate, or an extra amount of a product. The incentive may also be a free sample of the product, given in hopes of generating a future purchase, or a premium that serves as a reminder of the brand and reinforces its image, such as the miniature race car premium offer that ties into Tide's NASCAR sponsorship (Exhibit 16–1). Most sales promotion offers attempt to add some value to the product or service. While advertising appeals to the mind and emotions to give the consumer a reason to buy, sales promotion appeals more to the pocketbook and provides an incentive for purchasing a brand.

Sales promotion can also provide an inducement to marketing intermediaries such as wholesalers and retailers. A trade allowance or discount gives retailers a financial incentive to stock and promote a manufacturer's products. A trade contest directed toward wholesalers or retail personnel gives them extra incentive to perform certain tasks or meet sales goals.

A second point is that sales promotion is essentially an *acceleration tool,* designed to speed up the selling process and maximize sales volume.[2] By providing an extra incentive, sales promotion techniques can motivate consumers to purchase a larger quantity of a brand or shorten the purchase cycle of the trade or consumers by encouraging them to take more immediate action.

Companies also use limited-time offers such as price-off deals to retailers or a coupon with an expiration date to accelerate the purchase process.[3] Sales promotion attempts to maximize sales volume by motivating customers who have not responded to advertising. The ideal sales promotion program generates sales that would not be achieved by other means. However, as we shall see later, many sales promotion offers end up being used by current users of a brand rather than attracting new users.

A final point regarding sales promotion activities is that they can be *targeted to different parties* in the marketing channel. As shown in Figure 16–1, sales promotion can be broken into two major categories: consumer-oriented and trade-oriented promotions. Activities involved in **consumer-oriented sales promotion** include sampling, couponing, premiums, contests and sweepstakes, refunds and rebates, bonus packs, price-offs, and event marketing. These promotions are directed at consumers, the end purchasers of goods and services, and are designed to induce them to purchase the marketer's brand.

As discussed in Chapter 2, consumer-oriented promotions are part of a promotional pull strategy; they work along with advertising to encourage consumers to

Exhibit 16–1 Procter & Gamble offers a premium offer to provide extra incentive to purchase Tide and Downy

Figure 16–1 Types of sales promotion activities

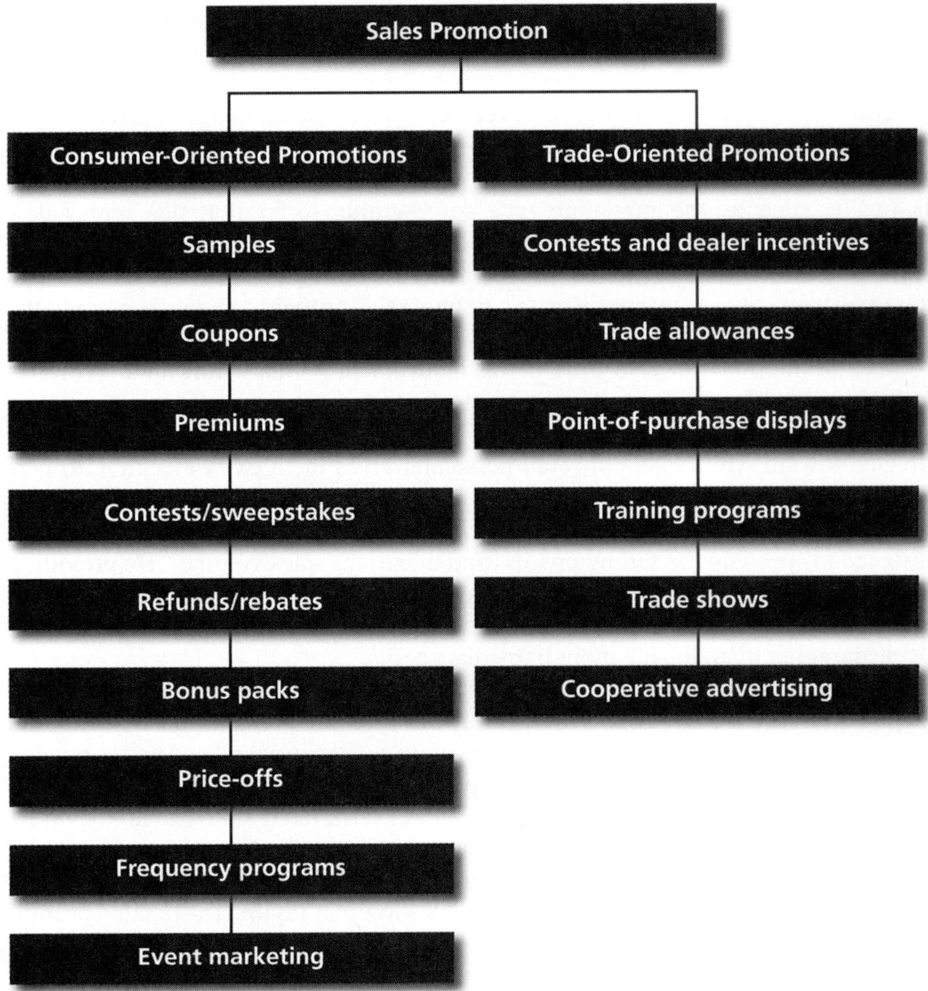

purchase a particular brand and thus create demand for it. Consumer promotions are also used by retailers to encourage consumers to shop in their particular stores. Many grocery stores use their own coupons or sponsor contests and other promotions to increase store patronage.

Trade-oriented sales promotion includes dealer contests and incentives, trade allowances, point-of-purchase displays, sales training programs, trade shows, cooperative advertising, and other programs designed to motivate distributors and retailers to carry a product and make an extra effort to push it to their customers. Nearly two-thirds of all sales promotion dollars are spent on trade promotions. Many marketing programs include both trade- and consumer-oriented promotions, since motivating both groups maximizes the effectiveness of the promotional program.

The Growth of Sales Promotion

While sales promotion has been part of the marketing process for a long time, its role and importance in a company's integrated marketing communications programs has increased dramatically over the past decade. The strong economy has resulted in massive consumer spending which has helped propel the sales promotion industry to an annual growth rate of 5 to 7 percent. In 1999 spending on promotion reached a record $93 billion, while another $155 billion was spent on promotions targeted at retailers and wholesalers. Consumer-package-goods firms continue to be the core users of sales promotion programs and tools. However, sales promotion activity is also increasing in new categories, including health care, computer hardware and software, electronics, and deregulated utilities.[4]

Not only has the total amount of money spent on sales promotion increased, but the percentage of marketers' budgets allocated to promotion has skyrocketed.

Figure 16–2 Long-term allocations to advertising, trade promotion, and consumer promotion

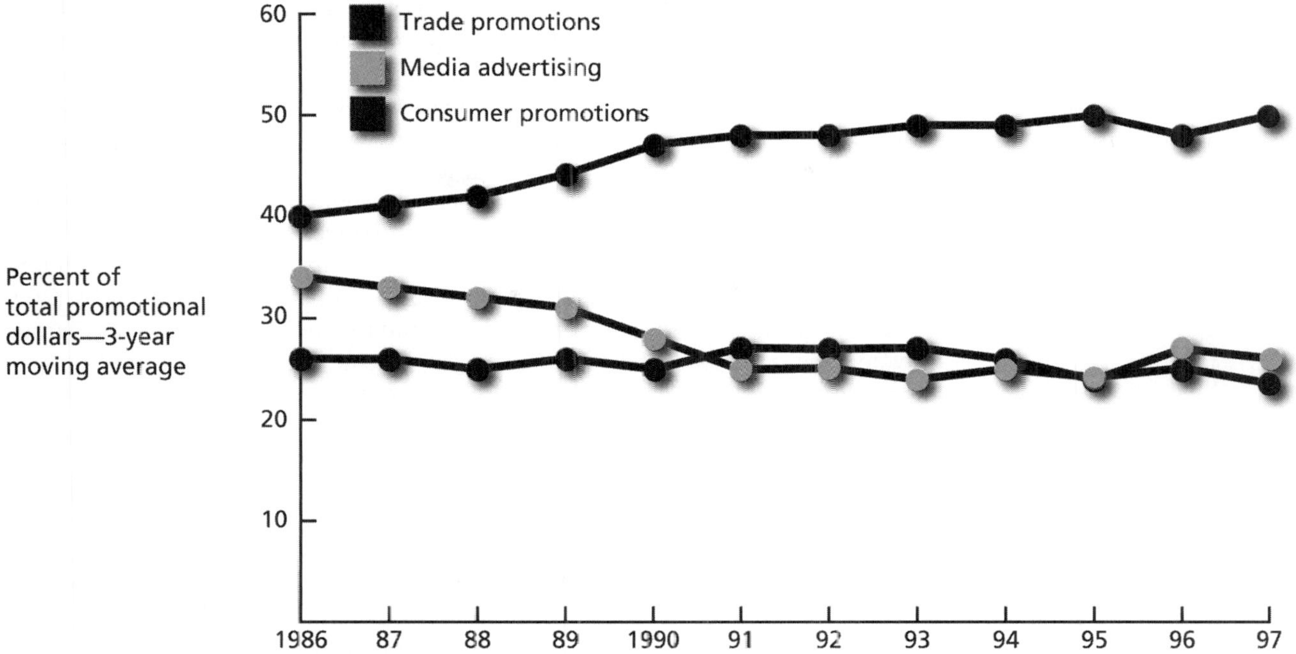

	1986	87	88	89	1990	91	92	93	94	95	96	97
Trade promotions	40	41	42	44	47	48	48	49	49	50	48	50
Media advertising	34	33	32	31	28	25	25	24	25	26	27	26
Consumer promotions	26	26	25	26	25	27	27	27	26	24	25	24

Annual studies by Carol Wright Promotions track the marketing spending of major package-goods companies in three categories: trade promotion, consumer promotion, and media advertising. Figure 16–2 shows the long-term trend of allocations to each category. The percentage of the marketing budget spent on consumer promotions has held steady over the past decade, while the allocation to trade promotions has risen dramatically.

This increase in trade promotion spending has come almost totally at the expense of media advertising. Marketers say they expect trade spending to decline somewhat in the future, with corresponding increases in consumer promotions and media advertising. However, many marketing people believe it will be difficult to reverse the flow of marketing dollars to the trade, for the reasons discussed next.

Reasons for the Increase in Sales Promotion

A number of factors have led to the shift in marketing dollars to sales promotion from media advertising. Among them are the growing power of retailers, declining brand loyalty, increased promotional sensitivity, brand proliferation, fragmentation of the consumer market, short-term focus, increased accountability, competition, and clutter.

The Growing Power of Retailers

One reason for the increase in sales promotion is the power shift in the marketplace from manufacturers to retailers. For many years, manufacturers of national brands had the power and influence; retailers were just passive distributors of their products. Consumer products manufacturers created consumer demand for their brands by using heavy advertising and some consumer-oriented promotions, such as samples, coupons, and premiums, and exerted pressure on retailers to carry the products. Retailers did very little research and sales analysis; they relied on manufacturers for information regarding the sales performance of individual brands.

In recent years, however, several developments have helped to transfer power from the manufacturers to the retailers. With the advent of optical checkout scanners and sophisticated in-store computer systems, retailers gained access to data concerning how quickly products turn over, which sales promotions are working, and which products make money.[5] Retailers use this information to analyze sales of manufacturers' products and then demand discounts and other promotional support from manufacturers of lagging brands. Companies that fail to comply with retailers' demands for more trade support often have their shelf space reduced or even their product dropped.

Another factor that has increased the power of retailers is the consolidation of the grocery store industry, which has resulted in larger chains with greater buying power and clout. These large chains have become accustomed to trade promotions and can pressure manufacturers to provide deals, discounts, and allowances. Consolidation has also given large retailers more money for advancing already strong private label initiatives, and sales promotion is the next step in the marketing evolution of private label brands. Private label brands in various package-good categories such as foods, drugs, and health and beauty care products are giving national brands more competition for retail shelf space and increasing their own marketing, including the use of traditional sales promotion tools. Well-marketed private label products are forcing national brand leaders, as well as second-tier brands, to develop more innovative promotional programs and to be more price-competitive.[6]

Declining Brand Loyalty Another major reason for the increase in sales promotion is that consumers have become less brand loyal and are purchasing more on the basis of price, value, and convenience. Some consumers are always willing to buy their preferred brand at full price without any type of promotional offer. However, many consumers are loyal coupon users and/or are conditioned to look for deals when they shop. They may switch back and forth among a set of brands they view as essentially equal. These brands are all perceived as being satisfactory and interchangeable, and consumers purchase whatever brand is on special or for which they have a coupon.

Increased Promotional Sensitivity Marketers are making greater use of sales promotion in their marketing programs because consumers respond favorably to the incentives it provides. A major research project completed by Promotion Decisions, Inc., in 1999 tracked the purchase behavior of over 33,000 consumers and their response to both consumer and trade promotions. The results showed that 42 percent of the total unit volume of the 12 package-good products analyzed was purchased with some type of incentive while 58 percent was purchased at full price. Coupons were particularly popular among consumers, as 24 percent of the sales volume involved the use of a coupon.[7]

An obvious reason for consumers' increased sensitivity to sales promotion offers is that they save money. Another reason is that many purchase decisions are made at the point of purchase by consumers who are increasingly time-sensitive and facing too many choices. Some studies have found that up to 70 percent of purchase decisions are made in the store, where people are very likely to respond to promotional deals.[8] Buying a brand that is on special or being displayed can simplify the decision-making process and solve the problem of overchoice. Professor Leigh McAlister has described this process:

> As consumers go down the supermarket aisle they spend 3 to 10 seconds in each product category. They often don't know the regular price of the chosen product. However, they do have a sense of whether or not that product is on promotion. As they go down the aisle, they are trying to pensively fill their baskets with good products without tiresome calculations. They see a "good deal" and it goes in the cart.[9]

Brand Proliferation A major aspect of many firms' marketing strategies over the past decade has been the development of new products. Consumer-product companies are launching nearly 20,000 new products each year, according to the trade publication *New Product News* (compared with only 2,689 in 1980).[10] The market has become saturated with new brands, which often lack any significant advantages that can be used as the basis of an advertising campaign. Thus, companies increasingly depend on sales promotion to encourage consumers to try these brands. In Chapter 4, we saw how sales promotion techniques can be used as part of the shaping process to lead the consumer from initial trial to repeat purchase at full price. Marketers are relying more on samples, coupons, rebates, premiums, and other innovative promotional tools to achieve trial usage of their new brands and encourage repeat purchase (Exhibit 16–2).

Promotions are also important in getting retailers to allocate some of their precious shelf space to new brands. The competition for shelf space for new products in stores is enormous. Supermarkets carry an average of 30,000 products (compared with 13,067 in 1982). Retailers favor new brands with strong sales promotion support that will bring in more customers and boost their sales and profits. Many retailers require special discounts or allowances from manufacturers just to handle a new product. These slotting fees or allowances, which are discussed later in the chapter, can make it expensive for a manufacturer to introduce a new product.

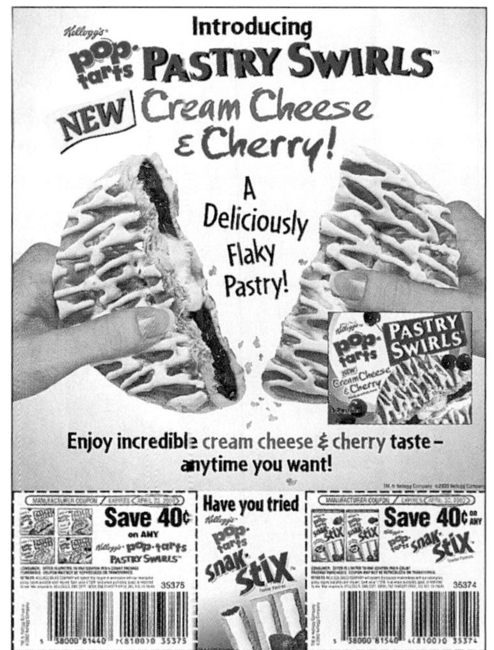

Exhibit 16–2 Sales promotion tools such as coupons are often used to encourage trial of a new brand

Fragmentation of the Consumer Market As the consumer market becomes more fragmented and traditional mass-media–based advertising less effective, marketers are turning to more segmented, highly targeted approaches. Many companies are tailoring their promotional efforts to specific regional markets. Sales promotion tools have become one of the primary vehicles for doing this, through programs tied into local flavor, themes, or events. For example, fast-food restaurants and take-out pizza chains such as Domino's spent a high percentage of their marketing budget on local tie-ins and promotions designed to build traffic and generate sales from their trade areas.[11]

A number of marketers are also using sales promotion techniques to target ethnic markets. For example, Sears targets the Hispanic market by hosting grassroots events at stores and tie-ins with local festivals using its "Fiestamobile," a 30-foot Winnebago party on wheels (Exhibit 16–3). The Fiestamobile is used for live remote broadcasts in Sears parking lots and brings games and live music to create a carnival atmosphere that drives traffic into the store.[12]

Marketers are also shifting more of their promotional efforts to direct marketing, which often includes some form of sales promotion incentive. Many marketers use information they get from premium offers, trackable coupons, rebates,

Exhibit 16–3 Sears uses its Fiestamobile for events targeting the Hispanic market

and sweepstakes to build databases for future direct-marketing efforts. As marketers continue to shift from media advertising to direct marketing, promotional offers will probably be used even more to help build databases. The technology is already in place to enable marketers to communicate individually with target consumers and transform mass promotional tools into ways of doing one-to-one marketing.[13]

Short-Term Focus Many businesspeople believe the increase in sales promotion is motivated by marketing plans and reward systems geared to short-term performance and the immediate generation of sales volume. Some think the package-goods brand management system has contributed to marketers' increased dependence on sales promotion. Brand managers use sales promotions routinely, not only to introduce new products or defend against the competition but also to meet quarterly or yearly sales and market share goals. The sales force, too, may have short-term quotas or goals to meet and may also receive requests from retailers and wholesalers for promotions. Thus, reps may pressure marketing or brand managers to use promotions to help them move the products into the retailers' stores.

Many managers view consumer and trade promotions as the most dependable way to generate short-term sales, particularly when they are price related. The reliance on sales promotion is particularly high in mature and slow-growth markets, where it is difficult to stimulate consumer demand through advertising. This has led to concern that managers have become too dependent on the quick sales fix that can result from a promotion and that the brand franchise may be eroded by too many deals.

Increased Accountability In addition to pressuring their marketing or brand managers and sales force to produce short-term results, many companies are demanding to know what they are getting for their promotional expenditures. Sales promotion is more economically accountable than advertising. In companies struggling to meet their sales and financial goals, top management is demanding measurable, accountable ways to relate promotional expenditures to sales and profitability. For example, Philip Morris's Kraft General Foods unit is using computerized sales information from checkout scanners in determining compensation for marketing personnel. Part of the pay managers receive depends on the sales a promotion generates relative to its costs.[14]

Managers who are being held accountable to produce results often use price discounts or coupons, since they produce a quick and easily measured jump in sales. It takes longer for an ad campaign to show some impact and the effects are more difficult to measure. Marketers are also feeling pressure from the trade as powerful retailers demand sales performance from their brands. Real-time data available from computerized checkout scanners make it possible for retailers to monitor promotions and track the results they generate on a daily basis.

Competition Another factor that led to the increase in sales promotion is manufacturers' reliance on trade and consumer promotions to gain or maintain competitive advantage. The markets for many products are mature and stagnant, and it is increasingly difficult to boost sales through advertising. Exciting, breakthrough creative ideas are difficult to come by, and consumers' attention to mass media advertising continues to decline. Rather than allocating large amounts of money to run dull ads, many marketers have turned to sales promotion.

Many companies are tailoring their trade promotions to key retail accounts and developing strategic alliances with retailers that include both trade and consumer promotional programs. A major development in recent years is **account-specific marketing** (also referred to as *comarketing*), whereby a manufacturer collaborates with an individual retailer to create a customized promotion that accomplishes mutual objectives. IMC Perspective 16–1 discusses an account-specific promotion Coppertone developed for Wal-Mart to promote its Kid Block sunscreen brand.

IMC Perspective 16–1

Coppertone and Wal-Mart Partner to Sell Sunscreen

Coppertone is the market leader in the sun care category and is known for being the inventor and innovator of sun care products. For more than 50 years Coppertone has pioneered sun care innovations that have helped define sun protection and that make time spent outdoors more fun and safe. Coppertone is positioned as the brand that "makes America fun in the sun," and it has very high brand awareness that is leveraged through the use of the well-known icon "Little Miss Coppertone." The blond pigtailed little girl with the black cocker spaniel tugging at her bathing suit has been associated with the Coppertone brand since the early 1950s and has become one of the world's most popular and recognizable trademarks. She has remained forever young over the years, reminding generations of people of the innocence and playfulness of youth.

Realizing how much of a cultural icon Little Miss Coppertone is, the company decided to feature her in advertising and national promotions during the summer of 1999. She was also the focus of the brand's first ever comarketing program, which Coppertone developed for Wal-Mart and which was run chainwide by the nation's largest retailer in June 1999. Coppertone's promotional agency DVC created the "Spot the Dog Scavenger Hunt" program, leveraging the high awareness and equity that Coppertone has behind the little girl and dog icon. The promotional theme was based on Little Miss Coppertone losing her dog in a Wal-Mart store. DVC developed an in-store scavenger hunt in which consumers were encouraged to find clues throughout the store, fill in a game piece, and receive a prize.

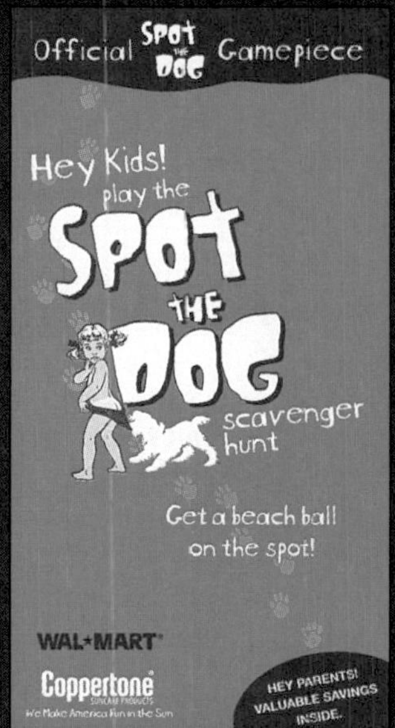

On event day, Wal-Mart greeters wore "Spot the Dog" buttons and distributed game pieces to children and their parents. The game piece explained the scavenger hunt and encouraged consumers to find clues located in sun care, lawn and garden, and pet food locations—categories not only related to Coppertone and outdoors but also important to Wal-Mart. The game piece also promoted Coppertone's innovative rub-free adult and children's sprays, contained valuable sun safety tips, and had a perforated $2 Wal-Mart-specific rebate coupon. Consumers followed the clues in the game piece to each location, and a shelf talker provided the answer to the clue. When all three answers were filled in, consumers turned in the game piece for a free beach ball at the "Scavenger Hunt Center" located near the store entrance.

The objectives for the account-specific program included building Coppertone and Wal-Mart sun care shoppers' loyalty; helping Wal-Mart keep consumers in the store longer; getting them to visit key destination departments and build sales; reinforcing the brand positioning for Coppertone, while educating consumers about the importance of sun safety; and increasing sunscreen sales for both Wal-Mart and Coppertone (specifically, for Kids Colorblock). The program was promoted to Wal-Mart associates over a period of several months using the retailer's internal communications channels, which include satellite TV, headquarters meetings, the annual shareholders' meeting, sell sheets, and a store manager carnival game themed to the "Spot the Dog" program.

The first ever comarketing event between Wal-Mart and Coppertone was a tremendous success on all fronts. Nearly 2,500 Wal-Mart stores participated in the one-day event and incremental displays were posted in 74 percent of the stores. Over 1.2 million prizes were delivered to an estimated 2 million consumers. Coppertone's share of sunscreen sales increased by 6 percent over that of the three weeks prior to the event, and Wal-Mart sales in other product categories increased as well. The program was well received by Wal-Mart managers who felt the promotional event was easy to execute and a success. Moreover, the success of the promotion led to additional plans for account-specific promotions between Coppertone and Wal-Mart in the future.

Source: "Coppertone & Wal-Mart 'Spot the Dog' Scavenger Hunt Promotion," DVC, Morristown, NJ.

Exhibit 16–4 Cox Target Media promotes its Carol Wright Account Specific marketing program

Estimates are that U.S. marketers will soon spend more than half of their promotion and advertising budgets on account-specific marketing.[15] Exhibit 16–4 shows an ad promoting the Carol Wright Account Specific marketing program offered by Cox Target Media.

Retailers may use a promotional deal with one company as leverage to seek an equal or better deal with its competitors. Consumer and trade promotions are easily matched by competitors, and many marketers find themselves in a promotional trap where they must continue using promotions or be at a competitive disadvantage. (We discuss this problem in more detail later in the chapter.)

Clutter A promotional offer in an ad can break through the clutter that is prevalent in most media today. A premium offer may help attract consumers' attention to an ad, as will a contest or sweepstakes. Some studies have shown that readership scores are higher for print ads with coupons than for ads without them.[16] However, more recent studies by Starch INRA Hooper suggest that magazine ads with coupons do not generate higher readership.[17]

Concerns about the Increased Role of Sales Promotion

Many factors have contributed to the increased use of sales promotion by consumer product manufacturers. Marketing and advertising executives are concerned about how this shift in the allocation of the promotional budget affects brand equity. As noted in Chapter 2, *brand equity,* or consumer franchise, is an intangible asset of added value or goodwill that results from consumers' favorable image, impressions of differentiation, and/or strength of attachment to a brand.

Some critics argue that sales promotion increases come at the expense of brand equity and every dollar that goes into promotion rather than advertising devalues the brand.[18] They say trade promotions in particular contribute to the destruction of brand franchises and equity as they encourage consumers to purchase primarily on the basis of price.

Proponents of advertising argue that marketers must maintain strong franchises if they want to differentiate their brands and charge a premium price for them. They say advertising is still the most effective way to build the long-term franchise of a brand: it informs consumers of a brand's features and benefits, creates an image, and helps build and maintain brand loyalty. However, many marketers are not investing in their brands as they take monies away from media advertising to fund short-term promotions. For example, H. J. Heinz Co., whose major products include ketchup and condiments, 9-Lives and Kibbles 'N Bits cat food, Star Kist tuna and Weight Watchers, allocated nearly all its marketing budget to trade promotions in the early to mid-'90s while cutting back substantially on advertising.[19] In 1996 Heinz had $9 billion in sales but spent only $90 million advertising its brands in the United States. Some analysts argued that the lack of ad spending was turning some Heinz brands into commodities, making it difficult for them to maintain prices. By the end of the decade Heinz had announced plans to increase advertising spending for its core business categories. Brands such as Heinz ketchup and Star-Kist tuna are being advertised more in an effort to rebuild their brand equity and make them less dependent on trade promotions.[20]

Marketing experts generally agree that advertising plays an important role in building and maintaining a brand's image and position, which are core components of its equity. Many are concerned that if the trend toward spending more on sales promotion at the expense of media advertising continues, brands may lose the equity that advertising helped create and be forced to compete primarily on the basis of price. Many of these concerns are justified, but not all sales promotion activities detract from the value of a brand. It is important to distinguish between consumer franchise-building and nonfranchise-building promotions.

Consumer Franchise-Building versus Nonfranchise-Building Promotions

Sales promotion activities that communicate distinctive brand attributes and contribute to the development and reinforcement of brand identity are **consumer franchise-building (CFB) promotions.**[21] Consumer sales promotion efforts cannot make consumers loyal to a brand that is of little value or does not provide them with a specific benefit. But they can make consumers aware of a brand and, by communicating its specific features and benefits, contribute to the development of a favorable brand image. Consumer franchise-building promotions are designed to build long-term brand preference and help the company achieve the ultimate goal of full-price purchases that do not depend on a promotional offer.

For years, franchise or image building was viewed as the exclusive realm of advertising, and sales promotion was used only to generate short-term sales increases. But now marketers are recognizing the image-building potential of sales promotion and paying attention to its CFB value. A survey of senior marketing executives found that 88 percent believe consumer promotions can help build a brand's equity and 58 percent think trade promotions can contribute.[22] One sales promotion expert says:

> Today's marketers who appreciate the potential of sales promotion as an ongoing strategy that works to build a brand's franchise recognize that promotion's potential goes well beyond mere quick-fix, price-off tactics. The promotion professional is familiar with a variety of approaches to generating consumer involvement—that is, sweepstakes, special events, premiums, or rebates—and understands that the given campaign must work in harmony with long-term goals and brand positioning.[23]

Many sales promotion agencies, such as Ryan Partnership, recognize the importance of developing consumer and trade promotions that can help build brand equity (Exhibit 16–5).

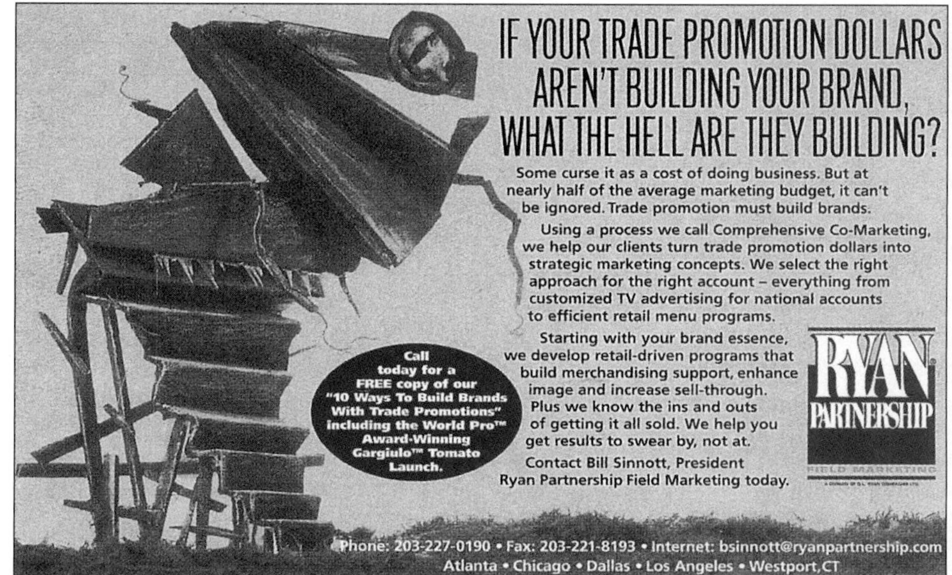

Exhibit 16–5 This promotion agency ad stresses the importance of using promotions to build brand equity

Companies can use sales promotion techniques in a number of ways to contribute to franchise building. Rather than using a one-time offer, many companies are developing frequency programs that encourage repeat purchases and long-term patronage. Many credit cards have loyalty programs where consumers earn bonus points every time they use their card to charge a purchase. These points can then be redeemed for various items. Most airlines and many hotel chains offer frequent flyer or guest programs to encourage repeat patronage. Many retail stores have also begun using frequency programs to build loyalty and encourage repeat purchases.[24]

Companies can also use sales promotion to contribute to franchise building by developing an offer consistent with the image of the brand. An example of a successful consumer brand-building promotion is the Search for 2000 Uses Sweepstakes promotion for WD-40, shown in Exhibit 16–6. The WD-40 Company positions its brand as the leading multipurpose problem solver that cleans, protects, penetrates, lubricates, and displaces moisture like no other product on earth. The marketing strategy for WD-40 is to continually promote the myriad of uses for the product. The Search for 2000 Uses Sweepstakes, which was launched to coincide with the new millennium, asked consumers to suggest their use for WD-40 in order to be entered for a chance to win various prizes such as WD-40 can radios, T-shirts, and baseball caps and a grand prize of $10,000 in company stock. The sweepstakes reinforced WD-40's image as a multipurpose problem solver and also encouraged consumers to visit the company's website to enter their use.

Exhibit 16–6 WD-40's Search for 2000 Uses Sweepstakes is an excellent example of a consumer brand-building promotion

Nonfranchise-building (non-FB) promotions are designed to accelerate the purchase decision process and generate an immediate increase in sales. These activities do not communicate information about a brand's unique features or the benefits of using it, so they do not contribute to the building of brand identity and image. Price-off deals, bonus packs, and rebates or refunds are examples of non-FB sales promotion techniques. Trade promotions receive the most criticism for being nonfranchise building—for good reason. First, many of the promotional discounts and allowances given to the trade are never passed on to consumers. Most trade promotions that are forwarded through the channels reach consumers in the form of lower prices or special deals and lead them to buy on the basis of price rather than brand equity.

Many specialists in the promotional area stress the need for marketers to use sales promotion tools to build a franchise and create long-term continuity in their promotional programs. Whereas non-FB promotions merely borrow customers from other brands, well-planned CFB activities can convert consumers to loyal customers. Short-term non-FB promotions have their place in a firm's promotional mix, particularly when competitive developments call for them. But their limitations must be recognized when a long-term marketing strategy for a brand is developed.

Consumer-Oriented Sales Promotion

In this section, we examine the various sales promotion tools and techniques marketers can use to influence consumers. We study the consumer-oriented promotions shown in Figure 16–2 and discuss their advantages and limitations. First, we consider some objectives marketers have for sales promotion programs targeted to the consumer market.

Objectives of Consumer-Oriented Sales Promotion

As the use of sales promotion techniques continues to increase, companies must consider what they hope to accomplish through their consumer promotions and how they interact with other promotional activities such as advertising, direct marketing, and personal selling. When marketers implement sales promotion programs without considering their long-term cumulative effect on the brand's image and position in the marketplace, they often do little more than create short-term spikes in the sales curve.

Not all sales promotion activities are designed to achieve the same objectives. As with any promotional mix element, marketers must plan consumer promotions by conducting a situation analysis and determining sales promotion's specific role in the integrated marketing communications program. They must decide what the promotion is designed to accomplish and to whom it should be targeted. Setting clearly defined objectives and measurable goals for their sales promotion programs forces managers to think beyond the short-term sales fix (although this can be one goal).

While the basic goal of most consumer-oriented sales promotion programs is to induce purchase of a brand, the marketer may have a number of different objectives for both new and established brands—for example, obtaining trial and repurchase, increasing consumption of an established brand, defending current customers, targeting a specific market segment, or enhancing advertising and marketing efforts.

Obtaining Trial and Repurchase One of the most important uses of sales promotion techniques is to encourage consumers to try a new product or service. While thousands of new products are introduced to the market every year, as many as 90 percent of them fail within the first year. Many of these failures are due to the fact that the new product or brand lacks the promotional support needed either to encourage initial trial by enough consumers or to induce enough of those trying the brand to repurchase it. Many new brands are merely new versions of an existing product without unique benefits, so advertising alone cannot induce trial. Sales promotion tools have become an important part of new brand introduction

Exhibit 16–7 Arm & Hammer used this FSI to promote a specific use for the product

strategies; the level of initial trial can be increased through techniques such as sampling, couponing, and refund offers.

The success of a new brand depends not only on getting initial trial but also on inducing a reasonable percentage of people who try the brand to repurchase it and establish ongoing purchase patterns. Promotional incentives such as coupons or refund offers are often included with a sample to encourage repeat purchase after trial. For example, when Lever Brothers introduced its Lever 2000 brand of bar soap, it distributed millions of free samples along with a 75-cent coupon. The samples allowed consumers to try the new soap, while the coupon provided an incentive to purchase it.

Increasing Consumption of an Established Brand

Many marketing managers are responsible for established brands competing in mature markets, against established competitors, where consumer purchase patterns are often well set. Awareness of an established brand is generally high as a result of cumulative advertising effects, and many consumers have probably tried the brand. These factors can create a challenging situation for the brand manager. Sales promotion can generate some new interest in an established brand to help increase sales or defend market share against competitors.

Marketers attempt to increase sales for an established brand in several ways, and sales promotion can play an important role in each. One way to increase product consumption is by identifying new uses for the brand. Sales promotion tools like recipe books or calendars that show various ways of using the product often can accomplish this. One of the best examples of a brand that has found new uses is Arm & Hammer baking soda. Exhibit 16–7 shows a clever freestanding insert (FSI) that promotes the brand's new fridge-freezer pack, which absorbs more odors in refrigerators and freezers.

Another strategy for increasing sales of an established brand is to use promotions that attract nonusers of the product category or users of a competing brand. Attracting nonusers of the product category can be very difficult, as consumers may not see a need for the product. Sales promotions can appeal to nonusers by providing them with an extra incentive to try the product, but a more common strategy for increasing sales of an established brand is to attract consumers who use a competing brand. This can be done by giving them an incentive to switch, such as a coupon, premium offer, bonus pack, or price deal. Marketers can also get users of a competitor to try their brand through sampling or other types of promotional programs.

One of the most successful promotions ever used to attract users of a competing brand was the Pepsi Challenge. In this campaign, Pepsi took on its archrival, industry leader Coca-Cola, in a hard-hitting comparative promotion that challenged consumers to taste the two brands in blind taste tests (Exhibit 16–8). The Pepsi

Exhibit 16–8 The Pepsi Challenge was a very successful promotion for attracting users of a competing brand

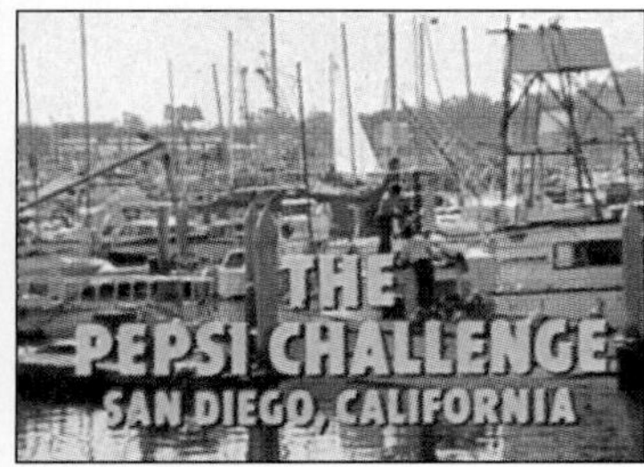

ANNCR: All across America people are taking the Pepsi Challenge. In California here's what they are saying.
TRACY KUERBIS: Pepsi really is the better drink.
DAVE JOHNSON: I've proven to myself now that I like Pepsi better.
ANNCR: Nationwide more people prefer the taste of Pepsi over Coca-Cola.
CHERIE BOOTH: I think today's test was very honest.
DAVE: Pepsi has a better product and that's probably why they are running a test like this because it's obvious how many people over here have picked Pepsi.
SUZANNE MACK: Being able to compare the two, I'd pick Pepsi.
CHERIE: If someone offered me either or, I choose the Pepsi.
ANNCR: What will you say? Take the Pepsi Challenge and find out.

Challenge promotion included national and local advertising, couponing, and trade support as part of a fully integrated promotional program. The campaign was used for several years and was instrumental in helping Pepsi move ahead of Coke to become the market share leader in supermarket sales. In response Coke launched a variety of counterattacks, including the controversial decision to change its formula and launch New Coke in 1986.

Defending Current Customers With more new brands entering the market every day and competitors attempting to take away their customers through aggressive advertising and sales promotion efforts, many companies are turning to sales promotion programs to hold present customers and defend their market share. A company can use sales promotion techniques in several ways to retain its current customer base. One way is to load them with the product, taking them out of the market for a certain time. Special price promotions, coupons, or bonus packs can encourage consumers to stock up on the brand. This not only keeps them using the company's brand but also reduces the likelihood they will switch brands in response to a competitor's promotion.

Targeting a Specific Market Segment Most companies focus their marketing efforts on specific market segments and are always looking for ways to reach their target audiences. Many marketers are finding that sales promotion tools such as contests and sweepstakes, events, coupons, and samplings are very effective ways to reach specific geographic, demographic, psychographic, and ethnic markets. Sales promotion programs can also be targeted to specific user-status groups such as nonusers or light versus heavy users.

Contests have become a popular sales promotion tool for targeting specific market segments. For example, Perdue Farms, Inc., the country's fourth-largest poultry producer, developed a contest to support its Fun Shapes line of breaded chicken nuggets among its core target of women between the ages of 25 and 49 and its secondary market of children age 2 to 12. The Fun Shapes line is a series of different and uniquely shaped nuggets including basketball, baseball, tic-tac-toe, dinosaur, and space-theme designs. Its promotion agency, DVC, developed a contest known as the Perdue "Masterpieces in Chicken" that invited children to design the nugget shape they would most like to see Perdue add to its line of fun shapes in the year 2000 (Exhibit 16–9). The grand-prize winner was designated "Artist of the Year" and received an all-expense paid family trip to Paris for a guided tour of the Louvre and passes to Euro-Disney. The winning design was also made into a shape by Perdue and introduced into its line in 2000. The program received thousands of entries and in the weeks during and after the promotion, sales volume increased by 10 percent.

Exhibit 16–9 Perdue Farms' "Masterpieces in Chicken" contest was targeted at mothers and their children

Enhancing Integrated Marketing Communications and Building Brand Equity A final objective for consumer-oriented promotions is to enhance or support the integrated marketing communications effort for a brand or company. Building brand equity and image has traditionally been done through advertising. However, sales promotion techniques such as contests or sweepstakes and premium offers are often used to draw attention to an ad, increase involvement with the message and product/service, and help build relationships with consumers. For example, one of the objectives of Perdue Farms' "Masterpiece in Chicken" promotion was to increase consumers' involvement level by encouraging them to interact with the brand. The promotion contributed to brand equity by using a contest that was fun and relevant to both mothers and children.

Career Profile

Stephanie Murrin

Executive Vice President, Chief Creative Officer at DVC

I graduated from the University of Hartford with a major in communications and a minor in marketing and advertising. As an undergraduate I took a variety of advertising, writing, and marketing classes. I also did an internship for the "Our Neighbors" telethon and I learned a great deal about creative ways to approach fund raising, advertising, and promotion.

My first job in advertising was at Saatchi & Saatchi Worldwide in New York City. I was very fortunate to be exposed to many different accounts and disciplines within the agency. I also worked with different creative directors and learned something from each, which helped me build my own creative style. During the 80s, working at a big agency in New York was seen as the only way to jumpstart a creative person's career. I don't think this is as true today, as you will find major accounts, outstanding creative talent, and opportunities to gain valuable experience in many different cities . . . and suburbs, for that matter.

After leaving Saatchi & Saatchi I moved to a small creative agency called CCM, where I did a short stint developing promotions and integrated marketing materials for a variety of companies. Following that, I took a job at DVC as a senior copywriter–creative supervisor. At the time, DVC was a very strategic promotion and marketing communications agency that was just building its Creative Department. I was then promoted to vice president, associate creative director and managed 20 people. After a few years I became executive creative director, managing the entire creative department. When I joined DVC in 1991 we had 25 employees. Today we have 325 employees and I manage nearly 100 people in four departments—Creative, Print Production, Art Buying, and Broadcast—so I am responsible for the entire execution phase of our work. Our clients include many major companies such as AT&T, Coca-Cola, Pillsbury, Perdue Farms, Hertz, and Johnson & Johnson.

Today, DVC is an integrated marketing communications and technology company that handles everything from advertising to Internet marketing solutions for our clients. However, developing sales promotion programs is a very important part of our business and promotional creative is no longer the forsaken stepchild of general advertising. This is a multibillion dollar industry as marketers recognize that 70 percent of all purchase decisions are now made in the store. Our clients demand the same high level of creative strategy and execution as they do from advertising, if not more. Promotional creative must work even harder than traditional advertising, as it has to bring the equity of the brand to life at the point-of-purchase and motivate consumers to take a desired action.

"Promotional creative must work even harder than traditional advertising."

The creative work we do for our clients must be smart as we constantly look for new formulas and try to blaze new trails. However, there must be a rationale for the creative and it must make an emotional connection with consumers. It has to move them. Our teams at DVC work closely with clients to immerse themselves in their business and develop a friendly and solutions-oriented partnership. Once that bond and trust is formed, it shows up in the promotional programs we develop for our clients.

In recent years, we have been entering our promotional work into award competitions just as we do with our creative for other communication disciplines such as advertising, interactive, and direct marketing. I am thrilled when I see our promotional work winning creative awards and standing up to the other disciplines as it is finally getting the respect it deserves and sharing the spotlight.

The favorite part of my job is making something from nothing. I enjoy taking the challenge of a client's marketing problem and solving it through the use of well-executed creative. I also enjoy developing young talent and watching these people grow and succeed. DVC was recently named Agency of the Decade by *PROMO Magazine,* the industry's leading trade publication. This means we have a lot of people growing and succeeding!

Sampling

Consumer-Oriented Sales Promotion Techniques

Marketers use various sales promotion techniques to meet the objectives just discussed. Figure 16–3 shows the extent to which these consumer promotions are used by package-goods companies.

Sampling involves a variety of procedures whereby consumers are given some quantity of a product for no charge to induce trial. Sampling is generally considered the most effective way to generate trial, although it is also the most expensive. As a sales promotion technique, sampling is often used to introduce a new product or brand to the market. However, as Figure 16–3 shows, sampling is also used for established products as well. Some companies do not use sampling for established products, reasoning that samples may not induce satisfied users of a competing brand to switch and may just go to the firm's current customers, who would buy the product anyway. This may not be true when significant changes (new and improved) are made in a brand.

Manufacturers of package-goods products such as food, health care items, cosmetics, and toiletries are heavy users of sampling since their products meet the three criteria for an effective sampling program:

1. The products are of relatively low unit value, so samples do not cost too much.
2. The products are divisible, which means they can be broken into small sample sizes that are adequate for demonstrating the brand's features and benefits to the user.
3. The purchase cycle is relatively short, so the consumer will consider an immediate purchase or will not forget about the brand before the next purchase occasion.

Benefits and Limitations of Sampling

Samples are an excellent way to induce a prospective buyer to try a product or service. One expert estimates approximately 75 percent of the households receiving a sample will try

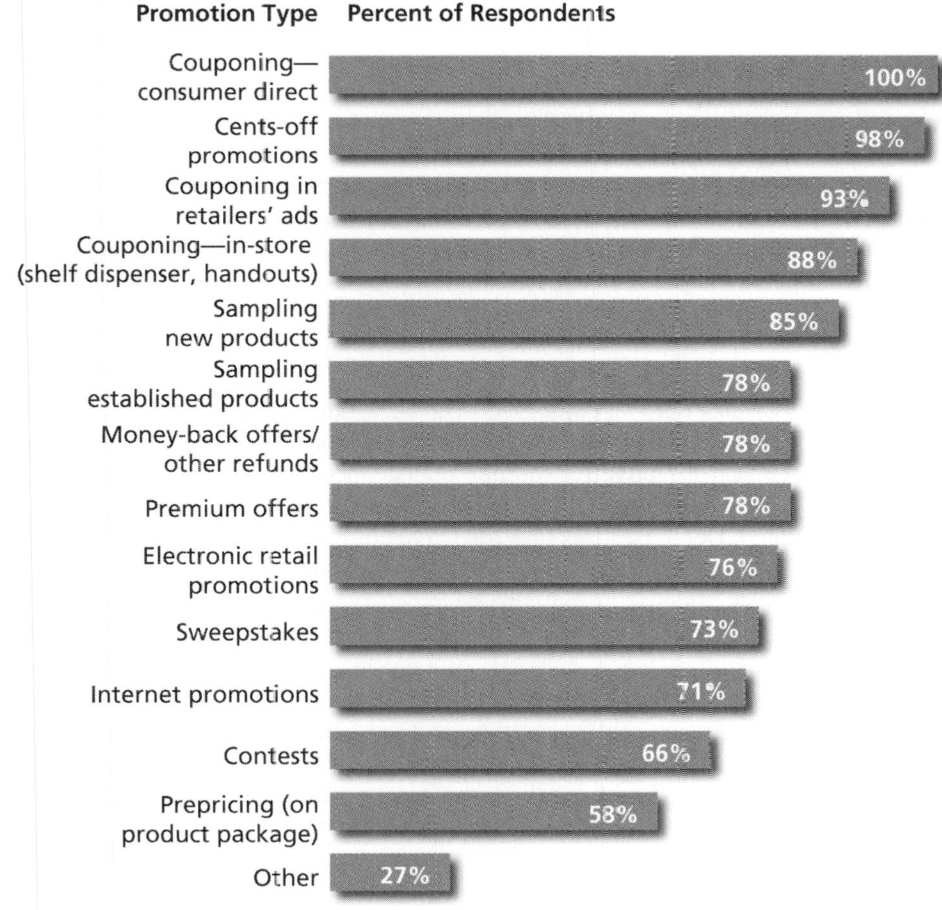

Figure 16–3 Types of consumer promotions used by package-goods manufacturers

it.[25] Sampling generates much higher trial rates than advertising or other sales promotion techniques.

Getting people to try a product leads to a second benefit of sampling: consumers experience the brand directly, gaining a greater appreciation for its benefits. This can be particularly important when a product's features and benefits are difficult to describe through advertising. Many foods, beverages, and cosmetics have subtle features that are most appreciated when experienced directly.

The brand must have some unique or superior benefits for a sampling program to be worthwhile. Otherwise, the sampled consumers revert back to other brands and do not become repeat purchasers. The costs of a sampling program can be recovered only if it gets a number of consumers to become regular users of the brand at full retail price.

Another possible limitation to sampling is that the benefits of some products are difficult to gauge immediately, and the learning period required to appreciate the brand may require supplying the consumer with larger amounts of the brand than are affordable. An example would be an expensive skin cream that is promoted as preventing or reducing wrinkles but has to be used for an extended period before any effects are seen.

Sampling Methods One basic decision the sales promotion or brand manager must make is how the sample will be distributed. The sampling method chosen is important not only in terms of costs but also because it influences the type of consumer who receives the sample. The best sampling method gets the product to the best prospects for trial and subsequent repurchase. Some basic distribution methods include door-to-door, direct-mail, in-store, and on-package approaches.

Exhibit 16–10 Product samples sent through the mail

Exhibit 16–11 Armor All uses on-package samples for related products

Door-to-door sampling, in which the product is delivered directly to the prospect's residence, is used when it is important to control where the sample is delivered. This distribution method is very expensive because of labor costs, but it can be cost-effective if the marketer has information that helps define the target market and/or if the prospects are located in a well-defined geographic area. Some companies have samples delivered directly to consumers' homes by including them with newspapers. Sunday papers have become an increasingly attractive way of mass distributing samples. However, there are also a number of newspapers that can now distribute a sample into a subscriber segment as small as 250 households with little increase in costs to marketers.[26]

Sampling through the mail is common for small, lightweight, nonperishable products such as those shown in Exhibit 16–10. A major advantage of this method is that the marketer has control over where and when the product will be distributed and can target the sample to specific market areas. Many marketers are using information from geodemographic target marketing programs such as Claritas's Prizm or Microvision to better target their sample mailings. The main drawbacks to mail sampling are postal restrictions and increasing postal rates.

In-store sampling is increasingly popular, especially for food products. The marketer hires temporary demonstrators who set up a table or booth, prepare small samples of the product, and pass them out to shoppers. The in-store sampling approach can be very effective for food products, since consumers get to taste the item and the demonstrator can give them more information about the product while it is being sampled. Demonstrators may also give consumers a cents-off coupon for the sampled item to encourage immediate trial purchase. While this sampling method can be very effective, it can also be expensive and requires a great deal of planning, as well as the cooperation of retailers.

On-package sampling, where a sample of a product is attached to another item, is another common sampling method (see Exhibit 16–11). This procedure can be very cost-effective, particularly for multiproduct firms that attach a sample of a new product to an existing brand's package. A drawback is that since the sample is distributed only to consumers who purchase the item to which it is attached, the sample will not reach nonusers of the carrier brand. Marketers can expand this sampling method by attaching the sample to multiple carrier brands and including samples with products not made by their company.

Event sampling has become one of the fastest-growing and most popular ways of distributing samples. Many marketers are using sampling programs that are part of integrated marketing programs that feature events, media tie-ins, and other activities that provide consumers with a total sense of a brand rather than just a few tastes of a food or beverage or a trial size of a package-goods product. Event sampling can take place in stores as well as at a variety of other venues such as concerts, sporting events, and other places.

Other Methods of Sampling

The four sampling methods just discussed are the most common, but several other methods are also used. Marketers may insert packets in magazines or newspapers (particularly Sunday supplements). Some tobacco and cereal companies send samples to consumers who call toll-free numbers to request them or mail in sample request forms. As discussed in Chapter 14, these sampling methods are becoming popular because they can help marketers build a database for direct marketing.

Many companies also use specialized sample distribution services such as Advo Inc., Carol Wright Promotions, and D. L. Blair. These firms help the company identify consumers who are nonusers of a product or users of a competing brand and develop appropriate procedures for distributing a sample to them. Many college students receive sample packs at the beginning of the semester that contain trial sizes of such products as mouthwash, toothpaste, headache remedies, and deodorant.

The Internet is yet another way companies are making it possible for consumers to sample their products, and it is adding a whole new level of targeting to the mix by giving consumers the opportunity to choose the samples they want. Catalina Marketing's ValuPage.com sampling and distribution service now has over 1 million members. The Sunflower Group has amassed over 50,000 members for its FreeSample-Club.com and is shooting to have a half million members by 2000.

Some companies cut back on their sampling programs in recent years because they felt they were too expensive, wasteful, and fraught with distribution problems. However, several factors have led to a resurgence in sampling recently. First, big companies like Advo and Time Warner have entered the sampling business, which creates more competition and helps keep sampling costs down. Also, a combination of technology and creativity is driving new sampling methods that let marketers target more efficiently. For example, Kendall-Futuro, the marketer of Curad adhesive strips, inserted kid-size bandage sample packs and coupons into 7.5 million McDonald's Happy Meals. The sampling promotion created so much exposure for the new brand, which was decorated with images of McDonald's characters, that the subsequent retail sell-in exceeded projections by 30 percent.[27]

Yet another factor may be the everyday low-pricing strategies that have prompted companies such as Procter & Gamble to move away from coupons and other price promotions in favor of samples. Many marketers are finding that sampling meets the complementary goals of introducing consumers to their products and getting retailers to support their promotional programs.

Couponing

The oldest, most widely used, and most effective sales promotion tool is the cents-off coupon. Coupons have been around since 1895, when the C. W. Post Co. started using the penny-off coupon to sell its new Grape-Nuts cereal. In recent years, coupons have become increasingly popular with consumers, which may explain their explosive growth among manufacturers and retailers that use them as sales promotion incentives. As Figure 16–3 showed, coupons are the most popular sales promotion technique. They are used by nearly all the package-goods firms in the Carol Wright Promotions survey.

Coupon distribution rose dramatically over the past 30 years. The number of coupons distributed by consumer package-goods marketers increased from 16 billion in 1968 to a peak of 310 billion in 1994. Since 1994 coupon distribution has been declining, but it leveled off in 1998 at 249 billion. According to NCH Promotional Services, a company that tracks coupon distribution and redemption patterns, over 80 percent of consumers in the United States use coupons and nearly 25 percent say they always use them when they shop. The average face value of coupons distributed increased from 21 cents in 1981 to 70 cents in 1998. Consumers generally seek out the coupons offering the highest savings, as the average face value of the 4.8 billion coupons that were redeemed in 1998 was 75 cents.[28]

Adding additional fuel to the coupon explosion of the past several decades has been the vast number of coupons distributed through retailers that are not even included in these figures. In most markets, a number of grocery stores make manufacturers' coupons even more attractive to consumers by doubling the face value.

Advantages and Limitations of Coupons

Coupons have a number of advantages that make them popular sales promotion tools for both new and established products. First, coupons make it possible to offer a price reduction only to those consumers who are price-sensitive. Such consumers generally purchase *because* of coupons, while those who are not as concerned about price buy the brand at full value. Coupons also make it possible to reduce the retail price of a product without relying on retailers for cooperation, which can often be a problem. Coupons are generally regarded as second only to sampling as a promotional technique for generating trial. Since a coupon lowers the price of a product, it reduces the consumer's perceived risk associated with trial of a new brand. Coupons can encourage repurchase after initial trial. Many new products include a cents-off coupon inside the package to encourage repeat purchase.

Coupons can also be useful promotional devices for established products. They can encourage nonusers to try a brand, encourage repeat purchase among current users, and get users to try a new, improved version of a brand. Coupons may also help coax users of a product to trade up to more expensive brands. The product category where coupons are used most is disposable diapers, with 43 percent of purchases being made with a coupon, followed by cereal (35 percent), detergents (29 percent), and deodorant (25 percent). Some of the product categories where coupons are used the least include carbonated beverages (8 percent), candy (7 percent), and gum (2 percent).

But there are a number of problems with coupons. First, it can be difficult to estimate how many consumers will use a coupon and when. Response to a coupon is rarely immediate; it typically takes anywhere from two to six months to redeem one. A study of coupon redemption patterns by Inman and McAlister found that many coupons are redeemed just before the expiration date rather than in the period following the initial coupon drop.[29] Many marketers are attempting to expedite redemption by shortening the time period before expiration. The average length of time from issue date to expiration date for coupons in 1998 was 3.1 months, for grocery products. However, coupons remain less effective than sampling for inducing initial product trial in a short period.

A problem associated with using coupons to attract new users to an established brand is that it is difficult to prevent the coupons from being used by consumers who already use the brand. For example, General Foods decided to reduce its use of coupons for Maxwell House coffee when research revealed the coupons were being redeemed primarily by current users. Rather than attracting new users, coupons can end up reducing the company's profit margins among consumers who would probably purchase the product anyway.

Other problems with coupons include low redemption rates and high costs. Couponing program expenses include the face value of the coupon redeemed plus costs for production, distribution, and handling of the coupons. Figure 16–4 shows the calculations used to determine the costs of a couponing program using an FSI (freestanding insert) in the Sunday newspaper and a coupon with an average face value of 67 cents. The marketer should track costs closely to ensure the promotion is economically feasible.

Figure 16–4 Calculating couponing costs

Cost per Coupon Redeemed: An Illustration	
1. Distribution cost 55,000,000 circulation × $6.25/M	$343,750
2. Redemptions at 1.8%	990,000
3. Redemption cost 990,000 redemptions × $.67 face value	$663,300
4. Retailer handling cost and processor fees 990,000 redemptions × $.10	$99,000
5. Total program cost Items 1 + 3 + 4	$1,106,050
6. Cost per coupon redeemed Cost divided by redemption	$1.12
7. Actual product sold on redemption (misredemption estimated at 20%) 990,000 × 80%	792,000
8. Cost per product moved Program cost divided by amount of product sold	$1.40

Another problem with coupon promotions is misredemption, or the cashing of a coupon without purchase of the brand. Coupon misredemption or fraud occurs in a number of ways, including:

- Redemption of coupons by consumers for a product or size not specified on the coupon.
- Redemption of coupons by salesclerks in exchange for cash.
- Gathering and redemption of coupons by store managers or owners without the accompanying sale of the product.
- Gathering or printing of coupons by criminals who sell them to unethical merchants, who in turn redeem them.

Estimates of coupon misredemption costs are as high as $500 million.[30] Many manufacturers hold firm in their policy to not pay retailers for questionable amounts or suspicious types of coupon submissions. However, some companies are less aggressive, and this affects their profit margins. Marketers must allow a certain percentage for misredemption when estimating the costs of a couponing program. Ways to identify and control coupon misredemption, such as improved coding, are being developed, but it still remains a problem.

Coupon Distribution Coupons can be disseminated to consumers in a number of ways, including freestanding inserts in Sunday newspapers, direct mail, newspapers (either in individual ads or as a group of coupons in a cooperative format), magazines, and packages. Distribution through newspaper *freestanding inserts* is by far the most popular method for delivering coupons to consumers, accounting for over 81 percent of all coupons distributed in 1998. This growth has come at the expense of vehicles such as manufacturers' ads in newspapers (newspaper ROP), newspaper co-op ads, and magazines.

There are a number of reasons why FSIs are the most popular way of delivering coupons, including their high-quality four-color graphics, competitive distribution costs, national same-day circulation, market selectivity, and the fact that they can be competition-free due to category exclusivity (by FSI company). Prices for a full-page FSI are currently about $6 to $7 per thousand, which makes FSI promotions very efficient and affordable. Because of their consumer popularity and predictable distribution, coupons distributed in FSIs are also a strong selling point with the retail trade.

Figure 16–5 Coupon redemption rates by media

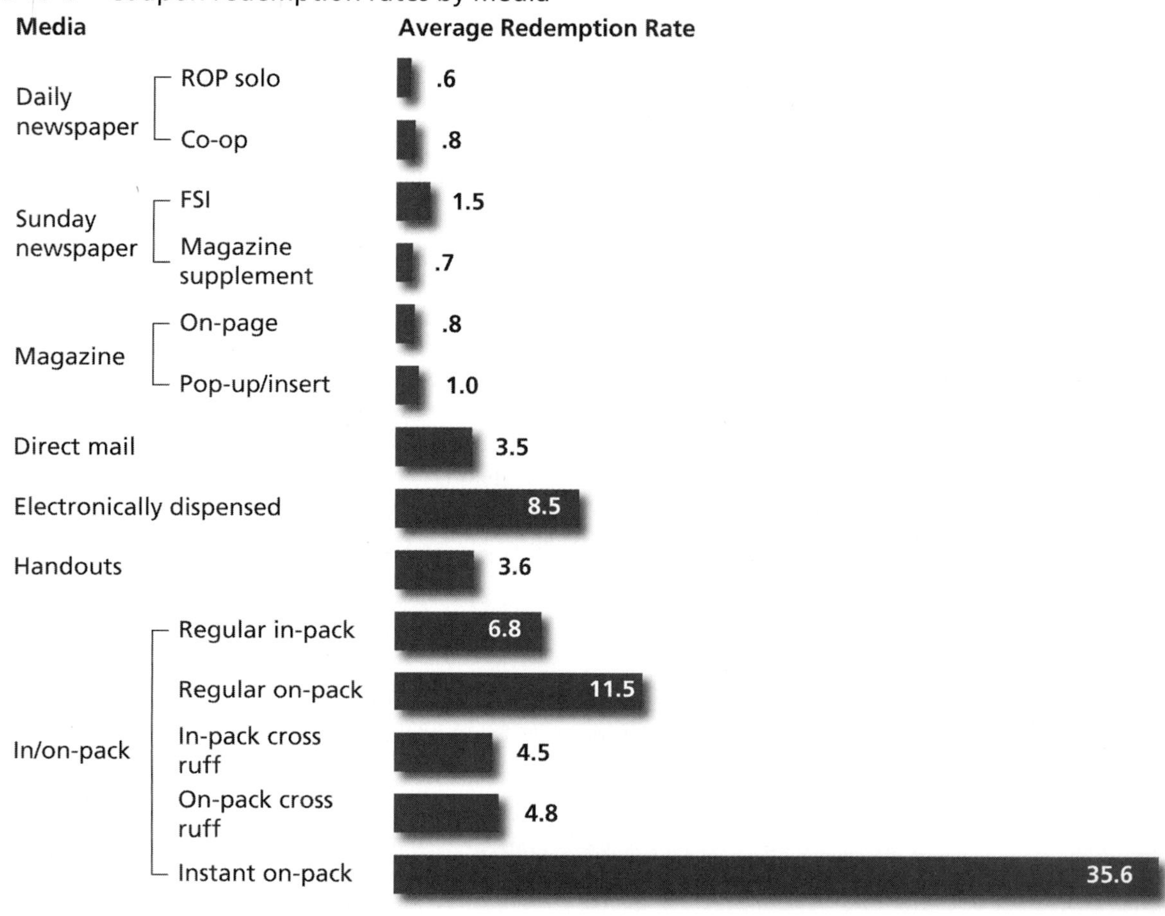

The increased distribution of coupons through FSIs has, however, led to a clutter problem. Consumers are being bombarded with too many coupons, and although each FSI publisher offers product exclusivity in its insert, this advantage may be negated when there are three inserts in a Sunday paper. Redemption rates of FSI coupons have declined from 4 percent to only 1.5 percent and even lower for some products (Figure 16–5). These problems are leading many marketers to look at ways of delivering coupons that will result in less clutter and higher redemption rates, such as direct mail.

Exhibit 16–12 Cox Target Media promotes its direct-mail couponing services

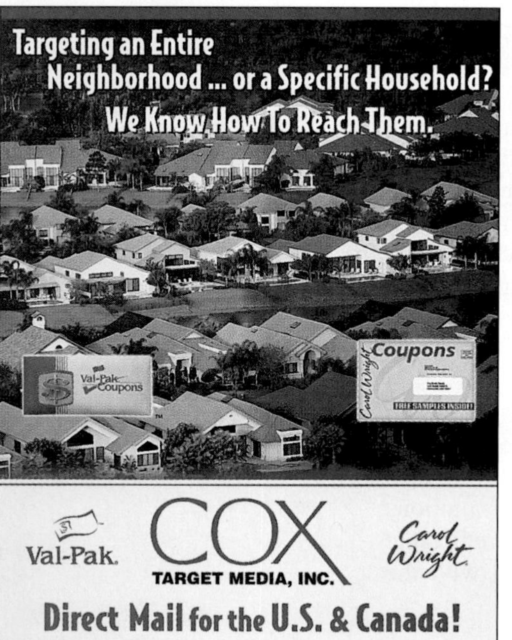

Targeting an Entire
Neighborhood ... or a Specific Household?
We Know How To Reach Them.
Coupons
Val-Pak Coupons
Val-Pak.
COX
TARGET MEDIA, INC.
Carol Wright
Direct Mail for the U.S. & Canada!

Direct mail accounts for about 2.3 percent of all coupons distributed. Most are sent by local retailers or through co-op mailings where a packet of coupons for many different products is sent to a household. These couponing programs include Metro-mail's Red Letter Day, Advo System's Mailbox Values, and Cox Target Media's Val-Pack and Carol Wright Systems. Exhibit 16–12 shows an ad promoting Cox Target Media's two programs.

Direct-mail couponing has several advantages. First, the mailing can be sent to a broad audience or targeted to specific geographic or demographic segments. Carol Wright Co-op, for example, has special mailings to teenagers, senior citizens, Hispanics, and other market segments. Firms that mail their own coupons can be quite selective about recipients. Another important advantage of direct-mail couponing is a redemption rate of nearly 4 percent, much higher than for FSIs. Direct-mail couponing can also be combined with a sample, which makes it a very effective way to gain the attention of consumers.

The major disadvantage of direct-mail coupon delivery is the expense relative to other distribution methods. The cost per thousand for distributing coupons through co-op mailings ranges from \$10 to \$15, and more targeted promotions can cost \$20 to \$25 or even more.

Also, the higher redemption rate of mail-delivered coupons may result from the fact that many recipients are already users of the brand who take advantage of the coupons sent directly to them.

The use of *newspapers* and *magazines* as couponing vehicles has declined dramatically since the introduction of FSIs. In 1998 only 1.5 percent of coupons were distributed via newspapers. The advantages of newspapers as a couponing vehicle include market selectivity, shorter lead times with timing to the day, cooperative advertising opportunities that can lead to cost efficiencies, and promotional tie-ins with retailers. Other advantages of newspaper-delivered coupons are the broad exposure and consumer receptivity. Many consumers actively search the newspaper for coupons, especially on Sundays or "food day" (when grocery stores advertise their specials). This enhances the likelihood of the consumer at least noticing the coupon. Problems with newspapers as couponing vehicles include higher distribution costs, poor reproduction quality, clutter, and declining readership of newspapers; all contribute to low redemption rates.

The use of magazines as a couponing vehicle has also declined steadily since the introduction of FSIs. Magazines now account for only about 2 percent of the total number of coupons distributed each year. Distribution of coupons through magazines can take advantage of the selectivity of the publication to reach specific target audiences, along with enhanced production capabilities and extended copy life in the home. However, the cost of distributing coupons through magazines is very high and redemption rates are low (just under 1 percent).

Placing coupons either *inside* or on the *outside* of the *package* is a distribution method that accounted for about 3 percent of the coupons distributed in 1998. The in/on package coupon has virtually no distribution costs and a much higher redemption rate than other couponing methods, averaging between 7 and 11 percent. An in/on pack coupon that is redeemable for the next purchase of the same brand is known as a **bounce-back coupon.** This type of coupon gives consumers an inducement to repurchase the brand.

Bounce-back coupons are often used with product samples to encourage the consumer to purchase the product after sampling. They may be included in or on the package during the early phases of a brand's life cycle to encourage repeat purchase, or they may be a defensive maneuver for a mature brand that is facing competitive pressure and wants to retain its current users. The main limitation of bounce-back coupons is that they go only to purchasers of the brand and thus do not attract nonusers. A bounce-back coupon placed on the package for Kellogg's Eggo brand waffles is shown in Exhibit 16–13.

Another type of in/on pack coupon is the **cross-ruff coupon,** which is redeemable on the purchase of a different product, usually one made by the same company but occasionally through a tie-in with another manufacturer. Cross-ruff coupons have a redemption rate of 4 to 5 percent and can be effective in encouraging consumers to

Exhibit 16–13 Kellogg's uses an on-package coupon to encourage repurchase

try other products or brands. Companies with wide product lines, such as cereal manufacturers, often use these coupons.

Yet another type of package coupon is the **instant coupon,** which is attached to the outside of the package so the consumer can rip it off and redeem it immediately at the time of purchase. Instant coupons have redemption levels of around 36 percent and give consumers an immediate point-of-purchase incentive. They can be selectively placed in terms of promotion timing and market region. Some companies prefer instant coupons to price-off deals because the latter require more cooperation from retailers and can be more expensive, since every package must be reduced in price.

Another distribution method that has experienced strong growth over the past 10 years or so is **in-store couponing,** which includes all co-op couponing programs distributed in a retail store environment. This medium now accounts for around 9 percent of total coupon distribution. Coupons are distributed to consumers in stores in several ways, including tear-off pads, handouts in the store (sometimes as part of a sampling demonstration), on-shelf dispensers, and electronic dispensers.

Most of the coupons distributed in stores are through ActMedia's Instant Coupon Machine. This coupon dispenser is mounted on the shelf in front of the product being promoted. It has blinking red lights to draw consumers' attention to the savings opportunity. These in-store coupons have several advantages: They can reach consumers when they are ready to make a purchase, increase brand awareness on the shelf, generate impulse buying, and encourage product trial. They also provide category exclusivity. In-store couponing removes the need for consumers to clip coupons from FSIs or print ads and then remember to bring them to the store. Redemption rates for coupons distributed by the Instant Coupon Machine are very high, averaging about 12 percent.

Another popular way to distribute in-store coupons is through electronic devices such as kiosks or at the checkout counter. Some electronically dispensed coupons, such as Catalina Marketing Corp.'s Checkout Coupon, are tied to scanner data at each grocery store checkout. When the specified product, such as a competitive brand, is purchased, the consumer receives a coupon at the checkout for the company's brand (Exhibit 16–14). Companies also use this system to link purchases of products that are related. For example, a consumer who purchases a caffeine-free cola might be issued a coupon for a decaffeinated coffee.

Major advantages of electronically dispensed checkout coupons are that they are cost-effective and can be targeted to specific categories of consumers, such as users of competitive or complementary products. Since 65 to 85 percent of a manufacturer's coupons are used by current customers, marketers want to target their coupons to users of competitive brands. Redemption rates are also high for electronically dispensed coupons, averaging around 8.5 percent.

Couponing Trends

Over the past four years the number of coupons distributed has declined by nearly 20 percent. While the average American household is still being barraged with nearly 3,000 coupons per year, many marketers have cut back on their use of coupons because of concerns over costs and effectiveness. Critics argue that coupons cost too much to print, distribute, and process and that they don't benefit enough consumers. Consumers redeemed only 2 percent of the 249 billion coupons distributed in 1998. Procter & Gamble CEO Durk Jager echoed the sentiment of many consumer-product companies when he said, "Who can argue for a practice that fails 98 percent of the time?"[31]

Jager's company has been leading the revolt against coupons; P&G has reduced its total spending on coupons by 50 percent.[32] Other consumer-product companies, such as Kimberly-Clark, Clorox, and Rubbermaid, have also been experimenting with ways to wean consumers from coupons. However, despite the growing sentiment among major marketers that coupons are inefficient and costly, very few companies, including Procter & Gamble, are likely to abandon them entirely. Although most coupons never get used, consumers use some of them and have come to expect them. More than 80 percent of consumers use coupons and nearly one-quarter say they use them every time they shop. With so many con-

Exhibit 16–14 Catalina Marketing promotes its checkout coupons

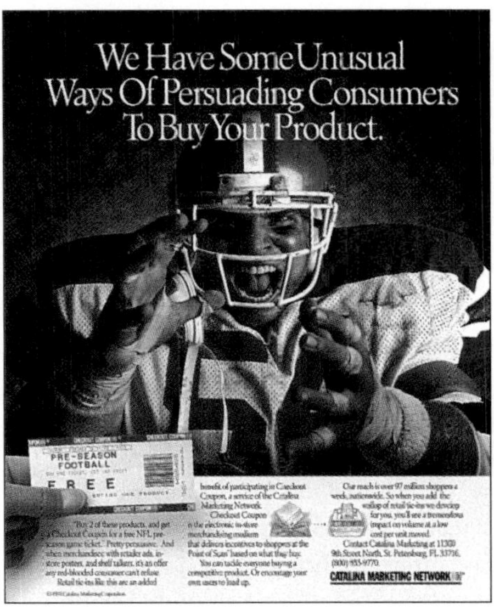

Exhibit 16–15 Coupons are now available online

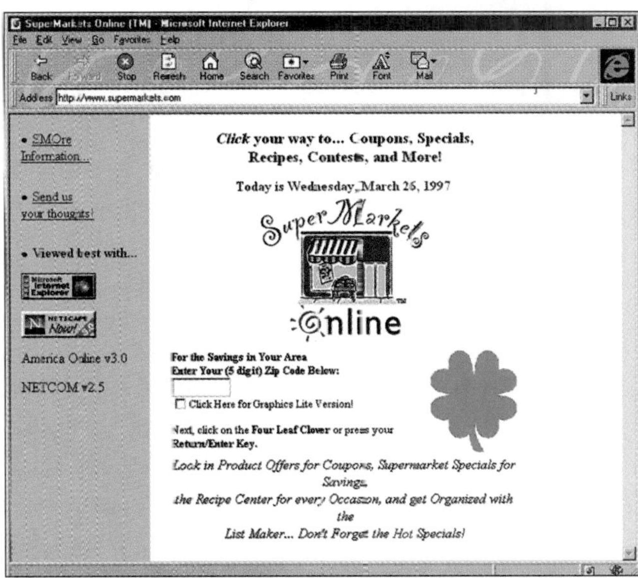

sumers eager for coupons, marketers will continue to accommodate them. However, companies as well as the coupon industry are looking for ways to improve on their use.

Marketers are continually searching for more effective couponing techniques. General Mills, Kellogg, and Post recently replaced brand-specific coupons with universal coupons good for any of their cereal brands. For example, to make its couponing spending more efficient, Post began using universal coupons worth $1.50 off two boxes (matching the average cereal-coupon discount of 75 cents) and cut coupon distribution in half. Even though Post dropped only half as many coupons, redemption rates reached 6 percent, far exceeding the FSI average of less than 2 percent.[33]

Some marketers are broadening their use of account-specific direct-mail couponing, in which coupons are cobranded with individual retailers but can be used by consumers at any retail store. Procter & Gamble began using account-specific couponing with Tide detergent and has broadened the program to include mailings for a number of other brands.[34]

Some marketers and retailers are looking to the Internet as a medium for distributing coupons.[35] Several companies now offer online couponing services. Catalina Marketing started SuperMarkets Online as a way for marketers to reach consumers at home with promotions traditionally offered in-store, including coupons. Consumers can log on to the website, type in their Zip code and choose from a list of participating grocery stores in their area and download manufacturer- and retailer-sponsored coupons (Exhibit 16–15). A number of retailers, particularly supermarkets, are also using the Internet to distribute coupons to encourage consumers to shop at their stores.

While many marketers are using the Internet for online promotions, online coupons account for less than 1 percent of all coupons distributed. One of the major problems that has kept marketers away from "e-couponing" is the risk of fraud, as it is too easy for consumers or unscrupulous retailers to mass-duplicate online coupons by printing out several, or by photocopying the black-and-white prints. There are ways to deal with this problem such as coding coupons and verifying them in-store when they are redeemed. However, this is time-consuming and not very popular with retailers. One way of getting around the problem is for marketers to offer their coupons on Planet U, a leading provider of Web-based consumer promotions. Planet U offers "U-pons" Internet coupons through a network of retailer, commercial, and marketer websites. After completing a short profile that includes an address or providing a supermarket frequent-shopper number, consumers can receive coupon savings in one of two ways. They can have the values electronically transferred to the stores where they normally shop and deducted when their frequent-shopper card is presented, or they can have the coupons mailed directly to them. Coupons sent via the mail are printed on copy-resistant paper and embedded with an extended UPC code with a unique identifier. U-pons are being used by a number of major supermarket and drugstore chains.[36]

Premiums

Premiums are a sales promotion device used by many marketers. A **premium** is an offer of an item of merchandise or service either free or at a low price that is an extra incentive for purchasers. Many marketers are eliminating toys and gimmicks in favor of value-added premiums that reflect the quality of the product and are consistent with its image and positioning in the market. Marketers spend nearly $5 billion a year on value-added premium incentives targeted at the consumer market. The two basic types of offers are the free premium and the self-liquidating premium.

Free Premiums

Free premiums are usually small gifts or merchandise included in the product package or sent to consumers who mail in a request along with a proof of purchase. In/on package free premiums include toys, balls, trading cards, or other items included in cereal packages, as well as samples of one product included with another. Surveys have shown that in/on package premiums are consumers' favorite type of promotion.[37]

Package-carried premiums have high impulse value and can provide an extra incentive to buy the product. However, several problems are associated with their use. First, there is the cost factor, which results from the premium itself as well as from extra packaging that may be needed. Finding desirable premiums at reasonable costs can be difficult, particularly for adult markets, and using a poor premium may do more harm than good.

Another problem with these premiums is possible restrictions from regulatory agencies such as the Federal Trade Commission and the Food and Drug Administration or from industry codes regarding the type of premium used. The National Association of Broadcasters has strict guidelines regarding the advertising of premium offers to children. There is concern that premium offers will entice children to request a brand to get the promoted item and then never consume the product. The networks' policy on children's advertising is that a premium offer cannot exceed 15 seconds of a 30-second spot, and the emphasis must be on the product, not the premium.

Since most free mail-in premium offers require the consumer to send in more than one proof of purchase, they encourage repeat purchase and reward brand loyalty. But a major drawback of mail-in premiums is that they do not offer immediate reinforcement or reward to the purchaser, so they may not provide enough incentive to purchase the brand. Few consumers take advantage of mail-in premium offers; the average redemption rate is only 2 to 4 percent.[38]

Exhibit 16–16 McDonald's Happy Meals use toys to help attract children

Free premiums have become very popular in the restaurant industry, particularly among fast-food chains such as McDonald's and Burger King, which use premium offers in their kids' meals to attract children.[39] McDonald's has become the world's largest toymaker on a unit basis, commissioning about 750 million toys per year for its Happy Meals (Exhibit 16–16). Many of the premium offers used by the fast-food giants have cross-promotional tie-ins with popular movies and can be very effective at generating incremental sales. McDonald's gained a major competitive advantage in the movie tie-in premium wars in 1996 when it signed an agreement with Disney giving McDonald's exclusive rights to promotional tie-ins with Disney movies for 10 years.[40] In late 1999 McDonald's won another round of the tie-in wars by signing an exclusive promotional deal with "Teletubbies," the popular PBS children's series which had previously partnered with Burger King for promotions.[41] Burger King's problems were compounded when its major promotion with the animated film *Pokemon: The First Movie,* had to be canceled after several young children suffocated on the plastic balls used as part of the giveaway.[42]

One of the fastest-growing types of incentive offers being used by marketers is airline miles, which have literally become a promotional currency. U.S. airlines make more than an estimated $2 billion each year selling miles to other marketers. Consumers are now choosing credit-card services, phone services, hotels, and many other products and services on the basis of mileage premiums for major frequent flyer programs such as American Airlines' AAdvantage program or United Airlines' Mileage Plus program. Exhibit 16–17 shows an ad promoting United's Mileage Plus Visa which allows users to earn miles in the airline's frequent flyer program when they use the credit card.

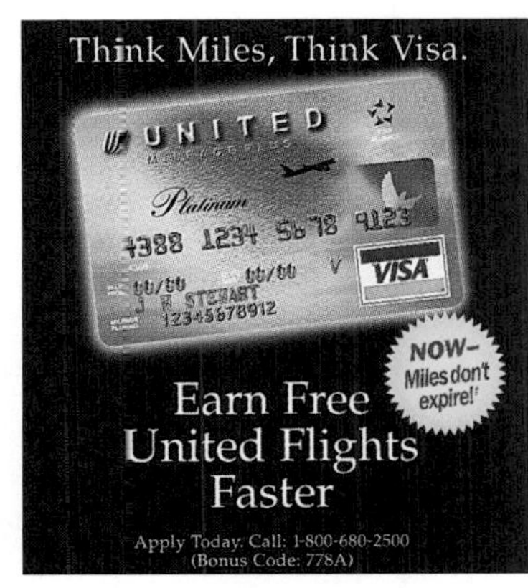

Exhibit 16–17 Many consumers now use credit cards that offer miles in frequent flyer programs, such as United's Mileage Plus, as an incentive

Self-Liquidating Premiums

Self-liquidating premiums require the consumer to pay some or all of the cost of the premium plus handling and mailing costs. The marketer usually purchases items used as self-liquidating premiums in large quantities and offers them to consumers at lower-than-retail prices. The goal is not to make a profit on the premium item but rather just to cover costs and offer a value to the consumer.

In addition to cost savings, self-liquidating premiums offer several advantages to marketers. Offering values to consumers through the premium products can create interest in the brand and goodwill that enhances the brand's image. These premiums can also encourage trade support and gain in-store displays for the brand and the premium offer. Self-liquidating premiums are often tied directly to the advertising campaign, so they extend the advertising message and contribute to consumer franchise building for a brand. For example, Philip Morris offers Western wear, outdoor items, and other types of Marlboro gear through its Marlboro Country catalog, which reinforces the cigarette brand's positioning theme.

Self-liquidating premium offers have the same basic limitation as mail-in premiums: a very low redemption rate. Fewer than 10 percent of U.S. households have ever sent for a premium, and fewer than 1 percent of self-liquidating offers are actually redeemed.[43] Low redemption rates can leave the marketer with a large supply of items with a logo or some other brand identification that makes them hard to dispose of. Thus, it is important to test consumers' reaction to a premium incentive and determine whether they perceive the offer as a value. Another option is to use premiums with no brand identification, but that detracts from their consumer franchise-building value.

Contests and Sweepstakes

Contests and sweepstakes are an increasingly popular consumer-oriented promotion. Marketers spent nearly $3 billion on these promotions in 1998. These promotions seem to have an appeal and glamour that tools like cents-off coupons lack. Contests and sweepstakes are exciting because, as one expert has noted, many consumers have a "pot of gold at the end of the rainbow mentality" and think they can win the big prizes being offered.[44] The lure of sweepstakes and promotions has also been influenced by the "instant-millionaire syndrome" that has derived from huge cash prizes given by many state lotteries in recent years. Marketers are attracted to contests and sweepstakes as a way of generating attention and interest among a large number of consumers. For example, a recent sweepstakes run by AT&T WorldNet generated more than 4 million entries and 70,000 new Internet subscriber services.[45]

There are differences between contests and sweepstakes. A **contest** is a promotion where consumers compete for prizes or money on the basis of skills or ability. The company determines winners by judging the entries or ascertaining which entry comes closest to some predetermined criteria (e.g., picking the winning teams and total number of points in the Super Bowl or NCAA basketball tournament). Contests usually provide a purchase incentive by requiring a proof of purchase to enter or an entry form that is available from a dealer or advertisement. Some contests require consumers to read an ad or package or visit a store display to gather information needed to enter. Marketers must be careful not to make their contests too difficult to enter, as doing so might discourage participation among key prospects in the target audience.

A **sweepstakes** is a promotion where winners are determined purely by chance; it cannot require a proof of purchase as a condition for entry. Entrants need only submit their names for the prize drawing. While there is often an official entry form, handwritten entries must also be permitted. One form of sweepstakes is a **game,** which also has a chance element or odds of winning. Scratch-off cards with instant winners are a popular promotional tool. Some games occur over a longer period and require more involvement by consumers. Promotions where consumers must collect game pieces are popular among retailers and fast-food chains as a way to build store traffic and repeat purchases. For example, McDonald's has used promotions based on the game *Monopoly* several times in recent years.

Because they are easier to enter, sweepstakes attract more entries than contests. They are also easier and less expensive to administer, since every entry does not have to be checked or judged. Choosing the winning entry in a sweepstakes requires only the random selection of a winner from the pool of entries or generation of a number to match those held by sweepstakes entrants. Experts note that the costs of mounting a sweepstakes are also very predictable. Companies can buy insurance to indemnify them and protect against the expense of awarding a big prize. In general, sweepstakes present marketers with a fixed cost, which is a major advantage when budgeting for a promotion.

Contests and sweepstakes can get the consumer involved with a brand by making the promotion product relevant. For example, contests that ask consumers to suggest a name for a product or to submit recipes that use the brand can increase involvement levels. Nabisco developed an "Open a box, make up a snack," promotional contest for its three top cracker brands—Ritz, Triscuit, and Wheat Thins. Consumers sent in their favorite recipes, which were then made available on a dedicated website and at a toll-free number.

Exhibit 16–18 The Gillette 3-Point Challenge sweepstakes is tied to a popular sporting event

Sweepstakes and games can also be used to generate excitement by involving people with a popular and timely event. For example, the Gillette 3-Point Challenge offers consumers a chance to win a trip to the NCAA Men's or Women's Final Four basketball tournament and take a three-point shot worth $1 million (Exhibit 16–18). Marketers can use contests and sweepstakes to build brand equity by connecting the prizes to the lifestyle, needs, or interests of the target audience. For example, the prize in the Gillette 3-Point Challenge sweepstakes would be very relevant to the interests of college basketball fans and thus would help Gillette build brand equity among this target audience.

Problems with Contests and Sweepstakes

While the use of contests and sweepstakes continues to increase, there are some problems associated with these types of promotions. Many sweepstakes and/or contest promotions do little to contribute to consumer franchise building for a product or service and may even detract from it. The sweepstakes or contest often becomes the dominant focus rather than the brand, and little is accomplished other than giving away substantial amounts of money and/or prizes. Many promotional experts question the effectiveness of contests and sweepstakes. Some companies have cut back or even stopped using them because of concern over their effectiveness and fears that consumers might become dependent on them.[46] The sweepstakes industry also received a considerable amount of negative publicity recently. Lawsuits were filed by a number of states against American Family Publishing for misleading consumers regarding their odds of winning large cash prizes in AFP's annual magazine subscription solicitation sweepstakes.[47]

Numerous legal considerations affect the design and administration of contests and sweepstakes.[48] These promotions are regulated by several federal agencies, and each of the 50 states has its own rules. The regulation of contests and sweepstakes has helped clean up the abuses that plagued the industry in the late 1960s and has improved consumers' perceptions of these promotions. But companies must still be careful in designing a contest or sweepstakes and awarding prizes. Most firms use consultants that specialize in the design and administration of contests and sweepstakes to avoid any legal problems, but they may still run into problems with promotions, as discussed in Global Perspective 16–2.

A final problem with contests and sweepstakes is participation by professionals or hobbyists who submit many entries but have no intention of purchasing the product or service. Because most states make it illegal to require a purchase as a qualification for a sweepstakes entry, consumers can enter as many times as they wish. Professional players sometimes enter one sweepstakes several times, depending on the nature of the prizes and the number of entries the promotion attracts. Newsletters are even available that inform them of all the contests and sweepstakes being held, the entry dates, estimated probabilities of winning for various numbers of entries, how to enter, and solutions to any puzzles or other information that might be needed. The presence of these professional entrants not only defeats the purpose of the promotion but may also discourage entries from consumers who think their chances of winning are limited.

Refunds and Rebates

Refunds (also known as rebates) are offers by the manufacturer to return a portion of the product purchase price, usually after the consumer supplies some proof of purchase. Consumers are generally very responsive to rebate offers, particularly as the size of the savings increases. Rebates are used by makers of all types of products, ranging from package goods to major appliances, cars, and computer software. Exhibit 16–19 shows an ad promoting a $30 rebate on Intuit's popular tax and financial software products, TurboTax and Quicken.

Exhibit 16–19 Intuit uses a rebate offer to promote its Quicken software products

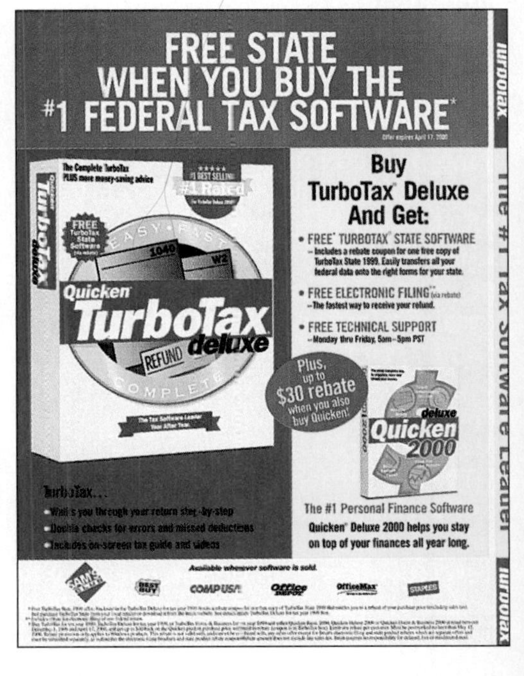

Package-goods marketers often use refund offers to induce trial of a new product or encourage users of another brand to switch. Consumers may perceive the savings offered through a cash refund as an immediate value that lowers the cost of the item, even though those savings are realized only if the consumer redeems the refund or rebate offer. Redemption rates for refund offers typically range from 1 to 3 percent for print and point-of-purchase offers and 5 percent for in/on package offers.

Refund offers can also encourage repeat purchase. Many offers require consumers to send in multiple proofs of purchase. The size of the refund offer may even increase as the number of purchases gets larger. Some package-goods companies are switching away from cash refund offers to coupons or cash/coupon combinations. Using coupons in the refund offer enhances the likelihood of repeat purchase of the brand.

Rebates have become a widely used form of promotion for consumer durables. Products such as cameras, sporting goods, appliances, televisions, audio and video equipment, computers, and cars frequently use rebate offers to appeal to price-conscious consumers. The use of rebates for expensive items like cars was begun by Chrysler Corp. in 1981 to boost sales and generate cash for the struggling company. Rebates are now common not only in the auto industry and other durable products but for package-goods products as well.

Evaluating Refunds and Rebates

Rebates can help create new users and encourage brand switching or repeat purchase behavior, or they can be a way to offer a temporary price reduction. The rebate may be perceived as an immediate

Global Perspective 16–2

Promotions Don't Always Go as Planned

Contests, sweepstakes, and other types of promotions are often used by marketers to give consumers an extra incentive to buy their products. However, when these promotions don't go as planned, they can embarrass a company or even create legal problems. Several major companies known for their marketing excellence have experienced major promotional blunders in recent years, both in the United States and abroad.

Coca-Cola lost millions of dollars and went through great turmoil in the summer of 1991 when its "Magi-can" promotion went awry. The liquid used to give the high-tech prize-bearing cans the same heft as Coke's regular cans leaked and the promotion had to be canceled. The Beatrice Co. ran into major legal problems when a computer buff cracked the contest code of a promotion tied to ABC's "Monday Night Football" and turned in 4,000 scratch-off cards worth $21 million in prize money. Millions of dollars in lawsuits were filed, although the case was eventually settled out of court.

Kraft also found out how expensive it can be when a promotion goes awry. A printing error resulted in tens of thousands of winning pieces being printed in a match-and-win sweepstakes for its cheese brands. Kraft canceled the promotion but still had to spend nearly $3.8 million to compensate the winners—versus the $36,000 budgeted for prizes. The snafu gave birth to what promotional professionals call "the Kraft clause," a disclaimer stating that a marketer reserves the right to cancel a promotion if there are problems and that a random drawing will be held if there are more winners than prizes.

These botched promotions were embarrassing for the companies and resulted in the loss of goodwill as well as money. But the consequences can be even worse, as PepsiCo discovered when a bottle-cap promotion went wrong in the Philippines. The local Pepsi bottler launched a Number Fever promotion offering a grand prize of 1 million pesos (about $36,000) to holders of bottle caps with the number 349 printed on them. Due to a computer glitch, the winning number appeared on more than 500,000 bottle caps, making the company liable for more than $18 billion in prize money.

When the error was discovered, Pepsi announced the problem and quickly offered to pay $19 for each winning cap. While more than 500,000 Filipinos have collected nearly $10 million from the company, thousands of others pursued the full amount in civil and criminal courts. The Filipino justice department found that Pepsi was not criminally liable and dismissed 7,000 lawsuits, but others are still pending. The furor caused by the botched promotion prompted anti-Pepsi rallies, death threats against Pepsi executives, and attacks on Pepsi trucks and bottling plants.

Sometimes marketers can run into problems when a promotion works too well. In Australia, a promotion for Sloggies pantyhose invited women to submit proofs of purchase from their packages in return for a free night at one of the 30 Best Western hotels in the country. The goal was to get them into the hotels and to encourage them to stay an extra night at their own expense. Problems arose when the brand didn't enforce an eligibility period or place promotion expiration dates on the pantyhose packages. Consumer response to the promotion was overwhelming and Best Westerns were overrun with calls from women wanting to book their free nights but very few asked for a second night. Thousands of consumers were turned away and many more were told rooms would not be available for months, and in some cases years, down the road.

Maytag Corp. also learned the hard way when it ran a promotion in the United Kingdom offering two free round-trip airline tickets with a purchase of a Hoover appliance for $150 or more. Nearly 100,000 consumers responded and it cost the company $48 million to cover the airfares. To make matters worse, Hoover's booking system couldn't order tickets fast enough, generating ill will among consumers and negative publicity for the company.

New technologies, especially the Internet, will provide new territory for various types of promotions. But as these examples show, marketers need to plan carefully when designing promotions at home or in foreign markets. Promotional blunders can cost companies millions of dollars in damages, as well as a slew of bad PR that will haunt it for years to come.

Sources: Amie Smith, "Learning from the Mistakes of Others," *Promo,* August 1998, pp. S8–9; Glenn Heitsmith and Betsy Spethmann, "The Perils of Promotion," *Promo,* November 1996, pp. 22, 134; "Botched Pepsi Promotion Prompts Terrorist Attacks," *Promo,* September 1993, p. 10.

savings even though many consumers do not follow through on the offer. This perception can influence purchase even if the consumer fails to realize the savings, so the marketer can reduce price for much less than if it used a direct price-off deal.

Some problems are associated with refunds and rebates. Many consumers are not motivated by a refund offer because of the delay and the effort required to obtain the savings. They do not want to be bothered saving cash register receipts and proofs of purchase, filling out forms, and mailing in the offer.[49] A study of consumer perceptions found a negative relationship between the use of rebates and the perceived difficulties associated with the redemption process.[50] The study also found that consumers perceive manufacturers as offering rebates to sell products that are not faring well. Nonusers of rebates were particularly likely to perceive the redemption process as too complicated and to suspect manufacturers' motives. This implies that companies using rebates must simplify the redemption process and use other promotional elements such as advertising to retain consumer confidence in the brand.

When small refunds are being offered, marketers may find other promotional incentives such as coupons or bonus packs more effective. They must be careful not to overuse rebate offers and confuse consumers about the real price and value of a product or service. Also, consumers can become dependent on rebates and delay their purchases or purchase only brands for which a rebate is available. Many retailers have become disenchanted with rebates and the burden and expense of administering them.[51]

Bonus Packs

Bonus packs offer the consumer an extra amount of a product at the regular price by providing larger containers or extra units (Exhibit 16–20). Bonus packs result in a lower cost per unit for the consumer and provide extra value as well as more product for the money. There are several advantages to bonus pack promotions. First, they give marketers a direct way to provide extra value without having to get involved with complicated coupons or refund offers. The additional value of a bonus pack is generally obvious to the consumer and can have a strong impact on the purchase decision at the time of purchase.

Bonus packs can also be an effective defensive maneuver against a competitor's promotion or introduction of a new brand. By loading current users with large amounts of its product, a marketer can often remove these consumers from the market and make them less susceptible to a competitor's promotional efforts. Bonus packs may result in larger purchase orders and favorable display space in the store if relationships with retailers are good. They do, however, usually require additional shelf space without providing any extra profit margins for the retailer, so the marketer can encounter problems with bonus packs if trade relationships are not good. Another problem is that bonus packs may appeal primarily to current users who probably would have purchased the brand anyway or to promotion-sensitive consumers who may not become loyal to the brand.

Exhibit 16–20 Bonus packs provide more value for consumers

Price-Off Deals

Another consumer-oriented promotion technique is the direct **price-off deal,** which reduces the price of the brand. Price-off reductions are typically offered right on the package through specially marked price packs, as shown in Exhibit 16–21. Typically, price-offs range from 10 to 25 percent off the regular price, with the reduction coming out of the manufacturer's profit margin, not the retailer's. Keeping the retailer's margin during a price-off promotion maintains its support and cooperation.

Marketers use price-off promotions for several reasons. First, since price-offs are controlled by the manufacturer, it can make sure the promotional discount reaches the consumer rather than being kept by the trade. Like bonus packs, price-off deals usually present a readily apparent value to shoppers, especially when they have a reference price point for the brand and thus recognize the value of the discount.[52] So

Exhibit 16–21 Examples of price-off packages

price-offs can be a strong influence at the point of purchase when price comparisons are being made. Price-off promotions can also encourage consumers to purchase larger quantities, preempting competitors' promotions and leading to greater trade support.

Price-off promotions may not be favorably received by retailers, since they can create pricing and inventory problems. Most retailers will not accept packages with a specific price shown, so the familiar X amount off the regular price must be used. Also, like bonus packs, price-off deals appeal primarily to regular users instead of attracting nonusers. Finally, the Federal Trade Commission has regulations regarding the conditions that price-off labels must meet and the frequency and timing of their use.

Frequency Programs

One of the fastest growing areas of sales promotion is the use of **frequency programs** (also referred to as *continuity* or *loyalty programs*). American Airlines was one of the first major companies to use loyalty programs when it introduced its AAdvantage frequent flyer program in 1981. Since then frequency programs have become commonplace in a number of product and service categories, particularly travel and hospitality, as well as among retailers. Virtually every airline, car rental company, and hotel chain has some type of frequency program. American Airlines has nearly 32 million members in its AAdvantage program, while Marriott International has enlisted more than 10 million business travelers into its Rewards program.

Many package-goods companies are also developing frequency programs. Pillsbury, Nestlé, Kraft, and others have recently introduced continuity programs that offer consumers the opportunity to accumulate points for continuing to purchase their brands; the points can be redeemed for gifts and prizes. For example, Gerber Baby Foods has developed a frequency program known as Gerber Rewards, in which consumers who purchase 16 or more Gerber products at one time automatically receive a game-piece coupon carrying a unique PIN number and an 800 phone number.[53] Customers call the phone number, punch in the PIN number, and receive points for entry into a sweepstakes giving away a $250,000 college scholarship. Consumers earn more points with subsequent purchases of Gerber products (Exhibit 16–22).

Exhibit 16–22 Gerber Rewards is an example of a loyalty program that helps build a customer database and encourages consumers to purchase more Gerber baby products

Frequency programs have become particularly popular among grocery stores.[54] Nearly 7,000 supermarkets now have loyalty programs that offer members discounts, a chance to accumulate points that can be redeemed for rewards, newsletters, and other special services. Loyalty programs are also used by a variety of other retailers, including department stores, home centers, bookstores, and even local bagel shops.

There are a number of reasons why frequency programs have become so popular. Marketers view these programs as a way of encouraging consumers to use their products or services on a continual basis and as a way of developing strong customer loyalty. Many companies are also realizing the importance of customer retention and understand that the key to retaining and growing market share is building relationships with loyal customers. Frequency programs also provide marketers with the opportunity to develop databases containing valuable information on their customers that can be used to better understand their needs, interests, and characteristics as well as to identify and track a company's most valuable customers. These databases can also be used to target specific programs and offers to customers to increase the amount they purchase and/or to build stronger relationships with them. For example, as part of the Gerber Rewards program discussed above, the company developed a database on those entering the sweepstakes that includes the ages of their children. Participants in the program periodically receive direct mail offers of discounts and deals on Gerber products that are based on the ages of their children.

As frequency programs become more common, marketers will be challenged to find ways to use them as a means of differentiating their product, service, business, or retail store. Marketers must find ways to make them true loyalty programs rather than just frequent-buyer programs. This will require the careful management of databases to identify and track valuable customers and their purchase history and the strategic use of targeted loyalty promotions.

Event Marketing

Another type of consumer-oriented promotion that has become very popular in recent years is the use of event marketing. It is important to make a distinction between *event marketing* and *event sponsorships,* as the two terms are often used interchangeably yet they refer to different activities. **Event marketing** is a type of promotion where a company or brand is linked to an event or where a themed activity is developed for the purpose of creating experiences for consumers and promoting a product or service. Marketers often do event marketing by associating their product with some popular activity such as a sporting event, concert, fair, or festival. However, marketers also create their own events to use for promotional purposes. For example, RC Cola staged events to launch RC Edge Maximum Power, a new soda targeted at teens that contains Indian ginseng and taurine in addition to caffeine. RC put together a 25-market tour that included radio tie-ins and "Edgy" events such as white-water rafting and skydiving at which samples of the product were distributed (Exhibit 16–23). The comarketing promotion Coppertone created for Wal-Mart, which was discussed in IMC Perspective 16–1, is an example of an in-store event marketing activity.

An **event sponsorship** is an integrated marketing communications activity where a company develops actual sponsorship relations with a particular event and provides financial support in return for the right to display a brand name, logo, or advertising message and be identified as a supporter of the event. Event marketing often takes place as part of a company's sponsorship of activities such as concerts, the arts, social causes, and sporting events. Decisions and objectives for event

Exhibit 16–23 RC Cola used event marketing to introduce Edge Maximum Power

sponsorships are often part of an organization's public relations activities and are discussed in the next chapter.

Event marketing has become very popular in recent years as marketers develop integrated marketing programs including a variety of promotional tools that create experiences for consumers in an effort to associate their brands with certain lifestyles and activities. Marketers use events to distribute samples as well as information about their products and services or to actually let consumers experience the product.

Summary of Consumer-Oriented Promotions and Marketer Objectives

The discussion of the various sales promotion techniques shows that marketers use these tools to accomplish a variety of objectives. As noted at the beginning of the chapter, sales promotion techniques provide consumers with an *extra incentive or reward* for engaging in a certain form of behavior such as purchasing a brand. For some types of sales promotion tools the incentive the consumer receives is immediate, while for others the reward is delayed and is not realized immediately. Marketers often evaluate sales promotion tools in terms of their ability to accomplish specific objectives and consider whether the impact of the promotion will be immediate or delayed. The chart in Figure 16–6 outlines which sales promotion tools can be used to accomplish various objectives of marketers and identifies whether the extra incentive or reward is immediate or delayed.[55]

It should be noted that in Figure 16–6 some of the sales promotion techniques are listed more than once because they can be used to accomplish more than one objective. For example, loyalty programs can be used to retain customers by providing both immediate and delayed rewards. Shoppers who belong to loyalty programs sponsored by supermarkets and receive discounts every time they make a purchase are receiving immediate rewards that are designed to retain them as customers. Some loyalty promotions such as frequency programs used by airlines, car rental companies, and hotels offer delayed rewards by requiring that users accumulate points to reach a certain level or status before the points can be redeemed. Loyalty programs can also be used by marketers to help build brand equity. For example, when an airline or car rental company sends its frequent users upgrade certificates, the practice helps build relationships with these customers and thus contributes to brand equity.

While marketers use consumer-oriented sales promotions to provide current and/or potential customers with an extra incentive, they also use these promotions

Figure 16–6 Consumer-oriented sales promotion tools for various marketing objectives

Consumer Reward Incentive	Marketing Objective: Induce trial	Customer retention/loading	Support IMC program/ build brand equity
Immediate	• Sampling • Instant coupons • In-store coupons • In-store rebates	• Price-off deals • Bonus packs • In- and on-package free premiums • Loyalty programs	• Events • In- and on-package free premiums
Delayed	• Media- and mail-delivered coupons • Mail-in refunds and rebates • Free mail-in premiums • Scanner- and Internet-delivered coupons	• In- and on-package coupons • Mail-in refunds and rebates • Loyalty programs	• Self-liquidating premiums • Free mail-in premiums • Contests and sweepstakes • Loyalty programs

as part of their marketing program to leverage trade support. Retailers are more likely to stock a brand, purchase extra quantities, or provide additional support such as end-aisle displays when they know a manufacturer is running a promotion during a designated period. The development of promotional programs targeted toward the trade is a very important part of the marketing process and is discussed in the next section.

Trade-Oriented Sales Promotion

Objectives of Trade-Oriented Sales Promotion

Like consumer-oriented promotions, sales promotion programs targeted to the trade should be based on well-defined objectives and measurable goals and a consideration of what the marketer wants to accomplish. Typical objectives for promotions targeted to marketing intermediaries such as wholesalers and retailers include obtaining distribution and support for new products, maintaining support for established brands, encouraging retailers to display established brands, and building retail inventories.

Obtain Distribution for New Products

Trade promotions are often used to encourage retailers to give shelf space to new products. Manufacturers recognize that only a limited amount of shelf space is available in supermarkets, drugstores, and other major retail outlets. Thus, they provide retailers with financial incentives to stock new products. For example, Lever Brothers used heavy sampling and high-value coupons in the successful introduction of Lever 2000 bar soap. However, in addition to these consumer promotions, the company used discounts to the trade to encourage retailers to stock and promote the new brand.

While trade discounts or other special price deals are used to encourage retailers and wholesalers to stock a new brand, marketers may use other types of promotions to get them to push the brand. Merchandising allowances can get retailers to display a new product in high-traffic areas of stores, while incentive programs or contests can encourage wholesale or retail store personnel to push a new brand.

Maintain Trade Support for Established Brands

Trade promotions are often designed to maintain distribution and trade support for established brands. Brands that are in the mature phase of their product life cycle are vulnerable to losing wholesale and/or retail distribution, particularly if they are not differentiated or face competition from new products. Trade deals induce wholesalers and retailers to continue to carry weaker products because the discounts increase their profit margins. Brands with a smaller market share often rely heavily on trade promotions, since they lack the funds required to differentiate themselves from competitors through media advertising.

Even if a brand has a strong market position, trade promotions may be used as part of an overall marketing strategy. As discussed previously, Heinz has relied heavily on trade promotions to hold its market share position for many of its brands. Many consumer-package-goods companies count on trade promotions to maintain retail distribution and support.

Encourage Retailers to Display Established Brands

Another objective of trade-oriented promotions is to encourage retailers to display and promote an established brand. Marketers recognize that many purchase decisions are made in the store and promotional displays are an excellent way of generating sales. An important goal is to obtain retail store displays of a product away from its regular shelf location. A typical supermarket has approximately 50 display areas at the ends of aisles, near checkout counters, and elsewhere. Marketers want to have their products displayed in these areas to increase the probability shoppers will come into contact with them. Even a single display can increase a brand's sales significantly during a promotion.

Exhibit 16–24 This brochure shows retailers the various promotions Chicken of the Sea planned to use in 2000 for its tuna brand

Manufacturers often use multifaceted promotional programs to encourage retailers to promote their products at the retail level. For example, Exhibit 16–24 shows a brochure that Chicken of the Sea International provided to retailers showing the various promotions the company planned to use during the year 2000 for its Chicken of the Sea brand tuna. The company used a variety of promotional tools to support the brand and increase retailer participation. These included advertising in local newspapers, FSI and direct mail coupons, in-store displays, premium offers, recipe handouts, Web support, contests, and a continuity program.

Build Retail Inventories

Manufacturers often use trade promotions to build the inventory levels of retailers or other channel members. There are several reasons manufacturers want to load retailers with their products. First, wholesalers and retailers are more likely to push a product when they have high inventory levels rather than storing it in their warehouses or back rooms. Building channel members' inventories also ensures they will not run out of stock and thus miss sales opportunities.

Some manufacturers of seasonal products offer large promotional discounts so that retailers will stock up on their products before the peak selling season begins. This enables the manufacturer to smooth out seasonal fluctuations in its production schedule and passes on some of the inventory carrying costs to retailers or wholesalers. When retailers stock up on a product before the peak selling season, they often run special promotions and offer discounts to consumers to reduce excess inventories.

Types of Trade-Oriented Promotions

Manufacturers use a variety of trade promotion tools as inducements for wholesalers and retailers. Next we examine some of the most often used types of trade promotions and some factors marketers must consider in using them. These promotions include contests and incentives, trade allowances, displays and point-of-purchase materials, sales training programs, trade shows, and co-op advertising.

Contests and Incentives

Manufacturers may develop contests or special incentive programs to stimulate greater selling effort and support from reseller management or sales personnel. Contests or incentive programs can be directed toward managers who work for a wholesaler or distributor as well as toward store or department managers at the retail level. Manufacturers often sponsor contests for resellers and use prizes such as trips or valuable merchandise as rewards for meeting sales quotas or other goals. Exhibit 16–25 shows a contest Chicken of the Sea sponsored for food-service distributors who call on restaurants.

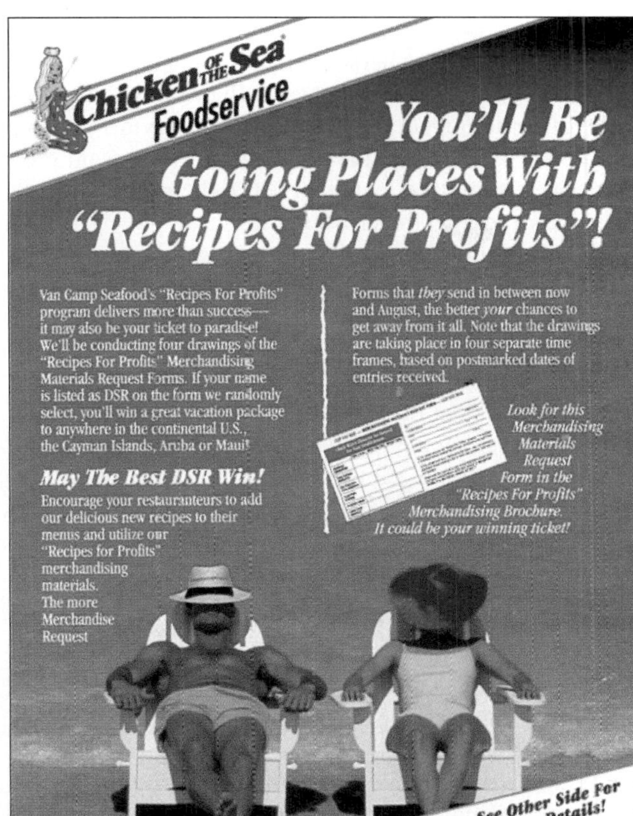

Exhibit 16–25 This contest sponsored by Chicken of the Sea was targeted toward food-service distributors

Contests or special incentives are often targeted at the sales personnel of the wholesalers, distributors/dealers, or retailers. These salespeople are an important link in the distribution chain because they are likely to be very familiar with the market, more frequently in touch with the customer (whether it be another reseller or the ultimate consumer), and more numerous than the manufacturer's own sales organization. Manufacturers often devise incentives or contests for these sales personnel. These programs may involve cash payments made directly to the retailer's or wholesaler's sales staff to encourage them to promote and sell a manufacturer's product. These payments are known as **push money** (pm) or *spiffs*. For example, an appliance manufacturer may pay a $25 spiff to retail sales personnel for selling a certain model or size. In sales contests, salespeople can win trips or valuable merchandise for meeting certain goals established by the manufacturer. As shown in Figure 16–7, these incentives may be tied to product sales, new account placements, or merchandising efforts.

- **Product or Program Sales**
  Awards are tied to the selling of a product, for example:
  - Selling a specified number of cases
  - Selling a specified number of units
  - Selling a specified number of promotional programs
- **New Account Placements**
  Awards are tied to:
  - The number of new accounts opened
  - The number of new accounts ordering a minimum number of cases or units
  - Promotional programs placed in new accounts
- **Merchandising Efforts**
  Awards are tied to:
  - Establishing promotional programs (such as theme programs)
  - Placing display racks, counter displays, and the like

Figure 16–7 Three forms of promotion targeted to reseller salespeople

While contests and incentive programs can generate reseller support, they can also be a source of conflict between retail sales personnel and management. Some retailers want to maintain control over the selling activities of their sales staff. They don't want their salespeople devoting an undue amount of effort to trying to win a contest or receive incentives offered by the manufacturer. Nor do they want their people becoming too aggressive in pushing products that serve their own interests instead of the product or model that is best for the customer.

Many retailers refuse to let their employees participate in manufacturer-sponsored contests or to accept incentive payments. Retailers that do allow them often have strict guidelines and require management approval of the program.

Trade Allowances

Probably the most common trade promotion is some form of **trade allowance,** a discount or deal offered to retailers or wholesalers to encourage them to stock, promote, or display the manufacturer's products. Types of allowances offered to retailers include buying allowances, promotional or display allowances, and slotting allowances.

Buying Allowances A buying allowance is a deal or discount offered to resellers in the form of a price reduction on merchandise ordered during a fixed period. These discounts are often in the form of an **off-invoice allowance,** which means a certain per-case amount or percentage is deducted from the invoice. A buying allowance can also take the form of *free goods;* the reseller gets extra cases with the purchase of specific amounts (for example, 1 free case with every 10 cases purchased).

Buying allowances are used for several reasons. They are easy to implement and are well accepted, and sometimes expected, by the trade. They are also an effective way to encourage resellers to buy the manufacturer's product, since they will want to take advantage of the discounts being offered during the allowance period. Manufacturers offer trade discounts expecting wholesalers and retailers to pass the price reduction through to consumers, resulting in greater sales. However, as discussed shortly, this is often not the case.

Promotional Allowances Manufacturers often give retailers allowances or discounts for performing certain promotional or merchandising activities in support of their brands. These merchandising allowances can be given for providing special displays away from the product's regular shelf position, running in-store promotional programs, or including the product in an ad. The manufacturer generally has guidelines or a contract specifying the activity to be performed to qualify for the promotional allowance. The allowance is usually a fixed amount per case or a percentage deduction from the list price for merchandise ordered during the promotional period.

Slotting Allowances In recent years, retailers have been demanding a special allowance for agreeing to handle a new product. *Slotting allowances,* also called *stocking allowances, introductory allowances,* or *street money,* are fees retailers charge for providing a slot or position to accommodate the new product. Retailers justify these fees by pointing out the costs associated with taking on so many new products each year, such as redesigning store shelves, entering the product into their computers, finding warehouse space, and briefing store employees on the new product.[56] They also note they are assuming some risk, since so many new product introductions fail.

Slotting fees can range from a few hundred dollars per store to $50,000 or more for an entire retail chain. Manufacturers that want to get their products on the shelves nationally can face several million dollars in slotting fees. Many marketers believe slotting allowances are a form of blackmail or bribery and say some 70 percent of these fees go directly to retailers' bottom lines.

Retailers can continue charging slotting fees because of their power and the limited availability of shelf space in supermarkets relative to the large numbers of products introduced each year. Some retailers have even been demanding **failure fees** if a new product does not hit a minimum sales level within a certain time. The fee is charged to cover the costs associated with stocking, maintaining inventories, and then pulling the product.[57] Large manufacturers with popular brands are less likely to pay slotting fees than smaller companies that lack leverage in negotiating with retailers.

In late 1999 the Senate Committee on Small Business began taking action against the practice of using slotting fees in the grocery, drugstore, and computer software industries because of the fees' negative impact on small business.[58] The committee recommended that the Federal Trade Commission and Small Business Administration take steps to limit the use of slotting fees because they are anticompetitive. A recent study by Paul Bloom, Gregory Gundlach, and Joseph Cannon found that the use of slotting fees places small marketers at a disadvantage, although it increases market efficiency.[59]

Problems with Trade Allowances Many companies are concerned about the abuse of trade allowances by wholesalers, retailers, and distributors. Marketers give retailers these trade allowances so that the savings will be passed through to consumers in the form of lower prices, but companies such as Procter & Gamble claim that only 30 percent of trade promotion discounts actually reach consumers because 35 percent is lost in inefficiencies and another 35 percent is pocketed by retailers and wholesalers. Moreover, many marketers believe that the trade is taking advantage of their promotional deals and misusing promotional funds.

For example, many retailers and wholesalers engage in a practice known as **forward buying,** where they stock up on a product at the lower deal or off-invoice price and resell it to consumers after the marketer's promotional period ends. Another common practice is **diverting,** where a retailer or wholesaler takes advantage of the promotional deal and then sells some of the product purchased at the low price to a store outside its area or to a middleperson who resells it to other stores.

Forward buying and diverting are widespread practices. Industry studies show that nearly 40 percent of wholesalers' and retailers' profits come from these activities. In addition to not passing discounts on to consumers, forward buying and diverting create other problems for manufacturers. They lead to huge swings in demand that cause production scheduling problems and leave manufacturers and retailers always building toward or drawing down from a promotional surge. Marketers also worry that the system leads to frequent price specials, so consumers learn to make purchases on the basis of what's on sale rather than developing any loyalty to their brands.

The problems created by retailers' abuse led Procter & Gamble, one of the country's most powerful consumer products marketers, to adopt **everyday low pricing (EDLP),** which lowers the list price of over 60 percent of its product line by 10 to 25 percent while cutting promotional allowances to the trade. The price cuts leave the overall cost of the product to retailers about the same as it would have been with the various trade allowance discounts.

P&G argues that EDLP eliminates problems such as deal buying, leads to regular low prices at the retail level, and helps build brand loyalty among consumers. Yet the EDLP strategy has caused great controversy in the trade, which depends heavily on promotions to attract consumers. Some retailers took P&G products off the shelf; others cut their ads and displays of the company's brands. Retailers prefer to operate on a *high/low strategy* of frequent price specials and argue that EDLP puts them at a disadvantage against the warehouse stores and mass merchandisers that already use everyday low pricing. They also say that some products, such as those that are bought on impulse, thrive on promotions and don't lend themselves to EDLP. Retailers rely on promotions like end-of-aisle displays and price discounts to create excitement and generate incremental sales and profits from products like soft drinks, cookies, and candy.[60]

Critics of EDLP also note that while the strategy may work well for market leaders whose brands enjoy high loyalty, it is not effective for marketers trying to build market share or prop up lagging products. Moreover, many consumers are still motivated more by promotional deals and specials than by advertising claims from retailers promoting everyday low prices.

Despite the criticism, P&G says EDLP is paying off and volume is growing faster in its brands that have switched to the new pricing strategy. And it claims that market share in two-thirds of these product categories has increased. P&G recently extended its use of everyday low pricing to international markets, including the United Kingdom and Italy.[61] IMC Perspective 16–3 discusses how P&G continues to make changes in the way sales promotions are being used by package-goods marketers.

IMC Perspective 16–3

Procter & Gamble Continues to Redefine Sales Promotion Strategy

For decades, Procter & Gamble and many other consumer-package-goods marketers prospered by bombarding both shoppers and retailers with promotional offers. The marketing system that developed during the 1980s and into the early 90s was based on the assumption that the best way to move products was through bigger and better promotions and pricing. Shoppers browsed through the aisles looking for specials, as popular brands would sell at full price one week and half-off the next. They clipped coupons, saved box tops, mailed in refund or rebate offers, and looked for packages with a toy or some other premium offer inside. Marketers pushed so many specials and price changes that it became difficult for them, as well as the retailers, to keep all the paperwork straight. P&G alone made an average of 55 price changes a day across 110 brands and offered over 400 different promotions a year.

But recently P&G, considered by many to be the world's preeminent consumer products company, discovered that the marketing system that had evolved over the years had forgotten someone very important: the consumer. Today's average consumer, more often than not a woman, takes just 21 minutes to do her shopping. In that time she buys an average of 18 items out of 30,000 choices in a supermarket. She spends 25 percent less time browsing than she did five years ago, and she often doesn't bother to check prices. She wants the same product at the same price in the same row and shelf position week after week. She is willing to pay more and be loyal to a store if it makes her shopping experience pleasant.

P&G began to simplify its promotional programs in the early 90s by moving many of its brands to an everyday-low-pricing (EDLP) strategy, which vastly reduced the number of deals offered to retailers and distributors in favor of lower list prices. P&G argues that all of the allowances and deals are costly and confusing for retailers. Moreover, they cause shelf prices to fluctuate weekly and train consumers to buy on price instead of perceived value, thereby undermining the development of brand loyalty. In 1996, P&G took its drive to simplify a step further by eliminating or cutting back on 27 different types of promotions, including the traditional bonus packs, premiums, cents-off packs, and refund offers. The company also cut back on its use of coupons, noting that with redemption rates declining, they are a less efficient way of attracting customers. P&G has put the money saved from these cutbacks into lower prices and other promotions such as sampling and in-store demonstrations.

Procter & Gamble has long been a bellwether for the package-goods industry, and its actions resulted in a broad movement by marketers to reduce the complexity of their sales promotion programs. However, when the changes were made, P&G's CEO Durk Jager noted there was little time to relax, as the company's rivals were working on how to better meet shoppers' needs and make things even simpler for them. In fact, P&G did not relax at all. In early 1999 a major restructuring initiative called "Organization 2005" was begun, and it is designed to double sales to $75 billion by 2005.

Better marketing is one of the major goals of the multifaceted initiative, and it will embrace promotion from a new perspective: strategic interaction between a brand and targeted consumers. P&G hopes to accomplish this through more consumer research, deeper retail partnerships, and more account-specific/local promotions. P&G has formed market development organizations (MDOs), which are regional teams staffed by brand and marketing managers that will act as experts on local consumers and retailers for P&G's seven global business units. The MDOs will become regional and local marketing experts on consumers and work with their retail partners to develop strategic marketing programs that meet consumer needs and sell more product more profitably.

Forming the MDOs was motivated in part by P&G's desire to develop stronger relationships with powerful retailers that are acquiring control of the marketplace, such as American Store, Safeway, and

Wal-Mart. P&G's long-time partnership with Wal-Mart continues to serve as a model for joint marketing programs. One promotional expert, noting that this comarketing program is two years ahead of P&G's relationships with the rest of the retail world, says, "Whatever they do with Wal-Mart is a poster-child of where they'll go with other retailers." It is estimated that P&G could have extensive comarketing programs with the top 10 retail chains by 2005 and spend as much as $1 billion on account-specific marketing through consumer and trade promotions.

As part of Organization 2005, P&G is re-evaluating its $1.6 billion consumer promotion budget and its $3.3 billion trade promotion budget. As the company reaches out to connect with consumers beyond the TV set, it is likely to shift some of its $1.7 billion advertising budget toward promotions, direct marketing, and event marketing. The implications of P&G's new strategy for the sales promotion business are huge and, as with the other areas in which the company has made the first move, will surely create a ripple effect among the other consumer-package-goods marketers.

Sources: Kerry J. Smith, "Procter Moves the Market, Again," *Promo Magazine,* July 1999, p. 6; Betsy Spethmann, "Procter's Gamble," *Promo Magazine,* July 1999, p. 6; "Make It Simple," *Business Week,* September 6, 1996, pp. 96–104.

Displays and Point-of-Purchase Materials The next time you are in a store, take a moment to examine the various promotional materials used to display and sell products. Point-of-purchase displays are an important promotional tool because they can help a manufacturer obtain more effective in-store merchandising of products. Companies in the United States spend more than $12 billion a year on point-of-purchase materials, including end-of-aisle displays, banners, posters, shelf cards, motion pieces, and stand-up racks, among others. Exhibit 16–26 shows an award-winning point-of-purchase display for Top-Flite golf balls.

Exhibit 16–26 Spalding uses point-of-purchase displays for Top-Flite golf balls to help generate in-store sales

Many manufacturers help retailers use shelf space more efficiently through **planograms,** which are configurations of products that occupy a shelf section in a store. Some manufacturers are developing computer-based programs that allow retailers to input information from their scanner data and determine the best shelf layouts by experimenting with product movement, space utilization, profit yields, and other factors.[62]

Sales Training Programs Another form of manufacturer-sponsored promotional assistance is sales training programs for reseller personnel. Many products sold at the retail level require knowledgeable salespeople who can provide consumers with information about the features, benefits, and advantages of various brands and models. Cosmetics, appliances, computers, consumer electronics, and sporting equipment are examples of products for which consumers often rely on well-informed retail sales personnel for assistance.

Manufacturers provide sales training assistance to retail salespeople in a number of ways. They may conduct classes or training sessions that retail personnel can attend to increase their knowledge of a product or a product line. These training sessions present information and ideas on how to sell the manufacturer's product and may also include motivational components. Sales training classes for retail personnel are often sponsored by companies selling high-ticket items or complex products such as personal computers, cars, or ski equipment.

Another way manufacturers provide sales training assistance to retail employees is through their own sales force. Sales reps educate retail personnel about their product line and provide selling tips and other relevant information. The reps can provide ongoing sales training as they come into contact with retail sales staff on a regular basis and can update them on changes in the product line, market developments, competitive information, and the like.

Manufacturers also give resellers detailed sales manuals, product brochures, reference manuals, and other material. Many companies provide videocassettes for retail sales personnel that include product information, product-use demonstrations, and ideas on how to sell their product. These selling aids can often be used to provide information to customers as well.

Trade Shows

Another important promotional activity targeted to resellers is the **trade show,** a forum where manufacturers can display their products to current as well as prospective buyers. According to the Trade Show Bureau, nearly 100 million people attend the 5,000 trade shows each year in the United States and Canada, and the number of exhibiting companies exceeds 1.3 million. In many industries, trade shows are a major opportunity to display one's product lines and interact with customers. They are often attended by important management personnel from large retail chains as well as by distributors and other reseller representatives.

A number of promotional functions can be performed at trade shows, including demonstrating products, identifying new prospects, gathering customer and competitive information, and even writing orders for a product. Trade shows are particularly valuable for introducing new products, because resellers are often looking for new merchandise to stock. Shows can also be a source of valuable leads to follow up on through sales calls or direct marketing. The social aspect of trade shows is also important. Many companies use them to entertain key customers and to develop and maintain relationships with the trade. A recent academic study demonstrated that trade shows generate product awareness and interest and can have a measurable economic return.[63]

Cooperative Advertising

The final form of trade-oriented promotion we examine is **cooperative advertising,** where the cost of advertising is shared by more than one party. There are three types of cooperative advertising. Although the first two are not trade-oriented promotion, we should recognize their objectives and purpose.

Horizontal cooperative advertising is advertising sponsored in common by a group of retailers or other organizations providing products or services to the market. For example, automobile dealers who are located near one another in an auto park or along the same street often allocate some of their ad budgets to a cooperative advertising fund. Ads are run promoting the location of the dealerships and encouraging car buyers to take advantage of their close proximity when shopping for a new automobile.

Ingredient-sponsored cooperative advertising is supported by raw materials manufacturers; its objective is to help establish end products that include the company's materials and/or ingredients. Companies that often use this type of advertising include Du Pont, which promotes the use of its materials such as Teflon, Thinsulate, and Kevlar in a variety of consumer and industrial products, and NutraSweet, whose artificial sweetener is an ingredient in many food products and beverages. Perhaps the best-known, and most successful, example of this type of cooperative advertising is the "Intel Inside" program, sponsored by Intel Corporation, which is discussed in IMC Perspective 16–4.

The most common form of cooperative advertising is the trade-oriented form, **vertical cooperative advertising,** in which a manufacturer pays for a portion of the advertising a retailer runs to promote the manufacturer's product and its availability in the retailer's place of business. Manufacturers generally share the cost of advertising run by the retailer on a percentage basis (usually 50/50) up to a certain limit.

The amount of cooperative advertising the manufacturer pays for is usually based on a percentage of dollar purchases. If a retailer purchases $100,000 of product from a manufacturer, it may receive 3 percent, or $3,000, in cooperative advertising money. Large retail chains often combine their co-op budgets across all of their stores, which gives them a larger sum to work with and more media options.

Cooperative advertising can take on several forms. Retailers may advertise a manufacturer's product in, say, a newspaper ad featuring a number of different products, and the individual manufacturers reimburse the retailer for their portion of the ad. Or the ad may be prepared by the manufacturer and placed in the local

IMC Perspective 16–4

Intel Inside: The Co-op Program That Changed the Computer Industry

If you were to ask most owners of personal computers what is inside their PCs, chances are they would respond by saying, "an Intel." And there's a good reason why. Over the past decade consumers have been exposed to hundreds of millions of dollars' worth of ads for personal computers each year that carry the "Intel Inside" logo. The logo has become ubiquitous in PC ads as a result of a landmark cooperative advertising program that is lauded as the most powerful ever and the definitive model for successful "ingredient" branding.

In 1989 Intel was the first computer chip manufacturer to advertise directly to consumers. Its goal was to persuade PC users to upgrade to Intel's 386SX chip from the 286. Known as the "Red X" campaign, the ads depicted the number 286 with a bold, spray-painted *X* over it. Dennis Carter, Intel's vice president and director of strategic marketing and the architect of the "Intel Inside" campaign, was a marketing manager at the time and was working with a tech ad shop on Intel's print, outdoor, radio, and in-store ads. He noticed that the ads were changing people's buying behavior and that the company had a model of something that was working, as Intel could communicate technical information in a basic way.

In 1909 Intel selected a new agency, Dahlin Smith White, Salt Lake City, which created the now-famous tagline "Intel. The Computer Inside." The goal of the campaign was to build awareness and position Intel as the real brains of the computer. In early 1991 Intel began pitching the program to PC makers, and IBM, creator of the first Intel-powered personal computer, became the first computer maker to use the logo. Intel then began talking to PC makers about the creation of a co-op fund in which Intel would take 5 percent of the purchase price of processors and put it in a pool to create funds for advertising.

The "Intel Inside" co-op program was officially launched in July 1991 and works as follows: In return for showing the logo in print ads and on the PCs, a computer maker can get back 5 percent of what it pays Intel for chips, with the money to be applied to ads paid for jointly by the PC vendor and Intel. More than 150 computer makers signed on to the program and began using the "Intel Inside" logo in their ads.

As the program began, Intel started playing up the logo in its own print ads as well. In November 1991 it moved the campaign to television with the classic "Power Source" spot, which magically took viewers on a whirlwind tour of the inside of a computer to show how the Intel chip streamlined upgrading of a PC. In 1993 Intel introduced the Pentium processor brand with a national TV campaign. However, the company was putting the bulk of its advertising budget into the "Intel Inside" co-op program. In 1995 Intel expanded the co-op program to include TV, radio, and in-flight ads. The move led to a boom in PC ads on television featuring the Intel auditory signature at the end of each commercial. In 1997 Intel expanded the co-op program to include Internet ads and provided incentives to PC makers to place ads on media-rich websites. Intel has also extended the co-op program into retail promotions as well.

Since the co-op program began, Intel has pumped into it an estimated $4 billion, and this has been an awfully smart investment. Intel's share of the microprocessor market has grown from 56 percent in 1989 to nearly 83 percent in 1999, and the company's revenue has gone from $3 billion to nearly $30 billion. Nearly 90 percent of the more than 17,000 PC print ads run in the United States for the first nine months of 1999 carried the "Intel Inside" logo. The program has influenced a generation of PC users and propelled growth of the entire computer industry.

According to positioning expert Al Ries, "Intel Inside" will go down in history as one of the more magnificent campaigns of the century. He notes, "It's brilliant, and, in a sense, it pre-empted the branding of personal computers." Branding guru Jack Trout notes, "They took an old idea—ingredient branding—which Du Pont pioneered, and took it into technology." Trout was an early believer in the program; he told *Advertising Age* in a 1991 interview that conceptually it was a good idea, although Intel would need consistent advertising over time for the logo to have much meaning.

How to spot the very best PCs.

In its early stages the program encountered criticism, as many advertising and computer marketing executives were skeptical about Intel's ability to differentiate its chips. The head of one agency noted: "Most people who buy computers don't even know that chip is there. They care about the performance of the computer. It really doesn't matter what the chip is." Well, they may not know exactly what a microprocessor chip does, but apparently it does matter if there is an "Intel Inside."

Sources: Tobi Elkin, "Co-op Crossroads," *Advertising Age*, November 15, 1999, pp. 1, 24, 26; Bradley Johnson, "Intel Inside Program Expands Global Reach," *Advertising Age*, January 29, 1996, p. 9.

media by the retailer. Exhibit 16–27 shows a cooperative ad format for New Balance athletic shoes that retailers in various market areas can use by simply inserting their store name and location.

Once a cooperative ad is run, the retailer requests reimbursement from the manufacturer for its percentage of the media costs. Manufacturers usually have specific requirements the ad must meet to qualify for co-op reimbursement, such as size, use of trademarks, content, and format. Verification that the ad was run is also required, in the form of a tearsheet (print) or an affidavit from the radio or TV station (broadcast) and an invoice.

As with other types of trade promotions, manufacturers have been increasing their cooperative advertising expenditures in recent years. Some companies have been moving money out of national advertising into cooperative advertising because they believe they can have greater impact with ad campaigns in local markets. There is also a trend toward more cooperative advertising programs initiated by retailers, which approach manufacturers with catalogs, promotional events they are planning, or advertising programs they have developed in conjunction with local media and ask them to pay a percentage of the cost. Manufacturers often go along with these requests, particularly when the retailer is large and powerful.[64]

Coordinating Sales Promotion and Advertising

Those involved in the promotional process must recognize that sales promotion techniques usually work best in conjunction with advertising and that the effectiveness of an ad campaign can be enhanced by consumer-oriented sales promotion efforts. Rather than separate activities competing for a firm's promotional budget, advertising and sales promotion should be viewed as complementary tools. When properly

Exhibit 16–27 This New Balance ad is an example of vertical cooperative advertising

planned and executed to work together, advertising and sales promotion can have a *synergistic effect* much greater than that of either promotional mix element alone.

Proper coordination of advertising and sales promotion is essential for the firm to take advantage of the opportunities offered by each tool and get the most out of its promotional budget. Successful integration of advertising and sales promotion requires decisions concerning not only the allocation of the budget to each area but also the coordination of the ad and sales promotion themes, the timing of the various promotional activities, and the target audience reached.

Budget Allocation

While many companies are spending more money on sales promotion than on media advertising, it is difficult to say just what percentage of a firm's overall promotional budget should be allocated to advertising versus consumer- and trade-oriented promotions. This allocation depends on a number of factors, including the specific promotional objectives of the campaign, the market and competitive situation, and the brand's stage in its life cycle.

Consider, for example, how allocation of the promotional budget may vary according to a brand's stage in the product life cycle. In the introductory stage, a large amount of the budget may be allocated to sales promotion techniques such as sampling and couponing to induce trial. In the growth stage, however, promotional dollars may be used primarily for advertising to stress brand differences and keep the brand name in consumers' minds.

When a brand moves to the maturity stage, advertising is primarily a reminder to keep consumers aware of the brand. Consumer-oriented sales promotions such as coupons, price-offs, premiums, and bonus packs may be needed periodically to maintain consumer loyalty, attract new users, and protect against competition. Trade-oriented promotions are needed to maintain shelf space and accommodate retailers' demands for better margins as well as encourage them to promote the brand. A study on the synergistic effects of advertising and promotion examined a brand in the mature phase of its life cycle and found that 30 percent of its sales at this stage were due to sales promotions. When a brand enters the decline stage of the product life cycle, most of the promotional support will probably be removed and expenditures on sales promotion are unlikely.

Coordination of Ad and Promotion Themes

To integrate the advertising and sales promotion programs successfully, the theme of consumer promotions should be tied in with the advertising and positioning theme wherever possible. Sales promotion tools should attempt to communicate a brand's unique attributes or benefits and to reinforce the sales message or campaign theme. In this way, the sales promotion effort contributes to the consumer franchise-building effort for the brand.

At the same time, media advertising should be used to draw attention to a sales promotion program such as a contest, sweepstakes, or event or to a special promotion offer such as a price reduction or rebate program. An example of this is the ad shown in Exhibit 16–28 for WD-40, which promotes the Search for 2000 Uses Sweepstakes that was discussed earlier and shown in Exhibit 16–6. Note how both the magazine ad and the sweepstakes promotion integrate the variety-of-uses positioning theme used for WD-40.

Exhibit 16–28 This WD-40 ad promotes the 2000 Uses Sweepstakes and is consistent with the positioning theme used for the brand

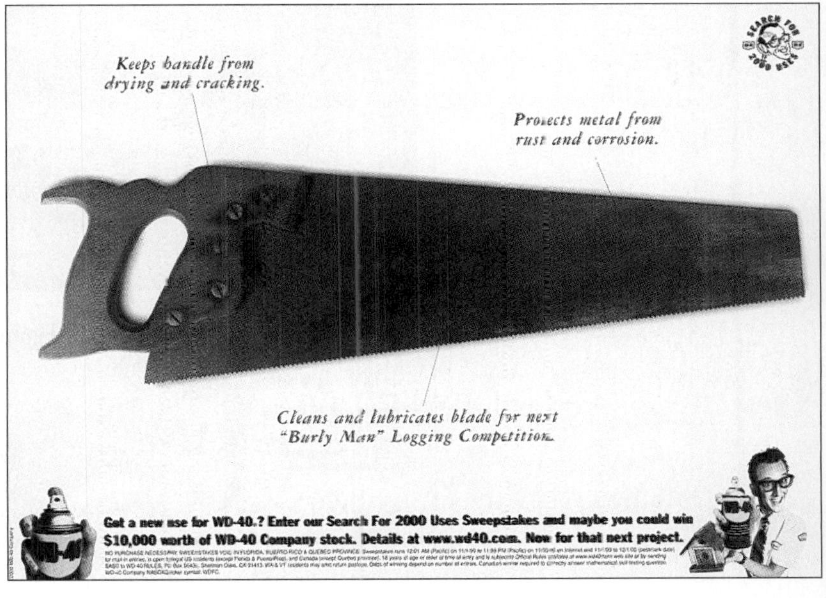

Keeps handle from drying and cracking.
Protects metal from rust and corrosion.
Cleans and lubricates blade for next "Burly Man" Logging Competition.
Got a new use for WD-40.? Enter our Search For 2000 Uses Sweepstakes and maybe you could win $10,000 worth of WD-40 Company stock. Details at www.wd40.com. Now for that next project.

Media Support and Timing

Media support for a sales promotion program is critical and should be coordinated with the media program for the ad campaign. Media advertising is often needed to deliver such sales promotion materials as coupons, sweepstakes, contest entry forms, premium offers, and even samples. It is also needed to inform consumers of a promotional offer as well as to create awareness, interest, and favorable attitudes toward the brand.

By using advertising in conjunction with a sales promotion program, marketers can make consumers aware of the brand and its benefits and increase their responsiveness to the promotion. Consumers are more likely to redeem a coupon or respond to a price-off deal for a brand they are familiar with than one they know nothing about. Moreover, product trial created through sales promotion techniques such as sampling or high-value couponing is more likely to result in long-term use of the brand when accompanied by advertising.[65]

Using a promotion without prior or concurrent advertising can limit its effectiveness and risk damaging the brand's image. If consumers perceive the brand as being promotion dependent or of lesser quality, they are not likely to develop favorable attitudes and long-term loyalty. Conversely, the effectiveness of an ad can be enhanced by a coupon, a premium offer, or an opportunity to enter a sweepstakes or contest.

An example of the effective coordination of advertising and sales promotion is the introductory campaign Lever Brothers developed for its Lever 2000 bar soap. As noted earlier in the chapter, Lever Brothers used high-value coupons, sent samples to half of U.S. households, and offered discounts to retailers as part of its introductory marketing blitz. These sales promotion efforts were accompanied by heavy advertising in print and TV with the tagline "Presenting some of the 2000 body parts you can clean with Lever 2000" (Exhibit 16–29).

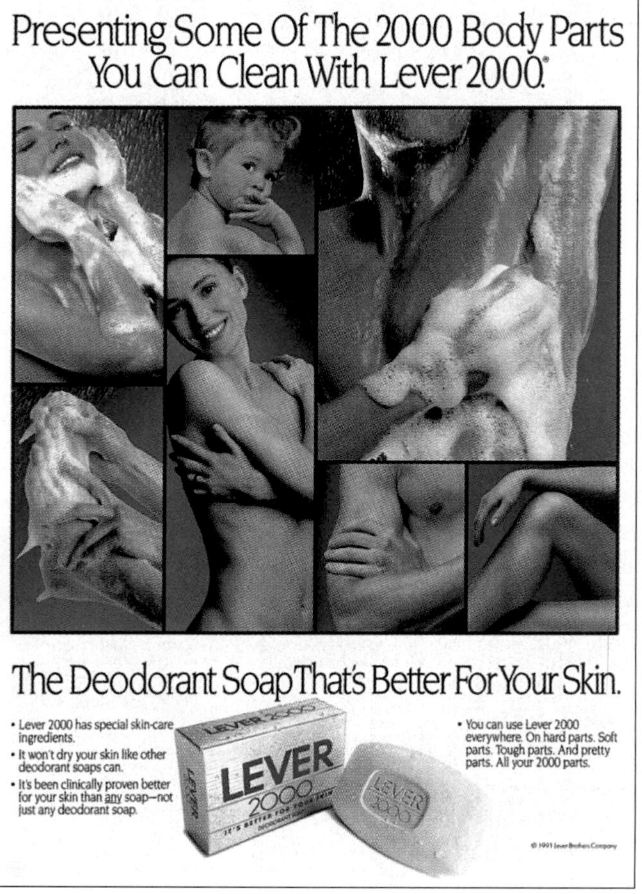

Exhibit 16–29 Creative advertising was coordinated with sales promotion in the successful introduction of Lever 2000 soap

Traditional	New and Improved
1. Primarily used to develop short-term tactics or concepts	1. Used to develop long- and short-term promotional strategies as well as tactics.
2. Hired/compensated on a project-by-project basis.	2. Contracted on annual retainer, following formal agency reviews.
3. Many promotion agencies used a mix—each one hired for best task and/or specialty.	3. One or two exclusive promotion agencies for each division or brand group.
4. One or two contact people from agency.	4. Full team or core group on the account.
5. Promotion agency never equal to ad agency—doesn't work up front in annual planning process.	5. Promotion agency works on equal basis with ad agency—sits at planning table up front.
6. Not directly accountable for results.	6. Very much accountable—goes through a rigorous evaluation process.

Figure 16–8 The shifting role of the promotion agency

Sales promotion was important in inducing trial for Lever 2000 and continued after introduction in the form of couponing. But it was the strong positioning created through effective advertising that converted consumers to regular users. Repeat sales of the brand were at about 40 percent even after heavy discounting ended. Just six months after its introduction, Lever 2000 became the number-2 deodorant soap in dollar volume, with an estimated 8.4 percent of the $1.5 billion bar-soap market.[66]

To coordinate their advertising and sales promotion programs more effectively, many companies are getting their sales promotion agencies more involved in the advertising and promotional planning process. Rather than hiring agencies to develop individual, nonfranchise-building types of promotions with short-term goals and tactics, many firms are having their sales promotion and advertising agencies work together to develop integrated promotional strategies and programs. Figure 16–8 shows how the role of sales promotion agencies is changing.

Sales Promotion Abuse

The increasing use of sales promotion in marketing programs is more than a passing fad. It is a fundamental change in strategic decisions about how companies market their products and services. The value of this increased emphasis on sales promotion has been questioned by several writers, particularly with regard to the lack of adequate planning and management of sales promotion programs.[67]

Are marketers becoming too dependent on this element of the marketing program? Consumer and trade promotions can be a very effective tool for generating short-term increases in sales, and many brand managers would rather use a promotion to produce immediate sales than invest in advertising and build the brand's image over an extended time. As the director of sales promotion services at one large ad agency noted:

> There's a great temptation for quick sales fixes through promotions. It's a lot easier to offer the consumer an immediate price savings than to differentiate your product from a competitor's.[68]

Overuse of sales promotion can be detrimental to a brand in several ways. A brand that is constantly promoted may lose perceived value. Consumers often end up purchasing a brand because it is on sale, they get a premium, or they have a coupon, rather than basing their decision on a favorable attitude they have developed. When the extra promotional incentive is not available, they switch to another brand. A recent study by Priya Raghubir and Kim Corfman examined whether price promotions affect pretrial evaluations of a brand.[69] They found that offering a price promotion is more likely to lower a brand's evaluation when the brand has not been promoted previously compared to when it has been frequently promoted; that price promotions are used as a source of information about a brand to a greater extent when the evaluator is not an expert but does have some product or industry knowledge; and that promotions are more likely to result in negative evaluations when they are uncommon in the industry. The findings from this study suggest that marketers must be careful in the use of price promotions as they may inhibit trial of a brand in certain situations.

Alan Sawyer and Peter Dickson have used the concept of *attribution theory* to examine how sales promotion may affect consumer attitude formation.[70] According to this theory, people acquire attitudes by observing their own behavior and considering why they acted in a certain manner. Consumers who consistently purchase a brand because of a coupon or price-off deal may attribute their behavior to the external promotional incentive rather than to a favorable attitude toward the brand. By contrast, when no external incentive is available, consumers are more likely to attribute their purchase behavior to favorable underlying feelings about the brand.

Another potential problem with consumer-oriented promotions is that a **sales promotion trap** or spiral can result when several competitors use promotions extensively.[71] Often a firm begins using sales promotions to differentiate its product or service from the competition. If the promotion is successful and leads to a differential advantage (or even appears to do so), competitors may quickly copy it. When all the competitors are using sales promotions, this not only lowers profit margins for each firm but also makes it difficult for any one firm to hop off the promotional bandwagon.[72] This dilemma is shown in Figure 16–9.

A number of industries have fallen into this promotional trap. In the cosmetics industry, gift-with-purchase and purchase-with-purchase promotional offers were developed as a tactic for getting buyers to sample new products. But they have become a common, and costly, way of doing business.[73] In many areas of the country, supermarkets have gotten into the trap of doubling or even tripling manufacturers' coupons, which cuts into their already small profit margins.

Fast-food chains have also fallen into the trap with promotions featuring popular menu items, such as Burger King's Whopper for 99 cents. McDonald's began another round of promotional wars with its Campaign 55, dropping the price of popular items like the Big Mac, Quarter Pounder, and Arch Deluxe to 55 cents with the purchase of french fries and a soft drink. If this promotion had been successful, the other fast-food chains may have had little choice but to match it.[74]

Marketers must consider both the short-term impact of a promotion and its long-term effect on the brand. The ease with which competitors can develop a retaliatory promotion and the likelihood of their doing so should also be considered. Marketers must be careful not to damage the brand franchise with sales promotions or to get the firm involved in a promotional war that erodes the brand's profit margins and threatens its long-term existence. Marketers are often tempted to resort to sales promotions to deal with declining sales and other problems when they should examine such other aspects of the marketing program as channel relations, price, packaging, product quality, or advertising.

Figure 16–9 The sales promotion trap

All Other Firms	Our Firm: Cut back promotions	Our Firm: Maintain promotions
Cut back promotions	Higher profits for all	Market share goes to our firm
Maintain promotions	Market share goes to all other firms	Market share stays constant; profits stay low

Summary

For many years, advertising was the major promotional mix element for most consumer product companies. Over the past decade, however, marketers have been allocating more of their promotional dollars to sales promotion. There has been a steady increase in the use of sales promotion techniques to influence consumers' purchase behavior. The growing power of retailers, erosion of brand loyalty, increase in consumers' sensitivity to promotions, increase in new product introductions, fragmentation of the consumer market, short-term focus of marketing and brand managers, and increase in advertising clutter are some of the reasons for this increase.

Sales promotions can be characterized as either franchise building or nonfranchise building. The former contribute to the long-term development and reinforcement of brand identity and image; the latter are designed to accelerate the purchase process and generate immediate increases in sales.

Sales promotion techniques can be classified as either trade or consumer oriented. A number of consumer-oriented sales promotion techniques were examined in this chapter, including sampling, couponing, premiums, contests and sweepstakes, rebates and refunds, bonus packs, price-off deals, frequency programs, and event marketing. The characteristics of these promotional tools were examined, along with their advantages and limitations. Various trade-oriented promotions were also examined, including trade contests and incentives, trade allowances, displays and point-of-purchase materials, sales training programs, trade shows, and cooperative advertising.

Advertising and sales promotion should not be viewed as separate activities but rather as complementary tools. When planned and executed properly, advertising and sales promotion can produce a synergistic effect that is greater than the response generated from either promotional mix element alone. To accomplish this, marketers must coordinate budgets, advertising and promotional themes, media scheduling and timing, and target audiences.

Sales promotion abuse can result when marketers become too dependent on the use of sales promotion techniques and sacrifice long-term brand position and image for short-term sales increases. Many industries experience sales promotion traps when a number of competitors use promotions extensively and it becomes difficult for any single firm to cut back on promotion without risking a loss in sales. Overuse of sales promotion tools can lower profit margins and threaten the image and even the viability of a brand.

Key Terms

sales promotion, 524
consumer-oriented sales promotion, 525
trade-oriented sales promotion, 526
account-specific marketing, 530
consumer franchise-building (CFB) promotions, 533
nonfranchise-building (non-FB) promotions, 535
sampling, 539
bounce-back coupon, 545
cross-ruff coupon, 545
instant coupon, 546
in-store couponing, 546
premium, 548
self-liquidating premiums, 549
contest, 549
sweepstakes, 550
game, 550
refund, 551
bonus packs, 553
price-off deal, 553
frequency programs, 554
event marketing, 555
event sponsorship, 555
push money, 559
trade allowance, 560
off-invoice allowance, 560
failure fees, 560
forward buying, 561
diverting, 561
everyday low pricing (EDLP), 561
planograms, 563
trade show, 564
cooperative advertising, 564
horizontal cooperative advertising, 564
ingredient-sponsored cooperative advertising, 564
vertical cooperative advertising, 564
sales promotion trap, 570

Discussion Questions

1. The opening vignette discusses how marketers are making sales promotion an integral part of their brand building strategies. Discuss how sales promotion can be used to help build brand equity.

2. What are the differences between consumer-oriented and trade-oriented sales promotion? Discuss the role of each in a marketer's IMC program.

3. Discuss how sales promotion can be used as an acceleration tool to speed up the sales process and maximize sales volume.

4. Discuss the various reasons marketers have been shifting their marketing dollars to sales promotion from media advertising. Discuss the pros and cons of this reallocation of marketers' advertising and promotion budgets.

5. What are the differences between consumer franchise-building and nonfranchise-building promotions? Find an example of a promotional offer you believe contributes to the equity of a brand and explain why.

6. Discuss how the Internet can be used for the distribution of various promotional offers such as samples, coupons, premiums, contests, and sweepstakes.

7. What steps might marketers take to avoid some of the major promotional blunders that are discussed in Global Perpsective 16–2?

8. IMC Perspective 16–3 discusses how Procter & Gamble (P&G) continues to redefine and simplify its sales promotion strategy in recent years. Evaluate the various changes P&G has made in its promotional strategy. Do you think other consumer-package-goods marketers will follow some of the moves made by P&G?

9. Why do you think the "Intel Inside" cooperative advertising program has been so successful? Can you think of another company that might be in a situation to benefit from this type of cooperative advertising program?

10. What is meant by a sales promotion trap? Find an example of an industry where a promotional war is currently taking place. What are the options for a marketer involved in such a situation?

Chapter Seventeen

Public Relations, Publicity, and Corporate Advertising

Chapter Objectives

- To recognize the roles of public relations, publicity, and corporate advertising in the promotional mix.
- To know the difference between public relations and publicity and demonstrate the advantages and disadvantages of each.
- To understand the reasons for corporate advertising and its advantages and disadvantages.
- To know the methods for measuring the effects of public relations, publicity, and corporate advertising.

The "Buzz"

You have probably seen the screensavers with the weird-looking dancing baby. You almost certainly have seen Taco Bell's Chihuahua and may even have a few Beanie Babies. But you probably didn't know what they all have in common—each has managed the "buzz."

It's hard to describe what exactly the "buzz" is. Nancy Austin of *Inc Magazine* describes it as "busy talk, the CNN of the street." "Buzz is what large numbers of people talk about. More than anything else, word of mouth stokes buzz and keeps it alive," she says. However you try to describe it, *buzz* is the discussion about whatever is hot in society, and it is powerful. Beanie Babies were the buzz for a long time, as was the dancing baby screensaver and the Taco Bell Chihuahua discussed earlier in the text. What may be the most interesting thing about buzz is that it can be created and managed and that there are even public relations companies out there that specialize in the process.

Consider the buzz around the dancing baby. Kinetix, the San Francisco–based division of Autodesk, Inc., developed the dancing baby and 11 other characters as a tutorial for its customers. The customers thought the boogying baby was so interesting that Kinetix modified the files and created a screensaver of the character and it spread quickly throughout the Internet via e-mail. That's where David Kelley, creator, producer, and writer of the TV show "Ally McBeal" first became aware of it. Kelley designed it into an episode in which lawyer McBeal worries about her biological clock, and the baby was big time. So as not to kill the buzz, Kinetix refrained from trying to promote the buzz with its own communications but made it extremely easy to copy the baby file and pass it on to others. Only after the baby had become enormously popular did Kinetix start to put together some public relations pieces to keep the craze alive. The baby buzz has been extremely beneficial to Kinetix. According to the former general manager of Kinetix, Jim Guerard, it has led to an increase in awareness and visibility (particularly in the entertainment community) and hits on the Kinetix website have surged—with very minimal marketing effort. Visits to the "unofficial Dancing Baby site" run by a

Seattle high school student have increased tremendously as well.

Then there is the incredible success of Ty, Inc., the producer of Beanie Babies. The miniature stuffed critters, which started off as toys for kids, became a rage and then collectors' items. There are websites devoted to selling and exchanging Beanie Babies, with people as far away as Europe and South America trading and buying from people in the United States; lines at stores when new ones are introduced; and near riots when consumers can't get the ones they want. McDonald's used mini Beanie Babies as a promotional item in Kids Meals, and supplies ran out so quickly the company had to place signs in front of its outlets saying the babies were out of stock to keep from angering parents who got there too late to get one. Ty controls when new babies are released, how many will be made, and when others will be retired (Bumble the Bee was retired in 1996)—with the utmost of secrecy—furthering the buzz and the value. Some hard-to-find Beanie Babies sell for $1,000 or more. When the company announced in 1999 that it was going to stop making Beanie Babies altogether (another publicity ploy), consumers practically begged Ty not to stop—and of course it didn't. The success of the Beanie Babies is incredible, with a 2,000 percent gain in sales from 1996 to 1997 and even higher growth since. The website averages 20,000 hits a day. Perhaps even more amazing, the company does no advertising!

Not all buzz is good, however, and not all is easily managed. The Taco Bell Chihuahua's success has led to complaints from Latino groups who have complained that the dog and its accent are demeaning. There is also a lawsuit against the company by a Michigan man who claims the dog idea was stolen from him. Odwalla, a California fresh-juice company, was the recipient of unwanted negative buzz when outbreaks of *E. coli* infections were linked to its unpasteurized apple drinks. The buzz was that the company was finished, and it almost was—sales dropped by 90 percent—had it not been for an extremely effective public relations campaign. Little Earth Productions, a Pittsburgh, Pennsylvania company, has managed the buzz to get exposure on the TV show "Home Improvement" and on the Miss USA pageant. Keep an ear out for it!

Sources: Greg Johnson, "Grooming an Icon for the Long Haul," *Los Angeles Times,* February 18, 1999, p. C1; Nancy Austin, "Buzz," *Inc Magazine,* May 1998, p. 44.

The attempt to generate buzz cited in the lead-in are just some examples of the many ways organizations integrate public relations programs with other elements of the promotional mix to market their products more effectively. These efforts have become such an integral part of the IMC mix that many agencies have formed departments within the public relations area specifically for this purpose. McCann-Erickson refers to it as experiential branding, while Puris Lintas calls it idea engineering. Whatever you call it, such efforts are clearly on the increase.[1] Besides generating increased sales, the good publicity provides long-term benefits.

Publicity, public relations, and corporate advertising all have promotional program elements that may be of great benefit to marketers. They are integral parts of the overall promotional effort that must be managed and coordinated with the other elements of the promotional mix. However, these three tools do not always have the specific objectives of product and service promotion, nor do they always involve the same methods you have become accustomed to as you have read this text. Typically, these activities are designed more to change attitudes toward an organization or issue than to promote specific products or affect behaviors directly (though you will see that this role is changing in some organizations). This chapter explores the roles of public relations, publicity, and corporate advertising, the advantages and disadvantages of each, and the process by which they are employed. Examples of such efforts—both successful and unsuccessful—are also included.

Public Relations

What is public relations? How does it differ from other elements of marketing discussed thus far? Perhaps a good starting point is to define what the term *public relations* has traditionally meant and then to introduce its new role.

The Traditional Definition of PR

A variety of books define **public relations,** but perhaps the most comprehensive definition is that offered by the *Public Relations News* (the weekly newsletter of the industry):

> the management function which evaluates public attitudes, identifies the policies and procedures of an organization with the public interest, and executes a program of action (and communication) to earn public understanding and acceptance.[2]

Public relations is indeed a management function. The term *management* should be used in its broadest sense; it is not limited to business managements but extends to other types of organizations, including nonprofit institutions.

In this definition, public relations requires a series of stages, including:

1. The determination and evaluation of public attitudes.
2. The identification of policies and procedures of an organization with a public interest.
3. The development and execution of a communications program designed to bring about public understanding and acceptance.

This process does not occur all at once. An effective public relations program continues over months or even years.

Finally, this definition reveals that public relations involves much more than activities designed to sell a product or service. The PR program may involve some of the promotional program elements previously discussed but use them in a different way. For example, press releases may be mailed to announce new products or changes in the organization, special events may be organized to create goodwill in the community, and advertising may be used to state the firm's position on a controversial issue.

The New Role of PR

In an increasing number of marketing-oriented companies, new responsibilities have been established for public relations. It takes on a much broader (and more marketing-oriented) perspective, designed to promote the organization as well as its products and/or services.

Figure 17–1 demonstrates four relationships that marketing and public relations can assume in an organization. These relationships are defined by the degree of use of each function.

Class 1 relationships are characterized by a minimal use of either function. Organizations with this design typically have very small marketing and/or public relations budgets and devote little time and effort to them. Small social service agencies and nonprofit organizations are typically class 1.

Organizations characterized by a *class 2* relationship have a well-established public relations function but do very little in the way of formal marketing. Colleges

	Public Relations	
Marketing	**Weak**	**Strong**
Weak	1 Example: Small social service agencies	2 Example: Hospitals and colleges
Strong	3 Example: Small manufacturing companies	4 Example: Fortune 500 companies

Figure 17–1 Four classes of marketing and public relations use

and hospitals typically have such a design, although in both cases marketing activities are increasing. Both of these groups have moved in the direction of class 4 organizations in recent years, though PR activities still dominate.

Many small companies are typified by a *class 3* organization, in which marketing dominates and the public relations function is minimal. Private companies (without stockholders) and small manufacturers with little or no public to appease tend to employ this design.

Class 4 enterprises have both strong marketing and strong public relations. These two departments often operate independently. For example, public relations may be responsible for the more traditional responsibilities described earlier, while marketing promotes specific products and/or services. Both groups may work together at times, and both report to top management. Many Fortune 500 companies employ multiple ad agencies and PR firms.

The new role of public relations might best be characterized as class 4, although with a slightly different relationship. Rather than each department operating independently, the two now work closely together, blending their talents to provide the best overall image of the firm and its product or service offerings. Public relations departments increasingly position themselves as a tool to both supplant and support traditional advertising and marketing efforts and as a key part of the IMC program.

Writing in *Advertising Age,* William N. Curry notes that organizations must use caution in developing class 4 relationships because PR and marketing are not the same thing, and when one becomes dominant, the balance required to operate at maximum efficiency is lost.[3] He says losing sight of the objectives and functions of public relations in an attempt to achieve marketing goals may be detrimental in the long run. Others take an even stronger view that if public relations and marketing distinctions continue to blur, the independence of the PR function will be lost and it will become much less effective.[4] In this book, we take the position that in a truly integrated marketing communications program, public relations must play an integral role.

Integrating PR into the Promotional Mix

Given the broader responsibilities of public relations, the issue is how to integrate it into the promotional mix. Philip Kotler and William Mindak suggest a number of alternative organizational designs: Either marketing or public relations can be the dominant function; both can be equal but separate functions; or the two can perform the same roles.[5] While each of these designs has its merits, in this text we consider public relations a promotional program element. This means that its broad role must include traditional responsibilities.

Whether public relations takes on a traditional role or a more marketing-oriented one, PR activities are still tied to specific communications objectives. Assessing public attitudes and creating a favorable corporate image are no less important than promoting products or services directly.

Marketing Public Relations (MPR) Functions

Thomas L. Harris has referred to public relations activities designed to support marketing objectives as **marketing public relations (MPR)** functions.[6] Marketing objectives that may be aided by public relations activities include raising awareness, informing and educating, gaining understanding, building trust, giving consumers a reason to buy, and motivating consumer acceptance. MPR adds value to the integrated marketing program in a number of ways:

- *Building marketplace excitement before media advertising breaks.* The announcement of a new product, for example, is an opportunity for the marketer to obtain publicity and dramatize the product, thereby increasing the effectiveness of ads.
- *Creating advertising news where there is no product news.* Ads themselves can be the focus of publicity. There seems to be as much hype about the ads on the Super Bowl as there is for the game itself.

- *Introducing a product with little or no advertising.* You will see later in this chapter that this strategy has been implemented successfully by Hewlett-Packard and No Excuses jeans, as well as by Kinetix and Ty. Crayon manufacturer Crayola has also used this approach to its advantage.
- *Providing a value-added customer service.* Butterball established a hotline where people can call in to receive personal advice on how to prepare their turkeys. The company handled 25,000 calls during one holiday season. Many companies provide such services on their Internet sites. Chicken of the Sea provides recipes to visitors of its site (which of course suggest using Chicken of the Sea tuna).
- *Building brand-to-customer bonds.* The Pillsbury Bake-Off has led to strong brand loyalty among Pillsbury customers, who compete by submitting baked goods. The winner now receives a one-million-dollar prize!
- *Influencing the influentials—that is, providing information to opinion leaders.*
- *Defending products at risk and giving consumers a reason to buy.* By taking constructive actions to defend or promote a company's products, PR can actually give consumers a reason to buy. Energizer's national education campaign that urges consumers to change the batteries in their fire alarms when they reset their clocks in the fall has resulted in a strong corporate citizen image and increased sales of batteries.

An excellent example of using MPRs in an integrated program is a strategy employed by Victoria's Secret. A spot ad that appeared on the Super Bowl in 1998 (cost, $1.5 million) announcing a live webcast of the Victoria's Secret fashion show that would appear a few days later generated mountains of publicity. An estimated 5 billion people worldwide were made aware of Victoria's Secret. The rush to view the show led to so many users signing on that servers throughout the world overloaded, causing many to crash—and this led to even more publicity. Combining these two events with in-store merchandising also paid off, as sales rose by 13 percent—making Victoria's Secret the most successful specialty retailer in 1999. The Web presence produced 600,000 new catalog requests, 1.1 million registrations for e-mail updates, and orders from 136 nations. The company has now increased its television budget, as well as its spending in magazines like *Elle* and *Vogue,* to broaden its integrated approach.[7] Additional successful implementations of MPRs are shown in Figure 17–2.

- *Wonderbra.* With almost no advertising support beyond billboards in major markets, Wonderbra created anticipation for the launch of the first Wonderbra in 1994. Already behind two major competitors, the company relied heavily on public relations coverage and media hype to create awareness and gain attention for the product launch. The same strategy has continued over the past five years, and Wonderbra has become the number 1 push-up bra in the United States.
- *Rockport.* Just another shoe company in the 1980s, Rockport was convinced by its public relations agency to promote the concept of "fitness walking" through a series of MPR initiatives. Rockport became known as the "Walking Shoe Company," achieving a tenfold increase in sales.
- *Arbor Mist Wine.* After several years of researching consumer trends and brand preferences for wine, Canandaigua found that younger women (among others) were dissatisfied with the choices of alcoholic beverages available to them. Positioning the product as "Snapple with an attitude," and as a fun wine, Arbor Mist used wine festivals and wine tastings for local media to achieve its success. By building one-on-one relationships with the media, Arbor Mist's PR team was able to generate significant publicity in New York, Chicago, Miami, and Los Angeles. The company became the first wine ever to ship 1 million cases in less than 100 days
- *California Kiwifruit Commission.* While the commission has been around since 1935, its public relations efforts have primarily focused on disseminating health and nutritional information about kiwis. Through a more marketing-oriented public relations campaign, the commission was able to increase sales by as much as 300 percent in stores and achieved a 12 percent increase in new users.

Figure 17–2 MPR adds value to the marketing program

Harris notes that there are a number of advantages of using MPR:[8]

- It is a cost-effective way to reach the market.
- It is a highly targeted way to conduct public relations.
- It benefits from the endorsement of independent and objective third parties who have no association with the product.
- It achieves credibility.
- It supports advertising programs by making messages more credible.
- It breaks through the clutter.
- It circumvents consumer resistance to sales efforts.

He also notes that there are disadvantages, including the following:

- There is a lack of control over the media.
- It is difficult to tie in slogans and other advertising devices.
- Media time and space are not guaranteed.
- There are no standard effectiveness measures.

One of the major threats expressed by Harris is that MPRs may lead to public relations' becoming subservient to marketing—a concern expressed by many opponents of MPR. However, if employed properly and used in conjunction with other traditional public relations practices as well as IMC elements, MPR can continue to be used effectively.

The Process of Public Relations

The actual process of conducting public relations and integrating it into the promotional mix involves a series of both traditional and marketing-oriented tasks.

Determining and Evaluating Public Attitudes

You've learned that public relations is concerned with people's attitudes toward the firm or specific issues beyond those directed at a product or service. The first question you may ask is why. Why is the firm so concerned with the public's attitudes?

One reason is that these attitudes may affect sales of the firm's products. A number of companies have experienced sales declines as a result of consumer boycotts. Procter & Gamble, Coors, Nike, and Bumble Bee Seafoods are just a few companies that responded to organized pressures. When high-ranking Texaco officials were caught on tape allegedly making racial slurs, the negative publicity led to public outrage. Texaco was hit with a $520 million racial discrimination lawsuit, as well as a second lawsuit by shareholders against Texaco directors and executives for failing to check racist attitudes and practices in the company. The city of Philadelphia voted to sell more than $5.6 million in Texaco stock as a protest.[9] Exhibit 17–1 shows an ad run by Texaco in response to the controversy.

Second, no one wants to be perceived as a bad citizen. Corporations exist in communities, and their employees may both work and live there. Negative attitudes carry over to employee morale and may result in a less-than-optimal working environment internally and in the community.

Due to their concerns about public perceptions, many privately held corporations, publicly held companies, utilities, and the media survey public attitudes. The reasons for conducting this research are many:

1. *It provides input into the planning process.* Once the firm has determined public attitudes, they become the starting point in the development of programs designed to maintain favorable positions or change unfavorable ones.
2. *It serves as an early warning system.* Once a problem exists, it may require substantial time and money to correct. By conducting research, the firm may be able

to identify potential problems and handle them effectively before they become serious issues.

3. *It secures support internally.* If research shows a problem or potential problem exists, it will be much easier for the public relations arm to gain the support it needs to address this problem.
4. *It increases the effectiveness of the communication.* The better it understands a problem, the better the firm can design communications to deal with it.[10]

Establishing a PR Plan

In a survey of 100 top and middle managers in the communications field, over 60 percent said their PR programs involved little more than press releases, press kits for trade shows, and new product announcements.[11] Further, these tools were not designed into a formal public relations effort but rather were used only as needed. In other words, no structured program was evident in well over half of the companies surveyed! As we noted earlier, the public relations process is an ongoing one, requiring formalized policies and procedures for dealing with problems and opportunities. Just as you would not develop an advertising and/or promotions program without a plan, you should not institute public relations efforts haphazardly. Moreover, the PR plan needs to be integrated into the overall marketing communications program. Figure 17–3 provides some questions marketers should ask to determine whether their PR plan is workable.

Cutlip, Center, and Broom suggest a four-step process for developing a public relations plan: (1) define public relations problems; (2) plan and program; (3) take action and communicate; and (4) evaluate the program.[12] The questions in Figure 17–3 and the four-step planning process tie in with the promotional planning process stressed throughout this text.

Where we go from here...

Texaco is facing a vital challenge. It's broader than any specific words and larger than any lawsuit.

We are committed to begin meeting this challenge swiftly through specific programs with concrete goals and measurable timetables.

Our responsibility is to eradicate discriminatory behavior wherever and however it surfaces within our company. Our challenge is to make Texaco a company of limitless opportunity for all men and women. Our goal is to broaden economic access to Texaco for women and minorities and to increase the positive impact our investments can have in communities across America.

We have started down this road by reaching out to prominent minority and religious leaders to explore ways to make Texaco a model of diversity and workplace equality.

It is essential to this urgent mission that we work together to help solve the problems we face as a company – which, after all, echo the problems faced in society as a whole.

Discrimination will be extinguished only if we tackle it together – only if we join in a unified, common effort.

Together we can take Texaco into the 21st century as a model of diversity.

We can make Texaco a company of limitless opportunity.

We can and must make Texaco a leader in according respect to every man and woman.

Peter I. Bijur
Chairman & CEO

Visit our Web site: http://www.texaco.com

Exhibit 17–1 Texaco responds to negative publicity

Developing and Executing the PR Program

Because of the broad role that public relations may be asked to play, the PR program may need to extend beyond promotion. A broader definition of the target market, additional communications objectives, and different messages and delivery systems may be employed. Let us examine this process.

1. Does the plan reflect a thorough understanding of the company's business situation?
2. Has the PR program made good use of research and background sources?
3. Does the plan include full analysis of recent editorial coverage?
4. Do the PR people fully understand the product's strengths and weaknesses?
5. Does the PR program describe several cogent, relevant conclusions from the research?
6. Are the program objectives specific and measurable?
7. Does the program clearly describe what the PR activity will be and how it will benefit the company?
8. Does the program describe how its results will be measured?
9. Do the research, objectives, activities, and evaluations tie together?
10. Has the PR department communicated with marketing throughout the development of the program?

Figure 17–3 Ten questions for evaluating public relations plans

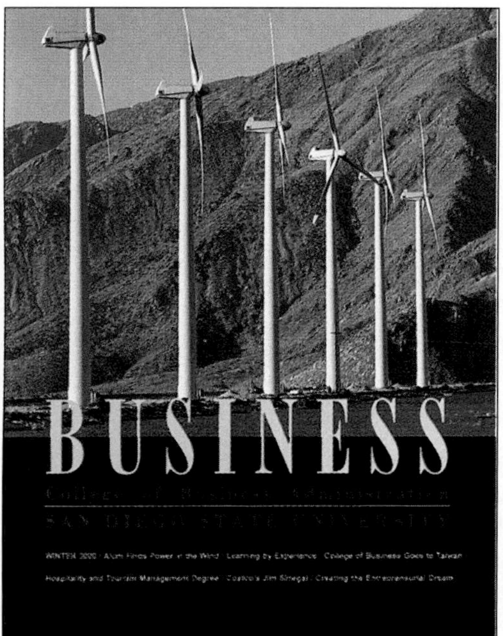

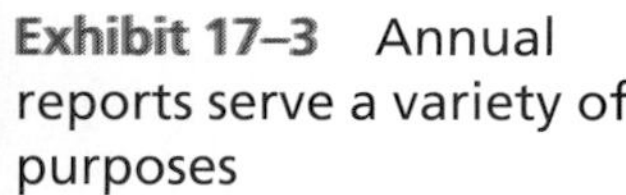

Exhibit 17–2 An example of a newsletter used for internal communication

Determining Relevant Target Audiences

The targets of public relations efforts may vary, with different objectives for each. Some may be directly involved in selling the product; others may affect the firm in a different way (e.g., they may be aimed at stockholders or legislators). These audiences may be internal or external to the firm.

Internal audiences may include the employees of the firm, stockholders and investors, members of the local community, suppliers, and current customers. Why are community members and customers of the firm considered internal rather than external? According to John Marston, it's because these groups are already connected with the organization in some way and the firm normally communicates with them in the ordinary routine of work.[13] **External audiences** are those people who are not closely connected with the organization (e.g., the public at large).

It may be necessary to communicate with these groups on an ongoing basis for a variety of reasons, ranging from ensuring goodwill to introducing new policies, procedures, or even products. A few examples may help.

Employees of the Firm Maintaining morale and showcasing the results of employees' efforts are often prime objectives of the public relations program. Organizational newsletters, notices on bulletin boards, paycheck envelope stuffers, direct mail, and annual reports are some of the methods used to communicate with these groups. Exhibit 17–2 shows one such internal communication used by the Business School at San Diego State University.

Personal methods of communicating may be as formal as an established grievance committee or as informal as an office Christmas party. Other social events, such as corporate bowling teams or picnics, are also used to create goodwill.

Stockholders and Investors You may think an annual report like the one in Exhibit 17–3 just provides stockholders and investors with financial information

Exhibit 17–3 Annual reports serve a variety of purposes

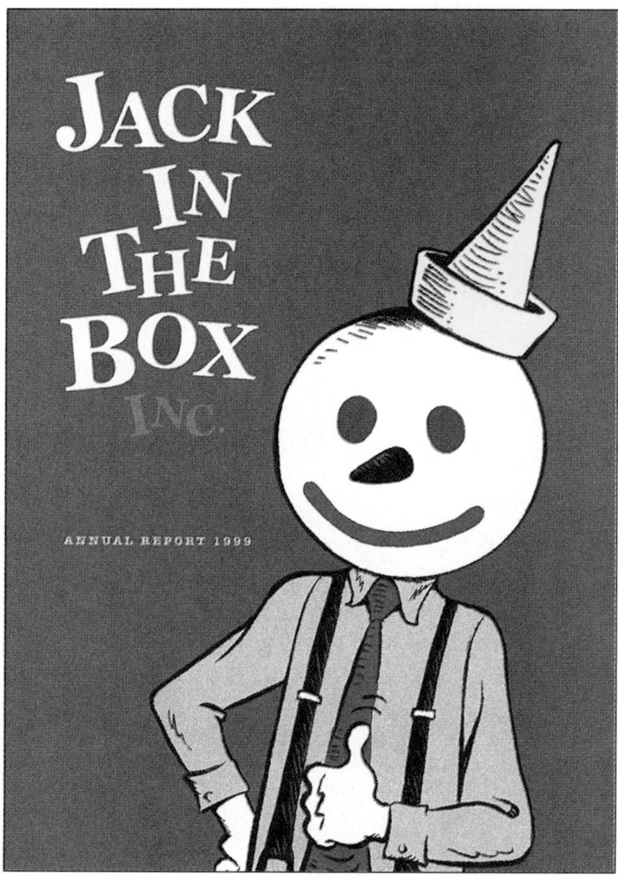

regarding the firm. While this is one purpose, annual reports are also a communications channel for informing this audience about why the firm is or is not doing well, future plans, and other information that goes beyond numbers.

For example, McDonald's has successfully used annual reports to fend off potential PR problems. One year the report described McDonald's recycling efforts to alleviate consumers' concerns about waste; another report included a 12-page spread on food and nutrition. Other companies use similar strategies, employing shareholders' meetings, video presentations, and other forms of direct mail. General Motors' annual public interest report is sent to shareholders and community members to detail the company's high standards of corporate responsibility. Companies have used these approaches to generate additional investments, to bring more of their stocks "back home" (i.e., become more locally controlled and managed), and to produce funding to solve specific problems, as well as to promote goodwill.

Community Members People who live and work in the community where a firm is located or doing business are often the target of public relations efforts. Such efforts may involve ads informing the community of activities that the organization is engaged in—for example, reducing air pollution, cleaning up water supplies, or, as shown in Exhibit 17–4, protecting turtles. (As you can see, the community can be defined very broadly.) Demonstrating to people that the organization is a good citizen with their welfare in mind may also be a reason for communicating to these groups.

Suppliers and Customers An organization wishes to maintain *goodwill* with its suppliers as well as its consuming public. If consumers think a company is not socially conscious, they may take their loyalties elsewhere. Suppliers may be inclined to do the same.

Sometimes sponsoring a public relations effort results in direct evidence of success. For example, the "Just say no" to drugs campaign was a boon to companies manufacturing drug testing kits, hospitals offering drug rehabilitation programs, and TV news programs' ratings.[14] Indirect indications of the success of PR efforts may include more customer loyalty, less antagonism, or greater cooperation between the firm and its suppliers or consumers.

Sometimes a public relations effort is targeted to more than one group. For example, San Diego Gas & Electric (SDGE), the public utility company for the San Diego area, has suffered from extreme negative attitudes among its customers due to its high rates. This problem was aggravated when a series of management blunders resulted in even higher rates and SDGE announced plans to build a nuclear plant in one of the lagoons near the ocean, resulting in protests from consumers and environmentalists. Stockholders and potential investors lacked trust, and employee

Exhibit 17–4 Chevron demonstrates concern for the public

morale was low. (Company cars with the SDGE logo on the doors were vandalized, and drivers were threatened to the point where the identifying logos had to be removed.)

The public relations plan developed to deal with these problems targeted a variety of publics and employed a number of channels. TV spots showed consumers how to save energy, print ads explained the reasons for the energy purchases made by management, and PR programs were developed to foster more community interaction. These programs have led to much more favorable attitudes among all the publics targeted. (At least employees can put the SDGE logo back on their cars.)

Relevant audiences may also include people not directly involved with the firm. The press, educators, civic and business groups, governments, and the financial community can be external audiences.

The Media Perhaps one of the most critical external publics is the media, which determine what you will read in your newspapers or see on TV, and how this news will be presented. Because of the media's power, they should be informed of the firm's actions. Companies issue press releases and communicate through conferences, interviews, and special events. The media are generally receptive to such information so long as it is handled professionally; reporters are always interested in good stories.

In turn, the media are concerned about how the community perceives them. Exhibit 17–5 is a public relations piece distributed by a San Diego TV station that describes a variety of ways the station benefits the community.

Educators A number of organizations provide educators with information regarding their activities. The Direct Marketing Association, the Promotional Prod-

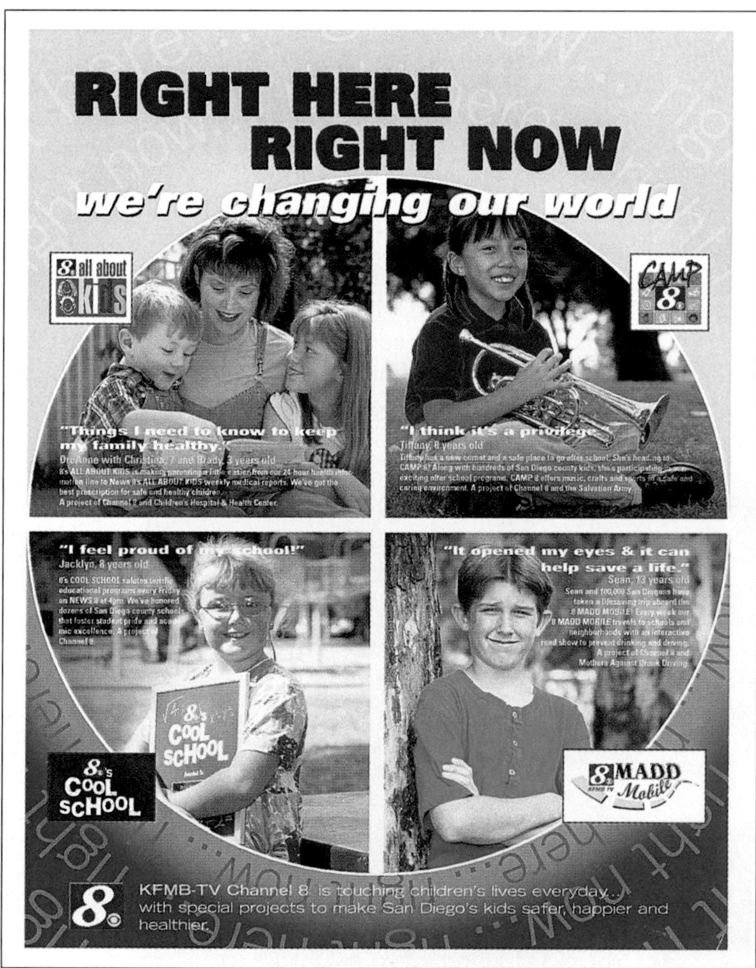

Exhibit 17–5 The media employ public relations to enhance their image in the community

ucts Association, and the Yellow Pages Publishers Association (YPPA), among others, keep educators informed in an attempt to generate goodwill as well as exposure for their causes. These groups and major corporations provide information regarding innovations, state-of-the-art research, and other items of interest (Exhibit 17–6). YPPA provides materials specifically designed for educators.

Educators are a target audience because, like the media, they control the flow of information to certain parties—in this case, people like you. *Business Week, Fortune,* and *Fast Company* magazines attempt to have professors use their magazines in their classes, as does *The Wall Street Journal, The New York Times,* and *Advertising Age,* among others. In addition to selling more magazines, such usage would also lend credibility to the mediums.

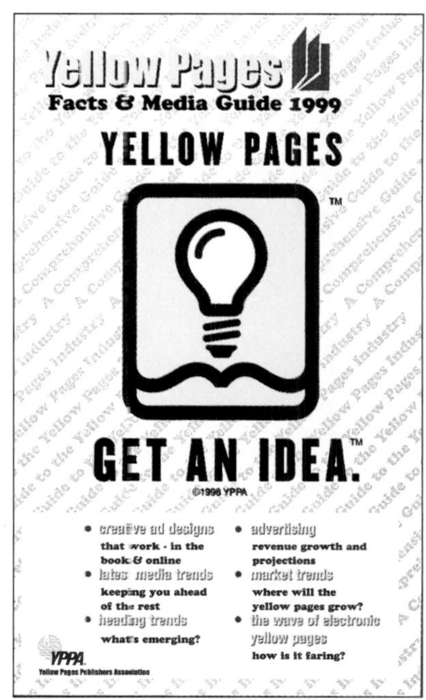

Exhibit 17–6 The Yellow Pages provide information about the medium

Civic and Business Organizations The local Jaycees, Kiwanis, and other nonprofit civic organizations also serve as gatekeepers of information. Companies' financial contributions to these groups, speeches at organization functions, and sponsorships are all designed to create goodwill. Corporate executives' service on the boards of nonprofit organizations also generates positive public relations.

Governments Public relations often attempts to influence government bodies directly at both local and national levels. Successful lobbying may mean immediate success for a product, while regulations detrimental to the firm may cost it millions. Imagine for a moment what FDA approval of NutraSweet meant to Searle or what could happen to the beer and wine industries if TV advertising were banned. The bicycle helmet industry sometimes experiences sales increases of 200 to 400 percent in a state when it passes a helmet law.

After decades of criticism from special-interest groups, the beer industry was forced to take steps to counteract legislation and other forms of government intervention similar to those affecting the cigarette and liquor industries. The beer industry's response was to support its political action committee, called Six-PAC, so that the committee could become more visible and active in its lobbying efforts in Washington, D.C. One of the first moves was to establish a new image for the industry, with a new slogan titled "Family businesses delivering America's beverage." Increased campaign contributions to candidates and pressures to investigate groups the industry felt were "gunning for beer" were also initiated. The lobby's efforts have paid off. While cigarettes and liquor continue to fall under attack and have had excise taxes levied on them, the beer industry remains unscathed and has a much more favorable reputation.[15]

Financial Groups In addition to current shareholders, potential shareholders and investors may be relevant target markets. Financial advisors, lending institutions, and others must be kept abreast of new developments as well as financial information, since they offer the potential for new sources of funding. Press releases and corporate reports play an important role in providing information to these publics.

Implementing the PR Program

Once the research has been conducted and the target audiences identified, the public relations program must be developed and delivered to the receivers. A number of PR tools are available for this purpose, including press releases, press conferences, exclusives, interviews, and community involvement.

The Press Release One of the most important publics is the press. To be used by the press, information must be factual, true, and of interest to the medium as well as to its audience. As shown in Figure 17–4, the source of the **press release** can do certain things to improve the likelihood that the "news" will be disseminated (Exhibit 17–7).

Figure 17–4 Getting the public relations story told

Jonathan Schenker of Ketchum Public Relations, New York, suggests four technological methods to make life easier for the press and to increase the likelihood that the media will use your story:

1. *Telephone press conferences.* Since reporters cannot always get to a press conference, use the telephone to call them for coverage.
2. *In-studio media tours.* Satellite communications providing a story, and a chance to interview, from a central location such as a TV studio save broadcast journalists time and money by eliminating their need to travel.
3. *Multicomponent video news releases (VNR).* A five-component package consisting of a complete script in print and on tape, a video release with a live reporter, a local contact source at which to target the video, and a silent video news release that allows the station to fill in with its own news reporter lend an advantage by saving the media money.
4. *Targeted newswire stories.* When the sender targets the public relations message, reporters are spared the need to read through volumes of news stories to select those of interest to their target audiences.

Exhibit 17–7 A Nortel press release

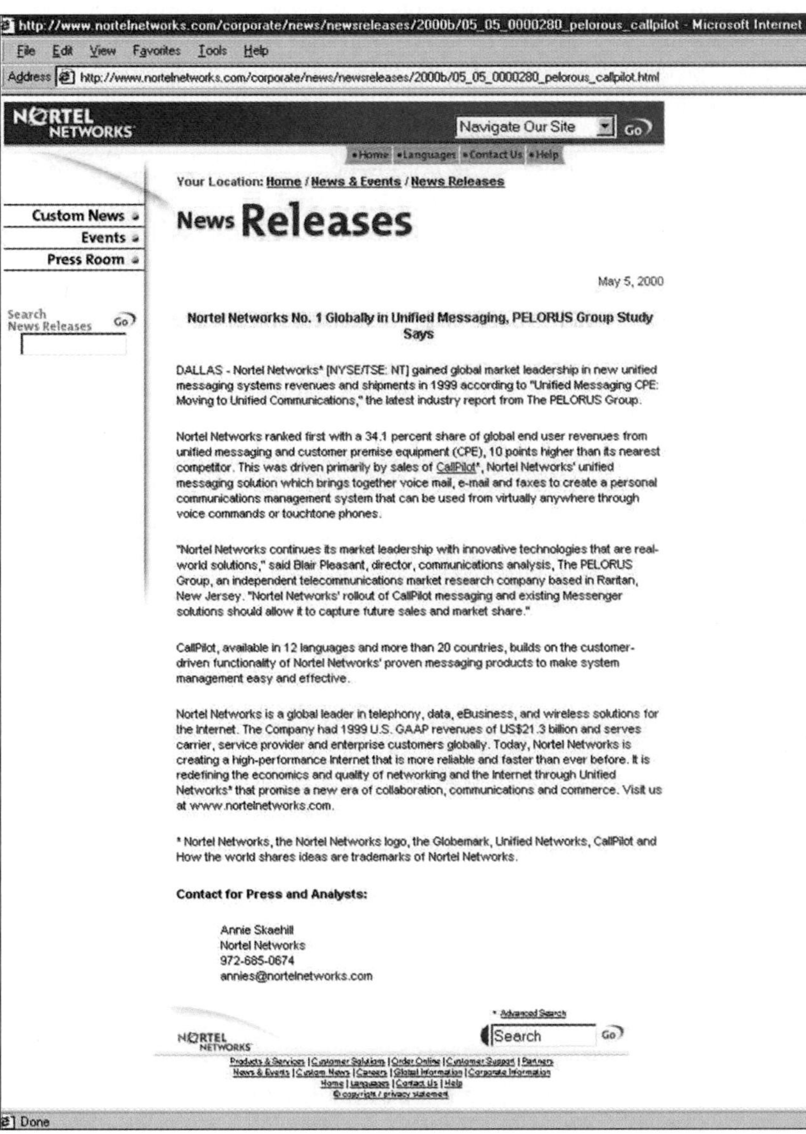

http://www.nortelnetworks.com/corporate/news/newsreleases/2000b/05_05_0000280_pelorous_callpilot - Microsoft Internet

File Edit View Favorites Tools Help

Address http://www.nortelnetworks.com/corporate/news/newsreleases/2000b/05_05_0000280_pelorous_callpilot.html

NORTEL NETWORKS

Navigate Our Site Go

•Home •Languages •Contact Us •Help

Custom News

Events

Press Room

Search News Releases Go

Your Location: Home / News & Events / News Releases

News Releases

May 5, 2000

Nortel Networks No. 1 Globally in Unified Messaging, PELORUS Group Study Says

DALLAS - Nortel Networks* [NYSE/TSE: NT] gained global market leadership in new unified messaging systems revenues and shipments in 1999 according to "Unified Messaging CPE: Moving to Unified Communications," the latest industry report from The PELORUS Group.

Nortel Networks ranked first with a 34.1 percent share of global end user revenues from unified messaging and customer premise equipment (CPE), 10 points higher than its nearest competitor. This was driven primarily by sales of CallPilot*, Nortel Networks' unified messaging solution which brings together voice mail, e-mail and faxes to create a personal communications management system that can be used from virtually anywhere through voice commands or touchtone phones.

"Nortel Networks continues its market leadership with innovative technologies that are real-world solutions," said Blair Pleasant, director, communications analysis, The PELORUS Group, an independent telecommunications market research company based in Raritan, New Jersey. "Nortel Networks' rollout of CallPilot messaging and existing Messenger solutions should allow it to capture future sales and market share."

CallPilot, available in 12 languages and more than 20 countries, builds on the customer-driven functionality of Nortel Networks' proven messaging products to make system management easy and effective.

Nortel Networks is a global leader in telephony, data, eBusiness, and wireless solutions for the Internet. The Company had 1999 U.S. GAAP revenues of US$21.3 billion and serves carrier, service provider and enterprise customers globally. Today, Nortel Networks is creating a high-performance Internet that is more reliable and faster than ever before. It is redefining the economics and quality of networking and the Internet through Unified Networks* that promise a new era of collaboration, communications and commerce. Visit us at www.nortelnetworks.com.

* Nortel Networks, the Nortel Networks logo, the Globemark, Unified Networks, CallPilot and How the world shares ideas are trademarks of Nortel Networks.

Contact for Press and Analysts:

Annie Skaehill
Nortel Networks
972-685-0674
annies@nortelnetworks.com

• Advanced Search

NORTEL NETWORKS

Search Go

Products & Services | Customer Solutions | Order Online | Customer Support | Partners
News & Events | Custom News | Careers | Global Information | Corporate Information
Home | Languages | Contact Us | Help
© copyright / privacy statement

Done

The information in a press release won't be used unless it's of interest to the readers of the medium it's sent to. For example, financial institutions may issue press releases to business trade media and to the editor of the business section of a general-interest newspaper. Information on the release of a new rock album is of more interest to radio disk jockeys than to TV newscasters; sports news also has its interested audiences.

Press Conferences We are all familiar with **press conferences** held by political figures. While used less often by organizations and corporations, this form of delivery can be very effective. The topic must be of major interest to a specific group before it is likely to gain coverage. Usually major accomplishments (such as the awarding of the next Super Bowl or Olympics location), major breakthroughs (such as medical cures), emergencies, or catastrophes warrant a national press conference. On a local level, community events, local developments, and the like may receive coverage. Companies often call press conferences when they have significant news to announce, such as the introduction of a new product or advertising campaign. Sports teams use this tool to attract fan attention and interest when a new star is signed. TV3, a Malaysian broadcast system, held an international press conference to announce its introduction of an interactive TV service. Hertz held two press conferences regarding O. J. Simpson when he was accused of murdering his wife—the first to announce that it would continue to support him as its spokesman, the second to announce that it would discontinue the relationship.

Exclusives Although most public relations efforts seek a variety of channels for distribution, an alternative strategy is to offer one particular medium exclusive rights to the story if that medium reaches a substantial number of people in the target audience. Offering an **exclusive** may enhance the likelihood of acceptance. As you watch television over the next few weeks, look for the various networks' and local stations' exclusives. Notice how the media actually use these exclusives to promote themselves.

Interviews When you watch TV or read magazines, pay close attention to the personal interviews. Usually someone will raise specific questions, and a spokesperson provided by the firm will answer them. For example, when four people died from eating tainted hamburgers at Jack in the Box restaurants, the company's president gave personal interviews with the press to detail the corrective actions the company would take. Microsoft's president, Steve Ballmer, appeared in a number of personal interviews to present the company's position in a legal case brought against it by the U.S. government. Monica Lewinsky's first TV interview with Barbara Walters of ABC was a major coup for the network, as the ratings were among the highest ever recorded. (The interview just happened to take place during "sweeps"!) Peter Bijur, the chair of Texaco, met with the press to discuss his plans to eliminate discriminatory practices within his corporation.

Community Involvement Many corporations enhance their public images through involvement in the local community. This involvement may take many forms, including membership in local organizations like the Kiwanis or Jaycees and contributions to or participation in community events. For example, after Hurricane Floyd created so much damage in the South, a number of companies came to the assistance of those experiencing losses. Retail Alliance provided $1 million in interest-free loans to small businesses. Lowe's stores contributed $5,000 and the Franciscus Company, a Virginia Beach condo developer, donated furnishings from professionally decorated model homes.[16] In addition, a local trade association raised $53,000 for victims in less than one week. A flood in Venezuela, which killed hundreds, brought aid from governments and businesses from around the world. Similar actions were taken after floods in the Midwest by Provident Bank, Parmalat USA (milk donations), and Wal-Mart, among others. The media also devoted free airtime to aid victims by coordinating activities, announcing programs and food drop-off points, and so on.

The Internet As mentioned briefly in Chapter 15, the Internet has become a means by which companies and organizations can disseminate public relations information. Just as in the print media, companies have used the Web to establish media relations and government, investor, and community relationships; deal with crises; and even conduct cause marketing. Companies have used their websites to address issues, as shown by the Odwalla example in Exhibit 17–8, as well as to provide information about products and services, archive press releases, link to other articles and sites, and provide lists of activities and events. Other Internet tools, including e-mails and e-mail newsletters, have also been used effectively.

Shel Holtz notes that while there are many similarities between public relations activities conducted in traditional media and those conducted on the Internet, three main elements account for the differences between the two:

1. The Internet offers a more limited opportunity to gain attention due to short exposure times.
2. The Internet offers the opportunity to build internal links that provide the media with instant access to additional sources of information on the issue.
3. The Internet offers the ability to provide much more substantial information. Print and broadcast materials are confined by time and space limitations, while

Exhibit 17–8 Odwalla Juice's website was established during its recall crisis

Questions and Answers
Odwalla Product Recall
November 3, 1996

Q: ***When was the Odwalla product recall announced and was it voluntary?***
A: Yes. The voluntary recall was announced by Odwalla on Wednesday, October 30, 1996, following notification by the Seattle-King County Department of Public Health in Washington State that several people diagnosed with the *E. coli* O157:H7 bacteria reported that they had consumed Odwalla apple juice.

Q: ***Which Odwalla products were recalled and why?***
A: All products containing apple juice have been recalled and as a further precautionary measure, carrot juice, organic carrot juice and vegetable cocktail, all of which are processed on the same line as the apple juice products, have been recalled.

Recalled products and approximate percentages of apple juice content (could contain less apple juice than percentages indicated):

Apple Juice 100%
Blackberry Fruitshake 40%
Mango Tango 30%
Super Protein 40%
Strawberry Banana Smoothie 10%
Raspberry Smoothie 20%
C-Monster 30%
Strawberry C Monster 10%
Mo' Beta 10%
Femme Vitale 40%
Superfood 50%
Serious Ginseng 20%
Deep in Peach 40%
Carrot Juice 0%
Organic Carrot Juice 0%
Vegetable Cocktail 0%

Q: ***Are any of the Odwalla citrus-based juices or the geothermal spring water associated with the E. coli O157:H7 bacteria?***
A: No. All Odwalla citrus-based juices and the geothermal spring water are not affected by the recall and are still being produced and distributed. These products include:

Orange Juice
Grapefruit Juice
Honey Lemonade
Strawberry Lemonade
Menage a Tropique
C Monster Light
Lemon Juice
Lime Juice
Geothermal Spring Water

Q: ***Have all recalled products been taken off the shelf?***
A: Yes. Odwalla has confirmed that all recalled products in its distribution system have been removed from store shelves. Consumers who purchased bottles of the recalled products are encouraged to return them to the store where purchased for a full refund.

Q: ***What are the symptoms of E. coli O157:H7 bacteria?***
A: Symptoms include diarrhea, abdominal cramps and visible blood in the stool. Usually, little or no fever is present. Anyone who has developed diarrheal illness within two weeks of consuming an Odwalla product containing apple juice may wish to consult a physician. Individuals who have consumed an Odwalla product and have not developed diarrheal illness are not at risk for complication and do not need to seek medical care.

Q: ***Is more Odwalla and recall-related information available?***
A: Yes. Odwalla has established a Web site at www.enw.com/odwalla. The company has also opened a hot line to answer consumer questions. The number is 1-800-639-2552.

This section will be updated regularly.

Back

the Internet can literally provide volumes of information at a fingertip—or click of a mouse.[17]

Holtz also notes that while public relations activities are increasing on the Internet, and will continue to do so, PR people have been some of the slowest to adopt the new technology. However, as more and more media people and PR people gain confidence, the Internet will become a major source of public relations activities.

Other methods of distributing information include photo kits, bylined articles (signed by the firm), speeches, and trade shows. Of course, the specific mode of distribution is determined by the nature of the story and the interest of the media and its publics.

Advantages and Disadvantages of PR

Like the other program elements, public relations has both advantages and disadvantages.

Advantages include the following:

1. *Credibility.* Because public relations communications are not perceived in the same light as advertising—that is, the public does not realize the organization either directly or indirectly paid for them—they tend to have more credibility. The fact that the media are not being compensated for providing the information may lead receivers to consider the news more truthful and credible. For example, an article in newspapers or magazines discussing the virtues of aspirin may be perceived as much more credible than an ad for a particular brand of aspirin.

Automotive awards presented in magazines such as *Motor Trend* have long been known to carry clout with potential car buyers. Now marketers have found that even lesser media mean a lot as well. General Motors' Pontiac division played up an award given to Pontiac as "the best domestic sedan" by *MotorWeek* in a 30-minute program carried by about 300 public broadcasting stations. Likewise, Chrysler trumpeted the awards given to its Jeep Cherokee by *4-Wheel & Off Road* magazine.[18] It has become a common practice for car companies to promote their achievements.

News about a product may in itself serve as the subject of an ad. Exhibit 17–9 demonstrates how Olympus used favorable publicity from a variety of sources to promote its digital camera. A number of auto manufacturers have also taken advantage in their ads of high customer satisfaction ratings reported by J. D. Powers & Associates, an independent research firm specializing in automotive research.

2. *Cost.* In both absolute and relative terms, the cost of public relations is very low, especially when the possible effects are considered. While a firm can employ public relations agencies and spend millions of dollars on PR, for smaller companies this form of communication may be the most affordable alternative available.

When Hewlett-Packard launched its new line of Pavilion PCs, the launch team was told that it would receive the $15 million advertising budget promised only if it first brought the HP name to consumers. Armed with only public relations and point-of-purchase materials, the team and its PR agency created the tagline "It's not just a PC. It's an HP," which appeared on all communications pieces, packaging, and product literature (Exhibit 17–10). Press releases and product information were then disseminated to many consumer and trade media. When it came time to seek the advertising dollars, the HP Pavilion (the name Pavilion never appeared alone) was firmly entrenched in the minds of the target market.[19]

Many public relations programs require little more than the time and expenses associated with putting the program together and getting it distributed, yet they still accomplish their objectives.

3. *Avoidance of clutter.* Because they are typically perceived as news items, public relations messages are not subject to the clutter of ads. A story regarding a new product introduction or breakthrough is treated as a news item and is likely to receive attention. When Steven Jobs (the founder of Apple Computer) announced

Exhibit 17–9 Olympus capitalizes on positive publicity in its advertising

Best Consumer Digital Camera
(MacUser EddyAwards, Jan.'97)
Product of the Year
(InfoWorld, Jan.'97)
Stellar
(Windows Sources, Jan.'97)
★★★★
(Computer Life, Feb.'97)

OLYMPUS

Any questions?
Plenty. How many pictures does the D-200L take?
Up to 80.
You're not sure?
You can shoot in both high-resolution or standard formats. And switch back and forth whenever you want. Even delete the shots you don't want at any time.
How do I know which ones to delete or keep?
You can instantly view the images you just captured.

72
73
74
75
76
77
78
79
80

Where?
On the color LCD screen. One at a time or nine at a time.
What's the resolution?
640 × 480. But you're not buying a pixel taker. It's pictures you're after. And picture quality is where the D-200L really outperforms the competition.
Who says?
InfoWorld, for one: "The image quality far surpassed any of the other digital cameras." And Windows Sources: "It delivers the best images we've seen from a consumer-level camera."
What about the lens?
It's a razor sharp, wide angle, macro, Olympus glass lens.
Flash?
With red-eye reduction, fill flash and auto mode.
But does it feel like a camera?
With an optical viewfinder and Olympus design, it follows in the footsteps of the Stylus series, the most successful line of 35mm cameras in the world.
Okay. I take a color shot. Now what?
Download the image into a computer, either Windows™ PC or a Mac® Then go to town.
Talk to me.
Create multiple images from one image. Or combine several. Add and subtract color. Retouch. Crop.
Go on.
E-mail it across the Internet. Put it on a Web page. Store it on disk.
Suppose I want to be creative?
With the included Adobe PhotoDeluxe™ software you can make greeting cards and real estate listings, design layouts, put together mail-order catalogs and newsletters. All in full living color.
Hold it! How much is all of this going to cost me?
$599.
That's it?
That's it.
There must be a science to all this.
And an art.
To learn more about the D-200L and how it completes the ideal home or office imaging system, contact your Olympus Marketing Represenative at 1-800-622-6372. They'll also tell you all about the new Olympus personal storage system and CD writer.

OLYMPUS
THE ART & SCIENCE OF IMAGING™
Visit us at http://www.olympus.com/digital
®and™ All trademarks and registered trademarks mentioned herein are the property of the respective holders.
The Art and Science of Imaging is a trademark of Olympus America Inc.
InfoWorld & MacUser awards received 1/97. ©1997 Olympus America Inc.

Exhibit 17–10 The HP Pavilion launch relied heavily on public relations activities

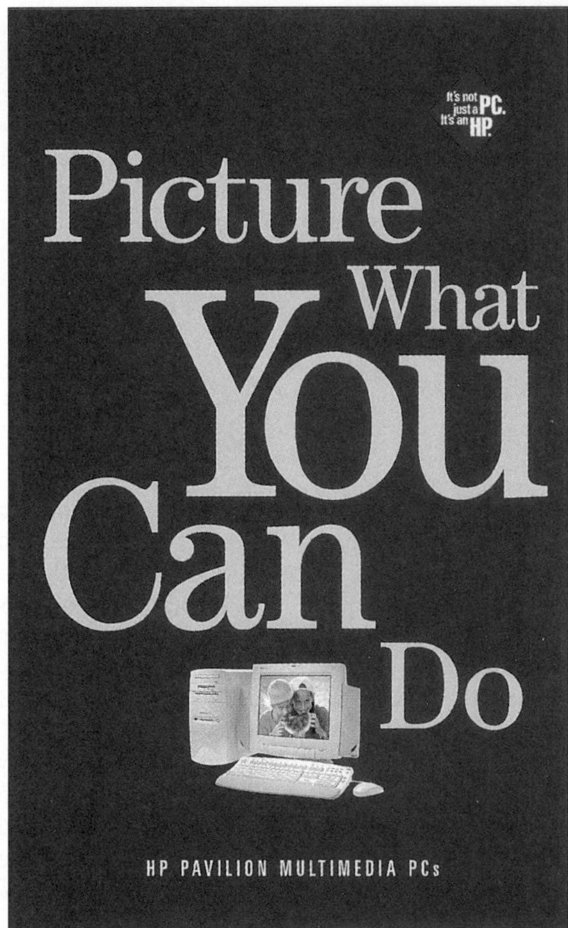

his return to Apple, all the networks covered it, as did major newspapers and magazines. Some (like CNN) devoted two- to three-minute segments to the story.

4. *Lead generation.* Information about technological innovations, medical breakthroughs, and the like results almost immediately in a multitude of inquiries. These inquiries may give the firm some quality sales leads. For example, when Tiger Woods, one of the longest drivers on the PGA tour, was seen using a Cobra golf club in the internationally televised U.S. Open, the club manufacturer received inquiries from all over the United States and as far away as Europe and Japan. When Dr. C. Everett Koop—the surgeon general in the Reagan administration—started a website called drkoop.com, it immediately became immensely popular as a source of health information. (Unfortunately for Dr. Koop, the popularity was short lived.)

5. *Ability to reach specific groups.* Because some products appeal to only small market segments, it is not feasible to engage in advertising and/or promotions to reach them. If the firm does not have the financial capabilities to engage in promotional expenditures, the best way to communicate to these groups is through public relations.

6. *Image building.* Effective public relations helps to develop a positive image for the organization. A strong image is insurance against later misfortunes. For example, in 1982, seven people in the Chicago area died after taking Extra Strength Tylenol capsules that had been laced with cyanide (after they reached the store). Within one week of the poisonings, Tylenol's market share fell from 35 to only 6.5 percent. Strong public relations efforts combined with an already strong product and corporate image helped the product rebound (despite the opinions of many

experts that it had no chance of recovering). A brand or firm with a lesser image would never have been able to come back. The ad in Exhibit 17–11 demonstrates the power of a strong image.

Perhaps the major disadvantage of public relations is the potential for not completing the communications process. While public relations messages can break through the clutter of commercials, the receiver may not make the connection to the source. Many firms' PR efforts are never associated with their sponsors in the public mind.

Public relations may also misfire through mismanagement and a lack of coordination with the marketing department. When marketing and PR departments operate independently, there is a danger of inconsistent communications, redundancies in efforts, and so on.

The key to effective public relations is to establish a good program, worthy of public interest, and manage it properly. To determine if this program is working, the firm must measure the effectiveness of the PR effort.

WHY A STRONG BRAND IMAGE GIVES YOU AN ALMOST UNFAIR ADVANTAGE.

[In a world of parity products and services, nothing can tilt things more dramatically in your favor than powerful brand and corporate advertising.]

A brand or corporate image is not something that can be seen, touched, tasted, defined, or measured. Intangible and abstract, it exists solely as an idea in the mind. Yet it is often a company's most precious asset.

When in the 1980s, corporations laid out billions for the companies that owned brands like Kraft, Jell-O, Del Monte, Maxwell House and Nabisco, it wasn't the products themselves they were after, but the enduring power of warm images, feelings, and impressions associated with the brand names. In fact, when the dust finally settles, it will become clear that the megamergers, takeovers, and leveraged buyouts of that decade were primarily about the acquisition of brands.

Yet despite their enormous value, brands are not immune to neglect, and in the face of a tough economy and strong competition, companies are often tempted to sacrifice brand and corporate advertising for short-term promotion. While such strategies can yield immediate results, over time they can weaken and tarnish the brand.

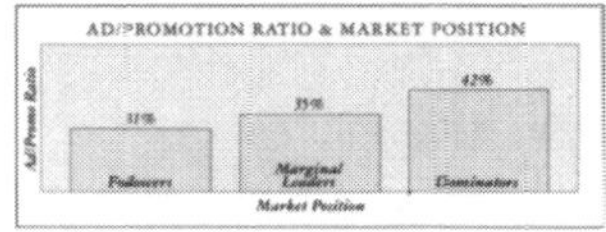

Studies conducted on the PIMS (Profit Impact on Market Strategy) data base prove that companies that put more money behind (their) image advertising are more likely to be market dominators, ranking first in a category and having sales volume one-and-a-half times greater than the nearest competitor. Moreover, the larger the ratio of brand advertising to promotion, the greater the return on investment (ROI). When only a quarter of a company's advertising/promotion budget is spent on brand advertising, the ROI is 18%. When the ratio is increased to 50/50, the return can be over 70% higher.

AD/PROMOTION RATIO & ROI

Return On Investment	18%	27%	31%
Ad/Promotion Ratio	Promo 76% / Ads 24%	Promo 56% / Ads 44%	Promo <50% / Ads >50%

Backing your brand in good times and bad—keeping that image in front of people—can mean higher profits as well as leadership.

PROTECTING AND NURTURING A brand is one of advertising's most important jobs. And that means choosing the media for your message with care. For more and more companies, the best environment is The Wall Street Journal. The Journal has always operated on the principle that there is a direct link between the quality of our editorial and the quality of the advertising we attract. Witness the impressive list of corporations appearing in any Journal issue.

In The Myers Marketing & Research survey of The Worldwide Marketing Leadership Panel, The Journal was awarded top honors in five separate categories, including editorial quality and reader involvement—more evidence of The Journal's unmatched stature and prestige.

If you're looking for a publication that can add value to your brand, there's no better brand than ours: The Wall Street Journal.

THE WALL STREET JOURNAL.
THE WORLD'S BUSINESS DAILY. IT WORKS.

Exhibit 17–11 This *Wall Street Journal* ad stresses the value of a strong brand and/or corporate image

Measuring the Effectiveness of PR

As with the other promotional program elements, it is important to evaluate the effectiveness of the public relations efforts. In addition to determining the contribution of this program element to attaining communications objectives, the evaluation offers other advantages:

1. It tells management what has been achieved through public relations activities.
2. It provides management with a way to measure public relations achievements quantitatively.
3. It gives management a way to judge the quality of public relations achievements and activities.

As shown in Figure 17–5, a number of criteria may be used to measure the effects of PR programs. Raymond Simon suggests additional means for accomplishing this evaluation process, including the following:

- *Personal observation and reaction.* Personal observation and evaluation by one's superiors should occur at all levels of the organization.
- *Matching objectives and results.* Specific objectives designed to attain the overall communications objectives should be related to actions, activities, or media coverage. For example, placing a feature story in a specific number of media is an objective, quantitative, and measurable goal.[20]
- *The team approach.* Harold Mendelsohn suggests that one way to achieve attitude and behavior modification through public information campaigns is the **team approach,** whereby evaluators are actually involved in the campaign.[21] By using research principles and working together, the team develops—and accomplishes—goals.
- *Management by objectives.* Executives and their managers act together to identify goals to be attained and the responsibilities of the managers. These goals are then used as a standard to measure accomplishments.
- *Public opinion and surveys.* Research in the form of public opinion surveys may be used to gather data to evaluate program goal attainment.
- *Audits.* Both internal and external audits may be used. **Internal audits** involve evaluations by superiors or peers within the firm to determine the performance of the employee (or his or her programs). **External audits** are conducted by consultants, the client (in the case of a PR agency), or other parties outside the organization.

A number of other bases for evaluation can be used. Walter Lindenmann says three levels of measures are involved: (1) the basic, which measures the actual PR activities undertaken; (2) the intermediate, which measures audience reception and

Figure 17–5 Criteria for measuring the effectiveness of PR

A system for measuring the effectiveness of the public relations program has been developed by Lotus HAL. The criteria used in the evaluation process follow:

- Total number of impressions over time
- Total number of impressions on the target audience
- Total number of impressions on specific target audiences
- Percentage of positive articles over time
- Percentage of negative articles over time
- Ratio of positive to negative articles
- Percentage of positive/negative articles by subject
- Percentage of positive/negative articles by publication or reporter
- Percentage of positive/negative articles by target audience

understanding of the message; and (3) the advanced, which measures the perceptual and behavioral changes that result.[22]

Some organizations may use a combination of measures, depending on their specific needs. For example, Hewlett-Packard uses impression counts, awareness and preference studies, in-house assessments, press clippings counts, and tracking studies.[23]

In summary, the role of public relations in the promotional mix is changing. As PR has become more marketing oriented, the criteria by which the programs are evaluated have also changed. At the same time, nonmarketing activities will continue to be part of the public relations department and part of the basis for evaluation.

Publicity

Publicity refers to the generation of news about a person, product, or service that appears in broadcast or print media. To many marketers, publicity and public relations are synonymous. In fact, publicity is really a subset of the public relations effort.

But there are several major differences. First, publicity is typically a *short-term* strategy, while public relations is a concerted program extending over a period of time. Second, public relations is designed to provide positive information about the firm and is usually controlled by the firm or its agent. Publicity, on the other hand, is not always positive and is not always under the control of, or paid for by, the organization. Both positive and negative publicity often originates from sources other than the firm.

In most organizations, publicity is controlled and disseminated by the public relations department. In this section, we discuss the role publicity plays in the promotional program and some of the ways marketers use and react to these communications.

The Power of Publicity

One of the factors that most sets off publicity from the other program elements is the sheer power this form of communication can generate. Unfortunately for marketers, this power is not always realized in the way they would like it to be. Publicity can make or break a product or even a company.

Earlier we discussed the substantial drop in Tylenol sales after extensive media coverage of the tampering with its products while on store shelves. The Johnson & Johnson marketing efforts (including a strong public relations emphasis) designed to aid recovery were a model in proficiency that will be studied by students of marketing (in both the classroom and the boardroom) for many years. By January 1983, almost 100 percent of the original brand share had been regained. When Odwalla's brand was threatened (see chapter lead-in) by negative publicity, the company immediately recalled the product, increased safety measures, and paid medical bills for those who had become ill. It also established a website and 800 numbers to make information easily available to concerned customers (Exhibit 17–12). The company has regained 100 percent of its market share as a result of these efforts. Unfortunately, a marketer cannot always capitalize on positive publicity or control the effects of negative publicity so effectively.

Why is publicity so much more powerful than advertising or sales promotion—or even other forms of public relations? First, publicity is highly credible. Unlike advertising and sales promotions, publicity is not usually perceived as being sponsored by the company (in the negative instances, it never is). So consumers perceive this information as more objective and place more confidence in it. In fact, *Consumer Reports,* the medium responsible for one of the examples previously cited, recently ran an ad campaign designed to promote its credibility by noting it does not accept advertising and therefore can be objective in its evaluations.

Exhibit 17–12 Odwalla assures customers of its quality

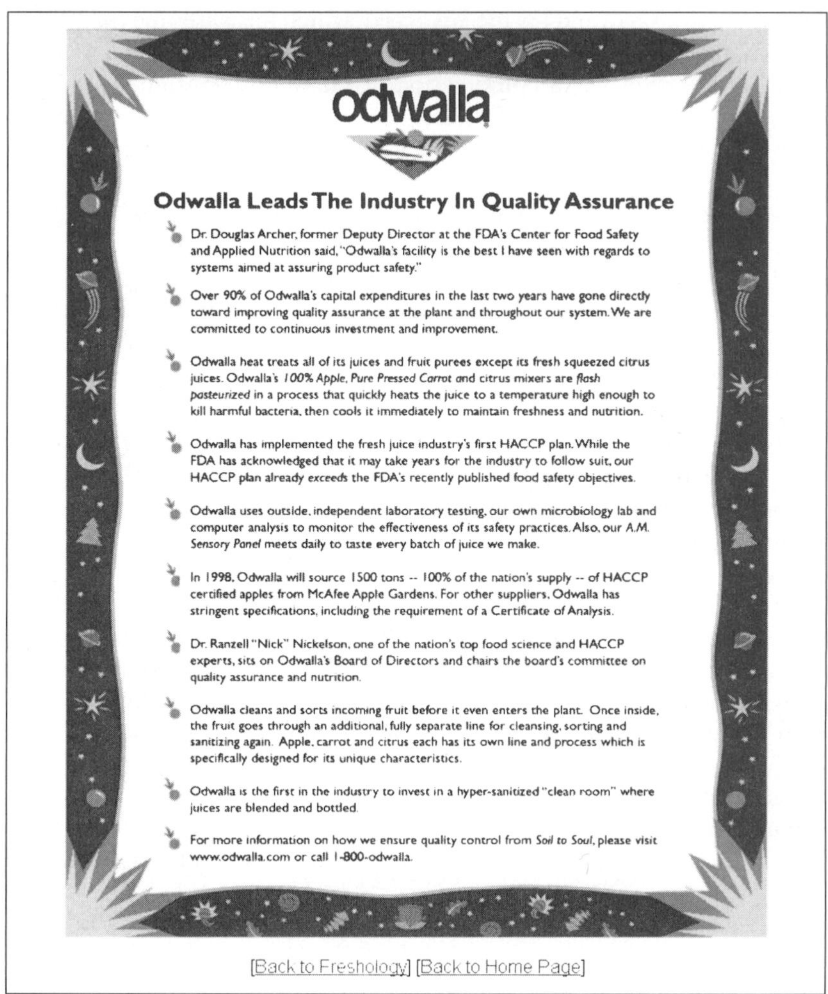

odwalla
Odwalla Leads The Industry In Quality Assurance
Dr. Douglas Archer, former Deputy Director at the FDA's Center for Food Safety and Applied Nutrition said, "Odwalla's facility is the best I have seen with regards to systems aimed at assuring product safety."
Over 90% of Odwalla's capital expenditures in the last two years have gone directly toward improving quality assurance at the plant and throughout our system. We are committed to continuous investment and improvement.
Odwalla heat treats all of its juices and fruit purees except its fresh squeezed citrus juices. Odwalla's *100% Apple, Pure Pressed Carrot* and citrus mixers are *flash pasteurized* in a process that quickly heats the juice to a temperature high enough to kill harmful bacteria, then cools it immediately to maintain freshness and nutrition.
Odwalla has implemented the fresh juice industry's first HACCP plan. While the FDA has acknowledged that it may take years for the industry to follow suit, our HACCP plan already *exceeds* the FDA's recently published food safety objectives.
Odwalla uses outside, independent laboratory testing, our own microbiology lab and computer analysis to monitor the effectiveness of its safety practices. Also, our *A.M. Sensory Panel* meets daily to taste every batch of juice we make.
In 1998, Odwalla will source 1500 tons -- 100% of the nation's supply -- of HACCP certified apples from McAfee Apple Gardens. For other suppliers, Odwalla has stringent specifications, including the requirement of a Certificate of Analysis.
Dr. Ranzell "Nick" Nickelson, one of the nation's top food science and HACCP experts, sits on Odwalla's Board of Directors and chairs the board's committee on quality assurance and nutrition.
Odwalla cleans and sorts incoming fruit before it even enters the plant. Once inside, the fruit goes through an additional, fully separate line for cleansing, sorting and sanitizing again. Apple, carrot and citrus each has its own line and process which is specifically designed for its unique characteristics.
Odwalla is the first in the industry to invest in a hyper-sanitized "clean room" where juices are blended and bottled.
For more information on how we ensure quality control from *Soil to Soul*, please visit www.odwalla.com or call 1-800-odwalla.
[Back to Freshology] [Back to Home Page]

Publicity information may be perceived as endorsed by the medium in which it appears. For example, publicity regarding a breakthrough in the durability of golf balls will go far to promote them if it is reported by *Golf* magazine. *Car & Driver*'s award for car of the year reflects the magazine's perception of the quality of the auto selected.

Still another reason for publicity's power is its news value and the frequency of exposure it generates. When basketball stars Larry Bird and Kareem Abdul-Jabbar appeared together in a commercial for Lay's potato chips, the ad appeared on every major TV network and many cable sports programs, both as a paid commercial and free as the media publicized the campaign. When Lay's introduced its campaign for Doritos Tortilla Thins featuring comedian Chevy Chase, TV reporters aired 1,734 stories about the ads using footage provided by Frito-Lay.[24]

The bottom line is that publicity is news, and people like to pass on information that has news value. Publicity thus results in a significant amount of free, credible, word-of-mouth information regarding the firm and its products.

The Control and Dissemination of Publicity

In some of the examples cited earlier, the control of publicity was not in the hands of the company. While in some instances it is the firm's own blunder to allow information to leak out, Texaco and Isuzu could do nothing to stop the media from releasing negative information. When publicity becomes news, it is reported by the media, sometimes despite the efforts of the firm. In these instances, the organization needs to react to the potential threat created by the news. As shown in IMC Perspective 17–1, this is not always an easy task.

Career Profile

Graham Hueber

Vice President, Director of Research and Measurement at Ketchum

I graduated from the University of Pennsylvania with a degree in modern European history. Fittingly, my career in public opinion analysis started as an editor at the American Enterprise Institute's magazine *Public Opinion.* The magazine tracked pre-election polls, analyzed voting patterns, and summarized a wide range of public policy issues for the legislative community in Washington, D.C. Part of my responsibilities consisted of doing secondary analysis on existing data. While doing this job I became interested in learning more about research methodology. I wanted to know how the data was actually gathered, how to develop a survey, design a questionnaire, and select a sample.

"There is never a dull moment in public relations research."

That initial training helped me get a research position with the Gallup Organization. Although I did not have a strong research background at the time, Gallup had a very open mind about hiring people with limited experience but a strong desire to learn. My experience with polling on public policy issues fit nicely with the needs of the company's well-known and respected research product, the Gallup Poll. Three times a week we wrote poll-based stories using data collected the previous weekend. The stories were sent to newspapers across the country and ultimately the Gallup Poll developed a partnership with *USA Today* for a wider distribution of its data. I remember a number of long nights completing surveys in a few hours and rushing the analysis off to the newspapers as the country anxiously awaited the beginning of the Gulf War.

The promise of a lackluster election year in 1992 prompted a career change from public opinion to public relations research. I accepted a position with Ketchum, which is the seventh largest public relations agency in the United States and has offices in more than 50 countries around the world. Their "best teams" approach to public relations includes having a full range of strategic counseling resources available to all staff members including: account planning, creative, information, communications and media strategy, research, and measurement.

Ketchum's Research Department was founded in 1987 and recently completed its 1,000th research project. The most interesting aspect of my job is having the opportunity to work with a wide range of clients who commission research studies. At any given time I may be managing projects from each of our six different practice areas—health care, food and nutrition, corporate, brand marketing, employee relations, and technology—and from offices around the world. The needs of these clients are very different and you are exposed to a wide range of research methodologies and every possible way to design a sample. The research department also specializes in projects designed to measure and evaluate the success of public relations projects. The Ketchum Effectiveness Yardstick, our proprietary approach, is discussed in this chapter of the book.

I am often asked to describe a typical project in a PR research department. There really isn't an answer to that question. Most of our surveys are quantitative in nature and most take place on the telephone, but beyond that very few generalizations can be made. In response to a client's crisis situation we can and have completed surveys overnight. Other projects take six months to a year to design, execute, and analyze. Some are done expressly for publicity purposes, which means the findings are released to the media. Other studies are done strictly for marketing and program development purposes, and the results are very closely guarded.

Our research department has designed surveys to determine the frequency with which auto mechanics disconnect catalytic converters, what frustrates people most when they shop online, and why people drink the brand of beer they do. We honestly live by the slogan "there is never a dull moment in public relations research." And now that I think about it, there really hasn't been one yet.

IMC Perspective 17–1

How Not to Handle Negative Publicity: 1999's Top 10 PR Blunders

While positive publicity can go a long way in helping a company achieve success, negative publicity is a manager's nightmare. It sometimes may seem difficult to get anyone to pay attention to positive things an organization is doing, but that certainly is not the case when a company does something wrong. How an organization responds to the "bad buzz" can have a long-term impact on its image and sales; if handled poorly, negative publicity can literally destroy a company.

Consider the examples set by Coca-Cola and Mobil. In the summer of 1999 a number of schoolchildren in Belgium and France became ill after drinking contaminated Coke. In the 30 days following the crisis, over 416 stories accounting for 297,248-plus words were devoted to the incident, and many of them focused on how poorly Coca-Cola handled the problem. Ultimately, the company's efforts were cited as one of the year's top 10 PR blunders. Mobil Corporation also received major coverage—not so much for what it did poorly as for what it didn't do. In the early 1990s the Indonesian government was allegedly running a torture site within a few hundred yards of a Mobil chemical plant. While Mobil employees and visiting advisors claimed to have no knowledge of the tortures, a coalition of 17 Indonesian human rights organizations claimed Mobil employees not only knew about the nature of the site but also may have provided logistical support to the army. Mobil flatly denied any complicity, but the bad press still resulted in major headlines in *Business Week*, *Time*, and other newsmagazines. (*Time* devoted five full pages to the story.) At the very least, the news stories said, Mobil could have said something about what was going on.

But Mobil and Coca-Cola are not the only major corporations with problems. Finneman Associates, a San Francisco–based public relations firm, publishes an annual "top 10" list of public relations disasters, which Finneman said involved "duplicity, myopia, paranoia, sloth, and overkill—cardinal sins when dealing with the public." Here are the winners for 1999:

- *Microsoft.* While spending the year fighting the federal government in an antitrust suit, Microsoft attempted to put a positive spin on each day's trial events and financially backed a think tank whose newspaper ads supported Microsoft's position. The company also placed ads in major newspapers around the United States defending its position—thereby initiating yet another government investigation.
- *RealNetworks.* RealNetworks made the list for developing "Big Brother" powers. The company got caught tracking the listening habits of 13 million users of its RealJukebox music-playing software without the listeners' consent.
- *Exxon.* The company lobbied, and then sued, to allow the *Exxon Valdez*—which 10 years ago spilled millions of gallons of oil into Prince William Sound—to return to the California-Alaska route from which it has been banned.
- *Coca-Cola.* Ten days into the crisis mentioned above, Coke's CEO Douglas Ivester flew to Brussels to apologize for the problem. His failure to respond immediately showed a lack of concern and further exacerbated the problem.
- *Great West Casualty.* After an 81-year-old woman stepped in front of a grain truck insured by Great West, the company sued her estate for negligence, asking $2,800 in damages.

Corporations were not the only ones to make the top 10:

- *Major League Baseball.* When 57 of the 68 major-league baseball umpires decided to quit in an attempt to force contract concessions, they expected the publicity to generate strong fan support—it didn't, and the owners called their bluff.
- *The Los Angeles Times.* When the newspaper devoted a Sunday magazine supplement section to coverage of the new Staples Arena, it failed to inform readers that the newspaper shared in the arena's advertising revenue.
- *The National Liberty Journal.* This newspaper received public criticism when it claimed that Tinky Winky of the Teletubbies was gay. The press depicted the paper's owner, evangelist Jerry Falwell, as "a paranoid, sexually obsessed Holy Roller." Whew!
- *Pat Robertson.* Robertson's financial service company lost a $3 billion deal with the Bank of Scotland after the conservative religious leader criticized Scotland's tolerance of homosexuals.
- *The American Medical Association.* The AMA fired the editor of the *Journal of the American Medical Association* after he published an article on college

students' views that oral sex didn't fit their definition of sex. The media hinted that the AMA was influenced by politics as a result of the Clinton scandal.

The above list is just a sampling of the many public relations disasters that occurred in 1999. The selection was based in part on the amount of attention that the organizations or individuals received as a result of their errors. Perhaps most interestingly, Finneman himself had a public relations disaster to deal with when the radio station he owns locked out its entire air staff, sparking weeks of street protests. Is that what they refer to as "what goes around comes around"?

Sources: Michelle Quinn, "Microsoft, RealNetworks Make Firm's Annual List of PR Blunders," *San Diego Union*, December 28, 1999, p. C4; Joe Mandese and Mark Weiner, "Coca-Cola's Belgian Crisis Dominates News," *Advertising Age*, July 12, 1999, p. 22; Michael Shari, Pete Engardio, and Sheri Prasso, "What Did Mobil Know?" *Business Week*, December 28, 1998, pp. 68–73.

A good example of one company's efforts to respond to adverse publicity is shown in Exhibit 17–13. Tree Top's problems began when all the major news media reported that the chemical Alar, used by some growers to regulate the growth of apples, might cause cancer in children. Despite published statements by reliable scientific and medical authorities (including the surgeon general) that Alar does not cause cancer, a few special-interest groups were able to generate an extraordinary amount of adverse publicity, causing concern among consumers and purchasing agents. A few school districts took apples off their menus, and even applesauce and juice were implicated. Tree Top ran the ad in Exhibit 17–13 to state its position and alleviate consumers' fears. It also sent a direct mailing to nutritionists and day care operators. The campaign was successful in assuring consumers of the product's safety and rebuilding their confidence.

In other instances, however, publicity must be managed like any other promotional tool. For example, when the FDA instructed P&G to stop using "fresh" claims in its Citrus Hill orange juice, the company refused to do so. After a lengthy confrontation, the FDA impounded thousands of gallons of the product, and the resulting publicity reflected negatively on both the brand and the organization.

Exhibit 17–13 Tree Top responds to the threat of negative publicity

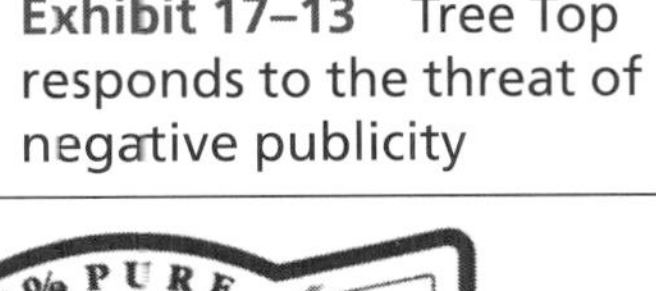

Publicity can also work for marketers. Pokemon, Tickle Me Elmo dolls, and Furbys all achieved significant sales due to high levels of positive publicity and word-of-mouth advertising. Sales of Cabernet Sauvignon increased an average of 45 percent in the month after a CBS "60 Minutes" report that daily moderate consumption of red wine can reduce the risk of heart disease. There are many more examples of the positive impact publicity can have.

Marketers like to have as much control as possible over the time and place where information is released. One way to do this is with the **video news release (VNR),** a publicity piece produced by publicists so that stations can air it as a news story. The videos almost never mention that they are produced by the subject organization, and most news stations don't mention it either. Zany Brainy, Experian, Consolidated Freightways, and Octavo Corp. are just a few of the companies that have used VNRs. Hewlett-Packard used this medium to introduce its new division, Agilent Technologies.[25] Many companies have made significant use of video news releases.

In their efforts to manage publicity and public relations, marketers are continuously learning more about these activities. Courses are offered and books written on how to manage publicity. These books cover how to make a presentation, whom to contact, how to issue a press release, and what to know about each medium addressed, including TV, radio, newspapers, magazines, and direct-response advertising. They discuss such alternative media as news conferences, seminars, events, and personal letters, as well as insights on how to deal with government and other legislative bodies. Because this information is too extensive to include as a single chapter in this text, we suggest you peruse one of the many books available on this subject for additional insights.

Advantages and Disadvantages of Publicity

Publicity offers the advantages of credibility, news value, significant word-of-mouth communications, and a perception of being endorsed by the media. Beyond the potential impact of negative publicity, two major problems arise from the use of publicity: timing and accuracy.

Timing Timing of the publicity is not always completely under the control of the marketer. Unless the press thinks the information has very high news value, the timing of the press release is entirely up to the media—if it gets released at all. Thus, the information may be released earlier than desired or too late to make an impact.

Accuracy A major way to get publicity is the press release. Unfortunately, the information sometimes gets lost in translation—that is, it is not always reported the way the provider wishes it to be. As a result, inaccurate information, omissions, or other errors may result. Sometimes when you see a publicity piece that was written on the basis of a press release, you wonder if the two are even about the same topic.

Measuring the Effectiveness of Publicity

The methods for measuring the effects of publicity are essentially the same as those discussed earlier under the broader topic of public relations. Rather than reiterate them here, we thought it would be more interesting to show you an actual example. Figure 17–6 is a model developed by Ketchum Public Relations for tracking the effects of publicity. (I guess we just provided Ketchum with some free publicity.)

Corporate Advertising

One of the more controversial forms of advertising is **corporate advertising.** Actually an extension of the public relations function, corporate advertising does not promote any one specific product or service. Rather, it is designed to promote the firm overall, by enhancing its image, assuming a position on a social issue or cause, or seeking direct involvement in something. Why is corporate advertising controversial? A number of reasons are offered:

1. *Consumers are not interested in this form of advertising.* A Gallup and Robinson study reported in *Advertising Age* found consumers were 35 percent less interested in corporate ads than in product-oriented advertising.[26] This may be because consumers do not understand the reasons behind such ads. Of course, much of this confusion results from ads that are not very good from a communications standpoint.
2. *It's a costly form of self-indulgence.* Firms have been accused of engaging in corporate image advertising only to satisfy the egos of top management. This argument stems from the fact that corporate ads are not easy to write. The message to be communicated is not as precise and specific as one designed to position a product, so the top managers often dictate the content of the ad, and the copy reflects their ideas and images of the corporation.
3. *The firm must be in trouble.* Some critics believe the only time firms engage in corporate advertising is when they are in trouble—either in a financial sense or in the public eye—and are advertising to attempt to remedy the problem. There are a

Figure 17–6 The Ketchum Effectiveness Yardstick (KEY); a strategic approach to the measurement of public relations results

At Ketchum, we believe strongly that it is possible to measure public relations effectiveness. We also believe strongly that measuring public relations results can be done in a timely and cost-efficient manner.

Our strategic approach to public relations measurement involves a two-step process:

1. Setting in advance very specific and clearly defined public relations goals and objectives, and,
2. Pinpointing those levels of measurement that are crucial to the organization in determining to what extent those specific public relations goals and objectives have been met.

In the model, there are three levels for measuring PR effectiveness:

- Level #1—the Basic level for measuring public relations OUTPUTS. This measures the amount of exposure an organization receives in the media, the total number of placements, the total number of impressions, and/or the likelihood of having reached specific target audience groups. Research tools often used when conducting Level #1 measurement include content analysis or publicity tracking studies, secondary analysis, segmentation analysis, and basic public opinion polls.
- Level #2—the Intermediate level for measuring public relations OUTGROWTHS. Outgrowths measure whether or not target audience groups actually received the messages directed at them, paid attention to them, understood the messages, and retained those messages in any shape or form. Research tools often used when conducting Level #2 measurement include focus groups; in-depth interviews; telephone, mail, face-to-face, or mall intercept surveys; testing techniques; and recall studies.
- Level #3—the Advanced level for measuring public relations OUTCOMES. This measures opinion, attitude, and/or behavior change to determine if there has been a shift in views and/or how people act when it comes to an organization, its products, or its services. Research tools often used when conducting Level #3 measurement include before-and-after studies, experimental and quasi-experimental research, ethnographic studies, communications audits, and multivariate analyses of data.
- The different levels of measuring public relations impact can be plotted on a yardstick in a hierarchial fashion. Here is a graphic displaying the KETCHUM EFFECTIVENESS YARDSTICK (KEY), which summarizes from left to right these levels of public relations measurement:

Level #1	**Level #2**	**Level #3**
Basic—Measuring OUTPUTS	Intermediate—Measuring OUTGROWTHS	Advanced—Measuring OUTCOMES
Media placements Impressions Targeted Audiences	Receptivity Awareness Comprehension Retention	Opinion change Attitude change Behavior change

More detailed information about Ketchum's strategic approach to measuring public relations effectiveness may be obtained by contacting Graham Hueber, Vice President and Director of Research at Ketchum.

number of forms of corporate advertising, each with its own objectives. These critics argue that these objectives have become important only because the firm has not been managed properly.

4. *Corporate advertising is a waste of money.* Given that the ads do not directly appeal to anyone, are not understood, and do not promote anything specific, critics say the monies could be better spent in other areas. Again, much of this argument has its foundation in the fact that corporate image ads are often intangible. They

typically do not ask directly for a purchase; they do not ask for investors. Rather, they present a position or try to create an image. Because they are not specific, many critics believe their purpose is lost on the audience and these ads are not a wise investment of the firm's resources.

Despite these criticisms and others, corporate advertising has increased in use. It's been estimated that more than 7 percent of all advertising dollars spent are for corporate advertising, meaning billions of dollars are spent on this form of communication.[27]

While corporate advertising has generally been regarded as the domain of companies such as USX, Phillips Petroleum, Aventis, and Deutsche Telekom (that is, companies that primarily sell directly to the consumer market), this is no longer the case. Beatrice Foods, BASF, and Procter & Gamble are just a few consumer products companies running corporate image ads, and Lucent Technologies, Microsoft, and Pfizer have also increased expenditures in this area.

Since the term *corporate advertising* tends to be used as a catchall for any type of advertising run for the direct benefit of the corporation rather than its products or services, much advertising falls into this category. For purposes of this text (and to attempt to bring some perspective to the term), we use it to describe any type of advertising designed to promote the organization itself rather than its products or services.

Objectives of Corporate Advertising

Corporate advertising may be designed with two goals in mind: (1) creating a positive image for the firm and (2) communicating the organization's views on social, business, and environmental issues. More specific applications include:

- Boosting employee morale and smoothing labor relations.
- Helping newly deregulated industries ease consumer uncertainty and answer investor questions.
- Helping diversified companies establish an identity for the parent firm rather than relying solely on brand names.[28]

As these objectives indicate, corporate advertising is targeted at both internal and external audiences and involves the promotion of the organization as well as its ideas. IMC Perspective 17–2 shows Nortel's efforts in this area.

Exhibit 17–14 Tyco uses image advertising to avoid confusion

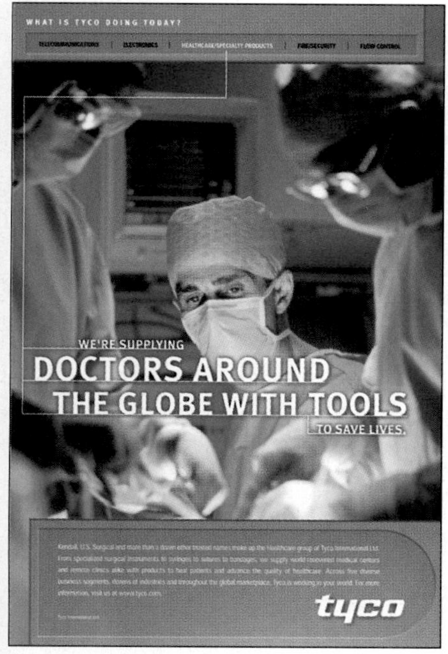

Types of Corporate Advertising

Marketers seek attainment of corporate advertising's objectives by implementing image, advocacy, or cause-related advertising. Each form is designed to achieve specific goals.

Image Advertising

One form of corporate advertising is devoted to promoting the organization's overall image. **Image advertising** may accomplish a number of objectives, including creating goodwill both internally and externally, creating a position for the company, and generating resources, both human and financial. A number of methods are used:

1. *General image or positioning ads.* As shown in Exhibit 17–14, ads are often designed to create an image of the firm in the public mind. The exhibit shows how Tyco is attempting to create an image of itself as a market leader and health care expert, not a *toy* company.

Other companies have used image advertising to attempt to change an existing image. The American Medical Association (AMA), responding to its less-than-positive image among many Americans who perceived doctors as "inattentive money-grubbers," ran a series of ads portraying doctors in a more sensitive light. It spent over $1.75 million to highlight the caring, sharing, and sensitive side of AMA members.[29] *Penthouse* magazine attempted

IMC Perspective 17–2

What Do You Want the Internet to Be? Nortel Wants to Know

If you ask most people outside of Canada to name a company that plays a major role in making the Internet work, they are likely to mention Microsoft, Cisco Systems, Lucent Technologies, or perhaps Intel. It is less likely they will name Nortel Networks, the Canadian-based telecommunications company that is the leading provider of integrated network solutions for the Internet. However, this is about to change, as Nortel has embarked on a $100 million global integrated marketing communications campaign to increase awareness of the company's leadership position at the heart of the Internet revolution.

Nortel Networks is a 103-year-old company based in Brampton, Ontario, that until recently operated under the name Northern Telecom Limited and was best known as a manufacturer of old-line telephone equipment. However, in March 1999 the company changed its name to Nortel Networks Corporation to reflect its position as a leading provider of integrated network solutions spanning data and telephony. Among other things, Nortel makes equipment that enables phone companies to transport voice, video, and data over a single network using a technology known as *Internet protocol,* or *IP.*

Nortel's new integrated marketing branding campaign is designed to play down its telephone roots and position the firm as a major Internet-related company. The theme chosen for the campaign, "Come Together," is based on the classic Beatles song from the popular "Abbey Road" album. The theme is a metaphor that underscores the company's commitment to unifying networks and bringing telephony, voice, data, video, and wireless together through the Internet.

The first phase of the campaign utilized 30- and 60-second television commercials that featured the well-known song against a backdrop of quick-cut visuals showcasing Nortel Network's innovative unified-networks solutions. The print ads used the refrain of the song as headlines: "Come Together," "Right Now," and "Over Me." The website also reprises the theme, and visitors can download and play the commercials or view the print advertising online at nortelnetworks.com.

The second phase of the campaign began in the fall of 1999 and shares the thoughts of celebrities, heroes, and everyday people on their vision of the Internet and what they see as its possibilities for commerce, communication, and collaboration. The print ads ask the eclectic list of celebrities, "What do you want the Internet to be?" and feature answers from them. For example, sprinter Michael Johnson, Olympic-gold-medal winner and world-record holder, answers by describing his vision of the Internet as "something that can keep up with me." Other celebrities featured in the campaign include former astronaut Buzz Aldrin, musician Curtis Mayfield, and author Kurt Vonnegut.

The third phase of the campaign began in early 2000 and is based on actual consumers' responses to the question, "What do you want the Internet to be?" As the bass line to the Beatles' "Come Together" plays in the background, a varied cast provides some answers. "I want it to be a new way of looking at things," says a man standing next to an upside-down chair. A hearing-impaired little girl answers in sign language, "I want it to be my voice." A voiceover explains that "Nortel is building the new, high-performance Internet and the networks' businesses need to take advantage of it."

Bill Conner, executive vice president of global marketing, notes that the "Come Together" campaign is a major investment for the company in building brand awareness for Nortel Networks. While the ads target decision makers who purchase equipment for their corporate computer and telephone networks, the media strategy is designed to also reach a broader audience. The corporate image campaign is being used to increase awareness and create a brand identity for Nortel Networks among customers, employees, and the financial community.

Nortel plans to run the global campaign throughout North America, as well as in the United

Kingdom, Germany, Brazil, Japan, and other countries for the next two years. By then it is very likely that nearly everyone will know what he or she wants the Internet to be and will recognize the role Nortel Networks plays in helping it all "come together."

Sources: "Nortel Networks Marketing Campaign Signals Aggressive Approach to Building a New Brand," News Releases, www.nortelnetworks.com; Stephanie N. Mehta, "Northern Telecom Plays Down Phone Roots, Embraces 'I Word,'" *The Wall Street Journal,* April 14, 1999, p. B10; Todd Wasserman, "Nortel Taps Rank and File," *Brandweek,* January 3, 2000.

to change its image with advertisers by running ads in trade magazines that showed *Penthouse* was not just a magazine with pictures of nude females. The ad for America's pharmaceutical companies (Exhibit 17–15) casts the industry in a very favorable light.

2. *Sponsorships.* A firm often runs corporate image advertising on TV programs or specials. For example, the Hallmark or IBM specials and documentaries on network TV and Mobil and Gulf Oil program sponsorships on public TV are designed to promote the corporation as a good citizen. By associating itself with high-quality or educational programming, the firm hopes for a carryover effect that benefits its own image.

Other examples of sponsorships include those run by Sara Lee Corp. to assist nonprofit organizations in the Chicago area, Dutch Boy paints and the National Basketball Association to raise funds to fight child abuse, *Family Circle* magazine and JCPenney to support "Sesame Street," State Farm's sponsorship of women's sports (Exhibit 17–16), Ben & Jerry's support of social and environmental programs, and AT&T's sponsorships of education, arts, and cultural programs.

Visa considers sponsorships an important part of its integrated marketing communications. It has sponsored the Olympics, the U.S. decathlon team, U.S. basket-

Exhibit 17–15 The pharmaceutical industry uses image advertising

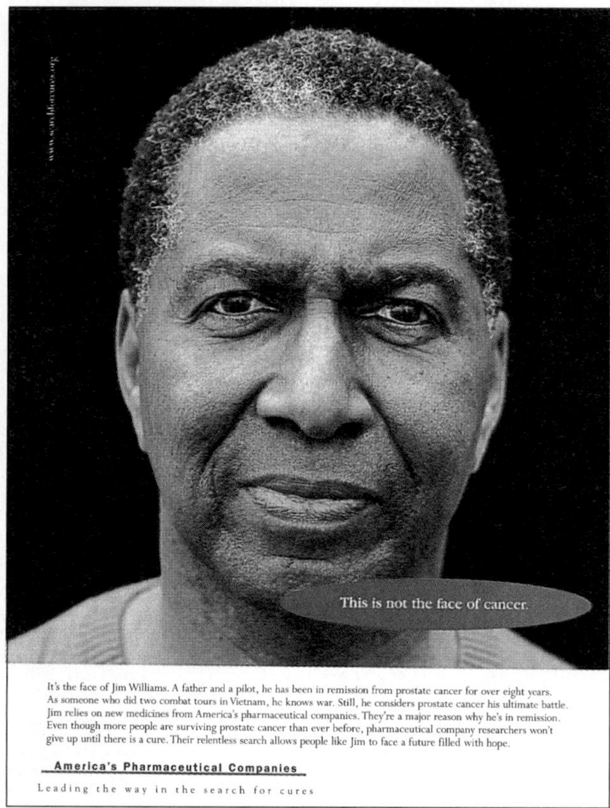

Exhibit 17–16 State Farm Insurance sponsors womens' sports

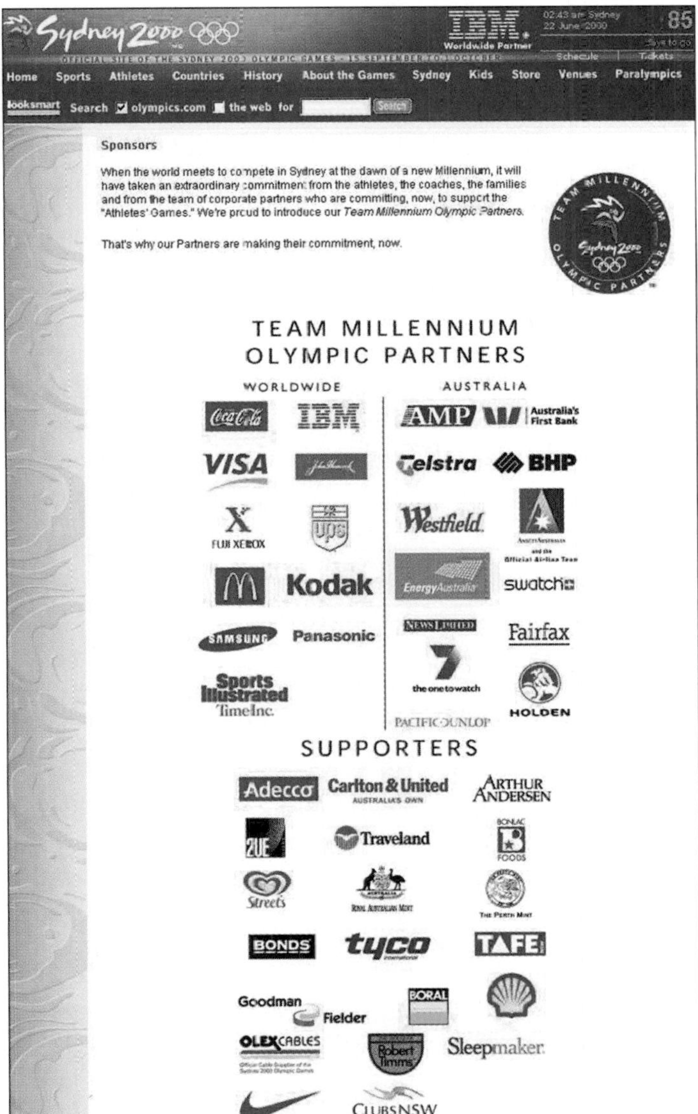

Figure 17–7 Some Olympic sponsors

ball's dream team, the U.S. Gymnastics Federation, the U.S. Open Tennis Championships, and Major League Baseball's All-Star game. According to John Bennett, senior VP for international marketing communications, the sponsorships are designed to fulfill specific business objectives while providing support for the recipients.[30] Figure 17–7 shows a few of the companies that decided an Olympic sponsorship would be good for them.

3. *Recruiting.* The promotional piece presented in Exhibit 17–17 is a good example of corporate image advertising designed to attract new employees. If you are a graduating senior considering a career in the new Internet economy, this ad, promoting a corporate image for the company, will interest you.

The Sunday employment section of most major metropolitan newspapers is an excellent place to see this form of corporate image advertising at work. Notice the ads in these papers and consider the images the firms are presenting.

4. *Generating financial support.* Some corporate advertising is designed to generate investments in the corporation. By creating a more favorable image, the firm makes itself attractive to potential stock purchasers and investors. More investments mean more working capital, more monies for research and development, and so on. In

Exhibit 17–17 An ad designed to attract new employees

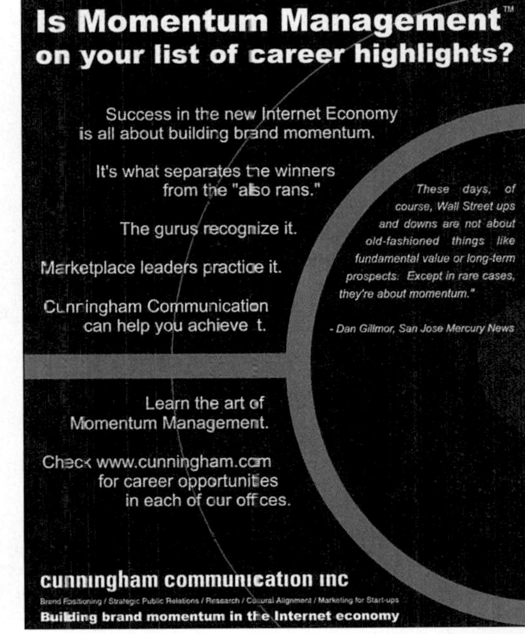

this instance, corporate image advertising is almost attempting to make a sale; the product is the firm.

While there is no concrete evidence that corporate image advertising leads directly to increased investment, at least one study shows a correlation between the price of stock and the amount of corporate advertising done.[31] Firms that spend more on corporate advertising also tend to have higher-priced stocks (though a direct relationship is very difficult to substantiate).

This thing called image is not unidimensional. Many factors affect it. Figure 17–8 shows the results of a survey conducted by Harris Interactive and the Rep-

Figure 17–8 The best corporate reputations in America

The Leaders

Top 30 companies, based on Reputation Quotient (RQ), a standardized instrument that measures a company's reputation by examining how the public perceives companies based on 20 attributes.

Rank	Company	RQ	Rank	Company	RQ	Rank	Company	RQ
1	Johnson & Johnson	83.4	11	Dell	78.4	21	FedEx	75.7
2	Coca-Cola	81.6	12	General Electric	78.1	22	Procter & Gamble	71.9
3	Hewlett-Packard	81.2	13	Lucent	78.0	23	Nike	71.3
4	Intel	81.0	14	Anheuser-Busch	78.0	24	McDonald's	71.2
5	Ben & Jerry's	81.0	15	Microsoft	77.9	25	Southwest Airlines	70.6
6	Wal-Mart	80.5	16	amazon.com	77.8	26	America Online	69.2
7	Xerox	79.9	17	IBM	77.6	27	DaimlerChrysler	69.1
8	Home Depot	79.7	18	Sony	77.4	28	Toyota	68.6
9	Gateway	78.8	19	Yahoo!	76.9	29	Sears	67.6
10	Disney	78.7	20	AT&T	75.7	30	Boeing	67.3

The Building Blocks

Twenty corporate attributes are classified into the following six elements of reputation. Top five companies in each category:

	Emotional Appeal[1]		Social Responsibility[2]		Products and Services[3]
1	Johnson & Johnson	1	Ben & Jerry's	1	Johnson & Johnson
2	Coca-Cola	2	amazon.com	2	Intel
3	Hewlett-Packard	3	Johnson & Johnson	3	Hewlett-Packard
4	Ben & Jerry's	4	Wal-Mart	4	Xerox
5	Xerox	5	Xerox	5	Ben & Jerry's

[1]How much the company is liked, admired, and respected

[2]Perceptions of the company as a good citizen in its dealings with communities, employees, and the environment

[3]Perceptions of the quality, innovation, value, and reliability of its products and services

	Workplace Environment[4]		Vision and Leadership[5]		Financial Performance[6]
1	Johnson & Johnson	1	Microsoft	1	Microsoft
2	Lucent	2	Intel	2	Wal-Mart
3	Ben & Jerry's	3	Anheuser-Busch	3	Coca-Cola
4	Hewlett-Packard	4	Coca-Cola	4	Johnson & Johnson
5	Intel	5	Dell	5	Intel

[4]Perception of how well the company is managed, how it is to work for, and the quality of its employees

[5]How much the company demonstrates a clear vision and strong leadership

[6]Perceptions of its profitability, prospects, and risk

utation Institute on the best corporate reputations in the United States. The most admired firms did not gain their positions merely by publicity and word of mouth (nor, we guess, did the least admired).

A positive corporate image cannot be created just from a few advertisements. Quality of products and services, innovation, sound financial practices, good corporate citizenship, and wise marketing are just a few of the factors that contribute to overall image. In addition, the type of product marketed and emotional appeal also contribute. The survey mentioned above demonstrated that profits and stock performances had little to do with reputation and that once a reputation is acquired, it has lasting power (Exxon can't shake its problems with the oil spill, yet Coca-Cola weathered the European crisis rather well). The study shows that companies are ranked differently on key corporate attributes including emotional appeal, social responsibility, workplace environment, and vision and leadership (among 16 others).[32] Another study, examining the best reputations in high technology, showed that the best-regarded companies (Microsoft, Intel, and Sony) do not necessarily receive similar ratings toward their stocks (Figure 17–9).[33]

Event Sponsorships As we noted in the last section, corporate sponsorships of charities and causes has become a popular form of public relations. While some companies sponsor specific events and/or causes with primarily traditional public

Figure 17–9 Relationship between reputation and stock purchases

Best-Regarded Companies		Attitudes toward Stocks	
Digital-technology companies that received the highest corporate reputation ratings among online computer users.		Percentage of respondents active in the stock market who said they will definitely or probably buy these stocks.	
Company	Reputation quotient*	Company	Will or may purchase stock
Microsoft	82.27	Dell	74%
Intel	81.50	Lucent	67
Sony	79.85	Gateway	63
Dell	79.62	Microsoft	63
Lucent	78.35	Sun Microsytems	62
Gateway	78.28	Intel	61
Eastman Kodak	78.23	Cisco Systems	59
Texas Instruments	77.57	IBM	54
Cisco Systems	77.23	Micron	53
Hewlett-Packard	77.20	Compaq	51
Xerox	77.17	Symantec	49
Symantec	76.73	Motorola	48
Intuit	76.70	Yahoo!	48
Sun Microsystems	76.58	Texas Instruments	47
IBM	76.02	Advanced Micro Devices	46
Motorola	75.84	Eastman Kodak	46
Red Hat	75.41	Novell	46
Yahoo!	74.91	Red Hat	46
3Com	74.89	Hewlett-Packard	45
Canon	74.86	E*Trade	44

*A standardized instrument that measures a company's reputation by examining how the public perceives companies based on 20 attributes.

Figure 17–10 Annual sponsorship spending in North America by property ($ millions)

	1996	1997	1998	1999*
Sports	$3,540	$3,840	$4,556	$5,100
Entertainment tours and attractions	566	650	680	756
Festivals, fairs, events	512	558	612	685
Causes	485	535	544	630
Arts	323	354	408	460
Total	$5,426	$5,937	$6,800	$7,631

*Projected.

relations objectives in mind, a separate and more marketing-oriented use of sponsorships is also on the increase. Such **event sponsorships** take on a variety of forms, as shown in Figure 17–10. Anything from golf apparel (Mossimo sponsors golfer David Duval) and equipment to concerts (Tommy Hilfiger's sponsorship of Lilith Fair) to naming stadiums (FedEx paid $200 million to change the name of Washington Redskins' Landover Stadium to "FedEx Field") is now a candidate for corporate sponsorship.

Companies spent over $7.6 billion on event sponsorships in 1999, with sports receiving the majority of event sponsorship monies. Among the most popular sporting events for sponsorship are auto racing, golf and tennis tournaments, and running events. Professional sports leagues and teams as well as Olympic teams and competitions also receive large amounts of sponsorship money. Bicycle racing, beach volleyball, skiing, and various water sports are also attracting corporate sponsorship. Traditionally, tobacco, beer, and car companies have been among the largest sports event sponsors. Now a number of other companies have become involved in event sponsorships, including beverage companies, airlines, telecommunications and financial services companies, and high-tech firms.

Many marketers are attracted to event sponsorship because it gets their company and/or product names in front of consumers. By choosing the right events for sponsorship, companies can get visibility among their target market. For example, RJR Nabisco is heavily involved in sponsoring auto racing under its Winston and Camel cigarette brands. The company's market research showed that racing fans fit the demographic profile of users of these brands and consumers would purchase a product that sponsored their favorite sport.[34] For tobacco companies, which are prohibited from advertising on radio and TV, event sponsorship is also a way to have their brand names seen on TV. However, President Clinton issued an executive order in 1996 that would prohibit any form of advertising of tobacco sponsorships at sporting events after 1998. The tobacco companies appealed this order in the courts on the grounds that to prohibit advertising a legal product violates free speech.[35]

Many companies are attracted to event sponsorships because effective IMC programs can be built around them and promotional tie-ins can be made to local, regional, national, and even international markets. Companies are finding event sponsorships an excellent platform from which to build equity and gain affinity with target audiences as well as a good public relations tool.

Most companies focus their marketing efforts on specific market segments and are always looking for ways to reach these target audiences. Many marketers are finding that sales promotion tools such as event sponsorships, contests and sweepstakes, and sampling are very effective ways to reach specific geographic, demographic, psychographic, and ethnic markets.

Event sponsorship has become a good sales promotion tool for reaching specific target markets. Golf tournaments are a popular event for sponsorship by marketers of luxury automobiles and other upscale products and services. The golf audience is affluent and highly educated, and marketers believe that golfers care passionately about the game, leading them to form emotional attachments to brands they associate with the sport.

Marketers can also turn their sponsorships into effective integrated marketing opportunities. For example, Cadillac is an umbrella sponsor of the Senior PGA Tour, which fits well with its attempt to target age 40-plus professionals with incomes exceeding $60,000. On-site signage and vehicle displays are part of the sponsorship deal. The 13 Team Cadillac golfers, including such notables as Lee Trevino and Arnold Palmer, wear the automaker's logo during tournaments and also help in public relations by giving media interviews and representing Cadillac at tie-in events. In the weeks preceding an event, dealers send out as many as 20,000 direct-mail pieces to owners and prospects inviting them to visit a dealership for a test drive and to pick up tournament tickets and hospitality passes. Response to the direct-mail offerings averages 16 percent. Cadillac also gets automotive advertising exclusivity on the ESPN telecasts and often airs commercials featuring the Team Cadillac members.

Cadillac attributes $250 million in vehicle sales directly to its involvement with the tour since 1990. The dollar figure comes from tracking sales to prospects who respond to Cadillac's direct-marketing programs built around the tournament.[36]

A major issue that continues to face the event sponsorship industry is incomplete research. As marketers become interested in targeted audiences, they will want more evidence that event sponsorship is effective and is a good return on their investment. Measuring the effectiveness of event sponsorships is discussed in Chapter 19.

Advocacy Advertising A third major form of corporate advertising addresses social, business, or environmental issues. Such **advocacy advertising** is concerned with propagating ideas and elucidating controversial social issues of public importance in a manner that supports the interests of the sponsor.[37]

While still portraying an image for the company or organization, advocacy advertising does so indirectly, by adopting a position on a particular issue rather than promoting the organization itself. An example is shown in Exhibit 17–18. Advocacy advertising has increased in use over the past few years and has also met with increased criticism. The ads may be sponsored by a firm or by a trade association and are designed to tell readers how the firm operates or management's position on a particular issue.

Exhibit 17–18 Advocacy ads take a position on an issue

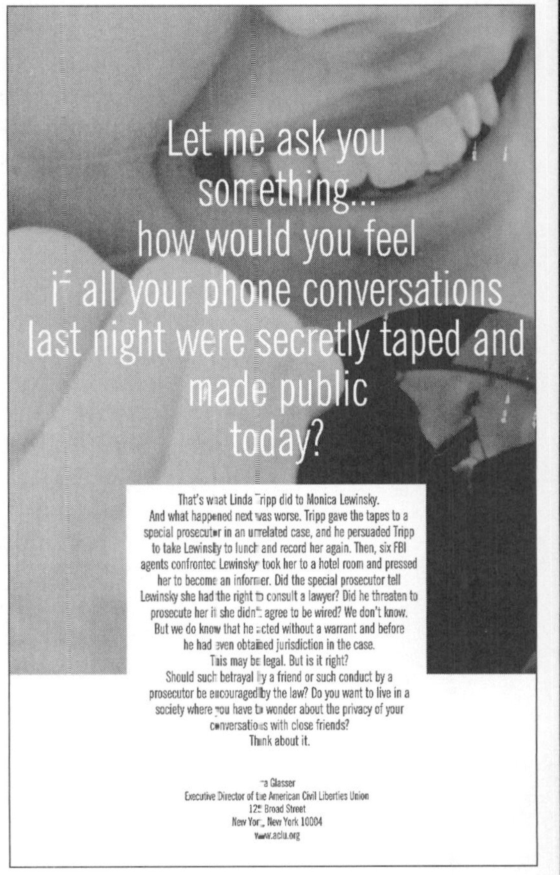

Let me ask you something...
how would you feel
if all your phone conversations
last night were secretly taped and
made public
today?
That's what Linda Tripp did to Monica Lewinsky.
And what happened next was worse. Tripp gave the tapes to a special prosecutor in an unrelated case, and he persuaded Tripp to take Lewinsky to lunch and record her again. Then, six FBI agents confronted Lewinsky, took her to a hotel room and pressed her to become an informer. Did the special prosecutor tell Lewinsky she had the right to consult a lawyer? Did he threaten to prosecute her if she didn't agree to be wired? We don't know. But we do know that he acted without a warrant and before he had even obtained jurisdiction in the case.
This may be legal. But is it right?
Should such betrayal by a friend or such conduct by a prosecutor be encouraged by the law? Do you want to live in a society where you have to wonder about the privacy of your conversations with close friends?
Think about it.
Glasser
Executive Director of the American Civil Liberties Union
Broad Street
New York 10004
aclu.org

Sometimes the advertising is a response to negative publicity or to the firm's inability to place an important message through public relations channels. Sometimes the firm just wants to get certain ideas accepted or have society understand its concerns.

Advocacy advertising has been criticized by a number of sources (including consumer advocate Ralph Nader). But as you can see in Exhibit 17–19, this form of communication has been around for a long time. AT&T engaged in issues-oriented advertising way back in 1908 and has continued to employ this form of communication throughout the 20th century. Critics contend that companies with large advertising budgets purchase too much ad space and time and that advocacy ads may be misleading, but the checks and balances of regular product advertising also operate in this area.

For example, an ad run by the seven regional Bell operating companies that addressed the threat of Japanese technologies in the telecommunications industry was perceived by some members of Congress (the group the ads were designed to influence) as Japan-bashing and offensive. When the ad backfired, the campaign was immediately halted and the agency that developed it was fired.[38] The ultimate judge, of course, is always the reader.

Cause-Related Advertising An increasingly popular method of image building is **cause-related marketing,** in which companies link with charities or nonprofit organizations as contributing sponsors. The company benefits from favorable publicity, while the charity receives much-needed funds. Spending on

SHE'S A PARTNER IN A GREAT AMERICAN BUSINESS
SHE is one of 850,000 owners of Bell System securities. They are typical Americans—some young, some middle age, some old. They live in every part of the nation.
One may be a housewife in Pennsylvania. Another a physician in Oregon—a clerk in Illinois—an engineer in Texas—a merchant in Massachusetts—a miner in Nevada—a stenographer in Missouri—a teacher in California—or a telephone employee in Michigan.
For the most part, Bell System stockholders are men and women who have put aside small sums for saving. More than half of them have held their shares for five years or longer. More than 650,000 of these 850,000 security holders own stock in the American Telephone and Telegraph Company—the parent company of the Bell System. More than 225,000 own five shares or less. Over fifty per cent are women. No one owns as much as one per cent of the stock of A. T. & T. In a very real sense, the Bell System is a democracy in business—owned by the people it serves.

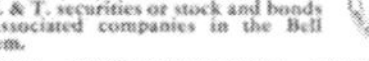

More than 270,000 men and women work for the Bell System. One person out of every 150 in this country owns A. T. & T. securities or stock and bonds of associated companies in the Bell System.
BELL TELEPHONE SYSTEM

Exhibit 17–19 Advocacy ads have been used for years

cause-related marketing has increased more than 300 percent since 1990, reaching $630 million in 1999. Proponents of cause marketing say that association with a cause may differentiate one brand or store from another, increase consumer acceptance of price increases, generate favorable publicity, and even win over skeptical officials who may have an impact on the company.[39] Cause marketing relationships can take a variety of forms. Making outright donations to a nonprofit cause, having companies volunteer for the cause, donating materials or supplies, running public service announcements, or even providing event refreshments are some of the ways companies get involved. Exhibit 17–20 shows Doug Flutie's support for the Doug Flutie, Jr., Foundation's attempts to find a cure for autism.

While companies receive public relations benefits from their association with causes (Wal-Mart and McDonald's are ranked as number 1 and 2 in regard to the nation's leading socially responsible companies, according to surveys conducted by Cone/Roper), with 80 percent of consumers saying they have a more positive impression of companies that support a cause, they sometimes receive financial rewards as well.[40] Visa's "Reading is Fundamental" campaign led to a 17 percent increase in sales, BMW saw sales increase when it sponsored a program to eradicate breast cancer, and Wendy's International in Denver saw sales increase by more than 33 percent when a portion of purchases was contributed to Denver's Mercy Medical Center.[41]

At the same time, not all cause marketing is a guarantee of success. Cause marketing requires more than just associating with a social issue, and it takes time and effort. Companies have gotten into trouble by misleading consumers about their relationships, and others wasted money by hooking up with a cause that offered little synergism. One survey showed that over 300 companies had associated themselves with breast cancer concerns, with most becoming lost in sponsorship clutter. Others have simply picked the wrong cause—finding that their customers and potential customers either have little interest in or don't like the cause. In some cases, cause marketing is considered nothing more than shock advertising. Finally, the results of cause-marketing efforts can sometimes be hard to quantify.

Advantages and Disadvantages of Corporate Advertising

A number of reasons for the increased popularity of corporate advertising become evident when you examine the advantages of this form of communication:

1. *It is an excellent vehicle for positioning the firm.* Firms, like products, need to establish an image or position in the marketplace. Corporate image ads are one way to accomplish this objective. A well-positioned product is much more likely to achieve success than is one with a vague or no image. The same holds true of the firm. Stop and think for a moment about the image that comes to mind when you hear the name IBM, Apple, Johnson & Johnson, or Procter & Gamble.

   Now what comes to mind when you hear Unisys, USX, or Navistar? How many consumer brands can you name that fall under ConAgra's corporate umbrella? (Swiss Miss, Wesson, La Choy, and many others.) While we are not saying these latter companies are not successful—because they certainly are—we are suggesting their corporate identities (or positions) are not as well

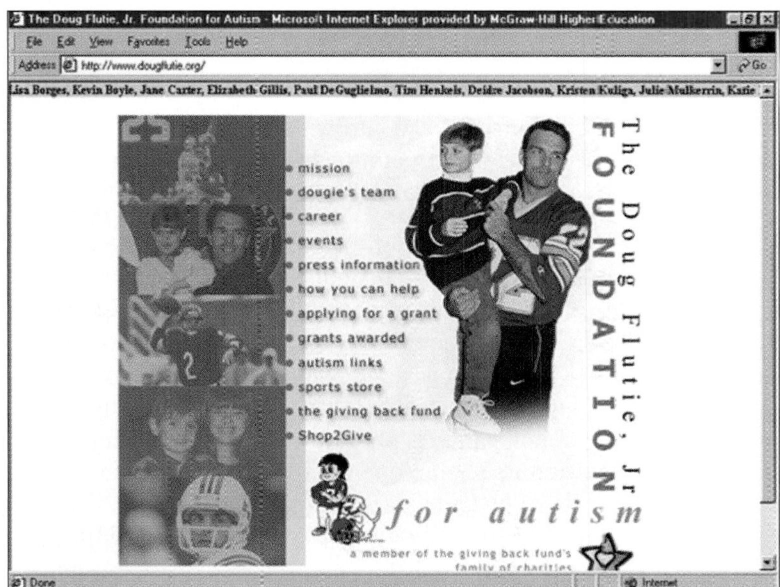

Exhibit 17–20 Doug Flutie's foundation cause is finding a cure for autism

entrenched as the identities of those first cited. Companies with strong positive corporate images have an advantage over competitors that may be enhanced when they promote the company overall.

2. *It takes advantage of the benefits derived from public relations.* As the PR efforts of firms have increased, the attention paid to these events by the media has lessened (not because they are of any less value, but because there are more events to cover). The net result is that when a company engages in a public relations effort, there is no guarantee it will receive press coverage and publicity. Corporate image advertising gets the message out, and though consumers may not perceive it as positively as information from an objective source, the fact remains that it can communicate what has been done.
3. *It reaches a select target market.* Corporate image advertising should not be targeted to the general public. It is often targeted to investors and managers of other firms rather than to the general public. It doesn't matter if the general public does not appreciate this form of communication, as long as the target market does. In this respect, this form of advertising may be accomplishing its objectives.

Some of the disadvantages of corporate advertising were alluded to earlier in the chapter. To these criticisms, we can add the following

1. *Questionable effectiveness.* There is no strong evidence to support the belief that corporate advertising works. Many doubt the data cited earlier that demonstrated a correlation between stock prices and corporate image advertising. A study by Bozell & Jacobs Advertising of 16,000 ads concluded that corporate advertising contributed to only 4 percent of the variability in the company's stock price, compared with a 55 percent effect attributable to financial factors.[42] A second study also casts doubts on earlier studies that concluded that corporate advertising worked.[43]
2. *Constitutionality and/or ethics.* Some critics contend that since larger firms have more money, they can control public opinion unfairly. This point was resolved in the courts in favor of the advertisers. Nevertheless, many consumers still see such advertising as unfair and immediately take a negative view of the sponsor.

A number of valid points have been offered for and against corporate advertising. Two things are certain: (1) no one knows who is right and (2) the use of this communications form continues to increase.

Measuring the Effectiveness of Corporate Advertising

As you can tell from our discussion of the controversy surrounding corporate advertising, there need to be methods for evaluating whether or not such advertising is effective:

- *Attitude surveys.* One way to determine the effectiveness of corporate advertising is conducting attitude surveys to gain insights into both the public's and investors' reactions to ads. The Phase II study conducted by market research firm Yankelovich, Skelly & White is one of the best-known applications of this measurement method.[44] The firm measured recall and attitudes toward corporate advertisers and found that corporate advertising is more efficient in building recall for a company name than is product advertising alone. Frequent corporate advertisers rated better on virtually all attitude measures than those with low corporate ad budgets.
- *Studies relating corporate advertising and stock prices.* The Bozell & Jacobs study is one of many that have examined the effect of various elements of corporate advertising (position in the magazine, source effects, etc.) on stock prices. These studies have yielded conflicting conclusions, indicating that while the model for such measures seems logical, methodological problems may account for at least some of the discrepancies.
- *Focus group research.* Focus groups have been used to find out what investors want to see in ads and how they react after the ads are developed. As with product-oriented advertising, this method has limitations, although it does allow for some effective measurements.

While the effectiveness of corporate advertising has been measured by some of the methods used to measure product-specific advertising, research in this area has not kept pace with that of the consumer market. (One study reported that only 35 of the Fortune 500 companies ever attempted to measure performance of their annual reports.[45]) The most commonly offered reason for this lack of effort is that corporate ads are often the responsibility of those in the highest management positions in the firm, and these parties do not wish to be held accountable. Interestingly, those who should be most concerned with accountability are the most likely to shun this responsibility!

Summary

This chapter examined the role of the promotional elements of public relations, publicity, and corporate advertising. We noted that these areas are all significant to the marketing and communications effort and are usually considered differently from the other promotional elements. The reasons for this special treatment stem from the facts that (1) they are typically not designed to promote a specific product or service and (2) in many instances it is harder for the consumer to make the connection between the communication and its intent.

Public relations was shown to be useful in its traditional responsibilities as well as in a more marketing-oriented role. In many firms, PR is a separate department operating independently of marketing; in others, it is considered a support system. Many large firms have an external public relations agency, just as they have an outside ad agency.

In the case of publicity, another factor enters the equation: lack of control over the communication the public will receive. In public relations and corporate advertising, the organization remains the source and retains much more control. Publicity often takes more of a reactive than a proactive approach, yet it may be more instrumental (or detrimental) to the success of a product or organization than all other forms of promotion combined.

While not all publicity can be managed, the marketer must nevertheless recognize its potential impact. Press releases and the management of information are just two of the factors under the company's control. Proper reaction and a strategy to deal with uncontrollable events are also responsibilities.

Corporate advertising was described as controversial, largely because the source of the message is top management, so the rules for other advertising and promoting forms are often not applied. This element of communication definitely has its place in the promotional mix. But to be effective, it must be used with each of the other elements, with specific communications objectives in mind.

Finally, we noted that measures of evaluation and control are required for each of these program elements, just as they are for all others in the promotional mix. We presented some methods for taking such measurements and some evidence why it is important to use them. As long as the elements of public relations, publicity, and corporate advertising are considered integral components of the overall communications strategy, they must respect the same rules as the other promotional mix elements to ensure success.

Key Terms

public relations, 577
marketing public relations (MPR), 578
internal audiences, 582
external audiences, 582
press release, 585
press conference, 587
exclusive, 587
team approach, 592
internal audits, 592
external audits, 592
publicity, 593
video news release (VNR), 597
corporate advertising, 598
image advertising, 600
event sponsorships, 606
advocacy advertising, 607
cause-related marketing, 607

Discussion Questions

1. Discuss the advantages that the Internet offers for those responsible for conducting public relations activities. Describe how these activities are different than traditional methods.

2. Discuss some of the advantages associated with the use of MPRs. What are some of the disadvantages?

3. Explain why traditional public relations practitioners might be unhappy with the organization's use of MPRs. Take a position as to whether this criticism is justified.

4. List and describe the advantages and disadvantages of the use of public relations in an IMC program. Provide an example of an appropriate use of public relations in this mix.

5. What is a video news release (VNR)? Provide an example of a situation in which a company might employ the use of a VNR. Discuss some of the ethical implications (if any) in using this tool.

6. Give examples of companies that are pursuing traditional public relations activities and those that are employing the new role.

7. Many companies are now taking the position that their charitable contributions should lead to something in return—for example, sales or increased visibility. Discuss the pros and cons of this position.

8. Many companies are now trying to generate as much free publicity as they can. Cite some examples of this, and discuss the advantages and disadvantages associated with this strategy.

9. Discuss the ethics involved in using situations like the O. J. Simpson case to gain publicity for one's products and services.

10. The text discussed the negative publicity and PR problem facing Texaco after executives were taped allegedly making discriminatory remarks about minorities. What would you do if you were the head of Texaco?

Chapter Eighteen

Personal Selling

Chapter Objectives

- To understand the role of personal selling in the integrated marketing communications program.
- To know the advantages and disadvantages of peronal selling as a promotional program element.
- To understand how personal selling is combined with other elements in an IMC program.
- To know ways to determine the effectiveness of the personal selling effort.

Death of the Sales Force?—Selling in the New Millennium

Not that long ago personal selling meant cold calling, finding prospects, demonstrating your product (hopefully), and taking the order (if you were successful). Selling strategies meant keeping a personal diary on the buyer, delivering specialty products with your company's name on them, providing tickets to sporting and/or entertainment events, and "outselling" your competition. Some companies—particularly those selling media time and space—offered (and still do offer) incentive trips to the buyer meeting a certain purchase plateau.

For most industries, those days are gone. Changes in the marketplace, including more sophisticated and better-educated buyers, new technologies (particularly the Internet), and increased regulations, have led to a whole new business model. The sales rep of the new millennium will have to adapt or die. Businesses are evolving.

Today's successful salesperson is really more of a marketer than a salesperson. She or he is armed with a laptop and planograms rather than pens, desk calendars, and baseball and football tickets. Successful salespeople are solution providers and problem solvers, not time consumers and/or "snake-oil" sellers.

With Boise,
you'll notice a difference right away.
Boise Office Products
Boise Promotional Products
Boise Furniture
Boise Technology Products
Especially when we make a promise.
Boise Cascade Office Products
And we promise impressive ordering flexibility. Easy options that amount to significant time savings when your company selects and places orders with Boise Cascade Office Products. It all starts with our main catalog, clearly organized with a more comprehensive index than you'll find in any other office products catalog. If your people are wired for Internet transactions, you'll be glad to know Boise was the first contract stationer to develop an online catalog and ordering site for a seamless buying process. Other options include fax orders or phone calls to one of our national customer service centers. Your Boise sales professional can help you determine the options that work best for you. Lots of companies make promises – we deliver. Call 888-BOISE-88 to learn how we really can simplify the whole process…honest!
BOISE. IT COULDN'T BE EASIER.
OFFICE SUPPLIES • TECHNOLOGY PRODUCTS • FURNITURE • PROMOTIONAL PRODUCTS

What has caused this change in salespeople is the change in purchase behaviors. Buyers and the businesses they represent have more commerce power and are more flexible, more efficient, and more demanding. They are looking for solutions, not desk calendars. But above all, they are more informed.

The proliferation of media and the advent of the Internet have changed the balance in the buyer–seller relationship. Whereas the seller used to be the initial and primary source of information about innovations, programs, products, and so on, and the buyer depended upon the seller for such information, this is no longer the case. Today's buyers have more information—sometimes more than the salespersons—

expect more knowledge from the sellers, and have many more options available to them. More trade journals, more business-to-business ads on TV, and the Internet have increased buyers awareness of companies offering goods and services and provide buyers with detailed product pricing and information. Best of all, most information is only a mouse click away and can be accessed while the salesperson is in the waiting room.

Some companies believe that in the very near future there will no longer be a need for sales reps. Sellers can offer their products, along with pricing information, through online catalogs. Demonstrations can take place through the website, or a demo disk can be mailed to prospects. Orders can be placed instantaneously. And the best part of it all is that the selling organization will save money in the process.

Many others disagree, taking the position that the salesperson will have to evolve with the industry. One seller making this change is Boise Cascade's Office Products Division. Boise provides its accounts with a software product that purchasers can use to determine acquisition costs. The technology takes the buyer through a time and cost process that not only shows what happens from the time an employee requests a product until it arrives at the hands of the user, but also shows the costs involved at each step. Purchasers use the software to save money, and both Boise and the customer win. In another example, the Chamberlain Group—a manufacturer of garage door openers, headquartered in Illinois—uses the Internet to shop for suppliers around the world. Bell Atlantic does the same. A company without a website has lost its selling opportunity if buyers can't find the company. Sellers must also spend time updating their sites, following up on leads, and completing sales.

More and more, companies are integrating communications technology with personal selling as the technologies available continue to increase. One thing remains constant, however: Although fewer and fewer desk calendars and ballpoint pens are being distributed, salespeople still exist.

Sources: James Champy, "Selling to Tomorrow's Customer," *Sales & Marketing Management,* March 1999, p. 28; Sarah Lorge, "Purchasing Power," *Sales & Marketing Management,* June 1998, pp. 43–46.

The Scope of Personal Selling

The chapter opener demonstrates just a few of the ways organizations are having to adapt their personal selling strategies and how they are integrating the personal selling function into the overall marketing communications program. The changing marketplace has had a significant impact on how personal selling activities are conducted and how successful firms will compete in the future. In Chapter 1, we stated that while we recognize the importance of personal selling and the role it plays in the overall marketing and promotions effort, it is not emphasized in this text. Personal selling is typically under the control of the sales manager, not the advertising and promotions department. A study conducted by *Sales & Marketing Management* showed that in 46 percent of the companies surveyed, sales and marketing are totally separate departments.[1] But personal selling does make a valuable contribution to the promotional program. To develop a promotional plan effectively, a firm must integrate the roles and responsibilities of its sales force into the communications program. Strong cooperation between the departments is also necessary.

This chapter focuses on the role personal selling assumes in the IMC program, the advantages and disadvantages of this program element, and the basis for evaluating its contributions to attaining communications objectives. In addition, we explore how personal selling is combined with other program elements, both to support them and to receive support from them.

Personal selling involves selling through a person-to-person communications process. The emphasis placed on personal selling varies from firm to firm depending on a variety of factors, including the nature of the product or service being marketed, size of the organization, and type of industry. Personal selling often plays the dominant role in industrial firms, while in other firms, such as makers of low-priced consumer nondurable goods, its role is minimized. In many industries, these roles are changing to a more balanced use of promotional program elements. In an integrated marketing communications program, personal selling is a partner with, not a substitute for, the other promotional mix elements.

Figure 18–1 shows the results of a survey of marketing managers' perceptions of how the various elements of the promotional mix were expected to change over the

Figure 18–1 Change in relative importance of components of the promotional mix

Strategy Statement	Change in Relative Importance					
	Greatly Decreased	Moderately Decreased	Same	Moderately Increased	Greatly Increased	Mean Rating*
Promotional strategy						
Special promotional activities such as promotional warranties, trade shows, dealer aids, and product displays	0.0%	12.6%	48.5%	35.0%	3.9%	3.3
Public relations, public affairs, and community relations	0.0	7.8	43.7	33.8	9.7	3.5
Product branding and promotional packaging	0.0	8.7	47.6	35.0	8.7	3.4
Sales management and personal selling, including all sales management activities (e.g., training, supervision) and the sales efforts of company management personnel	1.0	2.9	28.4	52.9	14.7	3.8
Print media advertising in newspapers, magazines, and brochures	0.0	17.6	52.0	24.5	5.9	3.2
Broadcast media advertising on radio/TV	0.0	15.8	51.5	25.7	6.9	3.2
Media advertising on cable TV, over-the-air pay TV, and videodisk	1.0	7.9	29.7	49.5	11.9	3.6

*1 = Greatly decreased, 2 = Moderately decreased, 3 = Same, 4 = Moderately increased, 5 = Greatly increased.

years. The managers interviewed expect sales management and personal selling to increase in importance more than any other element of the promotional mix. Note, however, that other elements are expected to gain in importance as well, indicating an enhanced overall promotional program.

The Role of Personal Selling in the IMC Program

Manufacturers may promote their products *directly* to consumers through advertising and promotions and/or direct-marketing efforts or *indirectly* through resellers and salespeople. (A sales force may call on customers directly—for example, in the insurance industry or real estate. But this chapter focuses on the personal selling function as it exists in most large corporations or smaller companies—that is, as a link to resellers or dealers in business-to-business transactions.) Depending on the role defined by the organization, the responsibilities and specific tasks of salespeople may differ, but ultimately these tasks are designed to help attain communications and marketing objectives.

Personal selling differs from the other forms of communication presented thus far in that messages flow from a sender (or group of senders) to a receiver (or group of receivers) directly (usually face to face). This *direct* and *interpersonal communication* lets the sender immediately receive and evaluate feedback from the receiver. This communications process, known as **dyadic communication** (between two people or groups), allows for more specific tailoring of the message and more personal communications than do many of the other media discussed. The message can be changed to address the receiver's specific needs and wants.

In some situations, this ability to focus on specific problems is mandatory; a standard communication would not suffice. Consider an industrial buying situation in which the salesperson is an engineer. To promote the company's products and/or services, the salesperson must understand the client's specific needs. This may mean understanding the tensile strength of materials or being able to read blueprints or plans to understand the requirements. Or say a salesperson represents a computer graphics firm. Part of his or her responsibility for making a sale may involve the design of a software program to solve a problem unique to this customer. Mass communications cannot accomplish these tasks. Personal selling plays a critical role not just in industrial settings but in the consumer market as well.

The great entrepreneur Marshall Field said, "The distance between the salesperson and the potential buyer is the most important three feet in business."[2] Personal selling is important in selling to consumers and resellers. Consumer products companies must secure distribution, motivate resellers to stock and promote the product, and so on.

Why is personal selling so important? Let's examine its role with respect to other promotional program elements.

Determining the Role of Personal Selling

The first questions a manager needs to ask when preparing the promotional program are what the specific responsibilities of personal selling will be and what role it will assume relative to the other promotional mix elements. To determine its role, management should be guided by four questions:

1. What specific information must be exchanged between the firm and potential customers?
2. What are the alternative ways to carry out these communications objectives?
3. How effective is each alternative in carrying out the needed exchange?
4. How cost effective is each alternative?[3]

- *Determining the information to be exchanged.* In keeping with the objectives established by the communications models in Chapter 5, the salesperson may have a variety of messages to communicate, such as creating awareness of the product or service offering, demonstrating product benefits for evaluation, initiating trial, and/or closing the sale. It may also be necessary to answer questions, counter misconceptions, and discover potentially unmet needs.
- *Examining promotional mix alternatives.* In previous chapters, we discussed the roles of advertising and sales promotion, direct marketing, and public relations/publicity. Each of these program elements offers specific advantages and disadvantages, and each needs to be considered when the promotional mix is developed. Personal selling is an alternative that offers distinct advantages in some situations but is less appropriate in others, as evidenced in Figure 18–2.

Figure 18–2 When the sales force is a major part of the IMC mix

Product or Service	Channels
Complex products requiring customer application assistance (computers, pollution control system, steam turbines) Major purchase decisions, such as food items purchased by supermarket chains Features and performance of the product requiring personal demonstration and trial by the customer (private aircraft)	Channel system relatively short and direct to end users Product and service training and assistance needed by channel intermediaries Personal selling needed to push product through channel Channel intermediaries available to perform personal selling function for supplier with limited resources and experience (brokers or manufacturer's agents)
Price	**Advertising**
Final price is negotiated between buyer and seller (appliances, cars, real estate) Selling price or quality purchased enables an adequate margin to support selling expenses (traditional department store compared to discount house)	Advertising media do not provide effective link with market targets Information needed by buyer cannot be provided entirely through advertising and sales promotion (life insurance) Number and dispersion of customers will not enable acceptable advertising economies

- *Evaluating the relative effectiveness of alternatives.* The effectiveness of each program element must be evaluated based on the target market and the objectives sought. Personal selling is effective in many situations, but other program elements may be more attractive in other cases. For example, advertising may do a better job of repeating messages or reaching a large number of people with one distinct, consistent message.
- *Determining cost effectiveness.* One of the major disadvantages of personal selling is the cost involved. (Cahners Research estimates the average cost per sales call could be as high as $292.)[4] While the cost of a personal sales call may not be prohibitive in industrial settings where a single purchase can be worth millions of dollars, the same cost may be unfeasible in a consumer market. Other media may be able to communicate the required message at a much lower cost.

The Nature of Personal Selling

To integrate the personal selling effort into the overall promotional program, we must understand the nature of this tool. Let us look at how personal selling has evolved over the years and then examine some of its characteristics.

The personal selling task encompasses a variety of responsibilities (some of which we discuss in the next section). Like other aspects of the promotional mix, these responsibilities are constantly changing. As noted by Thomas Wotruba, the personal selling area is constantly evolving as the marketing environment itself evolves.[5] Wotruba identifies five distinct stages of personal selling evolution, shown in Figure 18–3.

1. **Provider stage.** Selling activities are limited to accepting orders for the supplier's available offering and conveying it to the buyer.

Figure 18–3 The stages in the evolution of selling

	Characteristics of Stages			
Stages and Description	Customer Needs	Type of Market	Nature and Intensity of Competition	Examples
1. *Provider:* accepts orders and delivers to buyer.	Assumed to exist; not a concern	Sellers'	None	Route salespeople/drivers; some retail salesclerks
2. *Persuader:* attempts to convince anyone to buy available offerings.	Created, awakened	Buyers'	Undifferentiated; slight intensity	Telemarketers for photo studio; many new car dealers
3. *Prospector:* seeks out prospects with need for available offering and resources to buy.	Considered but inferred	Segmented	Differentiated; growing	Car insurance salespeople calling on new car buyers; office supplies sellers calling on small businesses
4. *Problem solver:* matches available offerings to solve customer-stated problems.	Diagnosed, with attention to customer input	Participative	Responsive and counteractive with increasing resources	Communication systems salespeople for a telephone company; architectural services sellers calling on building contractors
5. *Procreator:* creates a unique offering to match the buyer's needs as mutually specified, involving any or all aspects of the seller's total marketing mix.	Mutually defined; matched with tailored offering	Coactive	Focused; growing in breadth of market and service offerings	Materials handling equipment salespeople who design and sell a system to fit a buyer's manufacturing facility

2. **Persuader stage.** Selling involves an attempt to persuade market members to buy the supplier's offerings.
3. **Prospector stage.** Activities include seeking out selected buyers who are perceived to have a need for the offering as well as the resources and authority to buy it.
4. **Problem-solver stage.** Selling involves obtaining the participation of buyers to identify their problems, which can be translated into needs, and then presenting a selection from the supplier's offerings that corresponds with those needs and can solve those problems.
5. **Procreator stage.** Selling defines the buyer's problems or needs and their solutions through active buyer-seller collaboration and then creates a market offering uniquely tailored to the customer.

According to Wotruba, firms evolving through these five stages have to assume different market orientations, as well as different organizational designs, staffing, and compensation programs. The different stages require different promotional strategies, each integrated with personal selling to achieve the maximum communications effect.

The New Role of Personal Selling As previously noted, the business world is going through a very rapid transition as (1) individuals and corporations gain more knowledge and economic power, (2) value is replacing efficiency, and (3) industry boundaries are changing—for example, competitors are joining forces to achieve more buying power.[6] As a result, the role of the sales force will also significantly change, according to Kevin Hoffberg and Kevin Corcoran. Along with retaining their traditional roles, described by Wotruba, salespeople will have to acquire new roles to remain effective. That is, in addition to being information providers, influencers through proximity (i.e., through personal contact), and demonstrators, salespeople will engage in:

- *Surveying.* Educating themselves more about their customers' businesses and regularly assessing these businesses and their customers to achieve a position of knowledgeable authority.
- *Mapmaking.* Outlining both an account strategy and a solutions strategy (for the customer). This means laying out a plan, discussing it with the customer, and revising it as changes require.
- *Guiding.* Bringing incremental value to the customer by identifying problems and opportunities, offering alternative options and solutions, and providing solutions with tangible value.
- *Fire starting.* Engaging customers and driving them to commit to a solution.[7]

This new role, say Hoffberg and Corcoran, will create added value and develop a relationship between buyer and seller.

Relationship Marketing As noted, personal selling is evolving from a focus on persuasive techniques used to sell a product or service to a much more marketing-oriented *partnership* with the customer. This new role requires much broader thinking and expertise on the part of the seller and a more extensive use of the various promotional tools. The modern salesperson is attempting to establish a long-term, symbiotic relationship with clients, working with them as a solutions provider.

Relationship marketing is defined as "an organization's effort to develop a long-term, cost-effective link with individual customers for mutual benefit."[8] Rather than focusing on a short-term sale, the sales rep tries to establish a long-term bond. And rather than just selling, the sales department works with marketing to use techniques like database marketing, message differentiation to different target markets, and tracking of promotional effects to improve the relationship. For example, customer relationship management (CRM) tools have been used by

Harris Bank and Bank One. Both make extensive uses of their databases on purchase behavior and frequency and duration of customer interactions to estimate profitability at the individual account level. AT&T builds databases of customers with similar profiles, flagging those with the most potential for up-selling. As noted by Copulsky and Wolf, such marketing uses a more personalized form of communication that crosses the previous boundaries between personal selling and the other promotional tools. Relationship building also requires trust, as noted by Pepper and Rodgers; if the customer does not trust the salesperson, there is no relationship and the sale will focus only on price. In a long-term relationship, the buyer and seller collaborate within the context of previous and future transactions.[9] Kimberly-Clark, Porsche, First USA, and MCI are just a few of the companies now involving the salesperson in the integrated marketing communications program.

The Costs of Personal Selling In some industries, personal selling constitutes a substantial portion of the communications effort and may account for most of the promotional budget. This is true because (1) much attention is devoted to this function due to its advantages over other communication methods and (2) it is an expensive form of communication. As demonstrated by Figure 18–4, the average cost per sales call varies by industry, ranging from a low of $235 to $332 in the manufacturing sector. Communication does not come cheap!

When the cost per sales call is compared with the cost per message delivered through other media, these figure seem outrageous. We saw in earlier chapters that these costs could be as low as 3 cents. But taking these numbers at face value may lead to unfair comparisons. In evaluating the costs of personal selling, we must consider the nature of the call, the objectives sought, and whether other program elements could deliver the message as effectively. It may be that the higher costs cannot be avoided.

The costs of personal selling are even higher when you consider that one sales call is not likely to be enough to close a deal. This is particularly true in building and construction; while it may take (on the average) only 3.14 sales calls to close a deal in a services industry, the same close in electronics and computer manufacturing may require 6.6 visits.[10] The industry average is 4.08. As you can see through simple multiplication, the cost per sale is now even more intimidating (though in industrial markets the returns may easily warrant the expense).

Overall, personal selling is an expensive way to communicate. Yet it does usually involve more than just communicating, and the returns (more direct sales) may be greater than those from the other program elements.

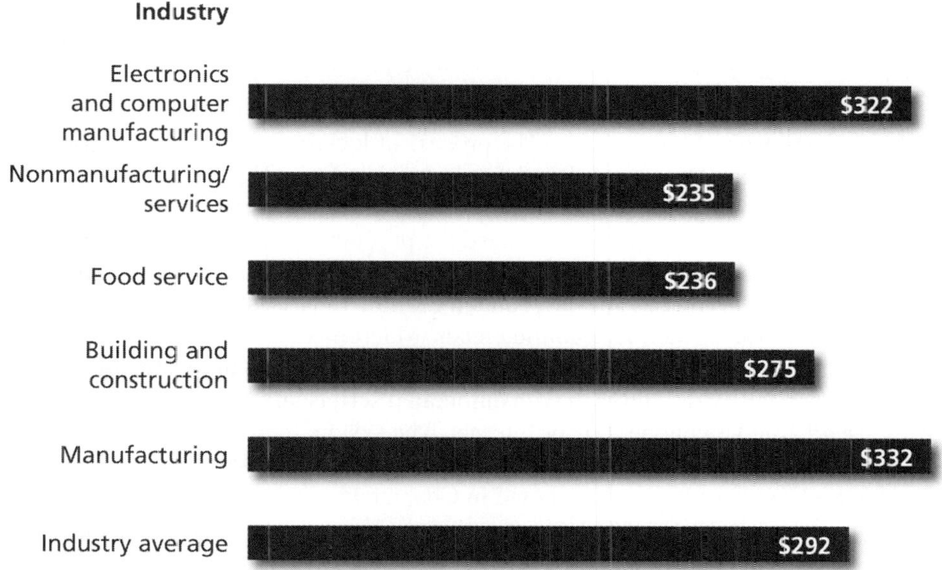

Figure 18–4 Average cost per sales call by industry

Figure 18–5 Types of sales jobs

Creative Selling
Creative selling jobs may require the most skill and preparation. In addition to prospecting, the salesperson must assess the situation, determine the needs to be met, present the capabilities for satisfying these needs, and get an order. The salesperson is often the "point person" who has established the initial contact on behalf of the firm and who is primarily responsibile for completing the exchange. He or she is, in fact, the order getter.
Order Taking
Once the initial sale has taken place, the creative seller may be replaced (not physically!) by an order taker, whose role is much more casual. It may simply involve a straight rebuy—that is, the order does not change much. (A bottled-water delivery person is an example.) When a slight change is considered, the order taker may be involved in a modified rebuy, which may require some creative selling (for example, a salesperson calling on a wholesale food company may have a list of products to sell). If a major purchase decision is required, however, the role of making the sale may again be turned over to the creative seller.
Missionary Sales Reps
The missionary representative is essentially a support role. While performing many of the tasks assumed in creative selling, the missionary rep may not actually take the order. He or she introduces new products, new promotions, and/or new programs, with the actual order to be taken by the company's order taker or by a distributor representing the company's goods. The missionary sales rep may have additional account service responsibilities. Missionary reps are most often employed in industries where the manufacturer uses a middleperson to distribute the product (for example, food products or pharmaceuticals).

Personal Selling Responsibilities *Sales & Marketing Management* uses three categories to classify salespeople: **order taking, creative selling,** and **missionary sales**[11] (see Figure 18–5). Of course, not all firms treat each of these responsibilities the same, nor are their salespeople limited to only these tasks. Personal selling has evolved responsibilities beyond these. Job requirements may include (1) locating prospective customers; (2) determining customers' needs and wants that are not being satisfied; (3) recommending a way to satisfy these needs and/or wants; (4) demonstrating the capabilities of the firm and its products for providing this satisfaction; (5) closing the sale and taking the order; and (6) following up and servicing the account. Let's discuss these job classifications and some of the responsibilities assigned to each:

1. *Locating prospective customers.* The process of locating new customers (often referred to as **prospecting**) involves the search for and qualification of prospective customers. Salespeople must follow up on **leads** (those who may become customers) and **prospects** (those who need the product or service). They must also determine whether these prospects are **qualified prospects**—that is, able to make the buying decision and pay for the product. Exhibit 18–1 is an ad for a company that helps sales forces identify qualified leads. Macromedia, a software company in San Francisco, uses an automated lead tracking system to help in this regard. The system gathers all leads, and then with automated scripts and questionnaires the leads are qualified by phone, fax, or Internet. The system then arranges each lead by "grade" and priority status and directs it to the appropriate salesperson. Dell and Cisco use a Web-based system, as noted in Chapter 15.[12]

2. *Determining customers' needs and wants.* At this stage, the salesperson gathers more information on the prospect and decides the best way to approach him or her.

Exhibit 18–1 Giltspur offers salespeople expertise on how to qualify leads

The rep must determine what the customer needs or wants and make certain the person being approached is capable of making the purchase decision. In some instances the salesperson may have to assist the customer in determining what he or she needs.

3. *Recommending a way to satisfy the customers' needs and wants.* Here the salesperson recommends a possible solution to the problem and/or needs of the potential customer. This may entail providing information the prospect had not considered or identifying alternative solutions that might work. As noted earlier, the salesperson acts as a systems provider.

4. *Demonstrating the capabilities of the firm and its products.* At this stage, the salesperson demonstrates the capabilities of the firm and shows the prospect why that firm is the obvious choice. As you might expect, corporate image (created through advertising and other promotional tools) is important to the salesperson.

5. *Closing the sale.* The key ingredient in any sales presentation is the **close**—getting the prospect's commitment. For many salespeople, this is the most difficult task. Many reps are adept at prospecting, identifying customer needs, and making presentations, but they are reluctant to ask for the sale. Most managers work with their sales forces to close the sale and help reluctant or uncertain buyers make a decision.

6. *Following up and servicing the account.* The responsibilities of the sales force do not end once the sale has been made. It is much easier to keep existing customers than to attract new ones. Maintaining customer loyalty, generating repeat sales, and getting the opportunity to **cross sell**—that is, sell additional products and services to the same customer—are some of the advantages of keeping customers satisfied through follow-up activities. In a relationship marketing versus selling orientation, follow-up is necessary and expected.

A primary advantage a salesperson offers is the opportunity to assess the situation firsthand and adapt the sales message accordingly (a *direct feedback* network).

No other promotional element provides this opportunity. The successful salesperson constantly analyzes the situation, reads the feedback provided by the receiver, and shapes the message to specifically meet the customer's needs.

While you might expect this to be an easy task, it isn't always the case. Sometimes buyers will not or cannot express their needs accurately. Other times, the salesperson must become a problem solver for the client. More and more, salespeople are being asked to assist in the buyers' decision-making process. The more salespeople can become involved in planning and decision making, the more confidence the buyer places in them, and the more bonding the relationship becomes.

Sometimes the true motivation for purchasing is not the one the customer gives. You might expect buyers to base their decisions on rational, objective factors, but this is not always the case. Even in industrial markets (where product specifications may be critical) or reseller markets (where product movements and/or profits are important), many purchase decisions are made on what might be called nonrational criteria (not irrational, but involving factors beyond cost or other product benefits). Since it is generally believed these purchase situations involve less emotion and more rational thinking than many consumer purchases, this is an important insight.

Consider the marketer's dilemma. If a firm provides advertising and promotions that speak only to the rational purchase motives, it may not be able to make the sale. On the other hand, how could an advertiser possibly know all the emotional or nonrational criteria influencing the decision, let alone integrate this information into its messages? The personal sales effort may be the only way to uncover the many motivations for purchasing and address them.

When you review this list of responsibilities, it becomes clear that the salesperson of today is no mere huckster. IMC Perspective 18–1 demonstrates the fact that selling in today's marketplace requires considerable sophistication, while Figure 18–6 provides a list of the 10 traits that are common to successful salespeople.

The importance of personal selling in the integrated marketing communications program should now be clear. This program element provides opportunities that no other form of message delivery does. But while the tasks performed by salespeople offer some distinct advantages to the marketing program, they may also constitute disadvantages, as you will now see.

Advantages and Disadvantages of Personal Selling

The nature of personal selling positions this promotional tool uniquely among those available to marketers. Its advantages include the following:

1. *Allowing for two-way interaction.* The ability to interact with the receiver allows the sender to determine the impact of the message.

Figure 18–6 Ten traits of effective salespeople

A *Sales & Marketing Management* survey of 209 salespeople representing 189 companies in 37 industries determined that the following traits characterize top sales performers:

1. *Ego strength:* a healthy self-esteem that allows one to bounce back from rejection.
2. *A sense of urgency:* wanting to get it done now.
3. *Ego drive:* a combination of competitiveness and self-esteem.
4. *Assertiveness:* the ability to be firm, lead the sales process, and get one's point across confidently.
5. *Willingness to take risk:* willing to innovate and take a chance.
6. *Sociable:* outgoing, friendly, talkative, and interested in others.
7. *Abstract reasoning:* ability to understand concepts and ideas.
8. *Skepticism:* a slight lack of trust and suspicion of others.
9. *Creativity:* the ability to think differently.
10. *Empathy:* the ability to place oneself in someone else's shoes.

IMC Perspective 18–1

America's Best Sales Forces—Innovative and Nimble

While a lot can be said about America's best sales forces, perhaps what describes them best is their ability to innovate and adapt to change. *Sales & Marketing Management* magazine and Dun & Bradstreet teamed up to determine the top 25 sales forces in the United States for 1999. While a number of different industries were included, several attributes were consistent across all the winners—basically, they think like marketers, not salespeople. The top three typify this quite well:

- *Enron.* If you live in Houston, or follow the Houston Astros baseball team, you are probably familiar with the name *Enron*—yes, it's the same Enron whose name adorns the baseball team's home stadium: Enron Field. But just as a stadium is anything but a field, Enron is anything but just a sales force. It is number 1! What's amazing is how quickly Enron got to the top. The energy services company was a start-up less than three years ago and now does $16 billion a year in sales. How does Enron do it? Rather than selling on a year-to-year basis, the sales force positions itself as a long-term energy solutions provider that works with companies to save them millions of dollars per year. Enron gains the trust of businesses and demonstrates the value they can provide through outsourcing energy management. All of it. If it heats, cools, boils, or ventilates, Enron wants to manage it—and free up the customers to attend to other problems. The savings Enron provides are attractive too, as Enron's customers now have money to invest in areas other than energy. Because negotiating each deal takes as long as 9 to 15 months, Enron has to be very careful who it deals with—spending that much time and not consumating an agreement is a waste of money and effort. To choose the right potential customers, Enron employs sound marketing strategies—segmentation, targeting marketing research, and positioning. Each salesperson is a marketer, providing insights and working with engineers and other divisions within the company to determine where Enron can deliver the best value. Most of Enron's customers will tell you that sometimes Enron knows their companies and their needs better than they do themselves. The salespeople do their homework and lay out a plan to get the business. And when they get it, they work to keep it—and they usually do.

- *Dell.* The small-business segment of the PC industry is the fastest-growing segment in the United States and it is the fastest-growing segment in Dell Computers as well. Part of the reason is that Dell's sales force has a number of marketing tools in its arsenal, which gives the sales reps a strong competitive edge. One is the Internet. Dell provides customers with a password-protected section on its site that allows them to access information on their account history and tune in to a weekly live webcast called "Breakfast with Dell" where they can learn more about business problems like Y2K, how to build an Internet business, and so on. The Internet saves Dell customers time and money and provides them with valuable information, while cementing their relationship with Dell.
- *Cisco.* In 1999, e-mail messages outnumbered regular mail by 10 to 1. And most of that e-mail was carried by a Cisco data-transferring system. The secret to Cisco's success is partnering. Like Enron, Cisco segments its market, determines which markets provide the best targets, and partners with resellers to market to segments that it was too thin-staffed to reach before. The new strategy has Cisco account reps and their channel members working together to provide solutions for companies—particularly small start-ups—with problems. In some cases, it is Cisco's channel member that finds and sells the companies' customers on Cisco products—now that is cost-effective selling!

The remaining 22 companies have similar success stories, most of which include finding innovative ways to adapt to the changing marketplace. GE Capital Services employs novel database management techniques, Pfizer focuses on research and new product development, Xerox trains its sales force to be "advanced solutions providers," and Federal Express attributes its success to understanding consumer behavior. If you examine the strategies of the remaining winners, you will see the same thing: the use of integrated marketing techniques to establish relationships and solve problems.

Source: Sara Lorge, "Here's to the Winners," *Sales & Marketing Management,* July 1999, pp. 46–70.

Problems in comprehension or objections can be resolved and in-depth discussions of certain selling points can be provided immediately. In mass communications this direct feedback is not available and such information cannot be obtained immediately (if at all).

2. *Tailoring of the message.* Because of the direct interaction, messages can be tailored to the receiver. This more precise message content lets the sender address the consumer's specific concerns, problems, and needs. The sales rep can also determine when to move on to the next selling point, ask for the sale, or close the deal.

3. *Lack of distraction.* In many personal selling situations, a one-to-one presentation is conducted. The likelihood of distractions is minimized and the buyer is generally paying close attention to the sales message. Even when the presentation is made by a group of salespeople or more than one decision maker is present, the setting is less distracting than those in which nonpersonal mass media are used.

4. *Involvement in the decision process.* Through consultative selling and relationship marketing, the seller becomes more of a partner in the buying decision process, acting in conjunction with the buyer to solve problems. This leads the buyer to rely more on the salesperson and his or her products and services. An added benefit may be increasing the involvement of the organization's own employees.

5. *Source of research information.* In a well-integrated marketing/sales department the sales force can be the "eyes and ears" of the firm. Sales reps can collect information on competitors' products and services, promotions, pricing, and so on, firsthand. In addition, they can learn about the buying needs and wants of customers and potential customers. The importance of conducting research is demonstrated in Global Perspective 18–2.

As you can see, the advantages of personal selling focus primarily on the dyadic communications process, the ability to alter the message, and the opportunity for direct feedback. Sometimes, however, these potential advantages are not always realized. In fact, they may become disadvantages.

Disadvantages associated with personal selling include the following:

1. *Inconsistent messages.* Earlier we stated that the ability to adapt the message to the receiver is a distinct advantage of personal selling. But the lack of a standardized message can become a disadvantage. The message to be communicated is generally designed by the marketing staff with a particular communications objective in mind. Once this message has been determined, it is communicated to all receivers. But the salesperson may alter this message in ways the marketer did not intend. Thus, the marketing staff is at the mercy of the sales force with respect to what exactly is communicated. (Sales communications aids can offset this problem to some degree, as you will see later in this chapter.)

2. *Sales force/management conflict.* Unfortunately, there are situations in even the best companies when one wonders if the sales staff and marketing staff know they work for the same company and for the same goals. Because of failure to communicate, corporate politics, and myriad other reasons, the sales force and marketing may not be working as a team. The marketing staff may not understand the problems faced by the sales staff, or the salespeople may not understand why marketing people do things the way they do. The result is that the sales force may not use materials provided from marketing, marketing may not be responsive to the field's assessment of customer needs, and so forth. The bottom line is that the communications process is not as effective as it could be due to faulty internal communications and/or conflicts.

3. *High cost.* We discussed earlier the high cost of personal selling. As the cost per sales call continues to climb, the marketer may find mass communications a more cost-effective alternative.

4. *Poor reach.* Personal selling cannot reach as many members of the target audience as other elements. Even if money were no object (not a very likely scenario!),

Global Perspective 18–2

So You Want to Sell Globally? Well Here's What It Takes

As the world gets smaller, it's not unusual for a company in Los Angeles to be buying from someone in Argentina, or for a Swedish company to be acquiring raw materials from Brazil. More and more companies are looking international to build their business. But it's not always as easy as it seems. Burt Cabanas, president and CEO of Benchmark Hospitality, Inc., found that out the hard way. Burt's company develops and manages conference centers, conference hotels, and resorts, and while based in Woodlands, Texas, it conducts business in Thailand, Japan, and the Philippines and soon may be in six more countries. Its first venture—in Thailand—was based on assumptions and no research, and that was a major mistake, says Cabanas. Taking other peoples' word as to what to do set Benchmark back a year and a half, he says.

Scott Haug of Towers Perrin Sales Management Practice in Los Angeles agrees. He notes that there are language and cultural issues and that to sell successfully, the salesperson has to tap into the psyche of the customer, and that psyche differs from one country to another. Like Cabanas, Haug feels that the only way to compete successfully in the international arena is to conduct extensive marketing research before you enter the foreign country.

But what kind of research is necessary, and how do you do it? Bill Edwards of Alphagraphics, a Tucson, Arizona, company currently operating in 24 countries in Asia, Europe, and Latin America, says that before his firm goes into any market, it conducts online research, searches U.S. Department of Commerce sources, and follows up on leads generated through the Internet. Only then will Alphagraphics visit the country to explore business opportunities. Burt Cabanas says he now tries to enlist the support of local talent to help him understand the market. He once hired a man who had written a book on Thai culture to help him understand the nuances of life there. When he goes into other countries, he splits the top management between U.S. and local employees to gain the knowledge that he feels can't be acquired by analyzing data.

Other companies have taken a very different approach to doing business internationally. Rather than conducting research and sending in expatriates to start a business, these companies are letting someone else do it for them. American Airlines and Westin Hotels are just two examples. When Internet company DoubleClick wanted to expand into Ireland but wasn't sure it wanted to build its own operations, it enlisted Eircom, a Dublin-based call-center provider. Rather than spending time and money on research, DoubleClick walked in and was ready to go in less than a month. Eircom is just one of the "incubator" call centers that has been established in Ireland and Scotland to provide companies with a temporary place to do business while they determine if they want to make a larger commitment and build their own operations (DoubleClick did after six months). Gateway has also used a call center in Ireland to conduct business in Europe, the Middle-East, and Africa, and IBM entered the market with a call center in Scotland. IBM's call center has grown to be massive, housing a direct-marketing service center as well as a central order and fulfillment center. Eight hundred employees offer support in 11 languages to IBM's Western European customers. IBM has been extremely satisfied with its decision, noting that customer satisfaction and perceptions of the company have both benefited as a result of the local presence.

So what is the right way to go? The best answer probably is that it depends. Is the company ready to make the commitment? Does it have the local knowledge required to compete successfully? Does it have the resources, financially and managerially, to compete successfully? One thing is certain, it better do its homework and acquire a local feel for the market. If not, it may end up like Burt Cabanas.

Sources: Erika Ramusson, "Global Sales on the Line," *Sales & Marketing Management*, pp. 76–82; Lambeth Hochwald, "Are You Smart Enough to Sell Globally?" *Sales & Marketing Management*, July 1998, pp. 53–56.

the sales force has only so many hours and so many people it can reach in a given time. Further, the frequency with which these accounts are reached is also low.

5. *Potential ethical problems.* Because the manager does not have complete control over the messages the salespeople communicate and because income and advancement are often directly tied to sales, sometimes sales reps bend the rules. They may say and do things they know are not entirely ethical or in the best interest of the firm in order to get a sale. The potential for this problem has led to a renewed emphasis on ethics in the marketplace.

Combining Personal Selling with Other Promotional Tools

Like the other program elements, personal selling is usually one component of the integrated marketing communications program. Rarely, if ever, is it used alone. Rather, this promotional tool both supports and is supported by other program elements.

Combining Personal Selling and Advertising

With specific market situations and communications objectives, the advantages of advertising make it more effective in the early stages of the response hierarchy (for example, in creating awareness and interest), whereas personal selling is more likely to be used in the later stages (for example, stimulating trial and getting the order). Thus, each may be more or less appropriate depending on the objectives sought. These elements can be combined in the promotional mix to compensate for each other's weaknesses and complement each other.

Consider a new product introduction. Given an adequate budget, the initial objective might be to reach as many people in the target market as quickly and cost effectively as possible. Since the primary objective is awareness and a simple message will suffice, advertising will likely be the most appropriate medium.

Now suppose specific benefits must be communicated that are not very obvious or easy to comprehend, and a product demonstration would be useful. Or consider a situation in which the objective is to ask for the sale and/or to establish a relationship. Here personal selling is a more appropriate tool than advertising. In common marketing situations like these, you can see how well advertising and personal selling work together to attain the objectives sought.

A number of studies bear out this complementary relationship. A study by Theodore Levitt showed that sales reps from well-known companies are better received than those from companies that do not spend advertising dollars to create awareness.[13] (Once they are in the door, however, the buyer expects the salesperson to perform better than those from lesser-known companies.) If a salesperson from a lesser-known company can get in to see the buyer, he or she is as likely to make the sale. But in risky situations, the well-advertised company rep has the advantage. Gateway recently embarked upon a $50 million IMC campaign (Exhibit 18–2) using advertising, direct marketing, sales promotion, and the Internet to create awareness that Gateway is interested in companies' business (Gateway has been perceived by many as being a consumer PC). The campaign is designed to position the company as a solutions provider and to assist and enhance the sales force's efforts.

In other studies, John Morrill found that selling costs were 2 to 28 percent lower if the buyer had received an advertising message before the salesperson's arrival.[14] McGraw-Hill Corp., in a review of 54 studies, concluded the combination of advertising and personal selling is important since "less than 10 percent of industrial decision makers had been called upon by a salesperson from a specific company about a specific product in the previous two months."[15]

Exhibit 18–2 Gateway's IMC campaign informs customers that Gateway is in the business-to-business market

The studies suggest that combining advertising and personal selling is likely to improve reach, reduce costs, and increase the probability of a sale (assuming the advertising is effective, a concern reflected in Exhibit 18–3).

Combining Personal Selling and Public Relations

The job descriptions presented earlier demonstrate that personal selling involves much more than just selling products and/or services. The personal selling agent is often the firm's best source of public relations. In their day-to-day duties, salespeople represent the firm and its products. Their personalities, servicing of the account, cooperation, and empathy not only influence sales potential but also reflect on the organizations they represent.

The salesperson may also be used directly in a PR role. Many firms encourage sales reps to participate in community activities like the Jaycees and Little League. Sometimes sales reps, in conjunction with the company, sacrifice time from their daily duties to help people in need. For example, after the Los Angeles earthquake, local companies donated food and their sales forces' time to aid quake victims. Computer salespeople devoted much of their time to getting customers and noncustomers back online. After a catastrophic flood, a beer company in the Northeast had its sales reps distribute water in its cans to flood victims. Coors provided free water in its cans to Pittsburghers when a barge break contaminated the drinking water. After floods ravished the Midwest, Provident Bank of Cincinnati, Ohio, had its tellers sell blue ribbons for $1 apiece, with proceeds going to flood victims. Thriftway Food Stores and a number of organizations also helped rebuild the ravaged community. Such actions result in goodwill toward both the company and its products while at the same time benefiting society.

Exhibit 18–3 Advertising and personal selling should be designed to work together

Combining Personal Selling and Direct Marketing

Companies have found that integrating direct marketing, specifically telemarketing, into their field sales operations makes their sales efforts more effective. The cost of a sales call and the cost associated with closing the sale are already very high and on the increase. Many marketers have reduced these costs by combining telemarketing and sales efforts (a typical telesales call costs about 11¢ for each $1.00 in revenue generated).[16] A number of companies now offer consulting services to help organizations in that endeavor, as shown in Exhibit 18–4.

The telemarketing department is used to screen leads and—after qualifying potential buyers on the basis of interest, credit ratings, and the like—pass them on to the sales force. The net result is a higher percentage of sales closings, less wasted time by the sales force, and a lower average cost per sale. For example, IBM teamed up with Zacson Corp. to open an integrated teleservices center for its Northern California territory. The group handles inquiries, lead generation, and qualification; develops promotional campaigns; distributes PR materials; and does problem solving for IBM clients. The new relationship reduced IBM's customer contact costs by 97 percent, lowered sales visit costs from $500 to $15, and exceeded customer expectations 78 percent of the time.[17]

As shown in Figure 18–7, there has been a rapid growth in the use of the telemarketing/ sales combination for other firms as well. They have determined the phone can be used effectively for service and follow-up functions as well as for growth-related activities. Supplementing personal selling efforts with phone calls frees the sales force to spend more time selling.

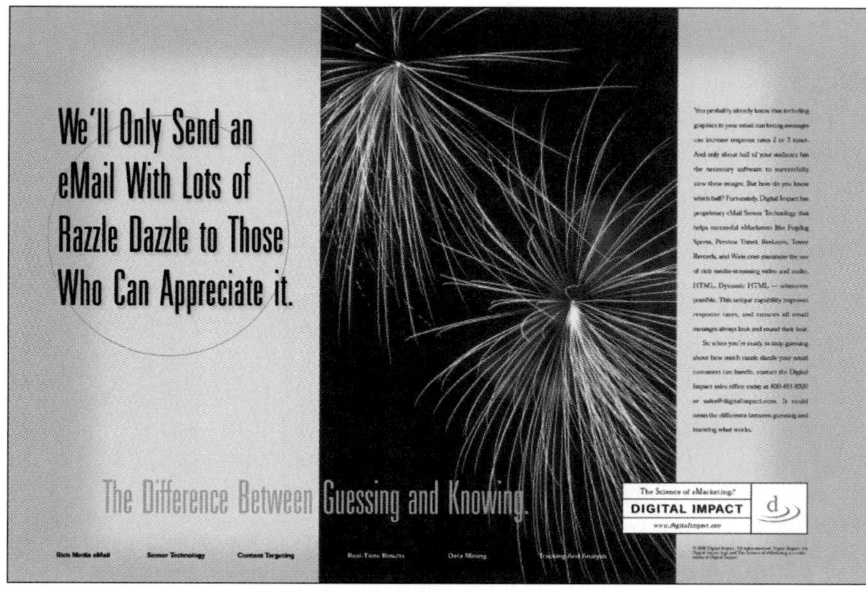

Exhibit 18–4 Research and consulting companies offer businesses direct-marketing services

Figure 18–7 The growth of telemarketing as a sales function: reasons for growth (in percent)

	Telephone Sales and Service	Field Sales
Total growth related	58.0	61.8
Overall business growth or expansion	44.7	43.1
Adding product lines	10.2	8.0
Adding territories	3.1	10.7
Total system related	20.8	7.5
Added centralized telemarketing dept.	11.5	1.8
Added/changed computer system	6.2	4.4
Centralized sales and marketing	3.1	1.3
Customer demand	10.5	10.2
Cost efficiencies	1.4	0
Other	2.0	2.2
Can't tell/no response	9.8	18.2

Note: Adds to more than 100 percent due to multiple mentions.

In addition to selling and supporting the sales efforts, the telemarketing staff provides a public relations dimension. Communicating with buyers more often creates goodwill, improving customer satisfaction and loyalty.

In addition to telemarketing, other forms of direct marketing have been combined successfully with personal selling. For example, many companies send out lead cards to screen prospective customers. The salesperson follows up on those who express a genuine interest, saving valuable time and increasing the potential for a sale. Exhibit 18–5 shows an example of a highly used software program available to assist marketers in creating and managing a database.

Combining Personal Selling and Sales Promotion

The program elements of sales promotion and personal selling also support each other. For example, many of the sales promotions targeted to resellers are presented by the sales force, who will ultimately be responsible for removing or replacing them as well.

While trade sales promotions are designed to support the reseller and are often targeted to the ultimate consumer, many other promotional tools are designed to assist the sales staff. Flip charts, leave-behinds, and specialty ads may be designed to assist salespeople in their presentations, serve as reminders, or just create goodwill. The number of materials available may range from just a few to hundreds, depending on the company. (If you ever get the chance, look into the trunk of a consumer products salesperson's car. You will find everything from pens to calendars to flip charts to samples to lost baseball mitts—all but the last of which are used in the selling effort.)

Likewise, many sales promotions are targeted at the sales force itself. Incentives such as free trips, cash bonuses, or gifts are often used to stimulate sales efforts. And, as we saw with resellers, contests and sweepstakes may also be used.

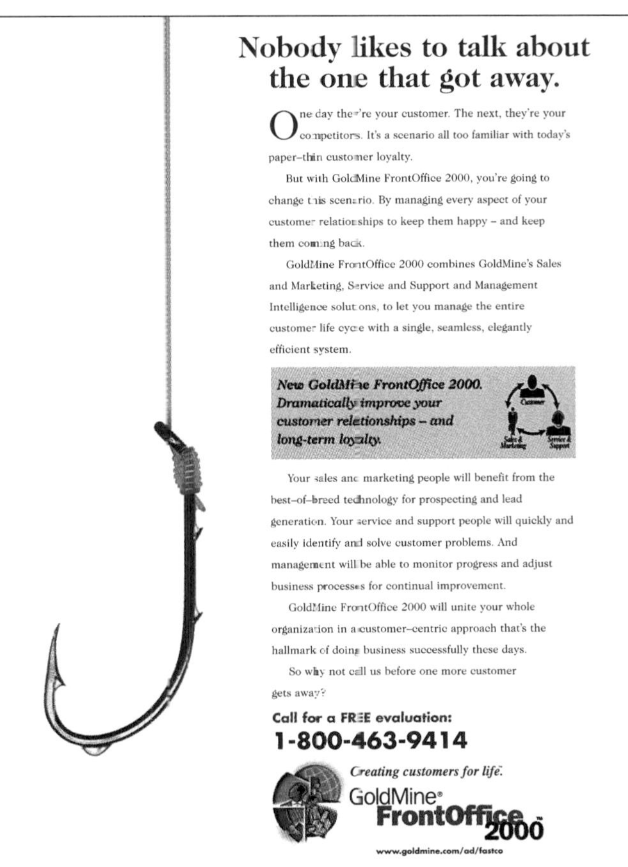

Exhibit 18–5 Goldmine is one of the more popular database management tools

Combining Personal Selling with the Internet

In the Internet chapter, we discussed the increasing use of the Internet as a replacement to personal selling. As noted, the Internet has been used to provide product information, generate leads, screen prospects, and build and market from databases. While many marketing managers see the Internet taking business away from channel members and direct sales, few are ready to relinquish their sales forces. Even though at least one study predicts that 98 percent of all large companies will be on the Internet by 2002, and that the ROI for direct sales on the Web is five times that for traditional direct marketing, most companies still see the sales force as an integral part of the IMC process—particularly for relationship building.[18] Many managers feel that the Web will be used to fulfill the more mundane tasks of order fulfillment and providing information. This in turn will allow the sales force to be more effective in closing orders, doing close selling, and focusing more attention on high-value and/or new customers. Future salespeople will do what is more profitable for the future—that is, sell, not take orders.

It is important that the elements of the promotional program work together, as each has its specific advantages and disadvantages. While personal selling is valuable in accomplishing certain objectives and supporting other promotional tools, it must be supported by the other elements. Ads, sales promotions, and the like may be targeted to the ultimate user, resellers, or the organization's sales force.

Evaluating the Personal Selling Effort

Like all other elements of the promotional mix, personal selling must be evaluated on the basis of its contribution to the overall promotional effort. The costs of personal selling are often high, but the returns may be just as high.

Because the sales force is under the supervision of the sales manager, evaluations are typically based on sales criteria. Sales may be analyzed by total sales volume, territories, product line, customer type, or sales rep.[19] Other sales-related criteria such as new account openings and personal traits are also sometimes considered, as shown in Figure 18–8.

From a promotional perspective, sales performance is important, as are the contributions of individuals in generating these sales. On the other hand, the promotions manager must evaluate the performance of personal selling as one program

Figure 18–8 Criteria used to evaluate sales forces

Quantitative Measures

Sales Results	Sales Efforts
Orders	**Sales calls**
Number of orders obtained	Number made on current customers
Average order size (units or dollars)	Number made on potential new accounts
Batting average (orders ÷ sales calls)	Average time spent per call
Number of orders canceled by customers	Number of sales presentations
Sales volume	Selling time versus nonselling time
Dollar sales volume	Call frequency ratio per customer type
Unit sales volume	**Selling expenses**
By customer type	Average per sales call
By product category	As percentage of sales volume
Translated into market share	As percentage of sales quota
Percentage of sales quota achieved	By customer type
Margins	By product category
Gross margin	Direct-selling expense ratios
Net profit	Indirect-selling expense ratios
By customer type	**Customer service**
By product category	Number of service calls
Customer accounts	Displays set up
Number of new accounts	Delivery cost per unit sold
Number of lost accounts	Months of inventory held, by customer type
Percentage of accounts sold	Number of customer complaints
Number of overdue accounts	Percentage of goods returned
Dollar amount of accounts receivable	
Collections made of accounts receivable	

Qualitative Measures

Sales Results	Sales Efforts
Selling skills	**Sales-related activities**
Knowing the company and its policies	Territory management: sales call preparation, scheduling, routing, and time utilization
Knowing competitors' products and sales strategies	Marketing intelligence: new product ideas, competitive activities, new customer preferences
Use of marketing and technical backup teams	Follow-ups: use of promotional brochures and correspondence with current and potential accounts
Understanding of selling techniques	Customer relations
Customer feedback (positive and negative)	Report preparation and timely submission
Product knowledge	Personal characteristics
Customer knowledge	Cooperation, human relations, enthusiasm, motivation, judgment, care of company property, appearance, self-improvement efforts, patience, punctuality, initiative, resourcefulness, health, sales management potential, ethical and moral behavior
Execution of selling techniques	
Quality of sales presentations	
Communication skills	

element contributing to the overall promotional program. So he or she needs to use different criteria in determining its effectiveness.

Criteria for Evaluating Personal Selling

A number of criteria may be used to evaluate the contribution of the personal selling effort to the promotional program. They include the following.

- *Provision of marketing intelligence.* The ability of the sales force to feed back information regarding competitive programs, customer reactions, market trends, and other factors that may be important in the development of the promotional program.
- *Follow-up activities.* The use and dissemination of promotional brochures and correspondences with new and existing customers; providing feedback on the effectiveness of various promotional programs.
- *Program implementations.* The number of promotional programs implemented; the number of shelf and/or counter displays used and so forth; the implementation and assessment of cooperative advertising programs.
- *Attainment of communications objectives.* The number of accounts to whom presentations were made (awareness, evaluation), the number of trial offers accepted, and the like.

Combining these criteria with those used by the sales department, the promotions manager should be able to accurately assess the effectiveness of the personal selling program. Making these evaluations requires a great deal of cooperation between the departments.

Summary

This chapter discussed the nature of personal selling and the role this program element plays in the promotional mix. The role of personal selling in the IMC program varies depending on the nature of the industry, competition, and market conditions. In many industries (for example, industrial markets) the personal selling component may receive the most attention, while in others (for example, consumer nondurables) it plays a minor role. However, managers in most industries believe the importance of this program element will continue to increase over the next few years.

Personal selling offers the marketer the opportunity for a dyadic communications process (a two-way exchange of information). The salesperson can instantly assess the situation and the effects of the communication and adapt the message if necessary.

While this exchange lets the sales rep tailor the message specifically to the needs and wants of the receiver, its disadvantage is a nonstandardized message, since the final message communicated is under the salesperson's control. In an attempt to develop a standard communication, marketers provide their reps with flip charts, leave-behinds, and other promotional pieces.

Evaluation of the personal selling effort is usually under the control of the sales department, since sales is the most commonly used criterion. The promotions manager must assess the contribution of personal selling with nonsales-oriented criteria as well.

Key Terms

personal selling, 614
dyadic communication, 615
provider stage, 617
persuader stage, 618
prospector stage, 618
problem-solver stage, 618
procreator stage, 618
relationship marketing, 618
order taking, 620
creative selling, 620
missionary sales, 620
prospecting, 620
leads, 620
prospects, 620
qualified prospects, 620
close, 621
cross sell, 621

Discussion Questions

1. One of the advantages of personal selling is the ability for dyadic communication. Explain what this term means. Why is this an advantage over other media?

2. Explain what is meant by "the new role of personal selling." How does this new role differ from what personal selling has involved in the past?

3. Give an example of how a personal salesperson might benefit from relationship marketing. How would the client benefit?

4. Explain why the high costs of personal selling might be warranted. Give a specific example of a situation where this is the case.

5. Explain why the salespersons' tailoring of the message can be both an advantage and a disadvantage to marketers.

6. Explain why the combination of personal selling and advertising may provide benefits that exceed just personal selling alone.

7. Describe some of the criteria used to evaluate qualitative aspects of the effectiveness of the salesperson. How might these be used to support the IMC program?

8. Give examples of companies' public relations efforts that may have required the efforts of their sales force.

9. Many marketing students' first job is in personal selling. Explain why Fortune 500 companies typically require entry-level marketing people to start off in sales.

10. Explain how a personal sales agent might use the Internet to become a more effective marketer.

Chapter Nineteen

Measuring the Effectiveness of the Promotional Program

Chapter Objectives

- To understand reasons for measuring promotional program effectiveness.
- To know the various measures used in assessing promotional program effectiveness.
- To evaluate alternative methods for measuring promotional program effectiveness.
- To understand the requirements of proper effectiveness research.

Measuring Effectiveness—Revolution or Evolution?

Perhaps one of the more frustrating issues in integrated marketing communications is how to measure the effectiveness of the IMC program. For years marketers have discussed, debated, and denigrated just about every technique that has been proposed. Many have given up the chase, concluding that establishing a direct relationship is like trying to find the proverbial needle in the haystack. Now, with the coming of the Internet, and all the new methods proposed to measure effectiveness on that medium, the task seems even more daunting. But wait, maybe there is hope after all. New technologies and new methodologies may offer help, if not an absolute solution.

One of the areas showing great promise is that of promotions. Just a short 20 years ago, computer methodologies for measuring effectiveness didn't even exist. To determine if a promotion was effective, marketers had to use store shelf audits (counting the movements of product during a promotion), warehouse withdrawal surveys, and/or consumer panels in which consumers kept track of their purchases over weeks or months. The diaries would then be turned over to a monitoring service, and a few more weeks or months would pass before results could be determined. In the 1980s, these methods were replaced by scanner data. While data were collected more quickly, the task of analyzing the data still took long periods of time. When automated checkouts arrived in the 90s, new opportunities for measurement were born—but unfortunately not recognized, as most managers focused on the checkout speed and error reduction benefits of the technology.

Once managers realized the capability of the new technology for building and analyzing databases, a revolution in the ability to measure promotions effectiveness was born. Marketers could track how much product was moved, compare promotional and nonpromotional sales, analyze demographic purchases, and do so on a store-by-store basis. And they could do it on a day-to-day basis! As noted by Paris Gogos, vice president of business development for Efficient Marketing Services, a Deerfield, Illinois, research firm, "Today's methods allow you to treat the illness while the patient is still alive."

The Internet has taken measuring effectiveness even further. Also using database analysis, the Net allows the marketer to measure promotional campaigns accurately and then use the resulting data to more effectively target. For example, Internet site CD-now ran a promotion in which each customer who made a purchase received an electronic "scratch and win" game card that instantly told the consumer if he or she had won anything. Using e-mail, the company was able to track the course of the promotion day by day. When sales increases were sought, e-mails were sent out with different offers. If the e-mails didn't increase sales, additional offers were sent out. Daily reports detailed the number of game plays and the corresponding purchases.

Eddie Bauer also employed the Internet to measure the effectiveness of both its list and the advertising message. By coding its e-mails, the company could tell on an individual basis who responded to a promotion for khaki pants. Another ad featured the khaki pants and 50 percent off on sweaters. By analyzing responses Eddie Bauer was able to see which promotions were driving traffic, as well as which part of the message was most exciting. The results were compiled, analyzed, and delivered within 36 hours.

Using yet another new technology, Pacific Bell was able to determine what kind of dialogue between customers and service reps would be most effective for cross selling additional phone services. For a price of more than $500,000 PacBell hired a company out of Tennessee called QualPro, which used advanced statistical techniques to determine what the service reps should say about the services and in what order they should present information. Was it worth the cost? By making changes based on the research, PacBell immediately increased its sales by four extra service features per day. Within four months the additional sales were in the teens.

These new technologies and others offer marketers a level of sophistication not previously available. More importantly, they offer the results in almost real time. It appears that measuring effectiveness is truly undergoing a revolution, not just an evolution!

Sources: Sarah Lorge, "Turning Small Ideas into Big Results," *Sales & Marketing Management,* December 1999, p. 79; Richard Sale, "Evaluation in Evolution," *Promo Magazine,* September 1998, pp. 63–68.

As marketers spend their communications dollars in diverse areas, the need to determine the effectiveness of these expenditures becomes increasingly important. As you can see by the lead-in to this chapter, several methods for evaluating the effectiveness of these programs are used. Both clients and agencies are continually striving to determine whether their communications are working and how well they are working relative to other options. Unfortunately, there seems to be little agreement on the best measures to use. Almost everyone agrees that research is required, but they disagree on how it should be conducted and how the results should be used.

Measuring the effectiveness of the promotional program is a critical element in the promotional planning process. Research allows the marketing manager to evaluate the performance of specific program elements and provides input into the next period's situation analysis. It is a necessary ingredient to a continuing planning process, yet it is often not carried out.

In this chapter, we discuss some reasons firms should measure the effectiveness of their IMC programs, as well as why many decide not to. We also examine how, when, and where such measurements can be conducted. Most of our attention is devoted to measuring the effects of advertising because much more time and effort have been expended developing evaluation measures in advertising than in the other promotional areas. We will, however, discuss measurement in other areas of the IMC program as well. (In some of these areas, the measures are more directly observable—for example, direct marketing and personal selling.) You'll recall that we addressed the methods used to evaluate many of the other promotional elements in previous chapters.

It is important to understand that in this chapter we are concerned with research that is conducted in an evaluative role—that is, to measure the effectiveness of advertising and promotion and/or to assess various strategies before implementing them. This is not to be confused with research discussed earlier in the text to help develop the promotional program, although the two can (and should) be used together. While evaluative research may occur at various times throughout the promotional process (including the development stage), it is conducted specifically to assess the effects of various strategies. We begin our discussion with the reasons effectiveness should be measured as well as some of the reasons firms do not do so.

Arguments for and Against Measuring Effectiveness

Almost any time one engages in a project or activity, whether for work or fun, some measure of performance occurs. In sports you may compare your golf score against par or your time on a ski course to other skiers' performance. In business, employees are generally given objectives to accomplish, and their job evaluations are based on their ability to achieve these objectives. Advertising and promotion should not be an exception. It is important to determine how well the communications program is working and to measure this performance against some standards.

Reasons to Measure Effectiveness

Assessing the effectiveness of ads both before they are implemented and after the final versions have been completed and fielded offers a number of advantages:

1. *Avoiding costly mistakes.* The top three advertisers in the United States spent over $7.5 billion in advertising and promotion in 1999. The top 10 spent a total of over $18 billion. This is a lot of money to be throwing around without some understanding of how well it is being spent. If the program is not achieving its objectives, the marketing manager needs to know so he or she can stop spending (wasting) money on it.

Just as important as the out-of-pocket costs is the opportunity loss due to poor communications. If the advertising and promotions program is not accomplishing its objectives, not only is the money spent lost but so too is the potential gain that could result from an effective program. Thus, measuring the effects of advertising does not just save money. It also helps the firm maximize its investment. For example, one mass merchant discovered that promoting Tide detergent generated more cross-selling opportunities than did promotions of nonpremium brands like Purex (Exhibit 19–1). At the same time, promotions of motor oil had no cross-selling impact.[1]

2. *Evaluating alternative strategies.* Typically a firm has a number of strategies under consideration. For example, there may be some question as to which medium should be used or whether one message is more effective than another. Or the decision may be between two promotional program elements. For example, should research be spent on sponsorships or on advertising? One retailer found that advertising do-it-yourself products on the radio was effective in rural areas but not in urban locales.[2] Research may be designed to help the manager determine which strategy is most likely to be effective. Companies often test alternate versions of their advertising in different cities to determine which ad communicates most effectively. They may also explore different forms of couponing.

Exhibit 19–1 Tide has been shown to be an effective promotional draw

3. *Increasing the efficiency of advertising in general.* You may have heard the expression "can't see the forest for the trees." Sometimes advertisers get so close to the project

they lose sight of what they are seeking, and because they know what they are trying to say, they expect their audience will also understand. They may use technical jargon that not everyone is familiar with. Or the creative department may get too creative or too sophisticated and lose the meaning that needs to be communicated. How many times have you seen an ad and asked yourself what it was trying to say, or how often have you seen an ad that you really like, but you can't remember the brand name? Conducting research helps companies develop more efficient and effective communications. An increasing number of clients are demanding accountability for their promotional programs and putting more pressure on the agencies to produce. As IMC Perspective 19–1 demonstrates, effective research can be used for both of these purposes.

Reasons Not to Measure Effectiveness

Companies give a number of reasons for not measuring the effectiveness of advertising and promotions strategies:

1. *Cost.* Perhaps the most commonly cited reason for not testing (particularly among smaller firms) is the expense. Good research can be expensive, in terms of both time and money. Many managers decide that time is critical and they must implement the program while the opportunity is available. Many believe the monies spent on research could be better spent on improved production of the ad, additional media buys, and the like.

While the first argument may have some merit, the second does not. Imagine what would happen if a poor campaign were developed or the incentive program did not motivate the target audience. Not only would you be spending money without the desired effects, but the effort could do more harm than good. Spending more money to buy media does not remedy a poor message or substitute for an improper promotional mix. For example, one of the nation's leading brewers watched its test-market sales for a new brand of beer fall short of expectations. The solution, it decided, was to buy all the TV time available that matched its target audience. After two months sales had not improved, and the product was abandoned in the test market. Analysis showed the problem was not in the media but rather in the message, which communicated no reason to buy. Research would have identified the problem, and millions of dollars and a brand might have been saved. The moral: spending research monies to gain increased exposure to the wrong message is not a sound management decision.

2. *Research problems.* A second reason cited for not measuring effectiveness is that it is difficult to isolate the effects of promotional elements. Each variable in the marketing mix affects the success of a product or service. Because it is rarely possible to measure the contribution of each marketing element directly, some managers become frustrated and decide not to test at all. They say, "If I can't determine the specific effects, why spend the money?"

This argument also suffers from weak logic. While we agree that it is not always possible to determine the dollar amount of sales contributed by promotions, research can provide useful results. As demonstrated by the Steel Alliance and Colgate examples in IMC Perspective 19–1, communications effectiveness can be measured and may carry over to sales.

3. *Disagreement on what to test.* The objectives sought in the promotional program may differ by industry, by stage of the product life cycle, or even for different people within the firm. The sales manager may want to see the impact of promotions on sales, top management may wish to know the impact on corporate image, and those involved in the creative process may wish to assess recall and/or recognition of the ad. Lack of agreement on what to test often results in no testing.

Again, there is little rationale for this position. With the proper design, many or even all of the above might be measured. Since every promotional element is designed to accomplish its own objectives, research can be used to measure its effectiveness in doing so.

IMC Perspective 19–1

Ogilvy Award Winners Rely on Research to Improve Their IMC Programs

One of the advertising industry's most prestigious awards is the Ogilvy Award. The award is given in honor of researcher-turned-adman David Ogilvy, whose own work always stressed the role of research in developing, evaluating, and improving advertising. To win an Ogilvy Award, the candidate must show how research was used in developing a program and demonstrate marketing success. Entries for the 1999 competition came from a variety of industries and included both consumer and business-to-business marketers. Here's what it takes to be an Ogilvy Award winner:

- *The Steel Alliance.* Research conducted in the steel industry in the 1990s showed that steel's image consisted of old stereotypes. While many in the industry recognized the need for improving this image, the lack of interest and cooperation among the industry's players resulted in a lack of cohesive effort. Seventy North American steel companies formed the Steel Alliance in 1997 to develop a communications program designed to make steel the "material of choice" for the packaging, automotive, housing construction, and appliance industries. The Alliance worked with Wirthlin Worldwide, as its research partner, and GSD&M advertising to implement a five-year $100 million program. Four specific goals were established: (1) Increase consumers' awareness of steel, (2) increase positive perceptions of steel and steel products, (3) improve attitudes toward steel relative to competitive products, and (4) increase purchases of steel as a result of the changed attitudes. In addition, the initial research was designed to serve as a benchmark for evaluating these changes over time.

  The positioning platform "The New Steel, Feel the Strength" led to the development of two initial spot ads. "Recycle Bin" presented steel as the product for future generations by stressing the fact that steel is the most recycled material on earth. The second, "Shark" combined the strength and environmental themes into one ad, in which a diver is seen in an underwater cage surrounded by sharks. Words flash on the screen to show the diver's thoughts, "Steel is the most recycled material on earth" and "Please, please let this thing be made of steel." Portions of the ads were strengthened on the basis of input from research, and tracking was used to measure effectiveness once changes were implemented. The tracking focused on various elements of the program, including the media strategy—continuity was more effective than heavy flighting—and media targeting women provided the greatest attitude shift. Research led to the conclusion in 1997 that attitudes toward steel could be made more positive, and in 1998 it proved that awareness and familiarity could be improved. More recent studies have shown that the image of the industry has changed significantly, as favorability (as measured on a scale of 0 to 100) moved from 58 to 82, positive mentions rose from 24 to 70 percent, and negative mentions fell from 37 to 5 percent. The campaign has proved to be successful in improving attitudes and behaviors of steel customers as well as those in the industry.

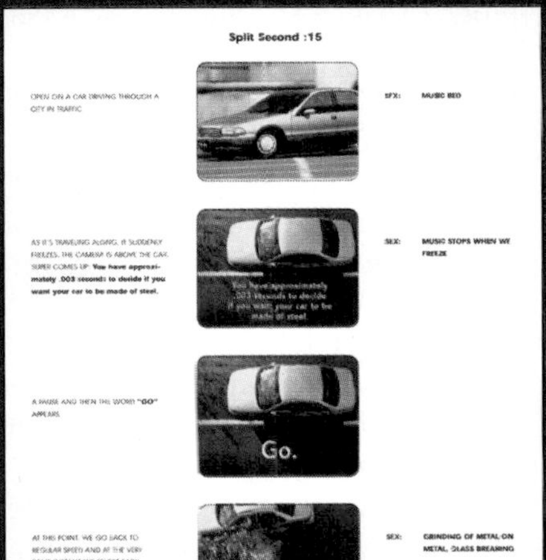

- *Colgate.* In the toothpaste market, Crest has been the leading brand for over 30 years, with Colgate a distant second. The introduction of a multitude of new brands stressing a variety of benefits, including whitening, tartar control, plaque management, and new formulas, eventually led to 16 new combinations of brand and benefits by 1998 and further eroded Colgate's market share in the early 1990s. In its quest for number 1, Colgate introduced Colgate Total—a unique and multidimensional benefit brand.

  Initial research indicated that positioning the Total brand as having a combination of benefits was well accepted by consumers. Putting the message into a spot advertisement constituted much more of a challenge. Focus groups and copy testing were employed to ensure successful campaign development. Nine ads were then developed and tested using animatics (cartoon roughs of the commercial), and measures of the "brand fit" of the celebrities to be used (Michael J. Fox and Michael Richards) were also undertaken.

Once the final commercial executions were determined, the product was launched on television and supported by public relations and promotions. Subsequent research indicated that the program was effective in generating high brand awareness and preference shifts. Nielsen market share data showed that the campaign led to higher shared gains than those of the competition and by the end of three months Colgate had done something it had been unable to do for 30 years—take over number 1 from Crest. Tracking conducted three months later showed that high levels of awareness and recognition remained, and they remained eight months later when promotions and public relations were reduced.

These are but two examples of how effective communications programs are developed and proved successful through research. The Chevy Venture minivan, Swanson Broth soup, Kraft salad dressing, and Miracle Whip are just a few of the other brands that have recently won Ogilvy Awards. While targeting different markets, and with different communications objectives in mind, all have one thing in common: their use of research to develop, guide, and measure the effectiveness of their efforts.

Sources: William A. Cook, "Ogilvy Winners Turn Research into Creative Solutions," *Journal of Advertising Research,* May/June 1999, pp. 59–65; "The ARF Names Ten Ogilvy Award–Winning Campaigns," *Journal of Advertising Research,* March/April 1998, pp. 57–62.

4. *The objections of creative.* It has been argued by many (and denied by others) that the creative department does not want its work to be tested and many agencies are reluctant to submit their work for testing. This is sometimes true. Ad agencies' creative departments argue that tests are not true measures of the creativity and effectiveness of ads; applying measures stifles their creativity; and the more creative the ad, the more likely it is to be successful. They want permission to be creative without the limiting guidelines marketing may impose. The Chiat/Day ad shown in Exhibit 19–2 reflects how many people in the advertising business feel about this subject.

Exhibit 19–2 Chiat/Day expresses their opinion of recall tests

To advertisers interested in 'day after recall', we submit a case history:
"My friends… each of you is a single cell in the great body of the State. And today, that great body has purged itself of parasites.
We have triumphed over the unprincipled dissemination of facts. The thugs and wreckers have been cast out. And the poisonous weeds of disinformation have
been consigned to the dustbin of history… Let each and every cell rejoice! For today we celebrate the first glorious anniversary of the Information Purification Directives.
We have created, for the first time in all history, a garden of pure ideology, where each worker may bloom secure from the pests of contradictory and confusing truths.
Our Unification of Thought is more powerful a weapon than any fleet or army on earth. We are one people. With one will.
One resolve. One cause. Our enemies shall talk themselves to death. And we will bury them with their own confusion.
We shall prevail!"
On January 24th, Apple Computer will introduce Macintosh. And you'll see why 1984 won't be like "1984"
Title and Voice Over: On January 24, Apple Computer will introduce Macintosh.
And you'll see why 1984 won't be like "1984"
On January 22, 1984, one commercial for Apple Computer ran on network television.
With all due respect to Burke, we didn't bother to test it.
Unlike a lot of advertising agencies, we prefer a different form of measurement:
When the product mentioned in the commercial, Apple's new Macintosh, was unveiled on January 24, over 200,000 people lined up to see it in person.
Within 6 hours, they bought $3,500,000 worth of Macintosh computers. And left cash deposits for $1,000,000 more.
ABC, CBS, NBC and CNN featured the commercial in network news segments.
Dan Rather covered it at night. Bryant Gumbel covered it at dawn.
The BBC ran it in England.
Associated Press put it on the wire.
27 TV stations in major U.S. markets ran it on local news programs.
Steven Spielberg called.
As did The New York Times, The Wall Street Journal, The Washington Post, the Philadelphia Inquirer, USA Today, the Boston Globe, the Los Angeles Times, the San Francisco Chronicle and, of course, the San Jose Mercury News.
Not to mention Time, Newsweek, Fortune, Forbes, Business Week and, of course, Advertising Age.
Apple is now producing one Macintosh every 27 seconds. And selling one every 20 seconds.
Not bad for one 60-second spot on the Super Bowl.
Chiat/Day
Los Angeles, San Francisco, New York

At the same time, the marketing manager is ultimately responsible for the success of the product or brand. Given the substantial sums being allocated to advertising and promotion, it is the manager's right, and responsibility, to know how well a specific program—or a specific ad—will perform in the market.

5. *Time.* A final reason given for not testing is a lack of time. Managers believe they already have too much to do and just can't get around to testing, and they don't want to wait to get the message out because they might miss the window of opportunity.

Planning might be the solution to the first problem. While many managers are overworked and time-poor, research is just too important to skip.

The second argument can also be overcome with proper planning. While timeliness is critical, getting the wrong message out is of little or no value and may even be harmful. There will be occasions where market opportunities require choosing between testing and immediate implementation. But even then some testing may help avoid mistakes or improve effectiveness. In most instances, proper planning and scheduling will allow time for research.

Conducting Research to Measure Advertising Effectiveness

What to Test

We now examine how to measure the effects of communications. This section considers what elements to evaluate, as well as where and how such evaluations should occur.

In Chapter 5, we discussed the components of the communications model (source, message, media, receiver) and the importance of each in the promotional program. Marketers need to determine how each is affecting the communications process. Other decisions made in the promotional planning process must also be evaluated.

Source Factors An important question is whether the spokesperson being used is effective and how the target market will respond to him or her. For example, Tiger Woods has proved to be a successful salesperson for Nike and Buick. Or a product spokesperson may be an excellent source initially but, owing to a variety of reasons, may lose impact over time. Michael Jordan is a spokesperson for Rayovac; but at one time or another, he has also done ads for Hanes, McDonald's, Gatorade, and MCI, among others—which might bring his credibility into question (as discussed in Chapter 6). In other instances, changes in the source's attractiveness or likability or other external factors may lead to changes in source effectiveness. (Recall the Dennis Rodman example cited earlier in the book.)

Message Variables Both the message and the means by which it is communicated are bases for evaluation. For example, in the beer example discussed earlier, the message never provided a reason for consumers to try the new product. In other instances, the message may not be strong enough to pull readers into the ad by attracting their attention or clear enough to help them evaluate the product. Sometimes the message is memorable but doesn't achieve the other goals set by management. One study showed that 7 of the 25 products that scored highest on interest and memorability in Video Storyboard Tests' ad test had flat or declining sales.[3] A number of factors regarding the message and its delivery may have an impact on its effectiveness, including the headline, illustrations, text, and layout.

Many ads are never seen by the public because of the message they convey. For example, an ad in which Susan Anton ate a slice of Pizza Hut pizza was considered too erotic for the company's small-town image. Likewise, an ad created for General Electric in which Uncle Sam got slapped in the face (to demonstrate our growing trade imbalance) was killed by the company's chair.[4]

Media Strategies Media decisions need to be evaluated. Research may be designed to determine which media class (for example, broadcast versus print), subclass (newspaper versus magazines), or specific vehicles (which newspapers or magazines) generate the most effective results. The location within a particular medium (front page versus back page) and size of ad or length of commercial also merit examination. For example, research has demonstrated that readers pay more attention to larger ads.[5] As shown in Chapter 15, a variety of methods have been employed to measure the effectiveness of advertising on the Internet. Similarly, direct-response advertisers on TV have found that some programs are more effective than others. One successful direct marketer found that old TV shows yield more responses than first runs:

> The fifth rerun of "Leave It to Beaver" will generate much more response than will the first run of a prime-time television program. Who cares if you miss something you have seen four times before? But you do care when it's the first time you've seen it.[6]

Another factor is the **vehicle option source effect,** "the differential impact that the advertising exposure will have on the same audience member if the exposure occurs in one media option rather than another."[7] People perceive ads differently depending on their context.[8]

A final factor in media decisions involves scheduling. The evaluation of flighting versus pulsing or continuous schedules is important, particularly given the increasing costs of media time. As discussed in Chapter 10 and IMC Perspective 19–1, there is evidence to support the fact that continuity may lead to a more effective media schedule than does flighting. Likewise, there may be opportunities associated with increasing advertising weights in periods of downward sales cycles or recessions. The manager experimenting with these alternative schedules and/or budget outlays should attempt to measure their differential impact.[9]

Budgeting Decisions

A number of studies have examined the effects of budget size on advertising effectiveness and the effects of various ad expenditures on sales. Many companies have also attempted to determine whether increasing their ad budget directly increases sales. This relationship is often hard to determine, perhaps because using sales as an indicator of effectiveness ignores the impact of other marketing mix elements. More definitive conclusions may be possible if other dependent variables, such as the communications objectives stated earlier, are used.

When to Test

Virtually all test measures can be classified according to when they are conducted. **Pretests** are measures taken before the campaign is implemented; **posttests** occur after the ad or commercial has been in the field. A variety of pretests and posttests are available to the marketer, each with its own methodology designed to measure some aspect of the advertising program. Figure 19–1 classifies these testing methods.

Pretesting

Pretests may occur at a number of points, from as early on as idea generation to rough execution to testing the final version before implementing it. More than one type of pretest may be used. For example, concept testing (which is discussed later in this chapter) may take place at the earliest development of the ad or commercial, when little more than an idea, basic concept, or positioning statement is under consideration. Ogilvy Award winner GM used focus groups to derive the concepts to promote its new minivan. In other instances, layouts of the ad campaign that include headlines, some body copy, and rough illustrations are used. For TV commercials, storyboards and animatics may be tested. The GM minivan research also involved the evaluation of six animatics. In these tests specific shortcomings were identified, and the ads were changed to enhance certain executional elements.

Figure 19–1 Classification of testing methods

Pretests		
Laboratory Methods		
Consumer juries	Theater tests	Readability tests
Portfolio tests	Rough tests	Comprehension and reaction tests
Physiological measures	Concept tests	
Field Methods		
Dummy advertising vehicles	On-air tests	
Posttests		
Field Methods		
Recall tests	Single-source systems	Recognition tests
Association measures	Inquiry tests	Tracking studies

The methodologies employed to conduct pretests vary. In focus groups, participants freely discuss the meanings they get from the ads, consider the relative advantages of alternatives, and even suggest improvements or additional themes. In addition to or instead of the focus groups, consumers are asked to evaluate the ad on a series of rating scales. (Different agencies use different measures.) In-home interviews, mall intercept, or laboratory methods may be used to gather the data.

The advantage of pretesting at this stage is that feedback is relatively inexpensive. Any problems with the concept or the way it is to be delivered are identified before large amounts of money are spent in development. Sometimes more than one version of the ad is evaluated to determine which is most likely to be effective.

A study of 4,637 on-air commercials designed to build normative intelligence conducted by McCollum Spielman Worldwide (MSW) found that only 19 percent were considered outstanding or really good. Nearly twice as many (34 percent) were failures. On the other hand, of those spots that were pretested before the final form was aired, the share of good to outstanding rose to 37 percent, while the failure rate fell to 9 percent.[10] This is certainly a testimonial to the value of pretesting.

The disadvantage is that mock-ups, storyboards, or animatics may not communicate nearly as effectively as the final product. The mood-enhancing and/or emotional aspects of the message are very difficult to communicate in this format. Another disadvantage is time delays. Many marketers believe being first in the market offers them a distinct advantage over competitors, so they forgo research to save time and ensure this position.

Posttesting Posttesting is also common among both advertisers and ad agencies (with the exception of testing commercials for wearout). Figure 19–2 presents the results of a study that examined ad agencies' and advertisers' use of various advertising research methods. The percentage of organizations that evaluate finished commercials and TV campaigns is very high. Posttesting is designed to (1) determine if the campaign is accomplishing the objectives sought and (2) serve as input into the next period's situation analysis. An excellent example of using research to guide future advertising strategies is reflected in an experiment conducted by Lowes, the nation's second-largest home improvement retailer. In a study designed to test 36 different versions of covers for its catalogs (which are sent to between 30 and 40 million homes per year), the company determined that by putting more products on the covers, using real pictures rather than cartoons, and reducing the size of the catalog, the catalogs were more effective. Other tests varying the number of TV spots, newspaper ads, and sports sponsorships led to increases in advertising spending and

Figure 19–2 General findings about copy research

	Total		Agencies		Advertisers	
	Number	Percent	Number	Percent	Number	Percent
Total respondents	112	100.0	39	100.0	73	100.0
Undertake preliminary, background, or strategic research in preparation for advertising campaigns	104	92.9	39	100.0	65	89.0
Evaluate copy ideas, storyboards, other formats before rough commercial	85	75.9	34	87.2	51	69.9
Evaluate rough commercial execution of other formats before finished commercial	102	91.1	38	97.4	64	87.7
Evaluate finished commercials	105	93.8	35	89.7	70	95.9
Evaluate TV campaigns	98	87.5	37	94.9	61	83.6
Test competitive commercials	73	65.2	27	69.2	46	63.0
Test commercials for wearout	29	25.9	9	23.1	20	27.4

affirmation of the company's sponsorship of NASCAR auto racing (Exhibit 19–3).[11] A variety of posttest measures are available, most of which involve survey research methods.

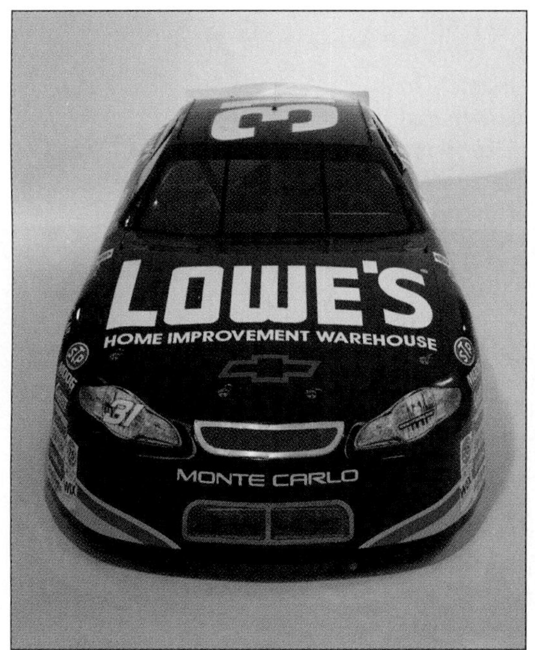

Exhibit 19–3 Research affirmed the value of a NASCAR sponsorship for Lowe's

Where to Test

In addition to when to test, decisions must be made as to *where.* These tests may take place in either laboratory or field settings.

Laboratory Tests

In **laboratory tests,** people are brought to a particular location where they are shown ads and/or commercials. The testers either ask questions about them or measure participants' responses by other methods—for example, pupil dilation, eye tracking, or galvanic skin response.

The major advantage of the lab setting is the *control* it affords the researcher. Changes in copy, illustration, formats, colors, and the like can be manipulated inexpensively and the differential impact of each assessed. This makes it much easier for the researcher to isolate the contribution of each factor.

The major disadvantage is the lack of *realism.* Perhaps the greatest effect of this lack of realism is a **testing bias.** When people are brought into a lab (even if it has been designed to look like a living room), they may scrutinize the ads much more closely than they would at home. A second problem with this lack of realism is that it cannot duplicate the natural viewing situation, complete with the distractions or comforts of home. Looking at ads in a lab setting may not be the same as viewing at home on the couch, with the spouse, kids, dog, cat, and parakeet chirping in the background. (A bit later you will see that some testing techniques have made progress in correcting this deficiency. No, they did not bring in the dogs and the parakeets.) Overall, however, the control offered by this method probably outweighs the disadvantages, which accounts for the frequent use of lab methods.

Field Tests

Field tests are tests of the ad or commercial under natural viewing situations, complete with the realism of noise, distractions, and the comforts of home. Field tests take into account the effects of repetition, program content, and even the presence of competitive messages.

The major disadvantage of field tests is the lack of control. It may be impossible to isolate causes of viewers' evaluations. If atypical events occur during the test, they may bias the results. Competitors may attempt to sabotage the research. And field tests usually take more time and money to conduct, so the results are not available to be acted on quickly. Thus, realism is gained at the expense of other important factors. It is up to the researcher to determine which trade-offs to make.

How to Test

Our discussion of what should be tested, when, and where was general and designed to establish a basic understanding of the overall process as well as some key terms. In this section, we discuss more specifically some of the methods commonly used at each stage. First, however, it is important to establish some criteria by which to judge ads and commercials.

Conducting evaluative research is not easy. In 1982, 21 of the largest U.S. ad agencies endorsed a set of principles aimed at "improving the research used in preparing and testing ads, providing a better creative product for clients, and controlling the cost of TV commercials."[12] This set of nine principles, called **PACT (Positioning Advertising Copy Testing),** defines *copy testing* as research "which is undertaken when a decision is to be made about whether advertising should run in the marketplace. Whether this stage utilizes a single test or a combination of tests, its purpose is to aid in the judgment of specific advertising executions."[13] The nine principles of good copy testing are shown in Figure 19–3.

1. Provide measurements that are relevant to the objectives of the advertising.
2. Require agreement about how the results will be used in advance of each specific test.
3. Provide multiple measurements (because single measurements are not adequate to assess ad performance).
4. Be based on a model of human response to communications—the reception of a stimulus, the comprehension of the stimulus, and the response to the stimulus.
5. Allow for consideration of whether the advertising stimulus should be exposed more than once.
6. Require that the more finished a piece of copy is, the more soundly it can be evaluated and require, as a minimum, that alternative executions be tested in the same degree of finish.
7. Provide controls to avoid the biasing effects of the exposure context.
8. Take into account basic considerations of sample definition.
9. Demonstrate reliability and validity.

Figure 19–3 Positioning Advertising Copy Testing (PACT)

As you can see, advertisers and their clients are concerned about developing *appropriate* testing methods. Adherence to these principles may not make for perfect testing, but it goes a long way toward improving the state of the art and alleviates at least one of the testing problems cited earlier.

The Testing Process

Testing may occur at various points throughout the development of an ad or a campaign: (1) concept generation research, (2) rough, prefinished art, copy, and/or commercial testing, (3) finished art or commercial pretesting, and (4) market testing of ads or commercials (posttesting).

Concept Generation and Testing

Figure 19–4 describes the process involved in advertising **concept testing,** which is conducted very early in the campaign development process in order to explore the targeted consumer's response to a potential ad or campaign or have the consumer evaluate advertising alternatives. Positioning statements, copy, headlines, and/or illustrations may all be under scrutiny. The material to be evaluated may be just a headline or a rough sketch of the ad. The colors used, typeface, package designs, and even point-of-purchase materials may be evaluated.

One of the more commonly used methods for concept testing is focus groups, which usually consist of 8 to 10 people in the target market for the product. Companies have tested everything from product concepts to advertising concepts using focus groups. For most companies, the focus group is the first step in the research process. The number of focus groups used varies depending on group consensus, strength of response, and/or the degree to which participants like or dislike the

Objective:	Explores consumers' responses to various ad concepts as expressed in words, pictures, or symbols.
Method:	Alternative concepts are exposed to consumers who match the characteristics of the target audience. Reactions and evaluations of each are sought through a variety of methods, including focus groups, direct questioning, and survey completion. Sample sizes vary depending on the number of concepts to be presented and the consensus of responses.
Output:	Qualitative and/or quantitative data evaluating and comparing alternative concepts.

Figure 19–4 Concept testing

Figure 19–5 Weaknesses associated with focus group research

- The results are not quantifiable.
- Sample sizes are too small to generalize to larger populations.
- Group influences may bias participants' responses.
- One or two members of the group may steer the conversation or dominate the discussion.
- Consumers become instant "experts."
- Members may not represent the target market. (Are focus group participants a certain type of person?)
- Results may be taken to be more representative and/or definitive than they really are.

concepts. Some companies use 50 or more groups to develop a campaign, although fewer than 10 are usually needed to test a concept sufficiently.

While focus groups continue to be a favorite of marketers, they are often overused. The methodology is attractive in that results are easily obtained, directly observable, and immediate. A variety of issues can be examined, and consumers are free to go into depth in areas they consider important. Also, focus groups don't require quantitative analysis. Unfortunately, many managers are uncertain about research methods that require statistics, and focus groups, being qualitative in nature, don't demand much skill in interpretation. Weaknesses with focus groups are shown in Figure 19–5. Clearly, there are appropriate and inappropriate circumstances for employing this methodology.

Another way to gather consumers' opinions of concepts is mall intercepts, where consumers in shopping malls are approached and asked to evaluate rough ads and/or copy. Rather than participating in a group discussion, individuals assess the ads via questionnaires, rating scales, and/or rankings. New technologies allow for concept testing over the Internet, where advertisers can show concepts simultaneously to consumers throughout the United States, garnering feedback and analyzing the results almost instantaneously.

Rough Art, Copy, and Commercial Testing

Because of the high cost associated with the production of an ad or commercial (many network commercials cost hundreds of thousands of dollars to produce), advertisers are increasingly spending more monies testing a rendering of the final ad at early stages. Slides of the artwork posted on a screen or animatic and photomatic roughs may be used to test at this stage. (See Figure 19–6 for an explana-

Figure 19–6 Rough testing terminology

A rough commercial is an unfinished execution that may fall into three broad categories:

Animatic Rough

Succession of drawings/cartoons

Rendered artwork

Still frames

Simulated movement:
Panning/zooming of frame/rapid sequence

Photomatic Rough

Succession of photographs

Real people/scenery

Still frames

Simulated movements:
Panning/zooming of frame/rapid sequence

Live-Action Rough

Live motion

Stand-in/nonunion talent

Nonunion crew

Limited props/minimal opticals

Location settings

A Finished Commercial Uses

Live motion/animation

Highly paid union talent

Full union crew

Exotic props/studio sets/special effects

Objective:	Potential viewers (consumers) are asked to evaluate ads and give their reactions to and evaluation of them. When two or more ads are tested, viewers are usually asked to rate or rank order the ads according to their preferences.
Method:	Respondents are asked to view ads and rate them according to either (1) the order of merit method or (2) the paired comparison method. In the former, the respondent is asked to view the ads, then rank them from one to *n* according to their perceived merit. In the latter, ads are compared only two at a time. Each ad is compared to every other ad in the group, and the winner is listed. The best ad is that which wins the most times. Consumer juries typically employ 50 to 100 participants.
Output:	An overall reaction to each ad under construction as well as a rank ordering of the ads based on the viewers' perceptions.

Figure 19–7 Consumer juries

tion of terminology.) Because such tests can be conducted for about $3,000 to $5,000, research at this stage is becoming ever more popular.

But cost is only one factor. The test is of little value if it does not provide relevant, accurate information. Rough tests must indicate how the finished commercial would perform. Some studies have demonstrated that these testing methods are reliable and the results typically correlate well with the finished ad.[14]

Most of the tests conducted at the rough stage involve lab settings, although some on-air field tests are also available. Popular tests include comprehension and reaction tests and consumer juries: Again, the Internet allows field settings to be employed.

1. *Comprehension and reaction tests.* One key concern for the advertiser is whether the ad or commercial conveys the meaning intended. The second concern is the reaction the ad generates. Obviously, the advertiser does not want an ad that evokes a negative reaction or offends someone. **Comprehension and reaction tests** are designed to assess these responses (which makes you wonder why some ads are ever brought to the marketplace).

Tests of comprehension and reaction employ no one standard procedure. Personal interviews, group interviews, and focus groups have all been used for this purpose, and sample sizes vary according to the needs of the client; they typically range from 50 to 200 respondents.

2. *Consumer juries.* This method uses consumers representative of the target market to evaluate the probable success of an ad. **Consumer juries** may be asked to rate a selection of layouts or copy versions presented in pasteups on separate sheets. The objectives sought and methods employed in consumer juries are shown in Figure 19–7.[15] Sample questions asked of jurists are shown in Figure 19–8.

While the jury method offers the advantages of control and cost effectiveness, serious flaws in the methodology limit its usefulness:

- *The consumer may become a self-appointed expert.* One of the benefits sought from the jury method is the objectivity and involvement in the product or service that the targeted consumer can bring to the evaluation process. Sometimes, however, knowing they are being asked to critique ads, participants try to become more *expert* in their evaluations, paying more

1. Which of these ads would you most likely read if you saw it in a magazine?
2. Which of these headlines would interest you the most in reading the ad further?
3. Which ad convinces you most of the quality or superiority of the product?
4. Which layout do you think would be most effective in causing you to buy?
5. Which ad did you like best?
6. Which ad did you find most interesting?

Figure 19–8 Questions asked in a consumer jury test

attention and being more critical than usual. The result may be a less than objective evaluation or an evaluation on elements other than those intended.

- *The number of ads that can be evaluated is limited.* Whether *order of merit* or *paired comparison* methods are used, the ranking procedure becomes tedious as the number of alternatives increases. Consider the ranking of 10 ads. While the top two and the bottom two may very well reveal differences, those ranked in the middle may not yield much useful information.

  In the paired comparison method, the number of evaluations required is calculated by the formula

$$\frac{n(n-1)}{2}$$

  If six alternatives are considered, 15 evaluations must be made. As the number of ads increases, the task becomes even more unmanageable.

- *A halo effect is possible.* Sometimes participants rate an ad good on all characteristics because they like a few and overlook specific weaknesses. This tendency, called the **halo effect,** distorts the ratings and defeats the ability to control for specific components. (Of course, the reverse may also occur—rating an ad bad overall due to only a few bad attributes.)
- *Preferences for specific types of advertising may overshadow objectivity.* Ads that involve emotions or pictures may receive higher ratings or rankings than those employing copy, facts, and/or rational criteria. Even though the latter are often more effective in the marketplace, they may be judged less favorably by jurists who prefer emotional appeals.

Some of the problems noted here can be remedied by the use of ratings scales instead of rankings. But ratings are not always valid either. Thus, while consumer juries have been used for years, questions of bias have led researchers to doubt their validity. As a result, a variety of other methods (discussed later in this chapter) are more commonly employed.

Pretesting of Finished Ads

Figure 19–2 showed that pretesting finished ads receives the most attention and participation among marketing researchers and their agencies. At this stage, a finished advertisement or commercial is used; since it has not been presented to the market, changes can still be made.

Many researchers believe testing the ad in final form provides better information. Several test procedures are available for print and broadcast ads, including both laboratory and field methodologies.

Print methods include portfolio tests, analyses of readability, and dummy advertising vehicles. Broadcast tests include theater tests and on-air tests. Both print and broadcast may use physiological measures.

Pretesting Finished Print Messages

A number of methods for pretesting finished print ads are available. One is *Diagnostic Research Inc.'s Copytest System,* described in Figure 19–9. The most common of these methods are portfolio tests, readability tests, and dummy advertising vehicles.

Portfolio Tests **Portfolio tests** are a laboratory methodology designed to expose a group of respondents to a portfolio consisting of both control and test ads. Respondents are then asked what information they recall from the ads. The assumption is that the ads that yield the *highest recall* are the most effective.

While portfolio tests offer the opportunity to compare alternative ads directly, a number of weaknesses limit their applicability:

1. Factors other than advertising creativity and/or presentation may affect recall. Interest in the product or product category, the fact that respondents know they

Objective:	Tests recall and readers' impressions of print ads.
Method:	Mall intercepts in two or more cities are used to screen respondents and have them take home "test magazines" for reading. Participants are phoned the next day to determine opinions of the ads, recall of ad contents, and other questions of interest to the sponsor. Approximately 225 people constitute the sample.
Output:	Scores reported include related recall of copy and visual elements, sales messages, and other nonspecific elements. Both quantitative (table) scores and verbatim responses are reported.

Figure 19–9 Diagnostic Research Inc.'s print test

are participating in a test, or interviewer instructions (among others) may account for more differences than the ad itself.

2. Recall may not be the best test. Some researchers argue that for certain types of products (those of low involvement) ability to recognize the ad when shown may be a better measure than recall.

One way to determine the validity of the portfolio method is to correlate its results with readership scores once the ad is placed in the field. Whether such validity tests are being conducted or not is not readily known, although the portfolio method remains popular in the industry.

Readability Tests The communications efficiency of the copy in a print ad can be tested without reader interviews. This test uses the **Flesch formula,** named after its developer, Rudolph Flesch, to assess readability of the copy by determining the average number of syllables per 100 words. Human interest appeal of the material, length of sentences, and familiarity with certain words are also considered and correlated with the educational background of target audiences. Test results are compared to previously established norms for various target audiences. The test suggests that copy is best comprehended when sentences are short, words are concrete and familiar, and personal references are drawn.

This method eliminates many of the interviewee biases associated with other tests and avoids gross errors in understanding. The norms offer an attractive standard for comparison.

Disadvantages are also inherent, however. The copy may become too mechanical, and direct input from the receiver is not available. Without this input, contributing elements like creativity cannot be addressed. To be effective, this test should be used only in conjunction with other pretesting methods.

Dummy Advertising Vehicles In an improvement on the portfolio test, ads are placed in "dummy" magazines developed by an agency or research firm. The magazines contain regular editorial features of interest to the reader, as well as the test ads, and are distributed to a *random sample* of homes in predetermined geographic areas. Readers are told the magazine publisher is interested in evaluations of editorial content and asked to read the magazines as they normally would. Then they are interviewed on their reactions to both editorial content and ads. Recall, readership, and interest-generating capabilities of the ad are assessed.

The advantage of this method is that it provides a more natural setting than the portfolio test. Readership occurs in the participant's own home, the test more closely approximates a natural reading situation, and the reader may go back to the magazine, as people typically do.

But the dummy magazine shares the other disadvantages associated with portfolio tests. The testing effect is not eliminated, and product interest may still bias the results. Thus, while this test offers some advantages over the portfolio method, it is not a guaranteed measure of the advertising's impact.

While all the previously described measures are available, the most popular form of pretesting of print ads now involves a series of measures. Companies like Gallup & Robinson and Ipsos-ASI offer copy testing services that have improved

Figure 19–10 Ipsos-ASI's Next*Print

Objective:	To assist advertisers in copy testing of print advertisements to determine (1) main idea communication, (2) likes and dislikes, (3) believability, (4) ad attribute ratings, (5) overall likability, and (6) brand attribute ratings.
Method:	Tests are conducted in current issues of newsstand magazines such as *People, Better Homes & Gardens,* and *Newsweek.* The recall measure consists of 150 responses. Diagnostic measures range from 105 to 150 responses. Highly targeted audiences are available through a version known as the Targeted Print Test.
Output:	Standard scores and specific diagnostics.

upon many of the shortcomings cited above. The tests can be used for rough and/or finished ads and are most commonly conducted in the respondents' homes. For example, Gallup & Robinson's Magazine Impact Research Service (MIRS) uses an at-home, in-magazine context, employing widely dispersed samples, and offers standardized measures as well as a variety of options. Ipsos-ASI's Next*Print methodology also offers multiple measures, as shown in Figure 19–10.

Pretesting Finished Broadcast Ads

A variety of methods for pretesting broadcast ads are available. The most popular are theater tests, on-air tests, and physiological measures.

Theater Tests In the past, one of the most popular laboratory methods for pretesting finished commercials was **theater testing.** In theater tests participants are invited by telephone, mall intercepts, and/or tickets in the mail to view pilots of proposed TV programs. In some instances, the show is actually being tested, but more commonly a standard program is used so audience responses can be compared with normative responses established by previous viewers. Sample sizes range from 250 to 600 participants.

On entering the theater, viewers are told a drawing will be held for gifts and asked to complete a product preference questionnaire asking which products they would prefer if they win. This form also requests demographic data. Participants may be seated in specific locations in the theater to allow observation by age, sex, and so on. They view the program and commercials, and a form asking for evaluations is distributed. Participants are then asked to complete a second form for a drawing so that changes in product preference can be noted. In addition to product/brand preference, the form may request other information:

1. Interest in and reaction to the commercial.
2. Overall reaction to the commercial as measured by an adjective checklist.
3. Recall of various aspects of the commercial.
4. Interest in the brand under consideration.
5. Continuous (frame-by-frame) reactions throughout the commercial.

The methods of theater testing operations vary, though all measure brand preference changes. For example, many of the services now use videotaped programs with the commercials embedded for viewing in one's office rather than in a theater. Others establish viewing rooms in malls and/or hotel conference rooms. Some do not take all the measures listed here; others ask the consumers to turn dials or push buttons on a keypad to provide the continual responses. An example of one methodology is shown in Figure 19–11.

Those opposed to theater tests cite a number of disadvantages. First, they say the environment is too artificial. The lab setting is bad enough, but asking respondents to turn dials or, as one service does, wiring people for physiological responses takes them too far from a natural viewing situation. Second, the contrived measure of brand preference change seems too phony to believe. Critics contend that participants will see through it and make changes just because they think they are sup-

Advertising Control for Television (ACT), a lab procedure of McCollum Spielman Worldwide, uses about 400 respondents representing four cities. It measures initial brand preference by asking participants which brands they most recently purchased. Respondents are then divided into groups of 25 to view a 30-minute program with seven commercials inserted in the middle. Four are test commercials; the other three are control commercials with established viewing norms. After viewing the program, respondents are given a recall test of the commercials. After the recall test, a second 30-minute program is shown, with each test commercial shown again. The second measure of brand preference is taken at this time, with persuasion measured by the percentage of viewers who switched preferences from their most recently purchased brand to one shown in the test commercials.

Figure 19–11 The ACT theater methodology

posed to. Finally, the group effect of having others present and overtly exhibiting their reactions may influence viewers who did not have any reactions themselves.

Proponents argue that theater tests offer distinct advantages. In addition to control, the established norms (averages of commercials' performances) indicate how one's commercial will fare against others in the same product class that were already tested. Further, advocates say the brand preference measure is supported by actual sales results.

Despite the limitations of theater testing, most major consumer product companies have used it to evaluate their commercials. This method may have shortcomings, but it allows them to identify strong or weak commercials and to compare them to other ads.

On-Air Tests Some of the firms conducting theater tests also insert the commercials into actual TV programs in certain test markets. Typically, the commercials are in finished form, although the testing of ads earlier in the developmental process is becoming more common. This is referred to as an **on-air test** and often includes single-source ad research (discussed later in this chapter). Information Resources, Ipsos-ASI, McCollum Spielman Worldwide (MSW), and Nielsen are well-known providers of on-air tests.

On-air testing techniques offer all the advantages of field methodologies, as well as all the disadvantages. Further, there are negative aspects to the specific measures taken through the on-air systems. One concern is associated with **day-after recall scores,** the primary measure used in these tests. Lyman Ostlund notes that measurement errors may result from the natural environment—the position of the ad in the series of commercials shown, the adjacent program content, and/or the number of commercials shown.[16] While the testing services believe their methods overcome many of these criticisms, each still uses recall as one of the primary measures of effectiveness. Since recall tests best reflect the degree of attention and interest in an ad, claims that the tests predict the ad's impact on sales may be going too far. (In 28 studies reviewed by Jack Haskins, only two demonstrated that factual recall could be related to sales.)[17] Joel Dubow's research indicates that recall is a necessary but not sufficient measure, while research by Jones and Blair was even more demonstrative, noting that "it is unwise to look to recall for an accurate assessment of a commercial's sales effect."[18]

On the plus side, most of the testing services have offered evidence of both validity and reliability for on-air pretesting of commercials. Both Ipsos-ASI and MSW claim their pretest and posttest results yield the same recall scores 9 out of 10 times—a strong indication of reliability and a good predictor of the effect the ad is likely to have when shown to the population as a whole.

In summary, on-air pretesting of finished or rough commercials offers some distinct advantages over lab methods and some indications of the ad's likely success. Whether the measures used are as strong an indication as the providers say still remains in question.

Physiological Measures A less common method of pretesting finished commercials involves a laboratory setting in which physiological responses are measured.

These measures indicate the receiver's *involuntary* response to the ad, theoretically eliminating biases associated with the voluntary measures reviewed to this point. (Involuntary responses are those over which the individual has no control, such as heartbeat and reflexes.) Physiological measures used to test both print and broadcast ads include pupil dilation, galvanic skin response, eye tracking, and brain waves:

1. *Pupil dilation.* Research in **pupillometrics** is designed to measure dilation and constriction of the pupils of the eyes in response to stimuli. Dilation is associated with action; constriction involves the body's conservation of energy.

Advertisers have used pupillometrics to evaluate product and package design as well as to test ads. Pupil dilation suggests a stronger interest in (or preference for) an ad or implies arousal or attention-getting capabilities. Other attempts to determine the affective (liking or disliking) responses created by ads have met with less success.

Because of high costs and some methodological problems, the use of pupillometrics has waned over the past decade. But it can be useful in evaluating certain aspects of advertising.

2. *Galvanic skin response.* Also known as **electrodermal response,** GSR measures the skin's resistance or conductance to a small amount of current passed between two electrodes. Response to a stimulus activates sweat glands, which in turn increases the conductance of the electrical current. Thus, GSR/EDR activity might reflect a reaction to advertising. In their review of the research in this area, Paul Watson and Robert Gatchel concluded that GSR/EDR (1) is sensitive to affective stimuli, (2) may present a picture of attention, (3) may be useful to measure long-term advertising recall, and (4) is useful in measuring ad effectiveness.[19] In interviews with practitioners and reviews of case studies, Priscilla LaBarbera and Joel Tucciarone also concluded that GSR is an effective measure and is useful for measuring affect, or liking, for ads.[20] While a number of companies have offered skin response measures, this research methodology is not commonly used now, and LaBarbera and Tucciarone believe that it is underused, given its potential.

3. *Eye tracking.* A methodology that is more commonly employed is **eye tracking** (Figure 19–12), in which viewers are asked to view an ad while a sensor aims a beam of infrared light at the eye. The beam follows the movement of the eye and shows the exact spot on which the viewer is focusing. The continuous reading of responses demonstrates which elements of the ad are attracting attention, how long the viewer is focusing on them, and the sequence in which they are being viewed.

Eye tracking can identify strengths and weaknesses in an ad. For example, attractive models or background action may distract the viewer's attention away from the brand or product being advertised. The advertiser can remedy this distraction before fielding the ad. In other instances, colors or illustrations may attract attention and create viewer interest in the ad.

4. *Brain waves.* **Electroencephalographic (EEG) measures** can be taken from the skull to determine electrical frequencies in the brain. These electrical impulses are used in two areas of research, alpha waves and hemispheric lateralization.

- **Alpha activity** refers to the degree of brain activation. People are in an alpha state when they are inactive, resting, or sleeping. The theory is that a person in

Figure 19–12 Eye movement research

Objective:	Tracks viewers' eye movements to determine what viewers read or view in print ads and where their attention is focused in TV commercials or billboards.
Method:	Fiber optics, digital data processing, and advanced electronics are used to follow eye movements of viewers and/or readers as they process an ad.
Output:	Relationship among what readers see, recall, and comprehend. Scan paths on print ads, billboards, commercials, and print materials. (Can also be used to evaluate package designs.)

an alpha state is less likely to be processing information (recall correlates negatively with alpha levels) and that attention and processing require moving from this state. By measuring a subject's alpha level while viewing a commercial, researchers can assess the degree to which attention and processing are likely to occur.

- **Hemispheric lateralization** distinguishes between alpha activity in the left and right sides of the brain. It has been hypothesized that the right side of the brain processes visual stimuli and the left processes verbal stimuli. The right hemisphere is thought to respond more to emotional stimuli, while the left responds to logic. The right determines recognition, while the left is responsible for recall.[21] If these hypotheses are correct, advertisers could design ads to increase learning and memory by creating stimuli to appeal to each hemisphere. However, some researchers believe the brain does not function laterally and an ad cannot be designed to appeal to one side or the other.

While EEG research has engaged the attention of academic researchers, it has been much less successful in attracting the interest of practitioners.

Market Testing of Ads

The fact that the ad and/or campaign has been implemented does not mean there is no longer a need for testing. The pretests were conducted on smaller samples and may in some instances have questionable merit, so the marketer must find out how the ad is doing in the field. In this section, we discuss methods for posttesting an ad. Some of the tests are similar to the pretests discussed in the previous section and are provided by the same companies.

Posttests of Print Ads

A variety of print posttests are available, including inquiry tests, recognition tests, and recall tests.

Inquiry Tests Used in both consumer and business-to-business market testing, **inquiry tests** are designed to measure advertising effectiveness on the basis of inquiries generated from ads appearing in various print media, often referred to as "bingo cards." The inquiry may take the form of the number of coupons returned, phone calls generated, or direct inquiries through reader cards. Exhibit 19–4 shows an example of a reader response card, while Figure 19–13 shows that this form is still the most commonly employed response to trade ads (pp. 654–655). For example, if you called in a response to an ad in a local medium recently, perhaps you were asked how you found out about the company or product or where you saw the ad. This is a very simple measure of the ad's or medium's effectiveness.

More complex methods of measuring effectiveness through inquiries may involve (1) running the ad in successive issues of the same medium, (2) running **split-run tests,** in which variations of the ad appear in different copies of the same newspaper or magazine, and/or (3) running the same ad in different media. Each of these methods yields information on different aspects of the strategy. The first measures the *cumulative* effects of the campaign; the second examines specific elements of the ad or variations on it. The final method measures the effectiveness of the medium rather than the ad itself.

While inquiry tests may yield useful information, weaknesses in this methodology limit its effectiveness. For example, inquiries may not be a true measure of the attention-getting or information-providing aspects of the ad. The reader may be attracted to an ad, read it, and even store the information but not be motivated to inquire at that particular time. Time constraints, lack of a need for the product or service at the time the ad is run, and other factors may limit the number of inquiries. But receiving a small number of inquiries doesn't mean the ad was not effective; attention, attitude change, awareness, and recall of copy points may all have been achieved. At the other extreme, a person with a particular need for the product may respond to any ad for it, regardless of specific qualities of the ad.

Exhibit 19–4 Inquiries may be measured through reader response cards

GET INFORMATION FROM BUSINESS WEEK ADVERTISERS.

Financial Products and Services
1/Dean Witter
2/Franklin/Templeton
3/Liberty Mutual
4/Merrill Lynch

Products/Services
5/American Institute of Architects
6/American Power Conversion (APC)
7/BREITLING WATCHES
8/Buick Motor Division
9/CABELTRON SYSTEM
10/Cessna Aircraft Company
11/Chevrolet Motor Division
12/Compaq
13/Control Data Systems
14/Corel Corporation
15/CyNet
16/Digital-SBU
17/Digital-PC
18/EMC Corporation
19/Exide Electronics
20/Fujitsu PC
21/Hilton Hotels & Resorts
22/Hyatt Hotel Corporation
23/IKON OFFICE SOLUTIONS
24/Johnson Controls
25/LG Group
26/Lucent Technologies
27/MCI
28/Minolta Copiers
29/NEC
30/Nortel
31/Packet Engines
32/Royal Insurance
33/SAP America, Inc.
34/SGS THOMSON MICROELECTRONICS S.p.A.
35/Sprint
36/Texas Instruments Digital Light Processing
37/Toshiba America Information Systems
38/Toyota
39/TSMC
40/USWEB
41/Virtual Office Solutions for AT&T
42/USPS
43/USPS Global Delivery Service
44/Westin Hotels & Resorts

Area Development
45/Bavarian Ministry for Economic Affairs
46/Fairfax County Economic Development Authority

Technology Guide
101/AGILE SOFTWARE CORPORATION
102/Digital Sound Corporation
103/Microrim Inc.
104/PORT INC.

BusinessWeek ONLINE **Reader Service Area**

Check out the latest offerings from Business Week advertisers and request information via the Electronic Reader Service Area on Business Week Online.

Look for the Electronic Reader Service Area behind the Offers & Info icon on the Business Week Online opening screen on America Online, or enter keyword: BW.

Please Print
Name
Business
❑ BUSINESS ❑ HOME
Address
City
State Zip
❑ BUSINESS ❑ HOME EXTENSION
Telephone

Please check one response for each following question.

1 What is your company's type of business?
1 ❑ Agriculture 2 ❑ Mining, Construction 3 ❑ Manufacturing, Processing
4 ❑ Wholesale, Retail Trade 5 ❑ Finance, Insurance, Real Estate
6 ❑ Government 7 ❑ Transportation, Public Utilities 8 ❑ Service Industries
9 ❑ Other - Please Specify:

2 What is your title?
A ❑ Chairman of the Board B ❑ President C ❑ Vice President D ❑ Treasurer, Secretary E ❑ General Manager F ❑ Division Manager G ❑ Department Manager H ❑ Other Manager I ❑ Student J ❑ Other - Please Specify:

3 How many employees in your company worldwide?
1 ❑ Under 100 2 ❑ 100-999 3 ❑ 1,000-2,499
4 ❑ 2,500-4,999 5 ❑ 5,000-9,999 6 ❑ 10,000 or more

BusinessWeek
Beyond news. Intelligence.

#970623
Requests will be honored until August 255,1997

Please circle advertisers' numbers

1	2	3	4	5
6	7	8	9	10
11	12	13	14	15
16	17	18	19	20
21	22	23	24	25
26	27	28	29	30
31	32	33	34	35
36	37	38		
101	102	103	104	

A Division of The McGraw-Hill Companies

For more information

PHONE
1-800-345-4331, or
FAX
1-609-786-4415, or
MAIL
the post-paid card

Order Code #970623

Major advantages of inquiry tests are that they are inexpensive to implement and they provide some feedback with respect to the general effectiveness of the ad or medium used. But they are usually not very effective for comparing different versions or specific creative aspects of an ad.

Recognition Tests Perhaps the most common posttest of print ads is the **recognition method,** most closely associated with Roper Starch Worldwide. The *Starch Readership Report* lets the advertiser assess the impact of an ad in a single issue of a magazine, over time, and/or across different magazines (see Figure 19–14). Starch measures over 75,000 ads in more than 1,000 issues representing more than 100 consumer, farm, and business magazines and newspapers per year and provides a number of measures of the ad's effectiveness. An example of a Starch-scored ad is shown in Exhibit 19–5.

Starch also offers the *Starch Impression Study* and the *Starch Ballot Readership Study.* The impression study provides consumers' qualitative impressions of ads

Figure 19–13 Ad response methods

Despite the rise in popularity of electronic response mechanisms, the traditional reader service, or "bingo card," remains the most common way to respond to trade publication advertising.

Ad Response Methods Used Frequently or Very Frequently*	
Indirect Methods	
Return reader service cards	41%
Save ads for reference	35
Discuss advertised products with others	30
Pass ads on to others for possible action	26
Direct Methods	
Send back reply cards/coupons	31%
Contact vendors' websites	28
Telephone manufacturers	23
Telephone local distributors/reps	22
Go to magazine websites	21
Stop at vendors' trade show exhibits	20
Discuss products with sales reps	20
Send faxes to vendors	17
Contact distributors' websites	15
Send e-mail messages	10
Mail notes to vendors	6

*The 2,705 respondents could name more than one method.

Figure 19–14 The *Starch Readership Report*

Objective:	Determining recognition of print ads and comparing them to other ads of the same variety or in the same magazine.
Method:	Samples are drawn from 20 to 30 urban areas reflecting the geographic circulation of the magazine. Personal interviewers screen readers for qualifications and determine exposure and readership. Samples include a minimum of 200 males and females, as well as specific audiences where required. Participants are asked to go through the magazines, looking at the ads, and provide specific responses.
Output:	*Starch Readership Reports* generate three recognition scores: • Noted score—the percentage of readers who remember seeing the ad. • Seen-associated score—the percentage of readers who recall seeing or reading any part of the ad identifying the product or brand. • Read-most score—the percentage of readers who report reading at least half of the copy portion of the ad.

(for example, company image and important features); the readership study measures readership in business magazines.

Starch claims that (1) the pulling power of various aspects of the ad can be assessed through the control offered, (2) the effectiveness of competitors' ads can be compared through the norms provided, (3) alternative ad executions can be tested, and (4) readership scores are a useful indication of consumers' *involvement* in the ad or campaign. (The theory is that a reader must read and become involved in the ad before the ad can communicate. To the degree that this readership can be shown, it is a direct indication of effectiveness.)

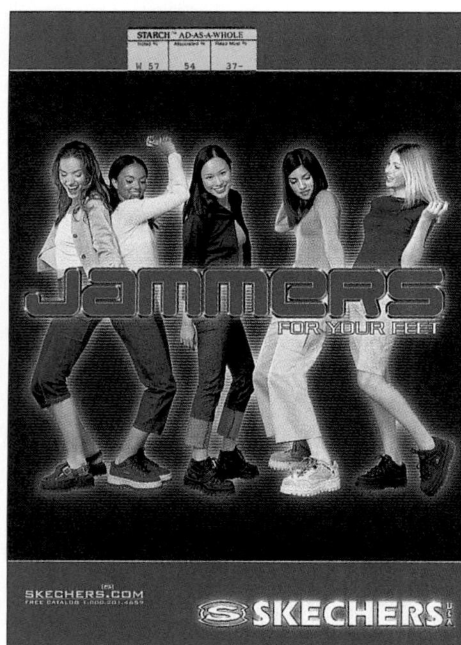

Exhibit 19–5 Example of a Starch-scored ad

Of these claims, perhaps the most valid is the ability to judge specific aspects of the ad. Many researchers have criticized other aspects of the Starch recognition method (as well as other recognition measures) on the basis of problems of false claiming, interviewer sensitivities, and unreliable scores:

1. *False claiming.* Research shows that in recognition tests, respondents may claim to have seen an ad when they did not. False claims may be a result of having seen similar ads elsewhere, expecting that such an ad would appear in the medium, or wanting to please the questioner. Interest in the product category also increases reporting of ad readership. Whether this false claiming is deliberate or not, it leads to an overreporting of effectiveness. On the flip side, factors such as interview fatigue may lead to an underreporting bias—that is, respondents not reporting an ad they did see.
2. *Interviewer sensitivities.* Any time research involves interviewers, there is a potential for bias. Respondents may want to impress the interviewer or fear looking unknowledgeable if they continually claim not to recognize an ad. There may also be variances associated with interviewer instructions, recordings, and so on, regardless of the amount of training and sophistication involved.
3. *Reliability of recognition scores.* Starch admits that the reliability and validity of its readership scores increase with the number of insertions tested, which essentially means that to test just one ad on a single exposure may not produce valid or reliable results.

In sum, despite critics, the Starch readership studies continue to dominate the posttesting of print ads. The value provided by norms and the fact that multiple exposures can improve reliability and validity may underlie the decisions to employ this methodology.

Recall Tests There are several tests to measure recall of print ads. Perhaps the best known of these are the Ipsos-ASI Next*Print test and the Gallup & Robinson Magazine Impact Research Service (MIRS) (described in Figure 19–15). These **recall tests** are similar to those discussed in the section on pretesting broadcast ads in that they attempt to measure recall of specific ads.

In addition to having the same interviewer problems as recognition tests, recall tests have other disadvantages. The reader's degree of involvement with the product and/or the distinctiveness of the appeals and visuals may lead to higher-than-accurate recall scores, although in general the method may lead to lower levels of recall than actually exist (an error the advertiser would be happy with). Critics contend the test is not strong enough to reflect recall accurately, so many ads may score as less effective than they really are, and advertisers may abandon or modify them needlessly.

On the plus side, it is thought that recall tests can assess the ad's impact on memory. Proponents of recall tests say the major concern is not the results themselves but how they are interpreted. In one very interesting study of the effects of brand name suggestiveness on recall, Kevin Keller, Susan Heckler, and Michael Houston found that suggestive brand names (those that convey relevant attribute or benefit information about the product) facilitate the initial recall of the brand's benefits but inhibit recall of subsequently advertised claims. These results would seem to indicate that a suggestive brand name could facilitate initial positioning of the brand but make it more difficult to introduce new attributes at a later time. The authors suggest that these results might be useful in explaining why Jack in the Box has had trouble developing a more adult image and why Old Spice and Oldsmobile have had difficulty with younger audiences.[22]

A very extensive longitudinal study was conducted by the Netherlands Institute of Public Opinion (NIPO) to assess the relationship between recall and recognition. The results indicated that the average correlation between recall and recognition in both newspapers and magazines was very high (r = .96 and .95, respectively). The

Objective:	Tracking recall of advertising (and client's ads) appearing in magazines to assess performance and effectiveness.
Method:	Test magazines are placed in participants' homes and respondents are asked to read the magazine that day. A telephone interview is conducted the second day to assess recall of ads, recall of copy points, and consumers' impressions of the ads. Sample size is 150 people.
Output:	Three measurement scores are provided: • Proven name registration—the percentage of respondents who can accurately recall the ad. • Idea communication—the number of sales points the respondents can recall. • Favorable buying attitude—the extent of favorable purchase reaction to the brand or corporation.

Figure 19–15 Gallup & Robinson Magazine Impact Research Service

study concluded that recall actually stems from recognition, in that 99 percent of 3,632 cases of recall also had recorded recognition. In addition, likable and interesting ads doubled the recall scores and increased the recall share of recognition. Creative advertising was much more effective for creating perceptions and recall than was the size of the ad.[23]

Posttests of Broadcast Commercials

A variety of methods exist for posttesting broadcast commercials. The most common provide a combination of day-after recall tests, persuasion measures, and diagnostics. Test marketing and tracking studies, including single-source methods, are also employed.

Day-After Recall Tests The most popular method of posttesting employed in the broadcasting industry for decades was the *Burke Day-After Recall test.* While a number of companies offered day-after recall methodologies, the "Burke test" for all intents and purposes became the generic name attached to these tests. While popular, day-after recall tests also had problems, including limited samples, high costs, and security issues (ads shown in test markets could be seen by competitors). In addition, the following disadvantages with recall tests were also suggested:

1. DAR tests may favor unemotional appeals because respondents are asked to verbalize the message. Thinking messages may be easier to recall than emotional communications, so recall scores for emotional ads may be lower.[24] A number of other studies have also indicated that emotional ads may be processed differently from thinking ones; some ad agencies, for example, Leo Burnett and BBDO Worldwide, have gone so far as to develop their own methods of determining emotional response to ads.[25]
2. Program content may influence recall. The programs in which the ad appears may lead to different recall scores for the same brand. The net result is a potential inaccuracy in the recall score and in the norms used to establish comparisons.[26]
3. A prerecruited sample (Gallup & Robinson) may pay increased attention to the program and the ads contained therein because the respondents know they will be tested the next day. This effect would lead to a higher level of recall than really exists.

The major advantage of day-after recall tests is that they are field tests. The natural setting is supposed to provide a more realistic response profile. These tests are also popular because they provide norms that give advertisers a standard for comparing how well their ads are performing. In addition to recall, a number of different measures of the commercial's effectiveness are now offered, including persuasive measures and diagnostics. (The Burke test itself no longer exists.)

Persuasive Measures As noted earlier in our discussion of pretesting broadcast commercials, a measure of a commercial's persuasive effectiveness is gathered by

Figure 19–16 Ipsos-ASI's Next*TV

Objectives:	To assist advertisers in copy testing of their commercials through multiple measures to determine (1) the potential of the commercial for impacting sales, (2) how the ad contributes to brand equity, (3) how well it is in line with existing advertising strategies and objectives, and (4) how to optimize effectiveness.
Method:	Consumers are recruited to evaluate a TV program, with ads embedded into the program as they would be on local prime-time television. Consumers view the program on a videotape in their homes to simulate actual field conditions. (The option to use local cable television programs with commercial inserts is also provided.)
Output:	Related recall (day-after recall) scores; persuasion scores, including brand preference shifts, purchase intent and frequency, brand equity differentiation, and relevance and communication; and reaction diagnostics to determine what viewers take away from the ad and how creative elements contribute to or distract from advertising effectiveness.

asking consumers to choose a brand that they would want to win in a drawing and then—after exposure to the ad—ask the question again. In theater settings this is accomplished by announcing a series of prize drawings, with viewers indicating which of the brands they would choose if they won. In field settings, it is accomplished by taking a brand preference measure when the video is delivered and then again the next day. Some of the services offer additional persuasion measures, including purchase-intent and frequency-of-purchase criteria.

Diagnostics In addition to measuring recall and persuasion, copy testing firms also provide diagnostic measures. These measures are designed to garner viewers' evaluations of the ads, as well as how clearly the creative idea is understood and how well the proposition is communicated. Rational and emotional reactions to the ads are also examined. A number of companies offer diagnostic measures, including Diagnostic Research, Inc., Gallup & Robinson, and Millward Brown.

Comprehensive Measures While each of the measures just described provides specific input into the effectiveness of a commercial, many advertisers are interested in more than just one specific input. Thus, some companies provide comprehensive approaches in which each of the three measures just described can be obtained through one testing program. Figure 19–16 describes one such comprehensive program, Ipsos-ASI's Next*TV test (Exhibit 19–6).

Test Marketing Many companies conduct tests designed to measure their advertising effects in specific test markets before releasing them nationally. The markets chosen are representative of the target market. For example, a company may test its ads in Portland, Oregon; San Antonio, Texas; or Buffalo, New York, if the demographic and socioeconomic profiles of these cities match the product's market. A variety of factors may be tested, including reactions to the ads (for example, alternative copy points), the effects of various budget sizes, or special offers. The ads run in finished form in the media where they might normally appear, and effectiveness is measured after the ads run.

The advantage of test marketing of ads is realism. Regular viewing environments are used and the testing effects are minimized. A high degree of control can be attained if the test is designed successfully. For example, an extensive test market study was designed and conducted by Seagram and Time, Inc., over three years to measure the effects of advertising frequency on consumers' buying habits. This study demonstrated just how much could be learned from research conducted in a field setting but with some experimental controls. It also showed that proper research can provide strong insights into the impact of ad campaigns. (Many advertising researchers consider this study one of the most conclusive ever conducted in the attempt to demonstrate the effects of advertising on sales.)

The Seagram study also reveals some of the disadvantages associated with test market measures, not the least of which are cost and time. Few firms have the luxury to spend three years and hundreds of thousands of dollars on such a test. In addition, there is always the fear that competitors may discover and intervene in the research process.

A number of companies, including AT&T, Clorox, Procter & Gamble, and Toyota, have participated in a test market of interactive commercials. The test, conducted in approximately 15,000 homes in Kingsport, Tennessee, asked viewers to answer questions about ads and made it possible for them to order brochures, coupons, and/or samples interactively. In return, the advertisers got the names and addresses of the consumers and their credit card information (with the consumer's permission) if they made a purchase. Information regarding the program, time of day, day of week, and network were also provided. If the test is successful, the interactive boxes will be expanded to 300,000 to 500,000 boxes nationwide.[27]

Test marketing can provide substantial insight into the effectiveness of advertising if care is taken to minimize the negative aspects of such tests.

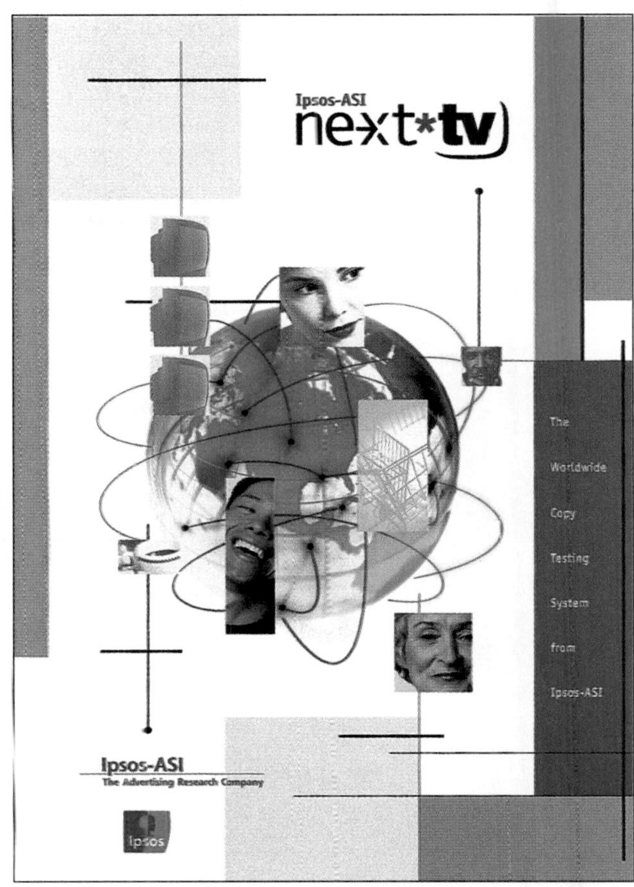

Exhibit 19–6 Ipsos-ASI offers a comprehensive testing measure

Single-Source Tracking Studies Since the 1980s the focus of many research efforts has been on single-source tracking methods. **Single-source tracking methods** track the behaviors of consumers from the television set to the supermarket checkout counter. Participants in a designated area who have cable TV and agree to participate in the studies are given a card (similar to a credit card) that identifies their household and gives the research company their demographics. The households are split into matched groups; one group receives an ad while the other does not, or alternate ads are sent to each. Their purchases are recorded from the bar codes of the products bought. Commercial exposures are then correlated with purchase behaviors.

Earlier we mentioned the use of single-source ad research in pretesting commercials and in the lead-in we discussed its use in evaluating sales promotions. One study demonstrated that the single-source method can also be used effectively to posttest ads, allowing for a variety of dependent measures and tracking the effects of increased ad budgets and different versions of ad copy—and even ad effects on sales.[28]

A 10-year study conducted by Information Resources' BehaviorScan service demonstrated long-term effects of advertising on sales. The study examined copy, media schedules, ad budgets, and the impact of trade promotions on sales in 10 markets throughout the United States and concluded that advertising can produce sales growth as long as two years after a campaign ends.[29] (The study also concluded that results of copy recall and persuasion tests were unlikely to predict sales reliably.) A number of single-source methods have been used, among them BehaviorScan (Information Resources) and MarketSource. The A.C. Nielsen company's Scantrack is another commonly employed single-source tracking system.

Many advertisers believe these single-source measures will change the way research is conducted due to the advantages of control and the ability to measure directly the ads' effects on sales. A number of major corporations and ad agencies are now employing this method, including Campbell Soup, Colgate-Palmolive, Nestlé, General Foods, P&G, Pepsi-Cola, Leo Burnett, and J. Walter Thompson. After using scanner data to review the advertising/sales relationship for 78 brands, John Jones concluded that single-source data are beginning to fulfill their promise now that more measurements are available.[30]

While single-source testing is a valuable tool, it still has some problems. One researcher says, "Scanner data focus on short-term sales effects, and as a result capture only 10 to 30 percent of what advertising does."[31] Others complain that the data are too complicated to deal with, as an overabundance of information is available. Still another disadvantage is the high cost of collecting single-source data. While the complexity of single-source data resulted in a slow adoption rate, this method of tracking advertising effectiveness became widely adopted in the 1990s by the research companies mentioned earlier (Gallup & Robinson, Millward-Brown, and Ipsos-ASI).

Tracking Print/Broadcast Ads One of the more useful and adaptable forms of posttesting involves tracking the effects of the ad campaign by taking measurements at regular intervals. **Tracking studies** have been used to measure the effects of advertising on awareness, recall, interest, and attitudes toward the ad and/or brand as well as purchase intentions. (Ad tracking may be applied to both print and broadcast ads but is much more common with the latter.) Personal interviews, phone surveys, mall intercepts, and even mail surveys have been used. Sample sizes typically range from 250 to 500 cases per period (usually quarterly or semiannually). Tracking studies yield perhaps the most valuable information available to the marketing manager for assessing current programs and planning for the future.

The major advantage of tracking studies is that they can be tailored to each specific campaign and/or situation. A standard set of questions can track effects of the campaign over time. The effects of various media can also be determined, although with much less effectiveness. Tracking studies have also been used to measure the differential impact of different budget sizes, the effects of flighting, brand or corporate image, and recall of specific copy points. Finally, when designed properly, as shown in Figure 19–17, tracking studies offer a high degree of reliability and validity.[32]

Some of the problems of recall and recognition measures are inherent in tracking studies, since many other factors may affect both brand and advertising recall. Despite these limitations, however, tracking studies are a very effective way to assess the effects of advertising campaigns.

In summary, you can see that each of the testing methods considered in this chapter has its strengths and its limitations. You may wonder: Can we actually test advertising effectiveness? What can be done to ensure a valid, reliable test? The next section of this chapter suggests some answers.

Figure 19–17 Factors that make or break tracking studies

1. Properly defined objectives
2. Alignment with sales objectives
3. Properly designed measures (e.g., adequate sample size, maximum control over interviewing process, adequate time between tracking periods)
4. Consistency through replication of the sampling plan
5. Random samples
6. Continuous interviewing (that is, not seasonal)
7. Evaluate measures related to behavior (attitudes meet this criterion; recall of ads does not)
8. Critical evaluative questions asked early to eliminate bias
9. Measurement of competitors' performance
10. Skepticism about questions that ask where the advertising was seen or heard (TV always wins)
11. Building of news value into the study
12. "Moving averages" used to spot long-term trends and avoid seasonality
13. Data reported in terms of relationships rather than as isolated facts
14. Integration of key marketplace events with tracking results (e.g., advertising expenditures of self and competitors, promotional activities associated with price changes in ad campaigns, introductions of new brands, government announcements, changes in economic conditions)

Establishing a Program for Measuring Advertising Effects

There is no surefire way to test advertising effectiveness. However, in reponse to pressures to determine the contribution of ads to the overall marketing effort, steps are being taken to improve this measurement task. Let's begin by reviewing the major problems with some existing methods and then examine possible improvements.

Problems with Current Research Methods

When current testing methods are compared to the criteria established by PACT (see Figure 19–3), it is clear that some of the principles important to good copy testing can be accomplished readily, whereas others require substantially more effort. For example, principle 6 (providing equivalent test ads) should require a minimum of effort. The researcher can easily control the state of completion of the test communications. Also fairly easy are principles 1 and 2 (providing measurements relative to the objectives sought and determining a priori how the results will be used).

We have seen throughout this text that each promotional medium, the message, and the budget all consider the marketing and communications objectives sought. The integrated marketing communications planning model establishes the roles of these elements. So by the time one gets to the measurement phase, the criteria by which these programs will be evaluated should simply fall into place.

Slightly more difficult are principles 3, 5, and 8, although again these factors are largely in the control of the researcher. Principle 3 (providing multiple measurements) may require little more than budgeting to make sure more than one test is conducted. At the most, it may require considering two similar measures to ensure reliability. Likewise, principle 5 (exposing the test ad more than once) can be accomplished with a proper research design. Finally, principle 8 (sample definition) requires little more than sound research methodology; any test should use the target audience to assess an ad's effectiveness. You would not use a sample of nondrinkers to evaluate new liquor commercials.

The most difficult factors to control—and the principles that may best differentiate between good and bad testing procedures—are PACT requirements 4, 7, and 9. Fortunately, however, addressing each of these contributes to the attainment of the others.

The best starting point is principle 4, which states the research should be guided by a model of human response to communications that encompasses reception, comprehension, and behavioral response. It is the best starting point, in our opinion, because it is the principle least addressed by practicing researchers. If you recall, Chapter 5 proposed a number of models that could fulfill this principle's requirements. Yet even though these models have existed for quite some time, few if any common research methods attempt to integrate them into their methodologies. Most current methods do little more than provide recall scores, despite the fact many researchers have shown that recall is a poor measure of effectiveness. Models that do claim to measure such factors as attitude change or brand preference change are often fraught with problems that severely limit their reliability. An effective measure must include some relationship to the communications process.

It might seem at first glance that principle 7 (providing a nonbiasing exposure) would be easy to accomplish. But lab measures, while offering control, are artificial and vulnerable to testing effects. And field measures, while more realistic, often lose control. The Seagram and Time study may have the best of both worlds, but it is too large a task for most firms to undertake. Some of the improvements associated with the single-source systems help to solve this problem. In addition, properly designed ad tracking studies provide truer measures of the impact of the communication. As technology develops and more attention is paid to this principle, we expect to see improvements in methodologies soon.

Last but not least is principle 9, the concern for reliability and validity. Most of the measures discussed are lacking in at least one of these criteria, yet these are two of the most critical distinctions between good and bad research. If a study is properly designed, and by that we mean it addresses principles 1 through 8, it should be both reliable and valid.

Essentials of Effective Testing

Simply put, good tests of advertising effectiveness must address the nine principles established by PACT. One of the easiest ways to accomplish this is by following the decision sequence model in formulating promotional plans.

- *Establish communications objectives.* We have stated that except for a few instances (most specifically direct-response advertising), it is nearly impossible to show the direct impact of advertising on sales. So the marketing objectives established for the promotional program are not good measures of communication effectiveness. For example, it is very difficult (or too expensive) to demonstrate the effect of an ad on brand share or on sales. On the other hand, attainment of communications objectives can be measured and leads to the accomplishment of marketing objectives.
- *Use a consumer response model.* Early in this text we reviewed hierarchy of effects models and cognitive response models, which provide an understanding of the effects of communications and lend themselves to achieving communications goals.
- *Use both pretests and posttests.* From a cost standpoint—both actual cost outlays and opportunity costs—pretesting makes sense. It may mean the difference between success or failure of the campaign or the product. But it should work in conjunction with posttests, which avoid the limitations of pretests, use much larger samples, and take place in more natural settings. Posttesting may be required to determine the true effectiveness of the ad or campaign.
- *Use multiple measures.* Many attempts to measure the effectiveness of advertising focus on one major dependent variable—perhaps sales, recall, or recognition. As noted earlier in this chapter, advertising may have a variety of effects on the consumer, some of which can be measured through traditional methods, others that require updated thinking (recall the discussion on physiological responses). For a true assessment of advertising effectiveness, a number of measures may be required. The Ogilvy Award winners mentioned earlier all employed multiple measures to track the effects on communications objectives. IMC Perspective 19–2 discusses some recent efforts to relate advertising to sales and market share.
- *Understand and implement proper research.* It is critical to understand research methodology. What constitutes a good design? Is it valid and reliable? Does it measure what we need it to? There is no shortcut to this criterion, and there is no way to avoid it if you truly want to measure the effects of advertising.

A major study sponsored by the Advertising Research Foundation (ARF), involving interviews with 12,000 to 15,000 people, addressed some of these issues.[33] While we do not have the space to analyze this study here, note that the research was designed to evaluate measures of copy tests, compare copy testing procedures, and examine some of the PACT principles. Information on this study has been published in a number of academic and trade journals and by the ARF.

Measuring the Effectiveness of Other Program Elements

Throughout this text, we have discussed how and when promotional program elements should be used, the advantages and disadvantages of each, and so on. In many chapters we have discussed measures of effectiveness used to evaluate these programs. In the final section of this chapter, we add a few measures that were not discussed earlier.

Measuring the Effectiveness of Sales Promotions

Sales promotions are not limited to retailers and resellers of products. Sports marketers have found them a very effective way to attract crowds and have been able to measure their relative effectiveness by the number of fans attending games. Major

IMC Perspective 19–2

Does Advertising Really Affect Sales?

The 2000 Super Bowl cost advertisers approximately $66,667 per second to air their spots—and that figure only includes the media costs. When costs of production are thrown in, the number more than doubles! Was it worth it? As you might imagine, an increasing number of businesses are asking the same question. Many of them want an answer to the question, "Does it lead to an increase in sales?"

This question is not a new one. For years advertisers have struggled with the fact that it is difficult to establish a direct relationship between advertising and sales. As ad budgets increase, so too does the pressure for accountability, as agencies and media-buying companies try to outdo each other to win increasingly sophisticated clients. Now, perhaps, there is some progress being made in this area.

One approach rapidly gaining acceptance is that of *econometrics.* Also known as *marketing mix modeling,* this method builds statistical models for predicting sales performance. As a result of previous successes in the financial and travel industries and advanced data collection capabilities, advertisers have turned their attention to these models in an attempt to satisfy their client's demands for accountability. One company, Media Market Assessment (MMA), has worked with Kraft to improve its ROI in the package-foods industry. Another promising effort is AdWorks2, a joint project undertaken by MMA and Information Resources and sponsored by ABC, CBS, Fox, and NBC. In the AdWorks2 study, actual sales and data for over 1,500 brands in over 200 categories are analyzed to determine incremental sales effects that may arise from TV advertising. Preliminary results show, for example, that brands with at least 30 percent of their impressions in prime time had higher sales than other brands. Another conclusion is that various forms of advertising support each other to achieve an overall greater effect; for example, magazine advertising enhances the impact of a television commercial, and vice versa. Another model is offered by Consumer Mix Modeling, which claims to be the first to integrate consumer targeting and response analysis and link it to marketing execution. In one analysis of an unidentified yogurt brand the model concluded that TV advertising contributed to about 5 percent of total sales, though sales impact differed by psychographic segments ("Downscale Urbans" showed almost zero impact, while "Metro Elites" showed a 30 percent increase).

Not all efforts to relate advertising to sales employ econometrics or new technologies. Advertising Research Systems (ARS) uses a variation of the traditional theater testing methodology to show the impact of a commercial on brand preference and selection. ARS takes the methodology a step further, however, and validates the impact on sales through Nielsen store audits, split cable tests, and scanner data modeling. After an analysis of 5,077 commercials representing 150 different strategic and executional elements including the use of humor, celebrity endorsements, and so on, the research firm was able to show that the factors that emphasize brand differentiation and specific product attributes are the most important in impacting sales. "New product/new feature" appeals were the most effective, and "brand differentiation" appeals were the second most effective. Another interesting finding is that "on the average, the more money spent on production, the less persuasive the commercial," as overproduced commercials often get in the way of the basic sales message. As of 1999, ARS had measured the sales effectiveness of more than 100,000 commercials.

While these methods have certainly advanced the understanding of the relationship between advertising and sales, there are still skeptics out there. Decades ago, John Wanamaker made the classic remark that half of his advertising was wasted and he just couldn't tell which half. Some advertisers today believe that a more accurate figure is 90 percent. Maybe they need to start modeling?

Source: Christina Merrill, "Machine Dreams," *American Demographics,* April 1999, pp. 28–31; Reginald B. Collier, "Predicting the Sales Effectiveness of Advertising," *Quirk's Marketing Research Review,* March 1998, pp. 36–39.

League Baseball teams have seen their attendance increase for those games in which promotions are offered.

A number of organizations measure sales promotions. One firm, MarketSource, provides marketers with a basis for measuring the effectiveness of their sampling programs. While too involved to discuss in detail here, the program calculates a

Figure 19–18 Measuring the effects of FSIs

A study by Promotion Decisions Inc. examined the actual purchase data of users and nonusers of 27 coupon promotions in its National Shopper Lab (75,000 households) over a period of 18 months. The findings:

- FSI coupons generated significant trial by new and lapsed users of a product (53%).
- Repeat purchase rates were 11.8% higher among coupon redeemers than nonredeemers.
- 64.2% of repeat volume among coupon redeemers was without a coupon.
- There was no significant difference in share of volume between buyers who used coupons and those who did not.
- Coupons returned between 71 and 79% of their cost within 12 weeks.
- Full-page ads provided higher redemption rates, incremental volume, redemption by new users, and a higher number of repeat buyers than half-page ads.
- Consumers who used coupons were brand loyal.

breakeven rate by dividing the sampling investment by the profit for the user. If the conversions exceed the breakeven rate, the sampling program is successful.[34] Promotion Decisions Inc. examines the impact of freestanding inserts (FSIs) (Figure 19–18).

Other measures of sales promotions are also available. Schnucks (St. Louis), Smitty's Super Valu (Phoenix), and Vons (Los Angeles) have all used pretests with effects measured through scanner data. Others have employed this methodology to examine brand and store switching, alternative promotions, price discounts, and merchandising techniques.[35] Other advertisers use awareness tracking studies and count the number of inquiries, coupon redemptions, and sweepstakes entries. They also track sales during promotional and nonpromotional periods while holding other factors constant.

One recent technological development designed to track the effectiveness of sales promotions at the point of sale is offered by Datatec Industries. This automated system, called Shopper Trak, places sensors in the store that track whether a person is coming or going, calculate the shopper's height (to differentiate between adults and children), and gauge traffic patterns. The system helps retailers evaluate the effectiveness of promotions or displays located throughout the store.[36]

Elizabeth Gardener and Minakshi Trivedi offer a communications framework to allow managers to evaluate sales promotion strategies over a given set of specific criteria. Borrowing from advertising applications, and using four communications goals—attention, comprehension (understanding), persuasion, and purchase—the researchers show the impact of four promotional tools and everyday low pricing (EDLP) on each goal (Figure 19–19). In addition, the impact of everyday low pric-

Figure 19–19 Conceptual framework analysis

		Communication Factors			
		Attention/ Impression	Communication/ Understanding	Persuasion	Purchase
Sales Promotions	FSI coupons	✓✓	✓✓✓	✓✓	✓✓
	On-shelf coupons	✓✓✓	✓✓✓	✓✓✓	✓✓✓
	On-pack promotions	✓	✓	✓✓	✓
	Bonus packs	✓✓✓	✓✓	✓✓	✓✓
	EDLP	✓	✓✓	✓✓	✓

Promotional tendency to fulfill factor: ✓✓✓ = Strong; ✓✓ = Moderate; ✓ = Weak ing, Procter & Gamble's strategy for discontinuing the use of sales promotions, is also discussed in the article.[37]

Measuring the Effectiveness of Nontraditional Media

In Chapter 13, we noted that one of the disadvantages of employing nontraditional media is that it is usually difficult to measure the effectiveness of the programs. But some progress has been made, as shown in these examples:

- *The effects of shopping cart signage.* Earlier we discussed sales increases that occurred when shopping cart signage was used. We have also noted throughout this chapter that while increasing sales is a critical goal, many other factors may contribute to or detract from this measure. (It should also be noted that these results are provided by the companies that sell these promotional media.) At least one study has examined the effectiveness of shopping cart signage on data besides sales.[38] This study used personal interviews in grocery stores to measure awareness of, attention to, and influence of this medium. Interestingly, it suggests shopping carts are much less effective than the sign companies claim.
- *The effectiveness of ski-resort-based media.* In Chapter 13, we discussed advertising on ski chair lifts and other areas to attempt to reach selective demographic groups. Now the Traffic Audit Bureau (TAB) is tracking the effectiveness of this form of advertising to give advertisers more reliable criteria on which to base purchase decisions. The TAB data verify ad placements, while the media vendors have employed Simmons Market Research Bureau and Nielsen Media Research to collect ad impressions and advertising recall information.[39] These measures are combined with sales tracking data to evaluate the medium's effectiveness.
- *Addressable commercials.* A test is underway of 2,000 homes receiving addressable commercials—that is, commercials targeted only to those expressing an interest in the products. The testing of the interactive advertisements will provide information on consumer viewing patterns and purchase behaviors.[40]

Measuring the Effectiveness of Sponsorships

In earlier chapters we discussed the growth in sponsorships and the reasons why organizations have increased their investments in this area. Along with the increased expenditures have come a number of methods for measuring the impact of sponsorships. Essentially, measures of sponsorship effectiveness can be categorized as exposure-based methods or tracking measures:[41]

- *Exposure methods.* Exposure methods can be classified as those that monitor the quantity and nature of the media coverage obtained for the sponsored event and those that estimate direct and indirect audiences. While commonly employed by corporations, scholars have heavily criticized these measures. For example, Pham argues that media coverage is not the objective of sponsorships and should not be considered as a measure of effectiveness. He argues that the measures provide no indication of perceptions, attitude change, or behavioral change and should therefore not be considered as measures of effectiveness.[42]
- *Tracking measures.* These measures are designed to evaluate the awareness, familiarity, and preferences engendered by sponsorship based on surveys. A number of empirical studies have measured recall of sponsors' ads, awareness of and attitudes toward the sponsors and their products, and image effect including brand and corporate images.

A number of companies now measure the effectiveness of sports sponsorships. For example, Events Marketing Research of New York specializes in custom research projects that perform sales audits in event areas, participant exit surveys, and economic impact studies. Joyce Julius & Associates of Ann Arbor, Michigan, assigns a monetary value to the amount of exposure the sponsor receives during the event. It reviews broadcasts and adds up the number of seconds a sponsor's product name or logo can be seen clearly (for example, on signs or shirts). A total of 30 seconds is considered the equivalent of a 30-second commercial. (Such measures are of questionable validity.)

Performance Research in Newport, Rhode Island, measures impact on brand awareness and image shifts. PS Productions, a Chicago-based research organization, provides clients with a measure of event sponsorships based on increased sales. PS calculates sales goals based on the cost of the event and the value of extras like donated media, customized displays, ads for key retailers, and tickets given away. An event is a success if it brings in at least that amount in additional sales (Figure 19–20).

While each of these measures has its advantages and disadvantages, we suggest using several in assessing the impact of sponsorships. In addition to those mentioned here, the eight-step process suggested in Figure 19–21 could be used to guide these evaluations.

Figure 19–20 Sales impact of concert sponsorships (average 4 to 6 weeks)

Product	Market	Sales during Event (Dollar or Volume)	Percent Change from Average Sales
Snacks	Louisville	$119,841	+52%
	Salt Lake City	$135,500	+47
	Indianapolis	$347,940	+105
Soap	Atlanta	950 cases	+375
	Minneapolis	880 cases	+867
	Cleveland	972 cases	+238
	Portland, OR	580 cases	+580
	St. Louis	1,616 cases	+1,454
Salad dressing	Atlanta	NA	+175
	Salt Lake City	NA	+143

Figure 19–21 Eight steps to measuring event sponsorship

1. Narrowly define objectives with specifics.
2. Establish solid strategies against which programming will be benchmarked and measure your programming and effectiveness against the benchmark.
3. Set measurable and realistic goals; make sure everything you do supports them.
4. Enhance, rather than just change, other marketing variables.
5. Don't pull Marketing Plan 101 off the shelf. Programming should be crafted to reflect the particulars of your company's constituencies and target audiences.
6. Define the scope of your involvement. Will it involve multiple areas within the company? Who internally and externally comprises the team?
7. Think "long term." It takes time to build brand equity. Also, think of leveraging your sponsorship through programming for as long as possible, before and after the event.
8. Build evaluation and a related budget into your overall sponsoring program. Include items such as pre- and post-event attitude surveys, media analysis, and sales results.

Measuring the Effectiveness of Other IMC Program Elements

Many of the organizations mentioned in this chapter offer research services to measure the effectiveness of promotional program elements. We do not have the space to discuss them all, but Figure 19–22 mentions a few to show you that these options exist.

All the advertising effectiveness measures discussed here have their inherent strengths and weaknesses. They offer the advertiser some information that may be useful in evaluating the effectiveness of promotional efforts. While not all promotional efforts can be evaluated effectively, at least the first step has been taken.

Company	Effectiveness Measure Provided
Perception Research Services, Inc.	Package design; out-of-home media; point-of-purchase displays; logos; corporate identity
McCollum Spielman Worldwide	Impact of celebrity presenters
Competitive Media Reporting	Business-to-business advertising; media effects
The PreTesting Company, Inc.	Package design; POP displays; billboards; direct mail
Gallup & Robinson	Radio advertising recall; trade show exhibit measures
TransWestern Publishing	Telephone directory advertising effectiveness

Figure 19–22 A sampling of measures of effectiveness of promotional program elements

Summary

This chapter introduced you to issues involved in measuring the effects of advertising and promotions. These issues include reasons for testing, reasons companies do not test, and the review and evaluation of various research methodologies. We arrived at a number of conclusions: (1) advertising research to measure effectiveness is important to the promotional program, (2) not enough companies test their ads, and (3) problems exist with current research methodologies. In addition, we reviewed the criteria for sound research and suggested some ways to accomplish effective studies.

All marketing managers want to know how well their promotional programs are working. This information is critical to planning for the next period, since program adjustments and/or maintenance are based on evaluation of current strategies. Problems often result when the measures taken to determine such effects are inaccurate or improperly used.

This chapter demonstrated that testing must meet a number of criteria (defined by PACT) to be successful. These evaluations should occur both before and after the campaigns are implemented.

A variety of research methods were discussed, many provided by syndicated research firms such as Ipsos-ASI, MSW, Arbitron, and A. C. Nielsen. Many companies have developed their own testing systems.

Single-source research data such as BehaviorScan, Scantrack, and Market Source were discussed for measuring the effects of advertising. These single-source systems offer strong potential for improving the effectiveness of ad measures in the future, since commercial exposures and reactions may be correlated to actual purchase behaviors.

It is important to recognize that different measures of effectiveness may lead to different results. Depending on the criteria used, one measure may show that an ad or promotion is effective while another states that it is not. This is why clearly defined objectives and the use of multiple measures are critical to determining the true effects of an IMC program.

Key Terms

vehicle option source effect, 641
pretests, 642
posttests, 642
laboratory tests, 644
testing bias, 644
field tests, 644
PACT (Positioning Advertising Copy Testing), 644
concept testing, 645
comprehension and reaction tests, 647
consumer juries, 647
halo effect, 648
portfolio tests, 648
Flesch formula, 649
theater testing, 650
on-air test, 651
day-after recall scores, 651
pupillometrics, 652
electrodermal response, 652
eye tracking, 652
electroencephalographic (EEG) measures, 652
alpha activity, 652
hemispheric lateralization, 653
inquiry tests, 653
split-run tests, 653
recognition method, 654
recall tests, 656
single-source tracking methods, 659
tracking studies, 660

Discussion Questions

1. Discuss some of the reasons why some companies decide not to measure the effectiveness of their promotional programs. Explain why this may or may not be a good strategy.

2. Discuss the differences between pretesting and posttesting. Give examples of each.

3. What is the difference between a lab test and a field test? When should each be employed?

4. Give examples of the various types of rough testing methodologies. Describe why a company might wish to test at this phase of the process. When might they wish to test only completed ads?

5. Major changes have taken place in the way that theater tests are conducted. Describe some of these changes and the changes in measures that have also occurred in this testing method.

6. Discuss some of the reasons copywriters and researchers are often at odds regarding the creative aspects of the campaign. What steps might be taken to reduce this conflict?

7. A great deal of money is being spent on sponsorships. Discuss why organizations are increasing their expenditures in this area and how they can measure the effectiveness of these investments.

8. The bottom line for advertisers is to evoke some behavior—for example, sales. Explain why it may be difficult to use sales to measure advertising effectiveness.

9. Describe some of the effectiveness measures that might be used to get at nonquantifiable aspects of advertising and promotions.

10. Describe some of the methods used to test other elements of the promotional mix.

Chapter Twenty

International Advertising and Promotion

Chapter Objectives

- To examine the importance of international marketing and the role of international advertising and promotion.
- To review the various factors in the international environment and how they influence advertising and promotion decisions.
- To consider the pros and cons of global versus localized marketing and advertising.
- To examine the various decision areas of international advertising.
- To understand the role of other promotional mix elements in the international marketing program.

Marketers Are Finding That It Is a Small World After All

In his classic 1983 book *The Marketing Imagination,* Harvard marketing professor Theodore Levitt argued that the world was becoming a common marketplace where people have the same basic needs, wants, desires, and taste no matter where they live. Levitt called on marketers to develop global marketing strategies and true global brands that could be sold the same way in every country, including the use of a standardized advertising approach. Many multinational companies heeded the call for global marketing and began consolidating their advertising by hiring large superagencies with international marketing capabilities rather than using local agencies in various countries. These agencies were given the charge of helping companies turn their products into global brands that could be promoted with the same advertising theme and approach worldwide.

While a number of companies, such as Gillette, Coca-Cola, and Nestlé, have been successful in turning many of their products into global brands, not everyone agreed with Levitt's call for globalization. Many companies abandoned their efforts to develop global brands through standardized advertising, dismissing it as impractical, and returned to more localized approaches that could be adapted to accommodate differences in culture, language, lifestyles, values, and other factors. However, as we enter the new millennium, global branding and advertising are alive and well, and every year more and more prestigious firms are among the converts.

Saab launched its first global advertising campaign in 1999 after spending a year and a half studying the brand before developing any ads. Saab asked owners around the world to define

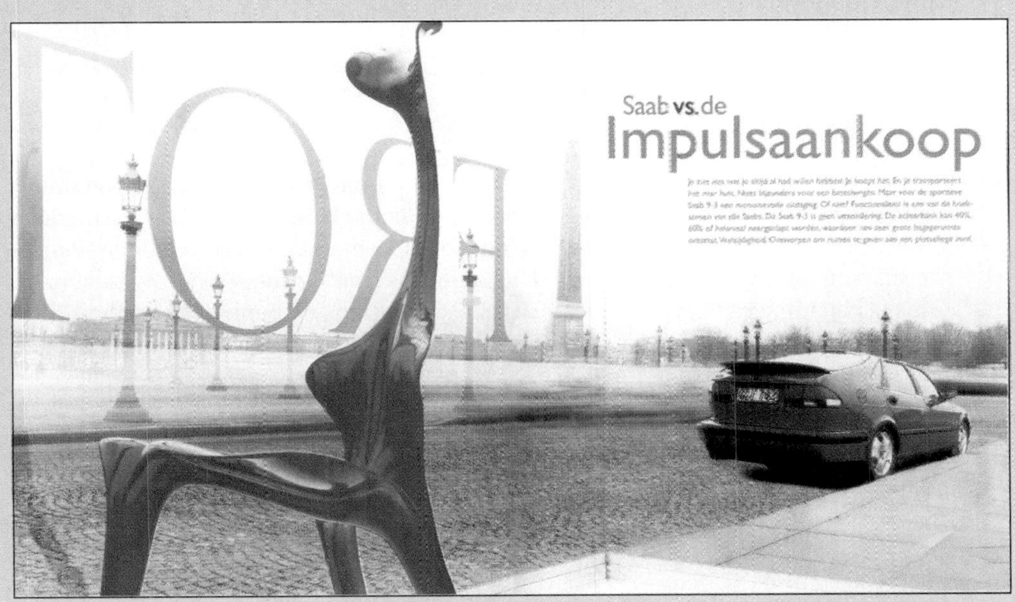

the brand as well as themselves. The findings revealed common owner psychographics, as Saab owners are active, affluent, and educated. They embrace technology, prefer educational TV, and shy away from conventional status symbols. The research also revealed that owners see Saabs as dynamic, distinctively styled, high performance, outstandingly safe, and inspired by Scandinavian heritage. However, according to the president of Saab Cars USA, Inc., the difference between his company and other automakers is how Saab fashions insightful solutions when developing its cars; he notes that the key to the brand is "the way we think." The global advertising campaign uses the "Saab vs." something theme. The executions pose riddles such as "Saab vs. Parenthood," "Saab vs. the Impulse Purchase," and "Saab vs. the Puritans," and the ad copy or voice-over in the TV commercials explains Saab's solutions.

Polaroid recently began a global advertising campaign for its new I-Zone Instant Pocket Camera, which is a petite camera about the size of a small cell phone and creates postage-stamp-size, self-developing color photos or stickers. Targeting Internet-savvy kids and teens around the world is part of the company's strategy to broaden its user base. A Polaroid executive notes, "We want new, younger users as we move into the digital world." The ads created for the global campaign highlight the photo-sticker feature, which Polaroid considers to be the biggest attraction for teens. One of the spots shows a bunch of teens snapping photos of each other making wacky faces and then cuts to reveal they've stuck them all over the faces of football players to make the match more interesting.

Some global marketers are now testing their global branding campaigns overseas before launching them in their home markets. Heinz tested its $50 million, teen-oriented ketchup campaign in Canada before taking it worldwide with only minor creative tweaks. A Heinz vice president noted that the way teens approach ketchup isn't that different across geographies and the only adaptation Heinz and its agency is making when the campaign goes into 75 countries is to customize the food teens are pouring the ketchup over, whether it be hot dogs, pasta, or hamburgers, depending upon primary usage in the local market.

Procter & Gamble tested several of its new products abroad as well as domestically in order to get them to market faster. Its new Dryel home dry-cleaning kit was tested in Columbus, Ohio, and Ireland, while its Swiffer, an electrostatic mop and cleaner cloth system, was test-marketed in Iowa and France. P&G's global business manager for new product development notes: "These are the first new-to-the-world brands that we've rolled out with a single brand name, package, marketing and advertising positioning from day one. In the old days we would have waited until it succeeded in the U.S. market before venturing abroad." P&G feels that the products are well suited to a fast, global launch because both solve universal cleaning needs.

Isn't it ironic that Ted Levitt was talking about universal needs and wants nearly 20 years ago. He would be happy to see that many companies have indeed heeded his call for creating true global brands. It appears that Levitt was right. It is a small world after all!

Sources: Jack Neff, "Test It in Paris France, Launch It in Paris Texas," *Advertising Age,* May 31, 1999, p. 28; Tara Parker-Pope, "P&G Cleaning Products Get on Fast Track," *The Wall Street Journal,* May 18, 1999, p. B6; Jean Haliday, "Saab's New Global Campaign Truly Global, Creatively," *Advertising Age,* April 19, 1999, p. 34; Cara Beardi, "Polaroid's Global Ads Get Daily Exposures," *Advertising Age,* October 19, 1999, pp. 3, 82.

The primary focus of this book so far has been on integrated marketing communications programs for products and services sold in the U.S. market. Many American companies have traditionally devoted most of their marketing efforts to the domestic market, since they often lack the resources, skills, or incentives to go abroad. This is changing rapidly, however, as U.S. corporations recognize the opportunities that foreign markets offer for new sources of sales and profits as well as the need to market their products internationally. Many companies are striving to develop global brands that can be advertised and promoted the world over.

In this chapter, we look at international advertising and promotion and the various issues marketers must consider in communicating with consumers around the globe. We examine the environment of international marketing and how companies often must adapt their promotional programs to conditions in each country. We reveiw the debate over whether a company should use a global marketing and advertising approach or tailor it specifically for various countries.

We also examine how firms organize for international advertising, select agencies, and consider various decision areas such as research, creative strategy, and media selection. While the focus of this chapter is on international advertising, we also consider other promotional mix elements in international marketing, including sales promotion, personal selling, publicity/public relations, and the Internet. Let's begin by discussing some of the reasons international marketing has become so important to companies.

The Importance of International Markets

One of the major developments in the business world during the decade of the 90s was the globalization of markets. The emergence of a largely borderless world has created a new reality for all types of companies. Today, world trade is driven by global competition among global companies for global consumers.[1] With the development of faster communication, transportation, and financial transactions, time and distance are no longer barriers to global marketing. Products and services developed in one country quickly find their way to other countries where they are finding enthusiastic acceptance. Consumers around the world wear Nike shoes and Calvin Klein jeans, eat at McDonald's, shave with Gillette razors, use Gateway and Dell computers, drink Coca-Cola and Pepsi Cola soft drinks and Starbucks coffee, talk on cellular phones made by Nokia and Motorola, and drive cars made by global automakers such as Ford, Honda, and Nissan.[2]

Companies are focusing on international markets for a number of reasons. Many companies in the U.S. and Western Europe recognize that their domestic markets offer them limited opportunities for expansion because of slow population growth, saturated markets, intense competition, and/or an unfavorable marketing environment. For example, U.S. tobacco companies face declining domestic consumption as a result of restrictions on their marketing and advertising efforts and the growing antismoking sentiment in this country. Companies such as R. J. Reynolds and Philip Morris are turning to markets outside the United States such as Asia and South America, where higher percentages of people smoke, nonsmokers are far more tolerant of the habit, opposition is less organized, and consumers are less litigious.[3] Many U.S.-based brewers, among them Anheuser-Busch, Miller, and Coors, are looking to international markets to sustain growth as beer sales in the United States decline and regulatory pressures increase.[4]

Many companies must focus on foreign markets to survive. Most European nations are relatively small in size and without foreign markets would not have the economies of scale to compete against larger U.S. and Japanese companies. For example, Swiss-based Nestlé and Unilever, which is based in the Netherlands, are two of the world's largest consumer-product companies because they have learned how to market their brands to consumers in countries around the world. Two of the world's major marketers of cellular telephones are from Scandinavian countries. Nokia is based in Finland and Ericsson is located in Sweden. Australia's tourist industry is a major part of its economy and relies heavily on visitors from other countries to visit the land down under. Exhibit 20–1 shows a direct-mail brochure used by the Australian Tourist Commission to attract visitors from abroad.

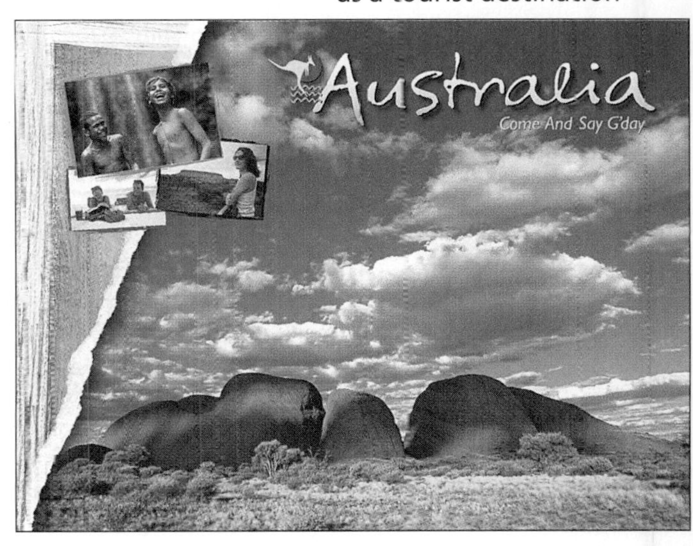

Exhibit 20–1 The Australian Tourist Commission promotes the country as a tourist destination

Companies are also pursuing international markets because of the opportunities they offer for growth and profits. The dramatic economic, social, and political changes around the world in recent years have opened markets in Eastern Europe and China. The World Trade Organization agreement signed in November 1999 by the United States, China, and other countries opens access to 1.2 billion potential Chinese consumers for Western marketers who are eager to sell them a variety of products and services.[5] The growing markets of the Far East, Latin America, and other parts of the world present tremendous opportunities to marketers of consumer products and services as well as business-to-business marketers.

Many companies in the United States as well as in other countries have long recognized the importance and potential profitability of international markets. General Electric, Ford, General Motors, Nike, Compaq, Nissan, Nestlé, and Procter & Gamble have made the world their market and generate much of their sales and profits from abroad. Gillette sells over 800 products in more than 200 countries. Colgate-Palmolive generates nearly 70 percent of its $10 billion in sales from outside the United States and Canada.[6] Kellogg earns 35 percent of its profits outside the United States and has over 40 percent of the ready-to-eat cereal market in Europe and Asia and more than 60 percent in Latin America. Coca-Cola, Pepsi, Nike, Sony, KFC, Dell, McDonald's, and many other U.S. companies and brands are known all over the world.

Exhibit 20–2 The WD-40 Co. gets much of its sales growth from foreign markets

Many U.S.-based companies have formed joint ventures or strategic alliances with foreign companies to market their products internationally. For example, General Mills and Swiss-based Nestlé entered into a joint venture to create Cereal Partners Worldwide (CPW), taking advantage of General Mills' popular product line and Nestlé's powerful distribution channels in Europe, Asia, Latin America, and Africa.[7] This global alliance now operates in 70 international markets and generated sales of nearly $850 million in 1999.[8] Nestlé also has entered into joint ventures with Coca-Cola to have the beverage giant distribute its instant coffee and tea throughout the world. Häagen-Dazs entered into a joint venture in Japan with Suntory Ltd., and its premium ice cream, frozen yogurt, and other brands are now sold throughout Asia.

International markets are important to small and mid-size companies as well as the large multinational corporations. Many of these firms can compete more effectively in foreign markets, where they may face less competition or appeal to specific market segments or where products have not yet reached the maturity stage of their life cycle. For example, the WD-40 Co. has saturated the U.S. market with its lubricant product and now gets much of its sales growth from Europe, Canada, and Japan (Exhibit 20–2).

Another reason it is increasingly important for U.S. companies to adopt an international marketing orientation is that imports are taking a larger and larger share of the domestic market for many products. The United States has been running a continuing **balance-of-trade deficit;** the monetary value of our imports exceeds that of our exports. American companies are realizing that we are shifting from being an isolated, self-sufficient, national economy to being part of an interdependent *global economy.* This means U.S. corporations must defend against foreign inroads into the domestic market as well as learn how to market their products and services to other countries.[9]

While many U.S. companies are becoming more aggressive in their pursuit of international markets, they face stiff competition from large multinational corporations from other countries. Some of the world's most formidable marketers are European companies such as Unilever, Nestlé, Siemens, Philips, and Renault, as well as the various Japanese car and electronic manufacturers and package-goods companies such as Suntory, Shiseido, and Kao.

The Role of International Advertising and Promotion

Advertising and promotion are important parts of the marketing program of firms competing in the global marketplace. An estimated $233 billion was spent on advertising in the United States in 2000, with much of this money being spent by multinational companies headquartered outside this country.[10] Advertising expenditures outside the United States have increased by nearly 60 percent since 1990, reaching an estimated $231 million in 2000 as global marketers based in the United States, as well as European and Asian countries increase their worldwide advertising spending.[11] Figure 20–1 shows the top 25 companies in terms of advertising spending outside the United States.

Figure 20–1 Top 25 companies by ad spending outside the United States, 1998

Rank	Advertiser	Headquarters	Ad Spending Outside the U.S.	U.S. Ad Spending	Worldwide Ad Spending
1	Procter & Gamble	Cincinnati, OH	$3,0812.2	$1,792.3	$4,747.5
2	Unilever	Rotterdam/London	2,737.3	691.2	3,428.5
3	Nestlé	Vevey, Switz.	1,559.3	273.8	1,833.0
4	Volkswagen	Wolfsburg, Germany	1,070.4	255.4	1,325.8
5	Ford Motor Co.	Dearborn, M	1,049.5	1,180.0	2,229.5
6	General Motors	Detroit	1,039.3	2,154.2	3,193.5
7	Toyota Motor Corp.	Toyota City, Japan	1,034.9	657.5	1,692.4
8	Coca-Cola Co.	Atlanta	1,011.5	315.8	1,327.3
9	Peugeot Citroen	Paris	854.9	0	855.0
10	L'Oreal	Paris	840.9	403.1	1,244.1
11	Mars Inc.	McLean, VA	793.0	275.6	1,069.6
12	Sony Corp.	Tokyo	775.1	562.6	1,337.7
13	Philip Morris Cos.	New York	715.8	1264.4	1,980.3
14	Henkel	Dusseldorf	699.2	1.3	700.5
15	Renault	Paris	688.2	.1	688.3
16	Nissan Motor Co.	Tokyo	663.6	461.3	1,124.9
17	Fiat	Turin, Italy	628.3	3.7	631.9
18	Honda Motor Co.	Tokyo	603.2	491.0	1,094.3
19	Colgate-Palmolive	New York	569.9	135.4	732.3
20	McDonald's Corp.	Oak Brook, IL	592.3	571.7	1,64.0
21	Ferrero	Perugia, Italy	558.7	22.6	581.2
22	Danone Group	Levallois-Perret, France	550.0	38.6	588.6
23	Daimler-Chrysler	Stuggart, Germany/ Auburn Hills, MI	522.4	1,399.7	1,922.2
24	Kao Corp.	Tokyo	511.8	71.7	583.4
25	BMW	Munich	455.9	106.1	562.0

Note: Numbers are in U.S. dollars.

In addition, estimates are that another $500 billion is spent on sales promotion efforts targeted at consumers, retailers, and wholesalers around the world. More than 90 percent of the money spent to advertise and promote goods and services is concentrated in the 30 or so industrialized countries of Western Europe, the Pacific Rim, and the United States and Canada. Advertising and promotional spending per person per year ranges from less than $1 in Third World countries such as Laos, Vietnam, and Nigeria to more than $2,100 in Japan, which has the most intensely advertised-to population.[12]

More and more companies recognize that an effective promotional program is important for companies competing in foreign markets. As one international marketing scholar notes:

> Promotion is the most visible as well as the most culture bound of the firm's marketing functions. Marketing includes the whole collection of activities the firm performs in relating to its market, but in other functions the firm relates to the market in a quieter, more passive way. With the promotional function, however, the firm is standing up and speaking out, wanting to be seen and heard.[13]

Many companies have run into difficulties developing and implementing advertising and promotion programs for international markets. Companies that promote their products or services abroad face an unfamiliar marketing environment and customers with different sets of values, customs, consumption patterns, and habits, as well as differing purchase motives and abilities. Languages vary from country to country and even within a country, such as India or Switzerland. Media options are quite limited in many countries, owing to lack of availability or limited effectiveness. These factors demand different creative and media strategies as well as changes in other elements of the advertising and promotional program for foreign markets.

The International Environment

Just as with domestic marketing, companies engaging in international marketing must carefully analyze the major environmental factors of each market in which they compete, including economic, demographic, cultural, and political/legal variables. Figure 20–2 shows some of the factors marketers must consider in each category when analyzing the environment of each country or market. These factors are important in evaluating the potential of each country as well as designing and implementing a marketing and promotional program.

The Economic Environment

A country's economic conditions indicate its present and future potential for consuming, since products and services can be sold only to countries where there is enough income to buy them. This is generally not a problem in developed countries such as the United States, Canada, Japan, and most of Western Europe, where consumers generally have higher incomes and standards of living. Thus, they can and want to purchase a variety of products and services. Developed countries have the **economic infrastructure** in terms of the communications, transportation, financial, and distribution networks needed to conduct business in these markets effectively. By contrast, many developing countries lack purchasing power and have limited communications networks available to firms that want to promote their products or services to these markets.

Figure 20–2 Forces in the international marketing environment

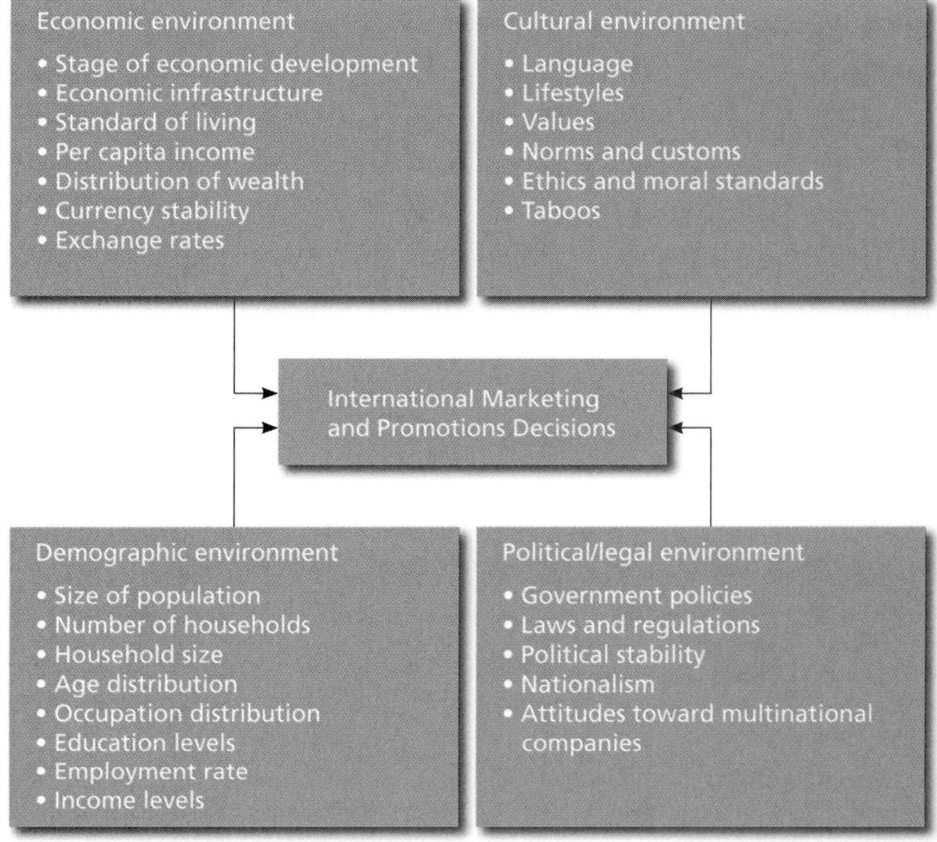

For most companies, industrialized nations represent the greatest marketing and advertising opportunities. But most of these countries have stable population bases, and their markets for many products and services are already saturated. Many marketers are turning their attention to parts of the world whose economies and consumer markets are growing. In the early to mid-1990s many marketers began turning their attention to the "four Tigers" of Asia—South Korea, Singapore, Hong Kong, and Taiwan—which were among the fastest-growing markets in the world.[14] However, in 1997 the Asian economic crisis hit, and these countries, as well as other parts of Asia, experienced a severe recession which resulted in major declines in consumer spending. Latin America also experienced a severe economic crisis and in countries such as Brazil the currency was devalued by 40 percent. Many companies reduced their advertising spending in Asia and Latin America as a result of the economic crises. However, by the beginning of the new millennium these regions appeared to be emerging from the recession.[15] High-tech brands in areas such as telecommunication products and services and computers have been leading the recovery in these markets. For example, Gateway, the computer manufacturer, has been aggressively opening markets in Asia using its multichannel business model and has been advertising heavily to build its brand and make its distinctive cow-spotted boxes a familiar sight in Asia.[16] Exhibit 20–3 shows a clever Gateway ad that covers Singapore's skyline in cow spots. Many other U.S. companies already have a strong presence in these countries, including Colgate-Palmolive, Du Pont, Procter & Gamble, and Coca-Cola.

Exhibit 20–3 This ad for Gateway Computer was used in Singapore; the headline reads: "Let's paint the town black and white this weekend"

Marketers are also focusing on developing countries that have expanding populations and future growth opportunities. For example, Nestlé, the world's largest food company, estimates that 20 percent of the world's population in Europe and North America consumes 80 percent of its products. While Nestlé continues to target the European and American markets with ads, it is also focusing on Third World nations as the market of tomorrow.[17]

The Demographic Environment

Major demographic differences exist among countries as well as within them. Marketers must consider income levels and distribution, age and occupation distributions of the population, household size, education, and employment rates. In some countries, literacy rates are also a factor; people who cannot read will not respond well to print ads. Demographic data can provide insight into the living standards and lifestyles in a particular country to help companies plan ad campaigns.

Demographic information can reveal the market potential of various foreign markets. India's census bureau estimates that the country's population will have topped 1 billion by May 2000. Only China, with 1.2 billion people, has a larger population.[18] Latin America remains one of the world's largest potential markets, although the meager income of most consumers in the region is still a problem. Brazil, the largest consumer market in South America, was expected to have a population of 200 million by the year 2000 and is a growing market for many products and services. More than 50 percent of the Latin American market is younger than age 26, and 30 percent is under 15. Moreover, children are the fastest-growing segment of that market. These numbers have caught the attention of international advertisers such as Mattel, Hasbro, Burger King, and others.[19] Indonesia also has a very young population with more people under the age of 16 than the United States, and they are very receptive to Western ways and products. For example, Tower

Records, a California-based chain of music stores, recently opened stores in Bangkok that are nearly identical to its U.S. outlets and are very popular with the youth in Thailand.[20]

The Cultural Environment

Another important aspect of the international marketing environment is the culture of each country. Cultural variables marketers must consider include language, customs, tastes, attitudes, lifestyles, values, and ethical/moral standards. Nearly every country exhibits cultural traits that influence not just the needs and wants of consumers but how they go about satisfying them.

Marketers must be sensitive not only in determining what products and services they can sell foreign cultures but also in communicating with them. Advertising is often the most effective way to communicate with potential buyers and create markets in other countries. But it can also be one of the most difficult aspects of the international marketing program because of problems in developing messages that will be understood in various countries.

International advertisers often have problems with language. The advertiser must know not only the native tongue of the country but also its nuances, idioms, and subtleties. International marketers must be aware of the connotations of words and symbols used in their messages and understand how advertising copy and slogans are translated. In Global Perspective 5–1, we discussed some of the problems marketers encounter in translating their advertising messages and brand names into various languages. The Heineken ad in Exhibit 20–4 is one example. Although this ad worked well in the United States and other English-speaking countries, the line "you don't have to make a great fuss" could not be translated in a meaningful way into many other languages.

Advertisers can also encounter problems with the connotative meaning of signs and symbols used in their messages. For example, Pepsodent toothpaste was unsuccessful in Southeast Asia because it promised white teeth to a culture where black and yellow teeth are symbols of prestige. An American ad campaign using various shades of green was a disaster in Malaysia, where the color symbolizes death and disease.

Problems arising from language diversity and differences in signs and symbols can usually be best solved with the help of local expertise. Marketers should consult local employees or use an ad agency knowledgeable in the local language that can help verify that the advertiser is saying what it wants to say. Many companies

Brewers don't have to be good talkers.
Heineken
When you make a great beer, you don't have to make a great fuss.

Exhibit 20–4 This Heineken ad did not translate well into some languages

turn to agencies that specialize in translating advertising slogans and copy into foreign languages.

Tastes, traditions, and customs are also an important part of cultural considerations. The customs of a society affect what products and services it will buy and how they must be marketed. In France, cosmetics are used heavily by men as well as women, and advertising to the male market is common. There are also cultural differences in grooming and hygiene habits of consumers in various countries. For example, though many U.S. consumers use products like deodorant and shampoo daily, consumers in many other Western countries are not as fanatical about personal hygiene, so consumption of products such as deodorants and mouthwash is much lower than in the United States.

Another aspect of culture that is very important for international marketers to understand is values. **Cultural values** are beliefs and goals shared by members of a society regarding ideal end states of life and modes of conduct. Society shapes consumers' basic values, which affect their behavior and determine how they respond to various situations. For example, cultural values in the United States place a major emphasis on individual activity and initiative, while many Asian societies stress cooperation and conformity to the group. Values and beliefs of a society can also affect its members' attitudes and receptivity toward foreign products and services.[21] Values such as *ethnocentrism,* which refers to the tendency for individuals to view their own group or society as the center of the universe, or nationalism often affect the way consumers in various countries respond to foreign brands or even advertising messages.[22] Global Perspective 20–1 discusses the changing attitudes of French consumers toward American products and how the athletic footwear company New Balance has capitalized on this trend.

Japan is one of the more difficult markets for many American advertisers to understand because of its unique values and customs.[23] For example, the Japanese have a very strong commitment to the group; social interdependence and collectivism are as important to them as individualism is to most Americans. Ads stressing individuality and nonconformity have traditionally not done well in Japan, but Westernized values have become more prevalent in Japanese advertising in recent years.[24] However, the Japanese dislike ads that confront or disparage the competition and tend to prefer soft rather than hard sells.[25] A recent study found that Japanese and American magazine ads tend to portray teenage girls in different ways and that the differences correspond to each country's central concepts of self and society. In many American ads teens are associated with images of independence, rebelliousness, determination, and even defiance that are consistent with the American value of individuality. In contrast, Japanese ads tend to portray a happy, playful, childlike, girlish image that is consistent with the Japanese culture's sense of self, which is more dependent on others.[26] Another recent study examined gender-role portrayals in Japanese magazine advertising and found that some of the previously used hard-line stereotyping of both men and women has softened considerably since the 1980s. Men are not associated as much with stereotypical male traits, while women are shown in more positive ways. The researchers suggest that this may reflect the Westernization of the depictions of men and women in Japan.[27]

Religion is another aspect of culture that affects norms, values, and behaviors. For example, in many Arab countries, advertisers must be aware of various taboos resulting from conservative applications of the Islamic religion. Alcohol and pork cannot be advertised. Human nudity is forbidden, as are pictures of anything sacred, such as images of a cross or photographs of Mecca. The faces of women may not be shown in photos, so cosmetics use drawings of women's faces in ads.[28] In conservative Islamic countries, many religious authorities are opposed to advertising on the grounds that it promotes Western icons and culture and the associated non-Islamic consumerism.[29] Procter & Gamble recently took on tradition in Egypt by underwriting a new groundbreaking TV talk show on feminine hygiene called "Frankly Speaking" that tackles some of the most sensitive issues facing women in an Islamic country. The program has the support of the Egyptian government, which has launched its own health education drive. P&G does not promote its products during the show, but the program does contain numerous commercials for its

Global Perspective 20–1

American Marketers Invade France

To many European consumers, "German made" is a sign of quality engineering, "made in Italy" signals style, and French products are synonymous with chic. If you asked a sample of European consumers what "made in U.S.A." conveys, you might not get a favorable answer. While Europeans showed interest in some American brands, for many years they were reluctant to buy American and there was even a backlash against American imagery. In fact, many U.S. companies doing business in Europe were careful not to flaunt their American roots.

One European country in particular where American products have not been prevalent, or even welcome, is France. Part of the problem stems from relations between the two countries. The United States and France have been at odds over a number of issues, including trade disputes on products ranging from Hollywood movies to imported French foods. Recently, angry farmers in France have been leading anti-American protests triggered by the World Trade Organization ruling ordering Europe to accept hormone-fed beef produced in the United States. In the fall of 1999 they seized on McDonald's as a symbol of American cultural imperialism and began staging protests against the company and vandalizing restaurants across the country.

According to Richard Pells, a historian at the University of Texas and author of *Not Like Us: How Europeans Have Loved, Hated and Transformed American Culture since Word War II,* the ongoing battle between the two countries is a matter of pride. After all, France is a country that punishes those who dare write advertising copy—or anything else for public consumption—in English without translating it to French. There are quotas for French-language shows on TV and music on the radio. Pells notes, "France, like the U.S, has traditionally seen itself as a country with a mission and a country whose culture and civilization is worthy of being exported around the world."

While the French may not like it, it appears that the United States is winning the export war in the marketing arena. Walk down the famed Champs-Elysees in Paris and you will see teenagers in cargo pants and athletic shoes made by American companies, sauntering in and out of McDonald's or standing in line to buy tickets for American-made movies. Instead of carrying traditional square book bags, they sport backpacks made by Jansport and many of them are on rollerblades. The Gap is opening retail stores all over Paris and had 45 shops in France in 2000. *Capital,* a major French business monthly, ran a 30-page cover story in June 1999 that warned: "Never has the United States so dominated the planet. From the Internet to pension funds, from Star Wars to genetically modified corn, America is on the brink of succeeding a gigantic IPO on the world."

A number of American companies are finding ways to narrow the cultural gap with French consumers and are making inroads into France like never before. In 1995 the French subsidiary of New Balance, the Boston-based company that makes high-tech running shoes targeted at serious runners, had sales of only about $3 million, less than 2 percent market share, and very little brand recognition. However, in 1997, New Balance struck gold. Almost overnight, the 576, a model designed for marathon runners, became *de rigueur*—not among marathoners and triathletes but among the Parisian fashion elite. Sales for the subsidiary more than doubled in 1998 to $7 million, and the few fashion boutiques that carried the shoe ran out within months as designers, fashionistas, film stars, and models rushed to buy the latest color. One French fashion writer stated in trendy *Biba* magazine: "This success should have an explanation, but it doesn't." However, there is an explanation according to Martin Journeau, the director of New Balance's subsidiary in France.

In late 1996, buyers from three of Paris's trendiest shops wanted to make a deal with the shoe manufacturer to make its shoes part of high fashion. Journeau's part of the deal was to limit distribution to a few elite stores and hike the price of the 576 in order to give the brand an aura of exclusivity. Then they let what the French call *la mode* work its magic. As sales took off, New Balance kept the nubuck shoes coming in a variety of solid colors. They sold them for almost twice the usual price, nearly 800 francs (about $130) a pair, to beef up the brand's image as a luxury item. They issued special, personalized 576s with the wearer's name stitched on the tongue as a "retro" fashion statement. And as the fashion mavens took the bait, sales skyrocketed.

New Balance plans to keep prices high and distribution limited to perpetuate the luxury-goods image of the 576. At the same time, the company is trying to tiptoe back toward its high-tech running gear image and plans to sell both trail and marathon models to a wider market in sports stores all over France. Executives in the company's home office were hesitant to position New Balance as fashion footwear. However, they eventually gave in and let the staff in France go with its instinct—a lesson any company wanting to woo the fickle French consumer must learn.

Sources: Shelly Pannill, "The Road to Richesse," *Sales & Marketing Management*, November 1999, pp. 89–96; Larry Speer, "McD's Self-Defense Is Its French Connection," *Advertising Age*, September 13, 1999, p. 26.

Always brand, which has 85 percent of the disposable sanitary pad market in the country.[30]

The Political/Legal Environment

The political and legal environment in a country is one of the most important factors influencing the advertising and promotional programs of international marketers. Regulations differ owing to economic and national sovereignty considerations, nationalistic and cultural factors, and the goal of protecting consumers not only from false or misleading advertising but, in some cases, from advertising in general. It is difficult to generalize about advertising regulation at the international level, since some countries are increasing government control of advertising while others are decreasing it. Government regulations and restrictions can affect various aspects of a company's advertising program, including:

- The types of products that may be advertised.
- The content or creative approach that may be used.
- The media that all advertisers (or different classes of advertisers) are permitted to employ.
- The amount of advertising a single advertiser may use in total or in a specific medium.
- The use of foreign languages in ads.
- The use of advertising material prepared outside the country.
- The use of local versus international advertising agencies.
- The specific taxes that may be levied against advertising.[31]

A number of countries ban or restrict the advertising of various products. Cigarette advertising is banned in some or all media in numerous countries besides the United States, including Argentina, Canada, France, Italy, Malaysia, Norway, Sweden, and Switzerland. In 1993 the Australian government limited tobacco advertising to point of purchase. The ban also excludes tobacco companies from sponsoring sporting events.[32] A ban on all tobacco advertising was enacted in the United Kingdom and was to begin in December 1999. However, the U.K.'s high court threw out the ban on the grounds that an appeal against a European Union directive to outlaw tobacco ads could succeed. It is expected that the U.K. government will appeal the decision in an effort to revive the ban.[33] In China, tobacco and liquor advertising are banned except in hotels for foreigners. In Hong Kong, which reverted to Chinese control in July 1997, a total ban on tobacco advertising is being considered, although it faces strong opposition from the tobacco and advertising industries.[34]

While international marketers are accustomed to restrictions on the advertising of cigarettes, liquor, and pharmaceuticals, they are often surprised by restrictions on other products or services. For example, margarine cannot be advertised in

France, nor can restaurant chains. For many years, the French government restricted travel advertising because it encourages the French to spend their francs outside the country.[35]

Many countries restrict the media advertisers can use. In 1999 the European Commission threw out an appeal against Greece's national ban on toy advertising on daytime television. Thus advertisers can advertise toys on TV only during the evening hours.[36] Sweden has a ban on all TV ads aimed at children, and Denmark is expected to make a similar move. Some of the most stringent advertising regulations in the world are found in Scandinavian countries. Commercial TV advertising did not begin in Sweden until 1992, and both Sweden and Denmark limit the amount of time available for commercials. Saudi Arabia opened its national TV system to commercial advertising in 1986, but advertising is not permitted on the state-run radio system. Advertising in magazines and newspapers in the country is subject to government and religious restrictions.[37]

Many governments have rules and regulations that affect the advertising message. For example, comparative advertising is legal and widely used in the United States and Canada but is illegal in some countries such as Korea and Belgium. In Europe, the European Union Commission has developed a directive to standardize the basic form and content of comparative advertising and develop a uniform policy.[38] Currently, comparative advertising is legal in many European countries, illegal in some, and legal and rarely used in others such as Great Britain. Many Asian and South American countries have also begun to accept comparative ads. However, Brazil's self-regulatory advertising codes are so strict that few advertisers have been able to create a comparative message that has been approved.[39] Many countries restrict the types of claims advertisers can make, the words they can use, and the way products can be represented in ads. In Greece, specific claims for a product, such as "20 percent fewer calories" are not permitted in an advertising message.[40] Copyright and other legal restrictions make it difficult to maintain the same name from market to market. For example, Diet Coke is known as Coca-Cola Light in Germany, France, and many other countries because of legal restrictions prohibiting the word *diet* (Exhibit 20–5).

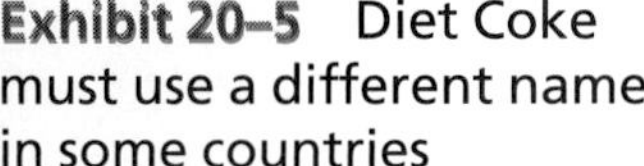
Exhibit 20–5 Diet Coke must use a different name in some countries

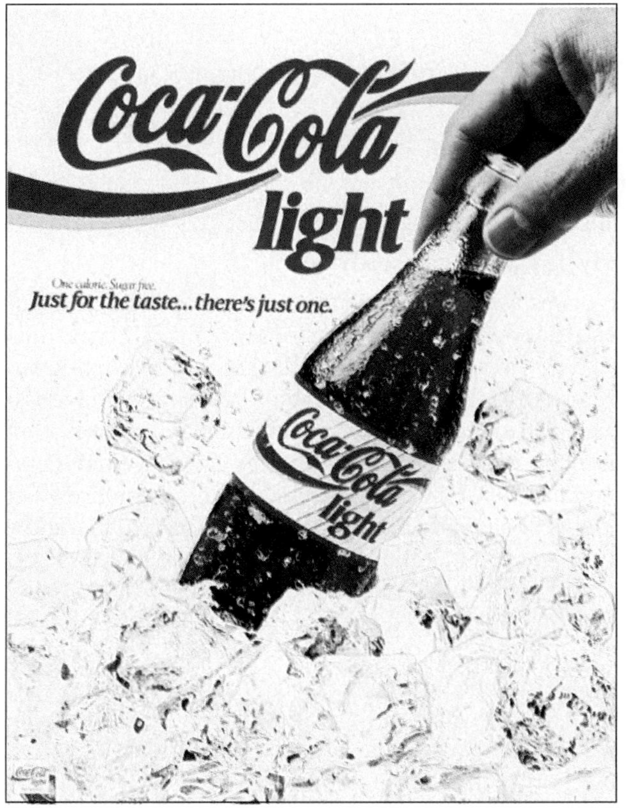

Government restrictions can influence the use of foreign languages in advertising as well as the production of the ad. Most countries permit the use of foreign languages in print ads and direct mail. However, some do not allow foreign-language commercials on TV or radio or in cinema ads, and some restrict foreign-language ads to media targeted to foreigners in their country.[41] Some countries also restrict the use of foreign-produced ads and foreign talent. For example, with few exceptions, such as travel advertising, all commercials aired on Malaysian television must be made in Malaysia. However, the Asian country is considering changing its rules to allow foreign commercials to air on the new legalized satellite signals into the country.[42]

These restrictions are motivated primarily by economic considerations. Many countries require local production of at least a portion of commercials to build local film industries and create more jobs for local producers of print and audiovisual materials. Nationalistic and cultural factors also contribute to these restrictions, along with a desire to prevent large foreign ad agencies from dominating the advertising business in a country and thus hampering its development. Restrictions affecting the advertising industry took a new twist recently in China when the government began strictly enforcing regulations governing licenses it requires of magazine publishers. Since the new enforcement took effect on January 1, 2000, Western publishers have been required to use a direct translation of the often-obscure name that appears on their license or use no English name at all. Thus, magazines such as *Cosmopolitan, Esquire,* and *Woman's Day* are not able to use their popular names.[43]

In some countries, steps are being taken to ease some of the legal restrictions and other barriers facing international advertisers. For example, the Maastricht Treaty was designed to create a single European market and remove many of the barriers to trade among the 12 member nations of the European Community. One of the goals of this plan was a single advertising law throughout the EC, but when the treaty was ratified in November 1993, many of the advertising directives were not agreed upon—so many advertising regulations are still decided by each country. A directive was passed by the European Commission banning all tobacco advertising, and most of the 15 European Union countries are expected to implement it in June 2001. However, an appeal of the initiative was filed by the tobacco industry and is expected to be heard in late 2000. Most ad industry leaders acknowledge that a ban on tobacco advertising is inevitable and expect that the European Commission may also take steps to restrict alcohol advertising and marketing.[44]

Global versus Localized Advertising

The discussion of differences in the marketing environments of various countries suggests that each market is different and requires a distinct marketing and advertising program. However, in recent years a great deal of attention has focused on the concept of **global marketing,** where a company uses a common marketing plan for all countries in which it operates, thus selling the product in essentially the same way everywhere in the world. **Global advertising** falls under the umbrella of global marketing as a way to implement this strategy by using the same basic advertising approach in all markets.

The debate over standardization versus localization of marketing and advertising programs began years ago.[45] But the idea of global marketing was popularized by Professor Theodore Levitt, who says the worldwide marketplace has become homogenized and consumers' basic needs, wants, and expectations transcend geographic, national, and cultural boundaries.[46] One writer described Levitt's position on global marketing as follows:

> Levitt's vision of total worldwide standardization is global marketing at the extreme. He argues that, thanks to cheap air travel and new telecommunications technology, consumers the world over are thinking—and shopping—increasingly alike. According to Levitt, the New Republic of Technology homogenizes world tastes, wants, and possibilities into global marketing proportions, which allows for world standardized products.[47]

Not everyone agrees with Levitt's global marketing theory, particularly with respect to advertising. Many argue that products and advertising messages must be designed or at least adapted to meet the differing needs of consumers in different countries.[48] We will consider the arguments for and against global marketing and advertising, as well as situations where it is most appropriate.

Advantages of Global Marketing and Advertising

A global marketing strategy and advertising program offer certain advantages to a company, including the following.

- Economies of scale in production and distribution.
- Lower marketing and advertising costs as a result of reductions in planning and control.
- Lower advertising production costs.
- Abilities to exploit good ideas on a worldwide basis and introduce products quickly into various world markets.
- A consistent international brand and/or company image.
- Simplification of coordination and control of marketing and promotional programs.

Advocates of global marketing and advertising contend that standardized products are possible in all countries if marketers emphasize quality, reliability, and low prices. They say people everywhere want to buy the same products and live the same way. Product standardization results in lower design and production costs as well as greater marketing efficiency, which translates into lower prices for consumers. Product standardization and global marketing also enable companies to roll out products faster into world markets, which is becoming increasingly important as product life cycles become shorter and competition increases.

A number of companies have been very successful using a global advertising approach, including Coca-Cola, Merrill Lynch, Xerox, American Express, and British Airways. Gillette used global advertising in the early 90s to launch its Sensor shaving system, which became one of the most successful products in the company's history. The advertising theme for the global campaign was "The Best a Man Can Get." In 1998 Gillette launched the Mach3, its new triple-bladed shaving system, and once again used a global campaign built around the high-tech theme of the product and retaining the same tagline.[49] Prior to the introduction of the new product, Gillette launched the Mach3.com website, which was supported by online advertising to educate prospective customers about the intricacies of the triple-bladed razor.[50] The Web campaign was followed by a $200 million global media blitz that helped make the Mach3 the number-1-selling shaving system after less than a year on the market. Exhibit 20–6 shows an ad for the Mach3 that was used in Spain.

Exhibit 20–6 Gillette used global advertising to launch its new Mach3 shaving system

Problems with Global Advertising

Opponents of the standardized global approach argue that very few products lend themselves to global advertising.[51] Differences in culture, market, and economic development; consumer needs and usage patterns; media availabilities; and legal restrictions make it extremely difficult to develop an effective universal approach to marketing and advertising. Advertising may be particularly difficult to standardize because of cultural differences in circumstances, language, traditions, values, beliefs, lifestyle, music, and so on. Moreover, some experts argue that cultures around the world are becoming more diverse, not less so. Thus, advertising's job of informing and persuading consumers and moving them toward using a particular brand can be done only within a given culture.

Consumer usage patterns and perceptions of a product may vary from one country to another, so advertisers must adjust their marketing and advertising approaches to different problems they may face in different markets. For example, when Nestlé introduced its Nescafé instant coffee brand, the company faced at least five different situations in various parts of the world:

1. In the United States, the idea of instant coffee had great penetration but Nescafé had the minor share.
2. In continental Europe, Nescafé had the major share of the market, but the idea of instant coffee was in the early stages.
3. In the tea-drinking countries, such as the United Kingdom and Japan, tea drinkers had to be converted not just to coffee but to instant coffee.
4. In Latin America, the preferred coffee was a heavy one that could not be duplicated with an instant version.
5. In Scandinavia, Nestlé had to deal with the ingrained custom of keeping a pot of coffee on the stove from early morning until late at night.

Nestlé had to use different advertising strategies for each market; a global campaign would not have been able to address the varying situations adequately. Exhibit 20–7 shows Nescafé ads used in Japan and Norway. Nestlé encountered yet another challenge when it entered the Israeli market in 1995. *Nescafé* was the generic word for instant coffee as Israelis assumed that it was an abbreviation of the Hebrew word *namess* (dissolving). Israeli consumers were also not very demanding with respect to the quality of their coffee and considered the low-quality powdered coffee, or *nescafé,* produced by a local company, suitable fare. To overcome the generic connotation of Nescafé, all of the advertising presented the Nescafé Classic brand as "Nescafé of Nestlé" and portrayed it as the coffee choice of people all around the world (Exhibit 20–8). The company also relied on taste-testing at the points of sale so consumers could experience Nescafé Classic's superior quality. Within one year Nestlé had 30 percent of the instant coffee market in Israel.[52]

Many experts believe that marketing a standardized product the same way all over the world can turn off consumers, alienate employees, and blind a company to

Exhibit 20–7

A. Nescafé instant coffee ad used in Japan

B. Nescafé instant coffee ad used in Norway

Exhibit 20–8 Nestlé had to reshape Israel's definition of instant coffee

diversities in customer needs. For example, when McDonald's expanded to Puerto Rico, it alienated consumers by using American TV ads dubbed in Spanish and then using Hispanic ads that were brought in from New York, which subsequent research showed looked too Mexican.[53]

Parker Pen also encountered problems when it attempted to use global advertising in the mid-1980s. Local managers in its foreign branches resented the home office centralizing the advertising function with one worldwide agency and mandating the type of advertising appeal used in their markets.[54]

Such problems have led some major companies to move away from a completely standardized approach. For example, the Colgate-Palmolive Co. has used global advertising for many of its brands, including the Colgate, Palmolive, Fab, and Ajax product lines, and continues to endorse the use of global appeals. Under its current marketing strategy, however, advertising is often modified for a specific country or region, particularly where local creativity can improve the advertising over the global standard.[55] An example of this approach is the advertising used for Colgate toothpaste (see Exhibit 20–9). The globe/smile image is used as the visual in nearly every country where Colgate is marketed, but the copy varies. This ad for the Russian market appeared in the Moscow edition of *Reader's Digest.*

Some marketing experts claim much of the attention to the advantages of global advertising stems from large ad agencies trying to increase business by encouraging clients to use one agency to handle their marketing communications worldwide.[56] Many large multinational companies are indeed consolidating their business with one or a few agencies who have offices around the world and offer international advertising capabilities. However, the consolidations are often driven by the client's increasing emphasis on global markets.[57]

When Is Globalization Appropriate?

While globalization of advertising is viewed by many in the advertising industry as a difficult task, some progress has been made in learning what products and services are best suited to worldwide appeals:[58]

1. Brands that can be adapted for a visual appeal, avoiding the problems of trying to translate words into dozens of languages.
2. Brands that are promoted with image campaigns that play to universal appeals such as sex or wealth.
3. High-tech products and new products coming to the world for the first time, not steeped in the cultural heritage of the country.
4. Products with nationalistic flavor if the country has a reputation in the field.
5. Products that appeal to a market segment with universally similar tastes, interests, needs, and values.

Many companies and brands rely heavily on visual appeals that are easily adapted for use in global advertising campaigns. For example, Nike used global advertising to launch the Air 180 running shoe, its first worldwide product launch.

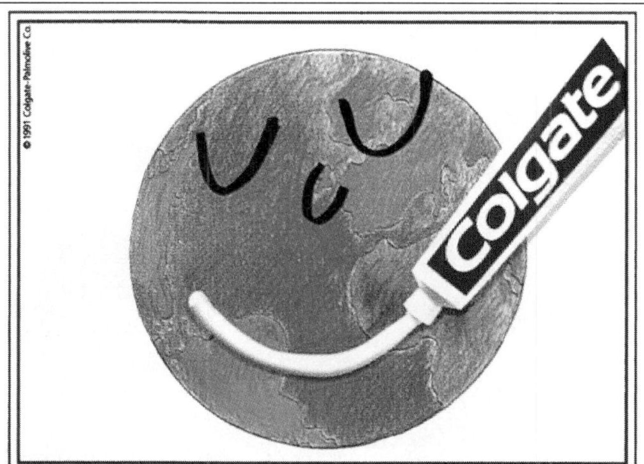

© 1991 Colgate-Palmolive Co.
Colgate

МИР ГОВОРИТ «КОЛГЕЙТ»–
ПОДРАЗУМЕВАЕТ ЗУБНАЯ ПАСТА.
МИР ГОВОРИТ ЗУБНАЯ ПАСТА–
ПОДРАЗУМЕВАЕТ «КОЛГЕЙТ».
Для людей в более чем 160 странах мира зубная паста «Колгейт» вот уже 100 лет является синонимом высочайшего качества. Люди больше доверяют пасте «Колгейт», чем другим пастам, потому что она содержит кальций и фтор, которые способствуют укреплению зубов и защищают их от кариеса.
С помощью пасты «Колгейт» вы и ваша семья смогут сохранить зубы здоровыми. Вашей семье также понравится освежающий вкус ментола.
Чистите зубы пастой «Колгейт» и вы убедитесь сами, что «Колгейт» означает качество.

ЗУБНАЯ ПАСТА НОМЕР ОДИН В МИРЕ.
Translation:
COLGATE. WHAT THE WORLD CALLS TOOTHPASTE.
THE WORLD SAYS COLGATE, THE WORLD MEANS TOOTHPASTE.
THE WORLD SAYS TOOTHPASTE, THE WORLD MEANS COLGATE.
In the 100 years since it was first introduced, Colgate toothpaste has come to mean superior quality to people in over 160 countries. In fact, more families trust Colgate than any other toothpaste in the world because it contains calcium and fluoride for stronger teeth and unsurpassed cavity protection. Colgate will also help keep your family's teeth healthy. And it has a fresh, minty taste they'll love. Brush with Colgate. And see for yourself that, when the world says "Colgate," they mean quality.
THE NUMBER ONE TOOTHPASTE IN THE WORLD.

Exhibit 20–9 Advertising for Colgate toothpaste uses a consistent visual image, but the copy may vary for different markets

The commercials contained no spoken language and relied on visual imagery. International airlines such as British Airways and Singapore Airlines also use global corporate image ads that rely heavily on visual appeals (Exhibit 20–10).

Products such as jewelry, liquor, cosmetics, and cigarettes can be promoted using image advertising, the second category. Marlboro uses its cowboy/western imagery around the world, and many cosmetic companies use similar image campaigns in different countries.

Levitt, like many advertisers, believes that joy, sentiment, excitement, and many other emotions are universal. Thus, it is common for global advertising campaigns to use emotional and image appeals. One advertising executive said:

> What it all boils down to is that we are all human. We share the gift of emotional response. We feel things. And we feel them in remarkably similar ways. We speak different languages, we observe different customs, but we are wired to each other and to an ultimate power source that transcends us in a way that makes us subject to a common emotional spectrum.[59]

An example of global advertising that appeals to universal emotions is the "Shadows" campaign that the J. Walter Thompson agency developed as part of the

Exhibit 20–10 Visual appeals work well in global advertising

"Diamonds are forever" branding concept for De Beers. The campaign captures the emotion of giving and receiving a diamond through the sophisticated and elegant "Shadows" photography, the classical music used in the commercials, and the anonymity/intrigue of the shadows themselves. De Beers has used the shadows campaign in 24 countries to communicate the idea that diamonds are a gift of enduring love.[60]

High-tech consumer products such as personal computers, calculators, VCRs, TVs, and audio equipment are in the third category, as are various types of business-to-business products and services such as computer systems. Business-to-business marketers like Digital Equipment Corp. and Xerox have begun using global advertising campaigns, as have Compaq and IBM.

Products in the fourth category are those whose national reputation for quality can be the basis for a global advertising campaign. Examples include Swiss watches, French wine, and German beer or automobiles. Many U.S. companies are taking advantage of the cachet American products have acquired among consumers in Europe and other international markets.[61] For example, Jeep promotes itself as "the American legend" in Europe and Japan. Brown-Forman has been using an American theme for its Jack Daniel's and Southern Comfort liquor brands since it began selling them in foreign markets more than two decades ago.

In the final category for which globalization is appropriate are products and services that can be sold to common market segments around the world, such as those identified by Salah Hassan and Lea Katsansis.[62] One such segment is the world's elite—people who, by reason of their economically privileged position, can pursue a lifestyle that includes fine jewelry, expensive clothing, quality automobiles, and the like. Marketers of high-quality products such as Bally leather goods, Cartier jewelry, Godiva chocolates, and Louis Vuitton luggage can use global advertising to appeal to the elite market segment around the world. Seagram launched a global billboard advertising campaign for its expensive Chivas Regal scotch based on the idea that "the rich all over the world will sip the tony brand, no matter where they made their fortune."[63] Well-known international brands competing in the luxury goods marketplace often present a singular image of prestige and style to the entire world.

Another segment of global consumers who have similar needs and interests and seek similar features and benefits from products and services is teenagers. There are more than 200 million teens in Europe, Latin America, and the Pacific Rim countries of Asia whose lifestyles are converging with those of the 40 million teens in the United States and Canada to create a vast, free-spending global market.[64] Teens now have intense exposure to television, magazines, movies, music, travel, and global advertising from companies such as Levi Strauss, Benetton, Motorola, Coca-

Cola, Pepsi, and many others. MTV is now seen in 136 countries. A recent study of 6,500 teens in 26 countries found an "Americanization" of fashion and culture. When teens were asked what country had the most influence on their attitudes and purchase behavior, the United States was named by 54 percent of the respondents from the United States, 87 percent of those from Latin America, and 80 percent of those from Europe and the Far East.[65]

Marketers are developing new products for the global teen market and many are tying into sports and music, which are universal languages for teens, in their IMC programs. For example, PepsiCo developed Pepsi Max, a sugar-free soft drink that it hopes will appeal to teens in Asian and European markets (Exhibit 20–11). Advertisers keen on reaching the teens around the world are also becoming involved with the development of television programming for this market segment. Swatch, Heineken, Levi Strauss, Philips, and Sony are among the companies that have recently directly invested in programming in areas such as music, fashion, alternative sports, and game shows that have been developed for the teen market.[66]

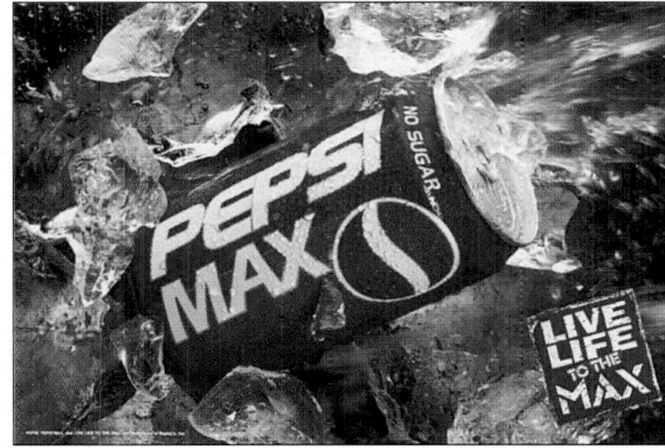

Exhibit 20–11 Pepsi Max is targeted at teens in Europe and Asia

Global Products, Local Messages

While the pros and cons of global marketing and advertising continue to be debated, many companies are taking an in-between approach by standardizing their products and basic marketing strategy but localizing their advertising messages. This approach recognizes similar desires, goals, needs, and uses for products and services but tailors advertising to the local cultures and conditions in each market. Some agencies call this approach "Think globally, act locally." Grey Advertising describes it as "global vision with a local touch."[67]

Although some marketers use global ads with little or no modification, most companies adapt their messages to respond to differences in language, market conditions, and other factors. Many global marketers use a strategy called **pattern advertising;** their ads follow a basic approach, but themes, copy, and sometimes even visual elements are adapted to differences in local markets. For example, Unilever's Dove soap uses the same basic advertising and positioning theme globally, but models from Australia, France, Germany, and Italy are used to appeal to women in those countries. Continental Airlines used pattern advertising to promote its BusinessFirst class of service in various countries. Exhibit 20–12 shows Continental ads used in Spain and France.

Exhibit 20–12 Continental Airlines uses pattern advertising to promote its BusinessFirst class in various countries

Another way global marketers adapt their campaigns to local markets is by producing a variety of ads with a similar theme and format and allowing managers in various countries or regions to select those messages they believe will work best in their markets. Coca-Cola used this approach when it launched its new "Coca-Cola Enjoy" global advertising theme in early 2000.[68] The company wanted a stronger emphasis on creative tailored to regional and local markets. To ensure that individual markets could easily adapt to the new global theme, local and international ad agencies were brought into the creative process early on to develop ads that augment the global campaign. The six agencies that work on the Coca-Cola Classic account around the world created spots for markets in China, Hong Kong, Europe, and Australia. According to the company's vice president and director of worldwide advertising, the agencies developed adaptations to the global campaign that "in local country terms reflect a deeper understanding of the human condition" (Exhibit 20–13).

Although many marketers are striving to develop global brands, research suggests most are doing so by using a localized approach. A study of international advertising strategies of successful U.S. multinational corporations found that only 9 percent used totally standardized global advertising for all foreign markets, while 37 percent used all localized advertising. The remaining 54 percent used a combination strategy, standardizing portions of their advertising but adapting it for local markets.[69] Marketers said a major risk of the global approach was a lack of communication owing to cultural differences. Another study found that most U.S. consumer durable goods manufacturers used a localized advertising approach—but most used some standardized messages.[70]

A more recent study of international advertising decision makers sponsored by *Advertising Age International* found that "think globally, act locally" still appears to be the dominant strategy of international advertisers, but with a slight revision: "Think globally, act regionally."[71] Most of the respondents in this survey said their companies' worldwide headquarters play a dominant role in determining their international advertising messages so they are consistent worldwide. However,

Exhibit 20–13 "Coca-Cola Enjoy" is the theme for the global ad campaign for Coke Classic but local adaptations are used to respond to conditions in various countries

there is a trend toward giving regional offices the autonomy to adapt the global theme for their local markets.

Most managers believe it is important to adapt components of their advertising messages—such as the language, models, scenic backgrounds, message content, and symbols—to reflect the culture and frame of reference of consumers in various countries. Many companies are making these tactical adjustments to their advertising messages while still pursuing global strategies that will help them project a consistent global image and turn their products and services into global brands.

Decision Areas in International Advertising

Companies developing advertising and promotional programs for international markets must make certain organizational and functional decisions similar to those for domestic markets. These decisions include organization style, agency selection, advertising research, creative strategy and execution, and media strategy and selection.

Organizing for International Advertising

One of the first decisions a company must make when it decides to market its products to other countries is how to organize the international advertising and promotion function. This decision is likely to depend on how the company is organized overall for international marketing and business. Three basic options are centralization at the home office or headquarters, decentralization of decision making to local foreign markets, or a combination of the two.

Centralization Many companies prefer to *centralize* the international advertising and promotion function so that all decisions about agency selection, research, creative strategy and campaign development, media strategy, and budgeting are made at the firm's home office.

Complete centralization is likely when market and media conditions are similar from one country to another, when the company has only one or a few international agencies handling all of its advertising, when the company can use standardized advertising, or when it desires a consistent image worldwide. Centralization may also be best when a company's international business is small and it operates through foreign distributors or licensees who do not become involved in the marketing and promotional process.

Many companies prefer the centralized organizational structure to protect their foreign investments and keep control of the marketing effort and corporate and/or brand image. Centralization can save money, since it reduces the need for staff and administration at the local subsidiary level. As the trend toward globalized marketing and advertising strategies continues, more companies are likely to move more toward centralization of the advertising function to maintain a unified world brand image rather than presenting a different image in each market. Some foreign managers may actually prefer centralized decision making, as it removes them from the burden of advertising and promotional decisions and saves them from defending local decisions to the home office.

However, many marketing and advertising managers in foreign markets oppose centralized control. They say the structure is too rigid and makes it difficult to adapt the advertising and promotional program to local needs and market conditions. As noted earlier, Parker Pen encountered such resistance when it attempted to implement a global advertising strategy.

Decentralization Under a *decentralized* organizational structure, marketing and advertising managers in each market have the authority to make their own advertising and promotional decisions. Local managers can select ad agencies, develop budgets, conduct research, approve creative themes and executions, and select advertising media. Companies using a decentralized approach put a great deal of faith in the judgment and decision-making ability of personnel in local markets. This approach is often used when companies believe local managers know the marketing situation in their countries the best. They may also be more effective and motivated when given responsibility for the advertising and promotional program in their markets. Decentralization also works well in small or unique markets where headquarters' involvement is not worthwhile or advertising must be tailored to the local market.

International fragrance marketer Chanel, Inc., uses a decentralized strategy. Chanel found that many of its fragrance concepts do not work well globally and decided to localize advertising. For example, the U.S. office has the option of using ads created by the House of Chanel in Paris or developing its own campaigns for the U.S. market. Chanel executives in the United States think that the French concept of prestige is not the same as Americans' and the artsy ads created in France do not work well in this country.[72]

Another company that uses a decentralized structure with multiple advertising agencies is Compaq Computer. When Compaq began its first global advertising campaign in 1996, it decided to have the agencies representing its two biggest regions—North America and Europe—develop distinct brand campaigns.[73] Compaq then gave the two agencies' work to managers in the other regions to test and decide which campaign they wanted to run.

Combination

While there is an increasing trend toward centralizing the international advertising function, many companies combine the two approaches. The home office, or headquarters, has the most control over advertising policy, guidelines, and operations in all markets. The international advertising manager works closely with local or regional marketing managers and personnel from the international agency (or agencies) and sets advertising and promotional objectives, has budgetary authority, approves all creative themes and executions, and approves media selection decisions, especially when they are made on a regional basis or overlap with other markets.

Advertising managers in regional or local offices submit advertising plans and budgets for their markets, which are reviewed by the international advertising manager. Local managers play a major role in working with the agency to adapt appeals to their particular markets and select media.

The combination approach allows for consistency in a company's international advertising yet permits local input and adaptation of the promotion program. Most consumer product companies find that local adaptation of advertising is necessary for foreign markets or regions, but they want to maintain control of the overall worldwide image they project. Eastman Kodak, for example, provides central strategy and support to local offices and acts as consultant to them. Although each country is autonomous, the main office controls the quality of advertising and advertising policy. Media buying is done on a local level, but the main office becomes involved in special media opportunities and overall strategy for events such as Olympic sponsorship and regionalized campaigns. Levi's created a centralized vice president of global marketing position to oversee the company's marketing in over 60 countries but still provides a great deal of autonomy to regional marketing directors.

Agency Selection

One of the most important decisions for a firm engaged in international marketing is the choice of an advertising agency. The company has three basic alternatives in selecting an agency to handle its international advertising. First, it can choose a major agency with both domestic and overseas offices. Many large agencies have offices all over the world and have become truly international operations. Some Western agencies have opened offices in Eastern Europe and Russia to create ads for the multinational companies participating in the free-market economies that are developing in these countries.[74]

Many American companies prefer to use a U.S.-based agency with foreign offices; this gives them greater control and convenience and also facilitates coordination of overseas advertising. For example, one of the reasons Colgate consolidated all of its worldwide advertising with Young & Rubicam was the unique fit with Y&R's worldwide agency network.[75] Young & Rubicam is one of the few U.S. agencies that owns agencies in virtually every country where they operate. Companies often use the same agency to handle international and domestic advertising. As discussed in Chapter 3, the flurry of mergers and acquisitions in the ad agency business in recent years, both in the United States and in other countries, has created large global agencies that can meet the international needs of global marketers. Global Perspective 20–2 disscusses how a number of multinational companies are consolidating their advertising with one large agency to develop a consistent global image.

A second alternative for the international marketer is to choose a domestic agency that, rather than having its own foreign offices or branches, is affiliated with agencies in other countries or belongs to a network of foreign agencies. An agency may acquire an interest in several foreign agencies or become part of an organization of international agencies. The agency can then sell itself as an international agency offering multinational coverage and contacts. For example, many U.S. agencies are expanding into Latin America by forming associations with regional agencies and acquiring partial or full ownership of agencies in various countries. Leo Burnett has majority stakes in agencies in 11 Latin American countries and minority ownership or associations in seven others.[76]

The advantage of this arrangement is that the client can use a domestic-based agency yet still have access to foreign agencies with detailed knowledge of market conditions, media, and so on in each local market. There may be problems with this approach, however. The local agency may have trouble coordinating and controlling independent agencies, and the quality of work may vary among network members. Companies considering this option must ask the local agency about its ability to control the activities of its affiliates and the quality of their work in specific areas such as creative and media.

The third alternative for the international marketer is to select a local agency for each national market in which it sells its products or services. Since local agencies often have the best understanding of the marketing and advertising environment in their country or region, they may be able to develop the most effective advertising.

Some companies like local agencies because they may provide the best talent in each market. In many countries, smaller agencies may, because of their independence, be more willing to take risks and develop the most effective, creative ads. Choosing local agencies also increases the involvement and morale of foreign subsidiary managers by giving them responsibility for managing the promotion function in their markets. Some companies have the subsidiary choose a local agency, since it is often in the best position to evaluate the agency and will work closely with it.

Criteria for Agency Selection

The selection of an agency to handle a company's international advertising depends on how the firm is organized for international marketing and the type of assistance it needs to meet its goals and objectives in foreign markets. Figure 20–3 lists some criteria a company might use in selecting an agency. In a study conducted among marketing directors of European

- Ability of agency to cover relevant markets
- Quality of agency work
- Market research, public relations, and other services offered by agency
- Relative roles of company advertising department and agency
- Level of communication and control desired by company
- Ability of agency to coordinate international campaign
- Size of company's international business
- Company's desire for local versus international image
- Company organizational structure for international business and marketing (centralized versus decentralized)
- Company's level of involvement with international operations

Figure 20–3 Criteria for selecting an agency to handle international advertising

Global Perspective 20–2

Global Marketers Go with One Image, One Agency

Traditionally, most large multinational corporations maintained a network of ad agencies around the world to handle their advertising in various countries. For example, Minnesota Mining & Manufacturing (3M), which operates in more than 70 countries, ran its global advertising through 34 separate agencies based in 23 countries. H. J. Heinz had 12 different agencies handling the advertising for its flagship ketchup brand in 30 countries. Recently, however, both 3M and Heinz consolidated their global advertising. 3M chose Grey Advertising, which has 278 offices in 70 countries, to handle most of its corporate and consumer advertising; Heinz placed its flagship ketchup brand into a single global advertising and brand-image account with Leo Burnett in 1998 and plans to consolidate worldwide advertising for all its businesses. In late 1999 Nissan Motor Co. consolidated its $1.1 billion global advertising account at TBWA Worldwide.

H. J. Heinz and 3M have joined a growing list of major companies that have recently pared their agency rosters to a single source. The consolidation trend began in May 1994 when IBM dismissed 40 agencies around the world and awarded its $450 million account to Ogilvy & Mather Worldwide. In late 1995 Colgate-Palmolive consolidated more than $500 million in global advertising with New York–based Young & Rubicam. The move, which followed the worldwide restructuring of Colgate's manufacturing and distribution system, marked the first time a large multibrand advertiser put all its billings with one agency.

IBM
BRAND
"NUNS"
TV :30 IMBR-5323

NUN 1:
I'm trying to get that new operating system, Chicago

but they keep pushing back the release date.

NUN 2:
That new OS/2 Warp from IBM sounds pretty hot.

NUN 1:
OS/2 Warp?

NUN 2:
I just read about it in "Wired."

You get true multitasking...

...easy access to the Internet.

NUN 1:
I'm dying to surf the 'net.

(SFX: Pager beeps)

NUN 1:
Whoops.

My beeper.

A number of factors are driving the consolidation trend. Most major corporations recognize they must develop a consistent global image for the company and/or its brands and speak with one coordinated marketing voice around the world. For example, IBM officials felt the company had been projecting too many images with its advertising divided among so many agencies. The consolidation enabled IBM to present a single brand identity across the world while taking advantage of one of the world's best-known brand names. Ogilvy & Mather's first global work for IBM was the popular "Solutions for a Small Planet" campaign, which delivered the message that IBM has solutions that are both simple and powerful enough to manage information anywhere, anytime, and for anyone. Recently the agency developed the award-winning "e-business" global campaign that has positioned IBM as the company to turn to for solutions to electronic commerce problems in the booming Internet era.

The Heinz CEO explained the consolidation move by saying, "It's the first time we're determining a positioning for ketchup so that we have a consistent message, much as Coca-Cola and McDonald's do world-wide." Nissan's consolidation grew out of a desire by the company's new chief operating officer to have one decision point for global account management and to build a global image for the automaker.

Companies are also consolidating their global advertising in an effort to increase efficiency and gain greater leverage over their agencies. Colgate notes that a major reason for its agency consolidation is to achieve greater cost efficiency. The company has moved into 25 new countries in recent years and its advertising spending has increased at a compounded rate of about 10 percent. The company feels consolidation will generate savings that can be invested in additional advertising.

3M's director of corporate advertising feels consolidation will help the company enhance its global competitive advantage in bringing new products to market quickly; the director notes, "Its difficult to roll out new products with one global voice when you have 25 different agencies." The chairman and CEO of Grey Advertising, 3M's agency, notes, "If a client wants to export a product it has already successfully launched in, say, the U.S., the client doesn't want to hire small agencies in country after country, each with their own egos who want to reinvent the creative."

Consolidation also gives advertisers greater leverage over their agencies. When a major client puts all its advertising with one agency, that company often becomes the agency's most important account. And, as one IBM executive notes, "You become a magnet for talent and attention."

Advertising executives also note that a major reason for all the account consolidation is that agencies now have the ability to communicate and manage globally. Fax machines, e-mail, and airline connections make it much easier to manage accounts around the globe. Of course, placing an entire global advertising account with one agency can be risky. If the agency fails to deliver an effective campaign, the client has no backup agency to make a fast rebound and the search for a new agency can be very time consuming. Clients that consolidate also face the problem of selling the idea to regional offices, which often previously enjoyed their own local agency relationships. However, it appears that more and more companies are willing to take these risks and rely on one agency to handle their advertising around the world.

Sources: Alice Z. Cuneo and Laura Petrecca, "Nissan Sizes up TBWA for $1 Billion Global Ad Prize," *Advertising Age,* December 6, 1999, pp. 1, 74; "Heinz Places Ketchup in Global Account," *The Wall Street Journal,* September 9, 1998, p. B10; Noreen O'Leary, "World Tours with a Single Client," *Adweek,* August 5, 1996, pp. 34–37; Sally Goll Beatty, "Young & Rubicam Is Only One for Colgate," *The Wall Street Journal,* December 1, 1995, p. B6; Kevin Goldman, "Global Companies Hone Agency Rosters," *The Wall Street Journal,* July 25, 1995, p. B8.

companies, creative capability was ranked the most important factor in selecting an advertising agency network, followed by understanding of the market, understanding of marketing goals, and ability to produce integrated communications. Size of the agency and agency reputation were cited as important criteria by less than 2 percent of the respondents.[77]

Some companies choose a combination of the three alternatives just discussed because their involvement in each market differs, as do the advertising environment and situation in each country. Several experts in international marketing and advertising advocate the use of international agencies by international companies, particularly those firms moving toward global marketing and striving for a consistent corporate or brand image around the world. The trend toward mergers and acquisitions and the formation of mega-agencies with global marketing and advertising capabilities suggests the international agency approach will become the preferred arrangement among large companies.

Advertising Research

Research plays the same important role in the development of international advertising and promotion programs that it does domestically—helping managers make better, more informed decisions. However, many companies do not conduct advertising research in international markets. Probably the main reason for this is the high cost of conducting research in foreign markets, coupled with the limited budgets many firms have for international advertising and promotion. When international markets represent a small percentage of overall sales, investments in research are difficult to justify. Rather than quality marketing information, generalizations based on casual observations of foreign markets have guided the promotional process.

As companies increase their investment in international marketing, they are recognizing the importance of conducting marketing and advertising research to better understand the characteristics and subtleties of consumers in foreign markets. There are a number of areas where research on foreign markets can help firms make better advertising decisions:

- Information on demographic characteristics of markets.
- Information on cultural differences such as norms, lifestyles, and values.
- Information on consumers' product usage, brand attitudes, and media preferences.

- Information on media usage and audience size.
- Copy testing to determine reactions to different types of advertising appeals and executions.
- Research on the effectiveness of advertising and promotional programs in foreign markets.

A great deal of information on international markets is available through secondary sources. One of the most valuable sources of information for companies based in this country is the U.S. Department of Commerce, which works closely with American companies to help them sell their products overseas through its International Trade Administration (ITA) division. The ITA publishes a series of *Overseas Business Reports* that provide valuable information on most major world markets, including economic and marketing data as well as laws and regulations. Information on markets is sometimes available from other countries' government agencies, embassies, or consulates. The Central Intelligence Agency (CIA) publishes the *World Fact Book,* which provides data on telephones, radios, television sets, and communication-satellite use for nearly every country in the world and usually updates its information annually. Circulation figures for the world's newspapers are published every year.

The *United Nations Statistical Yearbook,* which is published annually, provides demographic and economic data on more than 200 countries. Yearbooks and other reports are also available for regions such as Latin America, Europe, and Asia. Other international organizations that can provide valuable information on world markets include the International Monetary Fund and regional organizations like the Japanese External Trade Organization and the European Union. The World Bank's annual *World Development Reports* has many national statistics including per capita incomes, literacy rates, imports, exports, and a variety of other information.

Information on product and brand attitudes, usage patterns, and media habits is generally more difficult to find, particularly in developing countries. However, more information is becoming available. A. C. Nielsen has developed an international database that tracks purchase patterns of over 2,000 product classes in 25 countries, and Predicast has a foreign intelligence syndicated service. NCH Nù World Marketing Limited now collects information on coupon distribution and redemption patterns in the United States and a number of European countries (Exhibit 20–14). Data on media usage in European countries have increased tremendously over the past decade.[78] However, information on TV audiences is still lacking in many countries.

Exhibit 20–14 NCH Nù World is a source of information on coupon distribution and use in various countries

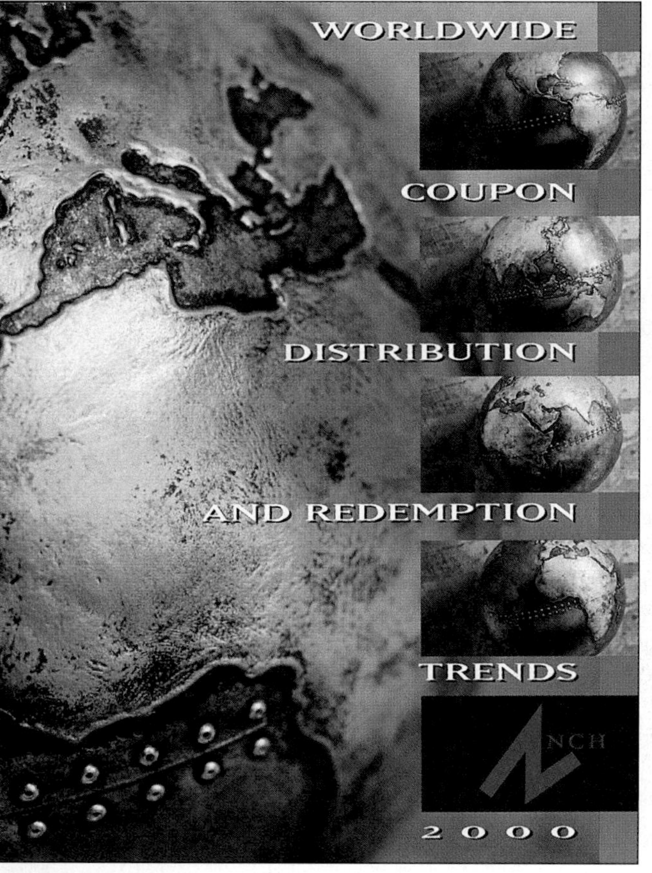

Much of the information advertisers need must be gathered from research generated by the company and/or ad agency. Consumer needs and wants, purchase motives, and usage patterns often vary from one country to another, and research is needed to understand these differences. Some companies and their agencies conduct psychographic research in foreign markets to determine activities, interests, and opinions as well as product usage patterns. A recent survey conducted by *Advertising Age International* and the research firm of Yankelovich, Clancy, Shulman looked at purchase habits and brand loyalty of consumers in the United Kingdom, France, and Germany. Consumers in all three countries said value for their money was the most important factor in their purchase decisions and were very open to buying products from other countries. The survey also found that consumers in the United Kingdom are most loyal to a brand.[79]

Global Perspective 20–3 discusses sources of information and specialized services available for companies that

Global Perspective 20–3

Integrated Marketing Communications North of the Border

If you ask people which nation is the largest trading partner of the United States, most are likely to name a European country or Japan. But Canada has been our largest trading partner for years, and the Canadian market has taken on even more importance with the passage of the North American Free Trade Agreement (NAFTA), which eliminated many of the trade barriers among the United States, Canada, and Mexico. And as more and more U.S. companies adopt the concept of integrated marketing communications, they are finding that the IMC approach works in the Canadian market as well as the U.S. market.

Companies hoping to use IMC in Canada will find that our northern neighbor has all the service technologies and message delivery systems needed to fully utilize this approach. Virtually every major U.S. ad agency has offices or affiliations in Canada. There are a number of excellent Canadian agencies throughout the country, which are particularly important in adapting IMC to the specialized needs of French Canada.

Direct marketing is becoming an integral part of successful IMC programs in Canada. Some direct marketers, knowledgeable about trends on both sides of the border, claim Canadians are not bombarded with as much direct mail as Americans. With less clutter in their mailboxes, Canadians respond better to mail solicitations. A number of companies provide special software and databases to target those of the Canada Post Corp.'s 25,000-plus mail walks that match a marketer's customer profile. There are also plenty of good mailing lists available. Much of the software used in the United States to support marketing databases can be used in Canada. Several U.S.-based database marketing companies have established a strong presence in Canada, and there are numerous Canadian direct-marketing agencies.

Canada offers broadcast and print media measurement services that closely resemble those used in the United States. For example, A. C. Nielsen and the Bureau of Broadcast Measurement in Toronto provide meter and diary results to subscribers for most broadcast programming, including U.S. stations that reach Canadians. PMB Print Measurement Bureau supplies national readership and product usage data in Canada and recently produced *The Canada/USA Report,* which compares Canadian and U.S. consumption in many product areas. For companies seeking information on the Canadian market, there are a number of professional survey research companies throughout Canada. Larger companies like Gallup of Canada and Market Facts of Canada offer syndicated tracking surveys similar to their U.S. counterparts. Canada's census bureau is also an excellent source of information. The bureau's *Statistics Canada's Survey of Family Expenditures* provides a wealth of detail on virtually all classes of consumer purchases across 17 metropolitan areas in Canada.

Canada has many demographic, cultural, and lifestyle diversities that must be recognized. Its 30.5 million people live in about 11 million households, and nearly 70 percent are within a two-hour drive of the U.S. border. About 40 percent of the Canadian population doesn't use English as its preferred language. Of the non-English speakers, about 60 percent are French Canadians, with the balance spread among a dozen or so other languages. Like the United States, Canada has seen the ethnic composition of its immigrants change. More than half of the country's immigrants now come from Asia and China in particular. By the year 2001, Canada's Chinese community will number nearly 1.2 million, with most settling in either Vancouver or Toronto. The Canadian Chinese are well educated, affluent, and easy to reach through Chinese-language media including TV, radio, and three major daily newspapers.

Companies doing business in Canada will find all the resources and services they need for customer-focused IMC. However, U.S. companies must not assume that Canadians are simply Americans living north of the 49th parallel and that what works in the United States should fit Canada. Canadians are different from their neighbors to the south and want that difference recognized. A major study was conducted recently comparing U.S. and Canadian consumers. The overall conclusion of the study was that there are many more differences between Canada and the United States than one would guess.

These differences in preference and consumption are driven by a number of factors such as disparities in income, especially after-tax disposable income, which is lower in Canada. Climatic conditions play a major role in creating differing leisure patterns, with winter activities such as skating and skiing being more popular in Canada. Differences in consumption are also driven by differences in the ethnic makeup of the two countries, as Canadians are more accepting of ethnic and cultural diversity. They also seem to be driven by a Canadian conservatism, in comparison with Americans, with respect to consuming new products and values such as materialism and conspicuous consumption. Americans think they are individual *because* of what they own; Canadians think they are individual *in spite of* what they own. It is important for marketers to understand these differences when marketing to Canadians.

Sources: Stephen Ferley, Tony Lea, and Barry Watson, "A Comparison of U.S. and Canadian Consumers," *Journal of Advertising Research,* September/October 1999, pp. 555–65; Stephen Barrington, "Canada Speaks to Chinese Markets," *Advertising Age International,* January 1997, pp. I12, 14; Jon Kalina, " 'Vive la Difference': Learning Trade North of the 49th Parallel," *Advertising Age International,* September 18, 1995, pp. i23, 30.

want to better understand and adapt their integrated marketing communications programs to the Canadian marketplace.

Advertisers should also research consumers' reactions to the advertising appeal and execution style they plan to use in foreign markets. One agency researcher recommends testing the basic premise and/or selling idea to be used in a global campaign first to be sure it is relevant to the target audiences in the markets where it will appear.[80]

Creative Decisions

Another decision facing the international advertiser is determining the appropriate advertising messages for each market. Creative strategy development for international advertising is basically similar in process and procedure to that for domestic advertising. Advertising and communications objectives should be based on the marketing strategy and market conditions in foreign markets. Major selling ideas must be developed and specific appeals and execution styles chosen.

An important factor in the development of creative strategy is the issue of global versus localized advertising. If the standardized approach is taken, the creative team must develop advertising that will transcend cultural differences and communicate effectively in every country. For example, Tropicana Products Inc. uses a global advertising campaign for its pure premium orange juice. Its ads, though tailored a bit for each market, stress the superior, nearly fresh-squeezed taste of its juice over local brands that are often reconstituted from concentrates.[81]

When companies follow a **localized advertising strategy,** the creative team must determine what type of selling idea, ad appeal, and execution style will work in each market. A product may have to be positioned differently in each market depending on consumers' usage patterns and habits. For example, General Foods found that in France, people drink very little orange juice and almost none at breakfast. Thus, when the company decided to market its Tang instant breakfast drink in France, the agency developed ads positioning the brand as a refreshment for any time of day rather than as a substitute for orange juice (the approach used in the United States).

Marketers must also figure out what type of advertising appeal or execution style will be most effective in each market. Emotional appeals such as humor may work well in one country but not in another because of differences in cultural backgrounds and consumer perceptions of what is or is not funny. While humorous appeals are popular in the United States and Britain, they are not used often in Germany, where consumers do not respond favorably to them. France, Italy, and Brazil are more receptive to sexual appeals and nudity in advertising than are most other societies.

International marketers sometimes find they can change consumer purchasing patterns by taking a creative risk. For example, Hãagen-Dazs broke through cultural barriers in Britain, where ice cream consumption is only a third as great as in the United States and consumers usually purchase low-grade, low-priced local brands. A sexy advertising campaign showing seminude couples feeding each other the ice cream helped get British consumers to pay premium prices for Hãagen-Dazs. The company also used an avant-garde billboard campaign in Japan showing a young couple kissing in public, a near-taboo. The posters were so popular that many were stolen[82] (Exhibit 20–15).

Another company that has used a creative promotion to change consumer purchase habits in a foreign market is Starbucks. In 1999 the Seattle-based coffee chain's United Kingdom subsidiary introduced its Frappuccino brand iced-coffee drink, which had been popular in the United States for several years, to Britain through the use of a humor-based promotional campaign. The drink was launched through ads based on "Billy," a mythical employee who comes up with the drink and is ridiculed by his co-workers for stupidity. The drink then becomes a success, and the newspaper, magazine, billboard, and transit ads that were used groveled with apologies, such as one acknowledging that the drink is "the work of a genius, not a loser." The promotion also was carried into the stores, as employees sported shirts pleading "Come Back Billy" and each store displayed a letter signed by every employee apologizing to Billy and asking him to return.[83]

Media Selection

One of the most challenging areas for international marketers is media strategy and selection. Companies generally find major differences in the media available outside their home markets, and media conditions may vary considerably from one country to another. In less developed countries such as Vietnam, Kenya, and Egypt, most consumers do not have contact with a marketer's advertising and promotion efforts until they enter a store. Packaging and other point-of-purchase elements, rather than media advertising, will have the greatest impact on purchase decisions. On the other hand, advertising bombards consumers in the more affluent countries of Europe, the Pacific Rim, and North America through a variety of print and broadcast as well as interactive media. Media planners face a number of problems in attempting to communicate advertising and promotional messages to consumers in

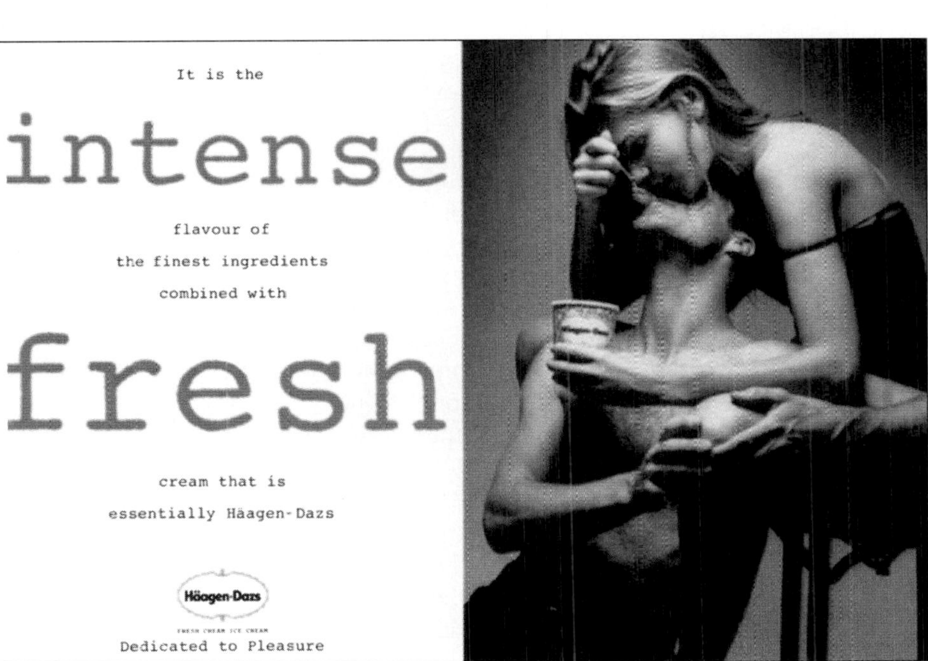

Exhibit 20–15 Häagen-Dazs used sexy ads to get attention in Britain

Career Profile

Jeffrey Beck

Vice President, Client Service Director at Vickers & Benson Direct and Interactive

I graduated from McGill University in Montreal with a BA in Economics and Political Science. I went on to graduate school and earned an MBA from Concordia University in Montreal with a concentration in marketing and finance. I then went to work for Air Canada as a strategy analyst. During my seven years at Air Canada I also worked as a manager of new product development and product manager for Europe, which involved being a liaison with European sales offices and managing a half-a-billion-dollar revenue budget. I was promoted to manager of direct marketing programs and cargo advertising, where my responsibilities included managing direct marketing programs with American Express in the U.S. and Europe and growing the airline's Aeroplan loyalty program. I was also the driving force behind the co-branded CIBC Aerogold Visa card becoming the number-one premium credit card in Canada.

"I understand the power of a strong brand."

I left Air Canada to join Gee, Jeffry and Partners Advertising, which had just won the Canadian airline's advertising account. I worked as an account supervisor and director of direct marketing, and was responsible for the development, execution, and implementation of the Canadian airline's new integrated marketing communications program. I then joined Vickers & Benson Direct and Interactive (VBDI). VBDI is one of Canada's fastest growing direct and interactive communications companies, committed to delivering online and offline solutions to build customer relationships. VBDI has won national and international marketing awards serving clients in sectors including finance, travel, retail, telecommunications, and e-commerce.

I joined VBDI as group account director with responsibility for the Canadian Tourism and British Airways accounts. I was subsequently promoted to my current position as Vice President, Client Services Director, where I am responsible for the profitability of VBDI's direct-marketing accounts. Most of my time involves general management of the direct agency, which includes staff hiring and training, budgeting, and strategic planning. I am also very active in new business development. I continue to oversee accounts where I am directly involved with senior clients, helping them formulate marketing strategy. I have expertise and a passion for developing relationship marketing programs by using various integrated marketing communication tools. I have also developed relationship marketing and IMC programs for clients such as Ralston Purina, British Airways, and Bell Express Vu.

My various positions on both the client and agency side of the business have helped me become a "complete marketer" with experience in advertising, direct marketing, strategic planning, customer loyalty management, new product development, and international marketing. I understand the power of a strong brand and the synergistic value of various integrated marketing communication tools such as advertising, direct marketing, and online/interactive marketing. My work has been recognized with a number of awards from various direct marketing associations in Canada, including the RSVP and Mobius Awards.

I really enjoy nurturing new talent within VBDI and teaching account executives how to incorporate strategic and integrated marketing communications thinking into every marketing challenge. I also enjoy having the opportunity to share my knowledge and experiences with students at Concordia University, where I have taught Management Strategy for seven years. My advice to students interested in a career in marketing communications is to never lose sight of the entire marketing mix. Synergy is truly derived by properly integrating brand and tactical activities through various communication channels.

various countries. First, the types of media available are different in different countries. Many homes in developing countries do not have TV sets. For example, in many South and Central African nations (such as Uganda, Tanzania, Kenya, and Zimbabwe), radio is the dominant medium and access to TV sets is very limited.[84] Vietnam's 71 million people own an estimated 7 million radios and 2.5 million television sets, and reported newspaper circulation is only 1.2 million copies. Outdoor advertising reaches the most Vietnamese (an estimated 14 million), followed by point-of purchase material, at 11 million.[85] Only one in three of the 151 million Russians has access to a television or radio, although Russians are better-educated than people in less developed nations and 26 million newspapers circulate throughout the country each day.

In some countries, TV advertising is not accepted or the amount of commercial time is severely limited. For example, in Germany, TV advertising is limited to 20 minutes a day on each of the government-owned channels (four 5-minute breaks) and banned on Sundays and holidays. Germany's privately-owned television stations, however, are permitted to devote up to 20 percent of their airtime to commercials. In the Netherlands, TV spots are limited to 5 percent of airtime and must be booked up to a year in advance. Programs also do not have fixed time slots for ads, making it impossible to plan commercial buys around desired programs. In some countries the limited number of channels and demand for commercial time result in extremely high levels of advertising clutter. Figure 20–4 shows one agency's estimate of the number of commercials shown per viewing hour in various countries around the world.

The number of TV sets is increasing tremendously, but there is still controversy over TV advertising. In India, for example, commercials are restricted to only 10 percent of programming time and must appear at the beginning or end of a program.[86] Australia just recently lifted a ban on cable TV advertising. However, some cable channels won't accept any advertising, and some media directors predict that Australian consumers will not tolerate as much advertising on cable channels as on free TV networks.[87]

The characteristics of media differ from country to country in terms of coverage, cost, quality of reproduction, restrictions, and the like. In some countries, media rates are negotiable or may fluctuate owing to unstable currencies, economic conditions, or government regulations. For example, in China TV stations charge a local rate for Chinese advertisers, a foreign rate, and a joint venture rate.[88]

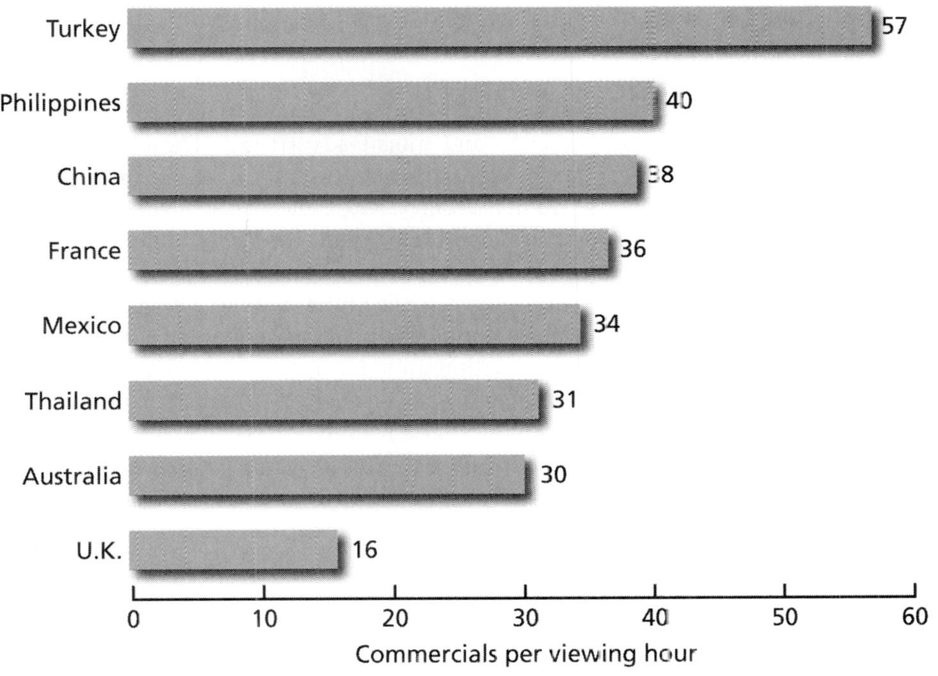

Figure 20–4 Commercials shown per hour in various countries

Another problem international advertisers face is obtaining reliable media information such as circulation figures, audience profiles, and costs. Many countries that had only state-owned TV channels are now experiencing a rapid growth in commercial channels, which is providing more market segmentation opportunities. However, reliable audience measurement data are not available, and media buyers often rely on their instincts when purchasing TV time. A number of research companies are developing audience measurement systems for countries in Eastern Europe, Russia, and China. In China, which has the largest television market in the world, with 300 million TV sets, A. C. Nielsen began using PeopleMeters in urban areas such as Shanghai and the southern city of Guangzhou. Television research also is available from China Sofres Media, a joint venture formed by the French company Sofres and the state-owned China Viewers Survey & Consulting Centre.[89] International advertising and television trade groups are also working to develop standardized measurement principles for global TV advertising.[90]

The goal of international advertisers is to select media vehicles that reach their target audience most effectively and efficiently. Media selection is often localized even for a centrally planned, globalized campaign. Local agencies or media buyers generally have more knowledge of local media and better opportunities to negotiate rates, and subsidiary operations can maintain control and adapt to media conditions and options in their market. Media planners have two options: using national or local media or using international media.

Local Media Many advertisers choose the local media of a country to reach its consumers. Print is the most used medium worldwide, since TV commercial time and the number of homes with TV sets are limited in many countries. Many countries have magazines that are circulated nationwide as well as national or regional newspapers that carry advertising directed to a national audience. Most countries also have magazines that appeal to special interests or activities, allowing for targeting in media selection.

Although restrictions and regulations have limited the development of TV as a dominant advertising medium in many countries, it is a primary medium for obtaining nationwide coverage in most developed countries and offers tremendous creative opportunities. Restrictions on television may be lessening in some countries, and time availability may increase. For example, the number of TV stations and television advertising in Italy have exploded in the past decade since government restrictions against private broadcasting were lifted. Advertising groups are using economic, legal, and political pressure to get more television commercial time from reluctant European governments. The increase in TV channels through direct broadcasting by satellite to many European households (discussed later in this section) is hastening this process.

In addition to print and television, local media available to advertisers include radio, direct mail, billboards, cinema, and transit advertising. These media give international advertisers great flexibility and the opportunity to reach specific market segments and local markets within a country. Most international advertisers rely heavily on national and local media in their media plans for foreign markets.

International Media The other way for the international advertiser to reach audiences in various countries is through international media that have multimarket coverage. The primary focus of international media has traditionally been magazines and newspapers. A number of U.S.-based consumer-oriented publications have international editions, including *Time, Newsweek, Reader's Digest,* and *National Geographic* as well as the newspaper *USA Today. Cosmopolitan* publishes 29 international editions that reach over 30 million readers in various countries (Exhibit 20–16). U.S.-based business publications with foreign editions include *Business Week, Fortune, Harvard Business Review,* and *The Wall Street Journal.*

International publications offer advertisers a way to reach large audiences on a regional or worldwide basis. Readers of these publications are usually upscale, high-income individuals who are desirable target markets for many products and services. There are, however, several problems with these international media that

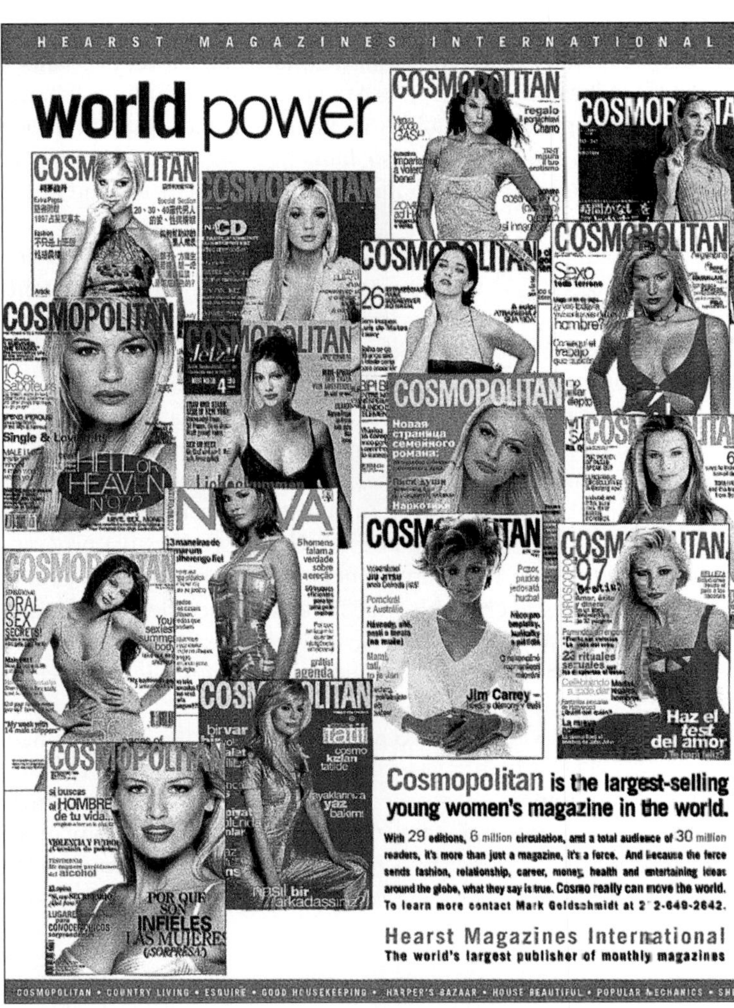

Exhibit 20–16 *Cosmopolitan* reaches women around the world with 29 international editions

can limit their attractiveness to many advertisers. Their reach in any one foreign country may be low, particularly for specific segments of a market. Also, while they deliver desirable audiences to companies selling business or upscale consumer products and services, they do not cover the mass consumer markets or specialized market segments very well. Other U.S.-based publications in foreign markets do offer advertisers ways to reach specific market segments.

While print remains the dominant medium for international advertising, many companies are turning their attention to international commercial TV. Package-goods companies in particular, such as Gillette, McDonald's, Pepsi, and Coca-Cola, view TV advertising as the best way to reach mass markets and effectively communicate their advertising messages. Satellite technology has helped spread the growth of cable TV in other countries and made global television networks a reality.

A major development affecting broadcasting in Europe, Asia, and Latin America is **direct broadcast by satellite (DBS)** to homes and communities equipped with small, low-cost receiving dishes. A number of satellite networks operate in these regions and beam entertainment programming across several countries. For example, media baron Rupert Murdoch's News Corp. owns 40 percent of British Sky Broadcasting (BSkyB), which was formed by the merger of Sky Television and British Satellite Broadcasting and beams 40 channels to 6 million subscribers in the United Kingdom. In 1993 News Corp. purchased Satellite Television Asian Region (STAR TV), which beams 15 advertising-supported channels and nine subscription movie channels to over 60 million Asian households, hotels, and restaurants equipped with satellite dishes. STAR TV has a potential market of 3 billion people (two-thirds of the world's population) as satellite dishes become more common in this region.[91] In 1996 Star entered into a partnership with two Hong Kong companies to launch the Phoenix Satellite Television Co. Along with airing reruns of popular American shows, the

Mandarin-language Phoenix channel offers a mix of locally produced sports, news, and talk shows. Phoenix has greater reach in China than any other foreign channel, particularly among upscale, educated viewers in urban areas such as Beijing, Shanghai, and Guangzhou. The favorable demographics make the channel popular among blue-chip advertisers.[92] In 1996 News Corp. also launched Sky Entertainment in Brazil and Mexico and expects to have nearly 5 million subscribers by the end of the decade in Brazil alone.[93]

The main incentive to the growth of these satellite networks has been the severely limited program choices and advertising opportunities on government-controlled stations in many countries. However, many European and Asian governments are moving to preserve cultural values and protect advertising revenues from going to foreign-based networks. In India, for example, advertising revenue has been shifting to ISkyB, a subsidiary of STAR TV, from Doordarshan, the state-run television network.[94] The Indian government is considering legislation that would regulate foreign satellite channels and advertisers and favor the Doordarshan. India's minister for information and broadcasting says foreign satellite channels are a threat to India's cultural fabric and should be curbed. He cites offensive program content and the amount of nudity on foreign channels as reasons why the Indian government needs to regulate satellite channels. In China, most people are officially barred from receiving foreign satellite broadcasts, but millions do anyway from unauthorized cable operators or through their satellite dishes. In 1999 the government did begin enforcing the ban, particularly in Beijing, but the Phoenix channel remains popular among Chinese viewers who want more options than China's state-run television.[95]

Advances in satellite and communications technology, the expansion of multinational companies with global marketing perspectives, and the development of global ad agencies mean advertisers' use of television as a global medium is likely to increase.

The Roles of Other Promotional Mix Elements in International Marketing

This chapter has focused on advertising, since it is usually the primary element in the promotional mix of the international marketer. However, as in domestic marketing, promotional programs for foreign markets generally include such other elements as sales promotion, personal selling, public relations, and websites on the Internet. The roles of these other promotional mix elements vary depending on the firm's marketing and promotional strategy in foreign markets.

Sales promotion and public relations can support and enhance advertising efforts; the latter may also be used to create or maintain favorable images for companies in foreign markets. For some firms, personal selling may be the most important promotional element and advertising may play a support role. This final section considers the roles of some of these other promotional mix elements in the international marketing program.

Sales Promotion

Sales promotion activity in international markets is growing due in part to the transfer of promotion concepts and techniques from country to country and in part to the proliferation of media. The growth also stems from the liberalization of trade, the rise of global brands, the spread of cable and satellite TV, and the deregulation and/or privatization of media. Sales promotion and direct-response agencies have been becoming more common, particularly in Europe and more recently in South American, Asian, and Middle Eastern countries. In many less developed countries, spending on sales promotion often exceeds media spending on TV, radio, and print ads.[96]

As we saw in Chapter 16, sales promotion is one of the fastest-growing areas of marketing in the United States. Companies increasingly rely on consumer- and trade-oriented sales promotion to help sell their products in foreign markets as well. Many of the promotional tools that are effective in the United States, such as free samples, premiums, event sponsorships, contests, coupons, and trade promotions, are also used in foreign markets. For example, Häagen-Dazs estimates it gave out more than 5 million free tastings of its ice cream as part of its successful strategy for entering the European market. Since taste is the major benefit of this premium product, sampling was an appropriate sales promotion tool for entering foreign markets.

A form of sales promotion that has become very popular in foreign markets is event sponsorship. Many companies sponsor sporting events, concerts, and other activities in foreign countries to promote their products and enhance corporate image. For example, aiming at an upscale international audience, Compaq Computer recently spent more than $7 million to sponsor rock star Sting's 80-city "Brand New Day" tour. The company also used the singer as the centerpiece of a worldwide advertising campaign, and he appeared in ads showing how he uses computers to compose and arrange music.[97] Visa sponsors World Cup Cricket matches as part of its promotional strategy for introducing its credit card to India; MasterCard, Gillette, and Canon sponsor Asian soccer.[98]

Unlike advertising, which can be done on a global basis, sales promotions must be adapted to local markets. Kamran Kashani and John Quelch noted several important differences among countries that marketers must consider in developing a sales promotion program.[99] They include the stage of economic development, market maturity, consumer perceptions of promotional tools, trade structure, and legal restrictions and regulations:

- *Economic development.* In highly developed countries such as the United States, Canada, Japan, and Western European nations, marketers can choose from a wide range of promotional tools. But in developing countries they must be careful not to use promotional tools such as in- or on-package premiums that would increase the price of the product beyond the reach of most consumers. Free samples and demonstrations are widely used, effective promotional tools in developing countries. But coupons, which are so popular with consumers in the United States, are rarely used because of problems with distribution and resistance from retailers. In the United States and Britain, most coupons are distributed through newspapers (including FSIs) or magazines. Low literacy rates in some countries make print media an ineffective coupon distribution method, so coupons are delivered door to door, handed out in stores, or placed in or on packages. Figure 20–5 shows the total number of coupons redeemed in various countries in 1998.

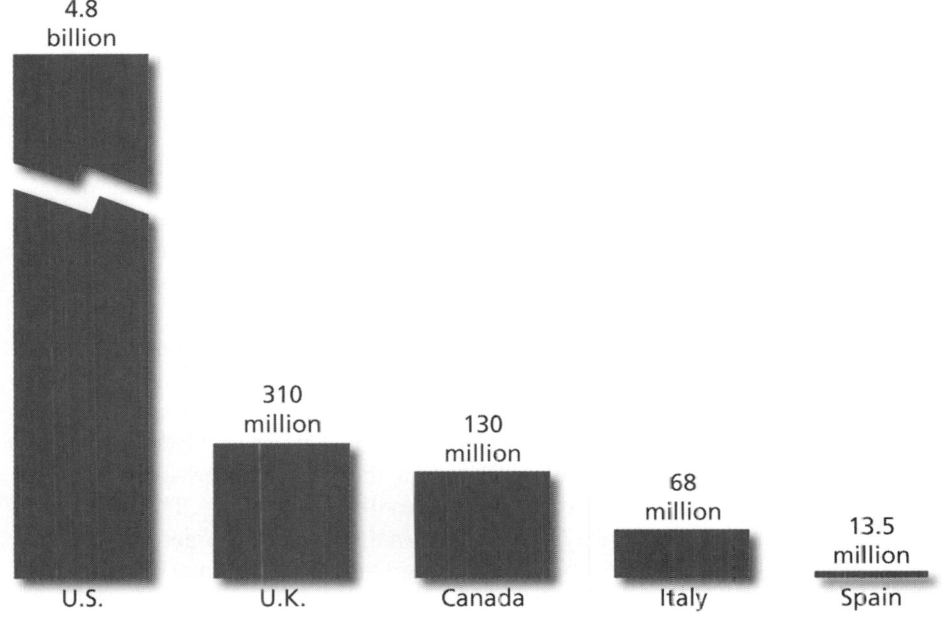

Figure 20–5 Number of coupons redeemed in various countries

- *Market maturity.* Marketers must also consider the stage of market development for their product or service in various countries when they design sales promotions. To introduce a product to a country, consumer-oriented promotional tools such as sampling, high-value coupons, and cross-promotions with established products and brands are often effective. The competitive dynamics of a foreign market are also often a function of its stage of development. More competition is likely in well-developed mature markets, which will influence the types of sales promotion tools used. For example, there may be competitive pressure to use trade allowances to maintain distribution or consumer promotions that will maintain customer loyalty, such as bonus packs, price-off deals, or coupons.
- *Consumer perceptions.* An important consideration in the design of sales promotion programs is how they are perceived by consumers as well as the trade. Consumer perceptions of various sales promotion tools vary from market to market. For example, Japanese women are less likely to take advantage of contests, coupons, or other promotions than are women in the United States.[100] Premium offers in particular must be adapted to the tastes of consumers in various markets. A recent study by Huff and Alden examined consumers' opinions toward the use of coupons and sweepstakes in three Asian countries: Taiwan, Malaysia, and Thailand. The study found differences among the three countries with consumers in Taiwan having more negative attitudes and lower levels of use of both sweepstakes and coupons than consumers in Malaysia and Thailand.[101]
- *Trade structure.* In areas with highly concentrated retailing systems, such as northern Europe, the trade situation is becoming much like the United States and Canada as pressure grows for more price-oriented trade and in-store promotions. In southern Europe, the retail industry is highly fragmented and there is less trade pressure for promotions. The willingness and ability of channel members to accommodate sales promotion programs must also be considered. Retailers in many countries do not want to take time to process coupons, post promotional displays, or deal with premiums or packaging that require special handling or storage. In countries like Japan or India, where retailing structures are highly fragmented, stores are too small for point-of-purchase displays or in-store sampling.
- *Regulations.* An important factor affecting the use of sales promotions in foreign countries is the presence of legal restrictions and regulations. Laws affecting sales promotions are generally more restrictive in other countries than in the United States. Some countries ban contests, games, or lotteries, while others restrict the size or amount of a sample, premium, or prize. For example, fair-trade regulations in Japan limit the maximum value of premiums to 10 percent of the retail price; in France the limit is 5 percent. Canada prohibits games of pure chance unless a skill element is used to determine the winner. In Japan the amount of a prize offer is limited to a certain percentage of the product tied to the promotion.[102] In some countries, a free premium must be related to the nature of the product purchased. Many countries have strict rules when it comes to premium offers for children, and some ban them altogether. The appendix at the end of this chapter shows the restrictions on various sales promotion tools in a number of different countries.

  Variations in rules and regulations mean marketers must often develop separate consumer sales promotion programs for each country. Many companies have found it difficult to do any promotions throughout Europe because sales promotion rules differ so from one country to another. While the treaty on European Union may result in a more standardized legal environment in Europe, laws regarding sales promotion are still likely to vary. This is why many companies use local agencies or international sales promotion companies to develop sales promotion programs for foreign markets.

Management of Sales Promotion in Foreign Markets Although sales promotion programs of multinational companies have traditionally been managed locally, this is changing somewhat as marketers create global brands. Many global marketers recognize the importance of giving local managers the autonomy to design and execute their own sales promotion programs. However, the ways local promotions influence and contribute to global brand equity must also be considered.

Kashani and Quelch developed a framework for analyzing the role of centralized (headquarters) versus local management in sales promotion decisions based on various stages of globalization (Figure 20–6). This model suggests headquarters' influence will be greatest for global brands and least for local brands. Since global brands require uniformity in marketing communications, the promotional program should be determined at the headquarters level. Decisions regarding overall promotional strategy—including international communications objectives, positioning, allocation of the communications budget to sales promotion versus advertising, and weight of consumer versus trade promotions—are made at the headquarters level.[103]

While the promotional strategy for global brands is determined by global product managers at headquarters, implementation of the programs should be left to local management. It is important to make the promotional strategy broad enough to allow for differences in diverse local markets. Headquarters is also responsible for encouraging the cross-fertilization of ideas and practices among local managers and facilitating the transfer of information.

Regional brands usually do not require the same level of standardization as global brands, and the promotional strategy can be developed by regional offices and carried out at the local level. However, regional promotions should avoid contradictory brand communications and promotional activities that might upset local activities in nearby markets. The role of national-level brand managers is adoption and adaptation. They determine what promotional ideas to adopt from the region and adapt them to local conditions.

For local brands, decisions regarding promotional strategy, program design, and execution are left to local managers. Of course, local managers may benefit from information about the promotions used in other local markets.

Personal Selling

As a company's most direct contact with its customers in foreign markets, personal selling is an important part of the marketing and promotional process. Companies selling industrial and high-tech products generally rely heavily on personal selling

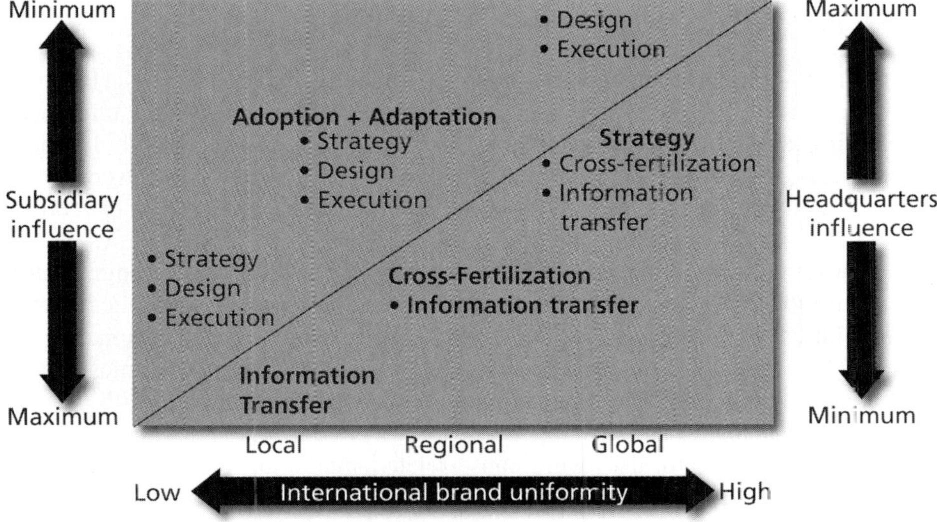

Figure 20–6 Central versus local roles in international sales promotion

as the primary method for communicating with their customers, internationally as well as domestically. Consumer products firms may also use personal selling to call on distributors, wholesalers, or major retailing operations in foreign markets. Due to low wages in many developing countries, some companies hire large sales staffs to perform missionary activities and support selling and advertising efforts. For example, Citibank launched its credit cards in many Asian countries using a multi-faceted marketing program that included advertising, direct mail, and personal selling. The company found personal selling a very focused and cost-effective way to reach prospective credit-card applicants in countries such as India, Malaysia, and Thailand. Citibank captured 40 percent of Thailand's credit-card market, relying primarily on a sales force of 600 part-timers who were paid a fee for each applicant approved.[104]

Because it involves personal contact and communication, personal selling is generally even more culture bound than advertising. So most companies use sales reps from the host country and adapt personal selling activities and sales programs to each market. Management of the sales force is usually decentralized to the local subsidiaries, although the international marketer sets the general sales policy and advises foreign managers on the role personal selling should play in their market, the development of the sales program, and various aspects of sales management.

Public Relations

Many companies involved in international marketing are recognizing the importance of using public relations to support and enhance their marketing and advertising efforts.[105] Public relations activities are needed to deal with local governments, media, trade associations, and the general public, any of which may feel threatened by the presence of a foreign multinational. The job of PR agencies in foreign markets is not only to help the company sell its products or services but also to present the firm as a good corporate citizen concerned about the future of the country.

Companies generally need a favorable image to be successful in foreign markets. Those perceived negatively may face pressure from the media, local governments, or other relevant publics, or even boycotts by consumers. Often, public relations is needed to deal with specific problems a company faces in international markets. For example, NutraSweet had problems getting its low-calorie sweetener into some markets because of strong sugar lobbies in Australia, Canada, and Europe. These lobbies encouraged the foreign press to pick up some unfavorable news about the product from the U.S. media. The company retained Burson-Marsteller, the second-largest PR company in the world, to help design factual ads about the product and to conduct other PR activities to counter the problems and get the facts out about NutraSweet. Global Perspective 20–4 discusses major public relations problems McDonald's and Coca-Cola faced recently in Europe.

Public relations can play an important role in helping companies pursue business in foreign markets. Acustar, Inc., a U.S. automotive component manufacturer, used its PR firm to increase its visibility before negotiating contracts with Japanese automakers. The PR campaign included an executive reception to introduce the company and its products, press interviews, and presentations to senior executives of several Japanese car manufacturers. The PR firm also distributed a news release to Japanese news media before the Acustar executives' visit and arranged interviews with the company's chair for the leading business and trade publications in Japan. Stories about Acustar appeared in more than 10 national and regional newspapers, *The Asian Wall Street Journal,* two TV networks, and several domestic publications. The PR campaign helped the company win contracts with several Japanese auto manufacturers.[106]

Some companies are also using cause-related marketing to develop stronger relations with consumers in foreign markets. For example, Microsoft recently launched a website in Singapore that tied the number of visits to the site to charity

Global Perspective 20–4

American Icons Face Public Relations Problems in Europe

One of the challenges facing multinational companies operating in foreign markets is that various groups such as consumers, government, the media, and other relevant publics may feel threatened by their presence. Resentment and concerns over their presence in a country can make public relations problems and crisis situations even more difficult for a multinational company, as McDonald's and Coca-Cola recently learned after encountering major public relations problems in Europe.

McDonald's has been receiving negative publicity from ongoing anti-American protests by angry French farmers. The farmers' movement was triggered by a World Trade Organization ruling ordering Europe to accept hormone-fed beef produced in the United States. The French farmers rejected the WTO decision and are equally opposed to sanctions the United States has imposed on a host of imported French foods, including Roquefort cheese, truffles, and Dijon mustard. The farmers' protests have included the dumping of tons of animal manure and rotting vegetables at McDonald's restaurants all over France and have attracted mass-media attention in the country.

Initially McDonald's took a low-key approach to the protest, declining to press charges for vandalism against its restaurants and placing posters in its restaurants explaining how McDonald's is a major partner of the French agricultural sector. However, in the fall of 1999 McDonald's France began countering the negative publicity by launching a "Made in France" corporate advertising campaign in 60 regional daily newspapers across the country. The ads inform consumers that while its brand may be American, the products served in France's 750 McDonald's outlets are French in origin. The ads underscore McDonald's policy of buying French products and its role in France's agricultural sector, while thanking consumers who have remained loyal. In response to the farmers' concerns, McDonald's also began substituting locally produced specialties targeted by the U.S. sanctions, such as duck breast and Roquefort cheese, for traditional ingredients in the company's Big Mac and cheeseburger menu items.

Coca-Cola has been dealing with a severe public relations crisis in Europe since June 1999, when several hundred Belgians, many of them schoolchildren, became ill after drinking Coke products. After Belgium and Luxembourg quickly banned all Coca-Cola products, the company traced the problem to bad carbon dioxide in its Antwerp, Belgium, bottler and to traces of fungicide on wooden pallets used in its Dunkirk, France, canning facility. France and the Netherlands then banned the sale of any products that came from those plants, and health ministers in other European countries issued warnings to consumers, even though Coke did not ship products to these countries from the plants in question.

In response to the crisis Coca-Cola ran full-page newspaper ads from its chairman in the countries where the company had to withdraw its products, apologizing for the quality-control problem. However, the media criticized the company's chairman at the time, Douglas Ivester, for not stepping forward and becoming involved in the handling of the crisis. In the ads apologizing for the problem Ivester acknowledged, "I should have spoken to you earlier." Facing a public relations crisis of global dimensions, Coca-Cola retained the European advertising and PR firm Publics, which had experience in handling crisis management situations for European companies such as Nestlé, Perrier, and Heineken.

Publics worked closely with executives at Coke's Atlanta headquarters to develop communication strategies and handle contacts with the media. When the ban on Coca-Cola products was lifted in Belgium, Coke and Publics hired several hundred thousand people to deliver vouchers and coupons for one free family-size bottle of Coke to each of the country's 4.4 million homes. The program was backed by newspaper ads developed by Publics. In France an existing commercial made by Coke's U.S. agency and adapted for France with the catchline

"Today more than ever, we thank you for your loyalty" was aired. In Poland newspaper ads were run guaranteeing the integrity of locally produced Coke products.

The crisis resulted in a drop of up to 7 percent in the number of unit cases sold in Europe during the second quarter of 1999. Coca-Cola gets a quarter of its sales revenue from greater Europe, and the financial impact of the crisis lingered into the third quarter of 1999 as well. Surveys have shown that Coca-Cola is the world's most valuable brand, and public relations experts have suggested that its brand equity will carry the company through the crisis. However, in the process the Coca-Cola Company has learned that even the most powerful brand in the world is not immune from a crisis.

Sources: Larry Speer, "McD's Self Defense Is Its French Connection," *Advertising Age*, September 13, 1999, p. 26; "Coke Marshals Forces after Crisis in Europe," *Advertising Age International*, July 1999, p. 3; Patricia Sellers, "Crunch Time for Coke," *Fortune*, July 19, 1999, pp. 72–78.

(Exhibit 20–17).[107] For every page hit within the Microsoft site (www.you-can-do-more.com.sq), the company donated one cent to three local charities, while showcasing inspirational stories about informational technology. The goal was to donate 3.5 million cents in total, one for each Singapore resident. The campaign culminated in a charity day when all the one-cent pieces were thrown into Singapore's Fountain of Wealth and a check was given to the local charities. The website was promoted with banner ads on other popular websites in Singapore as well as with print ads in newspapers and magazines. Visitors to the site were asked to nominate people for whom information technology has made a difference, and some of these stories were made into full-page print ads.

Like advertising, public relations is becoming more of a global activity. Like ad agencies, PR firms are merging with and/or acquiring overseas offices so clients can use one firm to communicate with appropriate parties all over the world.

The Internet

Worldwide Growth of the Internet

The Internet is coming of age as a global marketing medium and is becoming an important IMC tool for companies around the world, both large and small. Marketers are using the Internet to promote their companies, build their brands, and engage in e-commerce transactions in their own countries as well as across borders. As more homes and offices become connected to the Internet, its importance as an integrated marketing communications tool and way of transacting business will increase tremendously for companies selling consumer products and services as well as business-to-business marketers.

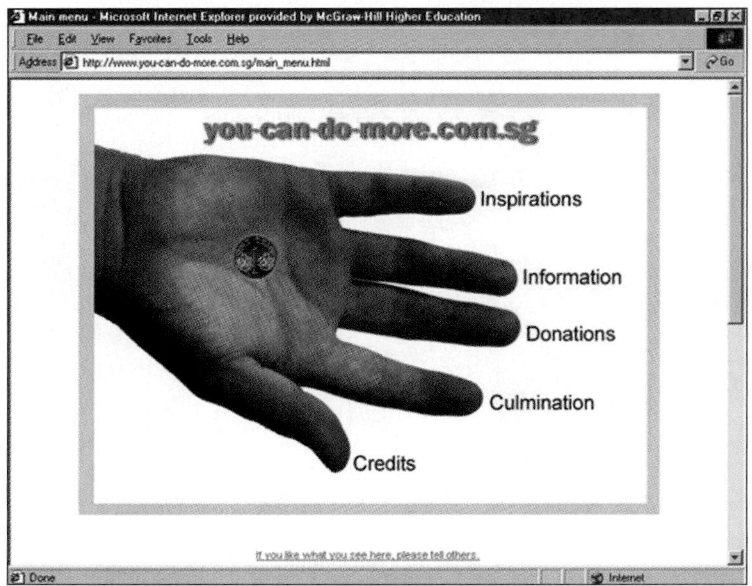

Exhibit 20–17 This ad was part of a cause-related marketing campaign used by Microsoft

During its formative years the Internet has largely been a North American phenomenon. English is the language used at 78 percent of all websites and 96 percent of all e-commerce sites, even though it is the primary language of only 8 percent of the world's population. By the end of the 90s nearly 54 percent of all online users were in North America, with most being in the United States. However, as can be seen in Figure 20–7, this is about to change, as Internet penetration is growing rapidly in other parts of the world. By the year 2002 it is estimated that there will be 61 million users in Asia/Pacific Rim, 84 million in Europe, and over 26 million in Latin America.[108]

While the use of the Internet around the globe continues to grow, there is tremendous variation in consumer usage as well as the level of marketing activity occurring on the World Wide Web. In the Asia/Pacific region, Internet use is high in places such as Hong Kong, Thailand, and Singapore. All three markets have considerable numbers of upscale users and several domestic service providers. By contrast, in India personal computer penetration is only 8 percent, and just 40 percent of the 750,000 households with PCs have Internet access.[109] The number of Internet users in China is expected to increase to 9.4 million by 2002, an increase of 571 percent from 1997, when the country had only 1.4 million users.[110] The number of Internet users in Latin

Figure 20–7 Number of Internet users in various regions

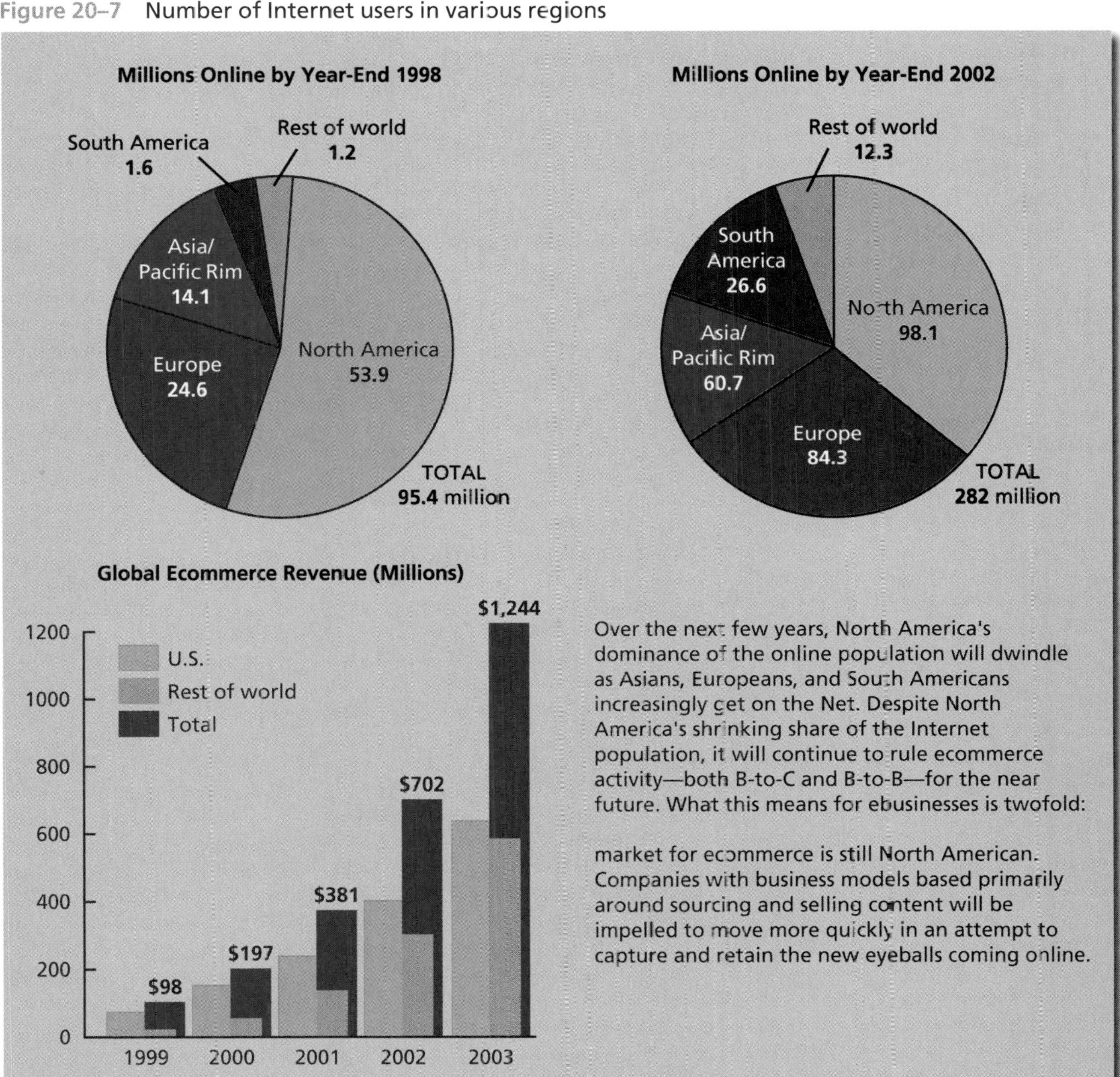

Exhibit 20–18 IBM offers country-specific information in several languages on its website

America is also growing rapidly, and the region is becoming one of the fastest-growing e-commerce markets in the world. However, factors such as unreliable delivery services, low usage of credit cards, security concerns, and customs duties are likely to be daunting obstacles to the growth of e-commerce in the region.[111]

Use of the Internet in International Marketing The use of the Internet as an IMC tool by companies in various countries is increasing as more marketers learn how to develop and maintain websites and improvements in the systems and technologies needed to support these sites occur. Many multinational companies are using the Internet to support their advertising and promotional programs. Anheuser-Busch, PepsiCo, Swatch, Lands' End, and Nike are among the global advertisers that are using mass-media advertising to drive consumers to their websites and provide them with detailed information about their products and services, encourage them to participate in online promotions, or allow them to make purchases.[112] A number of global business-to-business marketers such as Dell Computer, Nortel Networks, Xerox, and Hewlett-Packard are using websites to provide customers with information and conduct business with them. IBM has a multicultural website that offers country-specific information in several languages including Japanese (Exhibit 20–18).

As the digital revolution continues, marketers will be making greater use of the Internet in their global as well as local IMC programs. However, they will also face some challenges with respect to the way they approach global marketing and branding. As more consumers worldwide have access to the same information and same brands via the World Wide Web, many marketers will have to rethink their strategies of producing the same product under different names and tailoring promotions to local markets. It is predicted that marketers will use more global brands and promotional campaigns to take advantage of the worldwide exposure that will be available through the Internet.[113]

Summary

Many U.S. companies are recognizing not only the opportunities but also the necessity of marketing their products and services internationally because of saturated markets and intense competition from both domestic and foreign competitors. Advertising and promotion are important parts of the international marketing program of a multinational corporation. Advertising is generally the most cost-effective way to communicate with buyers and create a market in other countries.

International marketers must carefully analyze the major environmental forces in each market where they compete, including economic, demographic, cultural, and political/legal factors. These factors are important not only in assessing the potential of each country as a market but also in designing and implementing advertising and promotional programs.

In recent years, much attention has focused on global marketing, where a standard marketing program is used in all markets. Part of global marketing is global advertising, where the same basic advertising approach is used in all markets. Opponents of the global (standardized) approach argue that differences in culture, market and economic conditions, and consumer needs and wants make a universal approach to marketing and advertising impractical. Many companies use an in-between approach, standardizing their basic marketing strategy but localizing advertising messages to fit each market.

There are a number of important decision areas in the development of advertising and promotional programs for international markets. These include organization, agency selection, advertising research, creative strategy and execution, and media strategy and selection.

Sales promotion, personal selling, public relations, and Internet websites are also part of the promotional mix of international marketers. Sales promotion programs usually must be adapted to local markets. Factors to consider include stage of market development, market maturity, consumer perceptions of promotional tools, trade structure, and legal restrictions and regulations. Personal selling is the most important element of some companies' international marketing programs, since it is their main form of contact with foreign customers. PR programs are also important to help international marketers develop and maintain favorable relationships with governments, media, and consumers in foreign countries. The use of the Internet as a marketing tool varies by region. In many countries, there are few Internet users and few local companies with websites. But as the number of consumers online grows, so too does the number of large international marketers using the Internet to support their ad campaigns.

Key Terms

balance-of-trade deficit, 674
economic infrastructure, 676
cultural values, 679
global marketing, 683
global advertising, 683
pattern advertising, 689
localized advertising strategy, 698
direct broadcast by satellite (DBS), 703

Discussion Questions

1. The opening vignette describes how many large companies are using global advertising to develop their products and services into global brands that have a consistent image throughout the world. Discuss some of the reasons why companies such as Saab, Polaroid, Heinz, and others are using global branding campaigns.

2. Why are international markets becoming so important to U.S. companies such as Nike, McDonald's, and Coca-Cola, as well as to European companies such as Nestlé, Unilever, and Nokia? Discuss the role of advertising and other forms of promotion in these companies' international marketing programs.

3. Discuss the importance of the economic environment in evaluating a foreign market and how economic conditions and factors impact the type of integrated marketing communications program a company can use in various countries.

4. What are some of the cultural variables that are important in the development of advertising and promotional programs in various countries? Choose one of these cultural variables and discuss a specific example of how it has created a problem or challenge to an advertiser developing advertising in a foreign market.

5. Global Perspective 20–1 discusses how the New Balance 576 model running shoe has become very popular as a fashion brand in France. Do you think New Balance can maintain the popularity of its shoes as a fashion brand in the French market? What risk might this pose for the company regarding its positioning as a manufacturer of high-quality running shoes, both in France and in other countries?

6. Evaluate the arguments both for and against the use of global marketing and advertising, and discuss the types of products and services that lend themselves to global advertising. What developments have taken place in recent years that support the use of global advertising and what factors might make this approach more difficult to use effectively?

7. Discuss the concept of a global market segment. Provide several examples of companies that advertise their products and services the same way around the world to a global market segment.

8. Global Perspective 20–2 discusses how many large multinational companies are consolidating all of their worldwide advertising with one large agency. Evaluate the pros and cons of this approach.

9. What are some of the criteria a marketer can use in evaluating and selecting an agency to handle its international advertising and promotion programs? How might these factors differ for a large versus a smaller company?

10. What are some of the problems international marketers face in developing media strategies for foreign markets?

11. Discuss the various factors that marketers must consider in developing a sales promotion program in different countries.

12. Global Perspective 20–4 discusses the public relations problems McDonald's has been facing in France and the PR crisis Coca-Cola encountered in Europe during the summer of 1999. Evaluate the measures each company used to respond to its public relations problem in Europe.

Appendix C

Promoting Overseas: What's Legal and What's Not

The information contained in this chart has been abbreviated and is for general purposes only. If you're planning to run a promotion in any of these countries, be sure to contact the appropriate legal counsel in each country for more specific details on the restrictions there. You'll find a list of some promotion attorneys in this report, or you can contact www.gala-adlaw.com or one of the featured associations for additional information.

Country	Premiums	Home-Deliv. Coupons	Mail-Deliv. Coupons	Games	Contests
Argentina	Legal	Not in use.	Not in use.	Legal	Legal (if proof of purchase is required, free option must be fixed)
Australia	Legal	Legal, but third parties cannot put together coupon books or coupons from groups of companies.	Legal, but third parties cannot put together coupon books or coupons from groups of companies.	Legal	Legal
Belgium	Legal, but with many restrictions. Value may not exceed 5% of the main product value.	Legal	Legal	Legal, but not when linked with purchase.	Legal, but not when linked with purchase.
Brazil	Legal, very popular.	Legal, but not popular.	Legal, but not popular.	Legal, very popular. If requiring purchase or based on chance, approval from Consumer Defense Dept. required.	Legal, very popular. If requiring purchase or based on chance, approval from Consumer Defense Dept. required.
Chile	Legal	Not in use.	Not in use.	Legal	Legal
Columbia	Legal	Legal	Legal	Legal, but games based on chance or luck require authorization.	Legal, but contests based on chance or luck require authorization.
England	Legal	Legal	Legal	Subject to compliance with Lotteries & Amusements Act.	Subject to compliance with Lotteries & Amusements Act.
Finland	Legal, if gift has very small value or there is an evident material connection between the goods or services offered.	Legal, except coupons having a combined offer or connected to purchase, or containing illegal sweeps or lotteries.	Legal, except coupons having a combined offer or connected to purchase, or containing illegal sweeps or lotteries.	Legal, when based on skill, purchase can be required. When based on chance, free method of entry is required.	Legal, when based on skill, purchase can be required. When based on chance, free method of entry is required.
France	Legal, if gift has a very small value or is identical to the good purchased. Usually not allowed when the premium is free.	Legal, but only when offering discount on same product. Cross coupons forbidden.	Legal, but only when offering discount on same product. Cross coupons forbidden.	Legal, but must be absolutely free and not connected to a purchase.	Legal, but prize promotion must be skill, absolutely free, and not connected to a purchase.
Germany	Buy one get one free not allowed.	Legal, only for product samples. Price-off coupons not allowed.	Legal, only for product samples. Price-off coupons not allowed.	Legal, mechanics must be checked before practiced.	Legal, mechanics must be checked before practiced.

Sweeps	Rebates/ Refunds/	Gift W/ Purchase	Database Marketing	Product Sampling
Legal	Legal	Legal	Legal	Legal
Permit sometimes required. All states require compliance with special laws.	Legal	Legal	Legal, but state privacy laws shortly anticipated.	Legal, except therapeutics.
Usually not allowed.	Legal, but with many restrictions and conditions.	Legal, but with many restrictions and conditions.	Legal	Legal
Legal, very popular. If requiring purchase or based on chance, approval from Consumer Defense Dept. required.	Legal, but not popular.	Legal, popular.	Legal, very popular. Mail must be discontinued at receiver's request.	Legal, very popular.
Legal	All consumers must have the same discount based on volume bought.	Legal	Legal, but consumer can request to have names removed from database.	Legal
Legal, but sweeps based on chance or luck require authorization.	Legal, but not popular.	Legal	Legal	Legal
Subject to compliance with Lotteries & Amusements Act. Free prize draws & instant win must allow free entry.	Legal	Legal	Legal	Legal, but some restrictions on alcohol, tobacco, medicines, solvents, and some food.
Legal, when based on skill, purchase can be required. When based on chance, free method of entry is required.	Legal	Legal, if gift has very small value or there is an evident material connection between the goods or services offered.	Legal, with many restrictions.	Legal, some restrictions.
Legal, but must be absolutely free and not connected to a purchase.	Legal	Legal, if gift has a very small value or is identical to the good purchased. Usually not allowed when the premium is free.	Legal	Legal
Legal, should be checked with lawyer.	Legal, only to 3% maximum.	Usually not allowed. Some small-value giveaways are allowed. Lawyers usually can find a way around the law.	Legal, but consumer must consent first.	Usually legal when only samples are used. No regular original retail products.

Country	On-Pack Premiums	On-Pack Coupons	In-Pack Premiums	In-Pack Coupons	Near-Pack Premiums
Argentina	Legal	Not in use.	Legal	Not in use.	Legal
Australia	Legal	Legal, third party trading stamps not a problem.	Legal	Legal	Legal
Belgium	Legal, but with many restrictions.	Legal, but only when offering discount on same product. Cross coupons forbidden.	Legal, but with many restrictions.	Legal, but only when offering discount on same product. Cross coupons forbidden.	Legal, but with many restrictions.
Brazil	Legal, popular.	Legal, but not popular.	Legal, popular.	Legal, but not popular.	Legal, but not popular.
Chile	Legal	Not in use.	Legal	Not in use.	Legal
Colombia	Legal	Legal	Legal	Legal	Legal
England	Legal	Legal	Legal	Legal	Legal
Finland	Legal, if gift has very small value or there is an evident material connection between the goods or services offered. Restriction when directed to children.	Legal, if the good being offered free or at a discount has very small value and there is an evident material connection between the goods or services offered.	Legal, if gift has very small value or there is an evident material connection between the goods or services offered. Restriction when directed to children.	Legal, if the good being offered free or at a discount has very small value and there is an evident material connection between the goods or services offered.	Legal, if gift has very small value or there is an evident material connection between the goods or services offered. Restriction when directed to children.
France	Legal, if gift has a very small value or is identical to the good purchased. Usually not allowed when the premium is free.	Legal, but only when offering discount on same product. Cross coupons forbidden.	Legal, if gift has a very small value or is identical to the good purchased. Usually not allowed when the premium is free.	Legal, but only when offering discount on same product. Cross coupons forbidden.	Legal, if gift has a very small value or is identical to the good purchased. Usually not allowed when the premium is free.
Germany	Usually not allowed.	Retailers cannot make price reductions. Consumers must collect an on-pack code and mail it directly to the manufacturer.	Usually not allowed.	Usually not allowed. Must be checked with lawyer in every case.	Usually not allowed.

Self-Liquid. Premiums	Bonus Packs	Free in the Mail	Continuity/ Loyalty	Phone Cards	Freq. Shop. Cards
Legal	Legal	Not in use.	Legal	Not in use.	Legal
Legal, but exact nature of offer must be revealed (closing date, # of proofs required, etc.).	Legal, but some packaging restrictions.	Legal, except therapeutics, alcohol, cigarettes.	Legal, but many restrictions.	Lega	Legal
Legal, but with many restrictions.	Legal, but with many restrictions.	Legal	Legal	Legal	Legal
Legal, popular.	Legal, very popular.	Legal, but not popular.	Legal, popular.	Legal, but not popular.	Legal, popular.
Legal	Legal	Legal	Legal	Legal	Legal
Legal	Legal	Legal	Legal	Legal	Legal
Legal	Legal	Legal	Legal	Legal	Legal
Not in use.	Legal, as long as offer is not connected to a purchase.	Legal, as long as offer is not connected to a purchase.	Legal	Legal, but not in use.	Legal, as long as offer does not contain illegal benefits.
Legal	Legal	Legal, if gift has a very small value or is identical to the good purchased. Usually not allowed when the premium is free.	Legal	Legal, if gift has a very small value or is identical to the good purchased. Usually not allowed when the premium is free.	Legal
Legal	Legal, but many restrictions. Must be checked with lawyer in every case.	Usually not allowed.	No special refunds except a maximum discount of 3% when paying with cash.	Legal, but can't be combined with purchase.	Legal, members can buy exclusive offers. Advantages such as reduced prices only for members are not allowed.

Country	Premiums	Home-Deliv. Coupons	Mail-Deliv. Coupons	Games	Contests
Holland	Legal	Legal	Legal	Prize value not to exceed US$2,500. Regulations currently under review.	Prize value not to exceed US$2,500. Regulations currently under review.
Hungary	Legal, but only used between trade companies.	Legal, usually used in connection with fragile or large products.	Legal, must contain information as to where the advertiser's office is located.	Legal, must get approval from Gambling Supervision.	Legal, must get approval from Gambling Supervision.
Ireland	Legal	Legal	Legal	Legal, if based on chance free entry required. If winner is determined by skill, purchase can be required.	Legal, if based on chance free entry required. If winner is determined by skill, purchase can be required.
Israel	Legal	Legal, but not popular.	Legal, but not popular.	Legal, but proof of purchase may be required.	Legal, but proof of purchase may be required.
Italy	Legal, 20% tax on prize value. Government notification required.	Legal	Legal	Legal, 45% tax on prize value. Government notification required.	Legal, 45% tax on prize value. Government notification required.
Japan	Legal, but very strict restrictions apply.	Legal	Legal	Legal, but very strict restrictions apply.	Legal
Malaysia	Legal	Legal	Legal	Legal, but prize promotion must be skill, not chance.	Legal, but prize promotion must be skill, not chance.
Mexico	Legal	Legal	Legal	Legal	Legal
New Zealand	Legal	Legal	Legal	Legal	Legal
Poland	Legal	Legal	Legal	Legal, but games of chance restricted by Law on Games of Chance & Mutual Bets.	Legal, but games of chance restricted by Law on Games of Chance & Mutual Bets.
Singapore	Legal	Legal	Legal	Legal, may require permission from authorities.	Legal, may require permission from authorities.
Spain	Legal, but you must ask for permission.	Legal, but you must ask for permission.	Legal, but you must ask for permission.	Legal, you must register with the government.	Legal, you must register with the government.
Sweden	Legal, but exact details of offer must be revealed (closing date, conditions, value, etc.).	Legal, with some restrictions. Illegal to send to persons under age 16. Restrictions when sending to parent of newborns, relatives of deceased persons.	Legal, with some restrictions. Illegal to send to persons under age 16. Restrictions when sending to parent of newborns, relatives of deceased persons.	Legal, but government permit required.	Legal, but promotion must be skill, not chance. Some restrictions to connect to a purchase. Exact details of offer must be revealed (closing date, conditions, value, etc.).
United States	Legal, but all material terms and conditions must be disclosed.	Legal, with restrictions on alcohol, tobacco, drugs.	Legal, with restrictions on alcohol, tobacco, drugs.	Legal, but on-pack games subject to certain restrictions.	Legal, some states prohibit requiring consideration. Bona fide skill must dominate and control final result. Various state disclosure requirements.
Venezuela	Legal, some restrictions when with food. Must register with the government.	Legal, but only in use by very few retailers.	Legal, but only in use by very few retailers.	Legal, must register with the government.	Legal, must register with the government.

Sweeps	Rebates/ Refunds/	Gift W/ Purchase	Database Marketing	Product Sampling
Prize value not to exceed US$2,500. Regulations currently under review.	Rebates—Legal. Refunds—price restrictions.	Legal	Legal, with some restrictions. Consumers can request to have name removed from database.	Legal, except for alcohol, drugs and pharmaceuticals.
Legal, must get approval from Gambling Supervision.	Legal, but only used between trade companies.	Legal, as long as gift has a very small value.	Legal, consumers can request to have names removed from database.	Legal, except for pharmaceuticals, tobacco, alcohol, weapons, or explosives.
Legal, but purchase cannot be required.	Legal	Legal	Legal	Legal, but tobacco prohibited.
Legal, 180 days must be between each sweeps from the same company.	Legal, but not popular.	Legal	Legal, but can't use private data such as credit card, bank, healthcare, etc. info.	Legal
Legal, 45% tax on prize value. Government notification required.	Illegal	Legal, 20% tax on prize value. Government notification required.	Legal, but with use of personal data written permission of consumer required.	Legal
Legal, but very strict restrictions apply.	Legal	Legal, but very strict restrictions apply.	Legal	Legal, except medicine.
Illegal	Legal	Legal	Legal	Legal, except alcohol, cigarette to Muslims.
Legal	Legal	Legal	Legal	Legal
Legal	Legal, with restrictions.	Legal	Legal, but protected by consumer privacy act.	Legal
Legal, but restricted by Law on Games of Chance & Mutual Bets.	Legal, but rebates are not in use.	Legal	Legal, but significantly limited by the Law on Protection of Personal Data.	Legal, except pharmaceuticals, alcoholic beverages.
Legal, with many restrictions, and many require permission from authorities.	Legal	Legal	Legal	Legal
Legal, you must register with the government.	Legal, you must register with the government.	Legal, some restrictions.	Legal, you must register database with data protection agency.	Legal
Legal, but promotion must be skill, not chance. Some restrictions to connect to a purchase. Exact details of offer must be revealed (closing date, conditions, value, etc.).	Legal, but exact details of offer must be revealed (closing date, conditions, value, etc.).	Legal, but exact details of offer must be revealed (closing date, conditions, value, etc.).	Legal, with some restrictions and a permit to maintain a list. The marketing offer must state from where the address was obtained.	Legal
Legal, no consideration. Significant disclosure requirements by states. Some states prohibit everybody wins, direct mail sweeps subject to stringent disclosure requirements.	Legal, must not be coupons.	Legal, but cost of gift may not be built into the cost for purchased product.	Legal, consumers may request to have name removed from industry, state and company lists.	Legal, with restrictions on alcohol, tobacco, drugs and some agricultural products.
Legal, must register with the government.	Legal	Legal, some restrictions with food. Must register with the government.	Legal	Legal, except cigarettes and alcohol to minors. Must register with the government. Some restrictions when with food.

Country	On-Pack Premiums	On-Pack Coupons	In-Pack Premiums	In-Pack Coupons	Near-Pack Premiums
Holland	Legal	Legal	Legal	Legal	Legal
Hungary	Not in use.	Not in use.	Not in use.	Not in use.	Not in use.
Ireland	Legal	Legal	Legal	Legal	Legal
Israel	Legal	Legal, but not popular.	Legal	Legal, but not popular.	Legal
Italy	Legal, 20% tax on prize value. Government notification required.	Legal	Legal, 20% tax on prize value. Government notification required.	Legal, but cross coupons not permitted; 20% tax on redeemed value.	Legal, 20% tax on prize value. Government notification required.
Japan	Legal, but very strict restrictions apply.	Legal	Legal, but very strict restrictions apply.	Legal	Not in use.
Malaysia	Legal	Legal	Legal, must comply with safety requirements.	Legal	Legal
Mexico	Legal	Legal	Legal	Legal	Legal
New Zealand	Legal	Legal	Legal	Legal	Legal
Poland	Legal	Legal, not in use.	Legal	Legal, not in use.	Legal
Singapore	Legal	Legal	Legal	Legal	Legal
Spain	Legal, some restrictions.	Legal, you need permission from data protection agency.	Legal, some restrictions.	Legal, you need permission from data protection agency.	Legal, some restrictions.
Sweden	Legal	Legal	Legal	Legal	Legal
United States	Legal, with restrictions on alcohol, tobacco, drugs. Premium must be appropriate to targeted age group. Certain restrictions apply to premiums directed to children.	Legal, but all material terms must be disclosed. There must be a minimum six month redemption period.	Legal, with restrictions on alcohol, tobacco, drugs. Premium must be appropriate to targeted age group. Certain restrictions apply to premiums directed to children.	Legal, but all material terms must be disclosed. There must be a minimum six month redemption period.	Legal
Venezuela	Legal, must register with the government.	Not in use.	Legal, some sanitary restrictions with food. Must register with the government.	Not in use.	Legal, some restrictions with food. Must register with the government.

Self-Liquid. Premiums	Bonus Packs	Free in the Mail	Continuity/ Loyalty	Phone Cards	Freq. Shop. Cards
Legal	Legal	Legal	Legal, with some restrictions. Must conform with the Privacy Law.	Legal	Legal
Illegal	Not in use.	Legal, except pharmaceuticals, tobacco, alcohol, weapons or explosives.	Not in use.	Legal for use as a surface for advertising, very popular. If used as a credit card many restrictions.	Legal, not very popular.
Legal	Legal	Legal	Legal	Legal	Legal
Legal	Legal	Legal	Legal	Legal, but not popular.	Legal
Legal, but price of purchase must be more than price of base product alone.	Legal	Legal	Legal, 20% tax on prize value. Government notification required.	Legal, 20% tax on prize value. Government notification required.	Legal, 20% tax on prize value. Government notification required.
Legal, but very strict restrictions apply.	Legal, but very strict restrictions apply.	Legal	Legal, but very strict restrictions apply.	Legal	Legal, but very strict restrictions apply.
Legal	Legal	Legal	Legal	Legal	Legal
Legal	Legal	Legal	Legal	Legal	Legal
Legal	Legal	Legal	Legal	Legal	Legal
Legal	Legal	Not in use.	Legal	Not in use.	Legal
Legal	Legal	Legal	Legal	Legal	Legal
Legal	Legal, some restrictions.	Legal	Legal, you must register database with data protection agency.	Legal	Legal, you must register database with data protection agency.
Legal	Legal	Legal	Legal	Legal	Legal
Legal	Legal	Legal, unordered merchandise considered free gift.	Legal, but all items and conditions must be clearly disclosed and consumer expressly consents to join plan.	Legal, cannot be used to change customers long distance service without written authorization.	Legal
Legal, some restrictions with food. Must register with the government.	Legal, some restrictions with food. Must register with the government.	Legal, but not very common. Some restrictions when with food. Must register with the government.	— — — — —	— — — — —	— — — — —

Chapter Twenty-one

Regulation of Advertising and Promotion

Chapter Objectives

- To examine how advertising is regulated, including the role and function of various regulatory agencies.
- To examine self-regulation of advertising and evaluate its effectiveness.
- To consider how advertising is regulated by federal and state government agencies, including the Federal Trade Commission.
- To examine rules and regulations that affect sales promotion, direct marketing, and marketing on the Internet.

Just For Feet Sues Its Ad Agency for Malpractice

During the 1999 Super Bowl athletic shoe retailer Just For Feet ran a commercial that showed a barefoot Kenyan runner fleeing from hunters in a Humvee, who capture and drug him. When he awakes, he finds a pair of running shoes on his feet. The ad was supposed to be part of a brand-building campaign for the Alabama based retailer that would help move the company away from its "Where the 13th pair is free" positioning theme. However, rather than change the image of the company, the ad created a controversy that resulted in a lawsuit that may drastically change relationships between advertisers and their agencies.

Following the Super Bowl, critics lashed out at the commercial for its racial insensitivity. *Advertising Age* critic Bob Garfield not only said the ad was the worst on the big game but also described it as "neo-colonialist. And culturally imperialist. And probably racist. And certainly condescending." As a result of the fallout and criticism surrounding the ad, Just For Feet filed a lawsuit against its agency, Saatchi & Saatchi Business Communications, asking for more than $10 million in damages for advertising malpractice. In its lawsuit Just for Feet claims that the finished spot, called "Kenya," was entirely different from the concept the agency first presented. Moreover, the retailer's CEO claimed in news reports that he was forced into running the spot even though he personally disliked it.

According to the company, the original concept called for a Just For Feet team coming up to a runner whose shoelace had become untied. The team would tie the runner's shoelace and give him water and a towel, the company said. The commercial was one of two that Saatchi had been considering using until immediately before the Super Bowl. A second spot showed a geeky boy playing dodge ball in a school gymnasium where the Just For Feet team comes in and rescues the boy by giving him better shoes. Just For Feet preferred this spot, the lawsuit claims, but one network rejected it, saying it was "mean-spirited and promotes antisocial behavior."

As the Super Bowl approached, Saatchi presented the final "Kenya" spot to its client. Just For Feet said it "expressed strong misgivings and dissatisfaction over the spot," according to the lawsuit, but the agency "then reassured Just For Feet that the commercial would be well received based on Saatchi's expertise and experience with national advertising and marketing, and that having committed to advertise in the Super Bowl it was too late to develop and produce another commercial or to reshoot the dodge ball commercial." Since it had already spent $900,000 on production costs and $2 million for the Super Bowl time slot, Just For Feet said it had no choice but to run the "Kenya" spot.

In addition to its concerns over the creative work, Just For Feet ran into another major problem. The company planned a sweepstakes promotion, the "Just For Feet Third Quarter Super Bowl Win a Hummer Contest." In the weeks leading up to the game, Just For Feet spent $800,000 on promotional teaser spots during the National Football League conference championship games. These spots told viewers to watch the third quarter of the Super Bowl and find out how many times the Just For Feet name was mentioned. Viewers who wanted to participate in the contest could telephone or go to the company's website to enter their answers. However, the spot ran in the fourth quarter of the big game, making the contest's correct answer zero. The website would not accept zero as the answer, so "customers were left with the mistaken impression that Just For Feet was attempting to trick or deceive them," according to the lawsuit. The Super Bowl spot was bought by Zenith media, which is a sibling of Saatchi & Saatchi.

The litigation actually began just as the controversy from the spot was settling down, when Saatchi sued Just For Feet in late February 1999 for failing to pay its $3 million media bill. On March 1, Just For Feet filed its own suit against Saatchi and Fox Broadcasting. The retailer charged Saatchi with breach of guaranty and warranty, misrepresentation, breach of contract, and "professional negligence and malpractice." In the lawsuit the retailer claimed that its favorable reputation has come under attack and that it has been subjected to the entirely unfounded and unintended public perception that it is a racist or racially insensitive company.

The lawsuit has raised a troubling question for the advertising community as to whether ad agencies can be held liable for the ads they produce. In its legal papers Saatchi claims advertising is a business that has no explicit guidelines and standards and therefore that it cannot have committed malpractice. The agency also noted that the "Kenya" spot was presented to the networks and was not rejected. Many advertising executives argue that while Saatchi may have used bad judgment in developing the idea for the commercial and carrying it forward, Just For Feet is ultimately responsible because the company approved the spot and must take responsibility for it.

A ruling in favor of Just For Feet in the landmark case would create major problems for advertising agencies and could have a major impact on agencies' creative limits as they would have to be careful to avoid making ads that might result in a lawsuit. The matter may no longer be relevant to Just For Feet, as the company filed a motion in bankruptcy court in January 2000 to liquidate its assets. However, the outcome will be very important to the advertising industry.

Sources: Alice Z. Cuneo, "Can an Agency Be Guilty of Malpractice?" *Advertising Age,* January 31, 2000, pp. 24, 25; "Bad Ad Breeds Worse Lawsuit," *Advertising Age,* June 28, 1999, p. 30.

Suppose you are the advertising manager for a consumer products company and have just reviewed a new commercial your agency created. You are very excited about the ad. It presents new claims about your brand's superiority that should help differentiate it from the competition. However, before you approve the commercial you need answers. Are the claims verifiable? Did researchers use proper procedures to collect and analyze the data and present the findings? Do research results support the claims? Were the right people used in the study? Could any conditions have biased the results?

Before approving the commercial, you have it reviewed by your company's legal department and by your agency's attorneys. If both reviews are acceptable, you send the ad to the major networks, which have their censors examine it. They may ask for more information or send the ad back for modification. (No commercial can run without approval from a network's Standards and Practices Department.)

Even after approval and airing, your commercial is still subject to scrutiny from such state and federal regulatory agencies as the state attorney general's office and the Federal Trade Commission. Individual consumers or competitors who find the ad misleading or have other concerns may file a complaint with the National Advertising Division of the Council of Better Business Bureaus. Finally, disparaged competitors may sue if they believe your ad distorts the facts and misleads consumers. If you lose the litigation, your company may have to retract the claims and pay the competitor damages, sometimes running into millions of dollars.

After considering all these regulatory issues, you must ask yourself if the new ad can meet all these challenges and is worth the risk. Maybe you ought to continue with the old approach that made no specific claims and simply said your brand was great.

Regulatory concerns can play a major role in the advertising decision-making process. Advertisers operate in a complex environment of local, state, and federal rules and regulations. Additionally, a number of advertising and business-sponsored associations, consumer groups and organizations, and the media attempt to promote honest, truthful, and tasteful advertising through their own self-regulatory programs and guidelines. The legal and regulatory aspects of advertising are very complex. Many parties are concerned about the nature and content of advertising and its potential to offend, exploit, mislead, and/or deceive consumers.

Advertising has also become increasingly important in product liability litigation involving products that are associated with consumer injuries. In many of these cases the courts have been willing to consider the impact of advertising on behavior of consumers that leads to injury-causing situations. Thus advertisers must avoid certain practices and proactively engage in others to ensure that their ads are comprehended correctly and do not misrepresent their products or services.[1]

Numerous guidelines, rules, regulations, and laws constrain and restrict advertising. These regulations primarily influence individual advertisers, but they can also affect advertising for an entire industry. For example, cigarette advertising was banned from the broadcast media in 1970, and many groups are pushing for a total ban on the advertising of tobacco products.[2] Legislation now being considered would further restrict the advertising of alcoholic beverages, including beer and wine.[3] Advertising is controlled by internal self-regulation and by external state and federal regulatory agencies such as the Federal Trade Commission (FTC), the Federal Communications Commission (FCC), the Food and Drug Administration (FDA), and the U.S. Postal Service. And recently state attorneys general have become more active in advertising regulation. While only government agencies (federal, state, and local) have the force of law, most advertisers also abide by the guidelines and decisions of internal regulatory bodies. In fact, internal regulation from such groups as the media and the National Advertising Review Board probably has more influence on advertisers' day-to-day operations and decision making than government rules and regulations.

Decision makers on both the client and agency side must be knowledgeable about these regulatory groups, including the intent of their efforts, how they operate, and how they influence and affect advertising and other promotional mix elements. In this chapter, we examine the major sources of advertising regulation, including efforts by the industry at voluntary self-regulation and external regulation by government agencies. We also examine regulations involving sales promotion, direct marketing, and marketing on the Internet.

Self-Regulation

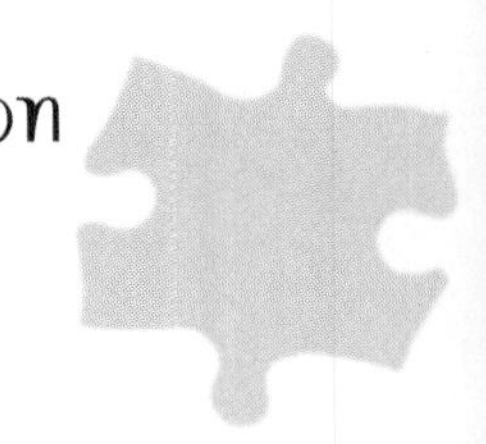

For many years, the advertising industry has practiced and promoted voluntary **self-regulation.** Most advertisers, their agencies, and the media recognize the importance of maintaining consumer trust and confidence. Advertisers also see self-regulation as a way to limit government interference, which, they believe, results in more stringent and troublesome regulations. Self-regulation and control of advertising emanate from all segments of the advertising industry, including individual advertisers and their agencies, business and advertising associations, and the media.

Self-Regulation by Advertisers and Agencies

Self-regulation begins with the interaction of client and agency when creative ideas are generated and submitted for consideration. Most companies have specific guidelines, standards, and policies to which their ads must adhere. Recognizing that their ads reflect the company, advertisers carefully scrutinize all messages to ensure they are consistent with the image the firm wishes to project. Companies also review their ads to be sure any claims made are reasonable and verifiable and do not mislead or deceive consumers. Ads are usually examined by corporate attorneys to avoid potential legal problems and their accompanying time, expense, negative publicity, and embarrassment.

Internal control and regulation also come from advertising agencies. Most have standards regarding the type of advertising they either want or are willing to produce, and they try to avoid ads that might be offensive or misleading. Most agencies will ask their clients to provide verification or support for claims the clients might want to make in their advertising and will make sure that adequate documentation or substantiation is available. However, agencies will also take formal steps to protect themselves from legal and ethical perils through agency-client contracts. For example, many liability issues are handled in these contracts. Agencies generally use information provided by clients for advertising claims, and in standard contracts the agency is protected from suits involving the accuracy of those claims. Contracts will also absolve the agency of responsibility if something goes wrong with the advertised product and consumers suffer damages or injury or other product liability claims arise.[4] However, agencies have been held legally responsible for fraudulent or deceptive claims and in some cases have been fined when their clients were found guilty of engaging in deceptive advertising.[5] Many agencies have a creative review board or panel composed of experienced personnel who examine ads for content and execution as well as for their potential to be perceived as offensive, misleading, and/or deceptive. Most agencies also employ or retain lawyers who review the ads for potential legal problems. Exhibit 21–1 shows an ad for a legal firm specializing in advertising law.

Exhibit 21–1 The Kinney & Lange firm specializes in advertising law

Most marketers and their agencies work closely with one another to develop advertising that adheres to legal and ethical standards. However, Just for Feet's lawsuit against its agency for advertising malpractice, which was discussed in the opening vignette, may redefine the relationships between advertisers and their agencies regarding responsibility for self-regulation of advertising.[6]

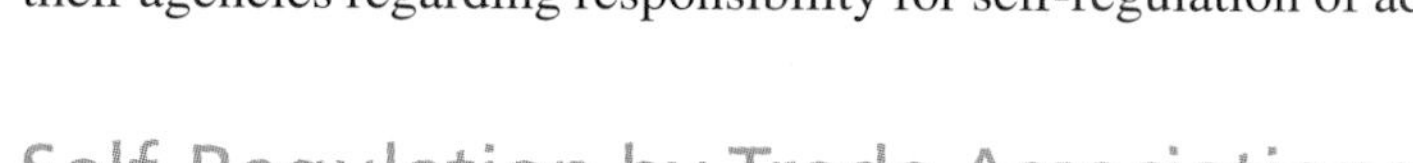

Self-Regulation by Trade Associations

Like advertisers and their agencies, many industries have also developed self-regulatory programs. This is particularly true in industries whose advertising is prone to controversy, such as liquor and alcoholic beverages, drugs, and various products marketed to children. Many trade and industry associations develop their own advertising guidelines or codes that member companies are expected to abide by.

The Wine Institute, the U.S. Brewers Association, and the Distilled Spirits Council of the United States all have guidelines that member companies are supposed to follow in advertising alcoholic beverages. No specific law prohibits the advertising of hard liquor on radio or television. However, such advertising was effectively banned for over five decades as a result of a code provision of the National Association of Broadcasters and by agreements of liquor manufacturers and their self-governing body, the Distilled Spirits Council. However, in November 1996 the Distilled Spirits Council amended its code of good practice and overturned its self-imposed ban on broadcast advertising.[7] Ethical Perspective 21–1 discusses the reasons why the council decided to overturn the ban, as well as the controversy that has resulted from its decision. Other industry trade associations with advertising guidelines and programs include the Toy Manufacturers Association, the Motion Picture Association of America, the Pharmaceutical Manufacturers Association, and the Proprietary Association (the trade association for nonprescription drug makers).[8]

Ethical Perspective 21–1

Liquor Advertising Returns to Television

For more than five decades, distilled spirits were not advertised on television or radio because of a self-imposed ban by members of the Distilled Spirits Council of the United States (DISCUS). Council members agreed in 1936 to avoid radio advertising and extended the ban to TV in 1948. But Seagram, the second-largest distiller in the world, ended the U.S. spirits industry's long-standing ban on broadcast advertising in June 1996 by airing commercials for its Crown Royal Canadian whiskey brand on an NBC affiliate in Corpus Christi, Texas.

Seagram issued a statement that it was ending the liquor industry's decades-old practice of not advertising on TV because DISCUS's voluntary code of good practice placed spirits at a competitive disadvantage to beer and wine. Seagram's vice president for marketing and strategy said, "Wine and beer face no restrictions on advertising. That inequity creates an unfair situation as far as promotion of spirits is concerned. We have a right to examine and test television as a viable communications medium." Seagram also argued that the ban has become outdated as radio and TV have become more targeted media, which means they can pinpoint their advertising message to people of legal drinking age.

Initial reactions within the liquor industry were mixed. Some companies were upset because Seagram made its move before the industry had time to reach a coordinated stand on the sensitive subject of TV advertising. The vice president of public relations for Heublin Inc. expressed concern that Seagram had acted rashly. He said, "We are not convinced that there has been enough research done into the attitudes of lawmakers, regulators, consumer groups, and the public at large regarding their attitudes toward distilled spirits broadcast advertising. We're concerned there could be backlash against the industry."

A number of distillers, eager to turn around the long, slow decline in hard liquor sales, watched Seagram test the water with its TV ads before rolling out their own commercials. Some, such as Hiram Walker and Brown-Forman, held discussions with broadcast outlets but waited for a formal amendment to the DISCUS code of good practice before proceeding. The amendment came on November 7, 1996, when DISCUS members voted unanimously to overturn the self-imposed ban on broadcast ads. DISCUS president and CEO Fred A. Meister noted that spirits marketers want to break down the public perception that spirits are stronger or more dangerous than beer and wine and thus deserving of harsher social and political treatment.

Since the DISCUS ban was lifted, the four major broadcast TV networks and many cable channels such as ESPN and MTV have continued to refuse liquor ads, and consumer and public-interest groups have applauded their actions. In fact, it has been argued that it is really the refusal by TV stations and networks to accept liquor advertising that has kept them off the air rather than the DISCUS code. However, the major networks cannot control the practices of affiliate stations they do not own, some of which are willing to accept liquor ads. A number of liquor companies have followed Seagram's lead and are running ads on these stations. Liquor commercials are also appearing on smaller cable TV networks, where guidelines are often looser and executives are hungrier for new sources of advertising revenue.

For now, liquor companies that want to air TV commercials do not face any serious government obstacles. Officials at the Federal Trade Commission, which oversees advertising, and the Bureau of Alcohol, Tobacco and Firearms, which regulates the spirits industry, say federal law does not give either agency the authority to ban liquor ads. In fact, the First Amendment protects this type of commercial speech.

The marketing of alcoholic beverages has come under increased scrutiny recently by the federal government as concern grows over underage drinking, advertising by wine makers increases, and liquor ads continue creeping into television. In 1998 the Federal Trade Commission opened up a broad new investigation of alcohol advertising and asked eight of the top U.S. marketers of beer, wine, and liquor for "special reports" on their advertising and marketing practices. The FTC wants to know how the companies are carrying out their own self-regulatory programs designed to prevent alcohol ads from reaching children and addressing complaints regarding violations of its self-regulatory programs. The agency investigation requests information on advertising and promotion on the Internet, product placement in movies, and other advertising techniques. The FTC's heightened interest in liquor advertising has also resulted in detailed reviews of commercials, including the judging of scenes, the age of actors, and overall themes of televised beer, wine, and hard-liquor ads. The goal is to ensure that these ads do not target underage drinkers or misrepresent the dangers involved when people perform certain activities while consuming alcoholic beverages.

It is likely that consumers will continue to see more ads for Crown Royal, Chivas Regal, Kahlua, and many other liquor brands on television. However, many experts argue that increased TV advertising by liquor companies will result in even more negative publicity and government scrutiny, which will more than offset any marketing gain, and say that these marketers might be better off sticking with print advertising.

Sources: Sally Beatty and John Simons, "FTC Eyes Liquor Ads' Kid-Appeal," *The Wall Street Journal,* August 7, 1998, pp. B1, 5; Herbert J. Rotfeld, "'Ban' on Liquor Ads Not What It Seems," *Marketing News,* May 26, 1997, p. 12; Ian P. Murphy, "Competitive Spirits: Liquor Industry Turns to TV Ads," *Marketing News,* December 2, 1996, pp. 1, 17; Sally Goll Beatty, "Seagram Flouts Ban on TV Ads Pitching Liquor," *The Wall Street Journal,* June 11, 1996, pp. B1, 6.

Many professions also maintain advertising guidelines through local, state, and national organizations. For years professional associations like the American Medical Association (AMA) and the American Bar Association (ABA) restricted advertising by their members on the basis that such promotional activities lowered members' professional status and led to unethical and fraudulent claims. However, such restrictive codes have been attacked by both government regulatory agencies and consumer groups. They argue that the public has a right to be informed about a professional's services, qualifications, and background and that advertising will improve professional services as consumers become better informed and are better able to shop around.[9]

In 1977, the Supreme Court held that state bar associations' restrictions on advertising are unconstitutional and that attorneys have First Amendment freedom of speech rights to advertise.[10] Many professional associations subsequently removed their restrictions, and advertising by lawyers and other professionals is now common (Exhibit 21–2).[11] In 1982, the Supreme Court upheld an FTC order permitting advertising by dentists and physicians.[12]

Research shows that consumers generally favor increased use of professional advertising. However, professionals continue to have reservations. They worry that advertising has a negative impact on their image, credibility, and dignity and see

Exhibit 21–2 Advertising by lawyers has become more common as the result of a 1977 Supreme Court ruling

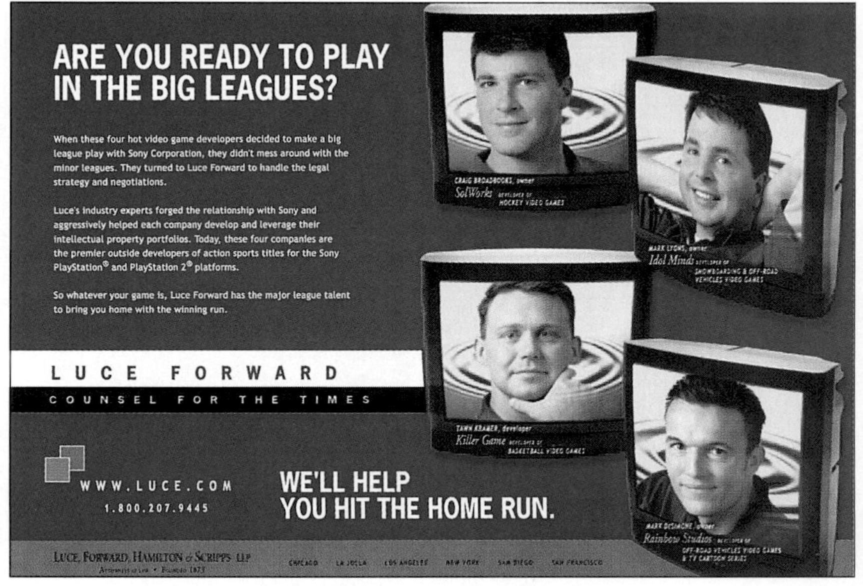

benefits to consumers as unlikely.[13] Still, advertising by professionals is increasing, particularly among newcomers to medicine, dentistry, and law. Associations such as the AMA and the ABA developed guidelines for members' advertising to help maintain standards and guard against misleading, deceptive, or offensive ads.

The issue of professional advertising, particularly by attorneys, is still hotly debated. Some traditional law firms resist using advertising, particularly on TV, due to concern that it might hurt the profession's image. Many in the legal profession worry that ads soliciting personal injury victims only worsen the public's perception of attorneys. A sizable faction within the American Bar Association blames the legal profession's image problem on sleazy ads. The ABA's Commission on Advertising recently held a series of public hearings on what, if any, restrictive measures to recommend to state ethics panels. Some states, such as Iowa and Florida, already restrict the content of attorney ads and the way they can be delivered. For example, Iowa lawyers are limited to "tombstone" print ads that merely list their name, location, and objective qualifications. And all ads require a disclaimer urging consumers not to base their attorney selection on an advertisement. Florida attorneys cannot use testimonials or endorsements, dramatizations, self-laudatory statements, illustrations, or photos.[14]

Many attorneys are incensed over efforts to restrict their rights to promote themselves because they use advertising to help build their practices. Several cases are currently being litigated, but ultimately the Supreme Court may have to decide just how far states can go in curtailing advertising.

Although industry associations are concerned with the impact and consequences of members' advertising, they have no legal way to enforce their guidelines. They can only rely on peer pressure from members or other nonbinding sanctions to get advertisers to comply.

Self-Regulation by Businesses

A number of self-regulatory mechanisms have been established by the business community in an effort to control advertising practices. The largest and best known is the **Better Business Bureau** (BBB), which promotes fair advertising and selling practices across all industries. The BBB was established in 1916 to handle consumer complaints about local business practices and particularly advertising. Local BBBs are located in most large cities throughout the United States and supported entirely by dues of the more than 100,000 member firms.

Local BBBs receive and investigate complaints from consumers and other companies regarding the advertising and selling tactics of businesses in their area. Each local office has its own operating procedures for handling complaints; generally, the office contacts the violator and, if the complaint proves true, requests that the practice be stopped or changed. If the violator does not respond, negative publicity may be used against the firm or the case may be referred to appropriate government agencies for further action.

While BBBs provide effective control over advertising practices at the local level, the parent organization, the **Council of Better Business Bureaus,** plays a major role at the national level. The council assists new industries in developing advertising codes and standards, and it provides information about advertising regulations and legal rulings to advertisers, agencies, and the media. The council also plays an important self-regulatory role through its National Advertising Division (NAD) and Children's Advertising Review Unit (CARU). The NAD works closely with the **National Advertising Review Board** (NARB) to sustain truth, accuracy, and decency in national advertising.

The NAD/NARB

In 1971 four associations—the American Advertising Federation (AAF), the American Association of Advertising Agencies (AAAA), the Association of National Advertisers (ANA), and the Council of Better Business Bureaus—joined forces to establish the **National Advertising Review Council** (NARC). The NARC's mission is to sustain high standards of truth, accuracy, and social responsibility in national advertising. The council has two operating arms, the National Advertising Division of the Council of Better Business Bureaus and the National Advertising Review Board. The NAD/NARB has become the advertising industry's primary self-regulatory mechanism.

The NAD's advertising monitoring program is the source of many of the cases it reviews (Figure 21–1). It also reviews complaints from consumers and consumer groups, local BBBs, and competitors. During the 1970s and 80s, many of the complaints to the NAD came from consumers. However, with the increased use of comparative advertising, nearly 90 percent of the complaints are now coming from marketers who are challenging competitors' comparisons with their brands.[15] For example, BMW filed a complaint with the NAD over a Volvo commercial claiming the Volvo 850 Turbo Sportswagon accelerates faster than a BMW 328I.[16] Procter & Gamble recently filed a challenge with the NAD over a TV commercial from Fort James Corp. that claimed Brawny paper towels were stronger than P&G's Bounty brand. The commercial in question was the popular "Grannies" spot that showed two grandmothers pushing over a refrigerator to make a mess that was more easily cleaned with Brawny paper towels than with Bounty.[17] The NAD acts as the investigative arm of the NARC. After initiating or receiving a complaint, it determines the issue, collects and evaluates data, and makes the initial decision on whether the advertiser's claims are substantiated. The NAD may ask the advertiser to supply substantiation for the claim in question. If the information provided is considered adequate to support the claim, the case is deemed substantiated. In the Volvo case, the NAD ruled that the company did have test results to support its superior-acceleration claim and the case was considered substantiated. If the substantiation is unsatisfactory, the NAD negotiates with the advertiser to modify or discontinue the advertising. For example, in the case involving Brawny and Bounty paper towels, the NAD found that several performance claims in the Brawny ads were substantiated. However, the NAD also found that the Brawny ads conveyed an overall-superiority claim that could not be supported, and it recommended that Fort James modify the spot or discontinue using it.

If the NAD and the advertiser fail to resolve the controversy, either can appeal to a five-person panel from the National Advertising Review Board. For example, Fort James Corp. chose to appeal the NAD decision regarding its overall-superiority claim for Brawny versus Bounty paper towels to the NARB rather than modify its ad. The NARB is composed of 85 advertising professionals and prominent public-interest members. If the NARB panel agrees with the NAD and rules against the advertiser, the advertiser must discontinue the advertising. If the advertiser refuses to comply, the NARB refers the matter to the appropriate government agency and indicates the fact in its public record. NAD/NARB decisions are released to the press and also are published in its monthly publication, *NAD Case Reports.* Figure 21–2 shows a flowchart of the steps in the NAD/NARB review process.

Although the NARB has no power to order an advertiser to modify or stop running an ad and no sanctions it can impose, advertisers who participate in an NAD investigation and NARB appeal rarely refuse to abide by the panel's decision.[18]

Figure 21–1 Sources of NAD cases and decisions, 1999

Sources	Number	Percent	Decisions	Number	Percent
Competitor challenges	88	91%	Modified/discontinued	56	57%
NAD monitoring	5	5	Administratively closed	22	23
Local BBB challenges	1	1	Substantiated	8	8
Consumer challenges	3	3	Compliance	6	6
Total	97	100%	Referred to government	5	5
			Total	97	100%

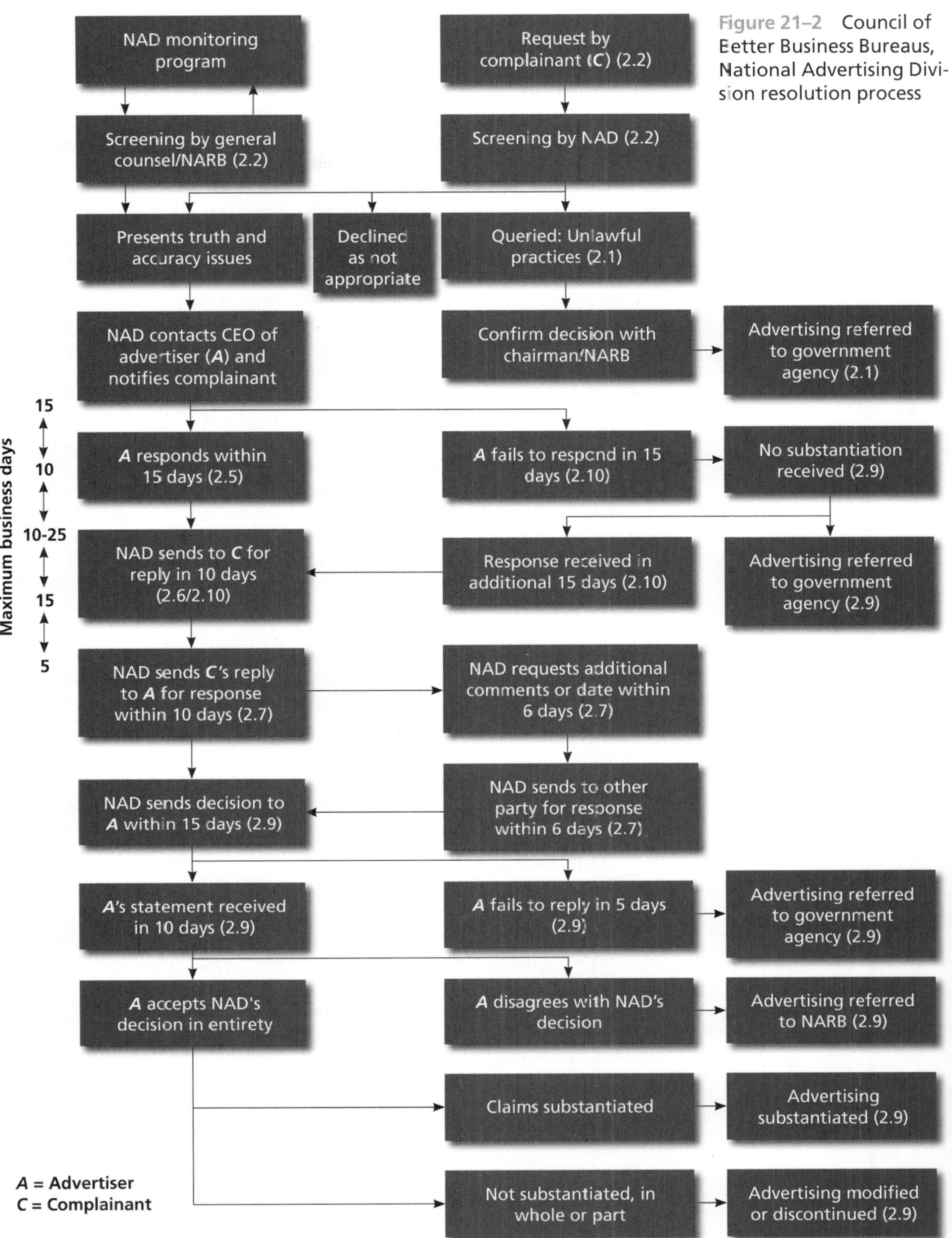

Figure 21–2 Council of Better Business Bureaus, National Advertising Division resolution process

Most cases do not even make it to the NARB panel. For example, in 1999, of the 97 NAD investigations, 8 ad claims were substantiated, 5 were referred to the government, and 56 were modified or discontinued (Figure 21–1). Of the 56 cases where the advertising claims were modified or discontinued, in only 4 did the advertiser appeal to the NARB for resolution.[19]

In 1993, for the first time in its history, the NARB referred a matter to the Federal Trade Commission following an advertiser's refusal to modify a commercial in accordance with an NARB decision. The case involved ads for Eggland's Best Eggs that claimed "You can eat eggs again and not increase your serum cholesterol," and "They're special eggs from specially fed hens." The NARB ruled that the company's ads and promotional materials misrepresented Eggland's eggs as not increasing consumers' serum cholesterol and as being superior to regular eggs in this respect. The Federal Trade Commission eventually ruled that Eggland's ads were deceptive and ordered the company to take steps to correct the misperception that had been created.[20]

The NAD/NARB is a valuable and effective self-regulatory body. Cases brought to it are handled at a fraction of the cost (and with much less publicity) than those brought to court and are expedited more quickly than those reviewed by a government agency such as the FTC. The system also works because judgments are made by the advertiser's peers, and most companies feel compelled to comply. Firms may prefer self-regulation rather than government intervention in part because they can challenge competitors' unsubstantiated claims through groups like the NARB.[21]

Advertising Associations Various groups in the advertising industry also favor self-regulation. The two major national organizations, the American Association of Advertising Agencies and the American Advertising Federation, actively monitor and police industrywide advertising practices. The AAAA, which is the major trade association of the ad agency business in the United States, has established standards of practice and its own creative code. It also issues guidelines for specific types of advertising such as comparative messages (Figure 21–3). The AAF

Figure 21–3 AAAA policy statement and guidelines for comparative advertising

The Board of Directors of the American Association of Advertising Agencies recognizes that when used truthfully and fairly, comparative advertising provides the consumer with needed and useful information.

However, extreme caution should be exercised. The use of comparative advertising, by its very nature, can distort facts and, by implication, convey to the consumer information that misrepresents the truth.

Therefore, the Board believes that comparative advertising should follow certain guidelines:

1. The intent and connotation of the ad should be to inform and never to discredit or unfairly attack competitors, competing products, or services.
2. When a competitive product is named, it should be one that exists in the marketplace as significant competition.
3. The competition should be fairly and properly identified but never in a manner or tone of voice that degrades the competitive product or service.
4. The advertising should compare related or similar properties or ingredients of the product, dimension to dimension, feature to feature.
5. The identification should be for honest comparison purposes and not simply to upgrade by association.
6. If a competitive test is conducted, it should be done by an objective testing source, preferably an independent one, so that there will be no doubt as to the veracity of the test.
7. In all cases the test should be supportive of all claims made in the advertising that are based on the test.
8. The advertising should never use partial results or stress insignificant differences to cause the consumer to draw an improper conclusion.
9. The property being compared should be significant in terms of value or usefulness of the product to the consumer.
10. Comparatives delivered through the use of testimonials should not imply that the testimonial is more than one individual's thought unless that individual represents a sample of the majority viewpoint.

consists of advertisers, agencies, media, and numerous advertising clubs. The association has standards for truthful and responsible advertising, is involved in advertising legislation, and actively influences agencies to abide by its code and principles.

Self-Regulation by Media

The media are another important self-regulatory mechanism in the advertising industry. Most media maintain some form of advertising review process and, except for political ads, may reject any they regard as objectionable. Some media exclude advertising for an entire product class; others ban individual ads they think offensive or objectionable. For example, *Reader's Digest* does not accept advertising for tobacco or liquor products. A number of magazines in the United States and other countries refused to run some of Benetton's shock ads (discussed in Ethical Perspective 8–4) on the grounds that their readers would find them offensive or disturbing (Exhibit 21–3).

Newspapers and magazines have their own advertising requirements and restrictions, which often vary depending on the size and nature of the publication. Large, established publications, such as major newspapers or magazines, often have strict standards regarding the type of advertising they accept. Some magazines, such as *Parents* and *Good Housekeeping,* regularly test the products they advertise and offer a "seal of approval" and refunds if the products are later found to be defective. Such policies are designed to enhance the credibility of the publication and increase the reader's confidence in the products it advertises.

Advertising on television and radio has been regulated for years through codes developed by the industry trade association, the National Association of Broadcasters (NAB). Both the radio code (established in 1937) and the television code (1952) provided standards for broadcast advertising for many years. Both codes prohibited the advertising of certain products, such as hard liquor. They also affected the manner in which products could be advertised. However, in 1982, the NAB suspended all of its code provisions after the courts found that portions (dealing with time standards and required length of commercials in the TV code) were in restraint of trade. While the NAB codes are no longer in force, many individual broadcasters, such as the major TV networks, have incorporated major portions of the code provisions into their own standards.[22]

The four major television networks have the most stringent review process of any media. All four networks maintain standards and practices divisions, which carefully review all commercials submitted to the network or individual affiliate stations. Advertisers must submit for review all commercials intended for airing on the network or an affiliate.

Exhibit 21–3 A number of magazines refused to run this Benetton ad

A commercial may be submitted for review in the form of a script, storyboard, animatic, or finished commercial (when the advertiser believes there is little chance of objection). Network reviewers consider whether the proposed commercial meets acceptable standards and is appropriate for certain audiences. For example, different standards are used for ads designated for prime-time versus late-night spots or for children's versus adults' programs (see Figure 21–4). Although most of these guidelines remain in effect, ABC and NBC loosened their rules on celebrity endorsements.[23]

The four major networks receive over 50,000 commercials a year for review; nearly two-thirds are accepted and only 3 percent are rejected. Most problems with the remaining 30 percent are resolved through negotiation, and the ads are revised and resubmitted.[24]

Network standards regarding acceptable advertising change constantly. The networks first allowed lingerie advertisers to use live models rather than mannequins in 1987. Advertising for contraceptives is now appearing on some stations. The networks also loosened long-standing restrictions on endorsements and competitive advertising claims.[25] Network standards will continue to change as society's values and attitudes toward certain issues and products change. Also, many advertising people believe these changes are a response to competition from independent and cable stations, which tend to be much less stringent in their standards and practices. However, since television is probably the most carefully scrutinized and frequently criticized of all forms of advertising, the networks must be careful not to offend their viewers and detract from advertising's credibility.

Appraising Self-Regulation

The three major participants in the advertising process—advertisers, agencies, and the media—work individually and collectively to encourage truthful, ethical, and responsible advertising. The advertising industry views self-regulation as an effec-

Figure 21–4 A sampling of the TV networks' guidelines for children's advertising

Each of the major TV networks has its own set of guidelines for children's advertising, although the basics are very similar. A few rules, such as the requirement of a static "island" shot at the end, are written in stone; others, however, can sometimes be negotiated. Many of the rules below apply specifically to toys. The networks also have special guidelines for kids' food commercials and for kids' commercials that offer premiums.

	ABC	CBS	NBC
Must not overglamorize product	✓	✓	✓
No exhortative language, such as "Ask Mom to buy..."	✓	✓	✓
No realistic war settings	✓		✓
Generally no celebrity endorsements	✓	Case-by-case	✓
Can't use "only" or "just" in regard to price	✓	✓	✓
Show only two toys per child or maximum of six per commercial	✓		✓
Five-second "island" showing product against plain background at end of spot	✓	✓	✓ (4 to 5)
Animation restricted to one-third of a commercial	✓		✓
Generally no comparative or superiority claims	Case-by-case	Handle w/care	✓
No costumes or props not available with the toy	✓		✓
No child or toy can appear in animated segments	✓		✓
Three-second establishing shot of toy in relation to child	✓	✓ (2.5 to 3)	
No shots under one second in length		✓	
Must show distance a toy can travel before stopping on its own		✓	

tive mechanism for controlling advertising abuses and avoiding the use of offensive, misleading, or deceptive practices, and it prefers this form of regulation to government intervention. Self-regulation of advertising has been effective and in many instances probably led to the development of more stringent standards and practices than those imposed by or beyond the scope of legislation.

In a speech to the American Advertising Federation, then FTC Commissioner Mary Azuenaga commented on the fact that the Eggland's Best Eggs case marked the first time in its 22-year history the NARB referred a matter to the FTC. She said, "Although it was unfortunate that such a referral was necessary, the very novelty of the referral underscores the important contribution of NARB and other self-regulatory groups in addressing questions of deceptive advertising."[26]

There are, however, limitations to self-regulation, and the process has been criticized in a number of areas. For example, the NAD may take six months to a year to resolve a complaint, during which time a company often stops using the commercial anyway. Budgeting and staffing constraints may limit the number of cases the NAD/NARB system investigates and the speed with which it resolves them.[27] And some critics believe that self-regulation is self-serving to the advertisers and advertising industry and lacks the power or authority to be a viable alternative to federal or state regulation.

Many do not believe advertising can or should be controlled solely by self-regulation. They argue that regulation by government agencies is necessary to ensure that consumers get accurate information and are not misled or deceived. Moreover, since advertisers do not have to comply with the decisions and recommendations of self-regulatory groups, it is sometimes necessary to turn to the federal and/or state government.

Federal Regulation of Advertising

Advertising is controlled and regulated through federal, state, and local laws and regulations enforced by various government agencies. The federal government is the most important source of external regulation since many advertising practices come under the jurisdiction of the **Federal Trade Commission.** In addition, depending on the advertiser's industry and product or service, other federal agencies such as the Federal Communications Commission, the Food and Drug Administration, the U.S. Postal Service, and the Bureau of Alcohol, Tobacco, and Firearms may have regulations that affect advertising. We will begin our discussion of federal regulation of advertising by considering the basic rights of marketers to advertise their products and services under the First Amendment.

Advertising and the First Amendment

Freedom of speech or expression, as defined by the First Amendment to the U.S. Constitution, is the most basic federal law governing advertising in the United States. For many years, freedom of speech protection did not include advertising and other forms of speech that promote a commercial transaction. However, the courts have extended First Amendment protection to **commercial speech,** which is speech that promotes a commercial transaction. There have been a number of landmark cases over the past three decades where the federal courts have issued rulings supporting the coverage of commercial speech by the First Amendment.

In a 1976 case, *Virginia State Board of Pharmacy* v. *Virginia Citizens Consumer Council,* the U.S. Supreme Court ruled that states cannot prohibit pharmacists from advertising the prices of prescription drugs, because such advertising contains information that helps the consumer choose between products and because the free flow of information is indispensable.[28] As noted earlier, in 1977 the Supreme Court ruled that state bar associations' restrictions on advertising are unconstitutional and attorneys have a First Amendment right to advertise their services and prices.[29] In a more recent case, the Supreme Court's 1996 decision in *44 Liquormart, Inc.* v. *Rhode Island* struck down two state statutes designed to support the state's interest in temperance. The first prohibited the advertising of alcoholic beverage prices in Rhode Island except on signs within a store, while the second prohibited the publication or broadcast of alcohol price ads. The Court ruled that the Rhode Island statutes were unlawful because they restricted the constitutional guarantee of freedom of speech, and the decision signaled strong protection for advertisers under the First Amendment.[30]

In the cases regarding advertising, the U.S. Supreme Court has ruled that freedom of expression must be balanced against competing interests. For example, the courts have upheld bans on the advertising of products that are considered harmful, such as tobacco. The Court has also ruled that only truthful commercial speech is protected, not advertising or other forms of promotion that are false, misleading, or deceptive. The job of regulating advertising at the federal level and determining whether advertising is truthful or deceptive is a major focus of the Federal Trade Commission. We now turn our attention to federal regulation of advertising and the FTC.

Background on Federal Regulation of Advertising

Federal regulation of advertising originated in 1914 with the passage of the **Federal Trade Commission Act** (FTC Act), which created the FTC, the agency that is today the most active in, and has primary responsibility for, controlling and regulating advertising. The FTC Act was originally intended to help enforce antitrust laws, such as the Sherman and Clayton acts, by helping to restrain unfair methods of competition. The main focus of the first five-member commission was to protect competitors from one another; the issue of false or misleading advertising was not even mentioned. In 1922, the Supreme Court upheld an FTC interpretation that false advertising was an unfair method of competition, but in the 1931 case *FTC* v. *Raladam Co.,* the Court ruled the commission could not prohibit false advertising unless there was evidence of injury to a competitor.[31] This ruling limited the power of the FTC to protect consumers from false or deceptive advertising and led to a consumer movement that resulted in an important amendment to the FTC Act.

In 1938, Congress passed the **Wheeler-Lea Amendment.** It amended section 5 of the FTC Act to read: "Unfair methods of competition in commerce and unfair or deceptive acts or practices in commerce are hereby declared to be unlawful." The amendment empowered the FTC to act if there was evidence of injury to the public; proof of injury to a competitor was not necessary. The Wheeler-Lea Amendment also gave the FTC the power to issue cease-and-desist orders and levy fines on violators. It extended the FTC's jurisdiction over false advertising of foods, drugs, cosmetics, and therapeutic devices. And it gave the FTC access to the injunctive power of the federal courts, initially only for food and drug products but expanded in 1972 to include all products in the event of a threat to the public's health and safety.

In addition to the FTC, numerous other federal agencies are responsible for, or involved in, advertising regulation. The authority of these agencies is limited, however, to a particular product area or service, and they often rely on the FTC to assist in handling false or deceptive advertising cases.

The Federal Trade Commission

The FTC is responsibile for protecting both consumers and businesses from anti-competitive behavior and unfair and deceptive practices. The major divisions of the FTC include the bureaus of competition, economics, and consumer protection. The Bureau of Competition seeks to prevent business practices that restrain competition and is responsible for enforcing antitrust laws. The Bureau of Economics helps the FTC evaluate the impact of its actions and provides economic analysis and support to antitrust and consumer protection investigations and rule makings. It also analyzes the impact of government regulation on competition and consumers. The Bureau of Consumer Protection's mandate is to protect consumers against unfair, deceptive, or fraudulent practices. This bureau also investigates and litigates cases involving acts or practices alleged to be deceptive or unfair to consumers. The Division of Advertising Practices of the Bureau of Competition protects consumers from deceptive and unsubstantiated advertising and enforces the provisions of the FTC Act that forbid misrepresentation, unfairness, and deception in general advertising at the national and regional level (Exhibit 21–4). The Division of Marketing Practices of the Bureau of Competition engages in activities that are related to various marketing and warranty practices such as fraudulent telemarketing schemes, 900-number programs, and disclosures relating to franchise and business opportunities.

The FTC has had the power to regulate advertising since passage of the Wheeler-Lea Amendment. However, not until the early 1970s—following criticism of the commission in a book by "Nader's Raiders" and a special report by the American Bar Association citing its lack of action against deceptive promotional practices—did the FTC become active in regulating advertising.[32] The authority of the FTC was increased considerably throughout the 1970s. The Magnuson-Moss Act of 1975, an important piece of legislation, dramatically broadened the FTC's powers and substantially increased its budget. The first section of the act dealt with consumers' rights regarding product warranties; it allowed the commission to require restitution for deceptively written warranties where the consumer lost more than $5. The second section, the FTC Improvements Act, empowered the FTC to establish **trade regulation rules** (TRR), industrywide rules that define unfair practices before they occur.

During the 1970s, the FTC made enforcement of laws regarding false and misleading advertising a top priority. Several new programs were instituted, budgets were increased, and the commission became a very powerful regulatory agency. However, many of these programs, as well as the expanded powers of the FTC to develop regulations on the basis of "unfairness," became controversial. At the root of this controversy is the fundamental issue of what constitutes unfair advertising.

The Concept of Unfairness

Under section 5 of the FTC Act, the Federal Trade Commission has a mandate to act against unfair or deceptive advertising practices. However, this statute does not define the terms *unfair* and *deceptive,* and the FTC has been criticized for not doing so itself. While the FTC has taken steps to clarify the meaning of *deception,* people have been concerned for years about the vagueness of the term *unfair.*

Controversy over the FTC's authority to regulate unfair advertising practices began in 1978, when the agency relied on this mandate to formulate its controversial "kid vid" rule restricting advertising to children.[33] This interpretation caused widespread concern in the business community that the term unfair could be used to encompass anything FTC commissioners might find objectionable. For example, in a 1980 policy statement the FTC noted that "the precise concept of consumer unfairness is one whose precise meaning is not immediately obvious." Consequently, in

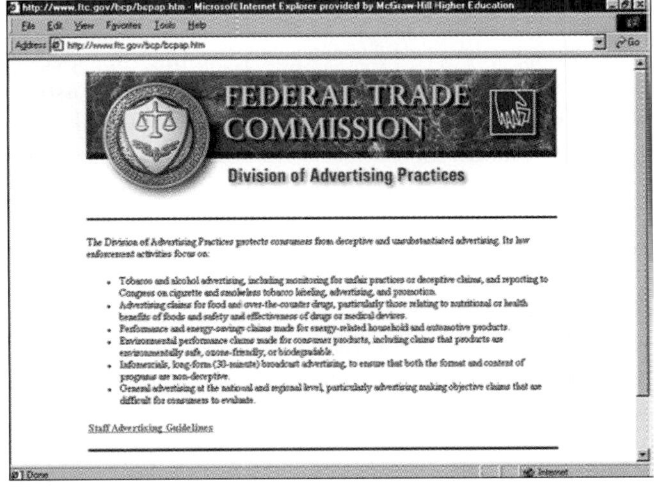

Exhibit 21–4 The Division of Advertising Practices protects consumers from deceptive and unsubstantiated advertising claims

1980 Congress responded by suspending the children's advertising rule and banning the FTC from using unfairness as a legal basis for advertising rulemaking.

The FTC responded to these criticisms in December 1980 by sending Congress a statement containing an interpretation of unfairness. According to FTC policy, the basis for determining **unfairness** is that a trade practice (1) causes substantial physical or economic injury to consumers, (2) could not reasonably be avoided by consumers, and (3) must not be outweighed by countervailing benefits to consumers or competition. The agency also stated that a violation of public policy (such as of other government statutes) could, by itself, constitute an unfair practice or could be used to prove substantial consumer injury. Practices considered unfair are claims made without prior substantiation, claims that might exploit such vulnerable groups as children and the elderly, and instances where consumers cannot make a valid choice because the advertiser omits important information about the product or competing products mentioned in the ad.[34]

The FTC's statement was intended to clarify its interpretation of unfairness and reduce ambiguity over what might constitute unfair practices. However, efforts by the FTC to develop industrywide trade regulation rules that would define unfair practices and have the force and effect of law were limited by Congress in 1980 with the passage of the FTC Improvements Act. Amidst calls to end the stalemate over the FTC's regulation of unfair advertising by having the agency work with Congress to define its advertising authority, in 1994 Congress and the advertising industry agreed on a definition of unfair advertising that is very similar to the FTC's 1980 policy statement discussed earlier. However, the new agreement requires that before the FTC can initiate any industrywide rule, it has to have reason to believe that the unfair or deceptive acts or practices are prevalent.[35]

The FTC does have specific regulatory authority in cases involving deceptive, misleading, or untruthful advertising. The vast majority of advertising cases that the FTC handles concern deception and advertising fraud, which usually involve knowledge of a false claim.

Deceptive Advertising

In most economies, advertising provides consumers with information they can use to make consumption decisions. However, if this information is untrue or misleads the consumer, advertising is not fulfilling its basic function. But what constitutes an untruthful or deceptive ad? Deceptive advertising can take a number of forms, ranging from intentionally false or misleading claims to ads that, although true, leave some consumers with a false or misleading impression.

The issue of deception, including its definition and measurement, receives considerable attention from the FTC and other regulatory agencies. One of the problems regulatory agencies deal with in determining deception is distinguishing between false or misleading messages and those that, rather than relying on verifiable or substantiated objective information about a product, make subjective claims or statements, a practice known as puffery. **Puffery** has been legally defined as "advertising or other sales presentations which praise the item to be sold with subjective opinions, superlatives, or exaggerations, vaguely and generally, stating no specific facts."[36] The use of puffery in advertising is common. For example, Bayer aspirin calls itself the "wonder drug that works wonders," Nestlé claims "Nestlé makes the very best chocolate," and Healthy Choice foods tell consumers "Never settle for less." Superlatives such as *greatest, best,* and *finest* are puffs that are often used.

Puffery has generally been viewed as a form of poetic license or allowable exaggeration. The FTC takes the position that because consumers expect exaggeration or inflated claims in advertising, they recognize puffery and don't believe it. But some studies show that consumers may believe puffery and perceive such claims as true.[37] One study found that consumers could not distinguish between a verifiable fact-based claim and puffery and were just as likely to believe both types of claims.[38] Ivan Preston argues that puffery has a detrimental effect on consumers' purchase decisions by burdening them with untrue beliefs and refers to it as "soft-core deception" that should be illegal.[39]

Advertisers' battle to retain the right to use puffery was supported in the latest revision of the Uniform Commercial Code in 1996. The revision switches the burden of proof to consumers from advertisers in cases pertaining to whether certain claims were meant to be taken as promises. The revision states that the buyer must prove that an affirmation of fact (as opposed to puffery) was made, that the buyer was aware of the advertisement, and that the affirmation of fact became part of the agreement with the seller.[40]

The use of puffery as a defense for advertising claims is periodically challenged in court. In one of the latest cases a suit was filed against the online brokerage firm E*Trade charging that it failed to keep promises of fast, reliable service made in its advertising campaign. The suit contends that several service outages cost clients of the online brokerage money when they could not complete trades quickly. E*Trade argues that the case is without merit and has moved to have the suit dismissed, citing other cases in which advertising claims were considered mere puffery or sales talk and immaterial. E*Trade also argues that it is acceptable for companies to extol the virtues of their products and services in an optimistic and positive tone and that its advertising is well within those bounds.[41]

Since unfair and deceptive acts or practices have never been precisely defined, the FTC is continually developing and refining a working definition in its attempts to regulate advertising. The traditional standard used to determine deception was whether a claim had the "tendency or capacity to deceive." However, this standard was criticized for being vague and all-encompassing.

In 1983 the FTC, under Chair James Miller III, put forth a new working definition of **deception:** "The commission will find deception if there is a misrepresentation, omission, or practice that is likely to mislead the consumer acting reasonably in the circumstances to the consumer's detriment."[42] There are three essential elements to this definition of deception.[43] The first element is that the representation, omission, or practice must be *likely to mislead* the consumer. The FTC defines *misrepresentation* as an express or implied statement contrary to fact, whereas a *misleading omission* occurs when qualifying information necessary to prevent a practice, claim, representation, or reasonable belief from being misleading is not disclosed.

The second element is that the act or practice must be considered from the perspective of *the reasonable consumer.* In determining reasonableness, the FTC considers the group to which the advertising is targeted and whether their interpretation of or reaction to the message is reasonable in light of the circumstances. The standard is flexible and allows the FTC to consider factors such as the age, education level, intellectual capacity, and frame of mind of the particular group to which the message or practice is targeted. For example, advertisements targeted to a particular group, such as children or the elderly, are evaluated with respect to their effect on a reasonable member of that group.

The third key element to the FTC's definition of deception is *materiality.* According to the FTC a "material" misrepresentation or practice is one that is likely to affect a consumer's choice or conduct with regard to a product or service. What this means is that the information, claim, or practice in question is important to consumers and, if acted upon, would be likely to influence their purchase decisions. In some cases the information or claims made in an ad may be false or misleading but would not be regarded as material since reasonable consumers would not make a purchase decision on the basis of this information.

Miller's goal was to help the commission determine which cases were worth pursuing and which were trivial. Miller argued that for an ad to be considered worthy of FTC challenge, it should be seen by a substantial number of consumers, it should lead to significant injury, and the problem should be one that market forces are not likely to remedy. However, the revised definition may put a greater burden on the FTC to prove that deception occurred and that the deception influenced the consumers' decision-making process in a detrimental way.

Determining what constitutes deception is still a gray area. Two of the factors the FTC considers in evaluating an ad for deception are (1) whether there are significant omissions of important information and (2) whether advertisers can substantiate the claims made for the product or service. The FTC has developed several programs to address these issues.

Affirmative Disclosure

An ad can be literally true yet leave the consumer with a false or misleading impression if the claim is true only under certain conditions or circumstances or if there are limitations to what the product can or cannot do. Thus, under its **affirmative disclosure** requirement, the FTC may require advertisers to include certain types of information in their ads so that consumers will be aware of all the consequences, conditions, and limitations associated with the use of a product or service. The goal of affirmative disclosure is to give consumers sufficient information to make an informed decision. An ad may be required to define the testing situation, conditions, or criteria used in making a claim. For example, fuel mileage claims in car ads are based on Environmental Protection Agency (EPA) ratings since they offer a uniform standard for making comparisons. Cigarette ads must contain a warning about the health risks associated with smoking.

An example of an affirmative disclosure ruling is the FTC's 1989 case against Campbell Soup for making deceptive and unsubstantiated claims. Campbell's ads, run as part of its "Soup is good food" campaign, linked the low fat and cholesterol content of its soup with a reduced risk of heart disease. However, the advertising failed to disclose that the soups are high in sodium, which may increase the risk of heart disease. In a consent agreement accepted in 1991, Campbell agreed that, for any soup containing more than 500 milligrams of sodium in an eight-ounce serving, it will disclose the sodium content in any advertising that directly or by implication mentions heart disease in connection with the soup. Campbell also agreed it would not imply a connection between soup and a reduction in heart disease in future advertising.[44]

Another area where the Federal Trade Commission is seeking more specificity from advertisers is in regard to country of origin claims. The FTC has been working with marketers and trade associations to develop a better definition of what the "Made in the USA" label means. The 50-year-old definition used until recently required full manufacturing in the United States, using U.S. labor and parts, with only raw materials from overseas.[45] Many companies argue that in an increasingly global economy, it is becoming very difficult to have 100 percent U.S. content and remain price-competitive. However, the FTC argues that advertising or labeling a product as "Made in the USA" can provide a company with a competitive advantage. For many products some consumers do respond to the claim, as they trust the quality of domestic-made products and/or feel patriotic when they buy American.

In December 1998 the FTC issued new guidelines for American-made products. The guidelines spell out what it means by "all or virtually all" in mandating how much U.S. content a product must have to wear a "Made in USA" label or be advertised as such. According to the new FTC guidelines, all significant parts and processing that go into the product must be of U.S. origin and the product should have no or very little foreign content. Companies do not have to receive the approval of the FTC before making a "Made in USA" claim. However, the commission does have the authority to take action against false and unsubstantiated "Made in USA" claims just as it does with other advertising claims.[46]

Advertising Substantiation

A major area of concern to regulatory agencies is whether advertisers can support or substantiate their claims. For many years, there were no formal requirements concerning substantiation of advertising claims. Many companies made claims without any documentation or support such as laboratory tests and clinical studies. In 1971, the FTC's **advertising substantiation** program required advertisers to have supporting documentation for their claims and to prove the claims are truthful.[47] Broadened in 1972, this program now requires advertisers to substantiate their claims before an ad appears. Substantiation is required for all claims involving safety, performance, efficacy, quality, or comparative price.

The FTC's substantiation program has had a major effect on the advertising industry, because it shifted the burden of proof from the commission to the advertiser. Before the substantiation program, the FTC had to prove that an advertiser's claims were unfair or deceptive.

Ad substantiation seeks to provide a basis for believing advertising claims so consumers can make rational and informed decisions and companies are deterred from making claims they cannot adequately support. The FTC takes the perspective that it is illegal and unfair to consumers for a firm to make a claim for a product without having a "reasonable basis" for the claim. In their decision to require advertising substantiation, the commissioners made the following statement:

> Given the imbalance of knowledge and resources between a business enterprise and each of its customers, economically it is more rational and imposes far less cost on society, to require a manufacturer to confirm his affirmative product claims rather than impose a burden on each individual consumer to test, investigate, or experiment for himself. The manufacturer has the ability, the know-how, the equipment, the time and resources to undertake such information, by testing or otherwise,...the consumer usually does not.[48]

Many advertisers respond negatively to the FTC's advertising substantiation program. They argue it is too expensive to document all their claims and most consumers either won't understand or aren't interested in the technical data. Some advertisers threaten to avoid the substantiation issue by using puffery claims, which do not require substantiation.

Generally, advertisers making claims covered by the substantiation program must have available prior substantiation of all claims. However, in 1984, the FTC issued a new policy statement that suggested after-the-fact substantiation might be acceptable in some cases and it would solicit documentation of claims only from advertisers that are under investigation for deceptive practices.

In a number of cases, the FTC orders advertisers to cease making inadequately substantiated claims. In 1993, the FTC obtained relief against Union Oil of California and its agency for making unsubstantiated claims in advertising for Unocal's 89 and 92 octane gasoline. According to the FTC complaint, Unocal lacked adequate scientific evidence for its claims that the higher-octane gasolines increased engine performance and longevity. Yet, the FTC argued many consumers believe that higher-octane gasoline improves an engine's performance and the advertising played into this belief. In settling with the FTC, Unocal and its agency agreed that, lacking better scientific evidence, they would stop making claims that drivers could get better performance by exceeding auto manufacturers' recommendations for fuel use.[49]

In the same year the FTC also took on the weight-loss industry when it filed a complaint charging that none of five large, well-known diet program marketers had sufficient evidence to back up claims that their customers achieved their weight-loss goals or maintained the loss (Exhibit 21–5). Three of the companies agreed to publicize the fact that most weight loss is temporary and to disclose how long their customers kept off the weight they lost. The agreement required the companies to substantiate their weight-loss claims with scientific data and to document claims that their customers keep off the weight by monitoring a group of them for two years.[50]

In 1997 the FTC challenged advertising claims made by Abbott Laboratories for its Ensure brand nutritional beverage. The FTC charged that Abbott made false and unsubstantiated claims that many doctors recommend Ensure as a meal supplement and replacement for healthy adults, including those in their 30s and 40s. The agency complaint said Abbott relied on a survey of doctors that wasn't designed to determine *whether* many doctors actually recommended Ensure as a meal replacement for healthy adults. Rather, according to the FTC complaint, the survey asked doctors to assume that they would recommend a supplement for adults who were not ill and then merely select which brand they would suggest. The FTC ruled that Abbott went too far when it suggested that doctors recommend Ensure for healthy, active people like those pictured in its ads, in order to stay healthy and active. Abbott agreed to settle the charges and stop using endorsements from medical professionals unless it could produce reliable scientific evidence to substantiate the claims.[51]

Exhibit 21–5 Weight-loss program marketers are now required to substantiate their claims as a result of an FTC ruling

Recently the FTC has stepped up its action against false and unsubstantiated claims in ads and infomercials. In 1999 the commission fined the Home Shopping Network $1.1 million for making unsubstantiated advertising claims for two weight-loss products, an acne treatment, and a dietary supplement for menopause and premenstrual syndrome. Under the settlement Home Shopping is enjoined from making product claims about curing and treating diseases without "reliable scientific evidence." Another company, e4L, formerly known as National Media Corp., also agreed to pay a $100,000 fine in an infomercial case involving unsubstantiated claims for its Motor Up Engine Treatment.[52]

The FTC's Handling of Deceptive Advertising Cases

Consent and Cease-and-Desist Orders Allegations of unfair or deceptive advertising come to the FTC's attention from a variety of sources, including competitors, consumers, other government agencies, or the commission's own monitoring and investigations. Once the FTC decides a complaint is justified and warrants further action, it notifies the offender, who then has 30 days to respond. The advertiser can agree to negotiate a settlement with the FTC by signing a **consent order,** which is an agreement to stop the practice or advertising in question. This agreement is for settlement purposes only and does not constitute an admission of guilt by the advertiser. Most FTC inquiries are settled by consent orders because they save the advertiser the cost and possible adverse publicity that might result if the case went further.

If the advertiser chooses not to sign the consent decree and contests the complaint, a hearing can be requested before an administrative law judge employed by the FTC but not under its influence. The judge's decision may be appealed to the full five-member commission by either side. The commission either affirms or modifies the order or dismisses the case. If the complaint has been upheld by the administrative law judge and the commission, the advertiser can appeal the case to the federal courts.

The appeal process may take some time, during which the FTC may want to stop the advertiser from engaging in the deceptive practice. The Wheeler-Lea Amendment empowers the FTC to issue a **cease-and-desist order,** which requires that the advertiser stop the specified advertising claim within 30 days and prohibits the advertiser from engaging in the objectionable practice until after the hearing is held. Violation of a cease-and-desist order is punishable by a fine of up to $10,000 a day. Figure 21–5 summarizes the FTC complaint procedure.

Corrective Advertising By using consent and cease-and-desist orders, the FTC can usually stop a particular advertising practice it believes is unfair or deceptive. However, even if an advertiser ceases using a deceptive ad, consumers may still remember some or all of the claim. To address the problem of residual effects, in the 1970s the FTC developed a program known as **corrective advertising.** An advertiser found guilty of deceptive advertising can be required to run additional advertising designed to remedy the deception or misinformation contained in previous ads.

The impetus for corrective advertising was another case involving Campbell Soup, which placed marbles in the bottom of a bowl of vegetable soup to force the solid ingredients to the surface, creating a false impression that the soup contained more vegetables than it really did. (Campbell Soup argued that if the marbles were not used, all the ingredients would settle to the bottom, leaving an impression of fewer ingredients than actually existed!) While Campbell Soup agreed to stop the practice, a group of law students calling themselves SOUP (Students Opposed to Unfair Practices) argued to the FTC that this would not remedy false impressions created by prior advertising and contended Campbell Soup should be required to run advertising to rectify the problem.[53]

Figure 21–5 FTC complaint procedure

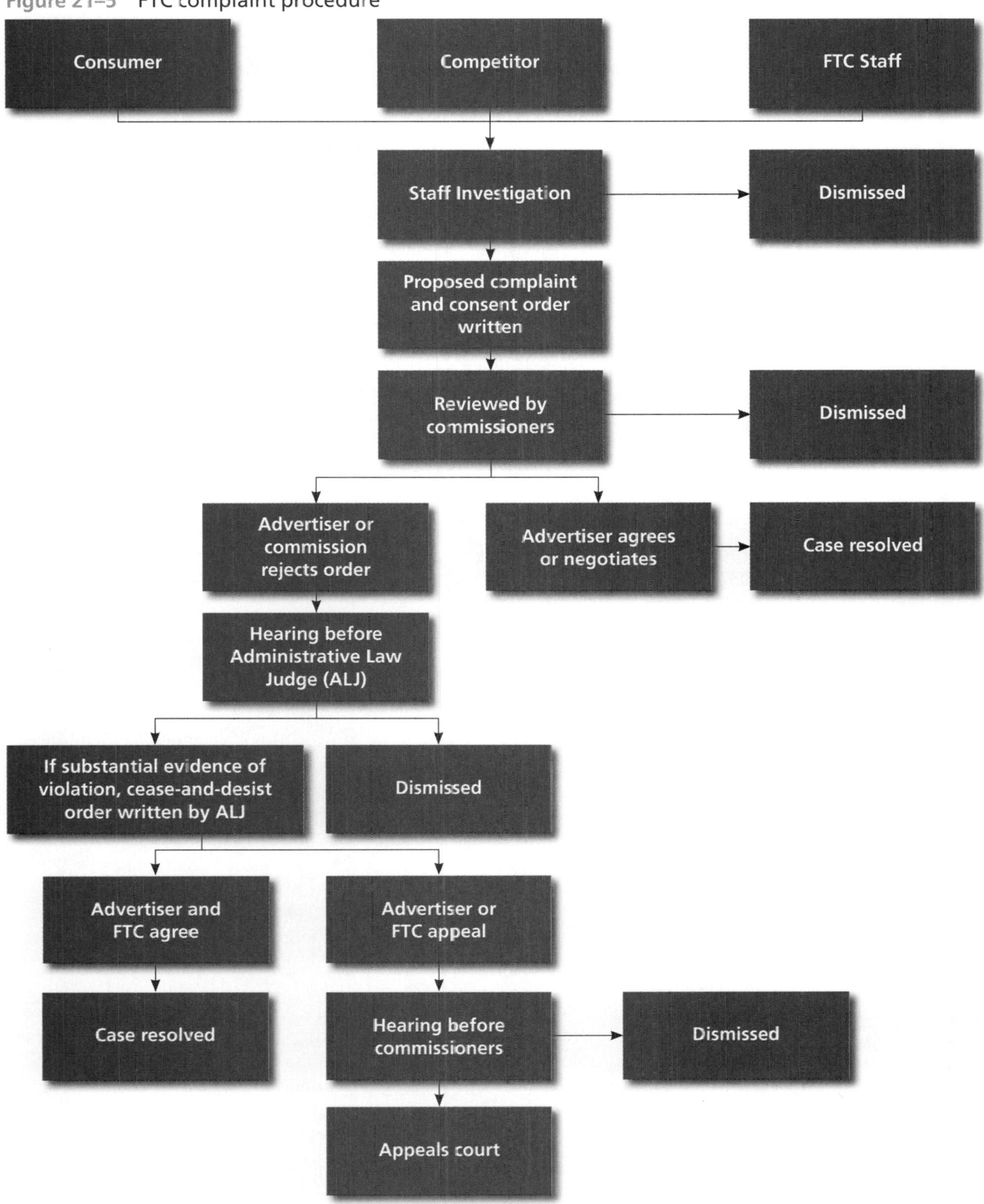

Although the FTC did not order corrective advertising in the Campbell case, it has done so in many cases since then. Profile Bread ran an ad stating each slice contained fewer calories than other brands—but the ad did not mention that slices of Profile bread were thinner than those of other brands. Ocean Spray cranberry juice was found guilty of deceptive advertising because it claimed to have more "food energy" than orange or tomato juice but failed to note it was referring to the technical definition of food energy, which is calories. In each case, the advertisers were ordered to spend 25 percent of their annual media budget to run corrective ads. The STP Corporation was required to run corrective advertising for claims regarding the ability of its oil additive to reduce oil consumption. Many of the corrective ads run in the STP case appeared in business publications to serve notice to other advertisers that the FTC was enforcing the corrective advertising program. The texts of the corrective messages required in each of these cases are shown in Figure 21–6.

The consent order signed by Unocal as part of its 1993 settlement with the FTC also included a corrective advertising provision. Unocal agreed to mail a corrective notice to all of its active credit-card customers in its primary marketing area stating that most cars do not need a high-octane gasoline to perform properly and reminding them to check their owner's manual for the recommended fuel octane level.

Corrective advertising is probably the most controversial of all the FTC programs. Advertisers argue that corrective advertising infringes on First Amendment rights of freedom of speech. The effectiveness of corrective advertising campaigns is also being questioned, as is the FTC's involvement in the business of creating ads through requiring particular content in corrective messages.[54] However, in a recent case involving Novartis Consumer Health Corp.'s Doan's Pills, the FTC sent a strong message to advertisers and agencies that it will require marketers to run corrective ads to remedy any misleading impressions that were created through unsubstantiated advertising claims.[55] In this case, Novartis was ordered to spend $8

Figure 21–6 Examples of corrective advertising messages

Profile Bread

"Hi, [celebrity's name] for Profile Bread. Like all mothers, I'm concerned about nutrition and balanced meals. So, I'd like to clear up any misunderstanding you may have about Profile Bread from its advertising or even its name.

"Does Profile have fewer calories than any other breads? No. Profile has about the same per ounce as other breads. To be exact, Profile has seven fewer calories per slice. That's because Profile is sliced thinner. But eating Profile will not cause you to lose weight. A reduction of seven calories is insignificant. It's total calories and balanced nutrition that count. And Profile can help you achieve a balanced meal because it provides protein and B vitamins as well as other nutrients.

"How does my family feel about Profile? Well, my husband likes Profile toast, the children love Profile sandwiches, and I prefer Profile to any other bread. So you see, at our house, delicious taste makes Profile a family affair."

(To be run in 25 percent of brand's advertising, for one year.)

Ocean Spray

"If you've wondered what some of our earlier advertising meant when we said Ocean Spray Cranberry Juice Cocktail has more food energy than orange juice or tomato juice, let us make it clear: we didn't mean vitamins and minerals. Food energy means calories. Nothing more.

"Food energy is important at breakfast since many of us may not get enough calories, or food energy, to get off to a good start. Ocean Spray Cranberry Juice Cocktail helps because it contains more food energy than most other breakfast drinks.

"And Ocean Spray Cranberry Juice Cocktail gives you and your family Vitamin C plus a great wake-up taste. It's ... the other breakfast drink."

(To be run in one of every four ads for one year.)

STP

As a result of an investigation by the Federal Trade Commission into certain allegedly inaccurate past advertisements for STP's oil additive, STP Corporation has agreed to a $700,000 settlement. With regard to that settlement, STP is making the following statement:

"It is the policy of STP to support its advertising with objective information and test data. In 1974 and 1975 an independent laboratory ran tests of the company's oil additive which led to claims of reduced oil consumption. However, these tests cannot be relied on to support the oil consumption reduction claim made by STP.

"The FTC has taken the position that, in making the claim, the company violated the terms of a consent order. When STP learned that the test did not support the claim, it stopped advertising containing that claim. New tests have been undertaken to determine the extent to which the oil additive affects oil consumption. Agreement to this settlement does not constitute an admission by STP that the law has been violated. Rather, STP has agreed to resolve the dispute with the FTC to avoid protracted and prohibitively expensive litigation."

million, or the equivalent of the average annual ad budget for Doan's Pills over an eight-year period, on corrective ads to remedy any impressions that might exist from previous advertising that the brand is more effective than other analgesics for relieving back pain. Novartis plans to appeal the decision, and this may, like the landmark Listerine mouthwash case in 1975, be a major test of the FTC's legal power to order corrective advertising. IMC Perspective 21–2 discusses the latest battle in the ongoing war over the FTC's authority to order corrective advertising.

Current Status of Federal Regulation by the FTC

By the end of the 1970s, the FTC had become a very powerful and active regulator of advertising. However, Congress was concerned about the FTC's broad interpretation of unfairness, which led to the restrictive legislation of the 1980 FTC Improvements Act. During the 1980s, the FTC became less active and cut back its regulatory efforts, due in large part to the Reagan administration's laissez-faire attitude toward the regulation of business in general. Some feared that the FTC had become too narrow in its regulation of national advertising, forcing companies and consumer groups to seek relief from other sources such as state and federal courts or through self-regulatory groups such as the NAD/NARB.[56]

In 1988–89, an 18-member panel chosen by the American Bar Association undertook a study of the FTC as a 20-year follow-up to the 1969 report used by President Richard Nixon to overhaul the commission. The panel's report expressed strong concern over the FTC's lack of sufficient resources and staff to regulate national advertising effectively and called for more funding.

After more than a decade of relative inactivity, the Federal Trade Commission has once again become active in the regulation of advertising. The commission has shown particular interest in cracking down on misleading advertising in areas such as health, nutrition, weight loss, and environmental claims as well as advertising directed to children and the elderly.[57] The FTC has also become more involved with potential fraud and deception through various other promotional methods such as telemarketing, 900 numbers, infomercials, and the Internet. For example, in 1999 the FTC charged iMall Inc. and two of the company's former presidents with misleading investors by making false claims for two Internet-based businesses they promoted from 1995 to 1998. The businesses involved putting up money for a chance to make, with little work, as much as $20,000 a month by selling Web pages on iMall's site or as much as $5,000 a month by selling ad space at another website. As part of the settlement, the company paid $750,000 and the two former executives paid a total of $3.25 million in investor restitution. In settling the case, the FTC's director of consumer protection stated: "A deceptive claim is a deceptive claim, whether it's on the Internet or in your local newspaper."[58] In addition to monitoring deceptive claims made over the Internet, the FTC has become very involved in privacy issues and the collection of personal information on websites. These issues are discussed later in the chapter.

While the FTC is the major regulator of advertising for products sold in interstate commerce, several other federal agencies and departments also regulate advertising and promotion.

Additional Federal Regulatory Agencies

The Federal Communications Commission

The FCC, founded in 1934 to regulate broadcast communication, has jurisdiction over the radio, television, telephone, and telegraph industries. The FCC has the authority to license broadcast stations as well as to remove a license or deny renewal to stations not operating in the public's interest. The FCC's authority over the airways gives it the power to control advertising content and to restrict what products and services can be advertised on radio and TV. The FCC can eliminate obscene and profane programs and/or messages and those it finds in poor taste. While the FCC can purge ads that are deceptive or misleading, it generally works closely with the FTC in the

IMC Perspective 21–2

The Latest Showdown over Corrective Advertising

One of the most publicized corrective advertising cases ever, and the first to test the FTC's legal power to order corrective messages, involved Warner-Lambert's Listerine mouthwash. For more than 50 years Warner-Lambert had advertised that gargling with Listerine helped prevent colds and sore throats or lessened their severity because it killed the germs that caused these illnesses. In 1975, the FTC ruled these claims could not be substantiated and ordered Warner-Lambert to stop making them. In addition, the FTC argued that corrective advertising was needed to rectify the erroneous beliefs that had been created by Warner-Lambert as a result of the large amount of advertising it had run for Listerine over the prior 50 years.

Warner-Lambert argued that the advertising was not misleading and, further, that the FTC did not have the power to order corrective advertising. Warner-Lambert appealed the FTC decision all the way to the Supreme Court, which rejected the argument that corrective advertising violates advertisers' First Amendment rights. The powers of the FTC in the areas of both claim substantiation and corrective advertising were upheld. Warner-Lambert was required to run $10 million worth of corrective ads over a 16-month period stating, "Listerine does not help prevent colds or sore throats or lessen their severity."

Since the Supreme Court ruling in the Listerine case, there have been several other situations where the FTC has ordered corrective advertising on the basis of the "Warner-Lambert test," which considers whether consumers are left with a latent impression that would continue to affect buying decisions and whether corrective ads are needed to remedy the situation. However, 25 years after this landmark case the FTC is once again facing a major court challenge to its authority to require corrective ads. The latest case testing the Federal Trade Commission's authority regarding corrective advertising involves Novartis Consumer Health and its product Doan's Pills. The FTC has argued that Doan's ads from 1987 to 1996 falsely presented the brand as better for back pain than other remedies. However, Novartis has argued that the ads were not misleading and no matter what they said they were unlikely to leave a sufficiently lasting impression to warrant corrective advertising.

In March 1998 an administrative law judge ruled that the claims for Doan's were misleading but said corrective advertising was not warranted. The judge considered the Warner-Lambert test and wrote: "Given the difference between the length of time that the false Doan's and Listerine ads ran, there is no certainty that the belief at issue required corrective advertising." However, the FTC appealed the decision to the full commission, and in May 1999 the judge's decision not to order corrective advertising was overturned. Novartis was ordered to run $8 million in corrective ads that state, "Although Doan's is an effective pain reliever, there is no evidence that it is more effective than other pain relievers for back pain." The FTC also ruled that those words must appear on packaging for one year. The $8 million figure matches the company's annual advertising spending on Doan's Pills.

Novartis has announced that it plans to appeal the FTC decision, and experts say the case will force the courts to determine how much evidence the FTC needs before it takes action. At issue in the appeal will be the FTC's standard for determining when a latent impression exists and whether the commission has to prove that advertising created a lingering false impression or whether it can assume that years of advertising would have created the misapprehension.

The Doan's case will have very important implications for the FTC as well as advertisers. A win by the FTC would reaffirm the agency's authority to order corrective advertising and give it greater freedom to use the remedy, but a loss could limit its ability to do so. The case will also have lasting repercussions for advertisers, who are concerned over an FTC commissioner's contention that "corrective advertising is not a drastic remedy" and is an appropriate method for restoring the status quo. Advertisers fear that this may indicate that the FTC will be more willing to apply the punishment in future cases. There is obviously a lot at stake in this case for advertisers. However, the case is also very important to the FTC in the ongoing battle over its authority to require corrective advertising.

Sources: Ira Teinowitz, "Doan's Decision Worries Marketers," *Advertising Age,* May 31, 1999, p. 74; Bruce Ingersoll, "FTC Orders Novartis Ads to Correct Claim," *The Wall Street Journal,* May 28, 1999, p. B2; Ira Teinowitz, "FTC Faces Test of Ad Power," *Advertising Age,* March 30, 1998, p. 26.

regulation of advertising. For example, in late 1999 the Federal Communications Commission and the FTC held a joint workshop and publicly accused long-distance phone marketers of deceiving consumers in their advertising. Officials of both commissions expressed concern over per-minute ads for long distance and so-called dial-around long-distance services. They also warned long-distance marketers that they would take action if steps were not taken to clean up their advertising.[59]

Many of the FCC's rules and regulations for TV and radio stations have been eliminated or modified. The FCC no longer limits the amount of television time that can be devoted to commercials. (But in 1991 the Children's Television Act went into effect. The act limits advertising during children's programming to 10.5 minutes an hour on weekends and 12 minutes an hour on weekdays.)

Under the Reagan administration, the controversial *Fairness Doctrine,* which required broadcasters to provide time for opposing viewpoints on important issues, was repealed on the grounds that it was counterproductive. It was argued that the Fairness Doctrine actually reduced discussion of important issues because a broadcaster might be afraid to take on a paid controversial message in case it might be required to provide equal free exposure for opposing viewpoints. It was under this doctrine that the FCC required stations to run commercials about the harmful effects of smoking before passage of the Public Health Cigarette Smoking Act of 1970, which banned broadcast advertising of cigarettes. Many stations still provide time for opposing viewpoints on controversial issues as part of their public service requirement, not necessarily directly related to fairness.

Several pieces of legislation passed in recent years involve the FCC and have an impact on advertising and promotion. The Cable Television Consumer Protection and Competition Act, passed in 1992, allows the FCC and local governments to regulate basic cable TV rates and forces cable operators to pay licensing fees for local broadcast programming they retransmit for free. One purpose of this bill is to improve the balance between cable rates and rapidly escalating advertising revenue. FCC rules affecting telemarketing will be discussed toward the end of this chapter.

The Food and Drug Administration Now under the jurisdiction of the Department of Health and Human Services, the FDA has authority over the labeling, packaging, branding, ingredient listing, and advertising of packaged foods and drug products. The FDA is authorized to require caution and warning labels on potentially hazardous products and also has limited authority over nutritional claims made in food advertising. This agency has the authority to set rules for promoting these products and the power to seize food and drugs on charges of false and misleading advertising.

Like the FTC, the Food and Drug Administration has become a very aggressive regulatory agency in recent years, particularly since David A. Kessler's stint as commissioner beginning in 1991. The FDA has cracked down on a number of commonly used descriptive terms it believes are often abused in the labeling and advertising of food products—for example, *natural, light, no cholesterol,* and *fat free.* The FDA has also become tougher on nutritional claims implied by brand names that might send a misleading message to consumers. For example, Great Foods of America was not permitted to continue using the HeartBeat trademark under which it sold most of its foods. The FDA argued the trademark went too far in implying the foods have special advantages for the heart and overall health. Recently the FDA forced Hoffman La-Roche to stop running a commercial for its much-hyped obesity drug Xenical. The FDA's Division of Drug Marketing, Advertising, and Communications charged that the commercial lacked fair balance and misled consumers in how it portrayed the drug's side effects and demonstrated who should use the product. However, the company quickly modified the spot in response to FDA concerns and was able to begin running it again.[60]

Many changes in food labeling are a result of the Nutritional Labeling and Education Act, which Congress passed in 1990. Under this law the FDA established legal definitions for a wide range of terms (such as *low fat, light,* and *reduced calories*) and required straightforward labels for all foods beginning in early 1994

Exhibit 21–6 The Nutritional Labeling and Education Act requires that labels be easy for consumers to understand

(Exhibit 21–6). In its current form the act applies only to food labels, but it may soon affect food advertising as well. The FTC would be asked to ensure that food ads comply with the new FDA standards.

In 1996 President Clinton signed an executive order declaring that nicotine is an addictive drug and giving the Food and Drug Administration broad jurisdiction to regulate cigarettes and smokeless tobacco. Many of the regulations proposed by the FDA are designed to keep teenagers from smoking. However, as discussed in IMC Perspective 21–3, a major legal battle has emerged between the government and the tobacco industry over whether the FDA has the authority to regulate the marketing and advertising of cigarettes.

The U.S. Postal Service

Many marketers use the U.S. mail to deliver advertising and promotional messages. The U.S. Postal Service has control over advertising involving the use of the mail and ads that involve lotteries, obscenity, or fraud. The regulation against fraudulent use of the mail has been used to control deceptive advertising by numerous direct-response advertisers. These firms advertise on TV or radio or in magazines and newspapers and use the U.S. mail to receive orders and payment. Many have been prosecuted by the Post Office Department for use of the mail in conjunction with a fraudulent or deceptive offer.

Bureau of Alcohol, Tobacco, and Firearms

The Bureau of Alcohol, Tobacco, and Firearms (BATF) is an agency within the Treasury Department that enforces laws, develops regulations, and is responsible for tax collection for the liquor industry. The BATF regulates and controls the advertising of alcoholic beverages. The agency determines what information can be provided in ads as well as what constitutes false and misleading advertising. It is also responsible for including warning labels on alcohol advertising and banning the use of active athletes in beer commercials. The BATF can impose strong sanctions for violators. As was discussed in Ethical Perspective 21–1, the advertising of alcoholic beverages has become a very controversial issue, with many consumer and public-interest groups calling for a total ban on the advertising of beer, wine, and liquor.

The Lanham Act

While most advertisers rely on self-regulatory mechanisms and the FTC to deal with deceptive or misleading advertising by their competitors, many companies are filing lawsuits against competitors they believe are making false claims. One piece of federal legislation that has become increasingly important in this regard is the Lanham Act. This act was originally written in 1947 as the Lanham Trade-Mark Act to protect words, names, symbols, or other devices adopted to identify and distinguish a manufacturer's products. The **Lanham Act** was amended to encompass false advertising by prohibiting "any false description or representation including words or other symbols tending falsely to describe or represent the same." While the FTC Act did not give individual advertisers the opportunity to sue a competitor for deceptive advertising, civil suits are permitted under the Lanham Act.

More and more companies are using the Lanham Act to sue competitors for their advertising claims, particularly since comparative advertising has become so common. For example, a U.S. district court fined Jartran a record $20 million in punitive damages on top of the $20 million awarded to U-Haul International to compensate for losses resulting from ads comparing the companies' prices and equipment that were ruled deceptive. In several recent cases, companies have sued a competitor for damages resulting from false advertising claims. A court ordered Ralston Purina to pay Alpo Petfoods $12 million for damages it caused by making

IMC Perspective 21–3

The FDA versus the Tobacco Industry

For more than 30 years the tobacco industry has been following a strategy of seeking compromise laws to avoid more stringent regulations. In the mid-1960s cigarette makers forestalled Federal Trade Commission regulations of their ads by agreeing to put warning labels on their packs. They also successfully weakened the FTC's proposed language. The labels became a powerful industry defense in liability lawsuits by smokers, as lawyers for tobacco companies argued that the risks of smoking were publicized. A few years later, the tobacco companies asked Congress to ban them from advertising on television. The ban reduced a wave of antismoking commercials that got on TV under the equal time provision of the Fairness Doctrine—and cigarette consumption rose.

Michael Pertschuk, a former FTC commissioner and longtime tobacco opponent, says the tobacco industry "has always had a strategy of giving just what they had to give to head off something worse." However, the tobacco industry has had to compromise over the latest round of regulation announced by the federal government. In August 1996, President Clinton signed an executive order that defines nicotine as an addictive drug and gives the Food and Drug Administration broad jurisdiction to regulate cigarettes and smokeless tobacco.

Under its new authority, the FDA proposed sweeping new rules designed to keep teenagers from smoking. The new rules include requiring that anyone younger than 27 show proof of age before buying cigarettes; banning most vending machine sales, except in places frequented by adults, such as bars; banning brand-name tobacco sponsorship of sporting events; eliminating brand-name tobacco logos on baseball caps, T-shirts, and other merchandise; and in the most controversial provision of all, restricting advertising in publications read by a significant number of young people to a black-and-white, text-only format with no photographs. This format also applies to billboards, which will be banned entirely within 1,000 feet of schools and playgrounds.

The tobacco industry immediately appealed the order giving the FDA the authority to regulate tobacco. The only two regulations currently in force, pending the outcome of the litigation, are a ban on sales to anyone under 18 years old and a requirement that anyone under 27 show photo identification to purchase cigarettes. In 1997, as part of a proposed resolution of lawsuits brought by individual states against the industry, tobacco makers agreed to provisions that would have limited FDA authority regulating tobacco products but not banning them. However, that accord collapsed when Congress failed to enact needed legislation.

While continuing to fight its legal battle with the federal government over the FDA regulations, the tobacco makers did agree to settlements of lawsuits brought by a number of states against the industry in late 1998, including New York and California. These settlements have been a better deal for the industry, as many of the onerous cigarette-marketing restrictions contained in the 1997 settlement are missing. The current pact allows large outdoor signs at retailers, whereas the original proposal banned all outdoor ads. The original deal banned all use of humans and cartoons in ads, while the current settlement bans only cartoons and even permits their use on cigarette packs. And while the original proposal eliminated sports sponsorships, the current agreement allows each company to continue one national sponsorship.

The tobacco companies also agreed to pay $145 million over the next five years to fund antismoking campaigns and $250 million more over 10 years to establish a national public-health foundation to reduce smoking among youths. However, as part of the settlement the tobacco companies would move closer to their long-cherished goal of no longer being held liable for tobacco-related illnesses and deaths.

Marketing 101:
Tobacco Ads Influence Children
Tobacco companies spend billions annually on cartoon ads, free clothing and other youth-oriented marketing. Yet they claim this has no effect on children. Research confirms what common sense tells us:
• Teens are twice as likely to be influenced by cigarette advertising as they are by peer pressure.[1]
• Teens are three times more sensitive to cigarette advertising than are adults.[2]
• 85% of kids who smoke (vs. just 35% of smokers overall) choose the three most advertised brands.[3]
Why are tobacco companies allowed to get away with marketing that clearly influences kids? They flood politicians with cash to block measures that would protect America's children.
To keep tobacco companies away from our kids, get tobacco cash out of politics. Ask your elected officials and all candidates to reject tobacco contributions. Tell them our children aren't for sale.
To contact your Members of Congress or to learn more, call 1-800-284-KIDS.
This ad sponsored by the National Association of Elementary School Principals, National Coalition of Hispanic Health and Human Services Organizations (COSSMHO), National Association of Secondary School Principals, National Association of County and City Health Officials, National Black Child Development Institute, Intercultural Cancer Council, and American Society of Addiction Medicine.
CAMPAIGN for TOBACCO-FREE Kids
[1] Pierce, L.P., Journal of the National Cancer Institute, October 18, 1995.
[2] Pollay, R.W. Journal of Marketing, April 1996.
[3] U.S. Centers for Disease Control and Prevention, August 1994.

The tobacco industry's latest settlement with the states does not address the issue of FDA regulation. Cigarette makers contend that FDA rules that go beyond what they agreed to with the states would limit their ability to fight for adult customers in the shrinking U.S. market. Domestic cigarette shipments fell 12 percent between 1989 and 1998 and were expected to drop by another 10 percent in 1999 because of higher taxes on cigarettes and the higher prices needed to pay for the massive legal settlements with the states.

In 1998 a U.S. Circuit Court of Appeals ruled that the FDA lacked the authority to regulate tobacco. However, the government has asked the Supreme Court to overturn that decision by deciding whether tobacco products are "drugs" and "medical devices" under the current Food, Drug and Cosmetic Act and thus fall under the FDA's jurisdiction. The case took yet another strange twist in late 1999 when the cigarette makers went before the Supreme Court to argue that if the Court gives the FDA the authority to regulate cigarettes, it will have no choice but to ban them. The argument is that under FDA rules, "failure to find that tobacco products are effective and safe for any intended use" means that it can't merely regulate them.

In March 2000 the Supreme Court ruled that the FDA has no power to regulate the manufacture and sale of cigarettes, noting that Congress never intended tobacco products to be treated as drugs under the Food, Drug and Cosmetic Act. The decision blocks the FDA rules that would have restricted tobacco advertising from taking effect. It is now up to Congress to decide whether it wants to enact legislation to grant the FDA the power to regulate the tobacco products. It is likely that there are still a number of battles to fight in the war over the marketing and advertising of tobacco products.

Sources: Ira Tenowitz, "Ad Groups Praise High Court Ruling on Tobacco Regulation," *Advertising Age,* March 27, 2000, pp. 4, 70; Robert S. Greenberger and Gordon Fairclough, "At High Court, a Showdown Over Tobacco," *The Wall Street Journal,* December 1, 1999, pp. B1, 4; Suein L. Hwang and Milo Geyelin, "Is Tobacco Settlement Good News for Industry?" *The Wall Street Journal,* November 17, 1998, pp. B1, 4.

false claims that its Purina Puppy Chow dog food could ameliorate and help prevent joint disease. The court ruled that the claim was based on faulty data and that the company continued the campaign after learning its research was in error. Alpo was awarded the money as compensation for lost revenue and for the costs of advertising it ran in response to the Puppy Chow campaign.[61]

Wilkinson Sword and its advertising agency were found guilty of false advertising and ordered to pay $953,000 in damages to the Gillette Co. Wilkinson had run TV and print ads claiming its Ultra Glide razor and blades produced shaves "six times smoother" than Gillette's Atra Plus blades. This case marked the first time an agency was held liable for damages in connection with false claims made in a client's advertising.[62] Although the agency was later found not liable, the case served as a sobering reminder to agencies that they can be drawn into litigation over advertising they create for their clients. To deal with this problem, many agencies insist on indemnification clauses in contracts with their clients.

Suing competitors for false claims was made even easier with passage of the Trademark Law Revision Act of 1988. According to this law, anyone is vulnerable to civil action who "misrepresents the nature, characteristics, qualities, or geographical origin of his or her or another person's goods, services, or commercial activities." This wording closed a loophole in the Lanham Act, which prohibited only false claims about one's own goods or services. While many disputes over comparative claims are never contested or are resolved through the NAD, more companies are turning to lawsuits for several reasons: the broad information discovery powers available under federal civil procedure rules, the speed with which a competitor can stop the offending ad through a preliminary injunction, and the possibility of collecting damages.[63] However, companies do not always win their lawsuits. Under the Lanham Act you are required to prove five elements to win a false advertising lawsuit containing a comparative claim.[64] You must prove that:

- False statements have been made about the advertiser's product or your product.
- The ads actually deceived or had the tendency to deceive a substantial segment of the audience.

- The deception was "material" or meaningful and is likely to influence purchasing decisions.
- The falsely advertised products or services are sold in interstate commerce.
- You have been or likely will be injured as a result of the false statements, either by loss of sales or loss of goodwill.

Marketers using comparative ads have to carefully consider whether their messages have the potential to mislead consumers or may overstate their brand's performance relative to that of competitors. A recent study by Michael J. Barone and his colleagues provides a framework for developing measures that provide an assessment of the misleading effects that may arise from various types of comparative advertising.[65] Over the past few years there has been a significant increase in the use of comparative advertising, and it has resulted in more and more companies suing one another under the Lanham Act. IMC Perspective 21–4 discusses some of the recent comparative advertising battles.

State Regulation

In addition to the various federal rules and regulations, advertisers must also concern themselves with numerous state and local controls. An important early development in state regulation of advertising was the adoption in 44 states of the *Printers Ink* model statutes as a basis for advertising regulation. These statutes were drawn up in 1911 by *Printers Ink,* for many years the major trade publication of the advertising industry. Many states have since modified the original statutes and adopted laws similar to those of the Federal Trade Commission Act for dealing with false and misleading advertising. For example, in California, the Business and Professional Code prohibits "unlawful, unfair, or fraudulent" business practices and "unfair, deceptive, untrue, or misleading advertising."

In addition to recognizing decisions by the federal courts regarding false or deceptive practices, many states have special controls and regulations governing the advertising of specific industries or practices. As the federal government became less involved in the regulation of national advertising during the 1980s, many state attorneys general (AGs) began to enforce state laws regarding false or deceptive advertising. For example, the attorneys general in New York and Texas initiated investigations of Kraft ads claiming the pasteurized cheese used in Cheez Whiz was real cheese.[66] The well-publicized "monster truck" deceptive advertising case involving Volvo and its advertising agency that occured in the early 90s was initiated by the attorney general's office in the state of Texas.

The **National Association of Attorneys General** (NAAG) moved against a number of national advertisers as a result of inactivity by the FTC during the Reagan administration. In 1987, the NAAG developed enforcement guidelines on airfare advertising that were adopted by more than 40 states. The NAAG has also been involved in other regulatory areas, including car-rental price advertising as well as advertising dealing with nutrition and health claims in food ads.[67] In the early 1990s, a group of attorneys general from various states reached an agreement with Pfizer Corp. and its ad agency to stop making deceptive claims regarding the ability of Pfizer's Plax mouthwash to reduce plaque.[68]

The NAAG's foray into regulating national advertising raises the issue of whether the states working together can create and implement uniform national advertising standards that will, in effect, supersede federal authority. An American Bar Association panel concluded that the Federal Trade Commission is the proper regulator of national advertising and recommended the state AGs focus on practices that harm consumers within a single state.[69] This report also called for cooperation between the FTC and the state attorneys general.

Advertisers are concerned about the trend toward increased regulation of advertising at the state and local levels because it could mean that national advertising campaigns would have to be modified for every state or municipality. Yet the FTC takes the position that businesses that advertise and sell nationwide need a national advertising policy. While the FTC recognizes the need for greater cooperation

IMC Perspective 21–4

Is It Time to Bring Back "Brand X"?

For many years marketers in the United States could not use advertisements that made direct, explicit comparisons between their brand and a competitor. Contrary to what many think, there were no explicit laws against comparative advertising, but the print and broadcast media would not accept ads that named a competing brand. The media defended their policies by arguing that the use of comparisons could lead to an environment of claims, counterclaims, and contradictions that would increase the likelihood of deceptive or misleading ads and would have a negative impact on the credibility of advertising in general.

In the early 1970s the Federal Trade Commission issued a set of guidelines encouraging the use of comparative advertising as a way of improving the information available to consumers. The FTC worked closely with the advertising industry and the media, and in 1974 the American Association of Advertising Agencies and National Association of Broadcasters approved the use of comparative advertising. This opened the door for marketers to compare their product to another brand rather than using blind comparisons with "brand X" representing the competition.

Since then, many marketers have used comparative ads to introduce a new product or service by positioning their brand directly against more established competitors or market leaders and claiming superiority. While comparative advertising has become commonplace over the past 25 years, recently there has been a great deal of concern that marketers are abusing the use of comparative claims. And rather than letting consumers decide whose advertising claims they want to believe, many marketers are turning to courtrooms and asking judges and juries to decide.

There have been a number of major legal battles over the use of comparative advertising in recent years. In the mid-90s the Campbell Soup Co. advertised that its Prego brand of spaghetti sauce was thicker than Van Den Bergh Food's Ragu brand. Van Den Bergh sued to have Campbell's comparative ads for Prego halted but lost the case in district as well as appeals court. Campbell capitalized on winning by creating an ad based on its legal victory. The ad tweaked Ragu by showing snippets of the comparison ads and then a shot of Prego with a breadstick standing up in the sauce. The tagline: "Ragu took us to court. We made our case stand. Just like our breadstick." The two companies finally declared a truce in the spaghetti sauce wars in late 1999.

Procter & Gamble took rival Johnson & Johnson to court for the latter's comparative ad showing P&G's Swiffer cleaner product and J&J's similar product in action. Both devices use detachable cloths and a long stick to sweep away dirt. However, in the ad, Swiffer was enlarged and shown to have gaping holes, allowing dust and other particles to escape, while J&J's Pledge Grab-It brand was depicted as less porous. The ad also showed a model whose white glove was sullied after handling Swiffer, while Grab-It, by contrast, left the glove clean. After viewing the ads and watching a demonstration, a U.S. District Court judge ruled that the J&J comparative ad was "false and misleading" and issued a temporary restraining order preventing the company from airing it.

The comparative advertising legal battle that has received the most attention recently is the nasty skirmish between upstart Papa John's International and its archrival Pizza Hut. Over the past four years, Papa John's, which has been growing rapidly and become the fourth-largest pizza chain in the United States, has been running ads comparing its product to market leader Pizza Hut and using the tagline "Better ingredients. Better pizza." The battle heated up in 1997 when Papa John's aired a TV spot featuring its brash founder, John Schnatter, claiming consumers preferred his chain's tomato sauce over Pizza Hut's. He said Pizza Hut used "remanufactured paste," while Papa John's used fresh tomatoes picked from the vine.

Pizza Hut filed suit against Papa John's for misleading and deceptive advertising and after more than three weeks of testimony in federal court, which included dough experts and sauce demonstrations, a jury sided with Pizza Hut. In January 2000, a federal judge upheld the decision and awarded Pizza Hut $468,000 in damages and ordered Papa John's to stop using the slogan. If the ruling survives in federal appeals court, Papa John's not only will have to change its advertising slogan but also will be forced to remove the slogan from its delivery boxes, napkins, uniforms, and signs outside its restaurants.

Many in the advertising industry are concerned that marketers are increasingly using comparative ads that are confusing and not very informative and that may undermine the potential benefits of comparisons. Nearly 80 percent of complaints to the National Advertising Division of the Council of Better Business Bureaus now come from marketers rather than consumers. However, many marketers will continue to turn to direct comparisons, particularly in crowded product categories where it is difficult to differentiate a brand.

Sources: Michael Fumento, "Free-a-the Papa!" *Forbes,* February 21, 2000, p. 53; Louise Kramer, "Jury Finds Papa John's Ads Misled," *Advertising Age,* November 22, 1999, p. 46; Jack Neff, "Household Brands Counterpunch," *Advertising Age,* November 1, 1999, p. 26.

with the states, the agency believes regulation of national advertising should be its responsibility.[70] Just in case, the advertising industry is still keeping a watchful eye on changes in advertising rules, regulations, and policies at the state and local levels.

Regulation of Other Promotional Areas

So far we've focused on the regulation of advertising. However, other elements of the promotional mix also come under the surveillance of federal, state, and local laws and various self-regulatory bodies. This section examines some of the rules, regulations, and guidelines that affect sales promotion, direct marketing, and marketing on the Internet.

Sales Promotion

Both consumer- and trade-oriented promotions are subject to various regulations. The Federal Trade Commission regulates many areas of sales promotion through the Marketing Practices Division of the Bureau of Consumer Protection. Many promotional practices are also policed by state attorneys general and local regulatory agencies. Various aspects of trade promotion, such as allowances, are regulated by the Robinson-Patman Act, which gives the FTC broad powers to control discriminatory pricing practices.

Contests and Sweepstakes As noted in Chapter 16, numerous legal considerations affect the design and administration of contests and sweepstakes, and these promotions are regulated by a number of federal and state agencies. There are two important considerations in developing contests (including games) and sweepstakes. First, marketers must be careful to ensure their contest or sweepstakes is not classified as a *lottery,* which is considered a form of gambling and violates the Federal Trade Commission Act and many state and local laws. A promotion is considered a lottery if a prize is offered, if winning a prize depends on chance and not skill, and if the participant is required to give up something of value in order to participate. The latter requirement is referred to as *consideration* and is the basis on which most contests, games, and sweepstakes avoid being considered lotteries. Generally, as long as consumers are not required to make a purchase to enter a contest or sweepstakes, consideration is not considered to be present and the promotion is not considered a lottery.

The second important requirement in the use of contests and sweepstakes is that the marketer provide full disclosure of the promotion. Regulations of the FTC, as well as many state and local governments, require marketers using contests, games, and sweepstakes to make certain all of the details are given clearly and to follow prescribed rules to ensure the fairness of the game.[71] Disclosure requirements include the exact number of prizes to be awarded and the odds of winning, the duration and termination dates of the promotion, and the availability of lists of

Exhibit 21–7 Marketers are required to provide consumers with full details of a contest or sweepstakes

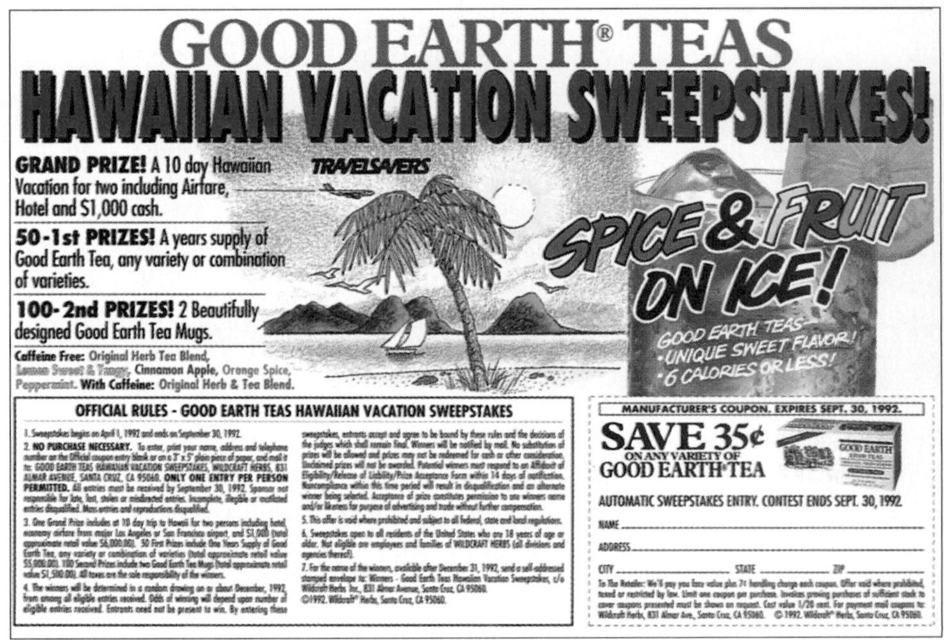

winners of various prizes (Exhibit 21–7). The FTC also has specific rules governing the way games and contests are conducted, such as requirements that game pieces be randomly distributed, that a game not be terminated before the distribution of all game pieces, and that additional pieces not be added during the course of a game.

Recently a number of states have responded to what they believe is widespread fraud on the part of some contest and sweepstakes operators. In 1995, at least 13 states either passed or tightened prize notification laws, requiring fuller disclosure of rules, odds, and the retail value of prizes. And many of the states are following through with tougher enforcement of these laws. For example, Publishers Clearing House, known for its million-dollar giveaways, agreed to pay $490,000 to 14 states and to change some of its language, better defining terms like "finalist" and "tie breaker." It also began to disclose the odds of winning prizes. More recently the controversy resulting from the lawsuits filed against American Family Publishing for misleading consumers regarding their odds of winning large cash prizes in its annual magazine subscription solicitation sweepstakes has led to investigations and stricter regulation of sweepstakes in a number of states.[72] For example, New York passed a law requiring the odds of winning a sweepstakes "must be conspicuously disclosed in the same type face, size and boldness and adjacent to the most prominent listing of the prizes on the front of the first page of the offer." The state law also prohibits statements that someone is a "winner" or that his or her name "has been selected" when no prize has been won. The law carries a fine of $1,000 per incident, which could be $1,000 per letter received by New York residents.[73] Some of the most ambitious legal actions are taking place in individual states such as West Virginia and Iowa, where prosecutors are taking sweepstakes and contest companies to court for misleading and deceptive practices.[74]

Premiums Another sales promotion area subject to various regulations is the use of premiums. A common problem associated with premiums is misrepresentation of their value. Marketers that make a premium offer should list its value as the price at which the merchandise is usually sold on its own. Marketers must also be careful in making premium offers to special audiences such as children. While premium offers for children are legal, their use is controversial; many critics argue that they encourage children to request a product for the premium rather than for its value. The Children's Advertising Review Unit has voluntary guidelines concerning the use of premium offers. These guidelines note that children have difficulty distinguishing a product from a premium. If product advertising contains a premium message, care should be taken that the child's attention is focused primarily on the product. The premium message should be clearly secondary. Conditions of a premium offer should be stated simply and clearly. "Mandatory" statements and disclosures should be stated in terms that can be understood by the child audience.[75] However, a recent study of children's advertising commissioned by CARU found the single most prevalent violation involved devoting virtually an entire commercial message to information about a premium. CARU guidelines state that advertising targeted to children must emphasize the product rather than the premium offer.[76]

Trade Allowances

Marketers using various types of trade allowances must be careful not to violate any stipulations of the Robinson-Patman Act, which prohibits price discrimination. Certain sections of the Robinson-Patman Act prohibit a manufacturer from granting wholesalers and retailers various types of promotional allowances and/or payments unless they are made available to all customers on proportionally equal terms.[77] Another form of trade promotion regulated by the Robinson-Patman Act is vertical cooperative advertising. The FTC monitors cooperative advertising programs to ensure that co-op funds are made available to retailers on a proportionally equal basis and that the payments are not used as a disguised form of price discrimination. As noted in Chapter 16, another trade promotion area where the FTC is becoming involved is the use of slotting fees or allowances paid to retailers for agreeing to handle a new product. In late 1999 the Senate Committee on Small Business charged retailers in the grocery, drugstore, and computer software industries with illegally using slotting fees to lock out competitors and prevent consumers from having their choice of the best products. Package-goods marketers and retailers have argued that examining slotting fees alone is unfair since they are just part of a wide variety of inducements marketers use to secure the best shelf space. The FTC plans to investigate the use of slotting fees as anticompetitive weapons that make it difficult for small-size companies to secure retail shelf space.[78]

Direct Marketing

As we saw in Chapter 14, direct marketing is growing rapidly. Many consumers now purchase products directly from companies in response to TV and print advertising or direct selling. The Federal Trade Commission enforces laws related to direct marketing, including mail-order offers, the use of 900 telephone numbers, and direct-response TV advertising. The U.S. Postal Service enforces laws dealing with the use of the mail to deliver advertising and promotional messages or receive payments and orders for items advertised in print or broadcast media.

A number of laws govern the use of mail-order selling. The FTC and the Postal Service police direct-response advertising closely to ensure the ads are not deceptive or misleading and do not misrepresent the product or service being offered. Laws also forbid mailing unordered merchandise to consumers, and rules govern the use of "negative option" plans whereby a company proposes to send merchandise to consumers and expects payment unless the consumer sends a notice of rejection or cancellation.[79] FTC rules also encourage direct marketers to ship ordered merchandise promptly. Companies that cannot ship merchandise within the time period stated in the solicitation (or 30 days if no time is stated) must give buyers the option to cancel the order and receive a full refund.[80]

Another area of direct marketing facing increased regulation is telemarketing. With the passage of the Telephone Consumer Protection Act of 1991, marketers who use telephones to contact consumers must follow a complex set of rules developed by the Federal Communications Commission. These rules require telemarketers to maintain an in-house list of residential telephone subscribers who do not want to be called. Consumers who continue to receive unwanted calls can take the telemarketer to state court for damages of up to $500. The rules also ban telemarketing calls to homes before 8:00 A.M. and after 9:00 P.M., automatic dialer calls, and recorded messages to emergency phones, health care facilities, and numbers for which the call recipient may be charged. They also ban unsolicited junk fax ads and require that fax transmissions clearly indicate the sender's name and fax number.[81]

The Federal Trade Commission has also been actively involved with the regulation of advertising that encourages consumers to call telephone numbers with a 900 prefix, whereupon they are automatically billed for the call. While there are many legitimate uses for 900-number technology, it has also been heavily used for sleazy sex operations, contest scams, and other unscrupulous activities.[82] One area of particular concern to the FTC has been ads targeting children and encouraging them to call 900 numbers. In 1993 the FTC issued its 900-Number Rule for advertising directed at children. The rule restricts advertisers from targeting children under the age of 12 with ads containing 900 numbers unless they provide a bona fide educational service. The rule also requires that 900-number ads directed at those under the age of 18 must contain a "clear and conspicuous" disclosure statement that requires the caller to have parental/guardian permission to complete the call. The rule also obligates advertisers to disclose the cost of the call and give the caller the opportunity to hang up without incurring any costs.[83]

The FTC enacted the 900-Number Rule under the premise that it would be reviewed within four years. This review, which was undertaken to obtain public comments about the costs and benefits of the 900-Number Rule, was recently completed, although the results have not been made available to the public. The FTC continues to use the rule to curb abuses associated with 900-number services.[84] A recent study by Russell Laczniak, Les Carlson, and Ann Walsh found that mothers of young children have positive attitudes toward the 900-Number Rule, particularly those who are more informed about it.[85]

The direct-marketing industry is also scrutinized by various self-regulatory groups, such as the Direct Marketing Association and the Direct Selling Association, that have specific guidelines and standards member firms are expected to adhere to and abide by. Exhibit 21–8 shows part of the Code of Ethics of the Direct Selling Association.

Exhibit 21–8 The Direct Selling Association has a Code of Ethics for companies engaged in direct selling

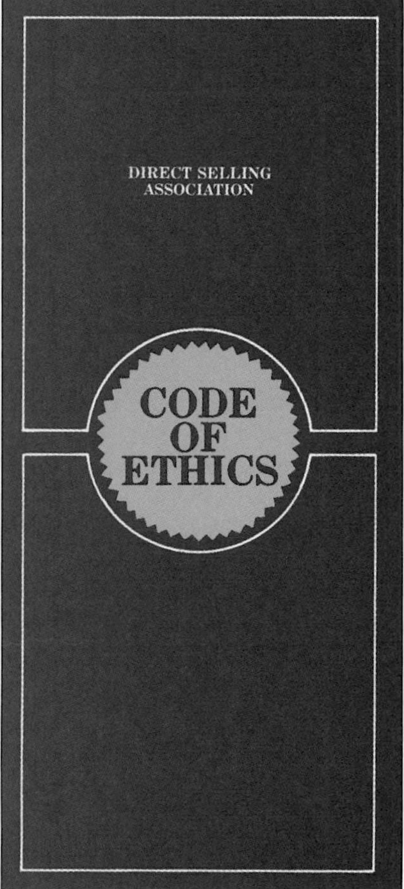

PREAMBLE

The Direct Selling Association, recognizing that companies engaged in direct selling assume certain responsibilities toward consumers arising out of the personal-contact method of distribution of their products and services, hereby sets forth the basic fair and ethical principles and practices to which member companies of the association will continue to adhere in the conduct of their business.

INTRODUCTION

The Direct Selling Association is the national trade association of the leading firms that manufacture and distribute goods and services sold directly to consumers. The Association's mission is "to protect, serve and promote the effectiveness of member companies and the independent businesspeople marketing their products and to assure the highest level of business ethics and service to consumers." The cornerstone of the Association's commitment to ethical business practices and consumer service is its Code of Ethics. Every member company pledges to abide by the Code's standards and procedures as a condition of admission and continuing membership in the Association. Consumers can rely on the extra protection provided by the Code when they purchase products or services from a salesperson associated with a member company of the Direct Selling Association. For a current list of Association members, contact DSA, 1776 K St., N.W., Washington, DC 20006, (202) 293-5760.

A. CODE OF CONDUCT

1. Deceptive or Unlawful Consumer Practices

No member company of the Association shall engage in any deceptive or unlawful consumer practice.

2. Products or Services

The offer of products or services for sale by member companies of the Association shall be accurate and truthful as to price, grade, quality, make, value, performance, quantity, currency of model, and availability.

3. Terms of Sale

A written order or receipt shall be delivered to the customer at the time of sale, which sets forth in language that is clear and free of ambiguity:

A. All the terms and conditions of sale, with specification of the total amount the customer will be required to pay, including all interest, service charges and fees, and other costs and expenses as required by federal and state law;

B. The name and address of the salesperson or the member firm represented.

4. Warranties and Guarantees

The terms of any warranty or guarantee offered by the seller in connection with the sale shall be furnished to the buyer in a manner that fully conforms to federal and state warranty and guarantee laws and regulations. The manufacturer, distributor and/or seller shall fully and promptly perform in accordance with the terms of all warranties and guarantees offered to consumers.

5. Pyramid Schemes

For the purpose of this Code, pyramid or endless chain schemes shall be considered consumer transactions actionable under this Code. The Code Administrator shall determine whether such pyramid or endless chain schemes constitute a violation of this Code in accordance with applicable federal, state and/or local law or regulation.

Marketing on the Internet

The rapid growth of the Internet as a marketing tool is creating a new area of concern for regulators. Currently marketing on the Internet is not subject to any formal government regulation, and many consumer and industry groups are concerned that some marketers will use the new medium to get around regulations and restrictions on other promotional areas. Following a Federal Trade Commission hearing in 1996, Chairman Robert Pitofsky issued a plea for voluntary industry codes rather than FTC rules and regulations.[86] He argued that the FTC's legal authority is limited to the areas of unfair or deceptive advertising and promotional practices and that many potential abuses of the Internet may not fall into these categories. Extending the FTC's legal authority would require congressional action. However, the results of the FTC's call for self-regulation of the Internet have been mixed. Two major areas of concern with regard to marketing on the Internet are privacy issues and online marketing to children.

With regard to privacy, several consumer and industry groups have proposed significant restrictions in the way marketers use the World Wide Web to get information from consumers, the types of information they can get, and what they do with this information.[87] The restrictions that have been proposed include:

- Banning unsolicited e-mail that cannot be automatically screened out. The Direct Marketing Association and the Interactive Services Association propose requiring marketers who send unsolicited e-mail messages to use coding that will allow mail systems to automatically remove such messages.
- Disclosing fully and prominently both the marketer's identity and the use for which information is being gathered in every communication.
- Giving consumers the right to bar marketers from selling or sharing any information collected from them as well as to review the personal information collected.

Recently the major privacy issue regarding the Internet that has emerged involves undisclosed profiling whereby Web marketers can profile a user on the basis of name, address, demographics, and online/offline purchasing data. Marketers have suggested that profiling offers them an opportunity to target specific niches and reach consumers with custom-tailored messages. However, FTC chairman Robert Pitofsky has stated that Internet sites that claim they don't collect information but permit advertisers to surreptitiously profile viewer sites are violating consumer protection laws and are open to a charge of deception.[88]

In response to the profiling controversy, 10 companies that collect data joined together in November 1999 under the banner of the Network Advertising Initiative to announce plans to develop a self-regulatory code that will require websites to disclose their use of ad servers and permit consumers to opt out of data collection that could be used for profiling. However, online privacy advocates and consumer groups planned to file a complaint with the FTC against DoubleClick, the company that is the largest Internet ad server and ad sales network provider and one of the leaders in tracking Web users.[89] The privacy debate is likely to escalate, and it is expected that legislation will be introduced to force companies to seek consumers' approval before sharing personal information captured from their websites.

While these proposals are aimed at protecting the privacy rights of adults, one of the biggest concerns is how to restrict marketers whose activities or websites are targeted at children. A number of children's advocacy groups have been critical of online marketing to children. In 1996 the Center for Media Education, in cooperation with the National Parent-Teachers Association (PTA), the Consumer Federation of America, and several other groups, issued a report entitled the "Web of Deception."[90] The report criticized marketers' online activities in a number of areas, including seeking household information from kids, sending direct mail, offering prizes, using advertising characters to reach children, and mixing advertising and nonadvertising content in websites.

Exhibit 21–9 The Children's Online Privacy Protection Act requires that websites targeted to children and teens have a privacy policy posted on their home page

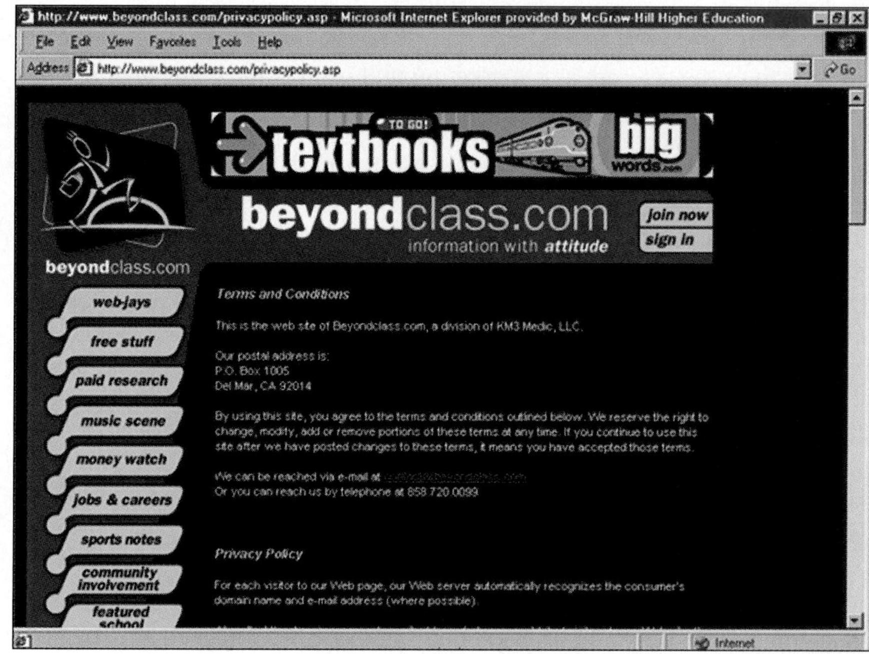

The report called for strict rules that would virtually eliminate the websites for children presently offered by some marketers and media companies and urged the FTC to adopt guidelines and restrictions. The restrictions being sought include prohibiting marketers from obtaining any personal information, including the age and e-mail address of children; forcing the clear labeling of advertising and promotion and its clear separation from other content; banning product mascots as spokespeople for websites; barring hypertext links jumping from content areas to advertising; and banning any microtargeting of children and direct-response marketing based on website-gathered data.

These concerns over online marketing to children led to the passage of the **Children's Online Privacy Protection Act of 1998,** which the FTC began enforcing in April 2000.[91] This act places tight restrictions on collecting information from children via the Internet and requires that websites directed at children and young teens have a privacy policy posted on their home page and areas of the site where information is collected (Exhibit 21–9). IMC Perspective 21–5 discusses how this new law will affect marketers with child-oriented websites.

As the use of the Internet as a commercial medium increases, the need for ethical standards by marketers and voluntary industry codes and guidelines will become greater. If they fail to respond, intervention by the FTC or other regulatory agencies is likely.

IMC Perspective 21–5

New Rules Will Protect Children's Online Privacy

One of the age cohorts of great interest to marketers over the next decade is Generation Y, the group generally described as born after 1979 and before 1994. This newest age cohort is an estimated 70 million strong and represents a huge opportunity that marketers are enthusiastically positioning themselves to exploit. However, many of the Gen Yers are still children, and regulators are working hard to protect these kids from the marketers who want to sell to them, including marketers trying to reach them over the Internet.

Government regulators recognize that today's young people are very comfortable with the Internet and seem to have no qualms about spending time or shopping online. A survey by Jupiter Communications of 600 teenagers (ages 13 to 18) and younger children (ages 5 to 12) found that 67 percent of teens and 37 percent of younger children with online access used the Internet to research or buy products online. Generation Y's presence on the Web is expected to go from an estimated 17 million in 1998 to 38.5 million by 2002—more than half of the 70 million in the age cohort. Jupiter estimates that the e-commerce dollar impact of spending by Generation Y will be $1.3 billion by 2002.

The federal government actually began taking steps to protect children a few years ago with the passage of the Children's Online Privacy Protection Act (COPPA) of 1998 which places tight restrictions on collecting information from children via the Internet. In April 2000 the Federal Trade Commission began enforcing the rules stemming from this legislation, which require posted privacy policies and verifiable parental consent before marketers can collect personally identifiable information from children, such as names and e-mail addresses. Congress passed the COPPA in response to parental concerns and a study by the FTC about the susceptibility of children to marketing tactics, especially with the new, interactive communications available on the Internet.

According to the FTC's rules, websites directed at children under 13 are required to prominently place a privacy policy, written in clear English rather than legalese, on the home page and in each area of the site where information is collected. The policy statement must list contact information, the kinds of information collected, collection techniques (cookies and questionnaires, for example), and the data's use. Finally, parents can review their child's information and either have it deleted or refuse permission to collect any further data.

The easy part of the FTC's new rules is the prominent posting of a privacy policy. For the trickier part—obtaining verifiable parental consent before collecting and using personally identifiable information from children—the FTC created a sliding scale to tell marketers what verification technique to use in different situations. If a marketer plans to use the information for internal use, such as marketing to children on the basis of their preference or e-mailing them messages about site content, an e-mail from a parent is considered sufficient as long as the site makes efforts to confirm the parent's wishes through a postal mailing or via e-mail. If a child's information will be sold to a third party or the data will be publicly available, the rules require a more reliable method of consent, such as a signed permission form that is mailed or faxed in, a phone call to a toll-free number, or a credit-card number. The sliding scale will expire in April 2002, at which point the FTC will determine if technology has progressed enough that more secure verification methods, such as digital signatures, are widely available and affordable.

The FTC has several options for enforcing the COPPA, but a partner with a law firm specializing in advertising and marketing law believes the most likely enforcement tool will be a federal lawsuit. The lawsuit would allow the FTC to seek a temporary injunction to stop a Web operator from collecting children's information until the lawsuit is settled. Websites found to be in violation of COPPA rules could be fined as much as $11,000 per violation per day.

The COPPA restrictions come at a time when Generation Y is starting to come into its own as a marketing target. Gen Yers' comfort level with the Internet and electronic communications technology is high, and they have money and the decision-making power to spend it. However, the government wants to make sure that the rules for the Internet age keep pace with the tools.

Sources: James Heckman, "COPPA to Bring No Surprises, Hefty Violation Fines in April," *Marketing News,* January 31, 2000, p. 6; James Heckman, "Today's Game is Keep-Away," *Marketing News,* July 5, 1999, pp. 1, 7.

Summary

Regulation and control of advertising stem from internal regulation or self-regulation as well as from external control by federal, state, and local regulatory agencies. For many years the advertising industry has promoted the use of voluntary self-regulation to regulate advertising and limit government interference with and control over advertising. Self-regulation of advertising emanates from all segments of the advertising industry, including advertisers and their agencies, business and advertising associations, and the media.

The NAD/NARB, the primary self-regulatory mechanism for national advertising, has been very effective in achieving its goal of voluntary regulation of advertising. Various media also have their own advertising guidelines. The major television networks maintain the most stringent review process and restrictions.

Traditionally, the federal government has been the most important source of external regulation, with the Federal Trade Commission serving as the major watchdog of advertising in the United States. The FTC protects both consumers and businesses from unfair and deceptive practices and anticompetitive behavior. The FTC became very active in the regulation of advertising during the 1970s when it began several new programs and policies, including affirmative disclosure, advertising substantiation, and corrective advertising. Since 1980 the FTC has not been allowed to implement industrywide rules that would define unfair advertising practices. However, the advertising industry and Congress are nearing agreement on a definition of unfairness, and this power may be restored to the FTC.

In 1983 the FTC developed a new working definition of deceptive advertising. Recently the FTC has become more active in policing false and deceptive advertising. Under the Lanham Act, many companies are taking the initiative by suing competitors that make false claims. Many states, as well as the National Association of Attorneys General, are also active in exercising their jurisdiction over false and misleading advertising.

A number of laws also govern the use of other promotional mix elements, such as sales promotion and direct marketing. The Federal Trade Commission regulates many areas of sales promotion as well as direct marketing. Various consumer-oriented sales promotion tools such as contests, games, sweepstakes, and premiums are subject to regulation. Recently many states have become very active in the regulation of contests and sweepstakes. Trade promotion practices, such as the use of promotional allowances and vertical cooperative advertising, are regulated by the Federal Trade Commission under the Robinson-Patman Act. The FTC also enforces laws in a variety of areas that relate to direct marketing and mail-order selling, while the FCC has rules governing telemarketing companies.

Currently there are no specific laws governing marketing practices on the Internet. However, two major areas of concern with regard to marketing on the Internet are privacy and online marketing to children. The Federal Trade Commission has called for voluntary industry codes rather than FTC rules to govern marketers' use of the Internet. Concerns over online marketing to children have led to the passage of the Children's Online Privacy Protection Act, which the FTC began enforcing in early 2000.

Key Terms

self-regulation, 725
Better Business Bureau, 729
Council of Better Business Bureaus, 729
National Advertising Review Board, 729
National Advertising Review Council, 730
Federal Trade Commission, 735
commercial speech, 735
Federal Trade Commission Act, 736
Wheeler-Lea Amendment, 736
trade regulation rules, 737
unfairness, 738
puffery, 738
deception, 739
affirmative disclosure, 740
advertising substantiation, 740
consent order, 742
cease-and-desist orders, 742
corrective advertising, 742
Lanham Act, 748
National Association of Attorneys General, 751
Children's Online Privacy Protection Act, 758

Discussion Questions

1. The opening vignette discusses the legal battle between Just For Feet and its advertising agency that developed from the controversial "Kenya" commercial that was run during the 1999 Super Bowl. Evaluate this controversy from the perspective of both Just For Feet and the Saatchi & Saatchi agency. With whom does the ultimate responsibility for the airing of this commercial lie, the client or the agency?

2. Ethical Perspective 21–1 discusses the decision by the Distilled Spirits Council of the United States (DISCUS) to overturn its self-imposed ban on broadcast advertising. Do you agree with the industry's argument that it is at a competitive disadvantage against beer and wine if hard liquor does not advertise on television? What are some of the possible negative outcomes of the DISCUS decision?

3. Discuss the pros and cons of self-regulation of advertising through organizations such as the NAD/NARB. What are the incentives for advertisers to cooperate with self-regulatory bodies?

4. Discuss the role the media play in the self-regulation of advertising. Do you think media self-regulation is an effective way of protecting consumers from offensive or misleading advertising?

5. How is advertising protected under the First Amendment? Do you feel advertising of controversial and/or harmful products such as tobacco should be protected by the First Amendment?

6. What is meant by puffery? Find examples of several ads that use puffery. Should advertisers be permitted to use puffery? Defend your position.

7. Discuss the three essential elements to the definition of deception adopted by the Federal Trade Commission in 1983.

8. What is corrective advertising? Why do you think this program is so controversial? Evaluate the argument for and against corrective advertising.

9. Discuss the Lanham Act and how it affects advertising. What elements are necessary to win a false advertising claim under the Lanham Act?

10. Discuss the various rules and regulations that affect the use of IMC tools such as sales promotion, direct marketing, and marketing on the Internet. Do these promotional areas require as much regulatory attention as advertising? Why or why not?

11. What are the two major areas of concern with regard to marketing on the Internet? What steps are being taken to address these concerns?

Chapter Twenty-two

Evaluating the Social, Ethical, and Economic Aspects of Advertising and Promotion

Chapter Objectives

- To consider various perspectives concerning the social, ethical, and economic aspects of advertising and promotion.
- To evaluate the social criticisms of advertising.
- To examine the economic role of advertising and its effects on consumer choice, competition, and product costs and prices.

Marketing to Kids in School—Is It Cool?

Nearly 10 years ago an entrepreneur named Chris Whittle created a national controversy and gave parents and educators fits because of a plan to put news programming and advertisements in high school classrooms all over America. In return for providing free TV sets for every classroom and a satellite hookup, Whittle's Channel One would be allowed to show a daily news program that contained two minutes of commercials for products such as acne medicine, electric razors, cereals, and candy. Channel One struggled in its early years, as many schools were reluctant to provide marketers with yet another way of reaching young people with their advertising messages. However, as the demand for upgraded technology in classrooms increased and funds available to pay for it decreased, many school districts became more receptive to Whittle. Today Channel One broadcasts into nearly 13,000 high schools, which is almost half of the nation's total, and some 8.3 million teenagers see its news show and commercials every school day.

Many educators, consumer activists, and parent groups feared letting Channel One into schools on the grounds that it would open the doors for corporate America to reach students in a place where they are supposed to be learning English and math rather than about Nike and Reebok. Marketers recognize that the youth market is a gold mine, as there are nearly 43 million U.S. children in kindergarten through high school and their purchasing power, as well as influence on their parents' purchases, is immense. Moreover, this is the only market segment whose members are held as a captive audience for six hours a day. The concern was that marketers would find all kinds of creative ways to reach a market that was entirely off-limits just a decade ago. Channel One has clearly helped spawn the new breed of in-school marketers that are taking advantage of the financial squeeze many schools are in and making them offers they find hard to resist.

ZapMe, a California-based computer marketing company, plans to give 120,000 top-of-the-line computers to 8,000 high schools, along with high-speed, broad-band Internet connections to reach a network of 11,000 preselected education websites.

The websites were originally set up by a 12-member committee, many of them former teachers, who studied online forums in education to determine what sites would be appropriate. In exchange, the schools agree to use the computers at least four hours a day, giving ZapMe a guaranteed audience for the commercials that run continuously on the lower left-hand corner of the computer screen, and the company gets permission to monitor the student's Web browsing habits. The ZapMe ad space is not the static banner ad Web browsers are used to. When students click on the ad space, an expanded version of the commercial fills the screen. By clicking on the commercial, students can go directly to the advertisers' home page. ZapMe funds the program by selling advertising from noncomputer companies and building the rotating ads into the Web browser.

High-tech companies are not the only ones finding their way into schools. For several years, General Mills' Box Tops for Education program has allowed students to earn cash by collecting box tops from General Mills' products. Individual schools are allowed to exchange up to $10,000 each year. Since the program began, more than 40,000 schools have been involved. Cover Concepts Marketing Services has quietly maneuvered corporate giants such as Nike, Calvin Klein, and Quaker Oats into over 30,000 schools via free textbook covers sporting trendy ads.

The two major soft-drink marketers, Coca-Cola and PepsiCo, have been especially aggressive in marketing to schools as well. Gone are the good old days when Coke and Pepsi could get into a school by providing a scoreboard and plastic coolers for the sports teams. Coca-Cola and PepsiCo are creating deals all over the country whereby they enter into agreements with districts to pay them large sums of money for exclusive vending rights in their schools. In the last 18 months the number of exclusive soda contracts in school districts has increased by 300 percent, with many of these being worth millions of dollars. Schools with exclusive beverage contracts sometimes find themselves inundated with promotional materials from the company.

As more schools open their doors to marketers, there is concern that the commercialization of our nation's classrooms has gone too far. Gary Ruskin, director of Commercial Alert, which is Ralph Nader's consumer advocacy group, says, "Kids are in school to learn to read and write and think, not to learn to desire products." David Walsh, president of the National Institute on Media & Family, is concerned about the increasingly sophisticated advertising in schools. He notes, "Kids are bombarded with commercial messages outside of school. The risk is that they will be treated increasingly as consumers in the one institution where they're supposed to be treated as learners."

The debate is likely to continue over the commercialization of classrooms. Many argue that these programs are corrupting young students and contaminating the educational process. However, others argue that they are legitimate activities of companies seeking to expand their markets while helping financially strapped schools pay for programs that help increase the quality of education

Sources: Peggy J. Faber, "Schools for Sale," *Advertising Age,* October 25, 1999, pp. 22–26; Richard Sale, "Lions among Lambs," *Promo Magazine,* February 1999, pp. 46–51.

> If I were to name the deadliest subversive force within capitalism, the single greatest source of its waning morality—I would without hesitation name advertising. How else should one identify a force that debases language, drains thought, and undoes dignity?[1]

The primary focus of this text has been on the role of advertising and other promotional variables as marketing activities used to convey information to, and influence the behavior of, consumers. We have been concerned with examining the advertising and promotion function in the context of a business and marketing environment and from a perspective that assumes these activities are appropriate. However, as you can see in this quote from economist Robert Heilbroner, not everyone shares this viewpoint. Advertising and promotion are the most visible of all business activities and are prone to scrutiny by those who are concerned about the methods marketers use to sell their products and services.

Proponents of advertising argue that it is the lifeblood of business—it provides consumers with information about products and services and encourages them to improve their standard of living. They say advertising produces jobs and helps new firms enter the marketplace. Companies employ people who make the products and provide the services that advertising sells. Free market economic systems are based on competition, which revolves around information, and nothing delivers information better and at less cost than advertising.

Not everyone, however, is sold on the value of advertising. Critics argue that most advertising is more propaganda than information; it creates needs and faults consumers never knew they had. Ads suggest that children won't succeed without a computer, that our bodies should be leaner, our faces younger, and our houses cleaner. They point to the sultry, scantily clad bodies used in ads to sell everything from perfume to beer to power tools and argue that advertising promotes materialism, insecurity, and greed.

One of the reasons advertising and other forms of integrated marketing communications are becoming increasingly criticized is because they are so prevalent. Not only are there more magazine, newspaper, outdoor, TV, and radio ads than ever, but more and more public space is becoming commercialized. Advertising professor David Helm notes: "Between the stickered bananas and the ads over the urinals and the ones on the floor of the supermarkets, we're exposed to 3,000 commercial messages a day. That's one every 15 seconds, assuming we sleep for 8 hours, and I'd guess right now there's someone figuring out how to get us while our eyes are closed."[2]

As marketers intensify their efforts to get the attention of consumers, resentment against their integrated marketing communications efforts is likely to increase. Concern is growing that there will be a consumer backlash as integrated marketing efforts move to new heights and marketers become increasingly aggressive. Diane Cook, a former advertising executive who founded the AdCenter at Virginia Commonwealth, says: "The growing practice of placing ads and logos everywhere seems a desperate last attempt to make branding work according to the old rules. As telemarketing, advertising, promotions and the rest continue at a frenzied pace, the value of the messages decrease. The system seems headed for a large implosion."[3]

Because of its high visibility and pervasiveness, along with its persuasive character, advertising has been the subject of a great deal of controversy and criticism. Numerous books are critical of not only advertising's methods and techniques but also its social consequences. Various parties—including scholars, economists, politicians, sociologists, government agencies, social critics, special-interest groups, and consumers—have attacked advertising for a variety of reasons, including its excessiveness, the way it influences society, the methods it uses, its exploitation of consumers, and its effect on our economic system.

Advertising is a very powerful force, and this text would not be complete without a look at the criticisms regarding its social and economic effects as well as some defenses against these charges. We consider the various criticisms of advertising and promotion from an ethical and societal perspective and then appraise the economic effects of advertising.

Advertising and Promotion Ethics

In the previous chapter, we examined the regulatory environment in which advertising and promotion operate. While many laws and regulations determine what advertisers can and cannot do, not every issue is covered by a rule. Marketers must often make decisions regarding appropriate and responsible actions on the basis of ethical considerations rather than on what is legal or within industry guidelines. **Ethics** are moral principles and values that govern the actions and decisions of an individual or group.[4]

A particular action may be within the law and still not be ethical. A good example of this involves target marketing. No laws restrict tobacco companies from targeting advertising and promotion for new brands to African-Americans. However, given the high levels of lung cancer and smoking-related illnesses among the black population, many people would consider this an unethical business practice.

Throughout this text we have presented a number of ethical perspectives to show how various aspects of advertising and promotion often involve ethical considerations. Ethical issues must be considered in integrated marketing communications decisions. And advertising and promotion are areas where a lapse in ethical standards or judgment can result in actions that are highly visible and often very damaging to a company.

The role of advertising in society is controversial and has sometimes resulted in attempts to restrict or ban advertising and other forms of promotion to certain groups or for certain products. College students are one such group. A study by Columbia University's Center on Addiction and Substance Abuse a few years ago concluded that America's colleges are witnessing a major increase in binge drinking, particularly among women, and as many as one in three students abuses alcohol. The study advocated a ban on alcohol-related advertising and promotions.[5] Many colleges and universities have imposed restrictions on the marketing of alcoholic beverages to their students. These restrictions include banning sponsorships or support of athletic, musical, cultural, or social events by alcoholic beverage companies and limiting college newspaper advertising to price and product information ads.

As was discussed in Chapter 21, many feel the liquor industry's push to join beer and wine advertisers on television is testing the public's attitudes and may lead to support for more governmental restrictions and regulations on alcohol advertising. Some feel that the FTC may use the protection of underage drinkers to justify a wider effort to curtail the advertising and promotion of alcoholic beverage ads in general.[6]

Companies marketing alcoholic beverages such as beer and liquor recognize the need to reduce alcohol abuse and drunken driving, particularly among young people. Many of these companies have developed programs and ads designed to address this problem. For example, Anheuser-Busch has been running a campaign that uses provocative ads such as the one shown in Exhibit 22–1 to encourage parents to talk to their kids about the risks of underage drinking. The company has also teamed up with parents, teachers, community organizations, law enforcement officials, and others to ensure progress in the fight against alcohol abuse.

Criticism often focuses on the actions of specific advertisers. Groups like the National Organization for Women and Women Against Pornography have been critical of advertisers such as Calvin Klein for promoting sexual permissiveness and

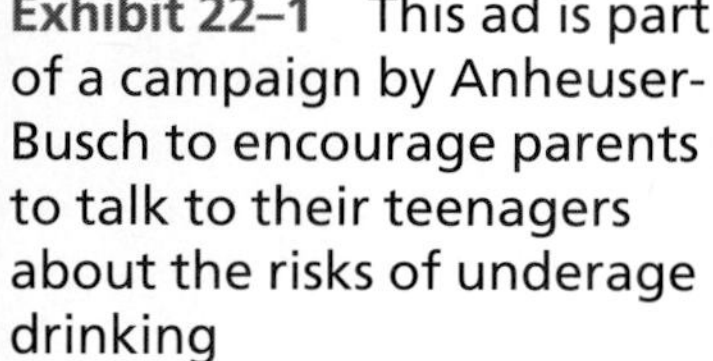

Exhibit 22–1 This ad is part of a campaign by Anheuser-Busch to encourage parents to talk to their teenagers about the risks of underage drinking

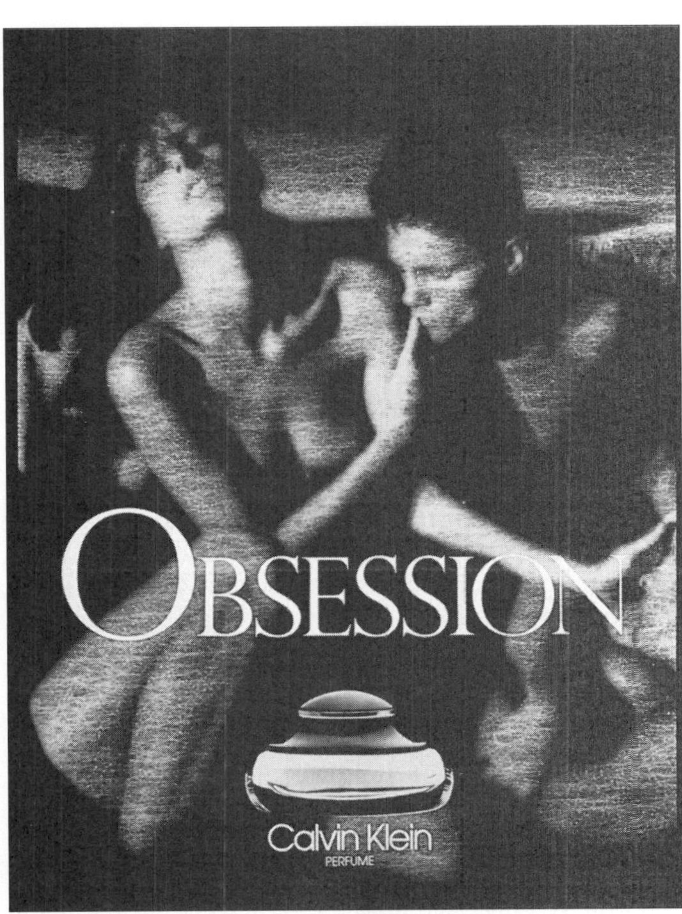

Exhibit 22–2 Ads by Calvin Klein have been the target of criticism by women's groups and others

objectifying women in their ads (Exhibit 22–2). The company was heavily criticized and even boycotted over the controversial "kiddie porn" ads it ran a few years ago featuring intimate snapshots of teenagers in provocative states of undress.[7]

Recently Nike has been criticized over a campaign for its Air Cross Trainer II shoes that directs consumers from their televisions to their computers to learn how a commercial ends.[8] The ads feature celebrities such as sprinter Marion Jones and baseball star Mark McGwire in dramatic situations, and as each spot ends, the words "Continued at Whatever.Nike.com" appear on the screen (Exhibit 22–3). At the website consumers may select various endings to the commercials. In the endings for one of the spots, the viewer dies. In three others the viewer has an arm severed, gets teeth knocked out, or suffers a facial injury that sends a nurse screaming

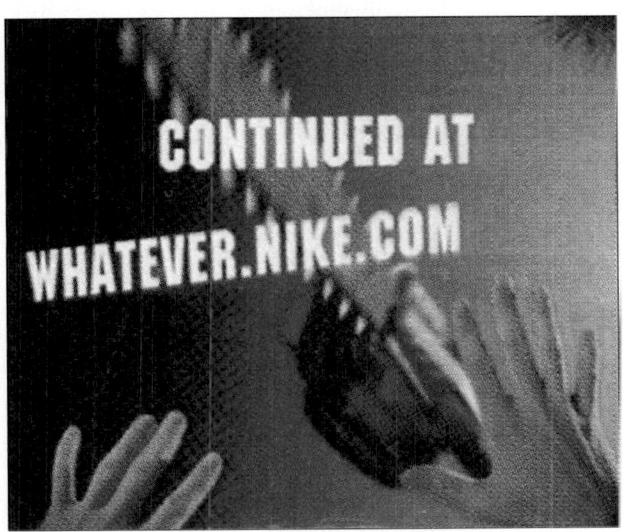

Exhibit 22–3 Some Nike TV commercials direct viewers to a website where they can select their own ending to the spot

out of the emergency room. Nike's vice president of marketing explains that the strategy is to intrigue people with the endings so that they will be motivated to linger on the website. He defends the ads by saying, "Most companies don't give teens enough credit for having perspective. Their ability to have a sense of humor about things and be sarcastic without losing perspective is really high." The campaign has been one of Nike's most successful in years and has helped make the Air Cross Trainer II Nike's best-selling shoe. It also has been recognized as an excellent example of combining television advertising with the Internet. Originally CBS and NBC asked Nike to cut the words "Continued at" from the spots, as they were concerned viewers would turn off the TV and log onto their computers. NBC reversed its decision a few weeks after the campaign began. However, despite the creative marriage of TV and the Internet, Nike's use of grisly outcomes to the spots on its website has been questioned.[9]

As you read this chapter, remember that the various perspectives presented reflect judgments of people with different backgrounds, values, and interests. You may see nothing wrong with the ads for cigarettes or beer or sexually suggestive ads. Other students, however, may oppose these actions on moral and ethical grounds. While we attempt to present the arguments on both sides of these controversial issues, you will have to draw your own conclusions as to who is right or wrong.

Social and Ethical Criticisms of Advertising

Much of the controversy over advertising stems from the ways many companies use it as a selling tool and from its impact on society's tastes, values, and lifestyles. Specific techniques used by advertisers are criticized as deceptive or untruthful, offensive or in bad taste, and exploitative of certain groups, such as children. We discuss each of these criticisms, along with advertisers' responses. We then turn our attention to criticisms concerning the influence of advertising on values and lifestyles, as well as charges that it perpetuates stereotyping and that advertisers exert control over the media.

Advertising as Untruthful or Deceptive

One of the major complaints against advertising is that many ads are misleading or untruthful and deceive consumers. A number of studies have shown a general mistrust of advertising among consumers.[10] A study by Banwari Mittal found that consumers felt that less than one-quarter of TV commercials are honest and believable.[11] Sharon Shavitt, Pamela Lowery, and James Haefner recently conducted a major national survey of over 1,000 adult consumers to determine the general public's current attitudes toward and confidence in advertising. They found that Americans generally do not trust advertising, although they tend to feel more confidence in advertising claims when focused on their actual purchase decisions.[12]

Attempts by industry and government to regulate and control deceptive advertising were discussed in Chapter 21. We noted that advertisers should have a reasonable basis for making a claim about product performance and may be required to provide evidence to support their claims. However, deception can occur more subtly as a result of how consumers perceive the ad and its impact on their beliefs.[13] The difficulty of determining just what constitutes deception, along with the fact that advertisers have the right to use puffery and make subjective claims about their products, tends to complicate the issue. But a concern of many critics is the extent to which advertisers are *deliberately* untruthful or misleading.

Sometimes advertisers have made overtly false or misleading claims or failed to award prizes promoted in a contest or sweepstakes. However, these cases usually involve smaller companies and a tiny portion of the hundreds of billions of dollars spent on advertising and promotion each year. Most advertisers do not design their messages with the intention to mislead or deceive consumers or run sweepstakes with no intention of awarding prizes. Not only are such practices unethical, but the culprits would damage their reputation and risk prosecution by regulatory groups or government agencies. National advertisers in particular invest large sums of money to develop loyalty to, and enhance the image of, their brands. These companies are not likely to risk hard-won consumer trust and confidence by intentionally deceiving consumers.

The problem of untruthful or fraudulent advertising and promotion exists more at the local level and in specific areas such as mail order, telemarketing, and other forms of direct marketing. Yet there have been many cases where large companies were accused of misleading consumers with their ads or promotions. Some companies test the limits of industry and government rules and regulations to make claims that will give their brands an advantage in highly competitive markets.

While many critics of advertising would probably agree that most advertisers are not out to deceive consumers deliberately, they are still concerned that consumers may not be receiving enough information to make an informed choice. They say advertisers usually present only information that is favorable to their position and do not always tell consumers the whole truth about a product or service.

Many believe advertising should be primarily informative in nature and should not be permitted to use puffery or embellished messages. Others argue that advertisers have the right to present the most favorable case for their products and services and should not be restricted to just objective, verifiable information.[14] They note that consumers can protect themselves from being persuaded against their will and that the various industry and government regulations suffice to keep advertisers from misleading consumers. Figure 22–1 shows the advertising principles of the American Advertising Federation, which many advertisers use as a guideline in preparing and evaluating their ads.

Advertising as Offensive or in Bad Taste

Another common criticism of advertising, particularly by consumers, is that ads are offensive, tasteless, irritating, boring, obnoxious, and so on. In the recent study by Shavitt and her colleagues, about half of the respondents reported feeling offended by advertising at least sometimes. A number of other studies have found that consumers feel most advertising insults their intelligence and that many ads are in poor taste.[15]

1. *Truth.* Advertising shall reveal the truth, and shall reveal significant facts, the omission of which would mislead the public.
2. *Substantiation.* Advertising claims shall be substantiated by evidence in possession of the advertiser and the advertising agency prior to making such claims.
3. *Comparisons.* Advertising shall refrain from making false, misleading, or unsubstantiated statements or claims about a competitor or his products or service.
4. *Bait advertising.* Advertising shall not offer products or services for sale unless such offer constitutes a bona fide effort to sell the advertised products or services and is not a device to switch consumers to other goods or services, usually higher priced.
5. *Guarantees and warranties.* Advertising of guarantees and warranties shall be explicit, with sufficient information to apprise consumers of their principal terms and limitations or, when space or time restrictions preclude such disclosures, the advertisement shall clearly reveal where the full text of the guarantee or warranty can be examined before purchase.
6. *Price claims.* Advertising shall avoid price claims that are false or misleading, or savings claims that do not offer provable savings.
7. *Testimonials.* Advertising containing testimonials shall be limited to those of competent witnesses who are reflecting a real and honest opinion or experience.
8. *Taste and decency.* Advertising shall be free of statements, illustrations, or implications that are offensive to good taste or public decency.

Figure 22–1 Advertising principles of the American Advertising Federation

Sources of Distaste Consumers can be offended or irritated by advertising in a number of ways. Some object when a product or service like contraceptives or personal hygiene products is advertised at all. Only in the last few years have media begun accepting ads for condoms, as the AIDS crisis forced them to reconsider their restrictions (Exhibit 22–4). The major TV networks gave their affiliates permission to accept condom advertising in 1987, but the first condom ad did not appear on network TV until 1991, when Fox broadcast a spot.

In 1994 the U.S. Department of Health's Centers for Disease Control and Prevention (CDC) began a new HIV prevention campaign that includes radio and TV commercials urging sexually active people to use latex condoms. The commercials prompted strong protests from conservative and religious groups, which argue that the government should stress abstinence in preventing the spread of AIDS among young people. NBC and ABC agreed to broadcast all the commercials, while CBS said it would air certain spots.[16]

A study of prime-time TV commercials found a strong product class effect with respect to the types of ads consumers perceived as distasteful or irritating. The most irritating commercials were for feminine hygiene products; ads for women's undergarments and hemorrhoid products were close behind.[17] Another study found that consumers are more likely to dislike ads for products they do not use and for brands they would not buy.[18] Ads for personal products have become more common on television and in print, and the public is more accepting of them.[19] However, advertisers must still be careful of how these products are presented and the language and terminology used. There are still many rules, regulations, and taboos advertisers must deal with to have their TV commercials approved by the networks.[20]

Another way advertising can offend consumers is by the type of appeal or the manner of presentation. For example, many people object to appeals that exploit

Exhibit 22–4 Many magazines and TV stations now accept ads for condoms

Exhibit 22–5 This Airwalk ad was criticized for being suggestive and symbolizing sexual submission

consumer anxieties. Fear appeal ads, especially for products such as deodorants, mouthwash, and dandruff shampoos, are criticized for attempting to create anxiety and using a fear of social rejection to sell these products. Some ads for home computers were also criticized for attempting to make parents think that if their young children couldn't use a computer, they would fail in school.

Sexual Appeals The advertising appeals that have received the most criticism for being in poor taste are those using sexual appeals and/or nudity. These techniques are often used to gain consumers' attention and may not even be appropriate to the product being advertised. Even if the sexual appeal relates to the product, people may be offended by it. Many people object to both nudity in advertising and sexually suggestive ads.

Advertising critics are particularly concerned about the use of sexual appeals to glorify the image of cigarettes, liquor, and beer or to suggest they can enhance one's own attractiveness. For example, the Center for Science in the Public Interest, a consumer advocacy group, gave one of its Lemon Awards to an ad for Kool cigarettes featuring attractive women dressed in provocative clothing and high heels next to the headline "Totally Kool." Center officials said the ad implies that smoking adds to sexual attraction.[21] Some women's groups criticized the Airwalk ad shown in Exhibit 22–5, arguing that it showed a submissive and sexually available woman. A critic argued that the ad contains a number of symbolic cues that are sexually suggestive and combine to reinforce an image of the woman's sexual submission to the man.[22]

Another common criticism of sexual appeals is that they can demean women (or men) by depicting them as sex objects (Exhibit 22–6). Ads for cosmetics, lingerie, beer, and liquor are among the most criticized for their portrayal of women as sex objects. Stroh Brewing Co. ignited a major

Exhibit 22–6 Sexual appeals are often criticized for portraying women as sex objects

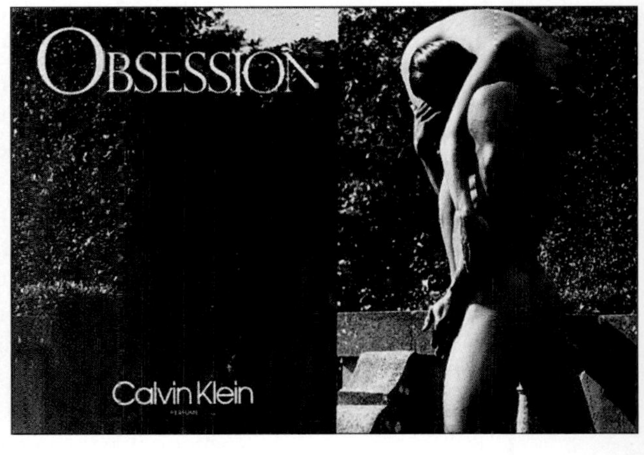

controversy a few years ago with an ad campaign for Old Milwaukee beer featuring the Swedish Bikini Team, a group of Scandinavian-looking women wearing blue bikinis who appeared out of nowhere in front of groups of beer-drinking men. A number of consumer groups were very critical of the ads, and female employees at the company even sued Stroh's because they said the ads contributed to an atmosphere that was conducive to sexual harassment in the workplace.[23]

Many advertisers are being much more careful not to portray women as sex objects. A few years ago Anheuser-Busch announced that it was committed to portraying women with more respect and in more equal roles with men. Other beer companies, such as Miller and Stroh's, are also more careful about the way they portray women in their ads.[24]

Some advertisers complain about the double standard: even the most suggestive commercials are bland compared with the content of many TV programs. The networks say they have to scrutinize commercials more carefully because ads encourage people to imitate behaviors, while programs are merely meant to entertain. Network executives also note the complaints of parents who are concerned about their children seeing these ads since they cannot always be there to change the channel or turn off the TV.

Because of the increasing clutter in the advertising environment, advertisers will probably continue to use sexual appeals and other techniques that offend many people but catch the attention of consumers in their target audience. How far the advertisers can go with these appeals will probably depend on the public's reactions. When consumers think they have gone too far, they are likely to pressure the advertisers to change their ads and the media to stop accepting them. Ethical Perspective 22–1 discusses how many marketers are using sexually oriented shock tactics to draw consumers' attention to their ads.

Advertising and Children

One of the most controversial topics advertisers must deal with is the issue of advertising to children. TV is a vehicle through which advertisers can reach children easily. Children between the ages of 2 and 11 watch an average of 21.5 hours of TV a week and may see between 22,000 and 25,000 commercials a year.[25] Studies show that television is an important source of information for children about products.[26] Concern has also been expressed about marketers' use of other promotional vehicles and techniques such as radio ads, point-of-purchase displays, premiums in packages, and the use of commercial characters as the basis for TV shows.

Critics argue that children, particularly young ones, are especially vulnerable to advertising because they lack the experience and knowledge to understand and evaluate critically the purpose of persuasive advertising appeals. Research has shown that preschool children cannot differentiate between commercials and programs, do not perceive the selling intent of commercials, and cannot distinguish between reality and fantasy.[27] Research has also shown that children need more than a skeptical attitude toward advertising; they must understand how advertising works in order to use their cognitive defenses against it effectively.[28] Because of children's limited ability to interpret the selling intent of a message or identify a commercial, critics charge that advertising to them is inherently unfair and deceptive and should be banned or severely restricted.

At the other extreme are those who argue that advertising is a part of life and children must learn to deal with it in the **consumer socialization process** of acquiring the skills needed to function in the marketplace.[29] They say existing restrictions are adequate for controlling children's advertising. A recent study by Tamara Mangleburg and Terry Bristol provided support for the socialization argument. They found that adolescents developed skeptical attitudes toward advertising that were learned through interactions with socialization agents such as parents, peers, and television. They also found that marketplace knowledge plays an important role in adolescents' skepticism toward advertising. Greater knowledge of the marketplace appears to give teens a basis by which to evaluate ads and makes them more likely to recognize the persuasion techniques used by advertisers.[30]

Ethical Perspective 22–1

Creating Sexy Ads That Are Hard to Ignore

In the good old days of advertising the most risqué image a consumer might see in an ad was Mr. Whipple squeezing a roll of Charmin toilet tissue. However, peruse through a magazine or fashion catalog today and you are likely to see ads featuring convicted killers gazing at you longingly to depict the "human face" of death row, fleshy photos of frat boys and coeds in compromising poses, a dog in a spiked leather collar licking the foot of a model, and very large, nude models being used to promote designer menswear.

Welcome to the brave new world of what is often referred to as "shock-vertising," where marketers use nudity, capital punishment, sadomasochism, bestiality, or whatever other startling image they can think of to get consumers' attention. Some consumers are excited by the new genre of shock ads, while others are likely to be offended or even outraged. However, almost everyone finds these ads very hard to ignore. Which is the whole point. With so many ads competing for consumers' attention today, marketers will go to great lengths to try to break through the clutter and ensure that their advertising gets noticed. However, many people feel that shock-vertising is finally pushing the envelope too far.

As was discussed earlier in Ethical Perspective 8–4, shock advertising is nothing new; companies such as Benetton and Calvin Klein have been using shock tactics in their ads since the 1980s. However, a number of other marketers have been causing a stir with their advertising. During the 1999 holiday season, it was retailer Abercrombie & Fitch's "Naughty & Nice" catalog that caused quite a stir.

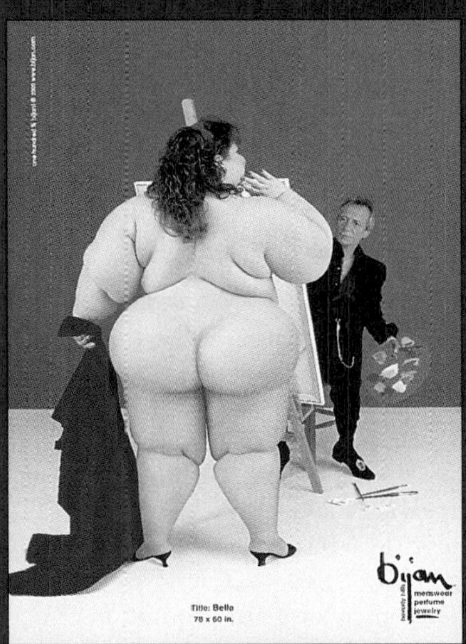

The catalog included sex tips from porn star Jenna Jameson, a spoof interview with a shopping mall Santa portrayed as a pedophile, and young models in various states of undress including a photo of a nude young woman on horseback. Officials in four states threatened or pursued legal action against the company, which responded by reiterating its plans to "card" would-be buyers of the catalog to ensure they were at least 18 years old.

A spokesman for the company said he was perplexed by the outcry over the catalog and added, "We really don't understand why people say this is shocking." He also defended the article on Santa by saying, "It was totally hysterical." The creative director at Abercrombie & Fitch's ad agency, Shahid & Co., also made no apologies, saying there is a double standard and hypocrisy in the shock-advertising debate: "When advertising uses sex, everybody complains. When editorial does it nobody cares. I'll tell you this. Everybody enjoys it. They love it." While young people may love the fleshy photos in Abercrombie & Fitch's quarterly catalogs, many consumer and public-interest groups do not like some of the articles that have appeared in them. One back-to-school catalog stirred outrage with a section titled "Drinking 101," which had detailed descriptions of drinking games and recipes for cocktails.

Advertisers seldom admit they are trying to use shock tactics in their ads. For example, Emanuel Ungaro, a French fashion company, has run the ad showing the dog in the spiked leather collar licking a model's foot and another featuring a large white dog in a leather mask dangling a paw inside a model's open blouse. The company says any S&M or bestiality connotations are the viewer's. A spokeswoman for the company says the ads were inspired by the film *Beauty and the Beast*—the French version, not Disney's. "It's about the purity and innocence of women," she explains. The white dog represents "purity," the leather mask symbolizes "the night." Regarding the ad showing the dog licking the model's foot, the creative director at Ungaro's ad agency explains: "I think all of us have been licked by dogs at one time or another." He says the "strong image" ads have been well received in Europe and in "high-end markets" in the United States.

Another company whose ads have been generating a great deal of discussion is Bijan, which decided to forgo the tall, thin, and glamorous supermodels typically used in fashion ads and use very large, naked women instead. The company's founder, Beverly Hills fashion maven Bijan, says his ads with high-heeled "Bella" in the buff are his homage to artists such as Rubens, who used full-figured models. He adds, "Women are beautiful in any size. I am receiving letters from all over America saying big is beautiful too."

Many advertising experts argue that what underlies all of the shock-vertising is the pressure on marketers and their agencies to do whatever it takes to get their ads noticed. Marketing strategist Al Ries notes: "The biggest danger in advertising is being ignored. People notice the shock message." However, critics argue that the more advertisers use the tactic, the more shocking it has to be. Says Ries: "We keep raising the shock bar. But it is very hard to shock anybody these days. Even Madonna hasn't shocked anybody for 10 years." He may be right about Madonna, but you can be sure that marketers will continue to find ways to shock people and in the process draw attention to their advertising.

Sources: Michael McCarthy, "Shockvertising Jolts Ad Viewers," *USA Today,* February 23, 2000, p. 6B; Rebecca Quick, "Is Ever-So-Hip Abercrombie & Fitch Losing Its Edge with Teens?" *The Wall Street Journal,* February 22, 2000, pp. B1, 4; Barbara Lipert, "Season's Meetings," *Adweek,* December 20, 1999, p. 5.

This issue received a great deal of attention in 1979 when the Federal Trade Commission held hearings on proposed changes in regulations regarding advertising to children. An FTC staff report recommended banning all TV advertising for any product directed to or seen by audiences composed largely of children under age eight because they are too young to understand the selling intent of advertising.[31]

The FTC proposal was debated intensely. The advertising industry and a number of companies argued strongly against it, based on factors including advertisers' right of free speech under the First Amendment to communicate with those consumers who make up their primary target audience.[32] They also said parents should be involved in helping children interpret advertising and can refuse to purchase products they believe are undesirable for their children.

The FTC proposal was defeated, and changes in the political environment resulted in less emphasis on government regulation of advertising. But parent and consumer groups like the Center for Science in the Public Interest are still putting pressure on advertisers regarding what they see as inappropriate or misleading ads for children. One activist group, Action for Children's Television (ACT), was disbanded in 1992, but first it was instrumental in getting Congress to approve the Children's Television Act in October 1990. The act limits the amount of commercial time in children's programming to 10.5 minutes per hour on weekends and 12 minutes on weekdays.[33]

In 1996 broadcasters, children's advocates, and the federal government reached an agreement requiring TV stations to air three hours of children's educational shows a week.[34] Many believe advertisers will play a major role in implementing the new initiative by providing financial backing for the educational shows—which have long had trouble luring sponsors.[35]

Children are also protected from the potential influences of commercials by network censors and industry self-regulatory groups such as the Council of Better Business Bureaus' Children's Advertising Review Unit (CARU). CARU has strict self-regulatory guidelines regarding the type of appeals, product presentation and claims, disclosures and disclaimers, the use of premiums, safety, and techniques such as special effects and animation. The CARU guidelines for advertising addressed to children under 12 are presented in Figure 22–2.

As we saw in Chapter 21, the major networks also have strict guidelines for ads targeted to children. For example, in network TV ads, only 10 seconds can be devoted to animation and special effects; the final 5 seconds are reserved for displaying all the toys shown in the ad and disclosing whether they are sold separately and whether accessories such as batteries are included. Networks also require 3 seconds of every 30-second cereal ad to portray a balanced breakfast, usually by showing a picture of toast, orange juice, and milk.[36]

While concerns over advertising and other forms of promotion directed at children diminished somewhat over the past decade, the issue has been receiving

Five basic principles underlie these guidelines for advertising directed to children:

1. Advertisers should always take into account the level of knowledge, sophistication, and maturity of the audience to which their message is primarily directed. Younger children have a limited capability for evaluating the credibility of what they watch. Advertisers, therefore, have a special responsibility to protect children from their own susceptibilities.
2. Realizing that children are imaginative and that make-believe play constitutes an important part of the growing-up process, advertisers should exercise care not to exploit that imaginative quality of children. Unreasonable expectations of product quality or performance should not be stimulated either directly or indirectly by advertising.
3. Recognizing that advertising may play an important part in educating the child, information should be communicated in a truthful and accurate manner with full recognition by the advertiser that the child may learn practices from advertising that can affect his or her health and well-being.
4. Advertisers are urged to capitalize on the potential of advertising to influence social behavior by developing advertising that, wherever possible, addresses itself to social standards generally regarded as positive and beneficial, such as friendship, kindness, honesty, justice, generosity, and respect for others.
5. Although many influences affect a child's personal and social development, it remains the prime responsibility of the parents to provide guidance for children. Advertisers should contribute to this parent-child relationship in a constructive manner.

Figure 22–2 Children's Advertising Review Unit principles

greater attention recently. Reasons for this growing concern include the increasing viewing options children have as a result of the growth of cable television, an increase in the number of ads encouraging children to call 900 numbers, the increase in the number of toy-based programs on TV, and general concerns over the content of children's programming, particularly with regard to violence. There is also growing concern over how marketers are using the Internet to communicate with and sell to children and, as was discussed in the opening vignette, the commercialization of schools.

Advertising to children will remain a controversial topic. Some groups feel that the government is responsible for protecting children from the potentially harmful effects of advertising and other forms of promotion, while others argue that parents are ultimately responsible for doing so. Various consumer groups have also urged the media, particularly television broadcasters, as well as marketers to assume responsibility for the programs and advertising and promotional messages they offer to children.[37] A study comparing the attitudes of business executives and consumers regarding children's advertising found that marketers of products targeted to children believe advertising to them provides useful information on new products and does not disrupt the parent–child relationship. However, the general public did not have such a favorable opinion. Older consumers and those from households with children had particularly negative attitudes toward children's advertising.[38]

It is important to many companies to communicate directly with children. However, only by being sensitive to the naiveté of children as consumers will they be able to do so freely and avoid potential conflict with those who believe children should be protected from advertising.

Social and Cultural Consequences

Concern is often expressed over the impact of advertising on society, particularly on values and lifestyles. While a number of factors influence the cultural values, lifestyles, and behavior of a society, the overwhelming amount of advertising and its prevalence in the mass media lead many critics to argue that advertising plays a major role in influencing and transmitting social values. In his book *Advertising and Social Change,* Ronald Berman says:

> The institutions of family, religion, and education have grown noticeably weaker over each of the past three generations. The world itself seems to have grown more complex. In the absence of traditional authority, advertising has become a kind of social guide. It depicts us in all the myriad situations possible to a life of free choice. It provides ideas about style, morality, behavior.[39]

Mike Hughes, president and creative director of the Martin Agency, notes that advertising has a major impact on society: "Ads help establish what is cool in society; their messages contribute to the public dialogue. Gap ads show white, black and Hispanic kids dancing together. Hilfiger ads showed it's cool for people to get along. Ikea showed a gay couple." He argues that advertising agencies have a social and ethical responsibility to consider the impact of the advertising messages they create for their clients.[40]

While there is general agreement that advertising is an important social influence agent, opinions as to the value of its contribution are often negative. Advertising is criticized for encouraging materialism, manipulating consumers to buy things they do not really need, perpetuating stereotypes, and controlling the media.

Advertising Encourages Materialism

Many critics claim advertising has an adverse effect on consumer values by encouraging **materialism,** a preoccupation with material things rather than intellectual or spiritual concerns. The United States is undoubtedly the most materialistic society in the world, which many critics attribute to advertising that

- Seeks to create needs rather than merely showing how a product or service fulfills them.
- Surrounds consumers with images of the good life and suggests the acquisition of material possessions leads to contentment and happiness and adds to the joy of living.
- Suggests material possessions are symbols of status, success, and accomplishment and/or will lead to greater social acceptance, popularity, sex appeal, and so on.

The ad shown in Exhibit 22–7 for Rolls-Royce automobiles is an example of how advertising can promote materialistic values.

Exhibit 22–7 Rolls-Royce appeals to consumers' materialism

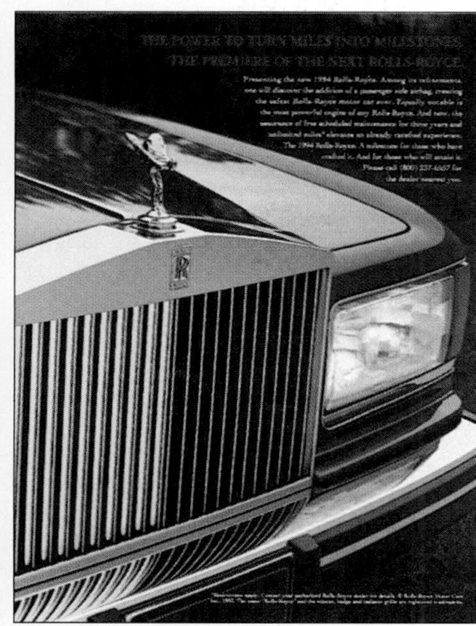

This criticism of advertising assumes that materialism is undesirable and is sought at the expense of other goals. But many believe materialism is an acceptable part of the **Protestant ethic,** which stresses hard work and individual effort and initiative and views the accumulation of material possessions as evidence of success. Others argue that the acquisition of material possessions has positive economic impact by encouraging consumers to keep consuming after their basic needs are met. Many Americans believe economic growth is essential and materialism is both a necessity and an inevitable part of this progress.

Economist John Kenneth Galbraith, often a vocal critic of advertising, describes the role advertising plays in industrialized economies by encouraging consumption:

> Advertising and its related arts thus help develop the kind of man the goals of the industrial system require—one that reliably spends his income and works reliably because he is always in need of more. In the absence of the massive and artful persuasion that accompanies the management of demand, increasing abundance might well have reduced the interest of people in acquiring more goods. Being not pressed by the need for these things, they would have spent less reliably to get more. The consequence—a lower and less reliable propensity to consume—would have been awkward for the industrial system.[41]

It has also been argued that an emphasis on material possessions does not rule out interest in intellectual, spiritual, or cultural values. Defenders of advertising say consumers can be more interested in higher-order goals when basic needs have been met. Raymond Bauer and Stephen Greyser point out that consumers may purchase material things in the pursuit of nonmaterial goals.[42] For example, a person may buy an expensive stereo system to enjoy music rather than simply to impress someone or acquire a material possession.

Even if we assume materialism is undesirable, there is still the question of whether advertising is responsible for creating and encouraging it. While many critics argue that advertising is a major contributing force to materialistic values, others say advertising merely reflects the values of society rather than shaping them.[43] They argue that consumers' values are defined by the society in which they live and are the results of extensive, long-term socialization or acculturation.

The argument that advertising is responsible for creating a materialistic and hedonistic society is addressed by Stephen Fox in his book *The Mirror Makers: A History of American Advertising and Its Creators.* Fox concludes advertising has become a prime scapegoat for our times and merely reflects society. Regarding the effect of advertising on cultural values, he says:

> To blame advertising now for those most basic tendencies in American history is to miss the point. It is too obvious, too easy, a matter of killing the messenger instead of dealing with the bad news. The people who have created modern advertising are not hidden persuaders pushing our buttons in the service of some malevolent purpose. They are just producing an especially visible manifestation, good and bad, of the American way of life.[44]

The ad shown in Exhibit 22–8 was developed by the American Association of Advertising Agencies and suggests that advertising is a reflection of society's tastes and values, not vice versa. The ad was part of a campaign that addressed criticisms of advertising.

Advertising does contribute to our materialism by portraying products and services as symbols of status, success, and achievement and by encouraging consumption. As Richard Pollay says, "While it may be true that advertising reflects cultural values, it does so on a very selective basis, echoing and reinforcing certain attitudes, behaviors, and values far more frequently than others."[45]

Individuals from a variety of backgrounds are concerned over the values they see driving our society. They believe that materialism, greed, and selfishness increasingly dominate American life and that advertising is a major reason for these undesirable values. The extent to which advertising is responsible for materialism

Exhibit 22–8 The advertising industry argues that advertising reflects society

and the desirability of such values are deep philosophical issues that will continue to be part of the debate over the societal value and consequences of advertising.

Advertising Makes People Buy Things They Don't Need A common criticism of advertising is that it manipulates consumers into buying things they do not need. Many critics say advertising should just provide information useful in making purchase decisions and should not persuade. They view information advertising (which reports price, performance, and other objective criteria) as desirable but persuasive advertising (which plays on consumers' emotions, anxieties, and psychological needs and desires such as status, self-esteem, and attractiveness) as unacceptable. Persuasive advertising is criticized for fostering discontent among consumers and encouraging them to purchase products and services to solve deeper problems. Critics say advertising exploits consumers and persuades them to buy things they don't need.

Defenders of advertising offer a number of rebuttals to these criticisms. First, they point out that a substantial amount of advertising is essentially informational in nature.[46] Also, it is difficult to separate desirable informational advertising from undesirable persuasive advertising. Shelby Hunt, in examining the *information-persuasion dichotomy,* points out that even advertising that most observers would categorize as very informative is often very persuasive.[47] He says, "If advertising critics really believe that persuasive advertising should not be permitted, they are actually proposing that no advertising be allowed, since the purpose of all advertising is to persuade."[48]

Defenders of advertising also take issue with the argument that it should be limited to dealing with basic functional needs. In our society, most lower-level needs recognized in Maslow's hierarchy, such as the need for food, clothing, and shelter, are satisfied for most people. It is natural to move from basic needs to higher-order ones such as self-esteem and status or self-actualization. Consumers are free to choose the degree to which they attempt to satisfy their desires, and wise advertisers associate their products and services with the satisfaction of higher-order needs.

Proponents of advertising offer two other defenses against the charge that advertising makes people buy things they do not really need. First, this criticism attributes too much power to advertising and assumes consumers have no ability to defend themselves against it.

Second, it ignores the fact that consumers have the freedom to make their own choices when confronted with persuasive advertising. While they readily admit the persuasive intent of their business, advertisers are quick to note it is extremely difficult to make consumers purchase a product they do not want or for which they do not see a personal benefit. For example, the "green" marketing movement has not gotten consumers to forgo low prices in favor of products that make environmental claims. The market research firm of Roper Starch Worldwide conducted an extensive study of 300 green ads that appeared in magazines between 1991 and 1994 and found that most were not effective. The study concluded that too many green ads failed to make the connection between what the company is doing for the environment and how it affects individual consumers.[49]

If advertising were as powerful as the critics claim, we would not see products with multimillion-dollar advertising budgets failing in the marketplace. The reality is that consumers do have a choice, and they are not being forced to buy. Consumers ignore ads for products and services they do not really need or that fail to interest them (see Exhibit 22–9).

Advertising and Stereotyping Advertising is often accused of creating and perpetuating stereotypes through its portrayal of women, ethnic minorities, and other groups.

Women The portrayal of women in advertising is an issue that has received a great deal of attention through the years.[50] Advertising has received much criticism for stereotyping women and failing to recognize the changing role of women in our society. Critics have argued that advertising often depicts women as preoccupied

Exhibit 22–9 The AAAA responds to the claim that advertising makes consumers buy things they do not need

with beauty, household duties, and motherhood or shows them as decorative objects or sexually provocative figures. The various research studies conducted through the years show a consistent picture of gender stereotyping that has varied little over time. Portrayals of adult women in American television and print advertising have emphasized passivity, deference, lack of intelligence and credibility, and punishment for high levels of efforts. In contrast, men have been portrayed as constructive, powerful, autonomous, and achieving.[51]

Research on gender stereotyping in advertising targeted to children has found a pattern of results similar to that reported for adults. A recent study found sex-role stereotyping in television advertising targeted at children in the United States as well as in Australia.[52] Boys are generally shown as being more knowledgeable, active, aggressive, and instrumental than girls. Nonverbal behaviors involving dominance and control are associated more with boys than girls. Advertising directed toward children has also been shown to feature more boys than girls, to position boys in more dominant, active roles, and to use male voiceovers more frequently than female ones.[53]

Feminist groups such as the National Organization for Women (NOW) and the Sexual Assault Prevention and Awareness Center argue that advertising that portrays women as sex objects contributes to violence against women. These groups often protest to advertisers and their agencies about ads they find insulting to women and have even called for boycotts against offending advertisers. NOW has also been critical of advertisers for the way they portray women in advertising for clothing, cosmetics, and other products. The organization feels that many of these ads contribute to the epidemic of eating disorders and smoking among women and girls who hope such means will help them control their weight.[54]

While sexism and stereotyping still exist, advertising's portrayal of women is improving in many areas. Many advertisers have begun to recognize the importance of portraying women realistically. The increase in the number of working women has resulted not only in women having more influence in family decision making but also in more single-female households, which mean more independent purchasers.

Researchers Steven Kates and Glenda Shaw-Garlock argue that the transformed social positioning of women in North American society is perhaps the most important social development of this century.[55] They note that as women have crossed the boundary from the domestic sphere to the professional arena, expectations and representations of women have changed as well. For example, a number of magazines, such as *MS* and *Working Woman,* now incorporate and appeal to the sociocultural shifts in women's lives. Many advertisers are now depicting women in a diversity of roles that reflect their changing place in society. In many ads, the stereotypic character traits attributed to women have shifted from weak and dependent to strong and autonomous.[56]

Some advertisers have found that being more sensitive to women customers can influence their purchase behavior. For example, a few years ago Maidenform began a campaign critical of negative stereotyping of women that significantly increased sales (Exhibit 22–10). Nike saw its sales to women increase 28 percent as a result of its "Empathy" campaign, which directly targeted women and issues that are relevant to them.[57]

Blacks and Hispanics African-Americans and Hispanics have also been the target of stereotyping in advertising. For many years, advertisers virtually ignored all nonwhite ethnic groups as identifiable subcultures and viable markets. Ads were rarely targeted to these ethnic groups, and the use of blacks and Hispanics as spokespeople, communicators, models, or actors in ads was very limited.[58]

Several studies in the late 1980s and early 90s examined the incidence of minorities in advertising. A study conducted in 1987 found that 11 percent of the people appearing in commercials were African-Americans.[59] Another study conducted two years later found that African-Americans appeared in 26 percent of all ads on network TV that used live models but Hispanics appeared in only 6 percent of the commercials with live models. The researchers also found that TV ads in which blacks appeared were overwhelmingly integrated and the blacks were likely to have played either minor or background roles in the majority of the ads.[60] A study conducted in 1995 found that 17 percent of prime-time network TV ads featured African-Americans as dominant characters and the majority of commercials featured them in minor roles.[61]

Exhibit 22–10 Maidenform's campaign lamenting the stereotyping of women resulted in a significant increase in sales

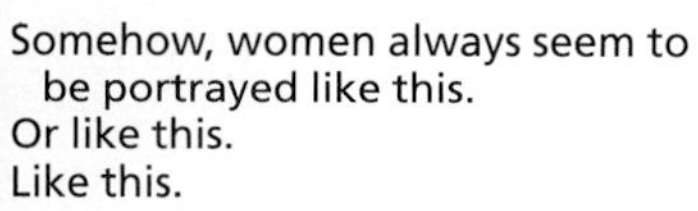

Somehow, women always seem to be portrayed like this.
Or like this.
Like this.

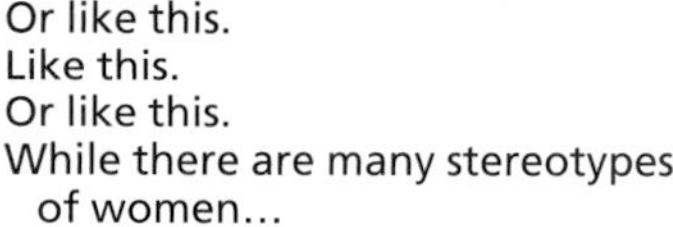

Or like this.
Like this.
Or like this.
While there are many stereotypes of women...

there aren't many women who fit them.
A simple truth known by all women . . . most men . . . and one lingerie company.

Exhibit 22–11 Ikea broke new ground with this ad showing an interracial couple shopping for furniture

Although research suggests that the number of African-Americans shown as dominant characters has not increased dramatically, many advertisers are changing blacks' social and role status in advertising. For example, blacks are increasingly being shown in executive positions in many ads. FedEx said that a commercial featuring a black female executive beating out her white male adversaries in a conference call showdown over a high-stakes business deal was one of its most successful ads in years.[62]

Ads are increasingly likely to be racially integrated. Recently some advertisers have begun breaking the taboo against suggesting interracial attraction. For example, furniture retailer Ikea ran a TV commercial showing an interracial couple shopping for a "daddy chair" and discussing their plans to conceive[63] (Exhibit 22–11). Advertisers are also finding that advertising developed specifically for the African-American market, such as the Mattel ad shown in Exhibit 22–12, is an effective way of reaching this ethnic market. A recent study by Corliss L. Green found that ads targeting African-Americans through racially targeted media, especially with race-based products, benefit from featuring African-American models with a dominant presence in the ad.[64]

Exhibit 22–12 Many marketers are creating ads specifically for the African-American market

Another minority group that has received attention recently from those researching advertising and stereotyping is Asian-Americans, whose affluence, high education, work ethic, and growth rate has made this group a popular target market. A recent study of prime-time TV commercials found that Asian male and female models are overrepresented in terms of their proportion of the U.S. population (3.6 percent), appearing in 8.4 percent of the commercials. However, Asian models were more likely than members of other minority groups to appear in background roles, and Asian women were rarely depicted in major roles. The study also found that portrayals of Asian-Americans put more emphasis on the work ethic and less on other aspects of their lives.[65]

There is little question that advertising has been guilty of stereotyping women and ethnic groups in the past and, in some cases, still does so. But as the role of women changes, advertisers are changing their portrayals to remain accurate and appeal to their target audience. Advertisers are also trying to increase the incidence of minority groups in ads while avoiding stereotypes and negative role portrayals. They are being careful to avoid ethnic stereotyping and striving to develop advertising that has specific appeals to various ethnic groups.

Other Groups While the focus here has been on women and ethnic minorities, some other groups feel they are victims of stereotyping by advertisers. For example, some advertisers have been criticized for portraying senior citizens as feeble, foolish, inept, or in desperate need of help.[66] A few years ago, advocates for the mentally ill objected to a Nike ad campaign that featured actor Dennis Hopper, who is best known for playing eccentric and sometimes violent characters. In the commercials he played the ultimate football fanatic—an ex-referee who is obsessed with the game—and his performance included twitches, tics, and maniacal laughter that some suggest portray a mentally ill person.[67]

Many groups in our society are battling against stereotyping and discrimination, and companies must consider whether their ads might offend them. It is increasingly difficult not to offend some segment of the public. Creative personnel in agencies are feeling restricted as their ideas are squelched out of concern that they might offend someone or be misinterpreted.[68] However, advertisers must be sensitive to the portrayal of specific types of people in their ads, for both ethical and commercial reasons.

One area where significant changes have taken place recently is in advertising targeted to gay consumers. In 1995 Ikea broke new ground with a TV commercial featuring a gay couple shopping for furniture. For years beer companies targeted this market by placing ads in local gay media to support or sponsor AIDS awareness, Gay Pride festivals, and the Gay Games. Recently a number of beer companies, including Anheuser-Busch and Miller Brewing Co., have begun placing gay-specific, brand-specific ads in national gay publications.[69]

A number of other companies, including IBM and United Airlines, have also begun to run ads with gay themes, although they generally confine them to magazines and newspapers targeting the gay market. While a TV commercial or print ad with a gay reference occasionally runs in the mainstream media, it usually is for a fashion brand and often is so subtle or ambiguous that many heterosexuals do not perceive it as a gay message. However, in early 2000 the Gay Financial Network, an online company (gfn.com) with a gay-friendly financial news and information website, became the first gay-oriented company to advertise in major U.S. business news and entertainment publications.[70] The gfn.com ads take a gentle swipe at homophobia in the business world (Exhibit 22–13).

Advertising and the Media

The fact that advertising plays such an important role in financing the media has led to concern that advertisers may influence or even control the media. It is well documented that *economic censorship* occurs, whereby the media avoid certain topics or even present biased news coverage, in acquiescence to advertiser demands.[71] In fact, Professors Lawrence Soley and Robert Craig say, "The assertion that advertisers attempt to influence what the public sees, hears, and reads in the mass media is perhaps the most damning of all criticisms of advertising, but this criticism isn't acknowledged in most advertising

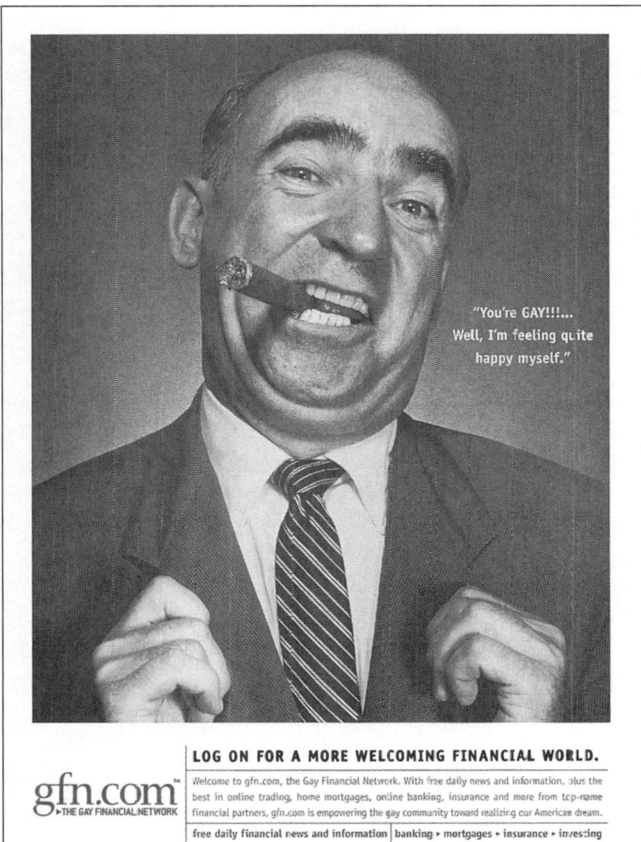

"You're GAY!!!... Well, I'm feeling quite happy myself."
LOG ON FOR A MORE WELCOMING FINANCIAL WORLD.
gfn.com™
▸THE GAY FINANCIAL NETWORK
Welcome to gfn.com, the Gay Financial Network. With free daily news and information, plus the best in online trading, home mortgages, online banking, insurance and more from top-name financial partners, gfn.com is empowering the gay community toward realizing our American dream.
free daily financial news and information
banking ▸ mortgages ▸ insurance ▸ investing

Exhibit 22–13 The Gay Financial Network broke barriers by becoming the first gay-oriented company to advertise in the mainstream media

textbooks."[72] We will address this important issue in this book by considering arguments on both sides.

Arguments Supporting Advertiser Control Some critics charge the media's dependence on advertisers' support makes them susceptible to various forms of influence, including exerting control over the editorial content of magazines and newspapers; biasing editorial opinions to favor the position of an advertiser; limiting coverage of a controversial story that might reflect negatively on a company; and influencing the program content of television. Ethical Perspective 22–2 considers whether the editorial content of newspapers and magazines is influenced by advertisers.

Newspapers and magazines receive nearly 70 percent of their revenue from advertising; commercial TV and radio derive virtually all their income from advertisers. Small, financially insecure newspapers, magazines, or broadcast stations are the most susceptible to pressure from advertisers, particularly companies that account for a large amount of the media outlet's advertising revenue. A local newspaper may be reluctant to print an unfavorable story about a car dealer or supermarket chain on whose advertising it depends. For example, a few years ago more than 40 car dealers canceled their ads in the *San Jose Mercury News* when the paper printed an article titled "A Car Buyer's Guide to Sanity." The dealers objected to the tone of the article, which they felt implied consumers should consider car dealers unethical adversaries in the negotiation process.[73] A survey of 147 daily newspapers found that more than 90 percent of editors have been pressured by advertisers and more than one-third of them said advertisers had succeeded in influencing news at their papers.[74]

While larger, more financially stable media should be less susceptible to an advertiser's influence, they may still be reluctant to carry stories detrimental to companies that purchase large amounts of advertising time or space.[75] For example, since cigarette commercials were taken off radio and TV in 1970, tobacco companies have allocated most of their budgets to the print media. The tobacco industry outspends all other national advertisers in newspapers, and cigarettes constitute the

Ethical Perspective 22–2

Is "The Wall" Falling Down?

Advertising is the primary source of revenue for nearly all of the news and entertainment media in the United States. And because advertising pays the bills, newspaper and magazine publishers as well as TV and radio networks and station executives must keep their advertisers happy. Professors Jef Richards and John Murphy call it a "task not unlike feeding crocodiles." They note the inherent danger is that advertisers might use their economic influence to act as unofficial censors of the media, banning them from publishing or broadcasting certain material.

It is well recognized that advertisers systematically avoid TV shows that deal with certain controversial issues, such as abortion and homosexuality. Most advertisers also have contract stipulations allowing them to cancel a media purchase if, after prescreening a show, they are uncomfortable with its content or feel it may reflect poorly on their company. And TV is not the only medium that must deal with the threats of advertiser defection or attempts to influence content. Advertisers can also influence the editorial content of magazines and newspapers by pressuring them to run only positive stories about their products or services.

Most magazine and newspaper publishers insist they do not allow advertiser pressure to influence their editorial content. They argue that they have long regarded the formal separation of their news and business departments as essential to their independence and credibility. This separation is often referred to as "The Wall" and is often spoken of with a mixture of reverence and trepidation. Many magazines and newspapers have traditionally discouraged employees on the publishing side, including advertising, circulation, and other business departments, from interacting with those on the editorial side who write and edit the articles. This can be done by separating editorial and advertising offices, barring the sales force from reading articles before they are printed, and prohibiting editorial employees from participating in advertising sales calls. For many years, the *Chicago Tribune* went so far as to program the elevators that went to the advertising and other business departments to bypass the fourth floor where the editorial staff worked.

Journalists agree that giving favorable editorial consideration to a company simply because it advertises in the publication would be a cardinal sin. Yet critics argue that this does sometimes occur. For example, a few years ago a controversy arose in business publishing when *Fortune* magazine published an article accusing its fierce rival *Forbes* of "turning downbeat stories into upbeat stories in order to keep advertisers happy—even at the risk of misleading their own readers." *Forbes* issued a statement saying, "The *Forbes* advertising department has no input into the *Forbes* editorial process."

There is also concern that the newspaper industry may be lowering The Wall in their search for new ways to increase readership and revenue as competition from TV, specialty magazines, and the Internet increases and newspaper readership continues to decline. At many newspapers these days, editors and business-side executives routinely meet to discuss readership, advertising, the creation of sections, and a wide range of other issues. This makes many journalists as well as others concerned, as they feel it is an issue that affects every citizen who wants honest and complete news and reporting that is not influenced by concerns over flattering or offending advertisers.

In October 1999 an assault on The Wall occurred when it was revealed that the Times Mirror Co.'s flagship newspaper, the *Los Angeles Times,* had made a secret deal to produce a special issue of the *Times* Sunday magazine devoted to the city's new Staples Center sports arena and had agreed to share the issue's ad revenues with the center. Times Mirror Co.'s CEO admitted that the advertising deal was a "mistake" but did not feel it had a significant effect on readers or advertisers. However, the move caused an outcry in the journalistic community as well as among the paper's own editorial staff. *Los Angeles Times* editor Michael Parks recently announced an investigation of the deal, calling the decision a key step to restoring the newspaper's credibility.

Magazines and newspapers are still very much concerned over maintaining the concept of The Wall and ensuring that decisions on the writing, editing, and publishing of stories are made on journalistic merit rather than whether they will attract or repel advertisers. However, the new economics of the publishing industry is making it difficult to keep The Wall standing. When the *Chicago Tribune* office was remodeled, the elevators were programmed to stop at every floor, and according to the paper's editor, "advertising people can come onto the fourth floor now and not get bitten or shot."

Sources: "'L.A. Times' Controversy Reflects Management 'Mindset' Problem," *Advertising Age,* November 15, 1999, p. 36; Lisa Bannon, "Times Mirror CEO Calls Ad Deal an Error," *The Wall Street Journal,* November 5, 1999; David Shaw, "An Uneasy Alliance of News and Ads," *Los Angeles Times,* March 29, 1998, pp. A1, 28.

second-largest category of magazine advertising (behind transportation). This has led to charges that magazines and newspapers avoid articles on the hazards of smoking to protect this important source of ad revenue.[76] A study by Joanne Lipman found that magazines relying on cigarette advertising are far less likely than others to publish stories about the health hazards associated with smoking.[77]

Individual TV stations and even the major networks also can be influenced by advertisers. Programming decisions are made largely on the basis of what shows will attract the most viewers and thus be most desirable to advertisers. Critics say this often results in lower-quality television as educational, cultural, and informative programming is usually sacrificed for shows that get high ratings and appeal to the mass markets.

Advertisers have also been accused of pressuring the networks to change their programming. Many advertisers have begun withdrawing commercials from programs that contain too much sex or violence, often in response to threatened boycotts of their products by consumers if they advertise on these shows. For example, groups such as the American Family Association have been fighting sex and violence in TV programs by calling for boycotts. Recently a number of companies, including Procter & Gamble, Mars Inc., and Kraft Foods, pulled their advertising from certain talk shows, like those of Jenny Jones and Ricki Lake, because of some of their incendiary topics.[78]

It has been speculated that the new rating system being considered by the networks may result in advertisers avoiding programs with adult content labels. This could result in a drop in advertising rates for these programs and greater demand for shows rated as suitable for family viewing.[79]

Arguments against Advertiser Control The commercial media's dependence on advertising means advertisers can exert influence on their character, content, and coverage of certain issues. However, media executives offer several reasons why advertisers do not exert undue influence over the media.

First, they point out it is in the best interest of the media not to be influenced too much by advertisers. To retain public confidence, they must report the news fairly and accurately without showing bias or attempting to avoid controversial issues. Media executives point to the vast array of topics they cover and the investigative reporting they often do as evidence of their objectivity. They want to build a large audience for their publications or stations so that they can charge more for advertising space and time.

Media executives also note that an advertiser needs the media more than they need any individual advertiser, particularly when the medium has a large audience or does a good job of reaching a specific market segment. Many publications and stations have a very broad base of advertising support and can afford to lose an advertiser that attempts to exert too much influence. This is particularly true for the larger, more established, financially secure media. For example, a consumer products company would find it difficult to reach its target audience without network TV and could not afford to boycott a network if it disagreed with a station's editorial policy or program content. Even the local advertiser in a small community may be dependent on the local newspaper, since it may be the most cost-effective media option available.

The media in the United States are basically supported by advertising; this means we can enjoy them for free or for a fraction of what they would cost without advertising. The alternative to an advertiser-supported media system is support by users through higher subscription costs for the print media and a fee or pay-per-view system with TV. The ad in Exhibit 22–14, part of a campaign by the International Advertising Association, explains how advertising lowers the cost of print media for consumers. Another alternative is government-supported media like those in many other countries, but this runs counter to most people's desire for freedom of the press. Although not perfect, our system of advertising-supported media provides the best option for receiving information and entertainment.

Exhibit 22–14 This ad points out how advertising lowers the cost of newspapers for consumers

WITHOUT ADVERTISING, YOUR NEWSPAPER WOULD COST YOU A BUNDLE.
Did you know that every ad in your newspaper helps pay for the rest of the essential pages? The fact is, your paper would cost you about $5.00 a day without advertisements. A price that would make news indeed.
Advertising. That's the way it works.

Summarizing Social Effects

We have examined a number of issues and have attempted to analyze the arguments for and against them. Many people have reservations about the impact of advertising and promotion on society. The numerous rules, regulations, policies, and guidelines marketers comply with do not cover every advertising and promotional situation. Moreover, what one individual views as distasteful or unethical may be acceptable to another.

Negative opinions regarding advertising and other forms of promotion have been around almost as long as the field itself, and it is unlikely they will ever disappear. However, the industry must address the various concerns about the effects of advertising and other forms of promotion on society. Advertising is a very powerful institution, but it will remain so only as long as consumers have faith in the ads they see and hear every day. Many of the problems discussed here can be avoided if individual decision makers make ethics an important element of the IMC planning process.

The primary focus of this discussion of social effects has been on the way advertising is used (or abused) in the marketing of products and services. It is important to note that advertising and other IMC tools, such as direct marketing and public relations, are also used to promote worthy causes and to deal with problems facing society (drunk driving, drug abuse, and the AIDS crisis, among others). For example, IMC Perspective 22–3 discusses how the Partnership for a Drug Free America and now the U.S. government are using advertising to help fight the war against drugs in the United States. Campaigns for nonprofit organizations and worthy causes are often developed pro bono by advertising agencies, and free advertising time and space are donated by the media.

Exhibit 22–15 shows an ad from a very successful public service campaign for the Boys & Girls Clubs of America featuring actor Denzel Washington. The campaign,

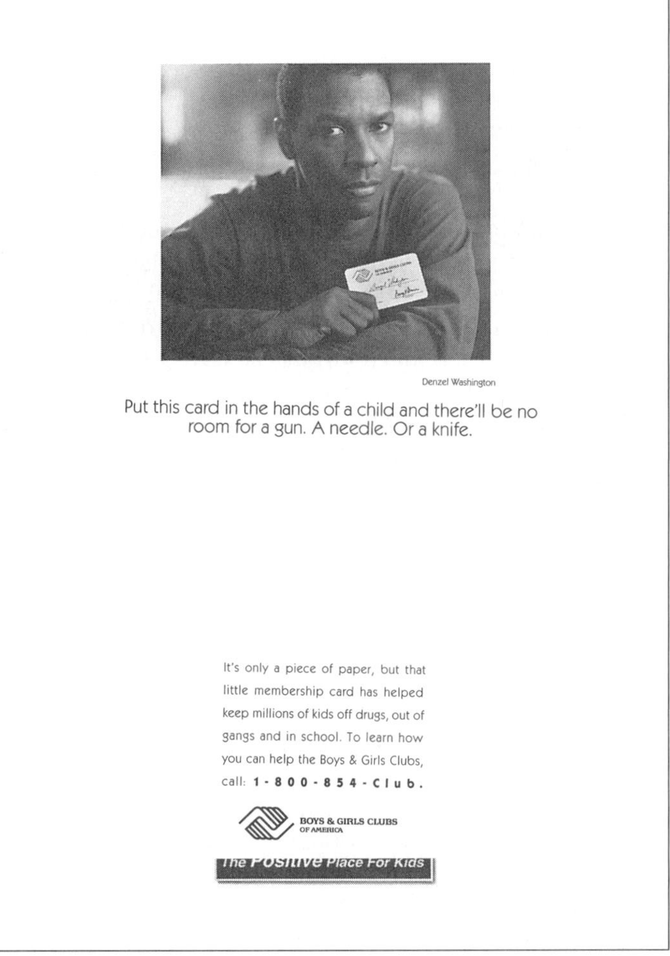

Denzel Washington
Put this card in the hands of a child and there'll be no room for a gun. A needle. Or a knife.
It's only a piece of paper, but that little membership card has helped keep millions of kids off drugs, out of gangs and in school. To learn how you can help the Boys & Girls Clubs, call: 1-800-854-Club.
BOYS & GIRLS CLUBS OF AMERICA
The Positive Place For Kids

Exhibit 22–15 This ad campaign for the Boys & Girls Clubs is an example of the pro bono work often done by advertising agencies for nonprofit organizations

IMC Perspective 22–3

Using Advertising to Fight the Drug War—and Making Sure It Works

Every day, in almost every city and town across America, children are deciding whether to try drugs. Drug abuse is a process that more often than not begins in childhood. The younger the person is when he or she begins using drugs, the more likely that other serious problems, including addiction, will follow. One method of preventing children from trying and using drugs is by helping them understand the dangers of using them.

For more than a decade the advertising industry has been tackling the problem of illicit drug use through the Partnership for a Drug Free America, which is a private, nonprofit coalition of professionals from the communications industry whose collective mission is to reduce demand for drugs in America through media communication. The Partnership was founded in 1986 as the advertising industry's affirmative response to the crack cocaine epidemic. Since its founding, more than 600 commercials have been created by advertising agencies that work on these ads on a pro bono basis, donating the time, talent, and services of their creative staff. More than $3 billion in media time also has been donated to the Partnership's national campaign, making it the single largest public service ad campaign in history.

In 1997 the U.S. government entered the media war on drugs when the Clinton administration announced a federally sponsored five-year campaign to keep kids from using drugs. Half the costs of this program are coming from contributions of advertising space and time by the media, and half from ads paid for by the government. While the PDFA receives no funding for its role in the campaign, the organization donates all of its advertising to the effort pro bono and serves as a primary strategic consultant (unpaid). One of the spots it has donated is an updated version of the famous "Fried Eggs" spot of the 80s, which showed an egg sizzling in a frying pan. In the new version, actress Rachael Leigh Cook, star of the movie *She's All That,* is shown using a frying pan to smash apart a kitchen as she shouts, "This is your brain. This is your brain on heroin."

The Partnership is continuing to work with the Office of National Drug Control Policy (ONDCP), which is the federal government office handling the program. However, the antidrug office also hired Ogilvy & Mather Worldwide to coordinate the campaign and place ads nationwide. U.S. drug czar Barry M. McCaffery, a retired four-star general, has indicated he plans to hold Madison Avenue accountable for showing results from the money being spent on the campaign. "There are no points for style," he says. "We've got to achieve an outcome. We have to change the way Americans act." McCaffery wants hard numbers to prove the campaign is working, so it is likely to become the most closely monitored campaign in U.S. advertising history. First, ads must pass a rigorous six-step evaluation. Then their real-world performance is put under a microscope. The government has hired scientific survey firm Westat to question about 20,000 children and parents every six months to measure the campaign's progress. Market researchers will also do telephone sampling every month or two for more immediate feedback.

Early results on the effectiveness of the campaign have been encouraging, according to officials of the ONDCP. Surveys in 12 test cities found that awareness of antidrug messages increased markedly during a six-month pilot program. The number of children who said the ads made them realize drugs are dangerous rose in the test cities,

while declining in the 12 cities used as a control group. Calls to antidrug hotlines also rose in the test cities.

Campaign planners have also commissioned ads to reach specific target groups, including Hispanics, African-Americans, and Asian-Americans, and Ogilvy has brought in a number of smaller agencies specializing in advertising for different ethnic groups. A panel of academic experts on human behavior reviews all spots. The two groups have provided advice ranging from the best way to reach Native American audiences (tribal newspapers and radio) to what kinds of images work with Chinese parents (most of whom have never seen a "joint" and have no idea what the word means).

Recently the campaign's effort to reach African-Americans ran into some problems when the cable network Black Entertainment Television (BET) refused to air ads for the initiative. BET argued that more money should be spent to run antidrug ads on the network because of its clout and efficiency in reaching African-Americans and charged the government with racial prejudice. The ONDCP denied the charge and argued that in addition to using targeted media such as BET, it uses a variety of mainstream media vehicles to reach African-Americans, such as MTV.

The government also came under fire in early 2000 for its policy of allowing TV networks that use antidrug themes in programs to run fewer public service ads, thereby giving them more time to sell to paying advertisers. Under the "match component" aspect of the government's program, media companies are required to provide a free antidrug ad or related antidrug programming for every ad paid for by the government.

Sources: Ira Teinowitz, "Black TV Network Rips White House Anti-drug Buy," *Advertising Age*, January 17, 2000, pp. 1, 50; Gordon Fairclough, "U.S. Antidrug Campaign to Be Closely Monitored," *The Wall Street Journal*, April 26, 1999, p. B10.

which was done by the New York agency Ammirati Puris Lintas, was designed to establish an image to distinguish the Boys & Girls Clubs from other public service groups and to encourage adults to organize clubs.[80]

Economic Effects of Advertising

Advertising plays an important role in a free-market system like ours by making consumers aware of products and services and providing them with information for decision making. Advertising's economic role goes beyond this basic function, however. It is a powerful force that can affect the functioning of our entire economic system.

Advertising can encourage consumption and foster economic growth. It not only informs customers of available goods and services but also facilitates entry into markets for a firm or a new product or brand; leads to economies of scale in production, marketing, and distribution, which in turn lead to lower prices; and hastens the acceptance of new products and the rejection of inferior products.

Critics of advertising view it as a detrimental force that not only fails to perform its basic function of information provision adequately but also adds to the cost of products and services and discourages competition and market entry, leading to industrial concentration and higher prices for consumers.

In their analysis of advertising, economists generally take a macroeconomic perspective: they consider the economic impact of advertising on an entire industry or on the economy as a whole rather than its effect on an individual company or brand. Our examination of the economic impact of advertising focuses on these broader macro-level issues. We consider its effects on consumer choice, competition, and product costs and prices.

Effects on Consumer Choice

Some critics say advertising hampers consumer choice, as large advertisers use their power to limit our options to a few well-advertised brands. Economists argue that advertising is used to achieve (1) **differentiation,** whereby the products or services of large advertisers are perceived as unique or better than competitors', and (2) brand loyalty, which enables large national advertisers to gain control of the market, usually at the expense of smaller brands.

Larger companies often end up charging a higher price and achieve a more dominant position in the market than smaller firms that cannot compete against them and their large advertising budgets. When this occurs, advertising not only restricts the choice alternatives to a few well-known, heavily advertised brands but also becomes a substitute for competition based on price or product improvements.

Heavily advertised brands dominate the market in certain product categories, such as soft drinks, beer, and cereals.[81] But advertising generally does not create brand monopolies and reduce the opportunities for new products to be introduced to consumers. In most product categories, a number of different brands are on the store shelves and thousands of new products are introduced every year. The opportunity to advertise gives companies the incentive to develop new brands and improve their existing ones. When a successful new product such as a personal computer is introduced, competitors quickly follow and use advertising to inform consumers about their brand and attempt to convince them it is superior to the original. Companies like Virgin Atlantic Airways recognize that advertising has been an important part of their success (Exhibit 22–16).

Effects on Competition

One of the most common criticisms economists have about advertising concerns its effects on competition. They argue that power in the hands of large firms with huge advertising budgets creates a **barrier to entry,** which makes it difficult for other firms to enter the market. This results in less competition and higher prices. Economists note that smaller firms already in the market find it difficult to compete against the large advertising budgets of the industry leaders and are often driven out of business. For example, in the U.S. beer industry, the number of national brewers has declined dramatically. In their battle for market share, industry giants Anheuser-Busch and Miller increased their ad budgets substantially and reaped market shares that total over 60 percent. Anheuser-Busch alone spent nearly $700

Exhibit 22–16 Virgin Atlantic Airways chair Richard Branson acknowledges the importance of advertising

million on advertising in 1999. However, these companies are spending much less per barrel than smaller firms, making it very difficult for the latter to compete.

Large advertisers clearly enjoy certain competitive advantages. First, there are **economies of scale** in advertising, particularly with respect to factors such as media costs. Firms such as Procter & Gamble and Philip Morris, which spend over $2 billion a year on advertising and promotion, are able to make large media buys at a reduced rate and allocate them to their various products.

Large advertisers usually sell more of a product or service, which means they may have lower production costs and can allocate more monies to advertising, so they can afford the costly but more efficient media like network television. Their large advertising outlays also give them more opportunity to differentiate their products and develop brand loyalty. To the extent that these factors occur, smaller competitors are at a disadvantage and new competitors are deterred from entering the market.

While advertising may have an anticompetitive effect on a market, there is no clear evidence that advertising alone reduces competition, creates barriers to entry, and thus increases market concentration. Lester Telser noted that high levels of advertising are not always found in industries where firms have a large market share. He found an inverse relationship between intensity of product class advertising and stability of market share for the leading brands.[82] These findings run contrary to many economists' belief that industries controlled by a few firms have high advertising expenditures, resulting in stable brand shares for market leaders.

Defenders of advertising say it is unrealistic to attribute a firm's market dominance and barriers to entry solely to advertising. There are a number of other factors, such as price, product quality, distribution effectiveness, production efficiencies, and competitive strategies. For many years, products such as Coors beer and Hershey chocolate bars were dominant brands even though these companies spent little on advertising. Hershey did not advertise at all until 1970. For 66 years, the company relied on the quality of its products, its favorable reputation and image among consumers, and its extensive channels of distribution to market its brands. Industry leaders often tend to dominate markets because they have superior product quality and the best management and competitive strategies, not simply the biggest advertising budgets.[83]

While market entry against large, established competitors is difficult, companies with a quality product at a reasonable price often find a way to break in. Moreover, they usually find that advertising actually facilitates their market entry by making it possible to communicate the benefits and features of their new product or brand to consumers. For example, Southern Korea's Daewoo Motor Co. entered the U.S. automotive market in 1998 and has recently begun a major national advertising campaign to create a brand identity for its cars. Exhibit 22–17 shows an ad for the company's flagship Leganza model, which is positioned as offering "affordable luxury."[84]

Exhibit 22–17 Advertising is very important to companies such as Daewoo Motor America as it enters the U.S. market

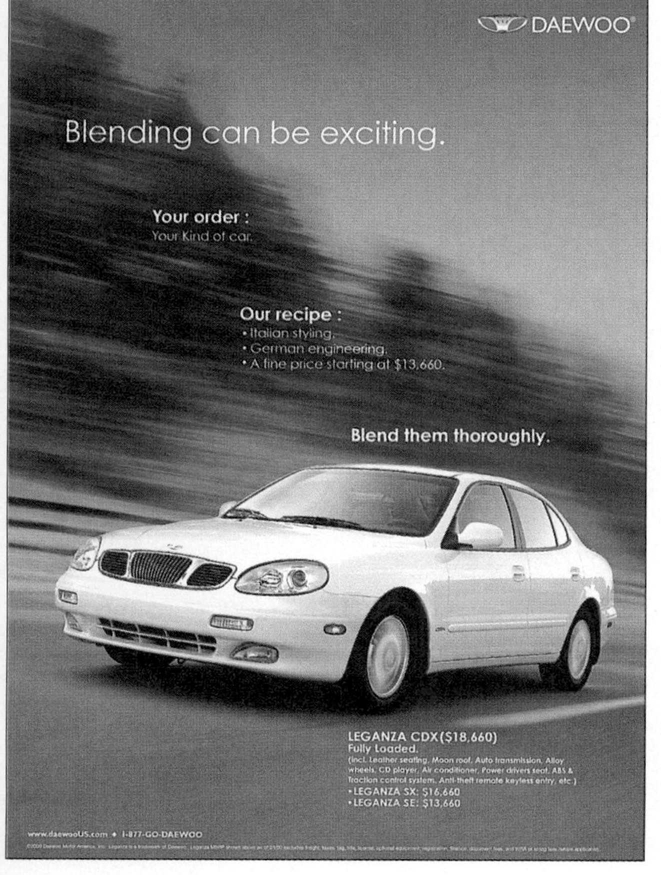

Effects on Product Costs and Prices

A major area of debate among economists, advertisers, consumer advocates, and policymakers concerns the effects of advertising on product costs and prices. Critics argue that advertising increases the prices consumers pay for products and services. First, they say the large sums of money spent advertising a brand constitute an expense that must be covered and the consumer ends up paying for it through higher prices. This is a common criticism from consumer advocates. Several studies show that firms with higher relative prices advertise their products more intensely than do those with lower relative prices.[85]

A second way advertising can result in higher prices is by increasing product differentiation and adding to the perceived value of the product in consumers' minds. Paul Farris and Mark Albion note that product differentiation occupies a central position in theories of advertising's economic effects.[86] The fundamental premise is that advertising increases the perceived differences between physically homogeneous products and enables advertised brands to command a premium price without an increase in quality.

Critics of advertising generally point to the differences in prices between national brands and private-label brands that are physically similar, such as aspirin or tea bags, as evidence of the added value created by advertising. They see consumers' willingness to pay more for heavily advertised national brands rather than purchasing the lower-priced, nonadvertised brand as wasteful and irrational. However, consumers do not always buy for rational, functional reasons. The emotional, psychological, and social benefits derived from purchasing a national brand are important to many people. Moreover, say Albion and Farris,

> Unfortunately there seems to be no single way to measure product differentiation, let alone determine how much is excessive or attributable to the effects of advertising . . . Both price insensitivity and brand loyalty could be created by a number of factors such as higher product quality, better packaging, favorable use experience and market position. They are probably related to each other but need not be the result of advertising.[87]

Proponents of advertising offer several other counterarguments to the claim that advertising increases prices. They acknowledge that advertising costs are at least partly paid for by consumers. But advertising may help lower the overall cost of a product more than enough to offset them. For example, advertising may help firms achieve economies of scale in production and distribution by providing information to and stimulating demand among mass markets. These economies of scale help cut the cost of producing and marketing the product, which can lead to lower prices—if the advertiser chooses to pass the cost savings on to the consumer. The ad in Exhibit 22–18, from a campaign sponsored by the American Association of Advertising Agencies, emphasizes this point.

Advertising can also lower prices by making a market more competitive, which usually leads to greater price competition. A study by Lee Benham found that prices of eyeglasses were 25 to 30 percent higher in states that banned eyeglass advertising than in those that permitted it.[88] Robert Steiner analyzed the toy industry and concluded that advertising resulted in lower consumer prices. He argued

Exhibit 22–18 This ad refutes the argument that reducing advertising expenditures will lead to lower prices

that curtailment of TV advertising would drive up consumer prices for toys.[89] Finally, advertising is a means to market entry rather than a deterrent and helps stimulate product innovation, which makes markets more competitive and helps keep prices down.

Overall, it is difficult to reach any firm conclusions regarding the relationship between advertising and prices. After an extensive review of this area, Farris and Albion concluded, "The evidence connecting manufacturer advertising to prices is neither complete nor definitive . . . consequently, we cannot say whether advertising is a tool of market efficiency or market power without further research."[90]

Economist James Ferguson argues that advertising cannot increase the cost per unit of quality to consumers because if it did, consumers would not continue to respond positively to advertising.[91] He believes advertising lowers the costs of information about brand qualities, leads to increases in brand quality, and lowers the average price per unit of quality.

Summarizing Economic Effects

Albion and Farris suggest that economists' perspectives can be divided into two principal schools of thought that make different assumptions regarding the influence of advertising on the economy.[92] Figure 22–3 summarizes the main points of the "advertising equals market power" and "advertising equals information" perspectives.

Advertising Equals Market Power The belief that advertising equals market power reflects traditional economic thinking and views advertising as a way to change consumers' tastes, lower their sensitivity to price, and build brand loyalty among buyers of advertised brands. This results in higher profits and market power for large advertisers, reduces competition in the market, and leads to higher prices and fewer choices for consumers. Proponents of this viewpoint generally have negative attitudes regarding the economic impact of advertising.

Figure 22–3 Two schools of thought on advertising's role in the economy

Advertising = Market Power		Advertising = Information
Advertising affects consumer preferences and tastes, changes product attributes, and differentiates the product from competitive offerings.	Advertising	Advertising informs consumers about product attributes but does not change the way they value those attributes.
Consumers become brand loyal and less price sensitive and perceive fewer substitutes for advertised brands.	Consumer buying behavior	Consumers become more price sensitive and buy best "value." Only the relationship between price and quality affects elasticity for a given product.
Potential entrants must overcome established brand loyalty and spend relatively more on advertising.	Barriers to entry	Advertising makes entry possible for new brands because it can communicate product attributes to consumers.
Firms are insulated from market competition and potential rivals; concentration increases, leaving firms with more discretionary power.	Industry structure and market power	Consumers can compare competitive offerings easily and competitive rivalry increases. Efficient firms remain, and as the inefficient leave, new entrants appear; the effect on concentration is ambiguous.
Firms can charge higher prices and are not as likely to compete on quality or price dimensions. Innovation may be reduced.	Market conduct	More informed consumers pressure firms to lower prices and improve quality; new entrants facilitate innovation.
High prices and excessive profits accrue to advertisers and give them even more incentive to advertise their products. Output is restricted compared with conditions of perfect competition.	Market performance	Industry prices decrease. The effect on profits due to increased competition and increased efficiency is ambiguous.

Advertising Equals Information The belief that advertising equals information takes a more positive view of advertising's economic effects. This model sees advertising as providing consumers with useful information, increasing their price sensitivity (which moves them toward lower-priced products), and increasing competition in the market. Advertising is viewed as a way to communicate with consumers and tell them about a product and its major features and attributes. More informed and knowledgeable consumers pressure companies to provide high-quality products at lower prices. Efficient firms remain in the market, whereas inefficient firms leave as new entrants appear. Proponents of this model believe the economic effects of advertising are favorable and think it contributes to more efficient and competitive markets.

It is unlikely the debate over the economic effects and value of advertising will be resolved soon. Many economists will continue to take a negative view of advertising and its effects on the functioning of the economy, while advertisers will continue to view it as an efficient way for companies to communicate with their customers and an essential component of our economic system. The International Advertising Association has been running a campaign for several years to convince consumers around the world of the economic value of advertising. Ads like the one shown in Exhibit 22–19 are used in countries such as China and Russia, where consumers are unfamiliar with the concept of advertising. The goal of the campaign is to get consumers in these countries to recognize the role advertising plays in contributing to their economic well-being.[93]

WHEN ADVERTISING DOES ITS JOB, MILLIONS OF PEOPLE KEEP THEIRS.

Good advertising doesn't just inform. It sells. It helps move product and keep businesses in business. Every time an ad arouses a consumer's interest enough to result in a purchase, it keeps a company going strong. And it helps secure the jobs of the people who work there.

Advertising. That's the way it works.

The global partnership of advertisers, agencies and media

Exhibit 22–19 This ad is part of a global campaign by the International Advertising Association to educate consumers about the economic value of advertising

Figure 22–4, excerpts from a speech given by famous adman Leo Burnett, summarizes the perspective of most advertising people on the economic effects of advertising. While many advertising and marketing experts agree that advertising and promotion play an important role in helping to expand consumer demand for new products, not everyone would agree that this is desirable. Ethical Perspective 22–4 discusses the issue of whether advertising is contributing to a problem of excess consumption, particularly among consumers in the wealthy industrialized countries such the United States, Japan, Australia, and nations in Western Europe.

To me it means that if we believe to any degree whatsoever in the economic system under which we live, in a high standard of living and in high employment, advertising is the most efficient known way of moving goods in practically every product class.

My proof is that millions of businessmen have chosen advertising over and over again in the operations of their business. Some of their decisions may have been wrong, but they must have thought they were right or they wouldn't go back to be stung twice by the same kind of bee.

It's a pretty safe bet that in the next 10 years many Americans will be using products and devices that no one in this room has even heard of. Judging purely by past performance, American advertising can be relied on to make them known and accepted overnight at the lowest possible prices.

Advertising, of course, makes possible our unparalleled variety of magazines, newspapers, business publications, and radio and television stations.

It must be said that without advertising we would have a far different nation, and one that would be much the poorer—not merely in material commodities, but in the life of the spirit.

Leo Burnett

These excerpts are from a speech given by Leo Burnett on the American Association of Advertising Agencies' 50th anniversary, April 20, 1967.

Figure 22–4 This message describes the positive economic effects of advertising

Ethical Perspective 22–4

Advertising's Role in the New Era of Sustainability

One of the newest movements attacking the basic tenets of marketing and advertising revolves around the issue of sustainable resources. Scientists and environmentalists have long argued that consumer-oriented countries, such as the United States, Japan, and the nations of Western Europe, are overusing the Earth's resources. But now, many critics are holding marketing and advertising as at least partially accountable for the problem. They argue that advertising and other forms of marketing convince people that consuming more products will bring them emotional rewards such as contentment.

David Jelly Helm, a former agency creative director who now teaches at Virginia Commonwealth University's AdCenter, notes that advertising "continues to perpetuate a world of continuous, unlimited and ever-expanding consumption." In a recent speech to the *Adweek* creative conference, he makes some very intriguing arguments to support his position. The 20 percent of the world's population in the wealthiest industrial countries—the United States, European nations, Japan, and Australia—account for 86 percent of total private consumption expenditures. The middle three-fifths account for 12.7 percent, while the bottom fifth accounts for just 1.3 percent. The richest fifth consume 58 percent of the world's energy, 65 percent of the electricity, 87 percent of the cars, 74 percent of the telephones, 46 percent of the meat, and 84 percent of the paper. In each of these areas the share of the bottom fifth is in single digits. Helm argues that if everyone consumed the way Americans do, we would need four more earths to support it.

Helm's refers to the 20 percent living in industrialized countries as *overconsumers* and argues that they are consuming at a rate that cannot be sustained. He calls the middle 60 percent sustainers. They have electricity, clean water, adequate food. They have fewer cars and depend on public transportation. They're not deprived, and their style of living does not threaten the earth. The bottom 20 percent are the *excluded,* who have very limited access or even no access to clean water, safe food, shelter, and health care. He argues that in order to create a sustainable system, the bottom 1.1 billion people must increase their consumption levels, the middle 3.3 billion must continue down the same road they are on now, and the top 1.1 billion need to consume in more appropriate, responsible ways.

Helm notes that despite being keenly aware that we live on a finite planet with a limited amount of resources, we continue to perpetuate a world-view of continuous, unlimited, and ever-expanding consumption. Advertising continues to encourage runaway spending, in direct opposition to the type of action needed to get the world out of the mess it is in. Advertising's goal, of course, is to make you want something. To create desire. That begins by making you unhappy with what you currently have or don't have. Advertising widens the gap between what you have and what you want. Its influence comes from the common theme underlying every ad, repeated thousands of times, day after day: *Buying things will make you happy.* According to Helm, it is on those emotions that a world economy and a dominant philosophy have been built, encouraging the act of spending to increase personal happiness, well-being, and, ultimately, one's identity.

Helm and others argue that a growing international movement to rein in unsustainable consumption will bode badly for the ad industry if it doesn't change its outlook. Mari Cortizo, a former account planner with TBWA/Chiat/Day's London office, agrees that sustainability is the next big thing. "It's the kind of issue that can sway the fortunes of international companies. But people want more than talk. They will want marketers to offer easy ways for them to do something about saving resources," she says. A 1999 survey sponsored by the Conference Board found that harming the environment is one of the main reasons American consumers would refuse to do business with a company. The international survey found that about half of U.S. respondents said they have punished a firm for not being socially responsible, which includes environmental responsibility.

Helm suggests that it is time for the advertising industry to revise its code of ethics and rejuvenate and reclarify those standards given what we now know about the state of the world and the relationship of advertising to it. He notes that the 1998 United Nations Human Development Report on Consumption may serve as a guide. It says: "Consumption clearly contributes to human development when it enlarges the capabilities and enriches the lives of people without adversely affecting the well-being of others, when it is as fair to future generations as it is to the present ones, when it respects the carrying capacities of the planet, and when it encourages lively, creative individuals and communities."

Sources: David Helm, "Advertising's Overdue Revolution," speech given to the *Adweek* creative conference, October 1, 1999; Joan Voight, "The Consumer Rebellion," *Adweek,* January 10, 2000, pp. 46–50.

Summary

Advertising is a very powerful institution and has been the target of considerable criticism regarding its social and economic impact. The criticism of advertising concerns the specific techniques and methods used as well as its effect on societal values, tastes, lifestyles, and behavior. Critics argue that advertising is deceptive and untruthful; that it is often offensive, irritating, or in poor taste; and that it exploits certain groups, such as children. Many people believe advertising should be informative only and advertisers should not use subjective claims, puffery, embellishment, or persuasive techniques.

Advertising often offends consumers by the type of appeal or manner of presentation used; sexually suggestive ads and nudity receive the most criticism. Advertisers say their ads are consistent with contemporary values and lifestyles and are appropriate for the target audiences they are attempting to reach. Advertising to children is an area of particular concern, since critics argue that children lack the experience, knowledge, and ability to process and evaluate persuasive advertising messages rationally. Although an FTC proposal to severely restrict advertising to children was defeated, it remains an issue.

The pervasiveness of advertising and its prevalence in the mass media have led critics to argue that it plays a major role in influencing and transmitting social values. Advertising has been charged with encouraging materialism, manipulating consumers to buy things they do not really want or need, perpetuating stereotypes through its portrayal of certain groups such as women, minorities, and the elderly, and controlling the media.

Advertising has also been scrutinized with regard to its economic effects. The basic economic role of advertising is to give consumers information that helps them make consumption decisions. Some people view advertising as a detrimental force that has a negative effect on competition, product costs, and consumer prices. Economists' perspectives regarding the effects of advertising follow two basic schools of thought: the advertising equals market power model and the advertising equals information model. Arguments consistent with each perspective were considered in analyzing the economic effects of advertising.

Key Terms

ethics, 765
consumer socialization process, 772
materialism, 776
Protestant ethic, 776
differentiation, 788
barrier to entry, 789
economies of scale, 790

Discussion Questions

1. The opening vignette discusses how many companies are targeting their promotional programs to schools as a way of reaching the youth market. Do you think schools should allow companies to reach students through programs such as Channel One or ZapMe's donation of computers and Internet access? Evaluate the arguments for and against these programs.

2. Discuss the role of ethics in advertising and promotion. How do ethical considerations differ from legal considerations?

3. Nike has received some criticism for the violence in the ending to the commercials for the Air Cross Trainer II that appear on its "Whatever.Nike.com" website. Do you think these commercial endings are too violent or do you agree with the company's vice president of marketing who argues that teens can keep them in perspective?

4. Evaluate the arguments for and against advertising to children. Do you feel restrictions are needed for advertising and other forms of promotion targeted to children?

5. Ethical Perspective 22–1 discusses the use of "shock-vertising" by companies such as Abercrombie & Fitch, Emanual Ungaro, Bijan, and others. Evaluate the arguments for and against shock ads that use sexual appeals. Do you think this type of advertising is effective?

6. A common criticism of advertising is that it stereotypes women. Discuss the ways this might occur. Do you think the Airwalk ad shown in Exhibit 22–5 is suggestive and symbolizes sexual submission?

7. With which position do you agree: "Advertising determines American consumers' tastes and values and is responsible for creating a materialistic society," or "Advertising is a reflection of society and mirrors its tastes and values"?

8. Ethical Perspective 22–2 discusses how "The Wall" that separates the news and editorial department of magazines and newspapers from the advertising and business side may be coming down. Discuss some of the reasons why this may be occurring and evaluate the implications.

9. Discuss how advertising can impact consumer choice, as well as its impact on product costs and the prices paid for products and services.

10. Discuss the two major perspectives of the economic impact of advertising: "advertising equals market power" versus "advertising equals information."

Glossary of Advertising and Promotion Terms

80/20 rule (2) The principle that 80 percent of sales volume for a product or service is generated by 20 percent of the customers.

5-W's model of communication (5) A model of the communications process that contains five basics elements: who? (source), says what? (message), in what way? (channel), to whom? (receiver), and with what effect? (feedback).

A

AIDA model (5) A model that depicts the successive stages a buyer passes through in the personal selling process including: attention, interest, desire, and action.

ASI Recall Plus Test (18) A day-after recall test of television commercials (formerly known as the Burke Test).

absolute costs (10) The actual total cost of placing an ad in a particular media vehicle.

account executive (3) The individual who serves as the liaison between the advertising agency and the client. The account executive is responsible for managing all of the services the agency provides to the client and representing the agency's point of view to the client.

account specific marketing (16) Development of customized promotional programs for individual retail accounts by marketers.

ad click rate (15) Often referred to as "click-through," this is the percentage of ad views that resulted in an ad click.

ad clicks (15) Number of times users click on a banner ad.

ad execution-related thoughts (5) A type of thought or cognitive response a message recipient has concerning factors related to the execution of the ad such as creativity, usual effects, color, and style.

adjacencies (11) Commercial spots purchased from local television stations that generally appear during the time periods adjacent to network programs.

advertising (1) Any paid form of nonpersonal communication about an organization, product, service, or idea by an identified sponsor.

advertising agency (3) A firm that specializes in the creation, production, and placement of advertising messages and may provide other services that facilitate the marketing communications process.

advertising appeal (9) The basis or approach used in an advertising message to attract the attention or interest of consumers and/or influence their feelings toward the product, service, or cause.

advertising campaign (8) A comprehensive advertising plan that consists of a series of messages in a variety of media that center on a single theme or idea.

advertising creativity (8) The ability to generate fresh, unique, and appropriate ideas that can be used as solutions to communication problems.

advertising manager (3) The individual in an organization who is responsible for the planning, coordinating, budgeting, and implementing of the advertising program.

advertising specialties (13) Items used as giveaways to serve as a reminder or stimulate remembrance of a company or brand such as calendars, T-shirts, pens, key tags, and the like. Specialties are usually imprinted with a company or brand name and other identifying marks such as an address and phone number.

advertising substantiation (21) A Federal Trade Commission regulatory program that requires advertisers to have documentation to support the claims made in their advertisements.

ad views (impressions) (15) Number of times a banner ad is downloaded (and presumably seen) by viewers.

advocacy advertising (17) Advertising that is concerned with the propagation of ideas and elucidation of social issues of public importance in a manner that supports the position and interest of the sponsor.

aerial advertising (13) A form of outdoor advertising where messages appear in the sky in the form of banners pulled by airplanes, skywriting, and on blimps.

affect referral decision rule (4) A type of decision rule where selections are made on the basis of an overall impression or affective summary evaluation of the various alternatives under consideration.

affiliates (11) Local television stations that are associated with a major network. Affiliates agree to preempt time during specified hours for programming provided by the network and carry the advertising contained in the program.

affiliation (15) A relationship with other websites in which a company can cross-promote and is credited for sales that accrue through their site.

affirmative disclosure (21) A Federal Trade Commission program whereby advertisers may be required to include certain types of information in their advertisements so consumers will be aware of all the consequences, conditions, and limitations associated with the use of the product or service.

affordable method (7) A method of determining the budget for advertising and promotion where all other budget areas are covered and remaining monies are available for allocation.

Note: Numbers in parentheses after term indicate chapter(s) where term is discussed.

agate line (12) Unit of newspaper space measurement, 1 column wide by 1/14 inch deep. (Thus, 14 agate lines = 1 column inch.)

agency evaluation process (3) The process by which a company evaluates the performance of its advertising agency. This process includes both financial and qualitative aspects.

alpha activity (19) A measure of the degree of brain activity that can be used to assess an individual's reactions to an advertisement.

alternative media (13) A term commonly used in advertising to describe support media.

animatic (8) A preliminary version of a commercial whereby a videotape of the frames of a storyboard is produced along with an audio soundtrack.

arbitrary allocation (7) A method for determining the budget for advertising and promotion based on arbitrary decisions of executives.

area of dominant influence (ADI) (11) A geographic survey area created and defined by Arbitron. Each county in the nation is assigned to an ADI, which is an exclusive geographic area consisting of all counties in which the home market stations receive a preponderance of viewing.

attitude toward the ad (5) A message recipient's affective feelings of favorability or unfavorability toward an advertisement.

attractiveness (6) A source characteristic that makes him or her appealing to a message recipient. Source attractiveness can be based on similarity, familiarity, or likability.

audimeter (11) An electric measurement device that is hooked to a television set to record when the set is turned on and the channel to which it is tuned.

audiotex (13) The use of telephone and voice information services to market, advertise, promote, entertain, and inform consumers.

average frequency (10) The number of times the average household reached by a media schedule is exposed to a media vehicle over a specified period.

average quarter-hour figure (AQH) (11) The average number of persons listening to a particular station for at least five minutes during a 15-minute period. Used by Arbitron in measuring the size of radio audiences.

average quarter-hour rating (11) The average quarter-hour figure estimate expressed as a percentage of the population being measured. Used by Arbitron in measuring the size of radio audiences.

average quarter-hour share (11) The percentage of the total listening audience tuned to each station as a percentage of the total listening audience in the survey area. Used by Arbitron in measuring the size of radio audiences.

B

balance-of-trade deficit (20) A situation where the monetary value of a country's imports exceeds its exports.

banner (15) An ad on a Web page that may be "hot-linked" to the advertiser's site.

barrier to entry (22) Conditions that make it difficult for a firm to enter the market in a particular industry, such as high advertising budgets.

barter syndication (11) The offering of television programs to local stations free or at a reduced rate but with some of the advertising time presold to national advertisers. The remaining advertising time can be sold to local advertisers.

behavioristic segmentation (2) A method of segmenting a market by dividing customers into groups based on their usage, loyalties, or buying responses to a product or service.

benchmark measures (7) Measures of a target audience's status concerning response hierarchy variables such as awareness, knowledge, image, attitudes, preferences, intentions, or behavior. These measures are taken at the beginning of an advertising or promotional campaign to determine the degree to which a target audience must be changed or moved by a promotional campaign.

benefit segmentation (2) A method of segmenting markets on the basis of the major benefits consumers seek in a product or service.

Better Business Bureau (BBB) (21) An organization established and funded by businesses that operates primarily at the local level to monitor activities of companies and promote fair advertising and selling practices.

big idea (8) A unique or creative idea for an advertisement or campaign that attracts consumers' attention, gets a reaction, and sets the advertiser's product or service apart from the competition.

billings (3) The amount of client money agencies spend on media purchases and other equivalent activities. Billings are often used as a way of measuring the size of advertising agencies.

bleed pages (12) Magazine advertisements where the printed area extends to the edge of the page, eliminating any white margin or border around the ad.

body copy (9) The main text portion of a print ad. Also often referred to as copy.

bonus packs (16) Special packaging that provides consumers with extra quantity of merchandise at no extra charge over the regular price.

bounce-back coupon (16) A coupon offer made to consumers as an inducement to repurchase the brand.

brand development index (BDI) (10) An index that is calculated by taking the percentage of a brand's total sales that occur in a given market as compared to the percentage of the total population in the market.

brand equity (2) The intangible asset of added value or goodwill that results from the favorable image, impressions of differentiation, and/or the strength of consumer attachment of a company name, brand name, or trademark.

brand loyalty (4) Preference by a consumer for a particular brand that results in continual purchase of it.

brand manager (3) The person responsible for the planning, implementation, and control of the marketing program for an individual brand.

broadcast media (12) Media that use the airwaves to transmit their signal and programming. Radio and television are examples of broadcast media.

build-up approach (7) A method of determining the budget for advertising and promotion by determining the specific tasks that have to be performed and estimating the costs of performing them. See objective and task method.

Burke Test (19) A method of posttesting television commercials using a day-after recall test (now known as Ipsos-ASI Recall Test).

business-to-business advertising (19) Advertising used by one business to promote the products and/or services it sells to another business.

buying center (5) A committee or group of individuals in an organization who are responsible for evaluating products and services and making purchase decisions.

C

cable television (11) A form of television where signals are carried to households by wire rather than through the airways.

carryover effect (7) A delayed or lagged effect whereby the impact of advertising on sales can occur during a subsequent time period.

category development index (CDI) (10) An index that is calculated by taking the percentage of a product category's total sales that occur in a given market area as compared to the percentage of the total population in the market.

category extension (2) The strategy of applying an existing brand name to a new product category.

category management (3) An organizational system whereby managers have responsibility for the marketing programs for a particular category or line of products.

cease-and-desist order (21) An action by the Federal Trade Commission that orders a company to stop engaging in a practice that is considered deceptive or misleading until a hearing is held.

central route to persuasion (5) One of two routes to persuasion recognized by the elaboration likelihood model. The central route to persuasion views a message recipient as very active and involved in the communications process and as having the ability and motivation to attend to and process a message.

centralized organizational structure (20) A method of organizing for international advertising and promotion whereby all decisions are made in a company's home office.

centralized system (3) An organizational system whereby advertising along with other marketing activities such as sales, marketing research, and planning are divided along functional lines and are run from one central marketing department.

channel (5) The method or medium by which communication travels from a source or sender to a receiver.

Children's Online Privacy Protection Act of 1998 (21) Federal legislation which places restrictions on information collected from children via the Internet and requires that websites directed at children have a privacy policy posted on their home page and areas of the site where information is collected.

city zone (12) A category used for newspaper circulation figures that refers to a market area composed of the city where the paper is published and contiguous areas similar in character to the city.

classical conditioning (4) A learning process whereby a conditioned stimulus that elicits a response is paired with a neutral stimulus that does not elicit any particular response. Through repeated exposure, the neutral stimulus comes to elicit the same response as the conditioned stimulus.

classified advertising (12) Advertising that runs in newspapers and magazines that generally contains text only and is arranged under subheadings according to the product, service, or offering. Employment, real estate, and automotive ads are the major forms of classified advertising.

clients (3) The organizations with the products, services, or causes to be marketed and for which advertising agencies and other marketing promotional firms provide services.

clipping service (7) A service which clips competitors' advertising from local print media allowing the company to monitor the types of advertising that are running or to estimate their advertising expenditures.

close (18) Obtaining the commitment of the prospect in a personal selling transaction.

clutter (6, 11) The nonprogram material that appears in a broadcast environment, including commercials, promotional messages for shows, public service announcements, and the like.

cognitive dissonance (4) A state of psychological tension or postpurchase doubt that a consumer may experience after making a purchase decision. This tension often leads the consumer to try to reduce it by seeking supportive information.

cognitive processing (4) The process by which an individual transforms external information into meanings or patterns of thought and how these meanings are used to form judgments or choices about behavior.

cognitive responses (5) Thoughts that occur to a message recipient while reading, viewing, and/or hearing a communication.

collateral services (3) Companies that provide companies with specialized services such as package design, advertising production, and marketing research.

combination rates (12) A special space rate or discount offered for advertising in two or more periodicals. Combination rates are often offered by publishers who own both morning and evening editions of a newspaper in the same market.

commission system (3) A method of compensating advertising agencies whereby the agency receives a specified commission (traditionally 15 percent) from the media on any advertising time or space it purchases.

communication (5) The passing of information, exchange of ideas, or process of establishing shared meaning between a sender and a receiver.

communication objectives (1, 7) Goals that an organization seeks to achieve through its promotional program in terms of communication effects such as creating awareness, knowledge, image, attitudes, preferences, or purchase intentions.

communication task (7) Under the DAGMAR approach to setting advertising goals and objectives, something that can be performed by and attributed to advertising such as awareness, comprehension, conviction, and action.

comparative advertising (6, 9) The practice of either directly or indirectly naming one or more competitors in an advertising message and usually making a comparison on one or more specific attributes or characteristics.

compensatory decision rule (4) A type of decision rule for evaluating alternatives where consumers consider each brand with respect to how it performs on relevant or salient attributes and the importance of each attribute. This decision rule allows for a negative evaluation or performance on a particular attribute to be compensated for by a positive evaluation on another attribute.

competitive advantage (2) Something unique or special that a firm does or possesses that provides an advantage over its competitors.

competitive parity method (7) A method of setting the advertising and promotion budget based on matching the absolute level of percentage of sales expenditures of the competition.

compliance (6) A type of influence process where a receiver accepts the position advocated by a source to obtain favorable outcomes or to avoid punishment.

computer simulation models (7) Quantitative-based models that are used to determine the relative contribution of advertising expenditures on sales response.

concave downward function (7) An advertising/sales response function that views the incremental effects of advertising on sales as decreasing.

concentrated marketing (2) A type of marketing strategy whereby a firm chooses to focus its marketing efforts on one particular market segment.

concept testing (19) A method of pretesting alternative ideas for an advertisement or campaign by having consumers provide their responses and/or reactions to the creative concept.

conditioned response (4) In classical conditioning, a response that occurs as a result of exposure to a conditioned stimulus.

conditioned stimulus (4) In classical conditioning, a stimulus that becomes associated with an unconditioned stimulus and capable of evoking the same response or reaction as the unconditioned stimulus.

conjunctive decision rule (4) A type of decision rule for evaluating alternatives where consumers establish minimally acceptable levels of performance for each important product attribute and accept an alternative only if it meets the cutoff level for each attribute.

consent order (21) A settlement between a company and the Federal Trade Commission whereby an advertiser agrees to stop the advertising or practice in question. A consent order is for settlement purposes only and does not constitute an admission of guilt.

consumer behavior (4) The process and activities that people engage in when searching for, selecting, purchasing, using, evaluating, and disposing of products and services so as to satisfy their needs and desires.

consumer franchise-building promotions (16) Sales promotion activities that communicate distinctive brand attributes and contribute to the development and reinforcement of brand identity.

consumer juries (19) A method of pretesting advertisements by using a panel of consumers who are representative of the target audience and provide ratings, rankings, and/or evaluations of advertisements.

consumer-oriented sales promotion (16) Sales promotion techniques that are targeted to the ultimate consumer such as coupons, samples, contests, rebates, sweepstakes, and premium offers.

consumer socialization process (22) The process by which an individual acquires the skills needed to function in the marketplace as a consumer.

content sponsorship (15) The sponsor not only provides dollars in return for name association on the Internet but participates in the provision of content itself.

contest (16) A promotion whereby consumers compete for prizes or money on the basis of skills or ability, and winners are determined by judging the entries or ascertaining which entry comes closest to some predetermined criteria.

continuity (10) A media scheduling strategy where a continuous pattern of advertising is used over the time span of the advertising campaign.

contribution margin (7) The difference between the total revenue generated by a product or brand and its total variable costs.

controlled circulation basis (12) Distribution of a publication free to individuals a publisher believes are of importance and responsible for making purchase decisions or are prescreened for qualification on some other basis.

cookie (15) An identifying string of text attached to a website visitor's computer for information-gathering purposes, such as how often they visit the site, what is looked at, and in what sequence.

cooperative advertising (2, 16) Advertising program in which a manufacturer pays a certain percentage of the expenses a retailer or distributor incurs for advertising the manufacturer's product in a local market area.

copy platform (8) A document that specifies the basic elements of the creative strategy such as the basic problem or issue the advertising must address, the advertising and communications objectives, target audience, major selling idea or key benefits to communicate, campaign theme or appeal, and supportive information or requirements.

copywriter (3, 8) Individual who helps conceive the ideas for ads and commercials and writes the words or copy for them.

corporate advertising (17) Advertising designed to promote overall awareness of a company or enhance its image among a target audience.

corrective advertising (21) An action by the Federal Trade Commission whereby an advertiser can be required to run advertising messages designed to remedy the deception or misleading impression created by its previous advertising.

cost per customer purchasing (14) A cost effectiveness measure used in direct marketing based on the cost per sale generated.

cost per order (CPO) (13) A measure used in direct marketing to determine the number of orders generated relative to the cost of running the advertisement.

cost per ratings point (10) A computation used by media buyers to compare the cost efficiency of broadcast programs that divides the cost of commercial time on a program by the audience rating.

cost per thousand (10) A computation used in evaluating the relative cost of various media vehicles that represents the cost of exposing 1,000 members of a target audience to an advertising message.

cost plus system (3) A method of compensating advertising agencies whereby the agency receives a fee based on the cost of the work it performs plus an agreed-on amount for profit.

Council of Better Business Bureaus (21) The parent office of local offices of the Better Business Bureau. The council assists in the development of codes and standards for ethical and responsible business and advertising practices.

counterargument (5) A type of thought or cognitive response a receiver has that is counter or opposed to the position advocated in a message.

coverage (10) A measure of the potential audience that might receive an advertising message through a media vehicle.

CPC (15) Cost-per-click is a marketing formula used to price ad banners. Some advertisers pay based on the number of clicks a specific banner gets.

creative boutique (3) An advertising agency that specializes in and provides only services related to the creative aspects of advertising.

creative execution style (9) The manner or way in which a particular advertising appeal is transformed into a message.

creative selling (18) A type of sales position where the primary emphasis is on generating new business.

creative strategy (8) A determination of what an advertising message will say or communicate to a target audience.

creative tactics (8) A determination of how an advertising message will be implemented so as to execute the creative strategy.

creativity (8) A quality possessed by persons that enables them to generate novel approaches, generally reflected in new and improved solutions to problems.

credibility (6) The extent to which a source is perceived as having knowledge, skill, or experience relevant to a communication topic and can be trusted to give an unbiased opinion or present objective information on the issue.

cross-media advertising (12) An arrangement where opportunities to advertise in several different types of media are offered by a single company or a partnership of various media providers.

cross/multimagazine deals (12) An arrangement where two or more publishers offer their magazines to an advertiser as one media package.

cross-ruff coupon (16) A coupon offer delivered on one product that is redeemable for the purchase of another product. The other product is usually one made by the same company but may involve a tie-in with another manufacturer.

cross sell (18) A term used in personal selling that refers to the sale of additional products and/or services to the same customer.

cultural values (20) Refers to beliefs and goals shared by members of a society regarding ideal end-states of life and modes of conduct.

culture (4) The complexity of learned meanings, values, norms, and customs shared by members of a society.

cume (11) A term used for cumulative audience, which is the estimated total number of different people who listened to a radio station for a minimum of five minutes during a particular daypart.

D

DAGMAR (7) An acronym that stands for defining advertising goals for measured advertising results. An approach to setting advertising goals and objectives developed by Russell Colley.

daily inch rate (10) A cost figure used in periodicals based on an advertisement placed one inch deep and one column wide (whatever the column inch).

database (14) A listing of current and/or potential customers for a company's product or service that can be used for direct-marketing purposes.

database marketing (14) The use of specific information about individual customers and/or prospects to implement more effective and efficient marketing communications.

day-after recall scores (19) A measure used in on-air testing of television commercials by various marketing research companies. The day-after recall score represents the percentage of viewers surveyed who can remember seeing a particular commercial.

dayparts (10, 11) The time segments into which a day is divided by radio and television networks and stations for selling advertising time.

decentralized organizational structure (20) A method of organizing for international advertising and promotion where managers in each market or country have decision-making authority.

decentralized system (3) An organizational system whereby planning and decision-making responsibility for marketing, advertising, and promotion lies with a product/brand manager or management team rather than a centralized department.

deception (21) According to the Federal Trade Commission, a misrepresentation, omission, or practice that is likely to mislead the consumer acting reasonably in the circumstances to the consumer's detriment.

decoding (5) The process by which a message recipient transforms and interprets a message.

demographic segmentation (2) A method of segmenting a market based on the demographic characteristics of consumers.

departmental system (3) The organization of an advertising agency into departments based on functions such as account services, creative, media, marketing services, and administration.

derived demand (19) A situation where demand for a particular product or service results from the need for other goods and/or services. For example, demand for aluminum cans is derived from consumption of soft drinks or beer.

designated market area (DMA) (11) The geographic areas used by the Nielsen Station Index in measuring audience size. DMAs are nonoverlapping areas consisting of groups of counties from which stations attract their viewers.

differentiated marketing (2) A type of marketing strategy whereby a firm offers products or services to a number of market segments and develops separate marketing strategies for each.

differentiation (22) A situation where a particular company or brand is perceived as unique or better than its competitors.

direct-action advertising (1) Advertising designed to produce an immediate effect such as the generation of store traffic or sales.

direct broadcast by satellite (DBS) (20) A television signal delivery system whereby programming is beamed from satellites to special receiving dishes mounted in the home or yard.

direct channel (2) A marketing channel where a producer and ultimate consumer interact directly with one another.

direct headline (9) A headline that is very straightforward and informative in terms of the message it is presenting and the target audience it is directed toward. Direct headlines often include a specific benefit, promise, or reason for a consumer to be interested in a product or service.

direct marketing (1, 14) A system of marketing by which an organization communicates directly with customers to generate a response and/or transaction.

direct-marketing media (14) Media that are used for direct-marketing purposes including direct mail, telemarketing, print, and broadcast.

direct-response advertising (1, 14) A form of advertising for a product or service that elicits a sales response directly from the advertiser.

direct-response agencies (3) Companies that provide a variety of direct-marketing services to their clients including database management, direct mail, research, media service, and creative and production capabilities.

direct selling (1, 14) The direct personal presentation, demonstration, and sale of products and services to consumers usually in their homes or at their jobs.

directional medium (13) Advertising media that are not used to create awareness or demand for products or services but rather to inform customers as to where purchases can be made once they have decided to buy. The Yellow Pages are an example of a directional medium.

display advertising (12) Advertising in newspapers and magazines that uses illustrations, photos, headlines, and other visual elements in addition to copy text.

dissonance/attribution model (5) A type of response hierarchy where consumers first behave, then develop attitudes or feelings as a result of that behavior, and then learn or process information that supports the attitude and behavior.

diverting (16) A practice whereby a retailer or wholesaler takes advantage of a promotional deal and then sells some of the product purchased at the low price to a store outside of their area or to a middleman who will resell it to other stores.

domain name (15) The unique name of an Internet site. There are six domains widely used in the U.S.: .com (commercial), .edu (education), .net (network operations), .gov (U.S. government), .mil (U.S. military), and .org (organization). Additional two letter domains specify a country, for example, .sp for Spain.

duplicated reach (10) Audience members' exposure to a message as a result of messages having appeared in two or more different media vehicles.

dyadic communication (18) A process of direct communication between two persons or groups such as a salesperson and a customer.

E

e-commerce (15) Direct selling of goods and services through the Internet.

economic infrastructure (20) A country's communications, transportation, financial, and distribution networks.

economies of scale (7, 22) A decline in costs with accumulated sales or production. In advertising, economies of scale often occur in media purchases as the relative costs of advertising time and/or space may decline as the size of the media budget increases.

effective reach (10) A measure of the percentage of a media vehicle's audience reached at each effective frequency increment.

elaboration likelihood model (ELM) (5) A model that identifies two processes by which communications can lead to persuasion—central and peripheral routes.

electrodermal response (19) A measure of the resistance the skin offers to a small amount of current passed between two electrodes. Used as a measure of consumers' reaction level to an advertisement.

electroencephalographic (EEG) measures (19) Measures of the electrical impulses in the brain that are sometimes used as a measure of reactions to advertising.

electronic teleshopping (14) Online shopping and information retrieval service that is accessed through a personal computer.

emotional appeals (6, 9) Advertising messages that appeal to consumers' feelings and emotions.

encoding (5) The process of putting thoughts, ideas, or information into a symbolic form.

ethics (22) Moral principles and values that govern the actions and decisions of an individual or group.

evaluative criteria (4) The dimensions or attributes of a product or service that are used to compare different alternatives.

event marketing (16) A type of promotion where a company or brand is linked to an event, or where a themed activity is developed for the purpose of creating experiences for consumers and promoting a product or service.

event sponsorship (17) A type of promotion whereby a company develops sponsorship relations with a particular event such as a concert, sporting event, or other activity.

evoked set (4) The various brands identified by a consumer as purchase options and that are actively considered during the alternative evaluation process.

exchange (1) Trade of something of value between two parties such as a product or service for money. The core phenomenon or domain for study in marketing.

exclusive (17) A public relations tactic whereby one particular medium is offered exclusive rights to a story.

expertise (6) An aspect of source credibility where a communicator is perceived as being knowledgeable in a given area or for a particular topic.

external analysis (1) The phase of the promotional planning process that focuses on factors such as the characteristics of an organization's customers, market segments, positioning strategies, competitors, and marketing environment.

external audiences (17) In public relations, a term used in reference to individuals who are outside of or not closely connected to the organization such as the general public.

external audits (17) Evaluations performed by outside agencies to determine the effectiveness of an organization's public relations program.

external search (4) The search process whereby consumers seek and acquire information from external sources such as advertising, other people, or public sources.

eye tracking (19) A method for following the movement of a person's eyes as he or she views an ad or commercial. Eye tracking is used for determining which portions or sections of an ad attract a viewer's attention and/or interest.

F

failure fee (16) A trade promotion arrangement whereby a marketer agrees to pay a penalty fee if a product stocked by a retailer does not meet agreed-upon sales levels.

Fairness Doctrine (21) A Federal Communications Commission program that required broadcasters to provide time for opposing viewpoints on important issues.

fear appeals (6) An advertising message that creates anxiety in a receiver by showing negative consequences that can result from engaging in (or not engaging in) a particular behavior.

Federal Trade Commission (FTC) (21) The federal agency that has the primary responsibility for protecting consumers and businesses from anticompetitive behavior and unfair and deceptive practices. The FTC regulates advertising and promotion at the federal level.

Federal Trade Commission Act (21) Federal legislation passed in 1914 that created the Federal Trade Commission and gave it the responsibility to monitor deceptive or misleading advertising and unfair business practices.

fee-commission combination (3) A type of compensation system whereby an advertising agency establishes a fixed monthly fee for its services to a client and media commissions received by the agency are credited against the fee.

feedback (5) Part of message recipient's response that is communicated back to the sender. Feedback can take a variety of forms and provides a sender with a way of monitoring how an intended message is decoded and received.

field of experience (5) The experiences, perceptions, attitudes, and values that senders and receivers of a message bring to a communication situation.

field tests (19) Tests of consumer reactions to an advertisement that are taken under natural viewing situations rather than in a laboratory.

financial audit (3) An aspect of the advertising agency evaluation process that focuses on how the agency conducts financial affairs related to serving a client.

first-run syndication (11) Programs produced specifically for the syndication market.

fixed-fee arrangement (3) A method of agency compensation whereby the agency and client agree on the work to be done and the amount of money the agency will be paid for its services.

flat rates (12) A standard newspaper advertising rate where no discounts are offered for large-quantity or repeated space buys.

Flesch formula (19) A test used to assess the difficulty level of writing based on the number of syllables and sentences per 100 words.

flighting (10) A media scheduling pattern in which periods of advertising are alternated with periods of no advertising.

focus groups (4)(8) A qualitative marketing research method whereby a group of 10–12 consumers from the target market are led through a discussion regarding a particular topic such as a product, service, or advertising campaign.

forward buying (16) A practice whereby retailers and wholesalers stock up on a product being offered by a manufacturer at a lower deal or off-invoice price and resell it to consumers once the marketer's promotional period has ended.

frequency (10) The number of times a target audience is exposed to a media vehicle(s) in a specified period.

frequency programs (16) A type of promotional program that rewards customers for continuing to purchase the same brand of a product or service over time (also referred to as continuity or loyalty programs).

full-service agency (3) An advertising agency that offers clients a full range of marketing and communications services including the planning, creating, producing, and placing of advertising messages and other forms of promotion.

functional consequences (4) Outcomes of product or service usage that are tangible and can be directly experienced by a consumer.

G

game (16) A promotion that is a form of sweepstakes because it has a chance element or odds of winning associated with it. Games usually involve game card devices that can be rubbed or opened to unveil a winning number or prize description.

gatefolds (12) An oversize magazine page or cover that is extended and folded over to fit into the publication. Gatefolds are used to extend the size of a magazine advertisement and are always sold at a premium.

general preplanning input (8) Information gathering and/or market research studies on trends, developments, and happenings in the marketplace that can be used to assist in the initial stages of the creative process of advertising.

geographical weighting (10) A media scheduling strategy where certain geographic areas or regions are allocated higher levels of advertising because they have greater sales potential.

geographic segmentation (2) A method of segmenting a market on the basis of different geographic units or areas.

global advertising (20) The use of the same basic advertising message in all international markets.

global marketing (20) A strategy of using a common marketing plan and program for all countries in which a company operates, thus selling the product or services the same way everywhere in the world.

green marketing (22) The marketing and promotion of products on the basis of environmental sensitivity.

gross ratings points (GRPs) (10) A measure that represents the total delivery or weight of a media schedule during a specified time period. GRPs are calculated by multiplying the reach of the media schedule by the average frequency.

group system (3) The organization of an advertising agency by dividing it into groups consisting of specialists from various departments such as creative, media, marketing services, and other areas. These groups work together to service particular accounts.

H

halo effect (19) The tendency for evaluations of one attribute or aspect of a stimulus to distort reactions to its other attributes or properties.

headline (9) Words in the leading position of the advertisement; the words that will be read first or are positioned to draw the most attention.

hemisphere lateralization (19) The notion that the human brain has two relatively distinct halves or hemispheres with each being responsible for a specific type of function. The right side is responsible for visual processing while the left side conducts verbal processing.

heuristics (4) Simplified or basic decision rules that can be used by a consumer to make a purchase choice, such as buy the cheapest brand.

hierarchy of effects model (5) A model of the process by which advertising works that assumes a consumer must pass through a sequence of steps from initial awareness to eventual action. The stages include awareness, interest, evaluation, trial, and adoption.

hierarchy of needs (4) Abraham Maslow's theory that human needs are arranged in an order or hierarchy based on their importance. The need hierarchy includes physiological, safety, social/love and belonging, esteem, and self-actualization needs.

hit (15) Each time a server sends a file to a browser it is recorded as a "hit." Hits are used to measure the traffic on a website.

horizontal cooperative advertising (16) A cooperative advertising arrangement where advertising is sponsored in common by a group of retailers or other organizations providing products or services to a market.

households using television (HUT) (11) The percentage of homes in a given area that are watching television during a specific time period.

I

identification (6) The process by which an attractive source influences a message recipient. Identification occurs when the receiver is motivated to seek some type of relationship with the source and adopt a similar position in terms of beliefs, attitudes, preferences, or behavior.

image advertising (8) Advertising that creates an identity for a product or service by emphasizing psychological meaning or symbolic association with certain values, lifestyles, and the like.

image transfer (11) A radio advertising technique whereby the images of a television commercial are implanted into a radio spot.

incentive-based system (3) A form of compensation whereby an advertising agency's compensation level depends on how well it meets predetermined performance goals such as sales or market share.

index numbers (10) A ratio used to describe the potential of a market. The index number is derived by dividing the percentage of users in a market segment by the percentage of population in the same segment and multiplying by 100.

indirect channels (2) A marketing channel where intermediaries such as wholesalers and retailers are utilized to make a product available to the customer.

indirect headlines (9) Headlines that are not straightforward with respect to identifying a product or service or providing information regarding the point of an advertising message.

in-flight advertising (13) A variety of advertising media targeting air travelers while they are in flight.

infomercials (11, 14) Television commercials that are very long, ranging from several minutes to an hour. Infomercials are designed to provide consumers with detailed information about a product or service.

information processing model (5) A model of advertising effects developed by William McGuire that views the receiver of a message as an information processor and problem solver. The model views the receiver as passing through a response hierarchy that includes a series of stages including message presentation, attention, comprehension, acceptance or yielding, retention, and behavior.

informational/rational appeals (9) Advertising appeals that focus on the practical, functional, or utilitarian need for a product or service and emphasize features, benefits, or reasons for owning or using the brand.

ingredient sponsored cooperative advertising (16) Advertising supported by raw material manufacturers with the objective being to help establish end products that include materials and/or ingredients supplied by the company.

inherent drama (8) An approach to advertising that focuses on the benefits or characteristics that lead a consumer to purchase a product or service and uses dramatic elements to emphasize them.

in-house agency (3) An advertising agency set up, owned, and operated by an advertiser that is responsible for planning and executing the company's advertising program.

ink-jet imaging (12) A printing process where a message is reproduced by projecting ink onto paper rather than mechanical plates. Ink-jet imaging is being offered by many magazines to allow advertisers to personalize their messages.

innovation-adoption model (5) A model that represents the stages a consumer passes through in the adoption process for an innovation such as a new product. The series of steps includes: awareness, interest, evaluation, trial, and adoption.

inquiry tests (19) Tests designed to measure advertising effectiveness on the basis of inquiries or responses generated from the ad such as requests for information, number of phone calls, or number of coupons redeemed.

inside cards (13) A form of transit advertising where messages appear on cards or boards inside of vehicles such as buses, subways, or trolleys.

instant coupon (16) Coupons attached to a package that can be removed and redeemed at the time of purchase.

in-store couponing (16) The distribution of coupons in retail stores through various methods such as tear-off pads, handouts, and on-shelf or electronic dispensers.

in-store media (13) Advertising and promotional media that are used inside of a retail store such as point-of-purchase displays, ads on shopping carts, coupon dispensers, and display boards.

integrated information response model (5) A model of the response process or sequence advertising message recipients go through which integrates concepts from the traditional and low-involvement response hierarchy perspectives.

integrated marketing communication objectives (7) Statements of what various aspects of the integrated marketing communications program will accomplish with respect to factors such as communication tasks, sales, market share, and the like.

integrated marketing communications (1) A concept of marketing communications planning that recognizes the added value of a comprehensive plan that evaluates the strategic roles of a variety of communication disciplines—for example, general advertising, direct response, sales promotion, and public relations—and combines these disciplines to provide clarity, consistency, and maximum communications impact.

integration processes (4) The way information such as product knowledge, meanings, and beliefs is combined to evaluate two or more alternatives.

interactive agency (3) An organization that specializes in the creation of interactive media such as CD-ROMs, kiosks, and websites.

interactive media (10) A variety of media that allows the consumer to interact with the source of the message, actively receiving information and altering images, responding to questions, and so on.

interconnects (11) Groups of cable systems joined together for advertising purposes.

internal analysis (1) The phase of the promotional planning process that focuses on the product/service offering and the firm itself including the capabilities of the firm and its ability to develop and implement a successful integrated marketing communications program.

internal audiences (17) In public relations, a term used to refer to individuals or groups inside of the organization or with a close connection to it.

internal audits (17) Evaluations by individuals within the organization to determine the effectiveness of a public relations program.

internalization (6) The process by which a credible source influences a message recipient. Internalization occurs when the receiver is motivated to have an objectively correct position on an issue and the receiver will adopt the opinion or attitude of the credible communicator if he or she believes the information from this source represents an accurate position on the issue.

internal search (4) The process by which a consumer acquires information by accessing past experiences or knowledge stored in memory.

international media (20) Advertising media that have multicountry coverage and can be used to reach audiences in various countries.

Internet (15) A worldwide means of exchanging information and communicating through a series of interconnected computers.

interstitial (15) An advertisement that appears in a window on your computer screen while you are waiting for a Web page to load.

J

jingles (9) Songs about a product or service that usually carry the advertising theme and a simple message.

L

laboratory tests (19) Tests of consumer reactions to advertising under controlled conditions.

Lanham Act (21) A federal law that permits a company to register a trademark for its exclusive use. The Lanham Act was recently amended to encompass false advertising and prohibits any false description or representation including words or other symbols tending falsely to describe or represent the same.

layout (9) The physical arrangement of the various parts of an advertisement including the headline, subheads, illustrations, body copy, and any identifying marks.

lexicographic decision rule (4) A type of decision rule where choice criteria are ranked in order of importance and alternatives are evaluated on each attribute or criterion beginning with the most important one.

link (15) An electronic connection between two websites.

local advertising (11) Advertising done by companies within the limited geographic area where they do business.

localized advertising strategy (20) Developing an advertising campaign specifically for a particular country or market rather than using a global approach.

low-involvement hierarchy (5) A response hierarchy whereby a message recipient is viewed as passing from cognition to behavior to attitude change.

M

magazine networks (12) A group of magazines owned by one publisher or assembled by an independent network that offers advertisers the opportunity to buy space in a variety of publications through a package deal.

mailing list (14) A type of database containing names and addresses of present and/or potential customers who can be reached through a direct-mail campaign.

major selling idea (8) The basis for the central theme or message idea in an advertising campaign.

marginal analysis (7) A principle of resource allocation that balances incremental revenues against incremental costs.
market opportunities (2) Areas where a company believes there are favorable demand trends, needs, and/or wants that are not being satisfied, and where it can compete effectively.
market segmentation (2) The process of dividing a market into distinct groups that have common needs and will respond similarly to a marketing action.
market segments (2) Identifiable groups of customers sharing similar needs, wants, or other characteristics that make them likely to respond in a similar fashion to a marketing program.
marketing (1, 2) The process of planning and executing the conception, pricing, promotion, and distribution of ideas, goods, and services to create exchanges that satisfy individual and organizational objectives.
marketing channels (2) The set of interdependent organizations involved in the process of making a product or service available to customers.
marketing mix (1, 2) The controllable elements of a marketing program including product, price, promotion, and place.
marketing objectives (1, 7) Goals to be accomplished by an organization's overall marketing program such as sales, market share, or profitability.
marketing plan (1) A written document that describes the overall marketing strategy and programs developed for an organization, a particular product line, or a brand.
marketing public relations function (MPR) (17) Public relations activities designed to support marketing objectives and programs.
mass media (5) Nonpersonal channels of communication that allow a message to be sent to many individuals at one time.
materialism (22) A preoccupation with material things rather than intellectual or spiritual concerns.
media buying services (3) Independent companies that specialize in the buying of media, particularly radio and television time.
media objectives (10) The specific goals an advertiser has for the media portion of the advertising program.
media organizations (3) One of the four major participants in the integrated marketing communications process whose function is to provide information or entertainment to subscribers, viewers, or readers while offering marketers an environment for reaching audiences with print and broadcast messages.
media plan (10) A document consisting of objectives, strategies, and tactics for reaching a target audience through various media vehicles.
media planning (10) The series of decisions involved in the delivery of an advertising message to prospective purchasers and/or users of a product or service.
media strategies (10) Plans of action for achieving stated media objectives such as which media will be used for reaching a target audience, how the media budget will be allocated, and how advertisements will be scheduled.
media vehicle (10) The specific program, publication, or promotional piece used to carry an advertising message.
medium (10) The general category of communication vehicles that are available for communicating with a target audience such as broadcast, print, direct mail, and outdoor.
message (5) A communication containing information or meaning that a source wants to convey to a receiver.
missionary sales (18) A type of sales position where the emphasis is on performing supportive activities and services rather than generating or taking orders.
mnemonics (4) Basic cues such as symbols, rhymes, and associations that facilitate the learning and memory process.
mobile billboards (13) An out-of-home medium in which advertisements are able to be transported to different locations (signs painted on automobiles, trailers pulling billboards, and the like).
motivation research (4) Qualitative research designed to probe the consumer's subconscious and discover deeply rooted motives for purchasing a product.
motive (4) Something that compels or drives a consumer to take a particular action.
multiattribute attitude model (4) A model of attitudes that views an individual's evaluation of an object as being a function of the beliefs that he or she has toward the object on various attributes and the importance of these attributes.
multimagazine deals (12) Arrangements whereby two to more publishers offer advertisers the opportunity to buy space in their magazines with one single media buy.
multiplexing (11) An arrangement where multiple channels are transmitted by one cable network.

N

narrowcasting (11) The reaching of a very specialized market through programming aimed at particular target audiences. Cable television networks offer excellent opportunities for narrowcasting.
national advertisers (2) Companies that advertise their products or services on a nationwide basis or in most regions of the country.
National Advertising Review Board (NARB) (21) A part of the National Advertising Division of the Council of Better Business Bureaus. The NARB is the advertising industry's primary self-regulatory body.
National Advertising Review Council (NARC) (21) An organization founded by the Council of Better Business Bureaus and various advertising industry groups to promote high standards of truth, accuracy, morality, and social responsibility in national advertising.
National Association of Attorneys General (21) An organization consisting of state attorneys general that is involved in the regulation of advertising and other business practices.
national spot (11) All non-network advertising done by a national advertiser in local markets.
negotiated commission (3) A method of compensating advertising agencies whereby the client and agency negotiate the commission structure rather than relying on the traditional 15 percent media commission.
noise (5) Extraneous factors that create unplanned distortion or interference in the communications process.
noncompensatory integration strategies (4) Types of decision rules used to evaluate alternatives that do not allow negative evaluation or performance on a particular attribute to be compensated for by positive evaluation or performance on some other attribute.
nonfranchise-building promotions (16) Sales promotion activities that are designed to accelerate the purchase decision process and generate an immediate increase in sales but do little or nothing to communicate information about a brand and contribute to its identity and image.
nonmeasured media (13) A term commonly used in the advertising industry to describe support media.
nonpersonal channels (5) Channels of communication that carry a message without involving interpersonal contact between sender and receiver. Nonpersonal channels are often referred to as mass media.
nontraditional media (13) A term commonly used in the advertising industry to describe support media.

O

objective and task method (7) A build-up approach to budget setting involving a three-step process: (1) determining objectives, (2) determining the strategies and tasks required to attain these objectives, and (3) estimating the costs associated with these strategies and tasks.

off-invoice allowance (16) A promotional discount offered to retailers or wholesalers whereby a certain per-case amount or percentage is deducted from the invoice.

off-network syndication (11) Reruns of network shows bought by individual stations.

on-air tests (19) Testing the effectiveness of television commercials by inserting test ads into actual TV programs in certain test markets.

one-sided message (6) Communications in which only positive attributes or benefits of a product or service are presented.

one-step approach (14) A direct-marketing strategy in which the medium is used directly to obtain an order (for example, television direct-response ads).

open rate structure (12) A rate charged by newspapers in which discounts are available based on frequency or bulk purchases of space.

operant conditioning (instrumental conditioning) (4) A learning theory that views the probability of a behavior as being dependent on the outcomes or consequences associated with it.

opt-in-e-mail (15) Lists where Internet users have voluntarily signed up to receive commercial e-mail about topics of interest.

order taking (18) A personal selling responsibility in which the salesperson's primary responsibility is taking the order.

out-of-home advertising (13) The variety of advertising forms including outdoor, transit, skywriting, and other media viewed outside the home.

outside posters (13) Outdoor transit posters appearing on buses, taxis, trains, subways, and trolley cars.

P

PACT (Positioning Advertising Copy Testing) (19) A set of principles endorsed by 21 of the largest U.S. ad agencies aimed at improving the research used in preparing and testing ads, providing a better creative product for clients, and controlling the cost of TV commercials.

page views (15) Number of times a user requests a page that contains a particular ad. Used to indicate the number of times an ad was potentially seen, or "gross impressions."

participations (11) The situation where several advertisers buy commercial time or spots on network television.

pass-along rate (10) An estimate of the number of readers of a magazine in addition to the original subscriber or purchaser.

pass-along readership (12) The audience that results when the primary subscriber or purchaser of a magazine gives the publication to another person to read, or when the magazine is read in places such as waiting rooms in doctors' offices, etc.

pattern advertising (20) Advertisements that follow a basic global approach although themes, copy, and sometimes even visual elements may be adjusted.

payout plan (7) A budgeting plan that determines the investment value of the advertising and promotion appropriation.

people meter (11) An electronic device that automatically records a household's television viewing, including channels watched, number of minutes of viewing, and members of the household who are watching.

percentage charges (3) The markups charged by advertising agencies for services provided to clients.

percentage of projected future sales method (7) A variation of the percentage of sales method of budget allocation in which projected future sales are used as the base.

percentage of sales method (7) A budget method in which the advertising and/or promotions budget is set based on a percentage of sales of the product.

perception (4) The process by which an individual receives, selects, organizes, and interprets information to create a meaningful picture of the world.

perceptual map (2) A "map" of perceptions of the positions of brands or products as received by consumers.

peripheral route to persuasion (5) In the elaboration likelihood model, one of two routes to persuasion in which the receiver is viewed as lacking the ability or motivation to process information and is not likely to be engaging in detailed cognitive processing.

personal selling (1) Person-to-person communication in which the seller attempts to assist and/or persuade prospective buyers to purchase the company's product or service or to act on an idea.

personalization (15) Individuals can request that specific information they are interested in viewing be sent to their computers.

persuasion matrix (6) A communications planning model in which the stages of the response process (dependent variables) and the communications components (independent variables) are combined to demonstrate the likely effect that the independent variables will have on the dependent variables.

phased processing strategy (4) An information processing strategy in which more than one decision rule is applied during the purchase decision process.

planograms (16) A planning configuration of products that occupy a shelf section in a store that is used to provide more efficient shelf space utilization.

pop-ups (15) Advertisement windows on the Internet usually larger than a banner ad and smaller than a full screen.

portfolio tests (19) A laboratory methodology designed to expose a group of respondents to a portfolio consisting of both control and test print ads.

positioning (2) The art and science of fitting the product or service to one or more segments of the market in such a way as to set it meaningfully apart from competition.

positioning strategies (2) The strategies used in positioning a brand or product.

posttests (19) Ad effectiveness measures that are taken after the ad has appeared in the marketplace.

preferred position rate (12) A rate charged by newspapers that ensures the advertiser the ad will appear in the position required and/or in a specific section of the newspaper.

premium (16) An offer of an item of merchandise or service either free or at a low price that is used as an extra incentive for purchasers.

preprinted inserts (12) Advertising distributed through newspapers that is not part of the newspaper itself, but is printed by the advertiser and then taken to the newspaper to be inserted.

press release (17) Factual and interesting information released to the press.

pretests (19) Advertising effectiveness measures that are taken before the implementation of the advertising campaign.

price elasticity (2) The responsiveness of the market to change in price.

price-off deal (16) A promotional strategy in which the consumer receives a reduction in the regular price of the brand.

primacy effect (6) A theory that the first information presented in the message will be the most likely to be remembered.

primary circulation (12) The number of copies of a magazine distributed to original subscribers.

problem detection (8) A creative research approach in which consumers familiar with a product (or service) are asked to generate an exhaustive list of problems encountered in its use.

problem recognition (4) The first stage in the consumer's decision-making process in which the consumer perceives a need and becomes motivated to satisfy it.

problem-solver stage (18) A stage of personal selling in which the seller obtains the participation of buyers in identifying their problems, translates these problems into needs, and then presents a selection from the supplier's offerings that can solve those problems.

procreator stage (18) A stage of personal selling in which the seller defines the buyer's problems or needs and the solutions to those problems or needs through active buyer-seller collaboration, thus creating a market offering tailored to the customer.

product manager (3) The person responsible for the planning, implementation, and control of the marketing program for an individual brand.

product placement (13) A form of advertising and promotion in which products are placed in television shows and/or movies to gain exposure.

product-specific preplanning input (8) Specific studies provided to the creative department on the product or service, the target audience, or a combination of the two.

product symbolism (2) The meaning that a product or brand has to consumers.

program rating (11) The percentage of TV households in an area that are tuned to a program during a specific time period.

promotion (1) The coordination of all seller-initiated efforts to set up channels of information and persuasion to sell goods and services or to promote an idea.

promotional management (1) The process of coordinating the promotional mix elements.

promotional mix (1) The tools used to accomplish an organization's communications objective. The promotional mix includes advertising, direct marketing, sales promotion, publicity/public relations, and personal selling.

promotional plan (1) The framework for developing, implementing, and controlling the organization's communications program.

promotional products marketing (13) The advertising or promotional medium or method that uses promotional products such as ad specialties, premiums, business gifts, awards, prizes, or commemoratives.

promotional pull strategy (2) A strategy in which advertising and promotion efforts are targeted at the ultimate consumers to encourage them to purchase the manufacturer's brand.

promotional push strategy (2) A strategy in which advertising and promotional efforts are targeted to the trade to attempt to get them to promote and sell the product to the ultimate consumer.

prospector stage (18) A selling stage in which activities include seeking out selected buyers who are perceived to have a need for the offering as well as the resources to buy it.

Protestant ethic (22) A perspective of life which stresses hard work and individual effort and initiative and views the accumulation of material possessions as evidence of success.

psychoanalytic theory (4) An approach to the study of human motivations and behaviors pioneered by Sigmund Freud.

psychographic segmentation (2) Dividing the product on the basis of personality and/or lifestyles.

psychosocial consequences (4) Purchase decision consequences that are intangible, subjective, and personal.

public relations (1, 17) The management function that evaluates public attitudes, identifies the policies and procedures of an individual or organization with the public interest, and executes a program to earn public understanding and acceptance.

public relations firm (3) An organization that develops and implements programs to manage a company's publicity, image, and affairs with consumers and other relevant publics.

publicity (1, 17) Communications regarding an organization, product, service, or idea that is not directly paid for or run under identified sponsorship.

puffery (21) Advertising or other sales presentations that praise the item to be sold using subjective opinions, superlatives, or exaggerations, vaguely and generally, stating no specific facts.

pulsing (10) A media scheduling method that combines flighting and continuous scheduling.

pupillometrics (19) An advertising effectiveness methodology designed to measure dilation and constriction of the pupils of the eye in response to stimuli.

purchase intention (4) The predisposition to buy a certain brand or product.

push money (16) Cash payments made directly to the retailers' or wholesalers' sales force to encourage them to promote and sell a manufacturer's product.

push technology (15) Allows a company to "push" a message to the consumer through the Internet rather than waiting for them to find it.

Q

qualified prospects (18) Those prospects that are able to make the buying decision.

qualitative audit (3) An audit of the advertising agency's efforts in planning, developing, and implementing the client's communications programs.

qualitative media effect (6) The positive or negative influence the medium may contribute to the message.

R

ratings point (11) A measurement used to determine television viewing audiences in which one ratings point is the equivalent of 1 percent of all of the television households in a particular area tuned to a specific program.

rational appeal (6) Communications in which features and/or benefits are directly presented in a logical, rational method.

reach (10) The number of different audience members exposed at least once to a media vehicle (or vehicles) in a given period.

readers per copy (10) A cost comparison figure used for magazines that estimates audience size based on pass-along readership.

recall tests (19) Advertising effectiveness tests designed to measure advertising recall.

receiver (5) The person or persons with whom the sender of a message shares thoughts or information.

recency effect (6) The theory that arguments presented at the end of the message are considered to be stronger and therefore are more likely to be remembered.

recognition method (19) An advertising effectiveness measure of print ads that allows the advertiser to assess the impact of an ad in a single issue of a magazine over time and/or across alternative magazines.

reference group (4) A group whose perspectives, values, or behavior is used by an individual as the basis for his or her judgments, opinions, and actions.

refutational appeal (6) A type of message in which both sides of the issure are presented in the communication, with arguments offered to refute the opposing viewpoint.

regional networks (11) A network that covers only a specific portion of the country. Regional network purchases are based in proportion to the percentage of the country receiving the message.

reinforcement (4) The rewards or favorable consequences associated with a particular response.

relationship marketing (1, 18) An organization's effort to develop a long-term, cost-effective link with individual customers for mutual benefit.

relative cost (10) The relationship between the price paid for advertising time or space and the size of the audience delivered; it is used to compare the prices of various media vehicles.

reminder advertising (9) Advertising designed to keep the name of the product or brand in the mind of the receiver.

repositioning (2) The changing of a product or brand's positioning.

resellers (2) Intermediaries in the marketing channel such as wholesalers, distributors, and retailers.

response (5) The set of reactions the receiver has after seeing, hearing, or reading a message.

retail trading zone (12) The market outside the city zone whose residents regularly trade with merchants within the city zone.

rich media (15) A term for advanced technology used in Internet ads, such as a streaming video which allows interaction and special effects.

ROI budgeting method (return on investment) (7) A budgeting method in which advertising and promotions are considered investments, and thus measurements are made in an attempt to determine the returns achieved by these investments.

rolling boards (13) Advertising painted or mounted on cars, trucks, vans, trailers, etc., so the exposure can be mobile enough to be taken to specific target market areas.

run of paper (ROP) (12) A rate quoted by newspapers that allows the ad to appear on any page or in any position desired by the medium.

S

S-shaped response curve (7) A sales response model that attempts to show sales responses to various levels of advertising and promotional expenditures.

sales-oriented objectives (7) Budgeting objectives related to sales effects such as increasing sales volume.

sales promotion (1, 16) Marketing activities that provide extra value or incentives to the sales force, distributors, or the ultimate consumer and can stimulate immediate sales.

sales promotion agency (3) An organization that specializes in the planning and implementation of promotional programs such as contests, sweepstakes, sampling, premiums, and incentive offers for its clients.

sales promotion trap (16) A spiral that results when a number of competitors extensively use promotions. One firm uses sales promotions to differentiate its product or service and other competitors copy the strategy, resulting in no differential advantage and a loss of profit margins to all.

salient beliefs (4) Beliefs concerning specific attributes or consequences that are activated and form the basis of an attitude.

sampling (16) A variety of procedures whereby consumers are given some quantity of a product for no charge to induce trial.

scatter market (11) A period for purchasing television advertising time that runs throughout the TV season.

schedules of reinforcement (4) The schedule by which a behavioral response is rewarded.

script (9) A written version of the commercial that provides a detailed description of its video and audio content.

selective attention (4) A perceptual process in which consumers choose to attend to some stimuli and not others.

selective binding (12) A computerized production process that allows the creation of hundreds of copies of a magazine in one continuous sequence.

selective comprehension (4) The perceptual process whereby consumers interpret information based on their own attitudes, beliefs, motives, and experiences.

selective demand advertising (2) Advertising that focuses on stimulating demand for a specific manufacturer's product or brand.

selective exposure (4) A process whereby consumers choose whether or not to make themselves available to media and message information.

selective learning (5) The process whereby consumers seek information that supports the choice made and avoid information that fails to bolster the wisdom of a purchase decision.

selective perception (4) The perceptual process involving the filtering or screening of exposure, attention, comprehension, and retention.

selective retention (4) The perceptual process whereby consumers remember some information but not all.

selectivity (12) The ability of a medium to reach a specific target audience.

self-liquidating premiums (16) Premiums that require the consumer to pay some or all of the cost of the premium plus handling and mailing costs.

self-paced media (6) Media that viewers and/or readers can control their exposure time to, allowing them to process information at their own rate.

self-regulation (21) The practice by the advertising industry of regulating and controlling advertising to avoid interference by outside agencies such as the government.

semiotics (5) The study of the nature of meaning.

sensation (4) The immediate and direct response of the senses (taste, smell, sight, touch, and hearing) to a stimulus such as an advertisement, package, brand name, or point-of-purchase display.

shaping (4) The reinforcement of successive acts that lead to a desired behavior pattern or response.

share-of-audience (11) The percentage of households watching television in a special time period that are tuned to a specific program.

showing (13) The percentage of supplicated audience exposed to an outdoor poster daily.

similarity (6) The supposed resemblance between the source and the receiver of a message.

single-source tracking (19) A research method designed to track the behaviors of consumers from the television set to the supermarket checkout counter.

situational determinants (4) Influences originating from the specific situation in which consumers are to use the product or brand.

sleeper effect (6) A phenomenon in which the persuasiveness of a message increases over time.

slotting allowance (16) Fees that must be paid to retailers to provide a "slot" or position to accommodate a new product on the store shelves.

social class (4) Relatively homogeneous divisions of society into which people are grouped based on similar lifestyles, values, norms, interests, and behaviors.

source (5, 6) The sender—person, group, or organization—of the message.

source bolsters (5) Favorable cognitive thoughts generated toward the source of a message.

source derogations (5) Negative thoughts generated about the source of a communication.

source power (6) The power of a source as a result of his or her ability to administer rewards and/or punishments to the receiver.

spam (15) Unsolicited commercial e-mail.

specialized marketing communication services (3) Organizations that provide marketing communication services in their areas of expertise including direct marketing, public relations, and sales promotion firms.

specialty advertising (13) An advertising, sales promotion, and motivational communications medium that employs useful articles of merchandise imprinted with an advertiser's name, message, or logo.

split runs (12) Two or more versions of a print ad are printed in alternative copies of a particular issue of a magazine.

split run test (19) An advertising effectiveness measure in which different versions of an ad are run in alternate copies of the same newspaper and/or magazine.

split 30s (11) 30-second TV spots in which the advertiser promotes two different products with two different messages during a 30-second commercial.

sponsorship (11) When the advertiser assumes responsibility for the production and usually the content of a television program as well as the advertising that appears within it.

sponsorships (15) When advertisers sponsor content on a website, it is considered a sponsorship.

spot advertising (11) Commercials shown on local television stations, with the negotiation and purchase of time being made directly from the individual stations.

standard advertising unit (SAU) (12) A standard developed in the newpaper industry to make newspaper purchasing rates more comparable to other media that sell space and time in standard units.

standard learning model (5) Progression by the consumers through a learn-feel-do hierarchical response.

station reps (11) Individuals who act as sales representatives for a number of local stations and represent them in dealings with national advertisers.

storyboard (8) A series of drawings used to present the visual plan or layout of a proposed commercial.

strategic marketing plan (2) The planning framework for specific marketing activities.

subcultures (4) Smaller groups within a culture that possess similar beliefs, values, norms, and patterns of behavior that differentiate them from the larger cultural mainstream.

subheads (9) Secondary headlines in a print ad.

subliminal perception (4) The ability of an individual to perceive a stimulus below the level of conscious awareness.

superagencies (3) Large external agencies that offer integrated marketing communications on a worldwide basis.

superstations (11) Independent local stations that send their signals via satellite to cable operators that, in turn, make them available to subscribers (WWOR, WPIX, WGN, WSBK, WTBS).

support advertising (14) A form of direct marketing in which the ad is designed to support other forms of advertising appearing in other media.

support argument (5) Consumers' thoughts that support or affirm the claims being make by a message.

support media (13) Those media used to support or reinforce messages sent to target markets through other more "dominant" and/or more traditional media.

sweeps periods (10) The times of year in which television audience measures are taken (February, May, July, and November).

sweepstakes (16) A promotion whereby consumers submit their names for consideration in the drawing or selection of prizes and winners are determined purely by chance. Sweepstakes cannot require a proof of purchase as a condition for entry.

syndicated programs (11) Shows sold or distributed to local stations.

T

target marketing (2) The process of identifying the specific needs of segments, selecting one or more of these segments as a target, and developing marketing programs directed to each.

target ratings points (TRPs) (10) The number of persons in the primary target audience that the media buy will reach—and the number of times.

team approach (17) A method of measuring the effectiveness of public relations programs whereby evaluators are actually involved in the campaign.

teaser advertising (9) An ad designed to create curiosity and build excitement and interest in a product or brand without showing it.

telemarketing (14) Selling products and services by using the telephone to contact prospective customers.

tele-media (14) The use of telephone and voice information services (800, 900, 976 numbers) to market, advertise, promote, entertain, and inform.

television households (11) The number of households in a market that own a television set.

television network (11) The provider of news and programming to a series of affiliated local television stations.

terminal posters (13) Floor dislays, island showcases, electronic signs, and other forms of advertisements that appear in train or subway stations, airline terminals, etc.

testing bias (19) A bias that occurs in advertising effectiveness measures because respondents know they are being tested and thus alter their responses.

tests of comprehension and reaction (19) Advertising effectiveness tests that are designed to assess whether the ad conveyed the desired meaning and is not reacted to negatively.

theater testing (19) An advertising effectiveness pretest in which consumers view ads in a theater setting and evaluate these ads on a variety of dimensions.

top-down approaches (7) Budgeting approaches in which the budgetary amount is established at the executive level and monies are passed down to the various departments.

total audience (television) (11) The total number of homes viewing any five-minute part of a television program.

total audience/readership (12) A combination of the total number of primary and pass-along readers multiplied by the circulation of an average issue of a magazine.

tracking studies (19) Advertising effectiveness measures designed to assess the effects of advertising on awareness, recall, interest, and attitudes toward the ad as well as purchase intentions.

trade advertising (2) Advertising targeted to wholesalers and retailers.

trademark (2) An identifying name, symbol, or other device that gives a company the legal and exclusive rights to use.

trade-oriented sales promotion (16) A sales promotion designed to motivate distributors and retailers to carry a product and make an extra effort to promote or "push" it to their customers.

trade regulation rules (TRRs) (21) Industrywide rules that define unfair practices before they occur. Used by the Federal Trade Commission to regulate advertising and promotion.

trade show (16) A type of exhibition or forum where manufacturers can display their products to current as well as prospective buyers.

transformational advertising (9) An ad that associates the experience of using the advertised brand with a unique set of psychological characteristics that would not typically be associated with the brand experience to the same degree without exposure to the advertisement.

transit advertising (13) Advertising targeted to target audiences exposed to commercial transportation facilities, including buses, taxis, trains, elevators, trolleys, airplanes, and subways.

trustworthiness (6) The honesty, integrity, and believability of the source of a communication.

two-sided message (6) A message in which both good and bad points about a product or claim are presented.

two-step approach (14) A direct-marketing strategy in which the first effort is designed to screen or qualify potential buyers, while the second effort has the responsibility of generating the response.

U

undifferentiated marketing (2) A strategy in which market segment differences are ignored and one product or service is offered to the entire market.

unduplicated reach (10) The number of persons reached once with a media exposure.

unfairness (21) A concept used by the Federal Trade Commission to determine unfair or deceptive advertising practices. Unfairness occurs when a trade practice causes substantial physical or economic injury to consumers, could not be avoided by consumers, and must not be outweighed by countervailing benefits to consumers or competition.

unique selling proposition (8) An advertising strategy that focuses on a product or service attribute that is distinctive to a particular brand and offers an important benefit to the customer.

unique users (15) The number of different individuals who visit a site within a specific time period.

up-front market (11) A buying period that takes place prior to the upcoming television season when the networks sell a large part of their commercial time.

V

valid hits (15) The number of hits that deliver all of the information to a user (excludes error messages, redirects, etc.).

values and lifestyles program (VALS) (2) Stanford Research Institute's method for applying lifestyle segmentation.

vehicle option source effect (19) The differential impact the advertising exposure will have on the same audience member if the exposure occurs in one media option rather than another.

vertical cooperative advertising (16) A cooperative arrangement under which a manufacturer pays for a portion of the advertising a retailer runs to promote the manufacturer's product and its availability in the retailer's place of business.

video advertising (13) Advertisements appearing in movie theaters and on videotapes.

video news release (16) News stories produced by publicists so that television stations may air them as news.

visits (15) A sequence of requests made by one user at one site.

voiceover (9) Action on the screen in a commercial that is narrated or described by a narrator who is not visible.

W

want (4) A felt need shaped by a person's knowledge, culture, and personality.

waste coverage (10) A situation where the coverage of the media exceeds the target audience.

webcasting (15) A system for pushing out site information to Web users rather than waiting for them to find the site on their own. (Often referred to as push technologies.)

website (15) The information made available to users of the Internet by the provider.

Wheeler-Lea Amendment (21) An act of Congress passed in 1938 that amended section 5 of the FTC Act to read that unfair methods of competition in commerce and unfair or deceptive acts or practices in commerce are declared unlawful.

word-of-mouth communications (5) Social channels of communication such as friends, neighbors, associates, coworkers, or family members.

World Wide Web (WWW) (15) Commonly referred to as the Web. The commercial component of the Internet.

Y

Yellow Pages advertising (13) Advertisements that appear in the various Yellow Pages-type phone directories.

Z

zapping (11) The use of a remote control device to change channels and switch away from commercials.

zero-based communications planning (7) An approach to planning the integrated marketing communications program that involves determining what tasks need to be done and what marketing communication functions should be used to accomplish them and to what extent.

zipping (11) Fast-forwarding through commercials during the playback of a program previously recorded on a VCR.

Endnotes

Chapter One

1. Robert J. Coen, *Insider's Report: Robert Coen Presentation on Advertising Expenditures* (New York: Universal McCann, McCann Erickson Worldwide, December 1999).
2. Ibid.
3. "AMA Board Approves New Marketing Definition," *Marketing News,* March 1, 1985, p. 1.
4. Richard P. Bagozzi, "Marketing as Exchange," *Journal of Marketing* 39 (October 1975), pp. 32–39.
5. Leonard L. Berry, "Relationship Marketing of Services—Growing Interest, Emerging Perspectives," *Journal of the Adademy of Marketing Science* 23, no. 4, 1995, pp. 236–45; Jonathan R. Capulsky and Michael J. Wolfe, "Relationship Marketing: Positioning for the Future," *Journal of Business Strategy,* July–August 1991, pp. 16–26.
6. James H. Gilmore and B. Joseph Pine II, "The Four Faces of Customization," *Harvard Business Review,* January–February 1997, pp. 91–101.
7. Robert J. Lavidge, "'Mass Customization' Is Not an Oxy-Moron," *Journal of Advertising Research,* July–August 1999, pp. 70–72.
8. B. Joseph Pine II, Don Peppers, and Martha Rogers, "Do You Want to Keep Your Customers Forever?" *Harvard Business Review,* March–April 1995, p. 103–14.
9. Adrienne Ward Fawcett, "Integrated Marketing—Marketers Convinced: Its Time Has Arrived," *Advertising Age,* November 6, 1993, pp. S1–2.
10. "Do Your Ads Need a Super-Agency?" *Fortune,* April 27, 1991, pp. 81–85; Faye Rice, "A Cure for What Ails Advertising?" *Fortune,* December 16, 1991, pp. 119–22.
11. Scott Hume, "Campus Adopts 'New' Advertising," *Advertising Age,* September 23, 1991, p. 17.
12. Don E. Schultz, "Integrated Marketing Communications: Maybe Definition Is in the Point of View," *Marketing News,* January 18, 1993, p. 17.
13. Ibid.
14. Tom Duncan and Sandra E. Moriarty, "A Communication-Based Model for Managing Relationships," *Journal of Marketing* 62 (April 1998), pp. 1–13.
15. Louise Lee, "Can Nike Still Do It?" *Business Week,* February 21, 2000, pp. 121–28.
16. Harlan E. Spotts, David R. Lambert, and Mary L. Joyce, "Marketing Déjà Vu: The Discovery of Integrated Marketing Communications," *Journal of Marketing Education,* 20, no. 3 (December 1998), pp. 210–18.
17. Kate Fitzgerald, "Beyond Advertising," *Advertising Age,* August 3, 1998, pp. 1, 14; Jane Smith, "Integrated Marketing," *Marketing Tools,* November/December 1995, pp. 63–70; Thomas R. Duncan and Stephen E. Everett, "Client Perception of Integrated Marketing Communications," *Journal of Advertising Research,* May/June 1993, pp. 30–39.
18. Anthony J. Tortorici, "Maximizing Marketing Communications through Horizontal and Vertical Orchestration," *Public Relations Quarterly* 36, no. 1 (1991), pp. 20–22.
19. Robert H. Ducoffe, Dennis Sandler, and Eugene Secunda, "A Survey of Senior Agency, Advertiser, and Media Executives on the Future of Advertising," *Journal of Current Issues and Research in Advertising* 18, no. 1 (Spring 1996).
20. Dave Guilford and Hillary Chura, "BMW Loads Up Bond Push to Precede Film Premiere," *Advertising Age,* November 1, 1999, p. 12.
21. Sergio Zyman, *The End of Marketing As We Know It* (New York: HarperBusiness, 1999); Joe Cappo, "Agencies: Change or Die," *Advertising Age,* December 7, 1992, p. 26.
22. Don E. Schultz, "Be Careful Picking Database for IMC Efforts," *Marketing News,* March 11, 1996, p. 14.
23. Michael L. Ray, *Advertising and Communication Management* (Englewood Cliffs, NJ: Prentice Hall, 1982).
24. Ralph S. Alexander, ed., *Marketing Definitions* (Chicago: American Marketing Association, 1965), p. 9.
25. "Trends in Media," Television Bureau of Advertising, New York.
26. Richard Lewis, "Absolut Vodka Case History," *A Celebration of Effective Advertising: 30 Years of Winning EFFIE Campaigns* (New York: American Marketing Association, 1999), pp. 20–23.
27. The 1999 Annual Report of the U.S. Promotion Industry, *Promo,* July 1999, p. S3.
28. *Cox Direct 20th Annual Survey of Promotional Practices* (Largo Lakes, FL: Cox Direct, 1998).
29. Jefferson Graham, "Abs Machine Sales Go Flabby," *USA Today,* October 22, 1996, p. D1.
30. H. Frazier Moore and Bertrand R. Canfield, *Public Relations: Principles, Cases, and Problems,* 7th ed. (Burr Ridge, IL: Irwin, 1977), p. 5.
31. Art Kleiner, "The Public Relations Coup," *Adweek's Marketing Week,* January 16, 1989, pp. 20–23.
32. Ronald Alsop, "The Best Corporate Reputations in America," *The Wall Street Journal,* September 29, 1999, pp. B1, 6.

Chapter Two

1. Joseph Periera, "Speaker Company Tags Out-of-Breath Baby Boomers," *The Wall Street Journal,* January 6, 1998, p. B1.

2. Wayne Friedman, "Casual K-Swiss' Refocuses on Performance Footwear," *Ad Age,* June 14, 1999, p. 8.
3. Spencer L. Hapoinen, "The Rise of Micromarketing," *The Journal of Business Strategy,* November/December 1990, pp. 37–42.
4. Dan Fost, "Growing Older, but Not Up," *American Demographics,* September 1998, pp. 58–65.
5. "What Happened to Advertising?" *Business Week,* September 23, 1991, pp. 66–72.
6. Judann Pollack, "Warner-Lambert to Roll Listerine Line Extension," *Ad Age,* September 28, 1998, p. 3.
7. Jim Henry, "BMW Evolves by Building a Brand within a Brand," *Ad Age,* April 6, 1998, p. 526.
8. David Leonhardt, "Sara Lee: Playing with the Recipe," *Business Week,* April 27, 1998, pp. 114–15.
9. Eric N. Berkowitz, Roger A. Kerin, and William Rudelius, *Marketing,* 6th ed. (Burr Ridge, IL: Irwin/McGraw-Hill, 2000).
10. Edward M. Tauber, "Research on Food Consumption Values Finds Four Market Segments: Good Taste Still Tops," *Marketing News,* May 15, 1981, p. 17; Rebecca C. Quarles, "Shopping Centers Use Fashion Lifestyle Research to Make Marketing Decisions," *Marketing News,* January 22, 1982, p. 18; and "Our Auto, Ourselves," *Consumer Reports,* June 1985, p. 375.
11. Judith Graham, "New VALS 2 Takes Psychological Route," *Advertising Age,* February 13, 1989, p. 24.
12. *Ayer's Dictionary of Advertising Terms* (Philadelphia: Ayer Press, 1976).
13. Davis A. Aaker and John G. Myers, *Advertising Management,* 3rd ed. (Englewood Cliffs, NJ: Prentice Hall, 1987), p. 125.
14. Jack Trout and Al Ries, "Positioning Cuts through Chaos in the Marketplace," *Advertising Age,* May 1, 1972, pp. 51–53.
15. Ibid.
16. David A. Aaker and J. Gary Shansby, "Positioning Your Product," *Business Horizons,* May–June 1982, pp. 56–62.
17. Aaker and Myers, *Advertising Management.*
18. Trout and Ries, "Positioning Cuts through Chaos."
19. Aaker and Myers, *Advertising Management.*
20. J. Paul Peter and Jerry C. Olson, *Consumer Behavior* (Burr Ridge, IL: Richard D. Irwin, 1987), p. 505.
21. Michael R. Solomon, "The Role of Products as Social Stimuli: A Symbolic Interactionism Perspective," *Journal of Consumer Research,* December 1983, pp. 319–29.
22. Don. E. Schultz, Stanley I. Tannenbaum, and Robert F. Lauterborn, "Integrated Marketing Communications: Putting It Together and Making It Work" (Lincolnwood, IL: NTC Publishing Group), p. 72.
23. Peter and Olson, *Consumer Behavior,* p. 571.
24. Paul W. Farris and David J. Reibstein, "How Prices, Ad Expenditures, and Profits Are Linked," *Harvard Business Review,* November–December 1979, pp. 172–84.
25. Berkowitz, Kerin, and Rudelius, *Marketing.*
26. David W. Stewart, Gary L. Frazier, and Ingrid Martin, "Integrated Channel Management: Merging the Communication and Distribution Functions of the Firm," in *Integrated Communication: Synergy of Persuasive Voices,* pp. 185–215, Esther Thorson & Jeri Moore (eds), Lawrence Earlbaum Associates, 1996, Mahwah, NJ.

Chapter Three

1. Jack Neff, "P&G Redefines the Brand Manager," *Advertising Age,* October 13, 1997, pp. 1, 18, 20.
2. Thomas J. Cosse and John E. Swan, "Strategic Marketing Planning by Product Managers—Room for Improvement?" *Journal of Marketing* 47 (Summer 1983), pp. 92–102.
3. "Behind the Tumult at P&G," *Fortune,* March 7, 1994, pp. 74–82; "Category Management: New Tools changing Life for Manufacturers, Retailers," *Marketing News,* September 25, 1989, pp. 2, 19.
4. Cosse and Swan, "Strategic Marketing Planning by Product Managers—Room for Improvement?"
5. Victor P. Buell, *Organizing for Marketing/Advertising Success* (New York: Association of National Advertisers, 1982).
6. M. Louise Ripley, "What Kind of Companies Take Their Advertising In-House?" *Journal of Advertising Research,* October/November 1991, pp. 73–80.
7. Bruce Horovitz, "Some Companies Say the Best Ad Agency Is No Ad Agency at All," *Los Angeles Times,* July 19, 1989, Sec IV, p. 5.
8. Bradley Johnson and Alice Z. Cuneo, "Gatey 2000 Taps DMB&B," *Advertising Age,* March 24, 1997, p. 2.
9. Anthony Vagnoni, "Gotham Regains Some Lost Luster as Center of U.S. Agency Creativity," *Advertising Age,* April 12, 1999, pp. 1, 10.
10. "Do Your Ads Need a Superagency?" *Fortune,* April 27, 1987, p. 81.
11. Sally Goll Beatty, "Global Needs Challenge Midsize Agencies," *The Wall Street Journal,* December 14, 1995, p. B9.
12. Kathryn Kranhold, "Fallon McElligott to Be Part of Publics," *The Wall Street Journal,* February 3, 2000, p. B5.
13. Gordon Fairclough, "Pace of Ad Mergers Is Expected to Continue," *The Wall Street Journal,* April 23, 1999, p. B2.
14. Bob Lammons, "A Good Account Exec Makes a Big Difference," *Marketing News,* June 3, 1996, p. 12.
15. Bradley Johnson, "Nestlé U.S. Units Join for Media Clout," *Advertising Age,* January 14, 1991, p. 3.
16. Sally Goll Beatty, "Media Planners to Draw Straws for Coke," *The Wall Street Journal,* February 14, 1996, p. B8; Kevin Goldman, "GM Merging Media Buying at Interpublic," *The Wall Street Journal,* December 8, 1993, p. B3.
17. Sally Goll Beatty, "Spike Lee, DDB Join to Create New Ad Agency," *The Wall Street Journal,* December 5, 1996, pp. B1, 13; Robert Frank, "Coca Cola Disney Venture Mines Creative Artists Agency Talent," *The Wall Street Journal,* November 10, 1995 p. B8.
18. Patricia Sellers, "Do You Need Your Ad Agency?" *Fortune,* November 15, 1993, pp. 47–61.
19. Judann Pollack, "ANA Survey: Under 50% Pay Agency Commissions," *Advertising Age,* June 15, 1998.
20. Ibid.
21. Kathryn Kranhold, "P&G Expands Its Program to Tie Agency Pay to Brand Performance," *The Wall Street Journal,* September 16, 1999, p. B12.
22. Sally Beatty, "P&G to Test Ad-Agency Pay Tied to Sales," *The Wall Street Journal,* November 9, 1998, p. B4.
23. Alice Z. Cuneo, "Nissan Ties TBWA's Pay to Car Sales," *Advertising Age,* June 7, 1999, pp. 1, 49.
24. Jean Halliday, "GM to Scrap Agency Commissions," *Advertising Age,* November 16, 1998, pp. 1, 57.
25. Joanne Lipman, "Study Shows Clients Jump Ship Quickly," *The Wall Street Journal,* May 21, 1992, p. B6.
26. Yumiko Ono, "TBWA Chiat/Day's Offbeat Style Helps It Win Levi's

Jeans Account," *The Wall Street Journal,* January 27, 1998, p. B7.

27. Sally Beatty, "Sprint Moves Creative Account to McCann," *The Wall Street Journal,* September 28, 1998, p. B9.
28. Fred Beard, "Marketing Client Role Ambiguity as a Source of Dissatisfaction in Client-Ad Agency Relationships," *Journal of Advertising Research,* September/October 1996, pp. 9–20; Paul Michell, Harold Cataquet, and Stephen Hague, "Establishing the Causes of Disaffection in Agency-Client Relations," *Journal of Advertising Research,* 32, 2, 1992, pp. 41–48; Peter Doyle, Marcel Corstiens, and Paul Michell, "Signals of Vulnerability in Agency-Client Relations," *Journal of Marketing* 44 (Fall 1980), pp. 18–23; and Daniel B. Wackman, Charles Salmon, and Caryn C. Salmon, "Developing an Advertising Agency-Client Relationship," *Journal of Advertising Research* 26, no. 6 (December 1986/January 1987), pp. 21–29.
29. Sally Goll Beatty, "AT&T Sends Agencies to Drawing Board," *The Wall Street Journal,* August 5, 1996, p. B6.
30. Sally Goll Beatty, "Blockbuster Puts Agencies in a Permanent Shootout," *The Wall Street Journal,* October 2, 1996, pp. B1, 8; and "Big Agencies Starting to Call for End to Costly Free Pitches," *The Wall Street Journal,* February 22, 1989, p. B7.
31. "A Potent New Tool For Selling: Database Marketing," *Business Week,* September 5, 1994, pp. 56–62.
32. Prema Nakra, "The Changing Role of Public Relations in Marketing Communications," *Public Relations Quarterly,* 1 (1991) pp. 42–45.
33. Mark Gleason and Debra Aho Williamson, "The New Interactive Agency," *Advertising Age,* February 2, 1996, pp. S1–11.
34. Sally Beatty, "Interpublic Buying Stake in Icon Medialab," *The Wall Street Journal,* March 25, 1999, p. B2.
35. Sally Goll Beatty, "Interpublic Diversifies Further with Purchase of Direct Marketer," *The Wall Street Journal,* May 17, 1996, p. B5.
36. Betsy Spethmann, "Sudden Impact," *PROMO Magazine,* April 1999, pp. 42–48.
37. Anders Gronstedt and Esther Thorson, "Five Approaches to Organize an Integrated Marketing Communications Agency," *Journal of Advertising Research,* March/April 1996, pp. 48–58.
38. "Ad Firms Falter on One-Stop Shopping," *The Wall Street Journal,* December 1, 1988, p. 81; and "Do Your Ads Need a Superagency?" *Fortune,* April 27, 1987, p. 81.
39. Faye Rice, "A Cure for What Ails Advertising?" *Fortune,* December 16, 1991, pp. 119–22.
40. Philip J. Kitchen and Don E. Schultz, "A Multi-Country Comparison of the Drive for IMC," *Journal of Advertising Research,* January/February 1999, pp. 21–38.
41. David N. McArthur and Tom Griffin, "A Marketing Management View of Integrated Marketing Communications," *Journal of Advertising Research,* 37, no. 5 (September/October) 1997, pp. 19–26; and Adrienne Ward Fawcett, "Integrated Marketing—Marketers Convinced: Its Time Has Arrived," *Advertising Age,* November 6, 1993, pp. S1–2.

Chapter Four

1. Russell W. Belk, "Possessions and the Extended Self," *Journal of Consumer Research,* September 1988, pp. 139–68.
2. Eric N. Berkowitz, Roger A. Kerin, Steven W. Hartley, and William Rudelius, *Marketing,* 6th ed. (Burr Ridge, IL: Irwin/McGraw-Hill, 2000), p. 14.
3. A. H. Maslow, "'Higher' and 'Lower' Needs," *Journal of Psychology* 25 (1948), pp. 433–36.
4. Morton Deutsch and Robert M. Krauss, *Theories in Social Psychology* (New York: Basic Books, 1965).
5. Jeffrey Ball, "But How Does It Make You Feel?" *The Wall Street Journal,* May 3, 1999, p. B1.
6. Jagdish N. Sheth, "The Role of Motivation Research in Consumer Psychology" (Faculty Working Paper, University of Illinois, Champaign: 1974); Bill Abrams, "Charles of the Ritz Discovers What Women Want," *The Wall Street Journal,* August 20, 1981, p. 29; and Ernest Dichter, *Getting Motivated* (New York: Pergamon Press, 1979).
7. Ronald Alsop, "Advertisers Put Consumers on the Couch," *The Wall Street Journal,* May 13, 1988, p. 19.
8. Ball, "But How Does It Make You Feel?"
9. For an excellent discussion of memory and consumer behavior, see James R. Bettman, "Memory Factors in Consumer Choice: A Review," *Journal of Marketing* 43 (Spring 1979), pp. 37–53.
10. Gilbert Harrell, *Consumer Behavior* (San Diego: Harcourt Brace Jovanovich, 1986), p. 66.
11. Raymond A. Bauer and Stephen A. Greyser, *Advertising in America: The Consumer View* (Boston: Harvard Business School, 1968).
12. Neal Santelmann, "Color That Yells 'Buy Me'," *Forbes,* May 2, 1988, p. 110.
13. J. Paul Peter and Jerry C. Olson, *Consumer Behavior,* 2nd ed. (Burr Ridge, IL: Irwin/McGraw-Hill, 1990), p. 73.
14. Gordon W. Allport, "Attitudes," in *Handbook of Social Psychology,* ed. C. M. Murchison (Winchester, MA: Clark University Press, 1935), p. 810.
15. Robert B. Zajonc and Hazel Markus, "Affective and Cognitive Factors in Preferences," *Journal of Consumer Research* 9 (1982), pp. 123–31.
16. Alvin Achenbaum, "Advertising Doesn't Manipulate Consumers," *Journal of Advertising Research,* April 2, 1970, pp. 3–13.
17. William D. Wells, "Attitudes and Behavior: Lessons from the Needham Lifestyle Study," *Journal of Advertising Research,* February–March 1985, pp. 40–44; and Icek Ajzen and Martin Fishbein, "Attitude-Behavior Relations: A Theoretical Analysis and Review of Empirical Research," *Psychological Bulletin,* September 1977, pp. 888–918.
18. For a review of multiattribute models, see William L. Wilkie and Edgar A. Pessemier, "Issues in Marketing's Use of Multiattribute Models," *Journal of Marketing Research* 10 (November 1983), pp. 428–41.
19. Joel B. Cohen, Paul W. Minniard, and Peter R. Dickson, "Information Integration: An Information Processing Perspective," in *Advances in Consumer Research,* vol. 7, ed. Jerry C. Olson (Ann Arbor, MI: Association for Consumer Research, 1980), pp. 161–70.
20. Peter and Olson, *Consumer Behavior,* p. 182.
21. Peter L. Wright and Fredric Barbour, "The Relevance of Decision Process Models in Structuring Persuasive Messages," *Communications Research,* July 1975, pp. 246–59.
22. James F. Engel, "The Psychological Consequences of a Major Purchase Decision," in *Marketing in Transition,* ed. William S. Decker (Chicago: American Marketing Association, 1963), pp. 462–75.
23. John A. Howard and Jagdish N. Sheth, *The Theory of Consumer*

Behavior (New York: John Wiley & Sons, 1969).

24. Leon G. Schiffman and Leslie Lazar Kannuk, *Consumer Behavior,* 4th ed. (Englewood Cliffs, NJ: Prentice Hall, 1991), p. 192.
25. I. P. Pavlov, *The Work of the Digestive Glands,* 2nd ed., trans. W. N. Thompson (London: Griffin, 1910).
26. Gerald J. Gorn, "The Effects of Music in Advertising on Choice: A Classical Conditioning Approach," *Journal of Marketing* 46 (Winter 1982), pp. 94–101.
27. James J. Kellaris, Anthony D. Cox, and Dena Cox, "The Effect of Background Music on Ad Processing: A Contingency Explanation," *Journal of Marketing,* 57, no. 4 (Fall 1993), p. 114.
28. Brian C. Deslauries and Peter B. Everett, "The Effects of Intermittent and Continuous Token Reinforcement on Bus Ridership," *Journal of Applied Psychology* 62 (August 1977), pp. 369–75.
29. Michael L. Rothschild and William C. Gaidis, "Behavioral Learning Theory: Its Relevance to Marketing and Promotions," *Journal of Marketing Research* 45, no. 2 (Spring 1981), pp. 70–78.
30. For an excellent discussion of social class and consumer behavior, see Richard P. Coleman, "The Continuing Significance of Social Class to Marketing," *Journal of Consumer Research* 10, no. 3 (December 1983), pp. 265–80.
31. Lyman E. Ostlund, *Role Theory and Group Dynamics in Consumer Behavior: Theoretical Sources,* ed. Scott Ward and Thomas S. Robertson (Englewood Cliffs, NJ: Prentice Hall, 1973), pp. 230–75.
32. James Stafford and Benton Cocanougher, "Reference Group Theory," in *Perspective in Consumer Behavior,* ed. H. H. Kassarjian and T. S. Robertson (Glenview, IL: Scott, Foresman, 1981), pp. 329–43.
33. Jagdish N. Sheth, "A Theory of Family Buying Decisions," in *Models of Buying Behavior,* ed. Jagdish N. Sheth (New York: Harper & Row, 1974), pp. 17–33.
34. Russell Belk, "Situational Variables and Consumer Behavior," *Journal of Consumer Research,* December 1975, pp. 157–64.

Chapter Five

1. Wilbur Schram, *The Process and Effects of Mass Communications* (Urbana: University of Illinois Press, 1955).
2. Ibid.
3. Joseph Ransdell, "Some Leading Ideas of Peirce's Semiotic," *Semiotica* 19 (1977), pp. 157–78.
4. Michael Solomon, *Consumer Behavior,* 4th ed. (Upper Saddle River, NJ: Prentice-Hall, 1999), p. 17.
5. Nina Munk, "Levi's Ongoing Quest for Street Cred," *Fortune,* February 1, 1999, p. 40.
6. For an excellent article on the application of semiotics to consumer behavior and advertising, see David G. Mick, "Consumer Research and Semiotics: Exploring the Morphology of Signs, Symbols, and Significance," *Journal of Consumer Research* 13, no. 2 (September 1986), pp. 196–213; see also Edward F. McQuarrie and David Glen Mick, "Figures of Rhetoric in Advertising Language," *Journal of Consumer Research* 22 (March 1996), pp. 424–38.
7. Barry L. Bayus, "Word of Mouth: The Indirect Effect of Marketing Efforts," *Journal of Advertising Research,* June/July 1985, pp. 31–39.
8. Quote by Gordon S. Bower in *Fortune,* October 14, 1985, p. 11.
9. Thomas V. Bonoma and Leonard C. Felder, "Nonverbal Communication in Marketing: Toward Communicational Analysis," *Journal of Marketing Research,* May 1977, pp. 169–80.
10. Jacob Jacoby and Wayne D. Hoyer, "Viewer Miscomprehension of Televised Communication: Selected Findings," *Journal of Marketing,* Fall 1982, pp. 12–26; Jacoby and Hoyer, "The Comprehension and Miscomprehension of Print Communications: An Investigation of Mass Media Magazines," Advertising Education Foundation study, New York, 1987.
11. E. K. Strong, *The Psychology of Selling* (New York: McGraw-Hill, 1925), p. 9.
12. Robert J. Lavidge and Gary A. Steiner, "A Model for Predictive Measurements of Advertising Effectiveness," *Journal of Marketing* 24 (October 1961), pp. 59–62.
13. Everett M. Rogers, *Diffusion of Innovations* (New York: Free Press, 1962), pp. 79–86.
14. William J. McGuire, "An Information Processing Model of Advertising Effectiveness," in *Behavioral and Management Science in Marketing,* ed. Harry J. Davis and Alvin J. Silk (New York: Ronald Press, 1978), pp. 156–80.
15. Michael L. Ray, "Communication and the Hierarchy of Effects," in *New Models for Mass Communication Research,* ed. P. Clarke (Beverly Hills, CA: Sage, 1973), pp. 147–75.
16. Herbert E. Krugman, "The Impact of Television Advertising: Learning without Involvement," *Public Opinion Quarterly* 29 (Fall 1965), pp. 349–56.
17. Scott A. Hawkins and Stephen J. Hoch, "Low-Involvement Learning: Memory without Evaluation," *Journal of Consumer Research* 19, no. 2 (September 1992), pp. 212–25.
18. Harry W. McMahan, "Do Your Ads Have VIP?" *Advertising Age,* July 14, 1980, pp. 50–51.
19. Robert E. Smith and William R. Swinyard, "Information Response Models: An Integrated Approach," *Journal of Marketing* 46, no. 2 (Winter 1982), pp. 81–93.
20. Ibid., p. 90.
21. Ibid., p. 86.
22. Robert E. Smith, "Integrating Information from Advertising and Trial: Processes and Effects on Consumer Response to Product Information," *Journal of Marketing Research* 30 (May 1993), pp. 204–19.
23. Harold H. Kassarjian, "Low Involvement: A Second Look," in *Advances in Consumer Research,* vol. 8 (Ann Arbor: Association for Consumer Research, 1981), pp. 31–34; also see Anthony G. Greenwald and Clark Leavitt, "Audience Involvement in Advertising: Four Levels," *Journal of Consumer Research* 11, no. 1 (June 1984), pp. 581–92.
24. Judith L. Zaichkowsky, "Conceptualizing Involvement," *Journal of Advertising* 15, no. 2 (1986), pp. 4–14.
25. Richard Vaughn, "How Advertising Works: A Planning Model," *Journal of Advertising Research* 20, no. 5 (October 1980), pp. 27–33.
26. Richard Vaughn, "How Advertising Works: A Planning Model Revisited," *Journal of Advertising Research* 26, no. 1 (February/March 1986), pp. 57–66.
27. Jerry C. Olson, Daniel R. Toy, and Phillip A. Dover, "Mediating Effects of Cognitive Responses to Advertising on Cognitive Structure," in *Advances in Consumer Research,* vol. 5, ed. H. Keith Hunt (Ann Arbor, MI: Association for Consumer Research, 1978), pp. 72–78.
28. Anthony A. Greenwald, "Cognitive Learning, Cognitive Response to

Persuasion and Attitude Change," in *Psychological Foundations of Attitudes,* ed. A. G. Greenwald, T. C. Brock, and T. W. Ostrom (New York: Academic Press, 1968); Peter L. Wright, "The Cognitive Processes Mediating Acceptance of Advertising," *Journal of Marketing Research* 10 (February 1973), pp. 53–62; Brian Wansink, Michael L. Ray, and Rajeev Batra, "Increasing Cognitive Response Sensitivity," *Journal of Advertising* 23, no. 2 (June 1994), pp. 65–76.

29. Peter Wright, "Message Evoked Thoughts, Persuasion Research Using Thought Verbalizations," *Journal of Consumer Research* 7, no. 2 (September 1980), pp. 151–75.
30. Scott B. Mackenzie, Richard J. Lutz, and George E. Belch, "The Role of Attitude toward the Ad as a Mediator of Advertising Effectiveness: A Test of Competing Explanations," *Journal of Marketing Research* 23 (May 1986), pp. 130–43; and Rajeev Batra and Michael L. Ray, "Affective Responses Mediating Acceptance of Advertising," *Journal of Consumer Research* 13 (September 1986), pp. 234–49.
31. Tim Ambler and Tom Burne, "The Impact of Affect on Memory of Advertising," *Journal of Advertising Research* 29, no. 3 (March/April 1999), pp. 25–34; Ronald Alsop, "TV Ads That Are Likeable Get Plus Rating for Persuasiveness," *The Wall Street Journal,* February 20, 1986, p. 23.
32. David J. Moore and William D. Harris, "Affect Intensity and the Consumer's Attitude toward High Impact Emotional Advertising Appeals," *Journal of Advertising* 25, no. 2 (Summer 1996), pp. 37–50; Andrew A. Mitchell and Jerry C. Olson, "Are Product Attribute Beliefs the Only Mediator of Advertising Effects on Brand Attitude?" *Journal of Marketing Research* 18 (August 1981), pp. 318–32.
33. David J. Moore, William D. Harris, and Hong C. Chen, "Affect Intensity: An Individual Difference Response to Advertising Appeals," *Journal of Consumer Research* 22 (September 1995), pp. 154–64; Julie Edell and Marian C. Burke, "The Power of Feelings in Understanding Advertising Effects," *Journal of Consumer Research* 14 (December 1987), pp. 421–33.
34. Richard E. Petty and John T. Cacioppo, "Central and Peripheral Routes to Persuasion: Application to Advertising," in *Advertising and Consumer Psychology,* ed. Larry Percy and Arch Woodside (Lexington, MA: Lexington Books, 1983), pp. 3–23.
35. David A. Aaker, Rajeev Batra, and John G. Myers, *Advertising Management,* 5th ed. (Upper Saddle River, NJ: Prentice Hall, 1996).
36. Richard E. Petty, John T. Cacioppo, and David Schumann, "Central and Peripheral Routes to Advertising Effectiveness: The Moderating Role of Involvement," *Journal of Consumer Research* 10 (September 1983), pp. 135–46.
37. Demetrios Vakratsas and Tim Ambler, "How Advertising Works: What Do We Really Know?" *Journal of Marketing* 63 (January 1999), pp. 26–43.

Chapter Six

1. William J. McGuire, "An Information Processing Model of Advertising Effectiveness," in *Behavioral and Management Science in Marketing,* ed. Harry J. Davis and Alvin J. Silk (New York: Ronald Press, 1978), pp. 156–80.
2. Herbert C. Kelman, "Processes of Opinion Change," *Public Opinion Quarterly* 25 (Spring 1961), pp. 57–78.
3. William J. McGuire, "The Nature of Attitudes and Attitude Change," in *Handbook of Social Psychology,* 2nd ed., ed. G. Lindzey and E. Aronson (Cambridge, MA: Addison-Wesley, 1969), pp. 135–214; Daniel J. O'Keefe, "The Persuasive Effects of Delaying Identification of High- and Low-Credibility Communicators: A Meta-Analytic Review," *Central States Speech Journal* 38 (1987), pp. 63–72.
4. Roobina Ohanian, "The Impact of Celebrity Spokespersons' Image on Consumers' Intention to Purchase," *Journal of Advertising Research,* February/March 1991, pp. 46–54.
5. "Business Celebrities," *Business Week,* June 23, 1986, pp. 100–07.
6. Bill McDowell, "Wendy's Won't Dump Dave Ads—for Now," *Advertising Age,* December 23, 1996, p. 8.
7. Erick Reidenback and Robert Pitts, "Not All CEOs Are Created Equal as Advertising Spokespersons: Evaluating the Effective CEO Spokesperson," *Journal of Advertising* 20, no. 3 (1986), pp. 35–50; Roger Kerin and Thomas E. Barry, "The CEO Spokesperson in Consumer Advertising: An Experimental Investigation," in *Current Issues in Research in Advertising,* ed. J. H. Leigh and C. R. Martin (Ann Arbor: University of Michigan, 1981), pp. 135–48; and J. Poindexter, "Voices of Authority," *Psychology Today,* August 1983.
8. A. Eagly and S. Chaiken, "An Attribution Analysis of the Effect of Communicator Characteristics on Opinion Change," *Journal of Personality and Social Psychology* 32 (1975), pp. 136–44.
9. For a review of these studies, see Brian Sternthal, Lynn Phillips, and Ruby Dholakia, "The Persuasive Effect of Source Credibility: A Situational Analysis," *Public Opinion Quarterly* 42 (Fall 1978), pp. 285–314.
10. Brian Sternthal, Ruby Dholakia, and Clark Leavitt, "The Persuasive Effects of Source Credibility: Tests of Cognitive Response," *Journal of Consumer Research* 4, no. 4 (March 1978), pp. 252–60; and Robert R. Harmon and Kenneth A. Coney, "The Persuasive Effects of Source Credibility in Buy and Lease Situations," *Journal of Marketing Research* 19 (May 1982), pp. 255–60.
11. For a review, see Noel Capon and James Hulbert, "The Sleeper Effect: An Awakening," *Public Opinion Quarterly* 37 (1973), pp. 333–58.
12. Darlene B. Hannah and Brian Sternthal, "Detecting and Explaining the Sleeper Effect," *Journal of Consumer Research* 11, no. 2 (September 1984), pp. 632–42.
13. H. C. Triandis, *Attitudes and Attitude Change* (New York: Wiley, 1971).
14. J. Mills and J. Jellison, "Effect on Opinion Change Similarity between the Communicator and the Audience He Addresses," *Journal of Personality and Social Psychology* 9, no. 2 (1969), pp. 153–56.
15. Arch G. Woodside and J. William Davenport, Jr., "The Effect of Salesman Similarity and Expertise on Consumer Purchasing Behavior," *Journal of Marketing Research* 11 (May 1974), pp. 198–202; and Paul Busch and David T. Wilson, "An Experimental Analysis of a Salesman's Expert and Referent Bases of Social Power in the Buyer-Seller Dyad," *Journal of Marketing Research* 13 (February 1976), pp. 3–11.
16. Sam Walker, "Michael Jordan Isn't Retiring from Hot Deals," *The Wall Street Journal,* February 15, 1999, pp. B1, 4.
17. Denise Gellene, "Bionic Woman Wired for Success with Region's

Ford Sales," *Los Angeles Times,* November 19, 1998, pp. C1, 7.

18. Valerie Folkes, "Recent Attribution Research in Consumer Behavior: A Review and New Directions," *Journal of Consumer Research* 14 (March 1988), pp. 548–65; John C. Mowen and Stephen W. Brown, "On Explaining and Predicting the Effectiveness of Celebrity Endorsers," in *Advances in Consumer Research,* vol. 8 (Ann Arbor, MI: Association for Consumer Research, 1981), pp. 437–41.
19. Stephen Rae, "How Celebrities Make Killings on Commercials," *Cosmopolitan,* January 1997, pp. 164–67.
20. Charles Atkin and M. Block, "Effectiveness of Celebrity Endorsers," *Journal of Advertising Research* 23, no. 1 (February/March 1983), pp. 57–61.
21. Ellen Neuborne, "Generation Y," *Business Week,* February 15, 1999, pp. 81–88.
22. Study by Total Research Corp. cited in Bruce Horowitz, "Wishing on a Star," *Los Angeles Times,* November 7, 1993, pp. D1, 7.
23. Jeff Jensen, "Performance, Shoe Tech Take Ad Stage for '98," *Advertising Age,* January 12, 1998, pp. 3, 36.
24. Brian D. Till and Terence A. Shimp, "Endorsers in Advertising: The Case of Negative Celebrity Information," *Journal of Advertising,* 27, no. 1, Spring 1998, pp. 67–82.
25. Greg Hernandez, "Carl's Jr. Execs Yank Rodman TV Ads, Again," *Los Angeles Times,* April 17, 1999, pp. C1, 8.
26. Mike Freeman, "Callaway Ends Deal with Golfer John Daly," *San Diego Union-Tribune,* September 16, 1999, pp. C1, 3.
27. Michael A. Kamins, "An Investigation into the 'Match-Up' Hypothesis in Celebrity Advertising," *Journal of Advertising* 19, no. 1 (1990), pp. 4–13.
28. Grant McCracken. "Who Is the Celebrity Endorser? Cultural Foundations of the Endorsement Process," *Journal of Consumer Research* 16, no. 3 (December 1989), pp. 310–21.
29. Ibid., p. 315.
30. Raymond Serafin, "Subaru Outback Taps 'Crocodile Dundee,'" *Advertising Age,* September 15, 1995, p. 38; Steve Geisi, "'Dundee' Returns to Extend Outback into Entry Level," *Brandweek,* September 2, 1996, pp. 1, 6.
31. For an excellent review of these studies, see Marilyn Y. Jones, Andrea J. S. Stanaland, and Betsy D. Gelb, "Beefcake and Cheesecake: Insights for Advertisers," *Journal of Advertising* 27, no. 2 (Summer 1998), pp. 32–51; and W. B. Joseph, "The Credibility of Physically Attractive Communicators," *Journal of Advertising* 11, no. 3 (1982), pp. 13–23.
32. Michael Solomon, Richard Ashmore, and Laura Longo, "The Beauty Match-Up Hypothesis: Congruence between Types of Beauty and Product Images in Advertising," *Journal of Advertising* 21, no. 4, pp. 23–34; M. J. Baker and Gilbert A. Churchill, Jr., "The Impact of Physically Attractive Models on Advertising Evaluations," *Journal of Marketing Research* 14 (November 1977), pp. 538–55.
33. Robert W. Chestnut, C. C. La Chance, and A. Lubitz, "The Decorative Female Model: Sexual Stimuli and the Recognition of the Advertisements," *Journal of Advertising* 6 (Fall 1977), pp. 11–14; and Leonard N. Reid and Lawrence C. Soley, "Decorative Models and Readership of Magazine Ads," *Journal of Advertising Research* 23, no. 2 (April/May 1983), pp. 27–32.
34. Herbert E. Krugman, "On Application of Learning Theory to TV Copy Testing," *Public Opinion Quarterly* 26 (1962), pp. 626–39.
35. C. I. Hovland and W. Mandell, "An Experimental Comparison of Conclusion Drawing by the Communicator and by the Audience," *Journal of Abnormal and Social Psychology* 47 (July 1952), pp. 581–88.
36. Alan G. Sawyer and Daniel J. Howard, "Effects of Omitting Conclusions in Advertisements to Involved and Uninvolved Audiences," *Journal of Marketing Research* 28 (November 1991), pp. 467–74.
37. Paul Chance, "Ads without Answers Make Brain Itch," *Psychology Today* 9 (1975), p. 78.
38. George E. Belch, "The Effects of Message Modality on One- and Two-Sided Advertising Messages," in *Advances in Consumer Research,* vol. 10, ed. Richard P. Bagozzi and Alice M. Tybout (Ann Arbor, MI: Association for Consumer Research, 1983), pp. 21–26.
39. Robert E. Settle and Linda L. Golden, "Attribution Theory and Advertiser Credibility," *Journal of Marketing Research* 11 (May 1974), pp. 181–85; and Edmund J. Faison, "Effectiveness of One-Sided and Two-Sided Mass Communications in Advertising," *Public Opinion Quarterly* 25 (Fall 1961), pp. 468–69.
40. Joel A. Baglole, "Cough Syrup Touts 'Awful Taste' in U.S.," *The Wall Street Journal,* December 15, 1999, p. B10.
41. Alan G. Sawyer, "The Effects of Repetition of Refutational and Supportive Advertising Appeals," *Journal of Marketing Research* 10 (February 1973), pp. 23–37; and George J. Szybillo and Richard Heslin, "Resistance to Persuasion: Inoculation Theory in a Marketing Context," *Journal of Marketing Research* 10 (November 1973), pp. 396–403.
42. Andrew A. Mitchell, "The Effect of Verbal and Visual Components of Advertisements on Brand Attitudes and Attitude toward the Advertisement," *Journal of Consumer Research* 13 (June 1986), pp. 12–24; and Julie A. Edell and Richard Staelin, "The Information Processing of Pictures in Advertisements," *Journal of Consumer Research* 10, no. 1 (June 1983), pp. 45–60; Elizabeth C. Hirschmann, "The Effects of Verbal and Pictorial Advertising Stimuli on Aesthetic, Utilitarian and Familiarity Perceptions," *Journal of Advertising* 15, no. 2 (1986), pp. 27–34.
43. Jolita Kisielius and Brian Sternthal, "Detecting and Explaining Vividness Effects in Attitudinal Judgments," *Journal of Marketing Research* 21, no. 1 (1984), pp. 54–64.
44. H. Rao Unnava and Robert E. Burnkrant, "An Imagery-Processing View of the Role of Pictures in Print Advertisements," *Journal of Marketing Research* 28 (May 1991), pp. 226–31.
45. Susan E. Heckler and Terry L. Childers, "The Role of Expectancy and Relevancy in Memory for Verbal and Visual Information: What Is Incongruency?" *Journal of Consumer Research* 18, no. 4 (March 1992), pp. 475–92.
46. Michael J. Houston, Terry L. Childers, and Susan E. Heckler, "Picture-Word Consistency and the Elaborative Processing of Advertisements," *Journal of Marketing Research,* November 1987, pp. 359–69.
47. William L. Wilkie and Paul W. Farris, "Comparative Advertising: Problems and Potential," *Journal of Marketing* 39 (1975), pp. 7–15.
48. For a review of comparative advertising studies, see Cornelia Pechmann and David W. Stewart, "The Psychology of Comparative Advertising," in

Attention, Attitude and Affect in Response to Advertising, ed. E. M. Clark, T. C. Brock, and D. W. Stewart (Hillsdale, NJ: Lawrence Erlbaum, 1994), pp. 79–96; and Thomas S. Barry, "Comparative Advertising: What Have We Learned in Two Decades?" *Journal of Advertising Research* 33, no. 2 (1993), pp. 19–29.
49. Michael L. Ray and William L. Wilkie, "Fear: The Potential of an Appeal Neglected by Marketing," *Journal of Marketing* 34 (January 1970), pp. 54–62.
50. Brian Sternthal and C. Samuel Craig, "Fear Appeals Revisited and Revised," *Journal of Consumer Research* 1 (December 1974), pp. 22–34.
51. Punam Anand Keller and Lauren Goldberg Block, "Increasing the Persuasiveness of Fear Appeals: The Effect of Arousal and Elaboration," *Journal of Consumer Research* 22, no. 4 (March 1996), pp. 448–60.
52. John F. Tanner, Jr., James B. Hunt, and David R. Eppright, "The Protection Motivation Model: A Normative Mode of Fear Appeals," *Journal of Marketing* 55 (July 1991), pp. 36–45.
53. Ibid.
54. Sternthal and Craig, "Fear Appeals Revisited and Revised."
55. Herbert Jack Rotfeld, "The Textbook Effect: Coventional Wisdom, Myth and Error in Marketing," *Journal of Marketing* 64 (April 2000), pp. 122–27.
56. For a discussion of the use of humor in advertising, see C. Samuel Craig and Brian Sternthal, "Humor in Advertising," *Journal of Marketing* 37 (October 1973), pp. 12–18.
57. Yong Zhang, "Response to Humorous Advertising: The Moderating Effect of Need for Cognition," *Journal of Advertising* 25, no. 1 (Spring 1996), pp. 15–32; Marc G. Weinberger and Charles S. Gulas, "The Impact of Humor in Advertising: A Review," *Journal of Advertising* 21 (December 1992), pp. 35–59.
58. Marc G. Weinberger and Leland Campbell, "The Use of Humor in Radio Advertising," *Journal of Advertising Research* 31 (December/January 1990–91), pp. 44–52.
59. Thomas J. Madden and Marc C. Weinberger, "Humor in Advertising: A Practitioner View," *Journal of Advertising Research* 24, no. 4 (August/September 1984), pp. 23–26.
60. Harold C. Cash and W. J. E. Crissy, "Comparison of Advertising and Selling: The Salesman's Role in Marketing," *Psychology of Selling* 12 (1965), pp. 56–75.
61. Marshall McLuhan, *Understanding Media: The Extensions of Man* (New York: McGraw-Hill, 1966).
62. Marvin E. Goldberg and Gerald J. Gorn, "Happy and Sad TV Programs: How They Affect Reactions to Commercials," *Journal of Consumer Research* 14, no. 3 (December 1987), pp. 387–403.
63. Andrew B. Aylesworth and Scott B. MacKenzie, "Context Is Key: The Effect of Program-Induced Mood on Thoughts about the Ad," *Journal of Advertising* 27, no. 2 (Summer 1998), pp. 17–32.
64. Michael T. Elliott and Paul Surgi Speck, "Consumer Perceptions of Advertising Clutter and Its Impact across Various Media," *Journal of Advertising Research* 38, no. 1 (January/February 1998), pp. 29–41; and Peter H. Webb, "Consumer Initial Processing in a Difficult Media Environment," *Journal of Consumer Research* 6, no. 3 (December 1979), pp. 225–36.
65. Alex Wallau, "And Now More Words from Our Sponsors—TV 'Clutter' Rises," *Los Angeles Times,* March 2, 2000, p. C1.
66. Chuck Ross, "TV Commercial Clutter Has Ad Buyers Worried," *Advertising Age,* December 6, 1999, p. 77.

Chapter Seven

1. Robert A. Kriegel, "How to Choose the Right Communications Objectives," *Business Marketing,* April 1986, pp. 94–106.
2. *1993 Effies.* (New York: New York Chapter of the American Marketing Association, 1993), p. 10.
3. Donald S. Tull, "The Carry-Over Effect of Advertising," *Journal of Marketing,* April 1965, pp. 46–53.
4. Darral G. Clarke, "Econometric Measurement of the Duration of Advertising Effect on Sales," *Journal of Marketing Research* 23 (November 1976), pp. 345–57.
5. Philip Kotler, *Marketing Decision Making: A Model Building Approach* (New York: Holt, Rinehart & Winston, 1971), ch. 5.
6. For a more detailed discussion of this, see William M. Weilbacher, *Advertising,* 2nd ed. (New York: Macmillan, 1984), p. 112.
7. Courtland I. Bovee and William F. Arens, *Advertising,* 3rd ed. (Burr Ridge, IL: Richard D. Irwin, 1989).
8. *1993 Effies,* p. 6.
9. Russell H. Colley, *Defining Advertising Goals for Measured Advertising Results* (New York: Association of National Advertisers, 1961).
10. Ibid., p. 21.
11. Don E. Schultz, Dennis Martin, and William Brown, *Strategic Advertising Campaigns,* 2nd ed. (Lincolnwood, IL: Crain Books, 1984).
12. Michael L. Ray, "Consumer Initial Processing: Definitions, Issues, Applications," in *Buyer/Consumer Information Processing,* ed. G. David Hughes (Chapel Hill: University of North Carolina Press, 1974); David A. Aaker and John G. Myers, *Advertising Management,* 2nd ed. (Englewood Cliffs, NJ: Prentice Hall, 1982), pp. 122–23.
13. Sandra Ernst Moriarty, "Beyond the Hierarchy of Effects: A Conceptual Framework," in *Current Issues and Research in Advertising,* ed. Claude R. Martin, Jr., and James H. Leigh (Ann Arbor, MI: University of Michigan, 1983), pp. 45–55.
14. Aaker and Myers, *Advertising Management.*
15. Kristian S. Palda, "The Hypothesis of a Hierarchy of Effects: A Partial Evaluation," *Journal of Marketing Research* 3 (February 1966), pp. 13–24.
16. Stewart H. Britt, "Are So-Called Successful Advertising Campaigns Really Successful?" *Journal of Advertising Research* 9, no. 2 (1969), pp. 3–9.
17. Steven W. Hartley and Charles H. Patti, "Evaluating Business-to-Business Advertising: A Comparison of Objectives and Results," *Journal of Advertising Research* 28 (April/May 1988), pp. 21–27.
18. Ibid., p. 25.
19. Study cited in Robert F. Lauterborn, "How to Know If Your Advertising Is Working," *Journal of Advertising Research* 25 (February/March 1985), pp. RC 9–11.
20. Don E. Schultz, "Integration Helps You Plan Communications from Outside-In," *Marketing News,* March 15, 1993, p. 12.
21. Thomas R. Duncan, "To Fathom Integrated Marketing, Dive!" *Advertising Age,* October 11, 1993, p. 18.
22. Robert L. Steiner, "The Paradox of Increasing Returns to Advertising," *Journal of Advertising Research,* February/March 1987, pp. 45–53.
23. Frank M. Bass, "A Simultaneous Equation Regression Study of Advertising and Sales of Cigarettes," *Jour-*

nal of Marketing Research 6, no. 3 (August 1969), p. 291.
24. David A. Aaker and James M. Carman, "Are You Overadvertising?" *Journal of Advertising Research* 22, no. 4 (August/September 1982), pp. 57–70.
25. Julian A. Simon and Johan Arndt, "The Shape of the Advertising Response Function," *Journal of Advertising Research* 20, no. 4 (1980), pp. 11–28.
26. Paul B. Luchsinger, Vernan S. Mullen, and Paul T. Jannuzzo, "How Many Advertising Dollars Are Enough?" *Media Decisions* 12 (1977), p. 59.
27. Paul W. Farris, *Determinants of Advertising Intensity: A Review of the Marketing Literature* (Report no. 77–109, Marketing Science Institute, Cambridge, MA, 1977).
28. Melvin E. Salveson, "Management's Criteria for Advertising Effectiveness" (Proceedings 5th Annual Conference, Advertising Research Foundation, New York, 1959), p. 25.
29. Robert Settle and Pamela Alreck, "Positive Moves for Negative Times," *Marketing Communications,* January 1988, pp. 19–23.
30. James O. Peckham, "Can We Relate Advertising Dollars to Market Share Objectives?" in *How Much to Spend for Advertising,* ed. M. A. McNiven (New York: Association of National Advertisers, 1969), p. 30.
31. George S. Low and Jakki Mohr, "Setting Advertising and Promotion Budgets in Multi-Brand Companies," *Journal of Advertising Research,* January/February 1999, pp. 667–78.
32. "Marketers Fuel Promotion Budgets," *Marketing and Media Decisions,* September 1984, p. 130.
33. Ibid.
34. Mary Welch, "Upbeat Marketers Wield Bigger Budgets, Shift Marketing Mix," *Business Marketing,* February 1993, p. 23.
35. John P. Jones, "Ad Spending: Maintaining Market Share," *Harvard Business Review,* January/February 1990, pp. 38–42; and James C. Schroer, "Ad Spending: Growing Market Share," *Harvard Business Review,* January/February 1990, pp. 44–48.
36. Randall S. Brown, "Estimating Advantages to Large-Scale Advertising," *Review of Economics and Statistics* 60 (August 1978), pp. 428–37.
37. Kent M. Lancaster, "Are There Scale Economies in Advertising?" *Journal of Business* 59, no. 3 (1986), pp. 509–26.
38. Johan Arndt and Julian Simon, "Advertising and Economics of Scale: Critical Comments on the Evidence," *Journal of Industrial Economics* 32, no. 2 (December 1983), pp. 229–41; Aaker and Carman, "Are You Overadvertising?"
39. George S. Low and Jakki J. Mohr, "The Budget Allocation between Advertising and Sales Promotion: Understanding the Decision Process," 1991 AMA Educators' Proceedings, Chicago, Summer 1991, pp. 448–57.

Chapter Eight

1. Jeanne Whalen, "BK Caters to Franchisees with New Review," *Advertising Age,* October 25, 1993, p. 3.
2. "Burger King Corporation Unveils New Advertising, *PR Newswire,* August 4, 1999.
3. Joshua Levine, "Fizz, Fizz—Plop, Plop," *Fortune,* June 21, 1993, p. 139.
4. Jean Halliday and Alice Z. Cuneo, "Nissan Reverses Course to Focus on the Product," *Advertising Age,* February 16, 1998, pp. 1, 39.
5. Bill Abrams, "What Do Effie, Clio, Addy, Andy and Ace Have in Common?" *The Wall Street Journal,* July 15, 1983, p. 1; Jennifer Pendleton, "Awards—Creatives Defend Pursuit of Prizes," *Advertising Age,* April 25, 1988, p. 1; David Herzbrun, "The Awards Awards," *Advertising Age,* May 2, 1988, p. 18.
6. Elizabeth C. Hirschman, "Role-Based Models of Advertising Creation and Production," *Journal of Advertising* 18, no. 4 (1989), pp. 42–53.
7. Ibid., p. 51.
8. Cyndee Miller, "Study Says 'Likability' Surfaces as Measure of TV Ad Success," *Marketing News,* January 7, 1991, pp. 6, 14; and Ronald Alsop, "TV Ads That Are Likeable Get Plus Rating for Persuasiveness," *The Wall Street Journal,* February 20, 1986, p. 23
9. For an interesting discussion on the embellishment of advertising messages, see William M. Weilbacher, *Advertising,* 2nd ed. (New York: Macmillan, 1984), pp. 180–82.
10. David Ogilvy, *Confessions of an Advertising Man* (New York: Atheneum, 1963); and Hanley Norins, *The Compleat Copywriter* (New York: McGraw-Hill, 1966).
11. Hank Sneiden, *Advertising Pure and Simple* (New York: ANACOM, 1977).
12. Quoted in Valerie H. Free, "Absolut Original," *Marketing Insights,* Summer 1991, p. 65.
13. Jeff Jensen, "Marketer of the Year," *Advertising Age,* December 16, 1996, pp. 1, 16; Cathy Taylor, "Risk Takers: Wieden & Kennedy," *Adweek's Marketing Week,* March 23, 1992, pp. 26, 27.
14. Ann-Christine P. Diaz, "No Washboard Stomachs in Gym Ad," *Advertising Age,* November 1, 1999, p. 18.
15. James Webb Young, *A Technique for Producing Ideas,* 3rd ed. (Chicago: Crain Books, 1975), p. 42
16. Debra Goldman, "Origin of the Species: Has the Planner Finally Evolved into the Agency's Most Potent Creature," *Adweek,* April 10, 1995, pp. 28–38.
17. Jon Steel, *Truth, Lies & Advertising: The Art of Account Planning* (New York: Wiley, 1998).
18. Sandra E. Moriarty, *Creative Advertising. Theory and Practice* (Englewood Cliffs, NJ: Prentice Hall, 1986).
19. E. E. Norris, "Seek Out the Consumer's Problem," *Advertising Age,* March 17, 1975, pp. 43–44.
20. Kathryn Kranhold, "Agencies Beefing Up on Brand Research," *The Wall Street Journal,* March 9, 2000, p. B14.
21. Thomas L. Greenbaum, "Focus Groups Can Play a Part in Evaluating Ad Copy," *Marketing News,* September 13, 1993, pp. 24–25.
22. A. Jerome Jeweler, *Creative Strategy in Advertising,* (Belmont, CA: Wadsworth, 1981).
23. John O'Toole, *The Trouble with Advertising,* 2nd ed. (New York: Random House, 1985), p. 131.
24. David Ogilvy, *Ogilvy on Advertising* (New York: Crown, 1983), p. 16.
25. Rosser Reeves, *Reality in Advertising* (New York: Knopf, 1961), pp. 47, 48.
26. Shelly Branch and Frances A. McMorris, "Irate Firms Take Comparisons to Court," *The Wall Street Journal,* December 22, 1999, p. B8.
27. Alecia Swasy, "How Innovation at P&G Restored Luster to Washed-Up Pert and Made It No. 1," *The Wall Street Journal,* December 6, 1990, p. B1.
28. Ogilvy, *Confessions.*
29. Martin Mayer, *Madison Avenue, U.S.A.* (New York: Pocket Books, 1958).
30. Jack Trout and Al Ries, "The Positioning Era Cometh," *Advertising Age,* April 24, 1972, pp. 35–38; May 1, 1972, pp. 51–54; May 8, 1972, pp. 114–16.

31. Rajeev Batra, John G. Myers, and David A. Aaker, *Advertising Management,* 5th ed. (Upper Saddle River, NJ: Prentice Hall, 1996).
32. Anthony Vagnoni, "They Might Be Giants," *Advertising Age,* April 27, 1998, pp. 1, 20, 24.
33. Anthony Vagnoni, "Goodby, Silverstein Do 'Intelligent Work' with a Sales Pitch," *Advertising Age,* April 27, 1998, pp. 20, 24.
34. Anthony Vagnoni, "Having Ad Bosses Focus on the Work Key to Cult of Clow," *Advertising Age,* April 27, 1998, pp. 22, 24.

Chapter Nine

1. Sandra E. Moriarty, *Creative Advertising: Theory and Practice,* 2nd ed. (Englewood Cliffs, NJ: Prentice Hall, 1991), p. 76.
2. William M. Weilbacher, *Advertising,* 2nd ed. (New York: Macmillan, 1984), p. 197.
3. William Wells, John Burnett, and Sandra Moriarty, *Advertising* (Englewood Cliffs, NJ: Prentice Hall, 1989), p. 330.
4. Stuart J. Agres, "Emotion in Advertising: An Agency Point of View," in *Emotion in Advertising: Theoretical and Practical Explanations,* ed. Stuart J. Agres, Julie A. Edell, and Tony M. Dubitsky (Westport, CT: Quorom Books, 1991).
5. Edward Kamp and Deborah J. Macinnis, "Characteristics of Portrayed Emotions in Commercials: When Does What Is Shown in Ads Affect Viewers?" *Journal of Advertising Research,* November/December 1995, pp. 19–28.
6. For a review of research on the effect of mood states on consumer behavior, see Meryl Paula Gardner, "Mood States and Consumer Behavior: A Critical Review," *Journal of Consumer Research* 12, no. 3 (December 1985), pp. 281–300.
7. Cathy Madison, "Researchers Work Advertising into an Emotional State," *Adweek,* November 5, 1990, p. 30.
8. Louise Kramer, "McDonald's Ad Goal: 'Touch People,'" *Advertising Age,* November 15, 1999, p. 22.
9. Christopher P. Puto and William D. Wells, "Informational and Transformational Advertising: The Different Effects of Time," in *Advances in Consumer Research,* Vol. 11, ed. Thomas C. Kinnear (Ann Arbor, MI: Association for Consumer Research, 1984), p. 638.
10. Ibid.
11. David Ogilvy and Joel Raphaelson, "Research on Advertising Techniques That Work and Don't Work," *Harvard Business Review,* July/August 1982, p. 18.
12. *Topline,* no. 4 (September 1989), McCann-Erickson, New York.
13. Eric Schmuckler, "Plan of the Year: Best Campaign Spending between $10 Million and $25 Million," *MediaWeek,* May 24, 1999.
14. Dottie Enrico, "Teaser Ads Grab Spotlight on Madison Ave.," *USA Today,* July 6, 1995, pp.1, 2B.
15. "Infiniti Ads Trigger Auto Debate," *Advertising Age,* January 22, 1990, p. 49.
16. Quote by Irwin Warren, cited in Enrico, "Teaser Ads Grab Spotlight."
17. Martin Mayer, *Madison Avenue, U.S.A.* (New York: Pocket Books, 1958), p. 64.
18. Sally Beatty, "P&G to Ad Agencies: Please Rewrite Our Old Formulas," *The Wall Street Journal,* November 5, 1998, pp. B1, 10; Alecia Swasy, "P&G Tries Bolder Ads—With Caution," *The Wall Street Journal,* May 7, 1990, pp. B1, 7.
19. *A Celebration of Effective Advertising: 30 Years of Winning EFFIE Campaigns* (New York: American Marketing Association, 1999), pp. 30–33.
20. Lynn Coleman, "Advertisers Put Fear into the Hearts of Their Prospects," *Marketing News,* August 15, 1988, p. 1.
21. Kevin Goldman, "Chips Ahoy! Ad Uses Spin on Claymation," *The Wall Street Journal,* February 9, 1994, p. B5.
22. Judann Pollack, "Charlie Rejoins Frenzied Tuna Wars," *Advertising Age,* May 31, 1999, p. 32.
23. Marla Matzer, "Alcohol Activists Want to Cage Bud's Lizards," *Los Angeles Times,* May 5, 1998, pp. D1, 17.
24. Barbara B. Stern, "Classical and Vignette Television Advertising: Structural Models, Formal Analysis, and Consumer Effects," *Journal of Consumer Research* 20, no. 4 (March 1994), pp. 601–15; and John Deighton, Daniel Romer, and Josh McQueen, "Using Drama to Persuade," *Journal of Consumer Research* 15, no. 3 (December 1989), pp. 335–43.
25. Moriarty, *Creative Advertising,* p. 77.
26. William F. Arens, *Contemporary Advertising,* 6th ed. (Burr Ridge, IL: Irwin/McGraw-Hill, 1998), p. 284.
27. W. Keith Hafer and Gordon E. White, *Advertising Writing,* 3rd ed. (St. Paul, MN: West Publishing, 1989), p. 98.
28. Carol Marie Cooper, "Who Says Talk Is Cheap," *New York Times,* October 22, 1998, pp. C1, 5; and Wendy Brandes, "Star Power Leaves Some Voice-Over Artists Speechless," *The Wall Street Journal,* June 2, 1995, p. B6.
29. Linda M. Scott, "Understanding Jingles and Needledrop: A Rhetorical Approach to Music in Advertising," *Journal of Consumer Research* 17, no. 2 (September 1990), pp. 223–36.
30. Ibid., p. 223.
31. Russell I. Haley, Jack Richardson, and Beth Baldwin, "The Effects of Nonverbal Communications in Television Advertising," *Journal of Advertising Research* 24, no. 4, pp. 11–18.
32. Gerald J. Gorn, "The Effects of Music in Advertising on Choice Behavior: A Classical Conditioning Approach," *Journal of Marketing* 46 (Winter 1982), pp. 94–100.
33. "A Few Rockers Give Ad Makers No Satisfaction," *The Wall Street Journal,* August 25, 1995, p. B1.
34. Stephanie N. Mehta, "Northern Telecom Plays Down Phone Roots, Embraces 'I Word,'" *The Wall Street Journal,* April 14, 1999, p. B10.
35. Stephanie Thompson, "Promotions: Nostalgia Bolognese," *Brandweek,* April 14, 1997.
36. Eleftheria Parpis, "Creative: Best Campaign," *Adweek,* January 24, 2000, p. 1.
37. Beatty, "P&G to Ad Agencies."
38. Eva Pomice, "Madison Avenue's Blind Spot," *U.S. News & World Report,* October 3, 1988, p. 49.
39. Bruce Horowitz, "TV Spots for Light Bulbs, Diet Pepsi This Year's Big Clio Award Winners," *Los Angeles Times,* June 21, 1988, pt. IV, p. 6.
40. Bob Garfield, "1999—the Year in Ad Review," *Advertising Age,* December 20, 1999, pp. 18, 20; Alice Z. Cuneo, "Can an Agency Be Guilty of Malpractice?" *Advertising Age,* January 31, 2000, pp. 24, 25.

Chapter Ten

1. John P Cortez, "Flowers Flourish through Interactive Media," *Advertising Age,* July 12, 1993, p. 12.
2. Patricia Sellers, "The Best Way to Reach Buyers," *Fortune,* Autumn/Winter 1993, pp. 14–17.
3. Chuck Ross, "Study Finds for Continuity vs. Flights," *Advertising Age,* April 19, 1999, p. 2.

4. Michael J. Naples, *Effective Frequency: The Relationship between Frequency and Advertising Effectiveness* (New York: Association of National Advertisers, 1979).
5. Joseph W. Ostrow, "Setting Frequency Levels: An Art or a Science?" *Journal of Advertising Research* 24 (August/September 1984), pp. i9–11.
6. David Berger, "How Much to Spend" (Foote, Cone & Belding Internal Report), in Michael L. Rothschild, *Advertising* (Lexington, MA: Heath, 1987), p. 468.
7. David W. Olson, "Real World Measures of Advertising Effectiveness for New Products," speech to the 26th Annual Conference of the Advertising Research Foundation, New York, March 18, 1980.
8. Naples, *Effective Frequency.*
9. Joseph W. Ostrow, "What Level Frequency?" *Advertising Age,* November 1981, pp. 13–18.
10. Jack Myers, "More Is Indeed Better," *Media Week,* September 6, 1993, pp. 14–18; and Jim Surmanek, "One-Hit or Miss: Is a Frequency of One Frequently Wrong?" *Advertising Age,* November 27, 1995, p. 46.
11. Ostrow, "What Level Frequency?"
12. Louisa Ha, "Media Models and Advertising Effects: Conceptualization and Theoretical Implications," *Journal of Current Issues and Research in Advertising,* Fall 1995, pp. 1–15.
13. Ibid.
14. Erwin Ephron, "Meet TV Planning's Whiz-Kid Brother," Television Bureau of Advertising, New York, NY, 1999, pp. 1–6.

Chapter Eleven

1. *Radio Marketing Guide and Fact Book for Advertisers,* Fall 1999 to Spring 2000 (New York: Radio Advertising Bureau, 1999).
2. *2000 Report on Television* (New York: Nielsen Media Research).
3. *Trends in Television* (New York: Television Bureau of Advertising, 1999).
4. Lex van Meurs, "Zapp! A Study on Switching Behavior during Commercial Breaks," *Journal of Advertising Research* January/February 1998, pp. 43–53; John J. Cronin, "In-Home Observations of Commercial Zapping Behavior," *Journal of Current Issues and Research in Advertising* 17, no. 2 (Fall 1995), pp. 69–75.
5. Laura Petrecca, "4A's: Production Costs for TV Spots Up by 6%," *Advertising Age,* August 18, 1997, p. 30.
6. Bruce Horovitz, "More Advertisers Are Tailoring TV Spots to Ethnicity of Viewers," *Los Angeles Times,* May 3, 1994, pp. D1, 3.
7. Chuck Ross, "TV Commercial Clutter Has Ad Buyers Worried," *Advertising Age,* December 6, 1999, p. 77.
8. Joe Flint, "Commercial Clutter on TV Networks Rises to Record," *The Wall Street Journal,* March 2, 2000, p. B18.
9. Dennis Kneal, "Zapping of TV Ads Appears Pervasive," *The Wall Street Journal,* April 25, 1988, p. 27.
10. John J. Cronin and Nancy Menelly, "Discrimination vs. Avoidance: 'Zipping' of Television Commercials," *Journal of Advertising* 21, no. 2 (June 1992), pp. 1–7.
11. Cronin, "In-Home Observations of Commercial Zapping Behavior."
12. Carrie Heeter and Bradley S. Greenberg, "Profiling the Zappers," *Journal of Advertising Research,* April/May 1985, pp. 9–12; Fred S. Zufryden, James H. Pedrick, and Avu Sandaralingham, "Zapping and Its Impact on Brand Purchase Behavior," *Journal of Advertising Research* 33 (January/February 1993), pp. 58–66; and Patricia Orsini, "Zapping: A Man's World," Spring Television Report, *Adweek's Marketing Week,* April 8, 1991, p. 3.
13. Lex van Meurs, "Zapp! A Study on Switching Behavior during Commercial Breaks," *Journal of Advertising Research,* January/February 1998, pp. 43–53.
14. Linda F. Alwitt and Parul R. Prabhaker, "Identifying Who Dislikes Television Advertising: Not by Demographics Alone," *Journal of Advertising Research* 32, no. 5 (1992), pp. 30–42.
15. Banwari Mittal, "Public Assessment of TV Advertising: Faint Praise and Harsh Criticism," *Journal of Advertising Research* no. 34, 1 (1994), pp. 35–53; Ernest F. Larkin, "Consumer Perceptions of the Media and Their Advertising Content," *Journal of Advertising* 8 (1979), pp. 5–7.
16. Lucy L. Henke, "Young Children's Perceptions of Cigarette Brand Advertising Symbols: Awareness, Affect, and Target Market Identification," *Journal of Advertising* 24, no. 4 (Winter 1995), pp. 13–28.
17. Joe Mandese, "Prime-Time Pricing Woes," *Advertising Age,* September 20, 1999, pp. 1, 12, 16.
18. "And Now, a Show from Your Sponsor," *Business Week,* May 22, 1995, pp. 100–102.
19. *2000 Cable TV Facts* (New York: Cable Advertising Bureau, 2000).
20. Sally Goll Beatty, "MSNBC Already Waging Marketing War," *The Wall Street Journal,* July 9, 1996, p. B8.
21. Leslie Cauley, "Buyers Turn to Cable as Ratings Gap Slims," *The Wall Street Journal,* October 5, 1998, p. B7.
22. Leslie Cauley, "Cable-TV Firms Pledge a Tight Rein on Price Increases," *The Wall Street Journal,* April 1, 1999, p. B12.
23. Kathy Chen, "Measure to Let Satellite TV Air Network Fare," *The Wall Street Journal,* November 22, 1999, p. B8.
24. Gary Levin, "Arbitron Exits from Ratings Race," *Advertising Age,* October 25, 1993, p. 4.
25. Chuck Ross, "Nielsen Defends Research Showing Drop in Key Demo," *Advertising Age,* January 18, 1999, pp. 3, 48; Elizabeth Jensen, "Networks Blast Nielsen, Blame Faulty Ratings for Drop in Viewership," *The Wall Street Journal,* November 22, 1996, pp. A1, 10.
26. David J. Wallace, "Changes at Oft-Maligned Nielsen," *Advertising Age,* July 22, 1996, p. S16.
27. Chuck Ross, "Nielsen Explores Switch to Continuous Measurement," *Advertising Age,* April 8, 1996, p. 10.
28. Chuck Ross, "Nielsen Out to Expand People Meters," *Advertising Age,* January 11, 1999, pp. 3, 40.
29. Chuck Ross, "Nielsen Readies Local Meters for Tryout in Boston," *Advertising Age,* December 6, 1999, p. 2.
30. David J. Wallace, "High Hopes for Smart Rating Service, but Promises Need to Be Fulfilled," *Advertising Age,* July 22, 1996, p. S16.
31. Chuck Ross, "Smart Demise Marks Setback for Nets, Shops," *Advertising Age,* May 31, 1999, pp. 3, 72.
32. "Nielsen Critics Collapse Again, *Advertising Age,* June 7, 1999, p. 22.
33. *Radio Marketing Guide and Fact Book.*
34. Ibid.
35. Suein L. Hwang, "Old Media Get a Web Windfall," *The Wall Street Journal,* September 17, 1999, p. B1.
36. Verne Gay, "Image Transfer: Radio Ads Make Aural History," *Advertising Age,* January 24, 1985, p. 1.
37. Avery Abernethy, "Differences Between Advertising and Program Exposure for Car Radio Listening," *Journal of Advertising Research* 31, no. 2 (April/May 1991), pp. 33–42.

38. Martin Peers, "Radio Produces Both Gains and Skeptics," *The Wall Street Journal,* January 1, 1999, p. B6.
39. Ibid.
40. Warren Cohen, "Radio Plays New Tricks," *U.S. News & World Report,* January 1, 2000, p. 42.
41. Katy Bachman, "Ratings Giants in Turf war," *Mediaweek,* February 15, 1999, p. 12.
42. Katy Bachman, "Radio/A New Ratings Stream," *Mediaweek,* December 13, 1999, p. 8.

Chapter Twelve

1. Herbert E. Krugman, "The Measurement of Advertising Involvement," *Public Opinion Quarterly* 30 (Winter 1966–67), pp. 583–96.
2. *The Magazine Handbook* (New York: Magazine Publishers of America, 1999).
3. Ann Marie Kerwin, "Sports Spawns Most Magazines," *Advertising Age,* January 10, 2000, p. 42.
4. Ann-Christine P. Diaz, "Weider Spinoff Targets Women Weight Lifters," *Advertising Age,* November 8, 1999, p. 22.
5. Scott Donaton and Pat Sloan, "Ad 'Printaculars' under Scrutiny," *Advertising Age,* February 12, 1990, p. 3.
6. *The Magazine Handbook.*
7. Ibid.
8. Steve Fajen, "Numbers Aren't Everything," *Media Decisions* 10 (June 1975), pp. 65–69.
9. *A Study of Media Involvement,* Vol. 7 (New York: Magazine Publishers of America, 1996).
10. Ibid.
11. *The Magazine Handbook.*
12. Christine Larson, "Made to Order," *Adweek,* October 25, 1999, pp. 64–70.
13. Sally Goll Beatty, "Philip Morris Starts Lifestyle Magazine," *The Wall Street Journal,* September 16, 1996, pp. B1, 8.
14. Study cited in Jim Surmanek, *Media Planning: A Practical Guide* (Lincolnwood, IL: Crain Books, 1985).
15. *How Advertising Readership Is Influenced by Ad Size,* Report no. 110.1, Cahners Advertising Research, Newton, MA; and *Larger Advertisements Get Higher Readership,* LAP Report no. 3102, McGraw-Hill Research, New York.
16. *Effect of Size, Color and Position on Number of Responses to Recruitment Advertising,* LAP Report no. 3116, McGraw-Hill Research, New York.
17. Ann-Christine Diaz, "Dot-Com Ads Help Power 5.2% Magazine Page Rise," *Advertising Age,* January 17, 2000, p. 48.
18. Matthew Rose, "In Print, a Shower of Dot-Com Ads," *The Wall Street Journal,* September 17, 1999, pp. B1, 4.
19. Ann Marie Kerwin, "MPA Members Aghast at Looming Postal Hike," *Advertising Age,* November 1, 1999, p. 66.
20. Carol Krol, "'Yahoo! Internet Life' Finds Real Success in Virtual World," *Advertising Age,* March 8, 1999, p. S8.
21. Ann Marie Kerwin, "Magazine Study Links Circ Woes to Sweepstakes Fall," *Advertising Age,* November 8, 1999, p. 3.
22. Sheree R. Curry, "A Blessing in Disguise," *Advertising Age,* October 25, 1999, pp. S2, 20.
23. Matthew Rose, "Deal May Help Magazines Add Subscribers," *The Wall Street Journal,* January 11, 1999, p. B8.
24. Richar Siklos and Catherine Yang, "Welcome to the 21st Century," *Business Week,* January 24, 2000, pp. 37–44.
25. *The Magazine Handbook.*
26. Junu Bryan Kim, "Cracking the Barrier of Two Dimensions," *Advertising Age,* October 6, 1991, pp. 32, 34.
27. *Facts about Newspapers 1999* (Vienna, VA: Newspaper Assocation of America, 1999).
28. Ann Marie Kerwin, "After a Long Lobbying Effort, 'New York Times' Wins New Ad Status," *Advertising Age,* February 22, 1999, p. 24.
29. Ann Marie Kerwin, "Big-City Dailies Eye National Stage," *Advertising Age,* February 22, 1999, p. 24.
30. Hanna Liebman, "NAA Network Ready to Roll," *Mediaweek,* December 13, 1993, p. 18.
31. Tony Case, "Reading the Numbers," *Mediaweek,* September 20, 1999, p. 64.
32. Robert Coen, *Insider's Report: Robert Coen Presentation on Advertising Expenditures* (New York: McCann-Erickson Worldwide, June 1999).
33. Michele Marchetti, "Extras!" *Sales and Marketing Management,* March 1996, pp. 56–61.
34. Studies cited in *Facts About Newspapers 1999.*
35. "Brandy, Bon Jovi, Barbara Bush, Elway, Hill and Streep Return for Fourth Flight of NAA National Ad Campaign," news release, Newspaper Association of America, 1999 (www.naa.org).
36. Bruce Bigelow, "Newspapers Plot Ways to End Slide in Readership," *San Diego Union-Tribune,* April 27, 1999, pp. C1, 5; "Newspaper Readership Initiative Information Site," www.naa.org/readership.
37. Ann Marie Kerwin, "Print's Power Play," *Advertising Age: The Next Century,* special issue, 1999.

Chapter Thirteen

1. "OAAA Special Report" (New York: Outdoor Advertising Association of America, 2000).
2. Ira Teinowitz, "Supreme Court's Inaction Opens Way for Outdoor Bans," *Advertising Age,* May 5, 1997, p. 58.
3. Maritz AmeriPoll, August 1998.
4. *Adweek,* August 25, 1997, p. 3.
5. Mukesh Bhargava and Naveen Donthu, "Sales Response to Outdoor Advertising," *Journal of Advertising Research,* August 1999, pp. 7–18.
6. Denise Henry, "Appeals on Wheels," *Business 99,* April/May 1999, pp. 28–31.
7. Amanda Beeter, "New Audit Gauges Impact of Truck-Side Advertising," *Advertising Age,* January 10, 2000, p. 43.
8. David Kalish, "Supermarket Sweepstakes," *Marketing & Media Decisions,* November 1988, p. 34.
9. Adam Snyder, "Outdoor Forecast: Sunny, Some Clouds," *Adweek's Marketing Week,* July 8, 1991, pp. 18–19.
10. Laurie Freeman and Alison Fahey, "Package Goods Ride with Transit," *Advertising Age,* April 23, 1990, p. 28.
11. *Advertisers Take the City Bus to Work* (New York: Winston Network, 1988), p. 13.
12. American Public Transit Authority, 2000 (www.apta.com).
13. Promotional Products Association International (Irving, TX), 1996.
14. Promotional Products Association International, 2000.
15. George L. Herpel and Steve Slack, *Specialty Advertising: New Dimensions in Creative Marketing* (Irving, TX: Specialty Advertising Association, 1983), pp. 76, 79–80.
16. Ibid., p. 78.
17. M. J. Caballero and J. B. Hunt, *Smilin' Jack: Measuring Goodwill,* unpublished research report from the Center for Professional Selling, Baylor University, 1989; M. J. Cooper

and J. B. Hunt, *How Specialty Advertising Affects Goodwill,* research report of Specialty Advertising Association International (now PPAI), Irving, TX, 1992.
18. George L. Herpel and Steve Slack, *Specialty Advertising: New Dimensions in Creative Marketing* (Irving, TX: Specialty Advertising Association, 1983), p. 75.
19. Yellow Pages Publishers Association, 2000.
20. Carol Hall, "Branding the Yellow Pages," *Marketing & Media Decisions,* April 1989, p. 59.
21. Ibid., p. 3.
22. Ibid.
23. Ibid., p. 5.
24. Ibid.
25. Yellow Pages Publishers Association, 2000.
26. Ibid., p. 8.
27. Joel J. Davis, *Understanding Yellow Pages* (Troy, MI: Yellow Pages Publishers Association, 1995).
28. Adam Snyder, "Are Spots on Home Video Badvertising?" *Brandweek,* January 29, 1996, p. 40.
29. Scott Hume, "Consumers Pan Ads on Video Movies," *Advertising Age,* May 28, 1990, p. 8.
30. Joanne Lipman and Kathleen A. Hughes, "Disney Prohibits Ads in Theaters Showing Its Movies," *The Wall Street Journal,* February 9, 1990, p. B1.
31. Snyder, "Are Spots on Home Video Badvertising?"
32. Ibid.
33. Motion Picture Association of America, 1999.
34. Betsy Baurer, "New Quick Flicks: Ads at the Movies," *USA Today,* March 13, 1986, p. D1.
35. Ibid.
36. Michael A. Belch and Don Sciglimpaglia, "Viewers' Evaluations of Cinema Advertising," Proceedings of the American Institute for Decision Sciences, March 1979, pp. 39–43.
37. Snyder, "Are Spots on Home Video Badvertising?"
38. Alice Cuneo, "Now Playing: Gap, Target Take Retail to the Movies," *Advertising Age,* June 9, 1997, p. 14.
39. "Hershey Befriends Extra-Terrestrial," *Advertising Age,* July 19, 1982, p. 1.
40. J. D. Reed, "Plugging Away in Hollywood," *Time,* January 2, 1998, p. 103.
41. Damon Darlin, "Highbrow Hype," *Forbes,* April 12, 1993, pp. 126–27.
42. Pola Gupta and Kenneth Lord, "Product Placement in Movies: The Effect of Prominence and Mode on Audience Recall," *Journal of Current Issues and Research in Advertising* 20, no. 1 (Spring 1998), pp. 1–29.
43. Pola B. Gupta and Stephen J. Gould, "Consumers' Perceptions of the Ethics and Acceptability of Product Placements in Movies: Product Category and Individual Differences," *Journal of Current Issues and Research in Advertising* 19, no. 1 (Spring 1997), pp. 40–49.
44. Randall Rothenberg, "Is It a Film? Is It an Ad? Harder to Tell," *The New York Times,* March 13, 1990, p. D23.
45. Laurie Mazur, "Screenland's Dirty Little Secret," *E* magazine, May/June 1996, p. 38.
46. "Consumer Products Become Movie Stars," *The Wall Street Journal,* February 29, 1988, p. 23.
47. Damon Darlin, "Highbrow Hype," *Forbes,* April 12, 1993, pp. 126–27.
48. *Hemispheres* magazine, 2000.
49. Jennifer Lawrence, "In-Flight Gets above Turbulence," *Advertising Age,* August 19, 1991, p. 32.
50. Ibid.
51. Joann S. Lublin, "In-Flight TV Commercials Are Booming," *The Wall Street Journal* September 19, 1990, p. B6.
52. Ira Teinowitz, "Channel One Criticized as 'Crass Commercialism,'" *Advertising Age,* May 21, 1999, p. 2.
53. Dean Takahashi, "Intel Plans a Major Blitz through Kiosks," *The Wall Street Journal,* August 30, 1996, p. B2.

Chapter Fourteen

1. Stan Rapp and Thomas I. Collins, *Maximarketing* (New York: McGraw-Hill, 1987).
2. Peter D. Bennett, ed., *Dictionary of Marketing Terms* (Chicago: American Marketing Association, 1988), p. 58.
3. *Direct Marketing Association Economic Impact,* 2000. (New York: Direct Marketing Association, 2000).
4. *Federal Reserve Bulletin—Annual Statistical Digest,* 1993, p. 516.
5. Jagdish N. Sheth, "Marketing Megatrends," *Journal of Consumer Marketing* 1, no. 1 (June 1983), pp. 5–13.
6. "Ladies First," *Life Insurance International,* August 31, 1999, www.Ads.com.
7. " A 15.6 Billion Home Shopping Spree by 2006," *Response TV,* December 1997, www.Ads.com.
8. William Dunn, "Pushing the Envelope," *Marketing Tools,* September 1995, pp. 20–23.
9. "Direct Mail by the Numbers," U.S. Postal Service, 1999.
10. "A Potent New Tool for Selling: Database Marketing," *Business Week,* September 5, 1994, pp. 56–59.
11. Herbert Kanzenstein and William S. Sachs, *Direct Marketing,* 2nd ed. (New York: Macmillan, 1992).
12. "Direct Mail by the Numbers."
13. *Direct Marketing Association Economic Impact,* 2000.
14. Ibid.
15. Ibid.
16. Cleveland Horton, "Porsche 300,000: The New Elite," *Advertising Age,* February 5, 1990, p. 8.
17. Jean Halliday, "Hyundai Fuels Up Heftier Direct Mail; New Funds Support Quarterly Efforts," *Advertising Age,* March 29, 1999, p. 54.
18. *Direct Marketing Association Economic Impact,* 2000.
19. Patricia O'Dell, "Mail's Last Call?" *Direct,* January 2000, pp. 63–64.
20. *Direct Marketing Association, 2000.*
21. Elaine Underwood, "Is There a Future for the TV Mall?" *Brandweek,* March 25, 1996, pp. 24–26.
22. *Direct Marketing Association, 2000.*
23. "Average Sales Figures for Infomercial products," *Response Magazine,* September 1999.
24. Chad Rubel, "Infomercials Evolve as Major Firms Join Successful Format," *Marketing News,* January 2, 1995, p. 1.
25. Anne-Marie Crawford, "Peugeot Develops First TV Advertorials for Cars," *Marketing,* December 9, 1999, p. 9.
26. "A 15.6 Billion Home Shopping Spree by 2006."
27. Underwood, "Is There a Future for the TV Mall?"
28. *Direct Marketing Association, 2000.*
29. *Direct Marketing Association, 2000.*
30. Ibid.
31. Ibid.
32. Ibid.
33. Tom Eisenhart, "Tele-media: Marketing's New Dimension," *Business Marketing,* February 1991, pp. 50–53.
34. *Direct Marketing Association 2000.*
35. Dana Blakenhorn, "Infomercial Sire Is QVC Leverages Its TV Brand," *Advertising Age,* March 1998, www.AdAge.com.
36. Bob Howard, "Successful K-Tel TV Strategy Doesn't Translate to Net," *Los Angeles Times,* January 31, 2000, p. C1.
37. Direct Selling Association, 2000, www.DSA.com.

38. Paul Hughes, "Profits Due," *Entrepreneur,* February 1994, pp. 74–78.
39. Patricia O'Dell, "Mail's Last Call?" *Direct,* January 2000, pp. 63–64.
40. "Bear Market," *Direct,* December 1999, p. 1+.

Chapter Fifteen

1. "Life on Campus: More Than Half of College Students Surf the Internet from Their Room," *Media Center,* August 25, 1999.
2. "Who's Online," *Business 2.0,* January 2000, p. 251
3. "The Lifestyles of Online Shoppers," www.cyberatlas.com, 2000.
4. Ibid.
5. Ibid.
6. Alexis Thomas, "Cyber Dialogue Study Shows U.S. Internet Growth Slowing," www.individual.com, December 1, 1999.
7. Michael Pastore, "Slowdown in Online as Growth Predicted," *Internet News.com,* December 9, 1999.
8. Cecile B. Corral, "Clicks & Mortar: Category Leaders in Cyber Retailing," *Discount Store News,* December 13, 1999, pp. 10–13.
9. Tom Hyland, "Web Advertising: A Year of Growth," Internet Advertising Bureau, February 9, 2000, pp. 1–4.
10. Michael Shirer, "eMarket Places Will Lead U.S. Business eCommerce to $2.7 Trillion in 2004, According to Forrester," www.individual.com, February 8, 2000.
11. Laurie Freeman, "HP Gambles $100 M on Securing Its Net Position," *Business Marketing,* June 1999, pp. 1+.
12. Melinda Ligos, "Point, Click, Sell," *Sales and Marketing Management,* May 1999, pp. 51–55.
13. Ibid.
14. William Holstein, "Let Them Have PC's," *U.S. News & World Report,* February 14, 2000.
15. "Life on Campus."
16. Lisa Hamm-Greenwalt, "Brokers Who Traffic in Eyeballs: What Advertising Networks Do and How to Approach Them," *Internet World,* December 15, 1999, pp. 1–4.
17. *Internet News,* December 14, 1999.
18. Kipp Cheng, "Online Ads on Superbowl.com: The Good, the Bad, and the Ugly," *Adweek,* February 7, 2000, pp. 52–54.
19. Kathryn Kranhold, "Banner Ads Are Driving Web Purchases," *The Wall Street Journal,* November 24, 1999, p. B9; and Beth Cox, "Peapod: Online Ads Yielding Up to 30% CTR," *Internet News.com,* April 16, 1999, p. 12.
20. "Online Media Strategies for Advertising," Internet Advertising Bureau, Spring 1999.
21. Helen D'Antoni, "NPD Online Research Finds More Individuals Are Pointing and Clipping with Online Coupons," www.individual.com, November 11, 1999.
22. Pamela Parker, "Webstakes, TKAI, Partner to Take Online Promotions to Japan," www.individual.com, February 2, 2000.
23. Chad Kaydo, "You've Got Sales," *Sales and Marketing Management,* October 1999, pp. 29–39.
24. Sean Donahue, "Hassle-Free Philanthropy," *Business 2.0,* October 1999, pp. 47–51.
25. Pamela Parker, "Direct E-Mail Promotions Best at Attracting Buyers," *Internet News.com,* December 22, 1999.
26. *Business Wire,* August 26, 1999, p. 1.
27. Ligos, "Point, Click, Sell."
28. Quentin Hardy, "Window Shopping," *Forbes,* January 24, 2000, p. 62.
29. Ellen Neuborne and Robert D. Hof, "Branding on the Net," *Business Week,* November 9, 1998, pp. 76–86.
30. Alexa Bezjian-Avery, "New Media Interactive Advertising vs. Traditional Advertising," *Journal of Advertising Research,* August 1998, pp. 23–32; Qimel Chen and William D. Wells, "Attitude toward the Site," *Journal of Advertising Research,* September 1999, pp. 27–38; Kim Bartel Sheehan and Sally J. McMillan, "Response Variation in E-Mail Surveys," *Journal of Advertising Research,* July 1999, pp. 45–54; and John Eighmey, "Profiling User Responses to Commercial Websites," *Journal of Advertising Research,* May 1997, pp. 59–66.
31. Leslie Singer, "NPD Study Finds Internet Users Multi-tasking during the Superbowl," www.individual.com, February 9, 2000.
32. San Brekke, "Jumpin' Jupiter," *Business 2.0,* October 1999, pp. 154–61.
33. Joseph Menn, "Web Firms May Vastly Inflate Claims of 'Hits'," *Los Angeles Times,* April 17, 2000, pp. 1–8.
34. Beth Cox, "Top 50 Web Sites Get 95 Percent of All Ad Dollars," *Internet News.com,* June 17, 1999.
35. Ben Hammer, "Interactive TV Takes Manhattan," *The Standard,* April 14, 2000, pp. 1–2.
36. Teresa Buyikan and Angela Dawson, "Dropping RPA, Web TV Puts Account in Play—Adweek," *Adweek.com,* May 10, 1999.
37. Partick Seitz, "Open TV Eyes an Opening in Interactive TV Market," *Investors Business Daily,* February 10, 2000, p. A6.

Chapter Sixteen

1. Louis J. Haugh, "Defining and Redefining," *Advertising Age,* February 14, 1983, p. M44.
2. Scott A. Nielsen, John Quelch, and Caroline Henderson, "Consumer Promotions and the Acceleration of Product Purchases," in *Research on Sales Promotion: Collected Papers,* ed. Katherine E. Jocz (Cambridge, MA: Marketing Science Institute, 1984).
3. J. Jeffrey Inman and Leigh McAlister, "Do Coupon Expiration Dates Affect Consumer Behavior?" *Journal of Marketing Research* 31, August 1994, pp. 423–28.
4. "Promotion Trends 2000," *Promo Magazine,* May 2000, p. A5.
5. Richard Sale, "Evaluation in Evolution," *Promo Magazine,* September 1998, pp. 63–68.
6. Richard Sale, "Attack," *Promo Magazine,* September 1999, pp. 79–84.
7. "The Effects of Promotion Stimuli on Consumer Purchase Behavior" (Glenview, IL: FSI Council, 1999).
8. "1996 Trend Report," Actmedia, Inc., Anaheim, CA.
9. Leigh McAlister, "A Model of Consumer Behavior," *Marketing Communications,* April 1987.
10. Study cited in "Make It Simple," *Business Week,* September 9, 1996, p. 98.
11. Betsy Spethmann, "Trading Newsprint for Pepperoni," *Promo Magazine,* August 1999, pp. 51–52.
12. Betsy Spethmann, "Here Comes the Neighborhood," *Promo Magazine,* January 1997, pp. 51–58.
13. Al Urbanski, "Techno Promo," *Promo Magazine,* August 1998, pp. 48–52, 146, 147.
14. Richard Gibson, "How Products Check Out Helps Determine Pay," *The Wall Street Journal,* August 1, 1991, p. B1.
15. Betsy Spethmann, "Account Specific Comes Due," *Promo Magazine,* November 1996, pp. 39–48.
16. *NCH Reporter,* no. 1 (Nielsen Clearing House, 1983).
17. *The Magazine Handbook,* no. 59 (New York: Magazine Publishers of America, 1991).

18. Judann Dagnoli, "Jordan Hits Ad Execs for Damaging Brands," *Advertising Age,* November 4, 1991, p. 47.
19. Judan Pollack, "Heinz to Pare Products While It Boosts Ads," *Advertising Age,* March 3, 1997, pp. 3, 37.
20. Judann Pollack, "Charlie Rejoins Frenzied Tuna Wars," *Advertising Age,* May 31, 1999, p. 32.
21. R. M. Prentice, "How to Split Your Marketing Funds Between Advertising and Promotion Dollars," *Advertising Age,* January 10, 1977, pp. 41–42, 44.
22. Betsy Spethmann, "Money and Power," *Brandweek,* March 15, 1993, p. 21.
23. Quote by Vincent Sottosanti, president of Council of Sales Promotion Agencies, in "Promotions That Build Brand Image," *Marketing Communications,* April 1988, p. 54.
24. "Calling All Shoppers," *Promo Magazine,* Special Report, April 1998, pp. S5, 6.
25. Reference cited in John P. Rossiter and Larry Percy, *Advertising and Promotion Management* (New York: McGraw-Hill, 1987), p. 360.
26. Peter Breen, "Sophisticated Sampling," *Promo Magazine,* September 1999, pp. 63–68.
27. Glenn Heitsmith, "Something for Nothing," *Promo Magazine,* September 1993, pp. 30–36.
28. *Worldwide Coupon Distribution & Redemption Trends,* (Lincolnshire, IL: NCH Promotional Services, 1999).
29. J. Jeffrey Inman and Leigh McAlister, "Do Coupon Expiration Dates Affect Consumer Behavior?"
30. Regina Eisman, "The Cutting Edge of Coupon Fraud," *Incentive,* January 1991, p. 40.
31. Raju Narisetti, "Many Companies Are Starting to Wean Consumers Off Coupons," *The Wall Street Journal,* January 22, 1997, pp. B1, 10.
32. "First Green Stamps, Now Coupons," *Business Week,* April 22, 1996, p. 68.
33. Betsy Spethmann, "A Wake-Up Call at Breakfastime," *Promo Magazine,* December 1996, pp. 27–28.
34. Jack Neff, "P&G Extends Co-branded Coupons," *Advertising Age,* June 3, 1996, p. 9.
35. Robert Storace, "Bringing Online in Line," *Promo Magazine,* April 1998, pp. 54–56, 155–56.
36. Richard Sale, "Not Your Mother's Coupon," *Promo Magazine,* April 1999, pp. 56–61.
37. Survey by Oxtoby-Smith, Inc., cited in "Many Consumers View Rebates as a Bother," *The Wall Street Journal,* April 13, 1989, p. B1.
38. William R. Dean, "Irresistable but Not Free of Problems," *Advertising Age,* October 6, 1980, pp. S1–12.
39. Eric Schmuckler, "Two Action Figures to Go, Hold the Burger," *Brandweek,* April 1, 1996, pp. 38–39.
40. "Mickey May Be the Big Winner in Disney–McDonald's Alliance," *The Wall Street Journal,* May 24, 1996, p. B5.
41. Louise Kramer, "McD's Steals Another Toy from BK," *Advertising Age,* November 15, 1999, pp. 1, 74.
42. "In Wake of Second Death, CPSC and Burger King Again Urge Consumers to Destroy and Discard Pokemon Balls," Burger King Press Release, January 27, 2000.
43. William A. Robinson, "What Are Promos' Weak and Strong Points?" *Advertising Age,* April 7, 1980, p. 54.
44. "Sweepstakes Fever," *Forbes,* October 3, 1988, pp. 164–66.
45. Richard Sale, "Serving Up Sweeps," *Promo Magazine,* August 1999, pp. 70–78.
46. Bob Woods, "Picking a Winner," *Promo Magazine,* August 1998, pp. 57–62.
47. Richard Sale, "Sweeping the Courts," *Promo Magazine,* May 1998, pp. 422–45, 148–52.
48. Maxine S. Lans, "Legal Hurdles Big Part of Promotions Game," *Marketing News,* October 24, 1994, pp. 15–16.
49. Survey by Oxtoby-Smith, Inc., "Many Consumers View Rebates."
50. Peter Tat, William A. Cunningham III, and Emin Babakus, "Consumer Perceptions of Rebates," *Journal of Advertising Research,* August/September 1988, pp. 45–50.
51. Martha Graves, "Mail-In Rebates Stirring Shopper, Retailer Backlash," *Los Angeles Times,* January 11, 1989, pt. IV, p. 1.
52. Edward A. Blair and E. Lair Landon, "The Effects of Reference Prices in Retail Advertisements," *Journal of Marketing* 45, no. 2 (Spring 1981), pp. 61–69.
53. Sale, "Not Your Mother's Coupon."
54. "Calling All Shoppers."
55. Adapted from Terrence A. Shimp, *Advertising, Promotion, and Supplemental Aspect of Integrated Marketing Communication,* 4th ed. (Fort Worth, TX: Dryden Press, 1997), p. 487.
56. Frank Green, "Battling for Shelf Control," *San Diego Union,* November 19, 1996, pp. C1, 6, 7.
57. "Want Shelf Space at the Supermarket? Ante Up," *Business Week,* August 7, 1989, pp. 60–61.
58. Ira Teinowitz, "Senators Berate Industry Abuse of Slotting Fees," *Advertising Age,* September 20, 1999, pp. 3, 66.
59. Paul N. Bloom, Gregory T. Gundlach, and Joseph P. Cannon, "Slotting Allowances and Fees: Schools of Thought and Views of Practicing Managers," *Journal of Marketing* 64, April 2000, pp. 92–108.
60. Melissa Campanelli, "What's in Store for EDLP?" *Sales & Marketing Management,* August 1993, pp. 56–59; "Procter & Gamble Hits Back," *Business Week,* July 19, 1993, pp. 20–22.
61. Amy Barone and Laurel Wentz, "Artzt Steering Barilla into EDLP Strategy," *Advertising Age,* February 26, 1996, p. 10.
62. Tom Steinhagen, "Space Management Shapes Up with Planograms," *Marketing News,* November 12, 1990, p. 7.
63. Srinath Gopalakrishna, Gary L. Lilien, Jerome D. Williams, and Ian K. Sequeria, "Do Trade Shows Pay Off?" *Journal of Marketing* 59, July 1995, pp. 75–83.
64. Cynthia Rigg, "Hard Times Means Growth for Co-op Ads," *Advertising Age,* November 12, 1990, p. 24.
65. Edwin L. Artzt, "The Lifeblood of Brands," *Advertising Age,* November 4, 1991, p. 32.
66. "Everyone Is Bellying Up to This Bar," *Business Week,* January 27, 1992, p. 84.
67. Jack Neff, "The New Brand Management," *Advertising Age,* November 8, 1999, pp. S2, 18; Benson P. Shapiro, "Improved Distribution with Your Promotional Mix," *Harvard Business Review,* March/April 1977, p. 116; and Roger A. Strang, "Sales Promotion—Fast Growth, Faulty Management," *Harvard Business Review,* July/August 1976, p. 119.
68. Quote by Thomas E. Hamilton, director of sales promotion service, William Esty Advertising, cited in Felix Kessler, "The Costly Couponing Craze," *Fortune,* June 9, 1986, p. 84.
69. Priya Raghubir and Kim Corfman, "When Do Price Promotions Affect Pretrial Brand Evaluations?" *Journal of Marketing Research* 36 (May 1999), pp. 211–22.
70. Alan G. Sawyer and Peter H. Dickson, "Psychological Perspectives on Consumer Response to Sales Promotion," in *Research on Sales Promotion: Collected Papers,* ed. Katherine E.

Jocz (Cambridge, MA: Marketing Science Institute, 1984).
71. William E. Myers, "Trying to Get Out of the Discounting Box," *Adweek,* November 11, 1985, p. 2.
72. Leigh McAlister, "Managing the Dynamics of Promotional Change," in *Looking at the Retail Kaleidoscope,* Forum IX (Stamford, CT: Donnelley Marketing, April 1988).
73. "Promotions Blemish Cosmetic Industry," *Advertising Age,* May 10, 1984, pp. 22–23, 26.
74. Richard Green, "Worried McDonald's Plans Dramatic Shifts and Big Price Cuts," *The Wall Street Journal,* February 26, 1997, pp. A1, 6.

Chapter Seventeen

1. Judann Pollack, "New Marketing Spin: The PR 'Experience,'" *Advertising Age,* August 5, 1996, p. 33.
2. Raymond Simon, *Public Relations, Concept and Practices,* 2nd ed. (Columbus, OH: Grid Publishing, 1980), p. 8.
3. William N. Curry, "PR Isn't Marketing," *Advertising Age,* December 18, 1991, p. 18.
4. Martha M. Lauzen, "Imperialism and Encroachment in Public Relations," *Public Relations Review* 17, no. 3 (Fall 1991), pp. 245–55.
5. Philip Kotler and William Mindak, "Marketing and Public Relations," *Journal of Marketing* 42 (October 1978), pp. 13–20.
6. Thomas L. Harris, "How MPR Adds Value to Integrated Marketing Communications," *Public Relations Quarterly,* Summer 1993, pp. 13–18.
7. Alice Z. Cuneo, "Victoria's Secret Web Plan Cuts Superbowl for Cannes," *Advertising Age,* November 22, 1999, p. 3.
8. Thomas L. Harris, "Marketing PR—The Second Century," Reputation Management, www.prcentral.com, January/February 1999, pp. 1–6.
9. Sally Goll Beatty, "Texaco's Effort to Repair Image Comes under Fire after First Ad," *The Wall Street Journal,* November 27, 1996, p. B7.
10. Simon, *Public Relations,* p. 164.
11. Bob Donath, "Corporate Communications," *Industrial Marketing,* July 1980, pp. 53–57.
12. Scott M. Cutlip, Allen H. Center, and Glenn M. Broom, *Effective Public Relations,* 6th ed. (Englewood Cliffs, NJ: Prentice Hall, 1985), p. 200.
13. John E. Marston, *Modern Public Relations* (New York: McGraw-Hill, 1979).
14. Joe Agnew, "Marketers Find the Antidrug Campaign Addictive," *Marketing News,* October 9, 1987, p. 12.
15. Michael J. McCarthy, "Inside the Beer Industry's Political Machine," *The Wall Street Journal,* August 18, 1997, pp. B1–2.
16. Susie Stoughton, "Recovering from Floyd," *Virginian-Pilot,* December 5, 1999, p. 6.
17. Shel Holtz, *Public Relations on the Internet* (New York: American Management Association, 1998).
18. Raymond Serafin, "Cars Squeeze Mileage from Awards," *Advertising Age,* June 4, 1990, p. 36.
19. Jeffrey M. O'Brien, "H-P Heads for Home," *Marketing Computers,* July/August 1996, pp. 55–58.
20. Raymond Simon, *Public Relations, Concepts and Practices,* 3rd ed. (New York: John Wiley & Sons, 1984), p. 291.
21. Harold Mendelsohn, "Some Reasons Why Information Campaigns Can Succeed," *Public Opinion Quarterly,* Spring 1973, p. 55.
22. Walter K. Lindenmann, "An Effectiveness Yardstick to Measure Public Relations Success," *Public Relations Quarterly* 38, no. 1 (Spring 1993), pp. 7–10.
23. Deborah Holloway, "How to Select a Measurement System That's Right for You," *Public Relations Quarterly* 37, no. 3 (Fall 1992), pp. 15–18.
24. J. Lawrence, "New Doritos Gets the Star Treatment," *Advertising Age,* March 29, 1993, p. 64.
25. "Zany Brainy, Experian and Consolidated Freightways Video News Releases," *PR Newsletter,* November 24, 1999, p. 1.
26. Jaye S. Niefeld, "Corporate Advertising," *Industrial Marketing,* July 1980, pp. 64–74.
27. Tom Garbett, "What Companies Project to Public," *Advertising Age,* July 6, 1981, p. 51.
28. Ed Zotti, "An Expert Weighs the Prose and Yawns," *Advertising Age,* January 24, 1983, p. M-11.
29. Bob Seeter, "AMA Hopes New Ads Will Cure Image Problem," *Los Angeles Times,* August 14, 1991, p. A-5.
30. John Burnett, "Shopping for Sponsorships? Integration Is Paramount," *Brandweek,* February 14, 1994, p. 18.
31. Ed Zotti, "An Expert Weighs the Prose and Yawns."
32. Ronald Alsop, "The Best Corporate Reputations in America," *The Wall Street Journal,* September 29, 1999, p. B1.
33. Ronald Alsop, "The Best Reputations in High Tech," *The Wall Street Journal,* November 18, 1999, p. B1.
34. Shav Glick, "Takeovers, Mergers Take Their Toll, Too," *Los Angeles Times,* March 27, 1989, pt. III, p. 14.
35. Brian Trusdell, "Will a Cigarette Ban Stall Nascar's Growth?" *Sales & Marketing Management,* February 1997, pp. 67–75.
36. Raymond Sefafin, "Upscale Drivers," *Advertising Age,* February 26, 1996, pp. 30–31.
37. Prakash Sethi, *Advertising and Large Corporations* (Lexington, MA: Lexington Books, 1977), pp. 7–8.
38. Janet Myers, "JWT Anti-Japan Ad Is a Bomb," *Advertising Age,* April 2, 1990, p. 4.
39. Harvey Meyer, "When the Cause Is Just," *Journal of Business Strategy,* November/December 1999, pp. 27–31.
40. Ibid., p. 28.
41. Ibid., p. 29.
42. Karen Benezra, "Cause and Effects Marketing," *Brandweek,* April 22, 1996, p. 38.
43. Donath, "Corporate Communications," p. 52.
44. Ibid., p. 53.
45. Ibid., p. 52.

Chapter Eighteen

1. Ginger Conlon, "Cornering the Market," *Sales & Marketing Management,* March 1997, pp. 74–76.
2. Carl G. Stevens and David P. Keane, "How to Become a Better Sales Manager: Give Salespeople How to, Not Rah Rah," *Marketing News,* May 30, 1980, p. 1.
3. Tom Wotruba and Edwin K. Simpson, *Sales Management* (Boston: Kent Publishing, 1989).
4. Cahners Publishing Co., a division of Reed Elsevier, Inc., www.cahners.com/research/5425d.htm (10/29/98).
5. Thomas R. Wotruba, "The Evolution of Personal Selling," *Journal of Personal Selling & Sales Management* 11, no. 3 (Summer 1991), pp. 1–12.
6. James Champy, "Selling to Tomorrow's Customer," *Sales & Marketing Management,* March 1999, p. 28.
7. Kevin Hoffberg and Kevin J. Corcoran, "Selling at the Speed of Change," *Customers 2000,* pp. S22–26.
8. Jonathan R. Copulsky and Michael J. Wolf, "Relationship Marketing: Positioning for the Future," *Journal of Business Strategy,* July/August 1990, pp. 16–20.

9. Don Pepper and Martha Rogers, "In Vendors They Trust," *Sales & Marketing Management,* November 1999, pp. 30–32.
10. Cahners Publishing Co., 1998, www.cahners.com/research/5425d.htm.
11. Thayer C. Taylor, "A Letup in the Rise of Sales Call Costs," *Sales & Marketing Management,* February 25, 1980, p. 24.
12. Laura Loro, "From Call Center Direct to Net," *Direct Marketing,* December 1997, p. 9.
13. Theodore Levitt, "Communications and Industrial Selling," *Journal of Marketing* 31 (April 1967), pp. 15–21.
14. John E. Morrill, "Industrial Advertising Pays Off," *Harvard Business Review,* March/April 1970, p. 4.
15. "Salespeople Contact Fewer than 10 Percent of Purchase Decision Makers over a Two-Month Period," McGraw-Hill LAP Report no. 1029.3 (New York: McGraw-Hill, 1987).
16. *Direct Marketing Association, 2000.*
17. Peggy Moretti, "Telemarketers Serve Clients," *Business Marketing,* April 1994, pp. 27–29.
18. Ginger Conlon, "Just Another Channel," *Wired Executive,* January 2000, pp. 23–26.
19. Rolph E. Anderson, Joseph F. Hair, and Alan J. Bush, *Professional Sales Management* (New York: McGraw-Hill, 1988).

Chapter Nineteen

1. Mary Tolan, "Holidays Are Here and So Is Ad Puzzle," *Advertising Age,* November 16, 1998, p. 36.
2. Ibid.
3. Laura Bird, "Loved the Ad. May (or May Not) Buy the Product," *The Wall Street Journal,* April 7, 1994, p. B1.
4. Bruce Horowitz, "TV Ads the Public Will Never See," *Los Angeles Times,* August 3, 1988, p. 1.
5. McGraw-Hill Lap Report no. 3151 (New York: McGraw-Hill, 1988); Alan D. Fletcher, *Target Marketing through the Yellow Pages* (Troy, MI: Yellow Pages Publishers Association, 1991), p. 23.
6. Personal interview with Jay Khoulos, president of World Communications, Inc., 1988.
7. David A. Aaker and John G. Myers, *Advertising Management,* 3rd ed. (Englewood Cliffs, NJ: Prentice Hall, 1987), p. 474.
8. Joel N. Axelrod, "Induced Moods and Attitudes toward Products," *Journal of Advertising Research* 3 (June 1963), pp. 19–24; Lauren E. Crane, "How Product, Appeal, and Program Affect Attitudes toward Commercials," *Journal of Advertising Research* 4 (March 1964), p. 15.
9. Robert Settle, "Marketing in Tight Times," *Marketing Communications* 13, no. 1 (January 1988), pp. 19–23.
10. "What Is Good Creative?" *Topline,* no. 41 (New York: McCollum Spielman Worldwide, 1994), p. 4.
11. James R. Hagerty, "Tests Lead Lowe's to Revamp Strategy," *The Wall Street Journal,* March 11, 1999, p. B18.
12. "21 Ad Agencies Endorse Copy-Testing Principles," *Marketing News* 15, no. 17 (February 19, 1982), p. 1.
13. Ibid.
14. John M. Caffyn, "Telepex Testing of TV Commercials," *Journal of Advertising Research* 5, no. 2 (June 1965), pp. 29-37; Thomas J. Reynolds and Charles Gengler, "A Strategic Framework for Assessing Advertising: The Animatic vs. Finished Issue," *Journal of Advertising Research,* October/November 1991, pp. 61–71; Nigel A. Brown and Ronald Gatty, "Rough vs. Finished TV Commercials in Telepex Tests," *Journal of Advertising Research* 7, no. 4 (December 1967), p. 21.
15. Charles H. Sandage, Vernon Fryburger, and Kim Rotzoll, *Advertising Theory and Practice,* 10th ed. (Burr Ridge, IL: Richard D. Irwin, 1979).
16. Lyman E. Ostlund, "Advertising Copy Testing: A Review of Current Practices, Problems and Prospects," *Current Issues and Research in Advertising,* 1978, pp. 87–105.
17. Jack B. Haskins, "Factual Recall as a Measure of Advertising Effectiveness," *Journal of Advertising Research* 4, no. 1 (March 1964), pp. 2–7.
18. John Philip Jones and Margaret H. Blair, "Examining 'Conventional Wisdoms' about Advertising Effects with Evidence from Independent Sources," *Journal of Advertising Research,* November/December 1996, pp. 37–52.
19. Paul J. Watson and Robert J. Gatchel, "Autonomic Measures of Advertising," *Journal of Advertising Research* 19 (June 1979), pp. 15–26.
20. Priscilla A. LaBarbera and Joel D. Tucciarone, "GSR Reconsidered: A Behavior-based Approach to Evaluating and Improving the Sales Potency of Advertising," *Journal of Advertising Research,* September/October 1995, pp. 33–40.
21. Flemming Hansen, "Hemispheric Lateralization: Implications for Understanding Consumer Behavior," *Journal of Consumer Research* 8 (1988), pp. 23–36.
22. Kevin Lane Keller, Susan E. Heckler, and Michael J. Houston, "The Effects of Brand Name Suggestiveness on Advertising Recall," *Journal of Marketing,* January 1998, pp. 48–57.
23. Jan Stapel, "Recall and Recognition: A Very Close Relationship," *Journal of Advertising Research,* July/August 1998, pp. 41–45.
24. Hubert A. Zielske, "Does Day-after Recall Penalize 'Feeling Ads'?" *Journal of Advertising Research* 22, no. 1 (1982), pp. 19–22.
25. Arthur J. Kover, "Why Copywriters Don't Like Advertising Research—and What Kind of Research Might They Accept," *Journal of Advertising Research,* March/April 1996, pp. RC8-RC10; Gary Levin, "Emotion Guides BBDO's Ad Tests," *Advertising Age,* January 29, 1990, p.12.
26. Terry Haller, "Day-after Recall to Persist Despite JWT Study; Other Criteria Looming," *Marketing News,* May 18, 1979, p. 4.
27. Chuck Ross, "Interactive Ads Ready for Test," *Advertising Age,* April 26, 1999, p. 2.
28. Dave Kruegel, "Television Advertising Effectiveness and Research Innovations," *Journal of Consumer Marketing* 5, no. 3 (Summer 1988), pp. 43–52.
29. Gary Levin, "Tracing Ads' Impact," *Advertising Age,* November 12, 1990, p. 49.
30. John Philip Jones, "Single-source Research Begins to Fulfill Its Promise," *Journal of Advertising Research,* May/June 1995, pp. 9–16.
31. Jeffrey L. Seglin, "The New Era of Ad Measurement," *Adweek's Marketing Week,* January 23, 1988, p. 24.
32. James F. Donius, "Marketing Tracking: A Strategic Reassessment and Planning Tool," *Journal of Advertising Research* 25, no. 1 (February/March 1985), pp. 15–19.
33. Russell I. Haley and Allan L. Baldinger, "The ARF Copy Research Validity Project," *Journal of Advertising Research,* April/May 1991, pp. 11–32.
34. Glenn Heitsmith, "Something for Nothing," *Promo,* September 1993, pp. 30, 31, 93.
35. Ibid.

36. "Journeying Deeper into the Minds of Shoppers," *Business Week,* February 4, 1991, p. 85.
37. Elizabeth Gardener and Minakshi Trivedi, "A Communications Framework to Evaluate Sales Promotion Strategies," *Journal of Advertising Research,* May/June 1998, pp. 67–71.
38. David W. Schumann, Jennifer Grayson, Johanna Ault, Kerri Hargrove, Lois Hollingsworth, Russell Ruelle, and Sharon Seguin, "The Effectiveness of Shopping Cart Signage: Perceptual Measures Tell a Different Story," *Journal of Advertising Research,* February/ March 1991, pp. 17–22.
39. June Bryan Kim, "Research Makes Ski Run Easier," *Advertising Age,* August 18, 1991, p. 30.
40. Steven Stark, "Advertising That Hits Home: Next Century Media Will Study Addressable Commercials," *Electronic Media,* August 30, 1999, p. 31.
41. Bettina Cornwell and Isabelle Maignan, "An International Review of Sponsorship Research," *Journal of Advertising,* March 1998.
42. Michel Tuan Pham, "The Evaluation of Sponsorship Effectiveness: A Model and Some Methodological Considerations," *Gestion 2000,* pp. 47–65.

Chapter Twenty

1. Ron Ashkneas, "Breaking through Global Boundaries, *Executive Excellence,*" July 1999, pp. 7, 8.
2. Normandy Madden, "Starbucks Ships Its Coffee Craze to Pacific Rim," *Advertising Age,* April 27, 1998, p. 28.
3. John A. Byrne, "Philip Morris: Inside America's Most Reviled Company," *Business Week,* November 29, 1999, pp. 176–92.
4. J. McCarthy, "Paring Bud with Sushi in South America," *The Wall Street Journal,* February 20, 1997, pp. B1, 6; "Anheuser-Busch Says Skoal, Salud, Prosit," *Business Week,* November 20, 1993, pp. 76–77.
5. Normandy Madden, "China Ad Opportunities to Grow with WTO Deal," *Advertising Age International,* January 2000, p. 6.
6. Linda Grant, "Outmarketing P&G," *Fortune,* January 12, 1998, pp. 150–52.
7. Christopher Knowlton, "Europe Cooks Up a Cereal Brawl," *Fortune,* June 3, 1991, pp. 175–78.
8. General Mills Annual Report, 1999.
9. Martha T. Moore, "New Breed CEO Markets Locally—Worldwide," *USA Today,* February 7, 1996, pp. 1, 2B.
10. *Insiders' Report, Robert Coen Presentation on Advertising Expenditures* (New York: McCann-Erickson Worldwide, December 1999), p. 10.
11. Laurel Wentz, "P&G Tops $3 Bil Mark in Non-U.S. Ad Spending," *Advertising Age,* November 8, 1999, p. 12.
12. Kip D. Cassino, "The World of Advertising," *American Demographics,* November 1997, pp. 57–60.
13. Vern Terpstra, *International Marketing,* 4th ed. (New York: Holt, Rinehart & Winston/Dryden Press, 1987), p. 427.
14. "Asian Horizons," *Sales & Marketing Management,* August 1996, pp. 64–68.
15. Julia Koranteng, "Ad Spending Seen Rising Worldwide," *Advertising Age International,* January 2000, pp. 1, 6, 34; Normandy Madden, "Ad Spending in South Korea Is Forecast to Reach $3.9 Billion in 1999, an 18% Increase from $3.3 Billion in 1998," *Advertising Age International,* July 1, 1999, pp. 1, 24.
16. Magz Osborne, "U.S. Gateway to Asia: Computer Seller Expands," *Advertising Age International,* December 1999, p. 7.
17. Carla Rapoport, "Nestlé's Brand Building Machine," *Fortune,* September 19, 1994, pp. 147–56.
18. Miriam Jordan, "Selling Birth Control to India's Poor," *The Wall Street Journal,* September 21, 1999, pp. B1, 4.
19. Anne Moncreiff Arrarte, "Advertisers Find Latin American Children's Media a Growing Market," *Miami Herald,* December 17, 1997.
20. G. Pascal Zachary, "Major U.S. Companies Expand Efforts to Sell to Consumers Abroad," *The Wall Street Journal,* June 13, 1996, pp. A1, 6.
21. George E. Belch and Michael A. Belch, "Toward Development of a Model and Scale for Assessing Consumer Receptivity to Foreign Products and Global Advertising," in *European Advances in Consumer Research,* vol. 1, ed. Gary J. Bamossy and W. Fred van Raaij (Provo, UT: Association for Consumer Research, 1993), pp. 52–57.
22. Subhash Sharma, Terrence Shimp, and Jeongshin Shin, "Consumer Ethnocentrism: A Test of Antecedents and Moderators," *Journal of the Academy of Marketing Science* (Winter 1995), pp. 26–37.
23. For an excellent discussion of various elements of Japanese culture such as language and its implications for promotion, see John F. Sherry, Jr., and Eduardo G. Camargo, "May Your Life Be Marvelous: English Language Labelling and the Semiotics of Japanese Promotion," *Journal of Consumer Research,* 14 (September 1987), pp. 174–88.
24. Barbara Mueller, "Reflections on Culture: An Analysis of Japanese and American Advertising Appeals," *Journal of Advertising Research,* June/July 1987, pp. 51–59.
25. Barbara Mueller, "Standardization vs. Specialization: An Examination of Westernization in Japanese Advertising," *Journal of Advertising Research,* January/February 1992, pp. 15–24; and Johny K. Johanson, "The Sense of Nonsense: Japanese TV Advertising," *Journal of Advertising* 23, no. 1 (March 1994), pp. 17–26.
26. Michael L. Maynard and Charles R. Taylor, "Girlish Images across Cultures: Analyzing Japanese versus U.S. *Seventeen* Magazine Ads," *Journal of Advertising* 28, no. 1 (Spring 1999), pp. 39–49.
27. John B. Ford, Patricia Kramer Voli, Earl D. Honeycutt, Jr., and Susan L. Casey, "Gender Role Portrayals in Japanese Advertising: A Magazine Content Analysis," *Journal of Advertising* 27, no. 1 (Spring 1998).
28. Marian Katz, "No Women, No Alcohol; Learn Saudi Taboos before Placing Ads," *International Advertiser,* February 1986, pp. 11–12.
29. Safran S. Al-Makaty, G. Norman van Tubergen, S. Scott Whitlow, and Douglas S. Boyd, "Attitudes toward Advertising in Islam," *Journal of Advertising Research,* May/June 1996, pp. 16–26.
30. Elizabeth Bryant, "P&G Pushes the Envelope in Egypt with TV Show on Feminine Hygiene," *Advertising Age International,* December 14, 1998, p. 2.
31. Dean M. Peebles and John K. Ryans, *Management of International Advertising* (Newton, MA: Allyn & Bacon, 1984).
32. Geoffrey Lee Martin, "Tobacco Sponsors Fear Aussie TKO," *Advertising Age,* April 27, 1992, p. I-8.

33. "U.K. Tobacco Ban Postponed Even as Companies Bid Farewell," *Advertising Age International,* December 1999, p. 9.
34. Jane Blennerhassett, "Hong Kong Ban May Be Tougher Than China's," *Advertising Age International,* July 1996, p. 16.
35. Laurel Wentz, "Local Laws Keep International Marketers Hopping," *Advertising Age,* July 11, 1985, p. 20.
36. Jeremy Slate, "EC Lets Stand Toy Ad Ban," *Advertising Age International,* August 1999, pp. 1, 11.
37. Al-Makatay et al., "Attitudes Toward Advertising in Islam."
38. Naveen Donthu, "A Cross-Country Investigation of Recall of and Attitude toward Comparative Advertising," *Journal of Advertising* 27, no. 2 (Summer 1998), pp. 111–122.
39. Derek Turner, "Coke Pops Brazilian Comparative Ad," *Advertising Age,* September 9, 1991, p. 24.
40. J.Craig Andrews, Steven Lysonski, and Srinivas Durvasula, "Understanding Cross-Cultural Student Perceptions of Advertising in General: Implications for Advertising Educators and Practitioners," *Journal of Advertising* 20, no. 2 (June 1991), pp. 15–28.
41. J. Boddewyn and Iris Mohr, "International Advertisers Face Government Hurdles," *Marketing News,* May 8, 1987, pp. 21–22.
42. Tze Yee-Lin, "Malaysia May Allow Foreign Commercials," *Advertising Age International,* March 1997, p. i22.
43. Matthew Rose and Leslie Chang, "Chinese Officials Force Magazines to Go without Famous Names," *The Wall Street Journal,* February 2, 2000, p. B1.
44. "U.K. Tobacco Ad Ban Postponed."
45. Robert D. Buzzell, "Can You Standardize Multinational Marketing?" *Harvard Business Review,* November/December 1968, pp. 102–13; and Ralph Z. Sorenson and Ulrich E. Wiechmann, "How Multinationals View Marketing," *Harvard Business Review,* May/June 1975, p. 38.
46. Theodore Levitt, "The Globalization of Markets," *Harvard Business Review,* May/June 1983, pp. 92–102; and Theodore Levitt, *The Marketing Imagination* (New York: Free Press, 1986).
47. Anne B. Fisher, "The Ad Biz Gloms onto Global," *Fortune,* November 12, 1984, p. 78.
48. Keith Reinhard and W. E. Phillips, "Global Marketing: Experts Look at Both Sides," *Advertising Age,* April 15, 1988, p. 47; and Anthony Rutigliano, "The Debate Goes On: Global vs. Local Advertising." *Management Review,* June 1986, pp. 27–31.
49. Sharon T. Klahr, "Gillette Puts $300 Mil Behind Its Mach3 Shaver," *Advertising Age,* April 20, 1998, p. 6.
50. Bernhard Warner, "IQ News: Gillette's Mach 3 Media Heft Hits Web: European Sites Next?" *Adweek Online,* August 24, 1998.
51. Kevin Goldman, "Professor Who Started Debate on Global Ads Still Backs Theory," *The Wall Street Journal,* October 13, 1992, p. B8.
52. Example from speech by Eugene H. Kummel, chairman emeritus, McCann-Erickson Worldwide, and Koji Oshita, president and CEO, McCann-Erickson, Hakuhodo, Japan, in San Diego, California, October 19, 1988; Margo Sugarman, "Nescafe Israel Entry Redefines Coffee Market," *Advertising Age International,* April 1997, p. i12.
53. Joanne Lipman, "Marketers Turn Sour on Global Sales Pitch," *The Wall Street Journal,* May 12, 1988, p. 1.
54. Joseph M. Winski and Laurel Wentz, "Parker Pens: What Went Wrong?" *Advertising Age,* June 2, 1986, p. 1.
55. Laurie Freeman, "Colgate Axes Global Ads, Thinks Local," *Advertising Age,* November 26, 1990, pp. 1, 59.
56. Lipman, "Marketers Turn Sour."
57. Sally Goll Beatty, "Global Needs Challenge Midsize Agencies," *The Wall Street Journal,* December 14, 1995, p. B9.
58. Criteria cited by Edward Meyer, CEO, Grey Advertising, in Rebecca Fannin, "What Agencies Really Think of Global Theory," *Marketing & Media Decisions,* December 1984, p. 74.
59. Quote cited in Reinhard and Phillips, "Global Marketing," p. 47.
60. J. Walter Thompson Total Branding, jwtworld.com; Laurel Wentz, "Millennium Marketer," *Advertising Age International,*" September 1999, p. 17.
61. Shelly Pannill, "The Road to Richesse," *Sales & Marketing Management,* November 1999, pp. 89–96.
62. Salah S. Hassan and Lea P. Katsansis, "Identification of Global Consumer Segments: A Behavioral Framework," *Journal of International Consumer Marketing* 3, no. 2, pp. 11–28.
63. Goldman, "Professor Who Started Debate."
64. "Ready to Shop until They Drop," *Business Week,* June 22, 1998, pp. 104–110.
65. "Teens Seen as the First Truly Global Consumers," *Marketing News,* March 27, 1995, p. 9; Shawn Tully, "Teens: The Most Global Market of All," *Fortune,* May 16, 1994, pp. 90–97.
66. "Teen-Brand Television," *Television Business International,* January 1998, pp. 1, 47.
67. Fannin, "What Agencies Really Think," p. 75.
68. Stephanie Thompson, "Coca-Cola Taps Local Pleasures to Push Classic," *Advertising Age,* January 17, 2000, p. 53.
69. Robert E. Hite and Cynthia L. Fraser, "International Advertising Strategies of Multinational Corporations," *Journal of Advertising Research,* August/September 1988, pp. 9–17.
70. Ali Kanso, "International Advertising Strategies: Global Commitment to Local Vision," *Journal of Advertising Research,* January/February 1992, pp. 10–14.
71. Jan Jaben, "Ad Decision-Makers Favor Regional Angle," *Advertising Age International,* May 1995, pp. i3, 16.
72. Penelope Rowlands, "Global Approach Doesn't Always Make Scents," *Advertising Age International,* January 17, 1994, pp. i-1, 38.
73. Bradley Johnson, "It's a Small World for Compaq Campaign," *Advertising Age International,* November 1996, p. i4.
74. Sergy Rybak, "Russian Ad Market Looks Up after Disastrous 1999 Drop," *Advertising Age International,* December 1999, p. 2; Tara Parker-Pope, "Ad Agencies Are Stumbling in Eastern Europe," *The Wall Street Journal,* May 10, 1996, pp. B1, 3.
75. Sally Goll Beatty, "Young & Rubicam Is Only One for Colgate," *The Wall Street Journal,* December 1, 1995, p. B6.
76. Calmetta Y. Coleman, "U.S. Agencies Expand in Latin America," *The Wall Street Journal,*" January 3, 1996, p. B8.
77. "Advertising Is Indeed Going Global," *Market Europe,* October 1997, pp. 8–10.

78. Normandy Madden and Sheryl R. Lee, "Demand for Viewer Data Going Up," *Advertising Age International,* July 1996, pp. i1, 26.
79. Nancy Giges, "Europeans Buy Outside Goods, but Like Local Ads," *Advertising Age International,* April 27, 1992, pp. i1, 26.
80. Joseph T. Plummer, "The Role of Copy Research in Multinational Advertising," *Journal of Advertising Research,* October/November 1986, p. 15.
81. Yumiko Ono, "Tropicana Is Trying to Cultivate a Global Taste for Orange Juice," *The Wall Street Journal,* March 28, 1994, p. B2.
82. "They're All Screaming for Häagen-Dazs," *Business Week,* October 14, 1991, p. 121.
83. Charles Goldsmith, "Starbucks Hits a Humorous Note in Pitching Iced Coffee to Brits," *The Wall Street Journal,* September 1, 1999, p. B7.
84. Karen Yates, "Advertising's Heart of Darkness," *Advertising Age International,* March 1997, p. i22.
85. Cassino, "The World of Advertising."
86. Mir Maqbool Alam Kahn, "TV Ad Spending Could Suffer under Pro-India Politicking," *Advertising Age International,* March 1997, p. i22.
87. Rochell Burbury, "Australia Ends Ban on Cable TV Spots," *Advertising Age International,* March 1997, p. i22.
88. Michael Laris, "China: The World's Most Populous Market," *Advertising Age,* May 15, 1996, p. 111.
89. "Seeing Is Believing," *Cable & Satellite Asia,* January 1998, pp. 1, 40; Fara Warner, "Sofres Group Faces Daunting Task of Rating China's TV Audience," *The Wall Street Journal,* August 1, 1996, p. B7.
90. Chuck Ross, "Global Rules Are Proposed for Measuring TV," *Advertising Age,* August 12, 1996, pp. 3, 28.
91. Thomas McCarroll, "New Star Over Asia," *Time,* August 9, 1993, p. 53.
92. Leslie Chang, "A Phoenix Rises in China," *The Wall Street Journal,* May 26, 1999, pp. B1, 4.
93. Juliana Koranteng, "Sky TV Tries to Repeat U.K. Success," *Advertising Age International,* March 1997, pp. i8, 20.
94. Alam Khan, "TV Ad Spending Could Suffer."
95. Frank Rose, "Think Globally, Script Locally," *Fortune,* November 8, 1999, pp. 156–60.
96. "Over There: 'Below-the-Line' Is Coming on Strong," *Promo Magazine,* Special Report, August 1998, pp. S12–13.
97. T. L. Stanley and Todd Wasserman, "Compaq's Brand New Day," *Brandweek,* August 9, 1999, pp. 1, 45.
98. "Stickey Wickets but What a Future," *Business Week,* August 7, 1995, pp. 72–73.
99. Kamran Kashani and John A. Quelch, "Can Sales Promotion Go Global?" *Business Horizons,* May/June 1990, pp. 37–43.
100. "What You Should Know About Advertising in Japan," *Advertising World,* April 1985, pp. 18–42.
101. Lenard C. Huff and Dana L. Alden, "An Investigation of Consumer Response to Sales Promotion in Developing Markets: A Three Country Analysis," *Journal of Advertising Research,* May/June 1998, pp. 47–56.
102. Douglas J. Wood and Linda A. Goldstein, "A Lawyer's Guide to Going Global," *Promo Magazine,* Special Report, August 1998, p. S11.
103. Kashani and Quelch, "Can Sales Promotion Go Global?"
104. Andrew Tanzer, "Citibank Blitzes Asia," *Forbes,* May 6, 1995, p. 44.
105. "Foreign Ads Go Further with PR," *International Advertiser,* December 1986, p. 30.
106. Anne Roman, "Ohio Firm Breaks International Ice," *Public Relations Journal* 47, no. 5 (May 1991), pp. 40–42.
107. Magz Osborne, "Microsoft's Singapore Site Ties Page View to Charity," *Advertising Age International,* October 1999, p. 4.
108. "Who's Online," *Business 2.0,* January 2000, pp. 251–52.
109. Indian Market Research Bureau, 2000.
110. Kathleen V. Schmidt, "Outlook 2000: Globalization," *Marketing News,* January 17, 2000, pp. 9, 16.
111. James F. Smith, "Latin America Is Online for an Internet Sales Explosion," *Los Angeles Times,* January 26, 1999, pp. C1, 6.
112. Jeffery D. Zbar, "A-B Pepsi Debut Latin Web Effort," *Advertising Age International,* July 1999, pp. 1, 4.
113. Schmidt, "Outlook 2000: Globalization."

Chapter Twenty-one

1. Fred W. Morgan and Jeffrey J. Stoltman, "Advertising and Product Liability Litigation," *Journal of Advertising* 26, no. 2 (Summer 1997), pp. 63–75.
2. Gordon Fairclough, "Philip Morris's Antismoking Campaign Draws Fire," *The Wall Street Journal,* April 7, 1999, p. B1; Suein L. Hwang and Milo Geyelin, "Is Tobacco Settlement Good News for Industry?" *Advertising Age,* November 18, 1998, pp. B1, 4.
3. Alice Mundy, "Trouble Brews for Booze," *Mediaweek,* August 10, 1998, p. 9.
4. Alice Z. Cuneo, "Of Contracts and Claims; Agencies Face Liability Issues," *Advertising Age,* January 31, 2000, p. 25.
5. Steven W. Colford and Raymond Serafin, "Scali Pays for Volvo Ad: FTC," *Advertising Age,* August 26, 1991, p. 4.
6. Alice Z. Cuneo, "Can an Agency Be Guilty of Malpractice?" *Advertising Age,* January 31, 2000, pp. 24–25.
7. Ian P. Murphy, "Competitive Spirits: Liquor Industry Turns to TV Ads," *Marketing News,* December 2, 1996, pp. 1, 17.
8. Priscilla A. LaBarbera, "Analyzing and Advancing the State of the Art of Advertising Self-Regulation," *Journal of Advertising* 9, no. 4 (1980), p. 30.
9. John F. Archer, "Advertising of Professional Fees: Does the Consumer Have a Right to Know?" *South Dakota Law Review* 21 (Spring 1976), p. 330.
10. *Bates* v. *State of Arizona,* 97 S.Ct. 2691. 45, *U.S. Law Week* 4895, (1977).
11. Charles Laughlin, "Ads on Trial," *Link,* May 1994, pp. 18–22; and "Lawyers Learn the Hard Sell—And Companies Shudder," *Business Week,* June 10, 1985, p. 70.
12. Bruce H. Allen, Richard A. Wright, and Louis E. Raho, "Physicians and Advertising," *Journal of Health Care Marketing* 5 (Fall 1985), pp. 39–49.
13. Robert E. Hite and Cynthia Fraser, "Meta-Analyses of Attitudes toward Advertising by Professionals," *Journal of Marketing* 52, no. 3 (July 1988), pp. 95–105.
14. Laughlin, "Ads on Trial."
15. Jack Neff, "Household Brands Counterpunch," *Advertising Age,* November 1, 1999, p. 26.
16. Jean Halliday, "BMW to Appeal NAD Vindication of Volvo Spot," *Advertising Age,* August 19, 1996, pp. 4, 32.
17. "NAD Urges in Brawny Ads," *Advertising Age,* November 3, 1999, p. 2.
18. Gary M. Armstrong and Julie L. Ozanne, "An Evaluation of NAD/NARB Purpose and Performance,"

Journal of Advertising 12, no. 3 (1983), pp. 15–26.
19. *NAD Case Reports,* 1999 Summary (National Advertising Division, Council of Better Business Bureaus) 30, no. 1 (January 2000), p. 1.
20. *NAD Case Reports* 23, no. 4 (June 1993), p. 23.
21. Dorothy Cohen, "The FTC's Advertising Substantiation Program," *Journal of Marketing* 44, no. 1 (Winter 1980), pp. 26–35.
22. Lynda M. Maddox and Eric J. Zanot, "The Suspension of the National Association of Broadcasters' Code and Its Effects on the Regulation of Advertising," *Journalism Quarterly* 61 (Summer 1984), pp. 125–30, 156.
23. Joe Mandese, "ABC Loosens Rules," *Advertising Age,* September 9, 1991, pp. 2, 8.
24. Eric Zanot, "Unseen but Effective Advertising Regulation: The Clearance Process," *Journal of Advertising* 14, no. 4 (1985), p. 48.
25. Mandese, "ABC Loosens Rules."
26. Azuenga quote cited in *Advertising Topics,* Supplement 533 (Council of Better Business Bureaus, Arlington, VA), March/April 1994, p. 3.
27. Steven W. Colford, "Speed Up the NAD, Industry Unit Told," *Advertising Age,* May 1, 1989, p. 3.
28. *Virginia State Board of Pharmacy* v. *Virginia Citizens Consumer Council,* 425 U.S. 748, 96 S.Ct. 1817, 48 L. Ed. 2d 346 (1976).
29. *Bates* v. *State of Arizona.*
30. *44 Liquormart, Inc.* v. *Rhode Island,* 517 U.S. 484 (1996).
31. *FTC* v. *Raladam Co.,* 258 U.S. 643 (1931).
32. Edward Cox, R. Fellmeth, and J. Schultz, *The Consumer and the Federal Trade Commission* (Washington, DC: American Bar Association, 1969); and American Bar Association, *Report of the American Bar Association to Study the Federal Trade Commission* (Washington, DC: The Association, 1969).
33. *FTC Staff Report on Advertising to Children* (Washington, DC: Government Printing Office, 1978).
34. Federal Trade Commission Improvements Act of 1980, P.L. No. 96-252, 94 Stat. 374 (May 28, 1980).
35. Bruce Silverglade, "Does FTC Have an 'Unfair' Future?" *Advertising Age,* March 26, 1994, p. 20.
36. Ivan L. Preston, *The Great American Blow-Up: Puffery in Advertising and Selling* (Madison: University of Wisconsin Press, 1975), p. 3.
37. Isabella C. M. Cunningham and William H. Cunningham, "Standards for Advertising Regulation," *Journal of Marketing* 41 (October 1977), pp. 91–97; and Herbert J. Rotfeld and Kim B. Rotzell, "Is Advertising Puffery Believed?" *Journal of Advertising* 9, no. 3 (1980), pp. 16–20.
38. Herbert J. Rotfeld and Kim B. Rotzell, "Puffery vs. Fact Claims—Really Different?" in *Current Issues and Research in Advertising,* ed. James H. Leigh and Claude R. Martin, Jr. (Ann Arbor: University of Michigan, 198[illegible]), pp. 85–104.
39. Preston, *The Great American Blow-Up.*
40. Chuck Ross, "Marketers Fend Off Shift in Rules for Ad Puffery," *Advertising Age,* February 19, 1996, p. 41.
41. Mercedes M. Cardona, "E*Trade Suit: Broker Fell Short of Ad Claims," *Advertising Age,* October 25, 1999, p. 12.
42. Federal Trade Commission, "Policy Statement on Deception," 45 ATRR 689 (October 27, 1983), at p. 690.
43. For an excellent discussion and analysis of these three elements of deception, see Gary T. Ford and John E. Calfee, "Recent Developments in FTC Policy on Deception," *Journal of Marketing* 50, no. 3 (July 1986), pp. 86–87.
44. Ray O. Werner, ed., "Legal Developments in Marketing," *Journal of Marketing* 56 (January 1992), p. 102.
45. Ira Teinowitz, "FTC Strives to Clarify 'Made in USA' Rules," *Advertising Age,* April 29, 1996, p. 12.
46. Kalpana Srinivasan, "FTC Spells Out Tough Standards for 'Made in USA,'" *Marketing News,* January 18, 1999, p. 18.
47. Cohen, "The FTC's Advertising Substantiation Program."
48. *Trade Regulation Reporter,* Par. 20,056 at 22,035, 1970–1973 Transfer Binder, Federal Trade Commission, July 1972.
49. Michael Parrish, "Unocal, FTC Settle over Premium Gas Claims," *Los Angeles Times,* December 31, 1993, p. D1.
50. John E. Califee, "FTC's Hidden Weight-Loss Ad Agenda," *Advertising Age,* October 25, 1993, p. 29.
51. Michael J. McCarthy, "Abbott Will Settle FTC Charges Linked to Ensure Endorsement," *The Wall Street Journal,* January 2, 1997, p. B2.
52. Bruce Ingersoll, "FTC Action Snares Home Shopping, iMall," *The Wall Street Journal,* April 16, 1999, p. B2.
53. For an excellent description of the Campbell Soup corrective advertising case, see Dick Mercer, "Tempest in a Soup Can," *Advertising Age,* October 17, 1994, pp. 25, 28–29.
54. William L. Wilkie, Dennis L. McNeill, and Michael B. Mazis, "Marketing's 'Scarlet Letter': The Theory and Practice of Corrective Advertising," *Journal of Marketing* 48 (Spring 1984), pp. 11–31.
55. Bruce Ingersoll, "FTC Orders Novartis to Correct Claims," *The Wall Street Journal,* May 28, 1999, p. B2.
56. "Deceptive Ads: The FTC's Laissez-Faire Approach Is Backfiring," *Business Week,* December 2, 1985, p. 136.
57. Joanne Lipman, "FTC Puts Advertisers on Notice of Crackdown on Misleading Ads," *The Wall Street Journal,* February 4, 1991, p. B6.
58. Ingersoll, "FTC Action Snares Home Shopping, iMall,"
59. Ira Teinowitz, "FCC, FTC Vow 'Action' Against Phone Ads," *Advertising Age,* November 8, 1999, p. 129.
60. David Goetzl, "Xenical Endures Ad Silence as FDA Forces Alterations," *Advertising Age,* November 8, 1999, p. 40.
61. Steven W. Colford, "$12 Million Bite," *Advertising Age,* December 2, 1991, p. 4.
62. Jan Joben, "A Setback for Competitive Ads?" *Business Marketing,* October 1992, p. 34.
63. Bruce Buchanan and Doron Goldman, "Us vs. Them: The Minefield of Comparative Ads," *Harvard Business Review,* May/June 1989, pp. 38–50.
64. Maxine Lans Retsky, "Lanham Have It: Law and Comparative Ads," *Marketing News,* November 8, 1999, p. 16.
65. Michael J. Barone, Randall L. Rose, Paul W. Minniard, and Kenneth C. Manning, "Enhancing the Detection of Misleading Comparative Advertising," *Journal of Advertising Research,* September/October 1999, pp. 43–50.
66. "Deceptive Ads: The FTC's Laissez-Faire Approach."
67. Jennifer Lawrence, "State Ad Rules Face Showdown," *Advertising Age,* November 28, 1988, p. 4.
68. "Ally in Plax Settlement," *The Wall Street Journal,* February 12, 1991, p. B4.
69. Steven Colford, "ABA Panel Backs FTC over States," *Advertising Age,* April 10, 1994, p.1.
70. S. J. Diamond, "New Director Putting Vigor Back into FTC," *Los Angeles Times,* March 29, 1991, pp. D1, 4.

71. Federal Trade Commission, "Trade Regulation Rule: Games of Chance in the Food Retailing and Gasoline Industries," 16 CFR, Part 419 (1982).
72. Richard Sale, "Sweeping the Courts," *Promo Magazine,* May 1998, pp. 42–45, 148–152.
73. Ira Teinowitz and Carol Krol, "Multiple States Scrutinize Sweepstakes Mailings," *Advertising Age,* February 9, 1998, p. 41.
74. Mark Pawlosky, "States Rein in Sweepstakes, Game Operators," *The Wall Street Journal,* July 3, 1995, pp. B1, 3.
75. *The Children Advertising Review Unit Self Regulatory Guidelines for Children's Advertising,* Council of Better Business Bureaus, 1999.
76. Steven W. Colford, "Top Kid TV Offender: Premiums," *Advertising Age,* April 29, 1991, p. 52.
77. Federal Trade Commission, "Guides for Advertising Allowances and Other Merchandising Payments and Services," 16 CFR, Part 240 (1983).
78. Ira Teinowitz, "Senators Berate Industry Abuse of Slotting Fees," *Advertising Age,* September 20, 1999, pp. 3, 66.
79. Federal Trade Commission, "Trade Regulation Rule: Use of Negative Option Plans by Sellers in Commerce," 16 CFR, Part 42 (1982).
80. For a more thorough discussion of legal aspects of sales promotion and mail-order practices, see Dean K. Fueroghne, *Law & Advertising* (Chicago: Copy Workshop, 1995).
81. Mary Lu Carnevale, "FTC Adopts Rules to Curb Telemarketing," *The Wall Street Journal,* September 18, 1992, pp. B1, 10.
82. Scott Hume, "900 Numbers: The Struggle for Respect," *Advertising Age,* February 18, 1991, p. S1.
83. *Federal Register,* "Rules and Regulations," August 9, 1993, 42364-42406.
84. "Commission to Seek Public Comment on 900-Number Rule Revisions," Federal Trade Commission Press Release, October 23, 1998.
85. Russell N. Laczniak, Les Carlson, and Ann Walsh, "Antecedents of Mothers' Attitudes toward the FTC's Rule for 900-Number Advertising Directed at Children," *Journal of Current Issues and Research in Advertising* 21, no. 2 (Fall 1999) pp. 49–58.
86. Ira Teinowitz, "FTC Chairman Seeking Voluntary Web Rules," *Advertising Age,* June 10, 1996, p. 42.
87. Ibid.
88. Ira Teinowitz and Jennifer Gilbert, "FTC Chairman: Stop Undisclosed Profiling on Net," *Advertising Age,* November 8, 1999, p. 2.
89. Jennifer Gilbert and Ira Teinowitz, "Privacy Debate Continues to Rage," *Advertising Age,* February 7, 2000, pp. 44, 46.
90. Ira Teinowitz, "FTC Plans to Zoom In on Kids Online Issues," *Advertising Age,* April, 1, 1996, p. 60.
91. James Heckman, "COPPA to Bring No Surprises, Hefty Violation Fines in April," *Marketing News,* January 31, 2000, p. 6.

Chapter Twenty-two

1. Robert L. Heilbroner, "Demand for the Supply Side," *New York Review of Books* 38 (June 11, 1981), p. 40.
2. David Helm, "Advertising's Overdue Revolution," speech given to the *Adweek* creative conference, October 1, 1999.
3. Joan Voight, "The Consumer Rebellion," *Adweek,* January 10, 2000, pp. 46–50.
4. Eric N. Berkowitz, Roger A. Kerin, Steven W. Hartley, William Rudedius, et al., *Marketing,* 5th ed. (Burr Ridge, IL: Irwin/McGraw-Hill, 1997), p. 102.
5. William J. Eaton, "College Binge Drinking Soars, Study Finds," *Los Angeles Times,* June 8, 1994, p. A21.
6. Ira Teinowitz, "FTC Governing of Beer Ads Expands to Miller, A-B," *Advertising Age,* April 17, 1997, pp. 1, 50.
7. "Calvin's World," *Newsweek,* September 11, 1995, pp. 60–66.
8. Louise Lee, "Take Our Swoosh. Please," *Business Week,* February 21, 2000, p. 128.
9. John Walters, "Nike Gets Kinky," *Sports Illustrated,* February 7, 2000, p. 24.
10. Stephanie O'Donohoe, "Attitudes to Advertising: A Review of British and American Research," *International Journal of Advertising* 14 (1995), pp. 245–61.
11. Banwari Mittal, "Public Assessment of TV Advertising: Faint Praise and Harsh Criticism," *Journal of Advertising Research* 34, no. 1 (1994), pp. 35–53.
12. Sharon Shavitt, Pamela Lowery, and James Haefner, "Public Attitudes toward Advertising; More Favorable Than You Might Think," *Journal of Advertising Research,* July/August 1998, pp. 7–22.
13. Gita Venkataramini Johar, "Consumer Involvement and Deception from Implied Advertising Claims," *Journal of Marketing Research* 32 (August 1995), pp. 267–79; J. Edward Russo, Barbara L. Metcalf, and Debra Stephens, "Identifying Misleading Advertising," *Journal of Consumer Research* 8 (September 1981), pp. 119–31.
14. Shelby D. Hunt, "Informational vs. Persuasive Advertising: An Appraisal," *Journal of Advertising,* Summer 1976, pp. 5–8.
15. Banwari Mittal, "Public Assessment of TV Advertising: Faint Praise and Harsh Criticism"; J. C. Andrews, "The Dimensionality of Beliefs toward Advertising in General," *Journal of Advertising* 18, no. 1 (1989), pp. 26–35; Ron Alsop, "Advertisers Find the Climate Less Hostile Outside the U.S.," *The Wall Street Journal,* December 10, 1987, p. 29.
16. Helen Cooper, "CDC Advocates Use of Condoms in Blunt AIDS-Prevention Spots," *The Wall Street Journal,* January 5, 1994, p. B1.
17. David A. Aaker and Donald E. Bruzzone, "Causes of Irritation in Advertising," *Journal of Marketing,* Spring 1985, p. 47–57.
18. Stephen A. Greyser, "Irritation in Advertising," *Journal of Advertising Research* 13 (February 1973), pp. 3–10.
19. Ron Alsop, "Personal Product Ads Abound as Public Gets More Tolerant," *The Wall Street Journal,* April 14, 1986, p. 19.
20. Joanne Lipman, "Censored Scenes: Why You Rarely See Some Things in Television Ads," *The Wall Street Journal,* August 17, 1987, p. 17.
21. Bruce Horowitz, "Taking Aim at the Bad Ads," *Los Angeles Times,* January 28, 1994, pp. D1, 4.
22. For an interesting analysis of an interpretation of this ad from a literary theory perspective see Aaron C. Ahuvia, "Social Criticism of Advertising: On the Role of Literary Theory and the Use of Data," *Journal of Advertising* 27, no. 1 (Spring 1998), pp. 143–62.
23. John P. Cortez and Ira Teinowitz, "More Trouble Brews for Stroh Bikini Team," *Advertising Age,* December 9, 1991, p. 45.
24. Ira Teinowitz, "Days of 'Beer and Babes' Running Out," *Advertising Age,* October 4, 1993, p. S-5.
25. David Lieberman, "Broadcasters Crowd the Playground," *USA Today,* February 7, 1996, pp. 1, 2B.
26. Scott Ward, Daniel B. Wackman, and Ellen Wartella, *How Children Learn*

to Buy: The Development of Consumer Information Processing Skills (Beverly Hills, CA: Sage, 1979).

27. Thomas S. Robertson and John R. Rossiter, "Children and Commercial Persuasion: An Attribution Theory Analysis," *Journal of Consumer Research* 1, no. 1 (June 1974), pp. 13–20; and Scott Ward and Daniel B. Wackman, "Children's Information Processing of Television Advertising," in *New Models for Communications Research,* ed. G. Kline and P. Clark (Beverly Hills, CA: Sage, 1974), pp. 81–119.
28. Merrie Brucks, Gary M. Armstrong, and Marvin E. Goldberg, "Children's Use of Cognitive Defenses against Television Advertising: A Cognitive Response Approach," *Journal of Consumer Research* 14, no. 4 (March 1988), pp. 471–82.
29. For a discussion on consumer socialization, see Scott Ward, "Consumer Socialization," *Journal of Consumer Research* 1, no. 2 (September 1974), pp. 1–14.
30. Tamara F. Mangleburg and Terry Bristol, "Socialization and Adolescents' Skepticism toward Advertising," *Journal of Advertising* 27, no. 3 (Fall 1998), pp. 11–21.
31. *FTC Staff Report on Advertising to Children* (Washington, DC: Government Printing Office, 1978).
32. Ben M. Enis, Dale R. Spencer, and Don R. Webb, "Television Advertising and Children: Regulatory vs. Competitive Perspectives," *Journal of Advertising* 9, no. 1 (1980), pp. 19–25.
33. Richard Zoglin, "Ms. Kidvid Calls It Quits," *Time,* January 20, 1992, p. 52.
34. Elizabeth Jensen and Albert R. Karr, "Summit on Kids' TV Yields Compromise," *The Wall Street Journal,* July 30, 1996, p. B12.
35. Sally Goll Beatty, "White House Pact on TV for Kids May Prove a Marketing Bonanza," *The Wall Street Journal,* August 2, 1996, p. B2.
36. Ronald Alsop, "Watchdogs Zealously Censor Advertising Targeted to Kids," *The Wall Street Journal,* September 5, 1985, p. 35.
37. Robert E. Hite and Randy Eck, "Advertising to Children: Attitudes of Business vs. Consumers," *Journal of Advertising Research,* October/November 1987, pp. 40–53.
38. Ann D. Walsh, Russell N. Laczniak, and Les Carlson, "Mother's Preferences for Regulating Children's Television," *Journal of Advertising,* 27, no. 3 (Fall 1998), pp. 23–36.
39. Ronald Berman, *Advertising and Social Change* (Beverly Hills, CA: Sage, 1981), p. 13.
40. Quote in Voight, "The Consumer Rebellion."
41. John K. Galbraith, *The New Industrial State* (Boston: Houghton Mifflin, 1967), cited in Richard W. Pollay, "The Distorted Mirror: Reflections on the Unintended Consequences of Advertising," *Journal of Marketing,* August 1986, p. 25.
42. Raymond A. Bauer and Stephen A. Greyser, "The Dialogue That Never Happens," *Harvard Business Review,* January/February 1969, pp. 122–28.
43. Morris B. Holbrook, "Mirror Mirror on the Wall, What's Unfair in the Reflections on Advertising," *Journal of Marketing* 5 (July 1987), pp. 95–103; and Theodore Levitt, "The Morality of Advertising," *Harvard Business Review,* July/August 1970, pp. 84–92.
44. Stephen Fox, *The Mirror Makers: A History of American Advertising and Its Creators* (New York: Morrow, 1984), p. 330.
45. Richard W. Pollay, "The Distorted Mirror: Reflections on the Unintended Consequences of Advertising," *Journal of Marketing* 50 (April 1986), p. 33.
46. Jules Backman, "Is Advertising Wasteful?" *Journal of Marketing* 32 (January 1968), pp. 2–8.
47. Hunt, "Informational vs. Persuasive Advertising."
48. Ibid., p. 6.
49. Kevin Goldman, "Survey Asks Which 'Green' Ads Are Read," *The Wall Street Journal,* April 11, 1994, p. B5.
50. Alice E. Courtney and Thomas W. Whipple, *Sex Stereotyping in Advertising* (Lexington, MA: Lexington Books, 1984).
51. Daniel J. Brett and Joanne Cantor, "The Portrayal of Men and Women in U.S. Television Commercials: A Recent Content Analysis and Trends of 15 Years," *Sex Roles* 18, no. 9/10 (1998), pp. 595–608; John B. Ford and Michael La Tour, "Contemporary Perspectives of Female Role Portrayals in Advertising," *Journal of Current Issues and Research in Advertising* 28, no. 1 (1996), pp. 81–93.
52. Beverly A. Browne, "Gender Stereotypes in Advertising on Children's Television in the 1990s: A Cross-National Analysis," *Journal of Advertising* 27, no. 1 (Spring 1998), pp. 83–96.
53. Richard H. Kolbe, "Gender Roles in Children's Advertising: A Longitudinal Content Analysis," in *Current Issues and Research in Advertising,* ed. James H. Leigh and Claude R. Martin, Jr. (Ann Arbor: University of Michigan, 1990), pp. 197–206.
54. Cate Terwilliger, "'Love Your Body Day' Auraria Event Takes Aim at 'Offensive' Images, Ads," *Denver Post,* September 23, 1999, p. E3.
55. Steven M. Kates and Glenda Shaw-Garlock, "The Ever Entangling Web: A Study of Ideologies and Discourses in Advertising to Women," *Journal of Advertising* 28, no. 2 (Summer 1999), pp. 33–49.
56. Basil Englis, Michael Solomon, and Richard Ashmore, "Beauty before the Eyes of Beholders: The Cultural Encoding of Beauty Types in Magazine Advertising and Music Television," *Journal of Advertising,* June 1994, pp. 49–64.
57. Cyndee Miller, "Liberation for Women in Ads," *Marketing News,* August 17, 1992, p. 1; Adrienne Ward-Fawcett, "Narrowcast in Past, Women Earn Revised Role in Advertising," *Advertising Age,* October 4, 1993, p. S1.
58. Thomas H. Stevenson, "How Are Blacks Portrayed in Business Ads?" *Industrial Marketing Management* 20 (1991), pp. 193–99; Helen Czepic and J. Steven Kelly, "Analyzing Hispanic Roles in Advertising," in *Current Issues and Research in Advertising,* ed. James H. Leigh and Claude Martin (Ann Arbor: University of Michigan, 1983), pp. 219–40; R. F. Busch, Allan S. Resnik, and Bruce L. Stern, "A Content Analysis of the Portrayal of Black Models in Magazine Advertising," in *American Marketing Association Proceedings: Marketing in the 1980s,* ed. Richard P. Bagozzi (Chicago: American Marketing Association, 1980); and R. F. Busch, Allan S. Resnik, and Bruce L. Stern, "There Are More Blacks in TV Commercials," *Journal of Advertising Research* 17 (1977), pp. 21–25.
59. James Stearns, Lynette S. Unger, and Steven G. Luebkeman, "The Portrayal of Blacks in Magazine and Television Advertising," in *AMA Educator's Proceedings,* ed. Susan P. Douglas and Michael R. Solomon (Chicago: American Marketing Association, 1987).

60. Robert E. Wilkes and Humberto Valencia, "Hispanics and Blacks in Television Commercials," *Journal of Advertising* 18, no. 1 (1989), pp. 19–26.
61. Julia Bristor, Renee Gravois Lee, and Michelle Hunt, "Race and Ideology: African American Images in Television Advertising," *Journal of Public Policy and Marketing* 14 (Spring 1995), pp. 48–59.
62. Leon E. Wynter, "Minorities Play the Hero in More TV Ads as Clients Discover Multicultural Sells," *The Wall Street Journal,* December 24, 1993, pp. B1, 6.
63. Bob Garfield, "Ikea Again Furnishes Ad Breakthrough," *Advertising Age,* April 1, 1996, p. 61.
64. Corliss Green, "Ethnic Evaluations of Advertising: Interaction Effects of Strength of Ethnic Identification, Media Placement, and Degree of Racial Composition," *Journal of Advertising* 28, no. 1 (Spring 1999), pp. 49–64.
65. Charles R. Taylor and Barbara B. Stern, "Asian-Americans: Television Advertising and the 'Model Minority' Stereotype," *Journal of Advertising* 26, no. 2 (Summer 1997), pp. 47–61.
66. Kevin Goldman, "Seniors Get Little Respect on Madison Avenue," *The Wall Street Journal,* September 20, 1993, p. B8.
67. Laura Bird, "Critics Cry Foul at Nike Spots with Actor," *The Wall Street Journal,* December 16, 1993, p. B8.
68. Jon Berry, "Think Bland," *Adweek's Marketing Week,* November 11, 1991, pp. 22–24.
69. Todd Pruzman, "Brewing New Ties with Gay Consumers," *Advertising Age,* April 8, 1996, p. 13.
70. Ronald Alsop, "Web Site Sets Gay-Themed Ad for Big, National Publications," *The Wall Street Journal,* February 17, 2000, p. B4.
71. Jef I. Richards and John H. Murphy, II, "Economic Censorship and Free Speech: The Circle of Communication between Advertisers, Media and Consumers," *Journal of Current Issues and Research in Advertising* 18, no. 1 (Spring 1996), pp. 21–33.
72. Lawrence C. Soley and Robert L. Craig, "Advertising Pressure on Newspapers: A Survey," *Journal of Advertising,* December 1992, pp. 1–10.
73. Mark Simon, "Mercury News Ad Dispute Cooling Off: Advertisers Return While Reporters Stew," *San Francisco Business Chronicle,* July 15, 1994, p. B1.
74. Soley and Craig, "Advertising Pressure on Newspapers."
75. David Shaw, "An Uneasy Alliance of News and Ads," *Los Angeles Times,* March 29, 1998, pp. A1, 28; Steven T. Goldberg, "Do the Ads Tempt the Editors?" *Kiplinger's,* May 1996, pp. 45–49.
76. Janet Guyon, "Do Publications Avoid Anti-Cigarette Stories to Protect Ad Dollars?" *The Wall Street Journal,* November 22, 1982, pp. 1, 20; Elizabeth M. Whelan, "When *Newsweek* and *Time* Filtered Cigarette Copy," *The Wall Street Journal,* November 1, 1984, p. 3; and "RJR Swears Off Saatchi and Nabisco Is in a Sweat," *Business Week,* April 18, 1988, p. 36.
77. Joanne Lipman, "Media Content Is Linked to Cigarette Ads," *The Wall Street Journal,* January 30, 1992, p. B5.
78. Laurie Freman, "Pillsbury Re-evaluates Ads on Violent Shows," *Advertising Age,* January 15, 1996, p. B6.
79. Sally Goll Beatty, "If TV Gets Ratings, Risqué Could Be Passe," *The Wall Street Journal,* February 16, 1996, p. B11.
80. Pamela Sebastian, "Boys & Girls Club Featuring Denzel Washington Is a Standout," *The Wall Street Journal,* July 8, 1996, p. B7.
81. For a discussion of monopolies in the cereal industry, see Paul N. Bloom, "The Cereal Industry: Monopolists or Super Marketers?" *MSU Business Topics,* Summer 1978, pp. 41–49.
82. Lester G. Telser, "Advertising and Competition," *Journal of Political Economy,* December 1964, pp. 537–62.
83. Robert D. Buzzell, Bradley T. Gale, and Ralph G. M. Sultan, "Market Share—A Key to Profitability," *Harvard Business Review,* January/February 1975, pp. 97–106.
84. Jean Halliday, "Daewoo's Ambitious Push: First National Ad Campaign," *Advertising Age,* January 17, 2000, p. 8.
85. Robert D. Buzzell and Paul W. Farris, *Advertising Cost in Consumer Goods Industries,* Marketing Science Institute, Report no. 76, August 1976, p. 111; and Paul W. Farris and David J. Reibstein, "How Prices, Ad Expenditures, and Profits Are Linked," *Harvard Business Review,* November/December 1979, pp. 173–84.
86. Paul W. Farris and Mark S. Albion, "The Impact of Advertising on the Price of Consumer Products," *Journal of Marketing* 44, no. 3 (Summer 1980), pp. 17–35.
87. Ibid., p. 19.
88. Lee Benham, "The Effect of Advertising on the Price of Eyeglasses," *Journal of Law and Economics* 15 (October 1972), pp. 337–52.
89. Robert L. Steiner, "Does Advertising Lower Consumer Price?" *Journal of Marketing* 37, no. 4 (October 1973), pp. 19–26.
90. Farris and Albion, "The Impact of Advertising," p. 30.
91. James M. Ferguson, "Comments on 'The Impact of Advertising on the Price of Consumer Products,'" *Journal of Marketing* 46, no. 1 (Winter 1982), pp. 102–5.
92. Farris and Albion, "The Impact of Advertising."
93. Cyndee Miller, "The Marketing of Advertising," *Marketing News,* December 7, 1992, pp. 1, 2.

Credits and Acknowledgments

Chapter 1

Chapter opening photo: Copyright 1999 Mazda Motor of America, Inc. Used by permission. **Exhibit 1-1:** Copyright 1999 Mazda Motor of America, Inc. Used by permission. **Global Perspective 1-1:** Courtesy Ford Motor Company. **Exhibit 1-2:** Courtesy American Red Cross. **Exhibit 1-3:** Courtesy Dell Computer Corporation. **Exhibit 1-4:** Courtesy of Montblanc, Inc. **Exhibit 1-5:** Courtesy American Airlines. **Figure 1-2:** Reprinted with permission from the September 27, 1999 issue of *Advertising Age.* Copyright, Crain Communications, Inc. 1999. **Exhibit 1-6:** Courtesy V&S Vin and Spirit AB. Imported by the House of Seagram, New York, NY. **Exhibit 1-7:** Used by permission of Eveready Battery Company, Inc. Eveready® is a registered trademark of Eveready Battery Company. **Exhibit 1-8:** Courtesy America's Dairy Farmers and Milk Processors. **Exhibit 1-9:** Courtesy Bose Corporation. **Exhibit 1-10:** Reprinted with permission by Lands' End, Inc. **IMC Perspective 1-2:** Courtesy HotJobs.com. **Exhibit 1-11:** Courtesy Johnson & Johnson Consumer Products, Inc. **Exhibit 1-12:** Courtesy E.I. du Pont de Nemours and Company. **Exhibit 1-13:** Courtesy Honeywell. **Exhibit 1-14:** Used with permission of Ben & Jerry's Homemade Holdings, Inc. 2000.

Chapter 2

Chapter opening photo: Courtesy Abercrombie & Fitch. **Exhibit 2-1:** Courtesy L.A. Gear. **Exhibit 2-2:** Courtesy Michelin North America. **Global Perspective 2-1:** Courtesy The Coca-Cola Company. "Coca-Cola" and the Dynamic Ribbon device are registered trademarks of The Coca-Cola Company. **Exhibit 2-3:** Courtesy Anheuser-Busch Companies, Inc. **Exhibit 2-4:** Courtesy Big Red, Incorporated. **Exhibit 2-5:** The iVillage.com home page made available courtesy iVillage Inc. ©2000 iVillage Inc. All rights reserved. iVillage and the iVillage logo are trademarks of iVillage Inc. **Exhibit 2-6:** Courtesy Cosmar Corporation, a Division of Renaissance Cosmetics, Inc. **Exhibit 2-7:** Courtesy Den-Mat Corporation. **Exhibit 2-8:** Courtesy Pfizer Inc. **Exhibit 2-9:** Courtesy Maxwell Business Systems. **Exhibit 2-10:** Courtesy Loro Piana. **Exhibit 2-11:** Courtesy Kimberly-Clark Corporation. **Exhibit 2-12:** Courtesy Oneida Ltd. All rights reserved. **Exhibit 2-13:** Courtesy Black & Decker. **Exhibit 2-14:** Courtesy Church & Dwight Co., Inc. **Exhibit 2-15:** Courtesy America's Dairy Farmers, National Dairy Board. **Exhibit 2-16:** Courtesy The Valvoline Company, a division of Ashland Inc. **Exhibit 2-17:** Courtesy The Pillsbury Company. **Exhibit 2-18:** Courtesy Fallon-McElligott for Rolling Stone. **IMC Perspective 2-3:** Courtesy of Volvo. **Exhibit 2-19:** Courtesy American Eagle Outfitters. **Exhibit 2-20:** Courtesy Rado Watch Co., Ltd. **Exhibit 2-21:** Courtesy Duracell. **Exhibit 2-22:** Designs copyrighted by Tiffany and Company. **Exhibit 2-23:** Courtesy McNeil Consumer Healthcare, 1999. **Exhibit 2-24:** Acushnet Company ©. Photography © Francine Zaslow.

Chapter 3

Chapter opening photo: Courtesy Apple Computer, Inc. **Exhibit 3-1:** Courtesy Link Magazine. **Exhibit 3-2:** © The Procter & Gamble Company. Used by permission. **IMC Perspective 3-1:** Copyright 1998—GM Corp. Used with Permission of GM Media Archives. All rights reserved. **Exhibit 3-3:** Courtesy No Fear. **Figure 3-6:** Reprinted with permission from the April 19, 1999 issue of *Advertising Age.* Copyright Crain Communications, Inc. 1999. **Exhibit 3-4:** Courtesy Quill Communications Inc. **IMC Perspective 3-2:** Courtesy J. Walter Thompson. **Exhibit 3-5:** Courtesy The Coca-Cola Company. "Coca-Cola" and the Dynamic Ribbon device are registered trademarks of The Coca-Cola Company. **Exhibit 3-6:** Courtesy Western International Media Corporation. **Exhibit 3-7:** Reprinted by permission of Borden Food Corporation. **Exhibit 3-8:** DR PEPPER® is a registered trademark of Dr Pepper/Seven Up, Inc. ©2000 Dr Pepper/Seven Up, Inc. **Page 92:** Tumbleweeds reprinted with special permission of NAS, Inc. **Exhibit 3-9:** Courtesy Marketing Computers ICON Awards. **Figure 3-9:** Reprinted with permission from the May 17, 1999 issue of *Advertising Age.* Copyright, Crain Communications, Inc. 1999. **IMC Perspective 3-3:** Courtesy DVC. **IMC Perspective 3-3:** Source: *PROMO,* Al Urbanski, "Agency of the Decade," pp. 67-69. © 1999 by PROMO. Used with permission. **Exhibit 3-10:** Reprinted with permission from the July 26, 1999 issue of *Advertising Age.* Copyright, Crain Communications, Inc. 1999. **Exhibit 3-10:** Courtesy AGENCY.COM. **Exhibit 3-11:** Courtesy Taylor Made.

Chapter 4

Chapter opening photo: The photograph of the PT Cruiser is used with permission from DaimlerChrysler Corporation. Emotional Rescue Ad—Mervin Franklin, photographer. **Exhibit 4-1:** Courtesy New Balance Athletic Shoe, Inc. **Exhibit 4-2:** Courtesy John Paul Mitchell Systems. **Exhibit 4-3:** Courtesy of Del Pharmaceuticals, Inc., a subsidiary of Del Laboratories, Inc. **Exhibit 4-4:** Courtesy Ericsson Inc. **Exhibit 4-5:** ©The Procter & Gamble Company. Used by permission. **Exhibit 4-6:** Courtesy Toyota Motor Sales, U.S.A. **Exhibit 4-7:** Courtesy Puig Beauty and Fashion North America. **Exhibit 4-8:** © American Association of Advertising Agencies. **Exhibit 4-9:** Courtesy Tropicana Products, Inc. **Exhibit 4-10:** Courtesy New Los Angeles Marketing Partnership. **Exhibit 4-11:** Courtesy Spalding & Evenflo Companies, Inc. **Exhibit 4-12:** The ad for JEEP GRAND CHEROKEE, with use of the QUADRA DRIVE name is used with permission from DaimlerChrysler Corporation. **Exhibit 4-13:** Courtesy The Pillsbury Company. **Exhibit 4-14:** Courtesy Anheuser-Busch Companies, Inc. **Exhibit 4-15:** Courtesy UUNET Technologies, Inc. a subsidiary of MCI WorldCom, Inc. **Exhibit 4-16:** Courtesy of International Business Machines Corporation. **Exhibit 4-17:** Courtesy of the Brita Products Company. **Exhibit 4-18:** Used by permission of Eveready Battery Company, Inc. Eveready® is a registered trademark of Eveready Battery Company. **Exhibit 4-19 (left):** Copyright 1998—GM Corp. Used with permission of GM Media Archives. All rights reserved. **(right):** Courtesy Bank One. **Exhibit 4-20:** Courtesy Countess Mara, Inc. **Exhibit 4-21 (left):** Courtesy of the U.S. Army. **(right):** Courtesy The Advertising Council, Inc.

Chapter 5

Chapter opening photo: Courtesy Hewlett-Packard Brand Advertising Dept. **Global Perspective 5-1:** Reproduced with permission of AT&T. **Exhibit 5-1:** Courtesy Hewlett-Packard Brand Advertising Dept. **Exhibit 5-2:** Courtesy Estee Lauder. **Exhibit 5-3:** © 1999 Time Inc. Reprinted by permission. **IMC Perspective 5-2:** Courtesy the Quaker Oats Company. **Exhibit 5-4:** Courtesy Johnson & Johnson Consumer Products, Inc **Exhibit 5-5:** Courtesy Panasonic Electronics Company. **Exhibit 5-6:** Courtesy of Canon. **Exhibit 5-7:** Courtesy Michelin North America. **Exhibit 5-8:** Courtesy Heinz U.S.A. **IMC Perspective 5-3:** Courtesy Taco Bell Corp. **Figure 5-8:** Reprinted by permission of Foote, Cone, and Belding Communications. **Exhibit 5-9:** Kenmore Elite™ ad, courtesy of Sears, Roebuck and Co. **Exhibit 5-10:** ©The Procter & Gamble Company. Used by permission. **Exhibit 5-11:** Courtesy The Gillette Company. **Figure 5-11:** *Journal of Marketing* 663, "How Advertising Works: What Do We Really Know?" p. 26, by Demetrios Vakratas and Tim Ambler. © 1999 by the American Marketing Association. Used by Permission.

Chapter 6

Chapter opening photo: Courtesy Jenny Craig, Inc. **Exhibit 6-1:** Courtesy Jim Beam Brands Co. **Exhibit 6-2:** Courtesy HEAD/Penn Raquet Sports. **Exhibit 6-3:** Courtesy of Lever Brothers Company. **Exhibit 6-4:** Courtesy Wendy's International, Inc. **IMC Perspective 6-2:** Courtesy King Stahlman Bail Bonds. **Exhibit 6-5:** American Isuzu Motors, Inc. and Goodby, Silverstein & Partners. **Exhibit 6-6:** Courtesy the Quaker Oats Company. **Exhibit 6-7:** Copyright 1998—GM Corp. Used with permission of GM Media Archives. All rights reserved. **Exhibit 6-9:** Courtesy The Coca-Cola Company. **Exhibit 6-10:** Courtesy Subaru of America and Temerlin McClain. **Exhibit 6-11:** Courtesy Revlon Consumer Products Corporation. **Exhibit 6-12:** Courtesy The Advertising Council, Inc. **Exhibit 6-13:** Courtesy of Hewlett-Packard Company. **Exhibit 6-14:** Courtesy W.K. Buckley Limited. **Exhibit 6-15:** Courtesy Apple Computer, Inc. and BBDO. **Exhibit 6-16:** Courtesy CamelBak Products, Inc. **IMC Perspective 6-4:** Courtesy Savin Corporation. **Exhibit 6-17:** Courtesy SmithKline Beecham. **Exhibit 6-18:** PayDay is a registered trademark. Used with permission of Hershey Foods Corporation. Photography © Howard Berman. **IMC Perspective 6-5:** Used with permission of Little Caesar Enterprises, Inc. © 1995, Little Caesar Enterprises, Inc. All rights reserved. **Exhibit 6-19:** Courtesy Travel & Leisure.

Chapter 7

Chapter opening photo: Courtesy Foster's Brewing Group. **Exhibit 7-1:** Courtesy Georgia-Pacific Corp. **Exhibit 7-2:** Courtesy Ford Motor. **Exhibit 7-3:** Courtesy Pace. **Exhibit 7-4:** Reprinted with permission of Del Monte Foods. **IMC Perspective 7-1:** Stone/David Young Wolff. **Exhibit 7-5:** Reuters/Jeff Vinnick/Archive Photos. **Exhibit 7-6:** Courtesy SkyTel Communications, SkyTel An MCI WorldCom Company. **Exhibit 7-7:** Courtesy Service Merchandise. **Exhibit 7-8:** Courtesy Waterford Wedgwood USA, Inc. **Exhibit 7-9:** Courtesy Midwest Express Airlines. **IMC Perspective 7-2:** Courtesy Subaru of America, Inc. **Exhibit 7-10:** Courtesy of the Zoological Society of San Diego. **Figure 7-7:** Reprinted Courtesy of San Diego Zoo. **Exhibit 7-11:** © American Association of Advertising Agencies. **Exhibit 7-8:** Reprinted by permission of the American Association of Advertising

Agencies. **Exhibit 7-12:** Courtesy Palm, Inc. Photography by Timothy Greenfield-Sanders. **Figure 7-15:** Schonfeld & Associates, Inc.

Chapter 8

Chapter opening photo: Courtesy Norwegian Cruise Line and Goodby, Silverstein & Partners. **Exhibit 8-1:** Courtesy Fallon McElligott for BMW of North America, Inc. **Figure 8-1:** "Burger King Corporation Unveils New Advertising, " PR Newswire, August 4, 1999. Reprinted by permission of PR Newswire. **Exhibit 8-2:** Courtesy Nissan North America, Inc. **Global Perspective 8-1:** Courtesy Lowe Lintas for The Independent. **Global Perspective 8-1:** Source: Reprinted with permission from the June 28, 1999 issue of *Advertising Age.* **Figure 8-2:** Reprinted with permission of D'Arcy, Masius, Benton & Bowles from website, © 2000. **Exhibit 8-3:** Courtesy V&S Vin and Spirit AB. Imported by the House of Seagram, New York, NY. **Exhibit 8-4:** Courtesy Crunch. **Exhibit 8-5:** Reprinted with permission from the February 21, 2000 issue of *Advertising Age.* Copyright, Crain Communications Inc. 2000. **Exhibit 8-6:** Courtesy Westin Hotels & Resorts. **IMC Perspective 8-2:** Courtesy California Milk Processor Board. **Exhibit 8-7:** Used by permission of San Diego Trust & Savings Bank. **Exhibit 8-8:** Courtesy Polaroid Corporation. **Exhibit 8-9:** Easterby & Associates. **Exhibit 8-10:** Courtesy Colgate-Palmolive Company. **Exhibit 8-11:** Courtesy No Fear. **Exhibit 8-12:** Courtesy Leo Burnett Company, Inc. as agent for Hallmark Cards, Incorporated. **Exhibit 8-13:** Courtesy 3M. **Ethical Perspective 8-4:** Concept: O. Toscani. Courtesy of United Colors of Benetton.

Chapter 9

Chapter opening photo: Courtesy Jack in the Box Inc. **Exhibit 9-1:** Courtesy The Quaker Oats Company. **Exhibit 9-2:** Courtesy Singapore Airlines. **Exhibit 9-3:** Courtesy of DFO, Inc. **Exhibit 9-4:** Courtesy Bristol-Myers Squibb Co. **Exhibit 9-5:** Courtesy Norwegian Cruise Line. **Exhibit 9-6:** Courtesy Team One Advertising for LEXUS. **Exhibit 9-7:** Courtesy MasterCard International Incorporated. **Exhibit 9-8:** Courtesy Leo Burnett Company, Inc. for Callard & Bowser-Suchard Inc. **Exhibit 9-9:** Courtesy Lee Jeans. **Exhibit 9-10:** © 1999 Castrol North America Inc. **IMC Perspective 9-1:** © Ameritrade. Ameritrade® is a registered trademark of Ameritrade Holding Corporation. **Exhibit 9-11:** The DERMASIL print ad was reproduced courtesy Chesebrough-Pond's USA Co. **Exhibit 9-12:** Courtesy DuPont. Teflon® is a registered trademark of DuPont. **Exhibit 9-13:** Courtesy Sybase, Inc. **Exhibit 9-14:** Courtesy AT&T and Young and Rubicam. **Exhibit 9-15:** Courtesy Hormel Foods, LLC. **Exhibit 9-16:** Courtesy Maytag Company. **Exhibit 9-17:** Courtesy Starkist Seafood, Pittsburgh, PA. **Exhibit 9-18:** Courtesy BASF Corporation. **Exhibit 9-19:** Courtesy Thomson Multimedia. Product photography by Thomas Card. Model photography by Dominick Guillemot. **Exhibit 9-20:** Courtesy The Coca-Cola Company. FRESCA is a trademark of The Coca-Cola Company. **Exhibit 9-21:** Courtesy AT&T Corp. Copyright 1997 AT&T Corp. All rights reserved. **Exhibit 9-22:** Courtesy Sims. **Exhibit 9-23:** Courtesy Volkswagen of America, Inc. and Arnold Communications. **IMC Perspective 9-3:** Courtesy Chevrolet Division General Motors and Campbell-Ewald Advertising. **IMC Perspective 9-4:** Courtesy Apple Computer, Inc. **Exhibit 9-24:** Courtesy Philips Lighting Company.

Chapter 10

Chapter opening photo: AP Photo/Stuart Ramson. **Figure 10-1:** Reprinted with permission from the September 27, 1999 issue of *Advertising Age.* Copyright, Crain Communications Inc. 1999. **Figure 10-4:** Simmons Market Research Bureau, Inc. 1997. **Figure 10-5:** MediaMark Research, Inc. **Figure 10-8:** Reprinted with permission from www.adage.com/dataplace. Copyright, Crain Communications, Inc. 1999. **Figure 10-9:** Reprinted with permission of Bill Communications, Inc. through the Copyright Clearance Center, from the 1996 "Buying Power Index," in *Sales & Marketing Management.* **Figure 10-10:** Reprinted with permission of Bill Communications, Inc. thorough the Copyright Clearance Center, from the 1996 "Brand Development Index," in *Sales & Marketing Management.* **Figure 10-11:** Reprinted with permission of Bill Communications, Inc. thorough the Copyright Clearance Center, from the 1996 "Brand Development Index," in *Sales & Marketing Management.* **Figure 10-12:** Reprinted with permission of Bill Communications, Inc. thorough the Copyright Clearance Center, from the 1996 "Brand Development Index," in *Sales & Marketing Management.* **Figure 10-15:** Simmons Market Research Bureau 1994. **Figure 10-18:** Who watches ads? December–January Ratings in New York Market, R.D. Percy & Co. **IMC Perspective 10-2:** Courtesy Outdoor Advertising Association of America, Inc. **IMC Perspective 10-2:** Source: Michael Freeman, "Media All-Stars: Jennifer Sparks," pp. 60-64; Verne Gray, "Media All-Stars: Peter Gardiner," pp. 12-18; Eric Schmuckler, "Media All-Stars: Mark Stewart," pp. 4-10. © 1999 ASM Communications. Used with permission from the December 6, 1999 issue of *Adweek.* **Exhibit 10-1:** Courtesy Scarborough Research. **Figure 10-28:** Reach and frequency analyses: San Diego Trust and Savings Bank. **Appendix A:** Adapted with permission from Arnold M. Bantam, Donald W. Jugenheimer, and Peter B. Burk, *Advertising Media Sourcebook,* 3rd edition (Lincolnwood, IL: NTC Business Books), pp. 8–9. **Appendix B:** Table on page 340: MRI Spring. Weighted by population © MRI All rights reserved. Appendix B: Table source: IMS Model reach and frequency report. Appendix B: IMS Net/Duplication Report © 1996 MRI. All rights reserved.

Chapter 11

Chapter opening photo: Bob D'Amico/ABC. Copyright 2000 ABC, Inc. **Exhibit 11-1:** Courtesy Porsche Cars North America, Inc. **Figure 11-1:** Reprinted with permission from the September 27, 1999 issue of *Advertising Age.* Copyright, Crain Communications Inc. 1999. **Exhibit 11-2:** Courtesy The Discovery Channel. **IMC Perspective 11-1:** Courtesy LifeMinders.com. **IMC Perspective 11-2:** Courtesy Tivo Inc. **Exhibit 11-3:** Courtesy United Paramount Network and World Wrestling Federation Entertainment, Inc. **Figure 11-3:** Reprinted with permission from the September 20, 1999 issue of *Advertising Age,* p. 12. Copyright, Crain Communications, Inc., 1999. **Exhibit 11-4:** Courtesy All American Television, Inc. **Exhibit 11-5:** © 2000 National Broadcasting Company, Inc. Used by permission. All rights reserved. **IMC Perspective 11-3:** Courtesy ESPN, Inc. **Exhibit 11-6:** Courtesy Viacom. **Exhibit 11-7:** © 1996 Cable News Network, Inc. A Time Warner Company. All Rights Reserved. Global Perspective **11-4:** Courtesy MTV, a division of Viacom. **Exhibit 11-8:** Courtesy A.C. Nielsen Company. **Exhibit 11-9:** Courtesy KFMB TV. **Figure 11-7:** Reprinted with permission of the Radio Advertising Bureau. **IMC Perspective 11-6:** Reprinted courtesy of The Richards Group. **Exhibit 11-10:** Courtesy Radio Advertising Bureau. **Exhibit 11-11:** Banana Boat of California, Inc. **Exhibit 11-12:** KCEO Radio. **Figure 11-8:** Reprinted from the *Radio Marketing Guide & Fact Book for Advertisers,* Fall 1999 to Spring 2000, p. 40, by permission of the Radio Advertising Bureau. **Figure 11-10:** Courtesy of Station XHTZ-FM, Chula Vista, California. **Figure 11-11:** Reprinted courtesy of Arbitron.

Chapter 12

Chapter opening photo: Cover image reproduced with permission of Fast Company Magazine. All rights reserved. **Exhibit 12-1:** Courtesy Virgo Publishing, Inc. **Figure 12-1:** Audit Bureau of Circulations. Reprinted by permission. **Exhibit 12-2**: Courtesy Powder Magazine. **Exhibit 12-3:** Courtesy Beef Magazine. **Exhibit 13-4:** Courtesy Weider Publications, Inc. **IMC Perspective 12-1:** TEEN PEOPLE Weekly is a registered trademark of Time Inc., used with permission. **Exhibit 12-5:** Courtesy *Philadelphia* Magazine. **Exhibit 12-6:** Courtesy *Newsweek* Magazine. **Exhibit 12-7:** Photography by Sharon Hoogstraten. **Exhibit 12-8:** Used by permission of WD-40 Company. **Figure 12-2:** Reprinted courtesy of Beta Research. **Exhibit 12-9:** Courtesy Magazine Publishers of America. **Figure 12-3:** Audit Bureau of Circulations. Reprinted by permission. **Exhibit 12-10:** Courtesy Bausch & Lomb Healthcare and Optics Worldwide. **Exhibit 12-11:** Courtesy Audit Bureau of Circulations. **Exhibit 12-12:** Courtesy Newsweek, Inc. All rights reserved. **Exhibit 12-13:** Courtesy Ivy League Network. **Exhibit 12-14:** Courtesy Yahoo! Internet Life. **IMC Perspective 12-2:** Source: *The Wall Street Journal,* "Magazines Seek to Demonstrate Efficacy of Ads," April 12, 1999, pp. B1, 3. © 1999 Dow Jones & Company, Inc. Used by permission of *The Wall Street Journal* through the Copyright Clearance Center. **Exhibit 12-15:** Courtesy *Newsweek,* Inc. All rights reserved. **Exhibit 12-16:** Reprinted from 5/1/200 Business Week Online by special permission, copyright © 2000 by The McGraw-Hill Companies. Inc. **Exhibit 12-17:** Copyright © 2000 by the New York Times Co. Reprinted by permission. **Exhibit 12-18:** Courtesy *The Daily Collegian.* **Exhibit 12-19:** Courtesy CompuServe, Inc. **Exhibit 12-20:** Courtesy *The Chicago Tribune.* **Exhibit 12-21:** Courtesy *San Diego Union-Tribune.* **Exhibit 12-22:** Courtesy *San Diego Union-Tribune.* **Figure 12-4:** National Newspaper Association Facts About Newspapers, 1999. Reprinted with permission. **Exhibit 12-23:** Courtesy Cathay Pacific Airways and McCann-Erickson. **Exhibit 12-24:** Courtesy Newspaper National Network. **Figure 12-5:** Courtesy Newspaper Advertising Bureau, Inc. **Exhibit 12-25:** Courtesy *Miami Herald/El Nuevo Herald.* **Exhibit 12-26:** Courtesy Newsweek, Inc. All rights reserved. **Exhibit 12-27:** Courtesy The Newspaper Association of America. **IMC Perspective 12-3:** Copyright 2000, Advance Magazine Publications, Inc. Reprinted with permission from *react* magazine.

Chapter 13

Chapter opening photos: Courtesy Princeton Video Image, Inc. **Figure 13-2:** http://www.oaaa.org//Marketing/cmr1999jansep.html, "Outdoor Advertising Expenditures, January–September 1999, Ranked by Dollar Growth. Reprinted by permission. **Exhibit 13-1:** Courtesy Outdoor Advertising Association of America, Inc. **Exhibit 13-2:** Courtesy Inflatable Design Group, El Cajon, California. ™ & © 1999 Saban. All Rights Reserved. **Figure 13-3:** Source: Outdoor Advertising Association of America. **Exhibit 13-4:** Courtesy AVIAD. **Exhibit 13-5:** AP Photo/Pizza Hut. **Exhibit 13-6 (right):** Courtesy Outdoor Advertising Association of America, Inc. **Exhibit 13-7:** Courtesy United Airlines, AT&T/Young & Rubicam. **Exhibit 13-8:** Courtesy TDI. **Exhibit 13-9:** Courtesy Outdoor Advertising Association of America, Inc. **Exhibit 13-10:** Courtesy Promotional Products Association International. **Figure 13-7:** http://www.ppa.org/industry_resources/sales_volume_98.html. Reprinted with permission of Promotional Products Association International. **IMC Perspective 13-1:** Courtesy Promotional Products Association International. **Figure 13-8:** http://www.ppa.org/industry_resources/sales_volume_98.html. Reprinted with permission of Promotional Products Association International. **Exhibit 13-11:** Courtesy Bell Atlantic Directory Services, Bell Atlantic Corporation. **Figure 13-9:** National Yellow Pages Monitor, a division of NFD Research, Inc. **Exhibit 13-12:** AP Photo/BMW, Stuart Ramson. Global Perspective **13-2:** Warren Miller Films/Photo by Mark Weaver. **Exhibit 13-13:** Courtesy *Hemispheres*—the magazine of United Airlines. **Exhibit 13-14:** Courtesy SKY Video LLC. **Figure 13-11:** Reprinted by permission of Halsey Publishing Co. **Exhibit 13-15:** AP Photo/Adam Butler.

Chapter 14

Chapter opening photo: © Millipore Corporation. Used with permission. **Figure 14-2:** "Direct Marketing . . . An Aspect of Total Marketing," by Martin Baier, Henry Hoke, Jr., and Robert Stone. Reprinted with permission from *Direct Marketing* magazine, 224 7th St., Garden City, NY 11530; 1-800-229-6700, 517-746-6700. **Exhibit 14-1:** Courtesy Cox Direct. **Exhibit 14-2:** Courtesy Texas Department of Economic Development. **Exhibit 14-3:** ©1999 Hertz System, Inc. Hertz is a registered service mark and trademark of Hertz System, Inc. **Figure 14-5:** Simmons Market Research Bureau, Inc. 1999. **Exhibit 14-4:** Courtesy Porsche Cars North America, Inc. **Exhibit 14-5:** Photography by Sharon Hoogstraten. **Exhibit 14-6:** Courtesy InfoUSA (NASDAQ:IUSA). **Exhibit 14-7:** Reprinted with permission of Lands' End, Inc. **Exhibit 14-8:** Courtesy Bennett Kuhn Varner, Inc. **Exhibit 14-9:** Courtesy Volvo Cars of North America. **Figure 14-6:** *Journal of Advertising Research,* 1996, p. 75. Reprinted by permission of the Advertising Research Foundation. **IMC Perspective 14-1:** Provided by the Arthritis Foundation. **Exhibit 14-10:** Courtesy The GM Card. **Figure 14-7:** Direct Marketing Association 1996 STATISTICAL FACT BOOK, p. 146. **Exhibit 14-11:** Courtesy Mary Kay Inc.

Chapter 15

Chapter opening photo: Courtesy beyondclass.com. **Figure 15-2:** Source http://www.adres.com. Reprinted by permission of Ad Resource. **Figure 15-3:** Reprinted courtesy of the Morgan Stanley Group, Inc. **Figure 15-4:** Reprinted by permission of Market Facts from "What do you do when you go online?" **Figure 15-5:** Reprinted with permission from the April 14, 2000 Special Issue of *Advertising Age,* "The Interactive Future." Copyright Crain Communications, Inc. 2000. **Figure 15-6:** Source: CyberAtlas (www.internet.com), "Internet User Profiles." Reprinted with permission. **Exhibit 15-1:** Reprinted from INC. Magazine by permission of Hot Hot Hot. **Exhibit 15-2:** Courtesy Kimberly-Clark Corporation. **Exhibit 15-3:** Courtesy General Mills. Inc. "Cheerios" is a registered trademark of General Mills, Inc. Used with permission. **Exhibit 15-4:** Courtesy Xerox Corporation. **Exhibit 15-5:** Amazon.com is a registered trademark or trademark of Amazon.com, Inc. in the U.S. and/or other countries. © 2000 Amazon.com. All rights reserved. **Exhibit 15-6:** These materials have been reproduced by McGraw-Hill Higher Education with the permission of eBay Inc. COPYRIGHT © EBAY INC. ALL RIGHTS RESERVED. **Figure 15-7:** Source: Competitive Media Reporting. Reprinted by permission. **Exhibit 15-7:** Courtesy of International Business Machines Corporation. **Exhibit 15-8:** Courtesy Yahoo! Inc. Exhibit 15-9: © Keebler Company. **IMC Perspective 15-2:** ©Procter & Gamble Company. Used by Permission. **Exhibit 15-10:** Courtesy DaimlerChrysler Corporation. **Exhibit 15-11:** Amazon.com is a registered trademark or trademark of Amazon.com, Inc. in the U.S. and/or other countries. © 2000 Amazon.com. All rights reserved. **IMC Perspective 15-3:** Courtesy of International Business Machines Corporation. **Figure 15-8:** Reprinted Courtesy of Jupiter Communication, Inc. **Exhibit 15-12:** Courtesy of WebTV Networks, Inc.

Chapter 16

Chapter opening photo: Courtesy The Coca-Cola Company. Chapter intro source: *PROMO,* "Sudden Impact," (April 1999), pp. 42-48; and "Is Advertising Dead" (September 1998), pp. 32-36, 159-162, by Betsy Spethmann. © 1998, 1999 by PROMO. Used with permission. **Exhibit 16-1:** © Procter & Gamble Company. Used by permission. **Figure 16-2:** Reprinted by permission from Cox Direct 20th Annual Survey of Promotional Practices, 1998: "Long-term allocations to advertising, trade promotion, and consumer promotion." **Exhibit 16-2:** KELLOGG'S POP-TARTS PASTRY SWIRLS™ and POP-TARTS SNAK-STIX™ are trademarks of Kellogg Company. All rights reserved. Used with permission. **Exhibit 16-3:** J.J. Warner/Courtesy Sears. **IMC Perspective 16-1:** Courtesy DVC **Exhibit 16-4:** Courtesy Cox Target Media, Inc. **Exhibit 16-5:** Courtesy Ryan Partnership. **Exhibit 16-6:** Courtesy WD-40 Company. **Exhibit 16-7:** Courtesy Burson Marsteller for Church & Dwight Company, Inc. **Exhibit 16-8:** Reproduced with permission of PepsiCo, Inc. 1994, Purchase, New York. **Exhibit 16-9:** Courtesy DVC. **Exhibit 16-10:** Sharon Hoogstraten. **Exhibit 16-11:** ArmorAll Products Corporation. **Exhibit 16-12:** Courtesy Cox Target Media, Inc. **Exhibit 16-13:** Courtesy Kellogg Company. Eggo®, Common Sense®, and Kellogg's® are registered trademarks of Kellogg Company. All rights reserved. **Exhibit 16-14:** Courtesy Catalina Marketing. **Exhibit 16-15:** Courtesy Catalina Marketing. **Exhibit 16-16:** Courtesy McDonald's Corporation. **Exhibit 16-17:** Courtesy First USA Bank, N.A. **Exhibit 16-18:** Courtesy The Gillette Company. **Exhibit 16-19:** Courtesy Intuit. Quicken® and TurboTax® are registered trademarks of Intuit Inc. **Exhibit 16-20:** ArmorAll Products Corporation. **Exhibit 16-21:** Courtesy Bristol-Myers Company. **Exhibit 16-22:** Courtesy Gerber Products Company. **Exhibit 16-23:** Courtesy Triarc Beverage Group. **Exhibit 16-24:** Courtesy Van Camp Seafood Company. **Exhibit 16-25:** Courtesy Van Camp Seafood Company. **IMC Perspective 16-3:** Reprinted from September 9, 1996 issue of *Business Week* by special permission, copyright © 1996 by The McGraw-Hill Companies, Inc. **Exhibit 16-26:** Courtesy Spalding Sports Worldwide. **IMC Perspective 16-4:** Courtesy Intel. **IMC Perspective 16-4:** source: Reprinted with permission from the November 15, 1999 and January 19, 1996 issues of *Advertising Age.* Copyright Crain Communications, Inc. 1996, 1999. **Exhibit 16-27:** Courtesy New Balance Athletic Shoe, Inc. **Exhibit 16-28:** Courtesy WD-40 Company. **Exhibit 16-29:** Courtesy Lever Brothers Company.

Chapter 17

Chapter opening photo: © Autodesk, Inc. and Unreal Pictures, Inc. Used by McGraw-Hill with permission. **Figure 17-2:** http://www.prcentral.com. Reprinted by permission. **Exhibit 17-1:** Courtesy Texaco. **Exhibit 17-2:** Courtesy College of Business Administration San Diego State University. **Exhibit 17-3:** Courtesy Jack in the Box Inc. **Exhibit 17-4:** Reprinted with permission of Chevron Corporation. **Exhibit 17-5:** Courtesy KFMB-TV, San Diego, CA. **Exhibit 17-6:** Courtesy Yellow Pages Publishers Association. **Exhibit 17-7:** Courtesy Nortel Networks Corporation. **Exhibit 17-8:** Courtesy Odwalla. **Exhibit 17-9:** CLIENT: Olympus America, Inc. AGENCY: McCaffrey & Ratner Gottlieb Lane. **Exhibit 17-10:** Courtesy HP—Home Products Division. **Exhibit 17-11:** © 1991 Dow Jones & Company, Publisher of *The Wall Street Journal.* All Rights Reserved. **Exhibit 17-12:** Courtesy Odwalla. **Exhibit 17-13:** Used by permission of Tree Top, Inc. **Figure 17-6:** Reprinted Courtesy of Ketchum Public Relations. **Exhibit 17-14:** Courtesy Tyco International. **IMC Perspective 17-2:** Courtesy Nortel Networks Corporation. **Exhibit 17-15:** Courtesy Pharmaceutical Research and Manufacturers of America. **Exhibit 17-16:** Copyright © State Farm Mutual Automobile Insurance Company, 1999. Used by permission. **Exhibit 17-17:** Courtesy Cunningham Communications. **Figure 17-8:** The September 29, 1999 issue of *The Wall Street Journal,* "The Best Corporate Reputations in America: The Leaders; The Building Blocks," p. B-1 (Illustrations by Mark Foster). © 1999 Dow Jones & Company, Inc. Reprinted by permission of *The Wall Street Journal* through the Copyright Clearance Center. **Figure 17-10:** *PROMO,* "Annual Sponsorship Spending," July, 1999. © 1999 by *PROMO.* Used with permission. **Exhibit 17-18:** Courtesy American Civil Liberties Union. **Exhibit 17-19:** Courtesy AT&T Advertising. **Exhibit 17-20:** Courtesy of The Doug Flutie, Jr. Foundation for Autism A member of The Giving Back Fund's Family of Charities.

Chapter 18

Chapter opening photo: Courtesy Boise Cascade Office Products. **Exhibit 18-1:** Courtesy Giltspur Inc./Haddon Advertising. **Figure 18-6:** *Sales and Marketing Management,* "The 20 Traits of Top Sales People," by Erika Rasmusson, August 1999, pp. 34-37. © 1999 by Bill Communications, Inc. Reprinted by permission of Bill Communications through the Copyright Clearance Center. **IMC Perspective 18-1:** Courtesy Enron Corporation. Enron Owned Photo. **IMC Perspective 18-1 source:** *Sales & Marketing Management,* "Here's to the Winners," by Sara Lorge, July 1999, pp 46-70. © 1999 by Bill Communications. Reprinted with permission of Bill Communications through the Copyright Clearance Center. **Exhibit 18-2:** Courtesy Gateway. **Exhibit 18-3:** Courtesy Gordon Publications, Inc. **Exhibit 18-4:** Courtesy Digital Impact, Inc. **Exhibit 18-5:** Courtesy GoldMine Software Corporation.

Chapter 19

Chapter opening photo: Stone/Phil Degginger. **Exhibit 19-1:** Churchill & Klehr/Liaison Agency Inc. **IMC Perspective 19-1:** Courtesy GSD&M for The Steel Alliance. **IMC Perspective 19-1 sources:** *Journal of Advertising Research,* William A. Cook, "Ogilvy Winners Turn Research Into Creative Solutions," May–June 1999. pp. 59–65; "The ARF Names Ten Ogilvy Award-Winning Campaigns," March–April, 1998, pp. 57–62. Used by Permission of the Advertising Research Foundation. **Exhibit 19-2:** Courtesy Chiat/Day/Mojo Inc. Advertising. **Exhibit 19-3:** Courtesy Lowe's Companies, Inc. **Exhibit 19-4:** Reprinted from *Business Week* by special permission © 1997 McGraw-Hill Companies, Inc. **Figure 19-13:** Reprinted with permission from BUSINESS MARKETING, "Ad Response Methods," page 41, March 1999. Copyright Crain Communications, Inc. 1999. All Rights Reserved. **Exhibit 19-5:** Courtesy Roper Starch Worldwide Inc. **Exhibit 19-6:** Courtesy Ipsos-ASI, Inc. **Figure 19-21:** © 1994 ASM Communications. Used with permission from the May 16, 1994 issue of *Brandweek.*

Chapter 20

Chapter opening photo: Courtesy Lowe & Partners Worldwide (The Martin Agency, Lowe Brindfars for Saab Automobile AB). **Exhibit 20-1:** Courtesy Australian Tourist Commission™ © The Brand Australia Trademark is the subject of copyright and is a trademark of the Australia Tourist Commission, 1995. **Exhibit 20-2:** Courtesy WD-40 Company. **Figure 20-1:** Reprinted with permission from the November 1999 issue of *Ad Age International.* Copyright Crain Communications, Inc. 1999. All rights Reserved. **Exhibit 20-3:** Courtesy Gateway. **Exhibit 20-4:** Courtesy Heineken Breweries. **Global Perspective 20-1:** Courtesy New Balance. **Exhibit 20-5:** Coca-Cola and Coca-Cola Light are registered trademarks of The Coca-Cola Company. Permission granted by the Coca-Cola Company. **Exhibit 20-6:** Illustrations appear with permission of The Gillette Company. **Exhibit 20-7:** Courtesy Nestlé. **Exhibit 20-8:** Courtesy Nestlé **Exhibit 20-9:** Courtesy The Colgate-Palmolive Company. **Exhibit 20-10:** Courtesy Singapore Airlines. **Exhibit 20-11:** Reproduced with permission of PepsiCo, Inc. 1997, Purchase, New York. **Exhibit 20-12:** Courtesy Continental Airlines. **Exhibit 20-13:** Courtesy The Coca-Cola Company. **Global Perspective 20-2:** Courtesy of International Business Machines Corporation. **Exhibit 20-14:** Courtesy NCH. **Global Perspective 20-3:** Courtesy of Vickers & Benson Advertising Ltd. for the Canadian Tourism Commission. **Exhibit 20-15:** Courtesy Häagen Daz. **Exhibit 20-16:** Courtesy of Hearst Magazines International. **Figure 20-5:** Reprinted with permission of NCH NuWorld Marketing Limited of Lincolnshire, IL. **Global Perspective 20-4:** AP Photo/Claude Paris. **Exhibit 20-17:** Courtesy Microsoft Singapore Pte Ltd. Figure 20-7: Reprinted with permission from Business 2.0, "Who's Online," p. 251, January 2000. **Exhibit 20-18:** Courtesy International Business Machines Corporation. **Appendix C:** *PROMO,* "Promoting Overseas: What's Legal and What's Not," pp. S14–S15. © 1998 by *PROMO.* Used with permission.

Chapter 21

Chapter opening photo: AP Photo/File. Chapter 21 vignette source: Reprinted with permission from the January 31, 2000, and June 28, 1999 issues of *Advertising Age.* Copyright Crain Communications, Inc. 1999, 2000. **Exhibit 21-1:** Reprinted with permission of Kinney & Lange. All rights reserved. **Ethical Perspective 21-1:** Courtesy Center for Science in the Public Interest. **Exhibit 21-2:** Courtesy Luce, Forward, Hamilton & Scripps LLP. **Figure 21-2:** Reprinted by permission of the Council of Better Business Bureaus. **Exhibit 21-3:** Courtesy Benetton Cosmetics Corporation. Photo by O. Toscani. **Exhibit 21-4:** Federal Trade Commission website. **Exhibit 21-5:** Courtesy Jenny Craig Weight Loss Centres, Inc. **Exhibit 21-6:** Courtesy Van Camp Seafood Company. **IMC Perspective 21-3:** Courtesy Campaign for Tobacco-Free Kids. **IMC Perspective 21-4:** Courtesy Campbell Soup Company. **Exhibit 21-7:** ©1992 Wildcraft® Herbs, Santa Cruz, CA 95060. **Exhibit 21-8:** Courtesy Direct Selling Association. **Exhibit 21-9:** Courtesy beyondclass.com. **IMC Perspective 21-5 sources:** *Marketing News,* James Heckman, "COPPA to Bring No Surprises, Hefty Violation Fines in April," January 31, 2000, p. 6; "Today's Game Is Keep-Away," July 5, 1999, pp. 1, 7. © 1999, 2000 by the American Marketing Association. Used by permission.

Chapter 22

Chapter opening photo: Carolyn Schaefer/Liaison Agency. **Exhibit 22-1:** Courtesy Anheuser-Busch Companies, Inc. **Exhibit 22-2:** Used by permission of Calvin Klein. **Exhibit 22-3:** Courtesy NIKE, Inc. **Exhibit 22-4:** Courtesy Ansell. **Exhibit 22-5:** Courtesy Airwalk. **Exhibit 22-6:** Used by permission of Calvin Klein. **Ethical Perspective 22-1:** Courtesy Bijan Designer for Men, Beverly Hills, California. **Figure 22-2:** Courtesy of the Council of Better Business Bureaus, Children's Advertising Review Unit. **Exhibit 22-7:** Reprinted by permission of Rolls Royce Motor Cars Inc. **Exhibit 22-8:** © American Association of Advertising Agencies. **Exhibit 22-9:** © American Association of Advertising Agencies. **Exhibit 22-10:** Courtesy Maidenform, Inc./Agency—Levine, Huntley, Schmidt & Beaver; Creative—Rochelle Klein, Michael Vitiello; Director—Mark Coppos, Copos Films. **Exhibit 22-11:** Courtesy IKEA and Deutsch Inc. **Exhibit 22-12:** Courtesy Mattel. **Exhibit 22-13:** Courtesy gfn.com, the Gay Financial Network, Inc. **Exhibit 22-14:** Courtesy International Advertising Association. **Exhibit 22-15:** Courtesy Boys & Girls Clubs of America. **IMC Perspective 22-3:** Courtesy Partnership For A Drug-Free America. **Exhibit 22-16:** © American Association of Advertising Agencies. **Exhibit 22-17:** Courtesy Daewoo Motor America, Inc. **Exhibit 22-18:** © American Association of Advertising Agencies. **Exhibit 22-19:** Courtesy International Advertising Association.

Name and Company Index

A

B

D

E

I

J

K

N

O

P

Q

R

X

Y

Z

Subject Index

A

B

C

J

K

L

M

N

O

P

S

T

U

V

W

Y

Z

www.mhhe.com/belch